WILEY

GAAP 99

Interpretation and Application of
GENERALLY ACCEPTED
ACCOUNTING PRINCIPLES
1999

SUBSCRIPTION NOTICE

This Wiley product is updated on an annual basis to reflect important changes in the subject matter. If you purchased this product directly from John Wiley & Sons, Inc., we have already recorded your subscription for this annual service.

If, however, you purchased this product from a bookstore and wish to receive revised volumes billed separately with a 30-day examination review, please send your name, company name (if applicable), address, and the title of the product to:

Supplement Department
John Wiley & Sons, Inc.
One Wiley Drive
Somerset, NJ 08875
1-800-225-5945

For customers outside the United States, please contact the Wiley office nearest you:

Professional & Reference Division
John Wiley & Sons Canada, Ltd.
22 Worcester Road
Rexdale, Ontario M9W 1L1
CANADA
(416) 675-3580
1-800-567-4797
FAX (416) 675-6599

Jacaranda Wiley Ltd.
PRT Division
P.O. Box 174
North Ryde, NSW 2113
AUSTRALIA
(02) 805-1100
FAX (02) 805-1597

John Wiley & Sons Ltd.
Baffins Lane
Chichester
West Sussex, PO19 1UD
UNITED KINGDOM
(44) (243) 779777

John Wiley & Sons (SEA) Pte. Ltd.
37 Jalan Pemimpin
Block B # 05-04
Union Industrial Building
SINGAPORE 2057
(65) 258-1157

WILEY GAAP 99

Interpretation and Application of GENERALLY ACCEPTED ACCOUNTING PRINCIPLES 1999

Patrick R. Delaney
Barry J. Epstein
James R. Adler
Michael F. Foran

JOHN WILEY & SONS, INC.
New York • Chichester • Weinheim • Brisbane • Singapore • Toronto

PERMISSIONS

This text is printed on acid-free paper. ♾

ISBN 0-471-29639-2

Printed in the United States of America
10 9 8 7 6 5 4 3 2 1

CONTENTS

ABOUT THE AUTHORS

Patrick R. Delaney, PhD, CPA, is the Arthur Andersen LLP Alumni Professor of Accountancy and Chair of the Department of Accountancy at Northern Illinois University. He received his PhD in Accountancy from the University of Illinois. Professor Delaney served as a Faculty Resident with Arthur Andersen LLP. He is the author of *CPA Examination Review*, 2-volume and 4-part sets, including the related components of the Wiley CPA preparation system. He is past president of the Rockford Chapter, Institute of Management Accountants; serves on Illinois CPA Society Committees (previously as Vice-President and member, Board of Directors; Chairman of Accounting Principles Committee; chair of the Relations with Accounting Educators and Students Committee; and chair of Educator CPA Issues Committee); and has served on numerous other professional committees. He is a member of the American Accounting Association, American Institute of Certified Public Accountants, and the Institute of Management Accountants. Professor Delaney has published in *The Accounting Review* and is the recipient of NIU's Excellence in Teaching Award and the Illinois CPA Society's Outstanding Educator Award.

James R. Adler, PhD, CPA, is a managing director with American Express Tax and Business Services Inc. and a senior partner at Checkers, Simon & Rosner LLP. He is a former member of both the Small Business Advisory Group at the Financial Accounting Standards Board Emerging Issues Task Force and the Board of Directors of the Illinois CPA Society. He earned his BS, MBA, and PhD at New York University, is a CPA in New Jersey and Illinois, and is a Certified Fraud Examiner. Dr. Adler has been an expert accounting witness and provided litigation and investigative services to various businesses and law firms. He has served as a consultant to public accounting firms, financial institutions, and other business enterprises and was a university professor. A frequent speaker and writer on accounting topics, he has authored articles in *Crain's Chicago Business* and *Cashflow* and won awards for teaching excellence.

Barry J. Epstein, PhD, CPA, is a partner in the Chicago office of the major international accounting firm BDO Seidman, LLP, where he specializes in litigation consulting and also is involved widely in technical accounting and auditing issues affecting the firm and its clients. In the litigation practice he is active principally in accountants' malpractice defense work and other matters, such as contractual disputes, which revolve around the interpretation of the professional accounting and auditing literature. Prior to joining BDO Seidman in 1997, he was partner in charge of quality control for several large regional CPA firms for over 15 years, was a technical manager in the national office of another large firm for over 8 years, taught at the college level for 5 years, and served a stint as a financial executive with a Fortune 250 Company. He has authored or coauthored six books (one of which, *Wiley IAS '98*, now in its second edition, is the first comprehensive practical book on the growing subject of international accounting standards), many professional articles, and a regular business column of a major newspaper. Dr. Epstein has served on numerous committees at the state and national levels and was a member of the AICPA's Board of Examiners for 5 years. He has lectured widely in the U.S., Canada, and the Middle East, and has been regularly involved in training professionals both for his firms and through continuing education programs in the community. Dr. Epstein holds a PhD in management information systems and finance from the University of Pittsburgh, a MBA from the University of Chicago, and a BSC in accountancy and finance from DePaul University.

Michael F. Foran, PhD, CPA, CMA, CIA, is a Professor of Accountancy at Wichita State University. He received his PhD in Accounting from the University of Washington. He is a member of the American Accounting Association, the Financial Executives Institute, the Institute of Internal Auditors (IIA), and the Institute of Management Accounting. He has served as chairman and/or a member of many national, regional, and local committees in these organizations. He has spoken on numerous occasions to various academic and professional groups. Dr. Foran has published in *The Accounting Review, Accounting Horizons, Journal of Accountancy, Management Accounting, The Tax Advisor, The National Public Accountant,* and many other academic and professional journals.

PREFACE

GAAP: Interpretation and Application provides an analytical explanation and illustration of generally accepted accounting principles. This book integrates the principles promulgated by the FASB, including Emerging Issues Task Force Consensus summaries and Statements of Position of the AICPA's Accounting Standards Executive Committee (AcSEC) into a usable topical format.

The focus of this book is on the practitioner and the practical problems faced in applying GAAP. However, a major strength of this book is its ability to address and explain the theory and application of GAAP in sufficient detail so as to supplement accounting textbooks. This book is not merely a reiteration of current promulgated GAAP. Using our combined expertise, we have addressed the problems faced by both the practitioner and the student in applying and understanding GAAP. Understandability is enhanced through the use of detailed examples, diagrams, and lucid explanations which emphasize the practical application of GAAP.

Each chapter (or major section therein) of this book provides a discussion of the perspective and issues relative to the topics covered; a listing of the sources of GAAP; and the promulgated concepts and rules with examples of implementation. Required financial statement disclosures under generally accepted accounting principles with additional required SEC disclosures are summarized in a simplified checklist at the back of this book. The book has a comprehensive index at the back and, following the Table of Contents, **a listing of pronouncements, each referenced to page(s) in this book and the location in the FASB's Current Text**. Thus, this listing of authoritative pronouncements serves as a reference to other sources of information on specific accounting problems, and it serves as an index to the FASB's system of coding pronouncements (i.e., the Current Text).

We hope that this book serves as a reliable reference tool for practitioners, faculty, and students in working through the complexities of the authoritative literature. Comments from users concerning materials contained in or omitted from this work would be appreciated. Please send them to Patrick R. Delaney, c/o John Wiley & Sons Inc., 155 N. 3rd Street, Suite 502, DeKalb, Illinois, 60115 before June 1, 1999, for inclusion in the 2000 Edition.

Patrick R. Delaney
James R. Adler
Barry J. Epstein
Michael F. Foran

September 1, 1998

CONTRIBUTORS

Michael L. Baker, MBA, CPA. He served as a major contributor to the first edition (1985). He prepared the chapters: Inventories, Accounting for Leases, Earnings Per Share, and Accounting Changes and Correction of Errors.

John C. Borke, MAS, CPA, Associate Professor of Accounting at the University of Wisconsin-Platteville. Professor Borke prepared the chapter: Interim and Segment Reporting.

Kathleen Duff, MAS, CPA, is employed with Sikich Gardner and Co., LLP.

Kendra Schoenholz, MAS, just finished a MAS degree at Northern Illinois University.

John R. Simon, PhD, CPA, Coopers and Lybrand LLP Professor of Accountancy and Presidential Teaching Professor at Northern Illinois University. He received his PhD from the University of Illinois and is a recipient of NIU's Excellence in Teaching Award. Professor Simon prepared the chapter: Foreign Currency.

Shannon Somers, BS, is working on a MAS degree at Northern Illinois University.

ACKNOWLEDGMENTS

The authors are deeply indebted to all of those who assisted in the production of this book, for without them there would be no book to publish. Our heartfelt thanks go out to Brenda Bannon, Lydia Gage, Margy Miller, Pam Miller, Kay Poormehr, and Toni Simmons for your many hours of dedication and effort.

Authoritative Accounting Pronouncements

Listed below are all of the authoritative accounting pronouncements **currently in effect** as we go to press. The current text refers to the FASB's *Accounting Standards - Current Text* which is divided into two volumes: General Standards and Industry Standards. These volumes as well as two volumes of Original Pronouncements may be ordered from the AICPA (800-862-4272) or FASB (203-847-0700). The Emerging Issues Task Force Abstracts, which are in a separate book, may be ordered from the FASB. AICPA Statements of Position by the Accounting Standards Executive Committee may be ordered from the AICPA. These are available individually or in the publication entitled *AICPA Technical Practice Aids*. Places in this text where the pronouncements are discussed may be found by referencing the last column in the listings below.

Pronouncement Abbreviations

The following is a key to the abbreviations used throughout the book to refer to authoritative pronouncements:

Pronouncement	*Abbreviation*
Accounting Principles Board Opinion	APB
Accounting Research Bulletin	ARB
Statements of Financial Accounting Concepts	SFAC
Statements of Financial Accounting Standards	SFAS
Financial Accounting Standards Board Interpretation	FASB I
FASB Technical Bulletin	FASB TB
AICPA Accounting Interpretation	AICPA AIN
Emerging Issues Task Force Issue	EITF
AICPA Audit and Accounting Guide	AICPA AAG
AICPA Statements of Position	SOP

Accounting Research Bulletins (ARB), Accounting Procedures Committee, AICPA (1953-1959)

Number *	*Title*	*Current text reference*	*GAAP Interp. & Applic. page reference*
43	Restatement and Revision of Accounting Research Bulletins Nos. 1-42 (originally issued 1939-1953)		
	Ch. 1 Prior Bulletins	A31, B50, CO8, C23, R36, R70, R75	1, 647
	Ch. 2 Form of Statements	F43	45
	Ch. 3 Working Capital	B05, I78	36, 38, 104, 133, 137, 437, 438
	Ch. 4 Inventory Pricing	I78	187, 192-197, 209, 210, 211, 219
	Ch. 7 Capital Accounts	C20, Q15	682
	Ch. 9 Depreciation	D40	298
	Ch. 10 Taxes	T10	441
	Ch. 11 Government Contracts	Co5	841
	Ch. 12 Foreign Operations and Foreign Exchange	C51, F65	

* *Missing numbers throughout this listing represent pronouncements that have been completely superseded.*

(FASB cont.)

Number	Title	Current text reference	GAAP Interp. & Applic. page reference
48	Revenue Recognition When Right of Return Exists	R75	188, 192, 260, 261
49	Accounting for Product Financing Arrangements	D18	188, 191, 192
50	Financial Reporting in the Record and Music Industry	Re4	884
51	Financial Reporting by Cable Television Companies	Ca4	817
52	Foreign Currency Translation	F60	132, 143, 162, 173, 175, 182, 472, 576, 650, 763, 764, 766, 777, 778, 781, 783, 785
53	Financial Reporting by Producers and Distributors of Motion Picture Films	Mo6	862
54	Financial Reporting and Changing Prices: Investment Companies	C27, In8	
55	Determining Whether a Convertible Security Is a Common Stock Equivalent	E09	
57	Related-Party Disclosures	R36	45, 507, 872
58	Capitalization of Interest Cost in Financial Statements That Include Investments Accounted for by the Equity Method	I67, A35, C51, I82	313
60	Accounting and Reporting by Insurance Enterprises	I42, In6, I25	758, 844, 845
61	Accounting for Title Plant	Ti7	892
62	Capitalization of Interest Cost in Situations Involving Certain Tax-Exempt Borrowings and Certain Gifts and Grants	I67	314
63	Financial Reporting by Broadcasters	Br5	812
64	Extinguishment of Debt Made to Satisfy Sinking Fund Requirements	D14, I17	71, 457
65	Accounting for Certain Mortgage Bank Activities	Mo4	135, 184, 855
66	Accounting for Sales on Real Estate	Re1, R10	264, 265, 267, 268, 271, 273, 274, 278, 279, 282, 287, 290, 291, 321, 493, 512, 513, 527
67	Accounting for Costs and Initial Rental Operations of Real Estate Projects	Re2, R10	282, 323
68	Research and Development Arrangements	R55	320, 321
69	Disclosures About Oil and Gas Producing Activities	C27, I73, Oi5, S20	226, 878
71	Accounting for the Effects of Certain Types of Regulation	Re6	887, 890
72	Accounting for Certain Acquisitions of Banking or Thrift Institutions	B50, Bt7, I60	798, 806, 807, 809, 810

(FASB cont.)

(FASB cont.)

(FASB cont.)

Number	Title	Current text reference	GAAP Interp. & Applic. page reference
114	Accounting by Creditors for Impairment of a Loan	C59, D22, I08, In6	290, 340, 447, 459, 463, 464, 465, 474, 797, 801
115	Accounting for Certain Investments in Debt and Equity Securities	B05, C25, F80, I08, I27, I80, I82, L20, Bt7, In6, Mo4	36, 37, 41, 92, 120, 129, 132, 140, 177, 185, 290, 326, 329-336, 339, 340, 345, 358, 459, 650, 689, 801, 804, 845
116	Accounting for Contributions Received and Contributions Made	C67, No5	643, 869, 875
117	Financial Statements of Not-for-Profit Organizations	C25, No5	85, 834, 869, 871, 872, 880
118	Accounting by Creditors for Impairment of a Loan--Income Recognition and Disclosures	I08	447, 459, 464
119	Disclosure About Derivative Financial Instruments and Fair Value of Financial Instruments (in effect until June 15, 1999)	F25	129, 140, 142, 148, 152, 156, 870
120	Accounting and Reporting by Mutual Life Insurance Enterprises and by Insurance Enterprises for Certain Long-Duration Participating Contracts	In6	844, 846
121	Accounting for the Impairment of Long-Lived Assets and for Long-Lived Assets to Be Disposed of	B50, Ca4, D22, I08, I17, I60, I67, In6, Oi5, R10, Re1, Re2, Re6, Ti7	287, 290, 297, 312, 321, 431, 464, 820, 825, 893
123	Accounting for Stock Compensation	C36, C44, C47, E09, F25	160, 634, 636, 637, 651-652, 656, 660-673, 689
124	Accounting for Certain Investments Held by Not-For-Profit Organizations	No5	326, 329, 869, 873
125	Transfers of Financial Assets and Extinguishment of Liabilities	F35, F38	103, 108, 109, 111, 122, 124, 129, 134, 140, 290, 367, 428, 432, 447, 457, 503, 504, 870

(FASB cont.)

Number	Title	Current text reference	GAAP Interp. & Applic. page reference
126	Exemption From Certain Required Disclosures About Financial Instruments for Certain Nonpublic Entities	F25	129, 331, 345, 870
127	Deferral of the Effective Date of Certain Provisions of FASB Statement 125	F38	103, 108, 130, 448, 870
128	Earnings per Share	E11	13, 72, 419, 694, 696, 697, 698, 710, 712, 742
129	Disclosures of Information About Capital Structure	C24	675, 680, 694, 870
130	Reporting Comprehensive Income	C49	62, 137, 138, 325, 326, 334, 616, 650, 834, 870, 880
131	Disclosures About Segments of Enterprise and Related Information	S30	9, 367, 725, 728, 730, 731, 733-735
132	Employers' Disclosures About Pensions and Other Postretirement Benefits	P16	600, 625-629
133	Accounting for Derivative Instruments and Hedging Activities		127, 140, 142, 146, 151, 154, 781

Financial Accounting Standards Board (FASB) Interpretations (1974-1998)

Number	Title	Current text reference	GAAP Interp. & Applic. page reference
1	Accounting Changes Related to the Cost of Inventory (APB 20)	A06	746
4	Applicability of FASB Statement No. 2 to Purchase Business Combinations	B50	432
6	Applicability of FASB Statement No. 2 to Computer Software	R50	821
7	Applying FASB Statement No. 7 in Statements of Established Enterprises	De4	81
8	Classification of a Short-Term Obligation Repaid Prior to Being Replaced by a Long-Term Security (SFAS 6)	B05	441
9	Applying APB Opinions 16 and 17 When a Savings and Loan or Similar Institution Is Acquired in a Purchase Business Combination (APB 16 and 17)	I60, B50, Bt7	798
14	Reasonable Estimation of the Amount of a Loss (SFAS 5)	C59	114, 444
18	Accounting for Income Taxes in Interim Periods (APB 28)	I73	583, 586, 595
19	Lessee Guarantee of the Residual Value of Leased Property (SFAS 13)	L10	478, 486
20	Reporting Accounting Changes Under AICPA Statements of Position (APB 20)	A06	746

(FASB I cont.)

Number	Title	Current text reference	GAAP Interp. & Applic. page reference
21	Accounting for Leases in a Business Combination (SFAS 13)	L10	478, 501
23	Leases of Certain Property Owned by a Governmental Unit or Authority (SFAS 13)	L10	478, 504
24	Leases Involving Only Part of a Building (SFAS 13)	L10	478, 516
26	Accounting for Purchase of a Leased Asset by the Lessee During the Term of the Lease (SFAS 13)	L10	478
27	Accounting for Loss on a Sublease (SFAS 13 and APB 30)	L10	478
28	Accounting for Stock Appreciation Rights and Other Variable Stock Option or Award Plans (APB 15 and 25)	C47, E09	656-658, 661, 677
30	Accounting for Involuntary Conversions of Nonmonetary Assets to Monetary Assets (APB 29)	N35	309
31	Treatment of Stock Compensation Plans in EPS Computations (APB 15 and FASB I 28)	E09	694
33	Applying FASB Statement No. 34 to Oil and Gas Producing Operations (SFAS 34)	I67	314, 878
35	Criteria for Applying the Equity Method of Accounting for Investments in Common Stock (APB 18)	I82	346, 569
36	Accounting for Exploratory Wells in Progress at the End of a Period	Oi5	878
37	Accounting for Translation Adjustment Upon Sale of Part of an Investment in a Foreign Entity	F60	677, 763, 774
38	Determining the Measurement Date for Stock Option, Purchase, and Award Plans Involving Junior Stock (APB 25)	C47, E09	
39	Offsetting of Amounts Related to Certain Contracts	B10	130, 143, 152, 184, 438
40	Applicability of Generally Accepted Accounting Principles to Mutual Life Insurance and Other Enterprises	A10, I89, In6, Re6	844
41	Offsetting of Amounts Related to Certain Repurchase and Reverse Repurchase Agreements	B10	438
42	Accounting for Transfers of Assets in Which a Not-for-Profit Organization Is Granted Variance Power	C67	870, 875

Financial Accounting Standards Board
FASB Technical Bulletins (1979-1998)

Number	Title	Current text reference	GAAP Interp. & Applic. page reference
79-1	Purpose and Scope of FASB Technical Bulletins and Procedures for Issuance	--	
79-3	Subjective Acceleration Clauses in Long-Term Debt Agreements	B05	448
79-4	Segment Reporting of Puerto Rican Operations	S20	732
79-5	Meaning of the Term "Customer" as It Applies to Health Care Facilities Under FASB Statement No. 14	S20	726

(FASB TB cont.)

Number	Title	Current text reference	GAAP Interp. & Applic. page reference
79-8	Applicability of FASB Statement 21 to Certain Brokers and Dealers in Securities	E09, S20	695
79-9	Accounting in Interim Periods for Changes in Income Tax Rates	I73	718
79-10	Fiscal Funding Clauses in Lease Agreements	L10	523
79-12	Interest Rate Used in Calculating the Present Value of Minimum Lease Payments	L10	523
79-13	Applicability of FASB Statement No. 13 to Current Value Financial Statements	L10	523
79-14	Upward Adjustment of Guaranteed Residual Values	L10	523
79-15	Accounting for Loss on a Sublease Not Involving the Disposal of a Segment	L10	524
79-16	Effect on a Change in Income Tax Rate on the Accounting for Leveraged Leases	L10	525
79-17	Reporting Cumulative Effect Adjustment From Retroactive Application of FASB No. 13	--	524
79-18	Transition Requirements of Certain FASB Amendments and Interpretations of FASB Statement No. 13	--	525
79-19	Investor's Accounting for Unrealized Losses on Marketable Securities Owned by an Equity Method Investee	I82, I89	
80-1	Early Extinguishment of Debt Through Exchange for Common or Preferred Stock	D14	448
80-2	Classification of Debt Restructurings by Debtors and Creditors	D22	459
81-6	Applicability of Statement 15 to Debtors in Bankruptcy Situations	D22	460
82-1	Disclosure of the Sale or Purchase of Tax Benefits Through Tax Leases	I25, I28	525
84-1	Accounting for Stock Issued to Acquire the Results of a Research and Development Arrangement	R55	
85-1	Accounting for the Receipt of Federal Home Loan Mortgage Corporation Participating Preferred Stock	Bt7	798
85-3	Accounting for Operating Leases With Scheduled Rent Increases	L10	485, 491, 526
85-4	Accounting for Purchases of Life Insurance	I50	
85-5	Issues Relating to Accounting for Business Combinations	B50	369, 430
85-6	Accounting for a Purchase of Treasury Shares at a Price Significantly in Excess of the Current Market Price of the Shares and the Income Statement Classification of Costs Incurred in Defending Against a Takeover Attempt	I60, C23, I17	71, 387

(FASB TB cont.)

Number	Issued	Current text reference	GAAP Interp. & Applic. page reference
86-2	Accounting for an Interest in the Residual Value of a Leased Asset: • Acquired by a Third Party or • Retained by a Lessor That Sells the Related Minimum Rental Payments	L10	504, 525, 526
87-2	Computation of a Loss on an Abandonment	I42, Re6	887
87-3	Accounting for Mortgage Servicing Fees and Rights	Mo4	798, 811, 855
88-1	Issues Relating to Accounting for Leases	L10	486, 491, 504
88-2	Definition of a Right of Setoff (Reference APB Opinion No. 10, para 7)	B10	250
90-1	Accounting for Separately Priced Extended Warranty and Product Maintenance Contracts	R75	250
94-1	Application of Statement 115 to Debt Securities in a Troubled Debt Restructuring	I80	130, 132, 340, 465
97-1	Accounting Under Statement 123 for Certain Employee Stock Purchase Plans With a Look-Back Option	C36	671, 689

Financial Accounting Standards Board (FASB) Statements of Financial Accounting Concepts (1978-1998)

	Issued		
1	Objectives of Financial Reporting by Business Enterprises	--	3, 22-24, 85
2	Qualitative Characteristics of Accounting Information	--	3, 24-26
4	Objectives of Financial Reporting by Nonbusiness Organizations	--	
5	Recognition and Measurement in Financial Statements of Business Enterprises		3, 27, 58, 61, 86, 226, 245, 324
6	Elements of Financial Statements	V18	3, 30, 31, 32, 56, 57, 59-62, 130, 324, 455, 535, 540, 541, 633

Emerging Issues Task Force Issues (1984-1998)

Issues Considered by the Emerging Issues Task Force

Issues Grouped by Type

Income taxes	34
Financial institutions	41
Financial instruments	72
Off-balance-sheet financing	6
Pensions/employee benefits	29
Business combinations/new basis	53
Inventory/fixed assets/leases	31
Real estate	15
Other	43
Total	324

Number	Topic	Status	GAAP Interp. & Applic. page reference
	INCOME TAXES (35)		
84-1	Tax Reform Act of 1984; Deferred Income Taxes of Stock Life Insurance Companies	Resolved by FAS 109.	
84-2	Tax Reform Act of 1984; Deferred Income Taxes Relating to Domestic International Sales Corporations	Resolved by FAS 109.	
84-27	Deferred Taxes on Subsidiary Stock Sales	Resolved by FAS 109.	
84-33	Acquisition of a Tax Loss Carryforward--Temporary Parent-Subsidiary Relationship	No resolution. Guidance provided by EITF.	423
84-43	Income Tax Effects of Asset Revaluations in Certain Foreign Countries	Consensus nullified by FAS 109.	
85-5	Restoration of Deferred Taxes Previously Eliminated by Net Operating Loss Recognition	Resolved by FAS 109.	
85-15	Recognizing Benefits of Purchased Net Operating Loss Carryforwards	Consensus nullified by FAS 96 which is superseded by FAS 109.	
86-1	Recognizing Net Operating Loss Carryforwards	Consensus nullified by FAS 109.	
86-3	Retroactive Regulations Regarding IRC Section 338 Purchase Price Allocations	Deemed no longer technically helpful.	
86-4	Income Statement Treatment of Income Tax Benefit for Employee Stock Ownership Plan Dividends	Consensus nullified by FAS 109.	
86-9	IRC Section 338 and Push-Down Accounting	Consensus reached. Additional guidance provided by FAS 109.	580
86-11	Recognition of Possible 1986 Tax Law Changes	Resolved by FAS 109.	
86-33	Tax Indemnifications in Lease Agreements	Consensus reached.	519
86-37	Recognition of Tax Benefit of Discounting Loss Reserves of Insurance Companies	Consensus nullified by FAS 109.	
86-41	Carryforward of the Corporate Alternative Minimum Tax Credit	Consensus nullified by FAS 109. Also see Issue 87-8.	
86-42	Effect of a Change in Tax Rates on Assets and Liabilities Recorded Net-of-Tax in a Purchase Business Combination	Consensus nullified by FAS 109.	
86-43	Effect of a Change in Tax Law or Rates on Leveraged Leases	Consensus reached. See Issue 87-8.	530, 580
86-44	Effect of a Change in Tax Law on Investments in Safe Harbor Leases	Consensus reached.	580
86-46	Uniform Capitalization Rules for Inventory Under the Tax Reform Act of 1986	Consensus reached.	194

(*EITF cont.*)

(EITF cont.)

Number	Topic	Status	GAAP Interp. & Applic. page reference
95-10	Accounting for Tax Credits Related to Dividend Payments in Accordance With FASB Statement No. 109	Consensus reached.	582
95-20	Measurement in the Consolidated Financial Statements of a Parent of the Tax Effects Related to the Operations of a Foreign Subsidiary That Receives Tax Credits Related to Dividend Payments	Consensus reached.	582
	FINANCIAL INSTITUTIONS (38)		
84-4	Acquisition, Development, and Construction Loans	Resolved by AICPA *Notice to Practitioners*, issued 2/10/86.	805
84-9	Deposit Float of Banks	Partial consensus reached.	805
84-19	Mortgage Loan Payment Modifications	Consensus reached.	805
84-20	GNMA Dollar Rolls	Partial consensus reached. Remaining issues resolved by AICPA Statement of Position 85-2, which has been incorporated in the AICPA *Guide on Savings Institutions*. After 12/31/97, Issue partially resolved by FAS 125.	805
84-21	Sale of a Loan With a Partial Participation Retained	Resolved by FAS 125.	805
84-22	Prior Years' Earnings per Share Following a Savings and Loan Association Conversion and Pooling	No resolution. Guidance provided by EITF.	805
84-31	Equity Certificates of Deposit	No resolution. Guidance provided by EITF.	806
85-3	Tax Benefits Relating to Asset Dispositions Following an Acquisition of a Financial Institution	Consensus nullified by FAS 109.	
85-7	Federal Home Loan Mortgage Corporation Stock	Resolved by FTB 85-1.	806
85-8	Amortization of Thrift Intangibles	Consensus reached. Additional guidance provided by SEC.	806
85-13	Sale of Mortgage Service Rights on Mortgages Owned by Others	Consensus reached.	806

(EITF cont.)

Number	Topic	Status	GAAP Interp. & Applic. page reference
87-5	Troubled Debt Restructurings: Interrelationship Between FASB Statement No. 15 and the AICPA Savings and Loan Guide	Consensus nullified by FAS 114.	
87-22	Prepayments to the Secondary Reserve of the FSLIC	Consensus reached.	808
87-34	Sale of Mortgage Servicing Rights With a Subservicing Agreement	Consensus reached.	808
88-17	Accounting for Fees and Costs Associated With Loan Syndications and Loan Participations	Consensus partially nullified by FAS 125.	809
88-19	FSLIC-Assisted Acquisitions of Thrifts	Consensus affected by FAS 109. Additional guidance provided by SEC *Staff Accounting Bulletin No. 82*.	809
88-20	Difference Between Initial Investment and Principal Amount of Loans in a Purchased Credit Card Portfolio	Consensus reached. Disclosure guidance in Issue 92-5.	809
88-25	Ongoing Accounting and Reporting for a Newly Created Liquidating Bank	Consensus reached. Additional guidance provided by SEC *Staff Accounting Bulletin No. 82*.	810
89-3	Balance Sheet Presentation of Savings Accounts in Financial Statements of Credit Unions	Consensus reached.	810
89-9	Accounting for In-Substance Foreclosures	Consensus affected by FAS 114.	473, 810
90-11	Accounting for Exit and Entrance Fees Incurred in a Conversion From the Savings Association Insurance Fund to the Bank Insurance Fund	Deemed no longer technically helpful.	
90-21	Balance Sheet Treatment of a Sale of Mortgage Servicing Rights With a Subservicing Agreement	Consensus reached. Additional guidance provided by SEC.	811
92-5	Amortization Period for Net Deferred Credit Card Origination Costs	Consensus reached.	811
92-10	Loan Acquisitions Involving Table Funding Arrangements	Consensus nullified by FAS 125.	
97-3	Accounting for Fees and Costs Associated With Loan Syndications and Loan Participations After the Issuance of FASB Statement No. 125, *Accounting for Transfers and Servicing of Financial Assets and Extinguishment of Liabilities*	Consensus reached.	125

(EITF cont.)

Number	Topic	Status	GAAP Interp. & Applic. page reference
	FINANCIAL INSTRUMENTS (86)		
84-3	Convertible Debt "Sweeteners"	Resolved by FAS 84.	
84-5	Sale of Marketable Securities With a Put Option	Consensus reached. See Issue 85-40.	361
84-7	Termination of Interest Rate Swaps	Consensus reached.	182
84-8	Variable Stock Purchase Warrants Given by Suppliers to Customers	Affected by FAS 123. See Issue 96-3.	
84-14	Deferred Interest Rate Setting	Consensus reached.	182
84-16	Earnings per Share Cash-Yield Test for Zero Coupon Bonds	Resolved by FAS 85.	
84-36	Interest Rate Swap Transactions	Partial consensus reached.	
84-40	Long-Term Debt Repayable by a Capital Stock Transaction	Consensus reached on Issue 1. Issue 2 resolved by SEC.	
85-6	Futures Implementation Questions	Resolved by FASB. See FASB *Highlights*, issued 6/85.	
85-9	Revenue Recognition on Options to Purchase Stock of Another Entity	Partial consensus reached. To be addressed in FASB project on financial instruments.	179
85-17	Accrued Interest Upon Conversion of Convertible Debt	Consensus reached.	472
85-23	Effect of a Redemption Agreement on Carrying Value of a Security	No resolution. Guidance provided by FASB staff. Affected by FAS 115.	
85-25	Sale of Preferred Stocks With a Put Option	Consensus partially nullified by FAS 125. See Issue 85-40. Affected by FAS 115.	684
85-28	Consolidation Issues Relating to Collateralized Mortgage Obligations	Resolved by FAS 94.	424
85-29	Convertible Bonds With a "Premium Put"	Consensus reached.	179
85-30	Sale of Marketable Securities at a Gain With a Put Option	Resolved by FAS 125. See Issue 85-40.	
85-34	Bankers' Acceptances and Risk Participations	Resolved by SEC and FAS 125.	
85-38	Negative Amortizing Loans	Deemed no longer technically helpful.	
85-39	Implications of SEC Staff Accounting Bulletin No. 59 on Noncurrent Marketable Equity Securities	Resolved by SEC.	

(EITF cont.)

(EITF cont.)

(EITF cont.)

Number	Topic	Status	GAAP Interp. & Applic. page reference
89-18	Divestitures of Certain Investment Securities to an Unregulated Commonly Controlled Entity Under FIRREA	Consensus affected by FAS 115.	185
90-2	Exchange of Interest-Only and Principal-Only Securities for a Mortgage-Backed Security	Consensus nullified by FAS 125.	
90-17	Hedging Foreign Currency Risks With Purchased Options	Consensus reached.	181
90-18	Effect of a "Removal of Accounts" Provision on the Accounting for a Credit Card Securitization	Consensus reached. Impact of FAS 125 on consensus pending.	811
90-19	Convertible Bonds With Issuer Option to Settle for Cash Upon Conversion	Consensus reached.	473
91-1	Hedging Intercompany Foreign Currency Risks	Consensus reached. Additional guidance in Issue 95-2.	783
91-4	Hedging Foreign Currency Risks With Complex Options and Similar Transactions	Guidance provided by SEC. Disclosure requirements of the consensus nullified by FAS 119.	
93-10	Accounting for Dual Currency Bonds	Resolved by SEC.	
93-18	Recognition of Impairment for an Investment in a Collateralized Mortgage Obligation Instrument or in a Mortgage-Backed Interest-Only Certificate	Consensus reached.	362
94-4	Classification of an Investment in a Mortgage-Backed Interest-Only Certificate as Held-to-Maturity	Resolved by FAS 125.	362
94-5	Determination of What Constitutes All Risks and Rewards and No Significant Unresolved Contingencies in a Sale of Mortgage Loan Servicing Rights Under Issue No. 89-5	Consensus rescinded. See Issue 95-5 for consensus reached on this issue. (95-5 states consensus reached.)	
94-7	Accounting for Financial Instruments Indexed to, and Potentially Settled in, a Company's Own Stock	Issue codified in Issue 96-13.	
94-8	Accounting for Conversion of a Loan Into a Debt Security in a Debt Restructuring	Consensus reached.	474
94-9	Determining a Normal Servicing Fee Rate for the Sale of an SBA Loan	Consensus nullified by FAS 125.	
95-2	Determination of What Constitutes a Firm Commitment for Foreign Currency Transactions Not Involving a Third Party	Consensus reached.	784

(EITF cont.)

Number	*Topic*	*Status*	*GAAP Interp. & Applic. page reference*
95-5	Determination of What Risks and Rewards, If Any, Can Be Retained and Whether Any Unresolved Contingencies May Exist in a Sale of Mortgage Loan Servicing Rights	Consensus reached.	185
95-11	Accounting for Derivative Instruments Containing Both a Written Option-Based Component and a Forward-Based Component	No resolution. May be addressed in FASB project on accounting for derivatives and hedging.	
95-13	Classification of Debt Issue Costs in the Statement of Cash Flows	Consensus reached.	102
95-15	Recognition of Gain or Loss When a Binding Contract Requires a Debt Extinguishment to Occur at a Future Date for a Specified Amount	Consensus reached.	474
96-1	Sale of Put Options on Issuer's Stock That Require or Permit Cash Settlement	Issue codified in Issue 96-13.	689
96-2	Impairment Recognition When a Nonmonetary Asset Is Exchanged or Is Distributed to Owners and Is Accounted for at the Asset's Recorded Amount	No resolution. To be addressed in FASB project on implementation issues related to FAS 121.	
96-3	Accounting for Equity Instruments That Are Issued for Consideration Other Than Employee Services Under FASB Statement No. 123	Superseded by Issue 96-18.	689
96-10	Impact of Certain Transactions on the Held-to-Maturity Classification Under FASB Statement No. 115	Consensus partially nullified by FAS 125.	
96-11	Accounting for Forward Contracts and Purchased Options to Acquire Securities Covered by FASB Statement No. 115	Consensus reached.	180
96-12	Recognition of Interest Income and Balance Sheet Classification of Structured Notes	Consensus reached.	180
96-13	Accounting for Derivative Financial Instruments Indexed to, and Potentially Settled in, a Company's Own Stock	Codifies Issues 87-13, 94-7, and 96-1. Consensuses reached. Partially resolved by FAS 128.	185
96-15	Accounting for the Effects of Changes in Foreign Currency Exchange Rates on Foreign-Currency-Denominated Available-for-Sale Debt Securities	Consensus reached.	180
96-18	Accounting for Equity Instruments With Variable Terms That Are Issued for Consideration Other Than Employee Services Under FASB Statement No. 123	Further discussion pending.	

(*EITF cont.*)

Number	Topic	Status	GAAP Interp. & Applic. page reference
96-22	Applicability of the Disclosures Required by FASB Statement No. 114 When a Loan Is Restructed in a Troubled Debt Restructuring Into Two (or More) Loans	Consensus reached.	474
97-5	Accounting for Delayed Receipt of Option Shares Upon Exercise Under APB Opinion No. 25, *Accounting for Stock Issued to Employees*	Resolved by FASB staff.	
97-7	Accounting for Hedges of Foreign Currency Risk Inherent in an Available-for-Sale Marketable Equity Security	Consensus reached.	363
98-5	Accounting for Convertible Securities With Beneficial Conversion Features or Contingently Adjustable Conversion Ratios	Further discussion pending.	475
98-7	Accounting for Exchanges of Similar Equity Method Investments	Further discussion pending.	363
98-12	Application of EITF Issue No. 96-13, *Accounting for Derivative Financial Instruments Indexed to, and Potentially Settled in, a Company's Own Stock*, to Certain Derivative Financial Instruments Issued With Other Instruments	Further discussion pending.	
	OFF-BALANCE-SHEET FINANCING (13)		
84-11	Offsetting Installment Note Receivables and Bank Debt ("Note Monetization")	Resolved by FIN 39.	472
84-15	Grantor Trusts Consolidation	Partially resolved by FTB 85-2.	
84-23	Leveraged Buyout Holding Company Debt	Guidance provided by SEC *Staff Accounting Bulletin No. 73*. Disclosure guidance provided by FAS 105. To be addressed in FASB project on consolidations.	
84-25	Offsetting Nonrecourse Debt With Sales-Type or Direct Financing Lease Receivables	Resolved by FTB 86-2 and SEC *Staff Accounting Bulletin No. 70*.	
84-26	Defeasance of Special-Purpose Borrowings	Resolved by FAS 125.	
84-30	Sales of Loans to Special-Purpose Entities	Disclosure guidance provided by SEC. To be addressed in FASB project on consolidations.	

(EITF cont.)

Number	Topic	Status	GAAP Interp. & Applic. page reference
84-41	Consolidation of Subsidiary After Instantaneous In-Substance Defeasance	Resolved by FAS 94.	
84-42	Push-Down of Parent Company Debt to a Subsidiary	Guidance provided by SEC *Staff Accounting Bulletin No. 73*. To be addressed in FASB project on consolidations.	
85-11	Use of an Employee Stock Ownership Plan in a Leveraged Buyout	No resolution.	
85-16	Leveraged Leases	Consensus reached. Partially resolved by FAS 98.	518
86-36	Invasion of a Defeasance Trust	Consensus reached.	472
87-7	Sale of an Asset Subject to a Lease and Nonrecourse Financing: "Wrap Lease Transactions"	Consensus reached. Partially resolved by FTB 88-1.	519
91-10	Accounting for Tax Increment Financing Entities and Special Assessments	Consensus reached.	322
	PENSION/EMPLOYEE BENEFITS (32)		
84-6	Termination of Defined Benefit Pension Plans	Consensus nullified by FAS 88.	
84-18	Stock Option Pyramiding	Consensus reached.	684
84-34	Permanent Discount Restricted Stock Purchase Plans	No resolution.	
84-44	Partial Termination of a Defined Benefit Pension Plan	Resolved by FAS 88.	
85-10	Employee Stock Ownership Plan Contribution Funded by a Pension Plan Termination	Consensus nullified by FAS 88.	
86-19	Change in Accounting for Other Postemployment Benefits	Resolved by FAS 106.	
86-27	Measurement of Excess Contributions to a Defined Contribution Plan or Employee Stock Ownership Plan	Consensus partially nullified by AICPA Statement of Position 93-6. See SOP 93-6 for transition provisions.	
87-13	Amortization of Prior Service Cost for a Defined Benefit Plan When There Is a History of Plan Amendments	Resolved by FAS 87 Q&A.	

(EITF cont.)

Number	Topic	Status	GAAP Interp. & Applic. page reference
87-23	Book Value Stock Purchase Plans	Consensus reached. Consensus on Issue 3 nullified by AICPA Statement of Position 93-6. See SOP 93-6 for transition provisions. Also see Issue 88-6.	676, 686
87-33	Stock Compensation Issues Related to Market Decline	Consensus reached.	686, 688
88-1	Determination of Vested Benefit Obligation for a Defined Benefit Pension Plan	Consensus reached.	631
88-5	Recognition of Insurance Death Benefits	Consensus reached on first issue. Second issue resolved by FAS 96 Q&A and by FAS 109 which superseded FAS 96.	631
88-6	Book Value Stock Plans in an Initial Public Offering	Consensus reached.	676, 686
88-23	Lump-Sum Payments Under Union Contracts	Consensus reached.	473
89-1	Accounting by a Pension Plan for Bank Investment Contracts and Guaranteed Investment Contracts	Resolved by FAS 110 and AICPA Statement of Position 94-4.	
89-8	Expense Recognition for Employee Stock Ownership Plans	Consensus nullified by AICPA Statement of Position 93-6. See SOP 93-6 for transition provisions.	
89-10	Sponsor's Recognition of Employee Stock Ownership Plan Debt	Consensus nullified by AICPA Statement of Position 93-6. See SOP 93-6 for transition provisions.	
89-11	Sponsor's Balance Sheet Classification of Capital Stock With a Put Option Held by an Employee Stock Ownership Plan	Consensus reached.	687
89-12	Earnings per Share Issues Related to Convertible Preferred Stock Held by an Employee Stock Ownership Plan	Consensus nullified by AICPA Statement of Position 93-6. See SOP 93-6 for transition provisions.	
90-3	Accounting for Employers' Obligations for Future Contributions to a Multiemployer Pension Plan	Consensus reached.	631

(EITF cont.)

Number	Topic	Status	GAAP Interp. & Applic. page reference
90-4	Earnings-per-Share Treatment of Tax Benefits for Dividends on Stock Held by an Employee Stock Ownership Plan	Partial consensus reached and partially nullified by FAS 128. Additional guidance in Issue 92-3.	
90-7	Accounting for a Reload Stock Option	Consensus reached.	687
90-9	Changes to Fixed Employee Stock Option Plans as a Result of Restructuring	Consensus reached.	687
91-7	Accounting for Pension Benefits Paid by Employers After Insurance Companies Fail to Provide Annuity Benefits	Consensus reached.	631
92-3	Earnings per Share Treatment of Tax Benefits for Dividends on Unallocated Stock Held by an Employee Stock Ownership Plan (Consideration of the Implications of FASB Statement 109 on Issue 2 of EITF Issue No. 90-4)	Consensus affected by AICPA Statement of Position 93-6.	711
92-12	Accounting for OPEB Costs by Rate-Regulated Enterprises	Consensus reached. Additional guidance provided by FAS 121.	891
92-13	Accounting for Estimated Payments in Connection With the Coal Industry Retiree Health Benefit Act of 1992	Consensus reached.	632
93-3	Plan Assets Under FASB Statement No. 106	Consensus reached.	632
94-6	Accounting for the Buyout of Compensatory Stock Options	Consensus reached.	688
95-16	Accounting for Stock Compensation Arrangements With Employer Loan Features Under APB Opinion No. 5	Consensus reached.	688
97-12	Accounting for Increased Share Authorizations in an IRS Section 423 Employee Purchase Plan Under APB Opinion 25, *Accounting for Stock Issued to Employees*	Consensus reached.	
97-14	Accounting for Deferred Compensation Arrangements Where Amounts Earned Are Held in a Rabbi Trust and Invested	Further discussion pending.	689

BUSINESS COMBINATIONS (49)

Number	Topic	Status	GAAP Interp. & Applic. page reference
84-13	Purchase of Stock Options and Stock Appreciation Rights in a Leveraged Buyout	Consensus reached.	386, 423, 424
84-35	Business Combinations: Sale of Duplicate Facilities and Accrual of Liabilities	Partially resolved by FAS 87, FAS 106, FTB 85-5, and SEC *Staff Accounting Bulletin No. 61*.	

(EITF cont.)

Number	Topic	Status	GAAP Interp. & Applic. page reference
84-38	Identical Common Shares for a Pooling of Interests	Consensus nullified by FTB 85-5.	
85-2	Classification of Costs Incurred in a Takeover Defense	Consensus nullified by FTB 85-6.	
85-4	Downstream Mergers and Other Stock Transactions Between Companies Under Common Control	Resolved by FTB 85-5.	
85-14	Securities That Can Be Acquired for Cash in a Pooling of Interests	Consensus reached.	424
85-21	Changes in Ownership Resulting in a New Basis of Accounting	To be addressed in FASB project on consolidations.	
85-45	Business Combinations: Settlement of Stock Options and Awards	Partial consensus reached.	386, 424
86-10	Pooling With 10 Percent Cash Payout Determined by Lottery	Consensus reached.	424
86-14	Purchased Research and Development Projects in a Business Combination	Resolved by FASB.	
86-16	Carryover of Predecessor Cost in Leveraged Buyout Transactions	Consensus superseded by Issue 88-16.	
86-20	Accounting for Other Postemployment Benefits of an Acquired Company	Consensus nullified by FAS 106.	
86-31	Reporting the Tax Implications of a Pooling of a Bank and a Savings and Loan Association	Consensus reached. Additional guidance provided by FAS 96 which is superseded by FAS 109.	808
87-11	Allocation of Purchase Price to Assets to Be Sold	Consensus reached.	385, 425
87-15	Effect of a Standstill Agreement on Pooling-of-Interests Accounting	Consensus reached.	425
87-16	Whether the 90 Percent Test for a Pooling of Interests Is Applied Separately to Each Company or on a Combined Basis	Consensus reached.	375, 425
87-21	Change of Accounting Basis in Master Limited Partnership Transactions	Consensus reached.	426
87-27	Poolings of Companies That Do Not Have a Controlling Class of Common Stock	Consensus reached.	426
88-14	Settlement of Fees With Extra Units to a General Partner in a Master Limited Partnership	No resolution. Related issues addressed in AICPA Statement of Position 92-1.	
88-16	Basis in Leveraged Buyout Transactions	Consensus reached.	413, 426
88-26	Controlling Preferred Stock in a Pooling of Interests	Consensus reached.	374, 426

(EITF cont.)

Number	Topic	Status	GAAP Interp. & Applic. page reference
	FINANCIAL INSTRUMENTS (86)		
84-3	Convertible Debt "Sweeteners"	Resolved by FAS 84.	
84-5	Sale of Marketable Securities With a Put Option	Consensus reached. See Issue 85-40.	361
84-7	Termination of Interest Rate Swaps	Consensus reached.	182
84-8	Variable Stock Purchase Warrants Given by Suppliers to Customers	Affected by FAS 123. See Issue 96-3.	
84-14	Deferred Interest Rate Setting	Consensus reached.	182
84-16	Earnings per Share Cash-Yield Test for Zero Coupon Bonds	Resolved by FAS 85.	
84-36	Interest Rate Swap Transactions	Partial consensus reached.	
84-40	Long-Term Debt Repayable by a Capital Stock Transaction	Consensus reached on Issue 1. Issue 2 resolved by SEC.	
85-6	Futures Implementation Questions	Resolved by FASB. See FASB *Highlights*, issued 6/85.	
85-9	Revenue Recognition on Options to Purchase Stock of Another Entity	Partial consensus reached. To be addressed in FASB project on financial instruments.	179
85-17	Accrued Interest Upon Conversion of Convertible Debt	Consensus reached.	472
85-23	Effect of a Redemption Agreement on Carrying Value of a Security	No resolution. Guidance provided by FASB staff. Affected by FAS 115.	
85-25	Sale of Preferred Stocks With a Put Option	Consensus partially nullified by FAS 125. See Issue 85-40. Affected by FAS 115.	684
85-28	Consolidation Issues Relating to Collateralized Mortgage Obligations	Resolved by FAS 94.	424
85-29	Convertible Bonds With a "Premium Put"	Consensus reached.	179
85-30	Sale of Marketable Securities at a Gain With a Put Option	Resolved by FAS 125. See Issue 85-40.	
85-34	Bankers' Acceptances and Risk Participations	Resolved by SEC and FAS 125.	
85-38	Negative Amortizing Loans	Deemed no longer technically helpful.	
85-39	Implications of SEC Staff Accounting Bulletin No. 59 on Noncurrent Marketable Equity Securities	Resolved by SEC.	

(EITF cont.)

(EITF cont.)

Number	Topic	Status	GAAP Interp. & Applic. page reference
	INVENTORY/FIXED ASSETS/LEASES (31)		
84-10	LIFO Conformity of Companies Relying on Insilco Tax Court Decision	Guidance provided by AICPA Issues Paper on LIFO Accounting, issued 11/30/84.	
84-12	Operating Leases With Scheduled Rent Increases	Consensus nullified by FTB 85-3. Additional guidance provided by FTB 88-1.	
84-24	LIFO Accounting Issues	Resolved by SEC *Staff Accounting Bulletin No. 58.*	
84-28	Impairment of Long-Lived Assets	Resolved by FAS 121.	
84-29	Gain and Loss Recognition on Exchanges of Productive Assets and the Effect of Boot	Resolved by Issue 86-29.	
84-37	Sale-Leaseback Transaction With Repurchase Option	Partially resolved by FAS 98.	
85-32	Purchased Lease Residuals	Consensus nullified by FTB 86-2.	
86-13	Recognition of Inventory Market Declines at Interim Reporting Dates	Consensus reached.	732
86-17	Deferred Profit on Sale-Leaseback Transaction With Lessee Guarantee of Residual Value	Consensus reached. Affected by FAS 98.	518
86-29	Nonmonetary Transactions: Magnitude of Boot and the Exceptions to the Use of Fair Value	Consensus reached. See Issue 87-29.	307, 321, 424
88-10	Costs Associated With Lease Modification or Termination	Partial consensus reached. Also see FTB 88-1.	519
88-21	Accounting for the Sale of Property Subject to the Seller's Preexisting Lease	Consensus reached.	519
89-7	Exchange of Assets or Interest in a Subsidiary for a Noncontrolling Equity Interest in a New Entity	Consensus reached.	427
89-16	Consideration of Executory Costs in Sale-Leaseback Transactions	Consensus reached.	509, 520
89-17	Accounting for the Retail Sale of an Extended Warranty Contract in Connection With the Sale of a Product	Consensus nullified by FTB 90-1.	
89-20	Accounting for Cross Border Tax Benefit Leases	Consensus reached.	520
90-14	Unsecured Guarantee by Parent of Subsidiary's Lease Payment in a Sale-Leaseback Transaction	Consensus reached.	520

(EITF cont.)

(EITF cont.)

OTHER (45)

(EITF cont.)

Number	Topic	Status	GAAP Interp. & Applic. page reference
85-12	Retention of Specialized Accounting for Investments in Consolidation	Consensus reached.	423
85-22	Retroactive Application of FASB Technical Bulletins	Deemed no longer technically helpful.	
85-35	Transition and Implementation Issues for FASB Statement No. 86	Resolved by FASB. See FASB *Highlights*, issued 2/86.	
85-36	Discontinued Operations With Expected Gain and Interim Operating Losses	Consensus reached. Partially resolved by FAS 121.	81
85-46	Partnership's Purchase of Withdrawing Partner's Equity	No resolution.	
86-2	Retroactive Wage Adjustments Affecting Medicare Payments	Deemed no longer technically helpful.	445
86-12	Accounting by Insureds for Claims-Made Insurance Policies	Consensus reached.	
86-22	Display of Business Restructuring Provisions in the Income Statement	Resolved by SEC *Staff Accounting Bulletin No. 67.*	
87-4	Restructuring of Operations: Implications of SEC *Staff Accounting Bulletin No. 67*	Consensus reached.	82
87-6	Adjustments Relating to Stock Compensation Plans	Consensus reached.	685
87-10	Revenue Recognition by Television "Barter" Syndicators	Consensus reached.	859
87-17	Spin-Offs or Other Distributions of Loans Receivable to Shareholders	Consensus reached.	425
87-24	Allocation of Interest to Discontinued Operations	Consensus reached.	82
88-3	Rental Concessions Provided by Landlord	Partially resolved by FTB 88-1 and Issues 88-10 and 94-3.	
88-15	Classification of Subsidiary's Loan Payable in Consolidated Balance Sheet When Subsidiary's and Parent's Fiscal Years Differ	No resolution. May be addressed in FASB project on consolidations.	
88-18	Sales of Future Revenues	Consensus reached.	472
89-2	Maximum Maturity Guarantees on Transfers of Receivables With Recourse	Consensus nullified by SFAS 125.	
89-13	Accounting for the Cost of Asbestos Removal	Consensus reached.	321
90-8	Capitalization of Costs to Treat Environmental Contamination	Consensus reached.	
90-16	Accounting for Discontinued Operations Subsequently Retained	Consensus affected by FAS 121.	82

(EITF cont.)

Number	Topic	Status	GAAP Interp. & Applic. page reference
90-22	Accounting for Gas-Balancing Arrangements	No resolution. Referred to AICPA industry group for consideration.	
91-6	Revenue Recognition of Long-Term Power Sales Contracts	Consensus reached.	242
91-9	Revenue and Expense Recognition for Freight Services in Process	Consensus reached.	244, 250
92-2	Measuring Loss Accruals by Transferors for Transfers of Receivables With Recourse	Consensus reached. Additional guidance provided by SEC. Issue affected by FAS 125.	103, 125
92-4	Accounting for a Change in Functional Currency When an Economy Ceases to Be Considered Highly Inflationary	Consensus reached.	783
92-7	Accounting by Rate-Regulated Utilities for the Effects of Certain Alternative Revenue Programs	Consensus reached.	891
93-5	Accounting for Environmental Liabilities	Consensus incorporated in and nullified by AICPA Statement of Position 96-1.	476
93-6	Accounting for Multiple-Year Retrospectively-Rated Contracts by Ceding and Assuming Enterprises	Consensus reached.	848
93-11	Accounting for Barter Transactions Involving Barter Credits	Consensus affected by FAS 121.	322
93-14	Accounting for Multiple-Year Retrospectively-Rated Insurance Contracts by Insurance Enterprises and Other Enterprises	Consensus reached.	849
94-3	Liability Recognition for Certain Employee Termination Benefits and Other Costs to Exit an Activity (Including Certain Costs Incurred in a Restructuring)	Consensus reached.	429
95-18	Accounting and Reporting for a Discontinued Business Segment When the Measurement Date Occurs After the Balance Sheet Date but Before the Issuance of Financial Statements	Consensus reached.	83
95-22	Balance Sheet Classification of Borrowings Outstanding Under Revolving Credit Agreements That Include Both a Subjective Acceleration Clause and a Lock-Box Arrangement	Consensus reached.	446, 838
96-4	Accounting for Reorganizations Involving a Non-Pro Rata Split-off of Certain Nonmonetary Assets to Owners	Consensus reached.	431

(*EITF cont.*)

Number	Topic	Status	GAAP Interp. & Applic. page reference
96-6	Accounting for the Film and Software Costs Associated With Developing Entertainment and Educational Software Products	Guidance provided by SEC.	
96-9	Classification of Inventory Markdowns and Other Costs Associated With a Restructuring	Guidance provided by SEC.	
96-14	Accounting for the Costs Associated With Modifying Computer Software for the Year 2000	Consensus reached.	323
96-17	Revenue Recognition Under Long-Term Power Sales Contracts That Contain Both Fixed and Variable Pricing Terms	Consensus reached.	242
96-19	Debtor's Accounting for a Substantive Modification and Exchange of Debt Instruments	Further discussion pending.	
97-4	Deregulation of the Pricing of Electricity--Issues Related to the Application of FASB Statement No. 71, *Accounting for the Effects of Certain Types of Regulation*, and No. 101, *Regulated Enterprises--Accounting for the Discontinuation of the Application of FASB Statement No. 71*	Consensus reached.	
97-13	Accounting for Costs Incurred in Connection With a Consulting Contract or an Internal Project That Combines Business Process Reengineering and Information Technology Transformation	Consensus reached.	833
98-2	Accounting by a Subsidiary for an Investment in Its Parent Company's Stock	Further discussion pending.	434, 689
98-10	Accounting for Energy Trading and Risk Management Activities	Further discussion pending.	

EITF DISCUSSION OF TECHNICAL MATTERS

Listed below are EITF documents that contain discussion by the Emerging Issues Task Force of technical matters that have long-term relevance and do not relate specifically to a numbered EITF Issue.

- D-1 Implications and Implementation of an EITF Consensus
- D-2 Applicability of FASB Statement No. 65 to Savings and Loan Associations
- D-4 Argentine Government Guarantee of US Dollar-Denominated Loans to the Argentine Private Sector
- D-5 Extraordinary Treatment Related to Abandoned Nuclear Power Plants
- D-8 Accruing Bad-Debt Expense at Inception of a Lease
- D-10 Required Use of Interest Method in Recognizing Interest Income
- D-11 Impact of Stock Market Decline
- D-12 Foreign Currency Translation--Selection of Exchange Rate When Trading Is Temporarily Suspended

Number	Topic
D-14	Transactions Involving Special-Purpose Entities
D-15	Earnings-per-Share Presentation for Securities Not Specifically Covered by APB Opinion No. 15
D-16	Hedging Foreign Currency Risks of Future Net Income, Revenues, or Costs
D-18	Accounting for Compensation Expense If Stock Appreciation Rights Are Cancelled
D-19	Impact on Pooling-of-Interests Accounting of Treasury Shares Acquired to Satisfy Conversions in a Leveraged Preferred Stock ESOP
D-21	Phase-in Plans When Two Plants Are Completed at Different Times But Share Common Facilities
D-22	Questions Related to the Implementation of FASB Statement No. 105
D-23	Subjective Acceleration Clauses and Debt Classification
D-24	Sale-Leaseback Transactions With Continuing Involvement
D-27	Accounting for the Transfer of Excess Pension Assets to a Retiree Health Care Benefits Account
D-30	Adjustment Due to Effect of a Change in Tax Laws or Rates
D-31	Temporary Differences Related to LIFO Inventory and Tax-to-Tax Differences
D-32	Intraperiod Tax Allocation of the Tax Effect of Pretax Income From Continuing Operations
D-33	Timing of Recognition of Tax Benefits for Pre-reorganization Temporary Differences and Carryforwards
D-34	Accounting for Reinsurance: Questions and Answers About FASB Statement No. 113
D-35	FASB Staff Views on Issue No. 93-6, *Accounting for Multiple-Year Retrospectively-Rated Contracts by Ceding and Assuming Enterprises*
D-36	Selection of Discount Rates Used for Measuring Defined Benefit Pension Obligations and Obligations of Postretirement Benefit Plans Other Than Pensions
D-39	Questions Related to the Implementation of FASB Statement No. 115
D-40	Planned Sale of Securities Following a Business Combination Expected to Be Accounted for as a Pooling of Interests
D-41	Adjustments in Assets and Liabilities for Holding Gains and Losses as Related to the Implementation of FASB Statement No. 115
D-42	The Effect on the Calculation of Earnings per Share for the Redemption or Induced Conversion of Preferred Stock
D-43	Assurance That a Right of Setoff Is Enforceable in a Bankruptcy Under FASB Interpretation No. 39
D-44	Recognition of Other-Than-Temporary Impairment Upon the Planned Sale of a Security Whose Cost Exceeds Fair Value
D-45	Implementation of FASB Statement No. 121 for Assets to Be Disposed Of
D-46	Accounting for Limited Partnership Investments
D-47	Accounting for the Refund of Bank Insurance Fund and Savings Association Insurance Fund Premiums

AICPA STATEMENTS OF POSITION (1974-1998)

(SOP cont.)

Audit and Accounting Guides

Agricultural Producers and Agricultural Cooperatives
Airlines
Banks and Savings Institutions
Brokers and Dealers in Securities
Casinos
Certain Nonprofit Organizations
Colleges and Universities
Common Interest Realty Associations
Construction Contractors
Credit Unions
Employee Benefit Plans
Entities With Oil and Gas Producing Activities
Federal Government Contractors
Finance Companies
Health Care Organizations
Investment Companies
Not-for-Profit Organizations
Personal Financial Statements Guide
Property and Liability Insurance Companies
State and Local Governmental Units
Voluntary Health and Welfare Organizations

OTHER GAAP SOURCES

Issues Papers of the Accounting Standards Division

Issues Papers of the AICPA's Accounting Standards Division primarily identify financial accounting and reporting issues that the Division believed needed addressing by the Financial Accounting Standards Board. These pronouncements constitute generally accepted accounting principles but are not mandatory.

Title	*Date Issued*
Accounting for Changes in Estimates	12/15/78
Joint Venture Accounting	7/17/79
Certain Issues That Affect Accounting for Minority Interest in Consolidated Financial Statements	3/17/81
Depreciation of Income Producing Real Estate	11/16/81
Accounting by Stock Life Insurance Companies for Annuities, Universal Life, and Related Products and Accounting for Nonguaranteed-Premium Products	11/5/84
Identification and Discussion of Certain Financial Accounting and Reporting Issues Concerning LIFO Inventories	11/30/84
Quasi Reorganizations	10/28/88

Practice Bulletins

1. Purpose and Scope of AcSEC Practice Bulletins and Procedures for Their Issuance

Title	*Date Issued*
ACRS Lives and GAAP	11/23/81
Accounting by Colleges and Universities for Compensated Absences	9/13/82
Mortgage Banking Activities	6/27/83
Interest as a Holding Cost	10/10/83
Bank Loan Disclosures	12/26/83
Accounting and Disclosures for Reinsurance Transactions	1/23/84
Deposit Float	9/24/84
Accounting for Foreign Loan Swaps	5/27/85
ADC Arrangements	2/10/86

2.	Elimination of Profits Resulting From Intercompany Transfers of LIFO Inventories	11/87
4.	Accounting for Foreign Debt/Equity Swaps	5/88
5.	Income Recognition on Loans to Financially Troubled Countries	7/88
6.	Amortization of Discounts on Certain Acquired Loans	8/89
8.	Application of FASB Statement 97 to Insurance Enterprises	11/90
11.	Accounting for Preconfirmation Contingencies in Fresh Start Reporting	3/94
12.	Reporting Separate Investment Fund Option Information of Defined Contribution Pension Plans	9/94
13.	Direct Response Advertising and Probable Future Benefits	12/94
14.	Accounting and Reporting by Limited Liability Companies and Limited Liability Partnerships	4/95
15.	Accounting by the Issuer of Surplus Notes	1/95

Web Sites

See pages 19-20.

1 RESEARCHING GAAP PROBLEMS

Accounting principles have developed through both official pronouncements by authoritative bodies empowered to create and select accounting principles and evolution by accepted historical practice. Accounting principles developed when rule-making bodies perceived a need and promulgated opinions and standards or, in their failure to act, when conditions arose requiring solutions, by practicing accountants and academicians.

DEVELOPMENT OF GAAP

Primarily as a result of external pressures, the American Institute of Accountants, later to become the American Institute of Certified Public Accountants (AICPA), created a committee in 1930 to cooperate with the New York Stock Exchange in creating standards for accounting procedures. The widespread growth in the activities of the Exchange had led to expanded ownership and trading activities by an underinformed public. This lack of information, more than the stock market crash of 1929, caused the accounting profession to become involved in the concept of generally accepted accounting principles. Although the profession had, through various committees, made previous contributions toward creating uniform accounting standards prior to 1930, the creation of this special committee was different because of the recognition that complexities in business activities and in ownership dispersion required consistency in accounting measurements and in the selection of accounting procedures. This special committee recommended five rules to the Exchange which later in 1938 were published as Accounting Research Bulletin (ARB) 1 of the Committee on Accounting Procedure.

The Committee published 51 such bulletins, including Accounting Research Bulletin 43 which consolidated and restated Bulletins 1-42. The Committee was also instrumental in attempting to make accounting terminology uniform. However, the Committee's method of operation came into question in the late 1950s as the need for research into accounting principles became obvious. The result was the substitution of the Accounting Principles Board (APB) for the Committee in order to promulgate principles based primarily on the research of the Accounting Research Division. The Division was to undertake extensive and exhaustive research, publish the results, and allow the Board to lead the discussions which would ensue concerning accounting principles and practices. The Board's authority was enforced primarily through prestige and Rule 203 of the Code of Professional Ethics. However, approval by the Securities and Exchange Commission (SEC) of Board issuances gave additional support to its activities. During the entire time period of the accounting profession's development of accounting principles, the SEC has often taken an active role, including issuing its own pronouncements, where it feels the public's interest demands action. The SEC has statutory authority to establish GAAP for publicly held entities, but has relied on the accounting profession for self-regulation.

During the 14 years of the Board, 31 opinions and 4 statements were issued. These dealt with amendments of Accounting Research Bulletins, opinions on the form and content of financial statements, and issuances requiring changes in both the measurement and disclosure policies of the profession. However, the Board did not utilize the Accounting Research Division, which published 15 research studies during its lifetime. Both the Board and the Division acted independently in selecting topics for their respective agendas. The Board issued pronouncements in areas where little research had been done, and the Division performed research studies without seeking to be all-inclusive or exhaustive in analysis. The Accounting Principles Board did not operate differently than the Committee on Accounting Procedure.

As a result of these operational problems and the conclusions of the Wheat Study Group, the Financial Accounting Standards Board (FASB) was formed in 1972. The Board consists of seven full-time members; they have diverse backgrounds with three coming from public accounting, two from private industry and one each from academia and government. The Board is assisted by a staff of professionals who conduct research and work directly with the Board. Although there is some controversy and disagreement as to its activities and pronouncements, the FASB continues to operate with the confidence of accounting practitioners and various business organizations.[*]

Conceptual Framework

The FASB has issued six pronouncements called Statements of Financial Accounting Concepts (SFAC) in a series designed to constitute a foundation of finan-

---

[*] *To date, the FASB has issued 133 Statements on Financial Accounting Standards, various Interpretations and Technical Bulletins, and devoted substantial time and resources towards developing a Conceptual Framework for Financial Accounting.*

cial accounting standards. The framework is designed to prescribe the nature, function, and limits of financial accounting and to be used as a guideline that will lead to consistent standards. These conceptual statements do not establish accounting standards or disclosure practices for particular items. They are not enforceable under the Rules of Conduct of the Code of Professional Ethics.

Of the six SFAC, the fourth, *Objectives of Financial Reporting by Nonbusiness Organizations*, is not covered here due to its specialized nature.

SFAC 1, *Objectives of Financial Reporting by Business Enterprises*, identified three objectives of financial reporting. These were to provide useful information for economic decisions, to provide understandable information capable of predicting cash flows, and to provide relevant information about economic resources and the transactions, events, and circumstances that change them.

SFAC 2, *Qualitative Characteristics of Accounting Information*, identifies the qualities which make information useful. Under a cost benefit constraint, the primary qualities of useful information are that it be relevant and reliable. Relevant information is timely and either aids in predicting the future or in providing knowledge of the past (feedback value). Reliable information is verifiable and neutral and it faithfully represents events. In addition, such information must be comparable, consistent, and understandable.

SFAC 3, *Elements of Financial Statements of Business Enterprises*, has been replaced by SFAC 6. This statement has been amended by SFAC 6 to include financial reporting by not-for-profit organizations.

SFAC 5, *Recognition and Measurement in Financial Statements of Enterprises*, sets forth recognition criteria which determines what information should be in financial statements and the timing of when that information will appear. A full set of such statements would show financial position at the end of a period, earnings, comprehensive income and cash flows for the period, and investments by and distributions to owners during the period.

SFAC 6, *Elements of Financial Statements*, defines 10 elements as the basic components of financial statements. Three of these elements (assets, liabilities, and equity) relate to the balance sheet and are discussed in depth in Chapter 2. The remaining elements (comprehensive income, revenue, expenses, gains, losses, investments by owners, and distributions to owners) relate to the performance of an entity over time and are discussed in Chapter 3. These would be displayed on the income statement, statement of changes in financial position, and statement of changes in equity.

The appendix to this chapter discusses SFAC 1, 2, and 5 in greater detail.

Generally Accepted Accounting Principles

Generally accepted accounting principles are concerned with the measurement of economic activity, the time when such measurements are made and recorded, the disclosures surrounding these activities, and the preparation and presentation of summarized economic activities in financial statements. These principles are a product of the economic environment in which they are developed. Complicated business activities usually result in complex accounting principles.

In APB Statement 4, the Accounting Principles Board stated

> ***Generally accepted accounting principles*** *therefore is a technical term in financial accounting. Generally accepted accounting principles encompass the conventions, rules, and procedures necessary to define accepted accounting practice at a particular time. The standard of "generally accepted accounting principles" includes not only broad guidelines of general application, but also detailed practices and procedures.*
>
> *Generally accepted accounting principles are conventional--that is, they become generally accepted by agreement (often tacit agreement) rather than by formal derivation from a set of postulates or basic concepts. The principles have developed on the basis of experience, reason, custom, usage, and, to a significant extent, practical necessity.*

Accounting principles are usually directed toward solutions that are objective, conservative, and verifiable. There are two broad categories of accounting principles--measurement and disclosure. Measurement principles determine the timing and basis of items which enter the accounting cycle and impact the financial statements. These are quantitative standards which require numerically precise answers to problems and activities subject to large amounts of uncertainty.

Disclosure principles deal with factors that are not always numerical. Such disclosures involve qualitative features that are essential ingredients of a full set of financial statements. Their absence would make the financial statements created by measurement principles misleading by themselves. Disclosure principles complement measurement standards by explaining these standards and giving other information on accounting policies, contingencies, uncertainties, etc., which are essential ingredients in the analytical process of accounting.

Hierarchy of GAAP

The Auditing Standards Board (ASB) is the senior authoritative organization in the promulgation of generally accepted auditing standards. These standards include, and the auditors' standard report specifically includes, the phrase "present fairly in conformity with generally accepted accounting principles." With this responsibility and authority, the ASB has undertaken to define the meaning of the above phrase and to delineate the sources of GAAP. The determination of which accounting principle is applicable under a particular set of conditions may be difficult or even impossible without such a determination of the hierarchy of GAAP by an authoritative body.

In AU 411 (SAS 69), the ASB identified the following as the sources of established generally accepted accounting principles:

A. Accounting principles promulgated by a body designated by the AICPA Council to establish such principles, pursuant to rule 203 [ET section 203.01] of the AICPA Code of Professional Conduct. An auditor should not express an unqualified opinion if the financial statements contain a material departure from such pronouncements unless, due to unusual circumstances, adherence to the pronouncements would make the statements misleading. Rule 203 implies that application of officially established accounting principles almost always results in the fair presentation of financial position, results of operations, and cash flows, in conformity with generally accepted accounting principles. Nevertheless, Rule 203 provides for the possibility that literal application of such a pronouncement might, in unusual circumstances, result in misleading financial statements.

B. Pronouncements of bodies, composed of expert accountants, that deliberate accounting issues in public forums for the purpose of establishing accounting principles or describing existing accounting practices that are generally accepted, provided those pronouncements have been exposed for public comment and have been cleared by a body referred to in category (A).

C. Pronouncements of bodies, organized by a body referred to in category (A) and composed of expert accountants, that deliberate accounting issues in public forums for the purpose of interpreting or establishing accounting principles or describing existing accounting practices that are generally accepted, or pronouncements referred to in category (B) that have been cleared by a body referred to in category (A) but have not been exposed for public comment.

D. Practices or pronouncements that are widely recognized as being generally accepted because they represent prevalent practice in a particular industry, or the knowledgeable application to specific circumstances of pronouncements that are generally accepted.

If the accounting treatment is not specified by a pronouncement covered by Rule 203, the accountant/auditor should proceed next to categories (B), (C), or (D) using the treatment specified by the source in the highest category.

For financial statements of entities other than governmental entities

a. Category (A), officially established accounting principles, consists of Financial Accounting Standards Board (FASB) Statements of Financial Accounting Standards and Interpretations, Accounting Principles Board (APB) Opinions, and AICPA Accounting Research Bulletins.

b. Category (B) consists of FASB Technical Bulletins and, if cleared by the FASB, AICPA Industry Audit and Accounting Guides and AICPA Statements of Position.

c. Category (C) consists of AICPA Accounting Standards Executive Committee (AcSEC) Practice Bulletins that have been cleared by the FASB and consensus positions of the FASB Emerging Issues Task Force.

d. Category (D) includes AICPA accounting interpretations and implementation guides ("Qs and As") published by the FASB staff, and practices that are widely recognized and prevalent either generally or in the industry.

In the absence of any source of established accounting principles, other accounting literature may be considered. These would include APB Statements, AICPA Issues Papers, AcSEC Practice Bulletins, FASB Statements of Financial Accounting Concepts, International Accounting Standards Committee Statements of International Accounting Standards, Governmental Accounting Standards Board Statements, Interpretations and Technical Bulletins, Technical Information Service Inquiries and Replies included in AICPA Technical Practice Aids, pronouncements of other professional associations or regulatory agencies, and accounting textbooks and articles. The use of these other sources depends upon their relevance to particular circumstances, the specificity of the guidance, and the general recognition of the author or issuing organization as an authority. This would mean that FASB issuances in this category would be more influential in establishing an acceptable accounting practice than would an accounting textbook. Guidance in this category would require more judgment and a broader search of literature than would be true in the other three categories.

For financial statements of state and local governmental entities

a. Category (A), officially established accounting principles, consists of GASB Statements and Interpretations, as well as AICPA and FASB pronouncements specifically made applicable to state and local governmental entities by GASB Statements and Interpretations. GASB Statements and Interpretations are periodically incorporated in the *Codification of Governmental Accounting and Financial Reporting Standards*.
b. Category (B) consists of GASB Technical Bulletins and, if specifically made applicable to state and local governmental entities by the AICPA and cleared by the GASB, AICPA Industry Audit and Accounting Guides and AICPA Statements of Position.
c. Category (C) consists of AICPA AcSEC Practice Bulletins if specifically made applicable to state and local governmental entities and cleared by the GASB, as well as consensus positions of a group of accountants organized by the GASB that attempts to reach consensus positions on accounting issues applicable to state and local governmental entities.
d. Category (D) includes implementation guides ("Qs and As") published by the GASB staff, as well as practices that are widely recognized and prevalent in state and local government.

Of course, in all accounting theory, the substance of a transaction rather than legal form should guide the accounting treatment, and materiality is a factor that must be considered in the selection of an appropriate principle.

The FASB

Since 1973 the FASB has been the designated authoritative organization that establishes standards of financial accounting and is recognized as authoritative through Financial Reporting Release No. 1 by the Securities and Exchange Commission and through Rule 203, Rules of Conduct by the AICPA.

The FASB is an independent body relying on the Financial Accounting Foundation for selection of its members and receipt of its budgets. Funds are raised from contributions made to the Foundation. The Board of Trustees of the Foundation is made up from members of

American Accounting Association
American Institute of Certified Public Accountants
Financial Analysts Federation
Financial Executives Institute
Government Finance Officers Association
Institute of Management Accountants
National Association of State Auditors, Comptrollers, and Treasurers
Securities Industry Association

There is also a Financial Accounting Standards Advisory Council that has responsibility for consulting with the Board on major areas of inquiry and analysis.

The Board issues several types of pronouncements. Statements of Financial Accounting Standards are the most important of these setting forth mandatory accounting principles. Interpretations are used to classify or elaborate on existing Standards or pronouncements of predecessor bodies. Interpretations are submitted for comment to the Standards Advisory Council. Technical Bulletins usually address issues not covered directly by existing standards and are primarily used to provide guidance where it is not expected to be costly or create a major change. Bulletins are discussed at Board meetings and subject to Board veto. Both Bulletins and Interpretations are designed to be responsive to implementation and practice problems on relatively narrow subjects.

In 1984, the Financial Accounting Foundation established the Governmental Accounting Standards Board to set financial accounting standards for state and local government entities.

Emerging Issues Task Force (EITF)

The Emerging Issues Task Force (EITF) was formed in 1984 by the FASB in order to assist the Board in identifying current or emerging issues and implementation problems that may need to be placed on the agenda of the Board. Membership on the Task Force consists of persons selected from wide ranging backgrounds who would be aware of issues and practices that should be considered by the group. The Task Force meets on almost a monthly basis throughout the year with persons representing the SEC and FASB in attendance for discussion but not voting purposes.

For each agenda item, an issues paper is developed by members, their firms, or the FASB staff. After discussion by the Task Force, a consensus can be reached on the issue, in which case further action by the FASB is not needed. However, the FASB may include a narrow issue in the scope of a broader project and reaffirm or supersede the work of the Task Force. If no consensus is reached, the problem may end up on the Board agenda or be resolved by the SEC or AICPA. It is also possible that no consensus is reached and the issue remains unresolved with no organization currently working on the problem. These may be in especially narrow areas having little broad-based interest.

The FASB publishes a volume of EITF Abstracts which are summaries of each issue paper and the results of Task Force discussion. The Status Report issued by the FASB on a recurring basis throughout the year follows up on the subsequent developments after a Task Force decision on an issue. A listing of the Issues considered by the Emerging Issues Task Force grouped by type in which the status concerning resolution of each issue is indicated appears in the front of this book immediately following the Table of Contents.

The EITF has been severely criticized for promulgating GAAP without sufficient due process procedures. Only a limited audience is aware of each issue, and the time period of exposure is often very brief, 1 month or so. However, the Task Force resolves problems in an environment where delay would often result in widespread divergent practices of accounting becoming entrenched. The guidance provided is often on narrow issues that are of immediate interest and importance.

Mandatory and Preferable GAAP

Category (A) specified by SAS 69 constitutes mandatory GAAP. This book is concentrated almost exclusively on GAAP in this category. Any deviation from accounting principles specified by the designated rule-making body would require an auditor to either qualify the opinion or explain in the body of the report the reasons and effects of the departures. Independent auditors agree on the existence of generally accepted accounting principles, but the determination that a particular accounting principle is generally accepted may be difficult because no single reference source exists for all such principles.

Departures from positions given by publications in the second and third categories would require auditors to document and justify their conclusions. Although the positions constitute GAAP, they represent preferable viewpoints, not mandatory ones. Preferable accounting principles have historically been specialized principles of particular industries which may not be transferable to other industries or to general business accounting policies.

Certain preferable accounting principles in the past have become mandatory principles by the actions of the FASB. In Statement 32, the Board indicated that accounting principles and practices in certain AICPA Statements of Position and Accounting and Auditing Guides were preferable accounting principles. This recognition by the Board raised the status of these pronouncements which at that time had been somewhat uncertain. Then the Board began to extract those principles and practices and issue Statements to adopt these preferable principles. Such steps by the Board had the effect of promoting principles from preferable to mandatory. The Board rescinded FASB 32 by issuing Statement 111 in 1992. There are questions when SAS 69 grants preferability status to the work of certain accounting bodies, since the Auditing Standards Board (ASB) is not empowered to create generally accepted accounting principles. The ASB, however, carefully defined such preferability in terms of the audit function in determining fairness in conformity with GAAP which is clearly within its authority.

The concept that auditors should express an opinion on the preferability of a change in accounting principles undertaken by an entity whose financial statements are being examined has been extremely controversial. Preferability in these circumstances has been sometimes modified in terms such as "preferable in the circumstances" or the term "preferability" is avoided altogether. When the Securities and Exchange Commission proposed making such a preferability statement mandatory, certain members of the profession actually filed suit to stop such a proposal from being implemented.

As accounting principles continue to be promulgated, developed, and evolved, other problems concerning preferability will surely surface again. Many accountants will argue that unless a definite stand on accounting principles is taken by an authoritative body, they will have no reason or justification for choosing one accounting procedure over another.

Materiality

Materiality as a concept has great significance in understanding, researching, and implementing GAAP. Each Statement of Financial Accounting Standards (SFAS) issued by the FASB concludes by stating that the provisions of the statement are not applicable to immaterial items.

Materiality is both a qualitative and quantitative concept. Certain events or transactions are material because of the nature of the item regardless of the dollar amounts involved. The enactment of prohibition outlawing the sale of most alcoholic beverages was a significant event to companies that produce and sell such products. Offers to buy or sell assets for more or less than book value, litigation proceedings against the company for price fixing or antitrust allegations, and active negotiations involving future profitability are all examples of items not capable of being evaluated for materiality based upon numerical calculations.

Quantitatively, materiality has been defined in many accounting standards. For example, in SFAS 131, *Disclosures about Segments of an Enterprise and Related Information*, a material segment or customer is defined as 10% or more of revenues.

The Securities and Exchange Commission has in several of its pronouncements defined materiality as 1% of total assets for receivables from officers and stockholders, 5% of total assets for separate balance sheet disclosure of items, and 10% of total revenues for disclosure of oil and gas producing activities.

Material information is that whose absence makes the financial statements misleading. This is not a definition of materiality nor does it sufficiently explain the concept to provide guidance in distinguishing material information from immaterial information. Until further research is performed or the FASB acts to provide such guidance, the individual accountant must exercise professional judgment in evaluating information and concluding on its materiality.

Standards Overload

Another complexity in the search for accounting principles has arisen in recent years with the complaint that there are too many accounting standards and too many organizations issuing pronouncements that create accounting standards. Solutions are needed to reduce and simplify existing GAAP either for all entities or at least for those entities where enforcement of such standards is not cost justified. Both the FASB and the AICPA have undertaken studies in order to seek to simplify or eliminate certain accounting principles.

A list of items identified as needing attention by standard setters will vary, depending upon personal preferences and problems. Generally, standards which are complicated, such as those on leases and income taxes, will find their way onto nearly everyone's list.

The search for simplicity is not an easy process. Complex business and economic activities may not lend themselves to simple accounting standards to measure and disclose them. If simplicity means having to make an incorrect measurement, many users will have to choose between erroneous financial statements, which do not reflect economic reality, and complicated accounting standards. A reduction in standards could ultimately reduce the quality of financial reporting.

Differential accounting principles for different entities may create additional complexities. Different disclosure standards may reduce the quantity of financial information available for certain entities selected, but this may also reduce the quality of such information. Different measurement standards again may create erroneous financial statements in terms of economic reality.

Differential standards require a selection of a system by which to categorize entities by the standards they should follow. Some recommend a size test with big firms following complete standards and small firms following a simpler set of standards. Size might be determined by assets, sales, net worth, or number of owners. Another possibility is an ownership test, with public companies following a different and more comprehensive set of standards than privately owned businesses. The difficulty in making such a selection and the added complexity caused by two sets of different standards obviously compounds the standard overload problem instead of reducing it.

The search for simpler accounting standards is not hopeless, however. Where research shows that disclosures are not utilized or understood by the users of financial data, such disclosures can easily be dropped. Where measurement standards are created to differentiate between events that are clearly not different from an economic viewpoint, such standards add nonessential complications and can be amended. For example, all business combinations constitute an economic union and the terms **purchase** and **pooling** have no meaning in economic theory. Also, all leases give rise to liabilities, as future obligations, and assets, as future economic benefits. The differentiation of some leases as capital and others as operating may be a highly subjective concept.

The search for easier, simpler, and fewer accounting standards will continue. Certain differential standards in terms of disclosures have already been adopted, allowing nonpublic entities to avoid disclosing earnings per share, segment data, and retroactive effects of a business combination. As the FASB considers future pronouncements on accounting standards, the issue of cost-benefit and applicability to all segments of the profession will be prime considerations. The standards overload issue will not fade away because there are numerous problems with the potential solutions that have been suggested.

RESEARCHING PUBLISHED GAAP

The search for written GAAP consists primarily of analysis of the publications of various organizations concerned with accounting principles and practices. Accounting policies are established by these authorities in order to limit discretion and create uniformity, to the extent practical, for information and reporting purposes.

The FASB publishes two sets of books (both looseleaf and bound) which can assist in researching accounting issues. The *Current Text* integrates all of the currently recognized standards in alphabetical order. The AICPA Research Bulletins, APB Opinions, and FASB Standards and Interpretations, and Emerging Issues Task Force Abstracts are combined in topical order. Supplemental guidance from the AICPA Accounting Interpretations and FASB Technical Bulletins are also incorporated. The materials have been edited down from the original pronouncements and may lack the clarity that can be obtained only from the unedited version. Descriptive material including reasons for conclusions are missing. Each paragraph in the current text is indexed back to the original pronouncement for research or follow-up referencing. The first volume of the *Current Text* deals with general standards while the second volume contains industry standards for specialized industries.

The *Original Pronouncements* contains all of the AICPA Accounting Research Bulletins, Interpretations and Terminology Bulletins, the APB Opinions, Statements and Interpretations, the FASB Standards, Interpretations, Concepts, Technical Bulletins, and Exposure Drafts. These are in two volumes in the order of their issuance. Paragraphs containing accounting principles that have been superseded or dropped are shaded in order to make the user aware. Such changes are identified in detail by a status page placed at the beginning of each pronouncement which can reference the user to other areas and pronouncements.

Essentially, if you need a quick answer to a specific question, the *Current Text* can be accessed very fast. If you need to understand the answer, the *Original Pronouncements* will afford you the opportunity to study the area in depth.

The Securities and Exchange Commission issues Staff Accounting Bulletins and makes rulings on individual cases that come before it, which create and impose accounting standards on those whose financial statements are submitted to the Commission. The SEC, through acts passed by Congress, has broad powers to prescribe accounting practices and methods for all statements filed with it. Although it has usually preferred to encourage the development of standards in the private sector by deferring to the AICPA and FASB, the SEC has occasionally adopted policies that conflict with established standards. In each case, the result has been a veto by the SEC of the standard, as the AICPA or FASB has withdrawn or amended the standard to conform to SEC policy. Usually SEC disclosure standards require far more information. However, the history of the SEC is one of cooperative assistance in the formulation of accounting standards. Congressional committees have been critical of the SEC in instances where they felt that too much power was ceded to the profession itself without adequate oversight by the Commission.

The search for authoritative guidance at the AICPA goes beyond Industry Audit and Accounting Guides and Statements of Position. The Auditing Standards Board may issue a pronouncement which affects GAAP similar to SAS 69 on the hierarchy of accounting principles. In its issuance of SAS 6, *Related-Party Transactions*, in July 1975, the ASB set standards for auditing and disclosing such related-party transactions. Not until the FASB issued Standard 57 in 1982, which was consistent with SAS 6, did the ASB amend its standard deferring to the FASB. Also, accounting interpretations are given by the AICPA Technical Information Service. Certain answers to inquiries made of it are published in a volume of Technical Practice Aids. These items constitute preferable GAAP to the extent that they are not amended or superseded by later pronouncements. Also, AICPA Issues Papers may be relied upon depending upon the circumstances to provide relevant information about alternative accounting treatments. Other publications of committees at the AICPA or information published in the *Journal of Accountancy* may give rise to understanding and interpreting accounting standards in areas where clarity is needed. The status of all AICPA publications not adopted by the FASB as mandatory or preferable is unclear. They are, however, issuances of the professional parent organization of the accounting profession and, therefore, must be considered as authoritative. Those who depart from them must be prepared to justify that departure based upon the facts and circumstances available in the particular situation.

The American Accounting Association is an organization consisting primarily of accounting educators. It is devoted to encouraging research into accounting theory and practice. The issuances of the AAA tend to be normative, that is, prescribing what GAAP ought to be like, rather than explaining current standards. However, the monographs, committee reports, and *The Accounting Review* published by the AAA may be useful sources for research into applicable accounting standards.

Other governmental agencies such as the Government Accounting Office and the Cost Accounting Standards Board have offered certain publications which may assist in researching written standards. Also, industry organizations and associations may be other helpful sources.

In the absence of any clear-cut and definite pronouncements covering the issues that require answers, a different approach may be useful. The AICPA publishes an annual survey of the accounting and disclosure policies of many public companies in *Accounting Trends and Techniques* and maintains a library of financial statements which can be accessed through a computerized search process (NAARS). Through selection of key words and/or topics, these services can provide information on whether other entities have had similar problems and the methods used in accounting for them.

The lack of specificity can create problems in attempting to adhere to a highly flexible standard. For example, in adhering to APB 28 on Interim Financial Reporting, assume a problem arises in how to account for an annual catalogue expense. The cost of the catalogue can be allocated based on a time expired basis, benefit received, or other activity to each interim period. However, the Opinion also states that an arbitrary allocation of costs should not be made. Since any method of allocation chosen may be deemed as arbitrary and since other allocation formulas would yield different results, the Opinion is not explicit. Therefore, different entities might expense the catalogue in different periods based upon different allocation schemes. The result is not uniform accounting or even faithfulness to the principles in APB 28. Obviously, almost any accounting for the catalogue could be justified as being consistent with that Opinion.

Extremely detailed standards can, on the other hand, lead to answers which are clearly misleading. SFAS 128, *Earnings per Share*, states that all warrants should be used in computing diluted earnings per share unless antidilutive. Assume that warrants issued contain a put option, whereby the holder of the warrant may either convert it into stock or put the warrant to the company at a defined price. If the economic situation was such that the holder would be better off financially to exercise the put rather than convert into common, then obviously the marketplace would treat the warrant as debt and not as a dilutive security. However, there is no alternative under SFAS 128 but to treat the warrant as dilutive in earnings per share calculations. An accountant may allow the entity to report on an economic basis rather than a GAAP basis, but clearly, whether justified or not, that would create a deviation from an accounting standard.

These are but two examples of the difficulties of dealing with written GAAP. Pronouncements may not be explicit enough, or they may be too explicit, to provide definitive answers to a particular accounting problem. Researching GAAP may not end with finding a pronouncement on the topic. Careful reading of the publication and analysis of the underlying rationale for the transaction and activity are essential to insure compliance with the spirit and intentions of GAAP and not just its written word.

Researching Using This Book

This book can assist in researching generally accepted accounting principles in order to find technical answers to specific inquiries. A listing of all Authoritative

Accounting Pronouncements **still in effect** appears in numerical order in the front of this book immediately following the table of contents. These are then referenced both to the *Current Text* published by the FASB and to pages in this book. Accordingly, the entire original pronouncement can be found in the FASB Original Pronouncement books or traced to or from this book to both the original pronouncements and/or the current text. The reader can therefore find more detail on each and every topic covered in this book and also be aware of which topics and pronouncements are not covered within this book at all. This should make research cross-referencing quick and reliable.

With respect to the EITF pronouncements, our listing appears in topic order and within that by date order. Each issues paper is then identified as to the current status whether superseded, resolved, or consensus reached by the EITF. Within each of the topical areas, the reader will be able to identify any or all of the EITF issues papers that would be relevant to the current research. We have included those EITF pronouncements for which a consensus was reached in this book at the end of the chapters to which they relate except for some pervasive ones that are included within the sections of the related chapters. This topical updating of the EITF pronouncements does not appear elsewhere in the accounting literature, including the looseleaf services by the FASB.

Although EITF pronouncements are deemed to be level C GAAP by SAS 69, they are nonetheless incorporated with level A GAAP in the Current Text by the FASB. Also, because EITF issues are topic specific, there is no level A or A GAAP which would apply. Accordingly, EITF consensus represent the highest level of GAAP available for each topic. Therefore, the inclusion in this book of EITF summaries is recognizing the relative importance of these issues.

The reader, therefore, can be directed by this book to the specific professional authoritative literature concerning the area of inquiry. In a like manner, the reader of the professional literature can use the listing of Authoritative Accounting Pronouncements to quickly locate the pages in this book relevant to each specific pronouncement.

Nonpromulgated GAAP

Not all GAAP came about because of a deliberation process and issuance of pronouncements by authoritative bodies. Certain principles and practices evolved into current acceptability without adopted standards. Depreciation methods such as straight-line and declining balance are both acceptable as are inventory costing methods such as LIFO and FIFO. There are, however, no definitive pronouncements that can be found to state this. There are many disclosure principles that evolved into general accounting practice because they were required by the SEC in documents submitted to them. Among these are reconciling the actual rate with the statutory rate used in determining income tax expense, when not otherwise obvious from the financial statements themselves. Even much of the form and content of balance sheets and income statements has evolved over the years.

The FASB through the Conceptual Framework Project, discussed more fully in the appendix of this chapter, has attempted to build a constitution of accounting theory for the evaluation of concepts by accounting principles researchers. Previously, the Accounting Principles Board in Statement 4 attempted to accomplish similar results. The underlying general standards from which all accounting concepts can be derived have proven to be elusive, but accounting standard authorities seem destined to continue their search for them.

Researching nonpromulgated GAAP consists of reviewing pronouncements in areas similar to those being researched, and careful reading of the relevant portions of the Conceptual Framework. Understanding concepts and intentions espoused by the deliberative authorities can give the essential clues to a logical formulation of alternatives and conclusions regarding problems that have not yet been addressed by these authorities.

Many of what are now promulgated accounting principles evolved through successful accounting practice. Two interesting and widely debated issues impact on this concept. First is the issue of whether promulgated GAAP consists of a codification of successful practice. In areas where a diversity of practice had previously existed, and pronouncements resolved the problem by selecting among the alternatives, the issue of which caused the success, practice or the pronouncement, is essentially unresolvable. The issue is certain to have supporters on both sides claiming that theory emulates practice or that successful practice came from the standards. In nonpromulgated GAAP, the methods may have evolved or may have benefited from other pronouncements in similar areas. The second issue is whether accounting research impacts on promulgated GAAP. Since its formation, the FASB has supported empirical research in an attempt to measure the cost and benefits of accounting pronouncements. Traditionally, research has been prescriptive in nature, describing what accounting could be under a different system. It, therefore, does not lend itself to impact technical pronouncements. However, research into capital markets and into social and economic consequences of accounting policy has impacted and will continue to impact future accounting principles. Unfortunately, the reverse will also become true. Accounting principles may be developed because of political, social, and economic reasons unrelated to accounting theory. The impact of such a development might well mean the end of the use of accounting theory as a problem-solving method.

Solving GAAP Problems

The methods that are employed in solving existing accounting problems can be summarized in the following steps:

1. Research published GAAP. A search should be initiated at the highest level of published accounting standards, following the levels and sources of principles according to Statement on Auditing Standards 69. The researcher should look for specific pronouncements and issuances level by level. In the absence of pronouncements directly applicable to the topic, the investigation should be broadened to include related and analogous topics. Analysis of the economic factors influencing the transaction will help in the broader search.

2. Research other literature. Other literature beyond that recognized by SAS 69 may consist of periodical literature and general industry publications. These may be important since not all principles are promulgated and successful practice is a source of accounting standards.

3. Research practice. Inquiries of other entities regarding the accounting practices they follow may indicate a potential solution or at least allow consideration of alternatives.

4. Use theory. When published standards, other literature, and practice fail to provide the answers to problems, the researcher must fall back on accounting theory. Textbooks, appendices to official pronouncements, FASB discussion memorandums, and the like are sources of theory to be analyzed. The use of theory constrained by the economic factors underlying the problem being researched may succeed in clarifying issues and alternatives when no other guidance is available.

Examples of unsolved accounting problems and potential solutions follow.

Example involving equity method

The equity method of accounting for investments in partnerships and significantly influenced and controlled corporations is in accordance with accounting principles stated in APB Opinion 18. However, there is no clearly defined solution to the problem of how to account for issuances of additional shares or interests by the investee. Assume the following:

A Company forms B Company by depositing $100,000. B then sells additional stock to outsiders, reducing A's percentage of ownership to 25%, for a total of $4,900,000. A under the equity method would see its investment account rise from $100,000 to $1,250,000 (or 25% of [$100,000 + $4,900,000]).

A did not do anything that constitutes an earning process. Furthermore, a capital transaction of an investee could have been a capital transaction by the investor. The increase in investment may be seen as a capital transaction and an increase in paid-in capital.

Another argument is that A owned 100% of an entity and now owns only 25%. Essentially, A could have sold its investment directly but chose instead to have the investment sold indirectly by the investee. Under this theory, the increase in investment may be seen as a sale by A of part of its investment, which resulted in a gain, or as a revenue transaction to be reported in the income statement.

There are various writings in accounting literature that speak on both sides of this question. Although, in general, most textbooks show the increase as a capital transaction, the Internal Revenue Service may tax it. The Securities and Exchange Commission in Staff Accounting Bulletin 51 states that it will accept both methods, and the AICPA in Issues Paper, Accounting in Consolidation for Issuances of a Subsidiary's Stock, states a preference for the revenue transaction method.

The issue is whether A's original acquisition was a bargain purchase (no revenue to be recognized) or the subsequent sale was an earning process (revenue is realized). The issue may revolve around what activities A pursued prior to B issuing its stock that may have caused the value of B's stock to rise. Such activities may qualify for revenue recognition.

Example involving consolidations

In consolidations of less than 100% ownership of a subsidiary, the question arises as to the use of the parent or entity theories of combination. Assume the following:

A Company purchases 80% of B Company for $46,000 when B has total book value of $50,000. Since 80% of $50,000 is $40,000, there is a $6,000 differential to be accounted for. Under the parent theory, since cost exceeds book value by $6,000, the entire amount represents either an identified or unidentified (goodwill) asset to be accounted for in the future. Under the entity theory, since 80% created a $6,000 value, then the entire value must be $7,500, of which $6,000 is attributed to the majority interest and $1,500 belongs to the minority interest.

Under the parent theory, the implied additional value is not acceptable because there is no cost associated with it. Under the entity theory, recognition of only the actual differential denies the market implication of value. There is no authoritative literature that speaks to these issues although the parent theory is derived from the proprietary theory (view everything from the standpoint of the owner), while the entity theory (view everything from the standpoint of the entity as a whole) is a predominant accounting concept.

Generally, if the additional value of $6,000 is unidentified (goodwill), the cost issue becomes persuasive because of the concept of acquisition of unidentifiable intangibles. If the additional value is identified, practice would push the value down to the subsidiary by entering the $7,500 increase in assets and increase in equity. B would then have a total book value of $57,500 and 80% of it would equal the investment of A of $46,000. The accounting then is B's accounting for its own asset. The argument justifying this is that the legal form of the various entities, A and B, is immaterial. A new economic entity began with A's purchase of the stock of B and the same thing could have been accomplished through a partnership to which assets were transferred or by a liquidation of B into a new corporation, with a stepped-up basis for assets. Substance over form would support equal accounting regardless of the form of the transaction.

There are, however, many who would support neither the push-down nor the implied value recognition. The answer is not definitive because there has yet to be a pronouncement on the parent and entity theories of consolidation.

Example involving cancelable leases

A lease which is cancelable is not covered by SFAS 13, *Accounting for Leases*. However, assume that a firm has no intention of canceling the lease; would this intention alone be sufficient to cause capitalization of the asset and obligation, assuming the criteria were met? Most accountants would probably agree that the intention of the pronouncement would be met by such capitalization.

In a peculiar situation, assume a construction company bidding for state projects must maintain a 2:1 current ratio in order to obtain such jobs. The company has various equipment subject to cancelable leases, which otherwise would qualify as capital leases. If the leases are capitalized, the ratio falls below 2 to 1 causing cancelation of the leases due to lack of construction jobs. If the leases are not capitalized, the ratio is above 2 to 1, and the company would intend to keep the equipment for the entire lease without cancelation. Such an accounting dilemma is conceivable, and the solution may not exist. However, since bidding does not guarantee getting a contract, the intention of the lessee with respect to cancelation is unclear at the time of bidding, and most likely, the leases would not be capitalized at that time.

Example involving employee capital accumulation plans

Such plans exist when companies reward employees by giving them stock or the right to benefit from the change in market price of the company's stock or both. There are two types of plans: (1) compensatory--the employee gets compensation and the company records an expense and liability, and (2) noncompensatory--no accounting recognition.

If a compensation plan is initiated at the then fair market value of the stock, no compensation can be reported because such compensation is measured only from the amount of the discount (market price less exercise price offered). Therefore, no discount means no accounting even though the plan is compensatory. So the difference between compensatory and noncompensatory plans can be meaningless (APB 25).

However, in practice many plans exist. These include incentive plans, option plans, stock appreciation rights plans, phantom stock plans, restricted plans, and others. Let's look at two examples.

1. A nonqualified stock option plan
2. A stock appreciation right plan

The substance of these two plans is essentially the same because economic benefits that may be received by the employee can be identical.

Assume that both plans are issued at an exercise price equal to the market price of the stock and that market price increases over time. Under the nonqualified plan, although compensatory, the compensation is measured at the date of grant which is the date of issuance. No compensation would ever be recorded and the increase in market value would be ignored. The employee could exercise the option and sell the stock, earning the profit while the corporation would ignore the "cost."

Under the stock appreciation right, the employee gets the profit directly from the corporation without buying and then selling the stock. However, when the amount of market appreciation is paid out, the corporation records the compensation as the excess of the market price over the exercise price of the SAR.

These two plans are virtually identical, yet the accounting for them is different. Furthermore, the first plan could give the employee a fixed number of shares while the second plan could be identical except the shares may be reduced based upon some contingency. Obviously, the first plan would be more valuable than the second because of no contingency in it to the employee. The stock plan is a more valuable award to the employee than the stock appreciation right. Under current accounting, the plan would cost zero while the right would cost the entire amount of the employee's gain.

Unfortunately, the form of the transaction prevails over the economic substance, although it clearly shouldn't. The corporation can influence its accounting recognized costs by how the plan is structured. The FASB is working on this problem.

Other examples

Other problems similar to the previous ones also exist. Should profit sharing and money purchase plans that are substitutes for pension plans be subjected to the accounting and disclosure requirements for pension plans? How should income tax expense allocated to individual companies in a consolidated group be accounted for? The expense could be allocated on the proportion of income or loss, on the proportion of income alone (no credit for losses to those entities that had losses), on the incremental basis of each company with the net benefit or cost of the consolidated tax return accruing to the parent company, or on any other basis. There are no pronouncements stating the methods that are acceptable.

Solutions to GAAP problems may not be definitive and may not be obtainable by looking up a pronouncement. The theory of accounting and analysis of the economic factors may be the path to their solution.

Accounting Web Sites

Illinois CPA Society	--http://www.icpas.org	--Includes information for members of the Illinois CPA Society; section for online CPE courses; Career Center; faculty resources; links to FASB, GASB, NASBA, and other sites
AICPA Online	--http://www.aicpa.org	--Includes accounting news section; CPE information; section on professional ethics; information on relevant Congressional/ Executive actions; online publications, such as the Journal of Accountancy; Accounting Standards Executive Committee; also has links to other organizations
FinanceNet	--http://www.financenet.gov	--Site is operated by the National Science Foundation, includes information on federal financial management; site is searchable for more information; includes links to other sites
IRS	--http://www.irs.ustreas.gov /prod/cover/html	--Has tax information for individuals and corporations; online tax forms; tax instructions; searchable for more information

Electronic Accountant	--http://www.electronicaaccountant.com	--Includes Internet Tax Research; Career Center; discussions on accounting. auditing, financial planning, and other topics; searchable
SEC	--http://www.sec.gov	--SEC digest and statements; EDGAR searchable database; information on current SEC rulemaking; links to other sites
Accounting Net	--http://www.accountingnet.com	--Includes news, research, products available for purchase; jobs database; online tax forms; John Wiley GAAP book will be searchable online soon; links to FASB and GASB
NASBA	--http://www.nasba.org	National State Boards of Accountancy; includes listings for all state organizations and publications
GASB	--http://www.rutgers.edu/accounting/raw/gasb/gasbhome.html	--Information on GASB; new GASB documents; summaries/status of all GASB statements; proposed statements; technical bulletins; interpretations
FASB	--http://raw.rutgers.edu/raw/fasb	--Information on FASB; includes list of new pronouncements/statements; summaries of selected projects; summaries/status of all FASB statements
Nonprofit Resource Center	--http://www.1800net.com/nprc	--Accounting standards and government regulations for nonprofits
American Accounting Association	--http://www.rutgers.edu/accounting/raw/aaa	--Accounting news; publications; faculty information; searchable; links to other sites

APPENDIX

CONCEPTUAL FRAMEWORK

In 1965, an AICPA Special Committee on Opinions of the Accounting Principles Board (APB) reported that the objectives, concepts, principles, and terminology of accounting should be enumerated and defined. In response to this recommendation, the APB published Statement 4, *Basic Concepts and Accounting Principles Underlying Financial Statements of Business Enterprises*. The purpose of this Statement was to increase the understanding of accounting fundamentals and to provide a basis for the development of accounting. This statement was descriptive, not prescriptive, because it identified and organized GAAP based on the observation of accounting practice. Although the statement was intended to contribute to the development of a "more consistent, comprehensive structure of useful financial information," it did not attempt to provide solutions to the problems of accounting nor did it attempt to determine what GAAP should be. In 1971, the AICPA established the Study Group on the Objectives of Financial Statements (known as the Trueblood Committee). This Committee identified 12 objectives of financial statements and seven qualitative characteristics of reporting. In 1976, based upon the Trueblood Report, the FASB issued *Tentative Conclusions on Objectives of Financial Statements of Business Enterprises* and later the same year issued *Conceptual Framework for Financial Accounting and Reporting: Elements of Financial Statements and Their Measurement*. These two pronouncements led to the establishment of Statements of Financial Accounting Concepts.

Components of the conceptual framework. The components of the conceptual framework for financial accounting and reporting include objectives, qualitative characteristics, elements, recognition, measurement, financial statements, earnings, funds flow, and liquidity. The relationship between these components is illustrated in the following diagram taken from a FASB Invitation to Comment, *Financial Statements and Other Means of Financial Reporting*.

In the diagram, components to the left are more basic and those to the right depend on components to their left. Components are closely related to those above or below them.

The most basic component of the conceptual framework is the objectives. The objectives underlie the other phases and are derived from the needs of those for whom financial information is intended. The qualitative characteristics are the criteria to be used in choosing and evaluating accounting and reporting policies.

Elements of financial statements are the components from which financial statements are created. They include assets, liabilities, equity, investments by owners, distributions to owners, comprehensive income, revenues, expenses, gains, and losses. In order to be included in financial statements, an element must meet criteria for recognition and possess a characteristic which can be reliably measured.

Conceptual Framework
For Financial Accounting and Reporting

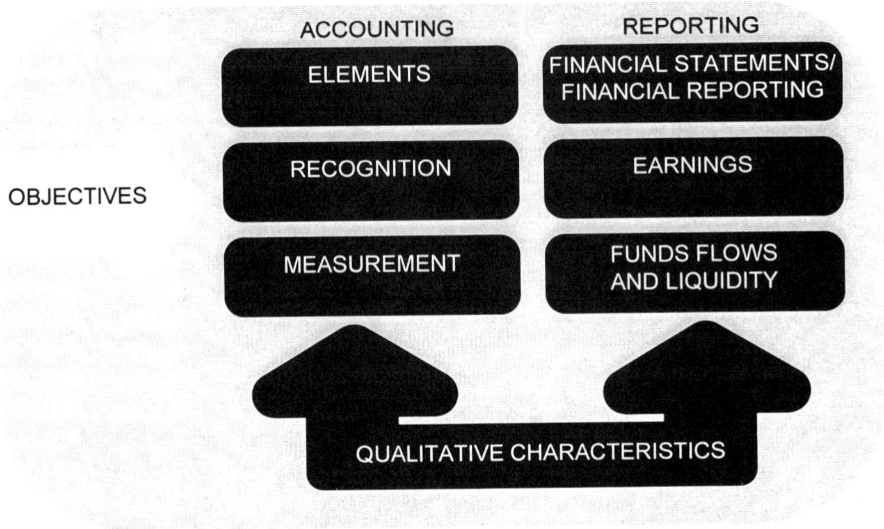

Reporting or display considerations are concerned with what information should be provided, who should provide it, and where it should be displayed. How the financial statements (financial position, earnings, and funds flow) are presented is the focal point of this part of the conceptual framework project.

Unlike a Statement of Financial Accounting Standards (SFAS), a Statement of Financial Accounting Concepts (SFAC) does not establish GAAP. Since GAAP may be inconsistent with the principles set forth in the conceptual framework, the FASB expects to reexamine existing accounting standards. Until that time, a SFAC does not require a change in existing GAAP. SFAC do not amend, modify, or interpret existing GAAP nor do they justify changing GAAP based upon interpretations derived from them.

SFAC 1: Objectives of Financial Reporting by Business Enterprises

SFAC 1 identifies the objectives (purposes) of financial reporting and indicates that these objectives apply to all financial reporting; they are not limited to financial statements. Financial reporting includes the financial statements and other forms of communication that provide accounting information (corporate annual reports, prospectuses, annual reports filed with the Securities and Exchange Commission, news releases, and management forecasts).

SFAC 1 identifies three objectives of financial reporting. The **first objective** of financial reporting is to provide information that is useful in making business and economic decisions. Financial information users are divided into internal and external groups. Internal users include management and directors of the business enterprise. Internal reports tend to provide information which is more detailed than the information available to or used by external users. External users include both those individuals who have or intend to have a direct economic interest in a business and those who have an indirect interest because they advise or represent those individuals with a direct interest. These users include owners, lenders, suppliers, potential investors and creditors, employees, customers, financial analysts and advisors, brokers, underwriters, stock exchanges, lawyers, economists, taxing authorities, regulatory authorities, legislators, financial press and reporting agencies, labor unions, trade associations, business researchers, teachers, students, and the public. SFAC 1 is directed at general purpose external financial reporting by a business enterprise as it relates to the ability of that enterprise to generate favorable cash flows. External users' needs are emphasized because these users lack the authority to obtain the financial information they want and need from an enterprise. Thus, external users must rely on the information provided to them by management.

The **second objective** of financial reporting is to provide understandable information which will aid investors and creditors in predicting the future cash flows of a firm. Investors and creditors want information about cash flows because the expectation of cash flows affects a firm's ability to pay interest and dividends, which in turn affects the market price of that firm's stocks and bonds.

The **third objective** of financial reporting is to provide information relative to an enterprise's economic resources, the claims to those resources (obligations), and the effects of transactions, events, and circumstances that change resources and claims to resources. A description of these informational needs follows:

- **Economic resources, obligations, and owners' equity.** Such information provides the users of financial reporting with a measure of future cash flows and an indication of the firm's strengths, weaknesses, liquidity, and solvency.
- **Economic performance and earnings.** Past performance provides an indication of a firm's future performance. Furthermore, earnings based upon accrual accounting provide a better indicator of economic performance and future cash flows than do current cash receipts and disbursements. Accrual basis earnings are a better indicator because charge for recovery of capital (depreciation/amortization) is made in determining these earnings. The relationship between earnings and economic performance results from the matching of the costs and benefits (revenues) of economic activity during a given period by means of accrual accounting. Over the life of an enterprise, economic performance can be determined by net cash flows or by total earnings since the two measures would be equal.
- **Liquidity, solvency, and funds flows.** Information about cash and other funds flows from borrowings, repayments of borrowings, expenditures, capital transactions, economic resources, obligations, owners' equity, and earnings may aid the user of financial reporting information in assessing a firm's liquidity or solvency.
- **Management stewardship and performance.** The assessment of a firm's management with respect to the efficient and profitable use of the firm's resources is usually made on the basis of economic performance as reported by periodic earnings. Because earnings are affected by factors other than current management performance, earnings may not be a reliable indicator of management performance.

- **Management explanations and interpretations.** Management is responsible for the efficient use of a firm's resources. Thus, it acquires knowledge about the enterprise and its performance which is unknown to the external user. Explanations by management concerning the financial impact of transactions, events, circumstances, uncertainties, estimates, judgments, and any effects of the separation of the results of operations into periodic measures of performance enhance the usefulness of financial information.

SFAC 2: Qualitative Characteristics of Accounting Information

The purpose of financial reporting is to provide decision makers with **useful** information. When accounting choices are to be made by individuals or by standard setting bodies, those choices should be based upon the **usefulness** of that information to the **decision making** process. This SFAC identifies the qualities or characteristics that make information useful in the decision making process. It also establishes a terminology and set of definitions to provide a greater understanding of the characteristics. The following diagram from SFAC 2 summarizes the qualitative characteristics of accounting information:

A Hierarchy Of Accounting Qualities

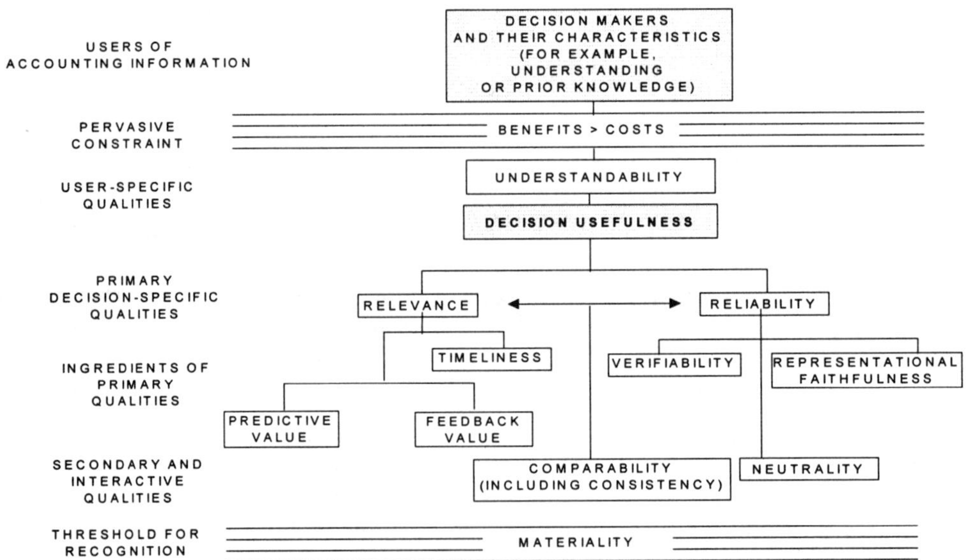

Usefulness for decision making. This is the most important characteristic of information. Information must be useful to be beneficial to the user. To be useful, accounting information must be both relevant and reliable. Both of these characteristics are affected by the completeness of the information provided.

Relevance. Information is **relevant** to a decision if it makes a difference to the decision maker in his/her ability to predict events or to confirm or correct expectations. Relevant information will reduce the decision maker's assessment of the uncertainty of the outcome of a decision even though it may not change the decision itself. Information is relevant if it provides knowledge concerning past events **(feedback value)** or future events **(predictive value)** and if it is **timely**. Disclosure requirement information such as segment reporting and interim earnings reports is relevant because it provides information about past events and it improves the predictability of future events. The predictive value of accounting information does not imply that such information is a prediction. The predictive value refers to the utility that a piece of information has as an input into a predictive model. Although timeliness alone will not make information relevant, information must be timely to be relevant. It must be available before it loses its ability to influence the decision maker.

Reliability. Financial statements are an abstraction of the activities of a business enterprise. They simplify the activities of the actual firm. To be **reliable**, financial statements must portray the important financial relationships of the firm itself. Information is reliable if it is verifiable and neutral and if users can depend on it to represent that which it is intended to represent (**representational faithfulness**).

Information may not be representationally faithful if it is biased. Bias is the tendency for an accounting measure to be consistently too high or too low. Bias may arise because the measurer does not use the measurement method properly or because the measurement method does not represent what it purports to represent.

Verifiability means that several independent measures will obtain the same accounting measure. An accounting measure that can be repeated with the same result (consensus) is desirable because it serves to detect and reduce measurer bias. Cash is highly verifiable. Inventories and depreciable assets tend to be less verifiable because alternative valuation methods exist. The direct verification of an accounting measure would serve to minimize measurer bias and measurement bias. The verification of the procedures used to obtain the measure would minimize measurer bias only. Finally, verifiability does not guarantee representational faithfulness or relevance.

The characteristic of **neutrality** means that accounting information should serve to communicate without attempting to influence behavior in a particular direction. This does not mean that accounting should not influence behavior or that it should affect everyone in the same way (e.g., differential disclosure requirements could be neutral). It does mean that information should not favor certain interest groups. The effect of lease capitalization on leasing firms would not be a valid argument to oppose the requirement that certain leases be recorded as direct financing-type leases.

To be useful, accounting information should be **comparable**. The characteristic of comparability allows the users of accounting information to assess the similarities and differences either among different entities for the same time period or for the same entity over different time periods. Comparisons are usually made on the basis of quantifiable measurements of a common characteristic. Therefore, to be comparable, the measurements used must be reliable with respect to the common characteristic. Noncomparability can result from the use of different inputs, procedures, or systems of classification. Noncomparability can also arise when the data measurements lack representational faithfulness.

The characteristic of **consistency** also contributes to information usefulness. Consistency is an interperiod comparison which requires the use of the same accounting principles from one period to another. Although a change of an accounting principle to a more preferred method results in inconsistency, the change is acceptable if the effect of the change is disclosed. Consistency does not insure comparability. If the measurements used are not representationally faithful, comparability will not be achieved.

Trade-offs. Although it is desirable that accounting information contain the characteristics that have been identified above, not all of these characteristics are compatible. Often, one characteristic may be obtained only by sacrificing another. The trade-offs that must be made are determined on the basis of the relative importance of the characteristics. This relative importance, in turn, is dependent upon the nature of the users and their particular needs.

Constraints. The qualitative characteristics of useful accounting information are subject to two constraints: the **materiality** and the **relative cost benefit** of that information. An item of information is material and should be reported if it is significant enough to have an effect on the decision maker. Materiality requires judgment. It is dependent upon the relative size of an item, the precision with which the item can be estimated, and the nature of the item. No general standards of materiality are provided (although an appendix to SFAC 2 lists several guidelines that have been applied).

Accounting information provides the user with certain benefits. Associated with this benefit, however, is the cost of using that information and of providing it to the user. Information should be provided only if its benefits exceed its cost. Unfortunately, it is difficult to value the benefit of accounting information. It is also difficult to determine whether the burden of the cost of disclosure and the benefits of such disclosure are distributed fairly.

Role of conservatism. Any discussion of the qualitative characteristics of accounting information would be incomplete without some reference to the doctrine of conservatism. Conservatism is a reaction to uncertainty. For many years, accountants have been influenced by conservatism. Conservatism in accounting may mislead users if it results in a deliberate understatement of net assets and net income. Such understatement is undertaken to minimize the risk of uncertainty to outside lenders. Unfortunately, such understatements often lead to overstatements in subsequent years, produce biased financial statements, and conflict with the characteristics of representational faithfulness, neutrality, and comparability.

SFAC 5: Recognition and Measurement in Financial Statements of Business Enterprises

SFAC 5 indicates that financial statements are the principal means of communicating useful financial information. A full set of such statements follows:

- Financial position at end of the period
- Earnings for the period
- Comprehensive income for the period
- Cash flows during the period
- Investments by and distributions to owners during the period

These statements result from simplifying, condensing, and aggregating transactions. Therefore, no one financial statement provides sufficient information by itself and no one item or part of each statement can summarize the information.

A statement of financial position provides information about an entity's assets, liabilities, and equity. Earnings is a measure of entity performance during a period. It is similar to net income but excludes accounting adjustments from earlier periods such as cumulative effect changes in accounting principles. Comprehensive income comprises all recognized changes in equity other than those arising from investments by and distributions to owners. The FASB has provided in SFAS 130 that comprehensive income be disclosed either as part of the income statement or in a separate statement of financial performance. A statement of cash flows reflects receipts and payments of cash by major sources and uses including operating, financing, and investing activities. The investments by and distributions to owners reflect the capital transactions of an entity during a period.

Income is determined by the concept of financial capital maintenance which means that only if the money amount of net assets increases during a period (excluding capital transactions) is there a profit. For recognition in financial statements, subject to both cost-benefit and materiality constraints, an item must meet the following criteria:

1. **Definition**--Meet the definition of an element in financial statements
2. **Measurability**--Have a relevant attribute measurable with sufficient reliability
3. **Relevance**
4. **Reliability**

Items reported in these statements are based on historical cost, replacement cost, market value, net realizable value, and present value of cash flows. Price level changes are not recognized in these statements and conservatism guides the application of recognition criteria.

2 BALANCE SHEET

PERSPECTIVE AND ISSUES

Balance sheets or statements of financial position present assets, liabilities, and shareholders' equity (net worth, partners' capital). They reflect the financial status of an enterprise in conformity with generally accepted accounting principles. The balance sheet reports the aggregate effect of transactions at a **point in time**, whereas the income statement, statement of retained earnings, and statement of cash flows report the effect of transactions over a **period of time.**

For years, users of financial statements put more emphasis on the income statement than on the balance sheet. Investors' main concern was the short-run maximization of earnings per share. During the late 1960s and early 1970s company growth and desirability was measured by earnings growth. But the combination of inflation and recession during the 1970's and the emphasis in the Conceptual Framework Project on the asset-liability approach to theory brought about a rediscovery of the balance sheet. This shift toward the balance sheet has marked a departure from the traditional transaction-based concept of income toward a capital maintenance concept proposed by economists. Under this approach to income measurement, the amount of beginning net assets would be compared to the amount of ending net assets, and the difference would be adjusted for dividends and capital transactions. Only to the extent that an entity maintained its net assets (after adjusting for capital transactions) would income be earned. By using a capital maintenance concept, investors can better predict the overall profit potential of the firm.

Financial statements should provide information that helps users make rational investment, credit, or economic decisions. The balance sheet must be studied in order to measure a firm's liquidity, financial flexibility and ability to generate profits, pay debts when due, and pay dividends. A firm's liquidity refers to the timing of cash flows in the normal course of business. Liquidity indicates the firm's ability to meet its obligations as they fall due. The concept of financial flexibility is broader than the concept of liquidity. Financial flexibility is the ability to take effective actions to alter the amounts and timing of cash flows so it can respond to unexpected needs and opportunities. Financial flexibility includes the ability to issue new capital or unused lines of credit.

One of the main objectives of financial reporting is to provide information that is useful in assessing the amounts, timing, and uncertainty of future cash flows. There have been two suggestions to make the balance sheet more useful in assessing a firm's liquidity. The first is to make alterations to the balance sheet's format. The second is to provide additional information about liquidity in the notes to the balance sheet.

In many industries, balance sheets are classified into categories. Assets are classified as "current" if they are reasonably expected to be converted into cash, sold, or consumed either in 1 year or in the operating cycle, whichever is longer. Liabilities are classified as "current" if they are expected to be liquidated through the use of current assets or the creation of other current liabilities.

In some industries, the concept of working capital has little importance and the balance sheet is not classified. Such industries are broker-dealer, investment companies, real estate companies, and utilities. Personal financial statements are unclassified for the same reason.

Sources of GAAP

ARB	*APB*	*SFAS*	*FASB I*	*TB*	*SFAC*
43, Ch. 2, 3A	6, 12, 21, 22	5, 6, 12, 57, 78, 95, 115, 130	8	79-3	6

DEFINITIONS OF TERMS

Statement of Financial Accounting Concepts 6 defines 10 elements of the financial statements of business enterprises and several other concepts that relate to those elements. Elements are the basic categories which appear on the financial statements. To be included in the financial statements, an item must meet the definitional requirements, recognition requirements, and measurement requirements. Although there may be other elements of the financial statements, this Statement defines only those elements that relate to the status and performance of a business and are relevant to decisions which would require the commitment of resources to the business. Three of the 10 elements (assets, liabilities, and equity) are related to the status of an entity at a particular point in time. The other 7 elements (comprehensive income, revenues, expenses, gains and losses, investments by owners, and distributions to owners) are related to the performance of an entity over a period of time. The two categories of elements **articulate**. That is, a change in one will affect the other.

Elements of balance sheets.

> ***Assets***--*Probable future economic benefits obtained or controlled by a particular entity as a result of past transactions or events (SFAC 6, para 25).*

The following three characteristics must be present for an item to qualify as an asset:

1. The asset must provide probable future economic benefit which enables it to provide future net cash inflows.
2. The entity is able to receive the benefit and restrict other entities' access to that benefit.
3. The event which provides the entity with the right to the benefit has occurred.

Assets remain an economic resource of an enterprise as long as they continue to meet the three requirements identified above. Transactions and operations act to change an entity's assets.

A valuation account is not an asset or a liability. It alters the carrying value of an asset and is not independent of that related asset. Assets have features that help identify them in that they are exchangeable, legally enforceable, and have future economic benefit (service potential). It is that potential that eventually brings in cash to the entity and that underlies the concept of an asset.

> ***Liabilities***--*Probable future sacrifices of economic benefits arising from present obligations of a particular entity to transfer assets or provide services to other entities in the future as a result of past transactions or events (SFAC 6, para 35).*

The following three characteristics must be present for an item to qualify as a liability:

1. A liability requires that the entity settle a present obligation by the probable future transfer of an asset on demand, when a specified event occurs or at a particular date.
2. The obligation cannot be avoided.
3. The event which obligates the entity has occurred.

Liabilities usually result from transactions which enable entities to obtain resources. Other liabilities may arise from nonreciprocal transfers such as the declaration of dividends to the owners of the entity or the pledge of assets to charitable organizations.

An entity may involuntarily incur a liability. A liability may be imposed on the entity by government or by the court system in the form of taxes, fines, or levies. A liability may arise from price changes or interest rate changes. Liabilities may be legally enforceable or they may be equitable obligations which arise from social, ethical, or moral requirements. Liabilities continue in existence until the entity is no longer responsible for discharging them. A valuation account is not an independent item. It alters the carrying value of a liability and is directly related to that liability.

Most liabilities stem from financial instruments, contracts, and laws which are legal concepts invented by a sophisticated economy. Enterprises incur liabilities primarily as part of their ongoing economic activities in exchange for economic resources and services required to operate the business. The end result of a liability is that it takes an asset or another liability to liquidate it. Liabilities are imposed by agreement, by law, by court, by equitable or constructive obligation, and by business ethics and custom.

> ***Equity***--*The residual interest in the assets that remains after deducting its liabilities. In a business enterprise, the equity is the ownership interest (SFAC 6, para 49).*

Equity arises from the ownership relation and is the source of enterprise distributions to the owners. Distributions of enterprise assets to owners are voluntary. Equity is increased by owners' investments and comprehensive income and is reduced by distributions to the owners. In practice, the distinction between equity and liabilities may be difficult to ascertain. Securities such as convertible debt and preferred stock may have characteristics of both equity (residual ownership interest) and liabilities (nondiscretionary future sacrifices).

The other elements which change assets, liabilities, and equities will be identified and defined in Chapter 3, Income Statement.

The diagram on the following page from SFAC 6 identifies the three classes of events which affect an entity.

CONCEPTS, RULES, AND EXAMPLES

Assets and liabilities are recorded in the financial statements under the historical cost principle. Historical exchange prices are used because they are objective and capable of being independently verified. One limitation of the balance sheet is that historical cost does not always reflect current value. When a balance sheet is presented, most assets are reported at cost. However, generally accepted accounting principles allow certain exceptions. Inventories may be reported at lower of cost or market, investments in debt and equity securities may be reported at amortized cost or market, and certain long-term investments may be reported under the equity method. Many accountants believe that the balance sheet would be more useful if the assets were restated in terms of current values. These current values may be market related or may simply be historical cost adjusted for the changing value of the dollar. Although assets are usually stated at historical cost, if market information indicates a permanent and material decline in value, recognition of the economic loss is immediate.

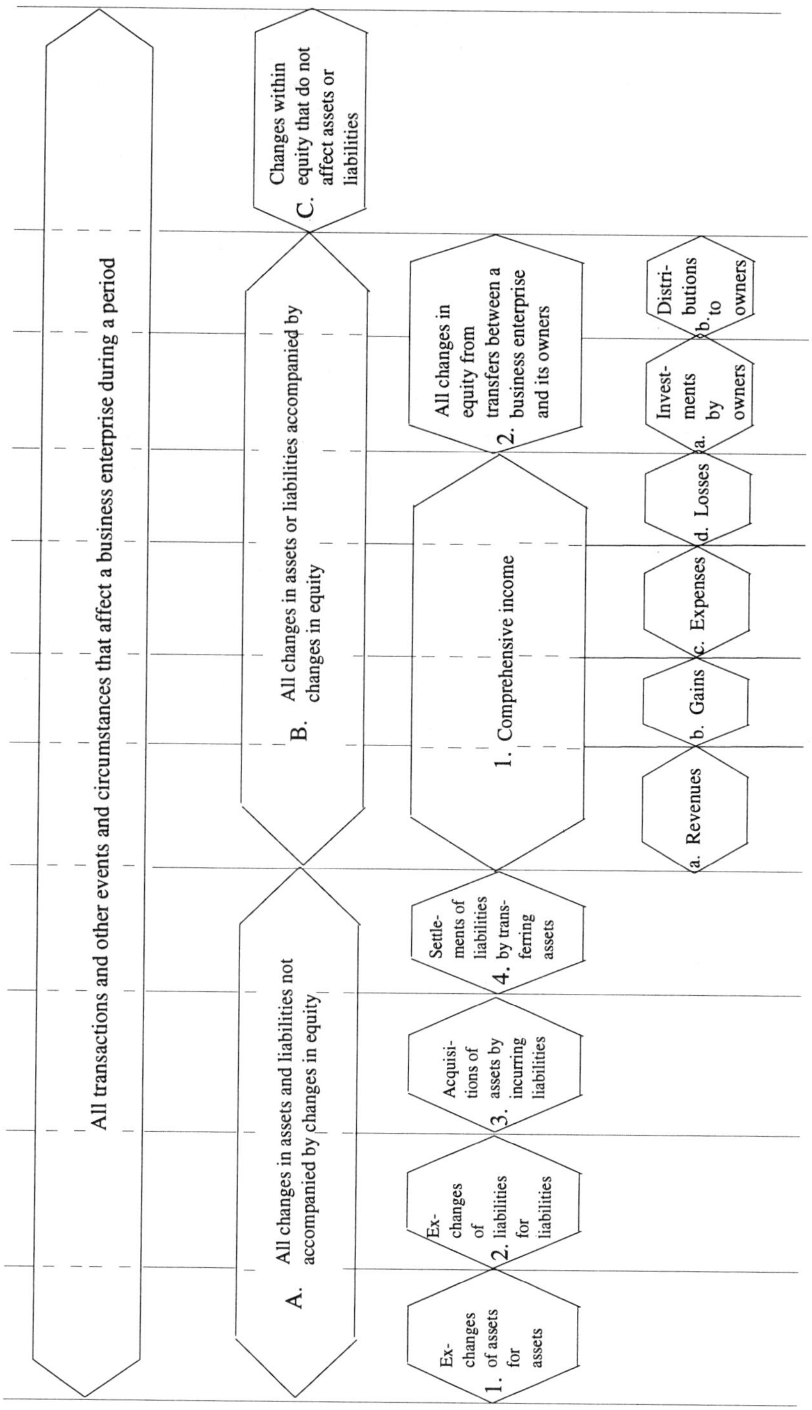
All transactions and other events and circumstances that affect a business enterprise during a period
A. All changes in assets and liabilities not accompanied by changes in equity
B. All changes in assets or liabilities accompanied by changes in equity
C. Changes within equity that do not affect assets or liabilities
1. Ex-changes of assets for assets
2. Ex-changes of liabilities for liabilities
3. Acquisi-tions of assets by incurring liabilities
4. Settle-ments of liabilities by trans-ferring assets
1. Comprehensive income
2. All changes in equity from transfers between a business enterprise and its owners
a. Revenues
b. Gains
c. Expenses
d. Losses
a. Invest-ments by owners
b. Distri-butions to owners

Another limitation of historical cost balance sheets is that estimates are used to determine the carrying/book values of many of the assets. Estimates are used in determining the collectibility of receivables, salability of inventory, and useful life of long-term assets. Depreciation, depletion, and amortization of long-term assets are acceptable practices, but appreciation of assets is not generally recorded. Appreciation of assets is usually recorded only when realized through an arm's-length transaction (sale). Estimates are necessary in order to divide and separate economic events occurring between two distinct accounting periods. However, such estimates require informed judgments for which there is little guidance in accounting literature.

An additional limitation of the balance sheet is that it ignores items that are of financial value to the firm but which cannot be objectively determined. For example, internally generated goodwill, human resources, and secret processes are of financial value, but since these values are not measurable under current accounting principles and practices, they are not recorded on the balance sheet. Only assets obtained in a market transaction are recorded on the books and records of an entity.

A final limitation of the balance sheet is that it ignores the time value of its elements. Although certain receivables and payables may be discounted (APB 21), most items are stated at face value regardless of the timing of the cash flows that they will generate.

The balance sheet has a mixture of historical cost and current value. For some assets and liabilities, cost is a close approximation of current value. Monetary assets such as cash, short-term investments, and receivables closely approximate current value. Current liabilities are payable in a short period, and closely approximate current value. If they were discounted, any discount value would be immaterial because of the short time period before payment. Current liabilities are not classified strictly on the basis of maturity value but on the concept that a current liability is one that requires either a current asset or another current liability to liquidate. Current liabilities should be shown on the balance sheet at face value. Productive assets such as property, plant, and equipment and intangibles are reported at cost less any reduction due to depreciation, depletion, or amortization. Long-term liabilities are recorded as the discounted value of future payments to be made under contract. On the date of issuance, the discount rate equals the market rate. Therefore, current value equals balance sheet cost. However, as time passes and the market rate fluctuates, the recorded cost will not necessarily approximate the current value.

The rights of the common shareholders of a firm and the rights of other capital-supplying parties (bondholders and preferred stockholders) of a firm are many and varied. Both sources of capital are concerned with two basic rights: the right to share in the cash or property disbursements (interest and dividends) and the right to share in the assets in the event of liquidation. The disclosure of these rights is an important objective in the presentation of financial statements.

Form of Balance Sheet

The use of the terms balance sheet, statement of financial position, or statement of financial condition denotes the use of generally accepted accounting principles. If some other comprehensive basis of accounting, such as income tax or cash, is used, the title of the financial statement must be adjusted to reflect this variation. Titles such as "Statements of Assets and Liabilities" would be necessary to differentiate the financial statement being presented from a balance sheet.

The three elements that are displayed in the heading of a balance sheet are

1. The entity whose financial position is being presented
2. The title of the statement
3. The date of the statement

The entity's name should appear exactly as written in the legal document which created it (e.g., the certificate of incorporation, partnership agreement, etc.). The title should also clearly reflect the legal status of the enterprise as a corporation, partnership, sole proprietorship, or divisions of some other entity. Where the entity's name does not disclose its legal status, supplemental information would have to be added to the title in order to clarify that status. A few examples are as follows:

ABC Company
(a partnership)

ABC Company
(a limited partnership)

ABC Company
(a sole proprietorship)

ABC Company
(a division of DEF, Inc.)

The title of the financial statement should be balance sheet unless another name is indicative of the terminology used in the industry. For example, in the securities industry, the title "Statement of Financial Condition" is used.

Finally, the last day of the month should be used as the statement date, unless the entity uses a fiscal reporting period always ending on a particular day of the week such as Friday or Sunday. In these cases, the balance sheet can appropriately be dated accordingly (i.e., December 26, October 1, etc.).

Balance sheets should generally be uniform in appearance from one period to the next. The form, terminology, captions, and pattern of combining insignificant items should be consistent.

Classification of Assets

Assets, liabilities, and stockholders' equity are separated in the balance sheet so that important relationships can be shown and attention can be focused on significant subtotals.

Current assets. Per ARB 43, Chapter 3, current assets are cash and other assets or resources commonly identified as those which are reasonably expected to be realized in cash or sold or consumed during the normal operating cycle of the business. When the cycle is less than 1 year, the 1-year concept is traditionally adopted. However, when the operating cycle exceeds 1 year, the operating cycle will serve as the proper measurement period for purposes of current asset classification. When the cycle is very long, the usefulness of the concept of current assets diminishes. The following items would be classified as current assets:

1. **Cash** and cash equivalents include cash on hand consisting of coins, currency, undeposited checks; money orders and drafts; and deposits in banks. Anything accepted by a bank for deposit would be considered as cash. Cash must be available for a demand withdrawal. Assets such as certificates of deposit would not be considered cash because of the time restrictions on withdrawal. Also, cash must be available for current use in order to be classified as a current asset. Cash which is restricted in use and whose restrictions will not expire within the operating cycle or cash restricted for a noncurrent use would not be included in current assets. Per SFAS 95, cash equivalents include short-term, highly liquid investments that (1) are readily convertible to known amounts of cash and (2) are so near their maturity (maturities of 3 months or less from the date of purchase by the enterprise) that they present negligible risk of changes in value because of changes in interest rates. Treasury bills, commercial paper, and money market funds are all examples of cash equivalents.
2. **Short-term investments** are readily marketable securities acquired through the use of temporarily idle cash. These securities are accounted for under SFAS 115. Under SFAS 115, the basis of reporting of these items need not be reported on the face of the balance sheet provided the different reporting classifications are reconciled in the notes. The balance sheet presentation would be as follows:

Marketable securities	$xxx

3. **Receivables** include accounts and notes receivable, receivables from affiliate companies, and officer and employee receivables. The term "accounts receivable" represents amounts due from customers arising from transactions in the ordinary course of business. Allowances due to uncollectibility and any amounts discounted or pledged should be clearly stated. The allowances may be based upon a relationship to sales or based upon direct

analysis of the receivables. If material, the receivables should be broken down into their component parts. The receivables section may be presented as follows:

Receivables:		
Accounts	$xxx	
Notes	xxx	
	xxx	
Less allowance for doubtful accounts	(xxx)	
	xxx	
Affiliate companies	xxx	
Officers and employees	xxx	$xxx

4. **Inventories** are goods on hand and available for sale. The basis of valuation and the method of pricing should be disclosed.

Inventories--at the lower of cost or market (specific identification)	$xxx

In the case of a manufacturing concern, raw materials, work in process, and finished goods should be disclosed separately on the balance sheet or in the footnotes.

Inventories:		
Finished goods	$xxx	
Work in process	xxx	
Raw materials	xxx	$xxx

5. **Prepaid expenses** are assets created by the prepayment of cash or incurrence of a liability. They expire and become expenses with the passage of time, usage or events (e.g., prepaid rent, prepaid insurance, and deferred taxes).

Long-term investments. Investments that are intended to be held for an extended period of time (longer than one operating cycle) would be classified as available-for-sale or held-to-maturity investments under SFAS 115. The following are the three major types of long-term investments:

1. **Debt and equity securities** are stocks, bonds, and long-term notes. Under SFAS 115, the basis of reporting of these items is not reported on the face of the balance sheet but should be reported in the notes.

Long-term investments:			
Investments in A company stock	$xxx		
Notes receivable	xxx		
Less discount on notes receivable	(xxx)	xxx	
Investment in B company bonds		xxx	$xxx

2. **Tangible assets** not currently used in operations.

3. **Investments held in special funds** (e.g., sinking funds, pension funds, amounts held for plant expansion, and cash surrender values of life insurance policies).

Property, plant, and equipment. Assets of a durable nature that are to be used in the production or sale of goods, sale of other assets, or rendering of services rather than being held for sale (e.g., machinery and equipment, buildings, furniture and fixtures, natural resources, and land). These should be disclosed with related accumulated depreciation/depletion as follows:

Machinery and equipment	$xxx	
Less accumulated depreciation	(xxx)	$xxx
or		
Machinery and equipment (net of $xxx accumulated depreciation)		$xxx

Accumulated depreciation may be shown in total or by major classes of depreciable assets. In addition to showing this amount on the balance sheet, the notes to the financial statements should contain balances of major classes of depreciable assets, by nature or function, at the balance sheet date and a general description of the method or methods used in computing depreciation with respect to major classes of depreciable assets (APB 12, para 5).

Intangible assets. Noncurrent, nonmaterialistic assets of a business, the possession of which provides anticipative benefits to the owner (e.g., goodwill, trademarks, patents, copyrights, organizational costs, etc.). Generally, the amortization of an intangible asset is credited directly to the asset account, although it is acceptable to use an accumulated amortization account.

Other assets. An all-inclusive heading for accounts that do not fit neatly into any of the other asset categories (e.g., long-term prepaid expenses, deferred taxes, bond issue costs, noncurrent receivables, and restricted cash).

Classification of Liabilities

The liabilities are displayed on the balance sheet in the order of payment.

Current liabilities. Per ARB 43, Chapter 3, obligations whose liquidation is reasonably expected to require the use of existing resources properly classifiable as current assets, or the creation of current obligations. Obligations that are due on demand or which are callable at any time by the lender are classified as current regardless of the intent of the entity or lender.

1. Obligations arising from the acquisition of goods and services entering the operating cycle (e.g., accounts payable, short-term notes payable, wages payable, taxes payable, and other miscellaneous payables).

2. Collections of money in advance for the future delivery of goods or performance of services, such as rent received in advance and unearned subscription revenues.
3. Other obligations maturing within the current operating cycle to be met through the use of current assets, such as the current maturity of bonds, and long-term notes.

In two cases, obligations to be paid in the next period should not be classified as current liabilities. Debt expected to be refinanced through another long-term issue and debt that will be retired through the use of noncurrent assets, such as a bond sinking fund, are treated as noncurrent liabilities because the liquidation does not require the use of current assets or the creation of other current liabilities.

The distinction between current and noncurrent liquid assets and liabilities generally rests upon both the ability of the entity and the intent of the entity to liquidate or not to liquidate within the traditional 1 year concept.

Noncurrent liabilities. Obligations that are not expected to be liquidated within the current operating cycle.

1. Obligations arising through the acquisition of assets, such as the issuance of bonds, long-term notes, and lease obligations.
2. Obligations arising out of the normal course of operations, such as pension obligations.
3. Contingent obligations involving uncertainty as to possible losses. These are resolved by the occurrence or nonoccurrence of one or more future events that confirm the amount payable, the payee, and/or the date payable, such as product warranties (see contingency section).

On all long-term liabilities the maturity date, nature of obligation, rate of interest, and any security pledged to support the agreement should be clearly shown. Also, on bonds and long-term notes, any premium or discount should be reported separately as an addition to or subtraction from the bond or note. Long-term obligations where certain covenants exist are classified as current liabilities if any of those covenants have been violated and the lender has the right to demand payment. Unless the lender expressly waives that right or the conditions causing the default are corrected, the obligation is current.

Other liabilities. Items that do not meet the definition of a liability, such as deferred income taxes or deferred investment tax credits. Many times these items will be included in current or noncurrent liabilities even though they technically are not similar.

Offsetting assets and liabilities. In general, assets and liabilities are not offset against each other. The reduction of accounts receivable by the allowance for doubtful accounts or property, plant, and equipment by the accumulated depreciation are acts which reduce these assets by the appropriate valuation accounts.

The right of setoff must exist for the offsetting in the financial statements to be a proper presentation. This right of setoff exists only when all the following conditions are met:

1. Each of the two parties owes the other determinable amounts (although they may be in different currencies and bear different rates of interest).
2. The entity has the right to setoff against the amount owed by the other party.
3. The entity intends to offset.
4. The right of setoff is legally enforceable.

In particular cases, state laws or bankruptcy laws may impose restrictions or prohibitions against the right of setoff. Furthermore, when maturities differ, only the party with the nearest maturity can offset because the party with the longer maturity must settle in the manner determined by the earlier maturity party.

The offsetting of cash or other assets against a tax liability or other amounts due to governmental bodies is also not acceptable except under limited circumstances. The only exception is when it is clear that the purchase of securities is in substance an advance payment of taxes payable in the near future and that the securities are acceptable for the payment of taxes. Primarily this occurs as an accommodation to governmental bodies.

For forwards, interest rate swaps, currency swaps, options, and other conditional or exchange contracts, the conditions for the right of offset must exist or the fair value of contracts in a loss position cannot be offset against the fair value of contracts in a gain position. Neither can accrued receivable amounts be offset against accrued payable amounts. If, however, there is a master netting arrangement, then fair value amounts recognized for forwards, interest or currency swaps, options, or other such contracts may be offset without respect to the conditions previously specified.

Classification of Stockholders' Equity

Stockholders' equity is the interest of the stockholders in the assets of a corporation. It shows the cumulative net results of past transactions and other events.

Capital stock. Stock which consists of the par/stated value of preferred and common shares. The number of shares authorized, the number issued, and the number outstanding should be clearly shown. For preferred stock, the preferences and features must also be stated as follows:

6% cumulative preferred stock, $100 par value, callable at $115, 10,000 shares authorized and outstanding	$xxx
Common stock, $10 par value per share, 2,000,000 shares authorized, 1,500,000 shares issued and outstanding	$xxx

Preferred stock which is redeemable at the option of the holder is not considered to be part of equity, but is usually shown in a separate caption between liabilities and equity.

Additional paid-in capital. There are two major categories of additional paid-in capital.

1. Paid-in capital in excess of par/stated value which is the difference between the actual issue price and par/stated value. Amounts in excess should be disclosed separately for common stock and each issue of preferred stock as follows:

Additional paid-in capital--6% preferred stock	$xxx
Additional paid-in capital--common stock	$xxx

2. Paid-in capital from other transactions which includes treasury stock, retirement of stock, stock dividends recorded at market, lapse of stock purchase warrants, conversion of convertible bonds in excess of the par value of the stock, and any other additional capital from the company's own stock transactions.

Donated capital. Donations of a noncash variety from either stockholders or outside parties, such as land, securities, buildings, and equipment.

Retained earnings. Accumulated earnings not distributed to the shareholders.

1. Appropriated, a certain amount of retained earnings that are not to be distributed to stockholders as dividends.
2. Unappropriated, earnings available to be distributed as dividends.

A balance sheet disclosure should reveal the pertinent provisions, source of restriction, amount subject to restriction, and restrictions on other items, such as working capital and additional borrowings. If a company appropriated retained earnings to satisfy bond indebtedness, the presentation would be as follows:

Retained earnings:		
Appropriated for bond indebtedness	$xxx	
Free and unappropriated	xxx	$xxx

Many corporations do not record the restrictions in appropriated and unappropriated accounts but merely explain the restrictions in the footnotes because financial statement users often believe the appropriation is held as cash. Also included in the equity section of the balance sheet is treasury stock representing issued shares reacquired by the issuer. These are generally stated at their cost of acquisition and as a reduction of shareholders' equity.

Accumulated other comprehensive income. Its components including net unrealized holding gains and losses on investments classified as available-for-sale securities (SFAS 115), the excess of minimum pension liability over unrecognized prior service cost, and unrealized gains (losses) on foreign currency translations shall be shown either in the statement of changes in stockholders' equity or in the stockholders' equity section (see pages 690-691).

Stockholders' equity		$xx
Common stock		xx
Paid in capital		xx
Retained earnings		xx
Accumulated other comprehensive income		
Foreign currency translation adjustments	$xx	
Pension liability adjustment	xx	
Unrealized gains on securities	xx	xx
Total stockholders' equity		$xx

Classification of Partners' Capital

In partnership entities, the balance sheet is the same as all other entities except for the net worth section. In a partnership, this section is usually referred to as partners' capital. In partnership accounting, the net worth section of the balance sheet includes the equity interests of the partners. Although each individual partner's capital need not be displayed, the totals for each class of partner, general or limited should be shown. Loans to or from partners should be displayed as assets and liabilities of the partnership and not as reductions or additions to partners (or stockholders in a corporation) although a separate line item on the balance sheet may be combined with net worth in a separately defined subtotal on the balance sheet. Payments to partners of interest on loans are properly classified as expenses on the income statement. Payments of interest on capital or salaries to partners are considered an allocation of profits and are usually not expensed on the income statement. However, in an attempt to emulate corporate financial reporting, some partnerships, with adequate disclosure, do display such payments as expenses.

Relation to the Income Statement

The balance sheet and income statement are interrelated through the changes that take place in each as a result of business transactions. Choosing a method of valuing inventory determines the method of calculating cost of goods sold. This articulation enables the users of financial information to use the statements as predictive indicators of future cash flows.

In assessing information about overall firm performance, users are interested in bringing together information in the income statement and the balance sheet. The balance sheet can also be used as a guide to give an indication of a firm's continuing ability to earn income and pay dividends. By combining the two statements, investors can develop some important financial ratios. For example, users may wish to express income as a rate of return on net operating assets.

Supplemental Disclosures

In addition to the measurement accounting principles which guide the values placed on the elements included in the balance sheet, there are disclosure accounting principles which are necessary to make the financial statements not misleading because of their omission.

The following are five techniques of disclosure:

1. Parenthetical explanations
2. Footnotes
3. Supporting schedules
4. Cross references
5. Valuation accounts

Parenthetical explanations. Supplemental information is disclosed by means of parenthetical explanations following the appropriate balance sheet items. For example

Common stock ($10 par value, 200,000 shares authorized, 150,000 issued)	$1,500,000

Parenthetical explanations have an advantage over both footnotes and supporting schedules. Parenthetical explanations place the disclosure in the body of the statement. The supplemental information tends to be overlooked when it is placed in a footnote.

Footnotes. If the additional information cannot be disclosed in a relatively short and concise parenthetical explanation, a footnote should be used. For example

Inventories (see note 1)	$2,550,000

The notes to the financial statements would contain the following:

Note 1: Inventories are stated at the lower of cost or market. Cost is determined on the first-in, first-out method and market is determined on the basis of estimated net realizable value. The market value of the inventory is $2,720,000.

Supporting schedules. In order to adequately present detail about certain balance sheet items, a supporting schedule may be used. Current receivables may be a single line item on the balance sheet, as follows:

Current receivables (see Schedule 2)	$2,500,000

A separate schedule for current receivables would then be presented as follows:

Schedule 2
Current Receivables

Customers' accounts and notes	$2,000,000
Associated companies	300,000
Nonconsolidated affiliates	322,000
Other	18,000
	2,640,000
Less allowance for doubtful accounts	(140,000)
	$2,500,000

Cross-references. Cross-referencing is used when there is a direct relationship between two accounts on the balance sheet. For example, among the current assets, the following might be shown if $1,500,000 of accounts receivable were required to be pledged as collateral for a $1,200,000 bank loan:

Accounts receivable pledged to bank	$1,500,000

Included in the current liabilities would be the following:

Bank loan payable-secured by accounts receivable	$1,200,000

Valuation accounts are used to reduce or increase the carrying amount of some assets and liabilities found in financial statements. Accumulated depreciation reduces the book value for property, plant, and equipment, and a bond premium (discount) increases (decreases) the face value of a bond payable as shown in the following illustrations:

Equipment	$18,000,000	
Less accumulated depreciation	(1,625,000)	$16,375,000
Bonds payable	$20,000,000	
Less discount on bonds payable	(1,300,000)	$18,700,000
Bonds payable	$20,000,000	
Add premium on bonds payable	1,300,000	$21,300,000

Accounting policies. There are many different methods of valuing assets and assigning costs. Financial statement users must be aware of the accounting policies used by enterprises so that sound economic decisions can be made. Per APB 22, the disclosures should identify and describe the accounting principles followed by the entity and methods of applying those principles that materially affect the determination of financial position, changes in cash flows, or results of operations. The accounting policies should encompass those accounting principles and methods that involve the following:

1. Selection from acceptable alternatives
2. Principles and methods peculiar to the industry
3. Unique applications of GAAP

The accounting policies should be in a separate section called "Summary of Significant Accounting Policies" or be the first note of the notes to the financial statements.

Related parties. According to SFAS 57, *Related Party Disclosures*, financial statements should include disclosure of material related party transactions other than compensation arrangements, expense allowances, or other similar items in the ordinary course of business.

A related party is essentially any party that controls or can significantly influence the management or operating policies of the company to the extent that the company may be prevented from fully pursuing its own interests. Such groups would include affiliates, investees accounted for by the equity method, trusts for the benefit of employees, principal owners, management, and immediate family members of owners or management.

Disclosures should take place even if there is no accounting recognition made for such transactions (e.g., a service is performed without payment). Disclosures should generally not imply that such related party transactions were on terms essentially equivalent to arm's-length dealings. Additionally, when one or more companies are under common control such that the financial statements might vary from those that would have been obtained if the companies were autonomous, the nature of the control relationship should be disclosed even if there are no transactions between the companies.

The disclosures generally should include

1. Nature of relationship.
2. Description of transactions and effects of such transactions on the financial statements for each period for which an income statement is presented.
3. Dollar amount of transactions for each period for which an income statement is presented and effects of any change in establishing the terms of such transactions differently than that used in prior periods.
4. Amounts due to and from such related parties as of the date of each balance sheet presented together with the terms and manner of settlement.

Comparative statements. In order to increase the usefulness of financial statements, many companies include in their annual reports 5 or 10-year summaries of condensed financial information. These comparative statements allow investment analysts and other interested readers to perform comparative analysis of pertinent information. ARB 43, Chapter 2 states the presentation of comparative financial statements in annual reports enhances the usefulness of such reports and brings out more clearly the nature and trends of current changes affecting the enterprise. Such presentation emphasizes the fact that the statements for a series of periods are far more significant than those for a single period and that the accounts for one period are but an installment of what is essentially a continuous history.

Subsequent events. The balance sheet is dated as of the last day of the fiscal period, but a period of time may elapse before the financial statements are issued. During this period, significant events or transactions may have occurred that materially affect the company's financial position. These events and transactions are called subsequent events. Significant events occurring between the balance sheet date and issue date could make the financial statements misleading if not disclosed.

There are two types of subsequent events (SAS 1, *Subsequent Events*). The first type consists of those events that provide additional evidence with respect to conditions that existed at the date of the balance sheet and affect the estimates inherent in the process of preparing financial statements. The second type consists of those events that provide evidence with respect to conditions that did not exist at the date of the balance sheet being reported on but arose subsequent to that date. The first type results in adjustments of the financial statements. The second type does not require adjustment of the financial statements but may require disclosure in order to keep the financial statements from being misleading. Disclosure can be made in the form of footnotes, supporting schedules, and pro forma statements.

Examples of subsequent events

1. A loss on an uncollectible trade account receivable as a result of a customer's deteriorating financial condition leading to bankruptcy subsequent to the balance sheet date would be indicative of conditions existing at the balance sheet date, thereby calling for adjustment of the financial statements before their issuance. On the other hand, a loss on an uncollectible trade account receivable resulting from a customer's major casualty, such as a fire or flood subsequent to the balance sheet date, would not be indicative of conditions existing at the balance sheet date and the adjustment of the financial statements would not be appropriate. However, if the amount is material, disclosure would be required.
2. A loss arising from the recognition after the balance sheet date that an asset such as plant and equipment had suffered a material decline in value arising out of reduced marketability for the product or service it can produce. Such a reduction would be considered an economic event in process at the balance sheet date and would require adjustment and recognition of the loss.
3. The second type of events (those not existing at the balance sheet date) which require disclosure but not adjustment include the following:

    a. Sale of a bond or capital stock issue
    b. Purchase of a business
    c. Settlement of litigation when the event giving rise to the claim took place subsequent to the balance sheet date. The settlement is an economic event which would be accounted for in the period of occurrence
    d. Loss of plant or inventories as a result of fire or flood
    e. Losses on receivables resulting from conditions (such as a customer's major casualty) arising subsequent to the balance sheet date
    f. Gains or losses on certain marketable securities

Contingencies. A contingency is defined in SFAS 5 as an existing condition, situation, or set of circumstances involving uncertainty as to possible gain or loss to an enterprise that will ultimately be resolved when one or more future events occur or fail to occur. Resolution of the uncertainty may confirm the acquisition of an asset, the reduction of a liability, the loss or impairment of an asset, or the incurrence of a liability.

An estimated loss from a **loss contingency** shall be accrued by a charge to income and the recording of a liability if **both** of the following conditions are met (SFAS 5, para 8):

1. Information available prior to issuance of the financial statements indicates that it is **probable** that an asset had been impaired or a liability had been incurred at the date of the financial statements.
2. The amount of loss can be **reasonably estimated.**

The likelihood of a loss on a contingency may be broken down into the following three classifications (SFAS 5, para 3):

1. Probable, the future event or events are likely to occur.
2. Reasonably possible, the chance of the future event or events occurring is more than remote but less than likely.
3. Remote, the chance of the future event or events occurring is slight.

If the loss contingency is probable but only a range of estimated values can be made, the minimum point of the range should be accrued and the maximum point should be disclosed.

If the loss contingency is at least reasonably possible, a liability should not be recorded but disclosure is required. If feasible, that disclosure should include an estimate of the loss or range of loss. If a reasonable estimate of the loss cannot be made, that fact should be disclosed.

Certain contingencies are remote, but their disclosure is expected in financial statements because a guarantee has been given. No disclosure is required for unasserted claims or assessments when no act by the potential claimant has transpired. In addition, general or unspecific business risks are neither accrued nor disclosed.

Examples of loss contingencies (SFAS 5, para 4)

1. Collectibility of receivables
2. Obligations related to product warranties and product defects
3. Risk of loss or damage of enterprise property by fire, explosion, or other hazards
4. Threat of expropriation of assets
5. Pending or threatened litigation
6. Actual or possible claims and assessments
7. Risk of loss from catastrophes assumed by property and casualty insurance companies including reinsurance companies

8. Guarantees of indebtedness of other entities
9. Obligations of commercial banks under standby letters of credit
10. Agreements to repurchase receivables (or to repurchase the related property) that have been sold

Accrual and disclosure of loss contingencies should be based on an evaluation of the facts in each particular case. Accrual is not a substitute for disclosure and disclosure is not a substitute for accrual.

An estimated gain from a **gain contingency** usually is not reflected in the accounts since to do so might be to recognize revenue prior to its realization. Adequate disclosure of the gain contingency shall be made, but care must be taken to avoid misleading implications as to the likelihood of realization.

Contracts and negotiations. All significant contractual agreements and negotiations should be disclosed in the footnotes to the financial statements. For example, lease contract provisions, pension obligations, requirements contracts, bond indenture convenants, and stock option plans should be clearly disclosed in the footnotes.

Risks and Uncertainties

AICPA Statement of Position 94-6 *Disclosure of Certain Significant Risks and Uncertainties* requires disclosure in financial statements about the risks and uncertainties existing as of the date of those statements. The four areas of disclosure are

1. Nature of operations
   a. Major products/services and principal markets served
   b. Industries operating within and relative importance of each industry including basis of determination (assets, revenue or earnings).

   NOTE: Quantification not required and words such as predominantly, equally, major, or other may be used.

2. Use of estimates in preparation of financial statements
   a. This fact must be disclosed as an explanation that management must use estimates
   b. Purpose is to clearly alert users to pervasiveness of estimates

3. Certain significant estimates
   a. Potential impact of estimates to value assets, liabilities, gains or losses when
      (1) Reasonably possible the estimate will change in the near term
      (2) Effect of change would be material to financial statements

      NOTE: Near term is defined as not to exceed 1 year from date of financial statements.

b. This is not a change in SFAS 5, *Accounting for Contingencies*
c. Disclosure of factors causing the estimate to be sensitive to change is encouraged, but not required
d. Materiality is measured by the effect of using a different estimate would have on the financial statements

Examples are "inventory subject to rapid technological obsolescence," "specialized equipment subject to technological obsolescence," "valuation allowances for deferred tax assets based on significant future income," "capitalized motion picture film production costs," "environmental remediation-related obligations," "litigation-related liabilities," "contingent liabilities for obligations of other entities," "provisions for restructurings," "estimated net proceeds recoverable, the provisions for expected loss incurred, or both, on disposition of a business or assets," "amounts reported for long-term contracts," "amounts reported for long-term obligations on a present-value basis, such as amounts reported for pensions and post employment benefits," and "assets subject to significant prepayment risk, such as investments in collateralized mortgage obligations."

4. Current vulnerability due to concentrations

a. Before issuance of financial statements, management knows that concentrations

(1) Exist at balance sheet date
(2) Make entity vulnerable to risk of near term severe impact
(3) Reasonably possible events could cause severe impact in near future

NOTE: Severe impact is defined as higher than materiality and would have a significant financially disruptive effect on the normal functioning of the entity.

b. Examples are concentrations in

(1) Volume of business transacted with a particular customer, supplier, lender, grantor, or contributor
(2) Revenue from particular products, services, or fund-raising events
(3) Available sources of supply of materials, labor, or services, or of licenses or other rights used in the entity's operations
(4) Market or geographical area in which an entity conducts its operations

c. Disclose the percentage of labor covered by a collective bargaining agreement and the percentage covered whose agreement expires within 1 year

d. Describe for operations outside of home country, the carrying value of net assets and location

Balance Sheet Format

The format of a balance sheet is not specified by any technical pronouncement but has become established as a matter of tradition and, in some circumstances, industry practices.

In general, the two types of format are the report form and the account form. In the report form the balance sheet continues line by line from top to bottom as follows:

Assets	$xxx
Liabilities	$xxx
Stockholders' equity	xxx
Total liabilities and stockholders' equity	$xxx

In the account form the balance sheet appears in a balancing concept with assets on the left and liabilities and equity amounts on the right as follows:

Assets	$ xxx	Liabilities	$ xxx
		Stockholders' equity	xxx
Total assets	$ xxx	Total liabilities & stockholders' equity	$ xxx

Example of balance sheet classification and presentation

The system of balance sheet classification and presentations is illustrated by the following comprehensive balance sheet:

ABC Corporation
Balance Sheet
December 31, 1999

Assets			
Current assets:			
Cash and bank deposits:			
Restricted to current bond maturity	$xxx		
Unrestricted	xxx	$xxx	
Short-term investments:			
Marketable equity securities (trading)		xxx	
Marketable debt securities (available-for-sale)		xxx	
Refundable income taxes		xxx	
Receivables from affiliates		xxx	
Accounts receivable	xxx		
Less allowance for doubtful accounts	(xxx)	xxx	
Notes receivable due in 2000	xxx		
Less notes receivable discounted	(xxx)	xxx	
Dishonored notes receivable		xxx	
Installment notes due in 2000		xxx	
Interest receivable		xxx	
Creditors' accounts with debit balances		xxx	
Advances to employees		xxx	
Inventories (carried at lower of cost or market by FIFO):			
Finished goods	xxx		
Work in process	xxx		
Raw materials	xxx	xxx	
Prepaid expenses:			
Prepaid rent	xxx		
Prepaid insurance	xxx	xxx	
Total current assets			$xxx
Long-term investments:			
Investments in equity securities (available-for-sale)		xxx	
Investments in bonds (held-to-maturity)		xxx	
Investments in equity securities (at cost, plus equity in undistributed net earnings since acquisition)		xxx	
Investments in unused land and facilities		xxx	
Cash surrender value of officers' life insurance policies		xxx	
Sinking fund for bond retirement		xxx	
Plant expansion fund		xxx	
Total long-term investments			$xxx

Property, plant, and equipment:			
Land		$xxx	
Buildings		xxx	
Machinery and equipment		xxx	
Furniture and fixtures		xxx	
Leasehold improvements		xxx	
Less accumulated depreciation and amortization		(xxx)	
Total property, plant, and equipment			xxx
Intangible assets net of amortization:			
Excess of cost over net assets of acquired businesses		$xxx	
Patents		xxx	
Trademarks		xxx	
Organization costs		xxx	
Total intangible assets, net			xxx
Other assets:			
Installment notes due after 2000		$xxx	
Unamortized bond issue costs		xxx	
Total other noncurrent assets			xxx
Total assets			$xxx
Liabilities and Stockholders' Equity			
Current liabilities:			
Commercial paper and other short-term notes	$xxx		
Accounts payable	xxx		
Salaries, wages, and commissions	xxx		
Taxes withheld from employees	xxx		
Income taxes payable	xxx		
Dividends payable	xxx		
Rent revenue collected in advance	xxx		
Other advances from customers	xxx		
Current portion of long-term debt	xxx		
Current obligations under capital leases	xxx		
Deferred tax liability	xxx		
Short-term portion of accrued warranty	xxx		
Other accrued liabilities	xxx		
Total current liabilities			$xxx

Noncurrent liabilities:			
Notes payable due after 2000	$xxx		
Plus unamortized note premium	xxx	$xxx	
Long-term bonds:			
10% debentures due 2012	xxx		
9-1/2% collateralized obligations maturing serially to 2003	xxx		
8% convertible subordinated debentures due 2017	xxx		
Less unamortized discounts net of premiums	(xxx)	xxx	
Accrued pension cost		xxx	
Obligations under capital leases		xxx	
Deferred tax liability		xxx	
Long-term portion of accrued warranty		xxx	
Total noncurrent liabilities			xxx
Total liabilities			$xxx
Capital stock:			
$12.50 convertible preferred stock, $100 stated value, 200,000 shares authorized, 175,000 outstanding	$xxx		
12% cumulative preferred stock, $100 stated value, callable at $115, 100,000 shares authorized and outstanding	xxx		
Common stock, $10 stated value, 500,000 shares authorized, 450,000 issued, 15,000 held in treasury	xxx		
Common stock subscribed 10,000 shares	xxx		
Less: Subscriptions receivable	(xxx)	$xxx	
Additional paid-in capital:			
From 12% cumulative preferred	xxx		
From common stock	xxx		
From treasury stock transactions	xxx		
From stock dividends	xxx		
From expiration of stock options	xxx		
Warrants outstanding	xxx	xxx	
Retained earnings:			
Appropriated for bond indebtedness	xxx		
Free and unappropriated	xxx	xxx	
Accumulated other comprehensive income			
Net unrealized loss on available-for-sale securities	(xxx)		
Unrealized loss from foreign currency translation	(xxx)		
Excess of minimum pension liability over unrecognized prior service cost	(xxx)	(xxx)	
Less: Treasury stock at cost		(xxx)	
Total stockholders' equity			$xxx
Total liabilities and stockholders' equity			$xxx

3 INCOME STATEMENT

PERSPECTIVE AND ISSUES

The income statement, also referred to as the statement of income, statement of earnings, or statement of operations, summarizes the results of an entity's economic activities for an accounting period. Since at least the early 1960s, the income statement has been widely perceived by investors, creditors, management, and other interested parties as the most important of an enterprise's basic financial statements. Investors consider the past income of a business as the most useful predictor of future earnings performance. Consequently, past income is generally considered the best indicator of future dividends and market stock price performance. Creditors look to the income statement for insight into the borrower's ability to generate the future cash flows needed to repay the obligations. Management must be concerned with the income statement by virtue of the fact that it is of concern to investors and creditors. Additionally, management uses the income statement as a gauge of its effectiveness and efficiency in combining the factors of production into the goods and/or services which it sells.

Much of current accounting theory is concerned with the measurement of income. Even with the renewed interest in the balance sheet, the income statement remains of paramount importance to the majority of financial statement users. This chapter will focus on key income measurement issues and on matters of income statement presentation and disclosure.

Sources of GAAP

ARB	*APB*	*SFAC*	*SFAS*	*TB*	*EITF*	*SOP*
43, Ch. 2	9, 11, 16, 18, 20, 30	5, 6	4, 7, 15, 16, 44, 64, 128, 130	85-6 87-4,	85-36, 87-4, 87-24, 90-16, 95-18	98-5

DEFINITIONS OF TERMS

Elements of Financial Statements

Comprehensive income. The change in equity of a business enterprise during a period from transactions and other events and circumstances from nonowner sources. It includes all changes in equity during a period, except those resulting from investments by owners and distributions to owners (SFAC 6).

Distribution to owners. Decreases in net assets of a particular enterprise resulting from transferring assets, rendering services, or incurring liabilities by the enterprise to owners.

Distributions to owners reduce the ownership interest of the receiving owners in the entity and reduce the net assets of the entity by the amount of the distribution. Such transactions are displayed in the statement of changes in equity.

Expenses. Decreases in assets or increases in liabilities during a period resulting from delivery of goods, rendering of services, or other activities constituting the enterprise's central operations (SFAC 6).

Gains. Increases in equity (net assets) from peripheral or incidental transactions of an entity and from all other transactions and other events and circumstances affecting the entity during a period except those that result from revenues or investments by owners (SFAC 6).

Investments by owners. Increases in net assets of a particular enterprise resulting from transfers to it of something valuable to obtain or increase ownership interests (or equity) in it.

Investments by owners may be in the form of assets, services, or the payment of entity liabilities. These investments are displayed in the statement of changes in equity. The purchase of an ownership interest from another owner is not a net investment because such a transfer does not increase the net assets of the entity.

Losses. Decreases in equity (net assets) from peripheral or incidental transactions of an entity from all other transactions and other events and circumstances affecting the entity during a period except those that result from expenses or distributions to owners (SFAC 6).

Revenues. Increases in assets or decreases in liabilities during a period from delivering goods, rendering services, or other activities constituting the enterprise's central operations (SFAC 6).

Other Terminology

Disposal date. The date of closing the sale if the disposal is by sale or the date that operations cease if disposal is by abandonment (APB 30).

Extraordinary item. Events and transactions that are distinguished by their unusual nature and by the infrequency of their occurrence (APB 30).

Measurement date. The date on which the management having the authority to approve the action commits itself to a formal plan to dispose of a segment of the business, whether by sale or abandonment (APB 30).

Realization. The process of converting noncash resources and rights into money or, more precisely, the sale of an asset for cash or claims to cash (SFAC 6).

Recognition. The process of formally recording or incorporating an item in the financial statements of an entity (SFAC 6).

Segment of a business. A component of an entity whose activities represent a major line of business or class of customer. A segment may be in the form of a subsidiary, a division, or a department, and in some cases, a joint venture or other nonsubsidiary investee. Its assets, results of operations, and activities can be clearly distinguished, physically and operationally, and for financial reporting purposes, from the other assets, results of operations, and activities of the entity (APB 30).

CONCEPTS, RULES, AND EXAMPLES

Concepts of Income

Economists have generally adopted a wealth maintenance concept of income. Under this concept, income is the maximum amount that can be consumed during a period and still leave the enterprise with the same amount of wealth at the end of the period as existed at the beginning. Wealth is determined with reference to the current market values of the net productive assets at the beginning and end of the period. Therefore, the economists' definition of income would fully incorporate market value changes (both increases and decreases in wealth) in the determination of periodic income.

Accountants, on the other hand, have generally defined income by reference to specific events which give rise to recognizable elements of revenue and expense during a reporting period. The events that produce reportable items of revenue and expense are a subset of economic events that determine economic income. Many changes in the market values of wealth components are deliberately excluded from the measurement of accounting income, but are included in the measurement of economic income.

The discrepancy between the accounting and economic measures of income are the result of a preference on the part of accountants and financial statement users for information which is reliable. Since many fluctuations in the market values of assets are matters of conjecture, accountants have retained the historical cost model which generally precludes the **recognition** of market value changes until realized by a transaction. Similarly, both accountants and economists realize that the earnings process occurs throughout the various stages of production, sales, and final delivery of the product. However, the difficulty in measuring the precise rate at which this earnings process is taking place has led accountants to conclude that income should normally be recognized only when it is fully realized. **Realization** generally implies that the enterprise producing the item has completed all of its obligations relating to the product and that collection of the resulting receivable is assured beyond reasonable doubt. For very sound reasons, accountants have developed a reliable system of income recognition which is based on generally accepted accounting principles applied consistently from period to period. The interplay between recognition and realization generally means that values on the balance sheet are recognized only when realized through an income statement transaction.

A separate, but equally important, reason for the disparity between the accounting and economic measures of income relates to the need for periodic reporting. The economic measure of income would be relatively simple to apply on a life cycle basis. Economic income would be measured by the difference between its wealth at the termination point versus its wealth at the origination date, plus withdrawals or other distributions and minus additional investments over the course of its life. However, applying the same measurement strategy to discrete fiscal periods, as accountants do, is much more difficult. The continual earnings process, in which the earnings of a business occur throughout the various stages of production and delivery of a product, is conceptually straightforward. Allocating those earnings to individual years, quarters, or months is substantially more difficult, requiring both estimates and judgment. Consequently, accountants have concluded that there must be unambiguous guidelines for revenue recognition. These have required recognition only at the completion of the earnings cycle.

The appropriate measurement of income is partially dependent upon the perspective of the party doing the measuring. From the perspective of the outside investors taken as a whole, income might be defined as earnings before any payments to those investors, including bondholders and preferred stockholders as well as common shareholders. On the other hand, from the perspective of the common shareholders, income might better be defined as earnings after payments to other investors, including creditors and preferred shareholders. Currently, net income is defined as earnings available for the preferred and common stockholders. However, in various statistics and special reports, a variety of these concepts is employed.

Recognition and Measurement

The definition of accounting income as a subset of economic income requires certain recognition criteria. The criteria are needed to assist accountants in determining which economic events are in the domain of items included in the measurement of income. SFAC 5 has identified four recognition criteria. They are the following:

1. **Definition**--To be recognized, the item must meet one of the definitions of an element of the financial statements. A resource must meet the definition of an asset; an obligation must meet the definition of a liability; and a change in equity must meet the definition of a revenue, expense, gain, loss, **investment by owner**, or **distribution to owner**.
2. **Measurability**--The item must have a relevant attribute that can be quantified in monetary units with sufficient reliability. Measurability must be considered in terms of both relevance and reliability, the two primary qualitative characteristics of accounting information.
3. **Relevance**--An item is relevant if the information about it has the capacity to make a difference in investors', creditors', or other users' decisions.
4. **Reliability**--An item is reliable if the information about it is representationally faithful, verifiable, and neutral. The information must be faithful in its representation, free of error, and unbiased.

In order to be given accounting recognition, an asset, liability, or change in equity would have to meet the four above-mentioned criteria.

Revenues. According to SFAC 6, para 78

> *Revenues are increases in assets or decreases in liabilities during a period from delivering goods, rendering services, or other activities constituting the enterprise's central operations. Characteristics of revenues (SFAC 6, para 79) include the following:*
>
> 1. *A culmination of the earnings process*
> 2. *Actual or expected cash inflows resulting from central operations*
> 3. *Inflows reported gross*

The realization concept stipulates that revenue is only recognized when the following occur:

1. The earnings process is complete or virtually complete.
2. Revenue is evidenced by the existence of an exchange transaction which has taken place.

The existence of an exchange transaction is critical to the accounting recognition of revenue. Generally, it means that a sale to an outside party has occurred, resulting in the receipt of cash or the obligation by the purchaser to make future payment for the item received.

However, an exchange transaction is viewed in a broader sense than the legal concept of a sale. Whenever an exchange of rights and privileges takes place, an exchange transaction is deemed to have occurred. For example, interest revenue and interest expense are earned or incurred ratably over a period without a discrete transaction taking place. Accruals are recorded periodically in order to reflect the interest realized by the passage of time. In a like manner, the percentage-of-completion method recognizes revenue based upon the measure of progress on a long-term construction project. The earnings process is considered to occur simultaneously with the measure of progress (e.g., the incurrence of costs).

The conditions for the timing of revenue recognition would also be varied if the production of certain commodities takes place in environments in which the ultimate realization of revenue is so assured that it can be recognized upon the completion of the production process. At the opposite extreme is the situation in which the exchange transaction has taken place, but significant uncertainty exists as to the ultimate collectibility of the amount. For example, in certain sales of real estate, where the down payment percentage is extremely small and the security for the buyer's notes is minimal, revenue is often not recognized until the time collections are actually received.

Expenses. According to SFAC 6, para 80:

> *Expenses are decreases in assets or increases in liabilities during a period resulting from delivery of goods, rendering of services, or other activities constituting the enterprise's central operations. Characteristics of expenses (SFAC 6, para 81) include the following:*
>
> 1. *Sacrifices involved in carrying out the earnings process*
> 2. *Actual or expected cash outflows resulting from central operations*
> 3. *Outflows reported gross*

Expenses are expired costs, or items which were assets but which are no longer assets because they have no future value. The matching principle requires that all expenses incurred in the generating of revenue should be recognized in the same accounting period as the revenues are recognized. The matching principle is broken down into three pervasive measurement principles: associating cause and effect, systematic and rational allocation, and immediate recognition.

Costs, such as materials and direct labor consumed in the manufacturing process, are relatively easy to identify with the related revenue elements. These cost elements are included in inventory and expensed as cost of sales when the product is sold and revenue from the sale is recognized. This is associating cause and effect.

Some costs are more closely associated with specific accounting periods. In the absence of a cause and effect relationship, the asset's cost should be allocated to benefiting accounting periods in a systematic and rational manner. This form of expense recognition involves assumptions about the expected length of benefit and the relationship between benefit and cost of each period. Depreciation of fixed assets, amortization of intangibles, and allocation of rent and insurance are examples of costs that would be recognized by the use of a systematic and rational method.

All other costs are normally expensed in the period in which they are incurred. This would include those costs for which no clear-cut future benefits can be identified, costs that were recorded as assets in prior periods but for which no remaining future benefits can be identified, and those other elements of administrative or general expense for which no rational allocation scheme can be devised. The general approach is first to attempt to match costs with the related revenues. Next, a method of systematic and rational allocation should be attempted. If neither of these measurement principles is beneficial, the cost should be immediately expensed.

Gains and losses. According to SFAC 6, paras 82 and 83

> *Gains (losses) are increases (decreases) in equity from peripheral transactions of an entity excluding revenues (expenses) and investments by owners (distribution to owners). Characteristics of gains and losses (SFAC 6, paras 84-86) include the following:*
>
> 1. *Result from peripheral transactions and circumstances which may be beyond entity's control*
> 2. *May be classified according to sources or as operating and nonoperating*

According to SFAC 5, the recognition of gains and losses should follow the principles stated below.

> 1. *Gains often result from transactions, and other events, that involve no "earnings process"; therefore, in terms of recognition, it is more significant that the gain be realized than earned.*
> 2. *Losses are recognized when it becomes evident that future economic benefits of a previously recognized asset have been reduced or eliminated, or that a liability has been incurred without associated economic benefits. The main difference between expenses and losses is that expenses result from ongoing major or central operations, whereas losses result from peripheral transactions that may be beyond the entity's control.*

Comprehensive income. SFAC 6, para 70 summarizes the income concept by defining comprehensive income as follows:

> *Comprehensive income is the change in equity of a business enterprise during a period from transactions and other events and circumstances from nonowner sources. It includes all changes in equity during a period, except those resulting from investments by owners and distributions to owners.*

Comprehensive income arises from the following:

1. Exchange transactions between the entity and entities other than the owners

2. Production, including manufacturing, storing, transporting, lending, insurance, and professional services
3. Environmental activities due to the economic, legal, social, political, and physical environment (price changes and casualties)

SFAS 130, *Reporting Comprehensive Income*, established standards for reporting and displaying comprehensive income and its components. Comprehensive income is the total of all components of comprehensive income, including net income, and other comprehensive income. Other comprehensive income represents revenues, expenses, gains, and losses that are included in comprehensive income but excluded from net income under generally accepted accounting principles. These terms, however, are not required to be used to meet the standard.

Note that SFAS 130 does not fully operationalize the definition in SFAC 6. It only addresses the reporting of changes in components that have been reported in stockholders' equity.

Comprehensive income should be reported in a financial statement that is displayed with the same prominence as other financial statements that are part of a full set of financial statements. Although no specific format is required by the standard, a preference was stated for the components of other comprehensive income and total comprehensive income to be displayed in the income statement (see page 79) or a separate statement of comprehensive income that begins with net income. Another alternative is to show the changes in the components of other comprehensive income in the statement of stockholders' equity (see pages 78 and 691). Components of other comprehensive income should also describe the amount of income tax expense or benefit for each component either on the face of the statement in which components are reported or in notes to the financials. Additionally, as items previously recognized in other comprehensive income as unrealized become realized they must be removed from other comprehensive income in the year such realization occurs. Balance sheet disclosure of accumulated other comprehensive income is shown on page 690.

Impact of Legal Form

Revenues and expenses of a corporation are easily identified and separated from the revenues and expenses of the stockholders. In both the sole proprietorship and partnership form of entity, the identification process can be more difficult. Items such as interest or salaries paid to partners or owners may be thought of as distributions of profits rather than expenses. However, many entities adopt the philosophy that income reporting should be the same regardless of legal form (economic substance takes precedence over legal form). Under the corporate form of business, interest on stockholder loans and salaries paid to stockholders are clearly classified as expenses and not as distributions. Accordingly, these items may be treated as expenses for both partnerships and sole proprietorships under this theory. However, full disclosure and consistency of financial reporting treatment would be required.

Circumstances may involve treating certain payments, such as guaranteed salaries, as expenses while classifying other "salaries" as profit distributions.

Income Statement Classification and Presentation

Income statements measure economic performance for a **period of time** and, except for this variation, follow the same basic rule for headings and titles as do balance sheets. The legal name of the entity must be used to identify the financial statements and the title "Income Statement" to denote preparation in accordance with generally accepted accounting principles. If another comprehensive basis of accounting is used, such as the cash or income tax basis, the title of the statement should be modified accordingly. "Statement of Revenue and Expenses--Income Tax Basis" or "Statement of Revenue and Expenses--Modified Cash Basis" are examples of such titles.

The date of an income statement must clearly identify the time period involved, such as "Year Ending March 31, 1999." This dating informs the reader of the length of the period covered by the statement and both the starting and ending dates. Dating such as "The Period Ending March 31, 1999" or "Through March 31, 1999" would be a violation of accounting principles because of the lack of precise definition in these titles. Income statements are rarely presented for periods in excess of 1 year but are frequently seen for shorter periods such as a month or a quarter. Entities whose operations form a natural cycle may have a reporting period end on a specific day (e.g., the last Friday of the month). These entities should head the income statement "For the 52 Weeks Ended March 28, 1999" (each week containing 7 days, beginning on a Saturday and ending on a Friday). Such entities' fiscal year only includes 364 days but is still considered an annual reporting period.

Income statements should be uniform both with respect to the appearance and the categories of income and expense accounts, from one time period through the next. Aggregation of items should not serve to conceal significant information, such as netting revenues against expenses or combining elements of interest to readers such as bad debts, depreciation, etc. The category "Other or Miscellaneous Expense" should contain, at maximum, an immaterial total amount of aggregated insignificant elements. Once this total approaches 10% of total expenses, some other aggregations with explanatory titles should be selected.

The major components and items required to be presented in the income statement are as follows:

1. Income from continuing operations
   a. Sales or revenues
   b. Cost of goods sold
   c. Operating expenses
   d. Gains and losses
   e. Other revenues and expenses
   f. Unusual or infrequent items
   g. Income tax expense related to continuing operations

2. Results from discontinued operations
   a. Income (loss) from operations of a discontinued segment (net of tax)
   b. Gain (loss) from disposal of discontinued segment (net of tax)
3. Extraordinary items (net of tax)
4. Cumulative effect of a change in accounting principles (net of tax)
5. Net income
6. Earnings per share

Income from continuing operations. This section summarizes the revenues and expenses of the company's central operations.

1. **Sales or revenues** are charges to customers for the goods and/or services provided during the period. This section should include information about discounts, allowances, and returns in order to determine net sales or net revenues.
2. **Cost of goods sold** is the cost of the inventory items sold during the period. In the case of a merchandising firm, net purchases (purchases less discounts, returns, and allowances plus freight-in) are added to beginning inventory to get cost of goods available for sale. From the cost of goods available for sale amount, the ending inventory is deducted to get cost of goods sold.

Example of schedule of cost of goods sold

ABC Merchandising Company
Schedule of Cost of Goods Sold
For the Year Ended 12/31/99

Beginning inventory				$xxx
Add:	Purchases		$xxx	
	Freight-in		xxx	
Cost of purchases			xxx	
Less:	Purchase discounts	$xx		
	Purchase R & A	xx	(xxx)	
Net purchases				xxx
Cost of goods available for sale				xxx
Less:	Ending inventory			(xxx)
Cost of goods sold				$xxx

A manufacturing company computes the cost of goods sold in a slightly different way. Cost of goods manufactured would be added to the beginning inventory to arrive at cost of goods available for sale. The ending inventory is then deducted from the cost of goods available for sale to determine the cost of goods sold. Cost of goods manufactured can be computed as follows:

Example of schedules of cost of goods manufactured and sold

XYZ Manufacturing Company
Schedule of Cost of Goods Manufactured
For the Year Ended 12/31/99

Direct materials inventory 1/1/99	$xxx	
Purchases of materials (including freight-in and deducting purchase discounts)	xxx	
Total direct materials available	$xxx	
Direct materials inventory 12/31/99	(xxx)	
Direct materials used		$xxx
Direct labor		xxx
Factory overhead:		
Depreciation of factory equipment	$xxx	
Utilities	xxx	
Indirect factory labor	xxx	
Indirect materials	xxx	
Other overhead items	xxx	xxx
Manufacturing cost incurred in 1999		$xxx
Add: Work in process 1/1/99		xxx
Less: Work in process 12/31/99		(xxx)
Cost of goods manufactured		$xxx

XYZ Manufacturing Company
Schedule of Cost of Goods Sold
For the Year Ended 12/31/99

Finished goods inventory 1/1/99	$xxx
Add: Cost of goods manufactured	xxx
Cost of goods available for sale	$xxx
Less: Finished goods inventory 12/31/99	(xxx)
Cost of goods sold	$xxx

3. **Operating expenses** are primary recurring costs associated with central operations (other than cost of goods sold) that are incurred in order to generate sales. Operating expenses are normally reported in the following two categories:

   a. Selling expenses
   b. General and administrative expenses

   Selling expenses are those expenses directly related to the company's efforts to generate sales (e.g., sales salaries, commissions, advertising, delivery expenses, depreciation of store furniture and equipment, and store supplies). General and administrative expenses are expenses related to the general administration of the company's operations (e.g., officers and office salaries, office supplies, depreciation of office furniture and fixtures, telephone, postage, accounting and legal services, and business licenses and fees).

4. **Gains and losses** stem from the peripheral transactions of the entity. These items are shown with the normal, recurring revenues and expenses. If they are material, they should be disclosed separately and shown above income (loss) from continuing operations before income taxes. Examples are write-downs of inventories and receivables, effects of a strike, and gains and losses from exchange or translation of foreign currencies.
5. **Other revenues and expenses** are revenues and expenses not related to the central operations of the company (e.g., gains and losses on the disposal of equipment, interest revenues and expenses, and dividend revenues).
6. **Unusual or infrequent** items are items which are either unusual or infrequent, but not both. They should be reported as a separate component of income from continuing operations.
7. **Income tax expense** related to continuing operations is that portion of the total income tax expense applicable to continuing operations.

Results from discontinued operations. Discontinued operations represent separately identifiable segments (components of a major class of business with separately identifiable assets, liabilities, revenues, and expenses) which are being disposed of. The discontinued operations section of an income statement consists of two components, the Income (loss) from operations and the Gain (loss) on the disposal. The first component, Income (loss) from operations, is disclosed for the current year only if the decision to discontinue operations is made after the beginning of the fiscal year for which the financial statements are being prepared. In the diagram below, the Income (loss) from operations component is determined for the time period designated by A--the period from the beginning of the year to the date the decision is made to discontinue a segment's operations (**measurement date**). The second component, Gain (loss) on disposal consists of the following two elements:

1. Income (loss) from operations during the phase-out period (the period between the measurement date and **disposal date**), B in the diagram below
2. Gain (loss) from disposal of segment assets

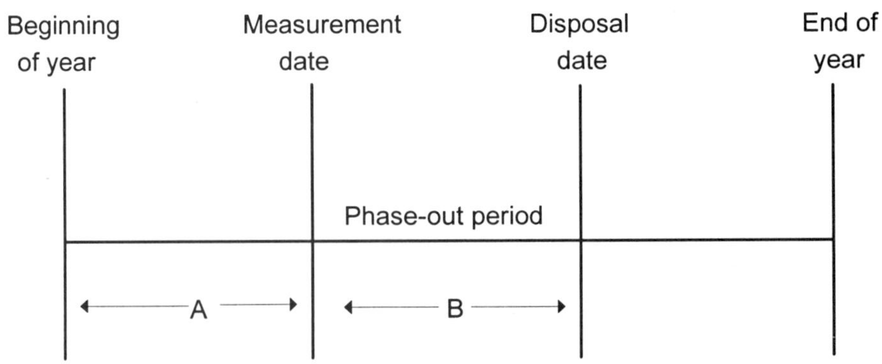

After it has been determined that certain discontinued operations constitute the disposal of a segment in accordance with APB 30, results of the discontinued segment must be segregated from normal, recurring operations. The allocation of interest to discontinued operations is permitted but not required. The maximum allocation cannot exceed the total of (a) interest on debt of the discontinued operation assumed by the buyer and (b) an allocated share of other interest not attributable to any other operations. If a loss is expected from the proposed sale or abandonment of a segment, the estimated loss should be provided for at the measurement date. If a gain is expected, it should be recognized when realized, which ordinarily is the disposal date. The results of discontinued operations should be disclosed separately as a component of income before extraordinary items and the cumulative effect of accounting changes (if applicable) as shown below.

Example of income statement presentation for discontinued operations

Income from continuing operations before income taxes		$xxxx
Provisions for income taxes		xxx
Income from continuing operations		$xxxx
Discontinued operations (Note _):		
Income (loss) from operations of discontinued Division X (less applicable income taxes of $_)	$xxxx	
Loss on disposal of Division X, including provision of $_ for operating losses during phase-out period (less applicable income taxes of $_)	(xxxx)	xxxx
Net income		$xxxx

There are special rules for situations in which the disposal date occurs in the year after the measurement date. The problem is one of estimating the unrealized Gain (loss) on disposal for that part of the phase-out period which is in the following year and comparing it to the actual Gain (loss) on disposal that has **already been realized** at the end of the preceding year for which the financial statements are being prepared. The following two rules apply to this situation:

1. A realized Loss on disposal may be increased by an estimated loss, or it may be reduced by an estimated gain (but only to zero).
2. A realized Gain on disposal may be reduced by an estimated loss but cannot be increased due to an estimated gain.

The diagram below depicts the relationships discussed above:

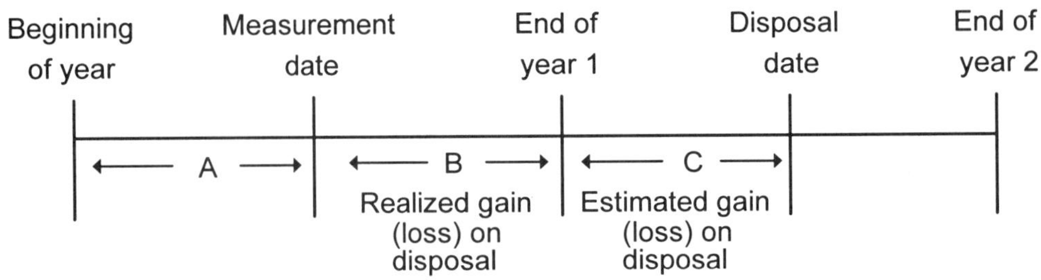

To find the year-end gain (loss), the amounts for B and C are compared and adjusted using the rules stated above.

Example of computing the year-end gain (loss) on disposal

Assume the following:

1. Loss from operations from beginning of year to the measurement date, \$699, net of taxes of \$466
2. Realized loss from operations from measurement date to end of current year, \$400, net of taxes of \$267
3. Estimated loss from operations from year end to disposal date, \$200, net of taxes of \$133
   Estimated gain from disposal of assets during next year, \$500, net of taxes of \$333

The loss from operations of the discontinued segment represents the first component of discontinued operations and is to be shown net of tax. Items 2 and 3 above are to be reported as the second component of discontinued operations: \$667 loss realized during phase-out period minus the \$300 estimated **net** gain to be realized in the next period (estimated gain on disposal less the estimated loss from operations). The income statement presentation would be as follows:

Income from continuing operations before provision for income taxes	\$598	
Provision for income taxes	239	
Income from continuing operations		\$359
Discontinued operations:		
Loss from operations of discontinued Division Z (less applicable taxes of \$466)	(699)	
Loss on disposal of Division Z including operating losses during phase-out period of \$1,000 and gain on disposal of assets of \$833, net of applicable taxes of \$67	(100)	(799)
Net loss		\$(440)

When discontinued operations are disclosed in a comparative income statement, the income statement presented for each previous year must be adjusted retroactively to enhance comparability with the current year's income statement. Accordingly, the revenues, cost of goods sold, and operating expenses (including income taxes) for the discontinued segment are removed from the revenues, cost of goods sold, and operating expenses of continuing operations. These items are netted into one figure [i.e., income (loss) from operations] which is disclosed under the discontinued operations section.

Example of comparative income statement disclosure

Assume the following:

1. The 1999 information is from the preceding example.
2. The 1998 information is given as shown.

	1999	*1998*
Discontinued operations:		
Loss from operations of discontinued Division Z, net of applicable taxes of $466	$699	$820
Loss on disposal of assets of discontinued Division Z, including loss during phase-out period, net of applicable taxes of $67	100	--

Example of computing and presenting income from discontinued operations

Assume the following:

1. Income from operations is $400,000
2. The following net of tax figures are given where:

A -- is the income (loss) **from operations** of Discontinued Segment X, net of taxes, in 1998.

B_1 -- is the gain (loss) on **disposal of assets** of Discontinued Segment X, net of taxes, **excluding operating** losses or gains during the phase-out period in 1998.

B_2 -- is the **operating** gain (loss) net of taxes, during the phase-out period in 1998.

C_1 -- is the gain (loss) on **disposal of assets** of Discontinued Segment X, net of taxes, **excluding operating** losses or gains during the phase-out period in 1999.

C_2 -- is the **operating** gain (loss) during the phase-out period in 1999, net of taxes.

	Case 1	*Case 2*	*Case 3*	*Case 4*	*Case 5*	*Case 6*
A	$ 50,000	$ 50,000	$ 50,000	$(50,000)	$(50,000)	$(50,000)
B_1	100,000	100,000	(100,000)	100,000	(100,000)	(100,000)
B_2	60,000	(110,000)	(60,000)	(40,000)	110,000	90,000
C_1	(80,000)	(80,000)	80,000	80,000	60,000	(10,000)
C_2	10,000	70,000	(70,000)	(70,000)	(80,000)	80,000

The trick is to net B_1 with B_2 and C_1 with C_2 before potential netting of the B's with the C's. Then the cases simplify, as follows:

	Case 1	*Case 2*	*Case 3*	*Case 4*	*Case 5*	*Case 6*
A	$ 50,000	$ 50,000	$ 50,000	$(50,000)	$(50,000)	$(50,000)
B	160,000	(10,000)	(160,000)	60,000	10,000	(10,000)
C	(70,000)	(10,000)	10,000	10,000	(20,000)	70,000

Note that in Case 4, the $10,000 expected gain cannot be recognized since it will not be realized until 1999. The gain was recognized in Case 3 because it offset the actual loss incurred. In Case 6 when the $70,000 anticipated gain is used to offset losses, only $10,000 can be used and $60,000 is delayed until the next year.

Now income statements can be readily prepared.

	Case 1	Case 2	Case 3	Case 4	Case 5	Case 6
Income from continuing operations (net of taxes)	$400,000	$400,000	$400,000	$400,000	$400,000	$400,000
Discontinued operations (net of taxes)						
Income (loss) from operations of discontinued Division X	$ 50,000	$ 50,000	$ 50,000	$ (50,000)	$ (50,000)	$ (50,000)
Gain (loss) on disposal of Division X, including provision for operating losses during phase-out period	90,000	(20,000)	(150,000)	60,000	(10,000)	--
Total	$140,000	$ 30,000	$(100,000)	$ 10,000	$ (60,000)	$ (50,000)
Net income (or income before extraordinary items and accounting changes) in 1998	$540,000	$430,000	$300,000	$410,000	$340,000	$350,000
Income to be reported in 1999	$ --	$ --	$ --	$ 10,000	$ --	$ 60,000

When amounts actually realized differ from estimates, differences between estimated and actual amounts shall be treated as changes in accounting estimates. These are reported net-of-tax on the appropriate line in the "discontinued operations" section of the income statement in the period realized. Amounts previously reported are not revised.

In addition to the amounts that should be disclosed in the financial statements, the notes to financial statements for the period encompassing the measurement date should disclose the following:

1. The identity of the **segment of business** that has been or will be discontinued
2. The expected disposal date
3. The expected manner of disposal
4. A description of the remaining assets and liabilities of the segment at the balance sheet date
5. The income or loss from operations and any proceeds from disposal of the segment during the period from the measurement date to the balance sheet date

Later periods, which include the period of disposal in financial statements, should disclose items 1, 2, 3, and 4.

Extraordinary items. Both of the following criteria must be met to classify an event or transaction as an extraordinary item. APB 30, para 20 defines these criteria as follows:

Unusual nature

> *The underlying event or transaction should possess a high degree of abnormality and be of a type clearly unrelated to, or only incidentally related to, the ordinary and typical activities of the entity, taking into account the environment in which the entity operates.*

Special characteristics of the entity include the following:

1. Type and scope of operations
2. Lines of business
3. Operating policies

Infrequency of occurrence

> *The underlying event or transaction should be of a type that would not reasonably be expected to recur in the foreseeable future, taking into account the environment in which the entity operates.*

In addition, accounting pronouncements have specifically required the following items to be disclosed as extraordinary, even though they do not meet the criteria stated above:

1. Material gains and losses from the extinguishment of debt (SFAS 4, para 8). Does not apply, however, to gains and losses from extinguishments of debt made to satisfy sinking-fund requirements that an enterprise must meet within 1 year of the date of extinguishment (SFAS 64, para 4).
2. Profit or loss resulting from the disposal of a significant part of the assets or a separable segment of previously separate companies, provided the profit or loss is material and the disposal is within 2 years after a pooling of interest (APB 16, para 60).
3. Write-off of operating rights of motor carriers (SFAS 44, para 6).
4. The investor's share of an investee's extraordinary item when the investor uses the equity method of accounting for the investee (APB 18, para 19).
5. Gains of a debtor related to a troubled debt restructuring (SFAS 15, para 21).

Per FASB Technical Bulletin 85-6, neither the cost incurred by a company to defend itself from a takeover attempt nor the cost incurred as part of a "standstill" agreement meet the criteria for extraordinary classifications as discussed in para 20, SFAS 30.

Extraordinary items should be segregated from the results of ordinary operations and be shown net of taxes in a separate section of the income statement, following "discontinued operations" and preceding "cumulative effect of a change in accounting principle," if any.

Example of the income statement presentation for extraordinary items

An extraordinary item would be presented as follows:

Income before extraordinary items	$xxx
Extraordinary items (less applicable income taxes of $_) (Note _)	xxx
Net income	$xxx

Accounting changes. A change in accounting principles results from adoption of a generally accepted accounting principle different from the one previously used for reporting purposes. The term **accounting principle** includes not only accounting principles and practices, but also the methods of applying them. Changes in accounting principles (or the method of applying them) must be justified by those who make the change (the firm's management), unless they are made in order to comply with a FASB position. (See Chapter 20 for a detailed discussion of accounting changes.)

Example of disclosure for a change in accounting principle

ABC Company
Income Statement
For the Year Ended December 31, 1999

	1999	1998
Income before cumulative effect of a change in accounting principle	$xxx	$xxx
Cumulative effect on prior years (to 12/31/98) of changing to (change described) (net of $_ tax)	xxx	
Net income	$xxx	$xxx
Per share amounts (simple capital structure)		
Income before cumulative effect of a change in accounting principle	$xxx	$xxx
Cumulative effect on prior years (to 12/31/98) of changing to (change described)	xxx	
Earnings per common share	$xxx	$xxx
Pro forma amounts assuming the new (change principle) is applied retroactively:		
Net income	$xxx	$xxx
Earnings per share	$xxx	$xxx

Earnings per share. Earnings per share is often used in evaluating a firm's stock price and in assessing the firm's future earnings and ability to pay dividends. Because of the importance of earnings per share, the profession has concluded that it should be disclosed on the face of the income statement.

Earnings per share is a very compact indicator of a company's performance. In order to assess quality of earnings, FASB 128 requires presentation of basic earnings per share on the face of the income statement for public-market issued common stock or potential common stock (such as options, warrants, convertible securities or contingent stock agreements). Shares outstanding are determined by the weighted average method. Earnings is defined as both income from continuing operations and net income available to common stockholders requiring the deduction of dividends declared on preferred stock and dividends for the period on cumulative preferred stock, whether or not earned or paid.

Diluted earnings per share is computed similarly to basic earnings per share by changing the number of shares outstanding to include the number of additional common shares that would be issued if the potentially dilutive shares had been issued.

Entities with simple capital structures, that is, only common stock, should display basic earnings per share for both continuing operations and net income on the face of the income statement. All other entities are required to display both basic and diluted per share amounts for both continuing operations and net income. For discontinued operations, extraordinary items, or cumulative effect of an accounting change, basic and diluted per share amounts may be described either on the face of the income statement or in the footnotes. More details on these calculations can be found in Chapter 18.

Example of the presentation and computation of earnings per share

Assume that 100,000 shares were outstanding throughout the year.

ABC Company
Income Statement
For the Year Ended December 31, 1999

Sales		$2,000,000
Cost of goods sold		750,000
Gross profit		$1,250,000
Selling and administrative expenses		500,000
Income from operations		$ 750,000
Other revenues and expense		
Interest income	$ 40,000	
Interest expense	(30,000)	10,000
Income before unusual or infrequent items and income taxes		$ 760,000
Unusual or infrequent items:		
Loss from permanent impairment of value of manufacturing facilities		(10,000)
Income from continuing operations before income taxes		$ 750,000
Income taxes		300,000
Income from continuing operations		$ 450,000
Discontinued operations:		
Income from operations of Division X, less applicable income taxes of $20,000	$ 30,000	
Loss on disposal of Division X, less applicable income taxes of $40,000	(60,000)	(30,000)

Income before extraordinary item and cumulative effect of accounting change	$ 420,000
Extraordinary item--loss from earthquake less applicable income taxes of $8,000	(12,000)
Cumulative effect in prior years of retroactive application of new depreciation method, less applicable income taxes of $40,000	(60,000)
Net income	$ 348,000

Basic EPS computation

Income from continuing operations	$4.50
Extraordinary items*	(0.12)
Accounting change*	(0.60)
Discontinued operations*	(0.30)
Net income available for common stockholders	$3.48

**May be shown in the notes to the financial statements.*

Format of Income Statement

There are two generally accepted formats for the presentation of income from continuing operations: the single-step and the multiple-step forms.

In the single-step form, items are classified into two groups: revenues and expenses. The operating revenues and other revenues are itemized and summed to determine total revenues. The cost of goods sold, operating expenses, and other expenses are itemized and summed to determine total expenses. The total expenses (including income taxes) are deducted from the total revenues to get net income (this title will vary depending upon the occurrence of discontinued operations, extraordinary items, or accounting changes).

Example of single-step income statement format

ABC Company
Income Statement
For the Year Ended 12/31/99

Revenues:		
Sales (net of discounts and returns and allowances)	$xxx	
Gain on sale of equipment	xxx	
Interest income	xxx	
Dividend income	xxx	$xxx
Expenses:		
Cost of goods sold	$xxx	
Selling expenses	xxx	
General and administrative expenses	xxx	
Interest expense	xxx	xxx

Income before unusual or infrequent items and income taxes	xxx
Unusual or infrequent items:	
Loss on sale of equipment	xxx
Income before income taxes	xxx
Income taxes	xxx
Net income	xxx
Earnings per share	$x.xx

Many accountants believe that intermediate groups and subtotals show significant relationships that assist in interpreting the income statement and advocate a multiple-step format. They believe that income statement users may be misled when operating and nonoperating activities are combined in a single-step income statement. In a multiple-step income statement, operating revenues and expenses are separated from nonoperating revenues and expenses to provide more information concerning the firm's primary activities. This format breaks the revenue and expense items into various intermediate income components so that important relationships can be shown and attention can be focused on significant subtotals. Some examples of common intermediate income components are as follows:

1. **Gross profit (margin)**--The difference between net sales and cost of goods sold.
2. **Operating income**--Gross profit less operating expenses.
3. **Income from operations before income taxes**--Operating income plus any other revenue items and less any other expense items.

Example of a multiple-step income statement format

ABC Company
Income Statement
For the Year Ended 12/31/99

Sales:				
Sales				$xxx
Less: Sales discounts			$xxx	
Sales returns and allowances			xxx	(xxx)
Net sales				$xxx
Cost of goods sold:				
Inventory, 1/1/99			$xxx	
Purchases		$xxx		
Add transportation-in		xxx		
Total cost of purchases		xxx		
Less: Purchase discount	$xxx			
Purchase returns and allowances	xxx	(xxx)		
Net purchases			xxx	
Cost of goods available for sale			$xxx	
Less inventory, 12/31/99			(xxx)	
Cost of goods sold				(xxx)
Gross profit				$xxx

Operating expenses:			
Selling expenses			
Sales salaries	$xxx		
Commissions	xxx		
Advertising expense	xxx		
Delivery expense	xxx		
Selling supplies expense	xxx		
Depreciation of store furniture and equipment	xxx	$xxx	
General and administrative expenses			
Officers' salaries	$xxx		
Office salaries	xxx		
Bad debts expense	xxx		
Office supplies expense	xxx		
Depreciation of office furniture and fixtures	xxx		
Depreciation of building	xxx		
Insurance expense	xxx		
Utilities expense	xxx	xxx	
Total operating expense			(xxx)
Operating income			$xxx
Other revenues:			
Dividend income		$xxx	
Interest income		xxx	xxx
Other expenses:			
Interest expense			(xxx)
Income before unusual or infrequent items and income tax			$xxx
Unusual or infrequent items:			
Write-down of inventory to market		$xxx	
Loss from permanent impairment of value of manufacturing facilities		xxx	(xxx)
Income from operations before income taxes			$xxx
Provision for income tax			(xxx)
Net income			$xxx
Earnings per share			$x.xx

4. **Net income**--Income from operations before income tax less the income tax provision. Only the final item in the income statement can be labeled "Net Income." Titles such as "Net Income Before Extraordinary Items" are incorrect and require removal of the word "Net."

Examples of the format for presentation of various income statement elements

Discontinued operations and an extraordinary item

Income (loss) from continuing operations		$xxx
Discontinued operations		
Income (loss) from operations of Division Z, less applicable income taxes of $xxx	$xxx	
Income (loss) on disposal of Division Z, less applicable income taxes of $xxx	xxx	xxx
Income (loss) before extraordinary item		$xxx
Extraordinary item, less applicable income taxes of $xxx (Note __)		xxx
Net income		$xxx
Per share of common stock*		
Income (loss) from continuing operations		$x.xx
Net income		$x.xx

Discontinued operations and a change in accounting principle

Income (loss) from continuing operations		$xxx

* *In these examples, assume per share amounts of discontinued operations, extraordinary items, and cumulative effect of a change in accounting principles are shown in the footnotes.*

Discontinued operations		
Income (loss) from operations of Division Z, less applicable income taxes of $xxx	$xxx	
Income (loss) on disposal of Division Z, less applicable income taxes of $xxx	xxx	xxx
Income (loss) before cumulative effect		$xxx
Cumulative effect on prior years (to **date of last year's income statement**) of changing to (change described), less applicable income taxes of $xxx (Note __)		xxx
Net income		$xxx
Per share of common stock		
Income (loss) from continuing operations		$x.xx
Net income		$x.xx

Extraordinary item and a change in accounting principle

Income (loss) before extraordinary item and cumulative effect of a change in accounting principle	$xxx
Extraordinary item, less applicable income taxes of $xxx (Note __)	xxx
Cumulative effect on prior years (to **date of last year's income statement**) of changing to (change described), less applicable income taxes of $xxx (Note __)	xxx
Net income	$xxx
Per share of common stock	
Income (loss) before extraordinary item and a change in accounting principle	$x.xx
Net income	$x.xx

Statement of Income, Other Comprehensive Income, and Retained Earnings

An acceptable practice is to combine the income statement and the statement of retained earnings into a single statement called the Statement of Income and Retained Earnings. Net income is computed in the same fashion as in a multiple- or single-step income statement. The beginning balance in retained earnings is added to the net income (loss) figure. Declared dividends are deducted to obtain the retained earnings ending balance.

Example of a comprehensive statement of income, other comprehensive income, and retained earnings

Baker, Inc.
Statement of Income, Other Comprehensive Income, and Retained Earnings
For the Year Ended December 31, 1999

Sales		$2,482
Cost of goods sold		1,489
Gross margin on sales		$ 993
Operating expenses		
Selling expenses	$ 220	
Administrative expenses	255	475
Income from operations		$ 518
Other revenues/gains (expenses/losses)		
Interest revenue (expense)--net	$ (40)	
Gain on sale of investment in ABC Company	100	
Gain on translation of foreign currencies	20	80
Income before unusual or infrequent items		$ 598
Unusual or infrequent items:		
Write-down of property and equipment	$ (20)	
Loss from permanent impairment of value of distributing facility	(50)	(70)
Income from continuing operations before provision for income taxes		$ 528
Provision for income taxes		211
Income from continuing operations		$ 317
Discontinued operations:		
Loss from operations of discontinued Division Z (less applicable taxes of $466)	$ (699)	
Loss on disposal of Division Z including operating losses during phase-out period (less applicable taxes of $67)	(100)	(799)
Loss before extraordinary items and cumulative effect of a change in accounting principle		$ (482)
Extraordinary loss from earthquake (less applicable income taxes of $30)		(45)
Cumulative effect on prior years of retroactive application of new depreciation method (less applicable income taxes of $80)		(120)
Net loss		$ (647)

Other comprehensive income, net of tax:		
Unrealized gains on securities:		
Unrealized holding gains that were identified this period	200	
Less: Reclassification adjustment for gains that are part of net income (less applicable income taxes of $40)	(60)	140
Comprehensive income		$ (507)
Retained earnings, January 1, 1999	$1,900	
Prior period adjustment:		
Correction of depreciation error (less applicable income taxes of $28)	(42)	
Adjusted retained earnings, January 1, 1999		1,858
Net loss		$ (647)
Deduct dividends:		
Preferred stock	$ (40)	
Common stock	(30)	(70)
Retained earnings, December 31, 1999		$1,141
Per share amounts (100 shares)		
Income from continuing operations		$ 3.17
Net loss		$(6.47)

Note:

1. Assumes a tax rate of 40% on applicable items
2. Footnote explanation would also be required for many of the above events and transactions.
3. Note the recycling/reclassification adjustment in other comprehensive income for the $100 realized gain shown under other revenue/gain in income from continuing operations. The adjustment removes the $60 unrealized gain, net of tax of $40 from other comprehensive income.

Prior Period Adjustments

SFAS 16 and APB 9 are the promulgated GAAP concerning the accounting for prior period adjustments. SFAS 16 was issued to define a prior period adjustment and clearly states that only the following shall be excluded from the determination of net income for the current period:

1. The correction of an error in the financial statements of a prior period
2. Adjustments that result from realization of income tax benefits of preacquisition operating loss carryforwards of purchased subsidiaries

APB 9 specifies the recording and presentation of a prior period adjustment. Accordingly, when prior period adjustments are recorded, the resulting effects on the net income of prior periods shall be disclosed in the year in which the adjustments are made. These effects shall be reported at both their gross amount and net of applicable income taxes. The proper presentation of these effects depends upon the nature of the statements presented. If the statements are presented for only a single period, then the beginning balance of retained earnings shall be restated to reflect the effects of the correction or change. When comparative statements are presented, corresponding adjustments should be made of the amounts of net income (and the components thereof) and retained earnings balance (as well as other affected balances) for all of the periods included in the financial statements.

An example of the accounting presentation for a prior period adjustment appears in Chapter 20, Accounting Changes and Error Correction.

Development Stage Enterprises (SFAS 7)

SFAS 7 defines a development stage enterprise as one which

> *is devoting substantially all of its efforts to establishing a new business and either of the following conditions exists:*
>
> *a. Planned principal operations have not commenced.*
> *b. Planned principal operations have commenced but there has been no significant revenue.*

SFAS 7 indicates that these enterprises should prepare their financial statements in accordance with the same GAAP applicable to established operating entities.

SFAS 7 indicated that specialized accounting practices are unacceptable and that development stage enterprises were to follow the same generally accepted accounting principles as those that applied to an established operating entity. SFAS 7 also provided that a development stage enterprise should disclose certain additional information which would alert readers to the fact that the company is in the development stage. Disclosure requirements include

1. All disclosures applicable to operating entities
2. Identification of the statements as those of a development stage enterprise
3. Disclosure of the nature of development stage activities
4. A balance sheet which, in the equity section, includes the cumulative net losses since inception
5. An income statement showing current period revenue and expense as well as the cumulative amount from the inception of the entity
6. A statement of cash flows showing cash flows for the period as well as those from inception
7. A statement of stockholders' equity showing the following from the enterprise's inception:
   a. For each issuance, the date and number of equity securities issued for cash or other consideration
   b. For each issuance, the dollar amounts per share assigned to the consideration received for equity securities
   c. For each issuance involving noncash consideration, the nature of the consideration and the basis used in assigning the valuation
8. For the first period in which an enterprise is no longer a development stage enterprise, it shall be disclosed that in prior periods the entity was a development

stage enterprise. If comparative statements are presented, the foregoing disclosure presentations (2-7) need not be shown.

FASB I 7 allows parent or equity method investor companies to defer some development stage company costs which would have to be expensed by the development stage company. Costs may be deferred if recoverable within the entire entity.

Reporting on the Costs of Start-up Activities

SOP 98-5 provides guidance on financial reporting of start-up costs and organization costs and requires such costs to be expensed as incurred. Start-up costs are defined as one-time activities related to opening a new facility or new class of customer, initiating a new process in an existing facility or some new operation. These are sometimes referred to as preopening costs, preoperating costs, organization costs, and start-up costs. Routine ongoing efforts to improve existing quality of products, services, or facilities are not start-up costs. Other costs related to specific activities listed below are excluded from this SOP and should be accounted for in accordance with other existing authoritative literature such as

1. Costs of acquiring or constructing long-lived assets and getting them ready for their intended uses. (However, the costs of using long-lived assets that are allocated to start-up activities [for example, depreciation of computers] are within the scope of this SOP.)
2. Costs of acquiring or producing inventory.
3. Costs of acquiring intangible assets. (However, the costs of using intangible assets that are allocated to start-up activities [for example, amortization of a purchased patent] are within the scope of this SOP.)
4. Costs related to internally developed assets (for example, internal-use computer software costs). (However, the costs of using those assets that are allocated to start-up activities are within the scope of this SOP.)
5. Costs that are within the scope of Financial Accounting Standards Board (FASB) Statement 2, *Accounting for Research and Development*, and FASB Statement 71, *Accounting for the Effects of Certain Types of Regulation*.
6. Costs of fund-raising incurred by not-for-profit organizations.
7. Costs of raising capital.
8. Costs of advertising.
9. Costs incurred in connection with existing contracts as stated in SOP 81-1, *Accounting for Performance of Construction-Type and Certain Production -Type Contracts*.

This SOP applies to all nongovernmental entities and is effective for financial statements for fiscal years beginning after December 15, 1998. Initial application should generally be reported as the cumulative effect of a change in accounting principle. Exclusion of certain costs from this SOP is not justification for their capitalization. Such costs should not be capitalized unless they qualify for such treatment under other generally accepted accounting principles.

EMERGING ISSUES TASK FORCE CONSENSUS SUMMARIES

85-36 Discontinued Operations With Expected Gain and Interim Operating Losses

A consensus was reached that estimated losses from operations during the period between the measurement date and the disposal date should be deferred until the disposal date, if there is reasonable assurance there will be a net gain on disposal. This consensus also applies to the sale of a significant portion of a line of business that is not considered a segment.

The Task Force also reached a consensus that a net gain resulting from the disposal of separate segments that are part of the same formal plan, whereby one results in a gain and one results in a loss should be reported net. The Task Force notes that the net gain treatment would not be appropriate for disposal of a portion of a line of business.

87-4 Restructuring of Operations: Implications of SEC Staff Accounting Bulletin 67

A consensus was reached that the provisions of SAB 67, requiring that restructuring charges be deducted in determining "income from operations" and prohibiting the presentation of "income before restructuring charges," are not required to be followed by nonpublic companies for a fair presentation of the results of operations in accordance with GAAP. The Task Force notes that nonpublic companies should exercise judgment in selecting the most meaningful presentation for the Income Statement.

87-24 Allocation of Interest to Discontinued Operations

A consensus was reached that the allocation of interest expense to discontinued operations is permitted but not required. If the corporation decides to allocate, the EITF provides guidance regarding the maximum amount and methods of allocation. Additionally, the Task Force reached a consensus that general corporate overhead may not be allocated to discontinued operations.

90-16 Accounting for Discontinued Operations Subsequently Retained

The Task Force reached consensus on two issues regarding how a company should properly account for the subsequent decision to retain a business segment, after the company had previously decided to dispose of the segment and had accounted for the disposal in accordance with APB 30. The first consensus was that if a company has accrued a loss on the disposal of segment in accordance with APB 30, the remaining estimated accrued loss should be reversed in the period the company subsequently decides to retain the segment. The second consensus was that the financial statements of the prior reporting period should not be restated. However, the prior period results of operations of the business segment should be reclassified from discontinued operations to continuing operations. The SEC Observer agreed with the consensus that this accounting treatment is required, not merely permitted. In addition to the disclosure requirements of APB 30, supplemental disclosures for when the consensus is applied are listed.

95-18 Accounting and Reporting for a Discontinued Business Segment When the Measurement Date Occurs After the Balance Sheet Date but Before the Issuance of Financial Statements

A consensus was reached that in accordance with APB 30 a presumption exists that estimated losses from the planned disposal of a segment should be recognized in the still-to-be-issued financial statements for the period prior to the measurement date. Additionally, the segment's operating results should be presented as a component of discontinued operations in the income statement of the still-to-be-released financial statements. Only an unexpected discrete and identifiable event such as an uncollected offer after the balance sheet date can overcome the presumption above. If the presumption is overcome, the estimated loss would be recognized in the period's financial statements that include the measurement date. In situations in which the presumption is overcome or a gain occurs, the still to be issued financial statements should show the segment's results as discontinued operations.

4 STATEMENT OF CASH FLOWS

PERSPECTIVE AND ISSUES

The FASB issued SFAS 95 entitled, *Statement of Cash Flows* superseding APB 19 and establishing standards for cash flow reporting effective for years ending after July 15, 1988. Additionally, the FASB issued SFAS 102 entitled *Statement of Cash Flows--Exemption of Certain Enterprises and Classification of Cash Flows from Certain Securities Acquired for Resale* and SFAS 104 entitled *Statement of Cash Flows--Net Reporting of Certain Cash Receipts and Cash Payments and Classification of Cash Flows from Hedging Transactions.* SFAS 117 amended SFAS 95 to extend its provisions to not-for-profit organizations.

The primary purpose of the statement of cash flows (SCF) is to provide information about the cash receipts and cash payments of an entity during a period. A secondary purpose is to provide information about the investing and financing activities of the entity during the period.

Specifically, the SCF should help investors and creditors assess

1. Ability to generate future positive cash flows
2. Ability to meet obligations and pay dividends
3. Reasons for differences between income and cash receipts and payments
4. Both cash and non-cash aspects of entities' investing and financing transactions

The FASB's Conceptual Framework Project, in particular SFAC 1, states that "financial reporting should provide information that is useful to present and potential investors, creditors, and other users for making rational investment and credit decisions." Since the ultimate objective of investment and credit decisions is the maximization of net cash inflows, information for assessing the amounts, timing, and uncertainty of prospective enterprise cash flows is needed. SFAC 5 gives particular attention to the statements of earnings and comprehensive income. It also addresses the question of which financial statements should be presented and the contribution of each statement to financial reporting. SFAC 5 concludes that financial statements must show cash flows during the period in order to be complete.

Sources of GAAP

SFAC	*EITF*	*SFAS*
1, 5	95-13	35, 95, 102, 104, 115, 117

DEFINITIONS OF TERMS

Cash equivalents. Short-term, highly liquid investments that (1) are readily convertible to known amounts of cash and (2) are so near their maturity (maturity of 3 months or less from the date of purchase by the enterprise) that they present negligible risk of changes in value because of changes in interest rates. Treasury bills, commercial paper, and money market funds are all examples of cash equivalents.

Direct method. A method which derives the net cash provided by operating activities from the components of operating cash receipts and payments as opposed to adjusting net income for items not affecting funds.

Financing activities. The transactions a firm engages in to acquire and repay capital (e.g., borrowings, sale of capital stock, repayments, etc.).

Indirect (reconciliation) method. A method which derives the net cash provided by operating activities by adjusting net income for revenue and expense items not resulting from cash transactions.

Investing activities. The transactions the firm engages in which affect their investments in assets (e.g., purchase, sale).

Operating activities. The transactions not classified as financing or investing activities, generally involving producing and delivering goods or providing services.

CONCEPTS, RULES, AND EXAMPLES

Cash Basis

The statement of cash flows shall include only inflows and outflows of cash and **cash equivalents**. Cash equivalents include any short-term highly liquid investments (see definition for criteria) used as a temporary investment of idle cash. The SCF shall exclude all transactions that do not directly affect cash receipts and payments. However, the effects of transactions not resulting in receipts or payments of cash shall be reported in a separate schedule. The reasoning for not including noncash items in the statement of cash flows and placing them in a separate schedule is that it preserves the statement's primary focus on cash flows from operating, investing, and financing activities.

Classification

The statement of cash flows requires classification into these three categories.

Investing activities include the acquisition and disposition of long-term productive assets or securities that are not considered cash equivalents. Investing activities also include the lending of money and collection on loans.

Financing activities include obtaining resources from and returning resources to the owners. Also included is obtaining resources from creditors and repaying the amount borrowed.

Operating activities include all transactions that are not investing and financing activities. Operating activities include delivering or producing goods for sale and providing services.

The following are examples of the statement of cash flows classification:

	Operating	*Investing*	*Financing*
Cash Inflows	• Receipts from sale of goods or services	• Principal collections from loans and sales of other entities' debt instruments*	• Proceeds from issuing stock
	• Sale of loans, debt, or equity instruments carried in trading portfolio	• Sale of equity instruments* of other enterprises and from returns of investment in those instruments	• Proceeds from issuing debt (short-term or long-term)
	• Returns on loans (interest) • Returns on equity securities (dividends)	• Sale of plant & equipment	• Not-for-profits' donor-restricted cash that is limited to long-term purposes
Cash Outflows	• Payments for inventory	• Loans made and acquisition of other entities' debt instruments*	• Payment of dividends
	• Payments to employees and other suppliers	• Purchase of equity instruments* of other enterprises	• Repurchase of entity's stock
	• Payments of taxes • Payments of interest • Purchase of loans, debt, or equity instruments carried in trading portfolio	• Purchase of plant & equipment	• Repayment of debt principal, including capital lease obligations

**Held in available-for-sale or held-to-maturity portfolios*

Noncash Investing and Financing Activities

(May be disclosed following statement or in the notes)

- Acquiring an asset through a capital lease
- Conversion of debt to equity
- Exchange of noncash assets or liabilities for other noncash assets or liabilities
- Isssuance of stock to acquire assets

Example of a classified SCF

Liquid Corporation
Statement of Cash Flows
For the Year Ended December 31, 1999

Net cash flows from operating activities		$ xxx
Cash flows from investing activities:		
Purchase of property, plant, and equipment	$(xxx)	
Sale of equipment	xx	
Collection of notes receivable	xx	
Net cash **used** in investing activities		(xx)
Cash flows from financing activities:		
Sale of common stock	xxx	
Repayment of long-term debt	(xx)	
Reduction of notes payable	(xx)	
Net cash **provided** by financing activities		xx
Effect of exchange rate changes on cash		xx
Net increase in cash		$ xxx
Cash and cash equivalents at beginning of year		xxx
Cash and cash equivalents at end of year		$xxxx
Schedule of noncash financing and investing activities:		
Conversion of bonds into common stock		$ xxx
Property acquired under capital leases		xxx
		$ xxx

Operating Activities Presentation

Direct vs. indirect. The operating activities section of the SCF can be presented under the direct or indirect method. However, the FASB has expressed a preference for the direct method of presenting net cash from operating activities.

The **direct method** shows the items that affected cash flow. Cash received and cash paid are presented, as opposed to converting accrual-basis income to cash flow information. Entities using the direct method are required to report the following classes of operating cash receipts and payments:

1. Cash collected from customers

2. Interest and dividends received
3. Cash paid to employees and other suppliers
4. Interest and income taxes paid
5. Other operating cash receipts and payments

The direct method allows the user to clarify the relationship between the company's net income and its cash flows. For example, payments of expenses are shown as cash disbursements and are deducted from cash receipts. In this way, the user is able to recognize the cash receipts and cash payments for the period. Formulas for conversion of various income statement amounts for the direct method presentation from the accrual basis to the cash basis are summarized below.

Accrual basis		*Additions*		*Deductions*		*Cash basis*
Net sales	+	Beginning AR	–	Ending AR AR written off	=	Cash received from customers
Cost of goods sold	+	Ending inventory Beginning AP	–	Depreciation and amortization* Beginning inventory Ending AP	=	Cash paid to suppliers
Operating expenses	+	Ending prepaid expenses Beginning accrued expenses	–	Depreciation and amortization Beginning prepaid expenses Ending accrued expenses payable Bad debts expense	=	Cash paid for operating expenses

**Applies to a manufacturing entity only*

Note that when the direct method is used, a separate schedule reconciling net income to net cash flows from operating activities must also be provided.

The **indirect method** is the most widely used presentation of cash from operating activities, primarily because it is easier to prepare. It focuses on the differences between net income and cash flows. The indirect format begins with net income, which can be obtained directly from the income statement. Revenue and expense items not affecting cash are added or deducted to arrive at net cash provided by operating activities. For example, depreciation and amortization would be added back because they reduce net income without affecting cash.

The statement of cash flows prepared using the indirect method emphasizes changes in the components of most current asset and current liability accounts. Changes in inventory, accounts receivable, and other current accounts are used to determine the cash flow from operating activities. It is important to note that the change in accounts receivable should be calculated using the balances net of the allowance account in order to assure write-offs of uncollectible accounts are treated properly. However, short-term borrowing used to purchase equipment would not be included since it is not related to operating activities. Instead, the short-term borrowing would be classified as a financing activity. Other adjustments under the indirect method include changes in the account balances of deferred income taxes and the income (loss) from investments under the equity method.

The following diagram may facilitate understanding of the adjustments to net income necessary for converting accrual-based net income to cash-basis net income when using the **indirect method**. The diagram is simply an expanded balance sheet equation.

	*Current assets**	–	*Fixed assets*	=	*Current liabilities*	+	*Long-term liabilities*	+	*Income*	*Accrual income adjustment to convert to cash flow*
1.	Increase			=					Increase	Decrease
2.	Decrease			=					Decrease	Increase
3.				=	Increase				Decrease	Increase
4.				=	Decrease				Increase	Decrease

**Other than cash and cash equivalents*

For example, using Row 1, a credit sale would increase accounts receivable and accrual-basis income but would not affect cash. Therefore, its effect must be removed from the accrual income in order to convert to cash income. The last column indicates that the increase in a current asset balance must be deducted from income to obtain cash flow.

Similarly, an increase in a current liability, Row 3, must be added to income to obtain cash flows (e.g., accrued wages are on the income statement as an expense, but they do not require cash; the increase in wages payable must be added back to remove this noncash flow expense from accrual-basis income).

If the **indirect method** is chosen, then the amount of interest and income tax paid shall be included in the related disclosures. Also with the indirect method, SFAS 95 permits, but does not require, separate disclosure of cash flows related to extraordinary items and discontinued operations. If an entity chooses to disclose this information, disclosure must be consistent for all periods affected.

The major drawback to the indirect method involves the user's difficulty in comprehending the information presented. This method does not show from where the cash was received or to where the cash was paid. Only adjustments to accrual basis net income are shown. In some cases the adjustments can be confusing. For instance, the sale of equipment resulting in an accrual-basis loss would require that the loss be added to net income to arrive at net cash from operating activities. (The loss was deducted in the computation of net income, but because the sale will be shown as an investing activity, the loss must be added back to net income.)

Although the **indirect method** is more commonly used in practice, the authors believe that the **direct method** is preferable. It portrays both the amounts of funds provided by and used in the firm's operations, instead of presenting net income and reconciling items. The direct method reports only the items that affect cash flow (inflows/outflows of cash) and ignores items that do not affect cash flow (depreciation, gains, etc.). Both the direct method and the indirect method are shown below.

Direct method

Cash flows from operating activities:		
Cash received from sale of goods	$xxx	
Cash interest received	xxx	
Cash dividends received	xxx	
Cash provided by operating activities:		$xxx
Cash paid to suppliers	(xxx)	
Cash paid for operating expenses	(xxx)	
Cash interest paid	(xxx)	
Cash paid for taxes	(xxx)	
Cash disbursed for operating activities		($xxx)
Net cash flows from operating activities		$xxx

Indirect method

Cash flows from operating activities:	
Net income	$ xx
Add/deduct items not affecting cash:	
Increase in accounts receivable	(xx)
Depreciation expense	xx
Increase in accounts payable	xx
Decrease in inventories	xx
Loss on sale of equipment	xx
Net cash flows from operating activities	$xxx

Other Requirements

Gross vs. net basis. The emphasis in the statement of cash flows is on gross cash receipts and cash payments. For instance, reporting the net change in bonds payable would obscure the financing activities of the entity by not disclosing separately cash inflows from issuing bonds and cash outflows from retiring bonds. The Board specifies a few exceptions where netting of cash flows is allowed. Items having quick turnovers, large amounts, and short maturities may be presented as net cash flows if the cash receipts and payments pertain to (1) investments (other than cash equivalents), (2) loans receivable, and (3) debts (original maturity of 3 months or less).

Exchange rate effects. Foreign operations must prepare a separate statement of cash flows, and translate the statement to the reporting currency using the exchange rate in effect at the time of the cash flow (a weighted-average exchange rate may be used if the result is substantially the same). This translated statement is then used in the preparation of the consolidated statement of cash flows.

Noncash exchange gains and losses recognized on the income statement should be reported as a separate item when reconciling net income and operating activities.

For a more detailed discussion about the exchange rate effects on the statement of cash flows, see Chapter 21.

Cash flow per share. This information shall **not** be reported in the financial statements of an enterprise.

Entities Exempt From Providing a SCF

Per SFAS 102, a statement of cash flows is not required for a defined benefit pension plan that presents the financial information under the guidelines of SFAS 35. Other employee benefit plans are exempted provided that the financial information presented is similar to the requirements of SFAS 35. Investment enterprises or a common trust fund held for the collective investment and reinvestment of moneys are not required to provide a statement of cash flows if the following conditions are met:

1. Substantially all of the entity's investments are highly liquid.
2. Entity's investments are carried at market value.
3. Entity had little or no debt, based on average debt outstanding during the period, in relation to average total assets.
4. Entity provides a statement of changes in net assets.

Investments Accounted for per SFAS 115

Per SFAS 102, as amended by SFAS 115, cash flows are classified as operating cash flows if originating from the purchase or selling of loans, debt, or equity instruments acquired specifically for resale and carried at market value in a trading account.

Cash flows from securities held in available-for-sale or held-to-maturity portfolios are disclosed gross in the investing activities section of the cash flow section.

Net Reporting by Financial Institutions

Per SFAS 104, banks, savings institutions, and credit unions are allowed to report net cash receipts and payments for the following:

1. Deposits placed with other financial institutions
2. Withdrawals of deposits
3. Time deposits accepted
4. Repayments of deposits
5. Loans made to customers
6. Principal collections of loans

Reporting Hedging Transactions

Per SFAS 104, providing the accounting method is disclosed, the cash flows resulting from futures contracts, forward contracts, options contracts, and swap contracts held for hedging may be classified as the same type of cash flows as the hedged items.

Preparation of the Statement

Under a cash and cash equivalents basis, the changes in the cash account and any cash equivalent account is the "bottom line" figure of the SCF. Using the 1998 and 1999 balance sheet shown below, an increase of $17,000 can be computed. This is the difference between the totals for cash and treasury bills between 1998 and 1999 ($33,000 – 16,000).

When preparing the statement of cash flows using the direct method, gross cash inflows from revenues and gross cash outflows to suppliers and for expenses are presented in the operating activities section.

In preparing the reconciliation of net income to net cash flow from operating activities (indirect method), changes in all accounts other than cash and cash equivalents that are related to operations are additions to or deductions from net income to arrive at net cash provided by operating activities.

A T-account analysis may be helpful when preparing the statement of cash flows. A T-account is set up for each account, and beginning (1998) and ending (1999) balances are taken from the appropriate balance sheet. Additionally, a T-account for cash and cash equivalents from operating activities and a master or summary T-account of cash and cash equivalents should be used.

Example of preparing a statement of cash flows

The financial statements below will be used to prepare the SCF.

Johnson Company
Balance Sheets
December 31, 1999 and 1998

	1999	*1998*
Assets		
Current assets:		
Cash	$ 29,000	$ 10,000
Treasury Bills	4,000	6,000
Accounts receivable--net	9,000	11,000
Inventory	14,000	9,000
Prepaid expenses	10,000	13,000
Total current assets	$ 66,000	$ 49,000

Noncurrent assets:		
Investment in XYZ (35%)	16,000	14,000
Patent	5,000	6,000
Leased asset	5,000	-0-
Property, plant, and equipment	39,000	37,000
Less accumulated depreciation	(7,000)	(3,000)
Total assets	$124,000	$103,000
Liabilities		
Current liabilities:		
Accounts payable	$ 2,000	$ 12,000
Notes payable--current	9,000	--
Interest payable	3,000	2,000
Dividends payable	5,000	2,000
Income taxes payable	2,000	1,000
Lease obligation	700	-0-
Total current liabilities	21,700	17,000
Noncurrent liabilities:		
Deferred tax liability	9,000	6,000
Bonds payable	10,000	25,000
Lease obligation	4,300	-0-
Total liabilities	$ 45,000	$ 48,000
Stockholders' equity		
Common stock, $10 par value	$ 33,000	$ 26,000
Additional paid-in capital	16,000	3,000
Retained earnings	30,000	26,000
Total stockholders' equity	$ 79,000	$ 55,000
Total liabilities and stockholders' equity	$124,000	$103,000

Johnson Company
Statement of Earnings
For the Year Ended December 31, 1999

Sales	$100,000
Other income	8,000
	$108,000
Cost of goods sold, excluding depreciation	60,000
Selling, general, and administrative expenses	12,000
Depreciation	8,000
Amortization of patents	1,000
Interest expense	2,000
	$ 83,000
Income before taxes	$ 25,000
Income taxes (36%)	9,000
Net income	$ 16,000

Additional information (relating to 1999)

1. Equipment costing $6,000 with a book value of $2,000 was sold for $5,000.
2. The company received a $3,000 dividend from its investment in XYZ, accounted for under the equity method and recorded income from the investment of $5,000 which is included in other income.
3. The company issued 200 shares of common stock for $5,000.
4. The company signed a note payable for $9,000.
5. Equipment was purchased for $8,000.
6. The company converted $15,000 bonds payable into 500 shares of common stock. The book value method was used to record the transaction.
7. A dividend of $12,000 was declared.
8. Equipment was leased on December 31, 1999. The principal portion of the first payment due December 31, 2000, is $700.

Summary of Cash and Cash Equivalents

	Inflows	Outflows	
(d)	5,000		
		8,000	(g)
(h)	5,000	9,000	(i)
(n)	9,000		
(s)	15,000		
	34,000	17,000	
		17,000	Net increase in cash
	34,000	34,000	

Cash and Cash Equivalents--Oper. Act.

	Debit	Credit	
(a)	16,000		
(b)	8,000		
(c)	1,000	3,000	(d)
(e)	3,000	5,000	(f)
(f)	3,000		
(j)	2,000		
(l)	3,000		
		5,000	(k)
(o)	1,000	10,000	(m)
(p)	1,000		
	38,000	23,000	
		15,000	(s)
	38,000	38,000	

Accounts Receivable (net)

	Debit	Credit	
	11,000		
		2,000	(j)
	9,000		

Inventory

	Debit	Credit
	9,000	
(k)	5,000	
	14,000	

Prepaid Expenses

Debit	Credit	
13,000		
	3,000	(l)
10,000		

Investment in XYZ

	Debit	Credit	
	14,000		
(f)	5,000	3,000	(f)
	16,000		

Patent

Debit	Credit	
6,000		
	1,000	(c)
5,000		

Leased Equipment

	Debit	Credit
(r)	5,000	
	5,000	

Prop., Plant, & Equip.

	Debit	Credit	
	37,000		
		6,000	(d)
(g)	8,000		
	39,000		

Accumulated Depr.

	Debit	Credit	
		3,000	
		8,000	(b)
(d)	4,000		
		7,000	

Accounts Payable

	Debit	Credit
		12,000
(m)	10,000	
		2,000

Notes Payable	
	9,000 (n)
	9,000

Interest Payable	
	2,000
(o) 1,000	2,000 (o)
	3,000

Dividends Payable	
	2,000
(i) 9,000	12,000 (i)
	5,000

Income Taxes Payable	
	1,000
(p) 5,000	6,000 (p)
	2,000

Deferred Tax Liability	
	6,000
	3,000 (e)
	9,000

Bonds Payable	
	25,000
(q) 15,000	
	10,000

Lease Obligation	
	5,000 (r)
	5,000

Common Stock	
	26,000
	2,000 (h)
	5,000 (q)
	33,000

Addl. Paid-in Capital	
	3,000
	3,000 (h)
	10,000 (q)
	16,000

Retained Earnings	
	26,000
	16,000 (a)
(i) 12,000	
	30,000

Explanation of entries

a. Cash and Cash Equivalents--Operating activities is debited for $16,000, and credited to Retained Earnings. This represents the net income figure.

b. Depreciation is not a cash flow; however, depreciation expense was deducted to arrive at net income. Therefore, Accumulated Depreciation is credited and Cash and Cash Equivalents--Operating activities is debited.

c. Amortization of patents is another expense not requiring cash; therefore, Cash and Cash Equivalents--Operating activities is debited and Patent is credited.

d. The sale of equipment (additional information, item 1) resulted in a $3,000 gain. The gain is computed by comparing the book value of $2,000 with the sales price of $5,000. Cash proceeds of $5,000 are an inflow of cash. Since the gain was included in net income, it must be deducted from net income to determine cash provided by operating activities. This is necessary to avoid counting the $3,000 gain both in cash provided by operating activities and in investing activities. The following entry would have been made on the date of sale:

Cash	5,000	
Accumulated depreciation (6,000 – 2,000)	4,000	
Property, plant, and equipment		6,000
Gain on sale of equipment (5,000 – 2,000)		3,000

Adjust the T-accounts as follows: debit Summary of Cash and Cash Equivalents for $5,000, debit Accumulated Depreciation for $4,000, credit Property, Plant, and Equipment for $6,000, and credit Cash and Cash Equivalents--Operating activities for $3,000. Note that per SFAS 95, the gross gain, not the net of tax gain, is removed from operating activities. The tax effect on this gain is left in operating activities.

e. The $3,000 increase in Deferred Income Taxes must be added to income from operations. Although the $3,000 was deducted as part of income tax expense in determining net income, it did not require an outflow of cash. Therefore, debit Cash and Cash Equivalents--Operating activities and credit Deferred Taxes.

f. Item 2 under the additional information indicates that the investment in XYZ is accounted for under the equity method. The investment in XYZ had a net increase of $2,000 during the year after considering the receipt of a $3,000 dividend. Dividends received (an inflow of cash) would reduce the investment in XYZ, while the equity in the income of XYZ would increase the investment without affecting cash. In order for the T-account to balance, a debit of $5,000 must have been made, indicating earnings of that amount. The journal entries would have been

Cash (dividend received)	3,000	
Investment in XYZ		3,000
Investment in XYZ	5,000	
Equity in earnings of XYZ		5,000

The dividend received ($3,000) is an inflow of cash, while the equity earnings are not. Debit Investment in XYZ for $5,000, credit Cash and Cash Equivalents--Operating activities for $5,000, debit Cash and Cash Equivalents--Operating activities for $3,000, and credit Investment in XYZ for $3,000.

g. The Property, Plant, and Equipment account increased because of the purchase of $8,000 (additional information, item 5). The purchase of assets is an outflow of cash. Debit Property, Plant, and Equipment for $8,000 and credit Summary of Cash and Cash Equivalents.

h. The company sold 200 shares of common stock during the year (additional information, item 3). The entry for the sale of stock was

Cash	5,000	
Common stock (200 shares x $10)		2,000
Additional paid-in capital		3,000

This transaction resulted in an inflow of cash. Debit Summary of Cash and Cash Equivalents $5,000, credit Common Stock $2,000, and credit Additional Paid-in Capital $3,000.

i. Dividends of $12,000 were declared (additional information, item 7). Only $9,000 was actually paid in cash resulting in an ending balance of $9,000 in the Dividends Payable account. Therefore, the following entries were made during the year:

Retained Earnings	12,000	
Dividends Payable		12,000
Dividends Payable	9,000	
Cash		9,000

These transactions result in an outflow of cash. Debit Retained Earnings $12,000 and credit Dividends Payable $12,000. Additionally, debit Dividends Payable

$9,000 and credit Summary of Cash and Cash Equivalents $9,000 to indicate the cash dividends paid during the year.

j. Accounts Receivable (net) decreased by $2,000. This is added as an adjustment to net income in the computation of cash provided by operating activities. The decrease of $2,000 means that an additional $2,000 cash was collected on account above and beyond the sales reported in the income statement. Debit Cash and Cash Equivalents--Operating activities and credit Accounts Receivable for $2,000.

k. Inventories increased by $5,000. This is subtracted as an adjustment to net income in the computation of cash provided by operating activities. Although $5,000 additional cash was spent to increase inventories, this expenditure is not reflected in accrual-basis cost of goods sold. Debit Inventory and credit Cash and Cash Equivalents--Operating activities for $5,000.

l. Prepaid Expenses decreased by $3,000. This is added back to net income in the computation of cash provided by operating activities. The decrease means that no cash was spent when incurring the related expense. The cash was spent when the prepaid assets were purchased, not when they were expended on the income statement. Debit Cash and Cash Equivalents--Operating activities and credit Prepaid Expenses for $3,000.

m. Accounts Payable decreased by $10,000. This is subtracted as an adjustment to net income. The decrease of $10,000 means that an additional $10,000 of purchases were paid for in cash; therefore, income was not affected but cash was decreased. Debit Accounts Payable and credit Cash and Cash Equivalents--Operating activities for $10,000.

n. Notes Payable increased by $9,000 (additional information, item 4). This is an inflow of cash and would be included in the financing activities. Debit Summary of Cash and Cash Equivalents and credit Notes Payable for $9,000.

o. Interest Payable increased by $1,000, but interest expense from the income statement was $2,000. Therefore, although $2,000 was expensed, only $1,000 cash was paid ($2,000 expense – $1,000 increase in interest payable). Debit Cash and Cash Equivalents--Operating activities for $1,000, debit Interest Payable for $1,000 and credit Interest Payable for $2,000.

p. The following entry was made to record the incurrence of the tax liability:

Income tax expense	9,000	
Income taxes payable		6,000
Deferred tax liability		3,000

Therefore, $9,000 was deducted in arriving at net income. The $3,000 credit to Deferred Income Taxes was accounted for in entry (e) above. The $6,000 credit to Taxes Payable does not, however, indicate that $6,000 cash was paid for taxes. Since Taxes Payable increased $1,000, only $5,000 must have been paid and $1,000 remains unpaid. Debit Cash and Cash Equivalents--Operating activities for $1,000, debit Income Taxes Payable for $5,000, and credit Income Taxes Payable for $6,000.

q. Item 6 under the additional information indicates that $15,000 of bonds payable were converted to common stock. This is a **noncash** financing activity and should be reported in a separate schedule. The following entry was made to record the transaction:

Bonds payable	15,000	
Common stock (500 shares x $10 par)		5,000
Additional paid-in capital		10,000

Adjust the T-accounts with a debit to Bonds Payable, $15,000; a credit to Common Stock, $5,000; and a credit to Additional Paid-in Capital, $10,000.

r. Item 8 under the additional information indicates that leased equipment was acquired on the last day of 1999. This is also a noncash financing activity and should be reported in a separate schedule. The following entry was made to record the lease transaction:

Leased asset	5,000	
Lease obligation		5,000

s. The cash and cash equivalents from operations ($15,000) is transferred to the Summary of Cash and Cash Equivalents.

Since all of the changes in the noncash accounts have been accounted for and the balance in the Summary of Cash and Cash Equivalents account of $17,000 is the amount of the year-to-year increase in cash and cash equivalents, the formal statement may now be prepared. The following classified SCF is prepared under the direct method and includes the reconciliation of net income to net cash provided by operating activities. The T-account, Cash and Cash Equivalents--Operating activities, is used in the preparation of this reconciliation. The calculations for gross receipts and gross payments needed for the direct method are shown below.

Johnson Company
Statement of Cash Flows
For the Year Ended December 31, 1999

Cash flow from operating activities		
Cash received from customers	$102,000 (a)	
Dividends received	3,000	
Cash provided by operating activities		$105,000
Cash paid to suppliers	$75,000 (b)	
Cash paid for expenses	9,000 (c)	
Interest paid	1,000 (d)	
Taxes paid	5,000 (e)	
Cash paid for operating activities		(90,000)
Net cash flow provided by operating activities		$ 15,000
Cash flow from investing activities		
Sale of equipment	5,000	
Purchase of property, plant, and equipment	(8,000)	
Net cash used in investing activities		(3,000)

Cash flow from financing activities

Sale of common stock	$ 5,000	
Increase in notes payable	9,000	
Dividends paid	(9,000)	
Net cash provided by financing activities		5,000
Net increase in cash and cash equivalents		$ 17,000
Cash and cash equivalents at beginning of year		16,000
Cash and cash equivalents at end of year		$ 33,000

Calculation of amounts for operating activities section of Johnson Co.'s SCF

(a) Net sales + Beginning AR – Ending AR = Cash received from customers

$100,000 + $11,000 – $9,000 = $102,000

(b) Cost of goods sold + Beginning AP – Ending AP + Ending inventory – Beginning inventory = Cash paid to suppliers

$60,000 + $12,000 – $2,000 + $14,000 – $9,000 = $75,000

(c) Operating expenses + Ending prepaid expenses – Beginning prepaid expenses – Depreciation expense (and other noncash operating expenses) = Cash paid for operating expenses

$12,000 + $10,000 – $13,000 = $9,000

(d) Interest expense + Beginning interest payable – Ending interest payable = Interest paid

$2,000 + $2,000 – $3,000 = $1,000

(e) Income taxes + Beginning income taxes payable – Ending income taxes payable + Beginning deferred income taxes – Ending deferred income taxes = Taxes paid

$9,000 + $1,000 – $2,000 + $6,000 – $9,000 = $5,000

Reconciliation of net income to net cash provided by operating activities

Net income	$16,000	
Add (deduct) items not using (providing) cash:		
Depreciation	8,000	
Amortization	1,000	
Gain on sale of equipment	(3,000)	
Increase in deferred taxes	3,000	
Equity in XYZ	(2,000)	
Decrease in accounts receivable	2,000	
Increase in inventory	(5,000)	
Decrease in prepaid expenses	3,000	
Decrease in accounts payable	(10,000)	
Increase in interest payable	1,000	
Increase in income taxes payable	1,000	
Net cash flow provided by operating activities		$15,000

Schedule of noncash transactions

Conversion of bonds into common stock	$15,000
Acquisition of leased equipment	$ 5,000

Disclosure of accounting policy

For purposes of the statement of cash flows, the Company considers all highly liquid debt instruments purchased with original maturities of 3 months or less to be cash equivalents.

Statement of Cash Flows for Consolidated Entities

A consolidated statement of cash flows must be presented when a complete set of consolidated financial statements is issued. The consolidated statement of cash flows would be the last statement to be prepared as the information to prepare it will come from the other consolidated statements (consolidated balance sheet, income statement, and statement of retained earnings). The preparation of these other consolidated statements is discussed in Chapter 11.

The preparation of a consolidated statement of cash flows involves the same analysis and procedures as the statement for an individual entity with a few additional items. The direct or indirect method of preparation may be used. When the indirect method is used, the additional noncash transactions relating to the business combination such as the differential amortization must also be reversed and all transfers to affiliates must be eliminated as they do not represent a cash inflow or outflow of the consolidated entity.

All unrealized intercompany profits should have been eliminated in preparation of the other statements; thus, no additional entry of this sort should be required. Any income allocated to noncontrolling parties would need to be added back as it would have been eliminated in computing consolidated net income but does not represent a true cash outflow. Finally, any dividend payments should be recorded as cash outflows in the financing activities section.

In preparing the operating activities section of the statement by the indirect method following a purchase business combination, the changes in assets and liabilities related to operations since acquisition should be derived by comparing the consolidated balance sheet as of the date of acquisition with the year-end consolidated balance sheet. These changes will be combined with those for the acquiring company up to the date of acquisition as adjustments to net income. The effects due to the acquisition of these assets and liabilities are reported under investing activities. Under the pooling-of-interests method the combination is treated as having occurred at the beginning of the year. Thus, the changes in assets and liabilities related to operations should be those derived by comparing the beginning of the year balance sheet amounts on a consolidated basis with the end of the year consolidated balance sheet amounts.

EMERGING ISSUES TASK FORCE CONSENSUS SUMMARIES

95-13 Classification of Debt Issue Costs in the Statement of Cash Flows

Cash paid for debt issue costs should be shown as a financing activity in the statement of cash flows.

5 CASH, RECEIVABLES, AND PREPAID EXPENSES

PERSPECTIVE AND ISSUES

One consequence of the concern with liquidity is the traditional presentation of a classified balance sheet. **Current assets** are defined as those assets which are or will become cash or will be consumed in normal business operations within a year or within one operating cycle if more than 1 year. **Current liabilities** are those obligations which will require the use of current assets or the incurrence of another current liability to liquidate them. Both the ratio of current assets to current liabilities (current ratio) or, alternatively, the excess of current assets over current liabilities (working capital) can be interpreted as a measure of an entity's liquidity. Generally, current assets are displayed in the balance sheet in the order of liquidity, beginning with cash on hand, continuing with temporary investments, receivables, inventories, and concluding with prepaid expenses.

SFAS 125 uses a financial-components approach that relies on control to establish standards for transfers and servicing of financial assets and extinguishments of liabilities. Derivatives and liabilities resulting from a transfer of financial assets are measured at fair value. In-substance defeasance does not result in the extinguishment of a liability. This statement is to be applied prospectively and is effective after December 31, 1996. Early or retroactive application is not permitted. SFAS 127 amends SFAS 125 to require deferral for 1 year of paragraph 15 (secured borrowings and collateral) and paragraphs 9-12 (dollar-rolls, repurchase agreements, securities lending, and similar transactions).

Sources of GAAP

ARB	*APB*	*SFAS*	*EITF*
43, Ch. 3A 43, Ch. 3	6, 20	6, 109, 125, 127	86-8, 88-22, 92-2

DEFINITIONS OF TERMS

Accounts receivable. Amounts due from customers for goods or services provided in the normal course of business operations.

Aging the accounts. Computation of the adjustment for uncollectible accounts receivable based upon the length of time the end-of-period outstanding accounts have been unpaid.

Assignment. The formal procedure for collateralization of borrowings through the use of accounts receivable. It normally does not involve debtor notification.

Cash. Coins and currency on hand and balances in checking accounts available for immediate withdrawal.

Cash equivalents. Short-term, highly liquid investments that are readily convertible to known amounts of cash. Examples include treasury bills, commercial paper, and money market funds.

Current assets. Those assets which are reasonably expected to be realized in cash or sold or consumed within a year or within the normal operating cycle of the entity.

Factoring. The outright sale of accounts receivable to a third-party financing entity. The sale may be with or without recourse.

Net realizable value. The amount of cash anticipated to be produced in the normal course of business from an asset, net of any direct costs of the conversion into cash.

Operating cycle. The average time between the acquisition of materials or services and the final cash realization from the sale of products or services.

Percentage-of-sales method. Computing the adjustment for uncollectible accounts receivable based on the historical relationship between bad debts and gross credit sales.

Pledging. Using an asset as collateral for borrowings. It generally refers to borrowings secured by accounts receivable.

Recourse. The right of the transferee (factor) of accounts receivable to seek recovery for an uncollectible account from the transferor. It is often limited to specific conditions.

Transfer. Conveyance of noncash financial asset by and to someone other than issuer of financial asset.

CONCEPTS, RULES, AND EXAMPLES

Cash

The promulgated GAAP for accounting for cash is ARB 43, Chapter 3. To be included as cash in the balance sheet, funds must be represented by actual coins and currency on hand or demand deposits available without restriction. It must be management's intention that the cash be available for current purposes. Cash in a demand deposit account which is being held for the retirement of long-term debts not maturing currently should be excluded from current assets and shown as a noncurrent investment. SFAS 6 identifies the intent of management as a key criterion in the classification of cash.

With the increased popularity of such instruments as NOW accounts and money market funds, it has become more common to see the caption "Cash and Cash Equivalents" in the balance sheet. This term includes other forms of near-cash as well as demand deposits and liquid, short-term securities. **Cash equivalents** must be available upon demand in order to justify inclusion.

Compensating balances. Pursuant to borrowing arrangements with lenders, an entity will often be required to maintain a minimum amount of cash on deposit (compensating balance). The purpose of this balance is to increase the yield on the loan to the lender. Since most organizations must maintain a certain working balance in their cash accounts simply to handle routine transactions and to cushion against unforeseen variations in the demand for cash, borrowers will often not find compensating balance arrangements objectionable. Nevertheless, the compensating balance is not available for unrestricted use and penalties will result if it is used. The portion of an entity's cash account which is a compensating balance must be segregated and shown as a noncurrent asset if the related borrowings are noncurrent liabilities. If the borrowings are current liabilities, it is acceptable to show the compensating balance as a **separately captioned** current asset.

Cash in savings accounts subject to a statutory notification requirement and cash in certificates of deposit maturing during the current **operating cycle** or within 1 year may be included as current assets but should be separately captioned in the balance sheet to avoid the misleading implication that these funds are available immediately upon demand. Typically, such items will be included in the **short-term investments** caption, but these could be labeled as time deposits or restricted cash deposits.

Petty cash and other imprest cash accounts are usually presented in financial statements with other cash accounts.

Receivables

Accounts receivable, open accounts, or trade accounts, are agreements by regular customers to pay for services received or merchandise obtained. Other categories of receivables include notes receivable, trade acceptances, third-party instruments, and amounts due from officers, stockholders, employees, or affiliated companies. Notes receivable are formalized obligations evidenced by written promissory notes. The latter categories of receivables generally arise from cash advances but could develop from sales of merchandise or the provision of services. The basic nature of amounts due from trade customers is often different from that of balances receivable from related parties, such as employees or stockholders. Thus, generally accepted accounting principles require that these different classes of receivables be separately identified either on the face of the balance sheet or in the notes.

Receivables should be presented at **net realizable** (realistically anticipated collectible) amounts. If the gross amount of receivables includes unearned interest or finance charges, these should be deducted in arriving at the net amount to be presented in the balance sheet (APB 6).

Deductions should be taken for amounts estimated to be uncollectible and also for the estimated returns, allowances, and other discounts to be taken by customers prior to or at the time of payment. In practice, the deductions that would be made for estimated returns, allowances, and trade discounts are usually deemed to be immaterial and such adjustments are rarely made. However, if it is known that sales are often recorded for merchandise which is shipped "on approval" and available data suggests that a **sizable** proportion of such sales are returned by the customers, then these estimated future returns must be accrued. Similarly, material amounts of anticipated discounts and allowances should be recorded in the period of sale.

The foregoing comments apply where revenues are recorded at the gross amount of the sale and subsequent sales discounts are recorded as debits (contra revenues). An alternative manner of recording revenue, which does away with any need to estimate future discounts, is to record the initial sale at the net amount; that is, at the amount that will be remitted if the customers take advantage of the available discount terms. If the customers pay the gross amount later (they fail to take the discounts), this additional revenue is recorded as income when it is remitted. The net method of recording sales, however, is rarely encountered in practice.

Bad Debts Expense

The recording of anticipated uncollectible amounts is almost always necessary. The direct write-off method, in which a receivable is charged off only when it is clear that it cannot be collected, is unsatisfactory since it results in a significant mismatching of revenues and expenses. Proper matching can only be achieved if bad debts expense is recorded in the same fiscal period as the revenues to which they are related. Since this expense is not known with certainty, an estimate must be made.

There are two popular estimation techniques. The **percentage-of-sales** method is principally oriented towards achieving the best possible matching of revenues and expenses. **Aging the accounts** is more oriented toward the presentation of the correct net realizable value of the trade receivables in the balance sheet. Both methods are acceptable and widely employed.

Percentage of sales. Historical data are analyzed to ascertain the relationship between bad debts and credit sales. The derived percentage is then applied to the current period's sales revenues in order to arrive at the appropriate debit to bad debts expense for the year. The offsetting credit is made to Allowance for Uncollectibles. When specific customer accounts are subsequently identified as uncollectible, they are written off against this allowance.

Example of percentage-of-sales method

Total **credit** sales for year:	$7,500,000
Bad debt ratio from prior years or other data source:	1.75% of credit sales
Computed year-end adjustment for bad debts expense:	$131,250 ($7,500,000 x .0175)

The entry required is

Bad debts expense	131,250	
Allowance for uncollectibles		131,250

Aging the accounts. An analysis is prepared of the customer receivables at the balance sheet date. These accounts are categorized by the number of days or months they have remained outstanding. Based on the entity's past experience or on other available statistics, historical bad debts percentages are applied to each of these aggregate amounts, with larger percentages being applicable to the older accounts. The end result of this process is a computed total dollar amount which is the proper balance in the allowance for uncollectibles at the balance sheet date. As a result of the difference between the previous years' adjustments to the allowance for uncollectibles and the actual write-offs made to the account, there will usually be a balance in this account. Thus, the adjustment needed will be an amount other than that computed by the aging.

Example of the aging method

		Age of accounts		
	Under 30 days	*30-90 days*	*Over 90 days*	*Total*
Gross receivables	$1,100,000	$425,000	$360,000	
Bad debt percentage	0.5%	2.5%	15%	
Provision required	$5,500	$10,625	$54,000	$70,125

The credit balance required in the allowance account is $70,125. Assuming that a **debit** balance of $58,250 already exists in the allowance account (from charge-offs during the year), the necessary entry is

Bad debts expense	128,375	
Allowance for uncollectibles		128,375

Both of the estimation techniques should produce approximately the same result. This will especially be true over the course of a number of years. Nonetheless, it must be recognized that these adjustments are based upon estimates and will never be totally accurate. When facts subsequently become available to indicate that the amount provided as an allowance for uncollectible accounts was incorrect, an adjustment classified as a change in estimate is made. Per APB 20, adjustments of this nature are never considered errors subject to subsequent correction or restatement. Only if an actual clerical or mechanical error occurred in the recording of allowance for uncollectibles would correction by means of a prior period adjustment be warranted.

Pledging, Assigning, and Factoring Receivables

An organization can alter the timing of cash flows resulting from sales to its customers by using its accounts receivable as collateral for borrowings or by selling the receivables outright. A wide variety of arrangements can be structured by the borrower and lender, but the most common are pledging, assignment, and factoring. SFAS 125 uses a financial-components approach that relies on control to establish standards for transfers and servicing of financial assets. It was effective after December 31, 1996. SFAS 127 amends SFAS 125 to require deferral for 1 year of paragraph 15 (secured borrowings and collateral) and paragraphs 9-12 (dollar-rolls, repurchase agreements, securities lending, and similar transactions).

Pledging of receivables. Pledging is an agreement where accounts receivable are used as collateral for loans. Generally, the lender has limited rights to inspect the borrower's records to achieve assurance that the receivables do exist. The customers whose accounts have been pledged are not aware of this event, and their payments are still remitted to the original obligee. The pledged accounts merely serve as security to the lender, giving comfort that sufficient assets exist which will generate cash flows adequate in amount and timing to repay the debt. However, the debt is paid by the borrower whether or not the pledged receivables are collected and whether or not the pattern of such collections matches the payments due on the debt.

The only accounting issue relating to pledging is that of adequate disclosure. The accounts receivable, which remain assets of the borrowing entity, continue to be shown as current assets in its financial statements but must be identified as having been pledged. This identification can be accomplished either parenthetically or by footnote disclosures. Similarly, the related debt should be identified as having been secured by the receivables.

Example of proper disclosure for pledged receivables

Current assets:	
Accounts receivable, net of allowance for doubtful accounts of $600,000 ($3,500,000 of which has been pledged as collateral for bank loans)	8,450,000
Current liabilities:	
Bank loans payable (secured by pledged accounts receivable)	2,700,000

A more common practice is to include the disclosure in the notes to the financial statements. Since the critical issue with SFAS 125 is the transfer of the asset and the associated release of control, normal business transactions involving pledging of accounts receivables will not be affected by the collateral provisions of the statement.

Assignment of receivables. The assignment of accounts receivable is a more formalized transfer of the asset to the lending institution. The lender will make an investigation of the specific receivables that are being proposed for assignment and will approve those which are deemed to be worthy as collateral. Customers are not usually aware that their accounts have been assigned and they continue to forward their payments to the original obligee. In some cases, the assignment agreement requires that collection proceeds be immediately delivered to the lender. The borrower is, however, the primary obligor and is required to make timely payment on the debt whether or not the receivables are collected as anticipated. The borrowing is with recourse, and the general credit of the borrower is pledged to the payment of the debt.

Since the lender knows that not all the receivables will be collected on a timely basis by the borrower, only a fraction of the face value of the receivables will be advanced as a loan to the borrower. Typically, this amount ranges from 70 to 90%, depending upon the credit history and collection experience of the borrower.

Assigned accounts receivable remain the assets of the borrower and continue to be presented in its financial statements, with appropriate disclosure of the assignment similar to that illustrated for pledging. Prepaid finance charges would be debited to a prepaid expense account and amortized to expense over the period to which the charges apply.

In the typical case involving the assignment of receivables, the assets will not be transferred and effective control will remain with the borrower. Thus, SFAS 125 will not be applicable. If the assigned receivables are transferred, a determination must be made as to whether to account for the transfer as a sale or as a secured borrowing under the criteria established by SFAS 125. In addition, a determination must be made as to whether new assets or liabilities have been created by the terms of the transfer and whether those new assets or liabilities are to be recorded at fair value or allocated cost.

Factoring of receivables. This category of financing is the most significant in terms of accounting implications. Factoring traditionally has involved the outright sale of receivables to a financing institution known as a factor. These arrangements involved (1) notification to the customer to forward future payments to the factor and (2) the transfer of receivables without recourse. The factor assumes the risk of an inability to collect. Thus, once a factoring arrangement was completed, the entity had no further involvement with the accounts, except for a return of merchandise.

In its simplistic form, the receivables are sold and the difference between the cash received and the carrying value is recognized as a gain or loss.

Example

Thirsty Corp., on July 1, 1999, enters into an agreement with Rich Company to sell a group of its receivables **without recourse**. A total face value of $200,000 accounts receivable (against which a 5% allowance had been recorded) are involved.

The entries required are as follows:

Cash	180,055	
Allowance for bad debts (200,000 x .05)	10,000	
Loss on sale of receivables	19,945	
Bad debts expense		10,000
Accounts receivable		200,000

The classical variety of factoring provides two financial services to the business: it permits the entity to obtain cash earlier and the risk of bad debts is transferred to the factor. The factor is compensated for each of the services. Interest is charged based on the anticipated length of time between the date the factoring is consummated and the expected collection date of the receivables sold. A fee is charged based upon the factor's anticipated bad debt losses.

Example

Thirsty Corp., on July 1, 1999, enters into an agreement with Rich Company to sell a group of its receivables **without recourse**. A total face value of $200,000 accounts receivable (against which a 5% allowance had been recorded) are involved. The factor will charge 20% interest computed on the weighted-average time to maturity of the receivables of 36 days plus a 3% fee.

The entries required are as follows:

Cash	180,055	
Allowance for bad debts (200,000 x .05)	10,000	
Interest expense (or prepaid) (200,000 x .20 x 36/365)	3,945	
Factoring fee (200,000 x .03)	6,000	
Loss on sale of receivables	10,000	
Bad debts expense		10,000
Accounts receivable		200,000

The interest expense, factor's fee and loss can be combined into a $19,945 loss on the sale of receivables.

Some companies continue to factor receivables as a means of transferring the risk of bad debts, but leave the cash on deposit with the factor until the weighted-average due date of the receivables, thereby avoiding interest charges. This arrangement is still referred to as factoring, since the customer receivables have been sold. However, the borrowing entity does not receive cash but creates a new receivable, usually captioned "Due From Factor." This receivable, in contrast to the original customer receivables, is essentially riskless and will be presented in the balance sheet without a deduction for estimated uncollectibles.

Merchandise returns will normally be the responsibility of the original vendor, who must then make the appropriate settlement with the factor. To protect against the possibility of merchandise returns which diminish the total of receivables to be collected, very often a factoring arrangement will **not** advance the full amount of the factored receivables (less any interest and factoring fee deductions). Rather, the factor will retain a certain fraction of the total proceeds relating to the portion of sales which are anticipated to be returned by customers. This sum is known as the factor's holdback. When merchandise is returned to the borrower, an entry is made offsetting the receivable from the factor. At the end of the return privilege period, any remaining holdback will become due and payable to the borrower.

Example of accounting for the transfer of receivables without recourse

1. Thirsty Corp., on July 1, 1999, enters into an agreement with Rich Company to sell a group of its receivables **without recourse**. A total face value of $200,000 accounts receivable (against which a 5% allowance had been recorded) are involved. The factor will charge 20% interest computed on the weighted-average time to maturity of the receivables of 36 days plus a 3% fee. A 5% holdback will also be retained.
2. Thirsty's customers return for credit $4,800 of merchandise.
3. The customer return privilege period expires and the remaining holdback is paid to the transferor.

The entries required are as follows:

1.	Cash	180,055	
	Allowance for bad debts (200,000 x .05)	10,000	
	Interest expense (or prepaid) (200,000 x .20 x 36/365)	3,945	
	Factoring fee (200,000 x .03)	6,000	
	Factor's holdback receivable (190,000 x .05)	9,500	
	Loss on sale of receivables (10,000 x .05)	500	
	Bad debts expense		10,000
	Accounts receivable		200,000

The interest expense, factor's fee and loss can be combined into a $10,445 charge to loss on the sale of receivables.

2.	Sales returns and allowances	4,800	
	Factor's holdback receivable		4,800
3.	Cash	5,200	
	Factor's holdback receivable		4,700
	Loss on sale of receivables		500

Notice that the factor's holdback receivable on the seller's books is required by SFAS 125 to be an allocation of the carrying value ($190,000) of the receivables retained. However, the factor will holdback 5% of the face value ($200,000) for a total of $10,000. Thus, upon settlement the recorded loss or gain may need to be adjusted.

Factoring does transfer title. Where there is a no recourse provision, the removal of these receivables from the borrower's balance sheet is clearly warranted.

Another variation is known as factoring with **recourse**. Some entities had such a poor history of uncollectible accounts that factors were only willing to purchase their accounts if a substantial fee were collected to compensate for the risk. When the company believed that the receivables were of a better quality, a way to avoid excessive factoring fees was to sell these receivables with recourse. This variation of factoring was really an assignment of receivables with notification to the customers.

In computing the gain or loss to be recognized at the date of the transfer of the receivables, the borrower (transferor) must take into account the anticipated chargebacks from the transferee for bad debts to be incurred. This action requires an estimate by the transferor, based on past experience. Adjustments should also be made at the time of sale for the estimated effects of any prepayments by customers (where the receivables are interest-bearing or where cash discounts are available), and for the effects of any defects in the eligibility of the transferred receivables.

Example of accounting for the transfer of receivables with recourse

1. Thirsty Corp., on July 1, 1999, enters into an agreement with Rich Company to sell a group of its receivables with a face value of $200,000 on which a 5% allowance had been recorded. Rich Company (the factor) will charge 20% interest computed on the weighted-average time to maturity of the receivables of 36 days and a 3% fee. A 5% holdback will also be retained.
2. Generally, 40% of Thirsty's customers take advantage of a 2% cash discount.
3. The factor accepts the receivables **subject to recourse** for nonpayment.

This situation qualifies as a sale because the Thirsty Corp. has surrendered control of the receivables, Thirsty's future obligation is reasonably estimable, and Rich Co. does not have a unilateral ability to require Thirsty to repurchase the receivables. Under SFAS 125, Thirsty must record a liability for the recourse liability. It has accepted the obligation for all credit losses and has, in effect, guaranteed the receivables.

The entries required to record the sale is

Cash	180,055	
Allowance for bad debts	10,000	
Interest expense	3,945	
Factoring fee	6,000	
Factor's holdback receivable (190,000 x .05)	9,500	
Loss on sale of receivables	2,100	
Due to factor (200,000 x .40 x .02)		1,600
Accounts receivable		200,000
Recourse obligation		10,000

Simplified, the entry is

Cash	180,055	
Allowance for bad debts	10,000	
Factor's holdback receivable (190,000 x .05)	9,500	
Loss on sale of receivables (3,945 + 6,000 + 2,100)	12,045	
Accounts receivable		200,000
Recourse obligation (10,000 + 1,600)		11,600

The accounts receivables and the allowance for bad debts (a contra asset) are removed from the transferor's books as these have been sold. Previously accrued bad debts expense is **not** reversed, however, as the transferor still expects to incur this through the recourse provision of the factoring agreement. (Alternatively, the bad debts expense could have been reversed and the charge to loss on sale increased by $10,000). The loss on sale of receivables is the sum of the interest charged by the factor ($3,945), the factor's fee ($6,000), the expected chargeback for cash discounts to be taken ($1,600), and the difference between the holdback receivable at face value and at carrying value ($500).

If, subsequent to the sale of the receivables, the actual experience relative to the recourse terms differs from the provision made at the time of the sale, a change in an accounting estimate results. It is reflected as an additional gain or loss in the subsequent period. These changes are not corrections of errors or retroactive adjustments.

Secured borrowings. If the above facts apply, but the transfer does not qualify as a sale, the borrower's entry will be

Cash	180,055	
Interest expense (or prepaid)	3,945	
Factoring fee	6,000	
Factor borrowing payable		190,000

The accounts receivable remain on the borrower's books. Both the accounts receivable and the factor borrowings payable should be cross-referenced in the balance sheet. Technically, the accounting for the collateral under SFAS 125 depends upon the terms of the collateral agreement. However, since the assets are not normally transferred and since a security interest is ordinarily not provided with borrowing transactions using accounts receivables as collateral, SFAS 125 collateral provisions are usually not applicable.

Transfers of Financial Assets Under SFAS 125

The FASB adopted a financial-components approach for SFAS 125. In doing so, the approach that views a financial asset as an indivisible unit has become obsolete. Financial assets are now to be viewed as a variety of components with a focus on who controls the components and on whether control has changed with a given transaction.

The basic accounting problem in this area involves instances of possible continuing involvement through recourse, repurchase agreements, options generated, servicing and collateral. The issue is whether the transfer has resulted in a sale or a secured borrowing. A sale results, to the extent that a consideration other than beneficial interests has been received, when the transferor gives up control.

Under SFAS 125, transfers of financial assets are disaggregated into separate assets and liabilities. Each entity involved in the transaction then

1. Recognizes only the assets controlled and liabilities incurred, and
2. Derecognizes assets where control has been given up or lost and liabilities where extinguishment has occurred.

Control is deemed to have been surrendered by the transferor only if **all** of the following conditions are met:

1. The assets transferred are beyond the reach of the transferor and its affiliates, its creditors, bankruptcy trustees or other receivers, except for an affiliate that is a qualifying special-purpose entity.
2. The transferee can pledge or exchange freely the assets transferred without unreasonable constraints or conditions imposed on its contractual right **or** the holders of beneficial interests in a qualifying special-purpose entity can pledge or exchange those interests freely without unreasonable constraints or conditions imposed on their right.
3. The transferor has not kept effective control of the financial assets transferred through a repurchase or redemption agreement that entitles and obligates repurchase or redemption before maturity at a determinable price **or** through an agreement (except for a cleanup call) to repurchase or redeem before maturity assets not readily obtainable elsewhere. To meet this condition, the transferor must have received cash or other collateral sufficient at all time to substantially fund repurchase or redemption.

Upon transfer, the transferor will allocate, based on relative fair values at the **date of transfer**, the previous carrying amount between the retained interests and the sale. Retained interests include undivided interests for which control has not been given up by the transferor, servicing (mortgages, credit card receivables, etc.) assets and liabilities and beneficial interests in transferred assets to a qualifying special-purpose entity in a securitization.

If a sale, the transferor should

1. Derecognize all assets sold
2. Recognize **all** assets (including cash, options, swaps, etc.) controlled and liabilities (including servicing liabilities) incurred in consideration as proceeds
3. Measure assets controlled and liabilities incurred at fair value initially. If it is not practicable to estimate the fair value of the assets, the transferor will record assets at zero. If it is not practical to estimate the fair value of the liabilities, the transferor will not recognize any gain and will record liabilities at the greater of
    a. Excess fair value of the assets obtained minus the fair value of the liabilities incurred over the carrying value of the assets transferred or
    b. The amount to be recorded in conjunction with SFAS 5 and FASB I 14.
4. Recognize gains or losses in earnings.

Example: Estimate of fair values is not practical

Entity A sells loans with a recourse obligation and retains the servicing which is expected to provide adequate compensation for performance.

	Asset fair value cannot be determined	*Liability fair value cannot be determined*
Loan's fair value	$16,500	$16,500
Loan's book value	15,000	15,000
Fair value of servicing asset	?	700
Fair value of recourse obligation	(900)	?

Proceeds

Cash	$16,500	$16,500
Less: Recourse obligation	(900)	?
Net cash received	$15,600	$16,500

Allocation of book value based on fair value of assets

	FV	*%*	*BV allocated*	*FV*	*%*	*BV allocated*
Loans sold	$15,600	100	$15,000	$16,500	96	$14,400
Servicing assets	0	0	0	700	4	600
	$15,600	100	$15,000	$17,200	100	$15,000

Journal Entries

Cash	16,500		16,500	
Servicing asset	0		600	
Loans		15,000		15,000
Recourse obligation		900		2,100
Gain		600		0

Example: Sale of loans

Facts Given

Loan's fair value	$16,500
Loan's book value	15,000
Fair value of recourse obligation	(900)
Fair value of call option	800
Fair value of interest rate swap	700

Seller's Journal Entries

1. Sale only

Cash	16,500	
Loans		15,000
Gain		1,500

2. Sale with recourse obligation

Cash	16,500	
Loans		15,000
Recourse obligation		900
Gain		600

3. Sale with recourse obligation and call option to purchase the loans sold or similar loans

Cash	16,500	
Call	800	
Loans		15,000
Recourse obligation		900
Gain		1,400

4. Sale with recourse obligation, call and swap (seller provides floating interest rate return although the basic sale is at fixed interest rate terms)

Cash	16,500	
Call	800	
Swap	700	
Loans		15,000
Recourse obligation		900
Gain		2,100

5. Partial sale with recourse obligation, call and swap. Seller sells 80% of loans.

	FV	*80% FV*	*20% FV*	*Allocated 80% BV*	*Allocated 20% BV*
Cash	$16,500	$13,200		$11,579	
Call	800	640		561	
Swap	700	560		491	
Recourse obligation	(900)	(720)		(631)	
Retained amount (20%)			$3,420		$3,000
	$17,100	$13,680	$3,420	$12,000	$3,000

Cash	13,200	
Call	640	
Swap	560	
Loans		12,000
Recourse obligation		720
Gain		1,680

Seller reports retained amount at $3,000.

If a sale, the transferee should recognize and initially measure assets controlled and liabilities incurred at fair value (in total, presumed to be the price paid). All financial asset transfers not meeting the sale criteria are required to be accounted for as secured borrowings with collateral (or other security interest) pledged.

Example: Secured borrowing (30 days)

Fair value of loaned security	$16,500
Book value of loaned security	16,500
Collateral (cash)	16,995
Seller's return from investing cash	5%
Seller's rebate to borrower	4%

Seller's Journal Entries

At Date of Loan:

	Debit	Credit
Loaned securities	16,500	
Securities		16,500
Cash	16,995	
Loan agreement payable		16,995
Money market	16,995	
Cash		16,995

At End of 30 Days:

	Debit	Credit
Cash	17,065	
Interest income		70
Money market		16,995
Securities	16,500	
Loaned securities		16,500
Loan agreement payable	16,995	
Interest rebate	56	
Cash		17,051

Retained Interests

In most cases, the outright transfer of assets and/or liabilities result(s) in changes in control that are obvious from the nature of the transaction. Problems generally occur when there is some sort of continuing involvement by the transferor. Retained interests include undivided interests for which control has not been given up by the transferor, servicing (mortgages, credit card receivables, etc.) assets and liabilities and beneficial interests in transferred assets to a qualifying special-purpose entity in a securitization. In general, the more that the transferor of assets retains an interest, the less likely the transaction will be classified as a sale and the more likely the transaction will be classified as a secured borrowing. The primary reason for this result is that in a sale, the transferor should give up control. If a determination cannot be made between classification as proceeds of a sale or as retained interests, the asset should be classified as proceeds and should be measured at fair value. Interests in transferred assets that are not a part of the proceeds are considered retained interests that are still under the control of the transferor.

Retained interests are to be measured at their previous carrying value before the transfer through an allocation at the date of sale based on relative fair values of the assets sold and the assets retained. This allocation is similar to that recommended in EITF 88-11 and must be applied to all transfers that have retained interests, regardless of whether or not they qualify as sales. It should be noted that this fair value allocation may result in a relative change in basis unless the fair values are proportionate to their carrying values. Thus, the gain or loss from any sale component could also be affected.

Example: Retained Interests

Sale of Receivable With Servicing

Facts Given:

Receivable's fair value	$16,500	
Receivable's book value	15,000	
Servicing asset		700

Partial sale of receivables with servicing asset retained. Seller sells 80% of receivables.

	FV	*80%FV*	*20%FV*	*Allocated 80%BV*	*Allocated 20%BV*
Receivables sold	$16,500	$13,200		$11,520	
Servicing asset	700	560		480	
Retained amount (20%)			$3,440		$3,000
	$17,200	$13,760	$3,440	$12,000	$3,000

Journal Entry

Cash	13,200	
Servicing asset	480	
Receivables		12,000
Gain		1,680

Seller reports retained amount at $3,000.

The retained interests continue to be the transferor's assets since control of these assets has not been transferred. They are carried at the allocated book value without recognition of any gain or loss. Thus, the retained interest is considered continuing control over a previous asset (although the form may have changed) and it should not be remeasured at fair value.

Servicing

Servicing of financial assets includes

1. Collecting payments
2. Paying taxes and insurance
3. Monitoring delinquencies
4. Foreclosing
5. Investing
6. Remitting fees
7. Accounting

Although inherent in transfers of most financial assets, servicing is a distinct asset or liability only when separated contractually from the underlying financial asset. The servicing asset usually results either from separate purchase or assumption of rights or from securitization with retained servicing. The servicer's obligations are specified in the contract.

Typically, the servicing contract results in an asset since the benefits are more than adequate compensation for the servicing. The benefits include

1. Fees
2. Late charges
3. Float
4. Other income

If the above benefits do not provide fair compensation, the contract results in a liability. With regard to the sale of assets, a servicing liability would reduce the net proceeds and would affect the gain or loss calculation.

Example: Sale of Receivable With Servicing

Facts Given:

Receivable's fair value	$16,500
Receivable's book value	15,000
Servicing liability	(500)

Partial sale of receivables with servicing liability retained. Seller sells 80% of receivables.

	FV	*80%FV*	*20%FV*	*Allocated 80%BV*	*Allocated 20%BV*
Receivables sold	$16,500	$13,200		$12,000	
Servicing asset	(500)	(400)			
Retained amount (20%)			$3,200		$3,000
	$16,000	$12,800	$3,200	$12,000	$3,000

Journal Entry

Cash	13,200	
Servicing liability	400	
Receivables		12,000
Gain		800

Seller reports retained amount at $3,000.

The fair value of a servicing contract is based on its value in the market and is not based on the internal cost structure of the servicer. Thus, the concept of adequate compensation is judged by requirements that would be imposed by a new or outside servicer. In cases where there are few servicing contracts that are purchased or sold, present value methods may be used for valuation.

In summary, the servicer should classify the components into one of the following categories:

1. More than adequate -- resulting in a recorded asset
2. Adequate compensation (no asset or liability)
3. Less than adequate -- resulting in a recorded liability

If, under a servicing contract, the transferor securitizes the assets, retains the securities and classifies them as held-to-maturity debt securities under SFAS 115, the asset or liability can be reported together with the asset being serviced. However, if the entity sells or securitizes with service retained or if the entity purchases or assumes servicing, a servicing asset or liability results. If servicing is retained, resulting assets are measured at book value based on relative fair value at the date of sale, if practical. Servicing liabilities undertaken, servicing assets purchased, and servicing liabilities assumed are measured at fair value.

Specifically, servicing assets or servicing liabilities are to be accounted for separately as follows:

1. Assets are to be reported separately from liabilities. They are not netted.
2. Initially measure retained servicing assets at allocated book value based on relative fair values at date of sale or securitization.
3. Initially measure at fair value all purchased assets, assumed liabilities, and liabilities undertaken in a sale or securitization.
4. Account separately for interest-only strips (future interest income from serviced assets that exceeds servicing fees).
5. Amortize assets in proportion to and over the period of net servicing income.
6. Evaluate and measure impairment as follows:
   a. Stratify recognized assets based on predominant risk (asset size, type, interest rate, terms, location, date of organization, etc.)
   b. Individual stratum should have impairment recognized through a valuation allowance in the amount of the excess of book value over fair value.
   c. Adjust the valuation allowances to reflect needed changes. Excess fair value for a stratum should not be recognized.
7. Amortize liabilities in proportion to and over the period of net servicing loss. In cases where changes have increased the fair value above the book value, an increased liability and a loss should be recognized.

Example: Sale of Receivable With Servicing

Receivable's fair value	$16,500
Receivable's book value	15,000
Servicing asset	(700)
Recourse obligaiton	(900)

1. Servicing asset retained

	FV	*%*	*BV Allocated*
Receivable sold	$16,500	96	$14,400
Servicing asset	700	4	600
	$17,200	100	$15,000

Journal Entry

Cash	16,500	
Servicing asset	600	
Receivables		15,000
Gain		2,100

2. Partial sale of receivables with servicing asset retained and recourse obligation. Seller sells 80% of receivables.

	FV	*80%FV*	*20%FV*	*Allocated 80%BV*	*Allocated 20%BV*
Receivables sold	$16,500	$13,200		$11,520	
Servicing asset	700	560		480	
Resource obligation	(900)	(720)			
Retained amount (20%)			$3,260		$3,000
	$16,300	$13,040	$3,260	$12,000	$3,000

Journal Entry

Cash	13,200	
Servicing asset	480	
Receivables		12,000
Recourse obligaiton		720
Gain		960

Seller reports retained amount at $3,000.

Securitizations

Securitization is the transformation of financial assets into securities (asset-backed securities). Various assets including mortgages, credit cards, trade receivables, loans, and leases are grouped and securitized. These groupings of relatively homogeneous assets are then pooled and divided into securities with cash-flows that can be quite different from those of the original assets. With an established market, most of these securities cost less than the alternative use of the assets as collateral for borrowing. Thus, the benefits of most securitizations include lower financing costs, increased liquidity, and lower credit risk.

The transferor (also called issuer or sponsor) forms a securitization mechanism (separate corporation or qualifying special-purpose entity [QSPE]) to buy the assets and to issue the securities. Sometimes, another transfer is made to a trust and the trust issues the securities. These different structures are generally referred to as one-tier or two-tier. The securitization mechanism then generates beneficial interests in the assets or resulting cash flows which are sold. The form of the securities chosen depends on such things as the nature of the assets, income tax considerations, and returns to be received.

Payments by the securitization mechanism are usually classified as **pay-through**, **pass-through** or **revolving-period**. In a **pay-through**, cash flows from the assets pay off the debt securities. The assets are essentially collateral. In a **pass-**

through, undivided interests are issued and the investors share in the net cash flows. In a **revolving-period**, undivided interests are issued, but until liquidation, the net cash flows are split between buying additional assets and paying off investors.

Various financial components arise from securitizations. Examples include servicing contracts, interest-only strips, retained interests, recourse obligations, options, swaps and forward contracts. All controlled assets and liabilities must be recognized under SFAS 125.

Example: Sale of Loans

Facts Given:

Loan's fair value	$16,500
Loan's book value	15,000
Fair value of recourse obligation	(900)
Fair value of call option	800
Fair value of interest rate swap	700

1. Sale with recourse obligation, call and swap (seller provides floating interest rate return although the basic sale is at fixed interest rate terms).

Journal Entry

Cash	16,500	
Call	800	
Swap	700	
Loans		15,000
Recourse obligation		900
Gain		2,100

2. Partial sale with recourse obligation, call and swap. Seller sells 80% of loans.

	FV	*80%FV*	*20%FV*	*Allocated 80%BV*	*Allocated 20%BV*
Cash	$16,500	$13,200		$12,000	
Call	800	640			
Swap	700	560			
Resource obligation	(900)	(720)			
Retained amount (20%)			$3,420		$3,000
	$17,100	$13,680	$3,420	$12,000	$3,000

Journal Entry

Cash	13,200	
Call	640	
Swap	560	
Loans		12,000
Recourse obligaiton		720
Gain		1,680

Seller reports retained amount at $3,000.

Example: Sale of Receivable With Servicing

Receivable's fair value	$16,500
Receivable's book value	15,000
Servicing asset	700
Interest-only strip receivable	600
Recourse obligation	(900)

Servicing asset retained with interest-only strip receivable.

	FV	*%*	*BV Allocated*
Receivable sold	$16,500	93	$13,950
Servicing asset	700	4	600
Interest-only strip receivable	600	3	450
	$17,800	100	$15,000

Journal Entry

Cash	16,500	
Servicing asset	600	
Interest-only strip receivable	450	
Receivables		15,000
Gain		2,550

If the interest-only strip was measured as an available-for-sale security, another entry would be

Interest-only strip	150	
Equity (or comprehensive income)		150

The credit would be to income if it was classified as a trading security.

The transferor generally desires for the assets to be taken off the balance sheet. This result can be accomplished if the transaction results in a sale. The key criterion in this case is to be sure that the assets are beyond control of the transferor even in bankruptcy.

Accounting for Collateral

Accounting for collateral depends both on control of the assets and on the liabilities incurred under the collateral agreement. Ordinarily, the transferor should carry the collateral as an asset and the transferee should not record the pledged asset.

If the transferee, however, has control and the transferor doesn't have the right or ability to redeem on short notice, the secured party should record the asset at fair value and also the liability to return it. The debtor should reclassify the asset (probably as a receivable) and report it separately in the balance sheet. If the debtor's rights to the collateral are impaired by the transferee's sale or repledge of the collateral without the right to get it back on short notice, the secured party should recognize the proceeds and also the liability to return the collateral to the extent it hasn't done so.

If the transferor defaults and is not entitled to the return of the collateral, it should be derecognized. If not already recognized, the transferee should record its asset at fair value.

Disclosures

SFAS 125 disclosures include

1. Policy for requiring collateral or other security under repurchase or securities lending agreements
2. Description of items for which it is not practicable to estimate fair value and reasons why it is not practicable
3. Servicing assets and liabilities

    a. Amounts recognized and amortized
    b. Fair value recognized, method and assumptions used to estimate fair value
    c. Risk characteristics used to stratify in order to measure impairments
    d. Valuation allowance for impairment activity for each period for which results of operations are given

Prepaid Expenses

Prepaid expenses are identified as a current asset by ARB 43, chapter 3A. They are considered current not because of their anticipated conversion to cash during the current operating cycle, but rather because if they were not prepaid they would require the use of current assets during the operating cycle. The account is to be amortized to expense on a ratable basis over the life of the asset.

EMERGING ISSUES TASK FORCE CONSENSUS SUMMARIES

86-8 Sale of Bad Debt Recovery Rights

The transaction is a secured borrowing from the seller's perspective. There was no consensus on whether the proceeds should reduce the loan-loss allowance.

88-22 Securitization of Credit Card Portfolios (affected by SFAS 125)

Amounts received from transferring to investors a participating interest in credit card receivables in a trust should be accounted for as a sale if the conditions in para 9 of SFAS 125 are met.

The type of liquidation method specified does not affect the accounting for the transfer unless the percentage of principal payments allocated exceeds the investors' ownership interest in the receivables in the trust at the beginning of the liquidation period. In this case, the transfer does not qualify as a sale under SFAS 125 because the investor has, in effect, the ability to require the seller to repurchase some of the receivables.

Gain on the sale of receivables should be limited to amounts related to receivables that exist at the sale date. The gain generally will not be material. Terms of the agreement should be examined to determine whether a loss should be recognized for expected costs to be incurred for future servicing obligations. Transaction costs relating to the sale may be recognized over the initial and reinvestment period in a rational and systematic manner unless a loss is indicated.

92-2 Measuring Loss Accruals by Transferors for Transfers of Receivables With Recourse

All probable credit losses (not only those recognized in accordance with SFAS 5) over the life of the receivables transferred should be included in the obligation recorded at the date of sale. The recourse obligation can be recognized on a present value (PV) basis if the cash flows can be reasonably estimated. If PV is used, the interest rate used in subsequent accruals should be the same rate used in determining the initial obligation. If the effect of discounting is material, the interest rate used and the recourse obligation's undiscounted amount should be disclosed.

The SEC will object to an interest rate higher than the rate on monetary assets that are essentially risk free and that have maturities similar to those of the recourse obligation. The recourse obligation is a liability and should not be offset unless a right of setoff exists (see FASB Interpretation 39).

If a right of setoff exists and the seller's recourse obligation is contractually limited to and paid from an escrow account (consisting of excess cash from the coupon interest on the receivables over the interest passed through to the buyer), the SEC observer stated that the value of the retained net asset should be determined as indicated in EITF 88-11. The interest rate used to discount would be that demanded by market participants unrelated to the seller and would generally be higher than the rate used to discount excess servicing. In this case, it is acceptable to measure the recourse liability separately before netting it and the excess servicing asset.

97-3 Accounting for Fees and Costs Associated With Loan Syndications and Loan Participation After the Issuance of FASB Statement No. 125

A consensus was reached that the accounting for financial asset transfers as described in SFAS 125 is applicable to loan participation, including those which are "in-substance loan syndications."

A consensus was also reached that all transactions legally structured as loan syndications including "in-substance loan participation," should be accounted for as loan syndications per SFAS 91.

6 SHORT-TERM INVESTMENTS AND FINANCIAL INSTRUMENTS

PERSPECTIVE AND ISSUES

SFAS 133, entitled *Accounting for Derivative Instruments and Hedging Activities*, was issued in June 1998. This standard is effective for all fiscal quarters of all fiscal years beginning after June 15, 1999. A calendar-year company would begin application in January 2000. Early application is encouraged but initial application must be at the beginning of a fiscal quarter after June 1998 when hedging relationships must be designated and documented according to SFAS 133. A calendar-year company would begin early application in January 1999. The standard cannot be applied retroactively.

SFAS 133 applies to all entities and requires that all derivative instruments (DI) be recognized as either assets or liabilities on the balance sheet at fair value. Gains and losses of DI not designated as hedges are recognized in earnings (or as a change in net assets for a not-for-profit).

After meeting specified conditions, a derivative may be specifically designated as a hedge of

1. Changes in fair value of

    a. A recognized asset or liability
    b. An unrecognized firm commitment

In a fair value hedge, all gains and losses (of both the DI and the hedged item) are recognized in earnings in the period of change.

2. Variable cash flows of a forecasted transaction

   In a cash flow hedge, the effective portion of the hedge is reported in comprehensive income and is reclassified into earnings when the forecasted transaction affects earnings. Hedge portions that are not effective are reported in earnings immediately.

3. Foreign currency exposure of

   a. A net investment in a foreign operation

      In a foreign currency net investment hedge, the gain or loss is reported in comprehensive income as part of the cumulative translation adjustment.

   b. An unrecognized firm commitment

      In a foreign currency unrecognized firm commitment hedge, the gain or loss is reported the same way as a fair value hedge (see category 1. above).

   c. An available for sale security

      In a foreign currency available-for-sale security hedge the gain or loss is reported the same way as a fair value hedge (see category 1. above).

   d. A foreign currency denominated forecasted transaction

      In a foreign currency denominated forecasted transaction hedge, the gain or loss is reported in the same way as a cash flow hedge (see category 2. above).

Not-for-profits (NFP) cannot use hedge accounting for forecasted transactions. A nonderivative financial instrument cannot generally be designated as a hedge. One exception, however, occurs when that instrument is denominated in a foreign currency and is designated as a hedge under 3.a. or 3.b. above.

The method used for assessing the effective and noneffective portions of a hedge must be determined at inception and must be consistent with the approach used for managing risk.

SFAS 133 affects the following pronouncements as indicated below:

Effect	*Pronouncement*
Supersedes	SFAS 80, 105, and 119
Amends	ARB 43 SFAS 52, 60, 65, 95, 107, 113, 115, 124, 125, and 126 TB 79-19
Nullifies or Modifies	Numerous EITF

SFAS 125 uses a financial-components approach that relies on control to establish standards for transfers and servicing of financial assets and extinguishments of liabilities. Derivatives and liabilities resulting from a transfer of financial assets are measured at fair value. In-substance defeasance does not result in the extinguishment of a liability.

SFAS 115 is GAAP regarding investments in all debt securities and in equity securities that have a readily determinable fair value. It classifies these securities into one of the following three categories:

1. Held-to-maturity – Debt securities reported at amortized cost
2. Trading – Debt and equity securities reported at fair value
3. Available-for-sale – Debt and equity securities not classified as 1 or 2, reported at fair value

SFAS 115 does not change the accounting for financial liabilities and does not apply to DI. In the case of an investment subject to this standard with an embedded derivative, the host instrument is accounted for under SFAS 115 and the embedded derivative is accounted for under SFAS 133.

SFAS 105 was the first in a series of disclosure statements about financial instruments. Its focus is on the extent, nature, and terms of financial instruments with **off-balance-sheet** credit or market risk. In addition, the statement addresses concentrations of credit risk for **all** financial instruments.

SFAS 107 requires entities to disclose the fair value of **all** (recognized and unrecognized) financial instruments that it is practicable to estimate, including liabilities. Pertinent descriptive information as to the fair value of the instrument is to be disclosed if an estimate of fair value cannot be made without incurring excessive costs. In paragraph 8, the statement excludes certain types of financial instruments including pensions, postretirement benefits, deferred compensation, defeased debt, insurance contracts, lease contracts, warranty obligations, and others. Fair value disclosure requirements specified by GAAP are acceptable for purposes of this statement. SFAS 107 was amended by SFAS 133 to include the disclosure requirements concerning concentrations of credit risk for **all** financial instruments from superseded SFAS 105.

SFAS 126 and SFAS 107 disclosures are optional for entities meeting the following criteria:

1. Enterprise is nonpublic.
2. Total enterprise assets are less than $100 million on financial statement date.
3. During the reporting period, enterprise has not held or issued any derivative financial instruments.

SFAS 119, entitled *Disclosure about Derivative Financial Instruments and Fair Value of Financial Instruments*, requires issuers and holders of derivative financial instruments (DFI) to disclose information about those instruments. It also amends the disclosure requirements of SFAS 105 and SFAS 107. The SEC has issued new qualitative and quantitative risk disclosure rules for derivatives. They are effective for filings after June 15, 1997, for banks, thrifts, and large companies (capitalization over $2.5 billion).

Although FASB Interpretation 39 makes an exception in the case of multiple forward, swap, and similar contracts executed with the same party under master netting arrangements, offsetting of assets and liabilities is improper except where a right of setoff exists. A right of setoff is a debtor's legal right to discharge debt owed to another party by applying against the debt an amount the other party owes to the debtor. The conditions to be met are

1. Each of the two parties owes the other determinable amounts.
2. The reporting party has the right to setoff.
3. The reporting party intends to setoff.
4. The right of setoff is enforceable at law.

Sources of GAAP

ARB	*APB*	*SFAS*	*FASB I*	*EITF*
43, Ch. 3A	22	52, 65, 80, 95, 102, 105, 107, 109, 111, 115, 119, 125, 126, 127, 130, 133	39 *FASB TB* 94-1	84-7, 84-14, 85-9, 85-29, 86-24, 86-25, 86-28, 86-34, 86-35, 86-40, 87-2, 87-12, 87-20, 87-26, 87-30, 87-31, 88-8, 88-11, 89-18, 90-17, 95-5, 96-11, 96-12, 96-13, 96-15

DEFINITIONS OF TERMS

Accounting loss. Accounting loss refers to the loss that may have to be recognized due to credit and market risk as a direct result of the rights and obligations of a financial instrument.

Carrying amount (value). The amount at which securities are being carried, net of allowances.

Contractual obligations. All contractual obligations that are financial instruments meet the definition of a liability set forth in FASB Concepts Statement 6, *Elements of Financial Statements*. Some may not be recognized as liabilities in financial statements--may be "off-balance-sheet"--because they fail to meet some other criterion for recognition. For some financial instruments, the obligation is owed to or by a group of entities rather than a single entity.

Contractual rights. All contractual rights that are financial instruments meet the definition of asset set forth in Concepts Statement 6. Some may not be recognized as assets in financial statements--may be "off-balance-sheet"--because they fail to meet some other criterion for recognition. For some financial instruments, the obligation is held by or due from a group of entities rather than a single entity.

Cost (of a security). The original purchase price plus all costs incidental to the acquisition (e.g., brokerage fees and taxes) unless a new cost basis is assigned as a result of a decline in market value which is other than temporary.

Credit risk. Credit risk is the possibility that a loss may occur from the failure of another party to perform according to the terms of a contract.

Equity instrument. Any evidence of an ownership interest in an entity.

Financial asset. Any asset that is (1) cash, (2) a contractual right to receive cash or another financial asset from another entity, (3) a contractual right to exchange other financial instruments on potentially favorable terms with another entity, or (4) an equity instrument of another entity.

Financial instrument. A financial instrument is cash, evidence of an ownership interest in an entity, or a contract that both

a. Imposes on one entity a contractual obligation (1) to deliver cash or another financial instrument to a second entity or (2) to exchange financial instruments on potentially unfavorable terms with the second entity.
b. Conveys to that second entity a contractual right (1) to receive cash or another financial instrument from the first entity or (2) to exchange other financial instruments on potentially favorable terms with the first entity.

Financial instrument with off-balance-sheet risk. A financial instrument has off-balance-sheet risk of accounting loss if the risk of accounting loss to the entity may exceed the amount recognized as an asset, if any, or if the ultimate obligation may exceed the amount that is recognized as a liability in the statement of financial position.

Financial liability. Any liability that is a contractual obligation (1) to deliver cash or another financial asset to another entity or (2) to exchange financial instruments on potentially unfavorable terms with another entity.

Market risk. Market risk is the possibility that future changes in market prices may make a financial instrument less valuable.

Marketable equity securities. Instruments representing actual ownership interest, or the rights to buy or sell such interests, and which are actively traded or listed on a national securities exchange.

Net realizable value. The amount of cash anticipated to be produced in the normal course of business from an asset, net of any direct costs of the conversion into cash.

Other-than-temporary decline. A downward movement in the value of a marketable equity security for which there are known causes. The decline indicates a remote likelihood of a price recovery.

Realized gain (loss). The difference between the cost or adjusted cost of a marketable security and the net selling price realized by the seller which is to be included in the determination of net income in the period of the sale.

Risk of accounting loss. The risk of accounting loss from a financial instrument includes the (1) possibility that a loss may occur from the failure of another party to perform according to the terms of a contract (credit risk), (2) the possibility that future changes in market prices may make a financial instrument less valuable (market risk), and (3) the risk of theft or physical loss. SFAS 105 addresses credit and market risk only.

Short-term investments. Securities or other assets acquired with excess cash, having ready marketability and intended by management to be liquidated, if necessary, within the current operating cycle.

Temporary decline. A downward fluctuation in the value of a marketable equity security that has no known causes that suggest the decline is of a permanent nature.

Unrealized gain (loss). The unrealized difference between the market value of short-term investments and their carrying value which is deemed not to be of a permanent nature.

Valuation allowance. An account used to value marketable equity securities at fair value. The offset is either a gain or loss account (for trading securities) or a contra equity account (for available-for-sale securities).

CONCEPTS, RULES, AND EXAMPLES

Short-Term Investments

Short-term (or temporary) investments usually consist of marketable debt and equity securities. Accordingly, investments that are held for purposes of control of another entity or pursuant to an ongoing business relationship, for example, stock held in a supplier, would be excluded from current assets and would instead be listed as **other assets** or **long-term investments** (see Chapter 10).

Debt securities and marketable equity securities. SFAS 115 is GAAP governing the accounting for all debt securities and for equity securities that have a readily determinable fair value. TB 94-1 includes restructured loans involving a modification of terms (even if a restructuring took place before the effective date of SFAS 114) under SFAS 115 if such loans meet the definition of a security. Equity securities include not only stock, but also the rights to purchase stock, such as warrants or call options, and the right to sell stock, such as put options. SFAS 115 does not apply to securities accounted for by the equity method. These securities are accounted for in accordance with APB 18 and are discussed in Chapter 10. This statement also does not apply to specialized industries that account for substantially all debt and equity securities at market or fair value with changes recognized in earnings or in the change in net assets. Not-for-profit organizations are excluded from the provisions of SFAS 115, but the statement does apply to cooperatives and mutual enterprises. In addition, unsecuritized loans are not covered, but mortgage-backed securities are covered. Accounting for financial liabilities is not changed.

The standard requires all debt securities and equity securities with readily determinable fair values to be classified into one of three categories.

Classification of Debt and Equity Securities

	Categories	*Type*	*Characteristics*	*Reported on balance sheet*	*Effect on income*
1.	Held-to-maturity	Debt	Positive intent and ability to hold until maturity	Amortized cost	Interest Realized gains and losses
2.	Trading	Debt & equity	Bought and held principally to sell short-term	Fair value	Interest and dividends Realized gains and losses Unrealized gains and losses
3.	Available-for-sale	Debt & equity	Neither held-to-maturity nor trading securities	Fair value Unrealized gains and losses to other comprehensive income	Interest and dividends Realized gains and losses

If a classified balance sheet is presented, the debt and equity securities owned by an entity should be grouped into current and noncurrent portfolios. All trading securities are classified as current assets. The determination of current or noncurrent status for individual held-to-maturity and individual available-for-sale securities is made on the basis of whether or not the securities are considered working capital available for current operations (ARB 43, ch 3A).

Fair value. SFAS 115 applies to equity securities if

1. Prices or bid-and-ask quotations are available on SEC registered exchanges or from the NASDAQ or the National Quotation Bureau. Unless qualified for sale within 1 year, restricted stock does not meet this definition.
2. Traded on a foreign market of comparable breadth and scope as the US markets identified above.
3. Fair value per unit (share) of a mutual fund is determined and published and is the basis for current transactions.

Classification. Classification is to be made at acquisition. The appropriateness of classification should be reassessed at each reporting date.

Held-to-maturity debt securities. If an entity has the **positive intent** and **ability** to hold debt securities to maturity, they are measured at amortized cost. All **transfers** or **sales** of securities in this category must disclose the following in the notes for each period for which the results of operations are presented:

1. Amortized cost
2. Realized or unrealized gain or loss

3. Circumstances leading to the decision

Isolated, nonrecurring, and unusual events that could not have been reasonably anticipated may cause a sale or transfer without calling intent or ability to hold into question. Other changes in circumstances that are not considered inconsistent include

1. Material deterioration in creditworthiness of the issuer
2. Elimination or reduction of tax-exempt status of interest through a change in tax law
3. Major business disposition or combination
4. Statutory or regulatory changes that materially modify what a permissable investment is or the maximum level of the security to be held
5. Downsizing in response to a regulatory increase in the industry's capital requirements
6. A material increase in risk weights for regulatory risk-based capital purposes

This category does not include securities available for sale in response to a need for liquidity or changes in

1. Market interest rates
2. Foreign currency risk
3. Funding sources and terms
4. Yield and availability of alternative investments
5. Prepayment risk

For asset-liability management purposes, similar or identical securities may be classified differently depending upon intent and ability to hold.

SFAS 125 amends SFAS 115 (effective for financial assets held or acquired after January 1, 1997) in a manner that may require reclassification of held-to-maturity securities. The held-to-maturity classification can no longer be used for securities that can be prepaid or settled in a manner where the recorded investments could not be substantially recovered. These kinds of securities (such as certain loans, interest-only strips, retained interests in securitizations, etc.) should be classified as trading or available-for-sale. Reclassifications based upon initial application of SFAS 125 will not call into question the intent to hold other debt to maturity.

SFAS 133 specifies that held-to-maturity debt security denominated in a foreign currency should be accounted for under SFAS 52.

Maturity date. The sale of a security within 3 months of its maturity meets the requirement to hold to maturity since the interest rate risk is substantially diminished. Likewise, if a call is considered probable, a sale within 3 months of that date meets the requirement. The sale of a security after collection of at least 85% of the principal outstanding at acquisition (due to prepayments or to scheduled payments of principal and interest in equal installments) also qualifies since the "tail" portion no longer represents an efficient investment due to the economic costs of accounting for the remnants. Scheduled payments are not required to be equal for variable-rate debt.

Example of held-to-maturity debt securities

The 12/31/99 debt security portfolio categorized as held-to-maturity is as follows:

Security	*Maturity value*	*Amortized cost*	*Assumed fair value*
DEF 12% bond, due 12/31/01	$ 10,000	$10,320	$10,200
PQR mortgage-backed debt, due 12/31/02	$100,000	$92,000	$90,000
JKL 8% bond, due 12/31/06	$ 10,000	$ 8,929	$ 9,100

The balance sheet would report all the securities in this category at amortized cost and would classify them as follows:

Security	*Maturity date*	*Balance sheet*	*Classification*
DEF	12/31/01	$10,320	Current
PQR	12/31/02	$92,000	Noncurrent
JKL	12/31/06	$ 8,929	Noncurrent

Interest income, including premium and discount amortization, is included in income. Any realized gains or losses are also included in income.

Trading securities. If an entity has debt and/or equity securities (with readily determinable fair value) that it intends to actively and frequently buy and sell for short-term profits, those securities are classified as trading securities. Unless classified as held-to-maturity securities, SFAS 65 mortgage-backed securities held for sale require classification as trading securities. The securities in this category are required to be carried at fair value on the balance sheet as current assets. All applicable interest and dividends, realized gains and losses, and unrealized gains and losses are included in income from continuing operations.

Example of accounting for trading securities

The year 1 current trading securities portfolio is as follows:

Security	*Cost*	*Market*	*Difference (Market minus cost)*
ABC	$1,000	$ 900	$(100)
MNO calls	1,500	1,700	200
STU	2,000	1,400	(600)
XYZ 7% bond	2,500	2,600	100
	$7,000	$6,600	$(400)

A $400 adjustment is required in order to recognize the decline in market value. The entry required is

Unrealized loss on trading securities	400	
Trading securities--MNO calls	200	
Trading securities--XYZ 7% bond	100	
Trading securities--ABC		100
Trading securities--STU		600

The unrealized loss would appear on the income statement as part of other expenses and losses. Dividend income and interest income (including premium and discount amortization) is included in income. Any realized gains or losses from the sale of securities are also included in income.

An alternative to direct write-up and write-down of securities is the use of an asset valuation allowance account to adjust the portfolio totals. In the above example, the entry would be

Unrealized loss on trading securities	400	
Valuation allowance		400

The valuation allowance of $400 would be deducted from historical cost to obtain a fair value of $6,600 for the trading securities on the balance sheet.

All trading securities are classified as current assets and the balance sheet would appear as follows:

Current assets:	
Trading securities at fair value (cost = $7,000)	$6,600

The year 2 current trading portfolio is as follows:

Security	New securities cost	Old securities X1 market	X2 market	*Difference
ABC		$ 900	$1,000	$100
DEF Puts	$1,500		1,500	0
STU		1,400	1,800	400
VWX	2,700		2,800	100
	$4,200	$2,300	$7,100	$600

**Difference = X2 market – (Cost or X1 market)*

A $600 adjustment is required in order to recognize the increase in market value. The entry required is

Trading securities--ABC	100	
Trading securities--STU	400	
Trading securities--VWX	100	
Unrealized gain on trading securities		600

The unrealized gain would appear on the income statement as part of other income.

Example of accounting for a realized gain

1. The same information as given in the above example for year 1

2. In year 2, the MNO calls are sold for $1,600 and the XYZ 7% bonds are sold for $2,700.

The entry required to record the sale is

Cash	4,300	
Realized loss on sale of trading securities	100	
Realized gain on sale of trading securities		100
Trading securities--MNO calls (X1 market)		1,700
Trading securities--XYZ 7% bonds (X1 market)		2,600

Under the valuation allowance method, the current trading portfolio would appear as follows:

Security	*Cost*	*X2 market*
ABC	$1,000	$1,000
STU	2,000	1,800
DEF Puts	1,500	1,500
VWX	2,700	2,800
	$7,200	$7,100

The required entries to recognize the increase in market value are

Valuation allowance	300	
Unrealized gain on trading securities		300
Cash	4,300	
Trading securities--MNO calls (Cost)		1,500
Trading securities--XYZ 7% bonds (Cost)		2,500
Realized gain on sale of trading securities		300

The balance sheet under both methods would appear as follows:

Current assets:	
Trading securities at fair value (cost = $7,200)	$7,100

Available-for-sale. Investments in debt securities and in equity securities with a readily determinable fair value that are **not** classified as either trading securities or held-to-maturity are classified as available-for-sale. The securities in this category are required to be carried at fair value on the balance sheet. The determination of current or noncurrent status for individual securities depends on whether the securities are considered working capital (ARB 43, chapter 3A).

Other than the possibility of having some noncurrent securities on the balance sheet, the major difference between trading securities and available-for-sale securities is the handling of unrealized gains and losses. Unlike trading securities, the **unrealized** gains and losses are excluded from net income. Instead, they are reported in other comprehensive income per SFAS 130. All applicable interest (including premium and discount amortization) and any realized gains or losses from the sale of securities are included in income from continuing operations.

Deferred tax effects. The recognition of unrealized gains and losses for financial purposes is likely to have deferred tax effects. See the discussion in Chapter 10, pages 337-338.

Transfers. Fair value is used for transfers between categories. When the security is transferred, any unrealized holding gains and losses are accounted for in the following manner:

1. **From trading**--Already recognized and should not be reversed
2. **Into trading**--Recognize immediately in income
3. **Available-for-sale debt security into held-to-maturity**--Continue to report the unrealized holding gain or loss at the transfer date as other comprehensive income and amortize the gain or loss over the investment's remaining life as an adjustment of yield in the same manner as a premium or discount. The transferred-in security will probably record a premium or discount since fair value is used. Thus, the two amortizations will tend to cancel each other on the income statement.
4. **Held-to-maturity debt security into available-for-sale**--Recognize in other comprehensive income per SFAS 130

Few transfers are expected from the held-to-maturity category.

Impairment. Other-than-temporary impairment (probable that all contractual amounts due won't be collected) of either the held-to-maturity or available-for-sale securities should be recognized as a realized loss. The cost basis should be written down to fair value and the write-down should be included in net income. The accounting should then proceed as required for the category. Subsequent recoveries will not change the new cost basis.

Cash flow statement. Cash flows resulting from sales, purchases or maturity of securities should be accounted for as follows:

1. Trading – Operating activity
2. Held-to-maturity – Investing activity
3. Available-for-sale – Investing activity

Cash flows from 2 and 3 above are required to be reported gross for each security classification.

Options

Call and put options can be effectively used as valuable hedging instruments or as highly leveraged speculative ventures. One call contract gives the **buyer** the right to **buy** 100 shares of the underlying security at a specific exercise price, regardless of the market price. The **seller** of the call, on the other hand, must **sell** the security to the buyer at that exercise price, regardless of the market price. For example, assume a Disney July 75 call has a quoted market price of $6 (per share or $600 per contract). These facts indicate that a buyer that pays $600 to a seller for a call has the right to purchase 100 shares of Disney at any time until July (typically the end of trading on the third Friday of the month quoted) for $75 per share. The buyer can exercise this right at any time until it expires. The seller of the call must stand ready to deliver 100 shares to the buyer for $75 per share until expiration. Typically, the buyer expects the market price to rise and the seller expects the market price to stay the same or to fall.

A put is the opposite of a call. A put gives the **buyer** the right to **sell** the underlying security at the exercise price regardless of the market price. It gives the **seller** the obligation to **buy** at the exercise price. Typically, the buyer expects the market price to fall and the seller expects the market price to stay the same or to rise. Strips, straps, straddles, and spreads are combinations and/or variations of the basic call and the basic put.

Example

Seller D owns 100 shares of Disney at a cost of $75 per share and sells 1 Disney July 75 call to Buyer E at $6. The following positions result if the market price:

	Position	
	Seller (D)	Buyer (E)
1. Stays at 75 and there is no exercise	+$600	–$600

D receives the $600 premium and E pays for the right to call the stock. If the market price doesn't move, the option expires and both parties remain as they started out.

2. Rises to 95 and there is an exercise and immediate sale	+$600 (0 + 600)	+$1,400 (2,000 – 600)

If the price rises to $95 per share and the security is called, D sells the security to E at $75 ($0 profit on the shares) and is effectively $600 (the amount of the premium) better off. E, however, buys the security at $75 per share and immediately sells it for $95 per share. E gains $2,000 from the security sale less the $600 premium and is $1,400 better off.

3. Falls to 55 and there is no exercise	–$1,400 (– 2,000 + 600)	–$600 (0 – 600)

If the market price falls to $55 per share, D incurs an effective $2,000 decrease in value of the shares held, less the $600 premium received. E does not exercise the option and loses the premium paid.

The accounting problems revolve around whether cost or market or some combination should be used in accounting for the option itself and/or the associated underlying security. For instance, assume M buys 100 shares of XYZ at $15 per share and the security price immediately moves to $25 per share. At this point, M **buys** a November 25 put contract at 1 ($100 per contract). M has effectively hedged and guaranteed a minimum profit of $900 [(100 shares x $10) – ($1 x 100 shares)] regardless of market price movement since XYZ can be **sold** for $25 per share until the third Friday in November. If the price continues upward, the put will expire unexercised and M will continue to benefit point for point. If the price stays the same, M locks in a profit of $900. If the price falls, M has locked in a profit of $900. The question is whether these facts can be accounted for by the cost principle for option and security, by the market principle for option and security, or by some combination.

Until SFAS 133, SFAS 115 was the only definitive guidance. Theoretically, that guidance only applies to purchased puts and calls since written options are liabilities, not investments. Likewise, cash settled options and equity indexed options do not represent ownership interests and debt securities options are not covered by SFAS 115. However, numerous aspects of the issue have been addressed by the EITF. The options are usually carried at market value. If hedge accounting is used, SFAS 80 probably provides the best guidance.

Financial Instruments

SFAS 133, entitled *Accounting for Derivative Instruments and Hedging Activities*, was issued in June 1998. This standard is effective for all fiscal quarters of all fiscal years beginning after June 15, 1999. A calendar-year company would begin application in January 2000. Early application is encouraged but initial application must be at the beginning of a fiscal quarter after June 1998 when hedging relationships must be designated and documented according to SFAS 133. A calendar-year company would begin early application in January 1999. The standard cannot be applied retroactively. It specifies recognition of all derivative instruments (not just derivative financial instruments) in the balance sheet as assets or liabilities measured at fair value. Derivatives can be specifically designated as hedges. SFAS 133, when effective, supersedes SFAS 80, 105, and 119. It amends numerous other SFAS and nullifies or modifies numerous EITF.

SFAS 125 uses a financial-components approach that relies on control to establish standards for transfers and servicing of financial assets and extinguishments of liabilities. Derivatives and liabilities resulting from a transfer of financial assets are measured at fair value. In-substance defeasance does not result in the extinguishment of a liability.

Derivative financial instruments (SFAS 119). This statement requires issuers and holders of derivative financial instruments (DFI) to disclose information about those instruments. It also amends the disclosure requirements of SFAS 105 and SFAS 107.

The derivatives market is extremely large as DFI are an important part of the operations of many institutions. Derivatives are financial instruments that derive their value from changes in a benchmark based on stock prices, interest rates, mortgage rates, currency rates, commodity prices or some other agreed upon base. Option contracts and forward contracts are the two basic forms of derivatives, and they can be either publicly or privately traded. Option contracts provide little or no exposure to losses (except for the premium paid) from unfavorable market movements, but can provide large benefits from potential favorable market movements. Forward contracts provide exposure to both losses and gains from market movements, but generally there is no initial premium paid. Forward contracts are usually settled on or near the delivery date by paying or receiving cash. However, they may also be settled by delivering or receiving assets.

DFI can be either on-balance-sheet or off-balance-sheet and include

1. Option contracts
2. Interest rate caps
3. Interest rate floors
4. Fixed-rate loan commitments
5. Note issuance facilities
6. Letters of credit
7. Forward contracts
8. Forward interest rate agreements
9. Interest rate collars
10. Futures
11. Swaps, and
12. Instruments with similar characteristics

It should be noted that DFI exclude all on-balance-sheet **receivables** and **payables** including

1. Mortgage-backed securities
2. Interest only obligations
3. Principal only obligations
4. Indexed debt
5. Other optional characteristics incorporated within those receivables and payables (such as convertible bond conversion or call terms)

In addition, DFI exclude contracts that either

1. Require exchange for a nonfinancial commodity or
2. Permit settlement by delivering a nonfinancial commodity

Thus, most product (petroleum, grain, etc.) future contracts would be excluded, while swaps (if settled in cash) would be included.

The basic purpose of DFI is to manage some kind of risk, such as stock price movements, interest rate variations, currency fluctuations, and commodity price volatility. The parties involved tend to be brokerage firms, financial institutions, insurance companies, and large corporations, although any two or more entities of any size can hold or issue derivatives. The DFI are contracts that are supposed to protect or hedge one or more of the parties from adverse movement in the underlying base. Unfortunately, these protections or hedges are rarely perfect and sometimes the hedge, once established, is removed in order to speculate. In this case, the DFI themselves can become risky and, if leveraged, small adverse price or interest rate variations can produce significant losses. Thus, instead of providing protection, many DFI have actually generated losses. Instruments such as interest rate swaps (exchanging variable or floating rate debt for fixed rate debt) and interest rate caps (limiting exposure to rising interest rates) have also resulted in losses along with mortgage-backed bonds, kitchen sink bonds, structured notes, inverse floaters, and interest-only bonds. Accounting concerns about these losses involve the off-balance-sheet nature of many DFI, the amount of capital that should be required for trading DFI, and the suitability of DFI for holders, given the risks that have resulted. Thus, users and issuers are now reassessing their policies regarding DFI and examining their internal controls to limit the risk.

Until SFAS 133, the FASB had not specified a preferred method of accounting for DFI. Therefore, the accounting for these complex instruments was not standardized. In many cases, the individual positions were accounted for separately at fair value with the gains or losses reported in operating income or in net income. In other cases, hedge accounting was used with its associated deferral of gains and losses. Numerous other methods of accounting for DFI were also used. In SFAS 119, the FASB (without specifying the accounting to be used) mandated disclosures in an attempt to require relevant information to be given to interested groups as an indication of the DFI's risk.

Currently, options held and other DFI are not disclosed under SFAS 105 because they are not off-balance-sheet and/or because they do not have off-balance-sheet risk of accounting loss. SFAS 119 amends SFAS 105 to replace the term "class of financial instrument" with the term "category of financial instrument." For DFI not included under the scope of SFAS 105, SFAS 119 requires disclosure by **category** of financial instrument of

1. Face, contract, or notional principal amount
2. Nature and terms including
   a. Credit risk
   b. Market risk
   c. Cash requirements
   d. APB 22 accounting policy
   e. Leverage features (or multipliers) and their general effects on each of the above

Category of financial instrument is the class, business activity, risk, or other category consistent with managing these instruments. Whenever **class** of DFI is not used as the category for the disclosure, the class of financial instruments included in the category must be described. All DFI are to be classified as (1) "trading" (including dealing and all activities measured at fair value and reported in a trading account) or (2) "other than trading."

For "traded" DFI, the required disclosures include

1. Net gains or losses (net trading revenue) reported in income by **category** of financial instrument and where the net gains or losses are reported.
2. Average fair value of DFI during the period, together with the related value at the end of the period, differentiating assets and liabilities. Disclosure of

this information is also encouraged for other types of financial instruments or nonfinancial assets that are traded.

For "other than traded" DFI, required disclosures include

1. A description, including the **class** of DFI used, of
    a. Objectives for holding
    b. Context required to understand the objectives
    c. Strategy for achieving the objectives
2. A description of how each **class** of DFI is reported in the statements including
    a. Recognition and measurement policies for DFI held or issued
    b. Location of DFI in the balance sheet and where the related gains or losses are reported in income
3. If held or issued and accounted for as hedges of anticipated transactions
    a. Information about the transaction being hedged and about the time period until occurrence
    b. Description of the **classes** of DFI used to hedge
    c. Amounts of **explicitly** deferred (i.e., in separate accounts as required by SFAS 52 and SFAS 80) hedging gains or losses
    d. Events that result in recognition in earnings of deferred items in c. above

Interest rate, commodity price, foreign exchange, or other market risk information which is useful for comparing strategic results with objectives of derivatives and which is consistent with the entity's management of risk is encouraged, but not required, to be disclosed. Different organizations will report this information in different ways. The development and evolution of effective ways of reporting the above data is encouraged.

The amendment of SFAS 107 by SFAS 119 requires that fair value information be presented along with the related carrying value so that it is clear whether the values represent assets or liabilities. If disclosed in more than one note, a summary table containing the above data is required in one of these notes, with a cross reference to the location of the other SFAS 107 notes. In addition, the relationship between the carrying amounts and what is reported in the balance sheet must be disclosed. "Traded" (including dealing and other activities measured at fair value with gains or losses recognized in earnings) financial instruments are to be distinguished from those that are categorized as "other than traded." In disclosing fair value of a DFI, that fair value should not be aggregated, netted or combined (even if considered related) with either the fair value of a nonderivative financial instrument or other DFI except as permitted by FASB Interpretation 39.

Example

Note 1: Summary of Accounting Policies

Financial Instruments and Risk Management

In the normal course of business, the Corporation enters into or is a party to the execution, settlement and financing of securities transactions involving derivative products, financial instruments, and nonfinancial instruments. These transactions are used in trading activities, hedging activities, and for other purposes.

Trading activities result from dealing, maintaining market liquidity, accommodating customers, and carrying out financial strategies associated with established business objectives approved by the Board of Directors. Financial instruments used in trading are recorded at fair value as either trading assets or trading liabilities. Gains and losses resulting from trading are categorized as net trading revenue in the income statement. Interest revenue and expense from trading are categorized as net interest and are included in other income or expense.

The Corporation enters into various contracts to hedge and manage interest rate and foreign exchange risks. Market value gains and losses are deferred for qualifying hedges and the resulting amounts either adjust carrying value when the transaction occurs or are taken into income. In certain cases, amounts resulting from premature terminations are deferred and amortized as yield adjustments over the time period remaining on the associated contracts.

Derivative products, other financial instruments, and other nonfinancial instruments are also used for nontrading purposes, including the management of foreign currency exposure, interest rate positions, and settlement of commodity future contracts. Asset amounts are reported as trading assets or other assets. Liability amounts are reported as trading liabilities, short-sale agreements, or as other liabilities. Gains or losses are taken into other income or expense currently or deferred if qualified as a hedge.

Note X: Trading Instruments

Trading activities are in accordance with established strategic business objectives that have been approved by the Board of Directors. Net trading revenues are a separate caption in the income statement and include

	(In millions)	
	19X8	*19X7*
Category	*Net gains (losses)*	*Net gains (losses)*
Foreign currency	xxx	yyy
Interest	xxx	yyy
Debt	xxx	yyy
Other	xxx	yyy
Net trading revenue	xxx	yyy

Foreign exchange instruments used include spots, forwards, options, swaps, and futures. Contracts utilized in interest management are forwards, options (including caps and floors), swaps, and futures. Debt instruments include a variety of corporate and government securities and securities sold but not yet purchased. Equity securities and commodity instruments are included in the "other" category.

Average fair value and end-of-the-period fair value of traded financial instruments are shown by category and class below.

		(In millions)			
		X8 Average fair value	*12/31/X8 Fair value*	*X7 Average fair value*	*12/31/X7 Fair value*
Derivatives					
Foreign Exchange					
Spot & forwards	– Assets	xxx	xxx	yyy	yyy
	Liabilities	(xxx)	(xxx)	(yyy)	(yyy)
Options	– Assets	xxx	xxx	yyy	yyy
	Liabilities	(xxx)	(xxx)	(yyy)	(yyy)
Swaps & futures	– Assets	xxx	xxx	yyy	yyy
	Liabilities	(xxx)	(xxx)	(yyy)	(yyy)
Interest					
Forwards	– Assets	xxx	xxx	yyy	yyy
	Liabilities	(xxx)	(xxx)	(yyy)	(yyy)
Options (including caps, floors)					
	– Assets	xxx	xxx	yyy	yyy
	Liabilities	(xxx)	(xxx)	(yyy)	(yyy)
Swaps & futures	– Assets	xxx	xxx	yyy	yyy
	Liabilities	(xxx)	(xxx)	(yyy)	(yyy)
Other Instruments					
Debt	– Assets	xxx	xxx	yyy	yyy
	Liabilities	(xxx)	(xxx)	(yyy)	(yyy)
Other	– Assets	xxx	xxx	yyy	yyy
	Liabilities	(xxx)	(xxx)	(yyy)	(yyy)

Estimated fair values are based on available quoted market prices, prices of similar instruments after considering risk, current interest rates and remaining maturities, present value calculations, and pricing models. In some cases, amounts to be paid or received to terminate agreements at reporting date were used. Leveraged swaps and items with embedded terms are not material.

Note Y: Other Than Trading Instruments

Various instruments, including derivatives, are used to manage risks associated with foreign currency, interest, and commodities. In addition, risk is actively managed through simulations, forecasts, pricing models, duration analysis, gap analysis, and value at risk analysis.

Nontraded derivative financial instruments are shown by category and class below

	(In millions) Contract or notational amount
Foreign Exchange	
Spot and forward	zzz
Options (includes caps and floors)	zzz
Swaps and futures	zzz
Interest	
Forwards	zzz
Options (includes caps and floors)	zzz
Swaps and futures	zzz

Foreign exchange contracts are used by the Corporation both to hedge net investment and to hedge currency commitments. Interest rate instruments are utilized to reduce or eliminate risk associated with specific assets or liabilities. Terms range to 5 years. Various nonfinancial commodity contracts are also used to hedge the business's long and short positions. The majority of these instruments are settled by delivery.

The following table details information on swaps. These contracts range up to 5 years. Swap fees adjust other income or expense.

	(In millions)	
	2000	1999
Pay--Fixed		
Average pay rate	x.xx%	y.yy%
Average receive rate	x.xx%	y.yy%
Receive--Fixed	x.xx%	y.yy%
Average receive rate	x.xx%	y.yy%
Average pay rate	x.xx%	y.yy%

Explicitly deferred hedging gains of xxx and yyy and losses of xxx and yyy were recorded in 2000 and 1999 respectively. Earnings are recognized upon collection, settlement, or expiration of the related contract, or upon disposition of the related asset or liability.

Off-balance-sheet and credit risk. SFAS 105 (which will be superseded by SFAS 133, when effective) requires disclosure of information (1) about financial instruments with off-balance-sheet risk of accounting loss that exceeds the amount required, if any, in the statement of financial position and (2) about **all** financial instruments with concentrations of credit risk. It addresses credit and market risks only.

Financial instruments include **cash**, ownership interest in an entity, or a contract that both

a. Imposes a contractual obligation on one entity (1) to surrender cash or another financial instrument to a second entity or (2) to exchange financial instruments on potentially unfavorable terms with the second entity.

b. Conveys a contractual right to the second entity (1) to receive from the first entity cash or another financial instrument or (2) to exchange with the first entity other financial instruments on potentially favorable terms.

SFAS 105 limits the definition of a financial instrument. It excludes many assets because their probable future economic benefit is receipt of goods or services instead of a right to receive cash or an ownership interest in another entity. Examples would be advances to suppliers and prepaid expenses. It also excludes many liabilities that contain contractual obligations because their probable economic sacrifice is delivery of goods or services instead of an obligation to deliver cash or an ownership interest in another entity. Examples include advances from suppliers, deferred revenues, and most warranty obligations. The definition also excludes contracts that either require or **permit** settlement by the delivery of commodities.

A **contractual obligation** whose economic benefit or sacrifice is receipt or delivery of a financial instrument other than cash is, however, considered a financial instrument. For example, a note that is payable in US Treasury bonds gives an issuer the contractual obligation to deliver and gives a holder the contractual right to receive bonds, not cash. But because the bonds represent obligations of the US Treasury to pay cash they are considered financial instruments. Therefore, the note is also a financial instrument to both the holder of the note and the issuer of the note.

Another type of financial instrument is one that gives an entity the **contractual right** or obligation to exchange other financial instruments on potentially favorable or unfavorable terms. An example of this type of financial instrument would be a call option to purchase a US Treasury note for $100,000 in 6 months. The option holder has a contractual right to exchange the financial instrument on potentially favorable terms. Six months later, if the market value of the note exceeds $100,000 the holder will exercise the option because the terms are favorable. The writer of the call option has contractual obligation to exchange financial instruments on potentially unfavorable terms if the holder exercises the option. The writer is normally compensated for this obligation. A put option to sell a Treasury note has similar but opposite effects. A bank's commitment to lend $100,000 to a customer at a fixed rate of 10% any time during the next 6 months at the customer's option is also a financial instrument.

An interest rate swap can be explained as a series of forward contracts to exchange, for example, fixed cash payments for variable cash receipts. The cash receipts would be computed by multiplying a floating-rate market index by a notional amount. An interest rate swap is both a contractual right and a contractual obligation to both parties.

Excluded from financial instrument classification are options and contracts that contain the right or obligation to exchange a financial instrument for a physical asset. For example, two entities enter a sale-purchase contract in which the purchaser agrees to take delivery of wheat or gold 6 months later and pay the seller $100,000 at the time of delivery. The contract is not considered a financial instrument because it requires the delivery of wheat or gold which are not considered financial instruments.

Also excluded from financial instrument classification are contingent items that may ultimately require the payment of cash but do not as yet arise from contracts. An example would be a contingent liability for tort judgments payable. However, when such an obligation becomes enforceable and is reduced to fixed payment schedules, it would then be considered a financial instrument.

SFAS 105 requires all entities to disclose in the body of the financial statements, or in footnotes, information about the financial instruments with off-balance-sheet risk. Disclosure by category of financial instrument must include the following information:

1. The face, contract, or notional principal amount
2. The nature and terms of the instruments including a discussion of (1) the credit and market risks, (2) the cash requirements, and (3) the related accounting policies (pursuant to APB 22)

In addition to disclosure of derivative financial instruments, SFAS 119 amends SFAS 105 to replace the term "**class** of financial instrument" with the term "**category** of financial instrument." It also requires that financial instruments with off-balance-sheet risk (held or issued) be classified as (1) trading or (2) "other than trading."

A financial instrument has off-balance-sheet risk of **accounting loss** if the risk of accounting loss to the entity may exceed the amount recognized as an asset or if the ultimate obligation may exceed the amount that is recognized as a liability in the statement of financial position. The risk of accounting loss includes the possibility that the loss may occur from credit risk or from market risk. Appendix B of SFAS 105 gives numerous examples of financial instruments that both have and do not have off-balance-sheet risk of accounting loss.

For financial instruments with off-balance-sheet credit risk, an entity must disclose in the body of the statement, or in notes to the statement, the following information by category of financial instrument:

1. The amount of accounting loss the entity would incur if any party to the financial instrument failed completely to perform according to the terms of the contract and if any collateral proved worthless
2. The entity's policy for requiring collateral on financial instruments subject to credit risks, information about access to that collateral, and the nature and brief description of collateral supporting financial instruments

Example

A Corporation might disclose the following:

Note 1: Summary of Accounting Policies

The Corporation does not deal or trade financial instruments. Derivatives are limited in use and leveraged swaps and items with embedded terms are not used.

Derivative products and other financial instruments are used for nontrading purposes including the management of foreign currency exposure and interest rate positions. Asset amounts are reported as other assets. Liability amounts are reported as other liabilities. Gains or losses are taken into other income or expense currently or deferred if qualified as a hedge.

Interest Rate Swap Agreements

The differential to be paid or received is accrued as interest rates change and is recognized over the life of the agreements.

Foreign Exchange Contracts

The Corporation enters into foreign exchange contracts as a hedge against foreign accounts payable or accounts receivables. Market value gains and losses are deferred, and the resulting credit or debit offsets foreign exchange losses or gains on those payables or receivables when recognized.

Note X: Financial Instruments With Off-Balance-Sheet Risk

In the normal course of business, the Corporation enters into or is a party to various financial instruments and contractual obligations that, under certain conditions, could give rise to or involve elements of market or credit risk in excess of that shown in the Statement of Financial Condition. These financial instruments and contractual obligations include interest rate swaps, forward foreign exchange contracts, financial guarantees, and commitments to extend credit. The Corporation monitors and limits its exposure to **market risk** through management policies designed to identify and reduce excess risk. The Corporation limits its credit risk through monitoring of client credit exposure, reviews, and conservative estimates of allowances for bad debt, and through the prudent use of collateral for large amounts of credit. The Corporation monitors collateral values on a daily basis and requires additional collateral when deemed necessary.

Interest rate swaps and forward exchange contracts. The Corporation enters into a limited amount of interest rate swaps and forward foreign exchange contracts. The primary use of these financial instruments is to reduce interest rate fluctuations and to stabilize costs or to hedge foreign currency liabilities or assets. Interest rate swap transactions involve the exchange of floating rate and fixed rate interest payment of obligations without the exchange of underlying notional amounts. The company is exposed to credit risk in the unlikely event of nonperformance by the counterparty. The differential to be received or paid is accrued as interest rates change and is recognized over the life of the agreement. Forward foreign exchange contracts represent commitments to exchange currencies at a specified future date. Gains (losses) on these contracts primarily serve to stabilize costs. Foreign currency exposure for the Corporation will result in the unlikely event that the other party fails to perform under the contract.

Nontraded derivative financial instruments are shown by category and class below.

	(In millions) Contract or notional amount
Foreign Exchange	
Forwards	zzz
Interest	
Swaps	zzz

Foreign exchange contracts are used by the Corporation to hedge currency commitments. Interest rate instruments are utilized to reduce or eliminate risk associated with specific assets or liabilities. Terms range up to 5 years.

The following table details information on swaps. These contracts range up to 5 years. Swap fees adjust other income or expense.

	(In millions) 2000	1999
Pay--Fixed		
Average pay rate	x.xx%	y.yy%
Average receive rate	x.xx%	y.yy%
Receive--Fixed	x.xx%	y.yy%
Average receive rate	x.xx%	y.yy%
Average pay rate	x.xx%	y.yy%

Explicitly deferred hedging gains of xxx and yyy and losses of xxx and yyy were recorded in 2000 and 1999 respectively. Earnings are recognized upon collection, settlement or expiration of the related contract or upon disposition of the related asset or liability.

Financial guarantees. Financial guarantees are conditional commitments to guarantee performance to third parties. These guarantees are primarily issued to guarantee borrowing arrangements. The Corporation's credit risk exposure on these guarantees is not material.

Commitment to extend credit. Loan commitments are agreements to extend credit under agreed-upon terms. The Corporation's commitment to extend credit assists customers to meet their liquidity needs. These commitments generally have fixed expiration or other termination clauses. The Corporation anticipates that not all of these commitments will be utilized. The amount of unused commitment does not necessarily represent future funding requirements.

The off-balance-sheet financial instruments are summarized as follows (in 000s):

Financial instruments whose notional or contract amounts exceed the amount of credit risk:

	Contract or notional amount
Interest rate swap agreements	$1,234
Forward foreign exchange contracts	2,345

Financial instruments whose contract amount represents credit risk:

	Contract or notional amount
Financial guarantees	$6,543
Commitments to extend credit	5,432

SFAS 105 also requires disclosure of information about significant concentrations of credit risk for **all** financial instruments. Both individual and group concentrations of credit risk are to be disclosed. The following should be disclosed about each significant concentration:

1. Information about the shared activity, region, or economic characteristic that identifies the concentration
2. The amount of accounting loss the entity would incur if any party to the financial instrument failed to completely perform and if any collateral proved worthless
3. The entity's policy for requiring collateral on financial instruments subject to credit risks, information about access to the collateral, and the nature and a brief description of collateral supporting financial instruments

Concentration of credit risk for certain entities. For certain corporations, industry or regional concentrations of credit risk may be disclosed adequately by a description of the business. Some examples are

1. Credit risk for these off-balance-sheet financial instruments is concentrated in North America and in the trucking industry.
2. All financial instruments entered into by the Corporation relate to US Government, international and domestic commercial airline customers.

Significant group concentrations of credit risk. The Corporation grants credit to customers throughout the nation. As of December 31, 1999, the five states where the Corporation had the greatest amount of credit risk were as follows:

California	$8,765
Florida	7,654
Texas	6,543
New York	5,432
Washington	4,321

All of the above disclosures are in addition to other disclosure requirements prescribed by GAAP.

The information required to be disclosed by SFAS 105 shall be included for each year for which a statement of financial position is presented for comparative purposes.

Fair value disclosures. SFAS 107 (which is amended by SFAS 133, when effective, to include the disclosure requirements of credit risk for **all** financial instruments from superseded SFAS 105) requires entities to disclose the fair value of **all** (recognized and unrecognized) financial instruments that it is practicable to estimate, including liabilities. Pertinent descriptive information as to the fair value of the instrument is to be disclosed if an estimate of fair value cannot be made without incurring excessive costs.

Some companies may combine the SFAS 105 and the SFAS 107 disclosures into one footnote. The emphasis of SFAS 105 tends to be on credit risk whereas the emphasis of SFAS 107 is on fair value disclosure.

The SFAS 119 amendment of SFAS 107 requires that fair value information be presented along with the related carrying value so that it is clear whether the values represent assets or liabilities. If disclosed in more than one note, a summary table containing the above data is required in one of these notes, with a cross reference to the location of the other SFAS 107 notes. In addition, the relationship between the carrying amounts and what is reported in the balance sheet must be disclosed. "Traded" financial instruments are to be distinguished from those that are categorized as "other than traded." In disclosing fair value of a DFI, that fair value should not be aggregated, netted or combined with either the fair value of a nonderivative financial instrument or other DFI except as permitted by FASB Interpretation 39.

Fair value is the exchange price in a current transaction (other than in a forced or liquidation sale) between willing parties. If a quoted market price is available, it should be used. If there is more than one market price, the one used should be the one from the most active market. The possible effect on market price from the sale of large holdings and/or from thinly traded issues can be disregarded for purposes of this statement.

If quoted market prices are unavailable, management's best estimate of fair value can be used. Some bases from which an estimate may be made include

1. Matrix pricing models
2. Option pricing models
3. Financial instruments with similar characteristics adjusted for risks involved
4. Financial instruments with similar valuation techniques (i.e., present value) adjusted for risks involved

Appendix A of SFAS 107 contains examples of procedures for estimating fair value.

If the **carrying amount** for trade receivables and payables approximates fair value, no disclosure is required.

If an estimate of fair value cannot be made without incurring excessive costs, disclose the following:

1. Information pertinent to estimating fair value such as carrying amount, effective interest rate, and maturity
2. Reasons why estimating fair values is not practicable

SFAS 107 does not change any other requirements of GAAP in regard to financial instruments. It applies to all entities and to all financial instruments except those listed in paragraph 8. In paragraph 8, the statement excludes certain types of financial instruments including pensions, postretirement benefits, deferred compensation, defeased debt, insurance contracts, lease contracts, warranty obligations and others. Despite possible variations in definitions, amounts computed under GAAP requirements satisfy the requirements of SFAS 107.

Disclosures are required for each year included for comparative purposes and may be in the body of the financial statements or in the notes. Methods and significant assumptions used should be disclosed.

Example

Note 1: Summary of Accounting Policies

The Corporation does not deal or trade financial instruments. Derivatives are limited in use and leveraged swaps and items with embedded terms are not used.

Derivative products and other financial instruments are used for nontrading purposes including the management of foreign currency exposure and interest rate positions. Asset amounts are reported as other assets. Liability amounts are reported as other liabilities. Gains or losses are taken into other income or expense currently or deferred if qualified as a hedge.

Note X: Financial Instruments Disclosures of Fair Value

The estimates of fair value of financial instruments are summarized as follows (in 000s):

Carrying amounts approximate fair values:

	Carrying amount
Cash	$987
Cash equivalents	876
Trade receivables	765
Trade payables	654

Fair values approximate carrying values because of the short time until realization.

Assets with fair values exceeding carrying amounts:

	Carrying amount	*Fair value*
Short-term securities	$876	$987
Long-term investments	765	876
Forward foreign exchange contracts	154	165

Estimated fair values are based on available quoted market prices, present value calculations and option pricing models.

Liabilities with carrying amounts exceeding fair values:

	Carrying amount	*Fair value*
Long-term debt	($543)	($432)

Estimated fair values are based on quoted market prices, present value calculations, and the prices of the same or similar instruments after considering risk, current interest rates, and remaining maturities.

Unrecognized financial instruments:

	Carrying amount	Fair value
Interest rate swap agreements		
Net receivable	$1,012	$1,865
Net payable	(1,753)	(1,543)
Commitments to extend credit	(5,432)	(4,321)
Financial guarantees	(6,543)	(7,654)

Estimated fair values after considering risk, current interest rates, and remaining maturities were based on the following:

Interest rate swaps--Amounts to be received or paid to terminate swap agreements at reporting date.

Credit commitments--Value of the same or similar instruments after considering credit ratings of counterparties.

Financial guarantees--Cost to settle or terminate obligations with counterparties at reporting date.

Fair value not estimated:

	Carrying amount	Fair value
Long-term investment	$1,234	--

Fair value could not be estimated without incurring excessive costs. Investment is carried at original cost and represents an 8% investment in the common stock of a privately held **untraded** company that supplies the corporation. Management considers the risk of loss to be negligible.

Accounting for Derivatives and Hedging Transactions Per SFAS 133*: An Overview

After a lengthy and controversial period of evolution, the FASB issued SFAS 133, *Accounting for Derivative Instruments and Hedging Activities*, in June 1998. SFAS 133 applies to all entities, and requires that all derivatives be recognized as assets or liabilities in the balance sheet, at fair values. Fair values are defined as they were in SFAS 107, *Disclosures About Fair Value of Financial Instruments*, which is amended by SFAS 133. The FASB's stated ultimate objective is to have all financial instruments measured at fair value; thus SFAS 133 can be seen as an intermediate step toward an all-encompassing standard on accounting for and reporting of financial instruments.

The new standard was issued to resolve a number of inconsistencies and other inadequacies in the existing literature, including the following:

* *Effective for all fiscal quarters of all fiscal years beginning after 6/30/99.*

- The effects of derivative instruments were not easily understood, were often not properly displayed in the financial statements, and, sometimes, were not even recognized in the financial statements.
- The available accounting guidance was incomplete. Many derivative instruments were carried off balance sheet.
- The accounting guidance was inconsistent. There was different measurement of various derivative instruments, and different qualifications for alternative types of hedging.
- The guidance which did exist was difficult to apply. There were a variety of sources and no single comprehensive approach.

SFAS 133 requires standardized accounting and reporting for all derivative instruments (including derivatives which are embedded in other instruments) and for hedging activities.

Underlying principles. There are four key principles underlying the new standard.

1. Derivative instruments are assets and liabilities.
2. The fair value of derivative instruments is the only relevant measure to be reported.
3. Only true assets and liabilities should be reported as such. Gains and losses from derivative instruments are not separate liabilities or assets and should not be reported as such.
4. Only designated qualifying items that are effectively offset by changes in fair value or cash flows during the term of the hedge should use the special accounting for hedging.

Derivative instuments represent rights and obligations, and these must be reported as assets and liabilities at fair value (which reflects the current cash equivalent). Gains and losses of derivative instruments not designated as hedges are recognized in earnings (or as a change in net assets, in the case of not-for-profit enterprises). The ability to apply hedge accounting requires that specified criteria be met, because of its elective nature and because of its reliance on management intent. Strategic risk hedges do not meet the qualifying criteria. Thus, hedge accounting is limited to relationships involving derivative instruments and certain foreign currency denominated instruments that are designated as hedges and meet the qualifying criteria.

Terminology

SFAS 133 defines a number of important terms which are used to describe various derivative instruments and hedging relationships. These include the following:

Derivative instruments. In SFAS 133, derivative instruments are defined by their three distinguishing characteristics. Specifically, derivative instruments are financial instruments or other contracts that have

1. One or more underlyings and one or more notional amounts (or payment provisions or both);
2. No initial net investment or a smaller net investment than required for contracts expected to have a similar response to market changes; and
3. Terms that require or permit
   a. Net settlement
   b. Net settlement by means outside the contract
   c. Delivery of an asset that results in a position substantially the same as net settlement

In contrast to SFAS 119, this standard defines derivative instruments by reference to specific characteristics rather than in terms of classes or categories of financial instruments. These distinctive features are believed to represent the fundamental nature of derivative instruments like options and futures.

Fair value. Defined as in SFAS 107 as the amount at which the asset or liability could be bought or settled in an arm's-length transaction; measured by reference to market prices or estimated by net present value of future cash flows, options pricing models, or by other techniques.

Financial instrument. Defined as it was in SFAS 105.

Firm commitment. An agreement with an unrelated party, binding on both, usually legally enforceable, specifying all significant terms and including a disincentive for nonperformance sufficient to make performance likely.

Forecasted transaction. A transaction expected to occur for which there is no firm commitment, and thus, which gives the entity no present rights or obligations. Under SFAS 133, forecasted transactions can be hedged and special hedge accounting can be applied.

Initial net investment. A derivative instrument is one where the initial net investment is zero or is less than the notional amount (possibly plus a premium or minus a discount). This characteristic refers to the relative amount of investment. Derivative instruments allow the opportunity to take part in the rate or price change without owning the asset or owing the liability. If an amount approximating the notional amount must be invested or received, it is not a derivative instrument. The two basic forms of derivative instruments are futures contracts and options. The futures contract involves little or no initial net investment. Settlement is usually near the delivery date. Call options, when purchased, require a premium payment that is less than the cost of purchasing the equivalent number of shares. Even though this distinguishing characteristic is the result of only one of the parties, it determines the application for both.

Net settlements. To qualify as a derivative instruments, one of the following settlement criteria must be met:

1. No delivery of an asset equal to the notional amount is required. For example, an interest rate swap does not involve delivery of the instrument in which the notional amount is expressed.
2. Delivery of an asset equal to the notional amount is required of one of the parties, but an exchange (or other market mechanism, institutional arrangement or side agreement) facilitates net settlement. For example, a call option has this attribute.
3. Delivery by one of the parties of an asset equal to the notional amount is required but the asset is either readily convertible to cash (as with a contract for the delivery of a marketable equity security), or is required but that asset is itself a derivative instrument (as is the case for a swaption [an option on a swap]).

This characteristic means that the derivative instrument can be settled by a net delivery of assets (the medium of exchange does not have to be cash). Contract terms based on changes in the price or rate of the notional that implicitly or explicitly require or permit net settlement qualify. Situations where one of the parties can liquidate their net investment or be relieved of the contract rights or obligations without significant transaction costs because of a market arrangement (broadly interpreted) or where the delivered asset can be readily converted to cash also meet the requirements for net settlement. It is assumed that an exchange traded security is readily converted to cash. Thus, commodity-based contracts for gold, oil, wheat, etc. are now included under this standard. The convertible to cash condition requires an active market and consideration of interchangeability and transaction volume. Determining if delivery of a financial asset or liability equal to the notional amount is a derivative instrument may depend upon whether it is readily convertible into cash. Different accounting will result if the notional is not readily converted to cash. Using the notional as collateral does not necessarily mean it is readily convertible to cash.

Notional amount. The notional amount (or payment provision) is the referenced associated asset or liability. A notional amount is commonly a number of units such as shares of stock, principal amount, face value, stated value, basis points, barrels of oil, etc. It may be that amount plus a premium or minus a discount. The interaction of the price or rate (underlying) with the referenced associated asset or liability (notional amount) determines whether settlement is required and, if so, the amount.

Underlyings. An underlying is commonly a specified price or rate such as a stock price, interest rate, currency rate, commodity price, or a related index. However, any variable (financial or physical) with (a) observable changes or (b) objectively verifiable changes such as a credit rating, insurance index, climatic or geological condition (temperature, rainfall) qualifies. Unless it is specifically excluded, a contract based on any qualifying variable is accounted for under SFAS 133 if it has distinguishing characteristics 2 and 3 above.

Contracts Not Subject to SFAS 133

The following contracts are considered exceptions and are not subject to the requirements of SFAS 133:

1. **Regular-way security trades**--Delivery of a security readily convertible to cash within the time period generally established by marketplace regulations or conventions where the trade takes place rather than by the usual procedure of an individual enterprise.

   For example, most trades of equity securities in the US require settlement in 3 business days. If an individual contract requires settlement in more than 3 business days (even if this is normal for a particular entity), this exception would not apply. This exception also applies to when-issued and to-be-announced securities, if there is no other way to purchase or sell them and if the trade will settle within the shortest period permitted.

   Based on the foregoing, the following may be excluded: forward purchases or sales of to-be-announced securities, and when-issued, as-issued, or if-issued securities.
2. **Normal purchases and normal sales**--Contracts for future delivery of assets (other than derivative instruments or financial instruments) that are readily convertible to cash and for which there is no net settlement provision and no market mechanism to ease net settlement. Terms must be consistent with normal transactions and quantities must be reasonable in relation to needs. All relevant factors are to be considered. An example would include contracts similar to a binding purchase orders. However, take or pay contracts that require little or no initial net investment, and that have products readily convertible to cash that do not qualify as normal purchases, would be a derivative instrument, and not an exception.

   Counter parties may reach different conclusions as to whether the contracts are a derivative instrument. Asymmetrical results are acceptable (i.e., the exception may apply to one party but not the other).
3. **Certain insurance contracts**--Contracts where the holder is only compensated when an insurable event (other than price or rate change) takes place and (a) the value of the holder's asset or liability is adversely changed or (b) the holder incurs a liability. For example, contracts generally not considered to be derivative instruments include those within the scope of SFAS 60, 97, and 113, traditional life insurance, and traditional property and casualty insurance policies.

   Most traditional insurance contracts will not be derivative instruments. Some, however, can include embedded derivatives that must be accounted for separately. For example, embedded derivatives may be found in annuity contracts, variable life and annuity contracts, and property and casualty contracts involving changes in currency rates.

4. **Certain financial guarantee contracts**--Contracts that call for payments only to reimburse for a loss from debtor failure to pay when due. However, a credit-indexed contract requiring payment for changes in credit ratings (an "underlying") would not be an exception.
5. **Certain contracts that are not exchange traded**--Contracts with underlyings based on one of the following:

   a. Climatic, geological or other physical variable: for example, inches of rain or heating-degree days;
   b. Value or price involving a nonfinancial asset not readily converted to cash or a nonfinancial liability that does not require delivery of an asset that is readily converted to cash; or
   c. Specified volumes of revenue of one of the parties: examples are royalty agreements or contingent rentals based on related sales.

   In the case of a mixture of underlyings, some of which are exceptions, the predominant characteristic of the combined variable of the contract is the determinant. If there is a high correlation with the behavior of the excepted variables above, it is an exception and if there is a high correlation with the nonexcepted variables, it is a derivative instrument.
6. **Derivatives that serve as impediments to sales accounting**--A derivative instrument that affects the accounting for the transfer of an asset. For example, a call option on transferred assets under SFAS 125 would prevent accounting for the transfer as a sale. This is necessary, since recognizing the call as a derivative instrument would result in double counting. For instance, a lessor guarantee of the residual value may prevent the accounting for a sales-type lease.

In addition to the foregoing, the following are not considered derivative instruments:

1. Contracts issued or held that are both

   a. Indexed to the enterprise's own stock, and
   b. Classified in shareholders' equity.

   Derivative instruments are assets or liabilities. Items properly accounted for in shareholders' equity are thus excluded from the definition of derivatives. Contracts that can or must be settled through issuance of an equity instrument but that are indexed in part or in full to something other than the enterprise's own stock are considered derivative instruments if they qualify and they are to be classified as assets or liabilities. Some of these kinds of items will be revisited later by the FASB.

2. Contracts issued in connection with SFAS 123.

   Many instruments under SFAS 123 are classified in shareholder equity. The FASB felt that those properly classified as liabilities have been adequately addressed.
3. Contracts issued as contingent consideration in a business combination under APB 16, using the purchase method.

   Contracts in a business combination that are similar to, but are not accounted for as contingent consideration under APB 16, are subject to this standard as derivative instruments or embedded derivative instruments.

The exceptions for the above three issued contracts are not applicable to the counterparties.

Embedded Derivative Instruments

An enterprise should not be allowed to circumvent the requirements of SFAS 133 recognition and measurement by embedding a derivative instrument in another contract. If these embedded derivative instruments would otherwise be subject to this standard, they are included in its scope. However, some common compound instruments that generally have been in existence for some time and that bear a close economic relationship to the host contract are excluded from SFAS 133 for practical reasons.

Embedded derivative instruments are defined as explicit or implicit terms affecting (a) the cash flows or (b) the value of other exchanges required by contract in a way similar to a derivative instrument (one or more underlying can modify the cash flows or exchanges). An embedded derivative instrument is to be separated out of the contract and accounted for separately as a derivative instrument by both parties **if and only if** all of the following three criteria are met:

1. Risks and economic characteristics are not clearly and closely related to those of the host contract;
2. The hybrid instrument is not required to be measured at fair value under GAAP with changes reported in earnings; and
3. A separate instrument with the same terms as the embedded derivative instrument would be accounted for as a derivative instrument. For this condition, the initial net investment of the hybrid instrument is not the same as that for the embedded derivative instrument.

These three conditions for the separate accounting for embedded derivatives are explained in the following paragraphs.

Risks and economic characteristics are not clearly and closely related to those of the host contract. If the underlying is an interest rate or interest rate index that changes the net interest payments of an interest-bearing contract, it is considered clearly and closely related **unless** one of the following conditions exist:

1. The hybrid instrument can be settled contractually in a manner that permits any possibility whatsoever that the investor would not recover **substantially all** of the initial recorded investment.
2. The embedded derivative instrument could under any possibility whatsoever (a) at least double the investor's initial rate of return (ROR) on the host contract and (b) could also result in a ROR at least twice the market return for a similar contract (same host contract terms and same debtor credit quality).

The date acquired (or incurred) is the assessment date for the existence of the above conditions. Thus, the issuer and an acquirer in a secondary market could account for the instrument differently because of different points in time.

Example of embedded instruments which are separately accounted for

Assuming that the host contract is a debt instrument, the following are considered not to be clearly and closely related and would normally have to be separated out as embedded derivatives:

1. Interest rate indexes, floors, caps and collars not meeting the criteria for exclusion (see below);
2. Leveraged inflation-indexed interest payments or rentals;
3. Calls and puts that do not accelerate repayment of the principal but require a cash settlement equal to the option price at date of exercise. Subsequently added options that cause one party to be exposed to performance or default risk by different parties for the embedded option than for the host contract;
4. Term extending options where there is no reset of interest rates;
5. Equity-indexed interest payments;
6. Commodity-indexed interest or principal payments;
7. A convertible debt conversion option for the investor if it qualifies as a derivative instrument (readily convertible to cash, etc.); and
8. A convertible preferred stock conversion option if the terms of the preferred stock (not the conversion option) are more similar to debt (a cumulative fixed rate with a mandatory redemption feature) than to equity (cumulative, participating, perpetual).

Example of embedded instruments which are not separately accounted for

Assuming that the host contract is a debt instrument, the following are considered to be clearly and closely related and would not normally have to be separated out as embedded derivative instruments:

1. Interest rate indexes (see below);
2. Interest rate floors, caps and collars, if **at issuance**
   a. The cap is at or above the current market price (or rate) and/or
   b. The floor is at or below the current market price (or rate).
3. Nonleveraged inflation-indexed interest payments or rentals.
4. Credit-sensitive payments (interest rate resets for debtor creditworthiness).

5. "Plain-vanilla" servicing rights not containing a separate embedded derivative instrument.
6. Calls and puts that can accelerate repayment of principal unless
   a. The debt involves substantial premium or discount (zero coupon) and
   b. The call or put is only contingently exercisable (not exercisable unless default occurs) and is indexed only to credit risk or interest rates.
7. Term-extending options if the interest rate is concurrently reset to approximately the current market rate for the extended term and the host contract had no initial significant discount.
8. Contingent rentals based on a variable interest rate.

Based on the foregoing, it can be stated that calls and puts on equity instruments are normally accounted for as follows:

1. **Investor**--Both the call and the put are embedded derivative instruments.
2. **Issuer**--Only the put could be an embedded derivative instrument. The put and the call would not be embedded derivative instruments if they are both
   a. Indexed to their own stock and
   b. Classified in shareholders' equity.

The hybrid instrument is not required to be measured at fair value under GAAP with changes reported in earnings. For example, most unsettled foreign currency transactions are subject to SFAS 52. Gains or losses are recognized in earnings and thus instruments of this nature are not considered embedded derivative instruments. Trading and available-for-sale securities that have cash flows denominated in a foreign currency also are not considered embedded derivative instruments.

A separate instrument with the same terms as the embedded derivative instrument would be accounted for as a derivative instrument. For this condition, the initial net investment of the hybrid instrument is not the same as that for the embedded derivative instrument.

To illustrate, a convertible debt conversion option for the **issuer** would not be an embedded derivative instrument since a separate option with the same terms would not be a derivative instrument because it is indexed to the issuer's own stock and would be classified in shareholders' equity.

Another example would involve convertible preferred stock. A convertible preferred stock conversion option would not be an embedded derivative instrument if the terms of the preferred stock (not the conversion option) are more similar to equity (cumulative, participating, perpetual) than to debt (a cumulative fixed rate with a mandatory redemption feature).

Interest-only strips and principal-only strips are specifically not subject to this standard assuming (1) the original financial instrument did not contain an embedded derivative instrument and (2) they don't incorporate any new terms from the original. In addition, foreign currency derivative instruments are specifically not separated from the host contract if (1) the currency of the primary economic environment is the functional currency of one of the parties or (2) the good or service price is routinely denominated in that currency in international commerce.

If an embedded derivative instrument is separated from the host, the accounting is as follows:

1. The embedded derivative instrument is accounted for based on SFAS 133; and
2. The host contract is accounted for based on GAAP for that instrument, without the embedded derivative instrument.

If the embedded derivative instrument cannot be reliably identified and measured separately, the entire contract must be measured at fair value with the gain or loss recognized in income. In this case, the contract cannot be designated as a hedging instrument.

Gains and losses of derivative instruments not designated as hedges are recognized in earnings or, for a not-for-profit organization, in the change in net assets.

Hedging Activities--General Requirements

Overview. Matters relating to hedging activities constitute the core of the new standard and represent the most difficult accounting issues. While the standard requires that all derivatives be reported at fair value in the balance sheet, the changes in fair value will be reported in different ways depending on the nature and effectiveness of the hedging activities to which they are related, if held for hedging purposes. SFAS 133 identifies changes in the fair values of derivatives as being the result of (1) effective hedging, (2) ineffective hedging, or (3) unrelated to hedging. Furthermore, the hedging itself can be related to the fair value of an existing asset or liability or of a firm commitment, the cash flow of forecasted transactions, or foreign currency exposures.

After meeting specified conditions, a qualified derivative may be specifically designated as a total or partial (expressed as a percentage where the risk exposure profile is the same as that in the whole derivative) hedge of

1. Changes in the fair value of

    a. A recognized asset or liability; or
    b. An unrecognized firm commitment.

    In a fair value hedge, all gains and losses (of both the derivative instrument and the hedged item) are recognized in earnings in the period of change.
2. Variable cash flows of a forecasted transaction.

    In a cash flow hedge, the effective portion of the hedge is reported in comprehensive income and is reclassified into earnings when the forecasted transaction affects earnings.

3. Foreign currency exposure of

   a. A net investment in a foreign operation

      In a foreign currency net investment hedge, the gain or loss is reported in comprehensive income as part of the cumulative translation adjustment to the extent that it is effective.

   b. An unrecognized firm commitment

      In a foreign currency unrecognized firm commitment hedge, the gain or loss is reported the same way as a fair value hedge (see category 1., above).

   c. An available-for-sale security

      In a foreign currency available for sale security hedge, the gain or loss is reported the same way as a fair value hedge (see category 1., above).

   d. A foreign currency denominated forecasted transaction.

      In a foreign currency denominated forecasted transaction hedge, the gain or loss is reported in the same way as a cash flow hedge (see category 2., above).

Hedge portions that are not effective are reported in earnings immediately.

A nonderivative financial instrument cannot generally be designated as a hedge. One exception, however, occurs when that instrument is denominated in a foreign currency and is designated as a hedge under 3a. or 3b. above. Not-for-profit enterprises cannot use hedge accounting for forecasted transactions.

Effectiveness--general observations. The method used for assessing the effective and noneffective portions of a hedge must be defined at the time of designation, must be used throughout the hedge period and must be consistent with the approach used for managing risk. Similar hedges should usually be assessed for effectiveness in a similar manner unless a different method can be justified. If an improved method is identified and is to be applied to an existing hedge, that hedge must be discontinued. The new method can then be designated and a new hedge relationship can be established.

Anything that is to be included in the effectiveness assessment must be specified. All excluded amounts and ineffective amounts are to be included in earnings. For example, if an option hedge is assessed for effectiveness based on changes in intrinsic value, the change due to the time value would be excluded and that amount would be included in earnings. As another example, differences in key terms between the hedged item and the hedging instrument such as notional amounts, maturities, quantities, location or delivery dates would cause ineffectiveness and that amount would be included in earnings.

Although there are specific conditions applicable to the hedge type (fair value or cash flow), in general, the assumption of no ineffectiveness in a hedging relationship between an interest bearing financial instrument and an interest rate swap can be assumed if **all** of the following conditions are met:

1. The principal amount and the notational amount of the swap match;
2. The fair value of the swap is zero at origin;
3. The net settlements under the swap are computed the same way each time;
4. The financial instrument is not prepayable; and
5. The terms are typical for those instruments and don't invalidate the assumption.

Fair Value Hedges

The change in the fair value of an entire financial asset or liability equals the fair value at the end of the period, adjusted to exclude changes in fair value (1) from payments received or made (partial recoveries or settlements) and (2) from the passage of time, minus the fair value at the beginning of the period.

To qualify as a fair value hedge, both the hedged items and the designated hedging instruments must meet **all** of the following criteria:

1. At the hedge's origin, formal documentation exists of the
   a. Hedging relationship;
   b. Risk management objectives;
   c. Strategy for undertaking the hedge;
   d. Identification of the hedged item, the hedging instrument, the nature of the risk, the method of assessing effectiveness and the components (if any) that are excluded (such as time value) from the assessment effectiveness; and the
   e. Reasonable method to be used in recognizing in earnings the asset or liability representing the gain or loss in the case of a hedged firm commitment.
2. The hedging relationship is expected to be highly effective in producing offsetting fair value changes throughout the hedge period. This relationship must be assessed at least every 3 months or when financial statements are reported.
3. If hedging with a **written** option, the combination must provide as much potential for gains from positive fair value changes as potential for losses from negative fair value changes. If a net premium is received, a combination of options is considered a written option. The combination of a written option and some other non option derivative is also considered a written option.

Unless foreign currency is involved, a nonderivative instrument cannot be a hedging instrument.

According to SFAS 133, an asset or liability will be eligible for designation as a hedged item in a fair value hedge (to which a hedging position will be related, for purposes of reporting gain or loss) if it is specifically identified as all or a specific portion of a recognized asset or liability, or an unrecognized firm commitment; is exposed to fair value changes that are attributable to the hedged risk such that earnings would be affected; and is not either remeasured at fair value for financial reporting purposes, or an equity method investment, or an equity method or minority interest in a consolidated subsidiary, a firm commitment related to the foregoing, or an equity instrument issued by the entity. Other limitations also apply, affecting held-to-maturity debt securities and nonfinancial assets.

More specifically, to be eligible for designation as a hedged item, an asset or liability must meet **all** of the following criteria:

1. The single item (or portfolio of similar items) must be specifically identified as hedging all or a specific portion.
   a. If similar items are aggregated and hedged, each item has to share the risk exposure that is being hedged (i.e. each individual item must respond in a proportionate manner to the change in fair value). Note that unrecognized firm commitments (noncancellable operating lease or mortgage servicing right) can be hedged items and hedged portfolios as described at SFAS 125, para. 37(q), do not automatically qualify.
   b. A specific portion must be one of the following:
      (1) A percentage of the total;
      (2) One or more selected contractual cash flows: for instance, the present value of the interest payments due in the first 2 years of a 4-year debt instrument;
      (3) An embedded put, call, cap, or floor that does not qualify as an embedded derivative in an existing asset or liability; or
      (4) Residual value in a lessor's net investment in a sales-type or direct financing lease.
2. The item has an exposure to fair value changes that could affect earnings (this doesn't apply to not-for-profit enterprises).
3. The item is **not**
   a. Remeasured with changes reported in earnings; for example, a foreign currency denominated item;
   b. An APB 18 equity method investment or an equity investment in a consolidated subsidiary;
   c. A minority interest;
   d. A firm commitment to enter a business combination or to acquire or dispose of
      (1) A subsidiary;
      (2) A minority interest; or
      (3) An equity method investee; or

e. An issued equity interest classified in stockholder's equity.

4. The item is not a held-to-maturity debt security (or similar portfolio) unless the hedged risk is for something other than for fair value changes in market interest rates or foreign exchange rates; examples include hedges of fair value changes in the obligor's creditworthiness, and hedges of fair value changes in a prepayment option component.
5. If the item is a nonfinancial asset or liability (other than a recognized loan servicing right or a nonfinancial firm commitment with financial components), the designated hedged risk is the fair value change of the total hedged item (at its actual location, if applicable); SFAS 133 stipulates that the price of a major ingredient cannot be used, and the price of a similar item at a different location cannot be used without adjustment.
6. If the item is a financial asset or liability, a recognized loan servicing right or a nonfinancial firm commitment with financial components, the designated hedge risk is the risk of changes in fair value from fair value changes in

   a. The total hedged item;
   b. Market interest rates;
   c. Related foreign currency rates;
   d. The obligor's creditworthiness; or
   e. Two or more of the above, other than a.

Prepayment risk for a financial asset cannot be hedged, but an option component of a prepayable instrument can be designated as the hedged item in a fair value hedge. Embedded derivatives have to be considered also in designating hedges. For instance, in a hedge of interest rates, the effect of an embedded prepayment option must be considered in the designation of the hedge.

Reporting gains and losses from fair value hedges. The accounting for qualifying fair value hedges' gains and losses is as follows:

- On the hedging instrument, gains and losses are recognized in earnings.
- On the hedged item, gains and losses are recognized in earnings, even if they would normally be included in other comprehensive income if not hedged. For example, gains and losses on an available-for-sale security would be taken into income, if this is being hedged. The carrying amount of the hedged item is adjusted by the gains and losses resulting from the hedged risk.

Differences between the gains and losses on the hedged item and the hedging instrument are either due to amounts excluded from the assessment of hedging effectiveness, or are due to ineffectiveness. These gains and losses are to be recognized currently in earnings.

Measuring the effectiveness of fair value hedges. In addition to the general effectiveness conditions discussed earlier, the assumption of no ineffectiveness in a fair value hedge only between an interest bearing financial instrument and an interest rate swap can be assumed if **all** of the following conditions are met:

1. The maturity date of the instrument and the expiration date of the swap match;
2. No floor or ceiling on the variable interest rate of the swap exists; and
3. The interval (3-6 months or less) between repricings is frequent enough to assume the variable rate is a market rate.

The fixed rate on the hedged item is not required to exactly match the fixed rate on the swap. The fixed and variable rates on the swap can be changed by the same amount. As an example, a swap payment based on LIBOR and a swap receipt based on a fixed rate of 5% can be changed to a payment based on LIBOR plus 1% and a receipt based on 6%.

Discontinuance of a fair value hedge. The accounting for a fair value hedge should not continue if any of the events below occur.

1. The criteria are no longer met;
2. The derivative instruments expire or are sold, terminated or exercised; and
3. The designation is removed.

If the fair value hedge is discontinued, a new hedging relationship may be designated with a different hedging instrument and/or a different hedged item, as long as the criteria established in SFAS 133 are met.

Noneffectiveness of a fair value hedging. If an assessment indicates the hedge is not effective, no adjustment of the carrying amount of the hedged item should be recognized from the date when effectiveness was last established. If the event that caused the change in effectiveness can be identified, then the carrying amount can be adjusted normally for the amount of fair value change that occurred prior to that event. If the fair value hedge is discontinued because a firm commitment doesn't qualify any longer, any recognized associated asset or liability must be derecognized, with the gain or loss recognized in earnings.

Impairment. All assets or liabilities designated as fair value hedges are subject to the normal GAAP requirements for impairment. Those requirements are to be applied, however, only after the carrying amounts have been adjusted for the period's hedge accounting. Since the hedging instrument is a separate asset or liability, its fair value is not considered in applying the impairment criteria to the hedged item.

Cash Flow Hedges

The second major subset of hedging arrangements relate to uncertain future cash flows, as contrasted with hedged items engendering uncertain fair values. A derivative instrument may be designated as a hedge to the exposure of fluctuating expected future cash flows produced by a particular risk. The exposure may be connected with an existing asset or liability or with a forecasted transaction. To qualify as a cash flow hedge, both the hedged items and the designated hedging instruments must meet **all** of the following criteria:

1. At the hedge's origin, formal documentation exists of the
   a. Hedging relationship;
   b. Risk management objectives;
   c. Strategy for undertaking the hedge; and
   d. Identification of the hedged transaction, the hedging instrument, the nature of the risk, the method of assessing effectiveness and the components (if any) that are excluded (such as time value) from the assessment effectiveness.
2. Documentation must include
   a. All relevant details;
   b. The specific nature of any asset or liability involved;
   c. When (date on or period within) a forecasted transaction is occurring; and
   d. The expected currency amount (exact amount of foreign currency being hedged) or expected quantity (specific physical quantities such as number of items, weight, etc.) of a forecasted transaction. If a price risk is being hedged in a forecasted sale or purchase, the hedged transaction **cannot**
      (1) Be specified solely in terms of expected currency amounts; or
      (2) Be specified as a percentage of sales or purchases.

   The current price of the transaction should be identified and the transaction should be described so that it is evident that a given transaction is or is not the hedged transaction. For instance, a forecasted sale of the first 2,000 units in January is proper, but the forecasted sale of the last 2,000 units is not because they can't be identified when they occur--the month has to end before the last units sold can be identified.
3. The hedging relationship is expected to be highly effective in producing offsetting cash flows throughout the hedge period. This relationship must be assessed at least every 3 months or when financial statements are reported.
4. If hedging with a **written** option, the combination must provide as much potential for gains from positive cash flow changes as potential for losses from negative cash flow changes. If a net premium is received, a combination of options is considered a written option. The combination of a written option and some other nonoption derivative is also considered a written option.

5. A link must be used to modify interest receipts or payments of a recognized financial asset or liability from one variable rate to another variable rate. It has to be between a designated asset (or group of similar assets) and a designated liability (or group of similar liabilities) and it has to be highly effective. A link occurs when the basis of one leg of an interest rate swap is the same as the basis of the interest rate receipt of a designated asset and the basis of the other leg of the swap is the same as the basis of the interest payments for a designated liability.

A nonderivative instrument cannot be designated as a hedging instrument for a cash flow hedge.

In addition to the above, to be eligible for designation as a hedged item, a forecasted transaction must meet **all** of the following criteria:

1. The single transaction (or group of individual transactions) must be specifically identified. If individual transactions are grouped and hedged, each has to share the risk exposure that is being hedged (i.e. each individual transaction must respond in a proportionate manner to the change in cash flow). Thus, a forecasted sale and a forecasted purchase cannot both be included in the same group.
2. The occurrence is probable.
3. It is a transaction with an external party (unless a foreign currency cash flow hedge) and it has an exposure to cash flow changes that could affect earnings.
4. The transaction is **not** to be remeasured with changes reported in earnings; for example, foreign currency denominated items would be excluded for this reason. Forecasted sales on credit and forecasted accrual of royalties on probable future sales are not considered the forecasted acquisition of a receivable. Also, if related to a recognized asset or liability, the asset or liability is not remeasured with changes in fair value resulting from the hedged risk reported in earnings.
5. The item is not a held-to-maturity debt security (or similar portfolio) unless the hedged risk is for something other than for cash flow changes in market interest rates, as for example, in a hedge of cash flow changes due to an obligor's creditworthiness or default.
6. It does **not** involve

   a. A business combination;
   b. A parent company's interest in consolidated subsidiaries;
   c. A minority interest;
   d. An equity method investment; or
   e. An equity interest classified in stockholder's equity.

7. If it involves a purchase or sale of a **nonfinancial** asset, the hedged risk is

a. The change in the functional-currency-equivalent cash flow resulting from changes in the related foreign currency rates; or
b. The change in cash flow relating to the total hedged price (at its actual location, if applicable); for example, the price of a similar item at a different location cannot be used without adjustment.

8. If it involves a purchase or sale of a **financial** asset or liability or the variable cash flow of an existing financial asset or liability, the hedged risk is the risk of changes in cash flow of

   a. The total hedged item;
   b. Market interest rates;
   c. Related foreign currency rates;
   d. Obligor's creditworthiness or default; or
   e. Two or more of the above, other than a.

Prepayment risk for a financial asset cannot be hedged.

Gains and losses from cash flow hedges. The accounting for qualifying cash flow hedges' gains and losses is as follows:

1. The effective portion of the derivative instrument is reported in other comprehensive income.
2. The ineffective portion of the derivative instrument is reported in earnings.
3. Any excluded component of the derivative instrument is reported in earnings.
4. Accumulated other comprehensive income from the hedged transaction should be adjusted to the lesser (in absolute amounts) of the following:

   a. The cumulative gain or loss on the derivative from the creation of the hedge minus any excluded component and minus any amounts reclassified from accumulated other comprehensive income into earnings;
   b. The portion of the cumulative gain or loss on the derivative needed to offset the cumulative change in expected cash flow on the transaction from the creation of the hedge minus any amounts reclassified from accumulated other comprehensive income into earnings.

   The adjustment of accumulated other comprehensive income should recognize in other comprehensive income either a part or all of the gain or loss on the adjustment of the derivative instrument to fair value.
5. Any remaining gain or loss is reported in earnings.

Reclassifications to earnings. In the period that the hedged forecasted transaction affects earnings, amounts in accumulated other comprehensive income should be reclassified into earnings. If the transaction results in an asset or liability, amounts in accumulated other comprehensive income should be reclassified into earnings when the asset or liability affects earnings through cost of sales, depreciation, interest expense, etc. Any time that a net loss on the combined derivative instrument and the hedged transaction is expected, the amount that isn't expected to be recovered should immediately be reclassified into earnings.

Effectiveness of cash flow hedges. In addition to the general effectiveness conditions discussed earlier, the assumption of no ineffectiveness in a cash flow hedge only between an interest-bearing financial instrument and an interest rate swap can be assumed if all of the following conditions are met:

1. All variable rate interest payments or receipts on the instrument during the swap term are designated as hedged and none beyond that term;
2. No floor or ceiling on the variable rate of the swap exists unless the variable rate instrument has one. If the instrument does, the swap must have a comparable (not necessarily equal) one;
3. Repricing dates match; and
4. The index base for the variable rates match.

The variable rate on the instrument is not required to exactly match the variable rate on the swap. The fixed and variable rates on the swap can be changed by the same amount.

Discontinuance of a cash flow hedge. The accounting for a cash flow hedge should not continue if any of the events below occur.

1. The criteria are no longer met;
2. The derivative instruments expire or are sold, terminated or exercised; or
3. The designation is removed.

The net gain or loss in accumulated other comprehensive income should remain there until it is properly reclassified when the transaction affects earnings. If it is probable that the original forecasted transactions won't occur, the net gain or loss in accumulated other comprehensive income should immediately be reclassified into earnings.

If the cash flow hedge is discontinued, a new hedging relationship may be designated with a different hedging instrument and/or a different hedged item as long as the criteria established in SFAS 133 are now met.

Impairment. All assets or liabilities designated as cash flow hedges are subject to normal GAAP requirements for impairment. Those requirements are to be applied, however, after hedge accounting has been applied for the period. Since the hedging instrument is a separate asset or liability, its expected cash flow or fair value is not considered in applying the impairment criteria to the hedged item. If an impairment loss or recovery on a hedged forecasting asset or liability is recognized, any offsetting amount should be immediately reclassified from accumulated other comprehensive income into earnings.

Foreign Currency Hedges

The FASB's basic objectives in hedge accounting for foreign currency exposure are

1. To continue to permit the hedge accounting required under SFAS 52; and
2. To increase the consistency of accounting guidance by broadening the scope of hedges that are eligible for this treatment.

Unlike SFAS 52, this standard allows hedges of forecasted foreign currency transactions, including some intercompany transactions. Hedging foreign currency intercompany cash flows with foreign currency options is a common practice that is allowed under certain conditions by EITF 91-1. SFAS 133 modifies that accounting to permit using other derivative instruments (forward contracts, etc.) because the accounting for all derivative instruments should be the same.

If an asset or liability is remeasured under SFAS 52 with the change reported in earnings, it cannot be a hedged item. If an intercompany foreign currency derivative is created, it can only be a hedging instrument in the **consolidated** statements if the other member is a party to an offsetting contract with an unrelated third party to hedge its exposure because the standard requires that some component that has foreign currency exposure has to be a party to the hedging transaction. However, the subsidiary could designate the intercompany derivative as a hedge in its **standalone** statements.

Foreign currency net investment hedge. Either a derivative instrument or a nonderivative financial instrument (that can result in a foreign currency transaction gain or loss under SFAS 52) can be designated as a hedge of a foreign currency net investment in a foreign operation. The gain or loss from the designated instrument to the extent that it is effective is reported as a translation adjustment. The hedged net investment is accounted for under SFAS 52.

Foreign currency unrecognized firm commitment hedge. Either a derivative instrument or a nonderivative financial instrument (that can result in a foreign currency transaction gain or loss under SFAS 52) can be designated as a fair value hedge of an unrecognized firm commitment (or a specific portion) attributable to foreign currency. If the criteria are met, this hedging relationship is accounted for as a fair value hedge.

Foreign currency available-for-sale security hedge. Only a derivative instrument can be designated as a fair value hedge of an available-for-sale debt security (or a specific portion) attributable to foreign currency. If the criteria are met, this hedging relationship is accounted for as a fair value hedge. For an available-for-sale **equity** security to be accounted for as a fair value hedge, it must meet all of the fair value criteria **and** the following two requirements:

1. The security **cannot** be traded on an exchange (or similar marketplace) denominated in the investor's functional currency; and

2. Dividends (or other cash flows) to the holders must be denominated in the same foreign currency as that expected to be received upon the sale of the security.

If the equity available-for-sale security qualifies as a foreign currency hedge, the change in fair value from foreign currency is reported in earnings and not in other comprehensive income.

Any gain or loss on a designated nonderivative hedging instrument from foreign currency is determined under SFAS 52 (as the increase or decrease in functional currency cash flows produced by the change in spot rates) and is reported in earnings along with the change in the carrying amount of the hedged firm commitment.

Foreign currency denominated forecasted transaction. Only a derivative instrument can be designated as a cash flow hedge of a foreign currency denominated forecasted transaction. The parties to this transaction can either be external or intercompany. To qualify for hedge accounting, **all** of the following criteria must be met:

1. An operating unit with foreign currency exposure is a party to the derivative instrument;
2. The transaction is denominated in a currency that is **not** the functional currency;
3. All of the criteria for a cash flow hedge are met (with the possible exception of allowing a qualifying intercompany transaction); and
4. If a group of individual transactions is involved, both an inflow and an outflow of foreign currency cannot be included in the same group.

If the foregoing criteria are met, this hedging relationship is accounted for as a cash flow hedge.

Organizations That Do Not Report Earnings

Not-for-profits or other organizations not reporting earnings should recognize gains or losses on nonhedging derivative instruments and hedging instruments as a change in net assets. Changes in the carrying amount of the hedged items are also recognized as a change in net assets.

Organizations which do not report earnings cannot use cash flow hedges. If the hedging instrument is a foreign currency net investment hedge, it is accounted for in that manner.

Disclosures

SFAS 133 requires certain disclosures for derivative instruments and nonderivative instruments designated and qualifying as hedging instruments. Specifically required are the objectives of the instruments, the context needed to understand them, the strategies for achieving them, the risk management policy and a description of items or transactions which are hedged for each of the following:

1. Fair value hedges;
2. Cash flow hedges;
3. Foreign currency net investment hedges; and
4. All other derivatives.

Derivative instruments not designated as hedges are to have the purpose of their activity disclosed. Qualitative disclosures concerning the use of derivative instruments are encouraged, particularly in a context of overall risk management. The FASB also encourages disclosure of similar quantitative information about financial instruments or nonfinancial assets and liabilities related by activity to derivative instruments.

Hedge disclosures. In addition to the above, for every reporting period that a complete set of financial statements is issued, there are required disclosures by hedge type.

Fair value hedges. For all designated and qualified instruments and hedged items that give rise to foreign currency transaction gains or losses under SFAS 52, disclosure is required of the net gain or loss in earnings, a description of where it is reported, and the amounts due to

1. Hedge ineffectiveness;
2. Components that were excluded from the assessment of effectiveness; and
3. Hedged firm commitments that no longer qualify as hedges.

Cash flow hedges. For all designated and qualified instruments and hedged items in cash flow hedges, the following are disclosed:

1. The net gain or loss in earnings, a description of where it is reported, and the amounts due to
   a. Hedge ineffectiveness; and
   b. Components that were excluded from the assessment of effectiveness;
2. A description of events that will result in reclassification of amounts in accumulated other comprehensive income to earnings and the net amount expected to be reclassified during the next 12 months;
3. The maximum length of time of any cash flow hedges of forecasted transactions (excluding those relating to payment of variable interest on existing financial instruments); and
4. The amount reclassified from accumulated other comprehensive income into earnings because it was probable that the original forecasted transactions wouldn't occur.

Foreign currency net investment hedges. For all designated and qualified instruments that give rise to foreign currency transaction gains or loses under SFAS 52, the net gain or loss that is included in the cumulative translation adjustment.

Comprehensive income. The net gain or loss from cash flow hedges on derivative instruments reported in other comprehensive income must be shown as a separate classification. Accumulated other comprehensive income disclosures should show separately the following:

1. Beginning and ending accumulated derivative instrument gain or loss;
2. Net change from hedging transactions; and
3. Net amount of reclassifications to earnings.

Other Pronouncements Affected by Issuance of SFAS 133

SFAS 133 has superseded SFAS 80, 105, and 119, and has amended ARB 43, and SFAS 52, 60, 65, 95, 107, 113, 115, 124, 125, and 126, as well as TB 79-19. It has nullified or modified a number of EITF consensuses.

SFAS 107 was amended by SFAS 133 to include the disclosure requirements concerning concentrations of credit risk for all financial instruments from superseded SFAS 105. The disclosure of the fair value of all financial instruments is still required, and SFAS 107 is relied on to provide valuation guidance for measuring fair value in the new standard.

SFAS 133 changes the scope of superseded SFAS 119 from derivative financial instruments to derivative instruments. The result is the inclusion of some contracts that are settled by a commodity or nonfinancial asset. In addition, the scope change means that certain contracts that were included under SFAS 119 may now be excluded and certain contracts that were excluded may now be included.

Effective Date

SFAS 133 is effective for all fiscal quarters of all fiscal years beginning after June 15, 1999. A calendar-year company would thus begin application in January 2000. Early application is encouraged, but initial application must be at the beginning of a fiscal quarter after June 1998, when hedging relationships must be designated and documented according to SFAS 133. Applying only selected provisions early is not permitted. The standard cannot be applied retroactively.

Transition

At initial application, the following is required:

1. All freestanding derivative instruments are recognized as assets or liabilities at fair value. At this date only, a compound derivative instrument composed of a foreign currency derivative and another can be separated into

two parts with each accounted for at fair value to the limit of the fair value of the compound derivative instrument.

2. Differences between fair value and carrying amounts of derivative instruments are reported as transition adjustments.
3. Offsetting gains and losses on hedged assets, liabilities, and firm commitments are recognized by adjusting carrying amounts.
4. Deferred losses or gains on derivative instruments that are reported as assets or liabilities are derecognized and reported as transition adjustments.
5. Gains or losses on derivative instruments reported in other comprehensive income because of fair value hedges of available-for-sale securities are reported as transition adjustments.
6. Gains or losses on derivative instruments reported in accumulated other comprehensive income because of cash flow hedges of a forecasted transaction related to available-for-sale securities should remain and are **not** reported as transition adjustments.
7. Gains or losses on derivative instruments prior to initial application are not affected and are **not** reported as transition adjustments.
8. Embedded derivatives are separated from the host contract and recognized as assets or liabilities if the host contract was issued, acquired, or substantively modified after December 31, 1997. For hybrid instruments issued or acquired before January 1, 1998, and not substantively modified after that date, there is a choice to either recognize the embedded derivatives as assets or liabilities under SFAS 133 or not apply the standard to these instruments. The choice must be on an all-or-none basis. If separated, the following should be considered in determining the transition adjustment:

    a. The host contract's carrying amount should be the fair value at date of issue or acquisition adjusted for subsequent activity (cash receipts or payments and/or amortization of premiums or discounts necessitated by the separation of the embedded derivative instrument).
    b. The embedded derivative instrument's carrying amount should be the fair value at initial application.
    c. The transition adjustment is the difference between the sum of the fair values in a. and b. above and the previous carrying amount of the hybrid instrument. If the embedded derivative instrument initially could have been accounted for separately from the host contract and wasn't, retroactively designating a hedging relationship is not permitted.

The transition adjustment is to be reported in net income or in other comprehensive income as required. It is considered to be a cumulative effect of a change in accounting principle under APB 20. The accounting for the derivative instrument under GAAP before the initial application of SFAS 133 is the determining factor for reporting the transition adjustment in earnings, in other comprehensive income, or in allocating it between both. Specifically, the transition adjustment to a derivative instrument should be reported as follows:

- If designated as a cash flow hedge of a forecasted transaction, it is reported as a cumulative effect adjustment of accumulated other comprehensive income.
- If designated as a fair value hedge, it is reported as a cumulative effect adjustment of net income. The gain or loss on the difference between the fair value of the hedged item and its carrying amount is recognized by adjusting the carrying amount at initial application to the extent of the offsetting transition amount for the derivative instrument. That adjustment is also reported as a cumulative effect adjustment of net income. In the case of a hedged available-for-sale security, the transition adjustment gain or loss on the derivative instrument reported in accumulated other comprehensive income together with the gain or loss on the security (to the extent of the offset) is reclassified to earnings as a cumulative effect adjustment of both net income and accumulated other comprehensive income.
- If designated in a multiple hedge of cash flow and fair value, it is allocated between them as a cumulative effect adjustment of both accumulated other comprehensive income and net income and is reported as in 1. and 2. above. Any gain or loss on the hedged item is reported as in 2. above.

All other transition adjustments are reported as cumulative effect adjustments of net income.

Transition adjustment amounts reported as cumulative effect adjustments of accumulated other comprehensive income are to be reclassified into earnings in the normal manner under SFAS 133. In the year of initial application, the amounts of gains or losses from the transition adjustment that are being reclassified into earnings during the next 12 months must be disclosed.

At initial application, held-to-maturity securities (including financial assets received or retained in a previous desecuritization) can be transferred to the available-for-sale or trading categories without calling into question the intent to hold to maturity. This movement may be desired so that the security or some component (interest rates, fair value, etc.) can be designated as the hedged item. The unrealized holding gain or loss is reported as required by SFAS 115 and is included in the transition adjustment discussed above.

At initial application, available-for-sale securities can be transferred to the trading category. After any related transition adjustment has been recognized, any remaining unrealized holding gain or loss is reclassified into earnings (not as a transition adjustment) as required by SFAS 115. If a derivative instrument was being used as a hedge and had reported a gain or loss in other comprehensive income, the gain or loss should be reclassified into earnings (not as a transition adjustment) upon transfer.

At initial application, servicing rights (SFAS 125, para. 37[g]) may be restratified so that individual strata will comply with the SFAS 133 requirements for a portfolio of similar assets. SFAS 125 designated hedged portfolios of aggregated servicing rights do not necessarily comply because of possible differences in the requirements for the risk stratum base. Restratification of servicing rights is reported as a cumulative effect transition adjustment.

EMERGING ISSUES TASK FORCE CONSENSUS SUMMARIES

Short-Term Investments

85-9 Revenue Recognition of Options to Purchase Stock of Another Entity

If debt is issued with detachable warrants to acquire the stock of **another** entity, no income should be recognized until the warrant is exercised or expires and a liability should be recorded for the value of the warrant. No consensus was reached on the accounting for exchangeable debt. In practice, most accountants follow APB 14. The SEC observer, however, did not believe APB 14 was applicable and thought that separation was required.

85-29 Convertible Bonds With a "Premium Put"

A liability for the put premium should be accrued over the period from the date of issuance to the initial put date. Accrual should continue regardless of market value changes. If the put expires unexercised and if the market value of the common stock exceeds the put price at expiration date, the put premium should be credited to additional paid-in capital. If the put expires unexercised and if the put price exceeds the market value of the common stock, the put premium should be amortized as a yield adjustment over the remaining term of the debt.

86-35 Debentures With Detachable Stock Purchase Warrants

The issue addressed senior subordinated notes with a detachable warrant giving both the right to purchase shares and a put with a price substantially higher than the value of the warrant without the put. In this case, there should be an allocation of the proceeds between the warrant and the debt liability. The carrying amount of the warrant should be accrued to the put price and reported as interest expense because the warrant is considered a debt instrument.

86-40 Investments in Open-End Mutual Funds That Invest in US Government Securities

The investment in the mutual fund should be at fair value per SFAS 115.

96-11 Accounting for Forward Contracts and Purchased Options to Acquire Securities Covered by FASB Statement 115

This issue addresses the accounting only when terms require physical settlement. Forward contracts and purchased options with no intrinsic value at acquisition should be designated and accounted for as prescribed in SFAS 115.

96-12 Recognition of Interest Income and Balance Sheet Classification of Structured Notes

When recognizing interest income on structured note securities in an available-for-sale or held-to-maturity portfolio, the retrospective interest method should be used if three conditions are satisfied. These are

1. Either the original investment amount or the maturity amount of the contractual principal is at risk
2. Return of investment on note is subject to volatility arising from
   a. No stated rate or stated rate is not a constant percentage or in same direction as changes in market-based interest rates or interest rate index, or
   b. Fixed or variable coupon rate is lower than that for interest for traditional notes with similar maturity and a portion of potential yield is based on occurrence of future circumstances or events
3. Contractual maturity of bond is based on a specific index or on occurrence of specific events or situations outside the control of contractual parties

96-15 Accounting for the Effects of Changes in Foreign Currency Exchange Rates on Foreign-Currency-Denominated Available-for-Sale Debt Securities (AFS)

Total changes in fair value of foreign-currency-denominated AFS debt securities should be reported in stockholders' equity.

Foreign currency transaction losses and gains arising from a foreign-currency-denominated liability or forward exchange contract should be reported in the SFAS 115 component of stockholders' equity. Then, it would offset the change in market value of a foreign-currency-denominated AFS debt security if the foreign-currency-denominated AFS debt security or forward exchange contract is either identified or does serve as a hedge of the foreign-currency-denominated AFS debt security.

Options

87-31 Sale of Put Options on Issuer's Stock

The provisions of ASR 268 provide guidance by analogy to public companies. Companies that sell puts should record the proceeds in permanent equity and transfer from permanent equity to temporary equity an amount equal to the redemption price of the common stock. Subsequent market value changes of the put are ignored. Only when the puts are exercised, redeemed or expire will the equity section be adjusted. If during a reporting period, the puts are "in the money" the potential dilutive effect on EPS should be computed using the reverse treasury stock method.

90-17 Hedging Foreign Currency Risks With Purchased Options

SFAS 52 foreign currency risk is risk associated with transactions and commitments in currencies other than the transacting entity's functional currency. Hedge accounting is appropriate for purchased foreign currency options used to hedge an anticipated transaction if the conditions of paras 4 and 9 of SFAS 80 are met. Specifically

1. The hedged item must expose the entity to foreign currency risks.
2. The option must be designated as a hedge and must reduce exposure to risk.
3. Expected terms and significant characteristics of the transaction must be identified.
4. It is probable that the transaction will occur.

Consensus was reached that purchased options having little or no intrinsic value at the time designated as a hedge and meeting the high correlation criteria **would** qualify for hedge accounting in the following situations:

1. Hedging foreign export sales
2. Hedging identifiable anticipated transactions with risk

The above options would **not** qualify for hedge accounting in the following situations:

1. Hedging foreign subsidiary sales
2. Hedging anticipated transactions with no enterprise risk
3. Hedging net income
4. Hedging competitive risk

The propriety of hedge accounting for "anticipated sales for several years" depends on the assessment of the transaction using SFAS 80 criteria. The further into the future the transaction is expected, the less likely it will meet the criteria.

Foreign Currency Forwards

86-25 Offsetting Foreign Currency Swaps

The currency swap accrual cannot be netted against the foreign currency debt. They are separate transactions without the right of setoff.

87-2 Net Present Value Method of Valuing Speculative Foreign Exchange Contracts

Discounting is allowed but not required in applying para 19 of SFAS 52.

87-26 Hedging of a Foreign Currency Exposure With a Tandem Currency

A tandem currency may not be used to hedge a net investment in a foreign subsidiary only because it is less expensive. SFAS 52 phrases "practical" or "feasible" refer to the availability of a hedging investment.

Swaps

84-7 Termination of Interest Rate Swaps

If accounted for as a hedge, terminated interest rate swaps should not be recognized immediately in income. Instead, the accounting should follow SFAS 80 and the gain or loss should be deferred until the offsetting gain or loss on the hedged transaction is recognized. No consensus was reached on nonhedge transactions.

88-8 Mortgage Swaps

The notional amount of mortgage-backed securities and the related debt in a mortgage swap are similar to an executory contract and should not be recognized at the inception of the transaction. Except for mortgage swaps that qualify for hedge accounting, it is appropriate to recognize subsequent changes in the market value (at market or the lower of cost or market) of the swap over its term in a manner consistent with the companies accounting for similar investment. Consensus was reached that hedge accounting is appropriate if hedge criteria under GAAP are met. The SEC observer noted that mortgage swap hedges should be accounted for by financial institutions in the trading account and would be recorded at market value.

Other Financial Instruments

84-14 Deferred Interest Rate Setting

If the deferred rate setting agreement is an integral part (i.e., must be with the underwriter of the debt) of the original issuance of debt, any cash receipt or cash payment should be accounted for over the term of the debt as a yield adjustment to interest expense.

86-24 Third-Party Establishment of Collateralized Mortgage Obligations

The sale of mortgages to an unrelated third party which then uses them as collateral to issue CMO should be accounted for as a sale. The gain or loss from the sale should be recognized in the period of the transaction and should include the present value of the residual interest if it can be reliably estimated. The recognition phase of the FASB's project on financial instruments will address this issue.

86-28 Accounting Implications of Indexed Debt Instruments

The issuer is required to allocate the proceeds between the investor's right to receive contingent payments and the debt instrument if the right is separable. No consensus was reached regarding a nonseparable right. As the index increases, a liability or an additional liability is required if the issuer must pay a contingent payment at maturity. The balance sheet date index value should be used and future changes should not be anticipated. If there were no proceeds initially allocated, any additional liability is an adjustment of the debt's carrying amount. Settlement by delivering the actual commodity fixes the issuer's cost of settlement. This issue is to be addressed as a part of the FASB's financial instrument project.

86-34 Futures Contracts Used as Hedges of Anticipated Reverse Repurchase Transactions

Gains or losses on futures contracts could qualify for SFAS 80 hedge accounting if they reduce the interest rate risk and if the criteria of para 9 of SFAS 80 is met. All relevant facts and circumstances should be considered.

Upon the sale of fixed-rate assets, if deferral criteria continue to be met, gains should be recognized while futures losses continue to be deferred. The future contracts were designated as hedges of the reverse repurchase liabilities.

If the hedge is terminated prior to the future issuance of short-term debt, the SFAS 80 high correlation requirement is not applicable after discontinuance.

87-12 Foreign Debt-for-Equity Swaps

If the foreign government requires the proceeds to be invested in that country, the difference between the US dollar values of the two transactions should be used, first, to reduce the basis of long-lived assets acquired in compliance with the arrangement and, second, to reduce the basis of existing long-lived assets (starting with the fixed asset with the longest remaining life and following that order to the shortest remaining life) other than goodwill. If all long-lived assets are reduced to zero, the remaining excess is reported as negative goodwill.

87-20 Offsetting Certificates of Deposit Against High Coupon Debt

Loss recognition is required when a company purchases a Certificate of Deposit from a bank in the amount of the par value of its bonds and the bank simultaneously purchases the company's bonds from third-party holders at a premium. FASB Interpretation 39 governs issues of setoff.

87-30 Sale of a Short-Term Loan Made Under a Long-Term Credit Commitment

If the long-term credit commitment contains a substantive **subjective** covenant, the transaction should be recorded as a sale. If it contains only **objective** covenants, it is only a sale if those covenants are substantive.

Substantive means that they are specific to the borrower and are expected to be meaningful and relevant. There was also consensus that long-term commitment fees should be recognized in accordance with SFAS 91.

88-11 Allocation of Recorded Investment When a Loan or Part of a Loan Is Sold

Relative fair values at acquisition (adjusted for payments and other activity from that date) should be used to allocate the recorded investment between the portion of the loan retained and the portion sold. If it is not practical to determine relative fair values at acquisition, relative fair value on date of sale may be used. Amounts in the allowance for loan losses should be excluded when considering the recorded investment to be allocated. Any gain recognized when selling a portion of the loan should not exceed that which would be recognized if the entire loan was sold. A portion of the recorded investment should be allocated to excess servicing if it is retained.

Para 5 of SFAS 77 should be used for transactions that provide for recourse to the seller. The adequacy of the allowance for credit losses should be evaluated by the seller in considering both the remaining recorded investment's collectibility and any recourse obligation for the portion sold in accordance with para 6 of SFAS 77.

For transactions after 4/6/89 involving sales with disproportionate credit **and** prepayment risk but with no disproportionate interest rates, the SEC requires the relative fair value method.

When an entire principal balance is sold at a price near par, including transactions where the seller passes through a rate of interest different from the coupon rate, the seller should measure excess servicing (or deficiency in normal servicing) in accordance with para 11 of SFAS 65. Under footnote 4 to that paragraph, the difference in fees should be calculated using prepayment, default and interest rate assumptions that market participants would use for similar financial instruments and should be discounted using an interest rate that an unrelated purchaser would demand.

89-18 Divestitures of Certain Investment Securities to an Unregulated Commonly Controlled Entity Under FIRREA

The transfer of securities to an affiliate at book value does **not** obviate the need for the savings association to account for the securities at fair value per SFAS 115. The SEC observer noted that gain recognition would not be appropriate when the securities are sold to the affiliate.

95-5 Determination of What Risks and Rewards, if Any, Can Be Retained and Whether Any Unresolved Contingencies May Exist in a Sale of Mortgage Loan Servicing Rights

This consensus supersedes the consensus reached in Issue 89-5. If substantially all risks and rewards of ownership have irrevocably passed to the buyer and any protection provisions retained by the seller are minor and can be reasonably estimated, then sales of rights to service mortgage loans should be recognized at the date title passes. If a sale is recognized and minor protection provisions exist, a liability should be accrued for the estimated obligation associated with those protection provisions. Protection provisions are considered to be minor if (1) the provisions are no more than 10% of the sales price and (2) the risk of prepayment is retained for no longer than 120 days. Additionally, temporary subservicing agreements in which the subservicing will be performed by the seller for a short period of time will not necessarily preclude recognizing a sale at the closing date.

96-13 Accounting for Derivative Financial Instruments Indexed To, and Potentially Settled In, a Company's Own Stock

The consensuses reached in this EITF involve detailed illustrations of models applied to freestanding contracts that are indexed to, and potentially settled in, a company's own stock. Refer to the original statement for detailed guidance.

7 INVENTORY

PERSPECTIVE AND ISSUES

The accounting for inventories is a major consideration for many entities because of its significance on both the income statement (cost of goods sold) and the balance sheet. Inventories are defined in ARB 43, Chapter 4 as

> *...those items of tangible personal property which are held for sale in the ordinary course of business, are in the process of production for such sale, or are to be currently consumed in the production of goods or services to be available for sale.*

The complexity of accounting for inventories arises from several factors.

1. The high volume of activity (or turnover) in the account
2. The various cost flow alternatives
3. The classification of inventories

There are two types of entities for which we must consider the accounting for inventories. The merchandising entity (generally a retailer or wholesaler) has a single inventory account which is usually titled merchandise inventory. These are the goods on hand which are purchased for resale. The other type of entity is the manufacturer. The manufacturer generally has three types of inventory: (1) raw materials, (2) work in process, and (3) finished goods. Raw materials inventory represents the goods purchased which will act as inputs in the production process leading to the finished product. Work in process (WIP) consists of the goods entered into production, but not yet completed. Finished goods inventory is the completed product which is on hand awaiting sale.

In the case of either type of entity we are concerned with satisfying the same basic questions.

1. At what point in time should the items be included in inventory (ownership)?
2. What costs incurred should be included in the valuation of inventories?
3. What cost flow assumption should be used?
4. At what value should inventories be reported (LCM)?

The promulgated GAAP which addresses these questions is ARB 43, Chapter 4. ARB 43, Chapter 4 discusses the definition, valuation, and classification of inventory. APB 28 addresses the measurement and classification of inventories during interim periods. Finally, SFAS 48 and SFAS 49 both deal with inventory-related topics; SFAS 48 concerns revenue recognition when the buyer has the right to return the product, and SFAS 49 addresses product financing arrangements.

Sources of GAAP

ARB	*APB*	*SFAS*	*EITF*
43, Ch. 4; 51	20, 28, 29	48, 49	86-46

DEFINITIONS OF TERMS

Absorption (full costing). Inclusion of all manufacturing costs (fixed and variable) in the cost of finished goods inventory, in accordance with GAAP.

Base stock. Based on the theory that a minimal level of inventory is a permanent investment, this amount is carried on the books at its historical cost.

Ceiling. In lower of cost or market computations, market is limited to net realizable value. Market (replacement cost) cannot be higher than the ceiling (net realizable value). Net realizable value is selling price less selling costs and costs to complete.

Consignments. A marketing method in which the consignor ships goods to the consignee, who acts as an agent for the consignor in selling the goods. The inventory remains the property of the consignor until sold by the consignee.

Direct (variable) costing. Inclusion of only variable manufacturing costs in the cost of ending finished goods inventory. This method is not acceptable for financial reporting purposes.

Dollar-value LIFO. A variation of conventional LIFO in which layers of inventory are priced in dollars adjusted by price indexes, instead of layers of inventory priced at unit prices.

Double-extension. A method used to compute the conversion price index. The index indicates the relationship between the base-year and current prices in terms of a percentage.

Finished goods. The completed, but unsold, products produced by a manufacturing firm.

First-in, first-out (FIFO). A cost flow assumption; the first goods purchased or produced are assumed to be the first goods sold.

Floor. In lower of cost or market computations, market is limited to net realizable value less a normal profit, called the floor. Market (replacement cost) cannot be below the floor.

Goods in transit. Goods being shipped from seller to buyer at year end.

Gross profit method. A method used to estimate the amount of ending inventory based on the cost of goods available for sale, sales, and the gross profit percentage.

Inventory. Those items of tangible property which are held for sale in the normal course of business, are in the process of being produced for such purpose, or are to be used in the production of such items.

Inventory layer. Under the LIFO method, an increase in inventory quantity during a period.

Last-in, first-out (LIFO). A cost flow assumption; the last goods purchased are assumed to be the first goods sold.

LIFO conformity rule. An IRS requirement that if the LIFO method is used for tax purposes, it must also be used for financial reporting purposes.

LIFO liquidation. Liquidation of the LIFO base or old inventory layers when inventory quantities decrease. This can distort income since old costs are matched against current revenues.

LIFO retail. An inventory costing method which combines the LIFO cost flow assumption and the retail inventory method.

Link-chain. Method of applying dollar-value LIFO by developing a single cumulative index. This method may be used instead of double-extension only when there are substantial changes in product lines over the years.

Lower of cost or market. Inventories must be valued at lower of cost or market (replacement cost). Market cannot exceed the ceiling (net realizable value) or be less than the floor (net realizable value less a normal markup).

Markdown. A decrease below original retail price. A markdown cancelation is an increase (not above original retail price) in retail price after a markdown.

Markup. An increase above original retail price. A markup cancelation is a decrease (not below original retail price) in retail price after a markup.

Moving average. An inventory costing method used in conjunction with a perpetual inventory system. A weighted-average cost per unit is recomputed after every purchase. Goods sold are costed at the most recent moving average cost.

Parking transaction. An arrangement which attempts to remove inventory and a current liability from the balance sheet. See **Product financing arrangement**.

Periodic. An inventory system where quantities are determined only periodically by physical count.

Perpetual. An inventory system where up-to-date records of inventory quantities are kept.

Product financing arrangement. An arrangement whereby a firm buys inventory for another firm which agrees to purchase the inventory over a certain period at specified prices which include handling and financing costs.

Purchase commitment. A noncancelable commitment to purchase goods. Losses on such commitments are recognized in the accounts.

Raw materials. For a manufacturing firm, materials on hand awaiting entry into the production process.

Replacement cost. The cost to reproduce an inventory item by purchase or manufacture. In lower of cost or market computations, the term market means replacement cost, subject to the ceiling and floor limitations.

Retail method. An inventory costing method which uses a cost ratio to reduce ending inventory (valued at retail) to cost.

Specific identification. An inventory system where the seller identifies which specific items are sold and which remain in ending inventory.

Standard costs. Predetermined unit costs, which are acceptable for financial reporting purposes if adjusted periodically to reflect current conditions.

Weighted-average. A periodic inventory costing method where ending inventory and cost of goods sold are priced at the weighted-average cost of all items available for sale.

Work in process. For a manufacturing firm, the inventory of partially completed products.

CONCEPTS, RULES, AND EXAMPLES

Ownership of Goods

The purpose of examining and determining the proper ownership of inventories is to assist in the determination of the actual physical quantity of inventory on hand. In general, a firm should record purchases and sales of inventory when legal title passes. While strict adherence to this rule is not as important in daily transactions, a proper inventory cutoff at the end of an accounting period is crucial. Thus, for accounting purposes, it is necessary to determine when title has passed in order to obtain an accurate measurement of inventory quantity. The most common error made in this area is to assume that the entity has title only to the goods on hand. This may be incorrect in two ways: (1) the goods on hand may not be owned, and (2) goods that are not on hand may be owned. There are four areas which create a question as to proper ownership: (1) goods in transit, (2) consignment sales, (3) product financing arrangements, and (4) sales made with the buyer holding the right of return.

At year end, any **goods in transit** from seller to buyer must be included in one of those parties' inventories based on the conditions of the sale. Such goods are included in the inventory of the firm financially responsible for transportation costs. This responsibility may be indicated by shipping terms such as FOB, which is used in overland shipping contracts, and by FAS, CIF, C&F, and ex-ship, which are used in maritime contracts.

The term FOB stands for "free on board." If goods are shipped FOB destination, transportation costs are paid by the seller and title does not pass until the carrier delivers the goods to the buyer; thus, these goods are part of the seller's inventory while in transit. If goods are shipped FOB shipping point, transportation costs are paid by the buyer and title passes when the carrier takes possession; thus, these goods are part of the buyer's inventory while in transit. The terms FOB destination and FOB shipping point often indicate a specific location at which title to the goods is transferred, such as FOB Cleveland. This means that the seller retains title and risk of loss until the goods are delivered to a common carrier in Cleveland who will act as an agent for the buyer.

A seller who ships FAS (free alongside) must bear all expense and risk involved in delivering the goods to the dock next to (alongside) the vessel on which they are to be shipped. The buyer bears the cost of loading and of shipment; thus, title passes when the carrier takes possession of the goods.

In a CIF (cost, insurance, and freight) contract the buyer agrees to pay in a lump sum the cost of the goods, insurance costs, and freight charges. In a C&F contract, the buyer promises to pay a lump sum that includes the cost of the goods and all freight charges. In either case, the seller must deliver the goods to the carrier and pay the costs of loading; thus, both title and risk of loss pass to the buyer upon delivery of the goods to the carrier.

A seller who delivers goods ex-ship bears all expense and risk until the goods are unloaded, at which time both title and risk of loss pass to the buyer.

In **consignments,** the consignor (seller) ships goods to the consignee (buyer) who acts as the agent of the consignor in trying to sell the goods. In some consignments, the consignee receives a commission; in other arrangements, the consignee "purchases" the goods simultaneously with the sale of the goods to the customer. Goods out on consignment are included in the inventory of the consignor and excluded from the inventory of the consignee.

SFAS 49 addresses the problems involved with **product financing arrangements.** A product financing arrangement is a transaction in which an entity sells and agrees to repurchase inventory with the repurchase price equal to the original sales price plus the carrying and financing costs. The purpose of this transaction is to allow the seller (sponsor) to arrange financing of his/her original purchase of the inventory. The substance of the transaction is illustrated by the diagram below.

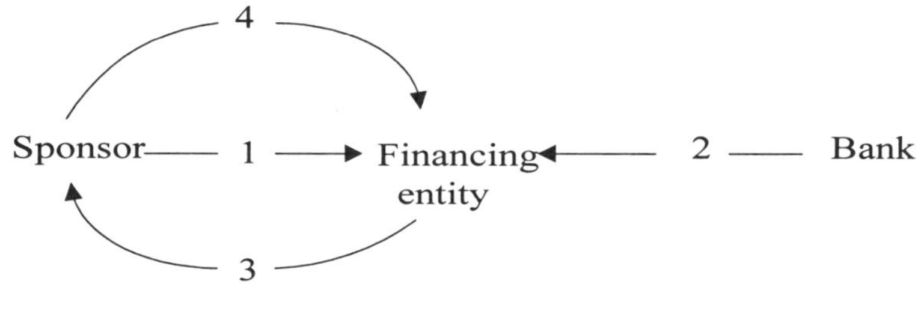

1. In the initial transaction the sponsor "sells" inventoriable items to the financing entity in return for the remittance of the sales price and at the same time agrees to repurchase the inventory at a specified price (usually the sales price plus carrying and financing costs) over a specified period of time.

2. The financing entity procures the funds remitted to the sponsor by borrowing from a bank (or other financial institution) using the newly purchased inventory as collateral.
3. The financing entity actually remits the funds to the sponsor and the sponsor presumably uses these funds to pay off the debt incurred as a result of the original purchase of the inventoriable debt.
4. The sponsor then repurchases the inventory for the specified price plus costs from the financing entity at a later time when the funds are available.

The purpose of this transaction was to enable the sponsor to acquire inventory and record sales without incurring additional reportable debt. The FASB ruled that the substance of this transaction is that of a borrowing transaction. That is, the transaction is, in substance, no different from the sponsor obtaining third-party financing to purchase his/her inventory. As a result, the FASB, in SFAS 49, ruled that the proper accounting is to record a liability when the funds are received for the initial transfer of the inventory in the amount of the selling price. The sponsor is then to accrue carrying and financing costs in accordance with his/her normal accounting policies. These accruals are eliminated and the liability satisfied when the sponsor repurchases the inventory. The inventory is **not** to be taken off the balance sheet of the sponsor and a sale is not to be recorded. Thus, although legal title has passed to the financing entity, for purposes of measuring and valuing inventory, the inventory is considered to be owned by the sponsor.

Another area which requires special consideration is the situation which exists when the buyer holds the **right of return**. SFAS 48 addresses the propriety of recognizing revenue at the point of sale under such a situation (this topic is discussed in detail in Chapter 8). Generally speaking, the sale is to be recorded if the future amount of the returns can be reasonably estimated. If the ability to make a reasonable estimate is precluded, then the sale is not to be recorded until the returns are unlikely. Thus, this too results in a situation where, although legal title has passed to the buyer, the seller must continue to include the goods in its measurement and valuation of inventory.

Accounting for Inventories

According to ARB 43, Chapter 4, a major objective of accounting for inventories is the matching of appropriate costs against revenues in order to arrive at the proper determination of periodic income. The accounting for inventories is done under either a periodic or perpetual system.

In a **periodic** inventory system, the inventory quantity is determined periodically by a physical count. The quantity so determined is then priced in accordance with the cost method used. Cost of goods sold is computed by adding beginning inventory and net purchases (or cost of goods manufactured) and subtracting ending inventory.

Alternatively, a **perpetual** inventory system keeps a running total of the quantity (and possibly the cost) of inventory on hand by recording all sales and purchases as they occur. When inventory is purchased, the inventory account (rather than purchases) is debited. When inventory is sold, the cost of goods sold and reduction of inventory are recorded. Periodic physical counts are necessary only to verify the perpetual records and to satisfy the tax regulations (tax regulations require that a physical inventory be taken, at least annually).

Valuation of Inventories

According to ARB 43, Chapter 4, the primary basis of accounting for inventories is cost. Cost is defined as the sum of the applicable expenditures and charges directly or indirectly incurred in bringing an article to its existing condition and location.

This definition allows for a wide interpretation of the costs to be included in inventory. For **raw materials** and merchandise inventory which are purchased outright, the identification of cost is relatively straightforward. The cost of these purchased inventories will include all expenditures incurred in bringing the goods to the point of sale and putting them in a salable condition. These costs include the purchase price, transportation costs, insurance, and handling costs.

It is important to note that purchases can be recorded at their gross amount or net of any allowable discount. If recorded at gross, the discounts taken represent a reduction in the purchase cost for purposes of determining cost of goods sold. On the other hand, if they are recorded at net, any lost discounts are treated as a financial expense, **not** part of cost of goods sold. The net method is considered to be theoretically preferable, but the gross method is simpler and, thus, more commonly used. Either method is acceptable under GAAP, provided that it is consistently applied.

The impact of interest costs as they relate to the valuation of inventoriable items (SFAS 34) is discussed in Chapter 8, Long-Lived Assets. Per APB 29, if similar items of inventory are exchanged with another entity, the earnings process is not culminated; the acquired items are recorded at the book value of the items given up.

Full absorption costing--GAAP. As we mentioned above, the basis for valuing any inventory is cost; the basis for establishing cost in a manufacturing firm is to include both acquisition and production costs. This concept is commonly referred to as absorption or full costing. As a result, the **WIP** and **finished goods** inventory accounts are to include an appropriate portion of direct materials, direct labor, and indirect production costs (both fixed and variable). The difficulty in determining the cost for these manufacturing inventory accounts is in the allocation of indirect costs. Prior to the Tax Reform Act of 1986, production costing for GAAP and for income tax purposes was very similar. However, the Act has changed inventory costing for tax purposes by requiring certain additional indirect costs which are listed below to be capitalized rather than expensed.

ARB 43, Chapter 4 indicates that, under some circumstances, expenses related to an idle facility, excessive spoilage, double freight, and rehandling costs may be abnormal and, therefore, require treatment as period costs. On the other hand, there may be instances in which certain general and administrative expenses are directly related to the production process and, therefore, should be allocated to the WIP and finished goods inventory. ARB 43 also points out the fact that selling costs do not constitute inventory costs. The chart below shows items which would ordinarily be included in inventory to the extent such costs are incident to and necessary for production.

Indirect production costs typically included in inventory under full absorption

- Repairs
- Maintenance
- Utilities
- Rent
- Indirect labor
- Production supervisory wages
- Indirect materials and supplies
- Quality control and inspection
- Small tools not capitalized

Full absorption costing--Income taxes. TRA 1986 requires that manufacturing firms capitalize rather than expense these additional items.

1. Depreciation and amortization in excess of that reported in financial statements.
2. Percentage depletion in excess of cost.
3. Rework labor, scrap, and spoilage costs.
4. Allocable general and administrative costs related to the production function.

For tax purposes, these costs, as well as the indirect production costs listed above for inventory costing under GAAP, will be allocated to the WIP and finished goods inventory. Examples of general and administrative costs that must be allocated include payroll department costs, wages of security guards, and the president's salary. These new capitalization rules apply to taxable years beginning after December 31, 1986. However, beginning inventories for the first year of the change must be restated as if the change had been in effect. Both the restatement of beginning inventory for tax purposes and temporary differences originating in subsequent periods will require interperiod income tax allocation.

Uniform capitalization rules--Tax vs. financial. The Tax Reform Act of 1986, which established new uniform capitalization rules for inventory costs for tax purposes, has raised new accounting issues. These issues were considered by the Emerging Issues Task Force (Issue no. 86-46) and involve whether the costs capitalized for tax purposes should also be capitalized under generally accepted accounting principles and if so, whether the new costing method would be preferable for purposes of justifying a change in accounting principle.

The Task Force reached a consensus that capitalizing a cost for tax purposes does not indicate that it is preferable or appropriate to capitalize the cost for financial reporting purposes. Although the cost may be capitalized for financial purposes, an enterprise must analyze its individual facts and circumstances and determine whether to capitalize based on the nature of its operations and industry practice.

Direct costing. The alternative to absorption costing is direct costing. Direct costing is also referred to as variable costing and requires classifying only direct materials, direct labor, and variable overhead related to production as inventory costs. All fixed costs are accounted for as period costs. ARB 43, Chapter 4 indicates that the exclusion of all overhead from inventory costs does not constitute an accepted accounting procedure. This has typically been interpreted to mean that direct costing is not allowable for GAAP. Treasury regulations require the inclusion of overhead for tax purposes.

Inventory capitalization for retailers/wholesalers--GAAP and income taxes. Retailers/wholesalers have previously recorded their inventory as the invoice price plus the cost of freight-in under both GAAP and tax law. However, the Tax Reform Act of 1986 now requires that additional costs be capitalized. These new uniform capitalization rules apply to all inventories except for the inventories of retailers/wholesalers whose average annual gross receipts do not exceed $10 million a year for the 3 preceding years. The costs which must be capitalized have been divided into two categories. The first category is direct costs and includes the inventory invoice price plus transportation. Also included in direct costs is the cost of labor for purchasing, storing, and handling inventory items. The second category is indirect costs and consists of any costs that directly benefit or are incurred because of the performance of a resale activity. The following types of indirect costs must be capitalized:

1. Off-site storage or warehousing
2. Purchasing
3. Handling, processing, assembly, and repackaging
4. Allocable general and administrative costs related to the above three functions

The indirect costs are allocated between inventory and cost of goods sold by using traditional methods (specific identification, standard costing methods, etc.) or one of three simplified methods. These new rules are effective for taxable years beginning after December 31, 1986, and require that the beginning inventory for the first year of application be restated to comply with the new capitalization rules. Both the restatement of beginning inventory for tax purposes and temporary differences originating in subsequent periods will require interperiod income tax allocation.

Specific identification. The theoretical basis for valuing inventories and cost of goods sold requires assigning the production and/or acquisition costs to the specific goods to which they relate. This method of inventory valuation is usually referred to as specific identification. Specific identification is generally not practical as the product will generally lose its separate identity as it passes through the production and sales process. Exceptions to this would arise in situations involving small inventory quantities with high unit value and low turnover rate. Because of the limited applicability of specific identification, it is necessary to make certain assumptions regarding the cost flows associated with inventory. These cost flows may or may not reflect the physical flow of inventory in the organization.

Cost Flow Assumptions

According to ARB 43, Chapter 4

> *...cost for inventory purposes shall be determined under any one of several assumptions as to the flow of cost factors; the major objective in selecting a method should be to choose the one which, under the circumstances, most clearly reflects periodic income.*

The most common cost flow assumptions used are (1) first-in, first-out (FIFO), (2) last-in, first-out (LIFO), and (3) weighted-average. Additionally, there are variations to each of these assumptions which are commonly used in practice.

In selecting the cost flow assumption to be used the entity should give thought to a variety of considerations. First, the industry norm should be examined as this will facilitate interfirm comparison. Recall that ARB 43 specified the major objective of such a selection "should be to choose the one which most clearly reflects periodic income." This will vary depending on the nature of the industry and the expected economic climate. The method which should be selected in a period of rising prices differs from that which is most applicable for declining prices. Each of the foregoing assumptions and their relative advantages or disadvantages are discussed below. Examples are provided to enhance the understanding of the application.

First-In, First-Out (FIFO)

The **FIFO method** of inventory valuation assumes that the first goods purchased are the first goods used or sold, regardless of the actual physical flow. This method is thought to most closely parallel the physical flow of the units in most industries. The strength of this cost flow assumption lies in the inventory amount reported on the balance sheet. Because the earliest goods purchased are the first ones removed from the inventory account, the remaining balance is composed of items at the latest cost. This yields results similar to those obtained under current cost accounting on the balance sheet. However, the FIFO method does not necessarily reflect the most accurate income figure as historical costs are being matched against current revenues.

The following example illustrates the basic principles involved in the application of FIFO:

	Units available	*Units sold*	*Actual unit cost*	*Actual total cost*
Beginning inventory	100	--	$2.10	$210
Sale	--	75	--	--
Purchase	150	--	2.80	420
Sale	--	100	--	--
Purchase	50	--	3.00	150
Total	300	175		$780

Given these data, the cost of goods sold and ending inventory balance are determined as follows:

	Units	*Unit cost*	*Total cost*
Cost of goods sold	100	$2.10	$210
	75	2.80	210
	175		$420
Ending inventory	50	3.00	$150
	75	2.80	210
	125		$360

Notice that the total of the units in cost of goods sold and ending inventory, as well as the sum of their total costs, is equal to the goods available for sale and their respective total costs.

The unique characteristic of the FIFO method is that it provides the same results under either the periodic or perpetual system.

Last-In, First-Out (LIFO)

The **LIFO method** of inventory valuation assumes that the last goods purchased are the first goods used or sold. This allows the matching of current costs with current revenue and, as proponents of the method argue, provides the best measure of periodic income which is the major objective stated in ARB 43. However, unless costs remain relatively unchanged, the LIFO method will usually misstate the ending inventory balance for balance sheet purposes because inventory usually consists of costs from earlier periods. Critics of the method also point out that LIFO does not usually follow the physical flow of merchandise or materials. However, this last argument should not affect the selection of a cost flow assumption, because the matching of physical flow is not considered to be an objective of accounting for inventories.

The LIFO method is not a promulgated accounting principle. Rather, the basis for LIFO is found in the Internal Revenue Code (the Code) §472 and, as such, is a tax concept. The treasury regulations indicate that any taxpayer who takes inventories may select LIFO application to any or all of his/her inventoriable items. This election is made with the taxpayer's tax return on Form 970 after the close of any taxable year. Partial adoption of LIFO is allowed for both accounting and tax purposes. (See the appendix to this chapter for a further discussion of partial adoption of LIFO for accounting purposes.)

Once elected, the LIFO method must continue to be used in future periods. In order to revert to another method, the taxpayer must apply for a change in accounting method on Form 3115 within the first 180 days of the taxable year during which the change is desired. A change to or from the LIFO method is an accounting change per APB 20 (see Chapter 20).

LIFO restrictions. In addition, for tax reporting purposes a taxpayer must adhere to the following two significant restrictions for the portions of its inventory valued under LIFO:

1. The inventory is to be valued at cost regardless of market value (i.e., application of the lower of cost or market rule is not allowed).
2. The taxpayer may not use a different inventory method in ascertaining profit or loss of the entity for external financial reports (i.e., if LIFO is elected for tax purposes, it must also be used for accounting purposes). This is known as the **LIFO conformity rule**. (See the appendix to this chapter for exceptions to this rule.)

The actual implementation of LIFO requires the valuation of the quantity of ending inventory at earlier prices. The quantity of ending inventory on hand in the year of election is termed the "base layer." This inventory is valued at actual (full absorption) cost, and unit cost is determined by dividing total cost by the quantity on hand. In subsequent periods, increases in the quantity of inventory on hand are referred to as increments, or **LIFO layers**. These increments are valued individually by applying one of the following costs to the quantity of inventory representing a layer:

1. The actual cost of the goods most recently purchased or produced.
2. The actual cost of the goods purchased or produced in order of acquisition.
3. An average unit cost of all goods purchased or produced during the current year.
4. A hybrid method which will more clearly reflect income (for tax purposes, this method must meet with the approval of the IRS Commissioner).

Thus, after using the LIFO method for 5 years, it is possible that an enterprise could have ending inventory consisting of the base layer and five additional layers (or increments) provided that the quantity of ending inventory increased every year.

The single goods (unit) LIFO approach is illustrated in the following example:

XYZ Co. is in its first year of operation and elects to use the periodic LIFO method of inventory valuation. The company sells only one product. XYZ will apply the LIFO method using the order of current year acquisition cost. The following data are given for years 1 through 3:

	Units	Unit cost	Total cost
Year 1			
Purchase	200	$2.00	$400
Sale	100	--	--
Purchase	200	3.00	600
Sale	150	--	--
Year 2			
Purchase	300	$3.20	$960
Sale	200	--	--
Purchase	100	3.30	330
Year 3			
Purchase	100	$3.50	$350
Sale	200	--	--
Sale	100	--	--

In year 1 the following occurred:

1. The total goods available for sale were 400 units.
2. The total sales were 250 units.
3. Therefore, the ending inventory was 150 units.

The ending inventory is valued at the earliest current year acquisition cost of $2.00 per unit. Thus, ending inventory is valued at $300 (150 x $2.00).

Another way to look at this is to analyze both cost of goods sold and ending inventory.

	Units	Unit cost	Total cost
Cost of goods sold	200	$3.00	$600
	50	2.00	100
	250		$700
Ending inventory	150	2.00	$300

Note that the base-year cost is $2.00 and that the base-year level is 150 units. Therefore, if ending inventory in the subsequent period exceeds 150 units, a new layer will be created.

Year 2	Units	Unit cost	Total cost
Cost of goods sold	100	$3.30	$330
	100	3.20	320
	200		$650
Ending inventory	150	2.00	$300
	200	3.20	640
	350		$940

Now, if ending inventory exceeds 350 units in the next period, a new layer will be created.

Year 3	*Units*	*Unit cost*	*Total cost*
Cost of goods sold	100	$3.50	$350
	200	3.20	640
	300		$990
Ending inventory base year	150	2.00	$300

Notice how the decrement of 200 units in year 3 eliminated the entire year 2 increment. Thus, any year 4 increase in the quantity of inventory would result in a **new** increment which would be valued at year 4 prices.

In situations where the ending inventory decreases from the level established at the close of the preceding year, the enterprise experiences a decrement or **LIFO liquidation**. Decrements will reduce or eliminate previously established LIFO layers. Once any part of a layer has been eliminated, it **cannot** be reinstated. For example, if in its first year after the election of LIFO an enterprise establishes a layer (increment) of 10 units, then in the next year inventory decreases by 4 units leaving the first layer at 6 units, the enterprise cannot reestablish the first layer (back up to 10 units) in the year that inventory next increases. Rather, it will be forced to create a new layer for the increase. The effect of LIFO liquidations in periods of rising prices is to release costs, which are significantly below the current cost being paid, into cost of goods sold from ending inventory. Thus, the resultant effect of a LIFO liquidation is to increase income for **both** accounting and tax purposes. Because of this, LIFO is most commonly used by industries in which inventories are maintained or increased.

LIFO liquidations can take two forms, voluntary or involuntary. A voluntary liquidation exists when an enterprise decides, for one reason or another, to let inventory levels drop. Such a liquidation occurs because current prices may be too high, less inventory is needed for efficient production, or maybe because of a transition in the product lines. Involuntary LIFO liquidations stem from reasons beyond the control of the enterprise, such as a strike, shortages, shipping delay, etc. Regardless of the reason, all liquidations result in a corresponding increase in income (assuming rising prices).

To compute the effect of the liquidation, the company must compute the difference between actual cost of sales and what cost of sales would have been had the inventory been reinstated. The Internal Revenue Service has ruled that this hypothetical reinstatement must be computed under the company's normal pricing procedures for valuing its LIFO increments. In the above example the effect of the year 3 LIFO liquidation would be computed as follows:

Inventory reinstatement:

200 units @ $3.50 – $3.20 = $60

Because the 200 units liquidated would have been stated at the year 3 price of $3.50 if there had been an increment, the difference between $3.50 and the actual amount charged to cost of sales for these units ($3.20) measures the effect of the liquidation.

The following is considered acceptable disclosure for both tax and financial reporting purposes in the event of a LIFO liquidation:

> During 1999, inventory quantities were reduced. This reduction resulted in a liquidation of LIFO inventory quantities carried at lower costs prevailing in prior years as compared with the cost of 1999 purchases, the effect of which decreased cost of goods sold by approximately $xxx and increased net income by approximately $xx or $x per share.

An inordinate amount of record keeping is required in applying the unit LIFO method. Remember that the illustration above involved only one product. The record keeping is much greater as the number of products increases. For this reason a "pooling" approach is generally applied to LIFO inventories.

Pooling is the process of grouping items which are naturally related and then treating this group as a single unit in determining the LIFO cost. Because the quantity of ending inventory includes many more items, decreases in one item can be made up for by increases in others, whereas under the single goods unit approach a decrease in any one item results in a liquidation of LIFO layers.

The problem in applying the pooling method emanates from the tax regulations, not the practical side of application. In applying LIFO, the tax regulations state that each type of good in the opening inventory must be compared with a similar type in the closing inventory. These items must be similar as to character, quality, and price. This qualification has generally been interpreted to mean identical. The effect of this statement is to require a separate pool for each item under the unit LIFO method. The need for a simpler, more practical approach to using the LIFO concept and allowing for a greater use of the pooling concept was met by dollar-value LIFO.

Dollar-Value LIFO

Use of dollar-value LIFO may be elected by any taxpayer. The dollar-value LIFO method of inventory valuation determines the cost of inventories by expressing base-year costs in terms of total dollars rather than specific prices of specific units. As discussed later, the dollar-value method also gives rise to an expanded interpretation of the use of pools. Increments and liquidations are treated the same, but are reflected only in terms of a **net** liquidation or increment for the entire pool.

Creating pools. Essentially three alternatives exist for determining pools under dollar-value LIFO: (1) the natural business unit, (2) multiple pools, and (3) pools for wholesalers, retailers, jobbers, etc.

The natural business unit is defined by the existence of separate and distinct processing facilities and operations and the maintenance of separate income (loss) records. The concept of the natural business unit is generally dependent upon the type of product, not the various stages of production for that project. Thus, the pool can (and will) contain raw materials, WIP, and finished goods. The three examples below, taken from the treasury regulations, illustrate the application of the natural business unit concept.

Example 1

A corporation manufactures, in one division, automatic clothes washers and dryers of both commercial and domestic grade as well as electric ranges, mangles, and dishwashers. The corporation manufactures, in another division, radios and television sets. The manufacturing facilities and processes used in manufacturing the radios and television sets are distinct from those used in manufacturing the automatic clothes washers, etc. Under these circumstances, the enterprise would consist of two business units and two pools would be appropriate: one consisting of all of the LIFO inventories involved with the manufacture of clothes washers and dryers, electric ranges, mangles, and dishwashers and the other consisting of all of the LIFO inventories involved with the production of radios and television sets.

Example 2

A taxpayer produces plastics in one of its plants. Substantial amounts of the production are sold as plastics. The remainder of the production is shipped to a second plant of the taxpayer for the production of plastic toys which are sold to customers. The taxpayer operates its plastics plant and toy plant as separate divisions. Because of the different product lines and the separate divisions, the taxpayer has two natural business units.

Example 3

A taxpayer is engaged in the manufacture of paper. At one stage of processing, uncoated paper is produced. Substantial amounts of uncoated paper are sold at this stage of processing. The remainder of the uncoated paper is transferred to the taxpayer's finishing mill where coated paper is produced and sold. This taxpayer has only one natural business unit since coated and uncoated paper are within the same product line.

The treasury regulations require that a pool shall consist of all items entering into the entire inventory investment of a natural business unit, unless the taxpayer elects to use the multiple-pooling method.

The multiple-pooling method is the grouping of substantially similar items. In determining substantially similar items, consideration should be given to the processing applied, the interchangeability, the similarity of use, and the customary practice of the industry. While the election of multiple pools will necessitate additional recordkeeping, it may result in a better estimation of periodic income.

According to Reg. §1.472-8(c), inventory items of wholesalers, retailers, jobbers, and distributors are to be placed into pools by major lines, types, or classes of goods. The natural business unit method may be used with permission of the commissioner.

All three methods of pooling allow for a change in the components of inventory. New items which properly fall within the pool may be added, and old items may disappear from the pool, but neither will necessarily effect a change in the total dollar value of the pool.

Computing dollar-value LIFO. The purpose of the dollar-value LIFO method of valuing inventory is to convert inventory which is priced at end-of-year prices to that same inventory priced at base-year (or applicable LIFO layer) prices. The dollar-value method achieves this result through the use of a conversion price index. The inventory at current year cost is divided by the appropriate index to arrive at the base-year cost. Thus, the main focus is on the determination of the conversion price index. There are four basic methods that can be used in the computation of the LIFO value of a dollar-value pool: (1) double-extension, (2) link-chain, (3) the index method, and (4) the alternative LIFO method for auto dealers. Each of these is discussed below with examples provided where appropriate.

Double-extension method. This was the method originally developed to compute the conversion price index. It involves extending the entire quantity of ending inventory for the current year at both base-year prices and end-of-year prices to arrive at a total dollar value for each, hence the title of double-extension. The end-of-year dollar total is then divided by the base-year dollar total to arrive at the index, usually referred to as the conversion price index. This index indicates the relationship between the base-year and current prices in terms of a percentage. Each layer (or increment) is valued at its own percentage. Although a representative sample is allowed (meaning that not all of the items need be double-extended; this is discussed in more detail under indexing), the recordkeeping under this method is very burdensome. The base-year price must be kept for each inventory item. Depending upon the number of different items included in the inventory of the company, the necessary records may be too detailed to keep past the first year.

The following example illustrates the double-extension method of computing the LIFO value of inventory. The example presented is relatively simple and does not attempt to incorporate all of the complexities of inventory accounting.

Example

ABC, Inc. uses the dollar-value method of LIFO inventory valuation and computes its price index using the double-extension method. ABC has a single pool which contains two inventory items, A and B. Year 1 is the company's initial year of operations. The following information is given for years 1 through 4:

Year	*Ending inventory current prices*	*Ending quantity (units) and current price*			
		A		*B*	
1	$100,000	5,000	$6.00	7,000	$10.00
2	120,300	6,000	6.30	7,500	11.00
3	122,220	5,800	6.40	7,400	11.50
4	133,900	6,200	6.50	7,800	12.00

In year 1 there is no computation of an index; the index is 100%. The LIFO cost is the same as the actual current year cost. This is our base year.

In year 2 the first step is to double extend the quantity of ending inventory at base-year and current year costs. This is illustrated below.

Item	*Quantity*	*Base-year cost/unit*	*Extended*	*Current year cost/unit*	*Extended*
A	6,000	$ 6.00	$ 36,000	$ 6.30	$ 37,800
B	7,500	10.00	75,000	11.00	82,500
			$111,000		$120,300*

* *When using the double-extension method and extending* ***all*** *of the inventory items to arrive at the index, this number must equal the ending inventory at current prices. If a sampling method is used (as discussed under indexing) this number* ***divided by*** *your ending inventory at current prices will give you the percentage sampled.*

Now we can compute the conversion price index which is

$$\frac{\text{Ending inventory at current year prices}}{\text{Ending inventory at base-year prices}}$$

In this case $\frac{120{,}300}{111{,}000}$ = 108.4% (rounded)

Next, compute the year 2 layer at the base-year cost by taking the current year ending inventory at base-year prices (if you only extend a sample of the inventory, this number is arrived at by dividing the ending inventory at current year prices by the conversion price index) of $111,000 and subtracting the base-year cost of $100,000. In year 2 we have an increment (layer) of $11,000 at base-year costs.

The year 2 layer of $11,000 at base-year cost must be converted so that the layer is valued at the prices in effect when it came into existence (i.e., at year 2 prices). This is done by multiplying the increment at base-year cost ($11,000) by the conversion price index (1.08). The result is the year 2 layer at LIFO prices.

Base-year cost	$100,000
Year 2 layer ($11,000 x 1.084)	11,924
	$111,924

In year 3 the same basic procedure is followed.

Item	*Quantity*	*Base-year cost/unit*	*Extended*	*Current year cost/unit*	*Extended*
A	5,800	$ 6.00	$ 34,800	$ 6.40	$ 37,120
B	7,400	10.00	74,000	11.50	85,100
			$108,800		$122,220

There has been a decrease in the base-year cost of the ending inventory which is referred to as a decrement. A decrement results in the decrease (or elimination) of previously provided layers. In this situation, the computation of the index is not necessary as there is no LIFO layer that requires a valuation. If a sampling approach has been used, the index is needed to arrive at the ending inventory at base-year cost and thus determine if there has been an increment or decrement.

Now the ending inventory at base-year cost is $108,800. The base-year cost is still $100,000, so the total increment is $8,800. Since this is less than the $11,000 increment of year 2, no additional increment is established in year 3. The LIFO cost of the inventory is as shown below.

Base-year cost	$100,000
Year 2 layer ($8,800 x 1.084)	9,539
	$109,539

The fourth year then follows the same steps.

Items	Quantity	Base-year cost/unit	Extended	Current year cost/unit	Extended
A	6,200	$ 6.00	$ 37,200	$ 6.50	$ 40,300
B	7,800	10.00	78,000	12.00	93,600
			$115,200		$133,900

The conversion price index is 116.2% (133,900/115,200).

A current year increment exists because the ending inventory at base-year prices in year 4 of $115,200 exceeds the year 3 number of $108,800. The current year increment of $6,400 must be valued at year 4 prices. Thus, the LIFO cost of the year 4 inventory is

Base-year layer	$100,000
Year 2 layer ($8,800 x 1.084)	9,539
Year 4 layer ($6,400 x 1.162)	7,437
	$116,976

It is important to point out that once a layer is reduced or eliminated it is never replaced (as with the year 2 increment).

Link-chain method. As seen in this example, the computations for application become arduous even if only a few items exist in the inventory. Also, consider the problems that arise when there is a constant change in the inventory mix or in situations in which the breadth of the inventory is large. The link-chain method of applying dollar-value LIFO was developed to combat these problems.

Another purpose served by the link-chain method is to eliminate the problem created by a significant turnover in the components of inventory. Under the double-extension or indexing method, the regulations require that any new products added to the inventory be costed at base-year prices. If these are not available, then the earliest cost available after the base year is used. If the item was not in existence in the base year, the taxpayer may reconstruct the base cost, using a reasonable method to determine what the cost would have been if the item had been in existence in the base year. Finally, as a last resort, the purchase price can be used. While this does not appear to be a problem on the surface, imagine a base period which is 25 to 50 years in the past. The difficulty involved with finding the base-year cost may require using a more current cost, thus eliminating some of the LIFO benefit. Also imagine a situation faced by a "hi-tech" industry where inventory is continually being replaced by newer, more advanced products. The effect of this rapid change under the double-extension method (because the new products didn't exist in the base period) is to use current prices as base-year costs. Thus, when inventory has such a rapid turnover, the LIFO advantage is nonexistent as current and base-year costs are sometimes synonymous. This is the major reason for the development of the link-chain method.

The link-chain method was originally developed for (and limited to) those companies that wanted to use LIFO but, because of a substantial change in product lines over time, were unable to recreate or keep the historical records necessary to make accurate use of the double-extension method. It is important to note that the double-extension and link-chain methods are not selective alternatives for the same situation. For tax purposes, the link-chain election **requires** that substantial change in product line be evident over the years, and it is not electable because of its ease of application. The double-extension and index methods must be demonstrated as impractical in order to elect the link-chain method. However, a company may use different computational techniques for financial reporting and tax purposes. Therefore, the link-chain method could be used for financial reporting purposes even if a different application is used for tax purposes.

The link-chain method is the process of developing a single cumulative index which is applied to the ending inventory amount priced at the beginning of the year costs. A separate cumulative index is used for each pool regardless of the variations in the components of these pools over the years. Technological change is allowed for by the method used to calculate each current year index. The index is derived by double extending a representative sample (generally thought to be between 50% and 75% of the dollar value of the pool) at both beginning-of-year prices and end-of-year prices. This annual index is then applied (multiplied) to the previous period's cumulative index to arrive at the new current year cumulative index.

An example of the link-chain method is shown below. Notice that the end-of-year costs and inventory quantity used are the same as those used in the double-extension example.

Assume the following inventory data for years 1-4. Year 1 is assumed to be the initial year of operation for the company. The LIFO method is elected on the first tax return. Assume that A and B constitute a single pool.

	Ending inventory	*Cost per unit*		*Extension*	
Product	*quantity*	*Beg. of yr.*	*End of yr.*	*Beginning*	*End*
Year 1:					
A	5,000	N/A	$ 6.00	N/A	30,000
B	7,000	N/A	10.00	N/A	70,000
Year 2:					
A	6,000	$ 6.00	6.30	36,000	37,800
B	7,500	10.00	11.00	75,000	82,500
Year 3:					
A	5,800	6.30	6.40	36,540	37,120
B	7,400	11.00	11.50	81,400	85,100
Year 4:					
A	6,200	6.40	6.50	39,680	40,300
B	7,800	11.50	12.00	89,700	93,600

The initial year (base year) does not require the computation of an index under any LIFO method. The base-year index will always be 1.00.

Thus, the base-year inventory layer is $100,000 (the end-of-year inventory restated at base-year cost).

The second year requires the first index computation. Notice that in year 2 our extended totals are:

	Beginning-of-year prices	*End-of-year prices*
A	$ 36,000	$ 37,800
B	75,000	82,500
	$111,000	$120,300

The year 2 index is 1.084 (120,300/111,000). This is the same as computed under the double-extension method because the beginning-of-the-year prices reflect the base-year price. This will not always be the case, as sometimes new items may be added to the pool, causing a change in the index.

Thus, the cumulative index is the 1.084 current year index multiplied by the preceding year index of 1.00 to arrive at a link-chain index of 1.084.

This index is then used to restate the inventory to base-year cost by dividing the inventory at end-of-year dollars by the cumulative index: $120,300/1.084 = $111,000. The determination of the LIFO increment or decrement is then basically the same as the double-extension method. In year 2 the increment (layer) at base-year cost is $11,000 ($111,000 – 100,000). This layer must be valued at the prices effective when the layer was created, or extended at the cumulative index for that year. This results in an ending inventory at LIFO cost of

	Base-year cost	*Index*	*LIFO cost*
Base year	$100,000	1.00	$100,000
Year 2 layer	11,000	1.084	11,924
	$111,000		$111,924

The index for year 3 is computed as follows:

	Beginning-of-year prices	*End-of-year prices*
A	$ 36,540	$ 37,120
B	81,400	85,100
	$117,940	$122,220

122,220/117,940 = 1.036

The next step is to determine the cumulative index which is the product of the preceding year's cumulative index and the current year index, or 1.123 (1.084 x 1.036). The new cumulative index is used to restate the inventory at end-of-year dollars to base-year cost. This is accomplished by dividing the end-of-year inventory by the new cumulative index. Thus, current inventory at base-year cost is $108,833. In this instance we have experienced a decrement (a decrease from the prior year's $111,000). The determination of ending inventory is

	Base-year cost	Index	LIFO cost
Base year	$100,000	1.00	$100,000
Year 2 layer	8,833	1.084	9,575
Year 3 layer	--	1.123	--
	$108,833		$109,575

Finally, perform the same steps for the year 4 computation. The current year index is 1.035 (133,900/129,380). The new cumulative index is 1.162 (1.035 x 1.123). The base-year cost of the current inventory is $115,232 (133,900/1.162). Thus, LIFO inventory at the end of year 4 is

	Base-year cost	Index	LIFO cost
Base year	$100,000	1.00	$100,000
Year 2 layer	8,833	1.084	9,575
Year 3	--	1.123	--
Year 4 layer	6,399	1.162	7,435
	$115,232		$117,010

Notice how even though the numbers used were the same as those used in the double-extension example, the results were different (year 4 inventory under double extension was $116,976), however, not by a significant amount. It is much easier to keep track of beginning-of-the-year prices than it is to keep base-year prices, but perhaps more importantly, it is easier to establish beginning-of-the-year prices for **new items** than to establish their base-year price. This latter reason is why the link-chain method is so much more desirable than the double-extension. However, before electing or applying this method, a company must be able to establish a sufficient need as defined in the treasury regulations.

Indexing. Indexing methods can basically be broken down into two types: (1) an internal index and (2) an external index.

The internal index is merely a variation of the double-extension method. The regulations allow for a representative sample (or some other statistical method) of the inventory to be double extended. The representative index computed from the sample is then used to restate the inventory to base-year cost and to value the new layer.

The external index method involves using an index published by the Bureau of Labor Statistics (BLS) and applying this index to the inventory figures. This method was primarily limited to retailers initially; however, new regulations issued in 1981 permit these various indices to be used by small businesses (defined as 3-year average sales of less than $5 million) to 100% of the change and any other businesses to 80% of the change. We do not propose to discuss this application in detail because of its complexity and limited application. The reader is referred to Reg. §1.472-8(e)(3). It should also be noted that application of the 80% method has not yet been addressed by the FASB, but the Accounting Standards Executive Committee (AcSEC) did not support its use for financial reporting purposes. Thus, larger businesses must still use one of the other alternatives in computing the dollar-value index.

Automobile Dealers' Alternative LIFO Method

Beginning in September 1992 a simplified dollar-value method became available for use by retail automobile dealers for valuing inventory of new automobiles and new light-duty trucks. The use of this method and its acceptance for tax purposes is conditioned on the application of several LIFO sub-methods, definitions and special rules. The reader is referred to Rev. Proc. 92-79 for a further discussion of this method.

The GAAP herein described for the application of LIFO has been based upon tax rules rather than on financial accounting pronouncements. ARB 43, Chapter 4 cites LIFO as an acceptable inventory method but does not provide any specific rules regarding its implementation. The tax regulations, on the other hand, do provide specific rules for the implementation of LIFO and require financial statement conformity. For this reason, tax rules have essentially defined the financial accounting treatment of LIFO inventories. In recognition of the lack of authoritative accounting guidelines in the implementation of LIFO, the AICPA's Accounting Standards Division has prepared an Issues Paper on this topic. "Identification and Discussion of Certain Financial Accounting and Reporting Issues Concerning LIFO Inventories," prepared by the Task Force on LIFO Inventory Problems, is to identify financial accounting issues resulting from the use of LIFO. This paper describes numerous accounting problems in the use of LIFO and includes advisory conclusions for these problems. Issues Papers, however, do not establish standards of financial accounting. This Issues Paper is detailed in an appendix to this chapter.

Interim Treatment of LIFO

Interim reporting problems associated with LIFO are discussed on pages 719-720.

Weighted-Average

Another method of inventory valuation involves averaging and is commonly referred to as the weighted-average method. The cost of goods available for sale (beginning inventory and net purchases) is divided by the units available for sale to obtain a weighted-average unit cost. Ending inventory and cost of goods sold are then priced at this average cost. For example, assume the following data:

	Units available	*Units sold*	*Actual unit cost*	*Actual total cost*
Beginning inventory	100	--	$2.10	$210
Sale	--	75	--	--
Purchase	150	--	2.80	420
Sale	--	100	--	--
Purchase	50	--	3.00	150
Total	300	175		$780

The weighted-average cost is $780/300, or $2.60. Ending inventory is 125 units at $2.60, or $325; cost of goods sold is 175 units at $2.60, or $455.

When the weighted-average assumption is applied to a perpetual inventory system, the average cost is recomputed after each purchase. This process is referred to as a moving average. Sales are costed at the most recent average. This combination is called the moving average method and is applied below to the same data used in the weighted-average example above:

	Units on hand	*Purchases in dollars*	*Sales in dollars*	*Total cost*	*Inventory unit cost*
Beginning inventory	100	$ --	$ --	$210.00	$2.10
Sale (75 units @ $2.10)	25	--	157.50	52.50	2.10
Purchase (150 units, $420)	175	420.00	--	472.50	2.70
Sale (100 units @ $2.70)	75	--	270.00	202.50	2.70
Purchase (50 units, $150)	125	150.00	--	352.50	2.82

Cost of goods sold is 75 units at $2.10 and 100 units at $2.70, or $427.50.

Comparison of Cost Assumptions

Of the three basic cost flow assumptions, LIFO and FIFO produce the most extreme results, while results from using the weighted-average method generally fall somewhere in between. The selection of one of these methods involves a detailed analysis including a determination of the organization's objectives and the current and future economic state.

As mentioned above, in periods of rising prices the LIFO method is generally thought to best fulfill the objective set forth in ARB 43, Chapter 4 of providing the clearest measure of periodic income. It does not provide an accurate estimate of the inventory value in an inflationary environment; however, this can usually be overcome by the issuance of supplementary data. In periods of rising prices a prudent business should use the LIFO method because it will result in a decrease in the current tax liability when compared to other alternatives. Yet, in a deflationary period, the opposite is true.

FIFO is a balance sheet oriented costing method as it gives the most accurate estimate of the current value of the inventory account during periods of changing prices. In periods of rising prices, the FIFO method will result in higher taxes than the other alternatives, while in a deflationary period FIFO provides for a lesser tax burden. However, a major advantage of the FIFO method is that it is not subject to all of the regulations and requirements of the tax code as is LIFO.

The average methods do not provide an estimate of current cost information on either the balance sheet or income statement. The average method will not serve to minimize the tax burden, nor will it result in the highest burden among the various alternatives.

Although price trends and underlying objectives are important in the selection of a cost flow assumption, other considerations such as the risk of LIFO liquidations, cash flow, capital maintenance, etc., are also important but were not mentioned above.

Lower of Cost or Market (LCM)

As stated in ARB 43, Chapter 4

> *...a departure from the cost basis of pricing the inventory is required when the utility of the goods is no longer as great as its cost.... Where there is evidence that the utility of goods...will be less than cost...the difference should be recognized as a loss of the current period.*

The utility of the goods in question is generally considered to be their market value, thus the term **lower of cost or market**. For purposes of this calculation the term market is taken to mean the current **replacement cost** not to exceed a **ceiling** of the net realizable value (selling price less reasonably estimable costs of completion and disposal) nor fall below a **floor** of net realizable value adjusted for a normal profit margin.

LCM is applied regardless of the method used to determine cost with one exception: LCM is not applied in conjunction with the LIFO method of inventory valuation for tax purposes. This is stated in the treasury regulations as a requirement upon the adoption of the LIFO method. However, it is important to note that LCM/LIFO may be applied for financial reporting purposes. Appendix B provides additional guidance on LCM/LIFO for financial reporting.

LCM may be applied to either the entire inventory as a whole or to each individual inventory item. The primary objective for selecting between the alternative methods of applying the LCM rule is to select the one which most clearly reflects periodic income. Generally speaking, the rule is most commonly applied to the inventory on an item-by-item basis. The reason for this application is twofold.

1. It is required by tax purposes unless it involves practical difficulties, and
2. It provides the most conservative valuation of inventories, because decreases in the value of one item are not offset by increases in the value of another.

The application of these principles is illustrated in the example below. Assume the following information for products A, B, C, D, and E:

Item	*Cost*	*Replacement cost*	*Est. selling price*	*Cost to complete*	*Normal profit percentage*
A	$2.00	$1.80	$ 2.50	$0.50	24%
B	4.00	1.60	4.00	0.80	24%
C	6.00	6.60	10.00	1.00	18%
D	5.00	4.75	6.00	2.00	20%
E	1.00	1.05	1.20	0.25	12.5%

In applying the foregoing principles, you must first determine the market value and then compare this to historical cost. Market value is equal to the replacement cost, but cannot exceed the net realizable value (NRV) nor be below net realizable value less the normal profit percentage.

Market Determination

Item	*Cost*	*Replacement cost*	*NRV (ceiling)*	*NRV less profit (floor)*	*Market*	*LCM*
A	$2.00	$1.80	$2.00	$1.40	$1.80	$1.80
B	4.00	1.60	3.20	2.24	2.24	2.24
C	6.00	6.60	9.00	7.20	7.20	6.00
D	5.00	4.75	4.00	2.80	4.00	4.00
E	1.00	1.05	0.95	0.80	0.95	0.95

In the second table, NRV (ceiling) equals selling price less costs of completion (e.g., item A: $2.50 – .50 = $2.00). NRV less profit (floor) is self-descriptive [e.g., $2.50 – .50 – (24% x $2.50) = $1.40]. Market is replacement cost unless lower than the floor or higher than the ceiling. Finally, LCM is the lower of cost or market value selected in the above algorithm. Note that market must be designated before LCM is determined.

Although the rules for determining the designated market value may seem needlessly complex, there is logic behind those rules. Replacement cost is a valid measure of the future utility of the inventory item since increases or decreases in the purchase price generally foreshadow related increases or decreases in the selling price.

The ceiling and the floor provide safeguards against the recognition of either excessive profits or excessive losses in future periods in those instances where the selling price and replacement cost do not move in the same direction in a proportional manner. The ceiling avoids the recognition of additional losses in the future when the selling price is falling faster than replacement cost. Without the ceiling constraint, inventories would be carried at an amount in excess of their net realizable value. The floor avoids the recognition of abnormal profits in the future when replacement cost is falling faster than the selling price. Without the floor, inventories would be carried at a value less than their net realizable value minus a normal profit.

The loss from writing inventories down to LCM is generally reflected on the income statement in cost of goods sold. If material, the loss should be separately disclosed in the income statement. The writedown is recorded with a debit to a loss account and a credit either to an inventory or an allowance account.

Special Valuation Methods

There are instances in which an accountant must estimate the value of inventories. Whether the reason be for interim financial statements or as a check against perpetual records, the need for an inventory valuation without an actual physical count is required. Some of the methods used, which are discussed below, are the retail method, the LIFO retail method, and the gross profit method.

Retail method. The conventional retail method is used by retailers as a method to estimate the cost of their ending inventory. The retailer can either take a physical inventory at retail prices or estimate ending retail inventory and then use the cost-to-retail ratio derived under this method to convert the ending inventory at retail to its estimated cost. This eliminates the process of going back to original invoices or other documents in order to determine the original cost for each inventoriable item. The retail method can be used under any of the three cost flow assumptions discussed earlier: FIFO, LIFO, or average cost. As with ordinary FIFO or average cost, the LCM rule can also be applied to the retail method when either one of these two cost assumptions is used.

The key to applying the retail method is determining the cost-to-retail ratio. The calculation of this number varies depending upon the cost flow assumption selected. Essentially, the cost-to-retail ratio provides a relationship between the **cost** of goods available for sale and the **retail** price of these same goods. This ratio is used to convert the ending retail inventory back to cost. The computation of the cost-to-retail ratio for each of the available methods is described below. The use of the LIFO cost flow assumption with this method is discussed in the next section and, therefore, is not addressed in this listing.

1. **FIFO cost**--The concept of FIFO indicates that the ending inventory is made up of the latest purchases; therefore, beginning inventory is excluded from the computation of the cost-to-retail ratio, and the computation becomes net purchases divided by their retail value adjusted for both net markups and net markdowns.
2. **FIFO (LCM)**--The computation is basically the same as FIFO cost except that markdowns are excluded from the computation of the cost-to-retail ratio.
3. **Average cost**--Average cost assumes that ending inventory consists of all goods available for sale. Therefore, the cost-to-retail ratio is computed by dividing the cost of goods available for sale (Beginning inventory + Net purchases) by the retail value of these goods adjusted for both net markups and net markdowns.
4. **Average cost (LCM)**--Is computed in the same manner as average cost except that markdowns are excluded for the calculation of the cost-to-retail ratio.

A simple example illustrates the computation of the cost-to-retail ratio under both the FIFO cost and average cost methods in a situation where no markups or markdowns exist.

	FIFO cost			*Average cost*		
	Cost		*Retail*	*Cost*		*Retail*
Beginning inventory	$100,000		$ 200,000	$100,000		$ 200,000
Net purchases	500,000 (a)		800,000 (b)	500,000		800,000
Total goods available for sale	$600,000		1,000,000	$600,000 (c)		1,000,000 (d)
Sales at retail			(800,000)			(800,000)
Ending inventory--retail			$ 200,000			$ 200,000
Cost-to-retail ratio	(a)500,000 / (b)800,000	=	62.5%	(c) 600,000 / (d)1,000,000	=	60%

Ending inventory--cost		
200,000 x 62.5%	$ 125,000	
200,000 x 60%		$ 120,000

Note that the only difference in the two examples is the numbers used to calculate the cost-to-retail ratio.

As shown above, the lower of cost or market aspect of the retail method is a result of the treatment of net markups and net markdowns. **Net markups** (markups less markup cancellations) are net increases above the original retail price, which are generally caused by changes in supply and demand. **Net markdowns** (markdowns less markdown cancellations) are net decreases below the original retail price. An approximation of lower of cost or market is achieved by including net markups but excluding net markdowns from the cost-to-retail ratio.

To understand this approximation, assume a toy is purchased for $6, and the retail price is set at $10. It is later marked down to $8. A cost-to-retail ratio including markdowns would be $6 divided by $8 or 75%, and ending inventory would be valued at $8 times 75%, or $6 (original cost). A cost-to-retail ratio excluding markdowns would be $6 divided by $10 or 60%, and ending inventory would be valued at $8 times 60%, or $4.80 (LCM). The write-down to $4.80 reflects the loss in utility which is evidenced by the reduced retail price.

The application of the lower of cost or market rule is illustrated for both the FIFO and average cost methods in the example below. Remember, if the markups and markdowns below had been included in the previous example **both** would have been included in the cost-to-retail ratio.

	FIFO cost (LCM)			*Average cost (LCM)*		
	Cost		*Retail*	*Cost*		*Retail*
Beginning inventory	$100,000		$ 200,000	$100,000		$ 200,000
Net purchases	500,000(a)		800,000(b)	500,000		800,000
Net markups	--		250,000(b)	--		250,000
Total goods available for sale	$600,000		1,250,000	$600,000 (c)		1,250,000(d)
Net markdowns			(50,000)			(50,000)
Sales at retail			(800,000)			(800,000)
Ending inventory--retail			$ 400,000			$ 400,000
Cost-to-retail ratio	(a) 500,000 / (b)1,050,000	=	47.6%	(c) 600,000 / (d)1,250,000	=	48%
Ending inventory--cost						
400,000 x 47.6%			$ 190,400			
400,000 x 48%						$ 192,000

Notice that under the FIFO (LCM) method all of the markups are considered attributable to the current period purchases. While this is not necessarily accurate, it provides the most conservative estimate of the ending inventory.

There are a number of additional inventory topics and issues which affect the computation of the cost-to-retail ratio and, therefore, deserve some discussion. Purchase discounts and freight affect only the cost column in this computation. The sales figure which is subtracted from the adjusted cost of goods available for sale in the retail column must be gross sales after adjustment for sales returns. If sales are recorded at gross, then deduct the gross sales figure. If sales are recorded at net, then both the recorded sales and sales discount must be deducted to give the same effect as deducting gross sales (i.e., sales discounts are not included in the computation). Normal spoilage is generally allowed for in the firm's pricing policies, and for this reason it is deducted from the retail column **after** the calculation of the cost-to-retail ratio. Abnormal spoilage, on the other hand, should be deducted from **both** the cost and retail columns **before** the cost-to-retail calculation as it could distort the ratio. It is then generally reported as a loss separate from the cost of goods sold section. Abnormal spoilage is generally considered to arise from a major theft or casualty, while normal spoilage is usually due to shrinkage or breakage. These determinations and their treatments will vary depending upon the firm's policies.

When applying the retail method, separate computations should be made for any departments which experience significantly higher or lower profit margins. Distortions arise in the retail method when a department sells goods with varying margins in a proportion different from that purchased, in which case the cost-to-retail percentage would not be representative of the mix of goods in ending inventory. Also, manipulations of income are possible by planning the timing of markups and markdowns.

The retail method is an acceptable method of valuing inventories for tax purposes. The regulations require valuation at lower of cost or market (except for LIFO) and an annual physical inventory.

LIFO retail method. As with other LIFO concepts, the treasury regulations are the governing force behind the LIFO retail method. The regulations differentiate between a "variety" store which is required to use an internally computed index and a "department" store which can use a price index published by the Bureau of Labor Statistics. The computation of an internal index was previously discussed in the dollar-value LIFO section. It involves applying the double-extension method to a representative sample of the ending inventory. Selection of a published index is to be in accordance with the regulations set forth by the treasury.

The steps used in computing the value of ending inventory under the LIFO retail method are listed below and then applied to an example for illustrative purposes.

1. Calculate (or select) the current year conversion price index. Recall that in the base year this index will be 1.00.
2. Calculate the value of the ending inventory at both cost and retail. Remember, as with other LIFO methods, tax regulations **do not** permit the use of LCM, so both markups and markdowns are included in the computation of the cost-to-retail ratio. However, the beginning inventory is excluded from goods available for sale at cost and at retail.

3. Restate the ending inventory at retail to base-year retail. This is accomplished by dividing the current ending inventory at retail by the current year index determined in step 1.
4. Layers are then treated in the same fashion as they were for the dollar-value LIFO example presented earlier. If the ending inventory restated to base-year retail exceeds the previous year's amount at base-year retail, a new layer is established.
5. The computation of LIFO cost is the last step and requires multiplying each layer at base-year retail by the appropriate price index and multiplying this product by the cost-to-retail ratio in order to arrive at the LIFO cost for each layer.

The following example illustrates a two-year period to which the LIFO retail method is applied. The first period represents the first year of operations for the organization and, thus, is its base year.

Year 1

Step 1 -- Because this is the base year, there is no need to compute an index, as it will always be 1.00.

Step 2 --

	Cost	*Retail*
Beginning inventory	$ --	$ --
Purchases	582,400	988,600
Markups	--	164,400
Markdowns	--	(113,000)
Subtotal	$582,400	$1,040,000
Total goods available for sale	$582,400	$1,040,000
Sales--at retail		840,000
Ending year 1 inventory--at retail		$ 200,000

Cost-to-retail ratio $\frac{582,400}{1,040,000} = 56\%$

Ending inventory at cost
$200,000 x 56% $112,000

Step 3 -- Because this is the base year, the restatement to base-year cost is not necessary; however, the computation would be $200,000/1.00 = $200,000.

Steps 4 and 5 -- The determination of layers is again unnecessary in the base year; however, the computation would take the following format.

	Ending inventory at base-year retail	*Conversion price index*	*Cost-to-retail ratio*	*LIFO cost*
Base year ($200,000/1.00)	$200,000	1.00	0.56	$112,000

Year 2

Step 1 -- We make the assumption that the computation of an internal index yields a result of 1.12 (obtained by double extending a representative sample).

Step 2 --

	Cost	*Retail*
Beginning inventory	$112,000	$ 200,000
Purchases	716,300	1,168,500
Markups	--	87,500
Markdowns	--	(21,000)
Subtotal	$716,300	$1,235,000
Total goods available for sale		$1,435,000
Sales--at retail		1,171,800
Ending year 2 inventory--at retail		$ 263,200

Cost-to-retail ratio $\frac{716,300}{1,235,000}$ = 58%

Step 3 -- The restatement of ending inventory at current year retail to base-year retail is done using the index computed in step 1. In this case it is $263,200/1.12 = $235,000.

Steps 4 and 5 -- We know that there is a LIFO layer in year 2 because the $235,000 inventory at base-year retail exceeds the year 1 amount of $200,000.

The computation of the LIFO cost for each layer is shown below.

	Ending inventory at base-year retail	*Conversion price index*	*Cost-to-retail ratio*	*LIFO cost*
Base year ($200,000/1.00)	$200,000	1.00	0.56	$112,000
Year 2 layer	35,000	1.12	0.58	22,736
	$235,000			
Ending year 2 inventory at LIFO cost				$134,736

The treatment of subsequent increments and decrements is the same for this method as it is for the regular dollar-value method.

Gross profit method. The gross profit method is used to estimate ending inventory when a physical count is not possible or feasible. It can also be used to evaluate the reasonableness of a given inventory amount. The cost of goods available for sale is compared with the estimated cost of goods sold. For example, assume the following data:

Beginning inventory	$125,000
Net purchases	450,000
Sales	600,000
Estimated gross profit	32%

Ending inventory is estimated as follows:

Beginning inventory	$125,000
Net purchases	450,000
Cost of goods available for sale	575,000
Cost of goods sold [$600,000 – (32% x $600,000)] or (68% x $600,000)	408,000
Estimated ending inventory	$167,000

The gross profit method is used for interim reporting estimates, analyses by auditors, and estimates of inventory lost in fires or other catastrophes. The method is not acceptable for either tax or annual financial reporting purposes. Thus, its major purposes are for internal and interim reporting.

Other Cost Topics

Base stock. The base stock method assumes that a certain level of inventory investment is necessary for normal business activities and is, therefore, permanent. The base stock inventory is carried at historical cost. Decreases in the base stock are considered temporary and are charged to cost of goods sold at replacement cost. Increases are carried at current year costs. The base stock approach is seldom used in practice since it is not allowed for tax purposes, and the LIFO method gives similar results.

Standard costs. Standard costs are predetermined unit costs used by manufacturing firms for planning and control purposes. Standard costs are often incorporated into the accounts, and materials, work in process, and finished goods inventories are all carried at standard costs. The use of standard costs in financial reporting is acceptable if adjustments are made periodically to reflect current conditions and if its use approximates one of the recognized cost flow assumptions.

Relative sales value. Relative sales (or net realizable) values are used to assign costs to inventory items purchased or manufactured in groups. This method is applicable to joint products, subdivided assets such as real estate lots, and basket purchases.

A frequently used example is the costing of a joint product. For example, products A and B have the same processes performed on them up to the split-off point. The total cost incurred to this point is $80,000. This cost can be assigned to products A and B using their relative sales value at the split-off point. If A could be sold for $60,000 and B for $40,000, the total sales value is $100,000. The cost would be assigned on the basis of each product's relative sales value. Thus, A would be assigned a cost of $48,000 (60,000/100,000 x 80,000) and B a cost of $32,000 (400,000/100,000 x 80,000).

Other Inventory Topics

Purchase commitments. Purchase commitments generally are not recorded in the accounts because they are executory in nature. However, footnote disclosure is required for firm purchase commitments which are material in amount (ARB 43, Chapter 4).

If at year end the contract price on these commitments exceeds the market value, the estimated loss should be recognized in the accounts and reported in the income statement. Note that this results in recognition of loss before the asset is recognized on the books.

Inventories valued at selling price. In exceptional cases, inventories may be reported at sales price less disposal costs. Such treatment is justified when cost is difficult to determine, quoted market prices are available, marketability is assured, and units are interchangeable. Precious metals, certain agricultural products, and meat are examples of inventories valued in this manner (ARB 43). When inventory is valued above cost, revenue is recognized before the point of sale. Full disclosure in the financial statements is required.

Interim reporting. The principles used to determine ending inventory and cost of goods sold in annual reports are also used in interim reports, although four exceptions are allowed (APB 28). These are

1. The gross profit method may be used to estimate cost of goods sold and ending inventory.
2. When LIFO layers are liquidated during the interim period but are expected to be replaced by year end, cost of goods sold should reflect current costs rather than old LIFO costs.
3. Temporary market decline need not be recognized if substantial evidence exists that market prices will recover. If LCM losses recorded in one interim period are recovered by year end, the recovery is recognized as a gain.
4. Planned standard cost variances expected to be offset by year end can be deferred.

APPENDIX A

LIFO CONFORMITY RULE

As stated earlier in this chapter, Treasury Regulations require that in order to take advantage of LIFO for tax purposes, a company must also use LIFO for determining income, profit, or loss for financial statement purposes. The regulations also cite certain exceptions to this general rule. Among the exceptions allowable under the regulations are the following:

1. The use of an inventory method other than LIFO in presenting information reported as a supplement to or explanation of the taxpayer's primary presentation of income in financial reports to outside parties. [Reg. §1.472-2(e)(1)(i)]
2. The use of an inventory method other than LIFO to determine the value of the taxpayer's inventory for purposes of reporting the value of such inventory as an asset on the balance sheet. [Reg. §1.472-2(e)(1)(ii)]
3. The use of an inventory method other than LIFO for purposes of determining information reported in internal management reports. [Reg. §1.472-2(e)(1)(iii)]
4. The use of an inventory method other than LIFO for financial reports covering a period of less than 1 year. [Reg. §1.472- 2(e)(1)(iv)]
5. The use of lower of LIFO cost or market to value inventories for financial statements while using LIFO cost for tax purposes. [Reg. §1.472-2(e)(1)(v)]
6. For inventories acquired in a section 351 transaction, the use of the transferor's acquisition dates and costs for book purposes while using redetermined LIFO layers for tax purposes. [Reg. §1.472-2(e)(1)(vii)]
7. The inclusion of certain costs (under full absorption) in inventory for tax purposes, as required by regulations, while not including those same costs in inventory under GAAP, (full absorption) for book purposes. [Reg. §1.472-2(e)(8)(i)]
8. The use of different methods of establishing pools for book purposes and tax purposes. [Reg. §1.472-2(e)(8)(ii)]
9. The use of different determinations of the time sales or purchases are accrued for book purposes and tax purposes. [Reg. §1.472-2(e)(8)(xii)]
10. In the case of a business combination, the use of different methods to allocate basis for book purposes and tax purposes. [Reg. §1.472-2(e)(8)(xiii)]

Another important consideration in applying the LIFO conformity rule is the new law concerning related corporations. The Tax Reform Act of 1984 added a rule which states that all members of the same group of financially related corporations shall be treated as a single taxpayer when applying the conformity rule. Previously, taxpayers were able to circumvent the conformity rule by having a subsidiary on LIFO, while the non-LIFO parent presented combined non-LIFO financial statements. This practice will now be considered a violation of the conformity requirement [Sec. 472(g)], effective for years beginning after July 18, 1984.

APPENDIX B

TASK FORCE ON LIFO INVENTORY PROBLEMS

Most of the prescribed rules concerning the implementation of LIFO have their origins in the Internal Revenue Code and Treasury Regulations. Because authoritative financial accounting pronouncements on implementing LIFO are virtually nonexistent, GAAP has followed tax. The AICPA Task Force on LIFO Inventory problems has developed an Issues Paper to discuss certain financial accounting issues related to LIFO. Issues Papers constitute generally accepted accounting principles but are not mandatory. The key conclusions from this Issues Paper (entitled "Identification and Discussion of Certain Financial Accounting and Reporting Issues Concerning LIFO Inventories") are described below.

1. **Specific goods vs. dollar value**. The Task Force believes that either the specific goods approach or dollar value approach to LIFO is acceptable for financial reporting. They also believe that it is not necessary to disclose whether the specific goods or dollar value approach is used. TRA 1986 provides an election for qualifying small businesses to account for their inventories using a simplified dollar-value LIFO method.
2. **Pricing current year purchases**. Three approaches to pricing LIFO inventory increments are available under tax regulations--earliest acquisition price, latest acquisition price, and average acquisition price. The Task Force believes that the earliest acquisition price approach is the most compatible with financial reporting objectives, but finds all three to be acceptable for financial reporting.
3. **Quantity to use to determine price**. The Task Force believes that the price used to determine the inventory increment should be based on the cost of the quantity or dollars of the increment rather than on the cost of the quantity or dollars equal to the ending inventory. They also believe that it is not necessary to disclose which approach is used.
4. **Disclosure of LIFO reserve or replacement cost**. The Task Force believes that either the LIFO reserve or replacement cost and its basis for determination should be disclosed for financial reporting.
5. **Partial adoption of LIFO**. The Task Force believes that if a company changes to LIFO, it should do so for all of its inventories. Partial adoption should only be allowed if there exists a valid business reason for not fully adopting LIFO. A planned gradual adoption of LIFO over several time periods is considered acceptable if valid business reasons exist (lessening the income statement effect of adoption in any one year is not a valid business reason). The Task Force also believes that where partial adoption of LIFO has been justified, the extent to which LIFO has been adopted should be disclosed. This can be disclosed by indicating either the portion of the

ending inventory priced on LIFO or the portion of cost of sales resulting from LIFO inventories.

6. **Methods of pooling**. The Task Force addressed several issues related to establishing pools. They believe that an entity should have valid business reasons for establishing its LIFO pools. Additionally, it is believed that the existence of a separate legal entity that has no economic substance is not reason enough to justify separate pools. It is also believed that an entity's pooling arrangements need not be disclosed.
7. **New items entering a pool**. The Task Force believes that new items should be added to the pool based on what the items would have cost had they been acquired in the base period (reconstructed cost) rather than based on their current cost. The reconstructed cost should be determined based on the most objective sources available including published vendor price lists, vendor quotes, and general industry indexes. The Task Force believes it is not necessary to disclose the way that new items are priced.

   It is also believed that, where necessary, the use of a substitute base year in making the LIFO computation is acceptable.
8. **Dollar value index**. The required index can be developed using two possible approaches, the unit cost method or the cost component method. The unit cost method measures changes in the index based on the weighted-average increase or decrease to the unit costs of raw materials, work in process, and finished goods inventory. The cost component method, on the other hand, measures changes in the index by the weighted-average increase or decrease in the component costs of material, labor, and overhead that make up ending inventory. The Task Force believes that either of these methods are acceptable.
9. **LIFO liquidations**. The Task Force believes that the effects on income of LIFO inventory liquidations should be disclosed in the notes to the financial statements. A replacement reserve for the liquidation should not be provided. When an involuntary LIFO liquidation occurs, the Task Force does not believe that the income effect of the liquidation should be deferred.

   When a LIFO liquidation occurs there are three possible ways to measure its effect on income.

   a. The difference between actual cost of sales and what cost of sales would have been had the inventory been reinstated under the entity's normal pricing procedure
   b. The difference between actual cost of sales and what cost of sales would have been had the inventory been reinstated at year-end replacement cost
   c. The amount of the LIFO reserve at the beginning of the year which was credited to income (excluding the increase in the reserve due to current year price changes)

The Task Force supports the first method. It is also believed that disclosure of the effect of the liquidation should give effect only to pools with decrements (i.e., there should be no netting against increments in other pools).

10. **Lower of cost or market**. The Task Force believes that the most reasonable approach to applying the lower of cost or market rules to LIFO inventory is to base the determination on groups of inventory rather than on an item by item approach. They believe that a pool constitutes a reasonable grouping for this purpose. They also believe, however, that an item by item approach is permitted by authoritative accounting literature, particularly for obsolete or discontinued items.

    For companies with more than one LIFO pool, it would be permissible to aggregate the pools in applying the lower of cost or market test if the pools are similar. It is believed that where the pools are significantly dissimilar, aggregating the pools is not appropriate.

    The Task Force also believes that previous writedowns to market value of the cost of LIFO inventories should be reversed after a company disposes of the physical units of the inventory for which reserves were provided. The reserves at the end of the year should be based on a new computation of cost or market.

11. **LIFO conformity and supplemental disclosures.** The Task Force believes that a company may present supplemental non-LIFO disclosures within the historical cost framework. If nondiscretionary variable expenses (i.e., profit sharing based on earnings) would have been different based on the supplemental information, then the company should give effect to such changes. Additionally, the supplemental disclosure should reflect the same type of tax effects as required by generally accepted accounting principles in the primary financial statements.

    The Task Force also believes a company may use different LIFO applications for financial reporting than it uses for income tax purposes. Any such differences should be accounted for as temporary differences with the exception of differences in the allocation of cost to inventory in a business combination. They further believe that any differences between LIFO applications used for financial reporting and those used for income tax purposes need not be disclosed beyond the requirements of APB 11.

12. **Interim reporting and LIFO**. The Task Force's conclusions on interim reporting of LIFO inventory is discussed on pages 719-720.

13. **Different financial and income tax years**. The Task Force believes that a company which has a year end for financial reporting different from that for income tax reporting should make a separate LIFO calculation for financial purposes using its financial reporting year as a discrete period for that calculation.

14. **Business combinations accounted for by the purchase method**. Inventory acquired in a business combination accounted for by the purchase method will be recorded at fair market value at the date of the combination.

The acquired company may be able to carryover its prior basis for that inventory for tax purposes, causing a difference between book and tax basis. The Task Force believes that an adjustment should be made to the fair value of the inventory only if it is reasonably estimated to be liquidated in the future. The adjustment would be for the income tax effect of the difference between tax and book basis.

The Task Force further believes that inventory acquired in such a combination should be considered the LIFO base inventory if the inventory is treated by the company as a separate business unit or a separate LIFO pool. If instead the acquired inventory is combined into an existing pool, then the acquired inventory should be considered as part of the current year's purchases.

15. **Changes in LIFO applications**. The Task Force believes that a change in a LIFO application is a change in accounting principle under APB 20. LIFO applications refer to the approach (i.e., dollar value or specific goods), computational technique, or the numbers or contents of the pools.

The AICPA Task Force did not include intercompany transfers in the 1984 Issues Paper; however, the AICPA issued Practice Bulletin 2 in 1987 to provide guidance for this complex area.

The focus of this bulletin is the LIFO liquidation effect caused by transferring inventories which in turn create intercompany profits. This liquidation can occur when (1) two components of the same taxable entity transfer inventory, for example, when a LIFO method component transfers inventory to a non-LIFO component, or (2) when two separate taxable entities that consolidate transfer inventory, even though both use the LIFO method.

According to Practice Bulletin 2, this LIFO liquidation creates profit which must be eliminated along with the other intercompany profits eliminated in accordance with ARB 51.

8 SPECIAL REVENUE RECOGNITION AREAS

Revenue should be recognized when (1) it is realized or realizable and (2) it has been earned. This is the conceptual guideline given by SFAC 5 for the recognition of revenue (see the discussion in Chapter 3). For some transactions (such as retail grocery sales) the realization principle is very easily applied. However, in some industries, accountants have a very difficult time applying these criteria. As a result, several of the professional pronouncements have concentrated on revenue recognition for certain special areas.

This chapter addresses seven areas for which the circumstances of the transaction do not allow for the clear application of the revenue realization principle. These are as follows:

1. Long-term construction contracts
2. Service sales transactions
3. Sales when collection is uncertain
4. Revenue recognition when right of return exists
5. Profit recognition on real estate
6. Real estate operations
7. Franchising

Each of these seven sections may be read as individual units.

LONG-TERM CONSTRUCTION CONTRACTS

PERSPECTIVE AND ISSUES

Accounting for long-term construction contracts involves questions as to when revenue should be recognized and how to measure the revenue to be recorded. The basic generally accepted accounting principles underlying these questions are covered in ARB 45, *Long-Term Construction-Type Contracts.* In 1981, the AICPA issued Statement of Position 81-1, *Accounting for Performance of Construction-Type* and *Certain Production-Type Contracts* and the *Audit and Accounting Guide for Construction Contractors.* These pronouncements were later deemed preferable accounting principles by SFAS 56 as an amendment to SFAS 32. Both of these pronouncements were superseded by SFAS 111 after SAS 69 was issued; it specifies that AICPA SOP are in category B of GAAP. The FASB has not yet considered adopting the accounting and reporting principles in those pronouncements as an amendment or replacement for ARB 45.

The accounting for long-term construction contracts is complicated by the need to rely upon estimates of revenues, costs and progress toward completion and the principle of recognition of losses when apparent.

Sources of GAAP

SFAC	ARB	APB	SFAS	Other	EITF
5	45	20	109	SOP 81-1	91-6, 96-17

DEFINITIONS OF TERMS

Back charges. Billings for work performed or costs incurred by one party that, in accordance with the agreement, should have been performed or incurred by the party billed.

Billings on long-term contracts. Accumulated billings sent to the purchaser at intervals as various points in the project are reached.

Change orders. Modifications of an original contract that effectively change the provisions of the contract without adding new provisions. (SOP 81-1, para 61)

Claims. Amounts in excess of the agreed contract price that a contractor seeks to collect from customers for customer-caused delays, errors in specifications and designs, unapproved change orders, or other causes of unanticipated costs. (SOP 81-1, para 61)

Combining contracts. Grouping two or more contracts into a single profit center for accounting purposes.

Completed-contract method. A method of accounting that recognizes income only after the contract is complete.

Construction-in-progress (CIP). An inventory account used to accumulate the construction costs of the contract project. For the percentage-of-completion method, the CIP account also includes the gross profit earned to date.

Cost-to-cost method. A percentage-of-completion method used to determine the extent of progress toward completion on a contract. The ratio of cost incurred to end of current year over total estimated costs of the project is used to recognize income.

Estimated cost to complete. The anticipated additional cost of materials, labor, subcontracting costs, and indirect costs (overhead) required to complete a project at a scheduled time.

Percentage-of-completion method. A method of accounting that recognizes income on a contract as work progresses.

Precontract costs. Costs incurred before a contract has been accepted (e.g., architectural designs, purchase of special equipment, engineering fees, and start-up costs).

Profit center. A unit for the accumulation of revenues and cost for the measurement of income.

Segmenting contracts. Dividing a single contract or group of contracts into two or more profit centers for accounting purposes.

Subcontractor. A second-level contractor who enters into a contract with a prime contractor to perform a specific part or phase of a construction project.

Substantial completion. The point at which the major work on a contract is completed and only insignificant costs and potential risks remain.

CONCEPTS, RULES, AND EXAMPLES

Long-term construction contract revenue may be recognized during construction rather than at the completion of the contract. This "as earned" approach to revenue recognition is justified because under most long-term construction contracts both the buyer and the seller (contractor) obtain enforceable rights. The buyer has the legal right to require specific performance from the contractor and, in effect, has ownership claim to the contractor's work in progress. The contractor, under most long-term contracts, has the right to require the buyer to make progress payments during the construction period. The substance of this business activity is that a continuous sale occurs as the work progresses (SOP 81-1).

ARB 45 describes the two generally accepted methods of accounting for long-term construction contracts.

> *The* ***percentage-of-completion method*** *recognizes income as work on a contract (or group of closely related contracts) progresses. The recognition of revenues and profits is generally related to costs incurred in providing the services required under the contract (para 4).*

Under this method, the **construction-in-progress (CIP)** account is used to accumulate costs and recognized income. When the CIP exceeds billings, the difference is reported as a current asset. If billings exceed CIP, the difference is reported as a current liability (para 5). Where more than one contract exists, the excess cost or liability should be determined on a project-by-project basis, with the accumulated costs and liabilities being separately stated on the balance sheet. Assets and liabilities should not be offset unless a right of offset exists. Thus, the net debit balances for certain contracts should not ordinarily be offset against net credit balances for other contracts. An exception may exist if the balances relate to contracts that meet the criteria for combining described in SOP 81-1.

Under the percentage-of-completion method, income should not be based on cash collections or interim billings. Cash collections and interim billings are based upon contract terms which do not necessarily measure contract performance. Costs and estimated earnings in excess of billings should be classified as a current asset. If billings exceed costs and estimated earnings, the difference should be classified as a current liability.

> *The* ***completed-contract method*** *recognizes income only when the contract is complete, or substantially complete (para 9).*

Under this method, the CIP account accumulates only the costs of contracts in process. The costs and related billings are reported as deferred items on the balance sheet until the project is complete or substantially complete. A contract can be regarded as substantially complete if remaining costs of completion are immaterial. When the accumulated costs (CIP) exceed the related billings, the excess should be shown as a current asset (inventory account). If billings exceed related costs, the difference should be shown as a current liability (para 12). This determination should also be made on a project-by-project basis with the accumulated costs and liabilities being separately stated on the balance sheet. An excess of accumulated costs over related billings should be shown as a current asset, and an excess of accumulated billings over related costs should be shown among the liabilities, in most cases as a current liability.

SOP 81-1 recommends the percentage-of-completion method as preferable when estimates are reasonably dependable and the following conditions exist:

1. Contracts executed by the parties normally include provisions that clearly specify the enforceable rights regarding goods or services to be provided and received by the parties, the consideration to be exchanged, and the manner and terms of settlement.
2. The buyer can be expected to satisfy his obligations under the contract.
3. The contractor can be expected to perform his contractual obligations.

SOP 81-1 presumes that contractors generally have the ability to produce estimates that are sufficiently dependable to justify the use of the percentage-of-completion method of accounting. Persuasive evidence to the contrary is necessary to overcome this presumption.

The principal advantage of the completed-contract method is that it is based on final results, whereas the percentage-of-completion method is dependent upon estimates for unperformed work. The principal disadvantage of the completed-contract method is that when the period of a contract extends into more than one period, there will be an irregular recognition of income (paras 13 and 14).

The Accounting Standards Division of the AICPA believes that these two methods should not be used as acceptable alternatives for the same set of circumstances. ARB 45, para 15 states that in general, when estimates of costs to complete and extent of progress toward completion of long-term contracts are reasonably dependable, the percentage-of-completion method is preferable. When lack of dependable estimates or inherent hazards cause forecasts to be doubtful, the completed-contract method is preferable.

The completed-contract method may also be acceptable when a contractor has numerous relatively short-term contracts and when the financial statement presentation does not vary materially from the presentation under the percentage-of-completion method.

Contract Costs

Contract costs are costs identifiable with or allocable to specific contracts. Generally, contract costs would include all direct costs such as direct materials, direct labor, and any indirect costs (overhead) allocable to the contracts. Contract costs can be broken down into two categories: costs incurred to date and estimated costs to complete.

The costs incurred to date would include **precontract costs** and costs incurred after contract acceptance. Precontract costs are costs incurred **before** a contract has been entered into, with the expectation of the contract being accepted and thereby recoverable through billings. Precontract costs would include architectural designs, costs of learning a new process, and any other costs which are expected to be recovered if the contract is accepted. Contract costs incurred after the acceptance of the contract are costs incurred towards the completion of the project and are also capitalized in the construction-in-progress (CIP) account.

The contract does not have to be identified before the capitalization decision is made; only the expectation of the recovery of the costs is necessary. Once the contract has been accepted, the precontract costs become contract costs incurred to date.

Certain costs (purchase of materials, equipment, supplies, etc.) may be deferred in anticipation of a specific contract, or for a number of identified related contracts. Precontract costs associated with a specific contract should **not** be included in contract costs or inventory unless the contract is accepted. These costs can be deferred; however, they are to be capitalized by the use of another account, such as Deferred Costs-Contract bid #97. Costs incurred on identified related contracts should be treated similarly to costs for a specific contract--capitalized outside of contract costs or inventory accounts.

The company may choose to defer costs related to producing excess goods in anticipation of future orders of the same item. Cost associated with excess production can be treated as inventory if the costs are considered recoverable.

A company may choose to defer the precontract costs for the learning, start-up, and mobilization (exclusive of R&D expenses) of an unidentified contract. These costs are treated differently than the previously mentioned precontract situations. If these costs are incurred with existing contracts and in anticipation of future contracts, these costs should be charged to existing contracts.

The existing contracts should absorb some portion of these precontract costs. Since the number of future contracts to benefit from the expenditures is unknown, the convention of conservatism prevails and the existing contracts will absorb all of the precontract costs incurred. If the costs were incurred for future contracts only, the costs should be accounted for as precontract costs for a number of contracts.

Once the outcome of the contract bid is known (acceptance or rejection), the precontract costs associated with it must be examined. If the contract was accepted, previously deferred precontract costs should be included in contract costs. If, however, precontract costs were charged to expense because recoverability was not probable, these costs can **not** be reinstated by crediting income. Precontract costs associated with rejected contracts should be expensed in the current period, unless recoverability is probable under other pending contracts.

Estimated costs to complete. These are the **anticipated costs** required to complete a project at a scheduled time. They would be comprised of the same elements as the original total estimated contract costs and would be based on prices expected to be in effect when the costs are incurred.

The latest estimates should be used to determine the progress towards completion. SOP 81-1 provides the practices to be followed when determining estimated costs to complete.

First of all, systematic and consistent procedures should be used. These procedures should be correlated with the cost accounting system and should be able to provide a comparison between actual and estimated costs. Additionally, the determination of estimated total contract costs should identify the significant cost elements.

Another procedure requires that the estimation of the costs to complete should include the same elements of costs included in accumulated costs. Additionally, the estimated costs should reflect any expected price increases. These expected price increases should not be "blanket provisions" for all contract costs, but rather specific provisions for each type of cost. Expected increases in each of the cost elements such as wages, materials, and overhead items should be taken into consideration separately.

Finally, estimates of costs to complete should be reviewed periodically to reflect new information. Estimates of costs should be examined for price fluctuations and also should be reviewed for possible future problems, such as labor strikes or direct material delays.

Accounting for contract costs is similar to accounting for inventory. Costs necessary to ready the asset for sale would be recorded in the construction-in-progress account, as incurred. CIP would include both direct and indirect costs but would usually not include general and administrative expenses or selling expenses since they are not normally identifiable with a particular contract and should therefore be expensed. However, general and administrative expenses **may** be included in contract costs under the completed contract method since a preferable allocation of revenues and costs might take place, especially in years when no contracts were completed (ARB 45, para 10).

Subcontractor costs. Since a contractor may not be able to do all facets of a construction project, a subcontractor may be engaged. The amount billed to the contractor for work done by the subcontractor should be included in contract costs. The amount billed is directly traceable to the project and would be included in the CIP account, similar to direct materials and direct labor.

Back charges. Contract costs may have to be adjusted for back charges. Back charges are billings for costs incurred, which the contract stipulated should have been performed by another party. These charges are often disputed by the parties involved.

Example of a back charge situation

The contract states the subcontractor was to raze the building and have the land ready for construction; however, the contractor/seller had to clear away debris in order to begin construction. The contractor wants to be reimbursed for the work; therefore, the contractor back charges the subcontractor for the cost of the debris removal.

The contractor should treat the back charge as a receivable from the subcontractor and should reduce contract costs by the amount recoverable. If the subcontractor disputes the back charge, the cost becomes a claim. Claims are an amount in excess of the agreed contract price or amounts not included in the original contract price that the contractor seeks to collect. Claims should only be recorded as additional contract revenue if the requirements set forth in SOP 81-1, para 65, are met.

The subcontractor should record the back charge as a payable and as additional contract costs if it is probable the amount will be paid. If the amount or validity of the liability is disputed, the subcontractor would have to consider the probable outcome in order to determine the proper accounting treatment.

Types of Contracts

Four types of contracts are distinguished based on their pricing arrangements: (1) fixed-price or lump-sum contracts, (2) time-and-materials contracts, (3) cost-type contracts, and (4) unit-price contracts.

Fixed-price contracts are contracts for which the price is not usually subject to adjustment because of costs incurred by the contractor.

Time-and-materials contracts are contracts that provide for payments to the contractor based on direct labor hours at fixed rates and cost of materials.

There are two cost-type contracts: **cost-without-fee contract**--contractor is reimbursed for costs with no provision for a fee, and **cost-plus-fixed-fee contract**--contractor is reimbursed for costs plus a provision for a fee. The contract price on a cost-type contract is determined by the sum of the reimbursable expenditures and a fee. The fee is the profit margin (revenue less direct expenses) to be earned on the contract. All reimbursable expenditures should be included in the accumulated contract costs account. If a contract cost was omitted from this account, a higher fee would result. The higher fee is a result of the contract price being fixed and the accumulated contract costs being understated. The reverse is also true. If unallocable costs (i.e., general and administrative expenses) are included in accumulated contract costs, the fee or profit margin declines.

Contract costs (incurred and estimated to complete) should be used to compute the gross profit or loss recognized. Under the percentage-of-completion method, gross profit or loss would be recognized each period. The revenue recognized would be matched against the contract costs incurred (similar to cost of goods sold) to determine gross profit/loss. Under the completed contract method, the gross profit/loss is determined at the **completion** of the contract, and no revenue or contract costs are recognized until this point.

Additionally, inventoriable costs (accumulated in the CIP account) should never exceed the net realizable value of the contract. When contract costs exceed their NRV, they must be written down, requiring a contract loss to be recognized in the current period (this will be discussed in greater detail later). This is similar to accounting for inventory.

Cost-type contracts provide for reimbursement of allowable or otherwise defined costs incurred plus a fee representing profits. Some variations of cost-plus contracts are (1) cost-without-fee: no provision for a fee, (2) cost-plus-fixed-fee: contractor reimbursed for costs plus provision for a fixed fee, and (3) cost-plus-award-fee: same as (2) plus provision for award based on performance.

Unit-price contracts are contracts under which the contractor is paid a specified amount for every unit of work performed.

Revenue Measurement

In practice, various methods are used to measure the extent of progress toward completion. The most common methods are the cost-to-cost method, efforts-expended method, units-of-delivery method, and units-of-work-performed method. All of these methods of measuring progress on a contract can be identified as either an input or output measure. The input measures attempt to identify progress in a contract in terms of the efforts devoted to it. The cost-to-cost and efforts-expended methods are examples of input measures. Under the cost-to-cost method, the percentage of completion would be estimated by comparing total costs incurred to date to total costs expected for the entire job. Output measures are made in terms of results by attempting to identify progress toward completion by physical measures. The units-of-delivery and units-of-work-performed methods are examples of output measures. Under both of these methods, an estimate of completion is made in terms of achievements to date. Output measures are usually not considered as reliable as input measures.

Both input and output measures have drawbacks in certain circumstances. A significant problem of input measures is that the relationship between input and productivity is only indirect; inefficiencies and other factors can cause this relationship to change. A particular drawback of the cost-to-cost method is that start-up costs, costs of uninstalled materials, and other up-front costs may produce higher estimates of completion because of their early incurrence. These costs may be excluded or allocated over the contract life when it appears that a better measure of periodic income will be obtained. A significant problem of output measures is that the cost, time, and effort associated with one unit of output may not be comparable to that of another. For example, because of the cost of the foundation, the costs to complete the first story of a 20-story office building can be expected to be greater than the costs of the remaining 19 floors.

Because ARB 45, para 4 recommends that "recognized income [should] be that percentage of estimated total income...that incurred costs to date bear to estimated total costs," the **cost-to-cost** method has become one of the most popular measures used to determine the extent of progress toward completion.

Under the cost-to-cost method, the percentage of **revenue** to recognize can be determined by the following formula:

$$\frac{\text{Cost to date}}{\text{Cumulative costs incurred + Estimated costs to complete}} \times \text{Contract price} - \text{Revenue previously recognized} = \text{Current revenue recognized}$$

By slightly modifying this formula, current **gross profit** can also be determined.

$$\frac{\text{Cost to date}}{\text{Cumulative costs incurred + Estimated costs to complete}} \times \text{Expected total gross profit} - \text{Gross profit previously recognized} = \text{Current gross profit}$$

Example of percentage-of-completion (cost-to-cost) and completed-contract methods with profitable contract

Assume a $500,000 contract that requires 3 years to complete and incurs a total cost of $405,000. The following data pertain to the construction period:

	Year 1	*Year 2*	*Year 3*
Cumulative costs incurred to date	$150,000	$360,000	$405,000
Estimated costs yet to be incurred at year end	300,000	40,000	--
Progress billings made during year	100,000	370,000	30,000
Collections of billings	75,000	300,000	125,000

Completed-Contract & Percentage-of-Completion Methods

	Year 1		*Year 2*		*Year 3*	
Construction in progress	150,000		210,000		45,000	
Cash, payables, etc.		150,000		210,000		45,000
Contract receivables	100,000		370,000		30,000	
Billings on contracts		100,000		370,000		30,000
Cash	75,000		300,000		125,000	
Contract receivables		75,000		300,000		125,000

Completed-Contract Method Only

Billings on contracts					500,000	
Cost of revenues earned					405,000	
Contracts revenues earned						500,000
Construction in progress						405,000

Percentage-of-Completion Method Only

Construction in progress	16,667		73,333		5,000	
Cost of revenues earned	150,000		210,000		45,000	
Contract revenues earned		166,667		283,333		50,000
Billings on contracts					500,000	
Construction in progress						500,000

Income Statement Presentation

	Year 1	Year 2	Year 3	Total
Percentage-of-completion				
Contract revenues earned	$166,667*	$283,333**	$ 50,000***	$ 500,000
Cost of revenues earned	(150,000)	(210,000)	(45,000)	(405,000)
Gross profit	$ 16,667	$ 73,333	$ 5,000	$ 95,000
Completed-contract				
Contract revenues earned	--	--	$ 500,000	$ 500,000
Cost of contracts completed	--	--	(405,000)	(405,000)
Gross profit	--	--	$ 95,000	$ 95,000

$$* \quad \frac{\$150{,}000}{450{,}000} \times 500{,}000 = \$166{,}667$$

$$** \quad \frac{\$360{,}000}{400{,}000} \times 500{,}000 - 166{,}667 = \$283{,}333$$

$$*** \quad \frac{\$405{,}000}{405{,}000} \times 500{,}000 - 166{,}667 - 283{,}333 = \$50{,}000$$

Balance Sheet Presentation

		Year 1	Year 2	Year 3
Percentage-of-completion				
Current assets:				
Contract receivables		$ 25,000	$ 95,000	*
Costs and estimated earnings in excess of billings on uncompleted contracts				
Construction in progress	166,667**			
Less billings on long-term contracts	(100,000)	$ 66,667		

	Year 1	Year 2	Year 3
Current liabilities:			
Billings in excess of costs and estimated earnings on uncompleted contracts, year 2 ($470,000*** – 450,000****)		$ 20,000	

Completed-contract

Current assets:				
Contract receivables		$ 25,000	$ 95,000	*
Costs in excess of billings on uncompleted contracts				
Construction in progress	150,000			
Less billings on long-term contracts	(100,000)	$ 50,000		
Current liabilities:				
Billings in excess of costs on uncompleted contracts, year 2 ($470,000 – 360,000)			$110,000	

* *Since the contract was completed and title was transferred in year 3, there are no balance sheet amounts. However, if the project is complete but transfer of title has not taken place, then there would be a balance sheet presentation at the end of the third year because the entry closing out the Construction in progress account and the Billings account would not have been made yet.*

** *$150,000 (Costs) + 16,667 (Gross profit)*

*** *$100,000 (Year 1 Billings) + 370,000 (Year 2 Billings)*

**** *$360,000 (Costs) + 16,667 (Gross profit) + 73,333 (Gross profit)*

Contract Losses

When the current estimate of total contract cost exceeds the current estimate of total contract revenue, a provision for the entire loss on the entire contract should be made. Provisions for losses should be made in the period in which they become evident under either the percentage-of-completion method or the completed-contract method (SOP 81-1, para 85). The loss provision should be computed on the basis of the **total** estimated costs to complete the contract, which would include the contract costs incurred to date plus estimated costs (use same elements as contract costs incurred) to complete. The provision should be shown separately as a current liability on the balance sheet.

In any year when a **percentage-of-completion** contract has an expected loss, the amount of the loss reported in that year can be computed as follows:

Reported loss = Total expected loss + All profit previously recognized

Example of percentage-of-completion and completed-contract methods with loss contract

Using the previous information, if the costs yet to be incurred at the end of year 2 were $148,000, the total expected loss is $8,000 [$500,000 – (360,000 + 148,000)], and the total loss reported in year 2 would be $24,667 ($8,000 + 16,667). Under the completed-contract method, the loss recognized is simply the total expected loss, $8,000.

Journal entry at end of year 2	*Percentage-of-completion*		*Completed-contract*	
Loss on uncompleted long-term contract	24,667		8,000	
Construction in progress (or estimated loss on uncompleted contract)		24,667		8,000

Profit or Loss Recognized on Contract
(Percentage-of-Completion Method)

	Year 1	*Year 2*	*Year 3*
Contract price	$500,000	$500,000	$500,000
Estimated total costs:			
Costs incurred to date	$150,000	$360,000	$506,000*
Estimated cost yet to be incurred	300,000	148,000	--
Estimated total costs for the 3-year period, actual for year 3	$450,000	$508,000	$506,000
Estimated income (loss), actual for year 3	$ 16,667	$ (8,000)	$ (6,000)
Less income (loss) previously recognized	--	16,667	(8,000)
Amount of estimated income (loss) recognized in the current period, actual for year 3	$ 16,667	$ (24,667)	$ 2,000

**Assumed*

Profit or Loss Recognized on Contract
(Completed-Contract Method)

	Year 1	*Year 2*	*Year 3*
Contract price	$500,000	$500,000	$500,000
Estimated total costs:			
Costs incurred to date	$150,000	$360,000	$506,000*
Estimated costs yet to be incurred	300,000	148,000	--
Estimated total costs for the 3-year period, actual for year 3	$ 50,000	$ (8,000)	$ (6,000)
Loss previously recognized	--	--	(8,000)
Amount of estimated income (loss) recognized in the current period, actual for year 3	$ --	$ (8,000)	$ 2,000

**Assumed*

Upon completion of the project during year 3, it can be seen that the actual loss was only $6,000 ($500,000 – $506,000); therefore, the estimated loss provision was overstated by $2,000. However, since this is a change of an estimate, the $2,000 difference must be handled prospectively; consequently, $2,000 of income should be recognized in year 3 ($8,000 previously recognized – $6,000 actual loss).

Combining and Segmenting Contracts

The profit center for accounting purposes is usually a single contract, but under some circumstances the profit center may be a combination of two or more contracts, a segment of a contract or of a group of combined contracts (SOP 81-1, para 17). The contracts must meet requirements in SOP 81-1 in order to combine, or segment; otherwise, each individual contract is presumed to be the profit center.

For accounting purposes, a group of contracts may be combined if they are so closely related that they are, in substance, parts of a single project with an overall profit margin. Per SOP 81-1, para 37, a group of contracts may be combined if the contracts

a. *Are negotiated as a package in the same economic environment with an overall profit margin objective.*
b. *Constitute an agreement to do a single project.*
c. *Require closely interrelated construction activities.*
d. *Are performed concurrently or in a continuous sequence under the same project management.*
e. *Constitute, in substance, an agreement with a single customer.*

Segmenting a contract is a process of breaking up a larger unit into smaller units for accounting purposes. If the project is segmented, revenues can be assigned to the different elements or phases to achieve different rates of profitability based on the relative value of each element or phase to the estimated total contract revenue. According to SOP 81-1, para 40, a project may be segmented if all of the following steps were taken and are documented and verifiable:

a. *The contractor submitted bona fide proposals on the separate components of the project and on the entire project.*
b. *The customer had the right to accept the proposals on either basis.*
c. *The aggregate amount of the proposals on the separate components approximated the amount of the proposal on the entire project.*

A project that does not meet the above criteria may still be segmented if all of the following (SOP 81-1, para 41) are applicable:

a. *The terms and scope of the contract or project clearly call for the separable phases or elements.*
b. *The separable phases or elements of the project are often bid or negotiated separately.*
c. *The market assigns different gross profit rates to the segments because of factors such as different levels of risk or differences in the relationship of the supply and demand for the services provided in different segments.*
d. *The contractor has a significant history of providing similar services to other customers under separate contracts for each significant seg-*

ment to which a profit margin higher than the overall profit margin on the project is ascribed.

e. *The significant history with customers who have contracted for services separately is one that is relatively stable in terms of pricing policy rather than one unduly weighted by erratic pricing decisions (responding, for example, to extraordinary economic circumstances or to unique customer-contractor relationships).*

f. *The excess of the sum of the prices of the separate elements over the price of the total project is clearly attributable to cost savings incident to combined performance of the contract obligations (for example, cost savings in supervision, overhead, or equipment mobilization). Unless this condition is met, segmenting a contract with a price substantially less than the sum of the prices of the separate phases or elements would be inappropriate even if the other conditions are met. Acceptable price variations should be allocated to the separate phases or elements in proportion to the prices ascribed to each. In all other situations a substantial difference in price (whether more or less) between the separate elements and the price of the total project is evidence that the contractor has accepted different profit margins. Accordingly, segmenting is not appropriate, and the contracts should be the profit centers.*

g. *The similarity of services and prices in the contract segments and services and the prices of such services to other customers contracted separately should be documented and verifiable.*

Note that the criteria for combining and segmenting should be applied consistently to contracts with similar characteristics and in similar circumstances.

Joint Ventures and Shared Contracts

Under many contracts that are obtained by long-term construction companies are those that are shared by more than one contractor. When the owner of the contract puts it up for bids, many contractors will form syndicates or joint ventures in order to bid on and successfully obtain a contract that each contractor individually could not perform under.

When this transpires, a separate set of books is maintained for the joint venture. If the percentages of interest for each of the ventures are identical in more than one contract, the joint venture might keep its records almost like another construction company. Usually, the joint venture is for a single contract and ends upon completion of that contract.

A joint venture is a form of a partnership, although a partnership for a limited purpose. An agreement of the parties and the terms of the contract successfully bid upon will determine the nature of the accounting records. Income statements are usually cumulative statements showing all totals from date of contract determination until reporting date. Each venturer records its share of the amount from the venture's income statement less its previously recorded portion of the venture's income as a single line item similar to the equity method for investments. Similarly, balance sheets of the venture give rise to a single line asset balance of investment and advances in joint ventures. In most cases, footnote disclosure is also similar to the equity method in displaying condensed financial statements of material joint ventures.

Accounting for Change Orders

Change orders are modifications of specifications or provisions of an original contract. Contract revenue and costs should be adjusted to reflect change orders that are approved by the contractor and customer. According to SOP 81-1, the accounting for the change order depends upon the scope and price of the change.

If the scope and price have both been agreed upon by the customer and contractor, contract revenue and cost should be adjusted to reflect the change order.

According to SOP 81-1, para 62, accounting for unpriced change orders depends on their characteristics and the circumstances in which they occur. Under the completed-contract method, costs attributable to unpriced change orders should be deferred as contract costs if it is probable that total contract costs, including costs attributable to the change orders, will be recovered from contract revenues. Recovery should be deemed probable if the future event or events are likely to occur.

Per SOP 81-1, para 62, the following guidelines should be followed when accounting for unpriced change orders under the percentage-of-completion method:

a. *Costs attributable to unpriced change orders should be treated as costs of contract performance in the period in which the costs are incurred if it is* ***not*** *probable that the costs will be recovered through a change in the contract price.*

b. *If it is probable that the costs will be recovered through a change in the contract price, the costs should be deferred (excluded from the cost of contract performance) until the parties have agreed on the change in contract price, or, alternatively, they should be treated as costs of contract performance in the period in which they are incurred, and contract revenue should be recognized to the extent of the costs incurred.*

c. *If it is probable that the contract price will be adjusted by an amount that exceeds the costs attributable to the change order and the amount of the excess can be reliably estimated, the original contract price should also be adjusted for that amount when the costs are recognized as costs of contract performance if its realization is probable. However, since the substantiation of the amount of future revenue is difficult, revenue in excess of the costs attributable to unpriced change orders should only be recorded in circumstances in which realization is assured beyond a reasonable doubt, such as circumstances in which an entity's historical experience provides such assurance or in which an entity has received a bona fide pricing offer from a customer and records only the amount of the offer as revenue.*

Accounting for Contract Options

Per SOP 81-1, para 64, an addition or option to an existing contract should be treated as a separate contract if any of the following circumstances exist:

a. *The product or service to be provided differs significantly from the product or service provided under the original contract.*
b. *The price of the new product or service is negotiated without regard to the original contract and involves different economic judgments.*
c. *The products or services to be provided under the exercised option or amendment are similar to those under the original contract, but the contract price and anticipated contract cost relationship are significantly different.*

If the addition or option does not meet the above circumstances, the contracts should be combined. However, if the addition or option does not meet the criteria for combining, they should be treated as change orders.

Accounting for Claims

These represent amounts in excess of the agreed contract price that a contractor seeks to collect from customers for unanticipated additional costs. The recognition of additional contract revenue relating to claims is appropriate if it is probable that the claim will result in additional revenue and if the amount can be reliably estimated. SOP 81-1, para 65 specifies that all of the following conditions must exist in order for the probable and estimable requirements to be satisfied:

a. *The contract or other evidence provides a legal basis for the claim; or a legal opinion has been obtained, stating that under the circumstances there is a reasonable basis to support the claim.*
b. *Additional costs are caused by circumstances that were unforeseen at the contract date and are not the result of deficiencies in the contractor's performance.*
c. *Costs associated with the claim are identifiable or otherwise determinable and are reasonable in view of the work performed.*
d. *The evidence supporting the claim is objective and verifiable, not based on management's "feel" for the situation or on unsupported representations.*

When the above requirements are met, revenue from a claim should be recorded only to the extent that contract costs relating to the claim have been incurred.

When the above requirements are not met, para 67 of SOP 81-1 states that a contingent asset should be disclosed in accordance with SFAS 5, para 17.

Accounting Changes

According to APB 20, a change in method of accounting for long-term construction contracts is a special change in principle requiring retroactive treatment and restatement of previous financial statements. (See Chapter 20 for further discussion.)

Revisions in revenue, cost, and profit estimates or in measurements of the extent of progress toward completion are changes in accounting estimates. Such changes should be accounted for prospectively in order for the financial statements to fully reflect the effects of the latest available estimates.

Deferred Income Taxes

Deferred taxes resulting from temporary differences should be classified in accordance with SFAS 109, *Accounting for Income Taxes*. Contract-related deferred taxes result from the use of a method of income recognition for tax purposes different from the method used for financial reporting purposes. (Refer to Chapter 15 on accounting for income taxes for further discussion of deferred taxes.)

EMERGING ISSUES TASK FORCE CONSENSUS SUMMARIES

91-6 Revenue Recognition of Long-Term Power Sales Contracts

A consensus was reached that Nonutility Generators (NUG) should recognize the lesser of (1) the amount billable under the contract or (2) a formula-based pricing arrangement, as revenue. The formula-based pricing arrangement is determined by the kwhs made available during the period multiplied by the estimated average revenue per kwh over the term of the contract for the fixed or scheduled price period of the contract. Revenue should not be recognized utilizing the formula-based pricing arrangement if its only purpose is to establish liquidating damages. Additionally, a receivable arises when the amounts billed are less than the amount computed pursuant to the formula-based pricing arrangement and if the contract requires a payment, probable of recovery, to the NUG at the end of the contract term.

96-17 Revenue Recognition Under Long-Term Power Sales Contracts That Contain Both Fixed and Variable Pricing Terms

This pronouncement extends the consensus of 91-6. Fixed price arrangements should be handled in accordance with 91-6. Variable price arrangements in which the rate is at least equal to expected costs should recognize revenue as billed, in accordance with the provisions of the contract for that variable price period. Long-term power sales contracts should be periodically reviewed to determine whether it is a loss contract in which the loss should be recognized immediately. Finally, the Task Force observed that any premium related to a contractual rate in excess of the current market rate should be amortized over the remaining portion of the contract for long-term power sales contracts acquired in a purchase business combination.

SERVICE SALES TRANSACTIONS

PERSPECTIVE AND ISSUES

Service sales transactions represent over half of the US economy's transactions; however, there are no official pronouncements that provide specific accounting standards for them. Accounting for service sales transactions has evolved primarily through industry practice. As a result, different accounting methods have developed to apply the fundamental principles of revenue and cost recognition. In fact, different accounting methods are used by similar entities for practically identical transactions. Because of these wide variations, the FASB and the AICPA combined efforts in an attempt to establish accounting standards for service transactions through their issuance of *Accounting for Certain Service Transactions*, FASB Invitation to Comment (the Invitation). The Invitation contained an AICPA draft Statement of Position that set forth conclusions on the following:

1. The guidelines to apply to transactions in which both services and products are provided
2. The appropriate manner of revenue recognition
3. The classification of costs as initial direct costs, direct costs, and indirect costs and the accounting for each
4. The accounting for initiation and installation fees

This section reflects the conclusions in the AICPA draft Statement of Position. Although no further progress has been made in this area, this section can still provide guidance in service industry issues.

Sources of GAAP

Other	EITF
*	90-1, 91-9

**FASB Invitation to Comment, Accounting for Certain Service Transactions.*

DEFINITIONS OF TERMS

Collection method. Revenue recognized upon the collection of cash.

Completed performance method. A method that recognizes revenue after the last significant act has been completed.

Direct costs. Costs that are directly related to the performance of services.

Indirect costs. Costs that are not directly related to the negotiation or consummation of service agreements and are not directly related to the performance of services.

Initial direct costs. Costs that are directly associated with the negotiation and consummation of service agreements.

Initiation fee. A one-time, up-front charge that gives the purchaser the privilege of using the service or the use of facilities.

Installation fee. A one-time, up-front charge for the installation of equipment essential to the provision of the service.

Product transaction. A transaction between a seller and a purchaser in which the seller supplies a product to the purchaser.

Proportional performance method. A method that recognizes revenue on the basis of the number of acts performed in relation to the total number of acts to be performed.

Service transaction. A transaction between a seller and a purchaser in which the seller provides a service, or agrees to maintain a readiness to perform a service, to the purchaser.

Specific performance method. A method that recognizes revenue after one specific act has been performed.

CONCEPTS, RULES, AND EXAMPLES

The AICPA has defined service transactions as follows:

> *...transactions between a seller and a purchaser in which, for a mutually agreed price, the seller performs, agrees to perform, agrees to perform at a later date, or agrees to maintain readiness to perform an act or acts, including permitting others to use enterprise resources that do not alone produce a tangible commodity or product as the principal intended result (the Invitation, para 7).*

Generally accepted accounting principles require that revenue should generally be recognized when: (1) it is **realized or realizable** and (2) it has been **earned** (SFAC 5, para 83). With respect to service transactions, the AICPA concluded

> *...revenue from service transactions should be based on performance, because performance determines the extent to which the earnings process is complete or virtually complete (the Invitation, para 10).*

In practice, performance may involve the execution of a defined act, a set of similar or identical acts, or a set of related but not similar or identical acts. Performance may also occur with the passage of time. Accordingly, one of the following four methods should serve as a guideline for the recognition of revenue from service transactions:

1. The specific performance method
2. The proportional performance method
3. The completed performance method
4. The collection method

Service vs. Product Transactions

Many transactions involve the sale of a tangible product and a service; therefore, for proper accounting treatment, it must be determined whether the transaction is primarily a service transaction accompanied by an incidental product, primarily a product transaction accompanied by an incidental service, or a sale in which both a service transaction and a product transaction occur. The following criteria are applicable:

1. If the seller offers both a service and a product in a single transaction and if the sale of the service is worded in such a manner that the inclusion or exclusion of the product would not change the total transaction price, the product is incidental to the rendering of the service; the transaction is a service transaction that should be accounted for in accordance with one of the four methods presented. For example, fixed price equipment maintenance contracts that include parts are service transactions.
2. If the seller offers both a service and a product in a single transaction and if the sale of the product is worded in such a manner that the inclusion or exclusion of the service would not change the total transaction price, the rendering of the service is incidental to the sale of the product; the transaction is a product transaction that should be accounted for as such. For example, the sale of a product accompanied by a guarantee or warranty for repair is considered a product transaction.
3. If the seller offers both a product and a service and the agreement states the product and service are separate elements such that the inclusion or exclusion of the service would vary the total transaction price, the transaction consists of two components: a product transaction that should be accounted for separately as such, and a service transaction that should be accounted for in accordance with one of the four accepted methods.

Revenue Recognition Methods

Once the sale has been identified as a service transaction, one of the following four methods should be used to recognize revenue. The method chosen should reflect the nature and extent of the service(s) to be performed.

1. **Specific performance method.** The specific performance method should be used when performance consists of the execution of a single act. Revenue is recognized at the time the act takes place. For example, a stockbroker should record sales commissions as revenue upon the sale of a client's investment.
2. **Proportional performance method.** The proportional performance method should be used when performance consists of a number of identical or similar acts.

a. If the service transaction involves a **specified number** of **identical** or **similar** acts, an equal amount of revenue should be recorded for each act performed. For example, a refuse disposal company would recognize an equal amount of revenue for each weekly removal of a customer's garbage.

b. If the service transaction involves a specified number of defined but **not** identical or similar acts, the revenue recognized for each act should be based on the following formula:

$$\frac{\text{Direct cost of individual act}}{\text{Total estimated direct costs of the transaction}} \times \text{Total revenues from complete transaction}$$

For example, a correspondence school that provides lessons, examinations, and grading should use this method. If the measurements suggested in the preceding equation are impractical or not objectively determinable, revenue should be recognized on a systematic and rational basis that reasonably relates revenue recognition to service performance.

c. If the service transaction involves an **unspecified** number of acts over a fixed time period for performance, revenue should be recognized over the period during which the acts will be performed by using the straight-line method unless a better method of relating revenue and performance is appropriate. For example, a health club might recognize revenue on a straight-line basis over the life of a member's membership.

3. **Completed performance method.** The completed performance method should be used when more than one act must be done and when the final act is so significant to the entire transaction taken as a whole that performance can't be considered to have taken place until the performance of that final act occurs. For example, a moving company packs, loads, and transports merchandise; however, the final act of delivering the merchandise is so significant that revenue should not be recognized until the goods reach their intended destination. If the services are to be performed in an **indeterminable** number of acts over an **indeterminable** period of time and if an objective measure for estimating the degree to which performance has taken place can't be found, the revenue should be recognized under the completed performance method.
4. **Collection method.** The collection method should be used in circumstances when there is a significant degree of uncertainty surrounding the collection of service revenue. Under this method, revenue should not be recorded until the cash is collected. For example, personal services may be provided to a customer whose ability to pay is uncertain.

Expense Recognition

GAAP, in general, requires that costs should be charged to expense in the period that the revenue with which they are associated is recognized. Costs should be deferred only when they are expected to be recoverable from future revenues. When applying these principles to service transactions, special consideration must be given to the different types of costs that may arise. The three major classifications of costs arising from service transactions are as follows:

1. Initial direct costs
2. Direct costs
3. Indirect costs

The three types of cost classifications arising from service transactions are defined as follows (the Invitation, para 15):

1. **Initial direct costs.** Costs that are directly associated with the negotiation and consummation of service agreements. They include, but are not limited to, legal fees, commissions, costs of credit investigations, installment paper processing fees, and the portion of salespersons' and other employees' compensation, other than commissions, that is applicable to the time spent on consummated agreements. They do not include costs allocable to time spent on service transactions that are not consummated or portions of supervisory, administrative, or other indirect costs, such as rent.
2. **Direct costs.** Costs that have a clear, beneficial, or causal relationship to the services or level of services performed. For example, servicemen's labor and repair parts on a fixed price maintenance contract are considered direct costs.
3. **Indirect costs.** All costs that cannot be classified as either an initial direct cost or a direct cost. They include provisions for uncollectible accounts, general and administrative expenses, advertising expenses, general selling expenses, the portion of salespersons' and other employees' compensation allocable to the time spent in negotiating service transactions that are not consummated, and all allocations of facility costs (depreciation, rent, maintenance, etc.).

Accounting treatment. The accounting treatment for indirect costs, initial direct costs and direct costs, and service transaction losses are discussed below.

1. **Indirect costs.** Regardless of the service revenue recognition method selected, indirect costs should always be charged to expense as incurred.
2. **Initial direct costs and direct costs.**

   a. ***Specific performance and completed performance methods.*** When service revenue is recognized under the **specific performance** or **completed performance** methods, all **initial direct costs** and **direct costs** should be recognized as expense at the time the related service revenue is recognized. Thus, any initial direct costs and direct costs incurred prior to the performance of the service should be deferred as prepayments and expensed at the time of service performance (i.e., at the point revenue is recognized).

b. ***Proportional performance method.*** When service revenue is recognized under the **proportional performance method, initial direct costs** should be charged to expense at the time revenues are recognized. Thus, any initial direct costs incurred prior to performance should be deferred as prepayments and allocated to expense over the length of service performance in proportion to the recognition of service revenue. **Direct costs**, on the other hand, should be charged to expense as incurred because, normally, there is a close correlation between the amount of direct costs incurred and the extent of performance achieved.

c. ***Collection method.*** When service revenue is recognized under the collection method (high uncertainty surrounding the realization of revenue), both **initial direct costs** and **direct costs** should be charged to expense as incurred.

3. **Service transaction losses.** A loss on a service transaction should be recognized when initial direct costs plus estimated total direct costs of performance exceed the current estimated realizable revenue. The loss (Initial direct costs + Estimated total direct costs – Estimated realizable revenue) should be first used to reduce any deferred costs. If an estimated loss remains, it should be credited to an estimated liability account.

Initiation and Installation Fees

Many service transactions also involve the charge of a nonrefundable initiation fee with subsequent periodic payments for future services and/or a nonrefundable fee for installation of equipment essential to the provision of future services with subsequent periodic payments for the services. These nonrefundable fees may, in substance, be partly or wholly advance charges for future services.

Initiation fees. If there is an objectively determinable value for the right or privilege granted by the initiation fee, that value should be recognized as revenue on the initiation date. Any related direct costs should be charged as expense on the initiation date. If the value of the right or privilege cannot be objectively determined, the fee should be recorded as a liability for future services and recognized as revenue in accordance with one of the recognition methods.

Installation fees. If the equipment and its installation costs are essential for the service to be provided and if customers cannot normally purchase the equipment in separate transactions, the installation fee should be considered an advance charge for future services. This fee should be recognized as revenue over the estimated service period. The costs of installation and installed equipment should be amortized over the period the installation is expected to provide revenue. If customers can normally purchase the equipment in a separate transaction, the installation fee is then a product transaction that should be accounted for separately as such.

Recommended Disclosures--Not Required by GAAP

1. The revenue recognition method used and its justification
2. Information concerning unearned revenues
3. Information concerning deferred costs
4. Periods over which services are to be performed

EMERGING ISSUES TASK FORCE CONSENSUS SUMMARIES

91-9 Revenue and Expense Recognition for Freight Services in Process

The Task Force discussed the appropriate accounting methods which could be used for recognizing revenue and expense related to a freight service company's freight-in-transit at the end of a reporting period. A consensus was reached that recognition of revenue when freight is received from the shipper or when freight leaves the carrier's terminal with expenses recognized as incurred is no longer acceptable.

FASB TECHNICAL BULLETINS

90-1 Accounting for Separately Priced Extended Warranty and Product Maintenance Contracts

Background: Extended warranties provide additional protection to that of manufacturer's original warranty or lengthen period of coverage specified in manufacturer's original warranty. A product maintenance contract is an agreement for services to maintain a product for a certain length of time.

Question: Recognition of revenue and costs from a separately priced extended warranty or product maintenance contract.

Response: Revenue from these contracts should be deferred and recognized on straight-line basis unless evidence exists that costs are incurred on other basis. If so, allocate revenue to each period in ratio of the period's cost to total cost. Direct costs of obtaining a contract should be capitalized and expensed in the ratio that revenue recognized each period bears to total revenue on that contract. Any other costs should be charged to expense as incurred. Losses on these contracts should be recognized if the future costs and remaining direct acquisition costs exceed the related unearned revenue.

SALES WHEN COLLECTION IS UNCERTAIN

PERSPECTIVE AND ISSUES

Under GAAP, revenue recognition does not depend upon the collection of cash. Accrual accounting techniques normally record revenue at the point of a credit sale by establishing a receivable. When uncertainty arises surrounding the collectibility of this amount, the receivable is appropriately adjusted by establishing a contra account. In some cases, however, the collection of the sales price may be so uncertain that an objective measure of ultimate collectibility cannot be established. When such circumstances exist, APB 10 permits the seller to use either the installment method or the cost recovery method to account for installment transactions. Both of these methods allow for a deferral of gross profit until cash has been collected.

An installment transaction occurs when a seller delivers a product or performs a service and the buyer makes periodic payments over an extended period of time. Under the installment method, income recognition is deferred until the period(s) of cash collection. The seller recognizes both revenues and cost of sales at the time of the sale; however, the related gross profit is deferred to those periods in which cash is collected. Under the cost recovery method, both revenues and cost of sales are recognized at the time of the sale, but none of the related gross profit is recognized until all cost of sales has been recovered. Once the seller has recovered all cost of sales, any additional cash receipts are included in income. APB 10 does not specify when one method is preferred over the other. However, the cost recovery method is more conservative than the installment method because gross profit is deferred until all costs have been recovered; therefore, it should be reserved for situations of extreme uncertainty.

Sources of GAAP

APB	*SFAC*
10	3

DEFINITIONS OF TERMS

Cost recovery method. The method of accounting for an installment basis sale whereby the gross profit is deferred until all cost of sales has been recovered.

Deferred gross profit. The gross profit from an installment basis sale that is deferred to future periods.

Gross profit rate. The gross profit on the installment sale divided by the revenue from the installment sale.

Installment method. The method of accounting for an installment basis sale whereby the gross profit is recognized in the period(s) the cash from the sale is collected.

Installment sale. A sales transaction for which the sales price is collected through the payment of periodic installments over an extended period of time.

Net realizable value. The fair market value of an asset less any costs of disposal.

Realized gross profit. The gross profit recognized in the current period.

Repossessions. Merchandise sold by a seller under an installment arrangement that is repossessed after the buyer defaults on the payments.

CONCEPTS, RULES, AND EXAMPLES

The **installment method** was developed in response to an increasing number of sales contracts that allowed buyers to make payments over several years. As the payment period becomes longer, the risk of loss resulting from uncollectible accounts increases; consequently, circumstances surrounding a receivable may lead to considerable uncertainty as to whether payments will actually be received. Under these circumstances, the uncertainty of cash collection suggests that revenue recognition should be deferred until the actual receipt of cash.

The installment method can be used in most sales transactions for which payment is to be made through periodic installments over an extended period of time and the collectibility of the sales price cannot be reasonably estimated. This method is applicable to the sales of real estate (covered in the last section of this chapter), heavy equipment, home furnishings, and other merchandise sold on an installment basis. Installment method revenue recognition is not in accordance with accrual accounting because revenue recognition should not normally be based upon cash collection; however, its use may be justified on the grounds that accrual accounting may result in "front-end loading" (i.e., all of the revenue from a transaction is recognized at the point of sale with an improper matching of related costs). For example, the application of accrual accounting to transactions that provide for installment payments over periods of 10, 20, or 30 years may underestimate losses from contract defaults and other future contract costs.

Accounting Treatment

When a seller uses the installment method, both revenue and cost of sales are recognized at the point of sale, but the related gross profit is deferred to those periods over which cash will be collected. As receivables are collected, a portion of the **deferred gross profit** equal to the gross profit rate times the cash collected is recognized as income. When this method is used, the seller must compute each year's **gross profit rate** and also must maintain installment accounts receivable and deferred revenue accounts that are identified by the year of sale. All other general and administrative expenses are normally expensed in the period incurred.

The steps to use in accounting for sales under the installment method are as follows:

1. During the current year, record sales revenue and cost of sales in the regular manner. Record **installment sales** transactions separately from other sales. Set up installment accounts receivable identified by the year of sale (e.g., Installment Accounts Receivable--1999).
2. Record cash collections from installment accounts receivable. Care must be taken so that the cash receipts are properly identified as to the year in which the receivable arose.
3. At the end of the current year, close out the installment sales revenue and installment cost of sales accounts into a deferred gross profit account that properly identifies the year of sale. Compute the current year's gross profit rate on installment sales as follows:

$$\text{Gross profit rate} = 1 - \frac{\text{Cost of installment sales}}{\text{Installment sales revenue}}$$

Alternatively, the gross profit rate can be computed as follows:

$$\text{Gross profit rate} = \frac{\text{Installment sales revenue - Cost of installment sales}}{\text{Installment sales revenue}}$$

4. Apply the current year's gross profit rate to the cash collections from the current year's installment sales to compute the realized gross profit from the current year's installment sales.

$$\text{Realized gross profit} = \text{Cash collections from the current year's installment sales} \times \text{Current year's gross profit rate}$$

5. Apply the previous years' gross profit rates to cash collections from previous years' installment sales to compute the realized gross profit from previous years' installment sales.

$$\text{Realized gross profit} = \text{Cash collections from the previous years' installment sales} \times \text{Previous years' gross profit rates}$$

6. Defer the current year's unrealized gross profit to future years. The deferred gross profit to carry forward to future years can be computed in the following manner:

$$\text{Deferred gross profit (1999)} = \text{Ending balance installment account receivable (1999)} \times \text{Gross profit rate (1999)}$$

Example of the installment method of accounting

	1999	*2000*	*2001*
Sales on installment	$ 400,000	$ 450,000	$ 600,000
Cost of installment sales	(280,000)	(337,500)	(400,000)
Gross profit on sales	$ 120,000	$ 112,500	$ 200,000

Cash collections:			
1999 sales	$ 150,000	$ 175,000	$ 75,000
2000 sales		$ 200,000	$ 125,000
2001 sales			$ 300,000

Journal entries would be made for steps 1, 2, and 3 above using this data; the following computations are required for steps 3-6:

Step 3 -- Compute the current year's gross profit rate.

	1999	*2000*	*2001*
Gross profit on sales	$120,000	$112,500	$200,000
Installment sales revenue	$400,000	$450,000	$600,000
Gross profit rate	30%	25%	33 1/3%

Step 4 -- Apply the current year's gross profit rate to cash collections from current year's sales.

Year	*Cash collections*		*Gross profit rate*		*Realized gross profit*
1999	$150,000	x	30%	=	$ 45,000
2000	200,000	x	25%	=	50,000
2001	300,000	x	33 1/3%	=	100,000

Step 5 -- Apply the previous years' gross profit rates to cash collections from previous years' installment sales.

In Year 2000

From year	*Cash collections*		*Gross profit rate*		*Realized gross profit*
1999	$175,000	x	30%	=	$52,500

In Year 2001

From year	*Cash collections*		*Gross profit rate*		*Realized gross profit*
1999	$ 75,000	x	30%	=	$22,500
2000	125,000	x	25%	=	31,250
					$53,750

Step 6 -- Defer the current year's unrealized gross profit to future years.

12/31/99

Deferred gross profit (1999) = ($400,000 – 150,000) x 30%	=	$ 75,000

12/31/00

Deferred gross profit (2000) = ($450,000 – 200,000) x 25%	=	$ 62,500
Deferred gross profit (1999) = ($400,000 – 150,000 – 175,000) x 30%	=	22,500
		$ 85,000

12/31/01

Deferred gross profit (2001) = ($600,000 – 300,000) x 33 1/3%	=	$100,000
Deferred gross profit (2000) = ($450,000 – 200,000 – 125,000) x 25%	=	31,250
		$131,250

Financial Statement Presentation

If installment sales transactions represent a significant portion of the company's total sales, the following three items of gross profit should, theoretically, be reported on the company's income statement:

1. Total gross profit from current year's sales
2. Realized gross profit from current year's sales
3. Realized gross profit from prior years' sales

An income statement using the previous example would be prepared as follows (assume all sales are accounted for by the installment method):

Thorsen Equipment Company
Partial Income Statement
For the Years Ending December 31

	1999	*2000*	*2001*
Sales	$400,000	$450,000	$600,000
Cost of sales	(280,000)	(337,500)	(400,000)
Gross profit on current sales	$120,000	$112,500	$200,000
Less deferred gross profit on current sales	(75,000)	(62,500)	(100,000)
Realized gross profit on current sales	$ 45,000	$ 50,000	$100,000
Plus realized gross profit on prior sales	--	52,500	53,750
Total gross profit on sales	$ 45,000	$102,500	$153,750

However, when a company recognizes only a small portion of its sales under the installment basis, the previous method of income reporting may be confusing. Therefore, in practice, some companies simply report the realized gross profit from installment sales by displaying it as a single line item on the income statement as follows:

Wisbrock Furniture Company
Partial Income Statement
For the Year Ended December 31, 1999

Sales	$ 2,250,000
Cost of sales	(1,350,000)
Gross profit on sales	$ 900,000
Realized gross profit on installment sales	35,000
Total gross profit on sales	$ 935,000

The balance sheet presentation of the installment accounts receivable will depend upon whether the installment sales are part of normal operations. If a company sells most of its products on an installment basis, the installment accounts receivable will be classified as a current asset because the operating cycle of the business is the average period of time covered by an installment contract. If the installment sales are not part of normal operations, installment accounts receivable that are not to be collected for a year or more should not be reported as current assets. In all cases, to avoid any confusion, it is generally desirable to fully disclose the year of maturity next to each set of installment accounts receivable as illustrated by the following example:

Current assets:		
Cash		$ 56,682
Receivables:		
Trade customers	$180,035	
Less allowance for uncollectible accounts	(4,200)	
	$175,835	
Installment accounts--collectible in 2000	26,678	
Installment accounts--collectible in 2001	42,234	$244,747

The accounting for the deferred gross profit account(s) is addressed in SFAC 3 which states that the deferred gross profit account is not a liability. The reason is that the seller company is not obligated to pay cash or provide services to the customer. Rather, the account arose because of the uncertainty surrounding the collectibility of the sales price. SFAC 3 goes on to say, "deferred gross profit on installment sales is conceptually an asset valuation--that is, a reduction of an asset." However, in practice, the deferred gross profit account is generally presented as either an unearned revenue classified as a current liability or a deferred credit displayed between liabilities and equity. Following the guideline given by SFAC 3, the current asset section would be presented as follows (using information from the Thorsen Equipment example and assuming a 12/31/01 balance sheet):

Installment accounts receivable	(2000)	$125,000		
Installment accounts receivable	(2001)	300,000	$ 425,000	
Less: Deferred gross profit	(2000)	$ 31,250		
Deferred gross profit	(2001)	100,000	(131,250)	$293,750

Interest on Installment Contracts

The previous examples ignored interest, a major component of most installment sales contracts. It is customary for the seller to charge interest to the buyer on the unpaid installment receivable balance. Generally, installment contracts call for equal payments, each with an amount attributable to interest on the unpaid balance and the remainder to the installment receivable balance. As the maturity date nears, a smaller amount of each installment payment is attributable to interest and a larger amount is attributable to principal. Therefore, to determine the amount of gross profit to recognize, the interest must first be deducted from the installment payment and then the difference is multiplied by the gross profit rate as follows:

Realized gross profit = (Installment payment – Interest portion) x Gross profit rate

The interest portion of the installment payment should be recorded as interest revenue at the time of the cash receipt. Appropriate adjusting entries are required to accrue interest revenue when the collection dates do not correspond with the year end.

To illustrate the accounting for installment sales contracts involving interest, assume that Babich Equipment Company sold a piece of machinery on January 1, 1999, to a customer with a dubious credit history. The equipment had a cost of $3,750 and a sales price of $5,000. Terms of the agreement required that a $1,000 down payment be made on the date of the sale and that the remaining balance ($4,000) plus 10% annual interest be paid in equal installments of $1,261.88 at the end of each of the next 4 years.

For each cash receipt Babich must determine the amount applicable to interest revenue and the value applicable to the installment account receivable balance because gross profit is recognized only on those amounts applicable to the installment receivable balance. It can be seen in the following schedule that gross profit is recognized on the entire down payment, whereas the annual installment payments are separated into their interest and receivable portions with gross profit only being recognized on the latter portion.

Schedule of Cash Receipts

Date	Cash (debit)	Interest revenue (credit)	Installment accounts receivable (credit)	Installment accounts receivable balance	Realized gross profit
1/1/99				$5,000.00	
1/1/99	$1,000.00	$ --	$1,000.00	4,000.00	$ 250.00[a]
12/31/99	1,261.88	400.00[b]	861.88[c]	3,138.12[d]	215.47[e]
12/31/00	1,261.88	313.81	948.07	2,190.05	237.02
12/31/01	1,261.88	219.01	1,042.87	1,147.18	260.72
12/31/02	1,261.88	114.70	1,147.18	-0-	286.79
		Total realized gross profit			$1,250.00

Gross profit rate = 1 – $3,750/5,000 = 25%

[a] $1,000 x 25% = $250
[b] $4,000 x 10% = $400
[c] $1,261.88 – 400 = $861.88
[d] $4,000 – 861.88 = $3,138.12
[e] $861.88 x 25% = $215.47

Bad Debts and Repossessions

The standard accounting treatment for uncollectible accounts is to accrue a bad debt loss in the year of sale by estimating the amount that is expected to be uncollectible. This treatment is in line with the concept of accrual. However, just as income recognition under the accrual basis is sometimes abandoned for certain installment basis sales, the accrual basis of recognizing bad debts is also often abandoned.

When the installment method is used, it is usually appropriate to recognize bad debts by the direct write-off method (i.e., bad debts are not recognized until the account has been determined to be uncollectible). This practice is acceptable because most installment contracts contain a provision that allows the seller to repossess the merchandise when the buyer defaults on the installment payments. The loss on the account may be eliminated or reduced because the seller has the option of reselling merchandise. When an installment account is written off, the following three things must be accomplished:

1. The installment account receivable and the deferred gross profit must be eliminated.
2. The repossessed merchandise must be recorded at its **net realizable value**. Net realizable value is the resale value less any sales or reconditioning costs. The repossessed asset is recorded at this fair value because any asset acquired should be put on the books at the best approximation of its fair value. Repossessed merchandise is inventory in the seller's hands and, therefore, should be presented in the inventory section of the balance sheet.
3. A bad debt expense, a repossession loss, or a repossession gain should be recognized. The bad debt expense or repossession gain or loss is the difference between the unrecovered cost (Installment account receivable – Deferred gross profit) and the net realizable value of the repossessed merchandise.

To illustrate, assume that the Fahey Company determined that a $3,000 installment receivable is uncollectible. The deferred gross profit ratio on the original sale was 30%; thus, $900 deferred gross profit exists ($3,000 x 30%). If the repossessed equipment has a $1,500 net realizable value, a $600 repossession loss (or bad debt expense) would need to be recorded.

Installment account receivable	$3,000
Less deferred gross profit	(900)
Unrecovered cost	$2,100
Less net realizable value	(1,500)
Repossession loss	$ 600

Fahey Company would record this loss by making the following entry:

Deferred gross profit	900	
Repossessed merchandise	1,500	
Repossession loss	600	
Installment account receivable		3,000

Cost Recovery

The cost recovery method does not recognize any income on a sale until the cost of the item has been recovered through cash receipts. Once the seller has recovered all costs, any subsequent cash receipts are included in income. The cost recovery method is used when the uncertainty of collection of the sale price is so great that even use of the installment method cannot be justified.

Under the cost recovery method, both revenues and cost of sales are recognized at the point of sale, but the related gross profit is deferred until all costs of sales have been recovered. Each installment must also be divided between principal and interest, but unlike the installment method where a portion of the principal recovers the cost of sales and the remainder is recognized as gross profit, all of the principal is first applied to recover the cost of the asset sold. After all costs of sales have been recovered, any subsequent cash receipts are realized as gross profit. The cost recovery method can be illustrated by using the information from the Babich Company example used in the interest on installment sales contract section. If Babich used the cost recovery method, gross profit would be realized as follows:

Schedule of Cash Receipts

Date	Cash (debit)	Deferred interest revenue (credit)*	Installment accounts receivable (credit)	Installment accounts receivable balance	Unrecovered cost	Realized gross profit	Realized interest revenue
1/1/99				$5,000.00	$3,750.00		
1/1/99	$1,000.00	$ --	$1,000.00	4,000.00	2,750.00	$ --	$ --
12/31/99	1,261.88	400.00	861.88	3,138.12	1,488.12	--	--
12/31/00	1,261.88	313.81	948.07	2,190.05	226.24	--	--
12/31/01	1,261.88	(713.81)	1,042.87	1,147.18	--	102.82	932.82**
12/31/02	1,261.88	--	1,147.18	-0-	--	1,147.18	114.70
	$6,047.52		$5,000.00			$1,250.00	$1,047.52

Interest received in 1999 and 2000 would be credited to deferred interest revenue since the cost of the asset was not recovered until 2001.

***Includes deferred interest revenue received in 1999 and 2000 [$713.81 (1999 and 2000) + $219.01 (2000)]. Interest revenue can only be realized after the cost of the asset is recovered (2001, in this example).*

REVENUE RECOGNITION WHEN RIGHT OF RETURN EXISTS

PERSPECTIVE AND ISSUES

In some industries it is common practice for customers to be given the right to return a product to the seller for a credit or refund. However, for companies that experience a high ratio of returned merchandise to sales, the recognition of the original sale as revenue is questionable. In fact, certain industries have found it necessary to defer revenue recognition until the return privilege has substantially expired. Sometimes the return privilege expires soon after the sale, as in the newspaper and perishable food industries. In other cases, the return privilege may last over an extended period of time, as in magazine and textbook publishing and equipment manufacturing. The rate of return normally is directly related to the length of the return privilege. An accounting problem arises when the recognition of the revenue occurs in one period while substantial returns occur in later periods.

SOP 75-1 was developed to reduce the diversity in the accounting for revenue recognition when the right of return exists. The FASB extracted the specialized accounting and reporting principles and practices from SOP 75-1 and reissued them through SFAS 48, *Revenue Recognition When Right of Return Exists*.

Sources of GAAP

SFAS

5, 48

DEFINITIONS OF TERMS

Deferred gross profit. The gross profit from a sale that is deferred to future periods because of the uncertainty surrounding the collection of the sales price.

Return privilege. A privilege granted to a buyer by express agreement with a seller or by practice of the industry that allows the buyer to return merchandise to the seller within a stated period of time.

CONCEPTS, RULES, AND EXAMPLES

SFAS 48 provides criteria for recognizing revenue on a sale in which a product may be returned (as a matter of contract or a matter of industry practice), either by the ultimate consumer or by a party who resells the product to others. Paragraph 6 states the following:

> *If an enterprise sells its product but gives the buyer the right to return the product, revenue from the sales transaction shall be recognized at time of sale only if all of the following conditions are met:*

a. The seller's price to the buyer is substantially fixed or determinable at the date of sale.

b. The buyer has paid the seller, or the buyer is obligated to pay the seller and the obligation is not contingent on resale of the product.

c. The buyer's obligation to the seller would not be changed in the event of theft or physical destruction or damage of the product.

d. The buyer acquiring the product for resale has economic substance apart from that provided by the seller.

e. The seller does not have significant obligations for future performance to directly bring about the resale of the product by the buyer.

f. The amount of future returns can be reasonably estimated. For purposes of this statement "returns" do not include exchanges by ultimate customers of one item for another of the same kind, quality, and price.

If all of the above conditions are met, the seller should recognize revenue from the sales transaction at the time of the sale and "any costs or losses that may be expected in connection with any returns shall be accrued in accordance with SFAS 5, *Accounting for Contingencies*" (para 7). SFAS 5 states that estimated losses from contingencies shall be accrued and charged to income when it is probable that an asset has been impaired or a liability incurred and the amount of loss can be reasonably estimated.

The interplay between SFAS 48 and SFAS 5 needs further explanation. Although SFAS 48 requires under condition f. that the amount of the returns be reasonably estimated, it does not reference the standard to the SFAS 5 loss accrual criteria. Accordingly, a strict interpretation of both SFAS 48 and SFAS 5 would indicate that only when the conditions for loss accrual under SFAS 5 are met would the condition f. above under SFAS 48 be also met, and both sales and estimated returns can be recorded. However, a more liberal interpretation of SFAS 48 would indicate that, by not cross-referencing SFAS 5, the FASB intended that the sole criterion for return accrual under SFAS 48 be the "reasonably estimated" condition f. Then, whether losses are probable or reasonably possible, they would be accrued under SFAS 48 and the sales could also be recognized. If the likelihood losses are remote, only a footnote would be required under SFAS 5 and condition f. under SFAS 48 would be achieved and sales recorded. Under this theory, only if returns cannot be reasonably estimated, regardless of whether losses are probable or reasonably possible, would accrual of sales under SFAS 48 be precluded.

Example of sale with right of return

Assume that Lee, Inc. began the sale of its new textbook on computer programming in 1999 with the following results: On December 1, 1999, 2,000 textbooks with a sales price of $45 each and total manufacturing costs of $30 each are delivered to school bookstores on account. The bookstores have the right to return the textbooks within 4 months of the delivery date. The bookstores remit cash payments when the books are sold. Payment and returns for the initial deliveries are as follows:

	Cash receipts		Returns	
	Units	Amount	Units	Amount
December 1999	600	$27,000	--	--
January 2000	500	22,500	40	$1,800
February 2000	400	18,000	90	4,050
March 2000	300	13,500	30	1,350
	1,800	$81,000	160	$7,200

Lee, Inc. has had similar agreements with the bookstores in the past and has experienced a 15% return rate on similar sales.

Requirements for revenue recognition met. If all six of the requirements were met, the following journal entries would be appropriate:

Date	Account	Debit	Credit
12/1/99	Accounts receivable	90,000	
	Sales (2,000 units x $45 per unit)		90,000
	(To record sale of 2,000 textbooks)		
12/31/99	Cash (600 units x $45 per unit)	27,000	
	Accounts receivable		27,000
	(To record cash receipts for the month)		
	Cost of sales	60,000	
	Inventory (2,000 units x $30 per unit)		60,000
	(To record cost of goods sold for the month)		
	Sales (15% x 2,000 units x $45 per unit)	13,500	
	Cost of sales (15% x 2,000 units x $30 per unit)		9,000
	Deferred gross profit on estimated returns (15% x 2,000 units x $15 per unit)		4,500
	(To record estimate of returns)		
1/1/00 to 3/31/00	Cash	54,000	
	Accounts receivable		54,000
	(To record cash receipts)		
	Inventory (160 units x $30 per unit)	4,800	
	Deferred gross profit on estimated returns	2,400	
	Accounts receivable (160 units x $45 per unit)		7,200
	(To record returns)		
3/31/00	Cost of sales (140 units x $30 per unit)	4,200	
	Deferred gross profit on estimated returns	2,100	
	Sales (140 units x $45 per unit)		6,300

The revenue and cost of goods sold recognized in 1999 are based on the number of units expected to be returned, 300 (15% x 2,000 units). The net revenue recognized is $76,500 (85% x 2,000 units x $45 per unit) and the cost of goods sold recognized is $51,000 (85% x 2,000 units x $30 per unit). The deferred gross profit balance is carried forward until the textbooks are returned or until the privilege expires.

Requirements for revenue recognition not met. If all six conditions are not met, revenue and cost of sales from the sales transactions must be deferred until either the return privilege has substantially expired or the point when all the conditions are subsequently met, whichever comes first (para 6).

In the Lee case, if any one of the six conditions is not met, the following entries would be required. The return privilege is assumed to be lost by the store when the books are sold to final customers.

Date	Account	Debit	Credit
12/1/99	Accounts receivable	90,000	
	Sales		90,000
	(To record sale of 2,000 units)		
12/31/99	Cash	27,000	
	Accounts receivable		27,000
	(To record cash receipts)		
	Cost of sales	60,000	
	Inventory		60,000
	(To record cost of goods sold)		
	Sales (1,400 units x $45 per unit)	63,000	
	Cost of sales (1,400 units x $30 per unit)		42,000
	Deferred gross profit		21,000
	(To defer revenue recognition on goods for which the right of return expires on 3/31/00)		
1/1/00 to 3/31/00	Cash	54,000	
	Accounts receivable (1,200 units x $45 per unit)		54,000
	(To record cash receipts)		
	Cost of sales (1,200 units x $30 per unit)	36,000	
	Deferred gross profit	18,000	
	Sales		54,000
	(To recognize revenue and cost of goods sold on cash receipts)		
	Inventory (160 units x $30 per unit)	4,800	
	Deferred gross profit	2,400	
	Accounts receivable		7,200
	(To record sales returns)		
3/31/00	Cost of sales (40 units x $30 per unit)	1,200	
	Deferred gross profit	600	
	Sales (40 units x $45 per unit)		1,800
	(To record revenue and cost of goods sold on products for which right of return expired)		

PROFIT RECOGNITION ON REAL ESTATE SALES

PERSPECTIVE AND ISSUES

The substance of a sale of any asset is that the transaction should transfer the risks and rewards of ownership to the buyer. However, the economic substance of many real estate sales is that the risks and rewards of ownership have not been clearly transferred. The turbulent environment in the real estate market over the last 15 years has led to the evolution of many complex methods of financing real estate transactions. For example, in some transactions the seller, rather than an independent third party, finances the buyer, while in others, the seller may be required to guarantee a minimum return to the buyer or operate the property for a specified period of time. In many of these complex transactions, the seller still has some association with the property even after the property has been sold. The question that must be answered in these transactions is: At what point does the seller become disassociated enough so that profit may be recognized on the transaction?

Accounting for sales of real estate is governed by SFAS 66. This statement adopts the specialized profit recognition principles in the AICPA Industry Accounting Guide, *Accounting for Profit Recognition on Sales of Real Estate* and AICPA Statements of Position 75-6, *Questions Concerning Profit Recognition on Sales of Real Estate*, and 78-4, *Application of the Deposit, Installment, and Cost Recovery Methods in Accounting for Sales of Real Estate*. Due to the complex nature of these real estate transactions, SFAS 66 is very detailed and complex. The purpose of this section is to present the guidelines that need to be considered when analyzing nonretail real estate transactions. SFAS 98 dealing with sales leaseback real estate transactions and sales-type real estate leases is covered by the lease chapter in this book on pages 482 and 492.

Sources of GAAP

SFAS
66, 98

DEFINITIONS OF TERMS

Continuing investment. Payments that the buyer is contractually required to pay on its total debt for the purchase price of the property.

Cost recovery method. A method which defers the recognition of gross profit on a real estate sale until the seller recovers the cost of the property sold.

Deposit method. A method which records payments by the buyer as deposits rather than a sale. The seller continues to report the asset and related debt on the balance until the contract is canceled or until the sale has been achieved.

First mortgage (primary debt). The debt the seller has on the property at the time the buyer purchases the property.

Full accrual method. A method which recognizes all profit from a real estate sale at the time of sale.

Initial investment. The sales value received by the seller at the point of sale. It includes cash down payment, buyer's notes supported by an irrevocable letter of credit and payment by the buyer to third parties to reduce seller indebtedness on the property.

Installment method. A method which recognizes income on the basis of payments made by the buyer on debt given to seller and payments by the buyer to the holder of primary debt. Each payment is apportioned between profit and cost recovery.

Lien. A claim or charge a creditor has on property for payment on debt by debtor.

Minimum initial investment. The minimum amount that an initial investment must equal or exceed so that the criterion for full accrual is met.

Partial sale. A sale in which the seller retains an equity interest in the property or has an equity interest in the buyer.

Property improvements. An addition made to real estate, usually consisting of buildings but may also include any permanent structure such as streets, sidewalks, sewers, utilities, etc.

Reduced profit method. A method which recognizes profit at the point of sale, but only a reduced amount. The remaining profit is deferred to future periods.

Release provision. An agreement that provides for the release of property to the buyer. This agreement releases the property to the buyer free of any previous liens.

Sales value. The sales price of the property increased or decreased for other consideration in the sales transaction that are, in substance, additional sales proceeds to the buyer.

Subordination. The process by which a person's rights are ranked below the rights of others.

CONCEPTS, RULES, AND EXAMPLES

Real Estate Sales Other Than Retail Land Sales

Profit from real estate sales may be recognized in full, provided the following:

1. The profit is determinable (i.e., the collectibility of the sales price is reasonably assured or the amount that will not be collectible can be estimated).
2. The earnings process is virtually complete, that is, the seller is not obliged to perform significant activities after the sale to earn the profit (SFAS 66, para 3).

When both of these conditions are satisfied, the method used to recognize profits on real estate sales is referred to as the **full accrual method.** If both of these conditions are not satisfied, recognition of all or part of the profit should be postponed.

For real estate sales, the collectibility of the sales price is reasonably assured when the buyer has demonstrated a commitment to pay. This commitment is supported by a substantial **initial investment**, along with **continuing investments** that give the buyer a sufficient stake in the property such that the risk of loss through default motivates the buyer to honor its obligations to the seller. Collectibility of the sales price should also be assessed by examining the conditions surrounding the sale (e.g., credit history of the buyer; age, condition, and location of the property; and history of cash flows generated by the property).

The full accrual method is appropriate and profit shall be recognized in full at the point of sale for real estate transactions when all of the following criteria are met:

1. A sale is consummated.
2. The buyer's initial and continuing investments are adequate to demonstrate a commitment to pay for the property.
3. The seller's receivable is not subject to future **subordination**.
4. The seller has transferred to the buyer the usual risks and rewards of ownership in a transaction that is, in substance, a sale and does not have a substantial continuing involvement in the property.

On sales in which an independent third party provides all of the financing for the buyer, the seller should be most concerned that criterion 1. is met. For such sales, the sale is usually consummated on the closing date. When the seller finances the buyer, the seller must analyze the economic substance of the agreement to ascertain that criteria 2., 3., and 4. are also met (i.e., whether the transaction clearly transfers the risks and rewards of ownership to the buyer).

On sales in which a buyer assumes debt on property, the FASB Emerging Issues Task Force (EITF) has reached a consensus (88-24) that if the seller is not released from its liability, the seller may use the full accrual method. Proceeds from incurrence of debts secured by the property are not to be included in computing either the buyer's initial investment or cash payments under nonfull accrual methods.

Consummation of a sale. A sale is considered consummated when the following conditions are met:

1. The parties are bound by the terms of a contract.
2. All consideration has been exchanged.
3. Any permanent financing for which the seller is responsible has been arranged.
4. All conditions precedent to closing have been performed.

When a seller is constructing office buildings, condominiums, shopping centers, or similar structures, item 4. may be applied to individual units rather than the entire project. These four conditions are usually met on or after closing, not at the point the agreement to sell is signed or at a preclosing. Closing refers to the final steps of the transaction (i.e., when consideration is paid, mortgage is secured, and the deed is delivered or placed in escrow). If the consummation criteria **have not** been satisfied, the seller should use the deposit method of accounting until the sale has been consummated.

Adequacy of the buyer's initial investment. Once it has been determined that the sale has been consummated, the next step is to determine whether the buyer's initial investment adequately demonstrates a commitment to pay for the property and the reasonable likelihood that the seller will collect it. This determination is made by comparing the buyer's initial investment to the sales value of the property. SFAS 66 specifically details items that are includable as the initial investment and the minimum percentages that the initial investment must bear as a percentage of the sales value of the property. In order to make the determination of whether the initial investment is adequate, the sale value of the property must also be computed.

Computation of sales value. The sales value of property in a real estate transaction can be computed by the following formula (SFAS 66, para 7):

	Stated sales price
+	Proceeds from the issuance of an **exercised** purchase option
+	Other payments that are, in substance, additional sales proceeds (e.g., management fees, points, or prepaid interest or fees required to be maintained in advance of the sale that will be applied against amounts due to the seller at a later point)
–	A discount that reduces the buyer's note to its present value
–	Net present value of services seller agrees to perform without compensation
–	Excess of net present value of services seller performs over compensation that seller will receive
=	Sales value of the property

Composition of the initial investment. Sales transactions are characterized by many different types of payments and commitments made between the seller, buyer, and third parties; however, the buyer's initial investment shall only include the following:

1. Cash paid to the seller as a down payment
2. Buyer's notes given to the seller that are supported by irrevocable letters of credit from independent lending institutions
3. Payments by the buyer to third parties that reduce existing indebtedness the seller has on the property
4. Other amounts paid by the buyer that are part of the sale value

5. Other consideration received by the seller that can be converted to cash without recourse to the seller for example, other notes of the buyer (SFAS 66, para 9)

SFAS 66 specifically states that the following items should not be included as initial investment (para 10):

1. Payments by the buyer to third parties for improvements to the property
2. A permanent loan commitment by an independent third party to replace a loan made by the seller
3. Funds that have been or will be loaned, refunded, or directly or indirectly provided to the buyer by the seller or loans guaranteed or collateralized by the seller for the buyer

Size of initial investment. Once the initial investment is computed, its size must be compared to the sales value of the property. To qualify as an adequate initial investment, the initial investment should be equal to at least a major part of the difference between usual loan limits established by independent lending institutions and the sales value of the property. The **minimum initial investment** requirements for real estate sales (other than retail land sales) vary depending upon the class of property being used. The following table from SFAS 66, Appendix A, provides the limits for the various properties:

Type of property	*Minimum initial investment expressed as a percentage of sales value*
Land	
Held for commercial, industrial, or residential development to commence within 2 years after sale	20
Held for commercial, industrial, or residential development to commence after 2 years	25
Commercial and Industrial Property	
Office and industrial buildings, shopping centers, and so forth:	
Properties subject to lease on a long-term lease basis to parties with satisfactory credit rating; cash flow currently sufficient to service all indebtedness	10
Single-tenancy properties sold to a buyer with a satisfactory credit rating	15
All other	20
Other income-producing properties (hotels, motels, marinas, mobile home parks, and so forth):	
Cash flow currently sufficient to service all indebtedness	15
Start-up situations or current deficiencies in cash flow	25

Multifamily Residential Property	
Primary residence:	
Cash flow currently sufficient to service all indebtedness	10
Start-up situations or current deficiencies in cash flow	15
Secondary or recreational residence:	
Cash flow currently sufficient to service all indebtedness	15
Start-up situations or current deficiencies in cash flow	25
Single-Family Residential Property (including condominium or cooperative housing)	
Primary residence of the buyer	5[a]
Secondary or recreational residence	10[a]

[a] *If collectibility of the remaining portion of the sales price cannot be supported by reliable evidence of collection experience, the minimum initial investment shall be at least 60% of the difference between the sales value and the financing available from loans guaranteed by regulatory bodies such as the Federal Housing Authority (FHA) or the Veterans Administration (VA), or from independent, established lending institutions. This 60% test applies when independent first-mortgage financing is not utilized and the seller takes a receivable from the buyer for the difference between the sales value and the initial investment. If independent first mortgage financing is utilized, the adequacy of the initial investment on sales of single-family residential property should be determined in accordance with paragraph 53.*

However, lenders' appraisals of specific properties often differ. Therefore, if the buyer has obtained a permanent loan or firm permanent loan commitment for maximum financing of the property from an independent lending institution, the minimum initial investment should be the greater of the following (SFAS 66, Appendix A):

1. The minimum percentage of the sales value of the property specified in the above table
2. The lesser of
   a. The amount of the sales value of the property in excess of 115% of the amount of a newly placed permanent loan or firm loan commitment from a primary lender that is an independent established lending institution
   b. 25% of the sales value

To illustrate the determination of whether an initial investment adequately demonstrates a commitment to pay for property, consider the following example:

Example determining adequacy of initial investment

Krueger, Inc. exercised a $2,000 option for the purchase of an apartment building from Gampfer, Inc. The terms of the sales contract required Krueger to pay $3,000 of delinquent property taxes, pay a $300,000 cash down payment, assume Gampfer's recently issued **first mortgage** of $1,200,000, and give Gampfer a second mortgage of $500,000 at a prevailing interest rate.

Step 1 -- Compute the sales value of the property.

Payment of back taxes to reduce Gampfer's liability to local municipality	$ 3,000
Proceeds from exercised option	2,000
Cash down payment	300,000
First mortgage assumed by Krueger	1,200,000
Second mortgage given to Gampfer	500,000
Sales value of the apartment complex	$2,005,000

Step 2 -- Compute the initial investment.

Cash down payment	$300,000
Payment of back taxes to reduce Gampfer's liability to local municipality	3,000
Proceeds from exercised option	2,000
	$305,000

Step 3 -- Compute the minimum initial investment required.

a. The minimum percentage of the sales value of the property as specified in the table is $200,500 ($2,005,000 x 10%).

b. 1. The amount of the sales value of the property in excess of 115% of the recently placed permanent mortgage is $625,000 (sales value of $2,005,000 – $1,380,000 [115% of $1,200,000]).

   2. 25% of the sales value ($2,005,000) is $501,250.

The lesser of b.1 and b.2 is b.2, $501,250. The greater of a. and b. is b., $501,250. Therefore, to record this transaction under the full accrual method (assuming all other criteria are met), the minimum initial investment must be equal to or greater than $501,250. Since the actual initial investment is only $305,000, all or part of the recognition of profit from the transaction must be postponed.

If the sale has been consummated but the buyer's initial investment does not adequately demonstrate a commitment to pay, the transaction should be accounted for by the **installment method** when the seller is reasonably assured of **recovering the cost** of the property if the buyer defaults. However, if the recovery of the cost of the property is not reasonably assured should the buyer default or if the cost has been recovered and the collection of additional amounts is uncertain, the cost recovery or deposit methods should be used (para 22).

Adequacy of the buyer's continuing investments. The collectibility of the buyer's receivable must be reasonably assured; therefore, for full profit recognition under the full accrual method, the buyer must be contractually required to pay each year on its total debt for the purchase price of the property an amount at least equal to the level annual payment that would be needed to pay that debt (both principal and interest) over a specified period. This period is no more than 20 years for land, and no more than the customary amortization term of a first mortgage loan by an independent lender for other types of real estate (SFAS 66, para 12). For continuing investment purposes, the contractually required payments must be in a form that is acceptable for an initial investment. If the seller provides funds to the buyer, either directly or indirectly, these funds must be subtracted from the buyer's payments in determining whether the continuing investments are adequate.

The indebtedness on the property does not have to be reduced proportionately. A lump-sum (balloon) payment will not affect the amortization of the receivable as long as the level annual payments still meet the minimum annual amortization requirement. For example, a land real estate sale may require the buyer to make level annual payments at the end of the first 5 years and then a balloon payment at the end of the sixth year. The continuing investment criterion is met provided the level annual payment required in each of the first 5 years is greater than or equal to the level annual payment that would be made if the receivable were amortized over the maximum 20-year (land's specified term) period.

Continuing investment not qualifying. If the sale has been consummated and the minimum initial investment criteria have been satisfied but the continuing investment by the buyer does not meet the stated criterion, the seller shall recognize profit by the **reduced profit method** at the time of sale if payments by the buyer each year will at least cover both of the following:

1. The interest and principal amortization on the maximum first mortgage loan that could be obtained on the property
2. Interest, at an appropriate rate, on the excess of the aggregate actual debt on the property over such a maximum first mortgage loan (para 23)

If the payments by the buyer do not cover both of the above, the seller may recognize profit by either the **installment** or **cost recovery** method.

Release provisions. An agreement to sell real estate may provide that part or all of the property sold will be released from liens by payment of an amount sufficient to release the debt or by an assignment of the buyer's payments until release. In order to meet the criteria of an adequate initial investment, the investment must be sufficient both to pay the release on property released and to meet the initial investment requirements on property not released. If not, profit is recognized on each released portion as if a separate sale when a sale has been deemed to have taken place.

Seller's receivable subject to future subordination. The seller's receivable should not be subject to future subordination. Future subordination by a primary lender would permit the lender to obtain a **lien** on the property, giving the seller only a secondary residual claim. This subordination criterion does not apply if either of the following occur:

1. A receivable is subordinate to a first mortgage on the property existing at the time of sale.

2. A future loan, including an existing permanent loan commitment, is provided for by the terms of the sale and the proceeds of the loan will be applied first to the payment of the seller's receivable (para 17).

If the seller's receivable is subject to future subordination, profit shall be recognized by the **cost recovery method**. The cost recovery method is justified because the collectibility of the sales price is not reasonably assured in circumstances when the receivable may be subordinated to other creditors.

Seller's continuing involvement. Sometimes sellers continue to be involved with property for periods of time even though the property has been legally sold. The seller's involvement often takes the form of profit participation, management services, financing, guarantees of return, construction, etc. The seller does not have a substantial continuing involvement with property unless the risks and rewards of ownership have been clearly transferred to the buyer.

If the seller has some continuing involvement with the property and does not clearly transfer substantially all of the risks and rewards of ownership, profit shall be recognized by a method other than the full accrual method. The method chosen should be determined by the nature and extent of the seller's continuing involvement. As a general rule, profit should only be recognized at the time of sale if the amount of the seller's loss due to the continued involvement with the property is limited by the terms of the sales contract. In this event, the profit recognized at this time should be reduced by the maximum possible loss from the continued involvement.

Profit-sharing, financing, and leasing arrangements. In real estate sales, it is often the case that economic substance takes precedence over legal form. Certain transactions, though possibly called sales, are in substance profit-sharing, financing, or leasing arrangements and should be accounted for as such. These include situations in which

1. The seller has an obligation to repurchase the property, or the terms of the transaction allow the buyer to compel the seller or give an option to the seller to repurchase the property (para 26).
2. The seller is a general partner in a limited partnership that acquires an interest in the property sold and holds a receivable from the buyer for a significant part (15% of the maximum first-lien financing) of the sales price (para 27).
3. The seller guarantees the return of the buyer's investment or a return on that investment for an **extended** period of time (para 28).
4. The seller is required to initiate or support operations, or continue to operate property at its own risk for an **extended** period of time (para 29).

Options to purchase real estate property. Often a buyer will buy an option to purchase land from a seller with the hopeful intention of obtaining a zoning change, building permit, or some other contingency specified in the option agreement. Proceeds from the issue of an option by a property owner (seller) should be accounted for by the **deposit method**. If the option is exercised, the seller should include the option proceeds in the computation of the sales value of the property. If the option is not exercised, the seller should recognize the option proceeds as income at the time the option expires.

Partial sales of property. Per SFAS 66, para 33, "a sale is a partial sale if the seller retains an equity interest in the property or has an equity interest in the buyer." Profit on a partial sale may be recognized on the date of sale if the following occur:

1. The buyer is independent of the seller.
2. Collection of the sales price is reasonably assured.
3. The seller will not be required to support the operations of the property on its related obligations to an extent greater than its proportionate interest (para 33).

If the buyer is not independent of the seller, the seller may not be able to recognize any profit that is measured at the date of sale.

If the seller is not reasonably assured of collecting the sales price, the **cost recovery** or **installment method** should be used to recognize profit on the partial sale.

A seller who separately sells individual units in condominium projects or time-sharing interests should recognize profit by the percentage-of-completion method on the sale of individual units or interests if all of the following criteria are met:

1. Construction is beyond a preliminary stage (i.e., engineering and design work, execution of construction contracts, site clearance and preparation, excavation, and completion of the building foundation have all been completed).
2. The buyer is unable to obtain a refund except for nondelivery of the units or interest.
3. Sufficient units have been sold to assure that the entire property will not revert to rental property.
4. Sales prices are collectible.
5. Aggregate sales proceeds and costs can be reasonably estimated.

The **deposit** method would be appropriate to account for these sales up to the point all the criteria are met for recognition of a sale.

Selection of method. If, however, a loss is apparent (e.g., the carrying value of the property exceeds the sum of the deposit, fair value of unrecorded note receivable, and the debt assumed by the buyer), then immediate recognition is required.

The installment method is appropriate if the full accrual method cannot be used due to an inadequate initial investment by the buyer provided that recovery of cost is reasonably assured if the buyer defaults. The cost recovery method or the deposit method are appropriate if such cost recovery is not assured.

The reduced profit method is appropriate when the buyer's initial investment is adequate but the continuing investment is not adequate, and payments by the buyer at least cover the sum of the amortization (principal and interest) on the maximum first mortgage that could be obtained on the property and the interest, at an appropriate rate, on the excess of aggregate debt over the maximum first mortgage.

Description of the Methods of Accounting for Real Estate Sales Other Than Retail Land Sales

Full accrual method. This method of accounting for nonretail sales of real estate is appropriate when all four of the recognition criteria have been satisfied. The full accrual method is simply the application of the revenue recognition principle. A real estate sale is recognized in full when the profit is determinable and the earnings process is virtually complete. The profit is determinable when the first three criteria have been met, the sale is consummated, the buyer has demonstrated a commitment to pay, and the seller's receivable is not subject to future subordination. The earnings process is virtually complete when the fourth criterion has been met, the seller has transferred the risks and rewards of ownership and does not have a substantial continuing involvement with the property. If all of the criteria have not been met, the seller should record the transaction by one of the following methods as indicated by SFAS 66:

1. Deposit
2. Cost recovery
3. Installment
4. Reduced profit
5. Percentage-of-completion (see the section on Long-Term Construction Contracts in this chapter)

Profit under the full accrual method is computed by subtracting the cost basis of the property surrendered from the sales value given by the buyer. Also, the computation of profit on the sale should include all costs incurred that are directly related to the sale, such as accounting and legal fees.

Installment method. Under the installment method, each cash receipt and principal payment by the buyer on debt assumed with recourse to the seller consists of part recovery of cost and part recovery of profit. The apportionment between cost recovery and profit is in the same ratio as total cost and total profit bear to the sales value of the property sold. Therefore, under the installment method, the seller recognizes profit on each payment that the buyer makes to the seller and on each payment the buyer makes to the holder of the primary debt. When a buyer assumes debt that is without recourse to the seller, the seller should recognize profit on each payment made to the seller and on the entire debt assumed by the buyer. The accounting treatment differs because the seller is subject to substantially different levels of risk under the alternative conditions. For debt that is without recourse, the seller recovers a portion, if not all, of the cost of the asset surrendered at the time the buyer assumes the debt.

Example of the installment method

Assume Benson sells to Golden a plot of undeveloped land for $2,000,000. Golden will assume, with recourse, Benson's existing first mortgage of $1,000,000 and also pay Benson a $300,000 cash down payment. Golden will pay the balance of $700,000 by giving Benson a second mortgage payable in equal installments of principal and interest over the 10-year period. The cost of the land to Benson was $1,200,000 and Golden will commence development of the land immediately.

1. Computation of sales value:

Cash down payment	$ 300,000
First mortgage	1,000,000
Second mortgage	700,000
Sales value	$2,000,000

2. Computation of the initial investment:

Cash down payment	$ 300,000

3. Computation of the minimum required initial investment:

   a. $400,000 ($2,000,000 x 20%)
   b. 1. $850,000 [$2,000,000 – (115% x 1,000,000)]
      2. $500,000 ($2,000,000 x 25%)

   The minimum initial investment is $500,000 since b.2. is less than b.1. and b.2. is greater than a.

The initial investment criterion has not been satisfied because the actual initial investment is less than the minimum initial investment. Therefore, assuming the sale has been consummated and Benson is reasonably assured of recovering the cost of the land from Golden, the installment method should be used. The gross profit to be recognized over the installment payment period by Benson would be computed as follows:

Sales value	$ 2,000,000
Cost of land	(1,200,000)
Gross profit	$ 800,000

The gross profit percentage to apply to each payment by Golden to Benson and the primary debt holder is 40% ($800,000/$2,000,000).

If Golden also pays $50,000 of principal on the first mortgage and $70,000 of principal on the second mortgage in the year of sale, Benson would recognize the following profit in the year of sale:

Profit recognized on the down payment ($300,000 x 40%)	$120,000

Profit recognized on the principal payments:	
First mortgage ($50,000 x 40%)	20,000
Second mortgage ($70,000 x 40%)	28,000
Total profit recognized in year of sale	$168,000

Note that Benson recognizes profit only on the **payment** applicable to the first mortgage. This is because Benson may be called upon to satisfy the liability on the first mortgage if Golden defaults.

If Benson's first mortgage was assumed without recourse, Benson would recognize the following profit in the year of sale:

Profit recognized on the down payment ($300,000 x 40%)	$120,000
Profit recognized on Golden's assumption of Benson's first mortgage without recourse ($1,000,000 x 40%)	400,000
Profit recognized on the principal payment of the second mortgage ($70,000 x 40%)	28,000
Total profit recognized in year of sale	$548,000

The income statement (or related footnotes) for the period of sale should include the sales value received, the gross profit recognized, the gross profit deferred, and the costs of sale. In future periods when further payments are made to the buyer, the seller should realize gross profit on these payments. This amount should be disclosed as a single line item in the revenue section of the income statement.

If, in the future, the transaction meets the requirements for the full accrual method of recognizing profit, the seller may change to that method and recognize the remaining deferred profit as income at that time.

Cost recovery method. When the cost recovery method is used (e.g., when the seller's receivable is subject to subordination or the seller is not reasonably assured of recovering the cost of the property if the buyer defaults), no profit is recognized on the sales transaction until the seller has recovered the cost of the property sold. If the buyer assumes debt that is with recourse to the seller, profit should not be recognized by the seller until the cash payments by the buyer, including both principal and interest on debt due the seller and on debt assumed by the buyer, exceed the seller's cost of the property sold. If the buyer assumes debt that is without recourse to the seller, profit may be recognized by the seller when the cash payments by the buyer, including both principal and interest on debt due the seller, exceed the difference between the seller's cost of the property and the nonrecourse debt assumed by the buyer.

For the cost recovery method, principal collections reduce the seller's related receivable, and interest collections on such receivable increase the deferred gross profit on the balance sheet (para 63).

Example of the cost recovery method

Assume that on January 1, 1999, Maher, Inc. purchased undeveloped land with a sales value of $365,000 from Bernard Co. The sales value is represented by a $15,000 cash down payment, Maher assumes Bernard's $200,000 first mortgage (10%, payable in equal annual installments over the next 20 years), and Maher gives Bernard a second mortgage of $150,000 (12%, payable in equal annual installments over the next 10 years). The sale has been consummated, but the initial investment is below the minimum required amount and Bernard is not reasonably assured of recovering the cost of the property if Maher defaults. The cost of the land to Bernard was $300,000. The circumstances indicate the cost recovery method is appropriate. The transaction would be recorded by Bernard as follows:

1/1/99	Notes receivable	150,000	
	First mortgage payable	200,000	
	Cash	15,000	
	Revenue from sale of land		365,000
	Revenue from sale of land	365,000	
	Land		300,000
	Deferred gross profit		65,000

Case 1 -- The first mortgage was assumed with recourse to Bernard. Immediately after the sale, the unrecovered cost of the land would be computed as follows:

Land	$300,000
Less: Cash down payment	(15,000)
Unrecovered cost	$285,000

The note (second mortgage) would be reported as follows:

Note receivable	$150,000	
Less: Deferred gross profit	(65,000)	$ 85,000

At the end of the year Maher would pay $26,547.64 ($8,547.64 principal and $18,000.00 interest) on the second mortgage note and $23,491.94 ($3,491.94 principal and $20,000.00 interest) on the first mortgage. At 12/31/99 the unrecovered cost of the land would be computed as follows:

Previous unrecovered cost		$285,000.00
Less: Note receivable payment	$26,547.64	
First mortgage payment	23,491.94	(50,039.58)
Unrecovered cost		$234,960.42

The receivable would be reported on the 12/31/99 balance sheet as follows:

Note receivable ($150,000 – 8,547.64)	$141,452.36	
Less: Deferred gross profit ($65,000 + 18,000)	83,000.00	$58,452.36

Case 2 -- The first mortgage was assumed without recourse to Bernard. The reporting of the note would be the same as Case 1; however, the unrecovered cost of the property would be different. Immediately after the sale, the unrecovered cost of the property would be computed as follows:

Land	$300,000
Less: Cash down payment	(15,000)
Nonrecourse debt assumed by Maher	(200,000)
Unrecovered cost	$ 85,000

After Maher makes the payments at the end of the year, the unrecovered cost would be computed as follows:

Previous unrecovered cost	$85,000.00
Less: Notes receivable payment	26,547.64
Unrecovered cost	$58,452.36

For the cost recovery method, the income statement for the year the real estate sale occurs should include the sales value received, the cost of the property given up, and the gross profit deferred. In future periods, after the cost of the property has been recovered, the income statement should include the gross profit earned as a separate revenue item.

If, after accounting for the sale by the cost recovery method, circumstances indicate that the criteria for the full accrual method are satisfied, the seller may change to the full accrual method and recognize any remaining deferred gross profit in full.

Deposit method. When the deposit method is used (e.g., when the sale is, in substance, the sale of an option and not real estate), the seller does not recognize any profit, does not record a receivable, continues to report in its financial statements the property and the related existing debt even if the debt has been assumed by the buyer, and discloses that those items are subject to a sales contract (SFAS 66, para 65). The seller also continues to charge depreciation expense on the property for which the deposits have been received. Cash received from the buyer (initial and continuing investments) is reported as a deposit on the contract. However, some amounts of cash may be received that are not subject to refund, such as interest on the unrecorded principal. These amounts should be used to offset any carrying charges on the property (e.g., property taxes and interest charges on the existing debt). If the interest collected on the unrecorded receivable is refundable, the seller should record this interest as a deposit before the sale is consummated and then include it as a part of the initial investment once the sale is consummated. For contracts that are cancelled, the nonrefundable amounts should be recognized as income and the refundable amounts returned to the depositor at the time of cancellation.

As stated, the seller's balance sheet should continue to present the debt assumed by the buyer (this includes nonrecourse debt) among its other liabilities. However, the seller should report any principal payments on the mortgage debt assumed as additional deposits, while correspondingly reducing the carrying amount of the mortgage debt.

Reduced profit method. The reduced profit method is appropriate when the sale has been consummated and the initial investment is adequate but the continuing investment does not clearly demonstrate the willing commitment to pay the remaining balance of the receivable. For example, a buyer may purchase land under an agreement in which the seller will finance the sale over a 30-year period. SFAS 66 specifically states 20 years as the maximum amortization period for the purchase of land; therefore, the agreement fails to meet the continuing investment criteria.

Under the reduced profit method, the seller recognizes a portion of the profit at the time of sale with the remaining portion recognized in future periods. The amount of reduced profit to be recognized at the time of sale is determined by discounting the receivable from the buyer to the present value of the lowest level of annual payments required by the sales contract over the maximum period of time specified for that type of real estate property (20 years for land and the customary term of a first mortgage loan set by an independent lending institution for other types of real estate). The remaining profit is recognized in the periods that lump-sum or other payments are made.

Example of the reduced profit method

Assume Zarembski, Inc. sells a parcel of land to Stees Co. Zarembski receives sales value of $2,000,000. The land cost $1,600,000. Stees gave Zarembski the following consideration:

Cash down payment	$ 500,000
First mortgage note payable to an independent lending institution (payable in equal installments of principal and 12% interest, $133,887 payable at the end of each of the next 20 years)	1,000,000
Second mortgage note payable to Zarembski (payable in equal installments of principal and 10% interest, $53,039 payable at the end of each of the next 30 years)	500,000
Total sales value	$2,000,000

The amortization term of the second mortgage (seller's receivable) exceeds the 20-year maximum permitted by the statement. It is assumed that the payments by the buyer will cover the interest and principal on the maximum first mortgage loan that could be obtained on the property and interest on the excess aggregate debt on the property over such a maximum first mortgage loan; consequently, the reduced profit method would be appropriate. It is also assumed that the market interest rate on similar agreements is 14%.

The present value of $53,039 per year for 20 years at the market rate of 14% is $351,278 ($53,039 x 6.623).

The gross profit on the sale ($400,000) is reduced by the difference between the face amount of the seller's receivable ($500,000) and the reduced amount ($351,278) or

$148,722. The profit recognized at the time of sale is the sales value less the cost of the land less the difference between the face amount of the receivable and the reduced amount. Therefore, the reduced profit recognized on the date of sale is computed as follows:

Sales value		$ 2,000,000
Less:	Cost of land	(1,600,000)
	Excess	(148,722)
Reduced profit		$ 251,278

Under the reduced profit method, the seller amortizes its receivable at the market rate, not the rate given on the second mortgage. The receivable's carrying balance is zero after the specified term expires (in this case, 20 years). The remaining profit of $148,722 is recognized in the years after the specified term expires as the buyer makes payments on the second mortgage (years 21 through 30).

Retail Land Sales

Recognition of profit. A single method of recognizing profit is applied to all sales transactions within a project that is consummated.

The full accrual method of accounting is applied if **all** of the following conditions are met and a sale can be recorded:

a. **Expiration of refund period.** The buyer has made the down payment and each required subsequent payment until the period of cancellation with refund has expired. That period is the longest period of those required by local law, established by the seller's policy, or specified in the contract.
b. **Sufficient cumulative payments.** The cumulative payments of principal and interest equal or exceed 10% of the contract sales price.
c. **Collectibility of receivables.** Collection experience for the project in which the sale is made or for the seller's prior projects indicates that at least 90% of the contracts in the project in which the sale is made that are in force 6 months after sale will be collected in full. The collection experience with the seller's prior projects may be applied to a new project if the prior projects have

    (1) The same characteristics (type of land, environment, clientele, contract terms, sales methods) as the new project
    (2) A sufficiently long collection period to indicate the percentage of current sales of the new project that will be collected to maturity

    A down payment of at least 20% is an acceptable indication of collectibility.
d. **Nonsubordination of receivables.** The receivable from the sale is not subject to subordination to new loans on the property except that subordination by an individual lot buyer for home construction purposes is permis-

sible if the collection experience on those contracts is the same as on contracts not subordinated.

e. **Completion of development.** The seller is not obligated to complete improvements of lots sold or to construct amenities or other facilities applicable to lots sold.

Percentage-of-completion. The percentage-of-completion method should be used if criteria a., b., c., and d. above are met, and full accrual criteria are not met (criterion e. is not satisfied). However, additional criteria (f. and g.) must be satisfied.

f. **There has been progress on improvements.** The project's improvements progressed beyond preliminary stages and the work apparently will be completed according to plan. Some indications of progress are

   (1) The expenditure of funds
   (2) Initiation of work
   (3) Existence of engineering plans and work commitments
   (4) Completion of access roads and amenities such as golf courses, clubs, and swimming pools

   Additionally, there should be no indication of significant delaying factors, such as the inability to obtain permits, contractors, personnel, or equipment. Finally, estimates of costs to complete and extent of progress toward completion should be reasonably dependable.

g. **Development is practical.** There is an expectation that the land can be developed for the purposes represented and the properties will be useful for those purposes restrictions, including environmental restrictions, will not seriously hamper development and that improvements such an access roads, water supply, and sewage treatment or removal are feasible within a reasonable time period.

Installment. The installment method is appropriate if criteria a. and b. are met, full accrual criteria are not met, and the seller is financially capable, as shown by capital structure, cash flow or borrowing capacity. This would be a change in accounting estimate. This method may be changed to the percentage-of-completion method when all of the criteria are met.

Other. If a retail land sale transaction does not meet any of the above, the deposit method is appropriate.

REAL ESTATE OPERATIONS

PERSPECTIVE AND ISSUES

SFAS 67, *Real Estate: Accounting for Costs and Initial Rental Operations of Real Estate Projects,* deals with the accounting for various costs in acquiring and developing real estate projects. It does not apply to

a. Real estate developed by an entity for its own use rather than sale or rental
b. Initial direct costs of leases
c. Costs directly related to manufacturing, merchandising or service activities rather than real estate activities
d. Rental operations in which the predominant rental period is less than a month

The standard does include accounting for costs of real estate whether rented or sold.

Sources of GAAP

SFAS	EITF	SOP
67, 121	84-17, 85-27, 86-6, 86-7, 87-9, 88-12, 88-24, 89-14, 90-20, 91-2, 94-2, 95-6, 95-7, 98-8	75-2, 78-9 92-1

DEFINITIONS OF TERMS

Amenities. Amenities include golf courses, utility plants, clubhouses, swimming pools, tennis courts, indoor recreational facilities, and parking facilities.

Common costs. Costs that relate to two or more units within a real estate project.

Costs incurred to rent real estate projects. Includes costs of model units and their furnishings, rental facilities, semipermanent signs, rental brochures, advertising, "grand openings," and rental overhead including rental salaries.

Costs incurred to sell real estate projects. Includes costs of model units and their furnishings, sales facilities, sales brochures, legal fees for preparation of prospectuses, semipermanent signs, advertising, "grand openings," and sales overhead including sales salaries.

Fair value. The amount in cash or cash equivalent value of other consideration that a real estate parcel would yield in a current sale between a willing buyer and a willing seller (other than in a forced or liquidation sale). The fair value of a parcel is affected by its physical characteristics, ultimate use, and the time required to make such use of the property considering access, development plans, zoning restrictions, and market absorption factors.

Incidental operations. Revenue-producing activities engaged in during the holding or development period to reduce the cost of developing the property for its intended use, as distinguished from activities designed to generate a profit or a return from the use of the property.

Incremental costs of incidental operations. Costs that would not be incurred except in relation to the conduct of incidental operations. Interest, taxes, insurance, security, and similar costs that would be incurred during the development of a real estate project regardless of whether incidental operations were conducted are not incremental costs.

Incremental revenue from incidental operations. Revenues that would not be produced except in relation to the conduct of incidental operations.

Indirect project costs. Costs incurred after the acquisition of the property, such as construction administration, legal fees, and various office costs, that clearly relate to projects under development or construction.

Net realizable value. The estimated selling price in the ordinary course of business less estimated costs of completion, holding, and disposal.

Phase. A parcel on which units are to be constructed concurrently.

Preacquisition costs. Costs related to a property that are incurred for the express purpose of, but prior to, obtaining that property. Examples may be costs of surveying, zoning or traffic studies, or payments to obtain an option on the property.

Project costs. Costs clearly associated with the acquisition, development, and construction of a real estate project.

Relative fair value before construction. The fair value of each land parcel in a real estate project in relation to the fair value of the other parcels in the project, exclusive of value added by on-site development and construction activities.

CONCEPTS, RULES, AND EXAMPLES

Preacquisition Costs

Payments are generally capitalized if they relate to an option to obtain the real property or if all of the following conditions are met:

a. Costs are directly identified with the property.
b. Costs would be capitalized if the property already were acquired.
c. Acquisition of the option or property is probable. The purchaser wants the property and believes it to be available for sale and has the ability to finance its acquisition.

Once capitalized, these costs are project costs which, if not receivable in the future, or if the property is not acquired should be charged to expense.

Taxes and Insurance

Real estate taxes and insurance are capitalized as property costs only when the property is undergoing activities necessary to get the property ready for its intended use. After the property is substantially complete and ready for its intended use are such items expensed.

Project Costs

Costs that are identifiable and clearly associated with acquisition, development, and construction of a real estate project are capitalized as a cost of the project.

Indirect costs that relate to several projects should be capitalized and allocated to these projects. Indirect costs that do not clearly relate to any project such as general administrative expenses should be expensed as incurred.

Amenities

Amenities that are to be sold or transferred in connection with the sale of individual units should have the costs in excess of anticipated proceeds treated as **common costs** of the project.

Amenities that are to be sold separately or retained by the developer should have the costs capitalized with those costs in excess of estimated fair value treated as common costs. **Fair value** is determined as of the expected date of substantial physical completion and the amounts allocated to the amenity should not be revised later. The sale of the amenity results in a gain or loss when the selling price differs from the fair value less accumulated depreciation.

Costs of amenities should be allocated among land parcels benefited for which development is probable. Before completion and availability for use, operating income or loss is an adjustment to common costs. After such date, operating income or loss is included in the income statement.

Incidental Operations

Revenue from incidental operations should be combined with the costs of such operations and any excess of incremental revenue over incremental costs should reduce capitalized project costs. If such costs exceed revenues they should be charged to expense as incurred.

Allocation of Costs

Capitalized costs should be allocated by specific identification. If this is not feasible, then for all costs prior to construction, the costs should be allocated by the relative fair value before construction and, for construction costs, allocated by the relative sale value of each unit.

If relative values are impractical then allocation may be square footage or other area method, or other values deemed appropriate.

Net Realizable Value

When real estate projects decline in value, the property is required to be written down either directly or by means of a reserve to net realizable value (NRV). This is defined as the selling price less the costs to complete and dispose of the property, net present value discounted, equivalent to the ceiling in lower of cost or market for inventory. After the write-down, property is expected to sell at a zero margin. Even though a property may be considered likely for a NRV adjustment, interest capitalization continues while the property is undergoing development activities. If such capitalization causes the property to be in excess of net realizable value, an adjustment is again required.

There are issues concerning the methods of applying a write-down to property. Generally, the rule is that NRV is measured project by project. Projects are not combined in order to offset a potential future profit on one project against other project losses that are required to be recognized currently. Also, once losses are taken on property, similar to inventory, a new cost basis is adopted and future recoveries in value are not recognized. Furthermore, if a project has identifiable elements with separate cash flows such as residential and commercial or houses and condominiums, then the NRV test should be made for each element separately and not combined for the whole project. The appropriate test is the similarity in nature, amount, and timing of cash flows.

In addition, there may be times that an NRV measurement differs from fair market value. Net realizable value assumes completion of the project and future revenue while fair market value represents current net selling price as is. To the extent that a project is yet to be developed, these two calculations may differ. If a company has the ability and intent to continue to hold and develop property, then the NRV calculation is proper. However, if there is a question about such ability, current sales price representing fair market value used in the NRV calculation usually results in a lower NRV and a more conservative option.

An NRV calculation, when the property is intended to be sold rather than developed, uses the expected "as is" selling price instead of a completed project selling price. If the time and expense necessary to sell "as is" is relatively long and high, NRV will also differ from appraisal estimates, which usually value a property against comparable sales, allowing a reasonable time frame (1 year) for a sale, and address gross sales pricing only.

Revisions of Estimates

Estimates made and cost allocations should be reviewed at least annually until the project is substantially complete and available for sale. Costs should be revised and reallocated as required for changes in current estimates.

Abandonment and Change in Use

Abandonment of a project requires all capitalized costs to be expensed and not reallocated to other components of the project or other projects. Real estate dedicated to governmental units is not deemed abandoned and should have its costs treated as project common costs.

Changes in use require that costs incurred and expected to be incurred that exceed the estimated value of the required project (when substantially complete and ready for intended use) should be charged to expense. If no formal plan for the project exists, then project costs in excess of current net realizable value should be expensed.

Selling Costs

Costs incurred to sell should be capitalized if they are

a. Reasonably expected to be recovered from sale of the project or from incidental operations, and
b. Incurred for tangible assets used directly throughout the selling period to assist the selling process or incurred for services required to obtain regulatory approval of sales.

Other costs may be capitalized as prepaid expenses if directly associated with sales, cost recovery is reasonably expected from sales and the full accrual method of sale cannot be used.

All other costs should be expensed in the period incurred. Capitalized costs are expensed in the period in which the related revenue is earned.

Rental Costs

Costs related to and reasonably expected to be recoverable from future rental operations should be capitalized. This excludes initial direct costs as defined and described in accounting for leases. Costs that cannot be capitalized should be expensed as incurred.

Capitalized costs should be amortized over the term of the lease, if directly related to a specific operating lease, or over the period of expected benefit. Amortization should begin when the project is substantially completed and available for occupancy. Estimated unrecoverable amounts should be expensed when it is probable that the lease will be terminated.

A project is substantially completed and available for occupancy when tenant improvements are completed or after 1 year from the end of major construction activity. Then normal operations take place with all revenues and costs (including depreciation and other amortized costs) recognized in the income statement. If part of a project is occupied but other parts are not yet complete, completed portions should be considered as separate projects.

Recoverability

Projects held for sale or development cannot be valued in excess of reductions in the carrying amounts of real estate assets prescribed by SFAS 121. Such projects, or parts thereof, that are substantially complete and ready for intended use shall be accounted for at the lower of carrying amount or fair value less cost to sell as described in paras 15-17 of SFAS 121. The recognition and measurement principles articulated in paras 4-7 of SFAS 121 apply to real estate held for development and sale as well as property to be developed in the future as well as property undergoing current development. Costs should, however, continue to be capitalized as required by the standards. Recoverability may be determined for each separate project. The determination of which components add up to a separate project may involve issues of homogeneity and other similarities.

Real estate rental projects which are valued in excess of that indicated by rental demand should be assessed in accordance with para 6 of SFAS 121. Para 5 of this statement also details other events or changes in circumstances that suggest that the recoverability of the carrying amount of an asset should be assessed.

EMERGING ISSUES TASK FORCE CONSENSUS SUMMARIES

84-17 Profit Recognition on Sales of Real Estate With Graduated Payment Mortgages and Insured Mortgages

Discusses the application of SFAS 66 to such mortgages. Graduated payment mortgages for which negative principal amortization is recognized do not meet the continuing investment tests in SFAS 66 and thus full profit shall **not** be recognized immediately. No consensus was reached regarding partially or fully insured mortgages. See EITF 87-9 for further discussion of the issue.

85-27 Recognition of Receipts From Made-up Rentals Shortfalls

When a seller of real estate agrees to make up any rental shortfalls for a period of time, the Task Force reached a consensus that payments to and receipts from the seller are adjustments to the cost of the property and will affect future depreciation.

86-6 Antispeculation Clauses in Real Estate Sales Contracts

Land sale agreements may contain an "antispeculation" clause requiring the buyer to develop the land in a specific manner or within a specific period of time or the seller has the right, but not the obligation, to reacquire the property. The Task Force concluded that this option would not preclude recognition of a sale if the probability of the buyer not complying is remote.

86-7 Recognition by Homebuilders of Profit From Sales of Land and Related Construction Contracts

A homebuilder enters into a contract to build a home on its own lot, relinquishing title to both the lot and the home at closing. The Task Force determined that SFAS 66 guidance provides that profit recognition is not appropriate until the conditions specified in paragraph 5 of that pronouncement are met. Deposit accounting should be used for both the land and building activity until that point.

87-9 Profit Recognition on Sales of Real Estate With Insured Mortgages or Surety Bonds

For sales of real estate, the EITF in 84-17 reached a consensus that a sale with a graduated payment mortgage that does not meet the continuing investment test in SFAS 66 should not result in full immediate profit recognition.

In 87-9, on a related matter, the Task Force reached a consensus that mortgage insurance should not be considered the equivalent of an irrevocable letter of credit in determining whether profit should be recognized. Purchase of such insurance is not in itself a demonstration of commitment by the buyer to honor its obligation to pay for the property. The sole exception to this rule is that for all FHA (Federal Housing Administration) and VA (Veteran's Administration) insured loans, profits may be recognized under the full accrual method.

88-12 Transfer of Ownership Interest as Part of Down Payment Under FASB Statement 66

The Task Force reached a consensus that the buyer's ownership interest in a purchased property that is pledged as security for a note cannot be included as part of the buyer's initial investment in determining whether profit can be recognized under SFAS 66.

88-24 Effect of Various Forms of Financing Under FASB Statement 66

The EITF reached a consensus that the following guidelines should be used in sales of real estate under SFAS 66:

1. The initial and continuing investment requirements of SFAS 66 for profit recognition are applicable unless the seller has unconditionally received all amounts due and is not at risk related to the financing.
2. Debt incurred by the buyer that is secured by the property, incurred from the seller or other parties, or by assumption is not part of an initial investment. The buyer must pay cash or other qualifying forms of investment (See paragraphs 9 and 10 of SFAS 66).
3. Such debt secured by the property is not part of the buyer's cash payments.

89-14 Valuation of Repossessed Real Estate

Foreclosed property should be recorded at the lower of the net receivable due to the seller at foreclosure or the fair value of the property. SOP 92-3 provides further guidance and states that, after foreclosure, foreclosed assets should be carried at the lower of fair value (less costs to sell) or cost.

90-20 Impact of an Uncollateralized Irrevocable Letter of Credit on a Real Estate Sale-Leaseback Transaction

The Task Force concluded that an uncollateralized irrevocable letter of credit is not a form of continuing involvement that precludes sale-leaseback accounting under SFAS 98. However, all written contracts between the seller-lessee and the issuer of the letter of credit must be evaluated since the latter may have other forms of collateral (e.g., right of offset of amounts on deposit).

91-2 Debtor's Accounting for Forfeiture of Real Estate Subject to a Nonrecourse Mortgage

The Task Force concluded that SFAS 15 applies when a nonrecourse borrower transfers property to lender in full satisfaction of the lien even though fair value of the property is less than the balance due the lender.

94-2 Treatment of Minority Interests in Certain Real Estate Investment Trusts

A sponsor's interest in an operating partnership should be reported as a minority interest in the REIT's consolidated financial statements. The net equity of the operating partnership (after the contributions of the sponsor and the REIT) multiplied by the sponsor's ownership percentage in the operating partnership represents the amount to be initially reported as the minority interest in the REIT's consolidated financial statements.

95-6 Accounting by a Real Estate Investment Trust for an Investment in a Service Corporation

Regardless of method of accounting by a REIT for its investment in a service corporation, the service corporation should not be considered an independent party. Thus, capitalized lease amounts should not exceed the allowable costs under SFAS 13.

Additionally, this EITF includes a list of factors that indicate that the equity method of accounting should be used.

95-7 Implementation Issues Related to the Treatment of Minority Interests in Certain Real Estate Investment Trusts

This is follow-up to Issue 94-2. If minority interest balance is negative, the related charge in REIT income statement would be greater of minority's share of current earnings or amount of distributions to minority during the year; any excess should be credited to equity directly. Other REIT accounting matters are also addressed; consensus that subsequent acquisitions of sponsor's minority interest should be accounted for consistent with accounting for formation of the partnership.

98-8 Accounting for Transfers of Investments That Are in Substance Real Estate

A consensus was reached that when investments in the form of financial assets that are in substance real estate are transferred, the accounting should follow SFAS 66. Per the EITF, the implications of this consensus are

1. Transfers of acquisition, development, and construction loans (ADC loans) deemed in substance real estate under Issue 84-4 are subject to this consensus.
2. Marketable investments in REIT accounted for under SFAS 115 should be accounted for per SFAS 125.

STATEMENTS OF POSITION ON REAL ESTATE

75-2 Accounting Practices of Real Estate Investment Trusts

Interest income should not be recorded when it is not reasonable to expect collection. Commitment fees should be amortized over the combined commitment and loan period. The provisions dealing with loan losses and property valuation have been effectively superseded by SFAS 114 and 121 respectively.

78-9 Accounting for Investments in Real Estate Ventures

Owners of real estate ventures should generally use the equity method of accounting to account for their investments. However, limited partners may have such a minor interest and have no influence or control, in which case, the cost method may be appropriate.

If there are losses in excess of investment, such losses should be recorded regardless of any increase in the estimated fair value of the venture's assets. Losses in excess of investment are a liability. Losses which cannot be borne by certain investors require the remaining investors to use SFAS 5, *Accounting for Contingencies*, to determine their share of any additional loss. Limited partners are not required to record losses in excess of investment. If investors do not recognize losses in excess of investment, the equity method should be resumed only after the share of net income exceeds net losses not recognized previously.

Venture agreements may designate different allocations for profits, losses, cash distributions and cash from liquidation. Accounting for equity in profits and losses requires careful consideration of allocation formulas because the substance over form concept requires equity accounting to follow the ultimate cash allocations.

Contributions of real estate to a venture as capital should be recorded by the investor at cost and should not result in recognition of a gain since a capital contribution is not the culmination of the earning process.

Interest on loans and advances that are in substance capital contributions should be accounted for as distributions and not interest income.

92-1 Accounting for Real Estate Syndication Income

This SOP applies to all income recognition from real estate syndication activities. SFAS 66 applies to profit and loss recognition on sales of real estate by syndicators to partnerships. This SOP requires that the same concepts be applied to syndicators even though they may have never owned the property.

All fees charged by syndicators are includable in determination of sales value as required by SFAS 66 except for syndication fees and fees for which future services must be performed. Syndication fees are recognized as income when the earning process is complete and collectibility is reasonably assured. If fees are unreasonable, they should be adjusted and the sale price of the real estate appropriately adjusted as well. If a partnership interest is received by the syndicator, the value should be included in the test of reasonableness of fees. If it is part of the fee, the syndicators should account for this interest as retained interest from partial sale of real estate in conformity with SFAS 66. Fees for future services should be recognized when the service is rendered.

Fees received from blind pool transactions should be recognized ratably as the syndication partnership invests in property but only to the extent that such fees are nonrefundable. If syndicators may incur future losses from material involvement or from uncertainties regarding collectibility, income should be deferred until the losses can be reasonably estimated. For purposes of determining the SFAS 66 requirement concerning the buyer's initial and continuing investment for profit recognition, cash received by syndicators should first be allocated to unpaid syndication fees and only after such fees are paid in full, then to fees for future services already performed before being allocated to the investment. If syndicators receive or retain partnership interests which are subordinated, these should be accounted for as participations in future profits without risk of loss.

FRANCHISING: ACCOUNTING BY FRANCHISORS

PERSPECTIVE AND ISSUES

Franchising has become one of the newest growth industries with many businesses seeking to sell franchises as their primary income source and individuals seeking to buy franchises and become an entrepreneur. How to recognize revenue on the individual sale of franchise territories and on the continuing relationship between the franchisor and franchisee are prime issues.

Originally, in 1973, the AICPA published an industry accounting guide, "Accounting for Franchise Fee Revenue" from which the FASB extracted the principles in SFAS 45 with the same title.

Sources of GAAP

SFAS
45

DEFINITIONS OF TERMS

Area franchise. An agreement that transfers franchise rights within a geographical area permitting the opening of a number of franchised outlets. The number of outlets, location, and so forth are decisions usually made by the franchisee.

Bargain purchase. A transaction in which the franchisee is allowed to purchase equipment or supplies for a price that is significantly lower than the fair value of the equipment or supplies.

Continuing franchise fee. Consideration for the continuing rights granted by the franchise agreement and for general or specific services during its life.

Franchise agreement. A written business agreement that meets the following principal criteria:

a. The relation between the franchisor and franchisee is contractual, and an agreement, confirming the rights and responsibilities of each party, is in force for a specified period.
b. The continuing relation has as its purpose the distribution of a product or service, or an entire business concept, within a particular market area.
c. Both the franchisor and the franchisee contribute resources for establishing and maintaining the franchise. The franchisor's contribution may be a trademark, a company reputation, products, procedures, manpower, equipment, or a process. The franchisee usually contributes operating capital as well as the managerial and operational resources required for opening and continuing the franchised outlet.

d. The franchise agreement outlines and describes the specific marketing practices to be followed, specifies the contribution of each party to the operation of the business, and sets forth certain operating procedures that both parties agree to comply with.
e. The establishment of the franchised outlet creates a business entity that will, in most cases, require and support the full-time business activity of the franchisee.
f. Both the franchisee and the franchisor have a common public identity. This identity is achieved most often through the use of common trade names or trademarks and is frequently reinforced through advertising programs designed to promote the recognition and acceptance of the common identity within the franchisee's market area.

Franchisee. The party who has been granted business rights (the franchise) to operate the franchised business.

Franchisor. The party who grants business rights (the franchise) to the party (the franchisee) who will operate the franchised business.

Initial franchise fee. Consideration for establishing the franchise relationship and providing some initial services. Occasionally, the fee includes consideration for initially required equipment and inventory, but those items usually are the subject of separate consideration. The payment of an initial franchise fee or a continuing royalty fee is not a necessary criterion for an agreement to be considered a franchise agreement.

Initial services. Common provision of a franchise agreement in which the franchisor usually will agree to provide a variety of services and advice to the franchisee, such as the following:

a. Assistance in the selection of a site. The assistance may be based on experience with factors such as traffic patterns, residential configurations, and competition.
b. Assistance in obtaining facilities, including related financing and architectural and engineering services. The facilities may be purchased or leased by the franchisee, and lease payments may be guaranteed by the franchisor.
c. Assistance in advertising, either for the individual franchisee or as part of a general program
d. Training of the franchisee's personnel
e. Preparation and distribution of manuals and similar material concerning operations, administration, and recordkeeping
f. Bookkeeping and advisory services, including setting up the franchisee's records and advising the franchisee about income, real estate, and other taxes, or about local regulations affecting the franchisee's business
g. Inspection, testing, and other quality control programs

CONCEPTS AND RULES

Franchise Sales

Franchise operations are generally subject to the same accounting principles as all regular enterprises. However, there are special issues which arise out of **franchise agreements** which require understanding and have special accounting rules.

Revenue should be recognized, with an appropriate provision for bad debts, when the franchisor has substantially performed all material services or conditions. Only when revenue is collected over an extended period of time and collectibility cannot be predicted in advance would the use of the cost recovery or installment methods of revenue recognition be appropriate. Substantial performance means

1. The **franchisor** has no remaining obligation to either refund cash or forgive any unpaid balance due.
2. Substantially all **initial services** required by the agreement have been performed.
3. No material obligations or conditions remain.

Even if the contract does not require initial services, the pattern of performance by the franchisor in other sales will impact the time period of revenue recognition. This can delay such recognition until services are either performed or can reasonably be assured will not be performed. The **franchisee** operations will be considered as started when such substantial performance has occurred.

If **initial franchise fees** are large compared to services rendered and **continuing franchise fees** are small compared to services to be rendered, then a portion of the initial fee should be deferred in an amount sufficient to cover the costs of future services and a reasonable profit, after considering the impact of the continuing franchise fee.

Area Franchise Sales

Sometimes franchisors sell territories rather than individual locations. In this event, the franchisor may render services to the area independent of the number of individual franchises to be established. Under this circumstance, revenue recognition for the franchisor is the same as stated above. If, however, substantial services are performed by the franchisor for each individual franchise established, then revenue should be recognized in proportion to mandatory service. The general rule is that when the franchisee has no right to receive a refund, all revenue should be recognized. It may be necessary for revenue recognition to treat a franchise agreement as a divisible contract and allocate revenue among existing and estimated locations. Future amendments to these estimates will require that remaining unrecognized revenue will be recorded in proportion to remaining services to be performed.

Other Relationships

Franchisors may guarantee debt of the franchisee, continue to own a portion of the franchise, or control the franchisee's operations. Revenue should not be recognized until all services, conditions and obligations have been performed.

In addition, the franchisor may have an option to reacquire the location. Accounting for initial revenue should consider the probability of exercise of the option. If the expectation at the time of the agreement is that the option is likely to be exercised, the entire franchise fee should be deferred and not recognized as income. Upon exercise, the deferral reduces the investment of the franchisor.

An initial fee may cover both franchise rights and property rights, including equipment, signs, and inventory. A portion of the fee applicable to property rights should be recognized to the extent of the fair value of these assets. However, fees relating to different services rendered by franchisors are generally not allocated to these different services because segregating the amounts applicable to each service could not be performed objectively. The rule of revenue recognition when all services are substantially performed is generally upheld. If objectively determinable separate fees are charged for separate services, then recognition of revenue can be determined and recorded for each service performed.

Franchisors may be an agent for the franchise by placing purchase orders for inventory and equipment. These should not be recorded as sales and purchases by the franchisor; instead, receivables and payables should be reported on the balance sheet of the franchisor.

Continuing Franchise and Other Fees

Continuing franchise fees are recognized as revenue as the fees become earned. Related costs are expensed as incurred. Regardless of the purpose of the fees, revenue is recognized when the fee is earned and receivable. The exception is when a portion of the fee is required to be segregated and used for a specific purpose, such as advertising. The franchisor should defer this amount and record it as a liability. This liability is reduced by the cost of the services received.

Sometimes, the franchisee has a period of time where **bargain purchases** of equipment or supplies are granted by the contract. If the bargain price is lower than other customers pay or denies a reasonable profit to the franchisor, a portion of the initial franchise fee should be deferred and accounted for as an adjustment of the selling price when the franchisee makes the purchase. The deferred amount should be either the difference in the selling price among customers and the bargain price or an amount sufficient to provide a reasonable profit to the franchisor.

Costs

Direct and incremental costs related to franchise sales should be deferred and recognized when revenue is recorded. However, deferred costs cannot exceed anticipated future revenue, net of additional expected costs.

Indirect costs are expensed as incurred. These usually are regular and recurring costs that bear no relationship to sales.

Repossessed Franchises

If, for any reason, the franchisor refunds the franchise fee and obtains the location, previously recognized revenue should be reversed in the period of repossession. If a repossession is made without a refund, there is no adjustment of revenue previously recognized. However, any estimated uncollectible amounts should be provided for and any remaining collected funds should be recorded as revenue.

Business Combinations

Business combinations where the franchisor acquires the business of a franchisee should be accounted for in accordance with the rules of APB 16.

If the transaction is deemed a pooling of interests, the financial statements are combined retroactively with franchise fee revenue and other sales eliminated in consolidation.

If the transaction is a purchase, no adjustment of prior revenue is made since the financial statements are not retroactively combined. Care must be taken to ensure that the purchase is not a repossession. If the transaction is deemed to be a repossession, it should be accounted for as described in the above section.

9 LONG-LIVED ASSETS

PERSPECTIVE AND ISSUES

Long-lived assets are those which provide an economic benefit to the enterprise for a number of future periods. GAAP regarding long-lived assets involves the determination of the appropriate cost at which to record the asset and the appropriate method to be used to allocate that cost over the periods benefiting.

These assets are primarily operational assets, and they are broken down into two basic types: tangible and intangible. Tangible assets have physical substance and are categorized as follows:

1. Depreciable
2. Depletable
3. Other tangible assets

Intangible assets have no physical substance. Their value is found in the rights or privileges which they grant to the business enterprise.

Most of the accounting problems involve proper measurement and timing of the transactions. Adequate consideration must be given to the substance of the transaction.

SFAS 121 applies to all entities. This statement requires long-lived assets and certain identifiable intangible assets and any goodwill related to those assets to be reviewed for impairment whenever circumstances and situations change such that there is an indication that the carrying amount may not be recoverable. If, upon review, the undiscounted future cash flows (without interest charges) are less than the carrying amount, the carrying amount is reduced to fair value and an impairment loss is recognized. This fair value is considered the new cost basis which is not subject to subsequent adjustment except for depreciation and further impairment. Thus, there is no restoration of recognized impairment losses.

Long lived assets and identifiable intangibles to be disposed of (except those covered by APB 30) would be carried at the lower of carrying value or fair value less the cost to sell. These assets should not be depreciated during the holding period.

With some exceptions, this standard applies to rate-regulated assets. Costs excluded by a regulator from the enterprise's rate base would be recognized as an impairment.

Sources of GAAP

ARB	*APB*	*SFAS*	*FASB I*	*EITF*	*SOP*
43, Ch. 9; 44	1, 6, 17, 29	2, 34, 42, 58, 62, 68, 109, 121	30, 33	86-29, 87-29, 89-13, 91-10, 93-11 95-23 96-14	88-1, 92-3, 93-7

Other: Accounting Research Monograph 1

DEFINITIONS OF TERMS

Boot. The monetary consideration given or received in an asset exchange.

Depreciation. The annual charge to income that results from a systematic and rational allocation of cost over the life of a tangible asset.

Exchange. A reciprocal transfer between an enterprise and another entity that results in the acquisition of assets or services, or the satisfaction of liabilities through a transfer of assets, services or obligations.

Fixed assets. Those assets which are used in a productive capacity, have physical substance, are relatively long-lived, and provide future benefit which is readily measurable.

Intangible assets. Those assets which provide future economic benefit but have no physical substance. Examples include goodwill, patents, copyrights, etc.

Monetary assets. Assets whose amounts are fixed in terms of units of currency. Examples are cash, accounts receivable, and notes receivable.

Nonmonetary assets. Assets other than monetary assets. Examples are inventories; investments in common stock; and property, plant, and equipment.

Nonmonetary transactions. Exchanges and nonreciprocal transfers that involve little or no monetary assets or liabilities.

Nonreciprocal transfer. A transfer of assets or services in one direction, either from an enterprise to its owners or another entity, or from owners or another entity to the enterprise. An enterprise's reacquisition of its outstanding stock is a nonreciprocal transfer.

Productive assets. Assets held for or used in the production of goods or services. Productive assets include an investment in another entity if the investment is accounted for by the equity method but exclude an investment not accounted for by that method.

Similar productive assets. Productive assets that are of the same general type, that perform the same function, or that are employed in the same line of business.

CONCEPTS, RULES, AND EXAMPLES

Fixed Assets

Fixed assets are tangible property used in a productive capacity which will benefit the enterprise for a period of more than one year.

Three problems in accounting for fixed assets are

1. The cost at which the assets should be recorded
2. The rate at which the cost should be allocated to future periods
3. The recording of the subsequent disposal of the assets

Recorded cost. Any reasonable cost involved in bringing the asset to the buyer and incurred prior to using the asset in actual production is capitalized. Examples include sales taxes, finders' fees, freight costs, installation costs, breaking-in costs, and set-up costs. These costs are **not** to be expensed in the period in which they are incurred.

Costs incurred subsequent to purchase. Costs which occur subsequent to the purchase such as repairs, maintenance, or betterments are treated in one of the following ways:

1. Expensed
2. Capitalized
3. Reduced accumulated depreciation

Ordinary maintenance and repair expenditures are charged to expense.

Extraordinary repairs or maintenance increase the value (utility) of the asset or increase the estimated useful life of the asset. Those costs which increase the value of the asset should increase the asset account, while those which extend the useful life of the asset should decrease the accumulated depreciation account.

The chart on the following page summarizes the treatment of expenditures subsequent to acquisition.

Construction of assets for self-use. All direct costs (labor, materials, and variable overhead) of constructing an entity's own fixed assets should be capitalized. However, a controversy exists regarding the proper treatment of fixed overhead. Two different views are

1. Charge the asset with its fair share of fixed overhead (i.e., use the same basis of allocation used for inventory).
2. Charge the fixed asset account with only the identifiable **incremental** amount of fixed overhead.

Costs Subsequent to Acquisition of Property, Plant, and Equipment

Type of expenditure	Characteristics	Normal accounting treatment: Expense when incurred	Capitalize: Charge to asset	Capitalize: Charge to accum. deprec.	Other
1. Additions	• Extensions, enlargements, or expansions made to an existing asset		X		
2. Repairs and maintenance a. Ordinary	• Recurring, relatively small expenditures				
	1. Maintain normal operating condition	X			
	2. **Do not** add materially to use value	X			
	3. **Do not** extend useful life	X			
b. Extraordinary (major)	• Not recurring, relatively large expenditures				
	1. Primarily increase the use value		X		
	2. Primarily extend the useful life			X	
3. Replacements and betterments	• Major component of asset is removed and replaced with the same type of component with comparable performance capabilities (replacement) or a different type of component having superior performance capabilities (betterment)				
a. Book value of old component is known					• Remove old asset cost and accum. deprec. • Recognize any loss (or gain) on old asset • Charge asset for replacement component
b. Book value of old component is not known	1. Primarily increase the use value		X		
	2. Primarily extend the useful life			X	
4. Reinstallations and rearrangements	• Provide greater efficiency in production or reduce production costs				
	1. Material costs incurred; benefits extend into future accounting periods		X		
	2. No measurable future benefit	X			

However, the AICPA in Accounting Research Monograph 1 has suggested that

> *...in the absence of compelling evidence to the contrary, overhead costs considered to have 'discernible future benefits' for the purposes of determining the cost of inventory should be presumed to have 'discernible future benefits' for the purpose of determining the cost of a self-constructed depreciable asset.*

While this treatment is not binding, it does provide guidance in establishing consistency.

If the total cost of the fixed asset contructed exceeds the fair market value, the asset should be written down to fair market value. The amount of the write-down is included in the determination of net income in the period that construction is completed.

Depreciation of fixed assets. The costs of fixed assets are allocated to the periods they benefit through depreciation. The method of depreciation chosen must result in a systematic and rational allocation of the cost of the asset (less its residual value) over the asset's expected useful life. The determination of useful life must take a number of factors into consideration, including technological change, normal deterioration, and actual physical usage. The method of depreciation is determined as a function of time (e.g., technological change or normal deterioration) or as a function of actual physical usage.

Depreciation methods based on time.

1. Straight-line--Depreciation expense is incurred evenly over the life of the asset.

$$\frac{\text{Cost less salvage value}}{\text{Estimated useful life}}$$

2. Accelerated methods--Depreciation expense is higher in the early years of the asset's useful life and lower in the later years.

   a. Declining balance--A multiple of the straight-line rate times the book value at the beginning of the year.

$$\text{Straight-line rate} = \frac{1}{\text{Estimated useful life}}$$

Example

Double-declining balance depreciation (stop when book value = estimated salvage value)

2 x Straight-line rate x Book value at beginning of year

b. Sum-of-the-years' digits (SYD) depreciation =
(Cost less salvage value) x Applicable fraction

$$\text{where applicable fraction} = \frac{\text{number of years of estimated life remaining as of the beginning of the year}}{\text{SYD}}$$

$$\text{and SYD} = \frac{n(n+1)}{2} \quad \text{where n = estimated useful life}$$

3. Present value methods--Depreciation expense is lower in the early years and higher in the later years. The rate of return on the investment remains constant over the life of the asset. Time value of money formulas are used.

   a. Sinking fund--Uses the future value of an annuity formula.
   b. Annuity fund--Uses the present value of an annuity formula.

Partial-year depreciation. When an asset is either acquired or disposed of during the year, the full-year depreciation calculation is prorated between the accounting periods involved.

Example of partial year depreciation

XYZ, a calendar year entity, acquired a machine on June 1, 1999, which cost $40,000 with an estimated useful life of 4 years and a $2,500 salvage value. The depreciation expense for each full year of the asset's life is calculated as

	Straight-line	*Double-declining balance*					*Sum-of-years' digits*				
Year 1	37,500* ÷ 4 = 9,375	50%	x	40,000	=	20,000	4/10	x	37,500*	=	15,000
Year 2	9,375	50%	x	20,000	=	10,000	3/10	x	37,500	=	11,250
Year 3	9,375	50%	x	10,000	=	5,000	2/10	x	37,500	=	7,500
Year 4	9,375	50%	x	5,000	=	2,500	1/10	x	37,500	=	3,750

**(40,000 – 2,500)*

Because the first full year of the asset's life does not coincide with the company's year, the amounts shown above must be prorated as follows:

	Straight-line	*Double-declining balance*					*Sum-of-years' digits*				
1999	7/12 x 9,375 = 5,469	7/12	x	20,000	=	11,667	7/12	x	15,000	=	8,750
2000	9,375	5/12	x	20,000	=	8,333	5/12	x	15,000	=	6,250
		7/12	x	10,000	=	5,833	7/12	x	11,250	=	6,563
						14,166					12,813
2001	9,375	5/12	x	10,000	=	4,167	5/12	x	11,250	=	4,687
		7/12	x	5,000	=	2,917	7/12	x	7,500	=	4,375
						7,084					9,062
2002	9,375	5/12	x	5,000	=	2,083	5/12	x	7,500	=	3,125
		7/12	x	2,500	=	1,458	7/12	x	3,750	=	2,188
						3,541					5,313
2003	5/12 x 9,375 = 3,906	5/12	x	2,500	=	1,042	5/12	x	3,750	=	1,562

As an alternative to proration, an entity may follow any one of several simplified conventions.

1. Record a full year's depreciation in the year of acquisition and none in the year of disposal.
2. Record one-half year's depreciation in the year of acquisition and one-half year's depreciation in the year of disposal.

Depreciation method based on actual physical usage--Units of production. Depreciation is based upon the number of units produced by the asset in a given year.

$$\text{Depreciation rate} = \frac{\text{Cost less salvage value}}{\text{Estimated number of units to be produced by the asset over its estimated useful life}}$$

$$\text{Units of production depreciation} = \text{Depreciation rate} \times \text{Number of units produced during the current year}$$

Other depreciation methods.

1. **Retirement method**--Cost of asset is expensed in period in which it is retired.
2. **Replacement method**--Original cost is carried in accounts and cost of replacement is expensed in the period of replacement.
3. **Group (Composite) method**--Averages the service lives of a number of assets using a weighted-average of the units and depreciates the group or composite as if it were a single unit. A group consists of similar assets, while a composite is made up of dissimilar assets.

   Depreciation rate:

$$\frac{\text{Sum of the straight-line depreciation of individual assets}}{\text{Total asset cost}}$$

   Depreciation expense:

$$\text{Depreciation rate} \times \text{Total group (composite) cost}$$

Gains and losses are not recognized on the disposal of an asset but are netted into accumulated depreciation.

Tax method. Assets placed in service prior to 1981 are depreciated based on the asset's useful life and cannot be depreciated below their salvage value. The depreciation method used depends upon the type of property and whether it was new or used when it was placed into service. Assets placed in service between 1981 and 1986 are depreciated under the Accelerated Cost Recovery System (ACRS). ACRS ignores salvage value. Thus, the asset's entire basis is depreciable over the specified recovery period to be used for each asset. Property is placed into classes and the depreciation method for each class is specified. Optional depreciation methods may be elected. In addition, Section 179 allows taxpayers to deduct, subject to limitations, an asset's entire cost in the year of acquisition. Depreciation deductions are calculated by multiplying the asset's unadjusted basis by the specified depreciation percentage for the related time period. The depreciation percentage will depend upon the asset's class, recovery year, depreciation method and convention. For assets placed into service after 1986, tax depreciation is calculated using the Modified Accelerated Cost Recovery System (MACRS) which also ignores salvage value and divides assets into classes. The asset's class and recovery period is specified in Rev. Proc. 87-56. Depreciation deductions are calculated by multiplying the asset's unadjusted basis by the appropriate depreciation percentage. Depreciation percentages are listed in Rev. Proc. 87-57. The percentages are based on the type of property, class life, depreciation method, and convention. Depreciation deductions are limited for certain assets such as listed property. Optional depreciation methods or Section 179 may also be elected.

Tax depreciation will differ in amount from financial depreciation because of the difference in treatment of salvage value, recovery methods, recovery periods, and the use of conventions. The difference between tax depreciation and financial depreciation is reported as a Schedule M-1 adjustment on a corporation's tax return.

MACRS is not considered to be in accordance with generally accepted accounting principles. Therefore, any differences between financial and tax depreciation must be used in the calculation of deferred taxes (Chapter 15).

Depletion

Depletion is the annual charge for the use of natural resources. The depletion base includes all development costs such as exploring, drilling, excavating, and other preparatory costs. The amount of the depletion base charged to income is determined by the following formula:

$$\frac{1}{\text{Total expected recoverable units}} \times \text{Depletion base} \times \text{Units sold}$$

The unit depletion rate is revised frequently due to the uncertainties surrounding the recovery of natural resources. The revision is made prospectively; the remaining undepleted cost is allocated over the remaining recoverable units.

Nonmonetary Transactions

APB 29 governs the accounting for nonmonetary transactions. It identifies the following three types of nonmonetary transactions:

1. Nonreciprocal transfers with owners
2. Nonreciprocal transfers with other than owners
3. Nonmonetary exchanges

The problem addressed by the opinion is the determination of the amount assigned to the nonmonetary asset transferred to or from the enterprise.

The general rule established by APB 29 is that the accounting for nonmonetary transactions should be based on the fair values of the assets involved. The fair value to be used is that of the asset surrendered unless the fair value of the asset received is "more clearly evident." Fair value is defined in APB 29 as

> *...the estimated realizable values in cash transactions of the same or similar assets, quoted market prices, independent appraisals, estimated fair values of assets or services received in exchange, and other available evidence.*

While this general rule is considered adequate for most situations, the Board noted that certain modifications should be made under two specific circumstances. If the fair value is not reasonably determinable, the recorded amount (i.e., book value) may be the only amount available to measure the transaction. According to the opinion, the fair value is to be considered not determinable within reasonable limits if

> *...major uncertainties exist about the realizability of the value that would be assigned to an asset received in a nonmonetary transaction accounted for at fair value.*

An exception to the rule is also required in the case of an exchange which is not essentially the culmination of the earnings process. The following two types of nonmonetary exchanges do not result in a culmination of the earnings process:

1. An exchange of a product or property held for sale in the ordinary course of business for a product or property to be sold in the same line of business to facilitate sales to customers other than the parties to the exchange.
2. An exchange of a productive asset not held for sale in the ordinary course of business for a similar productive asset or an equivalent interest in the same or similar productive asset in the same line of business.

EITF consensus (86-29) specifies that a product or property held for sale exchanged for a productive asset (even in the same line of business) should be recorded at fair value.

Nonreciprocal transfers. Examples of nonreciprocal transfers with owners would include dividends-in-kind, nonmonetary assets exchanged for common stock, split-ups, and spin-offs. An example of a nonreciprocal transaction with other than the owners is a donation of property either by or to the enterprise.

The valuation of most nonreciprocal transfers should be based upon the fair market value of the asset given (or received if the fair value of the nonmonetary asset is both objectively measurable and would be clearly recognizable). However, nonmonetary assets distributed to owners of an enterprise in a spin-off or other form of reorganization or liquidation should be based on the recorded amount. Where there is no asset given, the valuation of the transaction should be based upon the fair value of the asset received.

Example of accounting for a nonreciprocal transfer

1. XYZ donated property with a book value of $10,000 to a charity during the current year.
2. The property had a fair market value of $17,000 at the date of the transfer.

According to the opinion, the transaction is to be valued at the fair market value of the property transferred, and any gain or loss on the transaction is to be recognized. Thus, XYZ should recognize a gain of $7,000 ($17,000 – $10,000) in the determination of the current period's net income. The entry to record the transaction would be as follows:

Charitable donations	17,000	
Property		10,000
Gain on donation of property		7,000

Nonmonetary exchanges. An exchange of nonmonetary assets can take two basic forms:

1. Dissimilar assets may be involved in the exchange.
2. Similar assets may be involved in the exchange.

The recognition of a gain or loss on the exchange is dependent upon whether or not the gain or loss is deemed to be realized. If an exchange is considered to be the culmination of the earnings process, then the resulting gain or loss will be recognized. If the exchange is not considered to be the culmination of the earnings process, the resulting gain will not be recognized.

Dissimilar Assets

An exchange is the culmination of the earnings process when dissimilar assets are involved. The general rule is to value the transaction at the **fair market value** of the asset given up **(unless the fair value of the asset received is more clearly evident)** and to recognize the gain or loss.

Example of an exchange involving dissimilar assets and no boot

1. Gries, Inc. exchanges an automobile with a book value of $2,500 with Springsteen & Co. for a tooling machine with a fair market value of $3,200.
2. No boot is exchanged in the transaction.
3. The fair value of the automobile is not readily determinable.

In this case, Gries, Inc. has a realized gain of $700 ($3,200 – $2,500) on the exchange. Because the exchange involves dissimilar assets, the earnings process has culminated and the gain should be included in the determination of net income. The entry to record the transaction would be as follows:

Machine	3,200	
Automobile		2,500
Gain on exchange of automobile		700

Similar Assets

Similar assets are those that are used for the same general purpose, are of the same general type, and are employed in the same line of business. It is not necessary to exchange identical assets. The treatment described applies to those assets which are exchanged as a result of technological advancement as well as to those which are exchanged as a result of wearing out. The general rule involving the exchange of **similar** assets involving a gain is to value the transaction at the **book value** of the asset given up. In this situation, the gain is deferred over the life of the new asset by allowing a lower amount of annual depreciation.

A single exception to the nonrecognition rule for similar assets occurs when the exchange involves both a monetary and nonmonetary asset being exchanged for a similar nonmonetary asset. The monetary portion of the exchange is termed **boot**. The EITF has reached a consensus (86-29) that when boot is at least 25% of the fair value of the exchange, it is considered a monetary transaction and both parties should record the exchange at fair value. When boot less than 25% is received in exchange, only the boot portion of the earnings process is considered to have been culminated. The portion of the gain applicable to the boot is considered realized and should be recognized in the determination of net income for the period of the exchange.

The formula for the recognition of the gain in an exchange involving boot of less than 25% of fair value can be generalized as follows:

$$\frac{\text{Boot}}{\text{Boot + Fair value of nonmonetary asset received}} \times \text{Total gain indicated} = \text{Gain recognized}$$

In an exchange of similar real estate that is a monetary transaction under EITF 86-29 because boot is at least 25% of the fair value exchanged, the fair value would be allocated between the monetary and nonmonetary components based on relative fair values. The receiver of boot would have a sale under SFAS 66 and, for the nonmonetary portion, would account for it under paragraph 21 of APB 29, adjusted basis of the property. The payer of boot records the payment as a purchase of real estate and, for the nonmonetary portion, follows APB 29 and adjusts basis of the property.

Example of an exchange involving similar assets and boot

1. ABC exchanged a casting machine for a technologically newer model. The cost of the old machine was $75,000, and the accumulated depreciation was $5,000.
2. The fair value of the machine received was $90,000.

3. Boot was received in the amount of $10,000.

A total gain of $30,000 is created by the transaction. This amount is the difference between the fair value of the assets received and the cost of the assets surrendered ($100,000 – $70,000). The amount of the gain to be recognized can be computed as shown below.

$$\frac{\$10,000}{\$10,000 + \$90,000} \times \$30,000 = \$3,000$$

The entry required to record the transaction is as follows:

Cash	10,000	
New machine	63,000*	
Accumulated depreciation	5,000	
Old machine		75,000
Gain on exchange of machine		3,000

**The book value of the new machine is the book value of the old machine less the amount of boot received, plus the gain recognized.*

An exchange is the culmination of the earnings process when a loss is created as a result of the exchange of similar assets. While the earnings process is not generally considered complete when dealing with the exchange of similar assets, to record the asset at anything greater than the fair market value would be imprudent.

Summary. In some situations, the fair value of the asset cannot be determined. If the fair value is not determinable, the book values of the assets involved are to be used as the valuation measure.

The situations involving the exchange of nonmonetary assets can be summarized in the following diagram:

ACCOUNTING FOR NONMONETARY EXCHANGES

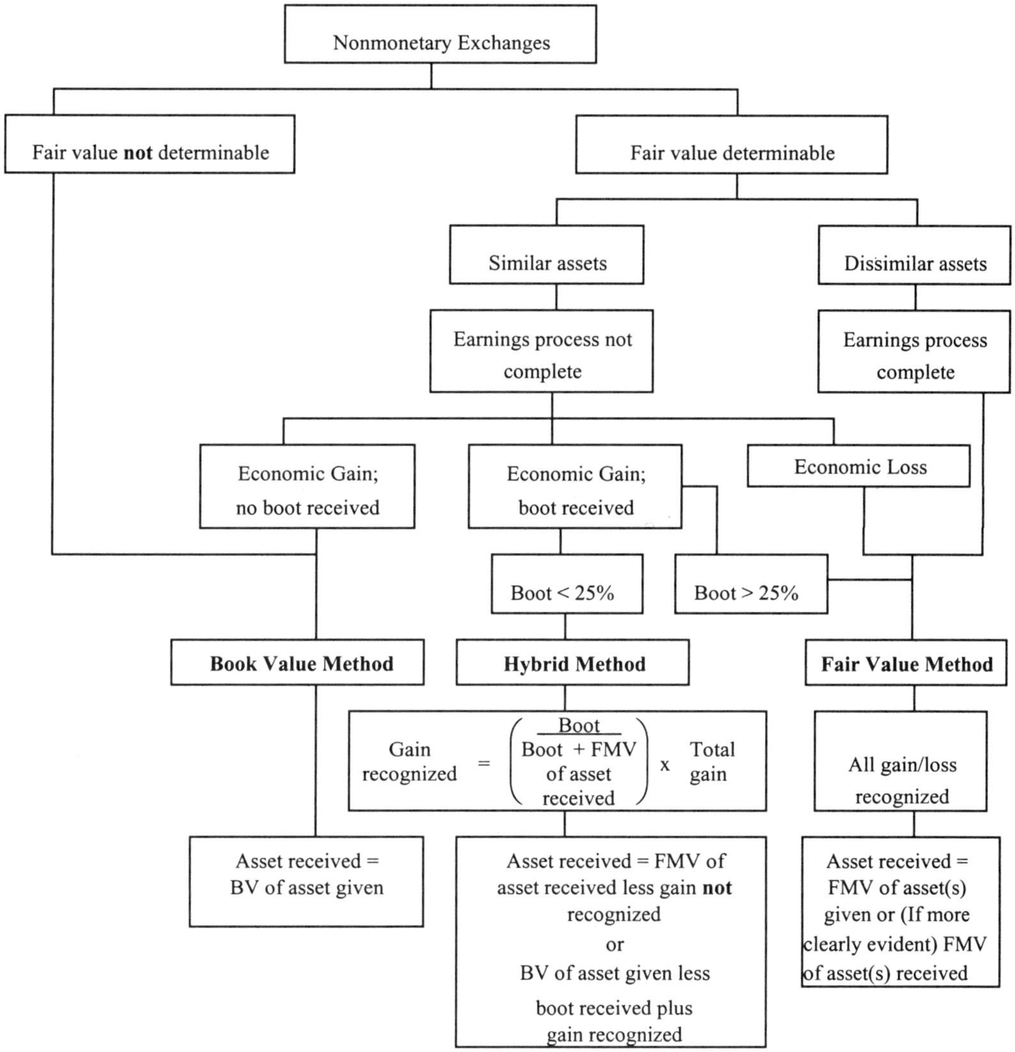

Involuntary Conversions

Certain conditions may occur that necessitate the involuntary conversion of a nonmonetary asset into a monetary asset. FASB Interpretation 30 is GAAP. Involuntary conversions of nonmonetary assets to monetary assets are monetary transactions, and the resulting gain or loss shall be recognized in the period of conversion. It makes no difference that the monetary assets received are immediately reinvested in nonmonetary assets. An example of an involuntary conversion would be the condemnation of property.

This interpretation does not apply to the involuntary conversion of LIFO inventories which are intended to be replaced but have not been replaced by the year end.

Deferred Taxes

A difference between the amount of gain or loss recognized for book purposes and that recognized for tax purposes constitutes a temporary difference. Under SFAS 109, the difference in the gain or loss will result in a difference in the basis of the asset received. The difference in the gain or loss reverses as a result of the annual charge to depreciation. The proper treatment of temporary differences is discussed in Chapter 15.

Impairment

Impairment occurs if the book value of fixed assets is determined not to be recoverable. In a **total impairment** the obsolete asset and related depreciation are removed from the accounts and a loss is recognized for the difference. If a **partial impairment** of a depreciable asset results, the asset should be written down to a new cost basis. That cost is then depreciated over the remaining life. The journal entry follows:

Accumulated depreciation	xxx	
Loss due to impairment	xxx	
Asset		xxx

The loss amount would appear in the income statement as a component of income from continuing operations before taxes or in a statement of activities (not-for-profit entity).

SFAS 121 requires long-lived assets and certain identifiable intangibles, and any goodwill related to those assets, to be reviewed for impairment whenever circumstances and situations change such that there is an indication that the carrying amount is not recoverable. Recoverability should be assessed under the following circumstances (among others):

1. The asset market value decreases significantly
2. The use of the asset is significantly changed in extent or manner
3. Legal factors or business climate changes adversely affect asset value
4. Regulator's adverse assessment or action
5. Original expected costs are significantly exceeded
6. A history of cash flow losses and continued asset losses are forecasted

The lowest level at which there are identifiable cash flows independent of cash flows from other groupings should be used to group assets for review. If, upon review, management's best estimate of the undiscounted future cash flows (without interest charges) is less than the carrying amount, the carrying amount is reduced to fair value and an impairment loss is recognized. This fair value is considered a new cost basis which is not subject to subsequent adjustment except for depreciation and further impairment. There is no restoration of recognized impairment losses.

If acquired as part of a business combination in which goodwill is associated, the tested (for recoverability) asset grouping should include an allocated amount of goodwill on a pro rata basis using fair values of the net assets acquired at acquisition, unless other evidence of association is more appropriate. A resulting impairment loss will reduce the associated goodwill carrying amount before the carrying amount of the long-lived assets and identifiable intangibles are reduced to fair value.

Example of impairment with goodwill

On 1/1/99, Parent Company purchased a wholly-owned Subsidiary Company for $1,300,000 cash. Book value of the equity acquired was $900,000. The relevant values at acquisition follow:

(In millions)

	1/1/99 Book value	*Excess*	*1/1/99 Fair value*
Cash	$ 200	---	$ 200
Accounts receivable	200	---	200
Inventory	100	$100	200
Net plant (20-yr. life)	500	100	600
Patents (5-yr. life)	100	100	200
Goodwill (10-yr. life)		100	100
Total	$1,100		$1,500
Current liabilities	$ 100	---	$ 100
Long-term debt	100	---	100
Common stock	200	---	---
Paid-in capital	300	---	---
Retained earnings	400	---	---
Total	$1,100		

On 1/1/01, there is an indication that the noncurrent assets may be impaired. Before testing for impairment of the plant and the patent, goodwill is allocated as indicated below. Future cash flows and fair values are then determined.

	*1/1/01 Book values**	*Allocated goodwill*	*Total carrying value 1/1/01*	*Expected future cash flows*	*1/1/01 Fair value*
Net plant (20-yr. life)	$540	$ 60**	$600	$800	$620
Patents (5-yr. life)	120	20***	140	120	105
Goodwill (10-yr. life)	80	(80)	-0-	-0-	-0-

* *1/1/99 fair values less depreciation/amortization for 2 years*
** *Plant $80 x $600/$800 = $60*
*** *Patent $80 x $200/$800 = $20*

The above analysis shows that there is no impairment loss recognized on the plant because the expected future cash flows ($800) exceed the adjusted carrying value of the plant ($600) on 1/1/01.

However, the patent's future cash flows ($120) are less than the carrying amount ($140). The amortization policy was reviewed and was found to be satisfactory. The patent's carrying value including the allocated goodwill is $140 ($120 + $20) and the fair value is $105. The adjusting journal entry is

Impairment Loss	35	
Goodwill		20
Patent		15

If the fair value of the patent was $130, the adjusting journal entry would be

Impairment Loss	10	
Goodwill		10

The resulting balances of the patent account and the goodwill account are amortized over their remaining life. If the fair value of the patent was above $140, there would be no impairment loss.

If an impairment loss is recognized, the following disclosures should be made:

1. Description of the impaired assets and the situation surrounding the impairment.
2. Amount of impairment loss and the method of determining fair value.
3. If the impairment losses are not reported separately or parenthetically, the caption where the losses are aggregated.
4. The business segment affected, if applicable.

SFAS 121 applies to all entities. However, it does **not** apply to

1. Financial instruments
2. Financial institutions' long-term customer relationships (core deposit intangibles, etc.)
3. Mortgage servicing rights
4. Deferred tax assets
5. Deferred policy acquisition costs
6. Assets whose accounting is prescribed by SFAS 50, 53, 63, 86, or 90 (as amended)

This standard applies to rate-regulated assets. Costs excluded by a regulator from the enterprise's rate base would be recognized as an impairment. Other pronouncements that apply the general impairment standard (SFAS 121) are SFAS 7, 34, 51, 61, 66, 67, 71, and 101. Pronouncements that apply existing requirements are APB 18, 30; SFAS 44, 50, 53, 63, 65, 86, 90, 97, 109, 114, and 115. Pronouncements that are split between the general and existing requirements follow:

Apply general impairment standard (SFAS 121):

APB 17	Identifiable intangibles not specifically excluded Goodwill identified with SFAS 121 assets

SFAS 13	Lessee capital leases Lessor assets subject to operating leases
SFAS 19	Proved properties and wells with related facilities and equipment
SFAS 60	All assets except deferred policy acquisition costs

Apply existing requirement:

APB 17	Identifiable intangibles specifically excluded Goodwill not identified with SFAS 121 assets
SFAS 13	Direct financing, sales-type, and leveraged leases of lessors
SFAS 19	Unproved properties
SFAS 60	Deferred policy acquisition costs

Resulting impairment losses are reported in the period when the recognition criteria are initially applied.

Assets To Be Disposed Of

Long-lived assets and identifiable intangibles to be disposed of (except those covered by APB 30) would be carried at the lower of cost or fair value less cost to sell. Expected costs to sell beyond 1 year should be discounted. If fair value less cost to sell is used, subsequent revisions in estimates should be reported as adjustments to the carrying amount. However, these adjustments cannot exceed the carrying value of the disposed asset (before adjustment) at the date of the decision to dispose. These assets should not be depreciated during the holding period.

Disclosures to be made in the case of assets to be disposed of are as follows:

1. The initial loss
2. Gains or losses resulting from subsequent revision in estimates of fair value less cost to sell
3. If they can be identified and to the extent they are included in the entity's operations for the period, the results of operations for the disposed assets
4. If not reported separately or parenthetically, the caption where the gains and losses are aggregated
5. Description of the assets and the situation surrounding the disposal, the carrying amount of the assets and the expected date of disposal
6. The business segment affected (for public companies)

Capitalization of Interest Costs

The cost of an asset should include all of the costs necessary to get the asset set up and functioning properly for its intended use. SFAS 34 is GAAP concerning the capitalization of interest. Other pronouncements have been issued (SFAS 42, 58,

62, and FASB Interpretation 33) which deal with the capitalization of interest in special situations.

The principal purposes to be accomplished by the capitalization of interest costs are

1. To get a more accurate original asset investment cost
2. To get a better matching of costs deferred to future periods with revenues of those future periods

All assets that require a time period to get ready for their intended use should include a capitalized amount of interest costs. However, accomplishing this level of capitalization would usually violate a reasonable cost/benefit test because of the added accounting and administrative costs generated. In many situations, the effect of interest capitalization would be immaterial. Thus, interest costs should only be capitalized as a part of the historical cost of the following qualifying assets when such costs are considered to be material:

1. Assets constructed for an entity's own use or for which deposit or progress payments are made.
2. Assets produced as discrete projects that are intended for lease or sale.
3. Equity method investments when the investee is using funds to acquire qualifying assets for its principal operations which have not yet begun.

Generally, inventories and land that are not undergoing preparation for intended use are not qualifying assets. When land is being developed, it is a qualifying asset. If land is developed for lots, the capitalized interest cost is added to the cost of the **land**. The interest is then matched against revenues when the lots are sold. If, however, the land is developed for a building, then the capitalized interest cost is added to the cost of the **building**. The interest is then matched against revenues as the building is depreciated.

The capitalization of interest costs does not apply to the following situations:

1. When routine inventories are produced in large quantities on a repetitive basis
2. When effects are not material, compared to the effect of expensing interest
3. When qualifying assets are already in use or ready for use
4. When qualifying assets are not being used and are not awaiting activities to get them ready for use
5. When qualifying assets are not included in a consolidated balance sheet
6. When principal operations of an investee accounted for under the equity method have already begun
7. When regulated investees capitalize both the cost of debt and equity capital
8. When assets are acquired with grants and gifts restricted by the donor to the extent that funds are available from those grants and gifts

The amount of interest capitalized. Interest cost includes the following:

1. Interest on debt having explicit interest rates

2. Interest related to capital leases
3. Interest required to be imputed on payables

The most appropriate rate to use as the capitalization rate is that rate which is applicable to specific new debt that resulted from the need to finance the acquired assets. If there was no specific new debt, the capitalization rate should be a weighted-average of the rates of the other borrowings of the entity. This latter case reflects the fact that the previous debt of the entity was indirectly incurred to finance the identified qualifying asset and its interest should be part of the cost of the new asset. The selection of borrowings to be used in the calculation of the weighted-average of rates requires judgment. The amount of interest to be capitalized is that portion which could have been avoided if the qualifying asset had not been acquired. Thus, the capitalized amount is the incremental amount of interest cost incurred by the entity to finance the acquired asset.

The base used to multiply the rate by is the average amount of accumulated net capital **expenditures** incurred for qualifying assets during the relevant time frame. Capitalized costs and expenditures are not the same terms. Theoretically, a capitalized cost financed by a trade payable for which no interest is recognized is not a capital expenditure to which the capitalization rate should be applied. Reasonable approximations of net capital expenditures are acceptable, however, and capitalized costs are generally used in place of capital expenditures unless there is a material difference.

If the average capitalized expenditures exceed the specific new borrowings for the time frame involved, then the **excess** expenditures should be multiplied by the weighted-average of rates and not by the rate associated with the specific debt. This requirement more accurately reflects the interest cost incurred by the entity to acquire the fixed asset.

The interest being paid on the debt may be simple or compound. Simple interest is computed on the principal alone, whereas compound interest is computed on principal **and** on any interest that has not been paid. Most fixed assets will be acquired with debt having interest compounded. Compound interest can be found by using the compound interest tables.

The total amount of interest actually incurred by the entity is the ceiling for the amount of interest cost capitalized. The amount capitalized cannot exceed the amount actually incurred during the period involved. On a consolidated basis, the ceiling is defined as the total of the parent's interest cost plus that of the consolidated subsidiaries. If financial statements are issued separately, the interest cost capitalized should be limited to the amount that the separate entity has incurred and that amount should include interest on intercompany borrowings. The interest incurred is a gross amount and is not netted against interest earned except in cases involving externally restricted tax exempt borrowings.

Example of accounting for capitalized interest costs

1. On January 1, 1999, Gemini Corp. contracted with Leo Company to construct a building for $2,000,000 on land that Gemini had purchased years earlier.
2. Gemini Corp. was to make five payments in 1999 with the last payment scheduled for the date of completion, December 31, 1999.
3. Gemini Corp. made the following payments during 1999:

January 1, 1999	$ 200,000
March 31, 1999	400,000
June 30, 1999	610,000
September 30, 1999	440,000
December 31, 1999	350,000
	$2,000,000

4. Gemini Corp. had the following debt outstanding at December 31, 1999:

a. A 12%, 4-year note dated 1/1/99 with interest compounded quarterly. Both principal and interest due 12/31/01 (relates specifically to building project).	$850,000
b. A 10%, 10-year note dated 12/31/95 with simple interest and interest payable annually on December 31.	$600,000
c. A 12%, 5-year note dated 12/31/97 with simple interest and interest payable annually on December 31.	$700,000

The amount of interest to be capitalized during 1999 is computed as follows:

Average Accumulated Expenditures

Date	Expenditure	Capitalization period*	Average accumulated expenditures
1/1/99	$ 200,000	12/12	$200,000
3/31/99	400,000	9/12	300,000
6/30/99	610,000	6/12	305,000
9/30/99	440,000	3/12	110,000
12/31/99	350,000	0/12	--
	$2,000,000		$915,000

**The number of months between the date expenditures were made and the date interest capitalization stops (December 31, 1999).*

Potential Interest Cost to be Capitalized

($850,000 x 1.12551)*	–	$850,000	=	$106,684
65,000 x .1108**			=	7,202
$915,000				$113,886

* *The principal, $850,000, is multiplied by the factor for the future amount of $1 for four periods at 3% to determine the amount of principal and interest due in 1999.*

** *Weighted-average interest rate:*

	Principal	*Interest*
10%, 10-year note	*$ 600,000*	*$ 60,000*
12%, 5-year note	*700,000*	*84,000*
	$1,300,000	*$144,000*

$$\frac{\textit{Total interest}}{\textit{Total principal}} = \frac{\$\ 144{,}000}{\$1{,}300{,}000} = \underline{\underline{11.08}}\%\ \textit{weighted-average interest rate}$$

The actual interest is

12%, 4-year note [(\$850,000 x 1.12551) – \$850,000]	=	\$106,684
10%, 10-year note (\$600,000 x 10%)	=	60,000
12%, 5-year note (\$700,000 x 12%)	=	84,000
Total interest		\$250,684

The interest cost to be capitalized is the lesser of \$113,886 (avoidable interest) or \$250,684 (actual interest), which is \$113,886. The remaining \$136,798 (\$250,684 – \$113,886) would be expensed.

Determining the time period for interest capitalization. Three conditions must be met before the capitalization period begins.

1. Necessary activities are in progress to get the asset ready to function as intended
2. Qualifying asset expenditures have been made
3. Interest costs are being incurred

As long as these conditions continue, interest costs can be capitalized.

Necessary activities are interpreted in a very **broad** manner. They start with the planning process and continue until the qualifying asset is substantially complete and ready to function. Brief, normal interruptions do not stop the capitalization of interest costs. However, if the entity intentionally suspends or delays the activities for some reason, interest costs should not be capitalized from the point of suspension or delay until substantial activities in regard to the asset resume.

If the asset is completed by parts, the capitalization of interest costs stops for each part as it becomes ready. An asset that must be entirely complete before the parts can be used capitalizes interest costs until the total asset becomes ready.

Interest costs should continue to be capitalized until the asset is ready to function as intended, even in cases where lower of cost or market rules are applicable and market is lower than cost. The required write-down should be increased accordingly.

Capitalization of interest costs incurred on tax-exempt borrowings. If qualifying assets have been financed with the proceeds from tax-exempt, **externally restricted** borrowings and if temporary investments have been purchased with those proceeds, a modification is required. The interest costs incurred from the date of borrowing must be reduced by the interest earned on the temporary investment in order to calculate the ceiling for the capitalization of interest costs. This procedure must be followed until the assets financed in this manner are ready. When the specified assets are functioning as intended, the interest cost of the tax-exempt borrowing becomes available to be capitalized by other qualifying assets of the entity. Portions of the tax-exempt borrowings that are not restricted are eligible for capitalization in the normal manner.

Assets acquired with gifts or grants. Qualifying assets which are acquired with externally restricted gifts or grants are not subject to capitalization of interest. The principal reason for this treatment is the belief that there is no economic cost of financing when a gift or grant is used in the acquisition.

Summary of interest capitalization requirements. The following diagram summarizes the accounting for "interest capitalization."

SUMMARY OF ACCOUNTING FOR INTEREST CAPITALIZATION

Capitalization of Interest During Construction

Qualifying assets

a. Assets constructed for use in operations
b. Assets for sale or lease which are constructed as discrete projects (ships, real estate), but not inventory
c. Certain equity method investments

When to capitalize interest (all three must be met)

a. Expenditures for asset have been made
b. Activities intended to get asset ready are in progress
c. Interest cost is being incurred

Applicable interest (net of discounts, premiums, and issue costs)

a. Interest obligations having explicit rates
b. Imputed interest on certain payables/receivables
c. Interest related to capital leases

Amount of interest to capitalize

Average accumulated expenditures

(Specific borrowings x Applicable interest rate) + (Other borrowings x Weighted-average interest rate*)

Qualifications

a. Amount of interest to be capialized cannot exceed total interest costs incurred during the period
b. Interest earned on temporarily invested borrowings may not be offset against interest to be capitalized (except externally restricted tax-exempt borrowings)

$$\text{*Weighted-average interest rate} = \frac{\text{Total interest on other borrowings}}{\text{Total principal on other borrowings}}$$

Intangible Assets

Intangible assets are noncurrent, nonphysical assets that entitle the enterprise to certain legal rights or competitive advantages. The noncurrent classification excludes such nonphysical assets as accounts receivable. Examples of intangible assets include copyrights, franchises, goodwill, leaseholds, organizational costs, patents, and trademarks. Intangibles are specifically covered by APB 17.

Intangible assets are acquired as follows:

1. They are purchased.
2. They are created internally.

When intangible assets are purchased, their cost should be the cash or fair market value disbursed or the present value of the liability assumed in conjunction with the exchange. This amount represents the potential earning power of the intangible asset as of the date of its acquisition.

When the intangible asset is created internally, the valuation of the asset can be very difficult. The costs involved are generally expensed. Where the intangible asset is identifiable and separable from the entity, their cost should be the cash or fair market value disbursed or the present value of the liability assumed in conjunction with the exchange.

The intangible asset should be amortized over the life of the asset on a straight-line basis unless some other method better matches revenues and expenses. The life to be used for the amortization period shall be the legal life if it is less than 40 years. Otherwise, it shall be determined based on numerous factors (some of which are listed below) but should not exceed 40 years.

1. Legal, regulatory, or contractual provisions
2. Provisions for renewal or extension
3. Obsolescence, demand, competition, etc.
4. Life expectancies of employees
5. Expected actions of competitors
6. Benefits may not be reasonably projected
7. Composite of many additional factors

Research and Development Costs

Research and development (R&D) are defined in SFAS 2 as follows:

> a. *Research is planned search or critical investigation aimed at the discovery of new knowledge with the hope that such knowledge will be useful in developing a new product or service or a new process or technique or in bringing about a significant improvement to an existing product or process.*
>
> b. *Development is the translation of research findings or other knowledge into a plan or design for a new product or*

process or for a significant improvement to an existing product or process whether intended for sale or use.

The following are three ways in which R&D costs are incurred by a business:

1. Through the purchase of R&D from other entities
2. Through an arrangement to develop R&D for other entities
3. Through R&D activities conducted for the benefit of the enterprise

The accounting treatment relative to R&D depends upon the nature of the cost.

SFAS 2 and SFAS 68 represent GAAP relative to research and development costs. SFAS 2 provides guidance for those R&D costs incurred in the ordinary course of operations. These costs consist of materials, equipment, facilities, personnel, and indirect costs which can be attributed to research or development activities. These costs are expensed in the period in which they are incurred unless they have alternative future uses.

Examples of R&D costs covered by SFAS 2 would include

1. Laboratory research to discover new knowledge
2. Formulation and design of product alternatives
    a. Testing for product alternatives
    b. Modification of products or processes
3. Preproduction prototypes and models
    a. Tools, dies, etc. for new technology
    b. Pilot plants not capable of commercial production
4. Engineering activity until the product is ready for manufacture

Examples of R&D costs which are **not** covered by SFAS 2 would include

1. Engineering during an early phase of commercial production
2. Quality control for commercial production
3. Troubleshooting during a commercial production breakdown
4. Routine, ongoing efforts to improve products
5. Adaptation of existing capacity for a specific customer or other requirements
6. Seasonal design changes to products
7. Routine design of tools, dies, etc.
8. Design, construction, startup, etc. of equipment except that used solely for R&D

Both R&D costs that are purchased from another enterprise and those that have alternative future uses are to be capitalized and amortized in accordance with APB 17. The amortization or depreciation of the asset is classified as a research and development expense. If purchased research is not determined to have future use, then its entire cost is to be expensed in the period incurred.

R&D costs incurred as a result of contractual arrangements are addressed in SFAS 68. This statement indicates that the nature of the agreement shall dictate the accounting treatment of the costs involved. The key determinant is the transfer of the risk associated with the R&D expenditures. If the business receives funds from another party to perform R&D and is obligated to repay those funds regardless of the outcome, a liability must be recorded and the R&D costs expensed as incurred. In order to conclude that a liability does not exist, the transfer of the financial risk must be substantive and genuine.

EMERGING ISSUES TASK FORCE CONSENSUS SUMMARIES

86-29 Nonmonetary Transactions: Magnitude of Boot and the Exceptions to the Use of Fair Value

When boot is at least 25% of the fair value of the exchange, it is considered a monetary transaction and both parties should record the exchange at fair value. When boot less than 25% is received in exchange, only the boot portion of the earnings process is considered to have been culminated. The portion of the gain applicable to the boot is considered realized and should be recognized in the determination of net income for the period of the exchange.

The formula for the recognition of the gain in an exchange involving boot of less than 25% of fair value can be generalized as follows:

$$\frac{\text{Boot}}{\text{Boot + Fair value of nonmonetary asset received}} \times \text{Total gain indicated} = \text{Gain recognized}$$

EITF consensus (86-29) specifies that a product or property held for sale exchanged for a productive asset (even in the same line of business) should be recorded at fair value.

87-29 Exchange of Real Estate Involving Boot

In an exchange of similar real estate that is a monetary transaction under EITF 86-29 because boot is at least 25% of the fair value exchanged, the fair value would be allocated between the monetary and nonmonetary components based on relative fair values. The receiver of boot would have a sale under SFAS 66 and, for the nonmonetary portion, would account for it under paragraph 21 of APB 29, adjusting basis of the property.

The payer of boot records the payment as a purchase of real estate and, for the nonmonetary portion, follows APB 29 and adjusts basis of the property.

89-13 Accounting for the Cost of Asbestos Removal

The cost of treating property acquired with a known asbestos problem should be capitalized. In the case of existing property, asbestos treating costs should be recorded as a betterment. Both capitalizations are subject to an impairment test.

When removal costs incurred due to the anticipation of the sale of property can be recovered from the sale, these costs should be deferred and recognized at the time of sale.

Expensed asbestos costs are not considered extraordinary items. SEC registrants should disclose any significant exposure for asbestos treatment in the MD&A.

91-10 Accounting for Special Assessments and Tax Increment Financing Entities

A property owner should recognize an obligation for special assessments levied by a municipality or by a Tax Increment Financing Entity (TIFE) that are for a fixed or determinable amount for a fixed or determinable period. A company may be contingently liable under SFAS 5 if

1. It must satisfy any shortfall in annual debt service
2. It has pledged its assets
3. It provides a letter of credit or other credit enhancements in support of the TIFE's debt.

If constructing facilities for its own use, the presence of these factors creates a presumption that the TIFE debt is a liability.

93-11 Accounting for Barter Transactions Involving Barter Credits

A consensus was reached that APB 29 applies to these kinds of transactions and that the basis for recording should be the fair value of the nonmonetary asset given up. Ordinarily, this fair value measurement should not be higher than its carrying value.

Impairment, if applicable, should be recorded before the exchange. Thus, a new cost basis is established and a loss is recognized on the income statement. If an operating lease is involved, impairment is measured as the amount of remaining lease costs in excess of fair value of the probable sublease rentals for the remaining lease term. Paragraph 13 of SFAS 15 should be helpful in defining fair value.

The value of barter credits should not be used to record fair value unless they can be converted to cash in the short term or there are independent existing market prices available for items to be received for the barter credits.

Impairment after the exchange should be recorded if the carrying amount exceeds the fair value of the barter credits or if the business determines that it won't be able to use the barter credits.

95-23 Treatment of Certain Site Restoration/Environmental Exit Costs When Testing a Long-Lived Asset for Impairment

For purposes of SFAS 121, site restoration/environmental exit costs that **have** been recorded as a liability are to be excluded from the undiscounted expected future cash flows used to test for recoverability. The intent of management determines whether exit costs that **have not** been recorded as a liability are to be excluded or included. In general, if disposition is not expected to incur exit costs or if the exit costs will not result in net cash outflow, the costs are excluded from the test; and if abandonment, sale, or closure are expected to incur exit costs, the costs are included in the test.

96-14 Accounting for the Costs Associated with Modifying Computer Software for the Year 2000

All specifically associated internal and external costs with modifying internal-use software should be expensed.

STATEMENTS OF POSITION

88-1 Accounting for Developmental and Preoperating Costs, Purchases and Exchanges of Take-off and Landing Slots, and Airframe Modifications

The Accounting Standards Division concluded that developmental costs related to the operation of new routes should not be capitalized, whereas preoperating costs related to the integration of new types of aircraft may be capitalized and amortized beginning on the date that the new aircraft is ready for use. In addition, take-off and landing slots purchased by an airline are recorded as identifiable intangible assets in accordance with APB 17, while slots acquired through exchange are non-monetary assets to be recorded as in APB 29 and amortized according to APB 17. The cost of modifications to an aircraft's interior which increase the usefulness of the craft are capitalized and depreciated over the lesser of the life of the aircraft or of the modifications. The net cost less salvage value of the replaced asset is charged to current income.

92-3 Accounting for Foreclosed Assets

This SOP applies to all reporting entities (except those that account for assets at fair value) and applies to all assets obtained through foreclosure or repossession (except inventories, marketable equity securities and real estate owned by the lender and acounted for under SFAS 67). Foreclosed assets held for sale should be measured on an individual asset basis on the balance sheet at the lower of (1) cost or (2) fair value less estimated selling costs. A valuation account should be used to show an amount less than cost.

If the asset is subject to senior debt, that debt should not be deducted from carrying value, but should be reported as a liability. Payments should be deducted from the liability. After foreclosure, accrued interest should be recognized as interest expense.

For foreclosed assets used in the production of income, the accounting should be the same as for any other nonforeclosed acquired asset in their category. If assets that have been foreclosed and classified as held for sale are to be used in the production of income, reclassification of the asset's carrying amount is required. The adjustment should be the amount necessary to get the asset to the value that it would have been if it had been used in the production of income since foreclosure. Selling costs in the valuation account should be reversed and the net effect should be reported in income from continuing operations in the period of reclassification.

If a change in accounting principle results, the nature of the change should be included in income from continuing operations. No restatement or cumulative-effect adjustment is permitted as of the beginning of the year this SOP is first applied.

93-7 Reporting on Advertising Costs

This SOP is an initial step in providing guidance concerning the financial reporting for the cost of activities such as advertising, start-up, and customer acquisition. The existing guidance is inconsistent and, as a result, there has been diversity in the accounting treatment of these costs.

The costs of advertising should be expensed either as incurred or the first time the advertising takes place. However, there are two exceptions: (1) direct-response advertising (a) whose primary purpose is to elicit sales to customers who could be shown to have responded specifically to the advertising and (b) that results in probable future economic benefits; and (2) expenditures for advertising costs that are made subsequent to recognizing revenues related to those costs.

Expenditures for direct-response advertising should be capitalized if both of the conditions listed above are met. The future benefits to be received are the future revenues arising from the advertising. The company is required to provide persuasive evidence that there is a linkage between the direct-response advertising and these future benefits. These costs are then amortized over the period in which the future benefits are to be received. The decision to capitalize direct-response advertising relied on the recognition criteria and the definition of an asset in FASB Concept Statements 5 and 6. On the other hand, the advertising expenditures made subsequent to the recognition of revenue should be accrued and these advertising costs should be expensed when the related revenues are recognized.

When the SOP is first applied, the financial statements should disclose the nature of the accounting change adopted to conform to the provisions of this SOP and their effect on income before extraordinary items, net income, and related per share amounts.

10 INVESTMENTS

PERSPECTIVE AND ISSUES

The appropriate accounting for noncurrent (or long term) investments in equity and debt securities is dependent upon the degree of marketability, management's intentions regarding the holding period, and (in the case of equity investments, only) the investor's ownership percentage.

For "passive" investments in marketable equity securities, generally defined as those circumstances where the investor holds less than a 20% interest in the investee, SFAS 115 (which superseded SFAS 12 in 1993) requires that the investment be reported at fair market value. Such equity investments must be classified at the acquisition date as being for "trading purposes" or as being "available-for-sale." While what is often called "mark-to-market" accounting is prescribed in either case, only in the "trading purposes" case will the change in fair value be reflected on the income statement in the current period. For investments in equity securities which are considered to be "available-for-sale," unrealized gains and losses are to be carried in a contra equity account, after being reported as a component of other comprehensive income per SFAS 130. However, if there is a permanent decline in the "available-for-sale" securities, this adjustment will be taken to income in the current period. Lower of cost or market accounting, as prescribed by SFAS 12, is no longer appropriate.

When an investor has **significant influence** over an investee, and thus is no longer a passive investor, the equity method must be used to account for the investment. Generally, significant influence is deemed to exist when the investor owns from 20 to 50% of the investee's voting shares, although APB 18 contemplates circumstances where such influence is present with under 20% ownership, or conversely is absent with holdings of 20% or greater. (Over 50%, of course, signals **control**, and under the provisions of SFAS 94, full consolidation of financial statements is mandatory unless one of the few exception conditions stipulated therein is met.) The equity method involves increasing the original cost of the investment by the investor's pro rata share of the investee's earnings, and decreasing it for the investor's share of the investee's losses and for dividends paid. Equity method accounting has been called "one-line consolidation," since the effect on the investor's net worth is the same as if full consolidation of the investee's financial results were accomplished. However, only a single line (or sometimes a few lines, as described later in this chapter) on the investor's statement of earnings is affected.

This chapter also discusses investments in marketable equity securities and in debt securities, as prescribed by SFAS 115. This standard replaced SFAS 12, which only addressed accounting for marketable equity securities, and created a new, tripartite classification scheme which supersedes the older "current vs. noncurrent" categorization of investments. Under SFAS 115 fair value reporting is embraced to a greater extent than it had been in the past, although there is still the use of the "contra equity" account to postpone income statement recognition of some changes in value, and debt securities which are being held to maturity are still accounted for at amortized historical cost. It should be noted that, beginning in 1998, changes to the contra equity (or additional equity) account will have to be reported in other comprehensive income, as described more fully in Chapter 3. While these changes will still be excluded from earnings, as such, they will be given much greater attention in the financial statements than had been the case prior to the promulgation of SFAS 130.

SFAS 115 applies to most industries and supersedes the specialized industry guidance (e.g., for the banking and thrift industries) previously found in AICPA audit and accounting guides. It does not apply to those industries for which fair value reporting is strictly required, such as brokers and dealers in securities. Furthermore, SFAS 115 does not apply to not-for-profits, which are governed by the provisions of recently issued SFAS 124, and which prescribes fair value reporting for all categories of investments, including those debt investments being held to maturity. (See Chapter 23 for a summary of this standard.)

The graphic on the following page summarizes the current distinctions for financial reporting purposes of varying levels of ownership in an investee entity. These requirements have not changed since the promulgation of SFAS 115; consolidation is still required when the parent owns over 50% of the subsidiary, regardless of actual control exerted. The FASB has, for several years, been considering abandoning a pure ownership test in favor of a new "control" criterion, which could result in full consolidation with only a minority share of ownership, but has yet to make this change. Thus the time-tested approach (under 20% ownership, cost or fair value accounting; 20% or greater, assume significant influence and apply the equity method; over 50%, fully consolidate) continues in effect. (See Chapter 11 for a discussion of the control criterion as a successor to majority ownership for purposes of determining whether consolidation should be effected.)

Percentage of Outstanding Voting Stock Acquired

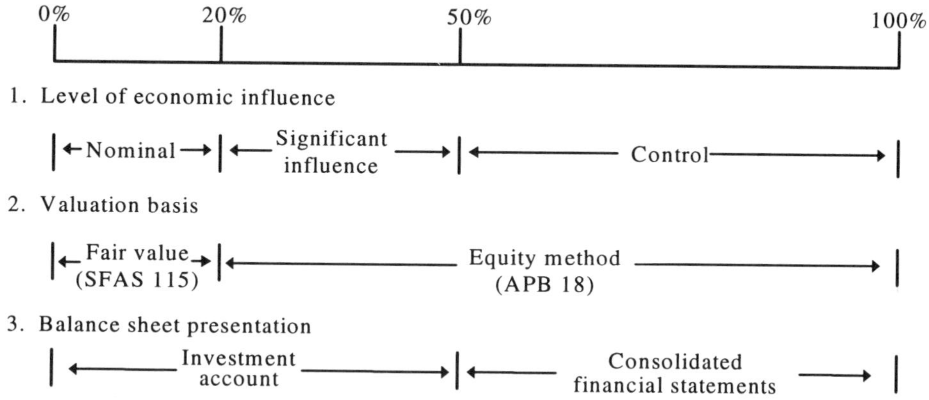

Sources of GAAP

APB	*ARB*	*SFAS*	*FASB I*	*EITF*
17, 18, 23, 24	43	52, 94, 107, 109, 115, 125, 126, 130, 133	35	84-5, 85-40 86-40, 89-4 93-18, 94-4 96-10, 97-7, 98-7

DEFINITIONS OF TERMS

Available-for-sale securities. Investments (debt or equity) which are not classifiable as held-to-maturity or as trading.

Corporate joint venture. A corporate business owned equally by two or more investor entities; it is typically accounted for by the equity method or, less commonly, by the proportional consolidation method by the investors.

Cost method. A method of accounting for investment whereby the investor recognizes only dividends received from investee as income.

Differential. The difference between the carrying value of common stock investment and book value of underlying net assets of the investee; it should be allocated between excess (deficiency) of fair value over (under) book value of net assets and goodwill (a negative goodwill) and amortized appropriately to earnings from investee.

Equity method. A method which includes recognition of a percentage share of income or loss, dividends, and any changes in the investment percentage in an investee by an investor. This method includes the amortization of the differential between the investment cost and book value of the investment and recognizes the effects of any intercompany transactions between the investor and investee.

Goodwill. The excess of the cost of the acquired enterprise over the sum of the amounts assigned to identifiable assets acquired less liabilities assumed.

Held-to-maturity securities. Investments in debt securities which the entity has the ability and intent to hold to maturity.

Investee. An enterprise that issued voting stock which is held by an investor.

Investee capital transaction. The purchase or sale by the investee of its own common shares, which alters the investor's ownership interest and is accounted for by the investor as if the investee were a consolidated subsidiary.

Investor. A business enterprise that holds an investment in voting stock of another enterprise.

Other comprehensive income. Revenues, expenses, gains and losses that under generally accepted accounting principles are included in comprehensive income but excluded from earnings.

Significant influence. The ability of the investor to affect the financial or operating policies of the investee; it is presumed to exist when there is at least 20% voting common stock ownership by the investor.

Trading securities. Investments (debt or equity) which the entity intends to sell in the near term, and which are usually acquired as part of an established strategy to buy and sell, thereby generating profits based on short-term price movements.

Undistributed investee earnings. The investor's share of investee earnings in excess of dividends paid.

CONCEPTS, RULES, AND EXAMPLES

Accounting for Marketable Equity Securities

The question of how to account for long-term investments in equity securities has been widely debated for many years. Historical cost was traditionally prescribed for investments where the **investor** did not exercise control (i.e., had no more than a 50% voting interest). The threshold for the use of historical cost was later reduced to only those circumstances where **significant influence** was not a factor, generally defined as under a 20% voting interest. The **equity method**, promulgated by APB 18, has since 1971 been the prescribed method of accounting for investments where significant influence over **investee** actions is held by the investor.

More recently, the trend in accounting thought has begun to favor a market (or fair) value approach. There are many reasons why users of financial statements as well as standard setters (including the SEC) have increasingly focused on the fair market value approach, including the enhanced availability of fair market value information, and the concern that the limitations of the historical cost model may have contributed to some of the more widely publicized business failures of recent years, particularly those of financial institutions. The current standard, SFAS 115, is the culmination of several years' study of and debate over these issues.

The former standard, SFAS 12, distinguished between current and noncurrent portfolios of marketable equity securities. For both portfolios, the basic accounting model was lower of cost or market. However, declines in value in the current portfolio were reflected directly in income, while declines in the noncurrent portfolio were reported only in a contra equity account, unless the declines were deemed to be "other than temporary" in nature. All investments in marketable equity securities were deemed noncurrent in the case of entities presenting unclassified balance sheets. SFAS 115 is applicable to almost all reporting entities, except those whose specialized accounting practice has already been to account for all investments at market value; it is also inapplicable to not-for-profit enterprises. (Under the provisions of SFAS 124, not-for-profits will have to account for all investments in debt and equity securities at fair value, with the changes in value taken into results from operations currently; see Chapter 23.) SFAS 115 completely revises the accounting standards for investments in marketable equity securities. The distinction between current and noncurrent portfolios is eliminated. All marketable equity securities (except those accounted for by the equity method, discussed later in this chapter) are to be classified at acquisition as being either for trading purposes or as available-for-sale. **Trading securities** are those which are bought with the intention of being sold in the near term with the general objective of realizing profits from short-term price movements. While a time criterion is not established, a persistent practice of active and frequent trading would be suggestive of the fact that new acquisitions of marketable equity securities are intended to be traded. If management does not admit an intention to trade, and it cannot be demonstrated that the securities are being held-for-trading, the investments are to be categorized as being **available-for-sale**.

The distinction between these classifications is important. While equity securities in either category are reported at fair market value (that is, they are marked-to-market), changes in the trading account are recognized in earnings in the current period. Thus, holding gains and losses are accounted for as if realized. This is a significant change from the accounting specified by SFAS 12, which only recognized declines in the current portfolio in current earnings (under the time-honored lower of cost or market concept). Under SFAS 115, however, increases as well as decreases are recognized currently, which for most entities has represented a major departure from past practice. The only exceptions will be the relatively few entities, such as securities broker-dealers, for which specialized industry accounting practices have long prescribed a pure mark-to-market approach.

Under SFAS 115, fair value of an equity security is considered to be determinable if it is quoted in an organized trading exchange or, generally, in over-the-counter trading. Restricted stock is, by definition, not traded and hence fair values are not readily determinable, but stock which is subject to "Rule 144" or similar restrictions, which are due to expire within 1 year, is not deemed to be restricted for purposes of applying SFAS 115. Stock traded only on foreign exchanges is included in the definition if the markets are comparable in breadth and scope to those in the US. Fair values for investments in mutual funds are generally considered to be determinable.

For equity securities which are defined as being available-for-sale, the same standard applies regarding the presentation of the investments on the balance sheet: they are marked to current fair market value as of the balance sheet date. However, except where permanent impairment has occurred, the adjustment to fair market value is recorded in a separate stockholders' equity account, with the current period's change in this account being included in other comprehensive income. This account, which may have a debit or credit balance, is conceptually similar to the (debit only) account specified by the now-superseded SFAS 12 for lower of cost or market adjustments for noncurrent investments in marketable equity securities. It is also similar to the accounting for translation gains or losses under SFAS 52.

The logic for this new approach is that the market value changes in investments intended to be held long-term are only temporary fluctuations which, over the long term, may tend to largely be offset. Thus, interim fluctuations in value would not necessarily be indicative of the long term economic impact from holding the investments. While others have argued that the goal of periodic financial reporting should be to report the economic events of the period being presented, without concealing or "smoothing" the results, the Board ultimately sided with those who favored the longer-term view. Although there had been substantial pressure to adopt a pure mark-to-market approach, with gains and losses on all holdings (not merely those in the trading portfolio) being taken into earnings in the current period, the outcome of the Board's deliberations on this matter did not greatly differ from the traditional historical cost concepts. The adoption of SFAS 130, requiring the display of comprehensive income, including current period changes in the contra or additional equity accounts relating to the changes in value of certain investments held in the available-for-sale portfolio, somewhat ameliorates the potentially misleading implications of omitting these changes from earnings.

As for the recognition of both unrealized holding gains and losses, the Board concluded that prior GAAP, requiring lower of cost or market accounting, had not been an evenhanded approach to measurement (nor was it intended to be, since lower of cost or market was designed as a "conservative" departure from strict adherence to historical cost accounting). Given the improved accuracy and wider availability of market value information, the arguably greater relevance of market value data, and the desire to "do something" to address the failings of the traditional financial reporting model, the decision to adopt a pure fair market value approach to the display of investments was not surprising. Thus, the decision to adopt mark-to-market for the assets, while maintaining a distinction between equity securities held for trading and those which are available for sale is both a reasonable compromise and a continuation of traditional accounting principles. The major concern with the Board's conclusion (which presents greater difficulties for independent auditors than it does for reporting entities) is that it continues to define accounting for certain transactions based on management intent, rather than on objectively verifiable circumstances. This has caused the profession problems in the past, not the least of which was the debate over so-called "gains trading," which led to this new pronouncement. The ultimate outcome of the Board's compromise approach will not become clear for several years.

It might also be noted that as it was developing SFAS 115 the Board had a number of related topics on its technical agenda, including matters relating to financial liabilities being marked-to-market. The Board concluded that it was unable to develop a workable methodology for measuring fair values of liabilities for inclusion in the balance sheet, but in the longer run it may well return to this project. Meanwhile, SFAS 107 requires disclosure of fair values for all financial instruments, including both assets and liabilities, subject to the exemption granted by SFAS 126 for nonpublic entities having total assets under $100 million and which have not held or issued derivative financial instruments during the most recent reporting period.

Example of accounting for investments in equity securities

Assume that Ralph Corporation purchases the following equity securities for investment purposes during 1999:

Security description	*Acquisition cost*	*Value at year end*
1,000 sh. Bell Steel common	$ 34,500	$ 37,000
2,000 sh. Whammer pfd. "A"	125,000	109,500
1,000 sh. Hilltopper common	74,250	88,750

Assume that, at the respective dates of acquisition, management of Ralph Corporation designated the Bell Steel and Hilltopper investments as being for trading purposes, while the Whammer shares were designated as having been purchased for long term investment purposes. Accordingly, the entries to record the purchases were as follows:

Investment in equity securities-- held-for-trading	108,750	
Cash		108,750
Investment in equity securities-- available-for-sale	125,000	
Cash		125,000

At year end, both portfolios are adjusted to fair market value; the decline in Whammer preferred stock, series A, is judged to be a temporary market fluctuation rather than a permanent decline. The entries to adjust the investment accounts at December 31, 1999, are

Investment in equity securities--held-for-trading	17,000	
Gain on holding equity securities		17,000
Unrealized loss on securities--available-for-sale (other comprehensive income)	15,500	
Investment in equity securities--available-for-sale		15,500

Thus, the change in value of the portfolio of trading securities is recognized in earnings, whereas the change in the value of the available-for-sale securities is reflected directly in stockholders' equity, after being reported in other comprehensive income.

Permanent Impairments of Investments Available for Sale

A permanent impairment in value of equity securities classified as available-for-sale must be reflected in earnings. The standard uses the term "other than temporary" rather than permanent to stress that the burden of proof is on those who believe a decline is only temporary. In other words, it is a refutable presumption that a decline in value is permanent in character. Absent an ability to demonstrate that a decline is temporary, the conclusion must be that the loss in value is other than temporary, in which case it must be recognized in income. Declines are measured at the individual security level and thus, losses in one security's value cannot be offset by gains in another's value.

Once a permanent impairment is recognized, the reduced carrying amount becomes the new cost basis from which other increases or decreases in value are measured. Increases or decreases in value which are temporary are recognized in other comprehensive income and then included in stockholders' equity, not in earnings. Further "other than temporary" declines in value are recognized in earnings. Recoveries in value in available-for-sale securities which have previously suffered a decline which was judged to be other than temporary cannot be recognized in earnings until the investment is liquidated. The fact that an equity investment has once suffered an other than temporary decline in value does not prevent a subsequent decline from being judged to be only temporary in character.

Assume now that in January 2000 new information comes to Ralph Corporation management regarding the viability of Whammer Corp. Based on this information, it is determined that the decline in Whammer preferred stock is probably not a temporary one, but rather is "other than temporary" (i.e., the asset is impaired).

SFAS 115 prescribes that such a decline be reflected in earnings, and the written down value be treated as the new cost basis. The fair value has remained at the amount last reported, $109,500. Accordingly, the entry to recognize the fact of the investment's permanent impairment is as follows:

Loss on holding equity securities	15,500	
Unrealized loss on securities--available-for-sale (other comprehensive income)		15,500

Any subsequent recovery in this value would not be recognized in earnings unless realized through a sale of the investment to an unrelated entity in an arm's-length transaction, as long as the investment continues to be categorized as "available-for-sale," as distinct from "held-for-trading." However, if there is an increase in value (not limited to just a recovery of the amount of the loss recognized above, of course) the increase will be added to the investment account and shown in a separate account in stockholders' equity, since the asset is to be marked to fair value on the balance sheet.

It should be noted that the issue of permanent impairment does not arise in the context of investments held-for-trading purposes, inasmuch as unrealized holding gains and losses are immediately recognized without limitation. In effect, the distinction between realized and unrealized gains or losses does not exist for trading securities. To illustrate this point, consider now that in March 1999 further information comes to management's attention, which now suggests that the decline in Whammer preferred was indeed only a temporary decline; in fact, the value of Whammer now rises to $112,000. Since the carrying value after the recognition of the impairment was $109,500, which is treated as the cost basis for purposes of measuring further declines or recoveries, the increase to $112,000 will be accounted for as an increase to be reflected in the additional stockholders' equity account, as follows:

Investment in equity securities--available-for-sale	2,500	
Unrealized gain on securities--available-for-sale (other comprehensive income)		2,500

Note that this increase in value is not taken into earnings, since the investment is still considered to be available-for-sale, rather than a part of the trading portfolio. Even though the previous decline in Whammer stock was realized in current earnings, because judged at the time to be a permanent impairment in value, the recovery cannot be recognized in earnings. Rather, the change in value will be included in other comprehensive income and then displayed in an additional equity account.

Transfers Between Available-for-Sale and Trading Investments

Under SFAS 115, transfers among portfolios are accounted for at fair value as of the date of the transfer. For investments in the trading category being transferred to available-for-sale, there is generally no further recognition of gain or loss at this point, as the investments have been marked to market value already. The only exception is that, if the investment accounts, as a practical matter, have not been updated for fair values since the latest balance sheet date, any changes since that time will need to be recognized at the date the transfer occurs. The fair value at the date of transfer becomes the new "cost" of the equity security to the available-for-sale portfolio.

To illustrate, consider Ralph Corporation's investment in Hilltopper common stock, which was assigned to the trading portfolio and at December 31, 1999, was marked to fair value of $88,750. Assume that in April 2000 management now determines that this investment will not be traded, but rather will continue to be held indefinitely. Under the criterion established by SFAS 115, this investment now belongs in the available-for-sale portfolio. Assume also that the value at the date this decision is made is $92,000, and that no book adjustments have been made since the one which recognized the value increase to $88,750. The entry to record the transfer from the trading to the available-for-sale portfolio is

Investment in equity securities--available-for-sale	92,000	
Investment in equity securities--held-for-trading		88,750
Gain on holding equity securities		3,250

Unrealized gains and losses on trading securities are always recognized in income, and in this example the additional increase in fair value since the last "mark-to-market" adjustment, $3,250, is recognized at the time of the transfer to the available-for-sale portfolio. Further gains after this date, however, will not be recognized in earnings, but rather will be included in other comprehensive income per SFAS 130.

For securities being transferred into the trading category, any unrealized gain or loss (recorded in an additional equity or contra equity account, as illustrated above) is deemed to be "realized" at the date of the transfer. Also, any fair value changes since the date of the most recent balance sheet may need to be recognized at this time. To illustrate, consider the investment in Whammer preferred stock, which was held in the available-for-sale portfolio, and which in March 2000 was adjusted to a fair value of $112,000 (as illustrated above). The increase from adjusted cost ($109,500, after a permanent impairment in value had been recognized) was reflected in other comprehensive income, rather than in earnings, given that the security was not at the time being held for trading. Now assume that, in June 2000, a decision is made to try to sell the investment in the short term. This means that the holding of Whammer stock will be treated as being in the trading portfolio. Further, the value of the shares held, at the date of this decision, is $114,700. The entry to record the transfer from available-for-sale to trading, and the "realization" of the increased value at that date, is as follows:

Investment in equity securities--held-for-trading	114,700	
Unrealized gain on securities--available-for-sale (other comprehensive income)	2,500	
Investment in equity securities--available-for-sale		112,000
Gain on holding equity securities (an income statement account)		5,200

The recognized gain at the time of transfer, in this case, is the sum of the previously unrecognized gain which had been recorded in the additional equity account ($2,500) plus the further gain not yet given any recognition in the investor's financial statements ($2,700). Note that the elimination of the additional equity representing the previously reported unrealized gain will be included in comprehensive income in the current period as a debit, since the additional equity account is being reversed at this time. On the other hand, had there been a decline since the date of the last balance sheet, the gain to be recognized at the date of this transfer would have been the net of the previous, unrecognized gain, and the later loss; if the loss exceeded the earlier gain, a net loss would be recognized at this point. Any further gains or losses after the transfer to the trading portfolio will be handled as earlier described (i.e., recognized in income currently).

Presentation of Investments in Marketable Equity Securities

Investments in equity securities which are held-for-trading should be presented as current assets in classified balance sheets. Investments which are available-for-sale may be either current or noncurrent, depending upon the reporting entity's intentions. For purposes of reporting in the statement of cash flows, all purchases and sales of trading securities must be included in the operations section, while those of available-for-sale investments are to be shown as part of investing activities.

SFAS 115 requires specific disclosures of the components of a reporting entity's portfolios of investments. For available-for-sale securities, a classification by type of security is necessary: equity securities will be grouped together in this disclosure, and thus distinguished from debt securities. Furthermore, aggregate fair values, gross unrealized holding gains and gross unrealized holding losses are also to be disclosed as of the date of each balance sheet being presented.

For each income statement presented, proceeds from the sales of available-for-sale securities and gross realized gains and losses must be disclosed. Further, the basis upon which the gains or losses were determined (e.g., average cost, specific identification, etc.) must be disclosed. In addition, the notes must identify gross gains or losses included in earnings resulting from transfers of securities from the available-for-sale to the trading portfolio, and the net change in unrealized gains or losses recognized by an adjustment of the contra equity account.

Changes in Fair Value After the Balance Sheet Date

Under GAAP, events occurring after the balance sheet date are generally not reflected in the balance sheet. However, disclosure may be necessary if, absent that information, the user of the financial statements would be misled. While not addressed explicitly by SFAS 115, presumably material changes in fair value occurring subsequent to the date of the balance sheet but prior to issuance of the financial statements should be disclosed.

Sometimes changes in value can be indicative of the underlying cause of the price fluctuations. Of most interest here would be declines in value of available-for-sale securities held at the balance sheet date which suggest that an "other than temporary" impairment has occurred. If the decline actually occurred after year end as evidenced by a bankruptcy filing, then the event would be disclosed but not reflected in the year-end balance sheet. However, in some instances, the subsequent decline would be seen as a "confirming event" which provided evidence that the classification or other treatment of an item on the balance sheet was incorrect. Thus, if a decline in the fair value of available-for-sale securities at the balance sheet date had been accounted for as temporary (and hence reported in other comprehensive income) a further decline after the balance sheet date might suggest that the decline **as of the balance sheet date** had, in fact, been a permanent impairment. Note that any further value decline after year end would not be recorded in the financial statements; the only question to be addressed is whether the decline which occurred **prior to year end** should have been treated as a permanent impairment rather than as a temporary market fluctuation.

If it is clear that the impairment at year end had, in fact, been permanent in nature, then the financial statements should be adjusted to reflect this loss in earnings. Absent sufficient basis to reach this conclusion, the appropriate course of action is to not adjust the statements, but merely to disclose the (material) change in fair value which occurred subsequent to year end including, if appropriate, a statement to the effect that the later decline was deemed to be a permanent impairment, and will be reflected in the earnings of the next year's financial statements. It should also be made clear that the decline occurring prior to year end was not considered to be a permanent impairment, at that time.

The FASB staff noted that when an entity has decided to sell a security classified as available-for-sale having a fair value less than cost at year end, and it does not reasonably expect a recovery in value before the sale is to occur, then a write-down for an other than temporary decline is prescribed. This would most obviously be necessary if the actual sales transaction, anticipated at year end, occurs prior to the issuance of the financial statements.

Deferred Tax Effects of Changes in Fair Value of Marketable Equity Securities

Unrealized gains or losses on holdings of marketable securities are not recognized for income tax purposes until realized through a sale. Thus, the gains or losses which are included in the financial statements (either in the income statement or in other comprehensive income) are temporary differences as defined by SFAS 109. Under this standard, the tax effects of all temporary differences are recognized in the financial statements as deferred tax benefits or deferred tax liabilities, with an additional requirement that an allowance be provided for deferred tax benefits which are "more likely than not" not going to be realized. Accordingly, adjustments to the carrying value of debt or equity investments included in either the trading or available-for-sale portfolios for changes in fair value will give rise to deferred taxes, as will any recognition of "other than temporary" declines in the value of debt securities being held-to-maturity.

For gains or losses recognized in connection with holdings of investments classified as trading, since the fair value changes are recognized in earnings currently, the deferred tax effects of those changes will also be presented in the income statement. For example, assume that Odessa Corp. purchased Zeta Company bonds as a short-term speculation, at a cost of $100,000. At year end, the bonds had a fair value of $75,000. Odessa has a 40% effective tax rate. The entries to record the fair value adjustment and tax effect thereof are

Loss on holding of trading securities	25,000	
Investment in debt securities-- trading portfolios		25,000
Deferred tax benefit	10,000	
Provision for income taxes		10,000

On the other hand, if the investment in Zeta Company bonds had been classified (at the date of acquisition, or subsequently if the intentions had been revised) as being available-for-sale, the adjustment to fair value would have been reported in other comprehensive income, and not included in earnings. Accordingly, the tax effect of the adjustment would also have been included in other comprehensive income. The entries would have been as follows:

Unrealized loss on securities-- available-for-sale	25,000	
Investment in debt securities-- available-for-sale (other comprehensive income)		25,000
Deferred tax benefit	10,000	
Unrealized loss on securities-- available-for-sale (other comprehensive income)		10,000

Finally, if the investment in Zeta Company bonds had been made with the intention and ability to hold to maturity, recognition of the decline in value would have depended upon whether it was judged to be temporary or other than temporary in nature. If the former, no recognition would be given to the decline, and hence there would be no deferred tax effect either. If deemed to be other than temporary, the investment would need to be written down, with the loss included in earnings. Accordingly, the tax effect would also be reported in the income statement. The entries would be as follows:

Loss on decline of securities--held-to-maturity	25,000	
Investment in debt securities--held-to-maturity		25,000
Deferred tax benefit	10,000	
Provision for income taxes		10,000

An other than temporary decline in value in securities available-for-sale would also have been recognized in earnings (not merely in other comprehensive income), and accordingly the tax effect of that loss would have been reported in earnings.

As with all other transactions or events giving rise to deferred tax assets, an evaluation must be made as to whether the entity would be "more likely than not" to ultimately realize the tax benefit so recorded. To the extent that it was concluded that some or all of the deferred tax asset would not be realized, an allowance would be recorded, with the offset being either to the current tax provision (if the tax effect of the timing difference was reported in earnings) or to other comprehensive income (if the tax effect had been reported there).

Deferred taxes will also be recorded in connection with unrealized gains recognized due to changes in the fair value of debt or equity investments. Deferred tax liabilities will be reported in the balance sheet, and the corresponding tax provision will be reported in the income statement (for fair value gains arising from holdings of securities in the trading portfolio) or in other comprehensive income (for value changes relative to available-for-sale investments).

Accounting for Investments in Debt Securities

Historically, accounting for marketable investments in debt securities was not well developed in the professional literature. In fact, the principal guidance concerning long-term investments in debt instruments was found in ARB 43, which stipulated that the amortized **cost method** be used, absent a substantial, other than temporary decline in value. However, in more recent years this topic has become highly controversial, largely due to the problems encountered by financial institutions, and to the popular belief that so-called "gains trading" had widely been abused, permitting entities to manipulate reported earnings almost at will.

Culminating several years of research and discussion, the FASB issued SFAS 115 in mid-1993. This standard applies to both equity and debt instruments held as investments, and prescribes fair market value accounting for all except debt instruments being held to maturity. For that limited category, amortized historical cost is generally preserved as the measurement principle.

SFAS 115 requires that investments in debt securities be classified upon acquisition as belonging to one of three portfolios: trading, available-for-sale, or held-to-maturity. The first of these is characterized by frequent purchase and sale activities, with the general objective of realizing profits from short-term price movements, which in the case of investments in debt instruments will largely be the result of changes in market interest rates but which may also be affected by market perceptions of credit risk. Since intention is the prime criterion applied, even a paucity of sales activity does not necessarily mean that specific debt securities acquired during a period do not belong in the trading portfolio.

The held-to-maturity category is the most restrictive of the three; debt instruments can be so classified only if the reporting entity has the positive intent and the ability to hold the securities for that length of time. A mere intent to hold an investment for an indefinite period is not adequate to permit such a classification. On the other hand, a variety of isolated causes may necessitate transferring an investment in a debt security from the held-for-investment category without calling into question the investor's general intention to hold other similarly classified investments to maturity. Among these are declines in the creditworthiness of a particular investment's issuer or a change in tax law or regulatory rules. On the other hand, sales of investments which were classified as held-to-maturity for other reasons will call into question the entity's assertions, both in the past and in the future, about its intentions regarding these and other similarly categorized securities. For this reason, transfers from or sales of held-to-maturity securities will be very rare, indeed.

If it cannot be established that a particular debt security held as an investment will be held for trading or held to maturity, it must be classed as available-for-sale. Whatever the original classification of the investment, however, transfers among the three portfolios will be made as intentions change.

Accounting for debt securities which are held for trading and those which are available for sale is based on fair value. For balance sheet purposes, increases or decreases in value are reflected by adjustments to the asset account; such adjustments are to be determined on an individual security basis. Changes in the values of debt securities in the trading portfolio are recognized in earnings immediately, while most changes in the values of debt securities in the available-for-sale category are reported in other comprehensive income rather than being included in earnings. The only exception is for declines which are deemed to be other than temporary, in which case the loss is recognized currently in earnings. Once the investment is written down for a decline which is other than temporary, subsequent increases are reported only in changes to the contra equity account; these cannot be accounted for as "recoveries" of previous permanent declines. (See **Permanent Impairments of Investments Available for Sale** in the discussion of equity investments, above, for an example.)

There had been some confusion regarding the applicability of SFAS 115, which has been resolved by the issuance of Technical Bulletin 94-1. The problem arose from the "grandfathering" provision of SFAS 114, permitting debt restructured prior to that standard's effective date to continue to be accounted for consistent with the provisions of SFAS 15, which SFAS 114 superseded. The concern was that this might have suggested that SFAS 115 could not be applied to restructured loans which qualified as debt securities. However, Bulletin 94-1 makes it clear that SFAS 115 applies to all loans which qualify as debt securities, and that the "grandfathering" provision would not be applicable in such circumstances. In other words, the provisions of SFAS 115 take precedence over those of SFAS 114, in situations where SFAS 115 applies.

Presentation in the Financial Statements

Trading securities must always be grouped with current assets in classified balance sheets, and held-to-maturity investments will be noncurrent (unless the maturity date is within 1 year). Available-for-sale securities may conceivably be classified as either current or noncurrent. Unlike under SFAS 12, classification as current or noncurrent no longer determines whether gains or losses are reported in earnings or are to be recognized at all. Instead, intent and ability to hold are the determinants of accounting and financial reporting treatment.

If declines in value are deemed to meet SFAS 115's definition of other than temporary, then these are to be included in earnings in the current period. However, subsequent recoveries cannot be recognized in earnings. If available-for-sale investments are written down for permanent impairments which later reverse, the recovery is accounted for as an increase in fair value to be reflected in other comprehensive income account on the balance sheet only. If held-to-maturity investments are similarly written down and later recover some or all of the lost value, the fair value increase will not be reported in the balance sheet at all, although disclosure will generally be made in the notes.

For purposes of reporting in the statement of cash flows, all purchases and sales of trading securities must be included in the operations section, while those of available-for-sale and held-to-maturity investments are to be shown as part of investing activities.

SFAS 115 requires specific disclosures of the components of a reporting entity's portfolios of investments. For available-for-sale securities and (separately) for **held-to-maturity securities**, classification by type of security is necessary; categories of issuers, such as US Treasury, other US agencies, state and municipal governmental units, foreign governmental units, corporations, mortgage backed, and others are suggested. Aggregate fair values, gross unrealized holding gains, and gross unrealized holding losses must also be disclosed, by major security type, as of the date of each balance sheet being presented.

For the available-for-sale and held-to-maturity portfolios, information about contractual maturities must be presented as of the date of the latest balance sheet presented and must be grouped into at least four categories: within 1 year; 1 to 5 years; 5 to 10 years; and, over 10 years. Both fair values and amortized cost of debt securities in each maturity category must be presented.

For each income statement presented, proceeds from the sales of available-for-sale securities, and the gross realized gains and losses therefrom, also must be disclosed. Further, the basis upon which the gains or losses were determined, (e.g., average cost, specific identification, etc.) must be disclosed. In addition, the notes must identify gross gains or losses included in earnings resulting from transfers of securities from the available-for-sale to the trading portfolio, and the net change in unrealized gains or losses recognized by an adjustment of the contra equity account.

For sales or transfers from securities categorized as held-to-maturity, the amortized cost amounts, the related gains or losses realized or unrealized, and the circumstances surrounding the decision to sell or to reclassify the investment, are all to be disclosed in the notes to the financial statements for each period for which an income statement is being presented. There is, of course, a presumption that sales or transfers from the held-to-maturity portfolio will be rare occurrences.

Transfers of Debt Securities Among Portfolios

Transfers of any given security between classifications is accounted for at fair market value. If the transfer is from the trading portfolio, there is no further income statement effect since the fair market value-based gains or losses have already been reported. If the transfer is to the trading portfolio, the unrealized gain or loss is recognized immediately; depending on whether the transfer is from the available-for-sale or the held-to-maturity category, such unrealized gain or loss would have been included in a contra equity account on the balance sheet, after having been reported as an element of other comprehensive income, or would not have been reported at all prior to the transfer.

If the debt security is being transferred from held-to-maturity to the available-for-sale portfolio, the unrealized gain or loss, not previously reflected in the investment account, will be added to the appropriate contra equity account at the date of transfer and reported in other comprehensive income. If a security is being transferred from available-for-sale to held-to-maturity, the unrealized holding gain or loss previously accrued will continue to be maintained in the contra equity account, but now will be amortized to income over the period until maturity as an adjustment of yield, using the effective interest method.

Example of accounting for debt securities

Marcy Corporation purchases the following debt securities as investments in 1998:

Issue	*Face value*	*Price paid**
Dukane Chemical 8% due 2002	$200,000	$190,000
Forwall Pharmaceutical 9.90% due 2014	500,000	575,000
Luckystrike Mining 6% due 1999	100,000	65,000

**Accrued interest is ignored in these amounts; the normal entries for interest accrual and receipt are assumed.*

Management has informed us that Marcy's objectives differed among the various investments; the Dukane bonds are considered to be suitable as a long-term investment, with the intention that they will be held until maturity. The Luckystrike bonds are a speculation; the significant discount from par value was seen as very attractive, despite the low coupon rate. Management believes the bonds were depressed because mining stocks and bonds have been out of favor, but believes the economic recovery will lead to a surge in market value, at which point the bonds will be sold for a quick profit. The Forwall Pharmaceutical bonds are deemed a good investment, but with a maturity date 16 years in the future, management is unable to commit to holding these to maturity.

Based on the foregoing, the appropriate accounting for the three investments in bonds would be as follows:

Dukane Chemical 8% due 2002

Account for these as held-to-maturity; maintain at historical cost, with discount ($10,000) to be amortized over term to maturity (assumed to be 4 years, for an amortization of $2,500 per year).

Forwall Pharmaceutical 9.90% due 2014

Account for these as available-for-sale, since neither the held-for-trading nor held-to-maturity criteria apply. These should be reported at fair market value at each balance sheet date, with any unrealized gain or loss included in the additional/contra equity account, unless an "other than temporary" decline occurs.

Luckystrike Mining 6% due 1999

As an admitted speculation, these should be accounted for as part of the trading portfolio, and also reported at fair market value on the balance sheet. All adjustments to carrying value will be included in earnings each year, whether the fluctuations are temporary or permanent in nature.

Accounting for Transfers Between Portfolios

Transfers between portfolio categories are to be accounted for at fair market value at the date of the transfer. Consider the following events.

1. Marcy management decides in 1999, when the Forwall bonds have a market (fair) value of $604,500, that the bonds will be disposed of in the short term, hopefully when the price hits $605,000. The bonds are presently car-

ried on the books at $580,000, which was the fair value at the time the year-end 1998 financial statements were being prepared. Based on this description of the decision, the bonds should be transferred to the trading portfolio at a "cost" of $604,500. The entry to record this would be the following:

Investment in debt securities--held-for-trading	604,500	
Unrealized gain on holding debt securities as investment	5,000	
Investment in debt securities--available-for-sale		580,000
Gain on holding debt securities		29,500

The previously unrealized gain (reflected in the write-up of the investment from original cost, $575,000, to the fair market value at year end 1998, $580,000) is now "realized" for financial reporting purposes, as is the further rise in value from $580,000 to $604,500 at the time the portfolio transfer takes place.

2. Assume that at year end 1998 the investment in the Forwall bonds is still held, and the fair value has declined to $602,000. Management's intentions regarding this holding have not changed since the decision to transfer to held-for-sale. The year-end adjustment will be

Loss on holding debt securities	2,500	
Investment in debt securities--held-for-trading		2,500

The market decline is reflected in earnings in 1999, since the bonds are in the held-for-trading portfolio.

3. Now, assume that in 2000, management determines that a major investment in plant renewal and expansion will likely be necessary by the year 2016, based on a detailed capital budget prepared. With this in mind, Marcy Corporation determines that the holding of Forwall Pharmaceutical bonds would be an excellent vehicle to provide for these future cash needs, and accordingly concludes to hold these to maturity. At the time this decision is made, the fair market value of the bonds is quoted at $603,000. The entry to record the transfer from held-for-trading to held-to-maturity is as follows:

Investment in debt securities--held-for-trading	1,000	
Gain on holding debt securities		1,000

The bonds are again transferred at fair market value, which in this case gives rise to a $1,000 recognized gain.

4. In 1999 Marcy management also made a decision about its investment in Dukane Chemical bonds. These bonds, which were originally designated as held-to-maturity, were accounted for at amortized historical cost. Assume the amortization in 1998 was $2,000 (because the bonds were not held for a full year), so that the book value of the investment at year end 1998 was $192,000. In 1999, at a time when the value of these bonds was $198,000, management concluded that it was no longer certain that they would be held to maturity, and therefore transferred this holding to the available-for-sale portfolio. The entry to record this would be

Investment in debt securities--available-for-sale	198,000	
Unrealized gain on holding debt securities as investment		6,000
Investment in debt securities--held-to-maturity		192,000

   The transfer is at fair market value, but since the bonds are being transferred into the available-for-sale category (for which unrealized gains and losses are recorded in an additional or contra equity account), the gain at this date, $6,000, is not recognized in earnings, but rather will be reported in other comprehensive income.

5. In 2000, for the same reason management determined to hold the Forwall Pharmaceuticals bonds to maturity, it also reverses its prior decision regarding the Dukane Chemical bond holding. It now professes an intention to hold these until their maturity, in 2002. At the date this decision is made, the Dukane bonds are quoted at $195,000. Assume that the fair market value at year-end 1999 was $198,000, so no adjustment was needed at that time to the carrying value of the investment. Again the transfer will be recorded at fair market value.

Investment in debt securities--held-to-maturity	195,000	
Unrealized gain on holding debt securities as investment	3,000	
Investment in debt securities--available-for-sale		198,000

The unrealized gain previously recognized in an equity account is partially eliminated, since fair value at the date of this transfer is less than the previously recorded amount. The change in this equity account must be reported as other comprehensive income for the period in which this portfolio reclassification occurs. The remaining balance in the additional/contra equity account (whether a net debit or credit) is accounted for as **additional** premium or discount, and is amortized over the remaining term to maturity. GAAP mandates that the effective yield method be used, but for this example, assume that the discount will be amortized over the remaining 2 years on the straight-line basis (if this difference from the effective yield method is not material, it is an acceptable practice). Thus, the actual discount as measured by the spread between the new carrying value, $195,000, and face value to be received at maturity, $200,000, **plus the additional discount** measured by the unrealized gain being reported currently in the equity section of $3,000, gives a total discount amounting to $8,000 to be amortized over the remaining 2 years. This $8,000, when added to the $2,000 discount amortized in 1999 (when the bonds were in the original held-to-maturity portfolio), equals $10,000, which is the discount between the face value, $200,000 and the price paid by Marcy Corporation ($190,000).

Disclosure of Fair Value Information (also see Disclosure Checklist at end of this book)

SFAS 107 requires disclosure of fair values for all financial instruments. The investments discussed in the foregoing sections of this chapter are included in the definition of financial instruments (whereas those investments accounted for by the equity method, as discussed below, are excluded). Since SFAS 115 goes beyond this requirement for investments held for trading purposes or available for sale, by mandating that the amounts presented in the balance sheet be adjusted to fair value, the only additional requirement imposed by SFAS 107 applies to investments in bonds being held to maturity. For these, supplementary disclosure of fair value would be required, unless the exceptions established by that standard (concerning the impracticality of obtaining fair value information) apply. The disclosure requirement has been eliminated by SFAS 126, however, for most nonpublic entities having less than $100 million in total assets.

The Equity Method of Accounting for Investments

The equity method, sometimes referred to as "one-line consolidation," permits an entity (investor) owning a percentage of the common stock of another entity (investee) to incorporate its pro rata share of the investee's operating results into its earnings. However, rather than include its share of each component (e.g., sales, cost of sales, operating expenses, etc.) in its financial statements, the **investor** shall only include its share of the investee's **net** income as a separate line item in its income. Note that there are exceptions to this one-line rule. The investor's share of **investee** extraordinary items and prior period adjustments retain their identities in the investor's income and retained earnings statements and are separately reported if material in relation to the investor's income. It should be noted that the final bottom-line impact on the investor's financial statements is **identical** whether the equity method or full consolidation is employed; only the amount of detail presented within the statements will differ.

The equity method is generally **not** a substitute for consolidation; it is employed where the investor has **significant influence** over the operations of the investee but lacks control. In general, significant influence is inferred when the investor owns between 20% and 50% of the investee's voting common stock. Any ownership percentage over 50% presumably gives the investor actual control, making full consolidation of financial statements necessary. The 20% threshold stipulated in APB 18 is not absolute; circumstances may suggest that significant influence exists even though the investor's level of ownership is less than 20%, or that it is absent despite a level of ownership above 20%. In considering whether significant influence exists, FASB Interpretation 35 identifies the following factors: (1) opposition by the investee, (2) agreements under which the investor surrenders shareholder rights, (3) majority ownership by a small group of shareholders, (4) inability to obtain desired information from the investee, (5) inability to obtain representation on investee board of directors, etc. Whether sufficient contrary evidence exists to negate the presumption of significant influence is a matter of judgment. Judgment requires a careful evaluation of all pertinent facts and circumstances, over an extended period of time in some cases.

Prior to the issuance of SFAS 94, some investors used the equity method in those rare instances in which the investor owned over 50% of the investee's voting common shares but consolidated statements were deemed to be inappropriate (usually because consolidated statements would mask important differences in the financial or operating characteristics of the investor-parent and investee-subsidiary). However, SFAS 94 eliminated this once popular "nonhomogeneity" justification for nonconsolidation. This leaves only temporary control, noncontrol, and foreign exchange restrictions and related reasons as justification for not consolidating majority-owned subsidiaries. The equity method continues to be used in accounting for nonconsolidated majority-owned subsidiaries (see Chapter 11). Furthermore, if the proposed FASB standard on consolidation policy and procedure is adopted (see discussion in Chapter 11), the upper threshold for the use of the equity method will no longer be 50% ownership, but instead will be the point at which control is achieved, which could be at a much lower level of ownership.

Complexities in the use of the equity method arise in two areas. First, the cost of the investment to the investor might not be equal to the fair value of the investor's share of investee net assets; this is analogous to the existence of **goodwill** in a purchase business combination. Or the fair value of the investor's share of the investee's net assets may not be equal to the book value thereof; this situation is analogous to the purchase cost allocation problem in consolidations. Since the ultimate income statement result from the use of equity method accounting must generally be the same as full consolidation, an adjustment must be made for each of these **differentials**.

The second major complexity relates to interperiod income tax allocation. The equity method causes the investor to reflect current earnings based on the investee's operating results; however, for income tax purposes the investor reports only dividends received and gains or losses on disposal of the investment. Thus, temporary differences result, and SFAS 109 provides guidance as to the appropriate method of computing the deferred tax effects of these differences.

In the absence of these complicating factors, the use of the equity method by the investor is straightforward: the original cost of the investment is increased by the investor's share of the investee's earnings and is decreased by its share of investee losses and by dividends received. The basic procedure is illustrated below.

Example of a simple case ignoring deferred taxes

Assume the following information. On January 2, 1999, R Corporation (the investor) acquired 40% of E Company's (the investee) voting common stock on the open market for $100,000. Unless demonstrated otherwise, it is assumed that R Corporation can exercise significant influence over E Company's operating and financing policies. On January 2, E's stockholders' equity consists of the following accounts:

Common stock, par $1, 100,000 shares authorized, 50,000 shares issued and outstanding	$ 50,000
Additional paid-in capital	150,000
Retained earnings	50,000
Total stockholders' equity	$250,000

Note that the cost of E Company common stock was equal to 40% of the book value of E's net assets. Assume also that there is no difference between the book value and the fair value of E Company's assets and liabilities. Accordingly, the balance in the investment account in R's records represents exactly 40% of E's stockholders' equity (net assets). Assume further that E Company reported a 1998 net income of $30,000 and paid cash dividends of $10,000. Its stockholders' equity at year end would be as follows:

Common stock, par $1, 100,000 shares authorized, 50,000 shares issued and outstanding	$ 50,000
Additional paid-in capital	150,000
Retained earnings	70,000
Total stockholders' equity	$270,000

R Corporation would record its share of the increase in E Company's net assets during 1999 as follows:

Investment in E Company	12,000	
Equity in E income		12,000
($30,000 x 40%)		
Cash	4,000	
Investment in E Company		4,000
($10,000 x 40%)		

When R's balance sheet is prepared at December 31, 1999, the balance reported in the investment account would be $108,000 ($100,000 + $12,000 – $4,000). This amount represents 40% of the book value of E's net assets at the end of the year (40% x

$270,000). Note also that the equity in E income is reported as one amount on R's income statement under the caption "Other income and expense."

In computing the deferred tax effects of income recognized by the equity method, the investor must make an assumption regarding the means by which the **undistributed earnings of the investee** will be realized by the investor. The earnings can be realized either through later dividend receipts or by disposition of the investment at a gain. The former assumption would result in taxes at the investor's marginal tax rate on ordinary income (net of the 80% dividends received deduction permitted by the Internal Revenue Code for intercorporate investments of less than 80% but at least 20%; a lower deduction of 70% applies if ownership is below 20%). The latter option would be treated as a capital gain, which is currently taxed at the full corporate tax rate, since the preferential capital gain rate was eliminated by the 1986 Tax Reform.

Example of a simple case including deferred taxes

Assume the same information as in the example above. In addition, assume that R Corporation has a combined (federal, state, and local) marginal tax rate of 34% on ordinary income and that it anticipates realization of E Company earnings through future dividend receipts. R Corporation's entries at year end 1999 will be as follows:

		Debit	Credit
1.	Investment in E Company	12,000	
	Equity in E income		12,000
2.	Income tax expense	816	
	Deferred taxes		816
	(Taxable portion of investee earnings to be received in the future as dividends times marginal tax rate: $12,000 x 20% x 34% = $816.)		
3.	Cash	4,000	
	Investment in E Company		4,000
4.	Deferred taxes	272	
	Taxes payable--current		272
	[Fraction of investee earnings currently taxed ($4,000/$12,000) x $816 = $272]		

Under prior GAAP (APB 11), the amount of deferred taxes provided ($816 in the above example) was not to be adjusted until such time as the "timing difference" reversed. At such time, any discrepancy would be adjusted through current tax expense. However, SFAS 109 is based upon an entirely different concept (the so-called "asset and liability approach"). The deferred tax liability is originally computed with reference to the **projected** tax effect of the "temporary difference reversal." It may be subsequently adjusted for a variety of reasons, including changed tax rates and altered management expectations (see Chapter 15 for a complete discussion).

Notwithstanding SFAS 109's requirement that deferred taxes be adjusted for changed expectations at each subsequent balance sheet date, the actual tax effect of the temporary difference reversal may still differ from the deferred tax provided. This difference may occur because the actual tax effect is a function of the entity's other current items of income and expense in the year of reversal (while SFAS 109 requires the use of a projected effective tax rate, actual rates may differ). It may also result from a realization of the investee's earnings in a manner other than anticipated (assuming that tax rates on "ordinary" income differ from those on capital gains).

To illustrate this last point, assume that in 1999, before any further earnings or dividends are reported by the investee, the investor sells the entire investment for $115,000. The tax impact is

Selling price	$115,000
Less cost	100,000
Gain	$ 15,000
Capital gain rate (marginal corporate rate)	x 34%
Tax liability	$ 5,100

The entries to record the sale, the tax thereon, and the amortization of previously provided deferred taxes on the undistributed 1999 earnings are as follows:

1.	Cash	115,000	
	Investment in E Company		108,000
	Gain on sale of investment		7,000
2.	Income tax expense	4,556	
	Deferred tax liability	544	
	Taxes payable--current		5,100

The income tax expense of $4,556 is the sum of two factors: (1) the capital gains rate of 34% applied to the actual **book** gain realized ($115,000 selling price less $108,000 carrying value), for a tax of $2,380, and (2) the difference between the capital gains tax rate (34%) and the effective rate on dividend income (20% x 34% = 6.8%) on the undistributed 1999 earnings of E Company previously recognized as ordinary income by R Corporation [$8,000 x (34% – 6.8%) = $2,176].

Note that if the realization through a sale of the investment had been anticipated at the time the 1999 balance sheet was being prepared, the deferred tax liability account would have been adjusted (possibly to reflect the entire $5,100 amount of the ultimate obligation), with the offset included in 1999's ordinary tax expense. The requirement that expected taxes be accrued for, mandated by SFAS 109, is radically different from the approach of APB 11. The above example explicitly assumes that the sale of the investment was **not** anticipated prior to 2000.

Accounting for a differential between cost and book value. The simple examples presented thus far avoided the major complexity of equity method accounting, the allocation of the **differential** between the cost to the investor and the investor's share in the net equity (net assets at book value) of the investee. Since the net impact of equity method accounting must equal that of full consolidation accounting, this differential must be analyzed into the following components and accounted for accordingly:

1. The difference between the book and fair values of the investee's net assets at the date the investment is made
2. The remaining difference between the fair value of the net assets and the cost of the investment, which is generally attributable to goodwill

According to APB 18, the difference between the book and fair value of the net assets should be identified and allocated to specific asset categories. These differences are then amortized to the income from investee account as appropriate, for example, over the economic lives of fixed assets whose fair values exceeded book values. The difference between fair value and cost will be treated like goodwill and, in accordance with the provisions of APB 17, amortized over a period not to exceed 40 years.

Example of complex case ignoring deferred taxes

Assume again that R Corporation acquired 40% of E Company's shares on January 2, 1999, but that the price paid was $140,000. E Company's assets and liabilities at that date had the following book and fair values:

	Book values	*Fair values*
Cash	$ 10,000	$ 10,000
Accounts receivable (net)	40,000	40,000
Inventories (FIFO cost)	80,000	90,000
Land	50,000	40,000
Plant and equipment (net of accumulated depreciation)	140,000	220,000
Total assets	$320,000	$400,000
Liabilities	$ (70,000)	$ (70,000)
Net assets (stockholders' equity)	$250,000	$330,000

The first order of business is the calculation of the differential, as follows:

R's cost for 40% of E's common	$140,000
Book value of 40% of E's net assets ($250,000 x 40%)	(100,000)
Total differential	$ 40,000

Next, the $40,000 is allocated to those individual assets and liabilities for which fair value differs from book value. In the example, the differential is allocated to inventories, land, and plant and equipment, as follows:

Item	*Book value*	*Fair value*	*Difference debit (credit)*	*40% of difference debit (credit)*
Inventories	$ 80,000	$ 90,000	$10,000	$ 4,000
Land	50,000	40,000	(10,000)	(4,000)
Plant and equipment	140,000	220,000	80,000	32,000
Differential allocated				$32,000

The difference between the allocated differential of $32,000 and the total differential of $40,000 is goodwill of $8,000. Goodwill, as shown by the following computation, represents the excess of the cost of the investment over the fair value of the net assets acquired.

R's cost for 40% of E's common	$140,000
40% of the fair value of E's net assets ($330,000 x 40%)	(132,000)
Excess of cost over fair value (goodwill)	$ 8,000

At this point, it is important to note that the allocation of the differential is not recorded formally by either R Corporation or E Company. Furthermore, R does not remove the differential from the investment account and allocate it to the respective assets, since the use of the equity method ("one-line consolidation") does not involve the recording of individual assets and liabilities. R leaves the differential of $40,000 in the investment account, as a part of the balance of $140,000 at January 2, 1999. Accordingly, information pertaining to the allocation of the differential is maintained by the investor, but this information is outside the formal accounting system, which is comprised of journal entries and account balances.

After the differential has been allocated, the amortization pattern is developed. To develop the pattern in this example, assume that E's plant and equipment have 10 years of useful life remaining and that E depreciates its fixed assets on a straight-line basis. Furthermore, assume that R amortizes goodwill over a 20-year period. R would prepare the following amortization schedule:

Item	*Differential debit (credit)*	*Useful life*	*Amortization 1999*	*2000*	*2001*
Inventories (FIFO)	$ 4,000	Sold in 1998	$4,000	$ --	$ --
Land	(4,000)	Indefinite	--	--	--
Plant and equipment (net)	32,000	10 years	3,200	3,200	3,200
Goodwill	8,000	20 years	400	400	400
Totals	$40,000		$7,600	$3,600	$3,600

Note that the entire differential allocated to inventories is amortized in 1999 because the cost flow assumption used by E is FIFO. If E had been using LIFO instead of FIFO, no amortization would take place until E sold some of the inventory that existed at January 2, 1999. Since this sale could be delayed for many years under LIFO, the differential allocated to LIFO inventories would not be amortized until E sold more inventory than it manufactured/purchased. Note, also, that the differential allocated to E's land is not amortized, because land is not a depreciable asset.

The **amortization** of the differential is recorded formally in the accounting system of R Corporation. Recording the amortization adjusts the equity in E's income that R recorded based upon E's income statement. E's income must be adjusted because it is based upon E's book values, not upon the cost that R incurred to acquire E. R would make the following entries in 1999, assuming that E reported net income of $30,000 and paid cash dividends of $10,000:

		Debit	Credit
1.	Investment in E Company	12,000	
	Equity in E income		12,000
	($30,000 x 40%)		
2.	Equity in E income (amortization of differential)	7,600	
	Investment in E Company		7,600
3.	Cash	4,000	
	Investment in E Company		4,000
	($10,000 x 40%)		

The balance in the investment account on R's records at the end of 1999 is $140,400 [$140,000 + $12,000 – ($7,600 + $4,000)], and E's stockholders' equity, as shown previously, is $270,000. The investment account balance of $140,000 is not equal to 40% of $270,000. However, this difference can easily be explained, as follows:

Balance in investment account at December 31, 1999		$140,400
40% of E's net assets at December 31, 1999		108,000
Difference at December 31, 1999		$ 32,400
Differential at January 2, 1999	$40,000	
Differential amortized during 1999	(7,600)	
Unamortized differential at December 31, 1999		$ 32,400

As the years go by, the balance in the investment account will come closer and closer to representing 40% of the book value of E's net assets. After 20 years, the remaining difference between these two amounts would be attributed solely to the original differential allocated to land (a $4,000 credit). This $4,000 difference would remain until E sold the property.

To illustrate how the sale of land would affect equity method procedures, assume that E sold the land in the year 2019 for $80,000. Since E's cost for the land was $50,000, it would report a gain of $30,000, of which $12,000 ($30,000 x 40%) would be recorded by R, when it records its 40% share of E's reported net income, ignoring income taxes. However, from R's viewpoint, the gain on sale of land should have been $40,000 ($80,000 – $40,000) because the cost of the land from R's perspective was $40,000 at January 2, 1999. Therefore, in addition to the $12,000 share of the gain recorded above, R should record an additional $4,000 gain [($40,000 – $30,000) x 40%] by debiting the investment account and crediting the equity in E income account. This $4,000 debit to the investment account will negate the $4,000 differential allocated to land on January 2, 1999, since the original differential was a credit (the fair market value of the land was $10,000 less than its book value).

Example of complex case including deferred taxes

The impact of interperiod income tax allocation in the foregoing example is similar to that demonstrated earlier in the simplified example. However, a complication arises with regard to the portion of the differential allocated to goodwill, since goodwill is not amortizable for tax purposes and, therefore, is a permanent (not a temporary) difference that does not give rise to deferred taxes. The other components of the differential in this example are all temporary differences.

The entries recorded by R Corporation in 1999 would be

1.	Investment in E Company	12,000	
	Equity in E income		12,000
2.	Income tax expense	816	
	Deferred tax liability		816
	($12,000 x 20% x 34%)		
3.	Cash	4,000	
	Investment in E Company		4,000
4.	Deferred tax liability	272	
	Taxes payable--current		272
	($4,000/$12,000 x $816)		
5.	Equity in E income	7,600	
	Investment in E Company		7,600
6.	Deferred tax liability	490	
	Income tax expense		490
	($7,200 x 20% x 34%)		

Note that the tax effect of the amortization of the differential is based on $7,200, not $7,600, since the $400 goodwill amortization would not have been tax deductible.

Intercompany transactions between investor and investee. Transactions between the investor and the investee **may** require that the investor make certain adjustments when it records its share of the investee earnings. According to the realization concept, profits can be recognized by an entity only when realized through a sale to outside (unrelated) parties in arm's-length transactions (sales and purchases) between the investor and investee. Similar problems, however, can arise when sales of fixed assets between the parties occur. In all cases, there is **no** need for any adjustment when the transfers are made at book value (i.e., without either party recognizing a profit or loss in its separate accounting records).

In preparing consolidated financial statements, all intercompany (parent-subsidiary) transactions are eliminated. However, when the equity method is used to account for investments, only the **profit component** of intercompany (investor-investee) transactions is eliminated. This is because the equity method does not result in the combining of all income statement accounts (such as sales and cost of sales), and therefore will not cause the financial statements to contain redundancies. In contrast, consolidated statements would include redundancies if the gross amounts of all intercompany transactions were not eliminated.

Another distinction between the consolidation and equity method situations pertains to the percentage of intercompany profit to be eliminated. In the case of consolidated statements, the entire intercompany profit is eliminated, regardless of the percentage ownership of the subsidiary. However, according to Accounting Interpretation 1 of APB 18, only the **investor's pro rata share** of intercompany profit would be eliminated in equity accounting, whether the transaction giving rise to the profit is "downstream" (a sale to the investee) or "upstream" (a sale to the investor). An exception is made when the transaction is not "arm's-length" or if the investee company was created by or for the benefit of the investor. In these cases, 100% profit elimination would be required, unless realized through a sale to a third party before year end.

Example of accounting for intercompany transactions

Continue with the same information from the previous example and also assume that E Company sold inventory to R Corporation in 1999 for $2,000 above E's cost. Thirty percent of this inventory remains unsold by R at the end of 2000. E's net income for 2000, including the gross profit on the inventory sold to R, is $20,000; E's income tax rate is 34%. R should make the following journal entries for 2000 (ignoring deferred taxes):

1. Investment in E Company	8,000	
Equity in E income		8,000
($20,000 x 40%)		
2. Equity in E income (amortization of differential)	3,600	
Investment in E Company		3,600
3. Equity in E income	158	
Investment in E Company		158
($2,000 x 30% x 66% x 40%)		

The amount in the last entry needs further elaboration. Since 30% of the inventory remains unsold, only $600 of the intercompany profit is unrealized at year end. This profit, net of income taxes, is $396. R's share of this profit ($158) is included in the first ($8,000) entry recorded. Accordingly, the third entry is needed to adjust or correct the equity in the reported net income of the investee.

Eliminating entries for intercompany profits in fixed assets are similar to those in the examples above. However, intercompany profit is realized only as the assets are depreciated by the purchasing entity. In other words, if an investor buys or sells fixed assets from or to an investee at a price above book value, the gain would only be realized piecemeal over the asset's remaining depreciable life. Accordingly, in the year of sale the pro rata share (based on the investor's percentage ownership interest in the investee, regardless of whether the sale is upstream or downstream) of the unrealized portion of the intercompany profit would have to be eliminated.

In each subsequent year during the asset's life, the pro rata share of the gain realized in the period would be added to income from the investee.

Example of eliminating intercompany profit on fixed assets

Assume that Investor Co., which owns 25% of Investee Co., sold to Investee a fixed asset, having a 5-year remaining life, at a gain of $100,000. Investor Co. is in the 34% marginal tax bracket. The sale occurred at the end of 1999; Investee Co. will use straight-line depreciation to amortize the asset over the years 2000 through 2004.

The entries related to the foregoing are

1999

1.	Gain on sale of fixed asset	25,000	
	Deferred gain		25,000
	(To defer the unrealized portion of the gain)		
2.	Deferred tax benefit	8,500	
	Income tax expense		8,500
	(Tax effect of gain deferral)		

Alternatively, the 1999 events could have been reported by this single entry.

Equity in investee income	16,500	
Investment in Investee Co.		16,500

2000 through 2004 (each year)

1.	Deferred gain	5,000	
	Gain on sale of fixed assets		5,000
	(To amortize deferred gain)		
2.	Income tax expense	1,700	
	Deferred tax benefit		1,700
	(Tax effect of gain realization)		

The alternative treatment would be

Investment in Investee Co.	3,300	
Equity in investee income		3,300

In the above example, the tax currently paid by Investor Co. (34% x $25,000 taxable gain on the transaction) is recorded as a deferred tax benefit in 1999 since taxes will not be due on the book gain recognized in the years 2000 through 2004. Under provisions of SFAS 109, deferred tax benefits are recorded to reflect the tax effects of all deductible temporary differences. Unless Investor Co. could demonstrate that future taxable amounts arising from existing temporary differences exist (or, alternatively, that a NOL carryback could have been elected), this deferred tax benefit will be offset by an equivalent valuation allowance in Investor Co.'s balance sheet at year-end 1999. Thus, the deferred tax benefit might not be recognizable, net of the valuation allowance, for financial reporting purposes unless other temporary differences not specified in the example provided future taxable amounts to offset the net **deductible** effect of the deferred gain (*NOTE: The deferred tax impact of an item of income for book purposes in excess of tax is the same as a deduction for tax purposes in excess of book*).

Investee income items separately reportable by investor. In the examples thus far, the investor has reported its share of investee income, and the adjustments to this income, as a single item described as equity in investee income. However, when the investee has extraordinary items and/or prior period adjustments that are material, the investor should report its share of these items separately on its income and retained earnings statements.

Example of accounting for separately reportable items

Assume that both an extraordinary item and a prior period adjustment reported in an investee's income and retained earnings statements are individually considered material from the investor's viewpoint.

Income statement	
Income before extraordinary item	$ 80,000
Extraordinary loss from earthquake (net of taxes of $12,000)	(18,000)
Net income	$ 62,000
Retained earnings statement	
Retained earnings at January 1, 1999, as originally reported	250,000
Add prior period adjustment--correction of an error made in 1998 (net of taxes of $10,000)	20,000
Retained earnings at January 1, 1999, restated	$270,000

If an investor owned 30% of the voting common stock of this investee, the investor would make the following journal entries in 1999:

1. Investment in investee company	24,000	
Equity in investee income before extraordinary item		24,000
($80,000 x 30%)		
2. Equity in investee extraordinary loss	5,400	
Investment in investee company		5,400
($18,000 x 30%)		
3. Investment in investee company	6,000	
Equity in investee prior period adjustment		6,000
($20,000 x 30%)		

The equity in the investee's prior period adjustment should be reported on the investor's retained earnings statement, and the equity in the extraordinary loss should be reported separately in the appropriate section on the investor's income statement.

Accounting for a partial sale or additional purchase of the equity investment. This section covers the accounting issues that arise when the investor sells some or all of its equity in the investee, or acquires additional equity in the investee.

Example of accounting for a discontinuance of the equity method

Assume that an investor owns 10,000 shares (30%) of XYZ Company common stock for which it paid $250,000 10 years ago. On July 1, 1999, the investor sells 5,000 XYZ shares for $375,000. The balance in the investment in XYZ Company account at January 1, 1999, is $600,000. Assume that all the original differential between cost and book value has been amortized. To calculate the gain (loss) upon this sale of 5,000 shares, it is first necessary to adjust the investment account so that it is current as of the date of sale. Assuming that the investee had net income of $100,000 for the 6 months ended June 30, 1999, the investor should record the following entries:

1. Investment in XYZ Company	30,000	
Equity in XYZ income		30,000
($100,000 x 30%)		
2. Income tax expense	2,040	
Deferred tax liability		2,040
($30,000 x 20% x 34%)		

The gain upon sale can now be computed, as follows:

Proceeds upon sale of 5,000 shares	$375,000
Book value of the 5,000 shares ($630,000 x 50%)	315,000
Gain from sale of XYZ common	$ 60,000

Two entries will be needed to reflect the sale: one to record the proceeds, the reduction in the investment account, and the gain (or loss) and the other to record the tax effects thereof. Remember that the investor must have computed the deferred tax effect of the undistributed earnings of the investee that it had recorded each year, on the basis that those earnings either would eventually be paid as dividends or would be realized as capital gains. When those dividends are ultimately received or when the investment is disposed of, the previously recorded deferred tax liability must be amortized.

To illustrate, assume that the investor in this example provided deferred taxes at an effective rate for dividends (considering the 80% exclusion) of 6.8%. The realized capital gain will be taxed at an assumed 34%. For tax purposes, this gain is computed as $375,000 – $125,000 = $250,000, yielding a tax effect of $85,000. For accounting purposes, the deferred taxes already provided are 6.8% x ($315,000 – $125,000), or $12,920. Accordingly, an **additional** tax expense of $72,080 is incurred upon the sale, due to the fact that an additional gain was realized for book purposes ($375,000 – $315,000 = $60,000; tax at 34% = $20,400) **and** that the tax previously provided for at dividend income rates was lower than the real capital gains rate [$190,000 x (34% – 6.8%) = $51,680 extra tax due]. The entries are as follows:

1. Cash	375,000	
Investment in XYZ Company		315,000
Gain on sale of XYZ Company stock		60,000

2. Deferred tax liability	12,920	
Income tax expense	72,080	
Taxes payable--current		85,000

The gains (losses) from sales of investee stock are reported on the investor's income statement in the "Other income and expense" section, assuming that a multistep income statement is presented.

In this example, the sale of investee stock reduced the percentage owned by the investor to 15%. In such a situation, the investor should discontinue use of the equity method. The balance in the investment account on the date the equity method is suspended ($315,000 in the example) will be accounted for on the basis of fair value, under SFAS 115; presumably being reported in the available-for-sale investment portfolio. This accounting principle change does **not** require the computation of a cumulative effect or any retroactive disclosures in the investor's financial statements. In periods subsequent to this principles change, the investor records cash dividends received from the investment as dividend revenue and places the security in its long-term marketable equity securities portfolio where it will be subjected to the lower of aggregate cost or market calculation. Any dividends received in excess of the investor's share of postdisposal earnings of the investee should be credits to the investment account, rather than to income.

The process of discontinuing the use of the equity method and adopting SFAS 115, as necessitated by a reduction in ownership below the significant influence threshold level, does not require a retroactive restatement. However, the opposite situation having the 20% ownership level equaled or exceeded again (or for the first time), is more complex. APB 18 stipulates that this change in accounting principle (**to** the equity method) requires that the investment account, results of operations (all periods being presented, current and prior), and retained earnings of the investor company be retroactively adjusted.

Example of accounting for a return to the equity method of accounting

Continuing the same example, XYZ Company reported earnings for the second half of 1999 and all of 2000, respectively, of $150,000 and $350,000; XYZ paid dividends of $100,000 and $150,000 in December of those years. In January 2001, the investor purchased 10,000 XYZ shares for $700,000, increasing its ownership to 45% and thereby necessitating a return for equity method accounting, including retroactive adjustment. The relevant entries are as follows:

1. Cash	15,000	
Income from XYZ dividends		15,000
2. Income tax expense	1,020	
Taxes payable--current		1,020
[To record dividend income and taxes thereon at current effective tax rate ($15,000 x .068) in 1999]		

		Debit	Credit
3.	Cash	22,500	
	Income from XYZ dividends		22,500
4.	Income tax expense	1,530	
	Taxes payable--current		1,530
	[To record dividend income and taxes thereon ($22,500 x .068) in 2000]		
5.	Investment in XYZ Company	700,000	
	Cash		700,000
6.	Investment in XYZ Company	37,500	
	Retained earnings		34,950
	Deferred tax liability		2,550

Entry 6. is the cumulative effect adjustment for 15% of XYZ Company's **undistributed** earnings for the second half of 1999 and all of 2000. This adjustment is computed as follows:

Income earned in 1999 subject to equity method	
1999 income ($100,000 + $150,000)	$250,000
Less income earned through June 30 which is reflected in the investment account through previous use of equity method	(100,000)
1999 income subject to equity method adjustment	$150,000
Income earned in 2000 subject to equity method	350,000
Total income subject to equity method	$500,000
Less dividends declared in 1999 and 2000	(250,000)
Increase in investee equity since suspension of equity method (undistributed income)	$250,000
Investor's equity during the period July 1, 1999, through December 31, 2000 (cumulative effect) ($250,000 x 15%)	$ 37,500

Besides showing the cumulative effect as a prior period adjustment on the retained earnings statement, the investor also must retroactively adjust the 1999 and 2000 financial statements to reflect use of the equity method. This means that the dividend income of $15,000 in 1999 and $22,500 in 2000 should be eliminated to reflect the equity method. Accordingly, the term "dividend income" is eliminated and "equity in investee income" is substituted. Since the equity method was used for half of the year 1999 and equity in investee income was accrued through June 30, the term should already appear on 1999's income statement. However, the equity in investee income should be increased by $22,500, the investor's share of the income for the last 6 months of 1999 ($150,000 x 15%). The net effect on 1999's income **before taxes** is a $7,500 increase ($22,500 increase in equity in investee income less a $15,000 decrease in dividend income). For 2000, the net effect on income before taxes is $30,000. This results from adding equity in investee income of $52,500 ($350,000 x 15%) and eliminating dividend income of $22,500. In addition to the income statement, the balance sheets at December 31, 1999 and 2000, are adjusted as follows (before income tax effects):

1. Add $7,500 to the investment in investee and the retained earnings balances at December 31, 1999.
2. Add $37,500 to the investment in investee and the retained earnings balances at December 31, 2000.

Investor accounting for investee capital transactions. According to APB 18, investee transactions of a capital nature that affect the investor's share of the investee's stockholders' equity shall be accounted for as if the investee were a consolidated subsidiary. These transactions principally include situations where the investee purchases treasury stock from, or sells unissued shares or shares held in the treasury to, outside shareholders. (If the investor participates in these transactions on a pro rata basis, its percentage ownership will not change and no special accounting will be necessary.) Similar results will be obtained when holders of outstanding options or convertible securities acquire investee common shares.

When the investee engages in one of the above capital transactions, the investor's ownership percentage is changed. This gives rise to a gain or loss, depending on whether the price paid (for treasury shares acquired) or received (for shares issued) is greater or lesser than the per share carrying value of the investor's interest in the investee. However, since no gain or loss can be recognized on capital transactions, these purchases or sales will affect paid-in capital and/or retained earnings directly, without being reflected in the investor's income statement. This method is consistent with the treatment that would be accorded to a consolidated subsidiary's capital transaction. An exception is that, under certain circumstances, the SEC will permit income recognition based on the concept that the investor is essentially selling part of its investment.

Example of accounting for an investee capital transaction

Assume R Corp. purchases, on 1/2/98, 25% (2,000 shares) of E Corp.'s outstanding shares for $80,000. The cost is equal to both the book and fair values of R's interest in E's underlying net assets (i.e., there is no differential to be accounted for). One week later, E Corp. buys 1,000 shares of its stock from other shareholders for $50,000. Since the price paid ($50/share) exceeded R Corp.'s per share carrying value of its interest, $40, R Corp. has in fact suffered an economic loss by the transaction. Also, its percentage ownership of E Corp. has increased as the number of shares held by third parties has been reduced.

R Corp.'s new interest in E's net assets is

$$\frac{\text{2,000 shares held by R}}{\text{7,000 shares outstanding}} \text{ x E Corp. net assets}$$

$$.2857 \text{ x } (\$320{,}000 - \$50{,}000) = \$77{,}143$$

The interest held by R Corp. has thus been diminished by $80,000 – $77,143 = $2,857.

Therefore, R Corp. should make the following entry:

Paid-in capital (or retained earnings)	2,857	
Investment in E Corp.		2,857

R Corp. should charge the loss against paid-in capital if paid-in capital from past transactions of a similar nature exists; otherwise the debit is to retained earnings. Had the transaction given rise to a gain it would have been credited to paid-in capital only (never to retained earnings) following the prescription in APB 6 that transactions in one's own shares cannot produce earnings.

Note that the amount of the charge to paid-in capital (or retained earnings) in the entry above can be verified as follows: R Corp.'s share of the posttransaction net equity (2/7) times the "excess" price paid ($50 – $40 = $10) times the number of shares purchased = 2/7 x $10 x 1,000 = $2,857.

EMERGING ISSUES TASK FORCE CONSENSUS SUMMARIES

84-5 Sale of Marketable Securities With a Put Option (affected by SFAS 125)

This consensus held that the proper accounting (as sale or as secured borrowing) would depend upon the assessed probability of the put being exercised by the holder. The effect of SFAS 125 is to replace this probability assessment with an evaluation of whether the transferor has surrendered control and whether it has received consideration other than a beneficial interest in the asset transferred. If control has been transferred, even a high likelihood of exercise of the put option would not result in secured borrowing accounting treatment. If accounted for as a sale, the gain is determined with reference to all assets received and liabilities incurred by transferor--including put option, which would be a liability, to be recorded at fair value, which would reflect likelihood of exercise. The original consensus called for continual reassessment of the likelihood of exercise of the put; SFAS 125, in contrast, does not mandate this, as there would be no accounting effect. If put option is exercised, investment is recorded in accordance with SFAS 115.

85-40 Comprehensive Review of Sales of Marketable Securities With Put Arrangements (affected by SFAS 125)

Former consensus 85-40 is nullified by SFAS 125; existence of put option does not affect accounting for sales of marketable securities, which are accounted for as sales if control is transferred, and as secured borrowings if control is not transferred. The criteria of SFAS 125 are to be applied to all transfers of financial assets. If put option is granted to transferee, it is recorded at fair value as a liability by the transferor, thus affecting the computation of gain or loss to be recognized on the sale.

86-40 Investments in Open-Ended Mutual Funds That Invest in US Government Securities

This consensus held that lower of cost or market accounting is required per SFAS 12 for investments in funds that invest in government bonds. Thus, the fact that the fund's holdings were debt instruments did not alter the fact that mutual fund shares are marketable equity security.

89-4 Accounting for Purchased Investment in Collateralized Mortgage Obligation Instrument or in Mortgage-Backed Interest-Only Certificate (affected by SFAS 125)

SFAS 125 amends this consensus by requiring that investments in financial assets, which can be prepaid or otherwise settled in a way which prevents the investor from fully recovering all of its investment, must be classified and measured as an available-for-sale or trading security. The other elements of the consensus, addressing classification of CMO investments as equity or nonequity, are not affected by SFAS 125; in general, the accounting should follow the form of the investment, although criteria set forth in EITF 89-4 indicate under which circumstances this would not hold.

93-18 Impairment Recognition for a Purchased Investment in a Collateralized Mortgage Obligation Instrument or in a Mortgage-Backed Interest-Only Certificate

The EITF agreed that SFAS 115 governs the measurement of impairment of mortgage-backed securities, based on fair value. An earlier consensus, 89-4, had held that impairment of mortgage-backed securities was indicated if the recalculated effective yield of the securities became negative; the new consensus holds that negative yield (using a risk-free discount rate) is presumptive evidence of an impairment which is other than temporary.

94-4 Classification of an Investment in a Mortgage-Backed Interest-Only Certificate as Held-to-Maturity

No concensus had been reached regarding whether interest-only strips could be classified as held-to-maturity under the criteria of SFAS 115. SFAS 125 has led to a resolution of this issue, as it amends SFAS 115 to prohibit the use of the held-to-maturity classification.

96-10 Impact of Certain Transactions on the Held-to-Maturity Classification Under FASB Statement No. 115

Transactions involving held to maturity investments which are not accounted for as sales (e.g., wash sales) do not call into question the classification of investments as held to maturity. A similar conclusion would result from bond swaps. however, if intent is to not hold new security received until maturity, then intent regarding other bond holdings, etc., is subject to being questioned. Issuance of SFAS 125 had the effect of partially nullifying this consensus: unless the closing side of the wash sale transaction is a concurrently entered contract, the opening side must be accounted for as a sale, which then would trigger the concern over the classification as held to maturity. SFAS 125 does not affect conclusion on desecuritizations, however.

97-7 Accounting for Hedges of the Foreign Currency Risk Inherent in an Available-for-Sale Marketable Equity Security

This issue relates to some investments, such as those registered on foreign exchanges, which have inherent foreign exchange risk associated with them. If these investments are categorized as available for sale, value changes may include the effects of both market and exchange rate changes. In some cases, the entity will enter into foreign exchange hedging to protect against exchange rate risk; the issue then is whether transaction gains or losses on forward contract should be included in contra equity account for available-for-sale securities' unrealized gains or losses. The consensus was in support of this treatment: The gain or loss should be shown in the same account if it is associated with the securities' price change. Foreign exchange risk is inherent only if two conditions are met: securities are not traded on exchange denominated in investor's functional currency; and dividends or other cash flows are all denominated in foreign currency.

98-7 Accounting for Exchanges of Similar Equity Method Investments

A consensus was reached that exchanges of similar equity method investments should be accounted for per APB 29. EITF 86-29 provides guidelines for determining similarity/nonsimilarity of productive assets.

11 BUSINESS COMBINATIONS AND CONSOLIDATED FINANCIAL STATEMENTS

PERSPECTIVE AND ISSUES

Business combinations may take a number of legal forms, but whatever the form, all combinations will be accounted for as either purchases or poolings of interest. A purchase occurs when one entity buys another; a pooling presumes that two or more entities combine in such a way as to preserve the ownership interests of substantially all the owners of the predecessor enterprises. A series of restrictive conditions must all be satisfied in order to account for a given transaction as a pooling of interests under existing GAAP; the FASB has recently begun a project which might eventually impose even stricter constraints on the use of the pooling method.

While logic suggests that few combinations would truly be poolings of interests, there exist strong motivations to qualify business combinations as poolings, and in fact a preponderance of acquisitions by large, publicly held companies are so accounted for. On the contrary, most combinations by smaller or privately held companies are purchases. This dichotomy is partly due to opportunity since poolings require exchanges of common stock, fewer nonpublic entities would be able to use the method, and partly due to motive since a primary driver in favor of pooling accounting is that it obviates recording goodwill and its subsequent amortization against earnings.

Purchase and pooling accounting procedures, as detailed in APB 16, are applicable to combinations of entities **not** under common control. If companies under common control are combined, the accounting is similar to that prescribed for a pooling of interests. Examples of companies under common control are parents and subsidiaries or brother-sister affiliates. An exception exists when a minority (outside) interest in a subsidiary is acquired, which is accounted for as a purchase. In other transfers among entities under common control, where accounting similar to that for a pooling is appropriate, any purchase cost in excess of historical cost should be charged against stockholders' equity.

When a combination is to be accounted for as a purchase, the assets acquired and liabilities assumed are recorded at their fair values. If the assets and liabilities net to an amount other than the total acquisition price, the excess (or deficiency) is generally referred to as goodwill (negative goodwill), which is accounted for in accordance with APB 17. Goodwill can arise only in the context of a purchase business combination, since in a pooling, the assets and liabilities of the combining entities are carried forward at precombination book values. This treatment follows from the theory that a pooling does not result in the acquisition of one business entity by another, and therefore a new basis of accountability cannot be established.

When the acquired entity is **merged** into the acquiring entity or when both entities are **consolidated** into a new (third) entity, all assets and liabilities are recorded directly on the books of the surviving organization. Depending upon whether the conditions stipulated by APB 16 are met, this transaction will be treated as either a pooling or a purchase. However, when the acquirer obtains a majority (or all) of the common stock of the acquired entity (which maintains a separate legal existence), the assets and liabilities of the acquired company will not be recorded on the acquirer's books. In this case, GAAP normally requires that consolidated financial statements be prepared (i.e., that an **accounting consolidation** be effected) and either pooling or purchase accounting used, depending upon the circumstances. In certain cases **combined** financial statements of entities under common control (but neither of which is owned by the other) are also prepared. This process is very similar to an accounting consolidation using pooling accounting, except that the equity accounts of the combining entities are carried forward intact.

The major accounting issues in business combinations and consolidated or combined financial statement preparation are as follows:

1. The proper accounting basis for the assets and liabilities of the combining entities
2. The decision to treat a combination as a pooling or as a purchase
3. The elimination of intercompany balances and transactions in the preparation of consolidated or combined statements

The Board has had a number of items dealing with consolidations and related matters on its agenda over the years, and a large fraction of EITF consensuses also deal with business combinations matters. It is further understood that the SEC devotes an inordinate amount of its time to ruling on whether specific transactions should be accounted for as poolings or as purchases, which has added to the Board's inclination to tackle this matter once again. The Board has lately decided to remove the so-called "push down" (new basis) accounting project from its agenda after a number of years of study, and has recently concluded another related agenda project, on disaggregated disclosures, with the issuance of SFAS 131 (discussed in Chapter 19). This leaves as its major project the matter of establishing a new criterion for requiring the presentation of consolidated financial statements. The Board expressed its intent to replace the ownership threshold test (50% + one share) with one based on the concept of control, and the expectation was that this should have been accomplished well before 1999. This project has proved to be more controversial than anticipated, however, and it is not clear that it will, in fact, result in adoption of a new standard. On the other hand, the use of control would be consistent with evolving standards in other matters (e.g., SFAS 125 uses a transfer of control criterion to determine whether sale treatment is warranted when there has been a transfer of financial assets), and a coherent approach to standard-setting would indicate that this change is also appropriate.

Assuming that the control criterion is ultimately adopted to distinguish when consolidated financial statements should be presented, control will be defined as the ability to derive benefits from the use of the individual assets of the controlled entity, in essentially the same way a controlling entity can direct the use of its own assets. It could be effected by establishing the controlled entity's policies as well as its capital and operating budgets, or by selecting, determining the compensation of, and terminating personnel responsible for implementing the entity's policies and decisions. Control would be exclusionary; however, only one entity could control another, although control could be delegated.

If adopted, the proposal would provide guidance to ascertain when control was present. Besides ownership of a large minority interest where there is no other party or organized group of parties having a significant interest, control could be suggested by such factors as

1. An ability, demonstrated by a recent election, to dominate the process of nominating candidates for the other entity's governing board, and to cast a majority of votes actually cast in an election for the board members;
2. A unilateral ability to obtain a majority voting interest through ownership of securities or other rights that may be converted into a majority voting interest at the option of the holder, without assuming risks in excess of the expected benefits from the conversion;
3. A relationship with an entity that it has established that has no voting stock or member voting rights and has no provision in its charter, bylaws, or trust instrument that

    a. Cannot be changed by entities other than its creator
    b. Limit the entity, including the powers of its board of directors or trustees, to activities that the creating entity can schedule or initiate to provide substantially all future net cash inflows or other future economic benefits to its creator;

4. A unilateral ability to dissolve an entity and assume control of its individual assets, subject to claims against those assets, without assuming economic costs in excess of the expected benefits from that dissolution; and
5. A sole general partnership interest in a limited partnership.

If adopted, the new standard would require that the noncontrolling interest in the subsidiary (presently known as the "minority interest") be shown on balance sheet in the equity section, whereas at present this is shown either in the debt section of the balance sheet, in equity, or in a special category between debt and equity. The separate components of the controlled entity's equity (e.g., common stock and retained earnings) could not be reported in the equity section of the controlling entity, however. Income attributable to the noncontrolling interest would not be reported as an expense or loss item, but rather as a deduction from consolidated net income to arrive at income available for the controlling interest (parent).

While the project discussed in the preceding paragraphs has progressed slowly to date, the Board has recently affirmed its commitment to the "control" criterion for consolidation of financial statements, but is still struggling with certain issues, particularly those involving so-called special purpose entities (SPE), which were addressed earlier by EITF 90-15. An exposure draft speaking to consolidation policy is promised for late 1998.

The proposed requirements discussed above are quite similar to the rules mandated by AICPA Statement of Position 94-3, which is applicable to not-for-profit organizations only. That standard introduced the notion of control as the critical threshold issue for consolidation or combination of the financial statements of two or more enterprises. This is discussed in Chapter 23.

Beginning in late 1997, the Board has been deliberating fundamental issues regarding the use of purchase and pooling of interests accounting and related issues pertaining to goodwill. Reportedly, most discussion to date has focused on accounting for goodwill arising from purchase business combinations, and the Board has reaffirmed that goodwill is an asset which is to be measured as set forth in APB 16 (excess of purchase price over fair value of net assets acquired), but only after first attempting to ascribe the price to tangible and identifiable intangible assets. The Board is apparently moving away form the current 40-year (APB 17-imposed) absolute limitation on useful life, however, in favor of a regularly scheduled series of reviews for possible impairment. As part of this same project, he Board will consider narrowing or eliminating the current gross differences between the purchase and pooling methods of accounting. An exposure draft addressing both of these important matters is promised for early 1999.

Sources of GAAP

APB	*ARB*	*SFAS*	*TB*	*EITF*
16, 17, 18, 29	51	38, 79, 94, 125	85-5, 85-6	84-13, 84-33, 85-12, 85-14, 85-28, 85-45, 86-10, 86-29, 86-32, 87-11, 87-15, 87-16, 87-17, 87-21, 87-27, 88-16, 88-26, 88-27, 89-7, 90-5, 90-6, 90-12, 90-13, 90-15, 91-5, 93-2, 93-7, 94-3, 95-3, 95-8, 95-12, 95-14, 95-19, 95-21, 96-4, 96-5, 96-7, 96-8, 96-20, 97-2, 97-6, 97-8, 97-9, 97-15, 98-1, 98-2, 98-3, 98-4

DEFINITIONS OF TERMS

Accounting consolidation. The process of combining the financial statements of a parent company and one or more legally separate and distinct subsidiaries.

Acquisition. One enterprise pays cash or issues stock or debt, for all or part of the voting stock of another enterprise. The acquired enterprise remains intact as a separate legal entity. If the parent-subsidiary relationship is accounted for as a purchase, it is called an acquisition. If pooling accounting is used, the term acquisition cannot be used and the result is called a combination of interests.

Combination. Any transaction whereby one enterprise obtains control over the assets and properties of another enterprise, regardless of the resulting form of the enterprise emerging from the combination transaction.

Combined financial statements. Financial statements presenting the financial position and/or results of operations of legally separate entities, related by common ownership, as if they were a single entity.

Consolidated financial statements. Consolidated statements present, primarily for the benefit of the shareholders and creditors of the parent company, the results of operations and the financial position of a parent company and its subsidiaries essentially as if the group were a single enterprise with one or more branches or divisions.

Consolidation. A new enterprise is formed to acquire two or more other enterprises through an exchange of voting stock. The acquired enterprises then cease to exist as separate legal entities.

Control. Ownership by one enterprise, directly or indirectly, of more than 50% of the outstanding voting shares of another enterprise.

Entity concept. A method of preparing consolidated financial statements of a parent and majority-owned subsidiary which involves restatement of net assets of the subsidiary to fair value at the date of acquisition for **both** majority and minority interests.

Goodwill. The excess of the cost of a business acquisition accounted for by the purchase method over the fair value of the net assets thereof; it must be amortized over a useful life of up to 40 years.

Merger. One enterprise acquires all of the net assets of one or more other enterprises through an exchange of stock, payment of cash or other property, or the issue of debt instruments.

Minority interest. Any remaining outstanding voting stock of a subsidiary not purchased by the acquiring enterprise.

Negative goodwill. Referred to as the "excess of fair value over cost of purchased business acquisition." This amount represents the **net** excess of fair value of the net assets of a business acquisition accounted for as a purchase, after offsetting the maximum amount against the fair value of all noncurrent assets acquired (except marketable securities).

Parent company concept. A method of preparing consolidated financial statements of a parent and majority-owned subsidiary which involves restatement of net assets of the subsidiary to fair value at the date of acquisition for **only** the majority interest.

Pooling-of-interests method. An accounting method used for a business combination which is predicated upon a mutual exchange and continuation of ownership interests in the combining entities. It does not result in the establishing of a new basis of accountability.

Preacquisition contingencies. Uncertainties existing at the date of an acquisition accounted for by the purchase method, which if resolved within 1 year of the acquisition result in a reallocation of the purchase price.

Purchase method. An accounting method used for a business combination which recognizes that one combining entity was acquired by another. It establishes a new basis of accountability for the acquiree.

Purchased preacquisition earnings. An account used to report the earnings of a subsidiary attributable to percentage ownership acquired at the interim date in the current reporting period.

Reverse acquisition. An acquisition when one entity, nominally the acquirer, issues so many shares to the former owners of the target entity that they become the majority owners of the successor entity.

Subsidiary. An enterprise that is controlled, directly or indirectly, by another enterprise.

Unrealized intercompany profit. The excess of the transaction price over the carrying value of an item (usually inventory or plant assets) transferred from (or to) a parent to (or from) the subsidiary (or among subsidiaries) and not sold to an outside entity. For purposes of consolidated financial statements, recognition must be deferred until subsequent realization through a transaction with an unrelated party.

CONCEPTS, RULES, AND EXAMPLES

Pooling of Interests

Business combinations have been accounted for as poolings since at least the early 1930s, although the term was not first applied until the mid-1940s. The early examples, however, generally involved affiliated entities (such as parents and subsidiaries), where the use of this method clearly made sense. The Federal Power Commission endorsed pooling accounting in 1943, and other agencies followed suit within a few years. Initially, pooling was accepted only for those mergers where the combining entities had roughly the same economic substance (so that it was difficult to discern which party was actually the acquirer). However, as time passed, pooling was accepted for a broad range of business combinations among economic unequals.

ARB 40 (1950) permitted pooling accounting when the shareholders of the combining entities continued forward as owners of the new or surviving business. This criterion remains one of the clearest tests of whether a combination should be accorded pooling treatment. ARB 40 also established comparable size and management continuity as criteria, but these terms were not quantitatively defined and a wide range of combinations continued to be accounted for as poolings of interests.

This situation continued with the subsequent issuances of ARB 43 and 48 (1953 and 1957, respectively), which failed to produce the strict guidelines that were needed. ARB 48 permitted pooling treatment even when the size relationship among the combining entities was as great as 19:1. As a result, accounting for business combinations as poolings became extremely popular in the early and mid-1960s. The major reason was that the true cost (measured by the market value of the consideration--usually the acquirer's stock or debt instruments) of the **acquisition** was concealed, with the lower carryforward basis of the assets acquired resulting in lower amortization expense and higher reportable earnings in future periods. Also, the acquirer could incorporate the acquired entity's retained earnings (subject to some limitations) into its financial statements, thereby providing further "window dressing."

The 12 Pooling of Interest Criteria

Abuses led to pressure to narrow the range of business combinations which could receive pooling treatment. APB 16 established 12 criteria, **all of which** must be met for pooling to be used. A failure to meet all of these 12 tests makes it mandatory to use the purchase accounting method. The criteria fall into three broad categories.

1. Those relating to the attributes of the combining entities
2. Those relating to the means by which the combination was effected
3. Those relating to the absence of specific postacquisition planned transactions

Combining companies. Independent ownerships are combined to continue previously separate operations.

1. "Each of the combining companies is autonomous and has not been a subsidiary or division of another corporation within 2 years before the plan of combination is initiated."

   a. Plan is initiated when announced publicly to stockholders
   b. A new company meets criterion as long as it is not a successor to a nonindependent company
   c. A previously owned company divested due to government order is exempted from this criterion

2. "Each of the combining companies is independent of the other combining companies."

   a. No more than 10% of any combining company is held by any other combining company(ies)

Combining of interest. The combination is effected through an exchange of stock.

3. "The combination is effected in a single transaction or is completed in accordance with a specific plan within 1 year after the plan is initiated."

   a. Must be completed in a year unless governmental proceeding or litigation prevents completion in 1 year

4. "A corporation offers and issues only common stock with rights identical to those of the majority of its outstanding voting common stock in exchange for substantially all of the voting common stock interest of another company at the date the plan of combination is consummated."

   a. Cash may be distributed for partial shares, but cash cannot be given pro rata to all stockholders. However, all holders of all outstanding shares may be offered cash. If 10% or less accept, then pooling treatment would still be allowed (if all other conditions are met). If more than 10% ask for cash but a lottery system is used to select the actual recipients of cash (no more than 10%), again pooling treatment would be permitted.
   b. 90% of the acquired entity's stock outstanding at consummation must be acquired by the issuing corporation. The following shares are excluded from the shares considered acquired at consummation:

      (1) Stock acquired before the plan was initiated and still owned by issuing corporation
      (2) Stock acquired by issuing corporation, other than by issuing its own, between initiation and consummation
      (3) Outstanding stock of the acquired corporation after consummation

(4) Shares of the issuing company held by a combining company. These shares are converted into an equivalent number of shares of the combining company and are deducted from the shares considered acquired at consummation.

c. When more than two companies are combined, the criteria must be met for each of them
d. An issuing company may acquire equity securities of the combining company other than common by any means **except those** issued for the combining company's stock within the prior 2 years (which must be acquired with common stock)
e. The foregoing requirement may extend to more than the actual outstanding common stock of the acquired entity. If it has outstanding stock purchase warrants, these too must (within the 90% rule) be exchanged for stock of the acquirer, since warrants are "substantially identical" to common shares. On the other hand, convertible debt may be exchanged for cash.

5. "None of the combining companies changes the equity interest of the voting common stock in contemplation of effecting the combination either within 2 years before the plan of combination is initiated or between the dates the combination is initiated and consummated. Changes in contemplation of effecting the combination may include distributions to stockholders and additional issues, exchanges, and retirements of securities."

   a. Normal dividend distributions (as determined by past dividends), however, are permitted

6. "Each of the combining companies reacquires shares of voting common stock only for purposes other than business combinations, and no company reacquires more than a normal number of shares between the dates the plan of combination is initiated and consummated."

   a. Normal treasury stock acquisitions (as determined by past acquisitions) are permitted
   b. Acquisition by other combining companies is the same as treasury stock acquisition

7. "The ratio of the interest of an individual common stockholder to those of other common stockholders in a combining company remains the same as a result of the exchange of stock to effect the combination."

   a. No stockholder denies or surrenders his/her potential share in the issuing corporation

8. "The voting rights to which the common stock ownership interests in the resulting combined corporation are entitled are exercisable by the stock-

holders. The stockholders are neither deprived of nor restricted in exercising those rights for a period."

   a. Stock cannot be put into a voting trust

9. "The combination is resolved at the date the plan is consummated and no provisions of the plan relating to the issue of securities or other consideration are pending."
   a. No contingent future issuances or other consideration is permitted (including any payable through a trustee)
   b. Later settlement of contingencies existing at the date of consummation, however, is permitted

Absence of planned transactions.

10. "The combined corporation does not agree directly or indirectly to retire or reacquire all or part of the common stock issued to effect the combination."
    a. The issuer may, however, retain the right of first refusal on a subsequent resale of the shares issued to effect the business combination without jeopardizing the pooling treatment
11. "The combined corporation does not enter into other financial arrangements for the benefit of the former stockholders of a combining company, such as a guaranty of loans secured by stock issued in the combination, which in effect negates the exchange of equity securities."
12. "The combined corporation does not intend or plan to dispose of a significant part of the assets of the combining companies within 2 years after the combination other than disposals in the ordinary course of business of the formerly separate companies and to eliminate duplicate facilities or excess capacity."

If a business combination (regardless of legal form) meets all of these 12 criteria, it must be accounted for as a pooling; otherwise, it must be treated as a purchase. A single business combination cannot be accounted for as part pooling, part purchase.

A pooling of interests should be recorded as of the date it is consummated. Therefore, if one of the combining entities has yet to issue its financial statements for a period which ended prior to the consummation of the pooling, those statements, when issued, should **not** reflect the pooling (although disclosure of the "subsequent event" should be provided in the notes to the financial statements). However, if, after the date the pooling is consummated, comparative financial statements are prepared, the effect of the pooling should be reflected in all the years presented.

The Emerging Issues Task Force (EITF) has reached a number of consensus positions interpreting the criteria enumerated above. In 88-26, the EITF stated that **common** stock, not preferred stock, of the acquirer must be issued to effect a pooling. When control originally resides with the acquirer's preferred shareholders, it must first arrange to exchange enough common for preferred to create a controlling class of common shareholders. On the other hand, where a controlling class of preferred shareholders exists in the acquiree company, there is no problem: the acquirer simply issues its common stock in exchange for both common and preferred shares of the entity being acquired. In all cases, the issuing (i.e., acquiring) entity must issue shares of its controlling class of common stock for at least 90% of the common stock of the other (i.e., acquired) entity. Additionally, the issuing entity must issue common and preferred stock (if any) for at least 90% of the aggregate common and preferred stock of the acquiree.

The APB's pooling criteria also established the so-called "90% test" for the minimum proportion of the acquired entity's shares being exchanged for the acquirer's common stock. In 87-16, the EITF has established a complex series of tests that apply to situations when several entities are acquired simultaneously, particularly when a new holding company is created as a merging of the other entities. When a new company is formed as a combination of two or more companies, the EITF concluded that pooling treatment is required if pooling would have been indicated had **any one** of the entities been the acquirer (the "issuing company," in the language of pooling accounting).

The EITF was inclined to encourage a case-by-case evaluation regarding the potential cash acquisition of securities other than common stock of an acquiree entity in a pooling of interests. Depending on the circumstances, these securities (warrants, options, convertible debt or convertible preferred) might be deemed common stock equivalents, and therefore subject to the 10% limits prescribed in APB 16 if pooling treatment is to be preserved. The SEC, on the other hand, applies a stricter criterion that treats warrants and options as common stock in all instances.

Similarly, the EITF reached a consensus that the "right of first refusal" by the issuing company of shares it issued to effect a pooling does not violate the rule concerning an absence of planned transactions to retire shares issued. Again, the SEC disagreed with the Task Force position. The pooling criterion would be clearly violated if the acquired company made an actual intention to tender shares it had received at the time of pooling.

According to the consensus in 93-2, unallocated shares of a sponsoring entity held by an ESOP are not deemed to be "tainted" treasury shares in determining whether pooling of interests accounting may be appropriate.

The EITF has considered a wide range of other purchase/pooling issues but generally has not reached consensus positions on them.

Accounting for a pooling. To illustrate the essential elements of the pooling-of-interests method of accounting, consider the following balance sheets of the combining entities:

Condensed Balance Sheets as of Date of Merger

	Company A	Company B	Company C
Assets	$30,000,000	$4,500,000	$6,000,000
Liabilities	$18,000,000	$1,000,000	$1,500,000
Common stock:			
$100 par	6,000,000	--	--
$10 par	--	3,000,000	--
$1 par	--	--	1,000,000
Additional paid-in capital	2,000,000	--	500,000
Retained earnings	4,000,000	500,000	3,000,000
Liabilities and stockholders' equity	$30,000,000	$4,500,000	$6,000,000

Company A will acquire companies B and C, and both B and C will tender 100% of their common shares. A will give 1 of its shares for each 15 shares of B stock and 1 of its shares for each 25 shares of C stock. Thus, A will issue 20,000 shares to acquire B and 40,000 shares to acquire C.

In a pooling of interests, the historical basis of the assets and liabilities of the combining entities is continued. No new basis of accountability is established. The assets of the combined (postacquisition) Company A will total $40,500,000; total liabilities will be $20,500,000. Total equity (net assets) will, therefore, equal $20,000,000.

While the total stockholders' equity of the postcombination entity will equal the sum of the combining entities' individual equity accounts, the allocation between paid-in capital and retained earnings can vary. Total (postcombination) retained earnings can be equal to **or less than** the sum of the constituent entities' retained earnings but cannot be more than that amount. Consider the cases of companies B and C.

Company A issues 20,000 shares of its stock, or an aggregate par value of $2,000,000, to substitute for Company B's $3,000,000 aggregate paid-in capital in effecting the merger with Company B. Therefore, the combined (postacquisition) balance sheet will include $2,000,000 of par value capital stock, **plus** $1,000,000 of additional paid-in capital. Even though only $2,000,000 of stock was issued to replace Company B's $3,000,000 of aggregate par, there **can be no increase in retained earnings and no decrease in contributed capital** as a consequence of the pooling.

The Company C merger presents the opposite situation; an aggregate of $4,000,000 of Company A stock is to be issued to supersede $1,000,000 of aggregate par and $500,000 of additional paid-in capital. To accomplish this, $2,500,000 of Company C retained earnings is "capitalized," leaving only $500,000 of Company C retained earnings to be carried **as retained earnings** into the postacquisition balance sheet. In reality, such a situation would not exist. If the pooling of interests took place simultaneously, APB 16 requires only that the combined contributed capital of all entities not be reduced. Therefore, the issuance of 60,000 shares would create an entry on A's books as follows:

Net assets	8,000,000	
Additional paid-in capital	1,500,000	
Common stock		6,000,000
Retained earnings		3,500,000

Note that the additional paid-in capital on the books of Company A is reduced by an amount sufficient to make the total increase in contributed capital of A $4,500,000 which equals the total contributed capital of both B ($3,000,000) and C ($1,500,000). In this way, all of the retained earnings of B and C are transferred to A. This accounting would hold even if A, B, and C simultaneously transferred their net assets to a new entity, D (a consolidation). The opening entry on the books of D would look the same as the consolidated balance sheet of A after the merger as presented below.

The balance sheet of Company A after the mergers are completed is as follows:

Assets	$40,500,000
Liabilities	$20,500,000
Common stock, $100 par	12,000,000
Additional paid-in capital	500,000
Retained earnings	7,500,000
Liabilities and stockholders' equity	$40,500,000

The historical basis of assets and liabilities is normally continued, but this rule has an exception: where different accounting principles were employed by the combining entities, these principles should be conformed, where possible, by retroactive adjustment. Prior period financial statements, when reissued on a pooled basis, should be restated for these changes.

When the pooling of interests method is used, it is necessary to report all periods presented on a combined basis. If only a single year is presented, the effect will be as if the combination occurred at the beginning of that year. If comparative statements are presented, the effect will be as if the combination occurred at the beginning of the earliest year being reported on. This is consistent with the concept of a pooling as not being a discrete economic event; but rather as a combining of common interests, such that the most meaningful reporting, **after the date of the combination,** is to present the financial position and results of operations of those entities as if they had always been combined. In order to present combined statements of financial position and results of operations, all intercompany balances and transactions should be eliminated, to the extent that this is practical to accomplish.

If any combining entity has a deficit in its retained earnings, that deficit is continued in the combined entity (and may even be increased as a consequence of the par value changeover, as illustrated above for a nondeficit situation). It cannot be reduced or eliminated as a consequence of the combination.

Any expenses relating to a business combination accounted for as a pooling of interests (e.g., stock registration costs, finders' fees, and costs of preparing stockholders' prospectuses) must be charged against income in the period in which the combination is effected. No new assets can arise from a pooling.

Example of pooling

To review the applicability of the pooling criteria set forth earlier and the accounting for poolings of interests, a comprehensive example will be developed here and continued in the subsequent discussion of purchase accounting.

Acquisitive Corporation (whose balance sheet is presented as Exhibit I) is about to acquire four other entities: Beta (Exhibit II), Gamma (Exhibit III), Delta (Exhibit IV), and Epsilon (Exhibit V).

1. The acquisitions will take place as follows:
   a. Beta is acquired by exchanging 1 Acquisitive common share for each 15 of Beta common shares
   b. Gamma is acquired by exchanging 1 Acquisitive common share for each 75 of Gamma common shares
   c. Delta is acquired by paying $4,250,000 in 90-day demand notes to retire the $4.5 million bank loan, and by exchanging 1 Acquisitive share for each 20 of Delta common shares (except as noted in 8. below)
   d. Epsilon is acquired by exchanging a new issue of $100 par, 7% preferred stock subject to a mandatory retirement plan (ending in 2001), plus common shares, for all Epsilon common stock. Shareholders of Epsilon will receive 1 share of Acquisitive preferred and 1 share of Acquisitive common for each 15 Epsilon common shares.
2. The appraised value of each acquired firm is given as follows (amounts in thousands):

	Assets acquired	*Liabilities assumed*	*Net asset value*
Beta Corporation	$78,500	$ 2,500	$76,000
Gamma Company, Inc.	42,500	6,500	36,000
Delta Corporation	37,000	2,500	34,500
Epsilon, Inc.	42,000	19,500	22,500

   In each case, current assets are appraised to be worth book values as per the acquired firms' balance sheets.
3. Epsilon originally issued 8% debentures on 1/1/95 at par value. Acquisitive purchased $5.0 million (face value) of these debentures on 1/1/98 at the market price of $97.60. The discount has been regularly amortized to earnings.
4. Investments by Beta and Gamma in the common shares of Acquisitive Corporation were recorded at cost.
5. Each of the five corporations in question has been in business for at least 5 years, and none has ever been a subsidiary of each other or any other company.
6. The acquisition agreement with Gamma provides that, if earnings of the acquired subsidiary exceed certain amounts in each or any of the following 5 years, additional shares of Acquisitive will be distributed to former Gamma shareholders. Specifically, for each 50% earnings advance over 1999 levels ($2,800,000 net), an additional 10% of shares are to be issued.
7. The agreement with Epsilon provides that the purchase price of $20,000,000 is protected against market declines for 2 years subsequent to the merger (i.e., if the value of securities distributed to Epsilon shareholders is below $20 million as of 12/31/01) additional Acquisitive Corporation common shares will be issued at that time, in an amount sufficient to bring the total value to the stipulated sum.

8. Holders of 5,000 shares of Delta stock angrily dissented to the merger plan, and Acquisitive agreed to pay them $25 for each share tendered instead of issuing common stock.
9. Common stock of the various firms traded on stock exchanges or were quoted in the over-the-counter market in 1999 at these prices.

	High	*Low*	*Average*	*Ending*
Acquisitive Corporation	$512	$388	$495	$492
Beta Corporation	51 7/8	28 1/2	35 1/4	35 3/4
Gamma Company, Inc.	8 3/4	7 1/2	8	8 1/8
Delta Corporation	28 1/2	14 3/8	20 1/8	20 1/2
Epsilon, Inc.	20 1/8	10 1/4	12 1/2	11 1/2

Exhibit I
Acquisitive Corporation
Condensed Balance Sheet
December 31, 1999

Sundry current assets		$ 75,000,000
Plant and equipment, net	$80,000,000	
Investment in Epsilon 8% debentures	4,900,000	84,900,000
Total assets		$159,900,000
Sundry liabilities		$ 87,000,000
Common stock, $100 par	$22,500,000	
Additional paid-in capital	12,200,000	
Retained earnings	38,200,000	72,900,000
Total liabilities and stockholders' equity		$159,900,000

Exhibit II
Beta Corporation
Condensed Balance Sheet
December 31, 1999

Sundry current assets		$ 3,900,000
Plant and equipment, net	$38,500,000	
Investment in Acquisitive common stock (11,250 shares)	9,800,000	48,300,000
Total assets		$52,200,000
Sundry liabilities		$ 2,500,000
Common stock, $10 par	$20,000,000	
Paid-in surplus	14,700,000	
Retained earnings	15,000,000	49,700,000
Total liabilities and stockholders' equity		$52,200,000

Exhibit III
Gamma Company, Inc.
Condensed Balance Sheet
December 31, 1999

Sundry current assets		$ 4,000,000
Plant and equipment, net	$17,400,000	
Investment in Acquisitive common stock (4,500 shares)	3,100,000	20,500,000
Total assets		$24,500,000
Sundry liabilities		$ 6,500,000
Common stock (no par), 3 million shares outstanding	$14,500,000	
Retained earnings	3,500,000	18,000,000
Total liabilities and stockholders' equity		$24,500,000

Exhibit IV
Delta Corporation
Condensed Balance Sheet
December 31, 1999

Sundry current assets		$ 4,000,000
Plant and equipment, net		24,000,000
Total assets		$28,000,000
Sundry liabilities		$ 2,500,000
Bank term loan due 2002 (6%)		4,500,000
Common stock, $1 par	$ 1,000,000	
Premium on common stock	3,500,000	
Retained earnings	16,500,000	21,000,000
Total liabilities and stockholders' equity		$28,000,000

Exhibit V
Epsilon, Inc.
Condensed Balance Sheet
December 31, 1999

Sundry current assets		$12,500,000
Plant and equipment, net		$22,000,000
Total assets		$34,500,000
Sundry liabilities		$ 7,000,000
8% debentures due 1/1/2010		12,500,000
Common stock, $10 par	$ 5,000,000	
Paid-in capital	6,200,000	
Retained earnings	3,800,000	15,000,000
Total liabilities and stockholders' equity		$34,500,000

All balance sheets are before recording mergers.

The first task is to determine which of the four mergers qualify for pooling treatment. The first company to be acquired, Beta Corporation, is to be obtained in exchange for **only** the issuing corporation's shares (which suggests a pooling); but prior to the merger Beta does own some of Acquisitive Corporation's shares, seemingly in violation of the second of APB 16's criteria. According to that requirement, each entity must be independent of the other.

An exception is provided for intercorporate investments of less than 10% of the total of outstanding voting shares. Therefore, the 5% of Acquisitive's shares held by Beta will not preclude the use of pooling accounting. Although in some instances an investment of **nominally** less than 10% will become an impediment (see discussion of the Gamma case, below), the situation with Beta poses no problem. Since all other pooling criteria are also satisfied, the Acquisitive-Beta merger must be handled as a pooling.

The Gamma Company, Inc. case is more complex. At first the 2% of Acquisitive shares owned by Gamma would appear, as in the Beta case, to be no problem since the 10% rule under the second pooling criterion is not violated. However, this requirement interacts with the fourth APB 16 pooling criterion (the rule that at least 90% of an acquired entity's common stock outstanding at the consummation date must be exchanged for the issuing corporation's shares, excluding shares that were acquired before the combination plan was initiated that are still owned by the acquired entity). Using the exchange ratio, the issuing company's shares held by the acquired entity are converted into the equivalent number of acquired entity shares. This number cannot exceed 10% of the total shares of the acquired entity being exchanged.

In the current example, Gamma holds 4,500 Acquisitive shares, which at the stated exchange ratio of 1:75, are equivalent to 337,500 Gamma shares, or 11.25% of Gamma's outstanding shares. In other words, a significant part of Gamma is being obtained by Acquisitive using Gamma's own asset (its investment in the acquirer company), rather than by issuing new shares. This violates the "all at one time for the issuer's stock" requirement embodied in the fourth criterion and precludes the application of pooling accounting.

(Incidentally, the same test applied to the Beta merger has this result: 11,250 shares x 1:15 exchange ratio = 168,750 equivalent Beta shares, which is only 8.44% of Beta's outstanding stock.)

The Gamma merger would also fail to qualify for pooling treatment because the agreement provides for contingent consideration based on future earnings (violating criterion 9.). Of course, as soon as any one of the 12 tests is failed, none of the others need to be applied.

The Delta Corporation merger involves both cash and stock, raising a possible red flag since poolings are, generally, purely stock swaps among the parties to the combination. However, the "only-stock" rule relates only to that which is issued by the acquirer for the acquired entity's **voting** stock; cash or other means of payment may be given in exchange for other securities (nonvoting equity or debt) of the acquired entity. Care must be exercised in dealing with this exception, since a transaction prohibited by the 12 pooling criteria cannot be finessed by making it a transaction with two steps. For example, if more than 10% of the acquired company's shares are retired in exchange for debt within 2 years before the merger, this debt cannot then be paid off in cash by the acquirer as part of the merger arrangement. Instead, the issuing company's common stock would have to be given to these creditors/ex-stockholders.

In the Delta case, cash is used to retire the bank loan, which was not incurred in connection with a repurchase of Delta common shares. Therefore, this is not a violation of any of the pooling criteria.

The cash exchanged for the 1/2% common stockholding of dissenting owners of Delta also poses no problem, since substantially all of Delta's common shares (i.e., at least 90%) are obtained in exchange for Acquisitive's common stock. Accordingly, the Delta merger qualifies for pooling treatment.

Finally, consider the Epsilon, Inc. merger. Common shares of Epsilon are being obtained in exchange for a package of preferred and common Acquisitive shares, and additional common shares may be issued in the future if the market value of the shares originally given falls below a specified threshold. Also, the acquirer owns a large block of the acquired entity's debentures prior to the initiation of the merger.

The debenture ownership is not a problem since it is not an intercorporate investment in the sense of a voting interest in the future merger partner. Pooling treatment is precluded by two other factors, though.

The issuance of preferred stock that is nonvoting violates the fourth criterion, which demands that only voting common stock be used as payment for substantially all the common shares of the acquired entity. Also, the contingent future share issuance, violating the ninth criterion, would be enough to obviate the pooling method. Thus, the Epsilon merger must be accounted for as a purchase.

The necessary entries to record the Beta and Delta mergers as poolings on Acquisitive's books are as follows:

		Debit	Credit
1.	Sundry current assets	3,900,000	
	Plant and equipment (net)	38,500,000	
	Treasury stock	9,800,000	
	Sundry liabilities		2,500,000
	Common stock, $100 par		13,333,300
	Additional paid-in capital		21,366,700
	Retained earnings		15,000,000
	(To record Beta acquisition by pooling)		
2.	Paid-in capital	475,000	
	Sundry current assets	4,000,000	
	Plant and equipment (net)	24,000,000	
	Sundry current assets (cash)		125,000
	Sundry liabilities		2,500,000
	Demand note payable		4,250,000
	Gain on retirement of debt		250,000
	Common stock, $100 par		4,975,000
	Retained earnings		16,375,000
	(To record Delta acquisition by pooling)		

If, instead of a merger, the combination (acquisition) form is utilized, whereby Acquisitive shares are exchanged directly for Beta and Delta shares held by the respective stockholders of those companies, Beta and Delta will continue their separate existence (albeit as wholly owned subsidiaries of Acquisitive Corporation). The entries to record the transactions assuming a pooling are as follows:

		Debit	Credit
1.	Investment in Beta common	49,700,000	
	Common stock, $100 par		13,333,300
	Additional paid-in capital		21,366,700
	Retained earnings		15,000,000
	(To record acquisition of Beta shares)		
2.	Investment in Delta common	21,000,000	
	Due from Delta	4,500,000	
	Paid-in capital	475,000	
	Notes payable		4,250,000
	Cash		125,000
	Gain on retirement of debt		250,000
	Common stock, $100 par		4,975,000
	Retained earnings		16,375,000
	(To record acquisition of Delta stock, payment of bank loan, and retirement of minority shares for cash)		

The purchase accounting entries will be presented in the following section, after the basic elements of this method of accounting for business combinations are discussed. Disclosure requirements for both purchases and poolings are set forth later in this chapter.

Purchase Accounting

Any business combination (of whatever legal form) involving unrelated entities (not previously under common control) **must** be treated as a purchase if it fails any of the 12 pooling criteria. Realistically, such transactions are often "purchases" as that term is commonly understood (i.e., one entity has bought another, and the buyer is the surviving entity). Purchase accounting is an application of the cost principle, whereby assets obtained are accounted for at the price that was paid. A purchase transaction gives rise to a **new basis of accountability** for the purchased assets (and liabilities).

The major accounting issue relates to the allocation of the purchase cost to the various assets and liabilities acquired. Where the legal form of combination is a merger or a consolidation, the acquirer records all the assets and liabilities purchased at their **fair market values** (**not** the book values of the acquired entity). If the actual cost exceeds the fair value of the identifiable net assets acquired, this excess is recorded as an intangible asset (**goodwill**). A deficiency of cost under fair value is first used to reduce the fair values of all noncurrent nonmonetary assets acquired, with any balance remaining recorded as a deferred credit (erroneously called **negative goodwill**). Both goodwill and the deferred credit (negative goodwill) must be amortized, generally by the straight-line method, to earnings over not more than 40 years, according to APB 17.

If the acquisition form of combination is used, the acquired entity maintains a separate legal and accounting existence and all assets and liabilities remain at their premerger book values. However, when an **accounting consolidation** is performed (i.e., when consolidated financial statements are prepared), exactly the same results are obtained as those outlined above (i.e., assets and liabilities are adjusted to fair values, and goodwill is recorded). When less than 100% of the stock of the acquired entity is owned by the acquirer, a complication arises in the preparation of consolidated statements, and a minority interest (discussed below) must be computed.

The other major distinguishing characteristic of the purchase accounting method is that none of the equity accounts of the acquired entity (including its retained earnings) will appear on the acquirer's books or on consolidated financial statements. In other words, ownership interests of the acquired entity's shareholders are **not** continued after the merger, consolidation, or combination (acquisition) takes place.

Determining fair market values. The purchase method requires a determination of the fair market value for each of the acquired company's identifiable tangible and intangible assets and for each of its liabilities at the date of combination. The determination of these fair market values is crucial for proper application of the purchase method. The list below indicates how this is done for various assets and liabilities.

1. **Marketable securities**--Current net realizable values
2. **Receivables**--Present values of amounts to be received determined by using current interest rates, less allowances for uncollectible accounts
3. **Inventories**

   a. Finished goods and merchandise inventories--Estimated selling prices less the sum of the costs of disposal and a normal profit
   b. Work-in-process inventories--Estimated selling prices less the sum of the costs of completion, costs of disposal, and a normal profit
   c. Raw material inventories--Current replacement cost

4. **Plant and equipment**

   a. If expected to be used in operations--Current replacement costs for similar capacity unless the expected future use of the assets indicates a lower value to the acquirer
   b. If expected to be sold--Fair value less cost to sell

5. **Identifiable intangible assets and other assets** (such as land, natural resources, and nonmarketable securities)--Appraised value
6. **Liabilities** (such as notes and accounts payable, long-term debt, pensions, warranties, claims payable)--Present value of amounts to be paid determined at appropriate current interest rates

Since aggregate purchase cost is allocated to the identifiable assets (and liabilities) according to their respective fair values to the acquirer, assets having no value are assigned no cost. For example, facilities of the acquired entity which duplicate those of the acquirer and which are to be disposed of should be assigned a cost equal to estimated net salvage value, or zero if no salvage is anticipated. In rare instances, a **negative** cost equal to the estimated costs of disposal is assigned. The EITF has approved the allocation of "holding costs" to assets to be disposed of when debt from the business acquisition is to be paid down from the proceeds of such asset sales. In effect, the value assigned to such assets to be sold is the present value of the estimated selling price; interest incurred on debt used to finance these assets is then charged to the asset rather than to interest expense until the disposition actually occurs. On the other hand, if facilities of the acquired entity duplicate and are superior to facilities of the purchaser, with the intention that the latter will be disposed of, fair value must be allocated to the former. Eventual disposition of the redundant facilities of the **acquirer** may later result in a recognized gain or loss. This would fall into the general category of indirect costs of acquisition, which are not capitalizable or allocable to assets acquired in the purchase business combination.

The EITF has reached a similar conclusion with regard to entire **subsidiaries** of acquired entities. (EITF 87-11 and 90-6.) In such situations, the expected cash flows from the subsidiary's operations, through the expected date of disposition (but not longer than 1 year from the acquisition date), are considered in the purchase price allocation process. Ideally, operations of the subsidiary, including the cost of borrowed funds, if relevant, will **not** impact the acquirer's income statement, absent changes in estimates or altered plans for its disposition. Failure to achieve the planned disposition within 1 year, however, will result in all further operating results, including borrowing costs, being reported in the consolidated statement of income for future periods. Any difference between the subsidiary's carrying value at the disposition date and the proceeds of the disposition should be treated as a reallocation of the original purchase price of the business combination. If, however, the difference arises from identifiable events which occur after the merger date, gain or loss would be reported at the disposition date.

Accounting for the tax implications of purchase business combinations has changed substantially with the issuance of SFAS 109. Under prior GAAP, any existing deferred tax benefits or liabilities of the acquired entity, or any deferred tax effects created by the purchase transaction itself (e.g., due to different tax and book bases of the acquired assets or liabilities), were not recognized **as such** in the post-acquisition consolidated balance sheet of the acquirer. Instead, these tax effects were deemed to be components of the valuation process whereby the total purchase cost was allocated to acquired identifiable assets and liabilities and, when necessary, to goodwill or negative goodwill. Accordingly, purchased assets and liabilities were recorded on a net-of-tax basis under APB 16.

SFAS 109 and its immediate predecessor, SFAS 96, have completely revised the approach under which values are assigned to purchased assets and liabilities. The net-of-tax method is prohibited; instead, values are assigned "gross," and tax effects, if any, are recorded in deferred tax accounts. Under the SFAS 109 "asset and liability" approach to deferred tax accounting (detailed in Chapter 15), deferred tax liabilities and assets are evaluated and adjusted at the date of each balance sheet. Therefore, any deferred taxes of an acquired entity, or any deferred taxes generated by the acquisition transaction itself, are now formally recognized in recording the purchase business combination. In fact, if an acquired entity has unrecorded deferred tax benefits which can be used to offset the acquirer's deferred tax liabilities, these benefits can also be recognized in the postacquisition balance sheet. Similarly, under the provisions of SFAS 109, the NOL benefits of an acquired entity will also be recognized in the balance sheet of the acquirer, if the acquirer can utilize those benefits under existing tax law. The gross amount of the tax benefits will always be recorded if the benefits are available to the acquirer. An offsetting valuation allowance will also be recorded if it is **more likely than not** that it will not be realized by the reporting entity (for example, if it is estimated that there will not be future taxable income against which to absorb the net operating losses).

Under APB 11, subsequent realization of unrecognized NOL benefits of an acquired entity necessitated reallocation of the purchase cost and possibly restatement of amortization and depreciation (and therefore net income) since the date of the purchase business combination. Under SFAS 109, only goodwill and other noncurrent intangible assets are adjusted (and then only **prospectively**, so prior earnings are never restated) for previously unrecognized (i.e., having a valuation allowance equal in amount to the deferred tax benefit) NOL benefits that are subsequently recognized. Benefits exceeding recorded goodwill and other tangibles are credited to income tax expense (not extraordinary income) in the period when first recognized. (See Chapter 15 for details.)

The 1993 Tax Reconciliation Act provides for amortization of goodwill over a 15-year period. Thus, if the management of an enterprise selects a longer or shorter amortization period, a temporary difference will result.

Direct costs of the acquisition (e.g., finders' fees) are part of the cost to be allocated to tangible and intangible assets, including goodwill. However, stock registration and related expenses are offset against the proceeds (credits) of the stock issuance. Indirect costs are simply expensed in the period when the combination is effected.

In some instances, there are alternative ways to handle certain costs, influencing their treatment as either direct or indirect costs of a business acquisition. For example, if a prospective acquiree company has employee stock options outstanding, and it pays the employees to settle the options prior to the acquisition, then (per APB 25, as later interpreted by the EITF in 84-13 and 85-45) compensation expense must be recognized. On the other hand, if the employees exercise their options and then have their shares purchased by the acquirer (or exchanged for stock in the acquirer), there is no compensation expense but instead an additional cost of the purchase.

In certain instances, allocation of purchase cost will be unclear. For example, if an acquired entity has a postretirement benefits program, under current GAAP no liability will have been accrued by that entity although a real economic obligation exists. It is likely, however, that this obligation will have been considered in arriving at the price paid for the purchase acquisition. Therefore, the fair value of the obligation should be recorded. However, the EITF failed to reach a consensus on this issue, noting that in practice, a liability may or may not be reflected. At the time, the Task Force determined that the allocation of purchase price to this previously unrecorded liability did not mean that the acquiree would have to use the accrual method thereafter; that conclusion is moot now that SFAS 106 has become fully effective. There will, however, continue to be other areas where the allocation of purchase costs are subject to varying interpretations.

Costs related to a takeover defense by a prospective acquiree company are not capitalized, but are expenses of the period incurred. However, the EITF has suggested that if the costs are related to a so-called "going private" transaction, these expenses may be classified as an extraordinary item in the statement of income.

In some takeover defense strategies, a target company will repurchase some of its own shares, generally at a price higher than that being offered by the prospective acquirer. Although generally the cost of repurchased stock is simply charged to the treasury stock account, there is the recognition that excessive repurchase costs are not always related to the "fair value" of the stock, per se. When the price paid explicitly contains consideration for the seller's agreement not to purchase any further shares (a so-called "standstill agreement"), this excess cost must be expensed (per Technical Bulletin 85-6), with only the fair market value of the shares themselves being charged to the treasury stock account. The EITF did not reach a consensus about the treatment of excessive costs of treasury shares absent explicit payment for other services. However, the SEC favors expensing any excess costs. As a general rule, judgment should be applied in evaluating each circumstance.

Example of accounting for a purchase

Continuing the acquisitive corporation example begun in the pooling-of-interests discussion (pages 375-383), the journal entries to record the purchase of the Gamma Company, Inc. and Epsilon, Inc. shares will be presented. Tax effects are ignored in these examples.

Using the fair market value information given earlier and assuming that a legal merger (or consolidation) form is used, Acquisitive makes these entries

1.	Sundry current assets	4,000,000	
	Plant and equipment	19,080,000	
	Treasury stock	3,100,000	
	Sundry liabilities		6,500,000
	Common stock, $100 par		4,000,000
	Additional paid-in capital		15,680,000
	(To record purchase of net assets of Gamma)		

2. Sundry current assets	12,500,000	
Plant and equipment	27,000,000	
Sundry liabilities		7,000,000
8% debentures		12,500,000
Preferred stock, $100 par		3,333,300
Premium on preferred		266,864
Common stock, $100 par		3,333,300
Additional paid-in capital		13,066,536
(To record purchase of net assets of Epsilon)		

The value of the Gamma purchase was determined by reference to the latest market value of the Acquisitive shares given ($492 per share). Notice that although the price paid was slightly greater than net **book** value ($19.68 million vs. $18 million), it was considerably less than estimated fair value ($36 million net). In other words, there was an excess of fair value over cost which, in accordance with the procedures specified by APB 16, was allocated against plant and equipment (the only noncurrent asset). Had this deficiency been large enough to reduce plant and equipment to zero, any remaining amount would have been recorded as a deferred credit (excess of fair value of net assets acquired over cost) and systematically amortized, like goodwill, over not more than 40 years (APB 17).

The total value of the Epsilon purchase was $20 million. Deducting the known market value of Acquisitive common shares from this purchase value revealed the apparent value assigned to the new Acquisitive preferred stock. The total price exceeded the net book value of Epsilon's identifiable assets but was lower than the fair value thereof, so again there is an excess of fair value over cost, and the noncurrent assets are recorded at less than their fair values.

If the acquisition form is used instead, the entries by the parent company would be as follows:

1. Investment in Gamma common	19,680,000	
Common stock, $100 par		4,000,000
Additional paid-in capital		15,680,000
2. Investment in Epsilon common	20,000,000	
Preferred stock, $100 par		3,333,300
Premium on preferred		266,864
Common stock, $100 par		3,333,300
Additional paid-in capital		13,066,536

Example of consolidation workpaper (date of acquisition, 100% ownership)

The worksheet for the preparation of a consolidated balance sheet for Acquisitive Corp. and its four wholly-owned subsidiaries at the date of the acquisitions is shown below. Remember that it is presumed that Acquisitive (the parent) acquired the common stock of each subsidiary; had it acquired the net assets directly (through a legal merger or a consolidation), this **accounting consolidation** would not be necessary.

Except for Epsilon, the entries are straightforward and need no further explanation, as they are necessary to eliminate the investment accounts of the parent and the equity accounts of the subsidiaries. Note that there are upward adjustments to the plant and equipment relative to the **purchases** of Gamma and Epsilon. The **poolings** of Beta and Delta result in their book values being carried forward.

Acquisitive Corporation and Subsidiaries
Workpapers for Consolidated Balance Sheet
As of December 31, 1999

	Acquisitive Corp.	*Beta Corp.*	*Gamma Co., Inc.*	*Delta Corp.*	*Epsilon, Inc.*	*Elimination entries*	*Consolidated balance sheet*
Current assets	$70,625,000	$ 3,900,000	$ 4,000,000	$ 4,000,000	$12,500,000	$ --	$ 95,025,000
Plant and equipment	80,000,000	38,500,000	17,400,000	24,000,000	22,000,000	1,680,000 [c]	188,580,000
						5,000,000 [f]	
Investments:							
Epsilon 8% debentures	4,900,000					(4,900,000) [g]	
Acquisitive stock		9,800,000	3,100,000			(9,800,000) [b]	
						(3,100,000) [d]	
Beta Corp.	49,700,000					(49,700,000) [a]	
Gamma Co., Inc.	19,680,000					(19,680,000) [c]	
Delta Corp.	25,500,000					(25,500,000) [e]	
Epsilon, Inc.	20,000,000					(20,000,000) [f]	
	$270,405,000	$52,200,000	$24,500,000	$28,000,000	$34,500,000		$283,605,000
Current liabilities	$ 87,000,000	$ 2,500,000	$ 6,500,000	$ 7,000,000	$ 7,000,000	$ (4,500,000) [e]	$105,500,000
8% debentures					12,500,000	(5,000,000) [g]	7,500,000
Preferred stock, $100 par	3,333,300						3,333,300
Premium on pfd. stock	266,864						266,864
Common stock							
$100 par	48,141,600						48,141,600
$10 par		20,000,000				(20,000,000) [a]	
No par			14,500,000			(14,500,000) [c]	
$1 par				1,000,000		(1,000,000) [e]	
$10 par					5,000,000	(5,000,000) [f]	
Additional paid-in capital, etc.	61,838,236	14,700,000		3,500,000	6,200,000	(14,700,000) [a]	61,838,236
						(3,500,000) [e]	
						(6,200,000) [f]	
Retained earnings	69,825,000	15,000,000	3,500,000	16,500,000	3,800,000	(15,000,000) [a]	
						(3,500,000) [c]	
						(16,500,000) [e]	69,925,000
						(3,800,000) [f]	
						100,000 [g]	
	$270,405,000	$52,200,000	$24,500,000	$28,000,000	$34,500,000		
Treasury stock (at cost)						(9,800,000) [b]	(12,900,000)
						(3,100,000) [d]	
							$283,605,000

The elimination of the investment in Epsilon debentures needs explanation. The parent paid $4,880,000 for debentures having a $5 million par on January 1, 1998. The discount has been properly amortized in 1998 and 1999, so that the carrying value at the date of acquisition of Epsilon is $4,900,000. Therefore, on a **consolidated** basis, debt of

$5 million has been extinguished at a cost of $4.9 million, for a gain on retirement of $100,000. Per APB 26, this gain will appear on the consolidated statement of income and will be classified as extraordinary (SFAS 4) if material. Since the workpapers shown are only for the preparation of a consolidated balance sheet, the gain has been credited to retained earnings. This gain could also be recorded on the books of the parent, Acquisitive Corp., which would make its retained earnings equal to consolidated retained earnings.

Minority Interests in Purchase and Pooling Combinations

When a company acquires some, but not all, of the voting stock of another entity, the shares held by third parties represent a **minority interest** in the acquired company. This occurs when the acquisition form is employed. A legal merger or consolidation would give the acquirer a 100% interest in whatever assets it obtained from the selling entity. Under GAAP, if a parent company owns more than half of another entity, the two should be consolidated for financial statement purposes (unless control is temporary or the parent company does not have control over the subsidiary). The minority interest in the assets and earnings of the consolidated entity must also be accounted for.

When consolidated statements are prepared, the full amount of assets and liabilities (in the balance sheet) and income and expenses (in the income statement) of the subsidiary are generally presented. Accordingly, a contra must be shown for the portion of these items that does not belong to the parent company. In the balance sheet this contra is normally a credit item shown between total liabilities and stockholders' equity, representing the minority interest in consolidated net assets equal to the minority's percentage ownership in the net assets of the subsidiary entity. Although less likely, a debit balance in minority interest could result when the subsidiary has a deficit in its stockholders' equity **and** when there is reason to believe that the minority owners will make additional capital contributions to erase that deficit. This situation sometimes occurs where the entities are closely held and the minority owners are related parties having other business relationships with the parent company and/or its stockholders. In most other circumstances, a debit in minority interest would be charged against parent company retained earnings under the concept that the loss will be borne by that company. Although some believe that this debit should be added to goodwill on the consolidated balance sheet instead, it might be difficult to demonstrate that this would not result in an overstatement of total assets.

In the income statement, the minority interest in the income (or loss) of a consolidated subsidiary is shown as a deduction from (or addition to) the consolidated net income account. As above, if the minority interest in the net assets of the subsidiary has already been reduced to zero, and if a net debit minority interest will **not** be recorded (the usual case), then the minority's interest in any further losses should **not** be recorded. (However, this must be explained in the footnotes.) Furthermore, if past minority losses have not been recorded, the minority's interest in current profits will not be recognized until the aggregate of such profits equals the aggregate unrecognized losses. This closely parallels the rule for equity method accounting recognition of profits and losses.

Example of consolidation process involving a minority interest

Assume the following:

Alto Company and Bass Company
Balance Sheets at 1/1/99
(Immediately before combination)

	Alto Company	*Bass Company*
Assets		
Cash	$ 30,900	$ 37,400
Accounts receivable (net)	34,200	9,100
Inventories	22,900	16,100
Equipment	200,000	50,000
Less accumulated depreciation	(21,000)	(10,000)
Patents	--	10,000
Total assets	$267,000	$112,600
Liabilities and stockholders' equity		
Accounts payable	$ 4,000	$ 6,600
Bonds payable, 10%	100,000	--
Common stock, $10 par	100,000	50,000
Additional paid-in capital	15,000	15,000
Retained earnings	48,000	41,000
Total liabilities and stockholders' equity	$267,000	$112,600

Note that the book value of the net assets of Bass Company may be computed by one of the following two methods:

1. Subtract the book value of the liability from the book values of the assets.

$112,600 – $6,600 = $106,000

2. Add the book values of the components of Bass Company stockholders' equity.

$50,000 + $15,000 + $41,000 = $106,000

At the date of combination, the fair values of all the assets and liabilities were determined by appraisal, as follows:

Bass Company Item	*Book value (BV)*	*Fair market value (FMV)*	*Difference between BV and FMV*
Cash	$ 37,400	$ 37,400	$ --
Accounts receivable (net)	9,100	9,100	--
Inventories	16,100	17,100	1,000
Equipment (net)	40,000	48,000	8,000
Patents	10,000	13,000	3,000
Accounts payable	(6,600)	(6,600)	--
Totals	$106,000	$118,000	$12,000

When a minority interest exists, as in this example, the concept employed will determine whether the consolidated balance sheet reflects the **full** excess of fair market values over book values of the subsidiary's net assets, or only the parent company's percentage share thereof. Under the **parent company** concept, only the parent's share of the revaluation is recognized, and minority interest is reported based on the book value of the subsidiary. If the **entity concept** is used, however, the full revaluation from book to fair value is recognized in the consolidated balance sheet, and the minority interest is based on the fair value of the subsidiary's net assets. Both techniques are acceptable.

Assume the following:

1. On January 1, 1999, Alto Company acquires a 90% interest in Bass Company in exchange for 5,400 shares of $10 par stock having a total market value of $120,600.
2. The purchase method of accounting is used for the combination.
3. Any goodwill resulting from the combination will be amortized over a period of 10 years.

The workpaper for a consolidated balance sheet at the date of acquisition is presented below. The first two columns are the trial balances from the books of Alto Company and Bass Company immediately following the acquisition.

Alto Company and Bass Company Consolidated Working Papers
For Date of Combination--1/1/99

Purchase accounting
90% interest

	Alto Company	*Bass Company*	*Adjustments and eliminations Debit*	*Credit*	*Minority interest*	*Consolidated balances*
Balance sheet, 1/1/99						
Cash	$ 30,900	$ 37,400				$ 68,300
Accounts receivable	34,200	9,100				43,300
Inventories	22,900	16,100	$ 900b			39,900
Equipment	200,000	50,000	9,000b			259,000
Accumulated depreciation	(21,000)	(10,000)		$ 1,800b		(32,800)
Investment in stock of Bass Company	120,600			120,600a		
Difference between cost and book value			25,200a	25,200b		
Excess of cost over fair value (goodwill)			14,400b			14,400
Patents	———	10,000	2,700b			12,700
Total assets	$387,600	$112,600				$404,800
Accounts payable	$ 4,000	$ 6,600				$ 10,600
Bonds payable	100,000					100,000
Capital stock	154,000	50,000	45,000a		$ 5,000	154,000
Additional paid-in capital	81,600	15,000	13,500a		1,500	81,600
Retained earnings	48,000	41,000	36,900a		4,100	48,000
Minority interest	———	———	———	———	$10,600	10,600 MI
Total liabilities and equity	$387,600	$112,600	$147,600	$147,600		$404,800

1. Investment on Alto Company's books

   The entry to record the 90% purchase-acquisition on Alto Company's books was

Investment in stock of Bass Company	120,600	
Capital stock		54,000
Additional paid-in capital		66,600

   (To record the issuance of 5,400 shares of $10 par stock to acquire a 90% interest in Bass Company)

   Although common stock is used for the consideration in our example, Alto Company could have used debentures, cash, or any other form of consideration acceptable to Bass Company's stockholders to make the **purchase** combination.

2. Difference between investment cost and book value

   The difference between the investment cost and the parent company's equity in the net assets of the subsidiary is computed as follows:

Investment cost		$120,600
Less book value % at date of combination		
Bass Company's		
Capital stock	$ 50,000	
Additional paid-in capital	15,000	
Retained earnings	41,000	
Total	$106,000	
Parent's share of ownership	x 90%	
Parent's share of book value		95,400
Excess of cost over book value		$ 25,200

This difference is due to several undervalued assets and to unrecorded goodwill. The allocation procedure is similar to that for a 100% purchase; however, in this case, the parent company obtained a 90% interest and, thus, will recognize 90% of the difference between the fair market values and book values of the subsidiary's assets, not 100%. The allocation is presented as follows:

Allocation of the Differential

Item	*Book value (BV)*	*Fair market value (FMV)*	*Difference between BV and (FMV)*	*Ownership percentage*	*Percentage share of difference between BV and FMV*
Cash	$ 37,400	$ 37,400	$ --		
Accounts receivable (net)	9,100	9,100	--		
Inventories	16,100	17,100	1,000	90%	$ 900
Equipment	50,000	60,000	10,000	90%	9,000
Accumulated depreciation	(10,000)	(12,000)	(2,000)	90%	(1,800)
Patents	10,000	13,000	3,000	90%	2,700
Accounts payable	(6,600)	(6,600)	--		
Total	$106,000	$118,000	$12,000		

Amount of difference between cost and book value share allocated to revaluation of net assets	$10,800
Total differential	25,200
Remainder allocated to goodwill	$14,400

The equipment has a book value of $40,000 ($50,000 less 20% depreciation of $10,000). An appraisal concluded that the equipment's replacement cost was $60,000 less 20% accumulated depreciation of $12,000 resulting in a net fair value of $48,000.

3. Elimination entries on workpaper

The basic reciprocal accounts are the investment in subsidiary account on the parent's books and the subsidiary's stockholders' equity accounts. Only the parent's share of the subsidiary's accounts may be eliminated as reciprocal accounts. The remaining 10% portion is allocated to the minority interest. The entries below include documentation showing the company source for the information. The workpaper entry to eliminate the basic reciprocal accounts is as follows:

Capital stock--Bass Co.	45,000	
Additional paid-in capital--Bass Co.	13,500	
Retained earnings--Bass Co.	36,900*	
Differential	25,200	
Investment in stock of Bass Co.--Alto Co.		120,600

**($41,000 x 90% = $36,900)*

Note that only 90% of Bass Company's stockholders' equity accounts are eliminated. Also, an account called differential is debited in the workpaper entry. The differential account is a temporary account to record the difference between the cost of the investment in Bass Company from the parent's books and the book value of the parent's interest (90% in our case) from the subsidiary's books.

The next step is to allocate the differential to the specific accounts by making the following workpaper entry:

Inventory	900	
Equipment	9,000	
Patents	2,700	
Goodwill	14,400	
Accumulated depreciation		1,800
Differential		25,200

This entry reflects the allocations prepared in step 2 on the previous page and recognizes the parent's share of the asset revaluations.

The minority interest column is the 10% interest of Bass Company's net assets owned by outside, third parties. Minority interest must be disclosed because 100% of the book values of Bass Company are included in the consolidated statements, although Alto Company controls only 90% of the net assets. An alternative method to prove minority interest is to multiply the net assets of the subsidiary by the minority interest share, as follows:

Stockholders' equity of Bass Company	x	Minority interest %	=	Minority interest
$106,000	x	10%	=	$10,600

The $10,600 would be reported on the credit side of the consolidated balance sheet between liabilities and stockholders' equity.

The **parent company concept** was used above to prepare the consolidated balance sheet. If the **entity concept** had been employed, minority interest would have been as follows:

Total fair market value of net assets of Bass Company	x	Minority percentage	=	Minority interest
$118,000	x	10%	=	$11,800

The example does not include any other intercompany accounts as of the date of combination. If any existed, they would be eliminated to fairly present the consolidated entity. Several examples of other reciprocal accounts will be shown later for the preparation of consolidated financial statements subsequent to the date of acquisition.

If the previous example were accounted for on a push-down basis, Bass would record the following entry on its books:

Inventories	1,000	
Equipment	10,000	
Patents	3,000	
Accumulated depreciation		2,000
Paid-in capital		12,000

As a result, Alto would have an investment of $120,600 in a company whose net equity was $118,000. Then 90% x $118,000 or $106,200 contrasted with the cost of $120,600 would mean the only number unaccounted for by Alto would be goodwill of $14,400. The elimination entry on the worksheet would change only with respect to the paid-in capital of Bass as follows:

Capital stock	45,000	
Paid-in capital	24,300	
Retained earnings	36,900	
Goodwill	14,400	
Investment		120,600

This would leave $5,000 of capital stock, $2,700 of paid-in capital, and $4,100 of retained earnings as minority interest or the same $11,800 as under the entity concept.

Example of consolidation for pooling involving minority interest

The foregoing entries are based on the combination being accounted for as a purchase. The same example will now be used to demonstrate the pooling-of-interests method applied to a minority interest situation. Assume the following:

1. On January 1, 1999, Alto Company acquired a 90% interest in Bass Company in exchange for 5,400 shares of $10 par value stock of Alto Company.
2. All criteria for a pooling have been met, and the combination is treated as a pooling of interests.

The workpaper for a consolidated balance sheet at the date of combination is presented below. Note that the first two columns are trial balances of Alto Company and Bass Company immediately after the combination was recorded by Alto Company.

1. Investment entry recorded on Alto Company's books
   The following entry was made by Alto Company to record its 90% acquisition-pooling of Bass Company:

Investment in stock of Bass Co.	95,400	
Capital stock, $10 par		54,000
Additional paid-in capital		4,500
Retained earnings		36,900

Alto Company and Bass Company Consolidated Working Papers
For Date of Combination--1/1/99

Pooling accounting
90% interest

	Alto Company	*Bass Company*	*Adjustments and eliminations* Debit	Credit	*Minority interest*	*Consolidated balances*
Balance sheet, 1/1/99						
Cash	$ 30,900	$ 37,400				$ 68,300
Accounts receivable	34,200	9,100				43,300
Inventories	22,900	16,100				39,900
Equipment	200,000	50,000				250,000
Accumulated depreciation	(21,000)	(10,000)				(31,000)
Investment in stock of Bass Company	95,400			$95,400a		
Patents		10,000				10,000
Total assets	$362,400	$112,600				$379,600
Accounts payable	$ 4,000	$ 6,600				$ 10,600
Bonds payable	100,000					100,000
Capital stock	154,000	50,000	45,000a		$ 5,000	154,000
Additional paid-in capital	19,500	15,000	13,500a		1,500	19,500
Retained earnings	84,900	41,000	36,900a		4,100	84,900
Minority interest					$10,600	10,600 MI
Total liabilities and equity	$362,400	$112,600	$95,400	$95,400		$379,600

The investment entry reflects the capital mix for a pooling of less than a 100% investment. The following schedule shows the mix for our 90% combination accomplished by the issuance of 5,400 shares of Alto Company's $10 par stock:

	Bass Company	*Alto Company's percentage share*	*Alto's share of Bass's equity*
Capital stock	$ 50,000	90%	$45,000
Additional paid-in capital	15,000	90%	13,500
Retained earnings	41,000	90%	36,900
	$106,000		$95,400

The $54,000 (5,400 shares x $10 par) in new capital issued by Alto Company represents $45,000 from Bass Company's capital stock and $9,000 of the $13,500 Bass Company's additional paid-in capital. Note that the remaining $4,500 of capital and $36,900 of Bass Company's retained earnings are carried over to Alto Company's books in the combination date entry. The $10,600 of Bass's capital that is not carried over to Alto will eventually be shown as minority interest on the consolidated balance sheet.

2. Elimination entry on workpaper

   Pooling accounting uses book values as a basis of valuation; therefore, no differential will ever occur in a pooling. The reciprocal accounts in a pooling consolidated balance sheet are in the investment in stock of Bass Company account from the parent's books and the stockholders' equity accounts from the subsidiary's books. Again, note that only 90% of the equity of Bass Company is being eliminated; the 10% remainder will be recognized as minority interest. The workpaper elimination entry is

Capital stock--Bass Co.	45,000	
Additional paid-in capital--Bass Co.	13,500	
Retained earnings--Bass Co.	36,900*	
Investment in stock of Bass Co.--Alto Co.		95,400

**($41,000 x 90% = $36,900)*

Consolidated Statements (Purchase and Pooling) in Subsequent Periods

The same concepts employed to prepare a consolidated balance sheet at the date of acquisition are applicable to later consolidated statements. Where a minority interest exists, income in subsequent periods must be allocated to it. The exact nature of the worksheet entries depends on whether the parent is maintaining the investment in subsidiary account on the cost, partial equity, or full equity basis (all of which are acceptable since the consolidated financial statements will be identical under any alternative). In practice, the cost and partial equity methods are most likely to be encountered. The partial equity method is used when separate, parent-only statements are expected to be prepared in addition to consolidated statements (which commonly is the case). Using the partial equity method, the parent records its share of the subsidiary's income or loss but does not amortize the differential between cost and book value against equity in the subsidiary's earnings.

In addition to the elimination entries for the parent investment account and subsidiary equity accounts, other eliminations will be needed when there are intercompany balances or transactions resulting from parent-subsidiary loans (advances), sales of inventory items (whether or not these occurred at a profit to the seller), sales of fixed assets at other than net book value, and bond transactions or transactions in stock other than voting common shares. The selected items in the following example will demonstrate the accounting issues applicable to all such intercompany items and the proper handling of these items in the consolidated workpapers.

Example of a consolidation in subsequent periods

The basic facts of the Alto Company-Bass Company case have already been presented; additional information is as follows:

1. Alto Company uses the partial equity method to record changes in the value of the investment account.
2. During 1999, Alto Company sold merchandise to Bass Company that originally cost Alto Company $15,000, and the sale was made for $20,000. On December 31, 1999, Bass Company's inventory included merchandise purchased from Alto Company at a cost to Bass Company of $12,000.
3. Also during 1999, Alto Company acquired $18,000 of merchandise from Bass Company. Bass Company uses a normal markup of 25% above its cost. Alto Company's ending inventory includes $10,000 of the merchandise acquired from Bass Company.
4. Bass Company reduced its intercompany account payable to Alto Company to a balance of $4,000 as of December 31, 1999, by making a payment of $1,000 on December 30. This $1,000 payment was still in transit on December 31, 1999.
5. On January 2, 1999, Bass Company acquired equipment from Alto Company for $7,000. The equipment was originally purchased by Alto Company for $5,000 and had a book value of $4,000 at the date of sale to Bass Company. The equipment had an estimated remaining life of 4 years as of January 2, 1999.
6. On December 31, 1999, Bass Company purchased for $44,000, 50% of the outstanding bonds issued by Alto Company. The bonds mature on December 31, 2004, and were originally issued at par. The bonds pay interest annually on December 31 of each year, and the interest was paid to the prior investor immediately before Bass Company's purchase of the bonds.

The worksheet for the preparation of consolidated financial statements as of December 31, 1999, is presented below, on the assumption that purchase accounting is used for the business combination.

The investment account balance at the statement date should be reconciled to ensure the parent company made the proper entries under the method of accounting used to account for the investment. Since the partial equity method is used by Alto, the amortizations of the excess of cost over book value will be recognized only on the worksheets.

An analysis of the investment account at December 31, 1999, is as follows:

	Investment in Stock of Bass Company (Dr.)	Investment in Stock of Bass Company (Cr.)	
Original cost	120,600		
% of Bass Co.'s income ($9,400 x 90%)	8,460	3,600	% of Bass Co.'s dividends declared ($4,000 x 90%)
Balance, 12/31/99	125,460		

Any errors will require correcting entries before the consolidation process is continued. Correcting entries will be posted to the books of the appropriate company; eliminating entries are **not** posted to either company's books.

The difference between the investment cost and the book value of the net assets acquired was determined and allocated in the preparation of the date of combination consolidated statements presented earlier. The same computations are used in preparing financial statements for as long as the investment is owned.

The following adjusting and eliminating entries will be required to prepare consolidated financials as of December 31, 1999. Note that a consolidated income statement is required and, therefore, the nominal accounts are still open. The number or letter in parentheses to the left of the entry corresponds to the key used on the worksheet.

Step 1 -- Complete the transaction for any intercompany items in transit at the end of the year.

(1)	Cash	1,000	
	Accounts receivable		1,000

This **adjusting** entry will now properly present the financial positions of both companies, and the consolidation process may be continued.

Step 2 -- Prepare the eliminating entries.

(a)	Sales	38,000	
	Cost of goods sold		38,000

Total intercompany sales of $38,000 include $20,000 in a downstream transaction from Alto Company to Bass Company and $18,000 in an upstream transaction from Bass Company to Alto Company.

(b)	Cost of goods sold	5,000	
	Inventory		5,000

The ending inventories are overstated because of the unrealized profit from the intercompany sales. The debit to cost of goods sold is required because a decrease in ending inventory will increase cost of goods sold to be deducted on the income statement. Supporting computations for the entry are as follows:

	In ending inventory of	
	Alto Company	Bass Company
Intercompany sales not resold, at selling price	$10,000	$12,000
Cost basis of remaining intercompany merchandise		
From Bass to Alto (÷ 125%)	(8,000)	
From Alto to Bass (÷ 133 1/3%)		(9,000)
Unrealized profit	$ 2,000	$ 3,000

When preparing consolidated workpapers for 2000 (the next fiscal period), an additional eliminating entry will be required if the goods in 1999's ending inventory are sold to outsiders during 2000. The additional entry will recognize the profit for 2000 that was eliminated as unrealized in 1999. This entry is necessary since the entry at the end of 1999 was made only on the worksheet. The 2000 entry will be as follows:

		Debit	Credit
	Retained earnings--Bass Co., 1/1/00	2,000	
	Retained earnings--Alto Co., 1/1/00	3,000	
	Cost of goods sold, 2000		5,000
(c)	Accounts payable	4,000	
	Accounts receivable		4,000

This entry eliminates the remaining intercompany receivable/payable owed by Bass Company to Alto Company. This eliminating entry is necessary to avoid overstating the consolidated entity's balance sheet. The receivable/payable is not extinguished, and Bass Company must still transfer $4,000 to Alto Company in the future.

		Debit	Credit
(d)	Gain on sale of equipment	3,000	
	Equipment		2,000
	Accumulated depreciation		250
	Depreciation expense		750

This entry eliminates the gain on the intercompany sale of the equipment, eliminates the overstatement of equipment, and removes the excess depreciation taken on the gain. Supporting computations for the entry are as follows:

	Cost	*At date of intercompany sale accum. depr.*	*1999 depr. ex.*	*End-of-period accum. depr.*
Original basis (to seller, Alto Co.)	$5,000	($1,000)	$ 1,000	($2,000)
New basis (to buyer, Bass Co.)	7,000	--	1,750	(1,750)
Difference	($2,000)		($ 750)	$ 250

If the intercompany sale had not occurred, Alto Company would have depreciated the remaining book value of $4,000 over the estimated remaining life of 4 years. However, since Bass Company's acquisition price ($7,000) was more than Alto Company's basis in the asset ($4,000), the depreciation recorded on the books of Bass Company will include part of the intercompany unrealized profit. The equipment must be reflected on the consolidated statements at the original cost to the consolidated entity. Therefore, the write-up of $2,000 in the equipment, the excess depreciation of $750, and the gain of $3,000 must be eliminated. The ending balance of accumulated depreciation must be shown at what it would have been if the intercompany equipment transaction had not occurred. In future periods, a retained earnings account will be used instead of the gain account; however, the other concepts will be extended to include the additional periods.

(e)	Bonds payable	50,000	
	Investment in bonds of Alto Company		44,000
	Gain on extinguishment of debt		6,000

This entry eliminates the book value of Alto Company's debt against the bond investment account of Bass Company. To the consolidated entity, this transaction must be shown as a retirement of debt even though Alto Company has the outstanding intercompany debt to Bass Company. SFAS 4 specifies that gains or losses on debt extinguishment, if material, should be shown as an extraordinary item. In future periods, Bass Company will amortize the discount, thereby bringing the investment account up to par value. A retained earnings account will be used in the eliminating entry instead of the gain account.

(f)	Equity in subsidiary's income--Alto Co.	8,460	
	Dividends declared--Bass Co.		3,600
	Investment in stock of Alto Co.		4,860

This elimination entry adjusts the investment account back to its balance at the beginning of the period and also eliminates the subsidiary income account.

(g)	Capital stock--Bass Co.	45,000	
	Additional paid-in capital--Bass Co.	13,500	
	Retained earnings--Bass Co.	36,900	
	Differential	25,200	
	Investment in stock of Bass Company--Alto Co.		120,600

This entry eliminates 90% of Bass Company's stockholders' equity at the beginning of the year, 1/1/99. Note that the changes **during** the year were eliminated in entry (f) above. The differential account reflects the excess of investment cost over the book value of the assets acquired.

(h)	Inventory	900	
	Equipment	9,000	
	Patents	2,700	
	Goodwill	14,400	
	Accumulated depr.		1,800
	Differential		25,200

This entry allocates the differential (excess of investment cost over the book values of the assets acquired). Note that this entry is the same as the allocation entry made to prepare consolidated financial statements for January 1, 1999, the date of acquisition.

		Debit	Credit
(i)	Cost of goods sold	900	
	Depreciation expense	1,800	
	Other operating expenses--patent amortization	270	
	Other operating expenses--goodwill amortization	1,440	
	Inventory		900
	Accumulated depr.		1,800
	Patents		270
	Goodwill		1,440

The elimination entry amortizes the revaluations to fair market value made in entry (h). The inventory has been sold and, therefore, becomes part of cost of goods sold. The remaining revaluations will be amortized as follows:

	Revaluation	*Amortization period*	*Annual amortization*
Equipment (net)	$7,200	4 years	$1,800
Patents	2,700	10 years	270
Goodwill	14,400	10 years	1,440

The amortizations will continue to be made on future worksheets. For example, at the end of the next year (2000), the amortization entry (i) would be as follows:

	Debit	Credit
Differential	4,410	
Depreciation expense	1,800	
Other operating expenses--patent amortization	270	
Other operating expenses--goodwill amortization	1,440	
Inventory		900
Accumulated depr.		3,600
Patents		540
Goodwill		2,880

The initial debit of $4,410 to differential is an aggregation of the prior period's charges to income statement accounts ($900 + $1,800 + $270 + $1,440). During subsequent years, some accountants prefer reducing the allocated amounts in entry (h) for prior period's charges. In this case, the amortization entry in future periods would reflect just that period's amortizations.

All the foregoing entries were based on the assumption that the acquisition was accounted for as a purchase. Had the pooling-of-interests method been used, however, book value rather than fair value would have been the basis for recording the accounting consolidation entries. Thus, entry (g) above would be different while entries (h) and (i) would **not** be made for a pooling. All other eliminating entries would be the same. The basic elimination entry (g) for a pooling, using the equity method of accounting for the investment, would be as follows:

Capital stock--Bass Co.	45,000	
Additional paid-in capital--Bass Co.	13,500	
Retained earnings--Bass Co.	36,900	
Investment in stock of Bass Co.		95,400

In adjusting for the minority interest in the consolidated entity's equity and earnings, the following guidelines should be observed:

1. Only the parent's share of the subsidiary's shareholders' equity is eliminated in the basic eliminating entry. The minority interest's share is presented separately.
2. The entire amount of intercompany reciprocal items is eliminated. For example, all receivables/payables and sales/cost of sales with a 90% subsidiary are eliminated.
3. For intercompany transactions in inventory and fixed assets, the possible effect on minority interest depends on whether the original transaction affected the subsidiary's income statement. Minority interest is adjusted only if the subsidiary is the selling entity. In this case, the minority interest is adjusted for its percentage ownership of the common stock of the subsidiary. The minority interest is **not** adjusted for unrealized profits on downstream sales. The effects of downstream transactions are confined solely to the parent's (i.e., controlling) ownership interests.

The minority interest's share of the subsidiary's income is shown as a deduction on the consolidated income statement since 100% of the sub's revenues and expenses are combined, even though the parent company owns less than a 100% interest. For our example, the minority interest deduction on the income statement is computed as follows:

Bass Company's reported income	$9,400
Less unrealized profit on an upstream inventory sale	(2,000)
Bass Company's income for consolidated financial purposes	$7,400
Minority interest share	x 10%
Minority interest on income statement	$ 740

The minority interest's share of the net assets of Bass Company is shown on the consolidated balance sheet between liabilities and controlling interest's equity. The computation for the minority interest shown in the balance sheet for our example is as follows:

Bass Company's capital stock, 12/31/99	$50,000	
Minority interest share	x 10%	$ 5,000
Bass Company's additional paid-in capital, 12/31/99	$15,000	
Minority interest share	x 10%	1,500
Bass Company's retained earnings, 1/1/99	$41,000	
Minority interest share	x 10%	4,100
Bass Company's 1999 income for consolidated purposes	$ 7,400	
Minority interest share	x 10%	740
Bass Company's dividends during 1999	$ 4,000	
Minority interest share	x 10%	(400)
Total minority interest, 12/31/99		$10,940

Alto Company and Bass Company Consolidated Working Papers
Year Ended December 31, 1999

Purchase accounting
90% owned subsidiary
subsequent year, partial equity method

	Alto Company	*Bass Company*	*Adjustments and eliminations* Debit	Credit	*Minority interest*	*Consolidated balances*
Income statements for year ended 12/31/99						
Sales	$750,000	$420,000	$ 38,000[a]			$1,132,000
Cost of sales	581,000	266,000	5,000[b] 900[i]	$ 38,000[a]		814,900
Gross margin	169,000	154,000				317,100
Depreciation and interest expense	28,400	16,200	1,800[i]	750[d]		45,650
Other operating expenses	117,000	128,400	1,710[i]			247,110
Net income from operations	23,600	9,400				24,340
Gain on sale of equipment	3,000		3,000[d]			
Gain on bonds				6,000[e]		6,000
Equity in subsidiary's income	8,460		8,460[f]			
Minority income ($7,400 x .10)					$ 740	(740)
Net income	$ 35,060	$ 9,400	$ 58,870	$ 44,750	$ 740	$ 29,600

	Alto Company	*Bass Company*	*Adjustments and eliminations* Debit	*Adjustments and eliminations* Credit	*Minority interest*	*Consolidated balances*
Statement of retained earnings for year ended 12/31/99						
1/1/99 retained earnings						
Alto Company	$ 48,000					$ 48,000
Bass Company		$ 41,000	$ 36,900[g]		$ 4,100	
Add net income (from above)	35,060	9,400	58,870	$ 44,750	740	29,600
Total	83,060	50,400			4,840	77,600
Deduct dividends	15,000	4,000		3,600[f]	400	15,000
Balance, 12/31/99	$ 68,060	$ 46,400	$ 95,770	$ 48,350	$ 4,440	$ 62,600
Balance sheet, 12/31/99						
Cash	$ 45,300	$ 6,400	$ 1,000[l]			$ 52,700
Accounts receivable (net)	43,700	12,100		$ 1,000[l] 4,000[c]		50,800
Inventories	38,300	20,750	900[h]	5,000[b] 900[i]		54,050
Equipment	195,000	57,000	9,000[h]	2,000[d]		259,000
Accumulated depreciation	(35,200)	(18,900)		250[d] 1,800[h] 1,800[i]		(57,950)
Investment in stock of Bass Company	125,460			4,860[f] 120,600[g]		
Differential			25,200[g]	25,200[h]		
Goodwill			14,400[h]	1,440[i]		12,960
Investment in bonds of Alto Company		44,000		44,000[e]		
Patents		9,000	2,700[h]	270[i]		11,430
	$412,560	$130,350				$382,990
Accounts payable	$ 8,900	$ 18,950	4,000[c]			$ 23,850
Bonds payable	100,000		50,000[e]			50,000
Capital stock	154,000	50,000	45,000[g]		$ 5,000	154,000
Additional paid-in capital	81,600	15,000	13,500[g]		1,500	81,600
Retained earnings (from above)	68,060	46,400	95,770	48,350	4,440	62,600
Minority interest					$10,940	10,940
	$412,560	$130,350	$261,470	$261,470		$382,990

The remainder of the consolidation process consists of the following worksheet techniques:

1. Take all income items across horizontally and foot the adjustments, minority interest, and consolidated columns down to the net income line.
2. Take the amounts on the net income line (on income statement) in the adjustments, minority interest, and consolidated balances columns **down to**

retained earnings items across the consolidated balances column. Foot and crossfoot the retained earnings statement.

3. Take the amounts of ending retained earnings in each of the four columns down to the ending retained earnings line in the balance sheet. Foot the minority interest column and place its total in the consolidated balances column. Take all the balance sheet items across to consolidated balances column.

Other Accounting Problems in Business Combinations

Contingent consideration. If the terms of the acquisition include contingent consideration, the combination must be treated as a purchase. Pooling accounting cannot be used. The accounting for the subsequent payment of the added consideration depends upon whether the contingency was related to the earnings of the acquired entity or to the market value of the original consideration package given by the acquirer.

In the former instance (exemplified by the purchase of Gamma Corp. in the example presented earlier), a later payment of added cash, stock, or any other valuable consideration will require a revaluation of the purchase price. This revaluation could alter the amounts allocable to noncurrent assets (where cost in the original purchase transaction was less than fair value acquired and the difference was offset against those assets), or could result in an increased amount of goodwill being recognized. The effects of a revaluation are handled prospectively (i.e., the additional amortization of goodwill and/or fixed assets is allocated to the remaining economic lives of those items) without adjustment of any postacquisition periods' results already reported.

In the latter case (exemplified by the Epsilon Co. merger in the earlier illustration), the event triggering the issuance of additional shares is a decline in market value of the original purchase package. The total value of the purchase ($20,000,000 in the Epsilon case) would **not** be changed and, thus, no alteration of allocated amounts would be needed. However, the issuance of extra shares of common stock will require that the allocation between the common stock and the additional paid-in capital accounts be adjusted. Had part of the original price been bonds or other debt, the reallocation could have affected the premium or discount on the debt, which would have an impact on future earnings as these accounts are subsequently amortized.

Net operating loss carryforward of acquired entity. An entity acquired in a purchase business combination may have a tax loss carryforward which will be available for use by the acquiring entity. Prior GAAP (APB 11 and SFAS 96) generally prohibited recognition of the tax benefit of NOL carryforwards, albeit for different reasons. Under APB 11, the subsequent realization of the NOL carryforward necessitated the reallocation of the purchase price. Reallocation was often accompanied by the restatement of the results of operations for the intervening years after the date of the purchase transaction. Under SFAS 96, subsequent realization of tax loss carryforward benefits was accounted for as a limited reallocation of the purchase transaction: only goodwill and other identifiable intangibles were to be restated, with any further tax benefit being reported in current period tax expense.

Essentially this same approach has been adopted by SFAS 109. As discussed more fully in Chapter 15, recognition **for the first time** of the benefits of NOL carryforwards (acquired in a purchase business combination at a date subsequent to the purchase) is accomplished by reducing recorded goodwill to zero. Next, other identifiable intangible assets acquired in the same transaction are reduced to zero. Any excess is reduced from current period tax expense. Under the provisions of SFAS 109 benefits related to acquired NOL are reported in the acquirer's balance sheet (as are benefits arising from any other deductible temporary differences). A valuation allowance is also recorded if realization is not considered **more likely than not. For the first time** means that the allowance account has been reduced or eliminated, either because the probability of realization has been reassessed or because the tax benefits have, in fact, been realized in the current period.

As to business combinations accounted for as poolings of interests, SFAS 109 stipulates that, if one of the combining entities has an unrecognized deferred tax benefit (i.e., the deferred tax benefit is offset by a valuation allowance), the benefits may or may not be reflected in the restated financials of prior periods. That is, the valuation allowance **may** be eliminated on a retrospective basis. This treatment depends upon whether the combined entity will be able, under provisions of the tax laws, to utilize the operating loss and tax credit carryforwards of the merged companies. If it can do so, then the deferred tax benefits should be given recognition in any restated prior period financial statements. On the other hand, if, under the law, the benefits cannot be utilized in a consolidated tax return or if a consolidated return is not expected to be filed, then the tax benefits would not be recognized in financial statements restated for the pooling of interests. If a benefit of a NOL carryforward is first recognized in a subsequent period (by reducing or eliminating the valuation allowance), the offsetting adjustment will be made to current period tax expense in all such cases.

Preacquisition contingencies. At the time a purchase business combination is consummated, the purchase price must be allocated to acquired assets and assumed liabilities in accordance with their respective fair values, with any excess purchase price being assigned to goodwill (if fair value exceeds cost, the cost deficiency is allocated against noncurrent assets, with any remainder treated as "negative goodwill"). In some cases, however, the fair values of certain assets (e.g., those to be disposed of) may not be known with precision, and the amounts of certain estimated or contingent liabilities (such as outstanding litigation claims) may also be subject to uncertainty. Since the promulgation of SFAS 16 (prior period adjustments) ended the earlier practice of restating prior period financial statements unless an "error" could be shown to have occurred, it became necessary to develop a new standard, SFAS 38, to provide for a "look back" to reallocate the purchase price when these contingencies are ultimately resolved. However, under SFAS 38 there is a limited period, usually deemed to be 1 year, during which a reallocation can be effected; thereafter, resolutions of preacquisition contingencies must be treated as current period events and reported in earnings.

An exception to this rule exists in the case of income tax uncertainties existing at the date of a purchase business combination. Resolution of these must be accounted for in accordance with SFAS 109, which stipulates that such adjustments are to be applied to increase or decrease the remaining balance of goodwill attributable to that business combination; if goodwill is reduced to zero, the remaining amount should be used to first reduce other noncurrent intangible assets from the same acquisition to zero, and any excess beyond that amount is to be taken into income. Thus, the resolution of these specific uncertainties cannot result in a general reallocation of the purchase price, as are other resolutions of preacquisition contingencies.

Changes in majority interest. The parent's ownership interest can change as a result of purchases or sales of the subsidiary's common shares by the parent, or as a consequence of capital transactions of the subsidiary. The latter circumstance is generally handled precisely as demonstrated in the equity method discussion in the previous chapter (see pages 345-347). If the parent's relative book value interest in the subsidiary has changed, then gains or losses are treated as incurred in an entity's own treasury stock transactions. Gains are credited to paid-in capital; losses are charged to any previously created paid-in capital or to retained earnings. However, the SEC requires that when a subsidiary sells shares to outside interests at a price greater than the parent's carrying amount, the parent company should recognize a gain on the transaction.

When the parent's share of ownership increases through a purchase of additional stock, simply debit investment and credit cash for the cost. A problem occurs with consolidated income statements when the change in ownership takes place in mid-period. Consolidated statements should be prepared based on the ending ownership level.

Example of a consolidation with a change in the majority interest

Assume that Alto Company increased its ownership of Bass Company from 90% to 95% on October 1, 1998. The investment was acquired at book value of $5,452.50 and is determined as follows:

Retained earnings at 10/1/98		$50,000
Additional paid-in capital, 10/1/98		15,000
Retained earnings at 10/1/98		
Balance, 1/1/98	$41,000	
Net income for 9 months ($9,400 x .75)	7,050*	
Preacquisition dividends	(4,000)	44,050
		$ 109,050
		x 5%
Book value acquired		$5,452.50

**Assumes income was earned evenly over the year.*

The consolidated net income should reflect a net of

90%	x	$9,400	x	12/12	=	$8,460.00
5%	x	$9,400	x	3/12	=	$ 117.50
95%						$8,577.50

The interim stock purchase will result in a new account being shown on the consolidated income statement. The account is **Purchased preacquisition earnings**, which represents the percentage of the subsidiary's income earned, in this case, on the 5% stock interest from January 1, 1998, to October 1, 1998. The basic eliminating entries would be based on the 95% ownership as follows:

Equity in subsidiary's income--Alto Co.	8,577.50	
Dividends declared--Bass Co.		3,600.00
Investment in stock of Bass Co.		4,977.50
Capital stock--Bass Co.	47,500.00	
Additional paid-in capital--Bass Co.	14,250.00	
Retained earnings--Bass Co.	38,750.00**	
Purchased preacquisition earnings	352.50***	
Differential	25,200.00	
Investment in stock of Bass Co.--Alto Co.		126,052.50

** *95% x $41,000 beginning 1998 balance*	*$38,950*
Less preacquisition dividend of 5% x $4,000	*(200)*
Retained earnings available, as adjusted	*$38,750*
*** *5% x $9,400 x 9/12 = $352.50*	

Purchased preacquisition earnings is shown as a deduction, along with minority interest, to arrive at consolidated net income. Purchased preacquisition earnings are used only with interim acquisition under the purchase accounting method; all poolings are assumed to take place at the beginning of the period regardless of when, during the period, the acquisition was actually made.

Requirement that all majority-owned subsidiaries be consolidated. GAAP has long held that when one entity is owned outright or controlled by another entity (the "parent company"), the most meaningful representation of the economic substance of the parent company will be through consolidated financial statements. This presumption dates from ARB 51, which did not, however, absolutely require that consolidated financial reporting be employed. Over the years since the issuance of ARB 51, a number of popular exceptions to the general rule have arisen, which eventually resulted in a substantial diversity of reporting practices. This lack of comparability led the FASB to reconsider the value of consolidated financial reporting; the issuance of SFAS 94 was the first (and thus far, only) result of the Board's announced three-phase project on the reporting entity, consolidated financial statements, and the equity method.

Varied reasons were given previously for excluding some or all subsidiaries from the parent company's financial statements. Lack of absolute control over the affairs of the subsidiary, whether because of legal restrictions or due to the relationship with minority owners, was often cited as a valid justification for not consolidating the subsidiary entity in the parent's financial statements. In other situations, control was present but expected to be only temporary; to prepare consolidated statements in one reporting period would likely cause comparability problems in later, postdivestment periods.

More controversial than the above were situations where so-called "off-balance-sheet financing" was accomplished through the use of majority or wholly-owned leasing, factoring, or other financing subsidiaries which were then excluded from the parent's financial statements. The actual justification given was that consolidation of such "nonhomogeneous" operations would distort the parent's key financial and operating statistics, such as the working capital ratio and gross profit margin. This situation was cited as the rationale for excluding highly leveraged financing subsidiaries.

The flaw in the above-noted argument is that the use of consolidated financial statements as the primary reporting vehicle never precluded the presentation of supplementary financial information, including separate subsidiary financial statements or **consolidating** financial statements if deemed necessary to convey the true essence of a company's operations. Also, since comparability of financial data across entities has always been an important underlying postulate of accounting theory, the lack of a standardized approach by diversified entities was a major hindrance to financial analysis.

SFAS 94 significantly narrows, but does not totally eliminate, the ability of entities to exclude majority owned subsidiaries from parent company financial statements. Most importantly, the "nonhomogeneity" argument cannot be employed any longer to exclude leasing, real estate, financing, insurance, or other subsidiary operations. Henceforth, unless one of the exceptions stated below applies, these operations must be included in consolidated financial statements.

The "consolidate everything" rule of SFAS 94 offers only the following exceptions:

- Control over the subsidiary is expected to be temporary in nature; or
- Control does not reside with the majority owner.

Absence of control is likely to occur only when a domestic subsidiary is in bankruptcy proceedings or when a foreign subsidiary operates in an environment of extreme exchange controls or restrictions on repatriation of earnings.

Separate financial statements of entities which are majority owned by other companies are still permitted. In fact, minority shareholders and other interested parties (creditors, vendors, or customers, as well as regulatory authorities) would receive little useful information from the parent company's consolidated financial statements in most instances. However, if the reporting subsidiary itself had one or more majority owned subsidiaries of its own, these would be consolidated in the financial statements of the first-tier subsidiary.

SFAS 94 does establish one somewhat unusual requirement. If subsidiaries were previously **not** consolidated, but were accounted for by the equity method, then the disclosure requirements of APB 18 are maintained **for those subsidiaries** that are later fully consolidated. Thus, summary balance sheet and income statement information must be provided notwithstanding the consolidation of these entities into the parent's balance sheet and income statement. In an extreme case, extensive detail could be provided on relatively insignificant (and, therefore, formerly unconsolidated) subsidiaries, while more significant subsidiaries, always consolidated in prior financial statements, will not necessarily have similar disclosures.

The Board's reason for adopting the aforementioned rule was essentially to avoid "information loss" during deliberations on the general need for disaggregated financial information in consolidated financial statements. This project might ultimately mandate any of the following: (1) full **consolidating** financial statements, (2) APB 18-like summarized data for all subsidiaries, (3) grouped disclosures on a line-of-business basis similar to that stipulated in SFAS 14 (no longer required for nonpublic entities, however), (4) some other mode of disclosure, or (5) none at all. Until then, extended disclosures will only be necessary for previously unconsolidated entities, although similar disclosures can be made on a voluntary basis for other subsidiaries as well.

Majority owned subsidiaries **not** consolidated (because one of the two available exception conditions applies) will generally be accounted for by the equity method. The Board's exposure draft preceding SFAS 94 would have proscribed the use of the equity method (i.e., would have required that the cost method of accounting for those investments be used). However, this requirement was dropped from the final standard. As a result, specific circumstances must determine whether the equity method is appropriate.

Combined Financial Statements

When a group of entities is under common ownership, control, or management, it is often useful to present combined (or combining--showing the separate as well as the combined entities) financial statements. In this situation, the economic substance of the nominally independent entities' operations may be more important to statement users than is the legal form of those enterprises. When consolidated statements are not presented, combined statements may be used to show the financial position, or operating results, of a group of companies which are each subsidiaries of a common parent.

According to ARB 51, the process of preparing combined statements is virtually the same as consolidations employing the pooling-of-interests method. The major exception is that the equity section of the combined balance sheet will incorporate the paid-in capital accounts of each of the combining entities. However, only a single combined retained earnings account need be presented.

Example of a combined financial statement

Adams Corporation and Benbow Company, Inc.
Combined Balance Sheet
December 31, 1999

Stockholders' equity	
Capital stock:	
Preferred, $100 par, authorized 90,000 shares, issued 5,000 shares	$ 500,000
Common, $50 par, authorized 100,000 shares, issued 60,000 shares	3,000,000
Common, $10 par, authorized 250,000 shares, issued 100,000 shares	1,000,000
Additional paid-in capital	650,000
Retained earnings	3,825,000
	$8,975,000

Combinations of Entities Under Common Control

APB 16 explicitly does **not** apply to entities under common control (brother-sister corporations, etc.). However, mergers among such affiliated entities must be accounted for "as if" poolings, per AICPA Interpretation 39. This treatment is consistent with the concept of poolings as combinations of common shareholder interests. A question arises, however, when a parent (Company P) transfers ownership in one of its subsidiaries (Company B) to another of its subsidiaries (Company A) in exchange for additional shares of Company A. If P's carrying value of its investment in B differs from B's book value, there appears to be a requirement under Interpretation 39 for A to reflect its new investment in B at B's book value, rather than at P's cost (or equity) basis.

EITF 90-5 has resolved this conflict by stating that A's carrying value for the investment in B should be P's basis, not B's book value. Furthermore, if A subsequently retires the interests of minority owners of B, the transaction should be accounted for as a purchase, whether it is effected through a stock issuance by A or by a cash payment to the selling shareholders.

The EITF further concluded (in 90-13) that when a purchase transaction is closely followed by a "sale" of the parent's subsidiary to the newly acquired ("target") entity, these two transactions should be viewed as a single transaction. Accordingly, and notwithstanding AICPA Interpretation 39 (above), the parent should recognize gain or loss on the sale of its subsidiary to the target company, to the extent of minority interest in the target entity. As a result, there will be a new basis ("step up") not only for the target company's assets and liabilities, but also for the subsidiary company's net assets. Basis is stepped up to the extent of minority participation in the target entity to which the subsidiary company was transferred.

Accounting for Leveraged Buyouts

Possibly one of the most complex accounting issues to have arisen over the past decade has been the appropriate accounting for so-called leveraged buyouts (LBO). At the center of this issue is the question of whether a **new basis** of accountability has been created by the LBO transaction. If so, then a step up in the reported value of assets and/or liabilities is warranted. If not, the carryforward bases of the predecessor entity should continue to be reported in the company's financial statements.

The EITF has addressed leveraged buyouts, first in 86-16, then in 88-16 and 90-12. The task force's conclusion was that partial or complete new basis accounting is appropriate only when the transaction is characterized by a **change in control of voting interest**. Consensus 88-16 established a series of mechanical tests by which this change in interest is to be measured. The EITF identified three groups of interests: shareholders in the newly created company, management, and shareholders in the old company (who may or may not also have an interest in the new company). Depending upon the relative interests of these groups in the old entity ("OLDCO") and in the new enterprise ("NEWCO"), there will be **either**, (1) a finding that the transaction was a purchase (new basis accounting applies) or (2) that it was a recapitalization or a restructuring (carryforward basis accounting applies).

Among the tests which the EITF decreed to determine proper accounting for any given LBO transaction is the "monetary test." This test requires that at least 80% of the net consideration paid to acquire OLDCO interests must be **monetary**. In this context, monetary means cash, debt, and the fair value of any equity by securities given by NEWCO to selling shareholders of OLDCO. Loan proceeds provided OLDCO to assist in the acquisition of NEWCO shares by NEWCO shareholders are excluded from this definition. If the portion of the purchase that is effected through monetary consideration is less than 80%, but other criteria of EITF 88-16 are satisfied, there will be a step up. This step up will be limited to the percentage of the transaction represented by monetary consideration.

EITF 88-16 presents an extensive series of examples illustrating the circumstances which would and would not meet the purchase accounting criteria to be employed in LBO. These examples should be consulted as needed when addressing an actual LBO transaction accounting issue.

Reverse Acquisitions

Reverse acquisitions occur when one entity (the nominal acquirer) issues so many shares to the former owners of another entity (the nominal acquiree) that they become the majority owners of the resultant combined enterprise. The result of this event is that the legal and accounting treatments of the transaction will diverge, with the nominal acquiree being the acquirer for financial reporting purposes. While often the nominal acquirer will adopt the acquiree's name, thus alerting users of the statements to the nature of the organizational change, this does not necessarily occur, and, in any event, it will be critical that the financial statements contain sufficient disclosure so that users are not misled. This will be important particularly in the periods immediately following the transaction, and especially when comparative financial statements are presented which include some periods prior to the acquisition, since comparability will be affected.

A typical reverse acquisition would occur when a so-called "shell" enterprise, which often is a publicly held but dormant company, merges with an operating company, which often will be nonpublic. The objective is for the operating entity to "go public" without the usual time consuming and expensive registration process. However, reverse acquisitions are not limited to such situations, and there have been many such transactions involving two public or two nonpublic companies, and the nominal acquirer may have substantial operations of its own, although of lesser scope or with lower growth prospects than those of the nominal acquiree.

A number of difficult questions arise in reverse acquisitions, and GAAP does not provide definitive guidance on these important issues. The SEC has provided some direction which, under the hierarchy of GAAP, should be viewed as definitive absent higher level "official" indicators from the profession. Among the matters to be considered, and which will be discussed in the following paragraphs, are these

1. What circumstances signal a reverse acquisition?
2. How should the consolidated financial statements be presented in the subsequent periods?
3. How should the purchase cost be computed and allocated in a reverse acquisition?
4. What would the shareholders' equity section of the balance sheet be immediately following the reverse acquisition?
5. What would be the impact on computation of earnings per share?
6. How will minority interest be presented in the financial statements?

As noted, reverse acquisitions occur when the former shareholders of the nominal acquiree become the majority owners of the postacquisition consolidated enterprise. Often, this will result when a stock-for-stock swap occurs; if all 12 conditions set forth in APB 16 are met, the transaction will be accounted for as a pooling and the concerns noted above will not be pertinent. However, if any of the 12 conditions for pooling of interests accounting are not met, the transaction will be accounted for as a purchase, and these reverse takeover issues will have to be resolved. Furthermore, some reverse acquisitions might involve the exchange of the nominal acquirer's shares for the net assets of the acquiree, with the nominal acquiree then liquidating by distributing the acquirer's shares to its stockholders. As with other business combinations under GAAP, if the entities were under common control before the transaction, APB 16 would not apply, and the combination would be accounted for similar to a pooling of interests (i.e., assets and liabilities would be carried forward at book values) per Interpretation 39, and thus reverse acquisition accounting would not be relevant.

It will be assumed in the following discussion of this topic that the transactions fail the pooling-of-interests tests for one or more reasons, and thus that reverse acquisition accounting will be necessary. If the former owners of the nominal acquiree in a purchase business combination become the majority owners of the consolidated enterprise following the transactions, it will be deemed to have been a reverse acquisition. If the FASB's project on consolidations results, as expected, in a new threshold, control instead of majority ownership, being defined, then the criterion for reverse acquisition accounting would be modified accordingly, if all other salient factors are held constant.

Following a business combination which in essence is a reverse acquisition, consolidated financial statements will be presented. While the statements will be identified as being those of the nominal acquirer, which is the legal owner of the nominal acquiree, the accounting substance will be that these are the financial statements of the acquiree company, with the assets and liabilities, and revenues and expenses of the nominal acquirer added effective with the date of the transaction. Put another way, the legal parent company will be deemed to be a continuation of the business of the legal subsidiary, notwithstanding the formal structure of the transaction or the name of the successor enterprise. If the legal parent (nominal acquirer) does not change its name, it would be appropriate if the financial statement titles were captioned in a way that the substance of the transaction is most clearly conveyed. For example, the statements may be headed "ABC Company, Inc.--successor to XYZ Corporation."

Given the foregoing, it is clear that the stockholders' equity section of the post-transaction consolidated balance sheet should be that of the acquiree, not the acquirer, with appropriate modification for the new shares issued in the transaction and ancillary adjustments, if any. Comparative financial statements for earlier periods, if presented, should be consistent, meaning that these would be the financial statements of the nominal acquiree. Since in some instances the acquiree's name is different than that shown in the heading, care must be taken to fully communicate with the readers. The fact that the prior period's financial information identified as being that of the legal parent is really that of the nominal acquiree obviously is extremely pertinent to a reader's understanding of these statements.

Consistent with the accounting imposed on other purchase business combinations, the cost of reverse acquisitions should be measured at the fair value of the net assets acquired, or the value of the consideration paid, if more apparent. A special rule is that, if fair market value cannot be determined for the issuer's stock, and the transaction is valued at the fair market value of the issuer's net assets, no goodwill should be recognized in the transaction. In addition, in the special case of a publicly held shell company and a privately held acquiree, the SEC has ruled that no goodwill can be recognized in any event. Clearly, in such instances there is substantial doubt about the true existence of goodwill and unusual difficulty in valuing the transaction, and this prohibition is prudent under the circumstances.

If the fair value of the shares of the nominal acquiree (which becomes the legal subsidiary after the transaction is completed) is used to determine the cost of the purchase, it is suggested that a calculation be made to determine the number of shares that the acquiree would have issued in order to provide the same level of ownership in the combined entity to the shareholders of the nominal acquirer as they have as a consequence of the reverse acquisition. The fair value of the number of shares thus determined is used to value the transaction, as illustrated later in this section.

In some instances, the market price of acquiree shares may not be fairly indicative of the value of the transaction. In such cases, the most feasible alternative would be to use the fair market value of all the outstanding shares of the ostensible acquirer, prior to the transaction, to value the purchase transaction. In some instances, adjustments would have to be made for trading volume, price fluctuations, etc., to most accurately reflect the substance of the acquisition.

In other cases, particularly where the acquirer is a dormant shell entity, market price of its shares may not be meaningful. If possible to determine, utilizing the fair value of the net assets of the acquirer may be a more meaningful technique.

Whatever specific technique is employed under the circumstances, the total purchase cost should be allocated to the net assets of the acquirer (not the acquiree) following the principles set forth in APB 16. If the purchase cost exceeds the fair value of net identifiable assets, the excess is allocated to goodwill, which will be amortized consistent with APB 17. The financial statements of the consolidated enterprise following the reverse acquisition would reflect the assets and liabilities of the nominal acquirer at fair value, and those of the nominal acquiree at historical cost.

Since for financial reporting purposes the nominal acquiree is the parent company, the retained earnings or deficit of the acquiree will be carried forward in the equity section of the successor entity's balance sheet. The retained earnings or deficit of the nominal acquirer will not be presented. The amount shown for paid-in capital would be valued in terms of the issued capital of the nominal acquiree (the new subsidiary), plus the cost of the acquisition as described above and illustrated below. However, in the actual financial statement, which must reflect the legal structure of the transaction, paid-in capital would be expressed in terms of the legal parent company, which was the nominal acquirer. An example of accounting for a reverse acquisition follows.

Assume that Agoura Corp., which is the nominal acquirer which becomes the legal parent company, issues shares in exchange for the outstanding common stock of Belmar Co., Inc., which is the nominal acquiree which becomes the legal subsidiary of Agoura. For accounting purposes, this will be a reverse acquisition such that Belmar is the actual acquirer.

The balance sheets of the two entities at the end of 1998 and as of September 30, 1999, the date of the transaction, are given as follows:

	Agoura Corporation	
	December 31, 1998	September 30, 1999
Current assets	$ 800,000	$1,000,000
Plant, property, and equipment, net	2,400,000	2,600,000
	$3,200,000	$3,600,000
Current liabilities	$ 400,000	$ 600,000
Long-term debt	600,000	400,000
Deferred tax liabilities	200,000	200,000
	1,200,000	1,200,000
Stockholders' equity		
8% redeemable preferred stock, 2,000 shs.	200,000	200,000
Common stock, 100,000 shs.	600,000	600,000
Retained earnings	1,200,000	1,600,000
	$3,200,000	$3,600,000

	Belmar Company, Inc.	
	December 31, 1998	September 30, 1999
Current assets	$2,500,000	$1,750,000
Plant, property and equipment, net	5,000,000	7,500,000
	$7,500,000	$9,250,000
Current liabilities	$1,250,000	$1,500,000
Long-term debt	1,750,000	2,000,000
Deferred tax liabilities	500,000	750,000
	3,500,000	4,250,000
Stockholders' equity		
Common stock, 60,000 shs.	1,500,000	1,500,000
Retained earnings	2,500,000	3,500,000
	$7,500,000	$9,250,000

Agoura had net income of $400,000 for the 9 months ended September 30, 1999, while Belmar Co. enjoyed earnings of $1,000,000 for that period. Neither company paid any dividends during this period.

The fair value of each share of Belmar common stock was $100 at the date of the acquisition. Agoura shares were quoted at $24 on the date.

Agoura's identifiable net assets had fair values equal to their respective book values, with the exception of the plant, property and equipment, which were appraised at $3,000,000 at September 30, 1999.

In effecting the acquisition, Agoura issues 150,000 new shares of its common stock to the owners of Belmar in exchange for all outstanding Belmar shares. Thus, former Belmar owners become the owners of a majority of the common stock of Agoura after this transaction.

To compute the cost of the reverse acquisition, the number of shares of the nominal acquiree entity, Belmar, which would have had to have been issued to acquire the nominal acquirer, Agoura, must be computed. This is done as follows:

Actual Agoura shares issued to former Belmar owners	150,000
Agoura shares outstanding prior to transaction	100,000
Total Agoura shares outstanding after transaction	250,000
Fraction held by former Belmar owners (150,000/250,000)	60%
Number of Belmar shares outstanding before transaction	60,000
Number of Belmar shares which could have been issued in transaction if 60% of total would have remained with original Belmar shareholders	40,000

If Belmar had issued 40,000 of its shares to effect the acquisition of Agoura, the cost would have been (given the fair value of Belmar shares at September 30, 1999) $100 x 40,000 = $4,000,000. This purchase cost would have been allocated to Agoura's assets and liabilities as follows:

Current assets		$1,000,000
Plant, property and equipment		3,000,000
		$4,000,000
Current liabilities	$600,000	
Long-term debt	400,000	
Deferred tax liabilities	200,000	1,200,000
		2,800,000
8% redeemable preferred stock, 2,000 shs.		200,000
		2,600,000
Cost of purchase (from above)		4,000,000
Goodwill to be recognized		$1,400,000

From the foregoing, the information needed to construct a consolidated balance sheet as of the date of the transaction, September 30, 1999, can be determined.

Agoura Corporation
Consolidated Balance Sheet
September 30, 1999

Current assets	$ 2,750,000
Plant, property and equipment, net	10,500,000
Goodwill	1,400,000
	$14,650,000
Current liabilities	$ 2,100,000
Long-term debt	2,400,000
Deferred tax liabilities	950,000
	5,450,000
Stockholders' equity	
8% redeemable preferred stock, 2,000 shs.	200,000
Common stock, 100,000 shs.	5,500,000
Retained earnings	3,500,000
	9,200,000
	$14,650,000

Computing earnings per share after a reverse acquisition poses special problems, particularly so in the year in which the transaction occurs and for any subsequent years when comparative financial statements are presented which include pretransaction periods. For this purpose, the number of shares outstanding for the period from the beginning of the current reporting year until the date of the reverse acquisition should be the number of shares issued by the nominal acquirer (the legal parent company) to the shareholders of the nominal acquiree. For the period after the transaction, the number of shares considered to be outstanding would be actual number of shares of the legal parent company outstanding during that period. The average number of shares outstanding for the full year being reported upon would be computed by averaging these two amounts. Other appropriate adjustments would be made to deal with changes in numbers of shares issued during the period, as is done under other circumstances (as described in Chapter 18), if necessary. Under the new standard for computing earnings per share (SFAS 128), the calculation of basic earnings per share (replacing the older measure, primary earnings per share) is simplified for all entities.

Earnings per share for any earlier periods presented for comparative purposes is likewise complicated by the occurrence of a reverse acquisition. The number of shares issued by the legal parent (nominal acquirer) in the reverse acquisition transaction would be used to make this calculation.

Continuing with the Agoura-Belmar acquisition example above, earnings per share can be computed. Assume that consolidated net income for the year ended December 31, 1999, after deducting preferred dividends, equals $1,600,000. This includes Belmar Co., Inc. earnings for the full year 1999, plus Agoura Corp. earnings from the date of acquisition, September 30, 1999, until year end. Remember that, notwithstanding that the new entity is called Agoura, from an accounting perspective this is Belmar Company.

Earnings per share would thus be computed as follows:

Number of shares outstanding from September 30, 1999	250,000
Number of shares deemed outstanding before September 30-- the number of Agoura shares issued to Belmar	150,000

Average number of shares

[(150,000 x 9) + (250,000 x 3)] ÷ 12 = 175,000

Earnings per share for 1998

$1,600,000 ÷ 175,000 = $9.14 per share

For 1998, assuming Belmar alone had earnings of $1,400,000 for the year, earnings per share would be

$1,400,000 ÷ 150,000 = $9.33 per share

Finally, there is the question of minority interest (which may become a matter of noncontrolling interest, if the FASB adopts the new standard setting control, rather than majority interest, as the criterion for consolidation). In a reverse acquisition situation, the minority is comprised of the former shareholders of the legal subsidiary who do not exchange their shares for those of the new parent company, but continue on as stockholders in the legal subsidiary entity. Note that this holds even though from the accounting perspective they are shareholders in an entity which acquired another company. In other words, the identity of the minority is determined by the legal structure of the transaction, not the accounting substance. Since the net assets of the legal subsidiary (but substantive parent) are included in the consolidated financial statements at the old book values, minority interest is likewise computed based on the book value of the legal subsidiary's net assets.

For example, in the present case all shareholders of Belmar might not agree to tender their shares in exchange for Agoura stock, and if so they will continue on as minority owners of the legal subsidiary, Belmar, after it is nominally acquired by Agoura Corp. To illustrate, consider these assumed facts.

Agoura offered 2.5 shares for each share of Belmar common stock. In the example above, 150,000 shares of Agoura were exchanged for 60,000 Belmar shares. Now, however, assume that owners of 4,000 Belmar shares decline to participate in this transaction, so Agoura issues only 140,000 shares in exchange for 56,000 Belmar shares. After the exchange, former Belmar owners hold 140,000 of a total of 240,000 Agoura Corp. shares, or 58.33% of the total outstanding; still a majority and thus enough to define this as a reverse acquisition.

The cost of the purchase is computed similar to what was illustrated above. Since the owners of 56,000 Belmar shares participated and the transaction resulted in these owners obtaining a 58.33% interest in the successor entity, the calculation of the number of Belmar shares which hypothetically would have had to have been issued in a "straight" acquisition of Agoura is as follows:

56,000 shares outstanding ÷ .5833 = 96,000 total shares after transaction

96,000 total shares – 56,000 shares outstanding = 40,000 new shares to be issued

Thus, it can be seen that the cost of the purchase, determined in the manner which is necessary when a reverse acquisition takes place, remains 40,000 x $100 = $4,000,000 even given the existence of the minority interest.

The minority interest is 4,000 shares ÷ 60,000 shares = 6.6667%. It consists, as of the acquisition date, of 6.6667% of the book value of Belmar common stock and retained earnings, as follows:

6.6667% x $1,500,000 =	$100,000
6.6667% x $3,500,000 =	233,310
Total minority interest	$333,310

The consolidated balance sheet at acquisition date would differ from that shown above only as follows: a minority interest of $333,310 would be presented (under current GAAP, as a liability, as equity, or in a semiequity account); common stock would be only $5,400,000, comprised of 93.33% (1 – 6.66667%) of Belmar's $1,500,000, plus the $4 million purchase cost); and retained earnings would be only 93.33% or Belmar's pretransaction balance of $3.5 million, or $3,266,655. All other asset and liability account balances would be identical to the presentation above.

Spin-Offs

Occasionally an entity disposes of a wholly or partially owned subsidiary or of an investee by transferring it unilaterally to the entity's shareholders. The proper accounting for such a transaction, generally known as a spin-off, depends upon the percentage of the company that is owned.

If the ownership percentage is relatively minor, 25% for example, the transfer to stockholders would be viewed as a "dividend in kind" and would be accounted for at the fair value of the property (i.e., shares in the investee) transferred.

However, when the entity whose shares are distributed is majority or wholly-owned, the effect is not merely to transfer a passive investment, but to remove the operations from the former parent and to vest them with the parent's shareholders. This transaction is a true spin-off transaction, not merely a property dividend. APB 29 requires that spin-offs and other similar nonreciprocal transfers to owners be accounted for at the recorded book values of the assets and liabilities transferred.

If the operations (or subsidiary) being spun off are distributed during a fiscal period, it may be necessary to estimate the results of operations for the elapsed period prior to spin-off in order to ascertain the net book value as of the date of the transfer. Stated another way, the operating results of the subsidiary to be disposed of should be included in the reported results of the parent through the actual date of the spin-off.

In most instances, the subsidiary being spun off will have a positive net book value. This net worth represents the cost of the nonreciprocal transfer to the owners, and, like a dividend, will be reflected as a charge against the parent's retained earnings at the date of spin-off. In other situations, the operations (or subsidiary) will have a net deficit (negative net book value). Since it is unacceptable to recognize a credit to the parent's retained earnings for other than a culmination of an earnings process, the spin-off should be recorded as a credit to the parent's paid-in capital. In effect, the stockholders (the recipients of the spun-off subsidiary) have made a capital contribution to the parent company by accepting the operations having a negative book value. As with other capital transactions, this would **not** be presented in the income statement, but only in the statement of changes in stockholders' equity (and in the statement of cash flows).

Push-Down Accounting

For a number of years the FASB had the matter of so-called "push-down" accounting (which it referred to as "new basis accounting") on its technical agenda, but in mid-1996 it was placed on a back burner by the Board, and has now officially been removed from the agenda altogether. However, this ongoing lack of official guidance does not mean that entities will not have to face the issue of applying this method of accounting, since it has been required by the SEC in some instances, and remains acceptable, if not mandated, under GAAP.

The concept of push-down (or new basis) accounting is to reflect a revaluation of the assets and/or liabilities of the acquired company **on its books** based on the price paid for some or all of its shares by the acquirer. Push-down accounting has no impact on the presentation of consolidated financial statements or on the separate financial statements of the parent (investor) company, which would continue to be based on the price paid for the acquisition and not on the acquired entity's book value. However, the use of this accounting technique represents a departure in the way separate financial statements of the acquired entity are presented.

Advocates of push-down accounting point out that in a purchase business combination a new basis of accounting is established. They believe that the new basis should be pushed down to the acquired entity and should be used when presenting its own separate financial statements.

While the push-down treatment has been used by a number of entities it remains controversial and lacks clear authoritative guidance. Although push-down makes some sense in the case where a major block of the investee's shares is acquired in a single free-market transaction, if new basis accounting were to be used in the context of a series of step transactions, continual adjustment of the investee's carrying values for assets and liabilities would be necessary. Furthermore, the price paid for a fractional share of ownership of an investee may not always be meaningfully extrapolated to a value for the investee company as a whole.

The profession's attempts to deal with push-down accounting can be traced back to an AICPA issues paper which preceded the FASB's 1991 discussion memorandum on the topic. While it remained on the Board's technical agenda for about 6 years, no visible progress was made during this time. Meanwhile, the SEC has permitted and, in some instances required, application of push-down accounting in separately filed financial statements of acquired subsidiaries, where the change in control resulted from a 100% change in common stock ownership. Push-down has not been required in instances where the change in ownership was less than complete, although conceptually it would be easy to argue that substantial changes in ownership of say, 80% or more provide sufficient information upon which to apply new basis accounting. The FASB's Emerging Issues Task Force has also discussed this matter, in Issue 85-21, without reaching any consensus, however.

Now that the "new basis" project has been shelved by the FASB, application of push-down accounting will remain largely a matter of professional judgment. While there is no requirement under GAAP to apply the push-down concept, the SEC position is substantial authoritative support and can be referenced even for nonpublic company financial reporting. It would be defensible in any instance where there is a change in control and/or a change in ownership of a majority of the common shares, when separate financial statements of the subsidiary are to be presented. Full disclosure should be made of the circumstances whenever push-down accounting is applied.

Non-Sub Subsidiaries

An issue that has recently concerned accountants and the Securities and Exchange Commission is the sudden popularity of what have been called "non-sub subsidiaries." This situation arises when an entity plays a major role in the creation and financing of what is often a start-up or experimental operation, but does not take an equity position at the outset. For example, the parent might finance the entity by means of convertible debt or debt with warrants for the later purchase of common shares. The original equity partner in such arrangements most often will be the creative or managerial talent, which generally exchanges its talents for a stock interest. If the operation prospers, the parent will exercise its rights to a majority voting stock position; if it fails, the parent presumably avoids reflecting the losses in its statements.

While this strategy may seem to avoid the requirements of equity accounting or consolidation, the economic substance clearly suggests that the operating results of the subsidiary should be reflected in the financial statements of the real parent, even absent stock ownership. Until formal requirements are established in this area, an approach akin to the preparation of combined statements would seem reasonable.

EMERGING ISSUES TASK FORCE CONSENSUS SUMMARIES

84-13 Purchase of Stock Options with Stock Appreciation Rights in a Leveraged Buyout

This pronouncement addressed the question of whether options and similar rights which are purchased by a target company before completion of a leveraged buyout, with or without funds advanced by acquirer, should be deemed as compensation or as part of cost of the buyout. The consensus was that GAAP (APB 25) requires that this be accounted for as compensation.

84-33 Acquisition of a Tax Loss Carryforward--Temporary Parent-Subsidiary Relationship

Assume that Company X has a large NOL carryforward while Company Y is profitable. In a highly leveraged purchase combination, Company X acquires 80% of Company Y while giving Y's owners the option to repurchase a 60% interest in Y at a fixed price. The Task Force concurred that in such a situation the companies' financial statements should not be consolidated and that income should be recognized on the equity method only until the carrying amount of the investment equals the probable repurchase price.

85-12 Retention of Specialized Accounting for Investments in Consolidation

A consensus was reached that specialized accounting principles which are appropriately applied at a subsidiary company level should also be used in the consolidated financial statements.

85-14 Securities that Can Be Acquired for Cash in a Pooling

This pronouncement addressed the issue of whether holders of options, warrants, convertible debt, etc., must be given an acquiring company's common stock or if cash can be paid. A consensus was reached that convertible securities must be considered on case by case basis, and not always deemed common stock equivalents. However, the SEC usually requires that these be treated as common stock equivalents.

85-28 Consolidation Issues Relating to Collateralized Mortgage Obligations

A special purpose subsidiary, created to originate collateralized mortgage obligations, must be consolidated, if it was formed by a parent company which normally originates mortgages and then transfers them to the subsidiary.

85-45 Business Combinations: Settlement of Stock Options and Awards

This pronouncement extends the consensus of 84-13. If a target company in an LBO (leveraged buyout) settles options voluntarily, the payments must be accounted for as compensation expense in the separate financial statement of the target company. However, no consensus was reached on how the target should account for a reimbursement of costs received from the acquirer.

86-10 Pooling with 10% Cash Payout Determined by Lottery

Under the provisions of APB 16, cash can be paid for up to 10% of the common stock of the acquired company without precluding pooling treatment. Often cash payouts are used to settle fractional shares and to eliminate dissenting stockholders. If more than 10% of the shares outstanding qualify, a lottery is sometimes used. This consensus stated that it is acceptable to use a lottery to allocate cash to be paid, without obviating the use of the pooling method of accounting for the combination.

86-29 Nonmonetary Transactions: Magnitude of Boot and the Exceptions to the Use of Fair Value

This consensus primarily addresses APB 29 issues, but also offers interpretation on exchanges of investments which are accounted for under the provisions of either APB 16 or APB 18. A consensus was reached that an entity should account for an exchange of securities in which it acquires control of a subsidiary as an acquisition to be accounted for per APB 16. If control is not achieved but the investment will be accounted for by the equity method, the exchange should be treated as a monetary transaction per APB 29. However, this accounting would not apply to the acquisition of a minority interest.

86-32 Early Extinguishment of a Subsidiary's Mandatorily Redeemable Preferred Stock

This extinguishment is a capital stock transaction with no gain or loss recognized. Dividends would be included in minority interest as a charge against income.

87-11 Allocation of Purchase Price to Assets to be Sold

A consensus was reached that earnings or losses of a division which is to be sold, as well as interest on any incremental debt used to acquire it, and the gain or loss on the ultimate sale of the division, should not be included in income, if the sale is within 1 year. Under the provisions of SFAS 38, these should be accounted for as reallocations of the purchase price, inasmuch as they effectively are resolutions of preacquisition contingencies.

87-15 Effect of Standstill Agreement on Pooling of Interests Accounting

This pronouncement addressed circumstances in which there is a standstill agreement with a more than 10% owner. If the entity is subsequently acquired, there is a question about the ability to apply pooling of interests accounting to the business combination. There was a consensus that, if the agreement was not made in anticipation of business combination, pooling accounting would not be precluded. However, if the agreement had been made in anticipation of such a transaction, it would preclude pooling accounting. If the agreement was made with an owner of under 10% of the shares, and made in anticipation of the acquisition, and there are other dissenters which brings the total over 10%, then pooling accounting would also be precluded.

87-16 Whether the 90% Test for a Pooling of Interests is Applied Separately to Each Company or on a Combined Basis

This pronouncement addressed several related questions about mergers among several entities, including those situations where a new entity is created to effect the mergers. A consensus was reached that pooling accounting was required in situations where a new entity was formed to effect the merger, if pooling would have been indicated had at least one of the combining companies acted as the issuer/acquirer. In other fact situations, a two step test was stipulated. Several detailed examples are provided.

87-17 The Spin-Offs or Other Distributions of Loans Receivable to Shareholders

A consensus was reached that a transfer of loans receivable to a newly formed subsidiary in consideration for stock of the subsidiary should be recorded at fair market value by the enterprise and the recipient. The transaction would be classified as a dividend-in-kind rather than a spin-off because the subsidiary is not an operating company.

87-21 Change of Accounting Basis in Master Limited Partnership Transactions

This pronouncement addressed the variety of transactions which are used to create master limited partnerships, and specifically was intended to specify when a new basis of accounting should be recognized. The consensus was that a new basis of accounting is not appropriate in so-called "roll-ups" where the general partner was the general partner in all of the predecessors. Similarly, new basis of accounting is not appropriate in a "drop down" in which the sponsor is the corporate parent which maintains effective control after the restructuring. Also, a new basis of accounting is not appropriate in a "roll out" or in a reorganization. Likewise, even if general partner was the general partner in only some of the predecessors, no new basis could be established. Transaction costs incurred in connection with a roll-up should be expensed, not capitalized, in a manner similar to the accounting for poolings under APB 16.

87-27 Poolings of Companies That Do Not Have a Controlling Class of Common Stock

Pooling accounting is acceptable only if the issuing company exchanges its common stock for substantially all the common and preferred stock of the other entity; the issuer must issue only common, not preferred stock. If the issuing company does not have a controlling class of common stock, but does have preferred, it must first exchange common for preferred stock to create a controlling class, then execute the pooling transaction.

88-16 Basis in Leveraged Buyout Transactions

One of the most complex accounting areas, first addressed in EITF 86-16, this pronouncement stipulates how to compute the new cost basis after an LBO transaction. A consensus was reached that a new basis is to be recognized only when there is a change in the voting control from the former entity to the post-LBO entity; that a "substance over form" rule applies when seeking to determine if there had in fact been a change in control; and that a "monetary test" is established whereby fair value can only be used if at least 80% of the fair value of consideration paid to make the acquisition is monetary in nature.

88-26 Controlling Preferred Stock in a Pooling of Interests

This pronouncement addressed several matters pertaining to the issuance of preferred stock in pooling transactions. A consensus was reached that, if one company issues voting preferred stock for voting preferred stock of the target company, and issues common stock for the target's common stock, then pooling treatment will be lost because common stock must be issued for overall controlling interest. In another fact situation, a consensus was reached that, if the merging companies both cause conversion of their preferred shares to common shares before the transaction is effected, then the use of pooling accounting can be preserved.

88-27 Effect of Unallocated Shares in ESOP on Accounting for Business Combinations

A consensus was reached that unallocated shares held by an Employee Stock Ownership Plan (ESOP) are not tainted unless there is more than a remote possibility that such shares could revert to the sponsor, or there exists an agreement (even a tacit one) for the sponsor to repurchase shares, or the shares were acquired to circumvent the rules of APB 16.

89-7 Exchange of Assets or Interest in a Subsidiary for a Noncontrolling Equity Interest in a New Entity

The Task Force analyzed two example transactions and reached a consensus that full gain recognition is not appropriate for either transaction. The specific facts of the transactions are described in the EITF. The Task Force did note that because of the many possible variations, the specific facts and circumstances of each transaction would affect gain or loss recognition.

90-5 Exchanges of Ownership Interests Between Entities Under Common Control

This consensus stipulates that there is no step up in a transfer of a subsidiary from a parent company to another of its subsidiaries, and that the subsidiary's basis in the new subsidiary will be the same as was the parent company's. However, a buyout of minority interests by the subsidiary should be accounted for as a purchase transaction, whether effected by cash or by a stock transaction.

90-6 Accounting for Certain Events Relating to an Acquired Operating Unit to Be Sold

This pronouncement addresses circumstances in which a division of an acquired company is expected to be sold within 1 year of the acquisition transaction, but the disposition doesn't occur in a timely manner. The consensus was that a strict interpretation of SFAS 38 should be applied; therefore, after 1 year, further changes must be included in earnings, and no longer by a reallocation of the purchase price. If the decision to sell is reversed, the accounting to be employed depends upon whether this occurs before or after the 1 year time horizon is reached. If before, a reallocation of the purchase price is prescribed, including a cumulative restatement for depreciation, etc. If the decision to sell is reversed after 1 year period elapses, then a fair value adjustment is to be made to the assets and liabilities as of the date of the decision: if this is a write-down, it is to be taken to income, while if it is a write-up, the adjustment will be to goodwill and amortization prospectively.

90-12 Allocating Basis to Individual Assets and Liabilities for Transactions Within the Scope of EITF 88-16

This consensus prescribes the use of the partial purchase (step acquisition accounting) method, even if retained earnings are eliminated as a consequence.

90-13 Accounting for Simultaneous Common Control Mergers

This consensus addresses situations in which a parent company obtains control of a target, then spins one of its previously owned subsidiaries off to the target in exchange for more shares in the target (i.e., the old subsidiary becomes a "grandson" after the series of transactions). A consensus was reached that this latter step must be viewed as an integral part of the acquisition, not as an "Interpretation 39" transfer among entities under common control. A step up in basis would be permitted to the extent of a change in control, both upon the acquisition of the target and on the sale of the subsidiary to the new target subsidiary. The accounting for a spin-off of the old subsidiary to the target company is to be accounted for as "reverse acquisition" of the target by the subsidiary, per para 70 of APB 16.

90-15 Impact of Nonsubstantive Lessors, Residual Value Guarantees, and Other Provisions in Leasing Transactions (as altered by SFAS 125, as it pertains to consolidation of SPE)

This important consensus requires consolidation of a special purpose entity (SPE)/lessor into the financial statements of the lessee when all these conditions are met: substantially all activities of the SPE involve assets leased to single lessee; expected substantive residual risks and substantially all residual rewards of leased assets and obligation imposed by underlying debt of the SPE reside with lessee through such means as terms of lease agreement, residual value guarantee (e.g., assumption of first dollar of loss provisions), guarantee of SPE's debt, or option granting lessee right to purchase leased asset at fixed or defined price other than fair market value, or to receive excess sales proceeds from lessor; and absence of substantive capital infusion by record owner of SPE which remains at risk for entire lease term.

91-5 Nonmonetary Exchanges of Cost-Method Investments

The Task Force reached consensus on three issues regarding how an investor should account for its investment in a company, subsequent to a business combination, if the cost method is used. The first consensus reached was that the cost-method investor in the acquired company would record the transaction at fair value. The second consensus reached was that the cost-method investor in the acquiring company would continue to carry the investment at historical cost. The third consensus was that if an investor in the acquired company also possessed a cost-method investment in the acquiring company, the first two conclusions would still apply.

93-2 Effect of Acquisition of Employer Shares for/by an Employee Benefit Trust on Accounting for Business Combinations

At issue was whether shares reacquired by either an employer or a benefit trust (e.g., an ESOP) to fund future commitments to employee benefit plans are deemed tainted under APB Opinion 16 re: pooling-of-interests accounting for a business combination. The SEC Observor's position was that any shares reacquired coincident to the establishment of the trust would be tainted. As a result, the EITF did not further consider the issue.

93-7 Uncertainties Related to Income Taxes in a Purchase Business Combination

The consensus was that all income tax uncertainties (such as uncertainties about the allocation of purchase price to individual assets and liabilities for tax purposes in a taxable business combination, uncertainties about carryforwards in a nontaxable combination, and uncertainties about preacquisition tax returns of the acquired entity) existing at the time of a purchase business combination are to be accounted for under the provisions of SFAS 109, not under the provisions of SFAS 38 (preacquisition contingencies). Any such adjustments are to be applied to increase or decrease the remaining balance of goodwill attributable to that business combination; if goodwill is reduced to zero, the remaining amount should be used to reduce other noncurrent intangible assets from the same acquisition to zero, with any excess taken to income.

94-3 Accounting for Restructuring Charges

The issue involves restructuring charges, which have been taken with increasing frequency by companies, and which typically include costs such as employee benefits, costs associated with product line elimination or relocation, costs for new systems development or acquisition, retraining costs, and losses on asset impairment and dispositions. Many of these are not addressed by existing accounting standards (some, like severance costs, are already dealt with in the literature, however), and it is not clear when such costs are to be recognized. A subconcern is the possible use of "big baths" to absorb some future costs, and to thereby ensure future profitability.

Two approaches were considered: one would analogize from APB 30 to require accrual of costs when management adopts a formal restructuring plan, the other would apply SFAS 5 as the determinant of the timing for an accrual. The issue was not resolved; however, the SEC argued that (in the context of employee termination costs) the mere announcement of a restructuring decision would not be sufficient to accrue a liability (until specific affected employees have been notified). See related item 95-14 below.

95-3 Recognition of Liabilities in Connection with a Purchase Business Combination

If costs to exit an activity of an acquiree and involuntary termination or relocation costs relative to employees of an acquiree are anticipated at or very shortly after the acquisition, they should be reflected in the allocation of the purchase price, unless the costs are not incurred to generate revenue of the combined entity after the acquisition, in which case these would be period costs. (This is analogous to Issue 94-3 and examples in that consensus apply here also.) If later settled for amounts are less than accrued, the savings should be used to reduce the purchase price of the entity, which usually means goodwill recorded on the acquisition would be reduced; these adjustments are **not** preacqusition contingencies as defined by SFAS 38, and thus the 1 year limit is probably not applicable. Costs not identified timely would be period costs of the postacquisition entity. Costs related to assets or employees of the acquirer are not costs of the acquisition and cannot be part of the purchase price allocation process; these must be reflected in the income statement in all cases. A number of restrictions on the use of accrued liability treatment are prescribed--generally, to avoid a "big bath" by anticipating vague future costs. Costs of activities or employees of the acquirer are not allocable to the purchase price, per FASB TB 85-5. The consensus also identified certain disclosures to be made under these circumstances, including a description of plans to exit activities, possible reallocation of purchase transaction, etc.

95-8 Accounting for Contingent Consideration Paid to the Shareholders of an Acquired Company in a Purchase Business Combination

Whether contingent consideration based on earnings should be accounted for as an adjustment of the purchase price or as compensation for services, for the use of property, or for profit sharing depends on the facts and circumstances of each case. Some of the factors which can assist in making this determination relate to the terms of continuing employment, components of shareholder group, reasons for the contingent payment provisions, the formula used for determining contingent consideration, and other agreements and issues. For example, if compensation other than contingent payments is set at a reasonable level, this supports treatment of the contingent payments as an additional purchase price.

95-12 Pooling of Interests with a Common Investment in a Joint Venture

A common investment amounting to joint control does not violate the independent entities criterion for application of the pooling of interests treatment unless the investment accounts for over 50% of fair value of one combining entity. The FASB apparently did not agree with the consensus, but the Task Force has thus far declined to revisit it.

95-14 Recognition of Liabilities in Anticipation of a Business Combination

The issue involves contingency plans for exiting businesses and/or terminating employees if a business combination is consummated. The specific questions are whether the conditions specified in Issue 94-3 will be met only if the combination does occur. The consensus was that the commitment date for exit plan costs, and the recognition date for involuntary termination benefits, cannot occur prior to consummation.

95-19 Determination of the Measurement Date for the Market Price of Securities Issued in a Purchase Business Combination

Where there is conflicting guidance on which market price is to be considered in determining cost of acquisition using stock, the guidance in APB 16, para 74, should be relied upon: market price for a reasonable period before and after the event should be considered, although this span is usually brief (i.e., a few days). If number of shares to be exchanged is subsequently changed, this creates a new measurement date for valuation.

95-21 Accounting for Assets to be Disposed of Acquired in a Purchase Business Combination

This involves the interaction among Issue 87-11 (allocation of purchase cost to assets to be sold), APB 16, SFAS 121, and a proposed standard on consolidation. There was no attempt to reach a consensus, and further consideration at a later date is likely. The key issue is whether expected cash flows from operation of assets to be sold off should be considered, per 87-11, or whether assets should simply be booked at fair value less costs to sell, as suggested by proposed SFAS on consolidations, which builds on the SFAS 121 rule.

96-4 Accounting for Reorganizations Involving a Non-Rata Split-Off of Certain Nonmonetary Assets to Owners

The EITF's consensus was that the accounting for a non-pro rata split-off in a corporate plan of organization should be at fair value. With regard to a pro rata basis distribution in the split-off of a targeted business, the distribution to holders of related targeted stock should be at historical cost.

96-5 Recognition of Liabilities for Contractual Termination Benefits or Changing Benefit Plan Assumptions in Anticipation of a Business Combination

Termination costs to be incurred from business combination should not be accrued when business combination is merely deemed probable, but only when it is actually consummated.

96-7 Accounting for Deferred Taxes on In-Process Research and Development Activities Acquired in a Purchase Business Combination

Per FASB Interpretation 4, the purchase price allocated in a purchase business combination to research and development costs must be expensed immediately. At issue is whether, under SFAS 109, a deferred tax liability must be allocated to the initial (pre-write-off) basis difference between tax and book bases. The consensus was that since write-off occurs prior to the measurement of deferred taxes, no deferred taxes should be assigned.

96-8 Accounting for a Business Combination When the Issuing Company Has Targeted Stock

In a business combination in which the issuing company has targeted stock, pooling of interests accounting is not precluded as long as the issuing company distributes its majority class of voting stock.

96-20 Impact of FASB Statement No. 125 on Consolidation of Special-Purpose Entities

This issue relates to consolidation of "qualifying" SPE (as the term is defined in SFAS 125) by transferors when all transfers of financial assets to the SPE have been accounted for as sales, secured borrowings, or transfers in exchange for beneficial interests in the transferred assets. The specific question raised was whether the financial components approach of SFAS 125 affected consolidation considerations? A consensus was reached to the effect that the definition of control in SFAS 125 should be applied to the matter of consolidation of a SPE only when all these criteria are met; SPE meets all criteria of SFAS 125, paragraph 26; assets held by SPE are financial assets; and assets held are not the result of a structured transaction that converts nonfinancial assets such as real estate into financial assets, or recognizes previously unrecognized financial assets. Also, in all other circumstances, a transferor would continue to apply consolidation criteria of D-14 and of EITF 90-15 as appropriate. Furthermore, this consensus only applies if all transfers of financial assets to SPE since its inception were within the scope of SFAS 125.

97-2 Application of FASB Statement No. 94 and APB Opinion No. 16 to Physician Practice Management Entities and Certain Other Entities with Contractual Management Arrangements

A physician practice management can establish a controlling financial interest in physician practices via contractual management agreement, and thus trigger SFAS 94 consolidation requirement, if six criteria are met: life of 10 years minimum or remaining life of entity; not terminable by physicians under normal conditions; control over all ongoing, major central operations except for dispensing medical services; control over compensation of professionals, hiring and firing, etc.; financial interest is salable or transferable; and right to receive income based on performance risk and change in fair value.

97-6 Application of Issue 96-20 to Qualifying Special-Purpose Entities Receiving Transferred Financial Assets Prior to the Effective Date of FASB Statement No. 125

This revises EITF 96-20 by making it applicable to qualifying SPE that either hold only financial assets obtained in transfers accounted for under SFAS 125, or that have substantial capital investments by third parties, per EITF 90-15.

97-8 Accounting for Contingent Consideration Issued in a Purchase Business Combination

This deal with indirect contingent considerations arrangements, such as when those which are embedded in a security or it part of separate financial instrument; the question is when to recognize this cost. A consensus was reached that the fair value of the instrument should be recognized at the date of acquisition as part of purchase cost to be allocated if the instrument is traded or indexed to one which is traded, with subsequent value changes ignored. If instrument is not traded, contingent cost would be measured when contingency is resolved, per APB 16, paragraph 79-83. Other accounting issues are addressed in EITF 96-13 and 86-28.

97-9 Effect of Pooling of Interest Accounting of Certain Contingently Exercisable Options or Other Equity Instruments

The issue relates to "lock up options" which are issued to assure negotiating parties that planned merger will occur, or else shares can be acquired at below-market price. Also this related to situation in which employees are given options which vest upon occurrence of events such as a planned merger. Questions relate to whether these "contingently exercisable instruments" affect use of pooling treatment. Consensus was that pooling is not precluded, but since alteration of equity interests in anticipation of combination would be bar to pooling and such arrangements would often meet the test, pooling might be ruled out as a practical effect. Consensus was that lock up options are the exception, in that alteration of equity interest will not occur if transaction goes forward, and thus do not affect use of pooling. However, any intervening deal would be affected, and thus could not be accounted for as pooling.

97-15 Accounting for Contingency Arrangements Based on Security Prices in a Purchase Business Combination

This issue relates to "below market" or "above market" guarantees of market value of securities issued in purchase transaction; under APB 16 the normal type of market value guarantee does not get reflected in purchase cost. The consensus is that for below market value guarantee, there would be no purchase cost adjustment, as cost is fair value of unconditional securities given at date of combination only. On the other hand, in an above market contingent issuance [e.g., issue more shares if price 3 years hence is not at least \$x, where \$x > \$y (price at deal date)], there will be a requirement to issue more shares if the price exceeds some defined threshold, perhaps with a declining number of shares up to price of \$z, where \$z > \$x. In these cases, the cost of the purchase is the maximum number of additional shares times price as of the date of transaction, with no later adjustments to be recognized.

98-1 Valuation of Debt Assumed in a Purchase Business Combination

APB 16 directs cost allocation based on fair values of assets and liabilities, with fair value of liabilities being computed using present value. Issue arises because present value ≠ fair value in some cases, such as when prepayment option affects fair value but present value would often ignore this contingent change in future cash flows. Consensus was to use fair value, even if ≠ present value of cash flows. Since market values may not be available, some use of present value method may be required, but the value of option features, etc. must be included in the calculation.

98-2 Accounting by a Subsidiary for an Investment in Its Parent Company's Stock

This issue relates to the display of an investment by subsidiary in parent's or joint venture partner's stock in separate statements of the subsidiary or the joint venture specifically, how; SFAS 115 rules affect this presentation. Questions to be answered are how to account for initial purchase and subsequent accounting for such investments. Possible answers are to account for the investment as an asset to be accounted for at fair value; a distribution to the parent or joint venture partner (similar to treasury stock); or as an asset measured by the equity method, with an elimination of reciprocal ownership investments. No consensus has been reached on this issue yet.

98-3 Determining Whether a Transaction Is an Exchange of Similar Productive Assets or a Business Combination

APB 29 states that nonmonetary exchanges should generally be reported at fair value, but exchange of productive assets are to be recorded at carrying value or assets relinquished. APB 16, however, uses a fair value approach. Some exchanges (e.g., of radio stations or other groups of operating assets) may be either nonmonetary exchanges or business combinations. No consensus yet achieved on this issue; the SEC favor APB 16 accounting, even for exchanges of entire similar businesses.

98-4 Accounting by a Joint Venture or Businesses Received at Its Formation

Issue is how a joint venture should record, in stand alone financials, businesses received from venture partner, in situations where either the relationship between joint venturer and venturers has none of the five attributes of a corporate joint venture set forth in APB 18, paragraph 3(d) but there is joint control, or where all five attributes exist and there is joint control. In common practice, the carryforward basis is used. A need for definition of joint control is noted, and this will be further pursued by EITF. SEC supports the APB 16 treatment for contributions to newly formed, jointly controlled entity if entity is not joint venture (presumably means carryforward basis); and also would object to the conclusion that joint control is the only defining characteristic of a joint venture. More discussion of these matters is anticipated.

12 CURRENT LIABILITIES AND CONTINGENCIES

PERSPECTIVE AND ISSUES

The division of assets and liabilities into current and noncurrent allows working capital (current assets minus current liabilities) to be calculated. Working capital, which is the relatively liquid portion of total enterprise capital, can be used to determine the ability of an enterprise to repay obligations. Working capital assumes a going-concern concept. If the enterprise is to be liquidated in the near future, classification of assets and liabilities is inappropriate.

ARB 43, Chapter 3 defines current liabilities as those enterprise obligations whose liquidation is reasonably expected to require the use of existing resources properly classifiable as current assets or the creation of other current liabilities. This definition excludes from the current liability classification any currently maturing obligations which will be satisfied by using long-term assets and currently maturing obligations expected to be refinanced.

Offsetting of assets and liabilities is improper except where a right of setoff exists. A right of setoff is a debtor's legal right to discharge debt owed to another party by applying against the debt an amount the other party owes to the debtor. Per FASB Technical Bulletin 88-2 the conditions to be met are as follows:

1. Each of the two parties owes the other determinable amounts.
2. The reporting party has the right to setoff.
3. The reporting party intends to setoff.
4. The right of setoff is enforceable at law.

FASB Interpretation No. 39 does permit the offsetting of fair value amounts recognized for multiple swap, forward, option and other conditional or exchange contracts with a single party executed under a master netting arrangement. FASB Interpretation No. 41 modifies this interpretation to provide guidance as to the circumstances in which amounts recognized as payables in repurchase agreements may be offset against amounts recognized as receivables in reverse repurchase agreements. The entity's choice to offset or not shall be applied consistently.

SFAS 5 and the issues related to the recognition of liabilities resulting from loss contingencies, SFAS 43, SFAS 78, and SFAS 112 are also discussed in this chapter.

Sources of GAAP

ARB	*APB*	*SFAS*	*FASB I*	*FASB TB*	*EITF*
43, Ch. 3, 10, 50	6, 21	5, 6, 11, 29, 43, 78, 112	8, 14, 34, 39, 41	79-3, 88-2	86-2, 86-5, 86-15, 86-30, 95-22

DEFINITIONS OF TERMS

Accumulated benefits. Employee benefits which can be carried over into the next year but which expire upon termination of employment.

Contingency. An existing condition, situation, or set of circumstances involving uncertainty as to possible gain or loss that will ultimately be resolved when one or more future events occur or fail to occur.

Current liabilities. Enterprise obligations whose liquidation is reasonably expected to require the use of existing resources properly classified as current assets or the creation of other current liabilities. Obligations that are due on demand or will be due on demand within 1 year or the operating cycle, if longer, are current liabilities. Long-term obligations callable because of the debtor's violation of a provision of the debt agreement are current liabilities unless specific SFAS 78 conditions are met.

FICA. Social security taxes levied upon both employees and employers.

FUTA. Social security tax levied upon employers to finance the administration of federal unemployment benefit programs.

Indirect guarantee of indebtedness of others. A guarantee under an agreement that obligates one enterprise to transfer funds to a second enterprise upon the occurrence of specified events under conditions whereby (1) the funds are legally available to the creditors of the second enterprise, and (2) those creditors may enforce the second enterprise's claims against the first enterprise.

Operating cycle. The average length of time necessary for an enterprise to convert inventory to receivables to cash.

CONCEPTS, RULES, AND EXAMPLES

ARB 43, Chapter 3 contains several examples of current liabilities. It also contains broad general descriptions of the types of items to be shown as current liabilities. These obligations can be divided into those where

1. Both the amount and the payee are known;

2. The payee is known but the amount may have to be estimated;
3. The payee is unknown and the amount may have to be estimated; and
4. The liability has been incurred due to a loss contingency.

Amount and Payee Known

Accounts payable arise primarily from the acquisition of materials and supplies to be used in the production of goods or in conjunction with the providing of services. APB 21, para 3a states that payables that arise from transactions with suppliers in the normal course of business, which are due in customary trade terms not to exceed 1 year, may be stated at their face amount rather than at the present value of the required future cash flows.

Notes payable are more formalized obligations which may arise from the acquisition of materials and supplies used in operations or from the use of short-term credit to purchase capital assets (APB 21, para 3a also applies to short-term notes payable).

Dividends payable become a liability of the enterprise when the board of directors declares a cash dividend. Since declared dividends are usually paid within a short period of time after the declaration date, they are classified as **current liabilities**.

Unearned revenues or advances result from customer prepayments of either performance of services or delivery of product. They may be required by the selling enterprise as a condition of the sale or may be made by the buyer as a means of guaranteeing that the seller will perform the desired service or deliver the product. Unearned revenues and advances should be classified as current liabilities at the balance sheet date if the services are to be performed or the products are to be delivered within 1 year or the **operating cycle**, whichever is longer.

Returnable deposits may be received to cover possible future damage to property. Many utility companies require security deposits. A deposit may be required for the use of a reusable container. Refundable deposits are classified as current liabilities if the firm expects to refund them during the current operating cycle or within 1 year, whichever is longer.

Accrued liabilities have their origin in the end-of-period adjustment process required by accrual accounting. Commonly accrued liabilities include wages and salaries payable, interest payable, rent payable, and taxes payable.

Agency liabilities result from the legal obligation of the enterprise to act as the collection agent for customer or employee taxes owed to various federal, state, or local government units. Examples of agency liabilities include sales taxes, income taxes withheld from employee paychecks, and employee **FICA** contributions. In addition to agency liabilities, an employer may have a current obligation for the **FUTA** (unemployment) tax. Payroll taxes are not legal liabilities until the associated payroll is actually paid.

Current maturing portion of long-term debt is shown as a current liability if the obligation is to be liquidated by using assets classified as current. However, if the currently maturing debt is to be liquidated by using other than current assets (i.e., by using a sinking fund which is properly classified as an investment), then these obligations should be classified as long-term liabilities.

Obligations that, by their terms, are due on demand (EITF 86-5) or will be due on demand within 1 year (or operating cycle, if longer) from the balance sheet date, even if liquidation is not expected to occur within that period, are classified as current liabilities. SFAS 78 also requires that long-term obligations which contain call provisions are to be classified as current liabilities, if as of the balance sheet date one of the following occurs:

1. The debtor is in violation of the agreement and this violation makes the obligation callable.
2. The debtor is in violation of the agreement and such violation, unless cured within the grace period specified in the agreement, makes the obligation callable.

Note, however, that if circumstances arise which effectively negate the creditor's right to call the obligation, then the obligation may be classified as long-term. Examples are

1. The creditor has waived the right to call the obligation caused by the debtor's violation or the creditor has subsequently lost the right to demand repayment for more than 1 year (or operating cycle, if longer) from the balance sheet date.
2. Obligations contain a grace period for remedying the violation, and it is probable that the violation will be cured within the grace period. In these situations, the circumstances must be disclosed.

Short-term obligations expected to be refinanced may be classified as noncurrent liabilities if certain conditions are met. If an enterprise intends to refinance the currently maturing portion of long-term debt or intends to refinance callable obligations by replacing them with either new long-term debt or with equity securities, SFAS 6 must be followed. SFAS 6 states that an enterprise may reclassify currently maturing debt (other than obligations arising from transactions in the normal course of business that are due in customary terms) as long-term provided that the enterprise intends to refinance the obligation on a long-term basis **and** its intent is supported by **either** of the following:

1. Post-balance-sheet-date issuance of a long-term obligation or equity securities. After the date of the enterprise's balance sheet but before that balance sheet is issued, long-term obligations or equity securities have been issued for the purpose of refinancing the short-term obligations on a long-term basis.

2. Financing agreement. Before the balance sheet is issued, the enterprise has entered into a financing agreement that clearly permits the enterprise to refinance the short-term obligation on a long-term basis on terms that are readily determinable.

If reclassification of the maturing debt is based upon the existence of a refinancing agreement, then SFAS 6 requires the following:

1. The agreement will not expire within 1 year or operating cycle of the balance sheet date and is noncancelable.
2. The replacement debt will not be callable except for violation of a provision of the agreement with which compliance is objectively determinable or measurable.
3. The enterprise is not in violation of the terms of the agreement.
4. The lender or investor is financially capable of honoring the agreement.

Under the provisions of SFAS 6, the amount of currently maturing debt to be reclassified cannot exceed the amount raised by the actual refinancing nor can it exceed the amount specified in the refinancing agreement. If the amount specified in the refinancing agreement can fluctuate, then the maximum amount of debt that can be reclassified is equal to a reasonable estimate of the minimum amount expected to be available on any date from the maturing date of the maturing obligation to the end of the fiscal year. If no estimate can be made of the minimum amount available under the financing agreement, then none of the maturing debt can be reclassified as long-term. FASB Interpretation 8 states that if an enterprise uses current assets after the balance sheet date to liquidate a current obligation, and replaces those current assets by issuing either equity securities or long-term debt before the issuance of the balance sheet, the current obligation must still be classified as a current liability.

Payee Known But Amount May Have to Be Estimated

Taxes payable include federal, state, and local income taxes. Due to frequent changes in the tax laws, the amount of income taxes payable may have to be estimated. That portion deemed currently payable must be classified as a current liability. The remaining amount is classified as a long-term liability.

Property taxes payable represent the unpaid portion of an entity's obligation to a state or other taxing authority which arises from ownership of real property. ARB 43, Chapter 10 indicates that the most acceptable method of accounting for property taxes is a monthly accrual of property tax expense during the fiscal period of the taxing authority for which the taxes are levied. The fiscal period of the taxing authority is the fiscal period which includes the assessment or lien date.

A liability for property taxes payable arises when the fiscal year of the taxing authority and the fiscal year of the entity do not coincide or when the assessment or lien date and the actual payment date do not fall within the same fiscal year. For example, XYZ Corporation is a calendar-year corporation which owns real estate in a state that operates on a June 30 fiscal year. In this state, property taxes are assessed and become a lien against property on July 1, although they are not payable until April 1 and August 1 of the next calendar year. XYZ Corporation would accrue an expense and a liability on a monthly basis beginning on July 1. At year end (December 31), the firm would have an expense for 6 months' property tax on their income statement and a current liability for the same amount.

Bonus payments may require estimation since the amount of the bonus payment may be affected by the amount of income taxes currently payable.

Compensated absences refer to paid vacation, paid holidays, and paid sick leave. SFAS 43 states that an employer must accrue a liability for employee's compensation of future absences if all of the following conditions are met:

1. The employee's right to receive compensation for future absences is attributable to employee services already rendered.
2. The right vests or accumulates.
3. Payment of the compensation is probable.
4. The amount of the payment can be reasonably estimated.

If an employer is required to compensate an employee for unused vacation, holidays, or sick days even if employment is terminated, then the employee's right to this compensation is said to vest. Accrual of a liability for nonvesting rights depends on whether the unused rights expire at the end of the year in which earned or accumulate and are carried forward to succeeding years. If the rights expire, a liability for future absences should not be accrued at year end because the benefits to be paid in subsequent years would not be attributable to employee services rendered in prior years. If unused rights accumulate and increase the benefits otherwise available in subsequent years, a liability should be accrued at year end to the extent that it is probable that employees will be paid in subsequent years for the increased benefits attributable to the accumulated rights and the amount can be reasonably estimated.

SFAS 43 allows an exception to the application of this statement to employee paid sick days which accumulate but do not vest. No accrued liability is required for sick days which only accumulate. However, an accrual may be made. The Board stated that these amounts are rarely material and the low reliability of estimates of future illness coupled with the high cost of developing these estimates indicates that accrual is not necessary. The required accounting should be determined by the employer's actual administration of sick pay benefits. If the employer routinely lets employees take time off and allows that time to be charged as sick pay, then an accrual should be made.

Pay for employee leaves of absence that represent time off for past services should be considered compensation subject to accrual. Pay for employee leaves of absence that will provide future benefits and that are not attributable to past services rendered would not be subject to accrual. SFAS 43 does not provide guidance as to whether accruals should be based on current pay rates or expected future rates of pay and does not provide guidance regarding discounting of the accrual amounts.

SFAS 112 uses the conditions of SFAS 43 to accrue an obligation for postemployment benefits other than pensions if employees' rights accumulate or vest, payment is probable, and the amount can be reasonably estimated. If these benefits do not vest or accumulate, SFAS 5 applies. If neither SFAS 43 nor SFAS 5 is applicable because the amount is not reasonably estimated, this fact must be disclosed.

Payee Unknown and the Amount May Have to Be Estimated

Premiums are usually offered by an enterprise to increase product sales. They may require the purchaser to return a specified number of box tops, wrappers, or other proofs of purchase. They may or may not require the payment of a cash amount. If the premium offer terminates at the end of the current period but has not been completely accounted for, or if it extends into the next accounting period, a current liability for the estimated number of redemptions expected in the future period will have to be recorded. If the premium offer extends for more than one accounting period, the estimated liability must be divided into a current portion and a long-term portion.

Product warranties providing for repair or replacement of defective products may be sold separately or may be included in the sale price of the product. If the warranty extends into the next accounting period, a current liability for the estimated amount of warranty expense expected in the next period must be recorded. If the warranty spans more than the next period, the estimated liability must be partitioned into a current and long-term portion.

Contingencies

SFAS 5 defines a **contingency** as an existing condition, situation, or set of circumstances involving uncertainty as to possible gain or loss. It will ultimately be resolved when one or more future events occur or fail to occur. SFAS 5 defines the different levels of probability as to whether or not future events will confirm the existence of a loss as follows:

1. **Probable**--The future event or events are likely to occur.
2. **Reasonably possible**--The chance of the future event or events occurring is more than remote but less than likely.
3. **Remote**--The chance of the future event or events occurring is slight.

Professional judgment is required to classify the likelihood of the future events occurring. All relevant information that can be acquired concerning the uncertain set of circumstances needs to be obtained and used to determine the classification.

SFAS 5 states that a loss must be accrued if **both** of the following conditions are met:

1. It is **probable** that an asset has been impaired or a liability has been incurred at the date of the financial statements.
2. The amount of loss can be reasonably estimated.

It is not necessary that a single amount be identified. A range of amounts is sufficient to indicate that some amount of loss has been incurred and should be accrued. The amount accrued is the amount within the range that appears to be the best estimate. If there is no best estimate, the minimum amount in the range should be accrued since it is probable that the loss will be at least this amount (FASB Interpretation 14, para 3). The maximum amount of loss should be disclosed. If future events indicate that the minimum loss originally accrued is inadequate, an additional loss should be accrued in the period when this fact becomes known. This accrual is a change in estimate, not a prior period adjustment.

When a loss is probable and no estimate is possible, these facts should be disclosed in the current period. The accrual of the loss should be made in the period in which the amount of the loss can be estimated. This accrual of a loss in future periods is a change in estimate. It is not a prior period adjustment.

If the occurrence of the loss is reasonably possible, the facts and circumstances of the possible loss and an estimate of the amount, if determinable, should be disclosed. If the occurrence of the loss is remote, no accrual or disclosure is usually required.

Guarantees. Guarantees of indebtedness (direct or indirect), obligations under standby letters of credit, guarantees to repurchase, and guarantees with similar circumstances should be disclosed even if the possibility of loss is remote.

Unasserted claims or assessments. It is not necessary to disclose loss contingencies for an unasserted claim or assessment where there has been no manifestation of an awareness of possible claim or assessment by a potential claimant unless it is deemed probable that a claim will be asserted and a reasonable possibility of an unfavorable outcome exists. Under the provisions of SFAS 5, general or unspecified business risks are not loss contingencies and, therefore, no accrual is necessary. In addition, no disclosure is required. Appropriations of retained earnings may be used for these risks as long as no charge to income is made to establish the appropriation.

Loss contingency. Loss contingencies are recognized only if there is an impairment of an asset or the incurrence of a liability as of the balance sheet date. Events which give rise to loss contingencies that occur after the balance sheet date (i.e., bankruptcy or expropriation) but before issuance of the financial statements may require disclosure so that statement users are not misled. Footnote disclosures or pro forma financial statements may be prepared as supplemental information to show the effect of the loss.

Gain contingency. SFAS 5 leaves unchanged the provisions of ARB 50 which state that gain contingencies should not be recorded before they have been realized but that adequate disclosure of the gain contingency should be made. Such disclosure should not contain misleading implications as to the likelihood of realization.

Estimate vs. contingency. Distinguishing between an estimate and a contingency can be difficult because both involve an uncertainty that will be resolved by future events. However, an estimate exists because of uncertainty about the amount of an event requiring an acknowledged accounting recognition. The event is known and the effect is known, but the amount itself is uncertain. For example, depreciation is an estimate, but not a contingency because the actual fact of physical depreciation is acknowledged, although the amount is obtained by an assumed accounting method.

In a contingency, the amount is also usually uncertain, although that is not an essential characteristic. Collectibility of receivables is a contingency because both the amount of loss and the identification of which customer will not pay in the future is unknown. Similar logic would hold for obligations related to product warranties. Both the amount and the customer are currently unknown.

Other contingencies are rarely recognized until specific events confirming their existence occur. Every business risks loss by fire, explosion, government expropriation or guarantees made in the ordinary course of business. These are all contingencies because of the uncertainty surrounding whether the future event confirming the loss will or will not take place. The risk of asset expropriation exists, but is more likely in an unfriendly foreign country than in the United States.

The most difficult area of contingencies is litigation. Accountants must rely on attorneys' assessments concerning the likelihood of such events. Unless the attorney indicates that the risk of loss is remote or slight, or that the loss if it occurs would be immaterial to the company, the accountant will add an explanatory paragraph regarding the contingency. In cases where judgments have been entered against the entity, or where the attorney gives a range of expected losses or other amounts, certain accruals of loss contingencies for at least the minimum point of the range must be made. In most cases, however, an estimate of the contingency is unknown and the contingency is reflected only in footnotes.

EMERGING ISSUES TASK FORCE CONSENSUS SUMMARIES

86-2 Retroactive Wage Adjustments Affecting Medicare Payments

Because of the uncertainty regarding these retroactive adjustments, an adjustment should not be recorded in the current period. However, if the amount of the adjustment is material, it should be disclosed in the financial statements.

86-5 Classifying Demand Notes with Repayment Terms

Obligations that, by their terms, are due on demand or will be due on demand within 1 year (or operating cycle, if longer) from the balance sheet date, even if liquidation is not expected to occur within that period, are classified as current liabilities.

86-15 Increasing-Rate Debt

Notes that mature in 3 months but can be continually extended for up to 5 years are known as "increasing-rate notes." The outstanding term of the debt should be estimated after considering plans, ability and intent to service the debt. Based upon this term, the borrower's periodic interest rate should be determined by the use of the interest method.

Debt interest costs should be amortized over the estimated outstanding term of the debt. Any excess accrued interest resulting from paying the debt before the estimated maturity date is an adjustment of interest expense. It is not an extraordinary item under SFAS 4.

The classification of the debt as to current or noncurrent should be based on the source of repayment. Thus, this classification need not be consistent with the period used to determine the periodic interest cost. For example, the time frame used for the estimated outstanding term of the debt could be a year or less but, because of a planned long-term refinancing agreement, the noncurrent classification could be used.

86-30 Classification of Obligations When a Violation is Waived by the Creditor

Except when indicated otherwise, the borrower's obligation is noncurrent unless the covenant violation has occurred at balance sheet date (or would have occurred except for a loan modification) and it is probable that the default will not be cured at measurement date within the next 12 months.

95-22 Balance Sheet Classification of Borrowings Outstanding Under Revolving Credit Agreements that Include Both a Subjective Acceleration Clause and a Lock-Box Agreement

These borrowings, where remittances reduce debt outstanding, are considered short-term obligations. Because of the subjective acceleration clause, the debt is classified as a current liability unless paragraphs 10 and 11 of SFAS 6, dealing with intent to refinance and ability to refinance, respectively, are met based on an agreement other than the revolving credit agreement.

13 LONG-TERM DEBT

PERSPECTIVE AND ISSUES

Long-term debt represents future sacrifices of economic benefits to be repaid over a period of more than one year or, if longer, the operating cycle. Long-term debt includes bonds payable, notes payable, lease obligations, pension and deferred compensation plan obligations, deferred income taxes, and unearned revenue. The accounting for bonds and long-term notes is covered in this chapter.

The proper valuation of long-term debt is the present value of future payments using the market rate of interest, either stated or implied in the transaction, at the date the debt was incurred. An exception to the use of the market rate of interest stated or implied in the transaction in valuing long-term notes occurs when it is necessary to use an imputed interest rate (APB 21).

SFAS 125 uses a financial-components approach that relies on control to establish standards for transfers and servicing of financial assets and extinguishments of liabilities. Derivatives and liabilities resulting from a transfer of financial assets are measured at fair value. In-substance defeasance does not result in the extinguishment of a liability.

Through-put and take-or-pay contracts are ways in which natural resource firms disguise debt. In these situations, capital projects (e.g., factories, plants, pipelines, etc.) are built through joint ventures with other firms. The joint venture incurs the debt while the firm(s) purchase the goods or services provided by the project. The payment for the goods and services must be made whether delivery is taken or not and is at some fixed or minimum amount which covers the interest. SFAS 47 sets forth the disclosure requirements for these contracts. This statement deferred the measurement and recognition problems until a future date.

SFAS 114 was amended by SFAS 118. Together, they specify the accounting by creditors for troubled debt restructurings involving a modification of terms.

Sources of GAAP

APB	*SFAS*	*FASB I*	*FASB TB*	*EITF*	*SOP*
14, 21, 26	4, 5, 6, 15, 47, 64, 84, 114, 118, 125, 127, 133	8, 14	79-3, 80-1, 80-2, 81-6	84-11, 85-17, 86-36, 87-19, 88-18, 88-23, 89-9, 89-15, 90-19, 94-8, 95-15, 96-22, 98-5	92-3, 96-1

DEFINITIONS OF TERMS

Amortization. The process of allocating an amount to expense over the periods benefited.

Bond. A written agreement whereby a borrower agrees to pay a sum of money at a designated future date plus periodic interest payments at the stated rate.

Bond issue costs. Costs related to issuing a bond (i.e., legal, accounting, underwriting fees, printing, and registration costs).

Bonds outstanding method. Accounting for serial bonds which assumes the discount or premium applicable to each bond of the issue is the same dollar amount per bond per year.

Book value approach. Recording the stock issued from a bond conversion at the carrying value of the bonds converted.

Callable bond. A bond in which the issuer reserves the right to call and retire the bond prior to its maturity.

Carrying value. The face amount of a debt issue increased or decreased by the applicable unamortized premium or discount plus unamortized issue costs.

Collateral. Asset(s) pledged to settle the obligation to repay a loan.

Convertible debt. Debt which may be converted into common stock at the holder's option after specific criteria are met.

Covenant. A clause in a debt contract written for the protection of the lender which outlines the rights and actions of the parties involved when certain conditions occur (e.g., when the debtor's current ratio declines beyond a specified level).

Debenture. Long-term debt not secured by collateral.

Defeasance. Extinguishment of debt by creating a trust to service it.

Discount. Created when a debt instrument sells for less than face value and occurs when the stated rate on the instrument is less than the market rate at the time of issue.

Effective interest method. Amortizing the discount or premium to interest expense so as to result in a constant rate of interest when applied to the amount of debt outstanding at the beginning of any given period.

Effective rate. See market rate.

Face value. The stated amount or principal due on the maturity date.

Imputation. The process of interest rate approximation which is accomplished by examining the circumstances under which the note was issued.

Long-term debt. Probable future sacrifices of economic benefits arising from present obligations that are not currently payable within 1 year or the operating cycle of the business, whichever is longer.

Market rate. The current rate of interest available for obligations issued under the same terms and conditions.

Market value approach. Recording the stock issued from a bond conversion at the current market price of the bonds converted or the stock issued.

Maturity date. The date on which the face value (principal) of the bond or note becomes due.

Maturity value. See face value.

Premium. Created when a debt instrument sells for more than its face value and occurs when the stated rate on the instrument is greater than the market rate at the time of issue.

Principal. See face value.

Secured debt. Debt which has collateral to satisfy the obligation (i.e., a mortgage on specific property) if not repaid.

Serial bond. Debt whose face value matures in installments.

Stated rate. The interest rate written on the face of the debt instrument.

Straight-line method. The method of amortizing the premium or discount to interest expense such that there is an even allocation of interest expense over the life of the debt.

Take-or-pay contract. A contract in which a purchaser of goods agrees to pay specified fixed or minimum amounts periodically in return for products, even if delivery is not taken. It results from a project financing arrangement where the project produces the products.

Through-put agreement. An agreement similar to a take-or-pay contract except a service is provided by the project under the financing arrangement.

Troubled debt restructure. Occurs when the creditor, for economic or legal reasons related to the debtor's financial difficulties, grants a concession to the debtor (deferment or reduction of interest or principal) that it would not otherwise consider.

Unconditional purchase obligation. An obligation to transfer a fixed or minimum amount of funds in the future or to transfer goods or services at fixed or minimum prices.

Yield rate. See market rate.

CONCEPTS, RULES, AND EXAMPLES

Notes and Bonds

Notes represent debt issued to a single investor without intending for the debt to be broken up among many investors. Their maturity, usually lasting 1 to 7 years, tends to be shorter than that of a bond. Bonds also result from a single agreement. However, a bond is intended to be broken up into various subunits, typically $1,000 each, which can be issued to a variety of investors.

Notes and bonds share common characteristics. These include a written agreement stating the amount of the **principal**, the interest rate, when the interest and principal are to be paid, and the **restrictive covenants**, if any, which must be met.

The interest rate is affected by many factors, including the cost of money, the business risk factors, and the inflationary expectations associated with the business.

The **stated rate** on a note or bond often differs from the **market rate** at the time of issuance. When this occurs, the present value of the interest and principal payments will differ from the maturity, or **face value**. If the market rate exceeds the stated rate, the cash proceeds will be less than the face value of the debt because the present value of the total interest and principal payments discounted back to the present yields an amount which is less than the face value. Because an investor is rarely willing to pay more than the present value, the bonds must be issued at a discount. The **discount** is the difference between the issuance price (present value) and the face, or stated, value of the bonds. This discount is then amortized over the life of the bonds to increase the recognized interest expense so that the total amount of the expense represents the actual bond yield.

When the stated rate exceeds the market rate, the bond will sell for more than its face value (at a **premium**) to bring the effective rate to the market rate and will decrease the total interest expense. When the market and stated rates are equivalent at the time of issuance, no discount or premium exists and the instrument will sell at its face value. Changes in the market rate subsequent to issuance are irrelevant in determining the discount or premium or their **amortization**.

Notes are a common form of exchange in business transactions for cash, property, goods, and services. Most notes carry a stated rate of interest, but it is not uncommon for noninterest notes or notes bearing an unrealistic rate of interest to be exchanged. Notes such as these, which are long-term in nature, do not reflect the economic substance of the transaction since the face value of the note does not represent the present value of the consideration involved. Not recording the note at its present value will misstate the cost of the asset or services to the buyer as well as the selling price and profit to the seller. In subsequent periods, both the interest expense and revenue will be misstated.

To remedy the situation APB 21 was issued. **All** commitments to pay (and receive) money at a determinable future date are subject to present value techniques and, if necessary, interest imputation with the exception of the following:

1. Normal accounts payable due within 1 year.
2. Amounts to be applied to purchase price of goods or services or that provide security to an agreement (e.g., advances, progress payments, security deposits, and retainages).
3. Transactions between parent and subsidiary.
4. Obligations payable at some indeterminable future date (warranties).
5. Lending and depositor savings activities of financial institutions whose primary business is lending money.

6. Transactions where interest rates are affected by prescriptions of a governmental agency (e.g., revenue bonds, tax exempt obligations, etc.).

Three categories of commitments subject to APB 21 are important.

Notes issued solely for cash. When a note is issued solely for cash, its present value is assumed to be equal to the cash proceeds. The interest rate is that rate which equates the cash proceeds to the amounts to be paid in the future (i.e., **no** interest rate is to be imputed). For example, a $1,000 note due in 3 years which sells for $889 has an implicit rate of 4% ($1,000 x .889, where .889 is the present value factor of a lump sum at 4% for 3 years). This rate is to be used when amortizing the discount.

Notes issued for cash and a right or privilege. Often when a note bearing an unrealistic rate of interest is issued in exchange for cash, an additional right or privilege is granted, such as the issuer agreeing to sell merchandise to the purchaser at a reduced rate. The difference between the present value of the receivable and the cash loaned is regarded as an addition to the cost of the products purchased for the purchaser/lender and as unearned revenue to the issuer. This treatment stems from the APB's attempt to match revenue and expense in the proper periods and to differentiate between those factors that affect income from operations and income or expense from nonoperating sources. In the situation above, the discount (difference between the cash loaned and the present value of the note) will be amortized to interest revenue or expense, while the unearned revenue or contractual right is amortized to sales and inventory, respectively. The discount affects income from nonoperational sources, while the unearned revenue or contractual right affects the gross profit computation. This differentiation is necessary because the amortization rates used differ for the two amounts.

Example of accounting for a note issued for both cash and a contractual right

1. Miller borrows $10,000 via a noninterest-bearing 3-year note from Krueger.
2. Miller agrees to sell $50,000 of merchandise to Krueger at less than the ordinary retail price for the duration of the note.
3. The fair rate of interest on a note such as this is 10%.

According to APB 21, para 7, the difference between the present value of the note and the face value of the loan is to be regarded as part of the cost of the products purchased under the agreement. The present value factor for an amount due in 3 years at 10% is .75132. Therefore, the present value of the note is $7,513 ($10,000 x .75132). The $2,487 ($10,000 – $7,513) difference between the face value and the present value is to be recorded as a discount on the note payable and as unearned revenue on the future purchases. The following entries would be made to record the transaction:

Miller			*Krueger*		
Cash	10,000		Note receivable	10,000	
Discount on note payable	2,487		Contract right with supplier	2,487	
Note payable		10,000	Cash		10,000
Unearned revenue		2,487	Discount on note receivable		2,487

The discount on note payable (and note receivable) is to be amortized using the effective interest method, while the unearned revenue account and contract right with supplier account are amortized on a pro rata basis as the right to purchase merchandise is used up. Thus, if Krueger purchased $20,000 of merchandise from Miller in the first year, the following entries would be necessary:

Miller			*Krueger*		
Unearned revenue	995		Inventory (or cost of sales)	995	
[$2,487 x (20,000/50,000)]			Contract right with supplier		995
Sales		995			
Interest expense	751		Discount on note receivable	751	
Discount on note payable			Interest revenue		751
($7,513 x 10%)		751			

The amortization of unearned revenue and contract right with supplier accounts will fluctuate with the amount of purchases made. If there is a balance remaining in the account at the end of the loan term, it is amortized to the appropriate account in that final year.

Noncash transactions. When a note is issued for consideration such as property, goods, or services, and the transaction is entered into at arm's length, the stated interest rate is presumed to be fair unless (1) no interest rate is stated; (2) the stated rate is unreasonable; or (3) the face value of the debt is materially different from the consideration involved or the current market value of the note at the date of the transaction. According to APB 21, when the rate on the note is **not** considered fair, the note is to be recorded at the "fair market value of the property, goods, or services received or at an amount that reasonably approximates the market value of the note, whichever is the more clearly determinable." When this amount differs from the face value of the note, the difference is to be recorded as a discount or premium and amortized to interest expense.

Example of accounting for a note exchanged for property

1. A sells B a machine which has a fair market value of $7,510.
2. A receives a 3-year noninterest-bearing note having a face value of $10,000.

In this situation, the fair market value of the consideration is readily determinable and, thus, represents the amount at which the note is to be recorded. The following entry is necessary:

Machine	7,510	
Discount on notes payable	2,490	
Notes payable		10,000

The discount will be amortized to interest expense over the 3-year period using the interest rate **implied** in the transaction.

If the fair market value of the consideration or note is not determinable, then the present value of the note must be determined using an **imputed** interest rate. This rate will then be used to establish the present value of the note by discounting all future payments on the note at this rate. General guidelines for imputing the interest rate, which are provided by APB 21, paras 13 and 14, include the prevailing rates of similar instruments from creditors with similar credit ratings and the rate the debtor could obtain for similar financing from other sources. Other determining factors include any collateral or restrictive covenants involved, the current and expected prime rate, and other terms pertaining to the instrument. The objective is to approximate the rate of interest which would have resulted if an independent borrower and lender had negotiated a similar transaction under comparable terms and conditions. This determination is as of the issuance date, and any subsequent changes in interest rates would be irrelevant.

Bonds represent a promise to pay a sum of money at a designated maturity date plus periodic interest payments at a stated rate. Bonds are primarily used to borrow funds from the general public or institutional investors when a contract for a single amount (a note) is too large for any one lender to supply. Dividing up the amount needed into $1,000 or $10,000 units makes it easier to sell the bonds.

In most situations, a bond is issued at a price other than its face value. The amount of the cash exchanged is equal to the total of the present value of the interest and principal payments. The difference between the cash proceeds and the face value is recorded as a premium if the cash proceeds are greater or a discount if they are less. The journal entry to record a bond issued at a premium follows:

Cash	(proceeds)	
Premium on bonds payable		(difference)
Bonds payable		(face value)

The premium will be recognized over the life of the bond issue. If issued at a discount, "Discount on bonds payable" would be debited for the difference. As the premium is amortized, it will reduce interest expense on the books of the issuer (a discount will increase interest expense). The premium (discount) would be added to (deducted from) the related liability when a balance sheet is prepared.

The **effective interest method** is the preferred method of accounting for a discount or premium arising from a note or bond, although some other method may be used (e.g., straight-line) if the results are not materially different. While APB 21 only mandated that the effective interest method be used on notes covered by that opinion, the profession has made the use of the effective interest method the only acceptable one. Under the effective interest method, the discount or premium is to be amortized over the life of the debt in such a way as to result in a constant rate of interest when applied to the amount outstanding at the beginning of any given period. Therefore, interest expense is equal to the market rate of interest at the time of issuance multiplied by this beginning figure. The difference between the interest expense and the cash paid represents the amortization of the discount or premium.

Interest expense under the **straight-line method** is equal to the cash interest paid plus the amortized portion of the discount or minus the amortized portion of the premium. The amortized portion is equal to the total amount of the discount or premium divided by the life of the debt from issuance in months multiplied by the number of months the debt has been outstanding that year.

Amortization tables are often created at the time of the bond's issuance to provide figures when recording the necessary entries relating to the debt issue. They also provide a check of accuracy since the final values in the unamortized discount or premium and carrying value columns should be equal to zero and the bond's face value, respectively.

Example of applying the effective interest method

1. A 3-year, 12%, $10,000 bond is issued at 1/1/X7, with interest payments semiannually.
2. The market rate is 10%.

The amortization table would appear as follows:

Date	*Credit cash*	*Debit int. exp.*	*Debit prem.*	*Unam. prem. bal.*	*Carrying value*
1/1/X7				$507.61	$10,507.61(a)
7/1/X7	$ 600.00(b)	$ 525.38(c)	$ 74.62(d)	432.99(e)	10,432.99(f)
1/1/X8	600.00	521.65	78.35	354.64	10,354.64
7/1/X8	600.00	517.73	82.27	272.37	10,272.37
1/1/X9	600.00	513.62	86.38	185.99	10,185.99
7/1/X9	600.00	509.30	90.70	95.29	10,095.29
1/1/X0	600.00	504.71(g)	95.29	--	10,000.00
	$3,600.00	$3,092.39	$507.61		

(a) PV of principal and interest payments

$10,000(.74622)	=	*$ 7,462.20*
$ 600(5.07569)	=	*3,045.41*
		$10,507.61

(b) $10,000.00 x .06

(c) $10,507.61 x .05
(d) $600.00 – 525.38
(e) $507.61 – 74.62
(f) $10,507.61 – 74.62
(or $10,000 + 432.99)
(g) Rounding error = $.05

When the interest date does not coincide with the year end, an adjusting entry must be made. The proportional share of interest payable should be recognized along with the amortization of the discount or premium. **Within** the amortization period, the discount or premium should be amortized using the straight-line method.

If the bonds are issued between interest dates, discount or premium amortization must be computed for the period between the sale date and the next interest date.

This is accomplished by "straight-lining" the period's amount calculated using the usual method of amortization. In addition, the purchaser prepays the seller the amount of interest that has accrued since the last interest date. This interest is recorded as a payable (or as a credit to interest expense) by the seller. At the next interest date, the buyer then receives the full amount of interest regardless of how long the bond has been held. This procedure results in interest being paid equivalent to the time the bond has been outstanding.

Costs may be incurred in connection with issuing bonds. Examples include legal, accounting, and underwriting fees; commissions; and engraving, printing, and registration costs. Although these costs should be classified as a deferred charge and amortized using the effective interest method, generally the amount involved is such that use of the simpler straight-line method would not result in a material difference. However, the FASB's position as stated in SFAC 6, para 237 is that the costs should be treated as either an expense in the period incurred or a reduction in the related amount of debt, in much the same manner as a discount. These costs do not provide any future economic benefit and, therefore, should not be considered an asset. Since these costs reduce the amount of cash proceeds, they in effect increase the effective interest rate and probably should be accounted for the same as an unamortized discount. However, because the SFACs do not constitute GAAP, bond issue costs are to be treated as deferred charges.

Short-term obligations which are expected to be refinanced and therefore classified as long-term debt per SFAS 6 are discussed in Chapter 12.

The diagram on the following page illustrates the accounting treatments for monetary assets (and liabilities) as prescribed by APB 21.

Extinguishment of Debt

Management may reacquire or retire outstanding debt before its scheduled maturity. This decision is usually caused by changes in present or expected interest rates or in cash flows.

SFAS 125 supersedes SFAS 76, SFAS 77, SFAS 122, FASB TB 84-4, and FASB TB 85-2. Among other aspects, it provides accounting and reporting standards for extinguishments of liabilities.

ACCOUNTING FOR MONETARY ASSETS AND LIABILITIES

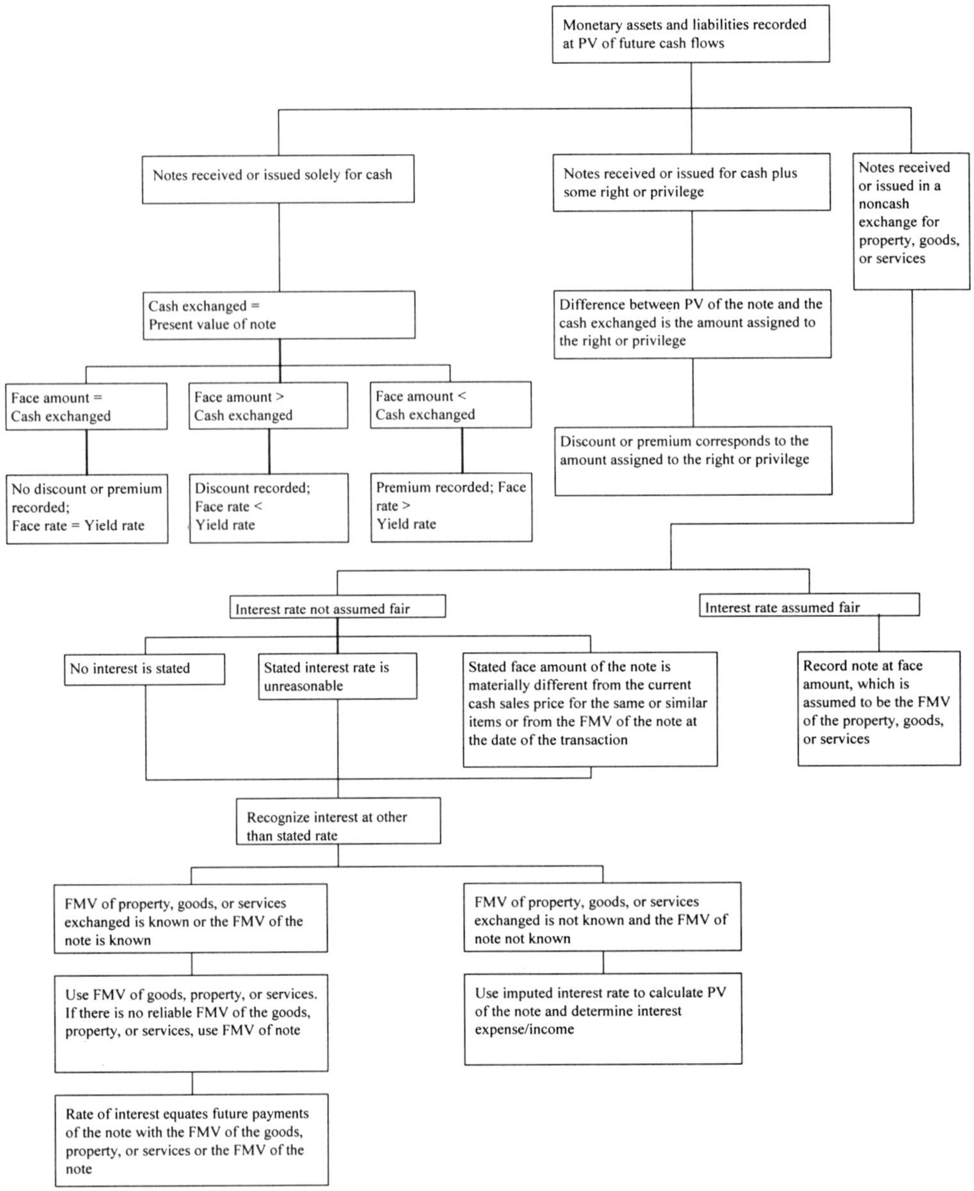

In a transfer of financial assets, any resulting liabilities or derivatives are to be measured initially at fair value. A servicing liability is to be amortized in proportion to and over the period of estimated net servicing loss or net servicing income. It should be assessed for increased obligation based on fair value.

In-substance defeasance does not result in the extinguishment of a liability. Except for items excluded by paragraph 4 in SFAS 125, a liability is derecognized only if

1. The creditor is paid and the debtor is relieved of the obligation.
2. The debtor is released legally either by the creditor or judicially from being the primary obligor.

Disclosure is required by SFAS 125 for in-substance defeased debt extinguished under SFAS 76 prior to December 31, 1996. The amount extinguished at the end of the period and a general description of the transaction must be given as long as the debt is outstanding. After the effective date of SFAS 125, the nature of any restrictions on assets set aside for making scheduled payments for specific liabilities must be disclosed.

If a debtor becomes secondarily liable, through a third-party assumption and a release by the creditor, the original party becomes a guarantor. A guarantee obligation, based on the probability that the third party will pay, is to be recognized and initially measured at fair value. The amount of guarantee obligation increases the loss or reduces the gain recognized on extinguishments.

Gain or loss. According to APB 26, para 20, the difference between the net carrying value and the acquisition price is to be recorded as a gain or loss. If the acquisition price is greater than the carrying value, a loss exists. A gain is generated if the acquisition price is less than the carrying value. These gains or losses are to be recognized in the period in which the retirement took place.

The unamortized premium or discount and issue costs should be amortized to the acquisition date and recorded **prior** to the determination of the gain or loss. If the extinguishment of debt does not occur on the interest date, the interest payable accruing between the last interest date and the acquisition date must also be recorded.

Except for any gains and losses resulting from satisfying sinking fund requirements within 1 year of the date of the extinguishment (SFAS 64), all gains and losses from extinguishment, if material in amount, receive extraordinary item treatment (SFAS 4, para 8).

Example of accounting for the extinguishment of debt

1. A 10%, 10-year, $200,000 bond is dated and issued on 1/1/96 at 98, with the interest payable semiannually.
2. Associated bond issue costs of $14,000 are incurred.
3. Four years later, on 1/1/00, the entire bond issue is repurchased at $102 per $100 face value and is retired.
4. The straight-line method of amortization is used since the result is not materially different from that when the effective interest method is used.

The gain or loss on the repurchase is computed as follows:

Reacquisition price [(102/100) x $200,000]		$204,000
Net carrying amount:		
Face value	$200,000	
Unamortized discount [2% x 200,000 x (6/10)]	(2,400)	
Unamortized issue costs [14,000 x (6/10)]	(8,400)	189,200
Loss on bond repurchase		$ 14,800

The loss on bond repurchase (debt extinguishment) is treated as an extraordinary item.

Defeasance. No controversy exists in practice regarding the extinguishment of debt through actual retirement. However, debt extinguishment discussed in SFAS 76, para 3c has caused some controversy. Defeasance is the retirement of debt in substance, but not in form. As mentioned previously, SFAS 125 (effective after December 31, 1996) supersedes SFAS 76 and does not allow in-substance defeasance to result in an extinguishment of a liability.

Example comparing the defeasance and retirement of a bond issue

1. On 1/1/96 a 9%, 20-year, $1,000 bond was issued at par.
2. On 1/1/00 the bond is trading at $800 due to an increase in interest rates and a deteriorating financial position.
3. On 1/1/00 a treasury bond with the same terms as the entity's bond can be purchased for $850. The greater price is due to the decreased risk associated with US Government instruments.

The following entries are required:

Defeasance			*Retirement (repurchase)*		
To purchase the bonds					
US treasury bond	850		Bonds payable	1,000	
Cash		850	Cash		800
			Extraordinary gain on extinguishment		200
To set up irrevocable trust					
Bonds payable	1,000				
US treasury bond		850			
Extrarodinary gain on extinguishment		150			

Notice the difference in the amount of the gain under each alternative. Actual retirement provides a $200 gain, while defeasance results in a $150 gain. Two other differences also exist, however: (1) the gain on extinguishment from the retirement of the bonds is currently taxable, whereas the gain on the extinguishment arising from defeasance is not currently taxable but represents a temporary difference, and (2) it is highly unlikely that all bondholders would be willing to voluntarily submit their bonds for repurchase at such a loss. Thus, the gain obtained through retirement may not be realistic. The gain recorded through defeasance is assured.

Critics of defeasance feel that gain or loss recognition should not be applicable to situations where the debtor is not legally released from being the primary obligor under the debt obligation (SFAS 76, para 3c). Recognizing these gains is merely window dressing.

The critics point out that a liability remains until it is satisfied by a future transaction or event. The creation of a trust, even for the sole purpose of repaying the debt, does not constitute the disposition of the trust assets or the satisfaction of the liability. It simply ensures the debt will be repaid by matching up the cash flows. The assets continue to be probable future economic benefits of the debtor until the debt is actually paid. They have not yet been used to eliminate, extinguish, or satisfy the obligation. Concurrently, the liability will continue to exist until satisfied by payment or by agreement with the creditor.

Troubled Debt Restructurings

Troubled debt restructurings are defined by SFAS 15, para 2, as situations where the creditor, for economic or legal reasons related to the debtor's financial difficulties, grants the debtor a concession that would not otherwise be granted. However, in any of the following four situations, a concession granted by the creditor does not automatically qualify as a restructuring:

1. The fair value of the assets or equity interest accepted by a creditor from a debtor in full satisfaction of its receivable is at least equal to the creditor's recorded investment in the receivable.
2. The fair value of the assets or equity interest transferred by a debtor to a creditor in full settlement of its payable is at least equal to the carrying value of the payable.
3. The creditor reduces the effective interest rate to reflect a decrease in current interest rates or a decrease in the risk, in order to maintain the relationship.
4. The debtor, in exchange for old debt, issues new debt with an interest rate that reflects current market rates.

A troubled debt restructuring can occur one of two ways. The first is a settlement of the debt at less than the carrying amount. The second is a continuation of the debt with a modification of terms (i.e., a reduction in the interest rate, face amount, accrued interest owed, or an extension of the payment date for interest or face amount). Accounting for such restructurings is prescribed for both debtors and creditors. FASB TB 80-2 points out that the debtor and creditor must individually apply SFAS 15 to the specific situation since the tests are not necessarily symmetrical and it is possible for one or the other, but not both, to have a troubled debt restructuring. SFAS 114 as amended by SFAS 118 specifies the accounting by creditors for troubled debt restructurings involving a modification of terms.

Debtors. If the debt is settled by the exchange of assets, an extraordinary gain is recognized in the period of transfer for the difference between the carrying amount of the debt (defined as the face amount of the debt increased or decreased by applicable accrued interest and applicable unamortized premium, discount, or issue costs) and the consideration given to extinguish the debt. A two-step process is used: (1) a revaluation of the noncash asset to FMV with an associated recognition of an ordinary gain or loss and (2) a determination of the extraordinary restructuring gain. EITF consensus 89-15, however, concluded that an exchange of existing debt for new debt with the same creditor and with a higher interest rate (but with the new rate less than the market rate for a company with a similar credit rating) does not result in a recognized gain or loss. In this circumstance, the terms of the exchange are not representative of and are less favorable to the creditor than prevailing terms for new borrowings by companies with similar credit ratings. The result is a concession by the creditor and should be accounted for by debtors as a modification of existing obligation under SFAS 15. If stock is issued to settle the liability, the stock is recorded at its FMV (SFAS 15, paras 13 through 21).

If the debt is continued with a modification of terms, it is necessary to compare the total future cash flows of the restructured debt (both principal and stated interest) with the prerestructured carrying value. If the total amount of future cash flows is greater than the carrying value, no adjustment is made to the carrying value of the debt. However, a new, lower effective interest rate must be computed. This rate makes the present value of the total future cash flows equal to the present carrying value of debt and is used to determine interest expense in future periods. The statement specifies that the effective interest method must be used to compute the expense. If the total future cash flows of the restructured debt are less than the present carrying value, the current debt should be reduced to the amount of the future cash flows and an extraordinary gain should be recognized. No interest expense would be recognized in subsequent periods, since only the principal is being repaid (paras 16-18 and 21).

If the restructuring consists of part settlement and part modification of payments, the part settlement is accounted for first and then the modification of payments (para 19).

FASB TB 81-6 notes that SFAS 15 generally does not apply to debtors in bankruptcy. There is an exception in the case of a restructuring that doesn't result in a general restatement of the debtor's liabilities in bankruptcy proceedings.

The following examples illustrate the accounting for debtors in troubled debt restructurings.

Example 1: Settlement of debt

Assume the debtor company transfers land having a book value of $70,000 and a FMV of $80,000 in full settlement of its note payable. The note has a remaining life of 5 years, a principal balance of $90,000, and related accrued interest of $10,000. The following entries are required to record the settlement:

<u>Debtor</u>

Land	10,000	
Gain on transfer of assets		10,000
Note payable	90,000	
Interest payable	10,000	
Land		80,000
Extraordinary gain on settlement of debt		20,000

Example 2: Restructuring with gain/loss recognized

Assume the interest rate on the above note is 5%. The interest rate is reduced to 4%, the principal is reduced to $72,500, and the accrued interest at date of restructure is forgiven.

Future cash flows (after restructuring):	
Principal	$ 72,500
Interest (5 years x $72,500 x 4%)	14,500
Total cash to be received	$ 87,000
Amount prior to restructure ($90,000 principal + $10,000 accrued interest)	(100,000)
Gain/loss to be recognized	
Debtor gain (**extraordinary**)	$ 13,000

The following entries need to be recorded to reflect the terms of the agreement:

<u>Debtor</u>

Beginning of Year 1		
Interest payable	10,000	
Note payable	3,000	
Extraordinary gain on restructure of debt		13,000
End of Years 1-5		
Note payable	2,900	
Cash		2,900

(Note: $14,500 ÷ 5 yrs. = $2,900; No interest expense is recorded in this case)

End of Year 5		
Note payable	72,500	
Cash		72,500

Example 3: Restructuring with no gain/loss recognized

Assume the $100,000 owed is reduced to a principal balance of $95,000. The interest rate of 5% is reduced to 4%.

Future cash flows (after restructuring):	
Principal	$ 95,000
Interest (5 years x $95,000 x 4%)	19,000
Total cash to be received	$ 114,000
Amount prior to restructure ($90,000 principal + $10,000 accrued interest)	(100,000)
Interest expense/revenue over 5 years	$ 14,000

In this example, a new effective interest rate must be computed such that the present value of the future payments equals $100,000. A trial and error approach is used to calculate the effective interest rate that discounts the $95,000 principal and the $3,800 annual interest payments to $100,000, the amount owed prior to restructuring.

Trial and Error Calculation

	(n = 5, i = 2.5%)	(n = 5, i = 3%)
PV of ordinary annuity	4.64583	4.57971
PV of 1	.88385	.86261

2.5%: (.88385 x $95,000) + (4.64583 x $3,800) = $101,620
3%: (.86261 x $95,000) + (4.57971 x $3,800) = $ 99,351

Interpolation:

$$\left[\frac{101{,}620 - 100{,}000}{101{,}620 - 99{,}351}\right] \times (3\% - 2.5\%) = .357$$

New effective rate = 2.5% + .357% = 2.857%

Interest amortization schedule:

Year	*Cash*	*Interest at effective rate*	*Reduction in carrying value*	*Carrying amount*
				$100,000
1	$ 3,800(a)	$2,857(b)	$ 943(c)	99,057
2	3,800	2,830	970	98,087
3	3,800	2,802	998	97,089
4	3,800	2,774	1,026	96,063
5	3,800	2,745	1,055	95,000*
	$19,000			

**Rounded*
(a) *$3,800 = $95,000 x .04*
(b) *$2,857 = $100,000 x 2.857%*
(c) *$943 = $3,800 – $2,857*

The following entries are made to recognize the cash payments in the subsequent periods:

<u>Debtor</u>

End of Year 1		
Note payable ($3,800 – $2,857)	943	
Interest expense ($100,000 x 0.2857)	2,857	
Cash		3,800
End of Year 5		
Note payable	95,000	
Cash		95,000

According to SFAS 15, a troubled debt restructuring which involves only a modification of terms is to be accounted for prospectively. The result of this treatment is to effect no change in the carrying value of the liability **unless** the carrying amount exceeds the total future cash payments specified by the new agreement.

When the total future cash payments **may** exceed the carrying amount of the liability, no gain or loss is recognized on the books of the debtor. Rather, a new effective interest rate should be determined which is to be the rate that equates the present value of the future cash payments with the carrying amount of the liability. Interest expense and principal reduction are then recognized as the future cash payments are made.

If the total cash payments are less than the carrying amount of the liability, the carrying amount of the liability should be written down to the total future cash payments and the amount of the write-down is to be recognized by the debtor as a gain. This gain is to be aggregated with other gains from restructuring, and the entire amount, if material, should be reported as an extraordinary item in accordance with SFAS 4. The liability shall be reduced as the payments are made and **no** interest expense shall be recognized on the liability for any period between the restructuring and the maturity of the liability (SFAS 15, para 17). An exception exists for contingent liabilities. They generally are not included in the carrying value of the original debt. Thus, for each period that a contingent liability is both probable and reasonably estimable, interest expense shall be recognized. However, to the extent that the contingent payments were included in the total future cash payments, the payment or accrual of these contingencies should be deducted from the restructured liability.

SFAS 15 Creditors. Accounting by creditors under SFAS 15 is similar to that by debtors for troubled debt restructurings involving a receipt of assets by the creditor. However, the loss to the creditor is ordinary, whereas the gain to the debtor is extraordinary. Troubled debt restructurings involving a modification of terms that were accomplished before the effective date of SFAS 114 and that are not impaired based on the terms of the restructuring agreement may be accounted for under the terms of SFAS 15.

1. Assets received in full settlement
   a. All assets which are not fixed assets are recorded at FMV.
   b. Fixed assets are recorded at FMV less cost to sell as defined in paras 15-17 of SFAS 121.
   c. Excess of receivable over the FMV of assets received (less cost to sell if a fixed asset) is an ordinary loss.
   d. Account for assets as if purchased for cash.

SFAS 114 Creditors. SFAS 114, as amended by SFAS 118, applies to all creditors, to all troubled debt restructurings involving a modification of terms, and to all loans except

1. Groups of similar small balance loans that are collectively evaluated
2. Loans measured at fair value or lower of cost or fair value
3. Leases
4. SFAS 115 debt securities

This standard attempts to make consistent the accounting by creditors for impaired loans.

If it is probable that a creditor will not collect all amounts (principal and interest) owed to the degree specified in the loan agreement, a loan is considered impaired. A delay, per se, does not impair the loan if the creditor collects all amounts due (including accrued interest during the delay at the contractual rate).

An impaired loan can be measured on a loan-by-loan basis in any of the following ways:

1. Present value of expected future cash flows using the loan's effective interest rate (the contractual interest rate adjusted for premium or discount and net deferred loan costs or fees at acquisition or origination)
2. Loans' observable market price
3. Fair value of the collateral if the loan is collateral dependent (repayment expected to be provided by the collateral). If foreclosure is probable, this measurement **must** be used.

Other measurement considerations include

1. Costs to sell on a discounted basis if they will reduce cash flows to satisfy the loan
2. Creation of or adjustment to a valuation allowance account with the offset to bad-debt expense if the recorded investment is greater than the impaired loan measurement
3. If the contractual interest rate varies based on changes in an independent factor, the creditor can choose between
   a. Calculating the effective interest on the factor as it changes over the loan's life, or

   b. Calculating the effective interest as fixed at the rate in effect at the date of impairment.

   The choice must be consistently applied. Projections of factor changes should not be made.

4. Cash flow estimates should be the creditors' best estimate based on reasonable and supportable assumptions
5. Significant changes occurring in measurement values require recalculation and adjustment of the valuation allowance. Net carrying amount of the loan should not exceed the recorded investment.

SFAS 118 changes the income recognition provisions of SFAS 114 so that it does not address the recognition, measurement, or display of interest income on unimpaired loans. Creditors can now use existing methods. In most cases, since it doesn't change the measurement of impairment, the amendment ordinarily will only affect how income or expense is classified. The total amount of income would not be affected. However, if the existing policy results in a recorded investment less than fair value, both the classification and the total amount could be affected.

The amended disclosures by creditors for impaired loans should include

1. Interest income recognition policy (include how cash receipts are recorded)
2. For every period the results of operations are given
   a. The amount of interest income recognized and the amount that would have accrued if the terms of the original loan agreement had been followed
   b. The total amount of cash receipts and the amount recorded as reduction in principal and the amount recorded as interest
   c. The average recorded investment
3. The recorded investments classified by whether there is a related allowance for credit losses

If they meet the definition of a security under SFAS 115, TB 94-1 includes under that statement restructured loans involving a modification of terms even if the restructuring took place before the effective date of SFAS 114.

Under SFAS 114, the above examples on pages 460-463 would be treated as follows:

SFAS 114 Creditor

Example 1

Land	80,000	
Bad debt expense	20,000	
Note receivable		90,000
Interest receivable		10,000

Example 2

Future cash flows (after restructuring)

		5% 5 yrs PV Factor
Principal	$ 56,806	($72,500 x .78353)
Interest	12,555	($ 2,900 x 4.32948)
Total present value	$ 69,361	
Amount prior to restructure ($90,000 principal + $10,000 accrued interest)	(100,000)	
Creditor loss	($ 30,639)	

	Debit	Credit
Beginning of Year 1		
Bad debt expense	30,639	
Interest receivable		10,000
Valuation allowance		20,639
End of Year 1		
Cash	2,900	
Valuation allowance	568	
Bad debt expense (or interest income)		3,468 (69,361 x .05)
End of Year 2		
Cash	2,900	
Valuation allowance	596	
Bad debt expense (or interest income)		3,496 [(69,361 + 568) = 69,929 x .05]
End of Year 3		
Cash	2,900	
Valuation allowance	626	
Bad debt expense (or interest income)		3,526 [(69,929 + 596) = 70,525 x .05]
End of Year 4		
Cash	2,900	
Valuation allowance	658	
Bad debt expense (or interest income)		3,558 [(70,525 + 626) = 71,151 x .05]
End of Year 5		
Cash	2,900	
Valuation allowance	691	
Bad debt expense (or interest income)		3,591 [(71,151 + 658) = 71,809 x .05]
Cash	72,500	
Valuation allowance	17,500	
Note receivable		90,000

Example 3

Future cash flows (after restructuring)

		5% 5 yrs PV Factor
Principal	$ 74,435	($95,000 x .78353)
Interest	16,452	($ 3,800 x 4.32948)
Total present value	$ 90,887	
Amount prior to restructure ($90,000 principal + $10,000 accrued interest)	(100,000)	
Creditor loss	($ 9,113)	

	Debit	Credit
Beginning of Year 1		
Bad debt expense	9,113	
Note receivable - new	95,000	
Note receivable - old		90,000
Interest receivable		10,000
Valuation allowance		4,113
End of Year 1		
Cash	3,800	
Valuation allowance	744	
Bad debt expense (or interest income)		4,544 (90,887 x .05)
End of Year 2		
Cash	3,800	
Valuation allowance	781	
Bad debt expense (or interest income)		4,581 [(90,887 + 744) = 91,631 x .05]
End of Year 3		
Cash	3,800	
Valuation allowance	821	
Bad debt expense (or interest income)		4,621 [(91,631 + 781) = 92,412 x .05]
End of Year 4		
Cash	3,800	
Valuation allowance	862	
Bad debt expense (or interest income)		4,662 [(92,412 + 821) = 93,233 x .05]
End of Year 5		
Cash	3,800	
Valuation allowance	905	
Bad debt expense (or interest income)		4,705 [(93,233 + 862) = 94,095 x .05]
Cash	95,000	
Note receivable		95,000

Convertible Debt

Bonds are frequently issued with the right to convert them into common stock of the company at the holder's option. **Convertible debt** is used for two reasons. First, when a specific amount of funds is needed, convertible debt often allows a lesser number of shares to be issued (assuming conversion) than if the funds were raised by directly issuing the shares. Thus, less dilution occurs. Second, the conversion feature allows debt to be issued at a lower interest rate and with fewer restrictive covenants than if the debt was issued without it.

This dual nature of debt and equity, however, creates a question as to whether the equity element should receive separate recognition. Support for separate treatment is based on the assumption that this equity element has economic value. Since the convertible feature tends to lower the rate of interest, a portion of the proceeds should be allocated to this equity feature. However, APB 14, para 7 argues that the debt and equity elements are inseparable. The instrument is either all debt or all equity.

Features of convertible debt typically include (1) a conversion price 15-20% greater than the market value of the stock when the debt is issued; (2) conversion features (price and number of shares) which protect against dilution from stock dividends, splits, etc.; and (3) a callable feature at the issuer's option that is usually exercised once the conversion price is reached (thus forcing conversion or redemption).

Convertible debt also has its disadvantages. If the stock price increases significantly after the debt is issued, the issuer would have been better off by simply issuing the stock. Additionally, if the price of the stock does not reach the conversion price, the debt will never be converted (a condition known as overhanging debt).

When convertible debt is issued, no value is apportioned to the conversion feature when recording the issue (APB 14, para 12). The debt is treated as nonconvertible debt. Upon conversion, the stock may be valued at either the book value or the market value of the bonds.

If the **book value approach** is used, the new stock is valued at the carrying value of the converted bonds. This method is widely used since no gain or loss is recognized upon conversion, and the conversion represents the transformation of contingent shareholders into shareholders. It does not represent the culmination of an earnings cycle. The primary weakness of this method is that the total value attributed to the equity security by the investors is not given accounting recognition.

Example of book value method

Assume that a $1,000 bond with an unamortized discount of $50 and a market value of $970 is converted into 10 shares of $10 par common stock whose market value is $97 per share. Conversion using the book value method is recorded as follows:

Bonds payable	1,000	
Discount on bonds payable		50
Common stock		100
Additional paid-in capital		850

The **market value approach** assumes the new stock issued is valued at its cost (i.e., the market price of the stock issued or the market price of the bonds converted, whichever is more easily determinable). A gain (loss) occurs when the market value of the stocks or bonds is less (greater) than the carrying value of the bond.

Example of the market value method

Assume the same data as the example above. The entry to record the conversion is

Bonds payable	1,000	
Loss on redemption (ordinary)	20	
Discount on bonds payable		50
Common stock		100
Additional paid-in capital		870

Since conversion is initiated by the bondholder and not the firm, the loss does not qualify as an extinguishment and is therefore considered ordinary.

That a gain or loss may be reported as a result of an equity transaction is the weakness of this method. Only the existing shareholders are affected, as their equity will increase or decrease, but the firm as a whole is unaffected. For this reason, the market value approach is not widely used.

When convertible debt is retired, the transaction is handled in the same manner as nonconvertible debt: the difference between the acquisition price and the carrying value of the bond is reported currently as a gain or loss. If material, the gain or loss is considered extraordinary.

Induced Conversion of Debt

A special situation exists in which the conversion privileges of convertible debt are modified **after** issuance. These modifications may take the form of reduced conversion prices or additional consideration paid to the convertible debt holder. The debtor offers these modifications or "sweeteners" to induce prompt conversion of the outstanding debt.

SFAS 84 specifies the accounting method used in these situations and only applies when the convertible debt is converted into equity securities. Upon conversion, the debtor must recognize an expense for the **excess** of the fair value of all the securities and other consideration given over the fair value of the securities specified in the original conversion terms. The reported expense should not be classified as an extraordinary item.

Example of induced conversion expense

1. January 1, 1995, XYZ Company issued 10 8% convertible bonds at $1,000 par value without a discount or premium, maturing December 31, 2005.
2. The bonds are initially convertible into no par common stock of XYZ at a conversion price of $25.
3. On July 1, 1999, the convertible bonds have a market value of $600 each.

4. To induce the convertible bondholders to quickly convert their bonds, XYZ reduces the conversion price to $20 for bondholders who convert before July 21, 1999 (within 20 days).
5. The market price of XYZ Company's common stock on the date of conversion is $15 per share.

The fair value of the incremental consideration paid by XYZ upon conversion is calculated for each bond converted before July 21, 1999.

Value of securities issued to debt holders:

Face amount	$1,000	per bond
÷ New conversion price	÷ $20	per share
Number of common shares issued upon conversion	50	shares
x Price per common share	x $15	per share
Value of securities issued	$ 750	(a)

Value of securities issuable pursuant to the original conversion privileges:

Face amount	$1,000	per bond
÷ Original conversion price	÷ $25	per share
Number of common shares issuable pursuant to original conversion privilege	40	shares
x Price per share	x $15	per share
Value of securities issuable pursuant to original conversion privileges	$ 600	(b)

Value of securities issued	$ 750	(a)
Value of securities issuable pursuant to the original conversion privileges	600	(b)
Fair value of incremental consideration	$ 150	

The entry to record the debt conversion for **each bond** is

Convertible debt	1,000	
Debt conversion expense	150	
Common stock--no par		1,150

Debt Issued with Stock Warrants

Warrants are certificates enabling the holder to purchase a stated number of shares of stock at a certain price within a certain time period. They are often issued with bonds to enhance the marketability of the bonds and to lower the bond's interest rate.

When bonds with **detachable** warrants are issued, the purchase price must be allocated between the debt and the stock warrants based on relative market values (APB 14, para 16). Since two separate instruments are involved, a market value must be determined for each. However, if one value cannot be determined, the market value of the other should be deducted from the total value to determine the unknown value.

Example of accounting for a bond with a detachable warrant

1. A $1,000 bond with a detachable warrant to buy 10 shares of $10 par common stock at $50 per share is issued for $1,025.
2. Immediately after the issuance the bonds trade at $980 and the warrants at $60.
3. The market value of the stock is $54.

The relative market value of the bonds is 94% (980/1,040) and the warrant is 6% (60/1,040). Thus, $62 (6% x $1,025) of the issuance price is assigned to the warrants. The journal entry to record the issuance is

Cash	1,025	
Discount on bonds payable	37	
Bonds payable		1,000
Paid-in capital--warrants (or "Stock options outstanding")		62

The discount is the difference between the purchase price assigned to the bond, $963 (94% x $1,025), and its face value, $1,000. The debt itself is accounted for in the normal fashion.

The entry to record the subsequent future exercise of the warrant would be

Cash	500	
Paid-in capital--warrants	62	
Common stock		100
Paid-in capital		462 (difference)

Assuming the warrants are not exercised, the journal entry is

Paid-in capital--warrants	62	
Paid-in capital--expired warrants		62

EMERGING ISSUES TASK FORCE CONSENSUS SUMMARIES

84-11 Offsetting Installment Note Receivables and Bank Debt ("Note Monetization")

The seller is not permitted to offset an installment note receivable with a bank debt with recourse even though the debt has a put option which effectively makes the debt a secured nonrecourse debt.

85-17 Accrued Interest Upon Conversion of Convertible Debt

If terms of the debt instrument provide that any accrued interest at the date of conversion is forfeited by the former debt holder, the accrued interest (net of income tax) from the last payment date to the conversion date should be charged to interest expense and credited to capital as a part of the cost of the securities issued.

86-36 Invasion of a Defeasance Trust

The basis for the consensus was a narrow, short-lived arbitrage of the 1986 tax rate differential between capital gains and ordinary income. The consensus was that removal of the assets from the trust does not affect the recognition of the extinguishment.

The purchase of the debenture is an investment and the receipt of the assets from the trust is accounted for as exchange of the investment for the assets received. The assets are to be recorded at their market value and any gain or loss would not be extraordinary.

87-19 Substituted Debtors in a Troubled Debt Restructuring

Given the sale of real estate collateral (present value less than the net investment) with the requirement for the purchaser to make direct payment to the creditor, the creditor is still required to recognize a loss in the amount by which the net investment in the loan exceeds the fair value of the payments to be received. The fair value of the payments should be recorded as an asset.

88-18 Sales of Future Revenue

Classification of the proceeds from an investor to obtain a right to a specified amount of revenues or a measure of income in the future would be classified as either debt or deferred income by the investee, based upon the specific facts and circumstances of the transaction. This EITF lists six factors that would cause the amounts to be recorded as debt.

Amounts recorded as debt should be amortized under the interest method and amounts recorded as deferred income should be amortized under the units-of-revenue method. Classification of proceeds as debt would not result in foreign exchange gains and losses if three criteria are met. If not met, the debt is a foreign currency transaction and SFAS 52 translation gains or losses are recognized.

Classification of the proceeds as deferred income would be a nonmonetary liability. Thus, no foreign exchange gains or losses would arise under SFAS 52. The Task Force did not address any situations when immediate income recognition would be appropriate.

88-23 Lump-Sum Payments Under Union Contracts

This EITF relates solely to union contracts and not to individual employment contracts. In negotiating union contracts, lump-sum cash payments made to employees in lieu of all or a portion of a base-wage rate increase may be deferred and amortized. The Task Force's consensus requires that (1) there is no evidence that the payment is related to past services, (2) the payment will benefit a future period in the form of a lower base wage rate, and (3) the amortization period not extend beyond the contract period. Facts surrounding the contract and negotiations must be reviewed to determine how to account for the payment.

89-9 Accounting for In-Substance Foreclosures

Collateral received in an in-substance foreclosure should be recorded at fair value, which establishes a new basis, similar to the accounting for a legal foreclosure. The collateral should not be accounted for as a valuation allowance and unrealized increases in the fair value subsequent to the in-substance foreclosure should not be recognized. Subsequent to the issuance of SFAS 114, the EITF decided not to change the provisions of this EITF consensus due to the practical problems of accounting for the operations of an asset the creditor does not possess.

89-15 Accounting for a Modification of Debt Terms When the Debtor is Experiencing Financial Difficulties

An exchange of existing debt for new debt with the same creditor and with a higher interest rate (but with the new rate less than the market rate for a company with a similar credit rating) does not result in a recognized gain or loss. In this circumstance, the terms of the exchange are not representative of and are less favorable to the creditor than prevailing terms for new borrowings by companies with similar credit ratings. The result is a concession by the creditor and should be accounted for by debtors as a modification of existing obligation under SFAS 15.

90-19 Convertible Bonds With Issuer Option to Settle for Cash Upon Conversion

Combined accounting for the debt obligation and the conversion feature is appropriate.

Accounting similar to indexed debt obligations should be used if the issuer must satisfy the obligation entirely in cash or if the issuer must satisfy the accreted value of the obligation in cash and may satisfy the conversion spread in either cash or stock. The carrying value should be adjusted in each reporting period to reflect the current stock price, but not below the accreted value. These adjustments are included currently in income.

If the issuer may satisfy the entire obligation in either stock or cash, it should be accounted for as conventional convertible debt. If the holder exercises the conversion and the issuer pays cash, the debt is extinguished and the issuer should account for the transaction in accordance with APB 26, para 20. Gain or loss should be classified in accordance with SFAS 4.

If the issuer must satisfy the obligation entirely with cash, the only EPS effect is the charge to income for the conversion spread. If the entire obligation may be satisfied in either stock or cash, the bond should be considered a common stock equivalent. If the issuer must satisfy the accreted value of the obligation in cash and may satisfy the conversion spread in either cash or stock, the only primary EPS effect is the charge to income for the conversion spread. This accounting is consistent with that of an indexed debt obligation. The APB 15 if-converted method is used for fully-diluted EPS. All other provisions of APB 15 must be considered also.

94-8 Accounting for Conversion of a Loan into a Debt Security in a Debt Restructuring

The initial cost basis of a debt security of the original debtor received as part of a debt restructuring should be the security's fair value at the date of the restructuring. Any excess fair value of the security over the net carrying amount of the loan should be recorded as a recovery on the loan. Any excess net carrying value amount of the loan over the fair value of the security should be recorded as a charge-off to the allowance for credit losses. Additionally, securities received in a restructuring for only past-due interest on a loan should be measured at the date of the restructuring and accounted for with the entity's policy for recognizing cash received for past-due interest. After the restructuring, the securities should be accounted for according to the provisions of SFAS 115.

95-15 Recognition of Gain or Loss When a Binding Contract Requires a Debt Extinguishment to Occur at a Future Date for a Specified Amount

If a debtor enters into a binding contract with a holder of its debt obligation to redeem the debt security at a future date within 1 year for a specified amount greater than (or less than) the debtor's carrying amount, the obligation should be classified as a current liability. An extraordinary loss (including deferred issue costs and unamortized premium or discount at the contract specified future date of exchange) is recognized by the debtor based on the terms of the contract at the date the contract becomes binding to both parties. A gain should not be recognized until redemption for the amount specified.

96-22 Applicability of the Disclosures Required by FASB Statement 114 When a Loan is Restructured in a Troubled Debt Restructuring into Two (or More) Loans

Since they are legally distinct from the original loan, restructuring loans should be considered separately in years after restructuring when addressing the applicability of disclosures. The measure of loan impairment would continue to be based on the terms of the original agreement. For SEC purposes, the impact of multiple loan structures on the disclosure of impaired loans should be made clear to users.

98-5 Accounting for Convertible Securities With Beneficial Conversion Features or Contingently Adjustable Conversion Ratios

A **tentative conclusion** was reached that beneficial embedded conversion features that exist at the security's issuance date should be valued separately.

STATEMENTS OF POSITION

96-1 Environmental Remediation Liabilities

This SOP includes accounting guidance, preceded by a very detailed description of relevant laws, remediation provisions, and other pertinent information useful to auditors as well as clients. Auditing guidance is limited to recitation of SFAS 5 concerns about reasonable estimation of loss accruals.

Accounting guidance includes the following provisions:

1. Interprets SFAS 5 in the context of environmental obligations (e.g., threshold for accrual of liability, etc.) and sets "benchmarks" for recognition.
2. Benchmarks for accrual and evaluation of estimated liability (stages which are deemed to be important to ascertaining the existence and amount of the liability) are
   a. Identification and verification of an entity as a potentially responsible party (PRP), since the proposal stipulated that accrual should be based on premise that expected costs will be borne by only the "participating potentially responsible parties" and that the "recalcitrant, unproven and unidentified" PRP will not contribute to costs of remediation
   b. Receipt of unilateral administrative order
   c. Participation, as a PRP, in the remedial investigation/feasibility study (RI/FS)
   d. Completion of the feasibility study
   e. Issuance of the Record of Decision (ROD)
   f. Remedial design through operation and maintenance, including post remediation monitoring
3. The amount of liability is affected by
   a. The entity's allocable share of liability for a specified site; and
   b. Its share of the amounts related to the site that will not be paid by the other PRP or the government

4. Costs to be included in the accrued liability are
    a. Incremental direct costs of the remediation effort itself; and
    b. Costs of compensation and benefits for employees directly involved in the remediation effort
    c. Costs are to be estimated based on existing laws and technologies, and not discounted to present value unless timing of cash payments is fixed or reliably determinable
5. Incremental direct costs will include such items as the following:
    a. Fees to outside law firms for work related to the remediation effort
    b. Costs relating to completing the RI/FS
    c. Fees to outside consulting and engineering firms for site investigations and development of remedial action plans and remedial actions
    d. Costs of contractors performing remedial actions
    e. Government oversight costs and past costs
    f. Cost of machinery and equipment dedicated to the remedial actions that do not have an alternative use
    g. Assessments by a PRP group covering costs incurred by the group in dealing with a site
    h. Costs of operation and maintenance of the remedial action, including costs of postremediation monitoring required by the remedial action plan

This SOP emphasizes the EITF 93-5, *Accounting for Environmental Liabilities*, consensus that potential recoveries cannot be offset against estimated liability, and further notes that any recovery recognized as an asset should be reflected at fair value, which implies that only the present value of future recoveries be recorded. It also stipulates that environmental cleanup costs are not unusual in nature, and thus cannot be shown as extraordinary items in the income statement. Furthermore, it is presumed that the costs are operating in nature, and thus cannot normally be included in "other income and expense" category.

Finally, this SOP calls for improved disclosure of accounting policies regarding recognition of a liability and related asset (for recoveries from third parties).

The standard is effective for years beginning after December 1996 (i.e., calendar 1997 and fiscal 1998 years).

Related guidance can also be found in SFAS 5, *Accounting for Contingencies*; FASB Interpretation 14, *Reasonable Estimation of the Amount of a Loss*; EITF 89-13, *Accounting for the Cost of Asbestos Removal*; EITF 90-8, *Capitalization of Costs to Treat Environmental Contamination*; and SOP 94-6, *Disclosure of Certain Significant Risks and Uncertainties*.

14 ACCOUNTING FOR LEASES

PERSPECTIVE AND ISSUES

Lease transactions have grown in popularity over the years as businesses look for new ways to finance their fixed asset additions. A lease agreement involves at least two parties, a lessor and a lessee, and an asset which is to be leased. The lessor, who owns the asset, agrees to allow the lessee to use it for a specified period of time in return for periodic rent payments.

There are many economic reasons why the lease transaction is considered. They are as follows:

1. The lessee (borrower) is able to obtain 100% financing
2. Flexibility of use for the tax benefits
3. The lessor receives the equivalent of interest as well as an asset with some remaining value at the end of the lease term

The lease transaction derives its accounting complexity from the number of alternatives available to the parties involved. Leases can be structured to allow manipulation of the tax benefits associated with the leased asset. They can be used to transfer ownership of the leased asset, and they can be used to transfer the risk of ownership. In any event, the substance of the transaction dictates the accounting treatment. The lease transaction is probably the best example of the accounting profession's substance over form argument. If the transaction effectively transfers ownership to the lessee, then the substance of the transaction is that of a sale and should be recognized as such even though the transaction takes the form of a lease.

SFAS 13 is the promulgated GAAP for lease accounting. Numerous pronouncements have followed which expand upon the base set by SFAS 13. As a result of the extensive additions to the principles related to lease accounting, the FASB issued a codified restatement of SFAS 13 in January 1990. This document reflected all pronouncements issued through that date. We have used the codified restatement as the basis for our discussion. Therefore, we generally do not cite the actual pronouncements. Rather, our citations refer to the codified restatement. The reason for our using the codified restatement is that the FASB is currently rewriting this restatement to both update it and put it in a more understandable form. Thus, the codified restatement of SFAS 13 will eventually be the only source of GAAP.

Sources of GAAP

SFAS	*FASB I*	*FASB TB*	*EITF*
13, 22, 23, 27, 28, 29, 77, 91, 98, 125	19, 21, 23, 24, 26, 27	79-10, 79-12, 79-13, 79-14, 79-15, 79-16, 79-17, 79-18, 82-1, 85-3, 86-2, 88-1	85-16, 86-17, 86-33, 87-7, 88-10, 88-21, 89-16, 89-20, 90-14, 90-15, 90-20, 92-1, 93-8, 95-1, 95-4, 95-17, 96-21, 97-1

DEFINITIONS OF TERMS

Bargain purchase option. A provision allowing the lessee the option of purchasing the leased property for an amount, exclusive of lease payments, which is sufficiently lower than the expected fair value of the property at the date the option becomes exercisable. Exercise of the option must appear reasonably assured at the inception of the lease. GAAP does not offer additional guidance defining "sufficiently lower," in which many factors such as time value of money, usage, and technological changes influence whether the option fulfills the criteria for a bargain.

Bargain renewal option. A provision allowing the lessee the option to renew the lease agreement for a rental payment sufficiently lower than the expected fair rental of the property at the date the option becomes exercisable. Exercise of the option must appear reasonably assured at the inception of the lease.

Contingent rentals. Rentals that represent the increases or decreases in lease payments which result from changes in the factors on which the lease payments are based occurring subsequent to the inception of the lease. However, changes due to the pass-through of increases in the construction or acquisition cost of the leased property or for increases in some measure of cost during the construction or preconstruction period should be excluded from contingent rentals. Also, provisions that are dependent only upon the passage of time should be excluded from contingent rentals. A lease payment that is based upon an existing index or rate, such as the consumer price index or the prime rate, is a contingent payment, and the computation of the minimum lease payments should be based upon the index or rate applicable at the inception of the lease.

Estimated economic life of leased property. The estimated remaining time which the property is expected to be economically usable by one or more users, with normal maintenance and repairs, for its intended purpose at the inception of the lease. The economic life may be determined by such factors as technological changes, normal deterioration, and physical usage. Judgment on these matters may be influenced by knowledge gained through previous experience. This estimated time period should not be limited by the lease term.

Estimated residual value of leased property. The estimated fair value of the leased property at the end of the lease term.

Executory costs. Those costs such as insurance, maintenance, and taxes incurred for leased property, whether paid by the lessor or lessee. Amounts paid by a lessee in consideration for a guarantee from an unrelated third party of the residual value are also executory costs. If executory costs are paid by the lessor, any lessor's profit on those costs is considered the same as executory costs.

Fair value of leased property. The property's selling price in an arm's-length transaction between unrelated parties.

When the lessor is a **manufacturer or dealer**, the fair value of the property at the inception of the lease will ordinarily be its normal selling price net of volume or trade discounts. In some cases, due to market conditions, fair value may be less than the normal selling price or even the cost of the property.

When the lessor is **not a manufacturer or dealer**, the fair value of the property at the inception of the lease will ordinarily be its costs net of volume or trade discounts. However, if a significant amount of time has lapsed between the acquisition of the property by the lessor and the inception of the lease, fair value should be determined in light of market conditions prevailing at the inception of the lease. Thus, fair value may be greater or less than the cost or carrying amount of the property.

Implicit interest rate. The discount rate that, when applied to the minimum lease payments, excluding that portion of the payments representing executory costs to be paid by the lessor, together with any profit thereon, and the unguaranteed residual value accruing to the benefit of the lessor, causes the aggregate present value at the beginning of the lease term to be equal to the fair value of the leased property to the lessor at the inception of the lease, minus any investment tax credit retained and expected to be realized by the lessor (and plus initial direct costs in the case of direct financing leases).

Inception of the lease. The date of the written lease agreement or commitment (if earlier) wherein all principal provisions are fixed and no principal provisions remain to be negotiated.

Incremental borrowing rate. The rate that, at the inception of the lease, the lessee would have incurred to borrow over a similar term (i.e., a loan term equal to the lease term) the funds necessary to purchase the leased asset.

Initial direct costs.* Only those costs incurred by the lessor that are (1) costs to originate a lease incurred in transactions with independent third parties that (a) result directly from and are essential to acquire that lease and (b) would not have been incurred had that leasing transaction not occurred and (2) certain costs directly related to specified activities performed by the lessor for that lease. Those activities are: evaluating the prospective lessee's financial condition; evaluating and recording guarantees, collateral, and other security arrangements; negotiating lease terms; preparing and processing lease documents; and closing the transaction. The costs directly related to those activities shall include only that portion of the employees' total compensation and payroll-related fringe benefits directly related to time spent performing those activities for that lease and other costs related to those activities that would not have been incurred but for that lease. Initial direct costs shall not include costs related to activities performed by the lessor for advertising, soliciting potential lessees, servicing existing leases, and other ancillary activities related to establishing and monitoring credit policies, supervision, and administration. Initial direct costs shall not include administrative costs, rent, depreciation, any other occupancy and equipment costs and employees' compensation and fringe benefits related to activities described in the previous sentence, unsuccessful origination efforts, and idle time.

Lease. An agreement conveying the right to use property, plant, or equipment (land or depreciable assets or both) usually for a stated period of time.

Lease term. The fixed noncancelable term of the lease plus the following:

1. Periods covered by bargain renewal options
2. Periods for which failure to renew the lease imposes a penalty on the lessee in an amount such that renewal appears, at the inception of the lease, to be reasonably assured
3. Periods covered by ordinary renewal options during which a guarantee by the lessee of the lessor's debt directly or indirectly related to the leased property is expected to be in effect or a loan from the lessee to the lessor directly or indirectly related to the leased property is expected to be outstanding
4. Periods covered by ordinary renewal options preceding the date that a bargain purchase option is exercisable
5. Periods representing renewals or extensions of the lease at the lessor's option

---

* *Initial direct cost shall be offset by nonrefundable fees that are yield adjustments as prescribed in SFAS 91,* ***Accounting for Nonrefundable Fees and Costs Associated with Originating or Acquiring Loans and Initial Direct Costs of Leases****.*

However, the lease term shall not extend beyond the date a bargain purchase option becomes exercisable.

Minimum lease payments. For the **lessee**: The payments that the lessee is or can be required to make in connection with the leased property. Contingent rental guarantees by the lessee of the lessor's debt, and the lessee's obligation to pay executory costs are excluded from minimum lease payments. Additionally, if a portion of the minimum lease payments representing executory costs is not determinable from the provisions of the lease, an estimate of executory costs shall be excluded from the calculation of the minimum lease payments. If the lease contains a bargain purchase option, only the minimum rental payments over the lease term and the payment called for in the bargain purchase option are included in minimum lease payments. Otherwise, minimum lease payments include the following:

1. The **minimum rental payments** called for by the lease over the lease term
2. Any **guarantee of residual value** at the expiration of the lease term made by the lessee (or any party related to the lessee), whether or not the guarantee payment constitutes a purchase of the leased property. When the lessor has the right to require the lessee to purchase the property at termination of the lease for a certain or determinable amount, that amount shall be considered a lessee guarantee. When the lessee agrees to make up any deficiency below a stated amount in the lessor's realization of the residual value, the guarantee to be included in the MLP is the stated amount rather than an estimate of the deficiency to be made up.
3. Any payment that the lessee must or can be required to make upon **failure to renew or extend** the lease at the expiration of the lease term, whether or not the payment would constitute a purchase of the leased property

For the **lessor**: The payments described above plus any guarantee of the residual value or of the rental payments beyond the lease term by a third party unrelated to either the lessee or lessor (provided the third party is financially capable of discharging the guaranteed obligation).

Noncancelable in this context is a lease which is cancelable only upon one of the following conditions:

1. The occurrence of some remote contingency
2. The permission of the lessor
3. The lessee enters into a new lease with the same lessor
4. Payment by the lessee of a penalty in an amount such that continuation of the lease appears, at inception, reasonably assured

Nonrecourse financing. Lending or borrowing activities in which the creditor does not have general recourse to the debtor but rather has recourse only to the property used for collateral in the transaction or other specific property.

Penalty. Any requirement that is imposed or can be imposed on the lessee by the lease agreement or by factors outside the lease agreement to pay cash, incur or assume a liability, perform services, surrender or transfer an asset or rights to an asset or otherwise forego an economic benefit, or suffer an economic detriment.

Related and unrelated parties in leasing transactions--Related parties. Entities that are in a relationship where one party has the ability to exercise significant influence over the operating and financial policies of the related party. Examples include the following:

1. A parent company and its subsidiaries
2. An owner company and its joint ventures and partnerships
3. An investor and its investees

The ability to exercise significant influence must be present before the parties can be considered related. Significant influence may also be exercised through guarantees of indebtedness, extensions of credit, or through ownership of debt obligations, warrants, or other securities. If two or more entities are subject to the significant influence of a parent, owner, investor, or common officers or directors, then those entities are considered related to each other.

Renewal or extension of a lease. The continuation of a lease agreement beyond the original lease term, including a new lease where the lessee continues to use the same property.

Sale-leaseback accounting. A method of accounting for a sale-leaseback transaction in which the seller-lessee records the sale, removes all property and related liabilities from its balance sheet, recognizes gain or loss from the sale, and classifies the leaseback in accordance with this section.

Sales recognition. Any method that is described in Section R10 in the current text of the accounting standard as a method to record a transaction involving real estate, other than the deposit method, or the methods to record transactions accounted for as financing, leasing, or profit-sharing arrangements. Profit recognition methods described in Section R10 commonly used to record transactions involving real estate include, but are not limited to, the full accrual method, the installment method, the cost recovery method, and the reduced profit method.

Unrelated parties. All parties that are not related parties as defined above.

Unguaranteed residual value. The estimated residual value of the leased property exclusive of any portion guaranteed by the lessee, by any party related to the lessee, or any party unrelated to the lessee. If the guarantor is related to the lessor, the residual value shall be considered as unguaranteed.

CONCEPTS, RULES, AND EXAMPLES

Classification of Leases--Lessee

For accounting and reporting purposes the lessee has two alternatives in classifying a lease.

1. Operating
2. Capital

The proper classification of a **lease** is determined by the circumstances surrounding the transaction. According to SFAS 13, if substantially all of the benefits and risks of ownership have been transferred to the lessee, the lease should be recorded as a capital lease. Substantially all of the risks or benefits of ownership are deemed to have been transferred if **any one** of the following criteria has been met:

1. The lease transfers ownership to the lessee by the end of the **lease term**
2. The lease contains a **bargain purchase option**
3. The lease term is equal to 75% or more of the **estimated economic life** of the leased property, and the beginning of the lease term does not fall within the last 25% of the total economic life of the leased property
4. The present value (PV) of the minimum lease payments at the beginning of the lease term is 90% or more of the fair market value to the lessor less any investment credit retained by the lessor. This requirement cannot be used if the lease's inception is in the last 25% of the useful economic life of the leased asset. The interest rate, used to compute the PV, should be the **incremental borrowing rate** of the lessee unless the **implicit rate** is available and lower.

If a lease agreement meets none of the four criteria set forth above, it is to be classified as an operating lease on the books of a lessee.

Classification of Leases--Lessor

The four alternatives a lessor has in classifying a lease are as follows:

1. Operating
2. Sales-type
3. Direct financing
4. Leveraged

The conditions surrounding the origination of the lease determine its classification on the books of the lessor. If the lease meets **any one** of the four criteria specified below and **both** of the qualifications set forth below, the lease is classified as either a sales-type lease, direct financing lease, or leveraged lease depending upon the conditions present at the inception of the lease.

Criteria:

The same four criteria used above to differentiate a capital lease and an operating lease on the books of the lessee. However, it should be noted that per SFAS 98, para 22c, a lease involving real estate must transfer title (i.e., criterion 1 above) by the end of the lease term for the lessor to classify the lease as a sales-type lease of real estate.

Qualifications:

1. Collectibility of the minimum lease payments is reasonably predictable
2. No important uncertainties surround the amount of unreimbursable costs yet to be incurred by the lessor under the lease

If a lease transaction does not meet the criteria for classification as a sales-type lease, a direct financing lease, or a leveraged lease as specified above, it is to be classified on the books of the lessor as an operating lease. This classification process must take place prior to considering the proper accounting treatment.

Distinction Between Sales-Type, Direct Financing, and Leveraged Leases

A lease is classified as a sales-type lease when the criteria set forth above have been met and the lease transaction is structured in such a way that the lessor (generally a **manufacturer or dealer**) recognizes a profit or loss on the transaction in addition to interest revenue. In order for this to occur, the **fair value of the property** must be different from the cost (carrying value). The essential substance of this transaction is that of a sale, and thus its name. Common examples of sales-type leases: (1) when an automobile dealership opts to lease a car to its customers in lieu of making an actual sale, and (2) the re-lease of equipment coming off of an expiring lease.

A direct financing lease differs from a sales-type lease in that the lessor does not realize a profit or loss on the transaction other than interest revenue. In a direct financing lease, the fair value of the property at the inception of the lease is equal to the cost (carrying value). This type of lease transaction most often involves entities engaged in financing operations. The lessor (a bank, or other financial institution) purchases the asset and then leases the asset to the lessee. This transaction merely replaces the conventional lending transaction where the borrower uses the borrowed funds to purchase the asset. There are many economic reasons why the lease transaction is considered. They are as follows:

1. The lessee (borrower) is able to obtain 100% financing
2. Flexibility of use for the tax benefits
3. The lessor receives the equivalent of interest as well as an asset with some remaining value at the end of the lease term

In summary it may help to visualize the following chart when considering the classification of a lease:

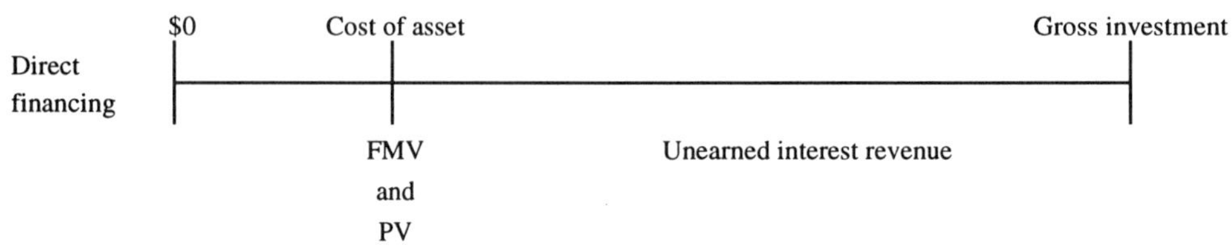

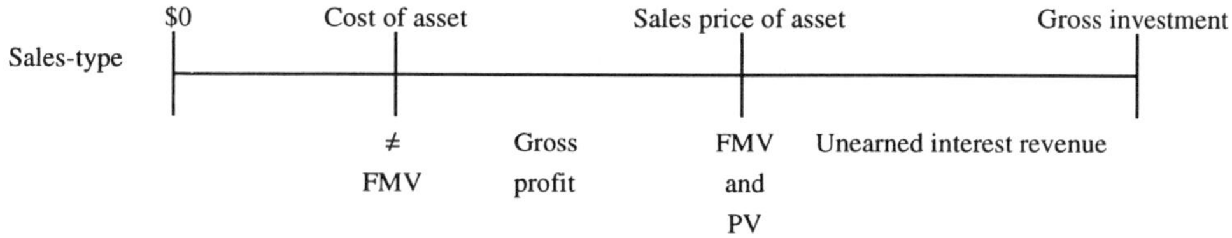

One form of a direct financing lease is a leveraged lease. This type is mentioned separately both here and in the following section on how to account for leases because it is to receive a different accounting treatment by a lessor. A leveraged lease meets all the definitional criteria of a direct financing lease, but differs because it involves at least three parties: a lessee, a long-term creditor, and a lessor (commonly referred to as the equity participant). Other characteristics of a leveraged lease are as follows:

1. The financing provided by the long-term creditor must be without recourse as to the general credit of the lessor, although the creditor may hold recourse with respect to the leased property. The amount of the financing must provide the lessor with substantial "leverage" in the transaction.
2. The lessor's net investment declines during the early years and rises during the later years of the lease term before its elimination (SFAS 13, para 42).

Accounting for Leases--Lessee

As discussed in the preceding section, there are two classifications that apply to a lease transaction on the books of the lessee. They are as follows:

1. Operating
2. Capital

Operating leases. The accounting treatment accorded an operating lease is relatively simple; the rental payment shall be charged to expense as the payments are made or become payable. This assumes that the lease payments are being made on a straight-line basis (i.e., an equal payment per period over the lease term). If the lease agreement calls for either an alternative payment schedule or a scheduled rent increase over the lease term, the lease expense should still be recognized on a straight-line basis unless another systematic and rational basis is a better representation of the actual physical usage of the leased property. In such an instance it will be necessary to create either a prepaid asset or a liability depending upon the structure of the payment schedule. Additionally, if the lease agreement provides for a scheduled increase(s) in contemplation of the lessee's increased physical use of the leased property, the total amount of rental payments, including the scheduled increase(s) shall be charged to expense over the lease term on a straight-line basis (TB 85-3). However, if the scheduled increase(s) is due to additional leased property, recognition should be proportional to the leased property with the increased rents recognized over the years that the lessee has control over the use of the additional leased property (TB 88-1).

Notice that in the case of an operating lease there is no balance sheet recognition of the leased asset because the substance of the lease is merely that of a rental. There is no reason to expect that the lessee will derive any future economic benefit from the leased asset beyond the lease term.

Capital leases. Recall that the classification of a lease must be determined prior to the consideration of the accounting treatment. Therefore, it is necessary to first examine the lease transaction against the four criteria (transfer of title, bargain purchase option, 75% of useful life, or 90% of net FMV). Assuming that the lease agreement satisfies one of these, it must be accounted for as a capital lease.

According to SFAS 13, para 10, the lessee shall record a capital lease as an asset and an obligation (liability) at an amount equal to the present value of the **minimum lease payments** at the beginning of the lease term. The asset should be recorded at the lower of the present value of the minimum lease payments or the fair market value of the asset. When the fair value of the leased asset is less than the present value of the minimum lease payments, the interest rate used to amortize the lease obligation will differ from the interest rate used in the 90% test as determined by the lessor. The interest rate used in the amortization will be the same as that used in the 90% test when the fair market value is greater than or equal to the present value of the minimum lease payments. For purposes of this computation, the minimum lease payments are considered to be the payments that the lessee is obligated to make or can be required to make excluding **executory costs** such as insurance, maintenance, and taxes. The minimum lease payments generally include the **minimum rental payments**, any **guarantee of the residual value** made by the lessee, and the **penalty** for **failure to renew** the lease, if applicable. If the lease includes a bargain purchase option (BPO), the amount required to be paid under the BPO is also included in the minimum lease payments. The present value shall be computed using the incremental borrowing rate of the lessee **unless** it is practicable for the lessee to determine the implicit rate computed by the lessor, **and** the implicit rate is less than the incremental borrowing rate. The lease term used in this present value computation is the fixed, **noncancelable** term of the lease plus the following:

1. All periods covered by **bargain renewal options**
2. All periods for which failure to renew imposes a penalty on the lessee
3. All periods covered by ordinary renewal options during which the lessee guarantees the lessor's debt on the leased property
4. All periods covered by ordinary renewals or extension up to the date a BPO is exercisable
5. All periods representing renewals or extensions of the lease at the lessor's option

Remember, if the amount computed as the present value of the minimum lease payments exceeds the fair value of the leased property at the **inception of the lease**, the amount recorded should be that of the fair value.

The amortization of the leased asset will depend upon how the lease qualified as a capital lease. If the lease transaction met the criteria as either transferring ownership, or containing a bargain purchase option, then the asset arising from the transaction is to be amortized over the estimated useful life of the leased property. If the transaction qualifies as a capital lease because it met either the 75% of useful life or 90% of FMV criteria, the asset must be amortized over the lease term. The conceptual rationale for this differentiated treatment arises because of the substance of the transaction. Under the first two criteria, the asset actually becomes the property of the lessee at the end of the lease term (or upon exercise of the BPO). In the latter situations, the title to the property remains with the lessor.

The leased asset is to be amortized (depreciated) over the lease term if title does not transfer to the lessee, while the asset is depreciated in a manner consistent with the lessee's normal depreciation policy if the title is to eventually transfer to the lessee. This latter situation can be interpreted to mean that the asset is depreciated over the useful economic life of the leased asset. The treatment and method used to amortize (depreciate) the leased asset is very similar to that used for any other asset. The amortization entry requires a debit to the lease expense and a credit to an accumulated amortization account. The leased asset shall not be amortized below the estimated residual value.

In some instances when the property is to revert back to the lessor, there may be a guaranteed residual value. This is an amount which the lessee guarantees to the lessor. If the FMV of the asset at the end of the lease term is greater than or equal to the guaranteed residual amount, the lessee incurs no additional obligation. On the other hand, if the FMV of the leased asset is less than the guaranteed residual value, then the lessee must make up the difference, usually with a cash payment. The guaranteed residual value is often used as a tool to reduce the periodic payments by substituting the lump-sum amount at the end of the term which results from the guarantee. In any event the amortization must still take place based on the **estimated residual value**. This results in a rational and systematic allocation of the expense through the periods and avoids a large loss (or expense) in the last period as a result of the guarantee.

The annual (periodic) rent payments made during the lease term are to be allocated between a reduction in the obligation and interest expense in a manner such that the interest expense represents a constant periodic rate of interest on the remaining balance of the lease obligation. This is commonly referred to as the effective interest method and was described in APB 21.

The following examples illustrate the treatment described in the foregoing paragraphs:

Example of accounting for a capital lease--Asset returned to lessor

1. The lease is initiated on 1/1/99 for equipment with an expected useful life of 3 years. The equipment reverts back to the lessor upon expiration of the lease agreement.
2. The FMV of the equipment is $135,000.
3. Three payments are due to the lessor in the amount of $50,000 per year beginning 12/31/99. An additional sum of $1,000 is to be paid annually by the lessee for insurance.
4. Lessee **guarantees** a $10,000 residual value on 12/31/01 to the lessor.
5. Irrespective of the $10,000 residual value guarantee, the leased asset is expected to have only a $1,000 salvage value on 12/31/01.
6. The lessee's incremental borrowing rate is 10%. (Lessor's implicit rate is unknown.)
7. The present value of the lease obligation is as follows:

PV of guaranteed residual value	=	$10,000 x	.7513*	=	$ 7,513
PV of annual payments	=	$50,000 x	2.4869**	=	124,345
					$131,858

The first step in dealing with any lease transaction is to classify the lease. In this case, the lease term is for 3 years which is equal to 100% of the expected useful life of the asset. Notice that the 90% test is also fulfilled as the PV of the minimum lease payments ($131,858) is greater than 90% of the FMV ($121,500). Thus, the lease is accounted for as a capital lease.

In number 7 (above) the present value of the lease obligation is computed. Note that the executory costs (insurance) are not included in the minimum lease payments and that the incremental borrowing rate of the lessee was used to determine the present value. This rate was used because the implicit rate was not determinable. (*NOTE: In order to have used the implicit rate it would have to have been less than the incremental borrowing rate.*) The entry necessary to record the lease on 1/1/99 is:

Leased equipment	131,858	
Lease obligation		131,858

Note that the lease is recorded at the present value of the minimum lease payments which, in this case, is less than the FMV. If the present value of the minimum lease payments had exceeded the FMV, the lease would be recorded at FMV.

The next step is to determine the proper allocation between interest and a reduction in the lease obligation for each lease payment. This is done using the effective interest method as illustrated below.

Year	*Cash payment*	*Interest expense*	*Reduction in lease obligation*	*Balance of lease obligation*
Inception of lease				$131,858
1	$50,000	$13,186	$36,814	95,044
2	50,000	9,504	40,496	54,548
3	50,000	5,452	44,548	10,000

* *The present value of an amount of $1 due in three periods at 10% is .7513.*

** *The present value of an ordinary annuity of $1 for three periods at 10% is 2.4869.*

The interest is calculated at 10% (the incremental borrowing rate) of the balance of the lease obligation for each period, and the remainder of the $50,000 payment is allocated to a reduction in the lease obligation. The lessee is also required to pay $1,000 for insurance on an annual basis. The entries necessary to record all payments relative to the lease for each of the 3 years are shown below.

	12/31/99		*12/31/00*		*12/31/01*	
Insurance expense	1,000		1,000		1,000	
Interest expense	13,186		9,504		5,452	
Lease obligation	36,814		40,496		44,548	
Cash		51,000		51,000		51,000

The lease equipment recorded as an asset must also be amortized (depreciated). The balance of this account is $131,858; however, as with any other asset it cannot be depreciated below the estimated residual value of $1,000 (note that it is depreciated down to the actual estimated residual value, **not** the guaranteed residual value). In this case, the straight-line depreciation method is applied over a period of 3 years. This 3-year period represents the lease term, **not** the life of the asset, because the asset reverts back to the lessor at the end of the lease term. Therefore, the following entry will be made at the end of each year:

Depreciation expense	43,619		
Accumulated depreciation		43,619	[($131,858 – 1,000) ÷ 3]

Finally, on 12/31/01 we must recognize the fact that ownership of the property has reverted back to the owner (lessor). The lessee made a guarantee that the residual value would be $10,000 on 12/31/01; as a result, the lessee must make up the difference between the guaranteed residual value and the actual residual value with a cash payment to the lessor. The following entry illustrates the removal of the leased asset and obligation from the books of the lessee:

Lease obligation	10,000	
Accumulated depreciation	130,858	
Cash		9,000
Leased equipment		131,858

The foregoing example illustrated a situation where the asset was to be returned to the lessor. Another situation exists (under BPO or transfer of title) where the asset is expected to remain with the lessee. Remember that leased assets are amortized over their useful life when title transfers or a bargain purchase option exists. At the end of the lease, the balance of the lease obligation should equal the guaranteed residual value, the bargain purchase option price, or a termination penalty.

Example of accounting for a capital lease--Asset ownership transferred to lessee

1. A 3-year lease is initiated on 1/1/99 for equipment with an expected useful life of 5 years.

2. Three annual lease payments of $52,000 are required beginning on 1/1/99 (note that the payment at the beginning of the year changes the PV computation). The lessor pays $2,000 per year for insurance on the equipment.
3. The lessee can exercise a bargain purchase option on 12/31/01 for $10,000. The expected residual value at 12/31/01 is $18,000.
4. The lessee's incremental borrowing rate is 10% (lessor's implicit rate is unknown).
5. The fair market value of the property leased is $140,000.

Once again, the classification of the lease must take place prior to the accounting for it. This lease is classified as a capital lease because it contains a BPO. In this case, the 90% test is also fulfilled.

The PV of the lease obligation is computed as follows:

PV of bargain purchase option	=	$10,000 x	.7513*	= $ 7,513
PV of annual payments	=	($52,000 – $2,000) x	2.7355**	= 136,755
				$144,288

Notice that the present value of the lease obligation is greater than the FMV of the asset. Since the lessor pays $2,000 a year for insurance, this payment is treated as executory costs and excluded from the calculation of the present value of annual payments. Because of this, the lease obligation must be recorded at the FMV of the asset leased.

1/1/99 Leased equipment	140,000	
Obligation under capital lease		140,000

According to SFAS 13, the allocation between interest and principal is to be such that interest recognized reflects the use of a constant periodic rate of interest applied to the remaining balance of the obligation. If the FMV of the leased asset is greater than or equal to the PV of the lease obligation, the interest rate used would be the same as that used to compute the PV (i.e., the incremental borrowing rate or the implicit rate). In cases such as this when the PV exceeds the FMV of the leased asset, a new rate must be computed through a series of trial and error calculations. In this situation the interest rate used was 13.265%. The amortization of the lease takes place as follows:

Date	*Cash payment*	*Interest expense*	*Reduction in lease obligation*	*Balance of lease obligation*
Inception of lease				$140,000
1/1/99	$50,000	$ --	$50,000	90,000
1/1/00	50,000	11,939	38,061	51,939
1/1/01	50,000	6,890	43,110	8,829
12/31/01	10,000	1,171	8,829	--

The following entries are required in years 99 through 01 to recognize the payment and amortization.

* *.7513 is the PV of an amount due in three periods at 10%.*

** *2.7355 is the PV of an **annuity due** for three periods at 10%.*

		99		*00*		*01*	
1/1	Operating expense	2,000		2,000		2,000	
	Obligation under capital lease	50,000		38,061		43,110	
	Accrued interest payable			11,939		6,890	
	Cash		52,000		52,000		52,000
12/31	Interest expense	11,939		6,890		1,171	
	Accrued interest payable		11,939		6,890		
	Obligation under capital lease						1,171
12/31	Depreciation expense	27,800		27,800		27,800	
	Accumulated depreciation ($139,000 ÷ 5 years)		27,800		27,800		27,800
12/31	Obligation under capital lease					10,000	
	Cash						10,000

Accounting for Leases--Lessor

As illustrated above, there are four classifications of leases with which a lessor must be concerned. They are as follows:

1. Operating
2. Sales-type
3. Direct financing
4. Leveraged

Operating lease. As in the case of the lessee, the operating lease requires a less complex accounting treatment. The payments received by the lessor are to be recorded as rent revenues in the period in which the payment is received or becomes receivable. As with the lessee, if either the rentals vary from a straight-line basis or the lease agreement contains a scheduled rent increase over the lease term, the revenue is to be recorded on a straight-line basis unless an alternative basis of systematic and rational allocation is more representative of the time pattern of physical usage of the leased property. Additionally, if the lease agreement provides for a scheduled increase(s) in contemplation of the lessee's increased physical use of the leased property, the total amount of rental payments including the scheduled increase(s) shall be allocated to revenue over the lease term on a straight-line basis (TB 85-3). However, if the scheduled increase(s) is due to additional leased property, recognition should be proportional to the leased property with the increased rents recognized over the years that the lessee has control over the use of the additional leased property (TB 88-1).

The lessor shall show the leased property on the balance sheet under the caption "Investment in leased property." This account should be shown with or near the fixed assets of the lessor, and depreciated in the same manner as the rest of the lessor's fixed assets.

Any **initial direct leasing costs** are to be amortized over the lease term as the revenue is recognized (i.e., on a straight-line basis unless another method is more representative). However, these costs may be charged to expense as they are incurred if the effect is not materially different from what would have occurred if the above method had not been used.

Any incentives made by the lessor to the lessee are to be treated as reductions of rent and recognized on a straight-line basis over the term of the lease (TB 88-1).

If, at the inception of the lease, the fair value of the property in an operating lease involving real estate that would have been classified as a sales-type lease except that it did not transfer title is less than its carrying amount, then the lessor must recognize a loss equal to that difference at the inception of the lease (SFAS 98, para 22j).

Sales-type lease. In the accounting for a sales-type lease, it is necessary for the lessor to determine the following amounts:

1. Gross investment
2. Fair value of the leased asset
3. Cost

From these amounts, the remainder of the computations necessary to record and account for the lease transaction can be made. The first objective is to determine the numbers necessary to complete the following entry:

Lease receivable	xx	
Cost of goods sold	xx	
Sales		xx
Inventory		xx
Unearned interest		xx

The gross investment (lease receivable) of the lessor is equal to the sum of the minimum lease payments (excluding executory costs) plus the **un**guaranteed residual value. The difference between the gross investment and the present value of the two components of gross investment (minimum lease payments and unguaranteed residual value) is recorded as the unearned interest revenue. The present value is to be computed using the lease term and implicit interest rate (both of which were discussed earlier). The resulting unearned interest revenue is to be amortized into income using the effective interest method. This will result in a constant periodic rate of return on the net investment (the net investment is the gross investment less the unearned income).

Recall from our earlier discussion that the fair market value (FMV) of the leased property is, by definition, equal to the normal selling price of the asset adjusted by any residual amount retained (this amount retained can be exemplified by an unguaranteed residual value, investment credit, etc.). According to SFAS 13, the adjusted selling price to be used for a sales-type lease is equal to the present value of the minimum lease payments. Thus, we can say that the normal selling price less the residual amount retained is equal to the PV of the minimum lease payments.

The cost of goods sold to be charged against income in the period of the sale is computed as the historic cost or carrying value of the asset (most likely inventory) plus any initial direct costs, less the present value of the unguaranteed residual value. The difference between the adjusted selling price and the amount computed as the cost of goods sold is the gross profit recognized by the lessor on the inception of the lease (sale). Thus, a sales-type lease generates two types of revenue for the lessor.

1. The gross profit on the sale
2. The interest earned on the lease receivable

It should be noted that if the sales-type lease involves real estate, the lessor must account for the transaction under the provisions of SFAS 66 in the same manner as a seller of the same property (SFAS 98, para 22g).

The application of these points is illustrated in the example below.

Example of accounting for a sales-type lease

XYZ Inc. is a manufacturer of specialized equipment. Many of its customers do not have the necessary funds or financing available for outright purchase. Because of this, XYZ offers a leasing alternative. The data relative to a typical lease are as follows:

1. The noncancelable fixed portion of the lease term is 5 years. The lessor has the option to renew the lease for an additional 3 years at the same rental. The estimated useful life of the asset is 10 years.
2. The lessor is to receive equal annual payments over the term of the lease. The leased property reverts back to the lessor upon termination of the lease.
3. The lease is initiated on 1/1/99. Payments are due on 12/31 for the duration of the lease term.
4. The cost of the equipment to XYZ Inc. is $100,000. The lessor incurs cost associated with the inception of the lease in the amount of $2,500.
5. The selling price of the equipment for an outright purchase is $150,000.
6. The equipment is expected to have a residual value of $15,000 at the end of 5 years and $10,000 at the end of 8 years.
7. The lessor desires a return of 12% (the implicit rate).

The first step is to calculate the annual payment due to the lessor. Recall that present value (PV) of the minimum lease payments is equal to the selling price adjusted for the present value of the residual amount. The present value is to be computed using the implicit interest rate and the lease term. In this case, the implicit rate is given as 12% and the lease term is 8 years (the fixed noncancelable portion plus the renewal period). Thus, the structure of the computation would be as follows:

Normal selling price – PV of residual value = PV of minimum lease payment

Or, in this case,

$$\$150{,}000 - (.40388^{*} \times \$10{,}000) = 4.96764^{**} \times \text{Minimum lease payment}$$

$$\frac{\$145{,}961.20}{4.96764} = \text{Minimum lease payment}$$

$$\$\ 29{,}382.40 = \text{Minimum lease payment}$$

Prior to examining the accounting implications of a lease, we must first determine the lease classification. Assume that there are no uncertainties regarding the lessor's costs, and the collectibility of the lease payments is reasonably assured. In this example, the lease term is 8 years (discussed above) while the estimated useful life of the asset is 10 years; thus, this lease qualifies as something other than an operating lease. [Note that it also meets the 90% of FMV criterion because the PV of the minimum lease payments of $145,961.20 is greater than 90% of the FMV which is $135,000, .90($150,000)]. Now it must be determined if this is a sales-type, direct financing, or leveraged lease. To do this, examine the FMV or selling price of the asset and compare it to the cost. Because the two are not equal, we can determine this to be a sales-type lease.

Next, obtain the figures necessary to record the entry on the books of the lessor. The gross investment is the total minimum lease payments plus the unguaranteed residual value or

$$(\$29{,}382.40 \times 8) + \$10{,}000 = \$245{,}059.20$$

The cost of goods sold is the historical cost of the inventory ($100,000) plus any initial direct costs ($2,500) less the PV of the unguaranteed residual value ($10,000 x .40388). Thus, the cost of goods sold amount is $98,461.20 ($100,000 + $2,500 – $4,038.80). Note that the initial direct costs will require a credit entry to some account, usually accounts payable or cash. The inventory account is credited for the carrying value of the asset, in this case $100,000.

The adjusted selling price is equal to the PV of the minimum payments, or $145,961.20. Finally, the unearned interest revenue is equal to the gross investment (i.e., lease receivable) less the present value of the components making up the gross investment (the minimum lease payment of $29,382.40 and the unguaranteed residual of $10,000). The present value of these items is $150,000 [($29,382.40 x 4.96764) + ($10,000 x .40388)]. Therefore, the entry necessary to record the lease is

Lease receivable	245,059.20	
Cost of goods sold	98,461.20	
Inventory		100,000.00
Sales		145,961.20
Unearned interest		95,059.20
Accounts payable (initial direct costs)		2,500.00

The next step in accounting for a sales-type lease is to determine the proper handling of the payment. Both principal and interest are included in each payment.

---

* *.40388 is the present value of an amount of $1 due in eight periods at a 12% interest rate.*

** *4.96764 is the present value of an annuity of $1 for eight periods at a 12% interest rate.*

According to SFAS 13, interest is recognized on a basis such that an equal rate is earned over the term of the lease. This will require setting up an amortization schedule as illustrated below.

Year	*Cash payment*	*Interest*	*Reduction in principal*	*Balance of net investment*
Inception of lease				$150,000.00
1	$ 29,382.40	$18,000.00	$ 11,382.40	138,617.00
2	29,382.40	16,634.11	12,748.29	125,869.31
3	29,382.40	15,104.32	14,278.08	111,591.23
4	29,382.40	13,390.95	15,991.45	95,599.78
5	29,382.40	11,471.97	17,910.43	77,689.35
6	29,382.40	9,322.72	20,059.68	57,629.67
7	29,382.40	6,915.56	22,466.84	35,162.83
8	29,382.40	4,219.57	25,162.83	10,000.00
	$235,059.20	$95,059.20	$140,000.00	

A few of the columns need to be elaborated upon. First, the net investment is the gross investment (lease receivable) less the unearned interest. Notice that at the end of the lease term, the net investment is equal to the estimated residual value. Also note that the total interest earned over the lease term is equal to the unearned interest at the beginning of the lease term.

The entries below illustrate the proper treatment to record the receipt of the lease payment and the amortization of the unearned interest in the first year.

Cash	29,382.40	
Lease receivable		29,382.40
Unearned interest	18,000.00	
Interest revenue		18,000.00

Notice that there is no entry to recognize the principal reduction. This is done automatically when the net investment is reduced by decreasing the lease receivable (gross investment) by $29,382.40 and the unearned interest account by only $18,000. The $18,000 is 12% (implicit rate) of the net investment. These entries are to be made over the life of the lease.

At the end of the lease term the asset is returned to the lessor and the following entry is required:

Asset	10,000	
Leased receivable		10,000

If the estimated residual value has changed during the lease term, then the accounting computations would have changed also to reflect this.

Direct financing lease. The accounting for a direct financing lease holds many similarities to that for a sales-type lease. Of particular importance is that the terminology used is much the same; however, the treatment accorded these items varies greatly. Again, it is best to preface our discussion by determining our objectives in the accounting for a direct financing lease. Once the lease has been classified, it must be recorded. In order to do this, the following numbers must be obtained:

1. Gross investment
2. Cost
3. Residual value

As mentioned earlier, a direct financing lease generally involves a leasing company or other financial institution and results in only interest revenue being earned by the lessor. This is because the FMV (selling price) and the cost are equal and, therefore, no profit is recognized on the actual lease transaction. Note how this is different from a sales-type lease which involves both a profit on the transaction and interest revenue over the lease term. The reason for this difference is derived from the conceptual nature underlying the purpose of the lease transaction. In a sales-type lease, **the manufacturer** (distributor, dealer) is seeking an alternative means to finance the sale of his product, whereas a direct financing lease is a result of the consumer's need to finance an equipment purchase. Because the consumer is unable to obtain conventional financing, he turns to a leasing company which will purchase the desired asset and then lease it to the consumer. Here the profit on the transaction remains with the manufacturer while the interest revenue is earned by the leasing company.

Like a sales-type lease, the first objective is to determine the amounts necessary to complete the following entry:

Lease receivable	xxx	
Asset		xxx
Unearned interest		xx

The gross investment is still defined as the minimum amount of lease payments exclusive of any executory costs plus the unguaranteed residual value. The difference between the gross investment as determined above and the cost (carrying value) of the asset is to be recorded as the unearned interest revenue because there is no manufacturer's/dealer's profit earned on the transaction. The following entry would be made to record initial direct costs:

Initial direct costs	xx	
Cash		xx

Net investment in the lease is defined as the gross investment less the unearned income plus the unamortized initial direct costs related to the lease. Initial direct costs are defined in the same way that they were for purposes of the sales-type lease; however, the accounting treatment is different. For a direct financing lease, the unearned lease (interest) income and the initial direct costs are to be amortized to income over the lease term so that a constant periodic rate is earned on the net investment. Thus, the effect of the initial direct costs is to reduce the implicit interest rate, or yield, to the lessor over the life of the lease.

An example follows which illustrates the preceding principles.

Example of accounting for a direct financing lease

XYZ needs new equipment to expand its manufacturing operation; however, it does not have sufficient capital to purchase the asset at this time. Because of this, XYZ has employed ABC Leasing to purchase the asset. In turn, XYZ will lease the asset from ABC. The following information applies to the terms of the lease:

Lease information

1. A 3-year lease is initiated on 1/1/99 for equipment costing $131,858 with an expected useful life of 5 years. FMV at 1/1/99 of equipment is $131,858.
2. Three annual payments are due to the lessor beginning 12/31/99. The property reverts back to the lessor upon termination of the lease.
3. The unguaranteed residual value at the end of year 3 is estimated to be $10,000.
4. The annual payments are calculated to give the lessor a 10% return (implicit rate).
5. The lease payments and unguaranteed residual value have a PV equal to $131,858 (FMV of asset) at the stipulated discount rate.
6. The annual payment to the lessor is computed as follows:

PV of residual value	=	$10,000 x .7513* = $7,513
PV of lease payments	=	Selling price – PV of residual value
	=	$131,858 – 7,513 = $124,345

$$\text{Annual payment} = \frac{\$124,345}{PV_{3,\ 10\%}} = \frac{\$124,345}{2.4869} = \$50,000$$

**.7513 is the PV of an amount due in three periods at 10%.*

7. Initial direct costs of $7,500 are incurred by ABC in the lease transaction.

As with any lease transaction, the first step must be to appropriately classify the lease. In this case, the PV of the lease payments ($124,345) exceeds 90% of the FMV (90% x $131,858). Assume that the lease payments are reasonably assured and that there are no uncertainties surrounding the costs yet to be incurred by the lessor.

Next, determine the unearned interest and the net investment in lease.

Gross investment in lease	
[(3 x $50,000) + $10,000]	$160,000
Cost of leased property	131,858
Unearned Interest	$ 28,142

The unamortized initial direct costs are to be added to the gross investment in the lease and the unearned interest income is to be deducted to arrive at the net investment in the lease. The net investment in the lease for this example is determined as follows:

Gross investment in lease	$160,000
Add:	
Unamortized initial direct costs	7,500
	$167,500
Less:	
Unearned interest income	28,142
Net investment in lease	$139,358

The net investment in the lease (Gross investment – Unearned revenue) has been increased by the amount of initial direct costs. Therefore, **the implicit rate is no longer 10%**. We must recompute the implicit rate. The implicit rate is really the result of an internal rate of return calculation. We know that the lease payments are to be $50,000 per annum and that a residual value of $10,000 is available at the end of the lease term. In return for these payments (inflows) we are giving up equipment (outflow) and incurring initial direct costs (outflows) with a net investment of $139,358 ($131,858 + $7,500). The only way to obtain the new implicit rate is through a trial and error calculation as set up below.

$$\frac{50{,}000}{(1+i)^1} + \frac{50{,}000}{(1+i)^2} + \frac{50{,}000}{(1+i)^3} + \frac{10{,}000}{(1+i)^3} = \$139{,}358$$

Where i = implicit rate of interest

In this case, the implicit rate is equal to 7.008%.

Thus, the amortization table would be set up as follows:

	(a) Lease payments	(b) Reduction in unearned interest	(c) PV x implicit rate (7.008%)	(d) Reduction in initial direct costs (b-c)	(e) Reduction in PVI net invest. (a-b + d)	(f) PVI net invest. in lease $(f)(n+1) = (f)n - (e)$
0						$139,358
1	$ 50,000	$13,186 (1)	$ 9,766	$3,420	$ 40,234	99,124
2	50,000	9,504 (2)	6,947	2,557	43,053	56,071
3	50,000	5,455 (3)	3,929	1,526	46,071	10,000
	$150,000	$28,145*	$20,642	$7,503	$129,358	

*Rounded

(b.1) $131,858 x 10% = $13,186
(b.2) [$131,858 - ($50,000 – 13,186)]x 10% = $9,504
(b.3) [$ 95,044 - ($50,000 – 9,504)] x 10% = $5,455

Here the interest is computed as 7.008% of the net investment. Note again that the net investment at the end of the lease term is equal to the estimated residual value.

The entry made to initially record the lease is as follows:

Lease receivable** [($50,000 x 3) + 10,000]	160,000	
Asset acquired for leasing		131,858
Unearned lease revenue		28,142

When the payment (or obligation to pay) of the initial direct costs occurs, the following entry must be made:

Initial direct costs	7,500	
Cash		7,500

Using the schedule above, the following entries would be made during each of the indicated years:

	Year 1		*Year 2*		*Year 3*	
Cash	50,000		50,000		50,000	
Lease receivable**		50,000		50,000		50,000
Unearned lease revenue	13,186		9,504		5,455	
Initial direct costs		3,420		2,557		1,526
Interest revenue		9,766		6,947		3,929

Finally, when the asset is returned to the lessor at the end of the lease term, it must be recorded on the books. The necessary entry is as follows:

Used asset	10,000	
Lease receivable**		10,000

****Also the "gross investment in lease."*

Leveraged leases. Leveraged leases are discussed in detail in the Appendix of this chapter because of the complexity involved in the accounting treatment.

Special Situations

Change in residual value. For any of the foregoing types of leases, the lessor is to review the estimated residual value on at least an annual basis. If there is a decline in the estimated residual value, the lessor must make a determination as to whether this decline is temporary or permanent. If temporary, no adjustment is required; however, if the decline is other than temporary, then the estimated residual value must be revised in line with the changed estimate. The loss that arises in the net investment is to be recognized in the period of decline. Under no circumstance is the estimated residual value to be adjusted to reflect an increase in the estimate.

Change in the provisions of a lease. In the case of either a sales-type or direct financing lease where there is a change in the provisions of a lease, the lease shall be accounted for as discussed below (by the lessor).

We are basically concerned with changes in the provisions that affect the amount of the remaining minimum lease payments. When a change such as this occurs, one of the following three things can happen:

1. The change does not give rise to a new agreement. A new agreement is defined as a change which, if in effect at the inception of the lease, would have resulted in a different classification.
2. The change does give rise to a new agreement which would be classified as a direct financing lease
3. The change gives rise to a new agreement classified as an operating lease

If either 1. or 2. occurs, the balance of the minimum lease payments receivable and the estimated residual value (if affected) shall be adjusted to reflect the effect of the change. The net adjustment is to be charged (or credited) to the unearned income account, and the accounting for the lease adjusted to reflect the change.

If the new agreement is an operating lease, then the remaining net investment (lease receivable less unearned income) is to be removed from the books and the leased asset shall be recorded at the lower of its cost, present fair value, or carrying value. The net adjustment resulting from these entries shall be charged (or credited) to the income of the period. Thereafter, the new lease shall be accounted for as any other operating lease.

Termination of a lease. The lessor shall remove the remaining net investment from his/her books and record the leased equipment as an asset at the lower of its original cost, present fair value, or current carrying value. The net adjustment shall be reflected in the income of the current period.

The lessee is also affected by the terminated agreement because s/he has been relieved of the obligation. If the lease is a capital lease, then the lessee should remove both the obligation and the asset from his/her accounts and charge any adjustment to the current period income. If accounted for as an operating lease, there is no accounting adjustment required.

Renewal or extension of an existing lease. The renewal or extension of an existing lease agreement affects the accounting of both the lessee and the lessor. SFAS 13 specifies two basic situations in this regard: (1) the renewal occurs and makes a residual guarantee or penalty provision inoperative, or (2) the renewal agreement does not do the foregoing and the renewal is to be treated as a new agreement. The accounting treatment prescribed under the latter situation for a lessee by SFAS 13 is as follows:

1. If the renewal or extension is classified as a capital lease, then the (present) current balances of the asset and related obligation should be adjusted by an amount equal to the difference between the present value of the future minimum lease payments under the revised agreement and the (present) current balance of the obligation. The present value of the minimum lease payments under the revised agreement should be computed using the interest rate that was in effect at the inception of the original lease.
2. If the renewal or extension is classified as an operating lease, then the current balances in the asset and liability accounts shall be removed from the books and a gain (loss) recognized for the difference. The new lease agreement resulting from a renewal or extension shall be accounted for in the same manner as other operating leases.

Under the same circumstances, SFAS 13 prescribes the following treatment to be followed by the lessor:

1. If the renewal or extension is classified as a direct financing lease, then the existing balances of the lease receivable and the estimated residual value accounts should be adjusted for the changes resulting from the revised agreement. (*NOTE: Remember that an upward adjustment to the estimated residual value is not allowed.*) The net adjustment should be charged or credited to an unearned income account.
2. If the renewal or extension is classified as an operating lease, then the remaining net investment under the existing sales-type lease or direct financing lease shall be removed from the books and the leased asset shall be recorded as an asset at the lower of its original cost, present fair value, or current carrying amount. The difference between the net investment and the amount recorded for the leased asset shall be charged to income of the period. The renewal or extension should then be accounted for as any other operating lease.
3. If the renewal or extension is classified as a sales-type lease **and** it occurs at or near the end of the existing lease term, then the renewal or extension should be accounted for as a sales-type lease. (*NOTE: A renewal or extension that occurs in the last few months of an existing lease is considered to have occurred at or near the end of the existing lease term.*)

If the renewal or extension causes the guarantee or penalty provision to be inoperative, the **lessee** shall adjust the current balance of the leased asset and the lease obligation **to** the present value of the future minimum lease payments (according to SFAS 13 "by an amount equal to the difference between the PV of future minimum lease payments under the revised agreement and the present balance of the obligation"). The PV of the future minimum lease payments shall be computed using the implicit rate used in the original lease agreement.

Given the same circumstances, the **lessor** shall adjust the existing balance of the lease receivable and estimated residual value accounts to reflect the changes of the revised agreement (remember, no upward adjustments to the residual value). The net adjustment shall be charged (or credited) to unearned income.

Leases between related parties. Leases between related parties shall be classified and accounted for as though the parties are unrelated, except in cases where it is certain that the terms and conditions of the agreement have been influenced significantly by the fact that the lessor and lessee are related. When this is the case, the classification and/or accounting shall be modified to reflect the true economic substance of the transaction rather than the legal form.

If a subsidiary's principal business activity is leasing property to its parent or other affiliated companies, consolidated financial statements shall be presented.

SFAS 57 requires that the nature and extent of leasing activities between related parties be disclosed.

Accounting for leases in a business combination. A business combination, in and of itself, has no effect upon the classification of a lease. However, if, in connection with a business combination, the lease agreement is modified to change the original classification of the lease, it should be considered a new agreement and reclassified according to the revised provisions.

In most cases, a business combination that is accounted for by the pooling-of-interest method or by the purchase method will not affect the previous classification of a lease unless the provisions have been modified as indicated in the preceding paragraph.

The acquiring company shall apply the following procedures to account for a leveraged lease in a business combination accounted for by the purchase method:

1. The classification of leveraged lease should be kept.
2. The net investment in the leveraged lease should be given a fair market value (present value, net of tax) based upon the remaining future cash flows. Also, the estimated tax effects of the cash flows should be given recognition.
3. The net investment shall then be broken down into three components: net rentals receivable, estimated residual value, and unearned income.
4. Thereafter, the leveraged lease should be accounted for as described above in the section on leveraged leases.

In a business combination where a lease is acquired that does not conform to SFAS 13 (pre-1979), the acquiring company should account for the lease by retroactively applying SFAS 13 at the date of combination.

Accounting for changes in lease agreements resulting from refunding of tax-exempt debt. If, during the lease term, a change in the lease results from a refunding by the lessor of tax-exempt debt (including an advance refunding) and (1) the lessee receives the economic advantages of the refunding and (2) the revised agreement can be classified as a capital lease by the lessee and a direct financing lease by the lessor, the change should be accounted for as follows:

1. If the change is accounted for as an extinguishment of debt

    a. Lessee accounting. The lessee should adjust the lease obligation to the present value of the future minimum lease payments under the revised agreement. The present value of the minimum lease payments should be computed by using the interest rate applicable to the revised agreement. Any gain or loss should be recognized currently as a gain or loss on the extinguishment of debt in accordance with the provisions of SFAS 4.
    b. Lessor accounting. The lessor should adjust the balance of the lease receivable and the estimated residual value, if affected, for the difference in present values between the old and revised agreements. Any resulting gain or loss should be recognized currently.

2. If the change is not accounted for as an extinguishment of debt

a. Lessee accounting. The lessee should accrue any costs in connection with the debt refunding that is obligated to be refunded to the lessor. These costs should be amortized by the interest method over the period from the date of refunding to the call date of the debt to be refunded.
b. Lessor accounting. The lessor should recognize any reimbursements to be received from the lessee, for costs paid in relation to the debt refunding, as revenue. This revenue should be recognized in a systematic manner over the period from the date of refunding to the call date of the debt to be refunded.

Sale or assignment to third parties; nonrecourse financing. The sale or assignment of a lease or of property subject to a lease that was originally accounted for as a sales-type lease or a direct financing lease will not affect the original accounting treatment of the lease. Any profit or loss on the sale or assignment should be recognized at the time of transaction except under the following two circumstances:

1. When the sale or assignment is between related parties, apply provisions presented above under "related parties"
2. When the sale or assignment is with recourse, it shall be accounted for using the provisions of SFAS 77 or 125

The sale of property subject to an operating lease shall not be treated as a sale if the seller (or any related party to the seller) retains "substantial risks of ownership" in the leased property. A seller may retain "substantial risks of ownership" by various arrangements. For example, if the lessee defaults upon the lease agreement or if the lease terminates, the seller may arrange to do one of the following:

1. Acquire the property or the lease
2. Substitute an existing lease
3. Secure a replacement lessee or a buyer for the property under a remarketing agreement

A seller will **not** retain substantial risks of ownership by arrangements where one of the following occurs:

1. A remarketing agreement includes a reasonable fee to be paid to the seller
2. The seller is not required to give priority to the releasing or disposition of the property owned by the third party over similar property owned by the seller

When the sale of property subject to an operating lease is not accounted for as a sale because the substantial risk factor is present, it should be accounted for as a borrowing. The proceeds from the sale should be recorded as an obligation on the seller's books. Rental payments made by the lessee under the operating lease should be recorded as revenue by the seller even if the payments are paid to the third-party purchaser. The seller shall account for each rental payment by allocating a portion to interest expense (to be imputed in accordance with the provisions of APB 21), and the remainder will reduce the existing obligation. Other normal accounting procedures for operating leases should be applied except that the depreciation term for the leased asset is limited to the amortization period of the obligation.

The sale or assignment of lease payments under an operating lease by the lessor should be accounted for as a borrowing as described above.

Nonrecourse financing is a common occurrence in the leasing industry, whereby the stream of lease payments on a lease is discounted on a nonrecourse basis at a financial institution with the lease payments collateralizing the debt. The proceeds are then used to finance future leasing transactions. Even though the discounting is on a nonrecourse basis, TB 86-2 prohibits the offsetting of the debt against the related lease receivable unless a legal right of offset exists or the lease qualified as a leveraged lease at its inception. The SEC in a recent Staff Accounting Bulletin has also affirmed this position.

Money-over-money lease transactions. In cases where a lessor obtains nonrecourse financing in excess of the leased asset's cost, FASB TB 88-1 states that the borrowing and leasing are separate transactions and should not be offset against each other unless a right of offset exists. Only dealer profit in sales-type leases may be recognized at the beginning of the lease term.

Transfers of residual value (SFAS 125 and TB 86-2). Recently, there has been an increase in the acquisition of interests in residual values of leased assets by companies whose primary business is other than leasing or financing. This generally occurs through the outright purchase of the right to own the leased asset or the right to receive the proceeds from the sale of a leased asset at the end of its lease term.

In instances such as these, the rights should be recorded by the purchaser at the fair value of the assets surrendered. Recognition of increases in the value of the interest in the residual (i.e., residual value accretion) to the end of the lease term are permitted for guaranteed residual values because they are financial assets. However, recognition of such increases are prohibited for unguaranteed residual values. A nontemporary write-down of a residual value interest (guaranteed/unguaranteed) should be recognized as a loss. This guidance also applies to lessors who sell the related minimum lease payments but retain the interest in the residual value. Guaranteed residual values also have no effect on this guidance.

Leases involving government units. Leases that involve government units (i.e., airport facilities, bus terminal space, etc.) usually contain special provisions which prevent the agreements from being classified as anything but operating leases. These special provisions include the governmental body's authority to abandon a facility at any time during lease term, thus making its economic life indeterminable. These leases also do not contain a BPO or transfer ownership. The fair market value is generally indeterminable because neither the leased property nor similar property is available for sale.

However, leases involving government units are subject to the same classification criteria as nongovernment units, except when the following six criteria are met (*NOTE: If all six conditions are met, the agreement shall be classified as an operating lease by both lessee and lessor*):

1. A government unit or authority owns the leased property
2. The leased property is part of a larger facility operated by or on behalf of the lessor
3. The leased property is a permanent structure or part of a permanent structure that normally cannot be moved to another location
4. The lessor, or a higher governmental authority, has the right to terminate the lease at any time under the lease agreement or existing statutes or regulations
5. The lease neither transfers ownership nor allows the lessee to purchase or acquire the leased property
6. The leased property or similar property in the same area cannot be purchased or leased from anyone else

Accounting for a sublease. A sublease is used to describe the situation where the original lessee re-leases the leased property to a third party (the sublessee), and the original lessee acts as a sublessor. Normally, the nature of a sublease agreement does not affect the original lease agreement, and the original lessee/sublessor retains primary liability.

The original lease remains in effect, and the original lessor continues to account for the lease as before. The original lessee/sublessor shall account for the lease as follows:

1. If the original lease agreement transfers ownership or contains a BPO and if the new lease meets any one of the four specified criteria (i.e., transfers ownership, BPO, 75% test, or 90% test) and both the collectibility and uncertainties criteria, then the sublessor shall classify the new lease as a sales-type or direct financing lease; otherwise as an operating lease. In either situation, the original lessee/sublessor should continue accounting for the original lease obligation as before.
2. If the original lease agreement does not transfer ownership or contain a BPO, but it still qualified as a capital lease, then the original lessee/sublessor should (with one exception) apply the usual criteria set by SFAS 13 in classifying the new agreement as a capital or operating lease. If the new lease qualifies for capital treatment, the original lessee/sublessor should account for it as a direct financing lease, with the unamortized balance of the asset under the original lease being treated as the cost of the leased property. The one exception arises when the circumstances sur-

rounding the sublease suggest that the sublease agreement was an important part of a predetermined plan in which the original lessee played only an intermediate role between the original lessor and the sublessee. In this situation, the sublease shall be classified by the 75% and 90% criteria as well as collectibility and uncertainties criteria. In applying the 90% criterion, the fair value for the leased property will be the fair value to the original lessor at the inception of the original lease. Under all circumstances, the original lessee should continue accounting for the original lease obligation as before. If the new lease agreement (sublease) does not meet the capitalization requirements imposed for subleases, then the new lease should be accounted for as an operating lease.

3. If the original lease is an operating lease, the original lessee/sublessor should account for the new lease as an operating lease and account for the original operating lease as before.

Sale-Leaseback Transactions

Sale-leaseback describes a transaction where the owner of property (seller-lessee) sells the property, and then immediately leases all or part of it back from the new owner (buyer-lessor). These transactions may occur when the seller-lessee is experiencing cash flow or financing problems or because the tax advantages are beneficial. The important consideration in this type of transaction is the recognition of two separate and distinct economic transactions. However, it is important to note that there is not a physical transfer of property. First, there is a sale of property, and second, there is a lease agreement for the same property in which the original seller is the lessee and the original buyer is the lessor. This is illustrated below.

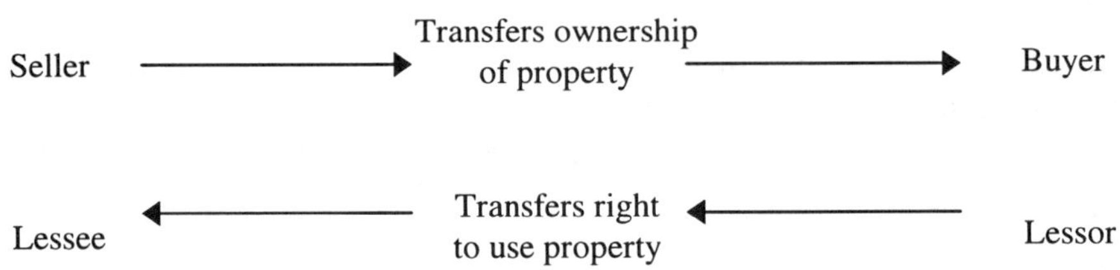

If an entity owns property and is also a lessee in it (e.g., entity invests in a partnership that owns this property), and sells the property while remaining a lessee, the transaction should be accounted for as a sale-leaseback, if the existing lease terms are modified. (FASB Emerging Issues Task Force [EITF] Consensus 88-21)

A sale-leaseback transaction is usually structured such that the sales price of the asset is greater than or equal to the current market value. The result of this higher sales price is a higher periodic rental payment over the lease term. The transaction is attractive usually because of the tax benefits associated with it. The seller-lessee benefits from the higher price because of the increased gain on the sale of the property and the deductibility of the lease payments which are usually larger than the depreciation that was previously being taken. The buyer-lessor benefits from both the higher rental payments and the larger depreciable basis.

The accounting treatment from the seller-lessee's point of view will depend upon the degree of rights to use retained by the seller-lessee. The degree of rights to use retained may be categorized as follows:

1. Substantially all
2. Minor
3. More than minor but less than substantially all

The guideline for the determination of substantially all is based upon the classification criteria presented for the lease transaction. For example, a test based upon the 90% recovery criterion seems appropriate. That is, if the present value of fair rental payments is equal to 90% or more of the fair value of the sold asset, the seller-lessee is presumed to have retained **substantially all** of the rights to use the sold property. The test for retaining **minor** rights would be to substitute 10% or less for 90% or more in the preceding sentence.

If substantially all the rights to use the property are retained by the seller-lessee, and the agreement meets at least one of the criteria for capital lease treatment, the seller-lessee should account for the leaseback as a capital lease and any profit on the sale should be deferred and either amortized over the life of the property or treated as a reduction of depreciation expense. If the leaseback is classified as an operating lease, it should be accounted for as one, and any profit or loss on the sale should be deferred and amortized over the lease term. Any loss on the sale would also be deferred unless the loss were perceived to be a real economic loss, in which case the loss would be immediately recognized and not deferred.

If only a **minor portion** of the rights to use are retained by the seller-lessee, the sale and the leaseback should be accounted for separately. However, if the rental payments appear unreasonable based upon the existing market conditions at the inception of the lease, the profit or loss should be adjusted so the rentals are at a reasonable amount. The amount created by the adjustment should be deferred and amortized over the life of the property if a capital lease is involved or over the lease term if an operating lease is involved.

If the seller-lessee retains **more than a minor portion but less than substantially all** the rights to use the property, any excess profit on the sale should be recognized on the date of the sale. For purposes of this paragraph, excess profit is derived as follows:

1. If the leaseback is classified as an operating lease, the excess profit is the profit which exceeds the present value of the minimum lease payments over the lease term. The seller-lessee should use its incremental borrowing rate to compute the present value of the minimum lease payments. If the

implicit rate of interest in the lease is known and lower, it should be used to compute the present value of the minimum lease payments.

2. If the leaseback is classified as a capital lease, the excess profit is the amount greater than the recorded amount of the leased asset.

When the fair value of the property at the time of the leaseback is less than its undepreciated cost, the seller-lessee should immediately recognize a loss for the difference. In the example below, the sales price is less than the book value of the property. However, there is no economic loss because the FMV is greater than the book value.

Sales price	Book value	FMV and PV
$85,000	$90,000	$100,000

($5,000)
Artificial loss

The artificial loss must be deferred and amortized as an addition to depreciation.

The diagram below summarizes the accounting for sale-leaseback transactions.

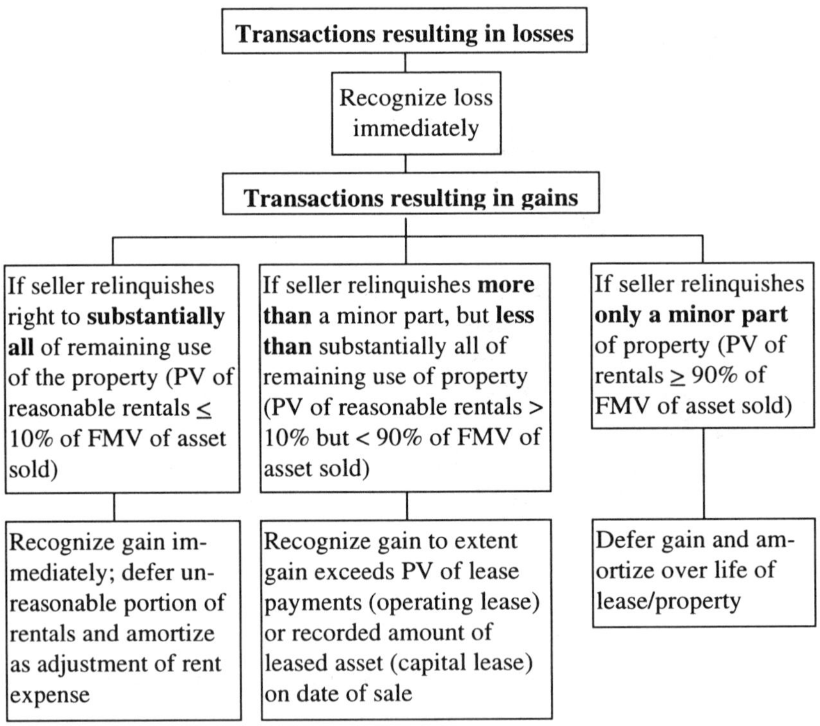

In the above circumstances, when the leased asset is land only, any amortization should be on a straight-line basis over the lease term, regardless of whether the lease is classified as a capital or operating lease.

Executory costs are not to be included in the calculation of profit to be deferred in a sale-leaseback transaction. (FASB Emerging Issues Task Force [EITF] Consensus 89-16.)

The buyer-lessor should account for the transaction as a purchase and a direct financing lease if the agreement meets the criteria of **either** a direct financing lease **or** a sales-type lease. Otherwise, the agreement should be accounted for as a purchase and an operating lease.

Sale-leaseback involving real estate. Three requirements are necessary for a sale-leaseback involving real estate (including real estate with equipment) to qualify for sale-leaseback accounting treatment. Those sale-leaseback transactions not meeting the three requirements should be accounted for as a deposit (see Chapter 8) or as a financing. The three requirements (SFAS 98, para 7) are

1. The lease must be a normal leaseback
2. Payment terms and provisions must adequately demonstrate the buyer-lessor's initial and continuing investment in the property
3. Payment terms and provisions must transfer all the risks and rewards of ownership as demonstrated by a lack of continuing involvement by the seller-lessee

A normal leaseback involves active use of the leased property in the seller-lessee's trade or business during the lease term.

The buyer-lessor's initial investment is adequate if it demonstrates the buyer-lessor's commitment to pay for the property and indicates a reasonable likelihood that the seller-lessee will collect any receivable related to the leased property. The buyer-lessor's continuing investment is adequate if the buyer is contractually obligated to pay an annual amount at least equal to the level of annual payment needed to pay that debt and interest over no more than (1) 20 years for land, and (2) the customary term of a first-year mortgage for other real estate.

Any continuing involvement by the seller-lessee other than normal leaseback disqualifies the lease from sale-leaseback accounting treatment (SFAS 98, para 10). Some examples of continuing involvement other than normal leaseback include

1. The seller-lessee has an obligation or option (excluding the right of first refusal) to repurchase the property
2. The seller-lessee (or party related to the seller-lessee) guarantees the buyer-lessor's investment or debt related to that investment or a return on that investment
3. The seller-lessee is required to reimburse the buyer-lessor for a decline in the fair value of the property below estimated residual value at the end of the lease term based on other than excess wear and tear
4. The seller-lessee remains liable for an existing debt related to the property
5. The seller-lessee's rental payments are contingent on some predetermined level of future operations of the buyer-lessor

6. The seller-lessee provides collateral on behalf of the buyer-lessor other than the property directly involved in the sale-leaseback
7. The seller-lessee provides nonrecourse financing to the buyer-lessor for any portion of the sales proceeds or provides recourse financing in which the only recourse is the leased asset
8. The seller-lessee enters into a sale-leaseback involving property improvements or integral equipment without leasing the underlying land to the buyer-lessor
9. The buyer-lessor is obligated to share any portion of the appreciation of the property with the seller-lessee
10. Any other provision or circumstance that allows the seller-lessee to participate in any future profits of the buyer-lessor or the appreciation of the leased property

Example of accounting for a sale-leaseback transaction

To illustrate the accounting treatment is a sale-leaseback transaction, suppose that Lessee Corporation sells equipment that has a book value of $80,000 and a fair value of $100,000 to Lessor Corporation, and then immediately leases it back under the following conditions:

1. The sale date is January 1, 1999, and the equipment has a fair value of $100,000 on that date and an estimated useful life of 15 years.
2. The lease term is 15 years, noncancelable, and requires equal rental payments of $13,109 at the beginning of each year.
3. Lessee Corp. has the option to annually renew the lease at the same rental payments upon expiration of the original lease.
4. Lessee Corp. has the obligation to pay all executory costs.
5. The annual rental payments provide the lessor with a 12% return on investment.
6. The incremental borrowing rate of Lessee Corp. is 12%.
7. Lessee Corp. depreciates similar equipment on a straight-line basis.

Lessee Corp. should classify the agreement as a capital lease since the lease term exceeds 75% of the estimated economic life of the equipment, and because the present value of the lease payments is greater than 90% of the fair value of the equipment. Assuming that collectibility of the lease payments is reasonably predictable and that no important uncertainties exist concerning the amount of unreimbursable costs yet to be incurred by the lessor, Lessor Corp. should classify the transaction as a direct financing lease because the present value of the minimum lease payments is equal to the fair market value of $100,000 ($13,109 x 7.62817).

Lessee Corp. and Lessor Corp. would normally make the following journal entries during the first year:

Upon Sale of Equipment on January 1, 1999

Lessee Corp.			*Lessor Corp.*		
Cash	100,000		Equipment	100,000	
Equipment*		80,000	Cash		100,000
Unearned profit on sale-leaseback		20,000			
Leased equipment	100,000		Lease receivable ($13,109 x 15 = $196,635)	196,635	
Lease obligations		100,000	Equipment		100,000
			Unearned interest		96,635

**Assumes new equipment*

To Record First Payment on January 1, 1999

Lessee Corp.			*Lessor Corp.*		
Lease obligations	13,109		Cash	13,109	
Cash		13,109	Lease receivable		13,109

To Record Incurrence and Payment of Executory Costs

Lessee Corp.			*Lessor Corp.*
Insurance, taxes, etc.	xxx		(No entry)
Cash (accounts payable)		xxx	

To Record Depreciation Expense on the Equipment, December 31, 1999

Lessee Corp.			*Lessor Corp.*
Depreciation expense	6,667		(No entry)
Accum. depr.--capital leases ($100,000 ÷ 15)		6,667	

To Amortize Profit on Sale-Leaseback by Lessee Corp., December 31, 1999

Lessee Corp.			*Lessor Corp.*
Unearned profit on sale-leaseback	1,333		(No entry)
Depr. expense ($20,000 ÷ 15)		1,333	

To Record Interest for 1999, December 31, 1999

Lessee Corp.			*Lessor Corp.*		
Interest expense	10,427		Unearned interest income	10,427	
Accrued interest payable		10,427	Interest income		10,427

Partial Lease Amortization Schedule

Date	*Cash payment*	*Interest expense*	*Reduction of obligation*	*Lease obligation*
Inception of lease				$100,000
1/1/99	$13,109	$ --	$13,109	86,891
1/1/00	13,109	10,427	2,682	84,209

Leases Involving Real Estate

Leases involving real estate can be divided into the following four categories:

1. Leases involving land only
2. Leases involving land and building(s)
3. Leases involving real estate and equipment
4. Leases involving only part of a building

Leases involving land only--Lessee accounting. If the lease agreement transfers ownership or contains a bargain purchase option, the lessee should account for the lease as a capital lease, and record an asset and related liability in an amount equal to the present value of the minimum lease payments. If the lease agreement does not transfer ownership or contain a bargain purchase option, the lessee should account for the lease as an operating lease.

Lessor accounting. If the lease gives rise to dealer's profit (or loss) and transfers ownership (i.e., title), SFAS 98 requires that the lease shall be classified as a sales-type lease and accounted for under the provisions of SFAS 66 in the same manner as a seller of the same property. If the lease transfers ownership, both the collectibility and no material uncertainties criteria are met, but does not give rise to dealer's profit (or loss), the lease should be accounted for as a direct financing or leveraged lease as appropriate. If the lease contains a bargain purchase option and both the collectibility and no material uncertainties criteria are met, the lease should be accounted for as a direct financing, leveraged, or operating lease as appropriate. If the lease does not meet the collectibility and/or no material uncertainties criteria, the lease should be accounted for as an operating lease.

Leases involving land and building--Lessee accounting. If the agreement transfers title or contains a bargain purchase option, the lessee should account for the agreement by separating the land and building components and capitalize each separately. The land and building elements should be allocated on the basis of their relative fair market values measured at the inception of the lease. The land and building components are separately accounted for because the lessee is expected to own the real estate by the end of the lease term. The building should be depreciated over its estimated useful life without regard to the lease term.

When the lease agreement neither transfers title nor contains a bargain purchase option, the fair value of the land must be determined in relation to the fair value of the aggregate properties included in the lease agreement. If the fair value of the land is less than 25% of the fair value of the leased properties in aggregate, then the land is considered immaterial. Conversely, if the fair value of the land is 25% or greater of the fair value of the leased properties in aggregate, then the land is considered material.

When the land component of the lease agreement is considered immaterial (FMV land < 25% total FMV), the lease should be accounted for as a single lease unit. The lessee should capitalize the lease if one of the following occurs:

1. The term of the lease is 75% or more of the economic useful life of the real estate
2. The present value of the minimum lease payments equals 90% or more of the fair market value of the leased real estate less any lessor investment tax credit

If neither of the above two criteria is met, the lessee should account for the lease agreement as a single operating lease.

When the land component of the lease agreement is considered material (FMV land ≥ 25% total FMV), the land and building components should be separated. By applying the lessee's incremental borrowing rate to the fair market value of the land, the annual minimum lease payment attributed to land is computed. The remaining payments are attributed to the building. The division of minimum lease payments between land and building is essential for both the lessee and lessor. The lease involving the land should **always** be accounted for as an operating lease. The lease involving the building(s) must meet either the 75% or 90% test to be treated as a capital lease. If neither of the two criteria is met, the building(s) will also be accounted for as an operating lease.

Lessor accounting. The lessor's accounting depends on whether the lease transfers ownership, contains a bargain purchase option, or does neither of the two.

If the lease transfers ownership and gives rise to dealer's profit (or loss), SFAS 98, para 1, requires that the lessor shall classify the lease as a sales-types lease and account for the lease as a single unit under the provisions of SFAS 66 in the same manner as a seller of the same property. If the lease transfers ownership, meets both the collectibility and no important uncertainties criteria, but does not give rise to dealer's profit (or loss), the lease should be accounted for as a direct financing or leveraged lease as appropriate.

If the lease contains a bargain purchase option and gives rise to dealer's profit (or loss), the lease should be classified as an operating lease. If the lease contains a bargain purchase option, meets both the collectibility and no material uncertainties criteria, but does not give rise to dealer's profit (or loss), the lease should be accounted for as a direct financing lease or a leveraged lease as appropriate.

If the lease agreement neither transfers ownership nor contains a bargain purchase option, the lessor should follow the same rules as the lessee in accounting for real estate leases involving land and building(s).

However, the collectibility and the no material uncertainties criteria must be met before the lessor can account for the agreement as a direct financing lease, and in no such case may the lease be classified as a sales-type lease (i.e., ownership must be transferred).

The treatment of a lease involving both land and building can be illustrated in the following examples.

Example of accounting for land and building lease containing transfer of title

1. The lessee enters into a 10-year noncancelable lease for a parcel of land and a building for use in its operations. The building has an estimated useful life of 12 years.
2. The FMV of the land is $75,000, while the FMV of the building is $310,000.
3. A payment of $50,000 is due to the lessor at the beginning of each of the 10 years of the lease.
4. The lessee's incremental borrowing rate is 10%. (Lessor's implicit rate is unknown.)
5. Ownership will transfer to the lessee at the end of the lease.

The present value of the minimum lease payments is $337,951 ($50,000 x 6.75902*). The portion of the present value of the minimum lease payments which should be capitalized for each of the two components of the lease is computed as follows:

FMV of land	$ 75,000
FMV of building	310,000
Total FMV of leased property	$385,000

Portion of PV allocated to land	$337,951 x	75,000 / 385,000	=	$ 65,835
Portion of PV allocated to building	$337,951 x	310,000 / 385,000	=	272,116
Total PV to be capitalized				$337,951

The entry made to initially record the lease is as follows:

Leased land	65,835	
Leased building	272,116	
Lease obligation		337,951

**6.75902 is the PV of an annuity due for 10 periods at 10%.*

Subsequently, the obligation will be decreased in accordance with the effective interest method. The leased building will be amortized over its expected useful life.

Example of accounting for land and building lease without transfer of title or bargain purchase option

Assume the same facts as the previous example except that title does not transfer at the end of the lease.

The lease is still a capital lease because the lease term is more than 75% of the useful life. Since the FMV of the land is less than 25% of the leased properties in aggregate, (75,000/385,000 = 19%), the land component is considered immaterial and the lease will be accounted for as a single lease. The entry to record the lease is as follows:

Leased property	337,951	
Lease obligation		337,951

Assume the same facts as the previous example except that the FMV of the land is $110,000 and the FMV of the building is $275,000. Once again title does not transfer.

Because the FMV of the land exceeds 25% of the leased properties in aggregate (110,000/385,000 = 28%), the land component is considered material and the lease would be separated into two components. The annual minimum lease payment attributed to the land is computed as follows:

$$\frac{\text{FMV of land}}{\text{PV factor}} \quad \frac{\$110,000}{6.75902^*} = \$16,275$$

The remaining portion of the annual payment is attributed to the building.

Annual payment	$50,000
Less amount attributed to land	(16,275)
Annual payment attributed to building	$33,725

The present value of the minimum annual lease payments attributed to the building is then computed as follows:

Minimum annual lease payment attributed to building	$ 33,725
PV factor	x 6.75902*
PV of minimum annual lease payments attributed to building	$227,948

The entry to record the capital portion of the lease is as follows:

Leased building	227,948	
Lease obligation		227,948

**6.75902 is the PV of an annuity due for 10 periods at 10%.*

There would be no computation of the present value of the minimum annual lease payment attributed to the land since the land component of the lease will be treated as an operating lease. For this reason, each year $16,275 of the $50,000 lease payment will be recorded as land rental expense. The remainder of the annual payment ($33,725) will be applied against the lease obligation using the effective interest method.

Leases involving real estate and equipment. When real estate leases also involve equipment or machinery, the equipment component should be separated and accounted for as a separate lease agreement by both lessees and lessors. "The portion of the minimum lease payments applicable to the equipment element of the lease shall be estimated by whatever means are appropriate in the circumstances" (SFAS 13, para 27). The lessee and lessor should apply the capitalization requirements to the equipment lease independently of accounting for the real estate lease(s). The real estate leases should be handled as discussed in the preceding two sections. In a sale-leaseback transaction involving real estate with equipment, the equipment and land are not separated (SFAS 98, para 6).

Leases involving only part of a building. It is common to find lease agreements that involve only part of a building, as, for example, when a floor of an office building is leased, or when a store in a shopping mall is leased. A difficulty that arises in this situation is that the cost and/or fair market value of the leased portion of the whole may not be objectively determinable.

Lessee accounting. If the fair value of the leased property is objectively determinable, then the lessee should follow the rules and account for the lease as described in "Leases involving land and building." If the fair value of the leased property cannot be determined objectively, but the agreement satisfies the 75% test, the estimated economic life of the building in which the leased premises are located should be used. If this test is not met, the lessee should account for the agreement as an operating lease.

Lessor accounting. From the lessor's position, **both the cost and fair value** of the leased property must be objectively determinable before the procedures described under "Leases involving land and building" will apply. If either the cost or the fair value cannot be determined objectively, then the lessor should account for the agreement as an operating lease.

Special Situations

Wrap lease transactions. A wrap lease transaction occurs when the lessor of an asset obtains nonrecourse financing using the lease rentals and asset as collateral, sells the underlying asset and nonrecourse debt and then leases the asset back while remaining the substantive lessor under the original lease. According to FASB TB 88-1, when this occurs and the asset is real estate, SFAS 98 applies, otherwise the transaction is treated as a sales-leaseback with the lease to the end user treated as a sublease under SFAS 13.

Summary of Accounting for Selected Items (See following page)

TREATMENT OF SELECTED ITEMS IN ACCOUNTING FOR LEASES

	Lessor: Operating	Lessor: direct financing and sales-type	Lessee: Operating	Lessee: capital
Initial direct costs	Capitalize and amortize over lease term in proportion to rent revenue recognized (normally SL basis)	Direct financing: Record in separate account Add to net investment in lease Compute new effective rate that equates gross amt. of min. lease payments and unguar. residual value with net invest. Amortize so as to produce constant rate of return over lease term Sales-type: Expense in period incurred	N/A	N/A
Investment tax credit retained by lessor	N/A	Reduces FMV of leased asset for 90% test	N/A	Reduces FMV of leased asset for 90% test
Bargain purchase option	N/A	Include in: Minimum lease payments 90% test	N/A	Include in: Minimum lease payments 90% test
Guaranteed residual value	N/A	Include in: Minimum lease payments 90% test Sales-type: Include PV in sales revenues	N/A	Include in: Minimum lease payments 90% test
Unguaranteed residual value	N/A	Include in: "Gross investment in lease" Not included in: 90% test Sales-type: Exclude from sales revenue Deduct PV from cost of sales	N/A	Include in: Minimum lease payments 90% test
Contingent rentals	Revenue in period earned	Not part of minimum lease payments; revenue in period earned	Expense in period incurred	Not part of minimum lease payments; expense in period incurred
Amortization period	Amortize down to estimated residual value over estimated economic life of asset	N/A	N/A	Amortize down to estimated residual value over lease term or estimated economic life[b]
Revenue (expense)[a]	Rent revenue (normally SL basis) Amortization depreciation expense)	Direct financing: Interest revenue on net investment in lease (gross investment less unearned interest income) Sales-type: Dealer profit in period of sale (sales revenue less cost of leased asset) Interest revenue on net investment in lease	Rent expense (normally SL basis)[c]	Interest expense and depreciation expense

[a]*Elements of revenue (expense) listed for the above items are not repeated here (e.g., treatment of initial direct costs).*

[b]*If lease has automatic passage of title or bargain purchase option, use estimated economic life; otherwise, use the lease term.*

[c]*If payments are not on a SL basis, recognize rent expense on a SL basis unless another systematic and rational method is more representative of use benefit obtained from the property, in which case, the other method should be used.*

Reporting of Current and Noncurrent Lease Receivable (Lessor) and Lease Obligations (Lessee)

The balance of lease payments receivable (lessor) and lease obligation (lessee) must be broken down between the current and noncurrent portions. First, the current portion is computed at the date of the financial statements as the present value of the next lease payment/receipt. The time period is from the date of the financial statements to the next lease payment. The noncurrent portion is computed as the difference between the current portion determined and the balance of the lease obligation at the end of the period. The conceptual justification for such treatment can be found in the fact that the total lease obligation is equal to the present value of the future minimum lease payments. Therefore, it follows that the current portion should be the present value of the next lease payment while the noncurrent portion should be the present value of all other remaining lease payments. In practice, however, the principal portion of the next payment is usually reported as current and the remaining amount of the obligation is reported as noncurrent without regard to the timing of the payment/receipt.

EMERGING ISSUES TASK FORCE CONSENSUS SUMMARIES

85-16 Leveraged Leases

- Real estate leases and sale-leaseback transaction
- Delayed equity contributions by lessors

Under the provisions of FASB Statement 13, real estate leases can be accounted for as a leveraged lease if the requirements are met in paragraph 42. Furthermore, the Task Force reached a consensus that recourse debt originating from the delayed equity investment can be accounted for as a leveraged lease if the other requirements excluding the nonrecourse statement are fulfilled. Finally, the lessor's related obligation should be accounted for at the present value on the inception of the lease as a liability.

86-17 Deferred Profit on Sale-Leaseback With Lessee Guarantee of Residual Value

A consensus was reached that the profit equal to the present value of periodic rents plus the gross amount of the guaranteed residual value should be deferred for sale-leaseback transactions classified as more than minor but less than substantially all the use of the property. The present value of the rents should be amortized over the lease term while the guaranteed residual should be deferred until resolution at the end of the lease term. SFAS 98 limits the use of sale-leaseback accounting to transactions in which all risks and rewards of ownership, other than the leaseback, are transferred to the buyer-lessor. SFAS 98 lists examples of continuing involvement by the seller-lessee which indicate the risks and rewards of ownership have not been transferred.

86-33 Tax Indemnification in Lease Agreements

A consensus was reached that tax indemnification payments do not meet the definition of contingent rentals. These payments should be allocated by lessors to: (1) amount resulting from any lost ITC and (2) amount linked to all other tax effects.

87-7 Sale of an Asset Subject to a Lease and Nonrecourse Financing: "Wrap Lease Transactions"

A consensus was reached that the original lessor should separate revenue directly associated with future remarketing rights and defer recognition of income until the remarketing services are performed. A consensus was also reached that the original lessor should record any retained interest in the residual value of the leased asset as an asset in their financial statements. No consensus was reached on how to account for the proceeds other than the revenue from the remarketing rights.

88-10 Costs Associated With Lease Modification or Termination

A consensus was reached regarding situations where a lessee enters into a new lease for replacement property prior to the expiration of a preexisting property lease. If the preexisting lease is terminated, all costs related to the preexisting lease should be expensed when the leased property has no future benefit to the lessee. When the lease is not terminated, the expense should be reduced by any actual or probable sublease income. In addition if the preexisting lease is assumed by the new lessor, any payments to the lessee or assumption of loss by the lessor should be considered incentives. These incentives should be amortized on a straight-line basis to rent expense or rent revenue over the life of the new lease. The amount of the incentive should be determined separately by the lessee and lessor. No consensus was reached on the issue of deferring the costs of moving from one lease to another (moving) however; generally moving costs must be expensed as incurred.

88-21 Accounting for the Sale of Property Subject to the Seller's Preexisting Lease

A consensus was reached regarding situations where an entity sells property in which it has an ownership interest, and continues to lease the property under a preexisting operating lease. The consensus requires recognition of a transaction as a sale-leaseback if the preexisting lease is modified in connection with the sale. If no changes are made or changes are insignificant, profit should be deferred and recognized in accordance with Statements 28, 66, or 98 as appropriate. Any deferred profit should not be affected by the seller-lessee's prior ownership. In addition, exercise of renewal options or sublease provisions contained in the preexisting lease should not affect the accounting for the transaction. Statement 98 only applies to renewal options not contained in the original lease term. Finally, leases between parties under common control are not considered preexisting leases and Statement 98 should apply unless one of the parties is a regulated enterprise.

89-16 Consideration of Executory Costs in Sale-Leaseback Transactions

A consensus was reached that executory costs in the calculation of deferred profit in a sale-leaseback transaction should be excluded from the calculation of deferred profit.

89-20 Accounting for Cross Border Tax Benefit Leases

A consensus was reached regarding the recognition of income for cash received by the US enterprise for the foreign investor's tax benefits in situations where a US enterprise gives ownership interest in an asset to a foreign investor to allow the foreign investor tax benefits. In exchange, the US enterprise receives cash for the fair value of the ownership interest plus consideration for the tax benefit. The US enterprise may agree to indemnify the foreign investor for future loss of the tax benefit. The income may be recognized immediately or deferred unless there is more than a remote possibility of loss of the cash consideration due to indemnification or other contingencies. In this case, income must be deferred.

90-14 Unsecured Guarantee by Parent of Subsidiary's Lease Payments in a Sale-Leaseback Transaction

The Task Force reached a consensus that when one member of a consolidated group provides an unsecured guarantee of lease payments for another member of the consolidated group, such additional collateral does not reduce the buyer-lessor's risk of loss, except in the event of the seller-lessee's bankruptcy. The unsecured guarantee would, therefore, not constitute a form of continuing involvement. Thus, sale-leaseback accounting under SFAS 98 would not be prohibited in the **consolidated financial statements.** The Task Force also reached a consensus that the unsecured guarantee represents additional collateral to buyer-lessor, which reduces the risk of loss, and so the seller-lessee would be prevented from applying sale-leaseback accounting under SFAS 98 in the **seller-lessee's** financial statements.

90-15 Impact of Nonsubstantive Lessors, Residual Value Guarantees, and Other Provisions in Leasing Transactions

A consensus was reached regarding the conditions which would require the lessee to consolidate the assets, liabilities, results of operations, and cash flows of a Special Purpose Entity (SPE) into the lessee's financial statements. These conditions are listed in the abstract. If these conditions are not met, the lease should be evaluated in accordance with Statement 13 to determine the appropriate lease classification. The abstract also contains SEC staff responses to various implementation questions.

90-20 Impact of an Uncollateralized Irrevocable Letter of Credit on a Real Estate Sale-Leaseback Transaction

A consensus was reached that an uncollateralized, irrevocable letter of credit is not considered a form of continuing involvement which would preclude sale-leaseback accounting unless a contract exists between the seller-lessee and third-party guarantor which would create collateral. The existence of collateral relating to the letter of credit is a form of continuing involvement that precludes sale-leaseback accounting under SFAS 98.

92-1 Allocation of Residual Value or First-Loss Guarantee to Minimum Lease Payments in Leases Involving Land and Building(s)

A consensus was reached that for both the lessor and lessee the portion of the minimum lease payment attributable to the land is the land's fair market value times the lessee's incremental borrowing rate. Therefore, the remaining part of the minimum lease payment, including the total guaranteed amount are assigned to the building.

93-8 Accounting for the Sale and Leaseback of an Asset That Is Leased to Another Party

A consensus was reached that when a leaseback involves an asset that is personal property falling outside coverage of SFAS 98 and (1) subject to an operating lease or (2) subleased or intended to be subleased to another entity under an operating lease, SFAS 13, paragraphs 32 and 33 as amended should be followed.

95-1 Revenue Recognition on Sales With a Guaranteed Minimum Resale Value

Transactions containing guarantees of resale value of equipment by a manufacturer should be accounted for as leases. Minimum lease payments used to determine if criteria not for sales-type lease equals the difference between proceeds from transfer of equipment and the amount of the residual value guarantee. Additionally, guidance is provided for those transfers that are accounted for as operating leases.

95-4 Revenue Recognition on Equipment Sold and Subsequently Repurchased Subject to an Operating Lease

This consensus determined that a manufacturer can recognize a sale at the time its product is transferred to a dealer for subsequent sale to a third-party customer even if this ultimate customer enters into an operating lease agreement with the same manufacturer or a finance affiliate thereof if four conditions exist: (1) The dealer must be an independent entity which conducts business separately with manufacturers and customers, (2) The passage of the product from the manufacturer to the dealer fully transfers ownership, (3) The manufacturer (or finance affiliate) has no obligation to provide a lease arrangement for the customer of the dealer, and (4) The customer is in control in selecting which of the many financing options available will be used.

95-17 Accounting for Modifications to an Operating Lease That Do Not Change the Lease Classification

A consensus was reached that when the lessee and the lessor agree to shorten the lease term and increase the lease payments over the lease period, the nature of the modification is a matter of judgment that depends on the relevant facts and circumstances. If the modification is deemed to be only a change in future lease payments, the increase should be amortized over the remaining term of the modified lease. On the other hand, the modification deemed a termination penalty should be recognized in the period of modification. Termination penalties should be calculated as the excess of the modified lease payments over the original lease payments that would have been required during the shortened lease term. To determine if the modification is a termination penalty, consider: (1) the length of the modified lease period compared to the remaining term of the original lease, and (2) the difference between the modified lease payments and comparable market rents.

96-21 Implementation Issues in Accounting for Leasing Transactions Involving Special Purpose Entities (SPE)

This is another follow-on to EITF Issue 90-15, this time dealing with the criteria concerning lessors with single lessees, and the failure of the owner of record of the SPE to have made a substantial initial investment in the entity. Consensuses were reached on a number of matters involving, among others, multi-tiered SPE structures, multiple leases within a single SPE, payments by the lessee prior to the beginning of the lease term, fees paid to owners of record of an SPE, and sources of initial investment in the SPE. This last item is a commonly encountered problem in related entity lessors. This consensus should be reviewed carefully, since it will be widely applicable.

97-1 Implementations Issues in Accounting for Lease Transactions, Including Those Involving Special Purpose Entities (SPE)

Yet another follow-up to Issue 90-15; this one is a follow-up to certain responses in Issue 96-21, and focuses on environmental risk indemnifications by lessees, nonperformance-related default covenants, and depreciation. Consensuses were reached on these, which impact upon determining whether consolidation of the SPE would be required under various circumstances. Further consideration of these items is also scheduled.

FASB TECHNICAL BULLETINS

79-10 Fiscal Funding Clauses in Lease Agreements (5 para)

Refers to SFAS 13.

Question: The effect a fiscal funding clause present in a lease agreement has on the classification of the lease under SFAS 13.

Background: Fiscal funding clauses are common in lease agreements with governmental units under which the lease is contingent upon fund appropriations.

Response: If the likelihood of a fiscal funding clause being exercised is remote, the lease agreement is considered noncancelable. Otherwise, the lease is considered cancelable and should be classified as an operating lease.

79-12 Interest Rate Used in Calculating the Present Value of Minimum Lease Payments (3 para)

Refers to SFAS 13.

Question: The allowability of the use of the secured borrowing rate by a lessee in computing the present value of minimum lease payments.

Background: SFAS 13 requires the lessee to use its incremental borrowing rate or the lessor's implicit rate if it is lower and known by the lessee.

Response: The lessee may use its secured borrowing rate as its incremental borrowing rate if that rate appears reasonable.

79-13 Applicability of FASB Statement No. 13 to Current Value Financial Statements (2 para)

Refers to SFAS 13.

Question: Applicability of SFAS 13 to current value financial statements.

Response: The provisions of SFAS 13 apply to current value financial statements.

79-14 Upward Adjustment of Guaranteed Residual Values (4 para)

Refers to SFAS 13.

Question: Allowability of upward adjustments resulting from renegotiations of guaranteed residual values.

Background: Upward adjustments of residual values are prohibited by SFAS 13.

Response: Upward adjustments of guaranteed residual values in lease agreements are not allowed.

79-15 Accounting for Loss on a Sublease Not Involving the Disposal of a Segment (3 para)

Refers to SFAS 13 and Interpretation 27.

Question: How to determine and whether to recognize a loss on a sublease.

Response: The general principles for recognition of losses should be followed with respect to expected losses on subleases.

79-16 Effect of a Change in Income Tax Rate on the Accounting for Leveraged Leases (4 para) (Revised)

Refers to SFAS 13.

Question: The effect of a change in income tax rate on the accounting for leveraged leases.

Background: SFAS 13 requires that rate of return and allocation of income be recalculated from the date of inception of a lease and a gain or loss recognized when an important assumption is changed.

Response: The income effect on a leveraged lease of a change in the income tax rate should be recognized as a gain or loss in the accounting period in which the rate changes. Deferred taxes relating to the change should be recognized in accordance with SFAS 109.

79-17 Reporting Cumulative Effect Adjustment From Retroactive Application of FASB Statement No. 13 (3 para)

Refers to SFAS 13.

Question: Requirement for including the cumulative effect of a retroactive application of SFAS 13 in the determination of net income for years presented in an annual report.

Background: SFAS 13 requires that the cumulative effect of the retroactive application of SFAS 13 be included in determining the net income of the earliest period restated.

Response: The cumulative effect of a retroactive application under SFAS 13 would not be included in net income of any period presented unless the year prior to the earliest year could not be restated, in which case the cumulative effect would be included in net income of the first year presented.

79-18 Transition Requirement of Certain FASB Amendments and Interpretations of FASB Statement No. 13 (6 para)

Refers to SFAS 17, 22, 23, 26, 27, 28, and 29 and Interpretations 19, 21, 23, 24, 26, and 27.

Question: The meaning of the phrase "have published annual financial statements" in applying transition requirements and the means of disclosing retroactive application of SFAS 13 without restatement due to immateriality.

Background: Enterprises that have published annual financial statements based on accounts restated under the retroactive application of SFAS 13 are not required to retroactively apply amendments and interpretations effective after the prior restatement.

Response: Clarifies the meaning of the term "have published annual financial statements" for determining the effective dates of SFAS 13 amendments and interpretations.

82-1 Disclosure of the Sale or Purchase of Tax Benefits Through Tax Leases (8 para)

Refers to ARB 43; APB 22 and 30; and SFAS 5.

Question: Required disclosures for the sale or purchase of tax benefits through tax leases.

Background: Disclosure is required for transactions involving solely the sale or purchase of tax benefits through tax leases until the related accounting issues are resolved.

Response: Information concerning tax leases must be disclosed under APB 22 (because alternative practices may exist until an SFAS is issued), SFAS 109 (due to a significant effect on income tax expense), APB 30 (if material and unusual or infrequent), SFAS 5 (if contingencies exist), and ARB 43 (if comparability is affected).

86-2 Accounting for an Interest in the Residual Value of a Leased Asset:

- Acquired by a Third Party or
- Retained by a Lessor that Sells the Related Minimum Rental Payments (21 para)

Refers to SFAS 13 and 33, SFAC 5, and APB 10.

Questions: Various questions concerning the accounting for and valuation of an interest in the residual value of a leased asset acquired by a third party or retained by a lessor that sells the related minimum lease payments.

Response: An interest in the residual value of a leased asset should be recorded as an asset at the amount of cash disbursed, the fair value of other consideration given, and the present value of liabilities assumed at the date the right is acquired, unless the fair value of the interest in the residual value is more clearly evident. A lessor retaining an interest in the residual value of the leased asset should not recognize increases in value, but should recognize other than temporary declines in value. (SFAS 125, which superseded only this provision of TB 86-2, permits recognition of such increases for guaranteed residual values, but not for unguaranteed residual values.)

88-1 Issues Relating to Accounting for Leases (36 para)

Provides guidance on five issues relating to leases.

1. Question: How to account for escalated rents when the physical use of the property changes under an operating lease.

Response: Refers to SFAS 13 and FTB 85-3.

When a lessee controls the use of the leased property, recognition of rental expense or rental revenue should not be affected by the extent to which the lessee utilizes that property. Escalated rents under agreements giving the lessee the right to control the use of the entire leased property at the beginning of the lease term should be included in the minimum lease payments and recognized on a straight-line basis over the term of the lease.

2. Question: How to account for lease incentives in an operating lease.

Response: Incentives paid to or incurred on behalf of the lessee by the lessor are an inseparable part of the new lease agreement. These costs must be recognized as reductions to rental expense or rental revenue on a straight-line basis over the term of a new lease.

3. Question: The applicability of leveraged lease accounting to existing assets of the lessor.

Response: Refers to SFAS 13 and 27.

At the inception of a lease, the cost or carrying value and the fair value of an asset must be the same for the lease to be classified as a direct financing lease. The carrying amount of an existing asset before any write-down must equal its fair value in order for the lease to be classified as a leveraged lease.

4. Question: Whether to recognize income on a money-over-money lease transaction.

Response: Refers to SFAS 13 and FTB 85-2 and 86-2.

If an enterprise manufactures or purchases an asset, leases the asset to a lessee and obtains nonrecourse financing in excess of the asset's cost using the leased asset and the future lease rentals as collateral (a money-over-money lease transaction), a lease broker may recognize income at the beginning of the lease term for the cash received in excess of the carrying amount of the leased asset provided four criteria are met. Some modification of the presentation of the nonrecourse debt and lease receivable is appropriate for leasing transactions meeting all of the criteria for leveraged leases.

5. Question: How to account for wrap lease transactions.

Response: Refers to SFAS 13, 28, 66, and 98.

If an enterprise purchases an asset, leases the asset to a lessee, obtains nonrecourse financing using the lease rentals or the lease rentals and the asset as collateral, sells the asset subject to the lease and the nonrecourse debt to a third-party investor, and leases the asset back while remaining the substantive principal lessor under the original lease, the transaction should be accounted for as a sale-leaseback transaction. The subleased asset and the related nonrecourse debt should not be offset in the statement of financial position unless a right of setoff exists.

APPENDIX

LEVERAGED LEASES

One of the more complex accounting subjects regarding leases is the accounting for a leveraged lease. Once again, as with both the sales-type and direct financing, the classification of the lease by the lessor has no impact on the accounting treatment accorded the lease by the lessee. The lessee simply treats it as any other lease and, thus, is only interested in whether the lease qualifies as an operating or capital lease. The lessor's accounting problem is substantially more complex than that of the lessee.

In order to qualify as a leveraged lease, a lease agreement must meet the following requirements, and the lessor must account for the investment tax credit (when in effect) in the manner described below (*NOTE: failure to do so will result in the lease being classified as a direct financing lease*):

1. The lease must meet the definition of a direct financing lease (the 90% of FMV criterion does not apply).*
2. The lease must involve at least three parties.
    a. An owner-lessor (equity participant)
    b. A lessee
    c. A long-term creditor (debt participant)
3. The financing provided by the creditor is nonrecourse as to the general credit of the lessor and is sufficient to provide the lessor with substantial leverage.
4. The lessor's net investment (defined below) decreases in the early years and increases in the later years until it is eliminated.

This last characteristic poses the accounting problem.

The leveraged lease arose as a result of an effort to maximize the tax benefits associated with a lease transaction. In order to accomplish this, it was necessary to involve a third party to the lease transaction (in addition to the lessor and lessee); a long-term creditor. The following diagram illustrates the existing relationships in a leveraged lease agreement:

* *A direct financing lease must have its cost or carrying value equal to the fair value of the asset at the lease's inception. So even if the amounts are not significantly different, leveraged lease accounting shall not be used (TB 88-1).*

The leveraged lease arrangement*

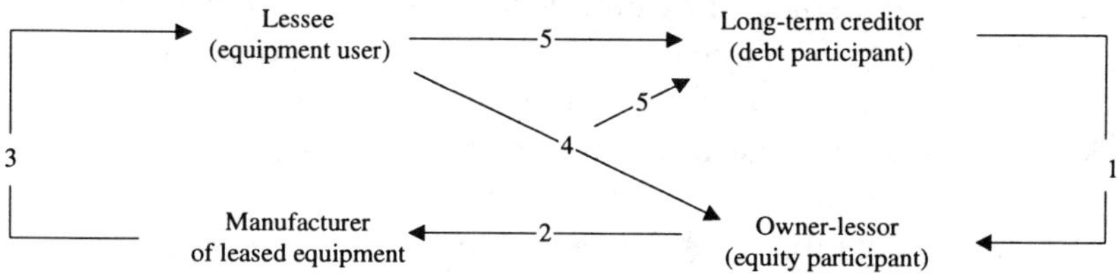

1. The owner-lessor secures long-term financing from the creditor, generally in excess of 50% of the purchase price. SFAS 13 indicates that the lessor must be provided with sufficient leverage in the transaction, therefore the 50%.
2. The owner then uses this financing along with his/her own funds to purchase the asset from the manufacturer
3. The manufacturer delivers the asset to the lessee
4. The lessee remits the periodic rent to the lessor
5. The debt is guaranteed by either using the equipment as collateral, the assignment of the lease payments, or both, depending on the demands established by the creditor

The FASB concluded in SFAS 13 that the entire lease agreement be accounted for as a single transaction and not a direct financing lease plus a debt transaction. The feeling was that the latter did not readily convey the net investment in the lease to the user of the financial statements. Thus, in accordance with SFAS 13, the lessor is to record the investment as a net amount. The gross investment is calculated as a combination of the following amounts:

1. The rentals receivable from the lessee, net of the principal and interest payments due to the long-term creditor
2. A receivable for the amount of the investment tax credit (ITC) to be realized on the transaction**
3. The estimated residual value of the leased asset
4. The unearned and deferred income consisting of

   a. The estimated pretax lease income (or loss), after deducting initial direct costs, remaining to be allocated to income
   b. The ITC remaining to be allocated to income over the remaining term of the lease**

* *Adapted from "A Straightforward Approach to Leveraged Leasing" by Pierce R. Smith,* ***The Journal of Commercial Bank Lending****, July 1973, pp. 40-47.*

** *The investment tax credit has been repealed, effective January 1, 1986. ITC will be relevant only for property placed in service prior to this date.*

The first three amounts described above are readily obtainable; however, the last amount, the unearned and deferred income, requires additional computations. In order to derive this amount, it is necessary to create a cash flow (income) analysis by year for the entire lease term. As described in 4. above, the unearned and deferred income consists of the pretax lease income (Gross lease rentals – Depreciation – Loan interest) and the unamortized investment tax credit. The total of these two amounts for all of the periods in the lease term represents the unearned and deferred income at the inception of the lease.

The amount computed as the gross investment in the lease (foregoing paragraphs) less the deferred taxes relative to the difference between pretax lease income and taxable lease income is the net investment for purposes of computing the net income for the period. In order to compute the periodic net income, another schedule must be completed which uses the cash flows derived in the first schedule and allocates them between income and a reduction in the net investment.

The amount of income is first determined by applying a rate to the net investment. The rate to be used is the rate which will allocate the entire amount of cash flow (income) when applied in the years in which the net investment is positive. In other words, the rate is derived in much the same way as the implicit rate (trial and error), except that only the years in which there is a positive net investment are considered. Thus, income is recognized only in the years in which there is a positive net investment.

The income recognized is divided among the following three elements:

1. Pretax accounting income
2. Amortization of investment tax credit
3. The tax effect of the pretax accounting income

The first two shall be allocated in proportionate amounts from the unearned and deferred income included in the calculation of the net investment. In other words, the unearned and deferred income consists of pretax lease accounting income and ITC. Each of these is recognized during the period in the proportion that the current period's allocated income is to the total income (cash flow). The last item, the tax effect, is recognized in the tax expense for the year. The tax effect of any difference between pretax lease accounting income and taxable lease income is charged (or credited) to deferred taxes.

When tax rates change, all components of a leveraged lease must be recalculated from the inception of the lease using the revised after-tax cash flows arising from the revised tax rates (EITF 86-43).

If, in any case, the projected cash receipts (income) are less than the initial investment, the deficiency is to be recognized as a loss at the inception of the lease. Similarly, if at any time during the lease period the aforementioned method of recognizing income would result in a future period loss, the loss shall be recognized immediately.

This situation may arise as a result of the circumstances surrounding the lease changing. Therefore, any estimated residual value and other important assumptions must be reviewed on a periodic basis (at least annually). Any change is to be incorporated into the income computations; however, there is to be no upward revision of the estimated residual value.

The following example illustrates the application of these principles to a leveraged lease:

Example of simplified leveraged lease

1. A lessor acquires an asset for $100,000 with an estimated useful life of 3 years in exchange for a $25,000 down payment and a $75,000 3-year note with equal payments due on 12/31 each year. The interest rate is 18%.
2. The asset has no residual value.
3. The PV of an ordinary annuity of $1 for 3 years at 18% is 2.17427.
4. The asset is leased for 3 years with annual payments due to the lessor on 12/31 in the amount of $45,000.
5. The lessor uses the ACRS method of depreciation for tax purposes and elects to reduce the ITC rate to 4% as opposed to reducing the depreciable basis.
6. Assume a constant tax rate throughout the life of the lease of 40%.

Chart 1 analyzes the cash flows generated by the leveraged leasing activities. Chart 2 allocates the cash flows between the investment in leveraged leased assets and income from leveraged leasing activities. The allocation requires finding that rate of return which when applied to the investment balance at the beginning of each year that the investment amount is positive, will allocate the net cash flow fully to net income over the term of the lease. This rate can be found only by a computer program or by an iterative trial and error process. The example which follows has a positive investment value in each of the 3 years, and thus the allocation takes place in each time period. Leveraged leases usually have periods where the investment account turns negative and is below zero.

Allocating principal and interest on the loan payments is as follows:

($75,000 ÷ 2.17427 = $34,494)

Year	*Payment*	*Interest 18%*	*Principal*	*Balance*
Inception of lease	$ --	$ --	$ --	$75,000
1	34,494	13,500	20,994	54,006
2	34,494	9,721	24,773	29,233
3	34,494	5,261	29,233	--

Chart 1

	A	B	C	D	E	F	G	H	I
	Rent	Depr.	Interest on loan	Taxable income (A-B-C)	Income tax payable (rcvbl.) Dx40%	Loan principal payments	ITC	Cash flow (A+G-C -E-F)	Cumulative cash flow
Initial	$ --	$ --	$ --	$ --	$ --	$ --	$ --	$(25,000)	$(25,000)
Year 1	45,000	25,000	13,500	6,500	2,600	20,994	4,000	11,906	(13,094)
Year 2	45,000	38,000	9,721	(2,721)	(1,088)	24,773	--	11,594	(1,500)
Year 3	45,000	37,000	5,261	2,739	1,096	29,233	--	9,410	7,910
Total	$135,000	$100,000	$28,482	$ 6,518	$ 2,608	$75,000	$4,000	$ 7,910	

The chart below allocates the cash flows determined above between the net investment in the lease and income. Recall that the income is then allocated between pretax accounting income and the amortization of the investment for credit. The income tax expense for the period is a result of applying the tax rate to the current periodic pretax accounting income.

The amount to be allocated in total in each period is the net cash flow determined in column H above. The investment at the beginning of year 1 is the initial down payment of $25,000. This investment is then reduced on an annual basis by the amount of the cash flow not allocated to income.

Chart 2

	1	2	3	4	5	6	7
		Cash Flow Assumption			Income Analysis		
	Investment beginning of year	Cash flow	Allocated to investment	Allocated to income	Pretax income	Income tax expense	Investment tax credit
Year 1	$25,000	$11,906	$ 7,964	$3,942	$3,248	$1,300	1,994
Year 2	17,036	11,594	8,908	2,686	2,213	885	1,358
Year 3	8,128	9,410	8,128	1,282	1,057	423	648
		$32,910	$25,000	$7,910	$6,518	$2,608	$4,000

Rate of return = 15.77%

1. Column 2 is the net cash flow after the initial investment, and columns 3 and 4 are the allocation based upon the 15.77% rate of return. The total of column 4 is the same as the total of column H in Chart 1.
2. Column 5 allocates column D in Chart 1 based upon the allocations in column 4. Column 6 allocates column E in Chart 1, and column 7 allocates column G in Chart 1 in the same basis.

The journal entries below illustrate the proper recording and accounting for the leveraged lease transaction. The initial entry represents the cash down payment, investment tax credit receivable, the unearned and deferred revenue, and the net cash to be received over the term of the lease.

The remaining journal entries recognize the annual transactions which include the net receipt of cash and the amortization of income.

	Year 1		*Year 2*		*Year 3*	
Rents receivable [Chart 1 (A-C-F)]	31,518					
Investment tax credit receivable	4,000					
Cash		25,000				
Unearned and deferred income		10,518				
[Initial investment, Chart 2 (5+7) totals]						
Cash	10,506		10,506		10,506	
Rent receivable		10,506		10,506		10,506
[Net for all cash transactions, Chart 1 (A-C-F) line by line for each year]						
Income tax receivable (cash)	4,000					
Investment tax credit receivable		4,000				
Unearned and deferred income	5,242		3,571		1,705	
Income from leveraged leases		5,242		3,571		1,705
[Amortization of unearned income, Chart 2 (5+7) line by line for each year]						

The following schedules illustrate the computation of deferred income tax amount. The annual amount is a result of the temporary difference created due to the difference in the timing of the recognition of income for book and tax purposes. The income for tax purposes can be found in column D in Chart 1, while the income for book purposes is found in column 5 of Chart 2. The actual amount of deferred tax is the difference between the tax computed with the temporary difference and the tax computed without the temporary difference. These amounts are represented by the income tax payable or receivable as shown in column E of Chart 1 and the income tax expense as shown in column 6 of Chart 2. A check of this figure is provided by multiplying the difference between book and tax income by the annual rate.

Year 1

Income tax payable	$ 2,600	
Income tax expense	(1,300)	
Deferred income tax (Dr)		$1,300
Taxable income	$ 6,500	
Pretax accounting income	(3,248)	
Difference	$ 3,252	
$3,252 x 40% = $1,300		

Year 2

Income tax receivable	$ 1,088	
Income tax expense	885	
Deferred income tax (Cr)		$1,973
Taxable loss	$ 2,721	
Pretax accounting income	2,213	
Difference	$ 4,934	
$4,934 x 40% = $1,973		

Year 3

Income tax payable	$ 1,096	
Income tax expense	(423)	
Deferred income tax (Dr)		$ 673
Taxable income	$ 2,739	
Pretax accounting income	(1,057)	
Difference	$ 1,682	
$1,682 x 40% = $673		

15 ACCOUNTING FOR INCOME TAXES

PERSPECTIVE AND ISSUES

From the late 1960s until the late 1980s, GAAP for interperiod income tax allocation was prescribed by APB 11, which mandated an income statement approach. However, this was obsoleted by the issuance of Statement of Financial Accounting Concepts (SFAC) 6, *Elements of Financial Statements*, which defined assets and liabilities in a way which seemingly excluded deferred tax assets and liabilities computed in accordance with that standard. To conform with SFAC 6 and adopt a balance sheet approach, APB 11 was superseded by the ill-fated SFAS 96 in late

1987. There was almost universal dissatisfaction with SFAS 96, because of its complex scheduling requirements and its ban on reporting most deferred tax benefits in the balance sheet. Due to the controversy, implementation of that standard was deferred three times, for a total of four years. Ultimately, it was superseded by the present standard, SFAS 109.

SFAS 109, which replaced SFAS 96 in 1992, continued the balance sheet orientation of its immediate predecessor. Under both of these standards, the principal objective is to report as of the balance sheet date the best estimate of the actual tax effects of the reporting entity's future deductible and taxable amounts. However, whereas application of SFAS 96 required a complex process of scheduling the expected reversals of temporary differences, SFAS 109 employs a simplified "tax rate convention" assumption which obviates the need for this. The result is that, in most instances, only a relatively straightforward, single set of computations is needed to determine deferred tax asset and liability balances.

Furthermore, all deferred taxes, asset as well as liability, are recorded and reported under SFAS 109, which represents an almost complete reversal of the logic applied by SFAS 96. However, the new standard does require an evaluation of the realizability of the deferred tax asset, and in many cases a valuation allowance will need to be provided against it.

Discounting of deferred taxes to present values is not permitted, even though the dates of ultimate realization of tax benefits or payment of obligations often lie far in the future. The Board has decreed that discounting should not be incorporated in any new accounting standards, pending resolution of its present value-based measurements in accounting project. Discounting was also generally prohibited by APB 11 and SFAS 96.

In accounting for purchase business acquisitions under APB 11, the timings of tax benefits or obligations attaching to assets and liabilities acquired were to be considered in allocating the purchase price (the "net of tax" method). SFAS 109, on the other hand, requires that purchased assets and liabilities be recorded gross of their tax effects, if any, and that the deferred taxes be reflected separately, without consideration of timing (i.e., without being discounted to present value).

SFAS 109 makes no distinction between operating losses and deductible temporary differences. Accordingly, the tax effects of both are reported as deferred tax assets. The requirement of APB 11, that realized tax benefits of previously unrecognized operating loss carryforwards be presented as extraordinary items in the income statement, has been eliminated.

The use of so-called tax planning strategies was a central concern under the provisions of SFAS 96, and this contributed substantially to the complexity of that standard. SFAS 109 has virtually dropped this requirement, except in the context of assessing the amount of allowance to be provided against the deferred tax asset being reported. The result is that computing deferred taxes under SFAS 109 will be significantly less difficult than it was under SFAS 96 in almost all cases.

When debating this replacement for SFAS 96, the Board had indicated that deferred taxes were to be measured with reference to the marginal rates expected to apply to the reversals of temporary differences existing at the balance sheet date. As promulgated, however, SFAS 109 requires measurement based on the entity's average (or effective) rate which is expected to apply in the periods of reversal. For many entities, this will result in lesser amounts of deferred taxes being recorded than would have been the case had the Board's original proposal been adopted. Deferred tax assets and liabilities must be classified as current or noncurrent consistent with the classification of the related asset or liability for financial reporting purposes. Deferred tax assets and liabilities that are not related to an asset or liability for financial reporting purposes should be classified according to the expected reversal date of the temporary difference pursuant to SFAS 37. In most cases, this should not require more than a minimal amount of scheduling, however.

Sources of GAAP

APB	SFAS	FASB I	FASB TB	EITF
11, 16, 17, 20, 23, 24, 28	5, 6, 12, 37, 52, 96, 109	18	83-1	86-9, 86-43, 86-44, 88-4, 93-12, 93-13, 93-16, 93-17, 94-10, 95-10, 95-20, 96-7

DEFINITIONS OF TERMS

Deductible temporary differences. Temporary differences that result in future tax deductions; these give rise to deferred tax assets.

Deferred tax asset. The deferred tax consequences of temporary differences that will result in net tax deductions in future years.

Deferred tax liability. The deferred tax consequences of temporary differences that will result in net taxable amounts in future years.

Gains and losses included in comprehensive income but excluded from net income. Certain items which, under GAAP, are events occurring currently but which are reported directly in equity, such as changes in market values of noncurrent portfolios of marketable equity securities.

Interperiod tax allocation. The process of apportioning income tax expense among reporting periods without regard to the timing of the actual cash payments for taxes. The objective is to reflect fully the tax consequences of all economic events reported in current or prior financial statements and, in particular, to report the expected tax effects of the reversals of temporary differences existing at the reporting date.

Intraperiod tax allocation. The process of apportioning income tax expense applicable to a given period between income before extraordinary items and those items required to be shown net of tax such as extraordinary items and prior period adjustments.

Operating loss carryback or carryforward. The excess of tax deductions over taxable income. To the extent that this results in a carryforward, the tax effect thereof is included in the entity's deferred tax asset.

Permanent differences. Differences between pretax accounting income and taxable income as a result of the treatment accorded certain transactions by the income tax regulations which differ from the accounting treatment. Permanent differences will not reverse in subsequent periods.

Pretax accounting income. Income or loss for the accounting period as determined in accordance with GAAP without regard to the income tax expense for the period.

Taxable income. The difference between the revenue and expenses as defined by the Internal Revenue Code for a taxable period without regard to the special deductions (e.g., net operating loss or contribution carrybacks and carryforwards).

Taxable temporary differences. Temporary differences that result in future taxable amounts; these give rise to deferred tax liabilities.

Tax credits. Reductions in the tax liability as a result of certain expenditures accorded special treatment under the Internal Revenue Code. Examples of such credits are: the Investment Tax Credit, investment in certain depreciable property; the Jobs Credit, payment of wages to targeted groups; the Research and Development Credit, an increase in qualifying R&D expenditures; and others.

Tax planning strategy. A representation by management of a planned transaction or series of transactions that would affect the particular future years in which temporary differences will result in taxable or deductible amounts.

Temporary differences. In general, differences between tax and financial reporting bases of assets and liabilities that will result in taxable or deductible amounts in future periods. Temporary differences include "timing differences" as defined by prior GAAP as well as certain other differences, such as those arising from business combinations. Some temporary differences cannot be associated with particular assets or liabilities, but nonetheless do result from events that received financial statement recognition and will have tax effects in future periods.

Unrecognized tax benefits. Deferred tax benefits against which a valuation allowance had been provided as of the date of the financial statements.

Valuation allowance. The contra asset which is to be reflected to the extent that it is "more likely than not" that the deferred tax asset will not be realized.

CONCEPTS, RULES, AND EXAMPLES

Interperiod Income Tax Allocation

Prior to the promulgation of APB 11, there had been a wide-ranging debate among proponents of no allocation (reporting taxes currently payable as income tax expense), partial allocation (providing deferred taxes only for those timing differences whose net reversal could be reasonably predicted), and comprehensive allocation. APB 11 endorsed comprehensive allocation, and this position also has been adopted by the FASB in both SFAS 96 and SFAS 109. (However, a major exception to comprehensive allocation, relating to unremitted earnings of subsidiaries, was created by APB 23, and was not amended by SFAS 96. The exception has, however, been altered under the provisions of SFAS 109, as described later in this chapter).

Comprehensive interperiod tax allocation requires the provision of income taxes for all items of income and expense reported in the statement of income, whether or not these items enter into the determination of taxes currently payable, with the exception of **permanent differences** for which deferred taxes are never provided. (An example of a permanent difference is officers' life insurance, when the cash surrender value is expected to be realized upon the death of the insured.) All **temporary differences** are subject to deferred tax accounting.

Under APB 11, the term "timing differences" referred to items of income or expense which entered into the determination of taxable income in periods different than financial reporting income. Common examples were depreciation, deferred compensation, prepaid income, bad debt reserves, and cash vs. accrual accounting. These items are included as "temporary differences" as defined by SFAS 96 and 109. However, the newer term is more inclusive than the one it replaces. It also connotes the effects of asset basis reductions for tax credits taken, asset basis increases resulting from inflation indexing, certain intercompany transfers among entities for which consolidated financial statements but not consolidated tax returns are prepared, and certain effects of accounting for purchase business combinations.

In analyzing an item's differential tax and financial reporting treatments, it is helpful to identify the periods of **origination** and periods of **reversal**. When a presumptive temporary difference does not appear to have an expected reversal, it is possible that the difference is actually a permanent one. This approach is particularly useful when dealing with new or complex differences, as witnessed by the accounting for the basis reduction for ITC taken under the 1982 tax act (TEFRA), which many incorrectly perceived to be a permanent difference until clarification was issued by the FASB in 1983.

While the requirement for comprehensive interperiod tax allocation appears to be well understood in practice, the appropriate measurement of tax expense, including the tax effects of temporary differences, is less clear. This will be addressed in the following section.

Measurement of Expense

A number of theories have been advanced over the years regarding the computation of income tax expense when temporary differences exist. The most popular have been the **deferred method** (which was GAAP under APB 11) and the **liability method** (prohibited by APB 11, but sanctioned by SFAS 96 and 109). A third approach, the **net of tax method**, has received a good deal of academic support but was less widely employed (or understood) by practitioners. Although the deferred method was soundly based on the matching principle, as defined by the APB, it was complex to apply and sometimes resulted in apparent distortion in the balance sheet. As attention in recent years has shifted again to the meaningful reporting of **financial position**, these issues have received renewed scrutiny. Following the promulgation of SFAC 6, it became inevitable that substantial changes in accounting for income taxes would be made. As defined in SFAC 6, the deferred charges and credits created by the proper application of APB 11 are generally **not** true assets or liabilities and do not belong on the balance sheet.

Deferred method. APB 11 required comprehensive interperiod income tax allocation. The conceptual justification supporting the deferred method of allocation appears to be found in the matching principle. Recall that the need for tax allocation is a result of differences between accounting and taxable income that will reverse. The deferred method determines the income tax expense for the period based on the accounting income while the current liability is based on taxable income. The difference between the actual current liability and the income tax expense is treated as either a deferred charge or credit which is amortized as the timing differences reverse. Timing differences that originate during the period are referred to as originating differences, while the reversal of tax effects arising from differences which originated in prior periods are referred to as reversing differences.

The tax computation which was used to determine the amount of deferred tax under APB 11 generally was referred to as the "with and without" or differential computation of income tax expense. According to APB 11, "the tax effect of a timing difference should be measured by the differential between income taxes computed with and without inclusion of the transaction creating the difference between taxable income and pretax accounting income." The purpose of the "with and without" computation was to take into account the effect of the graduated rate system. This required that the timing differences be added to (or subtracted from) taxable income and a tax on this amount was computed to determine the amount of tax had the timing difference not existed. The computation was relatively simple when there was only a single timing difference.

When many timing differences occurred in the same period, the calculation of the deferred tax adjustment became more complicated. If properly applied, APB 11 demanded that separate "with and without" computations be made for each "class" of timing difference (e.g., depreciation, prepaid income, etc.). Originating and reversing differences within a given class of timing difference could be considered together if the "net change" method were used, but if the more precise "gross change" method were employed, separate tax effects were to have been calculated. In practice, various shortcut methods were commonly used, often grouping **all** timing difference originations and reversals together. Frequently, the resultant deferred tax provision was different from the number prescribed by APB 11, often materially so.

In fact, many accountants employed as a shortcut computation a technique that approximated the "liability method" of the pre-APB 11 era. (Of course, this clearly contradicted the requirements of APB 11.) Although SFAS 96 reestablished the liability method as GAAP, the liability approach utilized most commonly as a shortcut under APB 11 is not appropriate under SFAS 96 and will not be appropriate under SFAS 109. The specific requirements of SFAS 109 are discussed in the following pages.

Liability method--An overview. The liability method is balance sheet oriented, in direct contrast to the deferred method which is income statement oriented. The primary goal of the liability method is to present the estimated actual taxes to be payable in future periods as the income tax liability on the balance sheet. In order to accomplish this goal, it is necessary to consider the effect of certain enacted future changes in the tax rates when computing the current period's tax provision. The computation of the amount of deferred taxes is based on the rate expected to be in effect when the temporary differences reverse. The annual computation is considered a tentative estimate of the liability (or asset) which is subject to change as the statutory tax rate changes or as the taxpayer moves into other tax rate brackets.

SFAC 6 defines liabilities as "probable future sacrifices of economic benefits arising from present obligations of a particular entity to transfer assets or provide services to other entities in the future as a result of past transactions." Assets, on the other hand, are defined as "probable future economic benefits obtained or controlled by a particular entity as a result of past transactions or events." According to SFAC 6, the deferred tax credits and debits that are generated by the liability method result in liabilities or assets that meet the definitions in the SFAC. The SFAC specifically states that the deferred debits and credits generated through the use of the deferred method do not meet the definitions of assets and liabilities prescribed by the SFAC. This lack of consistency was one of the primary reasons for the FASB's reconsideration of APB 11, which culminated in the issuance of SFAS 96 in December 1987, and the subsequent reconsideration of that standard, resulting in the issuance of SFAS 109 in February 1992.

Application of the liability method is, in concept at least, relatively simple in comparison to the deferred method. This is a balance sheet approach. The primary concern is to state the taxes payable account as accurately as possible. This is accomplished by multiplying the aggregate unreversed temporary differences including those originating this period by the expected future rate to determine the expected future liability. This expected liability is the amount presented on the balance sheet at the end of the period. The difference between this amount and the amount on the books at the beginning of the period is the deferred tax expense for the period. (Of course, this is a gross simplification of SFAS 109's requirements, but it serves to set forth the basic notion of the liability method. The complexities of SFAS 109 are discussed beginning on page 542.)

An example of application of the liability method of deferred income tax accounting follows.

Simplified example of interperiod allocation using the liability method

Gries International has no permanent differences in either years 1999 or 2000. The company has only two temporary differences, depreciation and prepaid rent. No consideration is given to the nature of the deferred tax account (i.e., current or long-term) as it is not considered necessary for purposes of this example. Gries has a credit balance in its deferred tax account at the beginning of 1999 in the amount of $180,000. This balance consists of $228,000 ($475,000 depreciation temporary difference x 48% tax rate) of deferred taxable amounts and $48,000 ($100,000 prepaid rent temporary difference x 48% tax rate) of deferred deductible amounts.

For purposes of this example, it is assumed that there was a constant 48% tax rate in all of the prior periods. The pretax accounting income and the temporary differences originating and reversing in 1999 and 2000 are as follows:

Gries International

		1999		*2000*
Pretax accounting income		$800,000		$1,200,000
Timing differences:				
Depreciation--originating	$(180,000)		$(160,000)	
reversing	60,000	(120,000)	100,000	(60,000)
Prepaid rental income--originating	75,000		80,000	
reversing	(25,000)	50,000	(40,000)	40,000
Taxable income		$730,000		$1,180,000

The tax rates for years 4 and 5 are 46% and 38%, respectively. These rates are assumed to be independent of one another and the 2000 change in the rate was not known until it took place in 2000.

Computation of tax provision--1999

Balance of deferred tax account, 1/1/99		
Depreciation ($475,000 x 48%)		$228,000
Prepaid rental income ($100,000 x 48%)		(48,000)
		$180,000
Aggregate temporary differences, 12/31/99		
Depreciation ($475,000 + 120,000)	$595,000	
Prepaid rental income ($100,000 + 50,000)	(150,000)	
	$445,000	
Expected future rate (1999 rate)	x 46%	
Balance required in the deferred tax account, 12/31/99		204,700
Required addition to the deferred tax account		$ 24,700
Income taxes currently payable ($730,000 x 46%)		335,800
Total tax provision		$360,500

Computation of tax provision--2000

Balance of deferred tax account, 1/1/00		
Depreciation ($595,000 x 46%)		$273,700
Prepaid rental income ($150,000 x 46%)		(69,000)
		$204,700
Aggregate timing differences, 12/31/00		
Depreciation ($595,000 + 60,000)	$655,000	
Prepaid rental income ($150,000 + 40,000)	(190,000)	
	$465,000	
Expected future rate (2000 rate)	x 38%	
Balance required in the deferred tax account, 12/31/00		176,700
Required reduction in the deferred tax account		$(28,000)
Income taxes currently payable ($1,180,000 x 38%)		448,400
Total tax provision		$420,400

SFAS 109 in Greater Detail

While conceptually the liability method is rather straightforward, in practice there are a number of complexities to be addressed. SFAS 109 presents fewer of these difficulties than existed under its ill-fated predecessor, SFAS 96, yet this subject still remains one of the more difficult areas of accounting practice. In the following pages, these measurement and reporting issues will be discussed in greater detail.

1. The nature of temporary differences
2. Treatment of operating loss carryforwards
3. The measurement of deferred tax assets and liabilities
4. The valuation allowance for deferred tax assets which are "more likely than not" to be not realizable
5. The effect of tax law changes on previously recorded deferred tax assets and liabilities
6. The effect of tax status changes on previously incurred deferred tax assets and liabilities
7. Tax effects of business combinations
8. Intercorporate income tax allocation
9. Exceptions to the general rules of SFAS 109

Detailed examples of deferred income tax accounting under SFAS 109 are presented throughout the following discussion of these issues.

The Nature of Temporary Differences

The majority of the typical reporting entity's transactions are treated identically for tax and financial reporting purposes. Some transactions and events, however, will have different tax and accounting implications. In many of these cases, the difference relates to the period in which the income or expense will be recognized. Under APB 11, these latter differences were referred to as "timing differences" and were said to **originate** in one period and to **reverse** in a later period. Common timing differences were those relating to depreciation methods, deferred compensation plans, percentage-of-completion accounting for long-term construction contracts, and cash vs. accrual accounting.

SFAS 96 introduced the concept of **temporary differences**, which is somewhat more comprehensive than that of timing differences. This concept is carried forward by SFAS 109 without alteration. Temporary differences include all the categories of the earlier concept, plus a number of additional items as well. **Temporary differences** include all differences between the tax and financial reporting bases of assets and liabilities, if those differences will result in taxable or deductible amounts in future years. The most common example of an item which did not represent a temporary difference, prior to the 1993 tax law changes, had been goodwill. Now, however, goodwill will be amortizable over 15 years, and thus (if the amortization period for financial reporting purposes is other then 15 years) this item will be a temporary difference as defined by SFAS 109. Organization costs, on the other hand, will remain a permanent difference. Deferred taxes are to be provided for all temporary differences.

Examples of temporary differences which were also timing differences under APB 11 are the following:

Revenue recognized for financial reporting purposes before being recognized for tax purposes. Revenue accounted for by the installment method for tax purposes, but reflected in income currently; certain construction-related revenue recognized on a completed-contract method for tax purposes, but on a percentage of completion basis for financial reporting; earnings from investees recognized by the equity method for accounting purposes but taxed only when later distributed as dividends to the investor. These are taxable temporary differences, which give rise to deferred tax liabilities.

Revenue recognized for tax purposes prior to recognition in the financial statements. Certain revenue received in advance, such as prepaid rental income and service contract revenue. These are deductible temporary differences in the terminology of SFAS 109, and give rise to deferred tax assets.

Expenses which are deductible for tax purposes prior to recognition in the financial statements. Accelerated depreciation methods or shorter useful lives used for tax purposes, while straight-line depreciation or longer useful economic lives are used for financial reporting; certain preoperating costs and certain capitalized interest costs which are currently tax deductible. These items are taxable temporary differences, and give rise to deferred tax liabilities.

Expenses which are reported in the financial statements prior to becoming deductible for tax purposes. Certain estimated expenses, such as warranty costs, as well as such contingent losses as accruals of litigation expenses, are not tax deductible until the obligation becomes fixed. These are deductible temporary differences, and accordingly give rise to deferred tax assets.

In addition to these familiar and well-understood timing differences, temporary differences include a number of other categories which also involve differences between the tax and financial reporting bases of assets or liabilities. These are

Reductions in tax deductible asset bases arising in connection with tax credits. Under the provisions of the 1982 tax act, taxpayers were permitted a choice of either full ACRS depreciation coupled with a reduced investment tax credit, or a full investment tax credit coupled with reduced depreciation allowances. If the taxpayer chose the latter option, the asset basis was reduced for tax depreciation, but was still fully depreciable for financial reporting purposes. Accordingly, this election was accounted for as a taxable timing difference, and gave rise to a deferred tax liability. This particular accounting treatment was first prescribed by FASB Technical Bulletin 83-1, and was later incorporated in SFAS 96. It has now been included in SFAS 109 as well.

Investment tax credits accounted for by the deferral method. Under GAAP, investment tax credits could be accounted for by either the "flow through" method (by far the most common method in practice), or by the "deferral" method. Under the latter method, the tax credit was reflected in income over the useful lives of the assets giving rise to the credit, although the benefit of the credit was fully received in the years the assets were placed in service. Thus, a deductible temporary difference existed, with which a deferred tax asset would be associated.

The two categories discussed immediately above are no longer of much interest since the investment tax credit was eliminated under current tax law. Of course, there remains the possibility that the ITC could be revived under a future revision of the income tax laws that are currently being discussed.

Increases in the tax bases of assets resulting from the indexing of asset costs for the effects of inflation. Occasionally proposed but never enacted, such a tax law provision would allow taxpaying entities to finance the replacement of depreciable assets through depreciation based on current costs, as computed by the application of indices to the historical costs of the assets being remeasured. This reevaluation of asset costs would give rise to deductible temporary differences that would be associated with deferred tax benefits.

Certain business combinations accounted for by the purchase method. Under certain circumstances, the costs assignable to assets or liabilities acquired in purchase business combinations will differ from their tax bases. Such differences may be either taxable or deductible and, accordingly, may give rise to deferred tax liabilities or assets. These differences now are explicitly recognized by the reporting of deferred taxes in the consolidated financial statements of the acquiring entity. Note that these differences are no longer allocable to the financial reporting bases of the underlying assets or liabilities themselves, as was the case under APB 11's **net of tax** method.

A financial reporting situation in which deferred taxes may or may not be appropriate would include life insurance (such as keyman insurance) under which the reporting entity is the beneficiary. Since proceeds of life insurance are not subject to income tax under present law, the excess of cash surrender values over the sum of premiums paid will **not** be a temporary difference under the provisions of SFAS 109, if the intention is to hold the policy until death benefits are received. On the other hand, if the entity intends to cash in the policy at some point (i.e., it is holding the insurance contract as an investment), which would be a taxable event, then the excess surrender value is in fact a temporary difference, and deferred taxes should be provided thereon.

Treatment of Operating Loss Carryforwards

One of the most significant distinctions among SFAS 109 and its predecessors, SFAS 96 and APB 11, lies in the recognition of the tax effects of operating loss carryforwards. Under APB 11, the presumption was that operating losses would not be realizable and, accordingly, the entity experiencing the loss would not provide for the tax effects of carryforwards in its financial statements until the benefits were in fact later realized for tax purposes. That is, the provision for income taxes in the loss year would not reflect benefits of the pretax accounting loss in excess of the amount available as a carryback (plus an amount equal to existing deferred tax liabilities, to the extent the timing differences related thereto were scheduled to reverse during the statutory carryforward period). The balance sheet likewise would not include a deferred tax benefit relating to the benefit carryforward. This rather conservative treatment was justified by the traditional test applied to the reporting for most assets: presentation should be at amounts equal to no more than net realizable value. In relatively rare cases, when realization of the future benefits was deemed to be assured beyond a reasonable doubt (usually justifiable only when losses were very unusual in the entity's experience), recognition in the loss period was permitted.

SFAS 96 took an even stricter approach to operating losses. Under that standard, the presentation of net deferred tax debits was prohibited, to the extent that they exceeded amounts which would be recoverable through operating loss carrybacks as of the date of the balance sheet. This prescription followed from SFAS 96's basic conception that no assumptions should be made about the future earnings of the reporting entity, apart from the effects of reversals of those temporary differences which are in existence at the reporting date. To do otherwise would have been, in that standard's view, tantamount to anticipating future income, which of course has long been proscribed by GAAP. Thus, even the narrow loophole provided under APB 11 (the "assured beyond a reasonable doubt" exception) was closed by SFAS 96.

SFAS 109 takes quite the opposite position, decreeing that all temporary differences are created equally and that the tax effects thereof are to be given equal recognition in the balance sheet. The tax effects of net operating loss carryforwards are equal to the tax effects of other deductible temporary differences: The once important distinction between the two has been eliminated. As with all other deferred tax assets, the need for a valuation allowance must be assessed (discussed below). This does not mean, however, that the deferred tax effects of operating losses should not first be computed and provided for.

Under SFAS 109, the tax effects of credit carryforwards are handled in precisely the same manner as are operating losses. Under both of the predecessor standards, recognition of the tax effects of credit carryforwards was absolutely prohibited unless available to offset existing deferred tax liabilities.

SFAS 109 provides that the tax benefits of operating loss carrybacks and carryforwards, with limited exceptions (discussed below), are to be reported in the same manner as either the source of income or loss in the current year. The tax benefits are not reported in the same manner as the source of the loss carryforward or taxes paid in a prior year, or as the source of the expected future income that will permit the realization of the carryforward. As used in the standard, the phrase **in the same manner** refers to the classification of the tax benefit in the income statement (i.e., as taxes on income from continuing operations, discontinued operations, extraordinary items, etc.) or as the tax effect of gains included in comprehensive income but excluded from the income statement.

For example, if the tax benefit of a loss, which arose in a prior year in connection with an extraordinary item, is first given recognition in the current year, the benefit would be allocated to taxes on income from continuing operations if they offset taxes on continuing operations in the current year. The expression **first given recognition** means that the **net** deferred tax asset, after deducting the valuation allowance, reflects the tax effect of the loss carryforward for the first time. Under SFAS 109, of course, the **gross** deferred tax asset will always reflect all deductible temporary differences, including loss carryforwards, in the periods they arise. Thus, **first given recognition** means that the valuation allowance is eliminated for the first time. If it offsets taxes on extraordinary income in the current year, then the benefits would be reported in extraordinary items. As another example, the tax benefit arising from the entity's loss from continuing operations in the current year would be allocated to continuing operations, regardless of whether it might be realized as a carryback against taxes paid on extraordinary items in prior years. The benefit would also be allocated to continuing operations in cases where it is anticipated that it will be realized through the reduction of taxes to be due on extraordinary gains in future years.

Thus, the general rule is that the reporting of tax effects of operating losses are driven by the source of the tax benefits in the current period. There are only two exceptions to the foregoing rule. The first exception relates to existing deductible temporary differences, including operating loss carryforwards, which arise in connection with purchase business combinations, and for which tax benefits are first recognized. This exception will be discussed below (see tax effects of business combinations). As in the preceding paragraph, **first recognized** means that a valuation allowance provided previously is being eliminated.

A second exception to the aforementioned general rule is that certain tax benefits allocable to stockholders' equity are **not** to be reflected in the income statement. Specifically, tax benefits arising in connection with contributed capital, employee stock options, dividends paid on unallocated ESOP shares, or temporary differences existing at the date of a quasi reorganization are reported in the stockholders' equity section, and are not included in results of operations.

Measurement of Deferred Tax Assets and Liabilities

The new standard eliminates the need to schedule reversals in all but the most exceptional circumstances. This change is in response to the outcry over SFAS 96's requirement that all reversals of temporary differences be scheduled, in order to identify the net annual taxable or deductible amounts upon which deferred tax effects would be computed. While the conceptual rationale for either the original approach, or for its replacement, can be debated at length, the primary objective in adopting SFAS 109 was the practical goal of streamlining the computation of deferred taxes. While scheduling is not prohibited, it will now be encountered mainly in the context of phased-in tax rate changes and other situations in which the reporting entity must identify particular years of temporary difference reversals in order to meaningfully calculate their expected tax effects.

Apart from the situations suggested above, scheduling will be encountered principally in the determination of the amount of the needed valuation allowance. The valuation allowance will be addressed in the following section of this chapter.

Since SFAS 109 has largely eliminated the need to schedule temporary difference reversals, it is no longer feasible to compute deferred taxes as prescribed by SFAS 96; applying graduated rates on a year-by-year basis, assuming no income or expense other than the reversals. Consequently, SFAS 109 mandates an alternative approach to this computation. At the exposure draft stage, the Board had indicated a preference for measuring the tax effects of temporary differences by applying the marginal tax rates applicable at the time of the expected reversals. Some respondents to the exposure draft argued that such an approach would often have the result of overstating the deferred tax assets and liabilities of those reporting entities which normally are affected by graduated rates. The Board saw the logic in these arguments, and opted to employ an **average (or graduated) rate** approach instead.

Under SFAS 96's methodology, computed deferred taxes for each year were based on the full application of the tax rate brackets each year for which reversals were scheduled. Thus, under present law, at least some and often most or even all, deferred taxes were provided at low tax rates. In fact, many reporting entities having large gross temporary differences were able to provide deferred taxes at an effective rate as low as 15%. This result was obtained because the temporary differences, while large in total, were scheduled to reverse over many years in modest annual amounts, with lower tax rates applied to each of these yearly amounts. The proposed replacement for SFAS 96 would have significantly increased the reported amounts of deferred tax liabilities by applying top **marginal** rates instead. SFAS 109 is somewhat of a compromise between these two extremes: deferred tax liabilities will generally be higher than under the SFAS 96 approach, but will often be lower than they would have been, had the Board's draft replacement for SFAS 96 been adopted. (Deferred tax assets will usually be greater under SFAS 109, but this result is due more to the fact that deferred tax assets were essentially prohibited by SFAS 96 than to the change in computational methodology.)

For reporting entities traditionally having taxable income over $335,000, the expected tax rate equals the 34% marginal rate, since the effect of the surtax exemption has phased out at that level, effectively resulting in a flat tax. Thus, the computation of deferred taxes is accomplished simply by applying the top marginal rate to all temporary differences outstanding as of the balance sheet date. This technique would be applied both to taxable temporary differences (producing deferred tax liabilities), and to deductible temporary differences (giving rise to deferred tax assets). The deferred tax **assets** computed must still be evaluated for realizability; some, or all, of the projected tax benefits may fail the "more likely than not" test and consequently may need to be offset by a valuation allowance account.

Other reporting entities will have historically been taxed at an effective federal rate below the top marginal rate. In such circumstances, deferred taxes should be computed with reference to the entity's expected, or **effective**, income tax rate. Consistent with its goal of simplifying the process of calculating deferred taxes, it appears that the Board is willing to have preparers apply a single, long-term expected tax rate, without attempting to differentiate among the years when the reversals are expected to occur. In the Board's view, the inherent imprecision of forecasting future income levels and the pattern of reversals makes a more sophisticated computational effort unlikely to be productive. Therefore, absent such factors as the phasing-in of new tax rates, it will not be necessary to consider whether the reporting entity's effective tax rate will vary from year to year.

The effective tax rate convention eliminates one of SFAS 96's least popular features: the requirement that alternative minimum tax (AMT) be calculated each year for which reversals of temporary differences were scheduled. Application of the AMT was necessary under SFAS 96 because that standard applied low statutory rates to at least some, and as much as all, of the taxable temporary differences. In many cases, as a consequence, the AMT would have applied and the reporting entity would have been obliged to pay the higher AMT rather than the lesser regular tax. The result was that reporting entities would need to compute both regular and alternative minimum taxes for **each** future year; the higher of these was then used as the necessary deferred tax provision for that future year. AMT credits were then carried forward to be utilized in later years, if any, when regular tax would exceed alternative minimum tax.

Under SFAS 109, there is no need to address the AMT in computing the amount of deferred taxes to be provided. By employing the expected tax rate, the number of computations is reduced to as few as one, compared to computing twice the number of future years over which temporary differences are expected to reverse. For example, under SFAS 96 an entity might have scheduled reversals over 40 years or longer (e.g., for depreciation on buildings being calculated by different methods for tax and financial reporting purposes), with the concomitant need to prepare 80 different tax computations in order to determine total deferred taxes needed at the balance sheet date. This is reduced to a single computation under SFAS 109, in the absence of any other complicating factors.

The Board's decision to delete consideration of the AMT, apart from the reporting entity's actual AMT credit carryforward at the balance sheet date, depends upon the application of rather subtle reasoning. If an entity is presently an AMT taxpayer due to the effect of temporary differences, over time those differences must reverse and, accordingly, the AMT credit carryforward will be utilized by the reporting entity. Thus, over its entire existence, the entity will pay taxes at its average **regular** tax rate, in the aggregate. To record deferred taxes at the AMT rate, therefore, would be to understate the entity's deferred tax liability. Accordingly, deferred taxes should be recorded based on the effective **regular** tax rates expected to apply to the entity.

The procedure to compute the **gross** deferred tax provision (i.e., before addressing the possible need for a valuation allowance) is as follows:

1. Identify all temporary differences existing as of the reporting date.
2. Segregate the temporary differences into those which are taxable and those which are deductible. This step is necessary because a valuation allowance may be provided against the tax effects of the **deductible** temporary differences, but not against the tax effects of the **taxable** temporary differences.

3. Accumulate information about the deductible temporary differences, particularly the net operating loss and credit carryforwards which have expiration dates or other types of limitations.
4. Measure the tax effect of aggregate taxable temporary differences by applying the appropriate expected tax rates (federal plus any state, local, and foreign rates which are applicable under the circumstances).
5. Similarly, measure the tax effects of deductible temporary differences, including net operating loss carryforwards.

It should be emphasized that separate computations should be made for each tax jurisdiction, since in assessing the need for valuation allowances it is necessary to consider the entity's ability to absorb deferred tax benefits against tax liabilities. Inasmuch as benefits in one tax jurisdiction will not reduce taxes payable in another jurisdiction, separate calculations will be needed. Also, for purposes of balance sheet presentation (discussed below in detail), offsetting of deferred tax assets and liabilities is only permissible within jurisdictions. Similarly, separate computations should be made for each taxpaying component of the business: if a parent company and its subsidiaries are consolidated for financial reporting purposes but file separate tax returns, the reporting entity comprises a number of components, and the tax benefits of any one will be unavailable to reduce the tax obligations of the others.

The principles set forth above are illustrated by the following examples:

Computation of deferred tax liability and asset--Basic example

Assume that Northern Company has pretax financial income of $250,000 in 1999, a total of $28,000 of taxable temporary differences, and a total of $8,000 of deductible temporary differences. There are no operating loss or tax credit carryforwards. The tax rate is a flat (i.e., not graduated) 40%. Also assume that there were no deferred tax liabilities or assets in prior years. Taxable income is computed as follows:

Pretax financial income	$250,000
Taxable temporary differences	(28,000)
Deductible temporary differences	8,000
Taxable income	$230,000

The journal entry to record required amounts is

Current income tax expense	92,000	
Deferred tax asset	3,200	
Income tax expense--deferred	8,000	
Deferred tax liability		11,200
Income taxes currently payable		92,000

Current income tax expense and income taxes currently payable are each computed as taxable income times the current rate ($230,000 x 40%). The deferred tax asset of $3,200 represents 40% of deductible temporary differences of $8,000. The deferred tax liability of $11,200 is calculated as 40% of taxable temporary differences of $28,000. The deferred tax expense of $8,000 is the **net** of the deferred tax liability of $11,200 and the deferred tax asset of $3,200.

In 2000 Northern Company has pretax financial income of $450,000, aggregate taxable and deductible temporary differences are $75,000 and $36,000, respectively, and the tax rate remains a flat 40%.

Taxable income is $411,000, computed as pretax financial income of $450,000 minus taxable differences of $75,000 plus deductible differences of $36,000. Current income tax expense and income taxes currently payable each are $164,400 ($411,000 x 40%).

Deferred amounts are calculated as follows:

	Deferred tax liability	*Deferred tax asset*	*Income tax expense--deferred*
Required balance at 12/31/00			
$75,000 x 40%	$30,000		--
$36,000 x 40%		$14,400	--
Balances at 12/31/99	11,200	3,200	--
Adjustment required	$18,800	$11,200	$7,600

The journal entry to record the deferred amounts is

Deferred tax asset	11,200	
Income tax expense--deferred	7,600	
Deferred tax liability		18,800

Because the **increase** in the liability in 2000 is larger (by $7,600) than the increase in the asset for that year, the result is a deferred tax **expense** for 2000.

The Valuation Allowance for Deferred Tax Assets Which Are "More Likely Than Not" to Be *Not* Realizable

Under prior GAAP, the reporting of deferred tax assets was severely constrained or prohibited entirely. In proposing what became SFAS 109, the Board originally considered mandating a threshold criterion for the recognition of these benefits. For example, the Board could have stipulated that deferred tax assets were to be recognized only if reasonably assured of realization. However, as ultimately promulgated, the approach to be employed is to record **all** deferred tax assets, and then, as a separate, secondary procedure, to provide a reserve against the assets thus computed, to the extent required under the circumstances.

One approach which the Board could have easily adopted is already widely applied. The accrual of the effects of asset impairments, if it is **probable** that such impairment has occurred and if the effects thereof can be measured, is to be recognized in the financial statements under the provisions of SFAS 5. Logically, this requirement could have been made applicable to deferred tax benefits. (The second recognition threshold of SFAS 5, for the disclosure of asset impairments which are **reasonably possible** to have occurred, also seems applicable to deferred tax assets.)

The Board rejected the notion of applying the SFAS 5 criteria to this problem, however, and instead developed a new measure, to be applied in this situation alone. This is the **more-likely-than-not** criterion. The Board has decreed that a valuation allowance is to be provided for that fraction of the computed year-end balances of the deferred tax assets for which it has been determined that it is more likely than not that the reported asset amount will not be realized. As used in this context, **more likely than not** represents a probability of just over 50%. Since it is widely agreed that the term **probable**, as used in SFAS 5, denotes a much higher probability, possibly a likelihood as high as 85% to 90%, the threshold for reflecting an asset impairment in the case of deferred tax assets is **much lower** than is the corresponding threshold for recognition of impairments of other assets.

The Board's action in developing this new criterion was the outcome of its deliberations over whether the threshold test should be applied to the deferred tax asset **recognition** decision or to the **derecognition** decision. If to the former, then a threshold criterion such as **assured beyond a reasonable doubt** (as applied to benefits of net operating losses under APB 11) could be seen as being too high; tax benefits which in fact are likely to be realized would be precluded from recognition by such a test. If the threshold criterion were to be applied to the **derecognition** decision, as would a strict application of the SFAS 5 test, then some tax benefits which were **not** likely to have been realizable would still have been reported, since they would fail the high threshold test of **probable** impairment.

The Board's solution was to devise a threshold test which would produce essentially the same result whether applied to the **recognition** or to the **derecognition** decision. Since the **more-likely-than-not** criterion implies a probability of about 50%, the same **net** deferred tax asset would result whether the approach taken was to record only those deferred tax assets which are more likely than not to be realized, or whether the measurement approach was to **derecognize** (that is, to reserve against) the asset to the extent that it was more likely than not that it would **not** be realized.

Establishment of a valuation allowance

Assume that Zebra Corporation has a deductible temporary difference of $60,000 at December 31, 1999. The tax rate is a flat 40%. Based on available evidence, management of Zebra Corporation concludes that it is more likely than not that all sources will not result in future taxable income sufficient to realize a tax benefit of more than $15,000 (25% of deductible temporary differences). Also assume that there were no deferred tax assets in previous years and that prior years' taxable income was inconsequential.

At 12/31/99 Zebra Corporation records a deferred tax asset in the amount of $24,000 ($60,000 x 40%) and a valuation allowance of $18,000 (40% of the difference between the $60,000 of deductible temporary differences and the $15,000 of expected future taxable income to absorb a portion of the tax benefit).

The journal entry at 12/31/99 is

Deferred tax asset	24,000	
Valuation allowance		18,000
Income tax benefit--deferred		6,000

The deferred income tax benefit of $6,000 represents that portion of the deferred tax asset (25%) that is more likely than not to be realized.

In 2000 assume that Zebra Corporation's results are

Pretax financial loss	$(32,000)
Reversing deductible differences from 1999	(10,000)
Loss carryforward for tax purposes:	$(42,000)

The total of the loss carryforward (computed above) plus the amount of deductible temporary differences from 1999 not reversing in 2000 ($50,000) is $92,000. A deferred tax asset of $36,800 ($92,000 x 40%) is recognized at the end of 1999. Also assume that management of Zebra Corporation concludes that it is more likely than not that $25,000 of the tax asset will **not** be realized. Thus, a valuation allowance in that amount is required, and the balance in the allowance account of $18,000 must be increased by $7,000 ($25,000 – $18,000).

The journal entry at 12/31/99 is

Deferred tax asset	12,800	
Valuation allowance		7,000
Income tax benefit--deferred		5,800

The deferred tax asset is debited $12,800 to increase it from $24,000 at the end of 1999 to its required balance of $36,800 at the end of 2000. Deferred tax **benefit** of $5,800 represents the **net** of the $12,800 increase in the deferred tax asset and the $7,000 increase in the valuation allowance account.

While the meaning of the **more-likely-than-not** criterion is clear, the practical difficulty of assessing whether or not this threshold test is met in a given situation remains. A number of positive and negative factors need to be evaluated in reaching a conclusion as to whether a valuation allowance is needed. Positive factors (those suggesting that a reserve is not necessary) include

1. Evidence of sufficient future taxable income, exclusive of reversing temporary differences and carryforwards, to realize the benefit of the deferred tax asset
2. Evidence of sufficient future taxable income arising from the reversals of existing taxable temporary differences (deferred tax liabilities) to realize the benefit of the tax asset
3. Evidence of sufficient taxable income in prior year(s) available for realization of an operating loss carryback under existing statutory limitations.
4. Evidence of the existence of prudent, feasible **tax planning strategies** under management control which, if implemented, would permit the realization of the tax asset
5. An excess of appreciated asset values over their tax bases, in an amount sufficient to realize the deferred tax asset
6. A strong earnings history exclusive of the loss which created the deferred tax asset

While the foregoing may suggest that the reporting entity will be able to realize the benefits of the deductible temporary differences outstanding as of the balance sheet date, certain negative factors must also be considered in determining whether a valuation allowance should be established against deferred tax assets. These factors include

1. A cumulative recent history of losses
2. A history of operating losses, or of tax operating loss or credit carryforwards which have expired unused
3. Losses which are anticipated in the near future years, despite a history of profitable operations

Thus, the process of evaluating whether a valuation allowance is needed involves the weighing of both positive and negative factors to determine whether, based on the preponderance of available evidence, it is more likely than not that the deferred tax assets will be realized.

To illustrate the computation of the valuation allowance required in a specific situation, assume the following facts:

1. Mary-lynn Corporation reports on a calendar year, and adopted SFAS 109 in 1999.
2. As of the December 31, 1999 balance sheet, it has taxable temporary differences of $85,000 relating to depreciation; deductible temporary differences of $12,000 relating to deferred compensation arrangements; a net operating loss carryforward (which arose in 1996) of $40,000; and a capital loss carryover of $10,000.
3. Mary-lynn's expected tax rate for future years is 40% for ordinary income, and 25% for net long-term capital gains. Capital losses cannot be offset against ordinary income.

The first steps are to compute the required balances of the deferred tax asset and liability accounts, without consideration of the possible need for a valuation allowance. The computations would proceed as follows:

Deferred tax liability:	
Taxable temporary difference (depreciation)	$85,000
Effective tax rate	x 40%
Required balance	$34,000
Deferred tax asset:	
Deductible temporary differences:	
Deferred compensation	$12,000
Net operating loss	40,000
	$52,000
Effective tax rate	x 40%
Required balance (a)	$20,800
Capital loss	$10,000
Effective tax rate	x 25%
Required balance (b)	$ 2,500

Total deferred tax asset:	
Ordinary	$20,800
Capital	2,500
Total required balance	$23,300

The next step would be to consider the need for a valuation allowance to partially or completely offset the deferred tax asset, based on an assessment that is "more likely than not" that the asset is not going to be realized. Mary-lynn management must evaluate both positive and negative evidence to determine the need for a valuation allowance, if any. Assume now that management identifies the following factors which may affect this need:

1. Before the net operating loss deduction, Mary-lynn reported taxable income of $5,000 in 1999. Management believes that taxable income in future years, apart from NOL deductions, should continue at approximately the same level experienced in 1999.
2. The taxable temporary differences are not expected to reverse in the foreseeable future.
3. The capital loss arose in connection with a transaction of a type which is unlikely to recur. The company does not generally engage in activities which have the potential to result in capital gains or losses.
4. Management estimates that certain productive assets have a fair value exceeding their respective tax bases by about $30,000. The entire gain, if realized for tax purposes, would be a recapture of depreciation previously taken. Since the current plans call for a substantial upgrading of the company's plant assets, management feels it could easily accelerate those actions in order to realize taxable gains, should it be desirable to do so for tax planning purposes.

Based on the foregoing information, Mary-lynn Corporation management concludes that a $2,500 valuation allowance is required. The reasoning is as follows:

1. There will be some taxable operating income generated in future years ($5,000 annually, based on the earnings experienced in 1999), which will absorb a modest portion of the reversal of the deductible temporary difference ($12,000) and net operating loss carryforward ($40,000) existing at year end 1999.
2. More importantly, the feasible tax planning strategy of accelerating the taxable gain relating to appreciated assets ($30,000) would certainly be sufficient, in conjunction with operating income over several years, to permit Mary-lynn to realize the tax benefits of the deductible temporary difference and NOL carryover.
3. However, since capital loss carryovers are only usable to offset future capital gains, and Mary-lynn management is unable to project future realization of capital gains, the associated tax benefit accrued ($2,500) will "more likely than not" **not** be realized, and thus must be reserved against.

Based on this analysis, an allowance for unrealizable deferred tax benefits in the amount of $2,500 should be established by a charge against the current (1999) tax provision.

Of the various positive and negative factors to be considered, perhaps the most difficult to fully grasp is the role to be played by available tax planning strategies. Under the provisions of SFAS 96, tax planning strategies were an important consideration in determining whether the tax benefits of deductible temporary differences would be available to be absorbed against taxes owed pursuant to taxable timing differences. SFAS 96 prohibited the "use" (for computation purposes) of any tax planning strategy which would have involved the incurrence of significant costs. This stance was logical in the framework of SFAS 96's requirement to not anticipate any future events which were not inherently assumed in the financial statements.

The role of tax planning strategies in SFAS 109 differs markedly from that in SFAS 96, however. Since SFAS 109 requires that all available evidence be assessed to determine the need for a valuation allowance, there is less concern about the cost of implementing those strategies. In fact, there is no limitation as there was under the prior standard regarding strategies which may involve significant costs of implementation. However, any costs of implementation must be netted against the benefits to be derived from such implementation in arriving at the measurement of the amount of valuation allowance needed. For example, if a gross deferred tax benefit of $50,000 is recorded, and certain strategies have been identified by management to protect realization of the future deductible item associated with the computed tax benefit at an implementation cost of $10,000, then the net amount of tax benefit which is more likely than not to be realizable would not be $50,000. Rather, it may be only $43,500, which is the gross benefit less the after-tax cost of implementation, assuming a 35% tax rate ($50,000 – [$10,000 x (1 – .35)]). Accordingly, a valuation allowance of $6,500 should be established in this example.

Impact of a qualifying tax strategy

Assume that Kruse Company has a $180,000 operating loss carryforward as of 12/31/99, scheduled to expire at the end of next year. Taxable temporary differences of $240,000 exist that are expected to reverse in approximately equal amounts of $80,000 in 2000, 2001, and 2002. Kruse Company estimates that taxable income for 1999 (exclusive of the reversal of existing temporary differences and the operating loss carryforward) will be $20,000. Kruse Company expects to implement a qualifying tax planning strategy that will accelerate the total of $240,000 of taxable temporary differences to 2000. Expenses to implement the strategy are estimated to approximate $30,000. The tax rate is 40%.

In the absence of the tax planning strategy, $100,000 of the operating loss carryforward could be realized in 2000 based on estimated taxable income of $20,000 plus $80,000 of the reversal of taxable temporary differences. Thus, $80,000 would expire unused at the end of 2000 and the net amount of the deferred tax asset at 12/31/99 would be recognized at $40,000, computed as $72,000 ($180,000 x 40%) minus the valuation allowance of $32,000 ($80,000 x 40%).

However, by implementing the tax planning strategy, the deferred tax asset is calculated as follows:

Taxable income for 2000:	
Expected amount without reversal of taxable temporary differences	$ 20,000
Reversal of taxable temporary differences due to tax-planning strategy, net of costs	210,000
	230,000
Operating loss to be carried forward	(180,000)
Operating loss expiring unused at 12/31/00	$ -0-

The gross deferred tax asset thus can be recorded at the full benefit amount of $72,000 ($180,000 x 40%). However, a valuation allowance is required for $18,000, representing the net-of-tax effect of the $30,000 in anticipated expenses related to implementation of the strategy. The **net** deferred tax asset at 12/31/99 is $54,000 ($72,000 – $18,000). Kruse Company will also recognize a deferred tax liability of $96,000 at the end of 1999 (40% of the taxable temporary differences of $240,000).

The adequacy of the valuation allowance must be assessed as of each balance sheet date. Adjustments of the amount of this valuation allowance are effected by a charge against, or a credit to, current earnings, via the current period tax provision. Thus, even if the gross amount of the deductible temporary differences has remained constant during a year, tax expense for that year might be increased or decreased as a consequence of reassessing the valuation allowance account at year end. It is important that these two computational steps be separately addressed: **first** the computation of the gross deferred tax benefits (the product of the expected tax rate and the total amount of deductible temporary differences) must be made; **then** the amount of the valuation allowance to be provided against the deferred tax asset must be assessed (using the criteria set forth above). Although changes in both the deferred tax asset and valuation allowance accounts affect current period tax expense, the process of measuring these two accounts is quite distinct. Furthermore, SFAS 109 requires disclosure of both the gross deferred tax asset (and also the gross deferred tax liability) and the change in the valuation allowance account for the year. These disclosure requirements underline the need to separately measure these items.

The Effect of Tax Law Changes on Previously Recorded Deferred Tax Assets and Liabilities

As it did under SFAS 96, the balance-sheet-oriented measurement approach of SFAS 109 necessitates the reevaluation of the deferred tax asset and liability balances at each year end. If changes to tax rates or other provisions of the tax law (e.g., deductibility of items) have been enacted, the effect of these changes must be reflected in the year-end deferred tax accounts; the offsetting adjustments are made through the current period tax provision.

While conceptually it could be argued that the increase or decrease in the deferred tax balances should be recognized when first anticipated, the Board concluded that it would be more meaningful to report the effects of such changes in the period when the changes are enacted into law. This approach provides the most reliable measure of the impact of such changes, and is most consistent with the informational needs of the statement users. Enactment is defined, for purposes of this requirement, as determined by the taxing jurisdictions (e.g., federal laws are enacted when the president signs the legislation into law). When revised tax rates are enacted, they may impact not only the unreversed effects of items which were originally reported in the continuing operations section of the income statement, but also the unreversed effects of items first presented as discontinued operations, extraordinary items, or in other income statement captions. Also, the impact of changes in tax rates on the accumulated balance of deferred tax benefits or obligations which arose through charges or credits to other comprehensive income (under SFAS 130) will be included in tax expense associated with continuing operations. For example, if an entity has unrealized gains on holding available-for-sale securities at a time when relevant income tax rates (presumably the capital gains rates) are lowered, the reduction in the tax obligation associated with these unrealized gains will reduce current period tax expense associated with continuing operations, despite the fact that the tax provision was originally reported in an additional equity account (and under recently promulgated GAAP, would be included in other comprehensive income, not earnings). It should be noted that the Board has been contemplating a limited-scope project on intraperiod tax allocation, particularly directed at the matter of reporting the effects of tax law changes, for over a year, but has yet to put this on its technical agenda. The Board considered whether to require (or permit) reporting the effects of tax law changes on such unreversed temporary differences in these same income statement captions, but concluded that the complexities of identifying the diverse treatments of these originating transactions or events made this requirement unworkable. Accordingly, remeasurements of the effects of tax law changes are to be reported in the tax provision associated with continuing operations.

With tax law changes being widely discussed in late 1996 and early 1997, and a tax reform act being enacted at midyear, there was additional attention given to the impact of this provision of SFAS 109. The popular business press, in fact, took to painting this GAAP requirement in somewhat negative terms, holding that to include the impact of lowered tax rates in current earnings would be a distortion which could disrupt the smooth functioning of the then-booming stock markets. In fact, if the average listed corporation had a net deferred tax liability position, the result of lowered rates would be to reduce the reported amount of this obligation currently, with the offset being against tax expense. However, SFAS 109 does require that such adjustments, if material, must be carefully and fully explained in the informative disclosures accompaning the financial statements. The problem, to the extent there might have been one, is mitigated by the fact that tax rate relief is minimal in the 1997 tax act, with most changes being targeted benefits not affecting business taxpayers, except that capital gains rates have been lowered.

SFAS 109 also follows the model of SFAS 96 with regard to the timing and method of recognition of the effects of tax law changes which occur during an interim reporting period. Under the provisions of both standards, the effects are to be reported in the interim period in which enactment occurs. The effects of the changes are included in continuing operations, despite the source of the temporary differences impacted currently by the tax law change. For example, if an entity accrued a loss relating to discontinued operations, which is not tax deductible until paid, the tax effect would be shown in the **discontinued operations** section of the income statement for the first quarter. If tax rates are changed in the third quarter of the same year, the deferred tax benefit recognized in connection with the discontinued operations would now need to be adjusted upward or downward, based on the newly enacted tax rate schedule. The income statement effect of this adjustment would be included with the tax provision on income from continuing operations in the third quarter. While this is consistent with practice under SFAS 96, it differs from that under APB 11, which handled this change by the prospective application of a revised effective tax rate to income being reported for remaining interim periods of the year during which enactment took place.

Computation of a deferred tax asset with a change in rates

Assume the Fantasy Company has $80,000 of deductible temporary differences at the end of 1999, which are expected to result in tax deductions of approximately $40,000 each on tax returns for 2000-2002. Enacted tax rates are 50% for years 1997-1999, and 40% for 2000 and thereafter.

The deferred tax asset is computed at 12/31/99 under each of the following independent assumptions:

1. If Fantasy Company expects to offset the deductible temporary differences against taxable income in years 2000-2002, the deferred tax asset is $32,000 ($80,000 x 40%).
2. If Fantasy Company expects to realize a tax benefit for the deductible temporary differences by loss carryback refund, the deferred tax asset is $40,000 ($80,000 x 50%).

Assume that Fantasy Company expects to realize a tax asset of $32,000 at the end of 1999. Also assume that taxes payable in **each** of the years 1997-1999 were $8,000 (or 50% of taxable income). Realization of $24,000 of the $32,000 deferred tax asset is assured through carryback refunds even if no taxable income is earned in years 2000-2002. Whether a valuation allowance for the remaining $8,000 is needed depends on Fantasy Company's assessment of the levels of future taxable earnings.

The foregoing estimate of the **certain** tax benefit, based on a loss carryback to periods of higher tax rates than are statutorily in effect for future periods, should only be utilized when future losses (for tax purposes) are expected. This restriction applies since the benefit thus recognized (net of the allowance) exceeds benefits which would be available in future periods, when tax rates will be lower.

Reporting the Effect of Tax Status Changes

Changes in the tax status of the reporting entity are reported in a manner which is entirely analogous to the reporting of enacted tax changes. When the tax status change becomes effective, the consequent adjustments to deferred tax assets and liabilities are reported in current tax expense, as part of the tax provision relating to continuing operations.

The most commonly encountered changes in status are those attendant to an S corporation election or the revocation thereof. When a previously taxable corporation (a C corporation) becomes an S corporation, the stockholders become personally liable for taxes on the company's earnings, whether the earnings are distributed to them or not (similar to the relationship among a partnership and its partners). Under prior practice, this event was accounted for in a variety of interesting ways, including the reclassification of deferred tax liabilities as paid-in capital, an approach which was justified on the basis that the shareholders were, by assuming personally what was formerly a corporate obligation, making a contribution to the company's equity. Others reported a direct charge or credit to retained earnings, such as might occur if recording a correction of an error. Under first SFAS 96 and now SFAS 109, these alternative interpretations are prohibited. Deferred taxes are to be eliminated by reversal through current period tax expense. For example, if an entity having a net deferred tax liability elects S corporation status, it will report a tax benefit in its current provision.

Similarly, if an S corporation becomes a C corporation, the effect is to assume a net tax benefit or obligation for unreversed temporary differences existing at the date the change becomes effective. Accordingly, the financial statements for the period of such a change will report the effects of the event in the current tax provision. If the entity had at that date many taxable temporary differences as yet unreversed, it would report a large tax expense in that period. Conversely, if it had a large quantity of unreversed deductible temporary differences, a substantial deferred tax benefit (subject to the more-likely-than-not criterion) would need to be recorded, with a concomitant credit to the current period's tax provision in the income statement. Whether eliminating an existing deferred tax balance or recording an initial deferred tax asset or liability, the income tax footnote to the financial statements will need to fully explain the nature of the events which had transpired.

Since S corporation elections are automatically effective when filed, if a reporting entity makes an election before the end of the current fiscal year, it is logical that the effects be reported in current-year income to become effective at the start of the following period. For example, an election filed in December 1999 would be reported in the 1999 financial statements to become effective at the beginning of the company's next fiscal year, January 1, 2000. No deferred tax assets or liabilities would appear on the December 31, 1999 balance sheet, and the tax provision for the year then ended would include the effects of any reversals that had been previously recorded.

Under existing tax law, a C corporation electing to become an S corporation may be found to have "built-in gains" which will result in a future tax liability, under defined circumstances. Temporary differences are defined by SFAS 109 and its precedent, SFAS 96, as differences in the tax and financial reporting bases of assets and liabilities. Accordingly, in such cases, the entity, which is now an S corporation, will continue to report a deferred tax liability related to this built-in gain. All other deferred taxes are eliminated upon election to be taxed as an S corporation.

Reporting the Effect of Accounting Changes for Tax Purposes

Occasionally, an entity will initiate or be required to adopt changes in accounting which affect income tax reporting, but which will not impact financial statement reporting. Examples include: the change to the direct write-off method of bad debt recognition mandated by changes in tax laws, while continuing to use the reserve method as required by GAAP for financial reporting; and the adoption of "full costing" for computing inventory valuations for tax purposes, while continuing to expense currently certain administrative costs not inventoriable under GAAP. Generally, these mandated changes really involve two distinct temporary differences. The first of these is the one-time, catch up adjustment which either immediately or over a prescribed time period impacts the **tax basis** of the asset or liability in question (net receivables or inventory, in the examples above), and which then reverses as these assets or liabilities are later realized or settled and are eliminated from the balance sheet. The second change is the ongoing differential in the amount of **newly** acquired assets or incurred liabilities being recognized for tax and accounting purposes; these differences also eventually reverse. This second type of change is the normal temporary difference which has already been discussed. It is the first change which differs from those previously discussed in this chapter.

As an example, consider that Leopold Corporation has, at December 31, 1998, gross receivables of $12,000,000 and an allowance for bad debts in the amount of $600,000. Also assume that expected future taxes will be at a 40% rate and that, effective January 1, 1999, the tax law is revised to eliminate deductions for accrued bad debts, with existing allowances to be taken into income ratably over 4 years (a "4-year spread"). A balance sheet of Leopold Corporation prepared on January 1, 1999, would report a deferred tax **benefit** in the amount of $240,000 (i.e., $600,000 x 40%, which is the tax effect of future deductions to be taken when specific receivables are written off and bad debts are incurred for tax purposes); a current tax liability of $60,000 (one fourth of the tax obligation); and a noncurrent tax liability of $180,000 (three fourths of the tax obligation).

The deferred tax benefit is **not** deemed to be identified with the contra asset allowance for doubtful accounts (if it were, it would all be reported as a current asset), but rather with the future specific bad debts expected to be incurred. Accordingly, the deferred tax benefit should be categorized as current and noncurrent according to Leopold Corporation's best estimate of the timing of those future bad debts (much or most of which will, in all likelihood, occur within 1 year).

Tax Effects of Dividends Paid on Shares Held by Employee Stock Ownership Plans (ESOP)

SFAS 109 has changed the way the tax benefits arising in connection with dividends paid on ESOP-held shares are recognized. Under APB 11, tax benefits relating to both allocated and unallocated shares were reported in the equity section (i.e., in retained earnings). SFAS 96 took the opposite approach, reporting such tax benefits in income.

SFAS 109 stakes out a middle ground. Tax benefits from deductible dividends paid on **unallocated** shares held by the ESOP are credited to retained earnings. However, benefits from dividends paid on **allocated** shares are included in the tax provision relating to continuing operations.

The Board's decision regarding ESOP dividends was based on its recognition that ESOP and other stock compensation plans are fully analogous. Given that both plans sometimes result in tax deductions for amounts not recognized under GAAP as compensation expense, the accounting treatment of the resulting tax benefits should be the same.

On the other hand, tax deductible dividends for **other** than unallocated ESOP-held shares represents, in the Board's view, an exemption from tax of an equivalent amount of the payor's earnings. For that reason, it concluded that the tax effects should be reported in continuing operations.

Accounting for Income Taxes: Business Combinations

One of the more complex aspects of interperiod income tax accounting, under both SFAS 96 and 109, occurs when business combinations treated as purchases, as defined by APB 16, are consummated. The principal complexity relates to the recognition, at the date of the purchase, of the deferred tax effects of the differences between the tax and financial reporting bases of assets and liabilities acquired. Further difficulties arise in connection with the recognition of goodwill and so-called negative goodwill. If the reporting entity expects that the ultimate tax allocation will differ from the initial one (such as when disallowance by the tax authorities of an allocation made to identifiable intangibles is anticipated by the taxpayer), then yet another complex accounting matter must be dealt with.

The major distinction between SFAS 96 and 109, on the other hand, and APB 11, as effectively amended by APB 16 (business combinations), is that APB 16 required the "net of tax" method of allocation of purchase cost to identifiable assets and liabilities. The net of tax method, which prior to the promulgation of APB 11 had been one of several alternative theories of comprehensive interperiod income tax allocation (albeit not widely employed in practice), considered the differences between tax and financial reporting bases of assets and liabilities to be attributes inferred in the valuations of the assets and liabilities themselves. If a given asset had a higher income tax basis than financial reporting basis, then that difference would represent an excess future tax deduction which would add to the value of the asset. For example: If an asset had a tax basis of $1,000, and a book basis before considering the tax effect of the basis difference of $800, and if the tax rates were a flat 30%, then the reportable amount of the asset would be $860 under the net of tax method [$800 + .30($200)], without considering the timing of the tax deductions.

In practice, the net of tax method was viewed as a somewhat "academic" alternative to the more popular deferred and liability methods, and was not commonly employed. APB 11 endorsed the deferred method of computing and reporting deferred income taxes, and prohibited the use of the net of tax method. APB 16, however, stipulated that tax-book differences in the bases of assets and liabilities acquired by means of purchase business combinations were not "timing differences" under APB 11 but were still determinants of fair value. Accordingly, it was the prescription of APB 16 that assets and liabilities so acquired were to be presented on a net of tax basis, as illustrated above. Furthermore, even though APB 11 prohibited presentation of deferred income taxes on a discounted present value basis, APB 16's net of tax requirement provided for discounting the valuation adjustment relating to the tax-book basis differences. This step acknowledges the importance of the timing of the expiration of those differences.

In actual practice, it appears that the process of allocating purchase cost to assets and liabilities acquired, including consideration of the effects of tax-book basis differences, was not always properly executed. Often the tax effects, in particular, were not measured with the precision contemplated in the standards. The failure to complete this calculation was explained frequently as an indirect attempt to address the discounting issue: since the tax-book differences were to "reverse" over an extended time period, the present values of the related tax benefits or obligations were likely to be judged immaterial, and thus not in need of measurement.

For example, LIFO inventories acquired in a purchase business combination would often have different tax and financial reporting bases; however, receipt or settlement of the related tax benefit or obligation would likely take place only upon liquidation of the company or of its inventories. Since these events were often assumed to be in the far off, indefinite future, the tax effects, discounted to present value, would only alter slightly the inventories reportable in the financial statements.

SFAS 96 eliminated the application of the net of tax method to purchase business combinations, and decreed instead that assets and liabilities so acquired be reported gross of tax effects. The tax effects of any differences in tax and financial reporting bases are to be reflected, from the date of the purchase, as deferred tax assets and liabilities in their own right. This requirement has been continued in SFAS 109.

Purchase business combinations can be either taxable or nontaxable in nature. In a taxable business combination, the total purchase price paid is allocated to assets and liabilities for both tax and financial reporting purposes, although under some circumstances these allocations may differ. In a nontaxable business combination, the predecessor entity's tax bases for the various assets and liabilities are carried forward, while for financial reporting the purchase price is allocated to the assets and liabilities acquired. Thus, in most cases, there will be significant differences between the tax and financial reporting bases. For this reason, both taxable and nontaxable purchase business combinations can involve the application of deferred income tax accounting.

Accounting for Purchase Business Combinations at Acquisition Date

SFAS 109, like SFAS 96 before it, requires that the tax effects of the tax-book basis differences of all assets and liabilities generally be presented as deferred tax assets and liabilities as of the acquisition date. In general, this "grossing up" of the balance sheet is a straightforward matter. An example, in the context of a nontaxable purchase business combination, follows:

Facts:

1. The income tax rate is a flat 40%.
2. The acquisition of a business is effected at a cost of $500,000.
3. The fair values of assets acquired total $750,000.
4. The carryforward tax bases of assets acquired total $600,000.
5. The fair and carryforward tax bases of the liabilities assumed in the purchase are $250,000.
6. The difference between the tax and fair values of the assets acquired, $150,000, consists of taxable temporary differences of $200,000 and deductible temporary differences of $50,000.
7. There is no doubt as to the realizability of the deductible temporary differences in this case.

Based on the foregoing facts, the allocation of the purchase price is as follows:

Gross purchase price	$500,000
Allocation to identifiable assets and (liabilities):	
Assets, other than goodwill and deferred tax benefits	750,000
Deferred tax benefits	20,000
Liabilities, other than deferred tax obligations	(250,000)
Deferred tax obligations	(80,000)
Net of the above allocations	440,000
Allocation to goodwill	$ 60,000

While it has yet to be officially interpreted, it is likely that goodwill (which under the 1993 tax act is now amortizable over 15 years for tax purposes) will not be "grossed up" in the balance sheet. There are two reasons for anticipating this. First, at the date on which the business combination is consummated, the tax and book bases of goodwill should generally be the same, inasmuch as amortization has yet to begin. Second, recognition of deferred taxes in connection with goodwill would have the effect of increasing the amount of goodwill to be reported in the financial statements in most cases, and this is not generally seen as being a desirable outcome.

Goodwill and negative goodwill. Goodwill arises when part of the price paid in a business combination accounted for as a purchase cannot be allocated to identifiable assets; "negative goodwill" results from so-called bargain purchases. Goodwill has now, with the passage of the 1993 tax act, become tax deductible, with a mandatory 15-year amortization period. Since under GAAP goodwill is to be amortized over its expected economic life (not to exceed 40 years, per APB 17), a temporary difference will often develop. Since negative goodwill is offset against all noncurrent assets (except long-term marketable securities) for financial reporting, differences between tax and book depreciation will result.

Temporary differences such as these will continue to occur relative to negative goodwill, under the provisions of the 1993 tax act. Furthermore, as regards unallocated negative goodwill (which is reported as a deferred credit in the balance sheet), temporary differences will now sometimes also occur.

The accounting for a taxable purchase business combination is essentially similar to that for a nontaxable one. However, unlike the previous example, in which there were numerous assets with different tax and financial reporting bases, there are likely to be only a few differences in the case of taxable purchases. Previously, because goodwill was not deductible, attempts were often made for tax purposes to allocate excess purchase cost to other intangibles, such as covenants not to compete. Since the 1993 tax act makes all such intangibles, including goodwill, amortizable over 15 years, this motive should no longer be encountered. Accordingly, tax-book differences in taxable business combinations are likely to be less common.

Accounting for Purchase Business Combinations After the Acquisition

A major distinction between SFAS 96 and 109 is that net deferred tax benefits (i.e., benefits which would not be offset by deferred tax liabilities or which would not be recoverable if they were loss carrybacks as of the balance sheet date) were not recognizable under the former but are fully recognized (subject to a valuation allowance) under the latter. This fundamental difference in approach has a major impact on the accounting for business combinations.

In the example above, it was specified that all deductible temporary differences were fully realizable, and therefore the deferred tax benefits associated with those temporary differences were recorded as of the acquisition date. In other situations, there may be substantial doubt concerning realizability (i.e., it may be **more likely than not** that the benefits will **not** be realized) and accordingly that a valuation allowance would be recognized, under SFAS 109, at the date of the purchase business combination. If so, then the allocation of the purchase price would reflect that fact, with the probability that more of the purchase cost would be allocated to goodwill than would otherwise be the case. If at a later date, it is decided that the valuation account should be reduced or eliminated, then the effect of that reduction is applied first to eliminate any goodwill recorded in connection with that business combination. The excess is applied to eliminate any identifiable intangibles acquired in that combination, and any further excess is reflected in the current period tax provision.

Subsequent realization of a deferred tax asset in a purchase business combination

Assume that Michael Company acquired another entity on January 1, 1999, for \$2,000,000. There was no goodwill in the transaction. The tax basis of the net assets is \$6,000,000 (i.e., deductible temporary differences equal \$4,000,000). The tax rate is 30% and the tax law restricts use of the acquired company's deductible temporary differences and carryforwards to future taxable income of the acquired entity itself. Pretax losses have been incurred in the past 3 years, and results for the acquired company in 1999 are also expected to be a deficit. Thus, Michael Company concludes that a valuation allowance for the full amount of the deferred tax asset is required. However, at the end of 2000, Michael Company decides that a valuation allowance is no longer necessary. Actual results for years 1999 and 2000 are as follows:

	1999	*2000*
Pretax financial income	$ 1,500,000	$ 1,000,000
Reversal of acquired deductible temporary differences	(1,500,000)	(1,000,000)
Taxable income	$ -0-	$ -0-

At the date of acquisition the deferred tax asset is recorded at $1,200,000 ($4,000,000 x 30%) but with a corresponding valuation allowance for the same amount. At the end of 1999, the deferred tax asset is $750,000 computed as 30% of $2,500,000 ($4,000,000 – $1,500,000), again with a corresponding valuation allowance. At the end of 2000, when management determines that a valuation allowance is no longer necessary, elimination of the valuation allowance results in a deferred tax benefit or in a reduction of deferred income tax expense. (Note that had goodwill arisen in the acquisition, the tax benefit would have first been applied to reduce goodwill to zero and then to reduce acquired intangible assets to zero).

Thus, journal entries related to deferred taxes are

At 1-1-99 (date of acquisition)		
Net assets	2,000,000	
Deferred tax asset	1,200,000	
Cash		2,000,000
Valuation allowance		1,200,000
At 12-31-99		
Valuation allowance	450,000	
Deferred tax asset		450,000
At 12-31-00		
Valuation allowance	750,000	
Deferred tax asset		300,000
Income tax benefit--deferred		450,000

Under SFAS 109, the tax benefits of net operating losses are not distinguished from those arising from temporary differences. Accordingly, the treatments set forth above hold here as well. If the benefits are recognized for the first time at a date after the acquisition (by reducing or eliminating the valuation allowance), then goodwill arising from the business combination is eliminated, other purchased intangibles are reduced to zero, and current tax expense is reduced. Negative goodwill is neither created nor increased in such circumstances, however.

Precisely the same approach is employed in connection with income tax credits which may have existed at the date of the business combination, but which may not have been given recognition due to doubtful realizability. While under APB 11 the treatments accorded net operating losses and tax credit carryforwards were dissimilar, under SFAS 109 they are identical. Under APB 11, recognition of benefits for operating loss carryforwards was possible under limited circumstances, while recognition of tax credit carryforwards was strictly prohibited.

In some instances, entities having unrecognized tax benefits of operating losses or tax credits arising in connection with a purchase business combination may generate other similar tax benefits after the date of the merger. A question in such a circumstance relates to whether a "FIFO" convention should be adopted to guide the recognition of these benefits. While in some instances tax law may determine the order in which the benefits are actually realized, in other cases the law may not do so. SFAS 109 provides that in those latter situations, the benefits realized should be apportioned, for financial reporting purposes, between pre- and postacquisition tax benefits. The former should be accounted for as above, and the latter reported as reductions of current period tax expense, consistent with the general rules of SFAS 109.

Purchase Business Combinations Consummated Prior to the Adoption of SFAS 109

SFAS 109 may be adopted either prospectively or retrospectively. If retrospectively, the financial statements of some or all consecutively occurring prior years may be restated. All purchase business combinations which took place after the beginning of the first of the restated years must be remeasured in accordance with the requirements of SFAS 109 (i.e., the assets and liabilities must be reported at gross allocated purchase cost) with the deferred tax assets and liabilities reported separately in the financial statements. In this regard, SFAS 109 is identical to SFAS 96. SFAS 109 differs from SFAS 96 with regard to restatement for differences in the tax and financial reporting bases of assets and liabilities acquired in purchase business combinations consummated **prior** to the beginning of the year for which the standard is first applied.

Whereas SFAS 96 prohibited adjustment of carrying values related to purchase business combinations occurring prior to the earliest application of that standard, SFAS 109 requires that any remaining balances of assets and liabilities (except those relating to leveraged leases) be restated from net of tax amounts to pretax amounts. The differences between those pretax amounts and the respective tax bases should be accounted for as temporary differences in accordance with SFAS 109.

The standard does, fortunately, recognize that for some assets and liabilities purchased long ago it may be extremely difficult to identify the gross of tax amounts remaining at the earliest date of application of SFAS 109's measurement principles. This would be particularly true if the net of tax measurements were applied improperly when the business combination originally took place. In such situations, the reporting entity may elect to omit the foregoing procedures for the remaining assets and liabilities of a given purchase business combination. Justification for not restating must be based either on the impracticability of doing so or on the fact that excessive costs would be incurred by the reporting entity in accomplishing the remeasurement. Remeasurement cannot be applied selectively, however if some assets or liabilities cannot be remeasured, then none of the assets and liabilities of that purchase can be remeasured. They must continue to be carried at their net of tax amounts. Any differences between such amounts and their respective tax bases are to be handled as temporary differences, as described above. Differences may result from, among other possible causes, discounting applied in the original application of the net of tax method and the prohibition against discounting in SFAS 109.

Finally, with regard to restatements of purchases prior to the date of first application of the measurement principles of SFAS 109, any remaining balances of either goodwill or so-called negative goodwill will **not** be adjusted to the amounts which would have existed at that date had the requirements of this standard been applied originally to that business combination.

Poolings of Interests

In poolings of interests, the combining entities generally do not adjust carrying values of assets and liabilities. Reissued or comparative financial statements of periods before the effective date of the combination are restated on a combined basis. SFAS 109 stipulates that, if one of the combining entities had an unrecognized deferred tax benefit (i.e., the deferred tax benefit was offset by a valuation allowance), the restated financials may or may not reflect the benefits. That is, the valuation allowance **may** be eliminated on a retrospective basis. This treatment depends upon whether the combined entity will be able, under provisions of the tax laws, to utilize the operating loss and tax credit carryforwards of the merged companies. If it can do so, then the deferred tax benefits should be recognized in any restated prior period financial statements. If, under the law, the benefits cannot be utilized in a consolidated tax return or if a consolidated return is not expected to be filed, then the tax benefits would not be recognized in financial statements restated for the pooling of interests.

Under some circumstances, poolings of interests are taxable, meaning that for tax purposes there will be a step up of the net assets of one of the merged entities. The differences between the new, stepped up tax bases and the carryforward book values utilized for financial reporting purposes are temporary differences giving rise to deferred tax benefits. Whether these benefits are given recognition is dependent upon whether the more likely than not criterion is met. If the test is not met, a valuation allowance must be established for some or all of the gross benefits recorded. If a valuation allowance is established, and it is later reduced or eliminated as the likelihood of ultimate realization exceeds the 50% probability threshold, the effect of eliminating the valuation allowance is reflected in tax expense for the current period.

Tax Allocation for Business Investments

As noted in Chapter 10, pending forthcoming Board actions that may alter or restrict use of the equity method, there are two basic methods for accounting for investments in the common stock of other corporations: (1) the cost method and

(2) the equity method. The cost method requires that the investing corporation (investor) record the investment at its purchase price, and no additional entry is made to the account over the life of the asset (this does not include any valuation contra accounts). The cost method is used in instances where the investor is not considered to have significant influence over the investee. The ownership threshold generally used is 20% of ownership. This figure is not considered an absolute (FASB Interpretation 35), but it will be used to identify the break between application of the cost and equity methods. Under the cost method, ordinary income is recognized as dividends are declared by the investee, and capital gains (losses) are recognized upon the disposal of the investment. For tax purposes, no provision is made during the holding period for the allocable undistributed earnings of the investee. There is no deferred tax computation necessary when using the cost method because there is no temporary difference.

The equity method is used whenever an investor owns more than 20% of an investee or has significant influence over its operations. The equity method calls for recording the investment at cost and then increasing this carrying amount by the allocable portion of the investee's earnings. The allocable portion of the investee's earnings is then included in pretax accounting income of the investor. Dividend payments are no longer included in pretax accounting income but are considered to be a reduction in the carrying amount of the investment. However, for tax purposes, dividends are the only revenue realized. As a result, the investor needs to recognize deferred income tax expense on the undistributed earnings of the investee that will be taxed in the future. The current promulgated GAAP in this area are APB 23 and SFAS 109, which supersedes APB 24 but which continues the principles set forth therein. These are discussed below.

GAAP distinguishes between an investee and a subsidiary and prescribes different accounting treatments for each. An investee is considered to be a corporation whose stock is owned by an investor who holds more than 20% but no greater than 50% of the outstanding stock. An investee situation occurs when the investor has significant influence but not control over the corporation invested in. A subsidiary, on the other hand, exists when more than 50% of the stock of a corporation is owned by another. This results in direct control over the corporation invested in. APB 23, as amended by SFAS 109, is the promulgated GAAP regarding the tax effects relating to the ownership of subsidiaries. APB 24 was the promulgated GAAP on the tax effects of investments in common stock of entities other than subsidiaries and corporate joint ventures which are accounted for by the equity method, until being superseded first by SFAS 96 and now by SFAS 109.

Subsidiary undistributed earnings. According to APB 23, the inclusion of undistributed earnings of a subsidiary in the pretax accounting income of a parent company through consolidation or equity reporting (or some combination of the two) would result in a temporary timing difference, albeit a difference that may not reverse until indefinite future periods. It is presumed that at some point in time all of the undistributed earnings of a subsidiary will be transferred to the parent. As such, the tax effect must be recognized on the temporary difference and treated as occurring either in the form of a dividend or a capital gain. The form that the temporary difference takes (dividend or capital transaction) is dependent upon the expectation in the situation.

The presumption that all undistributed income will eventually be transferred to the parent could, under APB 23, be overcome if sufficient evidence could be presented that the subsidiary would invest the undistributed earnings indefinitely or that the earnings would be distributed in a tax-free liquidation. Examples of such evidence would be the past experience of the companies involved or specific future plans of indefinite postponement. In such an instance, the opinion required that the following disclosures be made in the notes to the financial statements:

1. A declaration of an intention to reinvest the undistributed earnings of a subsidiary to support the contention that the distribution of those earnings has been indefinitely postponed or that the earnings will be distributed in the form of a tax-free liquidation.
2. The cumulative amount of undistributed earnings on which the parent company has not recognized taxes.

APB 23 provided that when a change occurred in the expectations regarding distributions of subsidiary earnings, the tax effects of the changed expectations were to be reflected in tax expense in the period the new information became available. In other words, the character of the change was that of an accounting estimate; it was not appropriate to treat it as either an extraordinary item or a correction of prior periods.

SFAS 96 left APB 23 in place, with minor amendments, as GAAP for accounting for the tax effects of investments in subsidiaries. The only real change was that changes in expected future tax effects were to be recognized currently (as set forth in SFAS 96), in contrast to APB 11's requirement that, once provided, deferred taxes were not subsequently revised for changes in tax rates, etc.

The Board's rationale for allowing the provisions of APB 23 to remain effective under SFAS 96 related to (1) the purported complexity of measuring deferred tax liabilities for foreign undistributed earnings, (2) a perceived need to compromise the principles of SFAS 96 to gain its acceptance, and (3) the prohibition against discounting. In SFAS 109, however, the Board has explicitly recognized that the timing (now temporary) differences of APB 23 do in fact give rise to recognizable deferred tax liabilities. While management may control the timing and circumstances of the recognition of earnings of nonconsolidated subsidiaries for tax purposes, ultimate occurrence is certain. The same logic also applies to the recognition of deferred tax assets (an issue which was not addressed earlier because of SFAS 96's prohibition against recognition of net deferred tax assets arising from **any** sources).

Nonetheless, SFAS 109 does offer a compromise approach to the adoption of comprehensive tax allocation. Deferred taxes are **not** to be provided for undistributed earnings of domestic subsidiaries or corporate joint ventures if they are essentially permanent in nature and arose in fiscal years beginning on or prior to December 15, 1992. Thus, the procedures of SFAS 109 are to be applied prospectively, but no adjustment needs to be made for temporary differences arising from ownership of subsidiaries prior to the effective date of the new standard.

The amount of tax to be provided depends upon specific application of the tax laws and management intent. If the law provides a mechanism under which the parent company can recover its investment tax free, no deferred taxes need to be provided. For example, an entity can elect to determine taxable gain or loss on the liquidation of an 80% or more owned subsidiary based on the tax basis of the subsidiary's net assets, rather than by reference to the parent's basis in its investment in the subsidiary. Also, under specified circumstances a parent company can effect a statutory merger, under which no gain or loss is recognized for tax purposes.

In other cases, options to minimize or avoid taxes are available only if the parent company owns a stipulated share of the subsidiary's stock. A parent company owning less than this threshold level may express its intent to utilize a **tax planning strategy** to acquire the necessary additional shares to realize this benefit. In evaluating this strategy, the cost of acquiring the additional shares must be considered and the benefits to be recognized (reduced deferred tax liability) must be offset by the cost of implementing the strategy.

Investee undistributed earnings. APB 24 promulgated GAAP for situations where there is significant influence but not control. It was the difference between these two degrees of power that was the catalyst for APB 24. The fact that an investor has significant influences in the operations of an investee is not enough to determine that distribution of the investee's earnings will be postponed indefinitely. As a result, the inclusion of undistributed earnings of an investee corporation in the pretax accounting income of the parent corporation will always result in a temporary difference. Again, the facts and circumstances involved in each situation will be the final determinant as to whether the temporary difference is treated as a dividend or a capital gain.

SFAS 109 has continued the approach set forth originally in APB 24, although of course the deferred tax provision is now computed by the liability method and no longer is determined by the "with and without" calculation of APB 11.

To illustrate the application of these concepts, assume Parent Company owns 30% of the outstanding common stock of Investee Company and 70% of the outstanding common stock of Subsidiary company. Additional data for Subsidiary and Investee companies for the year 1999 are as follows:

	Investee Company	*Subsidiary Company*
Net income	\$50,000	\$100,000
Dividends paid	20,000	60,000

The following sections illustrate how the foregoing data are used to recognize the tax effects of the stated events.

Income Tax Effects From Investee Company

The pretax accounting income of Parent Company will include equity in investee income equal to $15,000 ($50,000 x 30%). Parent's taxable income, however, will include dividend income of $6,000 ($20,000 x 30%), and a credit of 80% of the $6,000, or $4,800, will also be allowed for the dividends received. This 80% dividends received deduction is a permanent difference between pretax accounting and taxable income and is allowed for dividends received from domestic corporations in which the ownership is less than 80% but at least 20%; a lower dividend received deduction of 70% is permitted when the ownership is less than 20%. A 100% credit (dividends received deduction) is allowed for dividends received from domestic corporations in which the ownership is 80% to 100%. As discussed in APB 24, the originating temporary difference results from Parent's equity ($9,000) in Investee's undistributed income of $30,000. The amount of the deferred tax credit in 1999 depends upon the expectations of Parent Company as to the manner in which the $9,000 of undistributed income will be received. If the expectation of receipt is via dividends, then the temporary difference is 20% of $9,000, or $1,800, and the deferred tax credit for this originating temporary difference in 1999 is the current tax rate times $1,800. However, if the expectation is that receipt will be through future sale of the investment, then the temporary difference is $9,000 and the deferred tax credit is the current capital gains rate times the $9,000.

The entries below illustrate these alternatives. A tax rate of 34% is used for both ordinary income and for capital gains. Note that the amounts in the entries below relate only to Investee Company's incremental impact upon Parent Company's tax accounts.

	Expectations for undistributed income			
	Dividends		*Capital gains*	
Income tax expense	1,020		3,468	
Deferred tax liability		612[b]		3,060[c]
Income taxes payable		408[a]		408[a]

[a]Computation of income taxes payable:

Dividend income--30% x ($20,000)	$6,000
Less 80% dividends received deduction	(4,800)
Amount included in Parent's taxable income	$1,200
Tax liability--34% x ($1,200)	$ 408

[b]Computation of deferred tax liability (dividend assumption):

Originating temporary difference:	
Parent's share of undistributed income--30% x ($30,000)	$9,000
Less 80% dividends received deduction	(7,200)
Originating temporary difference	$1,800
Deferred tax liability--34% x ($1,800)	$ 612

[c]Computation of deferred tax liability (capital gain assumption):

Originating temporary difference: Parent's share of undistributed income--30% x ($30,000)	$9,000
Deferred tax liability--34% x ($9,000)	$3,060

Although APB 24 has been superseded by SFAS 109, the accounting procedures prescribed therein are continued essentially unchanged. The one difference, of course, is that under SFAS 109 the tax effect of this (and all other) temporary difference is measured by the tax impact of the future reversal of the difference, and **not** by the "with and without" method of APB 11. The example above therefore assumes that future taxes will continue at current rates.

Income Tax Effects From Subsidiary Company

The pretax accounting income of Parent Company will also include equity in Subsidiary income of $70,000 (70% x $100,000). This $70,000 will be included in pretax consolidated income if Parent and Subsidiary issue consolidated financial statements. For tax purposes, Parent and Subsidiary cannot file a consolidated tax return because the minimum level of control (i.e., 80%) is not present. Consequently, the taxable income of Parent will include dividend income of $42,000 (70% x $60,000), and there will be an 80% dividends received deduction of $33,600. The originating temporary difference discussed in APB 23 results from Parent's equity ($28,000) in the Subsidiary's undistributed earnings of $40,000. The amount of the deferred tax credit in 1999 depends upon the expectations of Parent Company as to the manner in which this $28,000 of undistributed income will be received. The same expectations can exist as previously discussed, for Parent's equity in Investee's undistributed earnings (i.e., through future dividend distributions or capital gains). In addition, however, under APB 23 if Parent could have demonstrated that its share of Subsidiary Company's earnings would have been permanently reinvested by Subsidiary, then APB 23 stated that no timing difference exists and, therefore, no deferred tax credits arose. This treatment was not available for stock investments between 20% and 50%. Whereas SFAS 96 explicitly preserved the "indefinite reversal" criterion contained in APB 23, SFAS 109 rejects this and requires, on a **prospective** basis, that deferred taxes be provided in such circumstances.

The entries below illustrate these alternatives. A marginal tax rate of 34% is assumed. The amounts in the entries below relate only to Subsidiary Company's incremental impact upon Parent Company's tax accounts.

	Expectations for undistributed income			
	Dividends		*Capital gains*	
Income tax expense	4,760		12,376	
Deferred tax liability		1,904[b]		9,520[c]
Income taxes payable		2,856[a]		2,856[a]

[a]Computation of income taxes payable:

Dividend income--70% x ($60,000)	$42,000
Less 80% dividends received deduction	(33,600)
Amount included in Parent's taxable income	$ 8,400
Tax liability--34% x ($8,400)	$ 2,856

[b]Computation of deferred tax liability (dividend assumption):

Originating temporary difference:	
Parent's share of undistributed income-- 70% x ($40,000)	$28,000
Less 80% dividends received deduction	(22,400)
Originating temporary difference	$ 5,600
Deferred tax liability--34% x ($5,600)	$ 1,904

[c]Computation of deferred tax liability (capital gain assumption):

Originating temporary difference: Parent's share of undistributed income--70% x ($40,000)	$28,000
Deferred tax liability--34% x ($28,000)	$ 9,520

If a parent company owns 80% or more of the voting stock of a subsidiary and the parent consolidates the subsidiary for both financial and tax reports, then no temporary differences exist between pretax consolidated income and taxable income. If, in the circumstances noted above, consolidated financial statements are prepared but a consolidated tax return is not, then it should be noted that a dividends received deduction of 100% is allowed. Accordingly, the temporary difference between pretax consolidated income and taxable income is zero if the parent assumes the undistributed income will be realized in dividends.

Summary of Temporary Differences of Investees and Subsidiaries

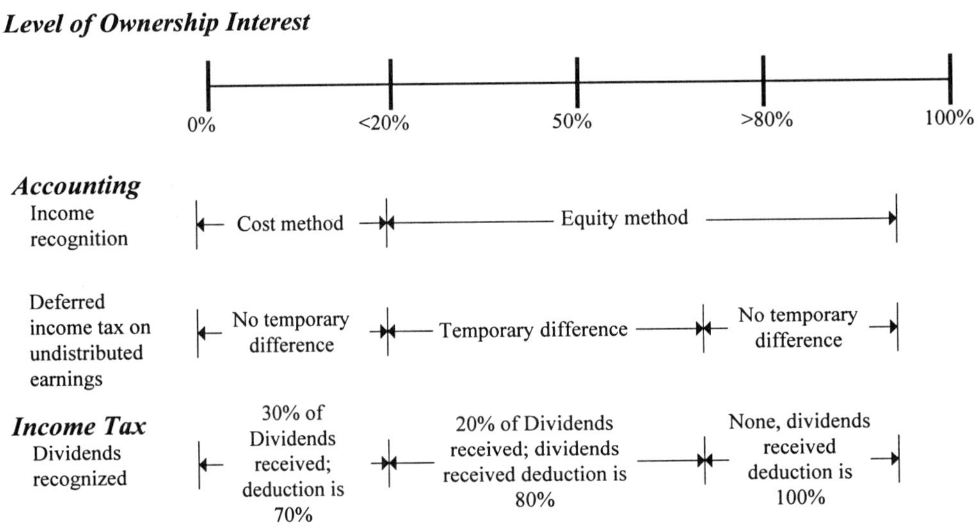

Accounting for Income Taxes: Intraperiod Tax Allocation

While SFAS 109 is predominantly concerned with the requirements of **inter**period income tax allocation (deferred tax accounting), it also addresses the questions of **intra**period tax allocation. Intraperiod tax allocation relates to the matching in the income (or other financial) statement of various categories of comprehensive income or expense (continuing operations, extraordinary items, corrections of errors, etc.) with the tax effects of those items. The general principle is that tax effects should follow the items to which they relate; in this regard, SFAS 109 follows the logical precedents of APB 11 and SFAS 96. A "with and without" series of computations is applied under each of these standards, in order to identify the marginal, or incremental, effects of items other than those arising from continuing operations. However, there are some significant differences in the most recent approach, as described in the following paragraphs.

Under APB 11, the "with and without" technique was applied in a step-by-step fashion proceeding down the face of the income statement. For example, an entity having continuing operations, discontinued operations, and extraordinary items would calculate tax expense as follows: (1) Tax would be computed for the aggregate results and for continuing operations. The difference between the two amounts would be allocated to the total of discontinued operations and extraordinary items. (2) Tax expense would be computed on discontinued operations. The residual amount (i.e., the difference between tax on the discontinued operations and the tax on the total of discontinued operations and extraordinary items) would then be allocated to extraordinary items. Thus, under the provisions of APB 11, the amount of tax expense allocated to any given classification in the statement of income (and the other financial statements, if relevant) was partially a function of the location in which the item was traditionally presented in the income and retained earnings statements.

SFAS 96 also utilized an incremental calculation of tax expense to be allocated to classifications other than continuing operations; however, rather than applying successive allocations on the "with and without" basis to determine tax provisions applicable to succeeding income and retained earnings statement captions, the tax effects of all items **other** than continuing operations were allocated pro rata. That is, once the tax provision allocable to continuing operations was determined, the residual tax expense or benefit was apportioned to all the other classifications (discontinued operations, et al.) in the ratios that those other items, on a pretax basis, bore to the total of all such items.

SFAS 109 adopts an approach essentially similar to that described above. Total income tax expense or benefit for the period is allocated among continuing operations, discontinued operations, extraordinary items, and stockholders' equity. However, as defined in SFAS 109, tax provisions on income from continuing operations include not only taxes on the income earned from continuing operations, as expected, but also the following items:

1. The impact of changes in tax laws and rates, which includes the effects of such changes on items which were previously reflected directly in stockholders' equity, as described more fully below
2. The impact of changes in tax status
3. Changes in estimates about whether the tax benefits of deductible temporary differences or net operating loss or credit carryforwards are more likely than not to be realizable (i.e., an adjustment to the valuation allowance account for such items)
4. The tax effects of tax-deductible dividends paid to stockholders, as discussed elsewhere in this chapter

Under SFAS 109, stockholders' equity is charged or credited with the initial tax effects of items which are reported directly in stockholders' equity. These items include the following:

1. Corrections of the effects of accounting errors of previous periods
2. Gains and losses which are defined under GAAP as being part of comprehensive income but which are not reported in the income statement, such as translation adjustments under SFAS 52, and the fair value adjustments applicable to available-for-sale portfolios of debt and marketable equity securities held as investments
3. Taxable or deductible increases or decreases in contributed capital, such as offering costs reported under GAAP as reductions of the proceeds of a capital stock offering, but which are either immediately deductible or amortizable for tax purposes
4. Increases in the tax bases of assets acquired in a taxable business combination accounted for as a pooling of interests under GAAP, if a tax benefit is recognized at the date of the business combination (i.e., if the tax effects of existing deductible temporary differences are not fully offset by a valuation account at that date)
5. Expenses incurred in connection with stock issued under provisions of compensatory option plans, which are recognized for tax purposes but which are reported for accounting purposes in stockholders' equity, under the provisions of APB 25
6. Dividends paid on unallocated shares held in an ESOP, and which are charged against retained earnings
7. Deductible temporary differences and operating loss and credit carryforwards which existed at the date of a quasi reorganization

The effects of tax rate or other tax law changes on items for which the tax effects were originally reported directly in stockholders' equity are reported in continuing operations, if they occur in any period after the original event. For example, assume the reporting entity recognized a tax benefit related to an employee stock option program amounting to $34,000 in 1999, based on the estimated future tax deduction it would receive at the then current and anticipated future tax rate of 34%.

If the statutory tax rate is lowered to 25% in 2001 before the temporary difference reverses, the adjustment to the deferred tax asset account ($34,000 – $25,000 = $9,000) will be reported in the tax provision applicable to income from continuing operations in 2001.

A comprehensive example of the intraperiod tax allocation process prescribed under SFAS 109 is presented below. Assume there was $50,000 in deductible temporary differences at 12/31/99; these remain unchanged during the current year, 2000.

Income from continuing operations	$400,000
Loss from discontinued operations	(120,000)
Extraordinary gain on involuntary conversion	60,000
Correction of error: understatement of depreciation in 1999	(20,000)
Tax credits	5,000

Tax rates are: 15% on first $100,000 of taxable income; 20% on next $100,000; 25% on next $100,000; 30% thereafter.

Expected future tax rates were 20% at December 31, 1999, but are judged to be 28% at December 31, 2000.

Retained earnings at December 31, 1999, totalled $650,000.

Intraperiod tax allocation proceeds as follows:

Step 1 -- Tax on total taxable income of $320,000 ($400,000 – $120,000 + $60,000 – $20,000) is **$61,000** ($66,000 based on rate structure, less tax credit of $5,000).

Step 2 -- Tax on income from continuing operations of $400,000 is **$85,000**, net of tax credit.

Step 3 -- The difference, $24,000, is allocated pro rata to discontinued operations, extraordinary gain, and correction of the error in prior year depreciation.

Step 4 -- The adjustment of the deferred tax asset, amounting to a $4,000 increase due to an effective tax rate estimate change [$50,000 x (.28 – .20)] is allocated to continuing operations, regardless of the source of the temporary difference.

A summary combined income and retained earnings statement is presented below.

Income from continuing operations, before income taxes		$400,000
Income taxes on income from continuing operations:		
Current	$90,000	
Deferred	(4,000)	
Tax credits	(5,000)	81,000
Income from continuing operations, net		319,000
Loss from discontinued operations, net of tax benefit of $36,000		(84,000)
Extraordinary gain, net of tax of $18,000		42,000
Net income		277,000
Retained earnings, January 1, 2000		650,000
Correction of accounting error, net of tax effects of $6,000		(14,000)
Retained earnings, December 31, 2000		$913,000

Classification of Deferred Taxes

An enterprise that presents a classified balance sheet will classify its deferred tax liabilities and assets as either current or noncurrent consistent with the classification of the related asset or liability. A deferred tax asset or liability that is not related to an asset or liability for financial reporting purposes, such as the deferred tax consequences related to an operating loss or tax credit carryforward, is classified based on the expected reversal or utilization date. These classifications must be made for each separate tax-paying component within each taxing jurisdiction. This approach is identical to that employed under APB 11 (as amended by SFAS 37), but differs from that under SFAS 96. The latter standard required that all deferred tax assets and liabilities be classified according to expected reversal or utilization date. Since SFAS 109 has dispensed with the detailed scheduling requirement or its predecessor, however, such a classification strategy would have been unworkable. Accordingly, the formerly employed approach has been reinstated.

Within each of the separate components, the current asset and liability are offset and presented as a single amount, with similar treatment for the noncurrent items. Understandably, offsetting is not permitted for different tax-paying components or for different tax jurisdictions. Thus, a balance sheet may present current and noncurrent deferred tax assets, along with current and noncurrent deferred tax liabilities, under certain circumstances.

If the enterprise has a valuation allowance, it must prorate the allowance between current and noncurrent according to the relative size of the gross deferred tax asset in each classification. The FASB mandated this approach to avoid the necessity of having to determine exactly which deferred tax assets would not be recovered.

Balance Sheet Disclosures

A reporting entity is required to disclose the components of the net deferred tax liability or asset recognized in the statement of financial position as follows:

1. Total of all deferred tax liabilities
2. Total of all deferred tax assets
3. Total valuation allowance
4. Net change in the valuation allowance for the year
5. Types of temporary differences and carryforwards that cause significant portions of deferred tax assets and liabilities. Disclosure of the approximate total tax effect (not the separate tax effect for each tax jurisdiction) of each of these is required only for publicly held companies.

When deferred tax liabilities are not recognized because of the exceptions provided under APB 23 the following information is to be provided:

1. The types of temporary differences and the events that would cause those temporary differences to become taxable

2. The cumulative amount of each type
3. The amount of unrecognized deferred tax liability for any undistributed foreign earnings, or a statement that such a determination is not practicable
4. The amount of unrecognized deferred tax liability for other temporary differences that arose prior to the period for which application of this statement is first required for each of those particular differences

Income Statement Disclosures

SFAS 109 places primary emphasis upon the income tax expense or benefit allocated to continuing operations. The following information must be disclosed about amounts allocated to continuing operations for each year for which an income statement is presented:

1. Current tax expense or benefit
2. Deferred tax expense or benefit (exclusive of the effects of other components listed below)
3. Investment tax credits
4. Government grants (to the extent recognized as a reduction of income tax expense)
5. The benefits of operating loss carryforwards
6. Tax expense that results either from allocating certain tax benefits directly to contributed capital or from allocating them to reduce goodwill or other noncurrent intangible assets of an acquired entity
7. Adjustments to the deferred tax liability or asset for enacted changes in tax laws or rates or a change in the tax status of the enterprise
8. Adjustments to the beginning of year balance of the valuation allowance because of a change in circumstances that causes a change in judgment about the realizability of the related deferred tax asset in future years

SFAS 109 also requires disclosure of the following:

1. The amounts of income tax expense or benefit allocated to financial statement elements other than continuing operations (e.g., discontinued operations, extraordinary items, and retained earnings)
2. The amounts and expiration dates of operating loss and tax credit carryforwards for tax purposes
3. The amount of the valuation allowance for which subsequently recognized tax benefits will reduce goodwill or other noncurrent intangible assets of an acquired entity, or will be allocated to the equity accounts
4. A reconciliation using percentages or dollar amounts of income tax expense or benefit attributable to continuing operations with the amount that would have resulted from applying regular federal statutory tax rates to pretax income from continuing operations is required for publicly held companies only. Other entities must, however, disclose the nature of significant reconciling items.

EMERGING ISSUES TASK FORCE CONSENSUS SUMMARIES

NOTE: Many other consensuses are deemed to have been made obsolete by the adoption of SFAS 109, and accordingly have been deleted from this listing.

86-9 IRC 338 and Push-Down Accounting

The EITF addressed a number of issues concerning whether the use of a step up in the tax basis of an acquired entity, as permitted by the 1982 tax law, mandated the use of push-down accounting; also the necessary allocation of the tax provision between parent and subsidiaries if a step up was not elected. There was a consensus that push-down is not required for non-SEC registrants. In addition, a consensus was reached that three different methods of tax allocation were acceptable: allocation to acquiree on preacquisition basis; crediting the tax benefit of tax basis step up to acquirer's capital surplus upon realization; and crediting the benefit to income of acquirer.

86-43 Effect of a Change in Tax Law or Rates on Leveraged Leases

All components of a leveraged lease must be recalculated from the inception of the lease based upon revised cash flows, resulting from change in the tax law, etc. Differences from original computation are included in income in the year in which the tax law changes are enacted. Later, EITF 87-8 stipulated that assumptions regarding the effect of alternative minimum tax must be included in lease computations.

86-44 Effect of a Change in Tax Law on Investments in Safe Harbor Leases

Related to proposed FASB Statements issued in 1981 and 1982, which were never finalized, concerning accounting for tax leases. Guidance is still valid, however, since it stipulates how recomputations are made analogously to leveraged leases case.

88-4 Classification of Payment Made to IRS to Retain Fiscal Year

There was a consensus that a tax payment is an asset (deposit), which is adjusted annually, and will be ultimately realized when entity liquidates (or law changes), income declines to zero, or conversion to calendar year takes place.

93-12 Recognition and Measurement of the Tax Benefit of Excess Tax-Deductible Goodwill Resulting From a Retroactive Change in Tax Law

Companies have the option of retroactively applying the goodwill amortization provisions of the 1993 tax act to business combinations which occurred after July 25, 1991. The consensus was that the benefit related to tax-deductible goodwill in excess of goodwill for financial reporting purposes is to be included in income from continuing operations in the period of enactment, **if** the entity expects to elect to retroactively amortize goodwill for tax purposes. A current tax benefit relates to the effect of retroactive amortization deducted from the combination date to the enactment date; a deferred tax benefit is related to the tax-deductible goodwill (less retroactive amortization to the enactment date) in excess of the reported amount of goodwill as of the enactment date.

93-13 Effect of a Retroactive Change in Tax Rates That Is Included in Income From Continuing Operations

The tax effect of a retroactive change in rates on current and deferred tax assets and liabilities should be determined at the enactment date (August 10, 1993), using temporary differences and currently taxable income existing as of the date of enactment. The cumulative tax effect is to be included in income from continuing operations. Furthermore, the tax effect of items not included in income from continuing operations (e.g., from discontinued operations) that arose during the current fiscal year and prior to enactment should be measured based on the enacted rate at the time the transaction was recognized for financial reporting purposes; the tax effect of a retroactive change in rates on current or deferred tax assets or liabilities is included in income from continuing operations.

93-16 Application of FASB Statement 109 to Basis Differences Within Foreign Subsidiaries That Meet the Indefinite Reversal Criterion of APB Opinion 23

The Task Force concluded that the APB 23 indefinite reversal criterion applies only to so-called "outside basis differences," and not to "inside basis differences" arising in connection with ownership of foreign subsidiaries. Furthermore, if deferred taxes had not previously been provided for the "inside basis differences," under SFAS 109 entities would be required to provide them for differences arising after December 15, 1992, but could elect not to provide them for temporary differences arising earlier, if this had not been done when SFAS 109 was adopted.

93-17 Recognition of Deferred Tax Asset on Discontinued Operations

This consensus relates to the disposal of the stock of a subsidiary which is accounted for as a discontinued operation under APB 30. Notwithstanding the rule in APB 30 that gain recognition at the measurement date is limited to the amount of the loss expected to be realized from the disposal, if the reporting entity has excess tax basis in the subsidiary, the gain recognition limitations under the standard should be applied on a pretax basis, and the deferred tax asset on the "outside basis difference" should be recognized as provided under SFAS 109 at the measurement date. This would only apply, of course, if the deferred tax asset is deemed more likely than not to be realized.

94-10 Accounting for the Income Tax Effect of Transactions Between (and With) Stockholders That Have Tax Effects for the Company

Certain transactions among stockholders, but outside the company, can affect the status of deferred taxes. The most commonly encountered of these is the change in ownership of over 50% of the company's stock, which limits or obviates the ability to utilize tax loss carryforwards, and accordingly will necessitate a write-off of deferred tax benefits previously recognized under SFAS 109. Changes in deferred taxes caused by transactions among stockholders are to be included in current period income tax expense in the income statement, since these are analogous to changes in expectations resulting from other external events (e.g., changes in tax rates). However, the tax effects of changes in the tax bases of assets or liabilities caused by transactions among stockholders would be included in equity, not in the income statement, although subsequent period changes in the valuation account, if any, would be reflected in income.

95-10 Accounting for Tax Credits Related to Dividend Payments in Accordance With FASB Statement No. 109

The accounting for a tax credit in the separate financials of the entity paying the dividend should be as a reduction of tax expense.

95-20 Measurement in the Consolidated Financial Statements of a Parent of the Tax Effects Related to the Operations of a Foreign Subsidiary That Receives Tax Credits Related to Dividend Payments

In consolidated statements of a parent company, a future tax credit related to dividends to be paid and related deferred taxes should be recognized based on the distributed rate if the parent is not invoking the indefinite reversal criteria of APB 23. However, the undistributed rate should be used if the parent has not provided deferred taxes.

96-7 Accounting for Deferred Taxes on In-Process Research and Development Activities Acquired in a Purchase Business Combination

In-process R&D acquired in a purchase business combination should be written off before the measurement of deferred taxes. Thus, no deferred taxes are provided on differences in initial bases for tax and financial reporting.

APPENDIX A

ACCOUNTING FOR INCOME TAXES IN INTERIM PERIODS

Interim Reporting

SFAS 109 essentially left unchanged the principles applicable to accounting for income taxes in financial statements covering interim periods, the accounting for which was established by APB 28 and FASB Interpretation 18. As set forth in those standards, the appropriate perspective for interim period reporting is to view the interim period as an integral part of the year, rather than as a discrete period. This objective is usually achieved by projecting income for the full annual period, computing the tax thereon, and applying the "effective rate" to the interim period income or loss, with quarterly (or monthly) revisions to the expected annual results and the tax effects thereof, as necessary.

While the Board chose to not comprehensively address interim reporting when promulgating SFAS 109, there were certain clear contradictions between APB 28 and the principles of SFAS 109, which the Board did address. As discussed in more detail below, these issues were (1) recognizing the tax benefits of losses based on expected earnings of later interim or annual periods, (2) reporting the benefits of net operating loss carryforwards in interim periods, and (3) reporting the effects of tax law changes in interim periods. Other matters requiring interpretation, which were left to the user to address without official guidance, included the classification of deferred taxes on interim balance sheets and allocation of interim period tax provisions between current and deferred expense.

While SFAS 109 is silent on the point, it would appear that the "with and without" methodology set forth in APB 28 and FASB Interpretation 18 (based on the now superseded APB 11) is no longer appropriate. The annual computation of tax expense is based upon the current tax provision as indicated in the tax return, plus or minus the adjustment necessary to bring the deferred tax asset and liability accounts to the proper balances as of the balance sheet date, thus a "with and without" approach focusing on the income statement is incorrect. Instead, the computation of interim period tax expense should be consistent with the asset and liability method set forth in SFAS 109.

Below is a relatively simple example which illustrates the basic principles of the opinion.

Basic example of interim period accounting for income taxes

Hartig, Inc. estimates that pretax accounting income for the full fiscal year ending June 30, 1999, will be $400,000. The company expects amortization of goodwill for the year to be $30,000, the annual premium on an officer's life insurance policy is $12,000, and dividend income (from a less than 20% ownership interest) is expected to be $100,000. The company recognized income of $75,000 in the first quarter of the year. The deferred tax liability arises solely in connection with depreciation temporary differences; these differences totaled $150,000 at the beginning of the year and are projected to equal $280,000 at year end. The effective rate expected to apply to the reversal at both year beginning and year end is 34%. The change in the taxable temporary difference during the current interim period is $30,000.

Hartig must first calculate its estimated effective income tax rate for the year. This rate is computed using all of the tax planning alternatives available to the company (e.g., tax credits, foreign rates, capital gains rates, etc.).

Estimated pretax accounting income		$ 400,000
Permanent differences:		
Add: Nondeductible officers' life insurance premium	$ 12,000	
Nondeductible amortization of organization costs	30,000	42,000
		442,000
Less: Dividends received deduction ($100,000 x 70%)		(70,000)
Estimated "book" taxable income		372,000
Less: Change in taxable temporary difference		(130,000)
Estimated taxable income for the year		$ 242,000
Tax on estimated taxable income (see below)		$ 70,530
Effective tax rate for **current** tax provision [$70,530/(400,000 – 130,000)]		26.1%

Tax rate schedule				
At least	*Not more than*	*Rate*	*Taxable income*	*Tax*
$ --	$ 50,000	15%	$ 50,000	$ 7,500
50,000	75,000	25%	25,000	6,250
75,000	--	34%	167,000	56,780
				$70,530

The deferred tax provision for the interim period should be based on the actual change in the temporary difference (depreciation, in this example) during the interim period. In this case, the depreciation temporary difference grew by $30,000 during the period, and the expected tax rate which will apply to the reversal, in future years, is the marginal rate of 34%. Accordingly, the tax provision for the period is as follows:

"Ordinary" income for the interim period	$75,000
Less: Change in temporary difference	30,000
Net "ordinary" income	45,000
Applicable tax rate	26.1%
Current tax provision	$11,755
Tax effect of temporary difference ($30,000 x 34%)	10,200
Total provision	$21,955

Therefore, the entry necessary to record the income tax expense at the end of the first quarter is as follows:

Income tax expense	21,955	
Income taxes payable--current		11,755
Deferred tax liability		10,200

The financial statement presentation would remain the same as has been illustrated in prior examples.

In the second quarter, Hartig, Inc. revises its estimate of income for the full fiscal year. It now anticipates only $210,000 of book income, including only $75,000 of dividend income, because of dramatic changes in the national economy. Other permanent differences are still expected to total $42,000.

Estimated pretax accounting income		$210,000
Permanent differences:		
Add: Nondeductible officers' life insurance premium	$12,000	
Nondeductible amortization of organization costs	30,000	42,000
		252,000
Less: Dividends received deduction ($75,000 x 70%)		(52,500)
Estimated "book" taxable income		199,500
Less: Change in taxable temporary difference		(130,000)
Estimated taxable income for the year		$ 69,500
Tax on estimated taxable income (see below)		$ 12,375
Effective tax rate for **current** tax provision [$12,375/(210,000 – 130,000)]		15.5%

Tax rate schedule				
At least	*Not more than*	*Rate*	*Taxable income*	*Tax*
$ --	$ 50,000	15%	$ 50,000	$ 7,500
50,000	75,000	25%	19,500	4,875
				$12,375

The actual earnings for the second quarter were $22,000, and the change in the temporary difference was only $10,000. The tax provision for the second quarter is computed as follows:

"Ordinary" income for the half year	$97,000
Less: Change in temporary difference	40,000
Net "ordinary" income	57,000
Applicable tax rate	15.5%
Current tax provision	$ 8,835
Tax effect of temporary difference ($40,000 x 34%)	13,600
Total provision	$22,435

Under APB 28, and also under the general principle that changes in estimate are reported prospectively (as stipulated by APB 20), the results of prior quarters are not restated for changes in the estimated effective annual tax rate. Given the provision for current and deferred income taxes which was made in the first interim period, shown above, the following entry is required to record the income taxes as of the end of the second quarter:

Income tax expense	480	
Income taxes payable--current	2,920	
Deferred tax liability		3,400

The foregoing illustrates the basic problems encountered in applying the promulgated GAAP to interim reporting. In the following paragraphs, we will provide a discussion relative to some of the items requiring modifications to the approach described above.

Net Operating Losses in Interim Periods

FASB Interpretation 18 set forth the appropriate accounting when losses were incurred in interim periods or when loss carryforward benefits were realized during an interim reporting period. Given that NOL benefits realized are no longer treated as extraordinary items under SFAS 109, and given that tax benefits of operating losses are fully recognized in the period of loss, subject to the possible need for a valuation allowance, the prescriptions set forth by FASB Interpretation 18 have been revised. The changes affect (1) the calculation of the expected annual tax rate for purposes of interim period income tax provisions, and (2) the recognition of an asset for the tax effects of a loss carryforward.

Carryforward from prior years. Loss carryforward benefits from prior years first given recognition (i.e., by reduction or elimination of a previously provided valuation allowance) in interim periods are now included in the ordinary tax provision, rather than as extraordinary gains. Interpretation 18 provided that an expected annual effective tax rate on **ordinary** income was to be calculated at each interim reporting date, and that this rate be used to provide income taxes on **ordinary** income on a cumulative basis at each interim date. The tax effects of extraordinary items, discontinued operations, and other nonoperating categories were excluded from this computation; those tax effects were separately determined on a "with and without" basis as explained later in this Appendix. Since, under APB 11, NOL benefit realization was not part of operating income, it was excluded from the estimation of the annual effective tax rate.

SFAS 109 amends Interpretation 18 to require that recognition of a previously unrecognized tax benefit be included in the tax provision of the interim period when the reduction or elimination of the valuation allowance is the result of a reevaluation of the likelihood of future tax benefits being realized. An increase in the valuation account resulting from a revised judgment that the benefits are more likely than not going to be unrealizable would cause a "catch up" adjustment to be included in the current interim period's ordinary tax provision. In either situation, the effect is **not** prorated to future interim periods by means of the effective tax rate estimate.

To illustrate, consider the following example:

Dillard Corporation has a previously unrecognized $50,000 net operating loss carryforward; a flat 40% tax rate for current and future periods is assumed. Income for the full year (before NOL) is projected to be $80,000; in the first quarter a pretax loss of $10,000 will be reported.

Projected annual income	$ 80,000
x Tax rate	40%
Projected tax liability	$ 32,000

Accordingly, in the income statement for the first fiscal quarter, the pretax operating loss of $10,000 will give rise to a tax **benefit** of $10,000 x 40% = $4,000.

In addition, a tax benefit of $20,000 ($50,000 loss carryforward x 40%) is given recognition, and is included in the current interim period tax provision relating to continuing operations. Thus, total tax benefit for the first fiscal quarter will be $24,000 ($4,000 + $20,000).

If Dillard's second quarter results in a pretax operating income of $30,000, and the expectation for the full year remains unchanged (i.e., operating income of $80,000), the second quarter tax provision is $12,000 ($30,000 x 40%).

The tax provision for the fiscal first half-year will be a **benefit** of $12,000, as follows:

Cumulative pretax income through second quarter ($30,000 – $10,000)	$20,000
x Effective rate	40%
Tax provision before recognition of NOL carryforward benefit	$ 8,000
Benefit of NOL carryforward first recognized in first quarter	(20,000)
Total tax provision (benefit)	$(12,000)

The foregoing example assumes that during the first quarter Dillard's judgment changed as to the full realizability of the previously unrecognized benefit of the $50,000 loss carryforward. Were this **not** the case, however, the benefit would have been recognized only as actual tax liabilities were incurred (through current period earnings) in amounts to offset the NOL benefit.

To illustrate this latter situation, assume the same facts about earnings for the first two quarters, and assume now that Dillard's judgment about realizability of prior period NOL does **not** change. Tax provisions for the first quarter and first half are as follows:

	First quarter	*First half-year*
Pretax income (loss)	$(10,000)	$ 20,000
x Effective rate	40%	40%
Tax provision before recognition of NOL carryforward benefit	$(4,000)	$ 8,000
Benefit of NOL carryforward recognized	-0-	(8,000)
Tax provision (benefit)	$(4,000)	-0-

Notice that recognition of a tax benefit of $4,000 in the first quarter is based on the expectation of at least a breakeven full year's results. That is, the benefit of the first quarter's loss was deemed **more likely than not**. Otherwise, no tax benefit would have been reported in the first quarter.

Estimated loss for the year. When the full year is expected to be profitable, it will be irrelevant that one or more interim periods results in a loss, and the expected effective rate for the full year should be used to record interim period tax benefits, as illustrated above. However, when the full year is expected to produce a loss, the computation of the expected annual tax benefit rate must logically take into account the extent to which a net deferred tax asset (i.e., the asset less any related valuation allowance) will be recordable at year end. For the first set of examples, below, assume that the realization of tax benefits related to operating loss carryforwards are **not entirely** more likely than not. That is, the full benefits will be recognized but will be offset partially or completely by the provision of the valuation allowance.

For each of the following examples we will assume that the Lori Corporation is anticipating a loss of $150,000 for the fiscal year. A deferred tax liability of $30,000 is currently recorded on the company's books; all of the credits will reverse in the 15-year carryforward period. Assume future taxes will be at a 40% rate.

Example 1

Assume that the company can carry back the entire $150,000 to the preceding 3 years. The tax potentially refundable by the carryback would (remember this is only an estimate until year end) amount to $48,000 (an assumed amount). The effective rate is then 32% ($48,000/150,000).

	Ordinary income (loss)		*Tax (benefit) expense*		
Reporting period	*Reporting period*	*Year-to date*	*Year-to date*	*Less previously provided*	*Reporting period*
1st qtr.	$ (50,000)	$ (50,000)	$(16,000)	$ --	$ (16,000)
2nd qtr.	20,000	(30,000)	(9,600)	(16,000)	6,400
3rd qtr.	(70,000)	(100,000)	(32,000)	(9,600)	(22,400)
4th qtr.	(50,000)	(150,000)	(48,000)	(32,000)	(16,000)
Fiscal year	$(150,000)				$ (48,000)

Note that both the income tax expense (2nd quarter) and benefit are computed using the estimated annual effective rate. This rate is applied to the year-to-date numbers just as in the previous examples, with any adjustment being made and realized in the current reporting period. This treatment is appropriate because the accrual of tax benefits in the first, third and fourth quarters is consistent with the effective rate estimated at the beginning of the year; in contrast to those circumstances in which a change in estimate is made in a quarter relating to the realizability of tax benefits not previously provided (or benefits which had been partially or fully reserved against).

Example 2

In this case assume that Lori Corporation can carry back only $50,000 of the loss and that the remainder must be carried forward. Realization of income to offset the loss is not deemed to be more likely than not. The estimated carryback of $50,000 would generate a tax refund of $12,000 (again assumed). The company is assumed to be in the 40% tax bracket (a flat rate is used to simplify the example). Although the benefit of the operating loss carryforward is recognized, a valuation allowance must be provided to the extent that it is more likely than not that the benefit will not be realized. In this example, management has concluded that only one-fourth of the gross benefit will be realized in future years. Accordingly, a valuation allowance of $30,000 must be established, leaving a net of $10,000 as an estimated recordable tax benefit related to the carryforward of the projected loss. Considered in conjunction with the carryback of $12,000, the company will obtain a $22,000 tax benefit relating to the projected current year loss, for an effective tax benefit rate of 14.7%. The calculation of the estimated annual effective rate is as follows:

Expected net loss			$150,000
Tax benefit from carryback		$12,000	
Benefit of carryforward ($100,000 x 40%)	$40,000		
Valuation allowance	(30,000)	10,000	
Total recognized benefit			$22,000
Estimated annual effective rate ($22,000 ÷ $150,000)			14.7%

	Ordinary income (loss)		*Tax (benefit) expense*			
			Year-to-date		*Less*	
Reporting period	*Reporting period*	*Year-to-date*	*Computed*	*Limited to*	*previously provided*	*Reporting period*
1st qtr.	$ 10,000	$ 10,000	$ 1,470	$ --	$ --	$ 1,470
2nd qtr.	(80,000)	(70,000)	(11,733)	--	1,470	(10,263)
3rd qtr.	(100,000)	(170,000)	(14,667)	(22,000)	(10,263)	(4,404)
4th qtr.	20,000	(150,000)	(22,000)	--	(22,000)	--
Fiscal year	$(150,000)					$(22,000)

In the foregoing, the tax expense (benefit) is computed by multiplying the year-to-date income or loss by the estimated annual effective rate, and then subtracting the amount of tax liability or benefit already provided in prior interim periods. It makes no difference if the current period indicates an income or a loss, assuming of course that the full year estimated results are not being revised. However, if the cumulative loss for the interim periods to date exceeds the projected loss for the full year upon which the effective tax benefit rate had been based, then no further tax benefits can be recorded, as is illustrated above in the provision for the third quarter.

The foregoing examples cover most of the situations encountered in practice. The reader is referred to paragraphs 49-55 in Appendix C of FASB Interpretation 18 for additional examples.

Operating loss occurring during an interim period. An instance may occur in which the company expects net income for the year and incurs a net loss during one of the reporting periods. In this situation, the estimated annual effective rate, which was calculated based upon the expected net income figure, is applied to the year-to-date income or loss to arrive at a total year-to-date tax provision. The amount previously provided is subtracted from the year-to-date figure to arrive at the provision for the current reporting period. If the current period operations resulted in a loss, then the tax provision for the period will reflect a tax benefit.

Tax Provision Applicable to Significant Unusual or Infrequently Occurring Items, Discontinued Operations, or Extraordinary Items Occurring in Interim Periods

Unusual, infrequent, or extraordinary items. The financial statement presentation of these items and their related tax effects are prescribed by SFAS 109. Extraordinary items and discontinued operations are to be shown net of their related tax effects. Unusual or infrequently occurring items that are part of continuing operations and will be separately disclosed in the fiscal year financial statements shall be separately disclosed as a component of pretax income, and the tax or benefit should be included in the tax provision for continuing operations.

The interim treatment accorded these items does not differ from the fiscal year-end reporting required by GAAP. However, according to APB 28, these items **are not** to be included in the computation of the estimated annual tax rate. The opinion also requires that these items be recognized in the interim period in which they occur. Examples of the treatment promulgated by the opinion follow later in this section.

Recognition of the tax effects of a loss due to any of the aforementioned situations is permitted if the benefits are expected to be realized during the year or if they will be recognizable as a deferred tax asset at year end under the provisions of SFAS 109.

If a situation arises where realization is not more likely than not in the period of occurrence but becomes assured in a subsequent period in the same fiscal year, the previously unrecognized tax benefit should be reported in income from continuing operations until it reduces the tax provision to zero, with any excess reported in other categories of income (e.g., discontinued operations) which provided a means of realization for the tax benefit.

The following examples illustrate the treatment required for reporting unusual, infrequently occurring, and extraordinary items. Again, these items are **not** to be used in calculating the estimated annual tax rate. For income statement presentation, the tax provision relating to unusual or infrequently occurring items is to be included with the tax provision for ordinary income. Extraordinary items are shown net of their applicable tax provision.

The following data apply to the next two examples:

1. Dynamix Company expects fiscal year ending June 30, 1999, income to be $96,000 and net permanent differences to reduce taxable income by $25,500.
2. Dynamix Company also incurred a $30,000 extraordinary loss in the second quarter of the year.

Example 1

In this case, assume that the loss can be carried back to prior periods and, therefore, the realization of any tax benefit is assured. Based on the information given earlier, the estimated annual effective tax rate can be calculated as follows:

Expected pretax accounting income	$96,000
Anticipated permanent differences	(25,500)
Expected taxable income	$70,500

Tax Calculation "Excluding" Extraordinary Item

$50,000	x	.15	=	$ 7,500
20,500	x	.25	=	5,125
$70,500				$12,625

Effective annual rate = 13.15% ($12,625 ÷ 96,000)

No adjustment in the estimated annual effective rate is required when the extraordinary, unusual, or infrequent item occurs. The tax (benefit) applicable to the item is computed using the estimated fiscal year ordinary income and an analysis of the incremental impact of the extraordinary item. The method illustrated below is applicable when the company anticipates operating income for the year. When a loss is anticipated but realization of benefits of loss carryforwards is **not** more likely than not, the company computes its estimated annual effective rate based on the amount of tax to be refunded from prior years. The tax (benefit) applicable to the extraordinary, unusual, or infrequent item is then the decrease (increase) in the refund to be received.

Computation of the tax applicable to the extraordinary, unusual, or infrequent item is as follows:

Estimated pretax accounting income	$96,000
Permanent differences	(25,500)
Extraordinary item	(30,000)
Expected taxable income	$40,500

Tax Calculation "Including" Extraordinary Item

$40,500 x .15 = $6,075

Tax "excluding" extraordinary item	$12,625
Tax "including" extraordinary item	6,075
Tax benefit applicable to extraordinary, unusual, or infrequent item	$ 6,550

			Tax (benefit) applicable to				
			Ordinary income (loss)		*Unusual, infrequent, or extraordinary item*		
Reporting period	*Ordinary income (loss)*	*Unusual, infrequent, or extraordinary item*	*Reporting period*	*Year-to-date*	*Year-to-date*	*Previously provided*	*Reporting period*
1st qtr.	$10,000	$ --	$ 1,315	$ 1,315	$ --	$ --	$ --
2nd qtr.	(20,000)	(30,000)	(2,630)	(1,315)	(6,550)	--	(6,550)
3rd qtr.	40,000	--	5,260	3,945	(6,550)	(6,550)	--
4th qtr.	66,000	--	8,680	12,625	(6,550)	(6,550)	--
Fiscal year	$96,000	$(30,000)	$12,625				$ (6,550)

Example 2

Again, assume that Dynamix Company estimates net income of $96,000 for the year with permanent differences of $25,500 which reduce taxable income. The extraordinary loss of $30,000 cannot be carried back and the ability to carry it forward is not **more likely than not**. Because no deferred tax credits exist, the only way that the loss can be deemed to be realizable is to the extent that current year ordinary income offsets the effect of the loss. As a result, realization of the loss is assured only as, and to the extent that, there is ordinary income for the year.

			Tax (benefit) applicable to				
			Ordinary income (loss)		Unusual, infrequent, or extraordinary item		
Reporting period	*Ordinary income (loss)*	*Unusual, infrequent, or extraordinary item*	*Reporting period*	*Year-to-date*	*Year-to-date*	*Previously provided*	*Reporting period*
1st qtr.	$ 5,000	$ --	$ 658	$ 658	$ --	$ --	$ --
2nd qtr.	20,000	(30,000)	2,630	3,288	(3,288)[a]	--	(3,288)
3rd qtr.	(10,000)	--	(1,315)	1,973	(1,973)[a]	(3,288)	1,315
4th qtr.	81,000	--	10,652	12,625	(6,550)[a]	(1,973)	(4,577)
Fiscal year	$96,000	$(30,000)	$12,625				$(6,550)

[a] *The recognition of the tax benefit to be realized relative to the unusual, infrequent, or extraordinary item is limited to the lesser of the total tax benefit applicable to the item or the amount available to be realized. Because realization is based upon the amount of tax applicable to ordinary income during the period, the year-to-date figures for the tax benefit fluctuate as the year-to-date tax expense relative to ordinary income fluctuates. Note that at no point does the amount of the tax benefit exceed what was calculated above as being applicable to the unusual, infrequent, or extraordinary item.*

Discontinued operations in interim periods. Discontinued operations, according to APB 28, are included as significant, unusual, or extraordinary items. Therefore, the computations described for unusual, infrequent, or extraordinary items will also apply to the income (loss) from the discontinued segment, including any provisions for operating gains (losses) subsequent to the measurement date.

If the decision to dispose of operations occurs in any interim period other than the first interim period, the operating income (loss) applicable to the discontinued segment has already been used in computing the estimated annual effective tax rate. Therefore, a recomputation of the **total tax** is not required. However, the total tax is to be divided into two components.

1. That tax applicable to ordinary income (loss)
2. That tax applicable to the income (loss) from the discontinued segment

This division is accomplished as follows: a revised estimated annual effective rate is calculated for the income (loss) from ordinary operations. This recomputation is then applied to the ordinary income (loss) from the preceding periods. The total tax applicable to the discontinued segment is then composed of two items.

1. The difference between the total tax originally computed and the tax recomputed on remaining ordinary income
2. The tax computed on unusual, infrequent, or extraordinary items as described above

Example

Realtime Corporation anticipates net income of $150,000 during the fiscal year. The net permanent differences for the year will be $10,000. The company also anticipates tax credits of $10,000 during the fiscal year. For purposes of this example, we will assume a flat statutory rate of 50%. The estimated annual effective rate is then calculated as follows:

Estimated pretax income	$150,000
Net permanent differences	(10,000)
Taxable income	140,000
Statutory rate	50%
Tax	70,000
Anticipated credits	(10,000)
Total estimated tax	$ 60,000
Estimated effective rate ($60,000 ÷ 150,000)	40%

The first two quarters of operations were as follows:

	Ordinary income (loss)		*Tax provision*		
Reporting period	*Reporting period*	*Year-to-date*	*Year-to-date*	*Less previously provided*	*Reporting period*
1st qtr.	$30,000	$30,000	$12,000	$ --	$12,000
2nd qtr.	25,000	55,000	22,000	12,000	10,000

In the third quarter, Realtime made the decision to dispose of Division X. During the third quarter, the company earned a total of $60,000. The company expects the disposal to result in a one-time charge to income of $50,000 and estimates that operating losses subsequent to the disposal will be $25,000. The company estimates revised ordinary income in the fourth quarter to be $35,000. The two components of pretax accounting income (discontinued operations and revised ordinary income) are shown below.

		Division X	
Reporting period	*Revised ordinary income*	*Loss from operations*	*Provision for loss on disposal*
1st qtr.	$ 40,000	$(10,000)	$ --
2nd qtr.	40,000	(15,000)	--
3rd qtr.	80,000	(20,000)	(75,000)
4th qtr.	35,000	--	--
Fiscal year	$195,000	$(45,000)	$(75,000)

Realtime must now recompute the estimated annual tax rate. Assume that all the permanent differences are related to the revised continuing operations. However, $3,300 of the tax credits were applicable to machinery used in Division X. Because of the discontinuance of operations, the credit on this machinery would not be allowed. Any recapture of prior period credits must be used as a reduction in the tax benefit from either operations or the loss on disposal. Assume that the company must recapture $2,000 of investment tax credit which is related to Division X.

The recomputed estimated annual rate for continuing operations is as follows:

Estimated (revised) ordinary income	$195,000
Less net permanent differences	(10,000)
	$185,000

Tax at statutory rate of 50%	$ 92,500
Less anticipated credits from continuing operations	(6,700)
Tax provision	$ 85,800
Estimated annual effective tax rate ($85,800 ÷ 195,000)	44%

The next step is to then apply the revised rate to the quarterly income from continuing operations as illustrated below.

	Ordinary income				*Tax provision*	
Reporting period	*Reporting period*	*Year-to-date*	*Estimated annual effective rate*	*Year-to-date*	*Less previously provided*	*Reporting period*
1st qtr.	$ 40,000	$ 40,000	44%	$17,600	$ --	$17,600
2nd qtr.	40,000	80,000	44%	35,200	17,600	17,600
3rd qtr.	80,000	160,000	44%	70,400	35,200	35,200
4th qtr.	35,000	195,000	44%	85,800	70,400	15,400
Fiscal year	$195,000					$85,800

The tax benefit applicable to the operating loss from discontinued operations and the loss from the disposal must now be calculated. The first two quarters are calculated on a differential basis as shown below.

	Tax applicable to ordinary income		
Reporting period	*Previously reported*	*Recomputed (above)*	*Tax (benefit) expense applicable to Division X*
1st qtr.	$12,000	$17,600	$ (5,600)
2nd qtr.	10,000	17,600	(7,600)
			$(13,200)

The only calculation remaining applies to the third quarter tax benefit pertaining to the operating loss and the loss on disposal of the discontinued segment. The calculation of this amount is made based on the revised estimate of annual ordinary income both including and excluding the effects of the Division X losses. This is shown below.

	Loss from operations of Division X	*Provision for loss on disposal*
Estimated annual income from continuing operations	$195,000	$195,000
Net permanent differences	(10,000)	(10,000)
Loss from Division X operations	(45,000)	--
Provision for loss on disposal of Division X	--	(75,000)
Total	$140,000	$110,000

Tax at the statutory rate of 50%	$ 70,000	$ 55,000
Anticipated credits (from continuing operations)	(6,700)	(6,700)
Recapture of previously recognized tax credits as a result of disposal	--	2,000
Taxes after effect of Division X losses	63,300	50,300
Taxes computed on estimated income before the effect of Division X losses	85,800	85,800
Tax benefit applicable to Division X	(22,500)	(35,500)
Amounts recognized in quarters one and two ($5,600 + $7,600)	(13,200)	--
Tax benefit to be recognized in the third quarter	$ (9,300)	$(35,500)

The quarterly tax provisions can be summarized as follows:

	Pretax income (loss)			*Tax (benefit) applicable to*		
Reporting period	*Continuing operations*	*Operations of Division X*	*Provision for loss on disposal*	*Continuing operations*	*Operations of Division X*	*Provision for loss on disposal*
1st qtr.	$ 40,000	$(10,000)	$ --	$17,600	$ (5,600)	$ --
2nd qtr.	40,000	(15,000)	--	17,600	(7,600)	--
3rd qtr.	80,000	(20,000)	(75,000)	35,200	(9,300)	(35,500)
4th qtr.	35,000	--	--	15,400	--	--
Fiscal year	$195,000	$(45,000)	$(75,000)	$85,800	$(22,500)	$(35,500)

The following income statement shows the proper financial statement presentation of these unusual and infrequent items. The notes to the statement indicate which items are to be included in the calculation of the annual estimated rate.

Income Statement
(FASB Interpretation 18, Appendix D)

* Net sales		$xxxx
* Other income		xxx
		xxxx
Costs and expenses		
* Cost of sales	$xxxx	
* Selling, general, and administrative expenses	xxx	
* Interest expense	xx	
* Other deductions	xx	
* Unusual items	xxx	
* Infrequently occurring items	xxx	xxxx
Income (loss) from continuing operations before income taxes and other items listed below		xxxx

* *Components of ordinary income (loss).*

+Provision for income taxes (benefit)		XXX
Income (loss) from continuing operations before items listed below		XXXX
Discontinued operations:		
Income (loss) from operations of discontinued Division X (less applicable income taxes of $xxxx)	XXXX	
Income (loss) on disposal of Division X, including provision of $xxxx for operating losses during phase-out period (less applicable taxes of $xxxx)	XXXX	XXXX
Income (loss) before extraordinary items and cumulative effect of a change in accounting principle		XXXX
Extraordinary items (less applicable income taxes of $xxxx)		XXXX
=Cumulative effect on prior years of a change in accounting principle (less applicable income taxes of $xxxx)		XXXX
Net income (loss)		$XXXX

+ *Consists of total income taxes (benefit) applicable to ordinary income (loss), unusual items and infrequent items.*
= *This amount is shown net of income taxes. Although the income taxes are generally disclosed (as illustrated), this is not required.*

APPENDIX B

SCHEDULE OF COMMON PERMANENT AND TEMPORARY DIFFERENCES

Permanent Differences

Dividends received deduction. Depending on ownership interest, a percentage of the dividends received by a corporation are nontaxable. Different rules apply to subsidiaries. See section in chapter.

Municipal interest income. 100% exclusion is permitted for investment in qualified municipal securities. Note that the capital gains applicable to these securities **are** taxable.

Officer's life insurance premiums. Premiums paid on an officer's life insurance policy on which the company is the beneficiary are not allowed as a taxable deduction, nor are any proceeds taxable.

Organization and start-up costs. Certain organization and start-up costs are not allowed amortization under the tax code. The most clearly defined are those expenditures relating to the cost of raising capital.

Fines and penalties. Any fine or penalty arising as a result of violation of the law is not allowed as a taxable deduction.

Percentage depletion. The excess of percentage depletion over cost depletion is allowable as a deduction for tax purposes.

The portion of wages or salaries used in computing the jobs credit is not allowed as a deduction for tax purposes.

Temporary Differences

Installment sale method. Use of the installment sale method for tax purposes generally results in a timing difference because that method is not used in accordance with GAAP.

Long-term construction contracts. A temporary difference will arise if different methods (e.g., completed-contract or percentage-of-completion) are used for book and tax purposes.

Depreciation. A temporary difference will occur unless the modified ACRS method is used for financial reporting.

Goodwill. The amortization of goodwill may be over a period greater than or less than the 15-year period mandated by the 1993 tax act.

Estimated costs (e.g., warranty expense). Estimates or provisions of this nature are not included in the determination of taxable income until the period in which they actually occur.

Accounting for investments. Use of the equity method for financial reporting while using the cost method for tax purposes.

Prepaid income (e.g., prepaid rent). Prepaid income of this nature is includable in taxable income in the period in which it is received, while for financial purposes, it is considered a liability until the revenue is earned.

Net capital loss. The loss is recognized currently for financial reporting purposes but is carried forward to be offset against future capital gains for tax purposes.

Accrued contingent liabilities. These cannot be deducted for tax purposes until the liability becomes fixed and determinable.

Excess charitable contributions. These can be carried over to future years for tax purposes.

Mandatory change from cash to accrual. Generally one-fourth of this adjustment is recognized for tax purposes each year.

Uniform cost capitalization adjustment to beginning inventories. This also is recognized over a 4-year period, with exceptions, for tax purposes.

Cash basis versus accrual basis. Use of the cash method of accounting for tax purposes and the accrual method for financial reporting is a temporary difference.

Deferred compensation. The present value of deferred compensation agreements must be accrued over the employee's remaining employment period, but cannot be deducted for tax purposes until actually paid.

16 ACCOUNTING FOR PENSIONS

PERSPECTIVE AND ISSUES

SFAS 87 and SFAS 88 are the sources of GAAP in the pension area. Single-employer defined benefit plans are the most affected. However, multiemployer plans and defined contribution plans are also affected by some provisions.

SFAS 87 specifies the accrual basis of accounting for pension costs. This standard is considered evolutionary and transitional in nature. However, it continues three primary characteristics of APB 8.

1. Delayed recognition (changes are not recognized immediately but are subsequently recognized in a gradual and systematic way)
2. Reporting net cost (aggregates of various items are reported as one net amount)
3. Offsetting assets and liabilities (assets and liabilities are sometimes shown net)

Estimates and averages may be used as long as material differences do not result. Explicit assumptions and estimates of future events must be used for each specified variable included in pension costs.

SFAS 87 focuses directly on the terms of the plan to assist in the recognition of compensation cost over the service period of the employees. It results in earlier recognition of significant liabilities and it recognizes a minimum liability in the case of plans that are underfunded by a material amount.

The principal emphasis of SFAS 87 is the present value of the pension obligation, the fair value of plan assets, and the disclosure of the makeup of net pension costs and of the projected benefit obligation. The main accounting problems revolve around the amount to be expensed on the income statement and the amount to be accrued on the balance sheet.

SFAS 88 is closely related to SFAS 87. It establishes standards to be followed by employers of defined benefit pension plans when obligations are settled, plans are curtailed, or benefits are terminated. Some previously unrecognized amounts are required to be immediately recognized by this standard.

Although there are some major differences in terminology and measurement, other postemployment benefits (OPEB) accounting basically follows the fundamental framework established for pension accounting and applies to all forms of postretirement benefits. However, in most cases, the material aspect will be the focus on postretirement health care benefits. SFAS 106 considers OPEB to be a form of deferred compensation and requires accrual accounting. The terms of the individual contract will govern the accrual of the employee's obligation for deferred compensation and the cost should be attributed over the employee service periods until full eligibility is attained. The employer's obligation for OPEB should be fully accrued when the employee attains full eligibility for all expected benefits.

SFAS 132, entitled *Employers' Disclosures About Pensions and Other Postretirement Benefits*, was issued in February 1998. It revises and standardizes these disclosures by using a separate but parallel format, eliminating less useful information, requiring some additional data deemed useful by analysts, and allowing some aggregation of presentation. Recognition and measurement aspects are not addressed. It amends only the disclosure requirements for SFAS 87, 88, and 106. The effective date is December 15, 1997, and earlier application is encouraged. Restatement for comparative purposes is required, unless the information is not readily available.

Sources of GAAP

APB	SFAS	EITF
12, 16, 30	5, 87, 88, 106, 112, 130, 132	88-1, 88-5, 90-3, 91-7, 92-13, 93-3

DEFINITIONS OF TERMS

Accrued pension cost. Cumulative net pension cost accrued in excess of the employer's contributions.

Accumulated benefit obligation. Actuarial present value of benefits (whether vested or nonvested) attributed by the pension benefit formula to employee service rendered before a specified date and based on employee service and compensation (if applicable) prior to that date. The accumulated benefit obligation differs from the projected benefit obligation in that it includes no assumption about future compensation levels. For plans with flat-benefit or no-pay-related pension benefit formulas, the accumulated benefit obligation and the projected benefit obligation are the same.

Accumulated postretirement benefit obligation. The actuarial present value of benefits attributed to employee service rendered to a particular date. Prior to an employee's full eligibility date, the accumulated postretirement benefit obligation as of a particular date for an employee is the portion of the expected postretirement benefit obligation attributed to that employee's service rendered to that date. On and after the full eligibility date, the accumulated and expected postretirement benefit obligations for an employee are the same.

Actual return on plan assets component (of net periodic pension cost). Difference between fair value of plan assets at the end of the period and the fair value at the beginning of the period, adjusted for contributions and payments of benefits during the period.

Actuarial present value. Value, as of a specified date, of an amount or series of amounts payable or receivable thereafter, with each amount adjusted to reflect (1) the time value of money (through discounts for interest) and (2) the probability of payment (by means of decrements for events such as death, disability, withdrawal, or retirement) between the specified date and the expected date of payment.

Amortization. Usually refers to the process of reducing a recognized liability systematically by recognizing revenues or reducing a recognized asset systematically by recognizing expenses or costs. In pension accounting, amortization is also used to refer to the systematic recognition in net pension cost over several periods of previously **unrecognized** amounts, including unrecognized prior service cost and unrecognized net gain or loss.

Annuity contract. Irrevocable contract in which an insurance company* unconditionally undertakes a legal obligation to provide specified benefits to specific individuals in return for a fixed consideration or premium. It involves the transfer of significant risk from the employer to the insurance company. Participating annuity contracts provide that the purchaser (either the plan or the employer) may participate in the experience of the insurance company. The insurance company ordinarily pays dividends to the purchaser. If the substance of a participating annuity contract is such that the employer remains subject to all or most of the risks and rewards associated with the benefit obligation covered or the assets transferred to the insurance company, the purchase of the contract does not constitute a settlement.

Assumptions. Estimates of the occurrence of future events affecting pension costs, such as mortality, withdrawal, disablement and retirement, changes in compensation and national pension benefits, and discount rates to reflect the time value of money.

Attribution. Process of assigning pension benefits or cost to periods of employee service.

---

* *If the insurance company is controlled by the employer or there is any reasonable doubt that the insurance company will meet its obligation under the contract, the purchase of the contract does not constitute a settlement for purposes of this chapter.*

Attribution period. The period of an employee's service to which the expected postretirement benefit obligation for that employee is assigned. The beginning of the attribution period is the employee's date of hire unless the plan's benefit formula grants credit only for service from a later date, in which case the beginning of the attribution period is generally the beginning of that credited service period. The end of the attribution period is the full eligibility date. Within the attribution period, an equal amount of the expected postretirement benefit obligation is attributed to each year of service unless the plan's benefit formula attributes a disproportionate share of the expected postretirement benefit obligation to employees' early years of service. In that case, benefits are attributed in accordance with the plan's benefit formula.

Career-average-pay formula. Benefit formula that bases benefits on the employee's compensation over the entire period of service with the employer. A career-average-pay plan is a plan with such a formula.

Contributory plan. Pension plan under which employees contribute part of the cost. In some contributory plans, employees wishing to be covered must contribute. In other contributory plans, employee contributions result in increased benefits.

Curtailment. Event that significantly reduces the expected years of future service of present employees or eliminates for a significant number of employees the accrual of defined benefits for some or all of their future services. Curtailments include (1) termination of employee's services earlier than expected, which may or may not involve closing a facility or discontinuing a segment of a business and (2) termination or suspension of a plan so that employees do not earn additional defined benefits for future services. In the latter situation, future service may be counted toward vesting of benefits accumulated based on past services.

Defined benefit pension plan. Pension plan that defines an amount of pension benefit to be provided, usually as a function of one or more factors such as age, years of service, or compensation. Any pension plan that is not a defined contribution pension plan is, for purposes of SFAS 87, a defined benefit pension plan.

Defined contribution pension plan. Plan that provides pension benefits in return for services rendered, provides an individual account for each participant, and specifies how contributions to the individual's account are to be determined instead of specifying the amount of benefits the individual is to receive. Under a defined contribution pension plan, the benefits a participant will receive depend solely on the amount contributed to the participant's account, the returns earned on investments of those contributions, and forfeitures of other participants' benefits that may be allocated to such participant's account.

Expected long-term rate of return on plan assets. Assumption as to the rate of return on plan assets reflecting the average rate of earnings expected on the funds invested or to be invested to provide for the benefits included in the projected benefit obligation.

Expected postretirement benefit obligation. The actuarial present value as of a particular date of the benefits expected to be paid to or for an employee, the employee's beneficiaries, and any covered dependents pursuant to the terms of the postretirement benefit plan.

Expected return on plan assets. Amount calculated as a basis for determining the extent of delayed recognition of the effects of changes in the fair value of assets. The expected return on plan assets is determined based on the expected long-term rate of return on plan assets and the market-related value of plan assets.

Explicit approach to assumptions. Approach under which each significant assumption used reflects the best estimate of the plan's future experience solely with respect to that assumption.

Fair value. Amount that a pension plan could reasonably expect to receive for an investment in a current sale between a willing buyer and a willing seller (i.e., in other than a forced or liquidation sale).

Final-pay formula. Benefit formula that bases benefits on the employee's compensation over a specified number of years near the end of the employee's service period or on the employee's highest compensation periods. For example, a plan might provide annual pension benefits equal to 1% of the employee's average salary for the last 5 years (or the highest consecutive 5 years) for each year of service. A final-pay plan is a plan with such a formula.

Flat-benefit formula. Benefit formula that bases benefits on a fixed amount per year of service, such as $20 of monthly retirement income for each year of credited service. A flat-benefit plan is a plan with such a formula.

Full eligibility (for benefits). The status of an employee having reached the employee's full eligibility date. Full eligibility for benefits is achieved by meeting specified age, service, or age and service requirements of the postretirement benefit plan.

Full eligibility date. The date at which an employee has rendered all of the service necessary to have earned the right to receive all of the benefits expected to be received by that employee (including any beneficiaries and dependents expected to receive benefits). Determination of the full eligibility date is affected by plan terms that provide incremental benefits expected to be received by or on behalf of an employee for additional years of service, unless those incremental benefits are trivial. Determination of the full eligibility date is **not** affected by plan terms that define when benefit payments commence or by an employee's current dependency status.

Fund. Used as a verb, to pay over to a funding agency (as to fund future pension benefits or to fund pension cost). Used as a noun, assets accumulated in the hands of a funding agency for the purpose of meeting pension benefits when they become due.

Funding policy. Program regarding the amounts and timing of contributions by the employer(s), participants, and any other sources (for example, state subsidies or federal grants) to provide the benefits a pension plan specifies.

Gain or loss. Change in the value of either the projected benefit obligation or the plan assets resulting from experience different from that assumed or from a change in an actuarial assumption. See also **Unrecognized net gain or loss**.

Gain or loss component (of net periodic pension cost). Sum of (1) the difference between the actual return on plan assets and the expected return on plan assets and (2) the amortization of the unrecognized net gain or loss from previous periods. The gain or loss component is the net effect of delayed recognition of gains and losses (the net change in the unrecognized net gain or loss) except that it does not include changes in the projected benefit obligation occurring during the period and deferred for later recognition.

Interest cost component (of net periodic pension cost). Increase in the projected benefit obligation due to passage of time.

Market-related value of plan assets. Balance used to calculate the expected return on plan assets. Market-related value can be either fair market value or a calculated value that recognizes changes in fair value in a systematic and rational manner over not more than 5 years. Different ways of calculating market-related value may be used for different classes of assets, but the manner of determining market-related value shall be applied consistently from year to year for each asset class.

Measurement date. Date as of which plan assets and obligations are measured.

Mortality rate. Proportion of the number of deaths in a specified group to the number living at the beginning of the period in which the deaths occur. Actuaries use mortality tables, which show death rates for each age, in estimating the amount of pension benefits that will become payable.

Net periodic pension cost. Amount recognized in an employer's financial statements as the cost of a pension plan for a period. Components of net periodic pension cost are service cost, interest cost, actual return on plan assets, gain or loss, amortization of unrecognized prior service cost, and amortization of the unrecognized net obligation or asset existing at the date of initial application of SFAS 87. The term **net periodic pension cost** is used instead of **net pension expense** because part of the cost recognized in a period may be capitalized as part of an asset such as inventory.

Plan amendment. Change in terms of an existing plan or the initiation of a new plan. A plan amendment may increase benefits, including those attributed to years of service already rendered. See also **Retroactive benefits**.

Postretirement benefits. All forms of benefits, other than retirement income, provided by an employer to retirees. Those benefits may be defined in terms of specified benefits, such as health care, tuition assistance, or legal services, that are provided to retirees as the need for those benefits arises or they may be defined in terms of monetary amounts that become payable on the occurrence of a specified event, such as life insurance benefits.

Prepaid pension cost. Cumulative employer contributions in excess of accrued net pension cost.

Prior service cost. Cost of retroactive benefits granted in a plan amendment. See also **Unrecognized prior service cost**.

Projected benefit obligation. Actuarial present value as of a date of all benefits attributed by the pension benefit formula to employee service rendered prior to that date. The projected benefit obligation is measured using assumptions as to future compensation levels if the pension benefit formula is based on those future compensation levels (pay-related, final-pay, final-average-pay, or career-average-pay plans).

Retroactive benefits. Benefits granted in a plan amendment (or initiation) that are attributed by the pension benefit formula to employee services rendered in periods prior to the amendment. The cost of the retroactive benefits is referred to as prior service cost.

Service. Employment taken into consideration under a pension plan. Years of employment before the inception of a plan constitute an employee's past service. Years thereafter are classified in relation to the particular actuarial valuation being made or discussed. Years of employment (including past service) prior to the date of a particular valuation constitute prior service.

Service cost component (of net periodic pension cost). Actuarial present value of benefits attributed by the pension benefit formula to services rendered by employees during the period. The service cost component is a portion of the projected benefit obligation and is unaffected by the funded status of the plan.

Settlement. Transaction that (1) is an irrevocable action, (2) relieves the employer (or the plan) of primary responsibility for a pension benefit obligation, and (3) eliminates significant risks related to the obligation and the assets used to effect the settlement. Examples include making lump-sum cash payments to plan participants in exchange for their rights to receive specified pension benefits and purchasing nonparticipating annuity contracts to cover vested benefits. A transaction must meet all of the above three criteria to constitute a settlement.

Substantive plan. The terms of the postretirement benefit plan as understood by an employer that provides postretirement benefits and the employees who render services in exchange for those benefits. The substantive plan is the basis for the accounting for that exchange transaction. In some situations an employer's cost-sharing policy, as evidenced by past practice or by communication of intended changes to a plan's cost-sharing provisions, or a past practice of regular increases in certain monetary benefits may indicate that the substantive plan differs from the extant written plan.

Transition obligation. The unrecognized amount, as of the date SFAS 106 is initially applied, of (1) the accumulated postretirement benefit obligation in excess of (2) the fair value of plan assets plus any recognized accrued postretirement benefit cost or less any recognized prepaid postretirement benefit cost.

Unfunded accumulated benefit obligation. Excess of the accumulated benefit obligation over plan assets.

Unfunded accumulated postretirement benefit obligation. The accumulated postretirement benefit obligation in excess of the fair value of plan assets.

Unrecognized net gain or loss. Cumulative net gain (loss) that has not been recognized as a part of net periodic pension cost. See **Gain or loss**.

Unrecognized prior service cost. Portion of prior service cost that has not been recognized as a part of net periodic pension cost.

CONCEPTS, RULES, AND EXAMPLES

The principal objective of SFAS 87 is to measure the compensation cost associated with employees' benefits and to recognize that cost over the employees' service period. This statement is concerned only with the accounting aspects of pension costs. The **funding** (amount paid) of the benefits is not covered and is considered to be a financial management matter.

When an entity provides benefits that can be estimated in advance to its retired employees and their beneficiaries, the arrangement is a pension plan. The typical plan is written and the amount of benefits can be determined by reference to the associated documents. The plan and its provisions can also be implied, however, from unwritten but established past practices. The accounting for most types of retirement plans is covered by SFAS 87 and 88. These plans include unfunded, insured, trust fund, **defined contribution** and **defined benefit plans**, and deferred compensation contracts, if equivalent. Independent deferred profit sharing plans and pension payments to selected employees on a case-by-case basis are not considered pension plans. SFAS 87 and SFAS 88 do not apply if a plan provides **only** life or health insurance benefits or both. Additionally, these statements do not **require** application to postemployment health care benefits. However, if the statements are not applied to postemployment health care benefits, related assets and obligations are excluded from consideration also.

The establishment of a pension plan represents a commitment to employees that is of a long-term nature. Although some corporations manage their own plans, this commitment usually takes the form of contributions to an independent trustee. These contributions are used by the trustee to obtain plan assets of various kinds (treasury bonds, treasury bills, certificates of deposit, annuities, marketable securities, corporate bonds, etc.). The plan assets are used to generate a return which generally is earned interest and/or appreciation in asset value. The return on the plan assets (and occasionally their liquidation) provides the trustee with cash to pay the benefits to which the employees are entitled. These benefits, in turn, are defined by the plan's benefit formula. The benefit formula incorporates many factors including employee compensation, employee service longevity, employee age, etc. and is considered to provide the best indication of pension obligations and costs. It is used as the basis for determining the pension cost recognized each fiscal year.

Net Periodic Pension Cost

It is assumed that a company will continue to provide retirement benefits well into the future. The accounting for the plan's costs should be reflected in the financial statements and these amounts should not be discretionary. All pension costs should be charged against income. No amounts should be charged directly to retained earnings.

The benefits earned and costs recognized over the employees' service period must be attributed by the pension plan's benefit formula. Net periodic pension cost consists of the sum of the following six components:

1. Service cost
2. Interest cost on projected benefit obligation
3. Actual return on plan assets
4. Gain or loss
5. Amortization of unrecognized prior service cost
6. Amortization of unrecognized net assets or net obligation existing at date of initial application of SFAS 87

Elements of pension plans that affect the determination of the above components of pension cost and amounts to be shown on the balance sheet are the **accumulated benefit obligation**, the **projected benefit obligation**, and plan assets. Both obligations are the **actuarial present value** of benefits attributed by the formula to service prior to a given date. The **accumulated** benefit obligation does **not** include an assumption about future compensation levels, whereas the **projected** benefit obligation does include such an assumption. Pay-related, **final-pay**, or **career-average-pay** plans are examples of plans based on future compensation levels. These plans measure benefits based on **service** to date but include **assumptions** as to compensation increases, turnover, etc. In non-pay-related or **flat-benefit plans**, both obligations are the same.

Example

	Start of year
Accumulated benefit obligation	$(1,500)
Progression of salary and wages	(400)
Projected benefit obligation	$(1,900)

> The expected progression of salary and wages is added to the accumulated benefit obligation to arrive at the projected benefit obligation. These amounts are provided by the actuary in a pension plan report.

Plan assets include contributions and asset earnings less benefits paid. They must be segregated and effectively restricted for pension benefits.

The amount of **vested** benefit obligation must be disclosed but it does not directly figure into any of the net periodic pension cost calculations.

Service costs. This component of net periodic pension cost is the actuarial present value of benefits attributed during the current period. Under SFAS 87, the plan's benefit formula is the key to attributing benefits to employee service periods. In most cases, this **attribution** is straightforward.

If the benefit formula is not straightforward, the accounting for pension service costs must be based on **substantive commitment**. In some cases, this means that if an employer has committed to make future **amendments** to provide benefits greater than those written in the plan, that commitment shall be the basis for the accounting. The relevant facts regarding that commitment shall be disclosed.

In other cases, a disproportionate share of benefits may be attributed to later years in order to delay vesting. In this situation, instead of the benefit formula, proportions or ratios need to be used to accumulate the total projected benefit in a manner that more equitably reflects the substance of the earning of the employee benefits. If the benefit formula does not specify a relationship between services and benefits, the following applies:

1. **Includable** in vested benefits (e.g., supplemental early retirement benefit)

$$\text{Benefit accumulation} = \frac{\text{Number of completed years of service}}{\text{Number of years when benefit first fully vests}}$$

2. **Not includable** in vested benefits (e.g., death or disability benefit)

$$\text{Benefit accumulation} = \frac{\text{Number of completed years of service}}{\text{Total projected years of service}}$$

SFAS 87 actuarial assumptions must reflect plan continuation, must be consistent as to future economic expectations, and must be the best estimate in regard to each individual assumption. It is not acceptable to determine that the aggregate assumptions are reasonable.

The discount rate used in the calculation of service costs should be the rate at which benefits could be settled. Examples include those rates in current **annuity contracts**, those published by Pension Benefit Guaranty Corporation (PBGC), and those that reflect returns on high quality, fixed income investments.

Future compensation will be considered in the calculation of the service cost component to the extent specified by the benefit formula. To the degree considered, future compensation would include changes due to advancement, longevity, inflation, etc. Indirect effects and automatic increases specified by the plan also need to be considered. The effect of **retroactive amendments** are included in the calculation when the employer has contractually agreed to them.

Example

	Start of year	*Service cost*
Accumulated benefit obligation	$(1,500)	$ (90)
Progression of salary and wages	(400)	(24)
Projected benefit obligation	$(1,900)	$(114) (a)*

**Component of net periodic pension cost*

The current period service cost component is found in the actuarial report.

Interest cost on projected benefit obligation. This component results from multiplying the assumed settlement discount rate times the projected benefit obligation as of the start of the year. The settlement rate should be determined by an annual review and represents the time value of money. The projected benefit obligation represents the discounted present value of employee benefits earned. The result is an accumulation of interest that increases the net periodic pension cost and the projected benefit obligation.

Example

	Start of year	*Service cost*	*Interest cost*
Accumulated benefit obligation	$(1,500)	$ (90)	$(120)
Progression of salary and wages	(400)	(24)	(32)
Projected benefit obligation	$(1,900)	$(114) (a)	$(152) (b)*

**Component of net periodic pension cost*

The **interest cost component** is calculated by multiplying the start of the year obligation balances by an assumed 8% settlement rate. This amount is found in the actuarial report.

Benefits paid to retirees are deducted from the above to arrive at the end of the year balance sheet figures for the accumulated benefit obligation and the projected benefit obligation.

Example

	Start of year	*Service cost*	*Interest cost*	*Benefits paid*	*End of year*
Accumulated benefit obligation	$(1,500)	$ (90)	$(120)	$160	$(1,550)
Progression of salary and wages	(400)	(24)	(32)	—	(456)
Projected benefit obligation	$(1,900)	$(114) (a)	$(152) (b)	$160	$(2,006)

Benefits of $160 were paid to retirees during the current year. This amount is found in the report of the pension plan trustee.

Actual return on plan assets. This component is the difference between the **fair value** of plan assets at the end of the period and the fair value of the plan assets at the beginning of the period adjusted for contributions and payments during the period. Another way to express the result is that it is total (realized and unrealized) appreciation and depreciation of plan assets plus earnings from the plan assets.

Example

	Start of year	*Actual return on plan assets*	*Funding*	*Benefits paid*	*End of year*
Plan assets	$1,400	$158 (c)*	$145	$(160)	$1,543

**Component of net periodic pension cost*

The actual return on plan assets of $158, cash deposited with the trustee of $145, and benefits paid ($160) are amounts found in the report of the pension plan trustee. These items increase the plan assets to $1,543 at the end of the year. The actual return on plan assets is adjusted, however, to the expected long-term rate (9% assumed) of return on plan assets ($1,400 x 9% = $126). The difference, $32, is a return on asset adjustment and is deferred as a gain (loss). The return on asset adjustment is a component of net periodic pension cost and is discussed in the following section.

Gain or loss. Gains (losses) result from (1) changes in plan assumptions, (2) changes in the amount of plan assets, and (3) changes in the amount of the projected benefit obligation. Immediate recognition of these gains (losses) is not acceptable. Also, SFAS 87 does not require that they be matched through recognition in net pension cost in the period of occurrence. Instead, **unrecognized net gain (loss)** is **amortized** if it meets certain criteria specified below.

Since actuarial cost methods are based on numerous assumptions (employee compensation, mortality, turnover, earnings of the pension plan, etc.), it is not unusual for one or more of these assumptions to be invalidated by changes over time. Adjustments will probably be necessary in order to bring prior estimates back in line with actual events. These adjustments are known as actuarial gains (losses). The accounting problem with the recognition of the actuarial adjustments is their timing. All pension costs must be charged to income. Thus, actuarial gains (losses) are not considered prior period adjustments but are considered changes in an estimate that should be recognized in current and future periods.

Plan asset gains (losses) result from both realized and unrealized amounts. They represent periodic differences between the actual return on assets and the expected return. The expected return is generated by multiplying the **expected long-term rate of return** and the **market-related value** of plan assets. This value is called market-related as opposed to fair value since it may be a calculated value. The purpose of allowing a calculated value was to enable the averaging or spreading of changes in fair value over not more than 5 years through a rational, systematic, and consistently applied method. Consistently applied means from year to year for each asset class (i.e., bonds, equities) since different classes of assets may have their market-related value calculated in a different manner (i.e., fair value in one case, moving average in another case). Thus, the market-related value may be fair value, but it also may be other than fair value if all or a portion results from calculation.

Plan asset gains (losses) include both (1) changes in the market-related value of assets (regardless of definition) from one period to another **and** (2) any changes that are not yet reflected in market-related value (i.e., the difference between the actual fair values of assets and the calculated market-related values). Only the former changes are recognized and amortized. The latter changes will be recognized over time through the calculated market-related values. Differences in the experienced amount of projected benefit obligation from that assumed will also result in gain (loss).

Since gains (losses) from one period may offset gains (losses) from another period, adjustments should not be recognized in a single accounting period. If they were recognized all at once, the result could be either unusually large increases or decreases (or even elimination of) net pension costs during the period. The long-term nature of pension costs must be considered, and these gains (losses) are to be accumulated as an unrecognized net gain (loss). If this unrecognized net gain (loss), however, exceeds a "corridor" of 10% of the greater of the beginning balances of the market-related value of plan assets or the projected benefit obligation, a minimum amortization is required. The **excess** over 10% should be divided by the average remaining service period of active employees and included as a component of net pension costs. Average remaining life expectancies of inactive employees may be used if that is a better measure.

Net pension costs will include only **expected return on plan assets**. While actual return is disclosed, any difference that results between actual and expected is deferred through the **gain (loss) component of net pension cost**. If actual returns are greater than expected returns, net pension costs are increased and an unrecognized gain results. If actual returns are less than expected returns, net pension costs are decreased and an unrecognized loss results. If the unrecognized net gain (loss) is large enough, it is amortized. Over the long-term, the expected return should be a fairly good indicator of performance, although in any given year an unusual or infrequent result may occur.

The expected long-term rate of return used to calculate the expected return on plan assets should be the average rate of return expected to provide for pension benefits. Present rates of return and expected future reinvestment rates of return should be considered in arriving at the rate to be used.

To summarize, the net periodic pension cost includes a gain (loss) component consisting of **both** of the following:

1. As a minimum, the portion of the unrecognized net gain (loss) from previous periods that exceeds the **greater** of 10% of the beginning balances of the market-related value of plan assets **or** the projected benefit obligation, usually amortized over the average remaining service period of active employees expected to receive benefits.
2. The difference between the expected return and the actual return on plan assets.

An accelerated method of amortization of unrecognized net gain (loss) is acceptable if it is applied consistently to both gains (losses) and if the method is disclosed. In all cases, at least the minimum amount discussed above must be amortized.

Example

	Start of year	*Return on asset adjustment*	*Amortization*	*End of year*
Unamortized actuarial gain (loss)	$(210)	$32 (d)*	$2(d)*	$(176)

**Components of net periodic pension cost*

The return on asset adjustment of $32 is the difference between the actual return of $158 and the expected return of $126 on plan assets. The actuarial loss at the start of the year ($210 assumed) is amortized if it **exceeds** a "corridor" of the larger of 10% of the projected benefit obligation ($1,900) or 10% of the fair value of plan assets ($1,400). In this example, $20 ($210 – $190) is amortized by dividing the years of average remaining service (12 years assumed), with a result rounded to $2. The straight-line method was used, and it was assumed that market-related value was fair value.

Amortization of unrecognized prior service cost. Prior service costs result from plan amendments and are accounted for as a change in estimate. These costs are measured at the amendment date by the increase in the projected benefit obligation. The service period of every active employee expected to receive benefits is to be determined, and then an equal amount of prior service cost should be assigned to each period. Consistent use of an accelerated amortization method is acceptable and must be disclosed if used.

If most of the plan's participants are inactive, remaining life expectancy should be used as a basis for amortization instead of remaining service life. If economic benefits will be realized over a shorter period than remaining service life, amortization of costs should be accelerated to recognize the costs in the periods benefited. If an amendment **reduces** the projected benefit obligation, unrecognized prior service costs should be reduced to the extent that they exist and any excess should be amortized as indicated above for benefit increases.

Example

	Start of year	*Amortization*	*End of year*
Unamortized prior service cost	$320	$(27) (e)*	$293

**Component of net periodic pension cost*

Unamortized prior service cost ($320) is amortized over the years of average remaining service (12 years assumed) at the amendment date with a result rounded to $27. The straight-line method was used. These amounts are found in the actuarial report.

Amortization of unrecognized amount at date of initial SFAS 87 application. Any difference between the projected benefit obligation and the fair value of plan assets minus recognized prepaid or plus accrued pension cost at the beginning of the fiscal year of the initial SFAS 87 application is to be amortized. The amortization is to be on a straight-line basis over the average remaining active employee service period. If the average remaining service period is less than 15 years, the employer may elect to use a 15-year period. If all or almost all of a plan's participants are inactive, the employer shall use the inactive participants' average remaining expectancy period.

Example

	Start of year	*Amortization*	*End of year*
Unamortized net obligation (asset) existing at SFAS 87 application	$(30)	$3 (f)*	$(27)

**Component of net periodic pension cost*

The unamortized net asset ($30) existing at SFAS 87 application is amortized over the average service remaining at date of application (12 years assumed) with a result rounded to $3. The straight-line method was used. These amounts are found in the actuarial report.

Summary of Net Periodic Pension Costs (required footnote disclosure)

The components that were identified in the above examples are summed to determine the one amount known as net periodic pension cost as follows:

Service cost	(a)	$114
Interest cost	(b)	152
Actual return on assets	(c)	(158)
Gain (loss)	(d)	34
Amortization of unrecognized prior service cost	(e)	27
Amortization of unrecognized net obligation (asset) existing at SFAS 87 application	(f)	(3)
Total net periodic pension cost		$166

One possible source of confusion is the return on plan assets ($158) and the unrecognized gain of $34 that total $124. The actual return on plan assets reduces pension cost. This reduction, however, is adjusted by increasing pension cost by the difference between actual and expected return of $32 and the amortization of the excess actuarial loss of $2 for a total of $34. The net result is to include the **expected** return of $126 ($158 – $32) less the amortization of the excess of $2 for a total of $124 ($158 – $34).

Employer's Liabilities and Assets

Any difference between the amount funded and the amount expensed should appear on the balance sheet as a prepaid pension cost or as a liability. An additional minimum liability is also required to be recognized under SFAS 87 when plans are materially underfunded. This minimum liability results when the accumulated benefit obligation exceeds the **fair value** (not the possible calculated market-related value used for determining plan asset gains or losses) of plan assets and a liability in the amount of the difference is not already recorded as unfunded accrued pension cost. The accumulated benefit obligation is based on history of service and compensation excluding future levels and indirect effects. Fair value is determined as of the financial statement date (or not more than 3 months prior to that date if used consistently), and in the amount that would result from negotiations between a willing buyer and seller not in a liquidation sale. Fair value is measured in preferred order by market price, selling price of similar investments, or discounted cash flows at a rate indicative of the risk involved.

In SFAS 87, the additional minimum liability is recognized by an offset to an intangible asset up to the amount of unrecognized prior service cost. Any additional debit needed is considered a loss and is shown net of tax benefits (subject to the restrictions on recognition of deferred tax assets per SFAS 109) as a separate component reducing equity.

Several points need to be remembered in regard to the additional minimum liability. First, an asset is **not** recorded if the fair value of the plan assets exceeds the accumulated benefit obligation. Second, the calculation of the minimum liability requires consideration of any already recorded prepaid or accrued pension cost. The net liability must be at least equal to the **unfunded accumulated benefit obligation** irrespective of the starting point. A **prepaid pension cost** will increase the amount of the recognized additional liability. An **accrued pension cost** will decrease it. Third, the intangible asset is **not** amortized. Fourth, at the time of the next calculation, the amounts are either added to or reversed out with no effect on the income statement. These balance sheet entries are entirely independent of the income statement and do not affect the calculation of net pension costs. Fifth, unless a significant event occurs or measures of obligations and assets as of a more current date become available, interim financials will show the year-end additional minimum liability adjusted for subsequent contributions and accruals. In this case, previous year-end assumptions regarding net pension cost would also carryover to the interim financials.

A schedule reconciling the balance sheet amounts with the funded status of the plan is shown below.

Required Footnote Disclosure

	Start	*End*
Change in benefit obligation		
Benefit obligation at beginning of year	$1,800	$1,900
Service cost	111	114
Interest cost	144	152
Amendment (prior service cost)	--	--
Actuarial loss (gain)	--	--
Benefits paid	(155)	(160)
Benefit obligation at end of year	$1,900	$2,006
Change in plan assets		
Fair value of plan assets at beginning of year	$1,265	$1,400
Actual return (loss) on plan assets	150	158
Employer contribution	140	145
Benefits paid	(155)	(160)
Fair value of plan assets at end of year	$1,400	$1,543
Funded status	$ (500)	$ (463)
Unrecognized loss on assets	210	176
Unrecognized prior service cost	320	293
Unamortized net obligation	(30)	(27)
Asset existing at SFAS 87 application (accrued)/prepaid pension cost	$ 0	$ (21)
Amounts recognized in the statement of financial position (balance sheet) consist of		
Accrued benefit liability	$ (100)	$ (21)
Intangible asset	100	0
Accumulated other comprehensive income	$ 0	$ 0
Net amount recognized	$ 0	$ (21)

The difference between the projected benefit obligation and the plan assets indicates that the plan in this example is underfunded by **$500** at the beginning of the year. Net actuarial losses, prior service costs, and the net asset existing when SFAS 87 was first applied are the remaining reconciling items to the zero amount shown on the balance sheet. **Conceptually**, the zero balance sheet amount is a journal entry netting of the following elements that would be recognized on the employer's books if accounting under SFAS 87 mirrored the pension plan's financial statements:

Investment	1,400	
Deferred actuarial loss	210	
Deferred prior service cost	320	
Deferred asset existing at SFAS 87 application		30
Projected benefit obligation		1,900

Only the additional minimum liability in the case of seriously underfunded plans will be required on the balance sheet. This amount is the difference between the accumulated benefit obligation ($1,500) and the plan assets ($1,400) plus prepaid pension cost ($0) or minus accrued pension cost ($0). In the above example, the result is $100 and the journal entry follows:

Intangible asset	100	
Pension liability		100

This journal entry is entirely independent of the calculation of pension cost and has no effect on that calculation. It only affects the balance sheet and remains until adjusted at the end of the next year. At that time, it will be decreased or increased to the extent required.

If the result of the minimum liability calculation exceeds the unamortized prior service cost, SFAS 130 requires the excess to be treated as other comprehensive income. For instance, assume that the required minimum liability in the above example is $350. In this case, the intangible asset would be recorded at the amount of the unamortized prior service cost and the **excess** would be recorded as other comprehensive income. The required journal entry would be

Other comprehensive income	30	
Intangible asset	320	
Pension liability		350

If not needed at the end of the next year, this entry would then be reversed.

Funding of $145, net periodic pension costs of $166, and benefit payments of $160 are used in order to arrive at the end of the year balance sheet amounts. An accrued pension cost of $21 ($166 – $145) is required. This difference results from funding $21 less than pension cost. **Conceptually**, this accrued amount is the netting of the following:

Investment	$1,543	
Deferred actuarial loss	176	
Deferred prior service cost	293	
Deferred assets existing at SFAS 87 application		$ 27
Projected benefit obligation		2,006
Totals	$2,012	$2,033

The excess credit is shown as an accrued pension liability of $21. Note that the additional minimum liability is no longer required since the accumulated benefit obligation ($1,550) and the plan assets ($1,543) differ by only $7 and there is already a pension liability on the balance sheet of $21. Thus, the additional minimum liability balances at the start of the year are reversed through the following journal entry:

Pension liability	100	
Intangible asset		100

This entry does not affect pension cost.

In summary, the only journal entries that are ordinarily required, if applicable, involve (1) the recording of net periodic pension cost and the associated accrued (or prepaid) pension cost, (2) the recording of the payment (funding) of the accrued (or prepaid) pension costs, and (3) the recording of any additional minimum liability and the associated intangible asset (and possible other comprehensive income entry). All of the other information used to determine these amounts are provided by the actuary or worksheet entries and do not appear on the books. Thus, accounts that reflect such things as the actuarial loss and prior service costs will usually not be found in the employer's ledger.

Other Pension Considerations

If an entity has more than one plan, SFAS 87 provisions should be separately applied to each plan. Offsets or eliminations are not allowed unless there clearly is the right to use the assets in one plan to pay the benefits of another plan.

If annuity contracts and other insurance contracts that are equivalent in substance are valid and irrevocable, if they transfer significant risks to an unrelated insurance company (not a captive insurer), and if there is no reasonable doubt as to their payment, they should be excluded from plan assets and their benefits should be excluded from the accumulated benefit obligation and from the projected benefit obligation. Most other contracts are not considered annuities for SFAS 87 purposes. If a plan's benefit formula specifies coverage by **nonparticipating** annuity contracts, the service component of net pension costs is the cost of those contracts. In the case of a **participating** annuity contract, the cost of the participation right is to be recognized as an asset and measured annually at its fair value. If fair value is unestimable, it should be systematically amortized and carried at amortized cost (not to exceed net realizable value). Benefits provided by the formula beyond those provided by annuities should be accounted for in the usual SFAS 87 manner. All other insurance contracts are considered investments and are usually measured at cash surrender value, conversion value, contract value, or some equivalent.

In the typical defined contribution plan, the contribution is derived from a formula, and that amount should be the expense for that year. Benefits are generally paid from the pool of accumulated contributions. If, however, the defined contribution plan has defined benefits, the provision is calculated in the usual manner.

Participation in a multiemployer plan (two or more unrelated employers contribute) requires that the contribution for the period be recognized as net pension cost and that any contributions due and unpaid be recognized as a liability. Assets in this type of plan are usually commingled and are not segregated or restricted. A Board of Trustees usually administers these plans, and multiemployer plans are generally subject to a collective-bargaining agreement. If there is a withdrawal from this type of plan and if an arising obligation is either probable or reasonably possible, SFAS 5 applies.

Some plans are, in substance, a pooling or aggregation of single employer plans and are ordinarily without collective-bargaining agreements. Contributions are usually based on a selected benefit formula. These plans are not considered multiemployer, and the accounting is based on the respective interest in the plan.

Non-US pension arrangements. The terms and conditions that define the amount of benefits and the nature of the obligation determine the substance of a non-US pension arrangement. If they are, in substance, similar to pension plans, SFAS 87 and 88 apply.

Business combinations. When an entity is purchased (APB 16) that sponsors a single employer defined benefit plan, the purchaser must assign part of the purchase price to an asset if plan assets exceed the projected benefit obligation or to a liability if the projected benefit obligation exceeds plan assets. The projected benefit obligation should include the effect of any expected plan curtailment or termination. This assignment eliminates any existing unrecognized components, and any future differences between contributions and net pension cost will affect the asset or liability recognized when the purchase took place.

Disclosures. See page 625.

SFAS 88

This statement is meant to be applied within the framework of SFAS 87. It describes the accounting to be followed by obligors when all or part of defined benefit pension plans have been settled or curtailed. It establishes employer accounting procedures in the case of benefits offered when employment is terminated.

Settlements include both the purchase of nonparticipating annuity contracts and lump-sum cash payments. The following three criteria must all be met in order to constitute a pension obligation settlement:

1. Must be irrevocable
2. Must relieve the obligor of primary responsibility
3. Must eliminate significant risks associated with elements used to effect it

A defeasance strategy does not constitute a settlement.

Under an annuity contract settlement, an unrelated insurance company unconditionally accepts an obligation to provide the required benefits. The following criteria must be met for this type of settlement:

1. Must be irrevocable

2. Must involve transfer of material risk to the insurance company

There can be no reasonable doubt as to the ability of the insurance company to meet its contractual obligation. The substance of any **participating** annuity contract must relieve the employer of most of the risks and rewards or it does not meet the criteria.

Curtailments include early discontinuance of employee services or cessation or suspension of a plan. Additional benefits may not be earned although future service time may be counted towards vesting. Curtailments must meet the following criteria:

1. Must materially diminish present employees' future service or
2. Must stop or materially diminish the accumulation of benefits by a significant number of employees

A curtailment and a settlement can occur separately or together.

Settlements. If the entire projected benefit obligation is settled, any SFAS 87 unrecognized net gain (loss) plus any remaining unrecognized net asset existing when SFAS 87 was initially applied is immediately recognized. A pro rata portion is used in the case of partial settlement. If the obligation is settled by purchasing **participating** annuities, the cost of the right of participation is deducted from the gain (but not from the loss) before recognition.

If the total of the interest cost and service cost components of the SFAS 87 periodic pension cost is greater than or equal to the settlement costs during a given year, the recognition of the above gain (loss) is not required, but is permitted. However, a consistent policy must be followed in this regard. The settlement cost is generally the cash paid or the cost of **nonparticipating** annuities purchased or the cost of **participating** annuities reduced by the cost of the right of participation.

Curtailments. A curtailment results in the elimination of future years of service. The pro rata portion of any (1) unrecognized cost of retroactive plan amendments and (2) remaining unrecognized net obligation existing when SFAS 87 was initially applied that is associated with the eliminated years of service is immediately recognized as a loss.

If curtailment results in a decrease in the projected benefit obligation, a gain is indicated. An increase in the projected benefit obligation (excluding termination benefits) indicates a loss. This indicated gain (loss) is then netted against the loss from unrecognized prior service cost recognized in accordance with the preceding paragraph. The net result is the **curtailment gain** or **curtailment loss**. This gain (loss) is accounted for as provided in SFAS 5. A gain is recognized upon actual employee termination or plan suspension. A loss is recognized when both the curtailment is probable and the effects are reasonably estimable.

After the curtailment gain (loss) is calculated, any remaining unrecognized net asset existing when SFAS 87 was initially applied is transferred from that category and combined with the gain (loss) arising after SFAS 87 application. It is subsequently treated as a component of the new gain (loss) category.

Termination benefits. Termination benefits are accounted for in accordance with SFAS 5. Special short time period benefits require that a loss and a liability be recognized when the offer is accepted and the amount can be reasonably estimated. Contractual termination benefits require that a loss and a liability be recognized when it is probable that employees will receive the benefits and the amount can be reasonably estimated. The cost of these benefits is the cash paid and the present value of future payments. Termination benefits and curtailments can occur together.

Segment disposal. Gains (losses), as calculated above, that result because of a disposal of a business segment should be recognized according to the provisions of APB 30.

Disclosures. See page 625.

Postretirement Benefits Other Than Pensions (OPEB)

SFAS 106 establishes the standard for employers' accounting for **other** (than pension) **postretirement employee benefits** (OPEB). This standard prescribes a single method for measuring and recognizing an employer's **accumulated postretirement benefit obligation** (APBO). It applies to all forms of postretirement benefits, although the most material benefit is usually postretirement health care. It uses the fundamental framework established by SFAS 87 and SFAS 88. To the extent that the promised benefits are similar, the accounting provisions are similar. Only when there is a compelling reason, is the accounting different.

SFAS 106 requires accrual accounting and adopts the three primary characteristics of pension accounting as follows:

1. Delayed recognition (changes are not recognized immediately but are subsequently recognized in a gradual and systematic way)
2. Reporting net cost (aggregates of various items are reported as one net amount)
3. Offsetting assets and liabilities (assets and liabilities are sometimes shown net)

SFAS 106 distinguishes between the **substantive** plan and the **written** plan. Although generally the same, the **substantive plan** (the one understood as evidenced by past practice or by communication of intended changes) is the basis for the accounting if it differs from the written plan.

SFAS 106 focuses on accounting for a single-employer plan that defines the postretirement benefits to be provided. A defined benefit postretirement plan defines benefits in terms of (1) monetary amounts or (2) benefit coverage to be provided. Postretirement benefits include tuition assistance, legal services, day-care, housing subsidies, health care (probably the most significant), and other benefits.

The amount of benefits usually depends on a benefit formula. OPEB may be provided to current employees, former employees, beneficiaries and covered dependents. This standard applies to **settlement** of the APBO and to **curtailment** of a plan as part of a **special termination** benefit offer. It also applies to deferred compensation contracts with individuals. Taken together, these contracts are **equivalent** to an OPEB plan. SFAS 106 does not apply to benefits provided through a pension plan. If part of a larger plan with active employees, the OPEB shall be segregated and accounted for in accordance with this standard. If not materially different, estimates, averages, and computational shortcuts may be used.

The basic tenet of SFAS 106 is that accrual accounting is better than cash basis accounting. Recognition and measurement of the obligation to provide OPEB is required in order to provide relevant information to financial statement users. Although funding and cash flow information is incorporated into the statement, the overall liability is the primary focus.

The standard attempts, in accordance with the terms of the substantive plan, to account for the exchange transaction that takes place between the employer, who is ultimately responsible for providing OPEB, and the employee who provides services, in part at least, to obtain those OPEB. SFAS 106 accounting requires that the liability for OPEB be fully accrued when the employee is **fully eligible** for all of the expected benefits. The fact that the employee may continue to work beyond this date is not relevant since the employee has already provided the services in order to earn the OPEB.

OPEB are considered to be deferred compensation earned in an exchange transaction during the time periods that the employee provides services. The expected cost generally should be attributed in equal amounts (unless the plan attributes a disproportionate share of benefits to early years) over the periods from the employee's hiring date (unless credit for the service is only granted from a later date) to the date that the employee attains full eligibility for all benefits expected to be received. This accrual should be followed even if the employee provides service beyond the **date of full eligibility**.

Accounting for Postretirement Benefits

The **expected postretirement benefit obligation** (EPBO) is the actuarial present value (APV) as of a specific date of the benefits expected to be paid to the employee, beneficiaries and covered dependents. This term is not used in SFAS 87. Measurement of the EPBO is based on the following:

1. Expected amount and timing of future benefits
2. Expected future costs
3. Extent of cost sharing (contributions, deductibles, coinsurance provisions, etc.) between employer, employee and others (i.e., government). The APV of employee contributions reduces the APV of the EPBO. Obligations to

return employee contributions, plus interest if applicable, should be recognized as a component of EPBO.

The EPBO includes an assumed salary progression for a pay-related plan. Future compensation levels should be the best estimate after considering the individual employees involved, general price levels, seniority, productivity, promotions, indirect effects, etc.

The APBO is the APV as of a specific date of all future benefits attributable to service by an employee to that date. It represents the portion of the EPBO earned to date. After full eligibility is attained, the APBO equals the EPBO.

The APBO also includes an assumed salary progression for a pay-related plan. Thus, this term is more comparable to the projected benefit obligation (PBO) under SFAS 87. The accumulated benefit obligation in SFAS 87 has no counterpart in SFAS 106.

Net periodic postretirement benefit costs include the following components:

1. Service cost--APV of benefits attributable to the current period (i.e., the portion of the EPBO earned this period)
2. Interest cost--Interest on the APBO
3. Actual return on plan assets
4. Gain or loss
5. Amortization of unrecognized prior service cost
6. Amortization of the transition asset or obligation

The **transition obligation**, under SFAS 106, is the unrecognized and **unfunded APBO** for all of the participants in the plan. This obligation can either (1) be recognized immediately as the effect of an accounting change, subject to certain limitations, or (2) be recognized on a delayed basis over future service periods with disclosure of the unrecognized amount. The delayed recognition has to result in, at least, as rapid a recognition as would have been recognized on a pay-as-you-go basis.

Service costs and interest costs are defined and measured in the same manner by SFAS 106 and SFAS 87. However, under SFAS 106, interest increases the APBO while under SFAS 87, interest increases the PBO.

Under SFAS 106, a single method is required to be followed in measuring and recognizing the net periodic cost and the liability involved. That method attributes the EPBO to employee service rendered to the full eligibility date.

Assumptions

SFAS 106 requires the use of explicit assumptions. Each should be the best estimate available of the plan's future experience, solely with regard to the individual assumption under consideration. Plan continuity can be presumed, unless there is evidence to the contrary. Principal actuarial assumptions include: discount rates, present value factors, retirement age, participation rates (**contributory plans**), salary progression (pay-related plans) and probability of payment (turnover, dependency status, mortality). Present value factors for health care OPEB include cost trend rates, medicare reimbursement rates and per capita claims cost by age.

Current interest rates, as of the **measurement date**, should be used for discount rates in present value calculations. Examples include high quality, fixed-income investments with similar amounts and timing and interest rates at which the postretirement benefit obligations could be settled. The EPBO, APBO, service cost and interest cost components use assumed discount rates.

The expected long-term rate of return on plan assets should be the average rate of earnings on contributions during the period and on qualifying existing plan assets. Current returns on plan assets and reinvestment returns should be given consideration in arriving at the rate to be used. Related income taxes, if applicable, should reduce the rate. Expected return on plan assets and the market-related value of plan assets use this rate in their calculation.

Example

A sample illustration of the basic accounting for OPEB as established by SFAS 106 follows. Firstime Accrual Co. plans to adopt accrual accounting for OPEB as of January 1, 1999. All employees were hired at age 30 and are fully eligible for benefits at age 60. There are no plan assets. This first calculation determines the unrecognized transition obligation (UTO).

Firstime Accrual
December 31, 1998

Employee	*Age*	*Years of service*	*Total years when fully eligible*	*Expected retirement age*	*Remaining service to retirement*	*EPBO*	*APBO*
A	35	5	30	60	25	$ 14,000	$ 2,333
B	40	10	30	60	20	22,000	7,333
C	45	15	30	60	15	30,000	15,000
D	50	20	30	60	10	38,000	25,333
E	55	25	30	65	10	46,000	38,333
F	60	30	30	65	5	54,000	54,000
G	65	RET	--		--	46,000	46,000
H	70	RET	--		--	38,000	38,000
					85	$288,000	$226,332

Explanations

1. EPBO (expected postretirement benefit obligation) is usually determined by an actuary, although it can be calculated if complete data is available.
2. APBO is calculated using the EPBO. Specifically, it is EPBO x (Years of service/Total years when fully eligible)
3. The unrecognized transition obligation (UTO) is the APBO at 12/31/98 since there are no plan assets to be deducted. The $226,332 can be amortized over the average

remaining service to retirement of 14.17 (85/6) years or an optional period of 20 years, if longer. Firstime Accrual selected the 20-year period of amortization.

4. Note that Employee F has attained full eligibility for benefits and yet plans to continue working.
5. Note that the above 1998 table is used in the calculation of the 1999 components of OPEB cost that follows.

After the establishment of the UTO, the next step is to determine the benefit cost for the year ended December 31, 1999. This calculation follows the framework established by SFAS 87. The discount rate is assumed to be 10%.

Firstime Accrual
OPEB Cost
December 31, 1999

1.	Service cost	$ 5,500
2.	Interest cost	22,633
3.	Actual return on plan assets	--
4.	Gain or loss	--
5.	Amortization of unrecognized prior service cost	--
6.	Amortization of UTO	11,317
	Total OPEB Cost	$39,450

Explanations

1. Service cost calculation uses only employees not yet fully eligible for benefits.

Employee	*12/31/98* *EPBO*	*Total years when* *fully eligible*	*Service cost*
A	$14,000	30	$ 467
B	22,000	30	733
C	30,000	30	1,000
D	38,000	30	1,267
E	46,000	30	1,533
			$5,000
	Interest for 1999 ($5,000 x 10%)		500
	Total service cost		$5,500

2. Interest cost is the 12/31/98 APBO of $226,332 x 10% = $22,633.
3. There are no plan assets so there is no return.
4. There is no gain (loss) since there are no changes yet.
5. There is no unrecognized prior service cost initially.
6. Amortization of UTO is the 12/31/98 UTO of $226,332/20-year optional election = $11,317.

After calculation of the 1999 benefit cost, the next step is to project the EPBO and APBO for December 31, 1999. Assuming no changes, it is based on the December 31, 1998 actuarial measurement and it is calculated as shown earlier in the determination of the UTO.

Firstime Accrual
December 31, 1999

Employee	*Age*	*Years of service*	*Total years when fully eligible*	*EPBO*	*APBO*
A	36	6	30	$ 15,400	$ 3,080
B	41	11	30	24,200	8,873
C	46	16	30	33,000	17,600
D	51	21	30	41,800	29,260
E	56	26	30	50,600	43,853
F	61	31	--	59,400	59,400
G	66	RET	--	44,620	44,620
H	71	RET	--	36,860	36,860
				$305,880	$243,546

Changes in experience or assumptions will result in gains (losses). The gain (loss) is measured by the difference resulting in the APBO or the plan assets from that projected. However, except for the effects of a decision to temporarily deviate from the substantive plan, these gains or losses have no impact in the year of occurrence. They are deferred and amortized as in SFAS 87. Amortization of unrecognized net gain (loss) is included as a component of net postretirement cost for a year if, as of the beginning of the year, it exceeds 10% of the **greater** of the APBO or the market-related value of plan assets. The minimum amortization is the **excess** divided by the remaining average service period of active plan participants. A systematic method of amortization that amortizes a greater amount, is applied consistently to both gains and losses and is disclosed may also be used. If gains (losses) are recognized immediately, special rules of offsetting may be required.

Disclosures

SFAS 132, entitled *Employers' Disclosures About Pensions and Other Postretirement Benefits*, was issued in February 1998. It revises and standardizes these disclosures by using a separate but parallel format, eliminating less useful information, requiring some additional data deemed useful by analysts, and allowing some aggregation of presentation. Recognition and measurement aspects are not addressed. It amends only the disclosure requirements for SFAS 87, 88, and 106. The effective date is December 15, 1997, and earlier application is encouraged. Restatement for comparative purposes is required, unless the information is not readily available.

SFAS 132 disclosures of pensions and other postretirement benefits (OPEB) show separate (pension and OPEB), but parallel.

1. Defined benefit plans

    a. Schedule reconciling beginning and ending balances of the benefit obligation, separately showing if applicable

        (1) Service cost

(2) Interest cost
(3) Contributions by plan participants
(4) Actuarial gains and losses
(5) Changes in foreign currency exchange rates
(6) Benefits paid
(7) Plan amendments
(8) Business combinations
(9) Divestitures
(10) Curtailments
(11) Settlements
(12) Special termination benefits

b. Schedule reconciling beginning and ending balances of the fair value of plan assets, separately showing if applicable

(1) Actual return
(2) Changes in foreign currency exchange rates
(3) Employer contributions
(4) Employee or retiree contributions
(5) Benefits paid
(6) Business combinations
(7) Divestitures
(8) Curtailments
(9) Settlements

c. Information on the funded status, amounts unrecognized in the balance sheet, and amounts recognized in the balance sheet including

(1) Unamortized prior service cost amount
(2) Unrecognized net gain (loss) amount (those not yet reflected in market-related value should also be included)
(3) Unamortized net obligation or net asset amount still remaining from that recorded at SFAS 87 and SFAS 106 date of initial application
(4) Accrued liabilities or prepaid assets, intangible asset and accumulated other comprehensive income (as a result of recording an additional minimum liability)

d. Net periodic benefit cost recognized, separately showing

(1) Service cost
(2) Interest cost
(3) Expected return on plan assets
(4) Amortization of unrecognized transition asset or obligation
(5) Recognized gains or losses
(6) Recognized prior service cost

(7) Recognized settlement or curtailment gain or loss

e. Amount in Other Comprehensive Income for the period due to a change in the additional minimum pension liability

f. Assumed weighted-average rates for

(1) Discount rate
(2) Expected long-term rate on plan assets
(2) Compensation rate increase (if applicable for pay-related plans)

g. Health care cost trend rate(s)

(1) Used to measure expected costs of benefits covered by the plan (gross eligible charges)
(2) Direction and pattern of change together with

(a) The ultimate trend rate(s)
(b) The time when that rate is expected to be achieved

h. The effect of both a 1% increase and a 1% decrease in the assumed health care cost trend rates on

(1) Service and interest cost components aggregated
(2) Health care APBO (based on the substantive plan and while holding all other assumptions constant)

i. Other, if applicable

(1) Employer and related parties

(a) Amounts and types of securities included in plan assets
(b) Approximate amount of annual benefits covered by annuity contracts issued by the above
(c) Any significant transactions with the plan

(2) Alternative amortization methods used
(3) Existence and nature of substantive commitments
(4) Termination benefits recognized

(a) Nature of event
(b) Cost

j. If not otherwise apparent, an explanation of matters of significance in regard to changes in

(1) Benefit obligation
(2) Plan assets

2. Two or more defined benefit plans (pension, postretirement, or both)

a. Should provide most useful information

(1) May be aggregated for pension and may be aggregated for postretirement plans

(a) If combined, plans where the accumulated benefit obligations are in excess of plan assets should show

1] Aggregate benefit obligation
2] Aggregate fair value of assets

(b) If combined, pension plans with APBO in excess of plan assets should show

1] Aggregate pension benefit obligation
2] Aggregate pension fair value of assets

(2) May be disaggregated in groups

b. Amounts recognized in the balance sheet separately

(1) Prepaid benefit costs
(2) Accrued benefit liabilities

c. US pension and OPEB plans and outside US plans may be combined unless benefit obligations outside the US are significant relative to the total and those plans use significantly different assumptions

3. Defined contribution plans

a. Amount of cost separate from defined benefit plans

(1) Pension
(2) Other postretirement

b. Description of nature and effect of significant changes affecting comparability

4. Multiemployer plans

a. Total amount of contributions without disaggregation
b. Description of nature and effect of significant changes affecting comparability
c. In case of withdrawal, SFAS 5 applies

5. Nonpublic entities may elect the following in lieu of required disclosures:

a. Benefit obligation, fair value of assets, funded status
b. Employer contributions, participant contributions, benefits paid
c. Amounts recognized in balance sheet

(1) Prepaid assets
(2) Accrued liabilities

(3) Intangible assets
(4) Other comprehensive income

d. Net periodic benefit cost

(1) Recognized in net income
(2) Recognized in other comprehensive income

e. Assumed weighted-average rates for

(1) Discount rate
(2) Expected long-term rate on plan assets
(3) Compensation rate increase (if applicable for pay-related plans)

f. Health care cost trend rate is

(1) Used to measure expected costs of benefits covered by the plan (gross eligible charges)
(2) Direction and pattern of change together with

(a) The ultimate trend rate(s)
(b) The time when that rate is expected to be achieved

g. Employer and related parties (if applicable)

(1) Amounts and types of securities included in plan assets
(2) Approximate amount of annual benefits covered by annuity contracts issued by the above
(3) Any significant transactions with the plan

h. If applicable, significant nonroutine events, such as amendments, curtailments, settlements, combinations, and divestitures.

SFAS 112. SFAS 112 uses the conditions of SFAS 43 to accrue an obligation for postemployment benefits other than pensions if employees' rights accumulate or vest, payment is probable, and the amount can be reasonably estimated. If these benefits do not vest or accumulate, SFAS 5 applies. If neither SFAS 43 nor SFAS 5 is applicable because the amount is not reasonably estimated, this fact must be disclosed.

Deferred compensation contracts. If the aggregate deferred compensation contracts with individual employees are equivalent to a pension plan, the contracts should be accounted for according to SFAS 87 and 88. All other deferred compensation contracts should be accounted for according to APB 12, para 6.

SFAS 106 states that the terms of the individual contract will govern the accrual of the employee's obligation for deferred compensation and the cost should be attributed over the employee service period until full eligibility is attained.

Per APB 12, the amount to be accrued should not be less than the present value of the estimated payments to be made. This estimated amount should be accrued in a systematic and rational manner. When elements of both current and future employment are present, only the portion attributable to the current services should be accrued. All requirements of the contract, such as the continued employment for a specified period and availability for consulting services and agreements not to compete after retirement, need to be met in order for the employee to receive future payments.

One benefit which may be found in a deferred compensation contract is the period payments to employees or their beneficiaries for life, with provisions for a minimum lump sum settlement in the event of early death of one or all of the beneficiaries. The estimated amount to be accrued should be based on the life expectancy of each individual concerned or on the estimated cost of an annuity contract, not on the minimum amount payable in the event of early death.

1974 Employee Retirement Income Security Act. Congress passed the Employee Retirement Income Security Act (ERISA) in 1974. The principal objectives of ERISA were to provide statutory law for pension plan requirements, to strengthen the financial soundness of private pension plans, to safeguard employees' pension rights, and to create the Pension Benefit Guaranty Corporation (PBGC).

Prior to ERISA, the Internal Revenue Code was the principal source of law for governing and managing pension plans. Unfortunately, the thrust of the Code was with tax considerations and the important nontax aspects of pension plans, such as vesting, funding, and employee participation were not addressed. ERISA filled the void by mandating minimum vesting, funding, employee participation, and other requirements. Virtually every private pension plan is affected by the provisions of ERISA.

The Act generally provides for full vesting of pension benefits after an employee has worked for the same employer for 15 years. Several different formulas can be used to determine when employee benefits vest. In addition, ERISA requires a minimum funding, in accordance with an acceptable actuarial method, for private pension plans. This requirement extends to the funding of past service costs over a period of 40 years or less. ERISA also established standards for employee participation and has made defined contribution plans more popular.

All of the above requirements strengthen the financial soundness of employee pension funds. To further ensure the ability of a plan to pay pension obligations and to safeguard employee rights, ERISA amended the Internal Revenue Code of 1954 to allow for the assessment of fines and the denial of tax deductions. The Act also requires that pension plans submit annual reports, provide a description of the plan, and make a full disclosure through the submission of various statements and schedules.

Prior to the enactment of ERISA, some employees lost pension benefits when plans were terminated because of bankruptcy or other reasons. In order to protect employee rights under these circumstances, ERISA created PBGC. The function of this agency is to guarantee employees, if the employer cannot pay, at least a minimum amount of benefits for their years of service. This guarantee is financed by an insurance premium charge which is levied on all employers with defined benefit plans. PBGC also has the right to administer terminated plans, to impose liens on employers' assets, and to take over employers' assets under certain specified circumstances.

For the most part, ERISA does not present any new or difficult accounting problems. It requires some additional disclosures and it has changed the tax law. Although the application of SFAS 87 is likely to produce more volatile differences than in the past between the amount shown as net periodic pension expense and the minimum or maximum (for tax purposes) amounts funded under ERISA, the Act per se has little effect on the accounting for pension plans.

EMERGING ISSUES TASK FORCE CONSENSUS SUMMARIES

88-1 Determination of Vested Benefit Obligation for a Defined Benefit Pension Plan

In situations not specifically addressed by SFAS 87, the vested benefit obligation can be (1) the actuarial present value of the vested benefits that the employee is entitled to if the employee separates immediately, or (2) the actuarial present value of the vested benefits to which the employee is currently entitled but based on the employee's expected date of separation or retirement. The FASB staff favored (1) but several task force members thought (2) was more consistent with SFAS 87. This issue is usually applicable to foreign defined benefit pension plans.

88-5 Recognition of Insurance Death Benefits

It is **not** appropriate for the purchaser of life insurance to recognize income from death benefits on an actuarially expected basis.

90-3 Accounting for Employers' Obligations for Future Contributions to a Multiemployer Pension Plan

Based on paragraph 68 of SFAS 87, the existence of an executed agreement does not require a liability beyond currently due and unpaid contributions.

91-7 Accounting for Pension Benefits Paid by Employers After Insurance Companies Fail to Provide Annuity Benefits

A consensus was reached that a loss should be recognized by the employer at the time the employer assumes the benefit obligation payments to retirees for an insolvent insurance company that held these pension obligations. The loss would be recognized as the lesser of any gain recognized in the original contract with the insurance company or the amount of benefit obligation payments assumed by the company. Any additional loss not recognized should be recorded as a plan amendment in accordance with SFAS 87.

92-13 Accounting for Estimated Payments in Connection With the Coal Industry Retiree Health Benefit Act of 1992

If the company is currently operating in the coal industry, it may account for this obligation as either part of its multiemployer plan participation or as a contingent extraordinary loss in accordance with SFAS 5. If the company is no longer operating in the coal industry, the entire obligation would be recorded as an extraordinary loss under SFAS 5.

93-3 Plan Assets Under FASB Statement No. 106

A trust established to pay postretirement benefits does not necessarily have to be "bankruptcy proof," or insulated completely from the claims of general creditors, in order to qualify as plan assets in accordance with FASB Statement 106. Plan assets held in a trust which explicitly makes them available to the general creditors in bankruptcy do not qualify as plan assets under SFAS 106.

17 STOCKHOLDERS' EQUITY

PERSPECTIVE AND ISSUES

SFAC 6 defines stockholders' equity as the residual interest in the assets of an entity after deducting its liabilities. Stockholders' equity is comprised of all capital contributed to the entity plus its accumulated earnings less any distributions that have been made. There are two major categories of stockholders' equity: paid-in capital and retained earnings.

It is conceptually clear that equity differs from liabilities insofar as the former represents an interest in net assets, while the latter are claims on those assets, and that claims have priority over residual interests. In practice, however, it has been well recognized that certain items, while nominally either equity or a liability, can have characteristics of both, making classification difficult and presentation on the balance sheet subject to controversy. Among such items are mandatorily redeemable preferred stock and shareholder interests subject to contingent repurchase arrangements (typically called "buy-sell agreements"). The FASB began to deliberate these issues about 10 years ago, and issued a discussion memorandum in 1990, but the project soon thereafter was stalled, partly because of concern over the far-reaching effects any changes to the definitions of liability and equity which had already been incorporated in SFAC 6. At that time, however, the Board agreed to address narrow issue projects pertaining to the distinction between liability and equity as the opportunity arose.

More recently, the FASB has developed an "obligation-based approach" which would require, if implemented, separate accounting for obligations and for certain types of options embodies therein. This would involve assessing the existence of a present obligation to another entity, understanding the type of performance required to discharge the obligation, and evaluating the risks and benefits of ownership vs. liability if performance involves share issuance. Instruments having defined characteristics of both would be accounted for piecemeal in accordance with those characteristics.

Using the obligation-based approach, all financial instruments requiring a transfer of entity assets to settle would be deemed liabilities. Those requiring settlement in equity or which provide the issuer the right to settle in equity would be deemed equity if the value were indexed to the fair value of the issuer's shares; if indexed to anything other than the fair value of the issuer's shares, initial classification would be as a liability. Financial instruments which impose on the issuer an obligation to transfer assets absent an election by the holder to receive equity, and also contain an option giving the holder the right to require share issuance, would be a compound instrument to be accounted for as both equity and debt. More recently, the Board has decided to extend the obligation-based approach to more complex arrangement as well. The plan is to conduct discussion of measurement issues and issue an exposure draft addressing both recognition and measurement matters in late 1998.

Earnings are not generated by transactions in an entity's own equity (e.g., by the issuance, reacquisition, or reissuance of its common or preferred shares). Depending on the laws of the jurisdiction of incorporation, distributions to shareholders may be subject to various limitations, such as to the amount of retained (accounting basis) earnings.

A major objective of the accounting for stockholders' equity is the adequate disclosure of the **sources** from which the capital was derived. For this reason, a number of different paid-in capital accounts may be presented in the balance sheet. The rights of each class of shareholder must also be disclosed. Where shares are reserved for future issuance, such as under the terms of stock option plans, this fact must also be made known.

The longstanding and very controversial stock compensation project finally was brought to completion with the issuance of SFAS 123. In something of a compromise, this standard urges, but does not require, that compensation cost be attributed to the granting of employee stock options, measured at fair value, although footnote disclosure of the impact of applying the new rules will be required if reporting entities choose to continue to employ the former standard, APB 25. This choice is limited to employee options; stock options issued in other transactions, such as to suppliers, must be measured at fair value in all cases. Fair value is measured by one of several available models, and nonpublic enterprises can use a somewhat simplified "minimum value" approach. The new requirements are effective for 1996, but comparative pro forma 1995 amounts must also be presented if comparative financial statements are issued.

SOP 93-6 revised the accounting for employers' contributions to employee stock ownership plans (ESOP), thereby superseding the former standards contained in SOP 76-3 as well as EITF 86-27, 89-8 and 89-10. The new standard does optionally permit "grandfathering" shares acquired prior to 1993. The major changes from the prior rules relate to the measurement of compensation cost, which must now be gauged by the fair value of the shares contributed, not their historical cost to the employer. Also, dividends on unallocated shares are now deemed to be part of compensation cost, and thus are reported on the income statement rather than being shown in equity.

Sources of GAAP

ARB	*APB*	*SFAS*	*FASB I*	*FASB TB*	*EITF*	*SOP*
43, Ch. 1A, 1B, 7A, 7B, 13B, 46	6, 12, 15, 25, 29	52,87, 115, 123, 129, 130	28, 31, 38	85-6	84-18, 85-1, 85-25, 87-6, 87-31, 87-33, 88-6, 89-11, 90-7, 90-9, 94-6, 95-16, 96-1, 96-3 97-14, 98-2	76-3, 90-7, 93-6

DEFINITIONS OF TERMS

Additional paid-in capital. Amounts received at issuance in excess of the par or stated value of capital stock and amounts received from other transactions involving the entity's stock and/or stockholders. It is classified by source.

Allocated shares. ESOP shares assigned to individual participants. These shares are usually based on length of service, compensation or a combination of both.

Appropriation (of retained earnings). A segregation of retained earnings to communicate the unavailability of a portion for dividend distributions.

Authorized shares. The maximum number of shares permitted to be issued by a corporation's charter and bylaws.

Callable. An optional characteristic of preferred stock allowing the corporation to redeem the stock at specified future dates and at specific prices. The call price is usually at or above the original issuance price.

Cliff vesting. A condition of an option or other stock award plan which provides that the employee becomes fully vested at a single point in time.

Combination plans. Awards consisting of two or more separate components, such as options and stock appreciation rights, each of which can be exercised. Each component is actually a separate plan and is accounted for as such.

Committed-to-be-released shares. ESOP shares that will be allocated to employees for service performed currently. They are usually released by payment of debt service.

Compensatory plan. A stock option or similar plan including elements of compensation which are recognized over the service period.

Constructive retirement method. Method of accounting for treasury shares which treats the shares as having been retired. The shares revert to authorized but unissued status. The stock and additional paid-in capital accounts are reduced, with a debit to retained earnings or a credit to a paid-in capital account for the excess or deficiency of the purchase cost over or under the original issuance proceeds.

Contributed capital. The amount of equity contributed by the corporation's shareholders. It consists of capital stock plus additional paid-in capital.

Convertible. An optional characteristic of preferred stock allowing the stockholders to exchange their preferred shares for common shares at a specified ratio.

Cost method. Method of accounting for treasury shares which presents aggregate cost of reacquired shares as a deduction from the total of paid-in capital and retained earnings.

Cumulative. An optional characteristic of preferred stock. Any dividends of prior years not paid to the preferred shareholders must be paid before any dividends can be distributed to the common shareholders.

Date of declaration. The date on which the board of directors votes that a dividend shall be paid. A legal liability (usually current) is created on this date in the case of cash, property, and scrip dividends.

Date of grant. The date on which the board of directors awards the stock to the employees in stock option plans.

Date of payment. The date on which the shareholders are paid the declared dividends.

Date of record. The date on which ownership of the shares is determined. Those owning stock on this date will be paid the declared dividends.

Deficit. A debit balance in the retained earnings account. Dividends may not generally be paid when this condition exists. Formally known as accumulated deficit.

Discount on capital stock. Occurs when the stock of a corporation is originally issued at a price below par value. The original purchasers become contingently liable to creditors for this difference.

Employee stock ownership plan (ESOP). A form of defined contribution employee benefit plan, whereby the employer facilitates the purchase of shares of stock in the company for the benefit of the employees, generally by a trust established by the company. The plan may be leveraged by borrowings either from the employer-sponsor or from third-party lenders.

Fair value. An estimate of the value of a stock option which takes into account exercise price, expected term, current stock price, expected volatility, expected dividend yield, and risk-free interest rate during expected term; used to measure compensation under SFAS 123.

Fixed options. Options which grant the holder the rights to a specified numbers of shares at fixed prices. They are not dependent upon achievement of performance targets.

Graded vesting. A vesting process whereby the employee becomes entitled to a stock-based award fractionally over a period of years.

Grant date. The date when the terms of a stock-based compensation award are mutually understood by both employer and employee.

Intrinsic value. The excess of the market price of an underlying stock over the exercise price of a related stock option; used to measure compensation under APB 25.

Issued stock. The number of shares issued by the firm and owned by the shareholders and the corporation. It is the sum of outstanding shares plus treasury shares.

Junior stock. Shares with certain limitations, often as to voting rights, which are granted to employees pursuant to a performance compensation program. Such shares are generally convertible to ordinary shares upon achievement of defined goals.

Legal capital. The aggregate par or stated value of stock. It represents the amount of owners' equity which cannot be distributed to shareholders. It serves to protect the claims of the creditors.

Liquidating dividend. A dividend distribution which is not based on earnings. It represents a return of contributed capital.

Measurement date. The date on which the price that enters into the computation of the fair value of an equity instrument granted as compensation is fixed.

Minimum value. As used in SFAS 123, a computed option value which does not take into account the effect of expected volatility of the price of the underlying stock.

Noncompensatory stock options. Options which do not include an element of compensation. Under APB 25, many stock option plans meet the prescribed criteria and thus are deemed noncompensatory; under SFAS 123 most stock plans will include an element of compensation to be measured and allocated over the service periods of the employees or to be disclosed as such in the notes to the financial statements.

No-par stock. Stock which has no par value. Sometimes a stated value is determined by the board of directors. In this case, the stated value is accorded the same treatment as par value stock.

Outstanding stock. Stock issued by a corporation and held by shareholders (i.e., issued shares which are not held in the treasury).

Par value method. A method of accounting for treasury shares which charges the treasury stock account for the aggregate par or stated value of the shares acquired and charges the excess of the purchase cost over the par value to paid-in capital and/or retained earnings. A deficiency of purchase cost is credited to paid-in capital.

Participating. An optional characteristic of preferred stock whereby preferred shareholders may share ratably with the common shareholders in any profit distributions in excess of a predetermined rate. Participation may be limited to a maximum rate or may be unlimited (full).

Performance based options. Options which are granted to employees conditional on the achievement of defined goals, such as market price of the underlying stock or earnings of the entity.

Phantom stock plan. A type of stock compensation arrangement which gives employees the right to participate in the increase in value of the company's shares (book value or market value, as stipulated in the plan), without being required to actually purchase the shares initially.

Quasi reorganization. A procedure which reclassifies amounts from contributed capital to retained earnings to eliminate a deficit in that account. All the assets and liabilities are first revalued to their current values. It represents an alternative to a legal reorganization in bankruptcy proceedings.

Retained earnings. The undistributed earnings of a firm.

Service period. The period over which a stock-based compensation award is earned by the recipient. If not otherwise defined in the plan, it is the vesting period. Under SFAS 123, if performance conditions affect either exercise price or date, then the service period must be consistent with the related assumption used in estimating fair value.

Stock-based compensation. Compensation arrangements under which employees receive shares of stock, stock options, or other equity instruments, or under which the employer incurs obligations to the employees based on the price of the company's shares.

Stock options. Enable officers and employees of a corporation to purchase shares in the corporation at a predetermined price for a defined period of time.

Stock rights. Enables present shareholders to purchase additional shares of stock of the corporation. It is commonly used if a preemptive right is granted to common shareholders by some state corporation laws.

Suspense shares. ESOP shares that usually collaterize ESOP debt. They have not been allocated or committed to be released.

Tandem plans. Compensation plans under which employees receive two or more components, such as options and stock appreciation rights, whereby the exercise of one component cancels the other(s). The accounting is based on the component which is more likely to be exercised.

Treasury stock. Shares of a corporation which have been repurchased by the corporation. This stock has no voting rights and receives no cash dividends. Some states do not recognize treasury stock. In such cases, reacquired shares are treated as having been retired.

Vesting. The process whereby the recipient of a stock-based compensation award earns the right to control or exercise the award.

CONCEPTS, RULES, AND EXAMPLES

Legal Capital and Capital Stock

Legal capital typically relates to that portion of the stockholders' investment in a corporation which is permanent in nature and which represents assets which will continue to be available for the satisfaction of creditor's claims. Traditionally, legal capital was comprised of the aggregate par or stated value of common and preferred shares issued. In recent years, however, many states have eliminated the requirement that corporate shares have a designated par or stated value. Also, some states have adopted provisions of the Model Business Corporation Act which eliminated the distinction between par value and the amount contributed in excess of par.

The specific requirements regarding the preservation of legal capital are a function of the corporation laws in the state in which a particular entity is incorporated. Accordingly, any action by the corporation that could affect the amount of legal capital (e.g., the payment of dividends in excess of retained earnings) must be considered in the context of the relevant laws of the state where the company is chartered.

Ownership interest in a corporation is made up of common and, optionally, preferred shares. The common shares represent the residual risk-taking ownership of the corporation after the satisfaction of all claims of creditors and senior classes of equity.

Preferred stock. Preferred shareholders are owners who have certain rights superior to those of common shareholders. These rights will pertain either to the earnings or the assets of the corporation. Preferences as to earnings exist when the preferred shareholders have a stipulated dividend rate (expressed either as a dollar amount or as a percentage of the preferred stock's par or stated value). Preferences as to assets exist when the preferred shares have a stipulated liquidation value. If a corporation were to liquidate, the preferred holders would be paid a specific amount before the common shareholders would have a right to participate in any of the proceeds.

In practice, preferred shares are more likely to have preferences as to earnings than as to assets. Some classes of preferred shares may have both preferential rights. Preferred shares may also have the following features: **participation** in earnings beyond the stipulated dividend rate; the **cumulative** feature affording the preferred shareholders the protection that their dividends in arrears, if any, will be fully satisfied before the common shareholders participate in any earnings distribution; and **convertibility** or **callability** by the corporation. Whatever preferences exist must be disclosed adequately in the financial statements, either on the face of the balance sheet or in the notes.

In exchange for the preferences, the preferred shareholders' rights or privileges are limited. For instance, the right to vote may be restricted to common shareholders. The most important right denied to the preferred shareholders, however, is the right to participate without limitation in the earnings of the corporation. Thus, if the corporation has exceedingly large earnings for a particular period, these earnings would tend to accrue to the benefit of the common shareholders. This is true even if the preferred stock is participating (a fairly uncommon feature) because even participating preferred stock usually has some upper limitation placed upon its degree of participation.

Occasionally, several classes of stock will be categorized as common (e.g., Class A common, Class B common, etc.). Since there can be only one class of shares that represents the true residual risk-taking investors in a corporation, it is clear that the other classes, even though described as common shareholders, must in fact have some preferential status. Typically, these preferences relate to voting rights. An example of this situation arises when a formerly closely held corporation sells shares to the public but gives the publicly held shares a disproportionately small capacity to exercise influence over the entity, thereby keeping control in the hands of the former majority owners even if they are reduced to the status of minority owners. The rights and responsibilities of each class of shareholder, even if described as common, must be fully disclosed in the financial statements.

Issuance of shares. The accounting for the sale of shares by a corporation depends upon whether the stock has a par or stated value. If there is a par or stated value, the amount of the proceeds representing the aggregate par or stated value is credited to the common or preferred stock account. The aggregate par or stated value is generally defined as legal capital not subject to distribution to shareholders. Proceeds in excess of par or stated value are credited to an additional paid-in capital account. The **additional paid-in capital** represents the amount in excess of the legal capital which may, under certain defined conditions, be distributed to shareholders. A corporation selling stock below par value credits the capital stock account for the par value and debits an offsetting **discount account** for the difference between par value and the amount actually received. If the discount is on original issue capital stock, it serves to notify the actual and potential creditors of the contingent liability of those investors. As a practical matter, corporations avoided this problem by reducing par values to an arbitrarily low amount. This reduction in par eliminated the chance that shares would be sold for amounts below par. Where the Model Business Corporation Act has been adopted or where corporation laws have embraced some of the attributes of that Act, there is often no distinction made between par value and amounts in excess of par. In those jurisdictions, the entire proceeds from the sale of stock may be credited to the common stock account without distinction between the stock and the additional paid-in capital accounts. The following entries illustrate these concepts:

Facts: A corporation sells 100,000 shares of $5 par common stock for $8 per share cash.

Cash	800,000	
Common stock		500,000
Additional paid-in capital		300,000

Facts: A corporation sells 100,000 shares of no-par common stock for $8 per share cash.

Cash	800,000	
Common stock		800,000

Preferred stock will often be assigned a par value because in many cases the preferential dividend rate is defined as a percentage of par value (e.g., 10%, $25 par value preferred stock will have a required annual dividend of $2.50).

If the shares in a corporation are issued in exchange for services or property rather than for cash, the transaction should be reflected at the fair value of the property or services received. If this information is not readily available, then the transaction should be recorded at the fair value of the shares that were issued. Where necessary, appraisals should be obtained in order to properly reflect the transaction. As a final resort, a valuation by the board of directors of the stock issued can be utilized (APB 29, paras 18 and 25). Stock issued to employees as compensation for services rendered should be accounted for at the fair value of the services performed, if determinable, or the value of the shares issued. If shares are given by a major shareholder directly to an employee for services performed for the entity, this exchange should be accounted for as a capital contribution to the company by the major shareholder and as compensation expense incurred by the company. Only when accounted for in this manner will there be conformity with the general principle that all costs incurred by an entity, including compensation, should be reflected in its financial statements.

In certain instances, common and preferred shares may be issued to investors as a unit (e.g., a unit of one share of preferred and two shares of common can be sold as a package). Where both of the classes of stock are publicly traded, the proceeds from a unit offering should be allocated in proportion to the relative market values of the securities. If only one of the securities is publicly traded, then the proceeds should be allocated to the one that is publicly traded based on its known market value. Any excess is allocated to the other. Where the market value of neither security is known, appraisal information might be used. The imputed fair value of one class of security, particularly the preferred shares, can be based upon the stipulated dividend rate. In this case, the amount of proceeds remaining after the imputing of a value of the preferred shares would be allocated to the common stock.

The foregoing procedures would also apply if a unit offering were made of an equity and a nonequity security such as convertible debentures.

Stock Subscriptions

Occasionally, particularly in the case of a newly organized corporation, a contract is entered into between the corporation and prospective investors, whereby the latter agree to purchase specified numbers of shares to be paid for over some installment period. These stock subscriptions are not the same as actual stock issuances and the accounting differs.

The amount of stock subscriptions receivable by a corporation is sometimes treated as an asset on the balance sheet and is categorized as current or noncurrent in accordance with the terms of payment. However, in accordance with SEC requirements, most subscriptions receivable are shown as a reduction of stockholders' equity in the same manner as treasury stock. Since subscribed shares do not have the rights and responsibilities of actual outstanding stock, the credit is made to a stock subscribed account instead of to the capital stock accounts.

If the common stock has par or stated value, the common stock subscribed account is credited for the aggregate par or stated value of the shares subscribed. The excess over this amount is credited to additional paid-in capital. No distinction is made between additional paid-in capital relating to shares already issued and shares subscribed for. This treatment follows from the distinction between legal capital and additional paid-in capital. Where there is no par or stated value, the entire amount of the common stock subscribed is credited to the stock subscribed account.

As the amount due from the prospective shareholders is collected, the stock subscriptions receivable account is credited and the proceeds are debited to the cash account. Actual issuance of the shares, however, must await the complete payment of the stock subscription. Accordingly, the debit to common stock subscribed is not made until the subscribed shares are fully paid for and the stock is issued.

The following journal entries illustrate these concepts:

1. 10,000 shares of $50 par preferred are subscribed at a price of $65 each; a 10% down payment is received.

Cash	65,000	
Stock subscriptions receivable	585,000	
Preferred stock subscribed		500,000
Additional paid-in capital		150,000

2. 2,000 shares of no-par common shares are subscribed at a price of $85 each, with one-half received in cash.

Cash	85,000	
Stock subscriptions receivable	85,000	
Common stock subscribed		170,000

3. All preferred subscriptions are paid, and one-half of the **remaining** common subscriptions are collected in full and subscribed shares are issued.

Cash [$585,000 + ($85,000 x .50)]	627,500	
Stock subscriptions receivable		627,500
Preferred stock subscribed	500,000	
Preferred stock		500,000
Common stock subscribed	127,500	
Common stock ($170,000 x .75)		127,500

When the company experiences a default by the subscriber, the accounting will follow the provisions of the state in which the corporation is chartered. In some jurisdictions, the subscriber is entitled to a proportionate number of shares based upon the amount already paid on the subscriptions, sometimes reduced by the cost incurred by the corporation in selling the remaining defaulted shares to other stockholders. In other jurisdictions, the subscriber forfeits the entire investment upon default. In this case, the amount already received is credited to an additional paid-in capital account that describes its source.

Additional Paid-in Capital

Additional paid-in capital represents all capital contributed to a corporation other than that defined as par or stated value. Additional paid-in capital can arise from proceeds received from the sale of common and preferred shares in excess of their par or stated values. It can also arise from transactions relating to the following:

1. Sale of shares previously issued and subsequently reacquired by the corporation (treasury stock)
2. Retirement of previously outstanding shares
3. Payment of stock dividends in a manner which justifies the dividend being recorded at the market value of the shares distributed
4. Lapse of stock purchase warrants or the forfeiture of stock subscriptions, if these result in the retaining by the corporation of any partial proceeds received prior to forfeiture
5. Warrants which are detachable from bonds
6. Conversion of convertible bonds
7. Other "gains" on the company's own stock, such as that which results from certain stock option plans

When the amounts are material, the sources of additional paid-in capital should be described in the financial statements.

Donated Capital

Donated capital should also be adequately disclosed in the financial statements. Donated capital can result from an outright gift to the corporation (e.g., a major shareholder donates land or other assets to the company in a nonreciprocal transfer) or may result when services are provided to the corporation. Under SFAS 116, such nonreciprocal transactions will be recognized as revenue in the period the contribution is received.

In these situations, historical cost is not adequate to properly reflect the substance of the transaction, since the historical cost to the corporation would be zero. Accordingly, these events should be reflected at fair market value (APB 29, para 18). If long-lived assets are donated to the corporation, they should be recorded at their fair value at the date of donation, and the amount so recorded should be depreciated over the normal useful economic life of such assets. If donations are conditional in nature, they should not be reflected formally in the accounts until the appropriate conditions have been satisfied. However, disclosure might still be required in the financial statements of both the assets donated and the conditions required to be met.

Retained Earnings

Legal capital, additional paid-in capital, and donated capital collectively represent the contributed capital of the corporation. The other major source of capital is retained earnings, which represents the accumulated amount of earnings of the corporation from the date of inception (or from the date of reorganization) less the cumulative amount of distributions made to shareholders and other charges to retained earnings (e.g., from treasury stock transactions). The distributions to shareholders generally take the form of dividend payments but may take other forms as well, such as the reacquisition of shares for amounts in excess of the original issuance proceeds.

Retained earnings are also affected by action taken by the corporation's board of directors. **Appropriation** serves disclosure purposes and serves to restrict dividend payments but does nothing to provide any resources for satisfaction of the contingent loss or other underlying purpose for which the appropriation has been made. Any appropriation made from retained earnings must eventually be returned to the retained earnings account. It is not permissible to charge losses against the appropriation account nor to credit any realized gain to that account. The use of appropriated retained earnings has diminished significantly over the years.

An important rule relating to retained earnings is that transactions in a corporation's own stock can result in a reduction of retained earnings (i.e., a deficiency on such transactions can be charged to retained earnings) but cannot result in an increase in retained earnings (any excesses on such transactions are credited to paid-in capital, never to retained earnings).

If a series of operating losses have been incurred or distributions to shareholders in excess of accumulated earnings have been made and if there is a debit balance in retained earnings, the account is generally referred to as **accumulated deficit**.

Dividends

Dividends are the pro rata distribution of earnings to the owners of the corporation. The amount and the allocation between the preferred and common shareholders is a function of the stipulated preferential dividend rate; the presence or absence of (1) a participation feature, (2) a cumulative feature, and (3) arrearages on the preferred stock; and the wishes of the board of directors. Dividends, even preferred stock dividends, where a cumulative feature exists, do not accrue. Dividends only become a liability of the corporation when they are declared by the board of directors.

Traditionally, corporations were not allowed to declare dividends in excess of the amount of retained earnings. Alternatively, a corporation could pay dividends out of retained earnings **and** additional paid-in capital but could not exceed the total of these categories (i.e., they could not impair legal capital by the payment of dividends). States that have adopted the Model Business Corporation Act grant more latitude to the directors. Corporations can now, in certain jurisdictions, declare and pay dividends in excess of the book amount of retained earnings if the directors conclude that, after the payment of such dividends, the fair value of the corporation's net assets will still be a positive amount. Thus, directors can declare dividends out of unrealized appreciation which, in certain industries, can be a significant source of dividends beyond the realized and recognized accumulated earnings of the corporation. This action, however, represents a major departure from traditional practice and demands both careful consideration and adequate disclosure.

Three important dividend dates are

1. The **declaration** date
2. The **record** date
3. The **payment** date

The declaration date governs the incurrence of a legal liability by the corporation. The record date refers to that point in time when a determination is made as to which specific registered stockholders will receive dividends and in what amounts. Finally, the payment date relates to the date when the distribution of the dividend takes place. These concepts are illustrated in the following example:

On May 1, 1999, the directors of River Corp. declared a $.75 per share quarterly dividend on River Corp.'s 650,000 outstanding common shares. The dividend is payable May 25 to holders of record May 15.

May 1	Retained earnings (or dividends)	487,500	
	Dividends payable		487,500
May 15	No entry		
May 25	Dividends payable	487,500	
	Cash		487,500

If a dividends account is used, it is closed to retained earnings at year end.

Dividends may be made in the form of cash, property, or scrip. Cash dividends are either a given dollar amount per share or a percentage of par or stated value. Property dividends consist of the distribution of any assets other than cash (e.g., inventory or equipment). Finally, scrip dividends are promissory notes due at some time in the future, sometimes bearing interest until final payment is made.

Occasionally, what appear to be disproportionate dividend distributions are paid to some, but not all, of the owners of closely held corporations. Such transactions need to be carefully analyzed. In some cases these may actually represent compensation paid to the recipients. In other instances, these may be a true dividend paid to all shareholders on a pro rata basis, which certain shareholders have waived their rights to. If the former, the distribution should not be accounted for as a dividend, but rather as compensation or some other expense category and included on the income statement. If the latter, the dividend should be "grossed up" to reflect payment on a proportional basis to all the shareholders, with an offsetting capital contribution to the company recognized as having been effectively made by those to whom payments were not made.

Property dividends. If property dividends are declared, the paying corporation may incur a gain or loss. Since the dividend should be reflected at the fair value of the assets distributed, the difference between fair value and book value is recorded at the time the dividend is declared and charged or credited to a loss or gain account.

Scrip dividends. If a corporation declares a dividend payable in scrip which is interest bearing, the interest is accrued over time as a periodic expense. The interest is **not** a part of the dividend itself.

Liquidating dividends. Liquidating dividends are not distributions of earnings, but rather a return of capital to the investing shareholders. A liquidating dividend is normally recorded by the declarer through charging additional paid-in capital rather than retained earnings. The exact accounting for a liquidating dividend is affected by the laws where the business is incorporated, and these laws vary from state to state.

Stock dividends. Stock dividends represent neither an actual distribution of the assets of the corporation nor a promise to distribute those assets. For this reason, a stock dividend is not considered a legal liability or a taxable transaction.

Despite the recognition that a stock dividend is not a distribution of earnings, the accounting treatment of relatively insignificant stock dividends (defined as being less than 20% to 25% of the outstanding shares prior to declaration) is consistent with it being a real dividend. Accordingly, retained earnings are debited for the fair market value of the shares to be paid as a dividend, and the capital stock and additional paid-in capital accounts are credited for the appropriate amounts based upon the par or stated value of the shares, if any. A stock dividend declared but not yet paid is classified as such in the stockholders' equity section of the balance sheet. Since such a dividend never reduces assets, it cannot be a liability.

The selection of 20% to 25% as the threshold for recognizing a stock dividend as an earnings distribution is arbitrary, but it is based somewhat on the empirical evidence that small stock dividends tend not to result in a reduced market price per share for outstanding shares. In theory, any stock dividend should result in a reduction of the market value of outstanding shares in an inverse relationship to the size of the stock dividend. The aggregate value of the outstanding shares should not change, but the greater number of shares outstanding after the stock dividend should necessitate a lower per share price. As noted, however, the declaration of small stock dividends tends not to have this impact, and this phenomenon supports the accounting treatment.

On the other hand, when stock dividends are larger in magnitude, it is observed that per share market value declines after the declaration of the dividend. In such situations, it would not be valid to treat the stock dividend as an earnings distribution. Rather, it should be accounted for as a split. The precise treatment depends upon the legal requirements of the state of incorporation and upon whether the existing par value or stated value is reduced concurrent with the stock split.

If the par value is not reduced for a large stock dividend and if state law requires that earnings be capitalized in an amount equal to the aggregate of the par value of the stock dividend declared, the event should be described as a stock split effected in the form of a dividend, with a charge to retained earnings and a credit to the common stock account for the aggregate par or stated value. When the par or stated value is reduced in recognition of the split and state laws do not require treatment as a dividend, there is no formal entry to record the split but merely a notation that the number of shares outstanding has increased and the per share par or stated value has decreased accordingly.

Treasury Stock

Treasury stock consists of a corporation's own stock which has been issued, subsequently reacquired by the firm and not yet reissued or canceled. Treasury stock does not reduce the number of shares issued but does reduce the number of shares outstanding, as well as total stockholders' equity. These shares are not eligible to receive cash dividends. Treasury stock is **not** an asset although, in some circumstances, it may be presented as an asset if adequately disclosed (ARB 43, ch 1A). Reacquired stock which is awaiting delivery to satisfy a liability created by the firm's compensation plan or reacquired stock held in a profit-sharing trust is still considered outstanding and would not be considered treasury stock. In each case, the stock would be presented as an asset with the accompanying footnote disclosure. Accounting for excesses and deficiencies on treasury stock transactions is governed by ARB 43, ch 1B, and APB 6, paras 12 and 13.

Three approaches exist for the treatment of treasury stock: the **cost, par value,** and **constructive retirement** methods.

Cost method. Under the cost method, the gross cost of the shares reacquired is charged to a contra equity account (treasury stock). The equity accounts which were credited for the original share issuance (common stock, paid-in capital in excess of par, etc.) remain intact. When the treasury shares are reissued, proceeds in excess of **cost** are credited to a paid-in capital account. Any deficiency is charged to retained earnings (unless paid-in capital from previous treasury share transactions exists, in which case the deficiency is charged to that account, with any excess charged to retained earnings). If many treasury stock purchases are made, a cost flow assumption (e.g., FIFO or specific identification) should be adopted to compute excesses and deficiencies upon subsequent share reissuances. The advantage of the cost method is that it avoids identifying and accounting for amounts related to the original issuance of the shares and is, therefore, the simpler, more frequently used method. The cost method is most consistent with the one-transaction concept. This concept takes the view that the classification of stockholders' equity should not be affected simply because the corporation was the middle "person" in an exchange of shares from one stockholder to another. In substance, there is only a transfer of shares between two stockholders. Since the original balances in the equity accounts are left undisturbed, its use is most acceptable when the firm acquires its stock for reasons other than retirement, or when its ultimate disposition has not yet been decided.

Par value method. Under the second approach, the par value method, the treasury stock account is charged only for the aggregate par (or stated) value of the shares reacquired. Other paid-in capital accounts (excess over par value, etc.) are relieved in proportion to the amounts recognized upon the original issuance of the shares. The treasury share acquisition is treated almost as a retirement. However, the common (or preferred) stock account continues at the original amount, thereby preserving the distinction between an actual retirement and a treasury share transaction.

When the treasury shares accounted for by the par value method are subsequently resold, the excess of the sale price over par value is credited to paid-in capital. A reissuance for a price **below** par value does not create a contingent liability for the purchaser. It is only the original purchaser who risks this obligation to the entity's creditors.

Constructive retirement method. The constructive retirement method is similar to the par value method, except that the aggregate par (or stated) value of the reacquired shares is charged to the stock account rather than to the treasury stock account. This method is superior when (1) it is management's intention not to reissue the shares within a reasonable time period or (2) the state of incorporation defines reacquired shares as having been retired. In the latter case, the constructive retirement method is probably the only method of accounting for treasury shares that is **not** inconsistent with the state Business Corporation Act, although the state law does not necessarily dictate such accounting. Certain states require that treasury stock be accounted for by this method.

The two-transaction concept is most consistent with the par value and constructive retirement methods. First, the reacquisition of the firm's shares is viewed as constituting a contraction of its capital structure. Second, the reissuance of the shares is the same as issuing new shares. There is little difference between the purchase and subsequent reissuance of treasury shares and the acquisition and retirement of previously issued shares and the issuance of new shares.

Treasury shares originally accounted for by the cost method can subsequently be restated to conform to the constructive retirement method. If shares were acquired with the intention that they would be reissued and it is later determined that such reissuance is unlikely (due, for example, to the expiration of stock options without their exercise), then it is proper to restate the transaction.

Example of accounting for treasury stock

1. 100 shares ($50 par value) which were originally sold for $60 per share are later reacquired for $70 each.
2. All 100 shares are subsequently resold for a total of $7,500.

To record the acquisition, the entry is

Cost method

Account	Debit	Credit
Treasury stock	7,000	
Cash		7,000

Par value method

Account	Debit	Credit
Treasury stock	5,000	
Additional paid-in capital--common stock	1,000	
Retained earnings	1,000	
Cash		7,000

Constructive retirement method

Account	Debit	Credit
Common stock	5,000	
Additional paid-in capital--common stock	1,000	
Retained earnings	1,000	
Cash		7,000

To record the resale, the entry is

Cost method

Account	Debit	Credit
Cash	7,500	
Treasury stock		7,000
Additional paid-in capital--treasury stock		500

Par value method

Account	Debit	Credit
Cash	7,500	
Treasury stock		5,000
Additional paid-in capital--common stock		2,500

Constructive retirement method

Account	Debit	Credit
Cash	7,500	
Common stock		5,000
Additional paid-in capital--common stock		2,500

If the shares had been resold for $6,500, the entry is

Cost method			*Par value method*			*Constructive retirement method*		
Cash	6,500		Cash	6,500		Cash	6,500	
*Retained earnings	500		Treasury stock		5,000	Common stock		5,000
Treasury stock		7,000	Additional paid-in capital--common stock		1,500	Additional paid-in capital--common stock		1,500

* *"Additional paid-in capital--treasury stock" or "Additional paid-in capital--retired stock" of that issue would be debited first to the extent it exists.*

Alternatively, under the par or constructive retirement methods, any portion of or the **entire** deficiency on the treasury stock acquisition may be debited to retained earnings without allocation to paid-in capital. Any excesses would always be credited to an "Additional paid-in capital--retired stock" account.

The laws of some states govern the circumstances under which a corporation may acquire treasury stock and they may prescribe the accounting for the stock. For example, a charge to retained earnings may be required in an amount equal to the treasury stock's total cost. In such cases, the accounting per the state law prevails. Also, some states (including those that have adopted the Model Business Corporation Act) define excess purchase cost of reacquired (i.e., treasury) shares as being "distributions" to shareholders which are no different in nature than dividends. In such cases, the financial statement presentation should adequately disclose the substance of these transactions (e.g., by presenting both dividends and excess reacquisition costs together in the retained earnings statement).

When a firm decides to formally retire the treasury stock, the journal entry is dependent on the method used to account for the stock. Using the original sale and reacquisition data from the illustration above, the following entry would be made:

Cost method			*Par value method*		
Common stock	5,000		Common stock	5,000	
Additional paid-in capital--common stock	1,000		Treasury stock		5,000
*Retained earnings	1,000				
Treasury stock		7,000			

* *"Additional paid-in capital--treasury stock" may be debited to the extent it exists.*

If the constructive retirement method were used to record the treasury stock purchase, no additional entry would be necessary upon the formal retirement of the shares.

After the entry is made, the pro rata portion of all paid-in capital existing for that issue (i.e., capital stock and additional paid-in capital) will have been eliminated. If stock is purchased for immediate retirement (i.e., not put into the treasury) the entry to record the retirement is the same as that made under the constructive retirement method.

In the case of donated treasury stock, the intentions of management are important. If the shares are to be retired, the capital stock account is debited for the par or stated value of the shares, "Donated capital" is credited for the fair market value, and "Additional paid-in capital--retired stock" is debited or credited for the difference. If the intention of management is to reissue the shares, then three methods of accounting are available. The first two methods, cost and par value, are analogous to the aforementioned treasury stock methods except that "Donated capital" is credited at the time of receipt and debited at the time of reissuance. Under the cost method, the current market value of the stock is recorded (an apparent contradiction), while under the par value method, the par or stated value is used. Under the last method, only a memorandum entry is made to indicate the number of shares received. No journal entry is made at the time of receipt. At the time of reissuance, the entire proceeds are credited to "Donated capital." The method actually used is generally dependent on the circumstances involving the donation and the preference of the firm.

Other Equity Accounts

While in theory, at least, modern accounting subscribes to the so-called "all inclusive" concept which mandates that all nonowner changes in equity should be reported in the statement of income, in fact a number of exceptions have evolved over the past 20 years. Unrealized losses on noncurrent investments in marketable equity securities were identified by SFAS 12 (now superseded) as among the first of the quasi income items to be removed from the current year's reported earnings. Later, SFAS 52, SFAS 87, and SFAS 115 (translation gains and losses, net actuarial loss not recognized in pension cost, and unrealized gains and losses on available-for-sale portfolios of debt securities and marketable equity securities, respectively) continued what has become something of a tradition in financial reporting. As a result, the income statement is no longer truly prepared in accordance with the all-inclusive concept, and the prospect of further moves to fair value accounting for financial assets and liabilities portends even greater departures from this venerable principle.

Prior to 1997, there was no financial statement which captured the changes in the accumulated balances of the various additional equity or contra equity accounts during the reporting period, although these often were included in a statement of changes in stockholders' equity, if one was presented (it is not mandatory that this be done, however). However, the newly prescribed concept of reporting comprehensive income (SFAS 130, described in detail in Chapter 3) will result in the changes in all these other equity accounts being reported either in a section of a combined statement of earnings and other comprehensive income, a separate statement of comprehensive income, or an expanded statement of changes in stockholders' equity. Changes can be presented gross or net of income tax effects; but if net, the missing details would have to be set forth in the notes to the financial statements. Since the particulars of the changes in these various additional or contra equity accounts will now be clearly set forth in a basic financial statement, it will be permissible for the end of period balances to be combined into a single amount on the balance sheet, captioned as "Accumulated other comprehensive income" (or, alternatively, still shown in detail).

Accounting for Stock Options and Related Plans

The subject of accounting for stock options, first addressed by ARB 43, later by APB 25 and several FASB interpretations of that standard, and most recently by SFAS 123, has long been controversial. The principal debate has been about whether such options represent compensation expense, and if so, how that cost should be measured and allocated. The FASB placed this topic on its technical agenda in early 1984, and issued a proposed standard in 1993, which was promptly targeted for massive opposition primarily by industries which made heavy use of options to compensate top executives. The stakes were raised even further when bills were introduced in the U.S. Congress to prohibit the implementation of any new standard which would make mandatory the recognition of compensation cost related to stock options. The outcome was a revised exposure draft, which was adopted in late 1995 as SFAS 123, which urges, but does not require, that compensation cost arising in connection with options granted to employees be measured and reported in the income statement.

As a result of the promulgation of SFAS 123, entities which grant options to employees will be able to freely choose from among two distinct methods of accounting and reporting. For those which adopt the new standard, all stock option and similar plans will give rise to compensation cost, which will be reflected in the income statement over the vesting period, as described below in greater detail. Entities which choose to not adopt SFAS 123, on the other hand, will continue to apply the provisions of APB 25 and related literature, which typically (although not always) will result in not recognizing compensation cost. However, SFAS 123 does require that footnote disclosures be presented in the financial statements of entities which do not adopt SFAS 123, which effectively will show what the effect of adoption would have been.

SFAS 123 has been designated as the preferable GAAP for purposes of applying the provisions of APB 20. Thus, if an enterprise adopts SFAS 123 it cannot later revert to using APB 25. An entity must employ only one set of rules, APB 25 or SFAS 123, for all stock compensation programs and plans in effect; it cannot use different rules to measure the impact of different plans.

APB 25 versus SFAS 123 in brief. APB 25 measured stock options by the **intrinsic value** method, under which compensation cost was limited to the excess of the quoted market price of the stock at the measurement date (generally, grant date) over the option exercise price. Since most so-called "qualified" fixed options (i.e., plans which for tax purposes qualified as deductible expenses) had exercise prices at least equal to present market values, there was no compensation cost to be recognized. Under SFAS 123, on the other hand, a **fair value** approach is prescribed for employee stock options and similar equity instruments which takes into account, among other factors, the time value of the option, that is, the value of being able to defer a decision on whether or not to exercise the option until the expiration date or some other date later in the life of the option. This generally will result in a compensation element being identified.

Under the prior rules variable or performance-based options were accounted for differently than fixed options. FASB Interpretations 28 and 38 addressed the accounting for such plans, including so-called junior stock plans. Compensation was recognized under these rules, and continues to be recognized under the requirements set forth in SFAS 123. However, the pattern of expense recognition will potentially differ as between these two alternative sets of standards. Entities which continue to adhere to APB 25 for fixed option plans will use the related literature (FASB Interpretations 28 and 38) as well; those which adopt SFAS 123 will be guided by it in accounting for all stock compensation arrangements.

In the following sections, the methodologies of both the old set of requirements (APB 25 et al.) and the new rules (SFAS 123) will be discussed and illustrated.

Accounting for Employee Stock Options Under APB 25

Under the provisions of APB 25, there are two types of stock option plans: compensatory and noncompensatory. To be classified as noncompensatory, the plan must meet all of the following four tests:

1. Substantially all full-time employees meeting limited employment qualifications must be eligible to participate;
2. Shares must be offered equally or proportionate to wages earned;
3. Time to exercise must be limited; and
4. There must be no more than a reasonable discount from market price, such as the discount which would be granted in a typical "rights offering."

Failing to meet even one of these criteria causes the stock option plan to be categorized as compensatory in nature. However, this does not necessarily mean that compensation expense will be recognized.

Logically, any stock option program conveys to the recipients something of value, namely, the time to decide whether or not to purchase the shares of stock at a price which was fixed at the date of the grant. However, because of the strong sentiment against the recognition of compensation, APB 25 continued the practice earlier established by ARB 43, which essentially eliminated compensation recognition from so-called fixed stock option plans. This result had been accomplished by defining compensation as the excess of the quoted market (or fair) value of the shares optioned over the amount to be paid by the employee, determined in most cases as of the grant date. That is, if the option price was equal to or greater than the market (or fair) value as of the date the option was granted, no compensation was to be recognized, regardless of the value of the shares at any later time. Since exercise price typically was fixed at or below the market price as of the grant date, compensation was rarely to be recognized under terms of the most common, fixed option plans.

The measurement date stipulated by APB 25 is the earliest date on which both the number of shares to which an individual employee is entitled is known, and the option price is fixed. For most fixed option plans, both of these data are known on the grant date. Note that the measurement date will be the grant date even if the employee must meet certain other conditions, such as continued employment for a specified period, before the options can be exercised. This later date, the vesting date, is used for purposes of allocating compensation, if any, but is not used to compute the amount of such compensation.

If an option plan is compensatory (because one or more of the four conditions are not met), compensation cost is measured by the difference between the **market price** (or the fair market value, for a nontraded stock) and the option price. The **cost** of the shares to the issuing corporation is not the relevant comparison, except in the very limited situation where the shares are specifically acquired to meet the requirements of the stock option plan and are delivered to option holders shortly after acquisition.

Furthermore, even if no compensation cost is deemed to have been incurred at the measurement date (usually the grant date), certain subsequent events may give rise to the recognition of compensation. The most important of these are

1. The renewal or extension of an option, in which case a new measurement date occurs, and if the market price or fair value at that date exceeds the option price, compensation cost will be recognized; and
2. The payment of cash to an employee to settle a previously made stock award or option grant, for which payment will be deemed compensation expense.

If a given option plan involves the payment of compensation to the employees, such compensation cost should be recognized in the period(s) in which the services being compensated are performed. If the grant is unconditional, which means it effectively is in recognition of past services rendered by the employees, then compensation is reported in the period of the grant. If the stock options are granted before some or all of the required services are performed, compensation cost should be recognized over the periods in which the performance is scheduled to occur. Whether compensation cost is recognized ratably over the periods or not is a function of the vesting provisions of the plan. If the plan provides for **cliff vesting**, compensation will be accrued on an essentially straight-line basis, while if it provides for **graded vesting** the pattern of recognition will be more complex.

Example of accounting for stock options--Measurement and grant date the same

Options are granted to corporate officers to purchase 10,000 shares of $1 par stock at a price of $52 per share, when the market price is $58. The options may not be exercised until 5 years from the grant date. The company has no reason to expect that any of the options will be forfeited by the employees to whom they are granted. The entry to record the granting of the options is

Deferred compensation expense	60,000	
Stock options outstanding		60,000

While deferred taxes are ignored for purposes of this example, in general the recognition of expense for tax purposes would be in a later period, necessitating the recording of a deferred tax benefit. Deferred compensation expense is subtracted from stock options outstanding in the paid-in capital section of owner's equity to indicate the amount of net contributed services on any date [i.e., on the grant date nothing has yet been contributed by the option holders ($60,000 – $60,000 = $0)]. As the employees provide services to earn the options, entries are made assigning compensation expense to years 1-5.

Compensation expense	12,000		($60,000 ÷ 5 years)
Deferred compensation expense		12,000	

When the option is exercised, cash is received and the stock is issued. The following entry is made (assume exercise after the 5-year period)

Cash	520,000		(option price)
Stock options outstanding	60,000		
Common stock		10,000	(par)
Additional paid-in capital		570,000	(excess)

If options are forfeited as a result of an employee failing to fulfill an obligation (e.g., staying with the company), under the provisions of APB 25 compensation expense is credited in the year of forfeiture. The amount credited reflects the total compensation expense previously charged to the income statement for the employee who forfeited the options. Assume that one officer, who was granted options for 1,000 shares, leaves the company in year 3, 2 years before the options can be exercised. The result is handled as a change in an accounting estimate and the following entry is made in year 3:

Stock options outstanding	6,000	
Deferred compensation expense		3,600
Compensation expense		2,400

If the measurement date follows the grant date, it is necessary to assume compensation expense based on the market values of the common stock that exist at the end of each period until the measurement date is reached. Per FASB Interpretation 28, changes in the market value of stock between the date of grant and the measurement date are adjustments to compensation expense in **the period the market value of the stock changes**. The effect of such changes is **not** spread over future periods.

Example of accounting for stock options--Measurement and grant date the same, with graded vesting

Assume the same facts as the previous example, except that rights to 2,000 shares vest each year (i.e., the officers can exercise options for a total of 2,000 shares after 1 year, a total of 4,000 shares after 2 years, etc.). Where the option program provides for such graded vesting (as contrasted with the cliff vesting of the prior example), the allocation of compensation expense to the period until full vesting has occurred (the end of year 5 in this example) is to be done in a manner proportional to the number of shares to which rights to exercise the option have vested. As explained in FASB Interpretation 28, the service period is determined separately for each portion of the option. Thus, the 20% which vests in the first year is deemed attributable to services performed in the first year only, while the 20% which vests in the second year is attributed to services performed in years 1 and 2, etc. The effect of this requirement is to heavily front-load the total compensation cost, as follows:

Fraction of options	*Allocation to years of service*				
	First	*Second*	*Third*	*Fourth*	*Fifth*
1st 20%	20 %	-	-	-	-
2nd 20%	10 %	10 %	-	-	-
3rd 20%	6.66%	6.66%	6.66%	-	-
4th 20%	5 %	5 %	5 %	5%	-
5th 20%	4 %	4 %	4 %	4%	4%
Total allocation	45.66%	25.66%	15.66%	9%	4%

Accordingly, the entries to record compensation in years 1 and 2, respectively, are

Compensation expense	27,396		($60,000 x .4566)
Deferred compensation expense		27,396	
Compensation expense	15,396		($60,000 x .2566)
Deferred compensation expense		15,396	

Example of accounting for stock options--Measurement and grant date different

1. On 1/1/99, a company grants an option to purchase 100 shares of common stock at 90% of the market price at 12/31/2001 and that the compensation period is **4 years**. The total compensation amount per share is represented by the difference between the current market price and the estimated purchase price granted by the option (90% x market price) or simply 10% of the current market price.
2. At 1/1/99, the number of shares is determinable, but the option price is unknown.
3. The market values of the common stock are as follows:

12/31/1999	$10
12/31/2000	13
12/31/2001	15

The following entries for compensation expense are recorded:

	1999		*2000*		*2001*		*2002*	
Compensation expense	25		40		47.50		37.50	
Stock options outstanding		25		40		47.50		37.50

1999: ($10 x 10% x 100 shares x 1/4) = $25
2000: ($13 x 10% x 100 shares x 2/4) – expense recognized to date = $40
2001: ($15 x 10% x 100 shares x 3/4) – expense recognized to date = $47.50
2002: ($15 x 10% x 100 shares x 4/4) – expense recognized to date = $37.50

The expense recorded from 2000 and 2001 results from a change in estimate. Note that the market value of the stock at the end of 1999 and 2000 is used as the estimate of the market price of the stock at 12/31/2001 and that the total amount of compensation expense previously accrued is subtracted from the latest estimate of cumulative expense.

A time line depicting the actual and estimated compensation expense would appear as follows:

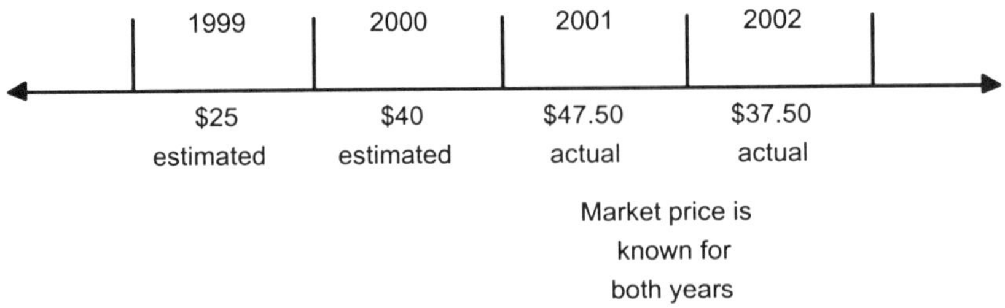

Stock Appreciation Rights Under APB 25

The previous section dealt with stock option plans, under which the employees are given the right to purchase shares either at advantageous (i.e., below market) prices or at the market price as of the date of the grant. Another type of stock-based compensation program gives the employees the opportunity to participate in any increase in value of the company's stock without having to incur the cost of actually purchasing the shares. Such plans may be referred to as phantom stock plans, stock appreciation rights, or variable stock award programs. A wide variety of such plans are found in practice: some provide for the payment of cash to the employees, while others reward participants with shares of the sponsor's stock. Often such plans are granted together with compensatory stock option plans as either combination or tandem plans: the former give the employees the rights to both the options and the phantom stock, while the latter require the employees to choose which they will exercise (simultaneously forfeiting the other).

Accounting for stock appreciation rights (SAR) and similar plans is prescribed by FASB Interpretation 28. There are significant distinctions between APB 25 and Interpretation 28, the most important of which is the method of computing the compensation cost to be allocated to the periods over which services are provided by the employees. Under APB 25, compensation cost (if any) is determined as of the measurement date (usually the grant date), and is not affected by changes in market price thereafter. By contrast, under Interpretation 28 compensation cost incurred in connection with stock appreciation rights or other variable awards is determined prospectively until full vesting is achieved, with future increases or decreases in market price resulting in charges or credits to periodic compensation expense.

Under both standards, however, total compensation cost is allocated ratably (if cliff vesting is provided by the plan) or proportionally (if graded vesting is provided). Likewise, both standards provide that when an employee forfeits options or rights for which compensation had previously been accrued, the accrual is to be reversed against compensation expense in the period of the forfeiture.

Accounting for compensation cost under SAR that provide graded vesting involves particularly complex allocations under the provisions of Interpretation 28. (If an enterprise adopts SFAS 123, the complexity of this computation is relaxed somewhat, but if the entity uses APB 25 for fixed option plans it must continue to apply Interpretations 28 and 38 as well, for variable plans.)

Performance based stock compensation plans often provide for payment in shares, instead of cash. For example, a stock appreciation rights plan may contain a provision that the increase in value will be distributed to the participant in the form of sufficient shares of the sponsor's stock to have an aggregate fair market value equal to the amount of the award. If the plan provides only for payment in shares (a plan which most often is referred to as a phantom stock plan), the offset to the periodic charge for compensation cost should be to paid-in capital accounts. If the award is payable at the participant's choice in either cash or stock, a liability should be accrued, since the sponsor cannot control the means by which the obligation will be settled. If the payment will be made in cash or stock at the option of the company, the offset to compensation should be either to a liability account or to equity accounts, based on the best available information concerning the sponsor's intentions. As these intentions change from one period to another, the amounts should be reclassified as necessary.

Example of accounting for SAR under Interpretation 28

1. A company grants 100 SAR, payable in cash, to an employee on 1/1/99.
2. The predetermined amount for the SAR plan is $50 per right, and the market value of the stock is $55 on 12/31/99, $53 on 12/31/00, and $61 on 12/31/01.

Compensation expense recorded in each year would be

			Total expense		*Expense previously accrued*		*Current expense*
1999	100 ($55 – $50)	=	$ 500	-	$ 0	=	$ 500
2000	100 ($53 – $50)	=	$ 300	-	$500	=	$(200)
2001	100 ($61 – $50)	=	$1,100	-	$300	=	$ 800

The total expense recognized over the 3-year period is $1,100 [100 x ($61 – $50)]. The required journal entries would be as follows:

1999		
Compensation expense	500	
Liability under SAR plan		500
2000		
Liability under SAR plan	200	
Compensation expense		200
2001		
Compensation expense	800	
Liability under SAR plan		800

If the SAR were to be redeemed in common stock, "Stock rights outstanding" (a paid-in capital account) would replace the liability account in the above entries.

The example assumes no service or vesting period, which is the period of time until the SAR become exercisable. If the above plan had a 2-year service period,

50% of the total expense would be recognized at the end of the first year and 100% at the end of the second year and thereafter until exercise. The compensation would be accrued as follows:

1999:	(\$ 500 x 50%)	= \$ 250	–	\$ 0	= \$250
2000:	(\$ 300 x 100%)	= \$ 300	–	\$250	= \$ 50
2001:	(\$1,100 x 100%)	= \$1,100	–	\$300	= \$800

Often stock option plans and SAR are joined in so-called tandem plans, under the terms of which the exercise of one (say, the SAR) automatically cancels the other (say, the option). This feature makes accounting for these types of arrangements more complex. Per FASB Interpretation 28, on the basis of the available facts each period, a determination must be made as to which one of the compensation plans has the higher likelihood of exercise. Once determined, this is the plan accounted for with the other plan being ignored. In the absence of evidence to the contrary, however, the presumption is that the SAR, not the options, will be exercised.

Example of accounting for a combined stock option and stock appreciation rights

To illustrate the accounting for a combined SAR and stock option plan, consider the following facts:

1/1/99 Plan adopted; market price is \$100, option price is \$95; 1,000 shares exercisable on 1/1/02 **or** 1,000 SAR payable in cash on 1/1/03 on increase over 1/1/99 market value.

Market prices are as follows:

12/31/99	\$ 98
12/31/00	110
12/31/01	108
12/31/02	125

Two cases are presented simultaneously, representing two alternative fact situations.

Case 1: It is assumed that only SAR will be exercised.
Case 2: It is assumed that 1/2 SAR, 1/2 options will be exercised.

The appropriate journal entries are as follows:

	Case 1	*Case 2*		
12/31/99	No entry	Compensation expense	625	
		Deferred compensation	1,875	
		Stock options outstanding (500 shares x \$5)		2,500
		Compensation expense is 1/4 of projected 4-year total relating to expected option exercise in Case 2.		

No SAR liability is accrued since the market price is below the base price. The compensatory part of the stock options, determined under the rules of APB 25, is $5 per share, which is allocated over the 4-year vesting period on a straight-line basis.

	Case 1			*Case 2*		
12/31/00	Compensation expense	10,000		Compensation expense	5,625	
	Liability under SAR plan ($10 x 1,000 SAR)		10,000	Deferred compensation		625
				Liability under SAR plan ($10 x 500 SAR)		5,000

Deferred compensation relating to options amortized ratably over option period ($2,500 x 1/4).

SAR liability recognized for difference between year-end market value and base price for number of expected SAR exercisable.

	Case 1			*Case 2*		
12/31/01	Liability under SAR plan	2,000		Liability under SAR plan	1,000	
	Compensation expense		2,000	Compensation expense		375
				Deferred compensation		625
12/31/02	Compensation expense	17,000		Compensation expense	9,125	
	Liability under SAR plan		17,000	Deferred compensation		625
				Liability under SAR plan ($12,500 - $5,000 + $1,000)		8,500

The option holders may exercise either the options or the SAR in ratios other than those presumed as the basis for the accounting. Assume that either (a) holders elect 100% SAR; (b) holders elect 50% SAR, 50% stock; or (c) they elect to exercise only the stock options. For each of the cases above, the entries under each assumed exercise ratio are as follows:

	Case 1			*Case 2*		
(a) (all cash)	Liability under SAR plan	25,000		Liability under SAR plan	12,500	
	Cash		25,000	Stock options outstanding	2,500	
				Compensation expense	10,000	
				Cash		25,000
(b) (1/2 cash, 1/2 stock)	Liability under SAR plan	25,000		Liability under SAR plan	12,500	
	Cash ($47,500 – $12,500)	35,000		Stock options outstanding	2,500	
	Common stock--$20 par		10,000	Cash	35,000	
	Additional paid-in capital		50,000	Common stock--$20 par		10,000
				Additional paid-in capital		40,000
(c) (all stock)	Liability under SAR plan	25,000		Liability under SAR plan	12,500	
	Cash	95,000		Stock option outstanding	2,500	
	Common stock--$20 par		20,000	Cash	95,000	
	Additional paid-in capital		100,000	Common stock--$20 par		20,000
				Additional paid-in capital		90,000

Notice that the proceeds of the stock issuance vary. When stock options are exercised but SAR were accrued, the cost of the shares includes the accrued SAR liability. On the other hand, when the expectation was that options would be exercised but SAR are exercised instead, additional compensation expense will be recorded (as in Case 2a). Since this is due to a change in estimate and not an accounting error, no prior period adjustment can be recorded.

An additional complication arises when there is not **cliff vesting**, as assumed here, but is graded over the years of the option/SAR plans. In such cases, the amount of compensation expense and/or liability under the SAR plan is based on the fraction of vesting at each reporting period. This has the effect of deferring much of the cost to later periods, as was illustrated earlier in the chapter for stock options with graded vesting provisions.

Essentially the same accounting procedures are employed for interim financial reporting. If in subsequent periods the presumed ratio of SAR exercise to stock option exercise in combination (or tandem) plans changes, compensation expense accrued in connection with the anticipated SAR exercise is **not** reduced even though the expected number of SAR to be exercised is diminished. On the other hand, a reduced expectation of stock option exercise may result in a reversal of compensation expense.

Other Interpretations of APB 25

When SFAS 123 was being developed, the expectation was that APB 25 would be superseded. However, as it turned out due to widespread opposition, compliance with SFAS 123 has been made optional (as described below), although expanded disclosures are required by those entities which eschew measurement based on the new standards. Since APB 25 continues in force for those reporting entities which elect to not fully embrace SFAS 123, certain open issues concerning interpretation of the earlier standard must now be resolved. Accordingly, the Board is currently pursuing a project to clarify how APB 25 is to be applied in the case of service providers which are treated not as employees but as independent contractors for tax purposes. It is also attempting to address an inconsistency arising from EITF 87-33 and 94-6, and SFAS 123, regarding cash settlements of nonvested options. The Board may also deal with the definition of "grant date"; accounting for plans which feature puts and/or calls; plan modifications, accelerated vesting, and cancellation and reissuance of stock-based awards; and accounting for the exchange of options in the context of poolings of interests and purchase business combinations.

Accounting for Employee Stock Options Under SFAS 123

In June 1993, the FASB exposed its long awaited proposal addressing stock options and other stock-based compensation arrangements. This proposal, if it had been adopted, would have replaced APB 25 with a fair value based measure of compensation cost for all fixed or variable stock award programs, with measurement based on the stock price as of grant date. Among the virtues of this proposal was the fact that this would have, for the first time, applied the same approaches to both fixed and variable (or performance) plans, thereby ending one of the most disturbing aspects of the present (APB 25 and FASB Interpretation 28) set of standards.

As noted above, however, the Board's original proposal met with such resistance that the FASB was pressured into proposing a more modest solution, which merely recommended that the fair value approach be adopted. Under this standard, SFAS 123, the method which would have been mandatory under the terms of the 1993 proposal has been retained but is no longer required, although designated as being preferable for purposes of adopting changes in accounting principle consistent with the provisions of APB 20.

The most significant departure from present practice prescribed by SFAS 123 is in the realm of fixed options granted at prices essentially equal to market price or fair value as of the grant date (or measurement date, if different). While under APB 25 typically no compensation is recognized even if the plan itself is deemed compensatory under its criteria, under SFAS 123 the value of these options must be measured, at the very least, at a so-called minimum value, which essentially will recognize the value of the right to defer payment of the exercise price until the end of the option period, net of missed dividends in the case of stock which is dividend paying. This minimum value is to be recognized as compensation expense over the service period. (For companies whose stock is publicly traded, the measure of fair value is more complicated, as discussed below.)

To illustrate this basic concept, assume that the present market price of underlying stock is $20 per share, and the option plan grants the recipient the right to purchase shares at today's market price at any time during the next 5 years. If a risk-free rate, such as that available on treasury notes having maturities of 5 years is 5%, then the present value of the future payment of $20 is $15.67 [$50 ÷ $(1.05)^5$], which suggests that the option has a value of $20 – $15.67 = $4.33 per share, before considering the value of lost dividends. If the stock is expected to pay a dividend of $.40 per share per year, the present value of the dividend stream which the option holder will forego until exercise 5 years hence is about $1.64, discounting again at 5%. Therefore, the **net** value of the option being granted, assuming it is expected to be held to the expiration date before being exercised, is $4.33 – $1.64 = $2.69 per share. (Although the foregoing computation was based on the full 5-year life of the option, the actual requirement is to use the **expected term** of the option, which may be shorter.)

SFAS 123 in Greater Detail

SFAS 123 applies, with only the exception described below, to all stock based compensation plans, by whatever name they are referred to as, and whether the employees receive stock or cash based on the price of the stock. This broad definition includes all stock purchase plans, fixed and variable option arrangements, restricted stock, and stock appreciation rights. It also applies to transactions in which stock is exchanged for goods and services in the normal course of business (e.g., for inventory), but the accounting for such transactions, using fair values, is essentially similar to what has long been considered GAAP.

As noted, the fair value of the equity instruments granted is used to measure each of these compensation arrangements. Fair value for publicly traded entities is to be measured by one of the recognized options pricing models, of which the Black-Scholes and binomial models are the universally recognized alternatives. These models take into consideration the term of the option (the longer the term, the greater will be the value of the right, all other factors remaining constant); the market price at grant date and the option exercise price (the greater the excess of the former over the latter, the greater will be the option value); the risk free interest rate, measured by the rate on zero coupon treasury debt with a term equal to the expected life of the option); the expected dividends to be paid on the stock (the option value is inversely related to expected dividends); and the expected volatility of the stock (the greater the expected volatility, the more valuable the option).

For nonpublicly traded companies, essentially the same approach is to be used, except that the measure of volatility which would be difficult to assess, or even meaningless, in the absence of an active market for the shares, is dispensed with. This truncated measure is referred to as the **minimum value** model. A full option pricing model approach including a factor for volatility can be used, however, if there is a desire to do so and a means of making that estimation.

Exception under SFAS 123 for stock purchase plans. SFAS 123 does provide an exemption for stock purchase plans which meet all of a set of defined conditions. If the plan does this, it will not be deemed to be a compensatory plan. The conditions are as follows:

1. The plan contains no option features **other** than permitting employees a very limited time, no longer than 31 days, to enroll in the plan after the purchase price has been fixed, or permitting employees to cancel participation in a program offering stock at the market price on the purchase date and obtaining a refund of moneys already withheld or paid.
2. Any discount from market price is limited to the greater of (a) that which would be reasonable in a recurring offer to existing shareholders or others or (b) stock issuance costs saved by not having a public offering. A 5% discount is assumed defensible; higher discounts would have to be justified.
3. Substantially all full-time employees, subject only to limited qualifications, are permitted to participate on an equitable basis.

With the sole exception of plans which comply with these restrictions, stock option and related programs are compensatory and subject to the measurement and disclosure requirements of SFAS 123. Thus, the new standard is far more restrictive than APB 25 was. For example, any program which offers employees the right to a lower price at exercise date based on the then-existing market value would be compensatory, as would be one which provided for a purchase price determined as of grant date but which gave participants the right to cancel before the exercise.

Measuring volatility. The volatility measure is the most difficult aspect of the option pricing model. SFAS 123 addresses this at great length, and should be consulted by those attempting to apply the Black-Scholes or binomial models. In general, volatility is a measure of the variation in prices of the security over a relevant period, projected to the future period which equals the expected term of the employee options. SFAS 123 stipulates that this is to be computed by reference to the annualized standard deviation of the differences in the natural logarithms of the possible future stock prices. Since future prices cannot be known, the standard suggests that historical volatility be used to forecast future volatility; in general, this will be achieved by using stock prices over a historical period of time equal to the expected life of the options being granted.

If the stock is expected to pay dividends (again, this can be anticipated based on historical experience, taking into account the frequency with which dividend rates have been adjusted and the amounts of such adjustments, modified to reflect future expectations), the volatility measure will also be affected. This is because the market price of the stock reflects the declaration of dividends, and this would distort the actual price volatility unless explicitly dealt with. The market price will reflect this event on the **ex dividend** date, which is the last date on which a seller of the shares will still have claim to the dividend; after this date, the buyer will own the dividend, therefore the price of the stock will typically drop by the per share amount of the dividend on this date).

A simple way of thinking about volatility is to relate it to the well understood concept of the "normal distribution" which governs such common phenomena as college grading systems. The expected annualized volatility is effectively the standard deviation of the expected price of the stock. One standard deviation plus or minus from the present price, adjusted for the expected (or average) change in price over the period, will have about a 67% probability of including the actual price at the end of the term of the option. For example, if the price per share is $40 currently, and the expected return (based on past price changes) is 10% and the computed volatility measure is 25%, the price of the stock 1 year hence which is determined at a 67% probability is from $34.43 to $56.76. This is computed as follows: The rate of return over 1 year, at 67% probability (i.e., one standard deviation plus or minus), is from –15% = (10% – 25%) to +35% = (10% + 25%). The natural logarithms $e^{-.15}$ and $e^{.35}$ equate to .8607 and 1.4191, respectively. Thus, the likely stock price 1 year hence ranges from $34.43 ($40 x .8607) to $56.76 ($40 x 1.4191).

The discount rate. SFAS 123 specifies the use of a risk-free rate, although the earlier proposal stipulated that a market rate determined with reference to similarly risky investments be used. The risk-free rate of return is easily ascertained as the rate on treasury bills or notes having a remaining term to maturity equal to the expected life of the options being computed. Reasonable approximations would be acceptable (e.g., it would be valid to interpolate a discount rate from published data).

The expected term of the options. The objective of SFAS 123 is to allocate compensation cost to the periods in which services are provided to the entity granting the options. If the award is for past services, as indicated when the options are immediately exercisable by the holders, compensation cost must be fully expensed at the date of the grant. More typically, however, the options will not be exercisable until some later date, called the vesting date, which often will be a few years after the grant date. In such a case, the compensation element is really intended to apply to some or all of the intervening period from grant to vesting dates, and should be accrued over that time, based either on an estimate of the number of options expected to vest or on an estimate of the number of options expected to be exercised.

In some instances there is a performance condition stipulated in the option agreement, and the options will not be exercisable until the condition is met. A variation of this has the number of options dependent upon the extent to which performance is achieved. Compensation cost associated with such option arrangements is to be accrued over the expected period until the conditions will be satisfied.

In the case of either service period-based or performance-based options, provision for forfeitures may be made either at inception or as forfeitures actually occur. The former method requires that compensation cost be accrued based on the number of options which are expected to vest less those which vest but are not, for whatever reason, subsequently exercised by the holders. For example, it may be estimated based on past behavior that of 100 options granted, only 85 will vest (due to employee turnover, failure to meet performance conditions, etc.) and only 78 will be exercised; compensation cost would be based on 78 options in such a case. The latter method would have compensation determined based on the 85 options expected to vest, with compensation cost adjusted if and when some of the 7 (85-78) options are forfeited.

If the former method, basing compensation on the number of options expected to be exercised, is utilized, then changes in that expectation during the period in which compensation is being accrued is to be accounted for as a change in an accounting estimate as defined in APB 20; the effect is reported in the period in which the change occurs. Under the alternative method, the effect of forfeitures is reported in compensation as they individually occur.

Payments in lieu of dividends on options. Normally dividends are not paid on shares which have not been issued; thus, unexercised options do not gain the benefit of any dividends declared on the underlying stock. However, an entity can choose to pay dividend equivalents on options. Under the provisions of SFAS 123, such dividends or dividend equivalents on options which vest are to be accounted for as other dividends, that is, charged against retained earnings, but those paid on options which do not vest are deemed to be compensation expense. The reporting entity can either estimate what fraction of options will vest, and allocate such dividend equivalents between retained earnings and compensation expense accordingly, or else can charge all to retained earnings and account for forfeitures as they occur, by reversing the charge from retained earnings to compensation cost.

Settlements of awards. Sometimes an entity which grants options to employees will repurchase the resulting shares after they are issued, or will purchase and cancel the options, by making a payment to the option holders. To the extent that shares are purchased for market value, the transaction is similar to any other treasury stock transaction, and equity accounts will be charged with the purchase price as described elsewhere in this chapter. If, however, the purchase price exceeds the market or fair value, the excess is deemed to be additional compensation expense. If the payment is made to cancel options which have not yet vested, the remaining unrecognized compensation cost must be expensed, as the options have effectively vested at that point in time. The additional compensation element, if any, is measured by the difference between the price paid and the value of the option repurchased, as computed using the methods prescribed by SFAS 123 (i.e., by the fair value method).

Examples of accounting for options under SFAS 123

Example where calculation of compensation expense does not consider expected forfeitures. Consider first the same facts as were presented earlier in this section, when APB 25 was being explained.

Options are granted to corporate officers to purchase 10,000 shares of $1 par stock at a price of $52 per share, when the market price is $58. The options may not be exercised until 5 years from the grant date. The company has no reason to expect that any of the options will be forfeited by the employees to whom they are granted. If the risk-free interest rate is 8% and the stock is expected to pay dividends of $2 annually, the minimum value as prescribed under SFAS 123 is as follows:

Current market	$58.00
Less:	
Present value of exercise price ($52 x .681)	35.39
Present value of expected dividends ($2 x 3.993)	7.99
	$14.62

Thus the 10,000 options have a value of $146,200 (10,000 x $14.62), to be recognized over 5 years, or $29,240 per year before considering forfeitures.

The entry to record the granting of the options is

Deferred compensation expense	146,200	
Stock options outstanding		146,200

As was the case under APB 25, deferred compensation expense is subtracted from stock options outstanding in the paid-in capital section of owner's equity to indicate the amount of net contributed services on any date [i.e., on the grant date nothing has yet been contributed by the option holders ($146,200 – $146,200 = $0)]. As the employees provide services to earn the options, entries are made assigning compensation expense to years 1-5.

Compensation expense	29,240	($146,200 ÷ 5 years)
Deferred compensation expense		29,240

When the option is exercised, cash is received and the stock is issued. The following entry is made (assume exercise after the 5-year period):

Cash	520,000		(option price)
Stock options outstanding	146,200		
Common stock		10,000	(par)
Additional paid-in capital		656,200	(excess)

If options are forfeited as a result of an employee failing to fulfill an obligation (e.g., staying with the company), under the provisions of SFAS 123 compensation expense is credited in the year of forfeiture. (This is assuming that compensation expense had not been based on the **net** number of options which were expected to be exercised, which is the alternative, acceptable method under this standard.) The amount credited reflects the total compensation expense previously charged to the income statement for the employee who forfeited the options. Assume that one officer, who was granted options for 1,000 shares, leaves the company in year 3, 2 years before the options can be exercised. The result is handled as a change in an accounting estimate and the following entry is made in year 3:

Stock options outstanding	14,620	
Deferred compensation expense		8,772
Compensation expense		5,848

Next consider the case of an option plan which features graded vesting, that is, where instead of having all options vest after 5 years, 20% of the options granted will vest each year. Under FASB Interpretation 28, which applies to entities which continue to adhere to APB 25, a rather complicated allocation pattern must be employed. Entities which adopt SFAS 123 can either continue the Interpretation 28 method, illustrated earlier in this section, or can recognize compensation on a straight-line basis. These are not freely selectable alternatives, however, if fair value is determined based on different expected lives for options which vest in different years, then the Interpretation 28 method is required. Straight-line compensation recognition can be used only if the expected lives of the award is determined in another manner. If the straight-line method is used, the compensation cost recognized to date must be at least equal to the value of the vested portion of the award at that date. SFAS 123 includes illustrations of the accounting required under such circumstances.

Accounting under SFAS 123 using expected number of options to be exercised. Assume most of the same facts as the example presented immediately above. The company's stock is not publicly traded, and therefore there will be no attempt to address volatility. The risk-free interest rate is now given as 6%. Based on past experience, the company estimates that 2% of the eligible officers will leave each year, thus forfeiting their options. SFAS 123 permits the computation of fair value based on the expected number of options which will vest (i.e., net of expected forfeitures). As noted above, the standard also permits accounting for forfeitures when they occur. With an annual forfeiture rate of 2%, the number of options expected to vest is given as

$$10{,}000 \times .98 \times .98 \times .98 \times .98 \times .98 = 9{,}039 \text{ options}$$

The fair value can be determined with reference to either the Black-Scholes option pricing model or a binomial model, or the minimum value model can be used. In the present example, assuming no dividends are expected to be paid on the underlying stock, and given the risk-free rate of 6%, the minimum value model would value each option as follows:

$$\$58 - (\$52 \div 1.06^5) = \$58 - \$38.86 = \$19.14 \text{ per option}$$

Accordingly, the total value of $173,006 (9,039 options x $19.14) will be recognized as compensation expense over the 5 years on a ratable basis. If the forfeiture rate changes, that would be treated as a change in an accounting estimate, and reflected in income on a prospective basis. The entry to record the granting of the options is

Deferred compensation expense	173,006	
Stock options outstanding		173,006

Stock options outstanding is an additional paid-in capital account. Deferred compensation expense is subtracted from stock options outstanding in the paid-in capital section of owners' equity to indicate the amount of net contributed services on any date [i.e., on the grant date nothing has yet been contributed by the option holders ($173,006 – $173,006 = $0)]. As the employees provide services to earn the options, entries are made assigning compensation expense to years 1-5.

Compensation expense	34,601		(173,006 ÷ 5 years)
Deferred compensation expense		34,601	

When the option is exercised, cash is received and the stock is issued. The following entry is made (assume exercise after the 5-year period, and that the number of forfeitures exactly equals the amount predicted):

Cash	470,028 (option price)	
Stock options outstanding	173,006	
Common stock		9,039 (par)
Additional paid-in capital		633,995 (excess)

Note that under this method the effect of forfeitures is reflected in income, that is, compensation cost is reduced, on a prospective basis. If the assumption regarding the number of forfeitures changed during the service period, compensation cost attributable to prior periods is effectively adjusted in the current period by making a "catch up" adjustment as illustrated in the following paragraph.

Assume that in year 3 of the preceding example the holders of 5% of the remaining options leave the company (the forfeiture rate in years 1 and 2 having equaled the expected 2%). Management believes that the rate in year 3 was unusually high, but now expects that the forfeiture rate over the full 5-year period will average 3%. Given this new insight, the number of options which it believes will eventually vest will be as follows:

$$10{,}000 \times .97 \times .97 \times .97 \times .97 \times .97 = 8{,}587 \text{ options}$$

The total compensation cost over 5 years, given this revised estimate, will be \$164,355 (8,587 options x \$19.14). Since aggregate compensation cost of \$69,202 (\$34,601 x 2) has already been recognized in years 1 and 2, and total compensation cost for years 1 through 3 under the revised assumption should be \$98,613 (3/5 x \$164,355), the difference of \$29,411 should be allocated to compensation expense in year 3. The entry in year 3 is

Compensation expense	29,411	
Deferred compensation expense		29,411

The entries in years 4 and 5, assuming no other changes in the forfeiture rate, are

Compensation expense	32,871	
Deferred compensation expense		32,871

Also, there should be an adjustment to reduce the amounts in the deferred compensation expense and stock options outstanding accounts, based on the new expected totals, as follows:

Stock options outstanding	8,651	
Deferred compensation expense		8,651

Assuming that the average forfeiture rate does indeed equal 3% over the vesting period, and that all options are exercised at the vesting date, the entry to be made at the end of year 5 will be

Cash	446,524		(option price)
Stock options outstanding	164,355		
Common stock		8,587	(par)
Additional paid-in capital		602,292	(excess)

On the other hand, if the options are not forfeited, but instead expire unexercised after first vesting with the grantees, then the accounting treatment under SFAS 123 would be different. The standard provides that previously recognized compensation cost is not to be reversed if vested options expire unexercised; thus, in such a circumstance the stock options outstanding would be closed to another paid-in capital account, such as "capital from unexercised options."

For example, given the facts in the immediately preceding discussion, assume now that at the time the options vest, only 8,000 are exercised, and that, per the terms of the option agreement, the remaining 587 expire 1 year later, unexercised. The entries would be as follows:

For the exercise:

Cash	416,000		(option price)
Stock options outstanding	153,120		
Common stock		8,000	(par)
Additional paid-in capital		561,120	(excess)

For the expiration 1 year later:

Stock options outstanding	11,235	
Additional paid-in capital from unexercised options		11,235

Accounting for stock appreciation rights (SAR) under SFAS 123. Under prior GAAP, accounting for stock appreciation rights was prescribed by FASB Interpretation 28, which differed significantly from the accounting for options under APB 25. However, one of the motivating reasons for developing SFAS 123 was to eliminate the disparate treatment applied to fixed options, variable (or performance) options and other stock based compensation schemes. Thus, under the new standard the measurement principles applicable to SAR is the same as for stock options.

One distinction which may arise in connection with SAR, however, is that the holder may have the ability to elect to receive cash in settlement of the award. In the case of such plans, the accrual of compensation expense will result in the recognition of a liability. (In some such plans, however, the settlement can only be made in shares of stock; in such cases, the accrual will be offset by paid-in capital.)

Accounting for tandem plans under SFAS 123. Accounting for tandem plans has been explained earlier in this section for situations where APB 25 and related standards are still being utilized. The concepts are the same for tandem plans by entities which adopt SFAS 123, but the accounting will be somewhat different, for several reasons. First, SFAS 123 requires that when an entity incurs a substantive liability, it must be reported as such; further, it states that when the employee has the right to receive payment in cash, a liability has been created. Only if the company can choose to settle tandem plans in stock, and past experience suggests that indeed it does choose to do so, will the compensation be based on the stock option part of the plan and will the offset to compensation expense be paid-in capital.

Second, cash SAR are measured with reference to the intrinsic value as of the exercise date, which differs from the fair value approach to measuring stock options under SFAS 123. Note that time value, which is typically a major component of total value assigned to options under the new standard, is not measured as part of intrinsic value as applied to SAR. For that reason, compensation cost as determined in the context of tandem plans may be significantly less than would be the case for the option portion of the plan on its own.

To illustrate, consider again the facts presented in the example of tandem plans earlier in this chapter when APB 25 was being discussed.

1/1/99 Plan adopted; market price is $100, option price is $95; 1,000 shares exercisable on 1/1/02 **or** 1,000 SAR payable in cash on 1/1/03 an increase over 1/1/99 market value.

Market prices are as follows:

12/31/99	$ 98
12/31/00	110
12/31/01	108
12/31/02	125

Assuming now a 6% risk-free rate and no dividend yield on the stock, the fair value of the options alone using the minimum value model is \$100 – (\$95 x .792) = \$24.75 x 1,000 = \$24,750. Were these options free-standing and not part of a tandem plan, compensation cost of \$6,187.50 would be accrued each year.

However, since the holders have the right to choose cash payments, under SFAS 123 it must be assumed that they will do this, and that the company has incurred a liability (not an equity instrument). Accordingly, compensation cost is debited or credited as the market price varies from the rights price (\$100), with the limitation that the cumulative compensation cost cannot be negative (as the employees obviously have no obligation to pay the company if the market declines from the \$100 per share level). Therefore the entries will be as follows:

12/31/99 No entry

No SAR liability is accrued since the market price is below the base price. The compensatory stock options are ignored since the holders have the right to demand a cash settlement.

12/31/00	Compensation expense	10,000	
	Liability under SAR plan (\$10 x 1,000 SAR)		10,000

SAR liability recognized for difference between year-end market value and base price for number of expected SAR exercisable.

12/31/01	Liability under SAR plan	2,000	
	Compensation expense		2,000
12/31/02	Compensation expense	17,000	
	Liability under SAR plan		17,000

Recall that the option holders may exercise either the options or the SAR, although the accrual under SFAS 123 was based on the presumption that 100% exercise of the SAR would occur. Assume that (a) holders elect 100% SAR; (b) holders elect 50% SAR, 50% stock; or (c) they elect to exercise only the stock options. For each of the cases above, the entries under each assumed exercise ratio are as follows:

(a)	Liability under SAR plan	25,000	
(all cash)	Cash		25,000
(b)	Liability under SAR plan	25,000	
(1/2 cash,	Cash (\$47,500 – \$12,500)	35,000	
1/2 stock)	Common stock--\$20 par		10,000
	Additional paid-in capital		50,000
(c)	Liability under SAR plan	25,000	
(all stock)	Cash	95,000	
	Common stock--\$20 par		20,000
	Additional paid-in capital		100,000

Reload options and other plan features. Some option arrangements permit the exercise price to be paid for by delivering shares already held by the grantee (these shares are referred to as "mature shares"), rather than with cash. These shares are valued at the market price as of the date of the exercise. Furthermore, there may be a so-called reload feature, which provides that the holder will be granted another option equal to the number of mature shares used in the exercise, and that the exercise price for the reload option will be equal to the market at the time of exercise of the original option. This feature obviously has value, and in a fair value approach as is adopted under SFAS 123 this feature should be considered in computing compensation cost. However, there are a number of subjective elements which would need to be addressed, including the expected market value at exercise and reload date and the number of options which would be exercised in this fashion. Due to this and the fact that valuation models dealing with reload features are not yet widely understood, SFAS 123 has stipulated that there be no additional value assigned for such options. Rather, if and when a reload option is granted (when mature shares are used to exercise the original option), it is to be accounted for as a new option.

Other modifications of options are accounted for prospectively as exchanges of the old options for a new equity instrument. Fair value is used to account for such transactions. For example, modification of the terms of an outstanding option would be accounted for based on a comparison of the fair value of the modified option at the date it is granted and at the date of the old option that is effectively repurchased, based on the shorter of (1) the remaining initially estimated expected life or (2) the expected life of the modified option. If the fair value of the modified option exceeds that of the option which is replaced, additional compensation cost must be recognized.

Other SFAS 123 Matters

The Board issued TB 97-1 which deals with "look back options" in the context of SFAS 123. Plans with this feature permit exercise at a price which is the lower of the market price at the grant date or at the date of exercise. This technical bulletin is applicable to stock-based awards with this feature which are granted, renewed, or modified after 1/1/98.

Disclosure requirements under SFAS 123. SFAS 123 significantly expands the disclosures which are required by entities having stock compensation arrangements, and this expansion applies as well, for the most part, to those companies which continue to employ APB 25 for financial statement purposes. For all entities, disclosures will include

1. A description of the plans, including terms of awards under each program (e.g., vesting requirements, maximum term of options granted, number of shares authorized or reserved, etc.);
2. For each year for which an income statement is presented, the following information is required to be disclosed:

a. The number and weighted-average exercise prices of options for each of these groups: (1) those outstanding at year beginning, (2) those outstanding at year end, (3) those exercisable at year end, (4) those granted during the year, (5) those exercised during the year, (6) those forfeited during the year, and (7) those expired during the year;
b. The weighted-average grant date fair value of options granted during the year. If exercise prices differ from market value as of grant date, the weighted-average exercise prices and weighted-average fair values of options shall be disclosed separately for options whose exercise price (1) equals, (2) exceeds, and (3) is less than market price of the stock as of the grant date.
c. The number and weighted-average grant date fair value of equity instruments other than options granted during the year (e.g., shares of nonvested stock).
d. A description of the method and significant assumptions used during the year to estimate fair values (e.g., Black-Scholes model), including the weighted-average (1) risk-free interest rate, (2) expected life, (3) expected volatility, and (4) expected dividends.
e. Total compensation cost recognized in income relating to stock-based compensation awards.
f. The terms of significant modifications of outstanding awards.

3. For options outstanding as of the date of the latest balance sheet, the range of exercise prices and weighted-average exercise price, and weighted-average remaining contractual life must be presented. If the range is wide, exercise prices should be grouped into ranges which are more meaningful for assessing the number and timing of additional share issuances and the cash which may be received as a result of such exercises (SFAS 123 suggests that the range is wide if the highest exercise price exceeds about 150% of the lowest). For each such range the following disclosures are required:

   a. The number, weighted-average exercise price, and weighted-average remaining contractual life of options outstanding.
   b. The number and weighted-average exercise price of options currently exercisable.

Furthermore, if the company grants options under a number of plans (e.g., fixed and variable plans), the income statement oriented disclosures should be appropriately segregated.

For entities which continue to apply APB 25, the company must also disclose for each year for which an income statement is provided the pro forma net income (and earnings per share, if required under APB 15 as amended by SFAS 21) as if fair value based measurements had been used. Thus, **all** entities will have to apply the Black-Scholes or binomial model (if publicly owned) or the minimum value model (if privately owned), whether SFAS 123 is adopted or not. It should be noted that, in determining the pro forma disclosures, the tax effect of compensation differences will also have to be considered, as discussed below. This particular pro forma disclosure cannot be merged with any other pro forma calculation; it must be possible for financial statement readers to understand the impact on earnings of the choice of accounting method for stock-based compensation alone.

Finally, enterprises that use equity instruments to acquire goods or services other than employee services must also provide disclosures similar to those above (e.g., number of shares, weighted-average prices, etc.).

Accounting for the Tax Effects of Options and SAR

Generally, amounts reported as compensation expense in connection with stock option and appreciation rights plans are deductible for tax purposes, but the timing and amounts of tax deductions may differ from the amounts reportable as expenses under GAAP. Thus, both temporary and permanent differences may occur, which are accounted for differently under GAAP (SFAS 109).

The timing difference occurs because, for tax purposes, the company will be entitled to a deduction in the period in which the employee reports the compensation as ordinary income, whereas for financial reporting purposes the compensation expense is accrued in the period(s) in which the services are provided. Since the tax deduction occurs in a period subsequent to the service provision periods, a deferred tax benefit will be recognizable by the sponsoring corporation. Under current GAAP, such benefits are to be recorded in every case, although when it is deemed "more likely than not" that the benefit will **not** be received by the reporting entity, an offsetting valuation account must also be recorded.

The permanent difference occurs because the amount of the compensation reportable for tax purposes differs from the amount which is to be recognized under GAAP for financial reporting. For tax purposes, the deduction available to the company (and the amount includable by the employee as ordinary income) is measured by the difference between the market price and the option price as of the **exercise** date. By contrast, for financial reporting purposes if APB 25 is being employed, compensation is defined as the spread between the market price and the option price as of the **measurement** date, which is almost always earlier than the exercise date, and is usually the grant date in the case of options. If SFAS 123 has been adopted, compensation is computed using the fair value approach, in accordance with a model such as Black-Scholes or by the minimum value method, as illustrated earlier in this chapter.

If the amount of compensation permitted as a tax deduction is greater than that reportable for financial reporting purposes, the tax effect of this difference is to be credited to paid-in capital. If the expense for financial reporting exceeds the tax deduction which is allowable, the tax effect of the difference may be debited to any paid-in capital accumulated from earlier transactions of like kind. Any excess debit should be taken directly to retained earnings, in the same manner as "deficiencies" on treasury stock transactions.

Example of accounting for the tax ramifications of stock options

An option to purchase 10 shares at $80 per share is granted to a key employee when the market price is $100 per share. The company is continuing to use APB 25 to account for such transactions. The following entry is made to record the deferred compensation:

Deferred compensation expense	200		[10 x ($100 – $80)]
Stock options outstanding		200	

Compensation is associated with employee service in years 1-4. The annual entry to recognize the expense is

Compensation expense	50	
Deferred compensation expense		50

Assume the tax rate remains constant at 40% and income before stock option compensation expense for years 1-5 is $400. The compensation expense is not deductible for tax purposes until the option is exercised. The entry to record the taxes and tax effects for years 1-4 is

Tax expense	140		($350 x .40)
Deferred tax asset	20		($50 x .40)
Tax payable		160	($400 x .40)

Under the provisions of SFAS 109, the deferred tax benefit of the foregoing transaction will always be recorded. There may also be recognition of a valuation allowance (contra to the deferred tax asset), depending upon the perceived likelihood of realization of the tax benefit. In the present example, it is presumed that no valuation allowance is deemed to be necessary in connection with the deferred tax asset arising from the compensation expense temporary difference. In year 5, the options are exercised at the option price of $80 per share when the market price per share is $115. Thus, the compensation expense deductible for tax purposes in year 5 is $350 [10 shares x ($115 – $80)]. No additional compensation expense is allowed as a deduction in the determination of net income. The result is a permanent difference of $150 ($350 – $200). The current year tax expense is $160 ($400 x 40%). The current year taxes payable is $20 [($400 – $350) x 40%]. The $140 difference represents the tax effects of the $200 reversing temporary difference ($80) and the $150 permanent difference ($60). The journal entry is as follows:

Tax expense	160		($400 x .40)
Paid-in capital		60	($150 x .40)
Deferred tax asset		80	($20 x 4 yrs.)
Tax payable		20	($50 x .40)

The same general approach approach is followed by an entity which has adopted SFAS 123; however the measure of compensation cost will differ, and thus will the measure of the deferred taxes related thereto.

Convertible Preferred Stock

The treatment of convertible preferred stock at its issuance is no different than that of nonconvertible preferred. When it is converted, the book value approach is used to account for the conversion. Use of the market value approach would entail a gain or loss for which there is no theoretical justification since the total amount of contributed capital does not change when the stock is converted. When the preferred stock is converted, the "Preferred stock" and related "Additional paid-in capital--preferred stock" accounts are debited for their original values when purchased, and "Common stock" and "Additional paid-in capital--common stock" (if an excess over par or stated value exists) are credited. If the book value of the preferred stock is less than the total par value of the common stock being issued, retained earnings is charged for the difference. This charge is supported by the rationale that the preferred shareholders are offered an additional return to facilitate their conversion to common stock. Many states require that this excess instead reduce additional paid-in capital from other sources.

Preferred Stock With Mandatory Redemption

A mandatory redemption clause requires the preferred stock to be redeemed (retired) at a specified date(s). This feature is in contrast to callable preferred stock, which is redeemed at the issuing corporation's option.

The mandatory redemption feature, when combined with a cumulative dividend preference, causes the preferred stock to have the characteristics of debt, especially when the stock is to be redeemed in 5-10 years. The dividend payments represent interest and redemption is the repayment of principal. However, there is one important difference. The dividend payments do not receive the same tax treatment as interest payments. They are not deductible in determining taxable income.

Despite the existence of characteristics similar to debt, under current GAAP preferred stock with mandatory redemption features are categorized with other equity issuances. It should be noted that the FASB did make some effort to address this issue in its 1990 discussion memorandum about distinguishing between liability and equity instruments, but this project was later placed on a back burner as more critical financial instruments-related topics were given more prominence. More recently, however, the Board has indicated that a very limited project will be undertaken, which will address mandatorily redeemable preferred stock and similar financial instruments, as well as compound instruments having characteristics of both liabilities and equity. Thus, it is possible that classification of redeemable preferred stock as a liability item may become a formal requirement within the near term. It is not clear whether such a requirement, if indeed it is forthcoming, would be accompanied by a rule classifying preferred dividends as an expense, similar to interest, to be reported in the income statement.

It should be noted that even under present GAAP, expanded disclosure of mandatorily redeemable preferred stock is required. This is pursuant to recently issued SFAS 129, which supersedes a virtually identical requirement established by SFAS 47. Specifically, the redemption requirements for each of the next 5 years must be set forth in the notes to the financial statements prepared in accordance with GAAP, if the amounts are either fixed or determinable on fixed or determinable dates. Thus readers can interpret the cash requirements on the reporting entity, in a manner similar to the drawing of inferences about other fixed commitments, such as maturities of long-term debt and lease obligations.

The SEC, conversely, does recognize the debt characteristics of mandatory redeemable preferred stock. According to SAR 268, the stock may not be presented under the heading "Stockholders' Equity." Rather, the amounts pertaining to this type of stock may be presented either as long-term debt or between long-term debt and stockholders' equity.

Book Value Stock Plans

Another type of stock purchase plan is referred to as a book value plan. It is intended also to be a compensation program for participating employees although there are important secondary motives in many such plans, such as the desires to generate capital and to tie the employees to the employer. Under the terms of typical book value plans, employees (or those attaining some defined level, such as manager) are given the opportunity or, in some cases, they are required to purchase shares in the company, which then must be sold back to the company upon termination of employment. EITF Issues 87-23 and 88-6 addressed different aspects of such plans.

In 87-23, a consensus was reached that, if the employees participating in a nonpublic company's book value stock plan have substantive investments in the company which are at risk, then the increases in book value during the period of ownership are not to be treated as compensation. However, if the employees are granted options to purchase shares at book value, compensation is to be recognized for value increases presumably because under the latter scenario the employee has no investment at risk and is only being given an "upside" opportunity. This interpretation is also applicable to book value options granted to employees of publicly held companies.

For accounting purposes, shares issued at book value to employees are simply recorded as a normal stock sale. To the extent that book value exceeds par or stated value, additional paid-in capital accounts may also be credited.

EITF 88-6 addresses the related question of book value stock plans of publicly held companies. In this consensus, the Task Force concluded that the plan was a performance plan akin to a SAR, and accordingly results in compensation expense recognition. This conclusion was reached at least in part due to SEC pressure, which arose largely in the context of initial public offerings (IPO).

Junior Stock

Another category of stock-based compensation program involves junior stock. Typically, such shares are subordinate to normal shares of common stock with respect to voting rights, dividend rate, or other attributes, and are convertible into regular common shares if and when stipulated performance goals are achieved. Like stock appreciation rights, grants of junior stock represent a performance-based program, in contrast to fixed stock options.

FASB Interpretation 38 specifies that compensation cost incurred in connection with grants of junior stock is generally to be accrued in accordance with the provisions of Interpretation 28. However, compensation is only to be recognized when it is deemed to be probable, as that term is defined by SFAS 5, that the performance goals will be achieved. It may be that achievement is not deemed probable at the time the junior stock is issued, but it later becomes clear that such achievement is indeed likely. In other circumstances, the ability to convert junior stock to regular stock is dependent upon the achievement of more than a single performance goal, and it is not probable that all such goals can be achieved, although some of them are deemed probable of achievement. In both scenarios, full accrual of compensation cost may be delayed until the estimated likelihood of achievement improves.

Interpretation 38 specifies that the measure of compensation is derived from the comparison of the market price of ordinary common stock with the price to be paid, if any, for the junior stock. Since the junior stock will be convertible to ordinary common stock if the defined performance goals are achieved, the compensation to be received by the employees participating in the plan is linked to the value of unrestricted common shares.

Put Warrant

A detachable put warrant can either be put back to the debt issuer for cash or can be exercised to acquire common stock. EITF 88-9 concluded that these instruments should be accounted for in the same manner as mandatory redeemable preferred stock. The proceeds applicable to the put warrant ordinarily are to be classified as equity and should be presented between the liability and equity sections in accordance with SEC SAR 268.

In the case of a warrant with a put price substantially higher than the value assigned to the warrant at issuance, however, the proceeds should be classified as a liability since it is likely that the warrant will be put back to the company.

The original **classification** should not be changed because of subsequent economic changes in the value of the put. The value assigned to the put warrant at issuance, however, should be adjusted to its highest redemption price, starting with the date of issuance until the earliest date of the warrants. Changes in the redemption price before the earliest put dates are changes in accounting estimates and changes after the earliest put dates should be recognized in income. If the put is classified as equity, the adjustment should be reported as a charge to retained earnings, and if the put is classified as a liability the adjustment is reported as interest expense.

Regardless of how the put is classified on the balance sheet, the primary and fully diluted EPS should be calculated on both an equity basis (warrants will be exercised) and on a debt basis (put will be exercised) and the more dilutive of the two methods should be used.

Accounting for Stock Issued to Employee Stock Ownership Plans

Increasingly, corporations have been availing themselves of favorable tax regulations which encourage the establishment of employee stock ownership plans (ESOP). The accounting for ESOP was first set forth in AICPA Statement of Position (SOP) 76-3, which has been superseded by SOP 93-6. However, employers may continue their current accounting methods for shares purchased prior to December 31, 1992.

Employee stock ownership plans (ESOP) are defined contribution plans in which shares of the sponsoring entity are given to employees as additional compensation. Subsequent to the inception of these types of plans some 40 years ago, these plans have grown enormously in popularity; in fact ever since the issuance of the previous guidance on accounting for these plans by the sponsoring employers, SOP 76-3, the number of such plans has approximately quadrupled. Importantly, ESOP have become popular vehicles for funding other employee benefits (such as the employer's matching contributions to savings [401(k)] plans). This type of usage had not been contemplated at the time GAAP in this area was first established. Additionally, major changes were made to the tax laws which favored creation of these plans. As a result, in 1993 the new accounting standard, SOP 93-6, was promulgated. It made significant changes to the employers' accounting for the costs associated with such plans.

In brief, ESOP are created by a sponsoring corporation which either funds the plan directly (unleveraged ESOP) or, as is more often the case, facilitates the borrowing of money either directly from an outside lender (directly leveraged ESOP) or from the employer, who in turn will borrow from an outside lender (indirectly leveraged ESOP). Borrowings from outside lenders may or may not be guaranteed by the sponsor. Since effectively the only source of funds for debt repayment are future contributions by the sponsor, GAAP requires that the ESOP's debt be considered debt of the sponsor. Depending on the reasons underlying the creation of the ESOP (estate planning by the controlling shareholder, expanding the capital base of the entity, rewarding and motivating the work force, etc.), the sponsor's shares may be contributed to the plan in annual installments, in a block of shares from the sponsor, or shares from an existing shareholder may be purchased by the plan.

Direct or indirect borrowings by the ESOP must be reported as debt in the sponsor's balance sheet. An offset to a contra equity account, not to an asset, is also reported since the plan represents a commitment (morally if not always legally) to make future contributions to the plan and **not** a claim to resources. This results in a "double hit" to the sponsor's balance sheet (i.e., the recording of a liability **and** the reduction of net stockholders' equity) which is often an unanticipated and unpleasant surprise. This contra equity account was called "unearned compensation" under SOP 76-3, but is now referred to as "unearned ESOP shares" under SOP 93-6. If the sponsor lends funds to the ESOP without a "mirror" loan from an outside lender, this loan should not be reported in the employer's balance sheet as debt, although the debit should still be reported as a contra equity account.

As the ESOP services the debt, using contributions made by the sponsor and/or dividends received on sponsor shares held by the plan, the sponsor reflects the reduction of the obligation by reducing the debt and the contra equity account on its balance sheet. Simultaneously, income and thus retained earnings will be impacted as the contributions to the plan are reported in the sponsor's current results of operations. Thus, the "double hit" is eliminated, but net worth continues to reflect the economic fact that compensation costs have been incurred. Both standards (SOP 76-3 and 93-6) require that the interest cost component be separated from the remaining compensation expense, that is, that the sponsor's income statement should reflect the true character of the expenses being incurred, rather than aggregating the entire amount into a category such as "ESOP contribution."

In a leveraged ESOP, shares held serve as collateral for the debt and are not allocated to employee until the debt is retired. In general, shares must be allocated by the end of the year in which the debt is repaid; however, in order to satisfy the tax laws, the allocation of shares may take place at a faster pace than the retirement of the principal portion of the debt.

While the sponsor's journal entries under SOP 93-6 differ from those under SOP 76-3, the net results are similar, with two important exceptions. First, under the new standard the cost of ESOP shares allocated is measured (for purposes of reporting compensation expense in the sponsor's income statements) based upon the fair value on the release date, in contrast to the actual historical cost of the shares to the plan. Second, dividends paid on unallocated shares (i.e., shares held by the ESOP) are no longer treated as dividends (that is, as charges against retained earnings), but rather must be reported in the sponsor's income statement as compensation cost and/or as interest expense. Of less significance to nonpublic companies is the fact that under the new rules only common shares released and committed to be released are treated as being outstanding, and thus are to be considered in both primary and fully diluted EPS calculations. Under prior GAAP, all ESOP-held shares were deemed to be outstanding for EPS computation purposes.

Prospective application of the rules is not required (but is permitted) for shares acquired by ESOP after December 31, 1992, but not previously committed to be released as of the beginning of the year of adoption. Thus, if it so desired, an entity could preserve the historical acquisition cost of these "grandfathered" shares as the measure of compensation cost in future years, until the supply of these pre-1993 shares was depleted.

Example of accounting for ESOP transactions under the new standard

Assume that Intrepid Corp. establishes an ESOP, which then borrows $500,000 from Second Interstate Bank. The ESOP then purchases 50,000 shares of Intrepid no-par shares from the company; none of these shares are allocated to individual participants. Under SOP 93-6, the entries would be

Cash	500,000	
Bank loan payable		500,000
Unearned ESOP shares (contra equity)	500,000	
Common stock		500,000

The ESOP then borrows an additional $250,000 from the sponsor, Intrepid, and uses the cash to purchase a further 25,000 shares, all of which are allocated to participants.

Compensation	250,000	
Common stock		250,000

Intrepid Corp. contributes $50,000 to the plan, which the plan uses to service its bank debt, consisting of $40,000 principal reduction and $10,000 interest cost. The debt reduction causes 4,000 shares to be allocated to participants at a time when the average market value had been $12 per share.

Interest expense	10,000	
Bank loan payable	40,000	
Cash		50,000
Compensation	48,000	
Additional paid-in capital		8,000
Unearned ESOP shares		40,000

Dividends of $.10 per share are declared (only the ESOP shares are represented in the following entry, but dividends are paid equally on all outstanding shares)

Retained earnings	2,900	
Compensation	4,600	
Dividends payable		7,500

Note that in all the foregoing illustrations the effect of income taxes is ignored. Since the difference between the cost and fair values of shares committed to be released is analogous to differences in the expense recognized for tax and accounting purposes with regard to stock options, the same treatment should be applied. That is, the tax effect should be reported directly in stockholders' equity, rather than in earnings.

Disclosure Requirements

Under recently issued SFAS 129, which consolidates requirements previously set forth in APB 10 and 15, and SFAS 47, certain disclosures of an entity's capital structure are required. Under this standard, the financial statements will be required to explain, in summary form, the pertinent rights and privileges of the various equity securities outstanding, including dividend and liquidation preferences, participation rights, call prices and dates, conversion and exercise prices or rates along with pertinent dates, sinking fund requirements, unusual voting rights, and significant terms of any contractual obligations to issue additional shares.

Furthermore, the number of shares issued upon conversion, exercise, or satisfaction of required conditions, during at least the most recent annual reporting period and any subsequent interim period which is presented, must be disclosed. If preference shares have a liquidation preference considerably in excess of par or stated value in the event of involuntary liquidation, the aggregate amount must be disclosed. The amount which would be paid upon exercise of call privileges applicable to preferred shares must be disclosed also, but in this case either per share or aggregate data can be given. Any dividend arrearages on cumulative preferred shares must be stated, this on **both** per share and aggregate bases. Finally, if redeemable preferred shares are outstanding, the amount of redemption requirements for each of the subsequent 5 years must be given, if fixed or determinable on fixed or determinable dates; if there are several series of such shares, this can be given in the aggregate.

The requirements of SFAS 129 are effective for years ending after December 1997.

Corporate Bankruptcy and Reorganizations

Entities operating under and emerging from protection of the bankruptcy laws. The going concern assumption is one of the basic postulates underlying generally accepted accounting principles and is responsible for, among other things, the historical cost convention in financial reporting. For entities which have entered bankruptcy proceedings, however, the going concern assumption will no longer be of central importance.

Traditionally, the basic financial statements (balance sheet, income statement, and statement of cash flows) presented by going concerns were seen as less useful for entities undergoing reorganization. Instead, the **statement of affairs,** reporting assets at estimated realizable values and liabilities at estimated liquidation amounts, was recommended for use by such organizations. In more recent years, use of the statement of affairs has not been frequently encountered in practice. In late 1990, the AICPA's Accounting Standards Executive Committee promulgated Statement of Position 90-7, setting forth certain financial reporting standards for entities undergoing, and emerging from, reorganization under the bankruptcy laws.

Under provisions of this SOP, assets are presented at estimated realizable values. Liabilities are set forth at the estimated amounts to be allowed in the balance sheet and liabilities subject to compromise are to be distinguished from those which are not. Furthermore, the SOP requires that in both the statements of income and cash flows, normal transactions be differentiated from those which have occurred as a consequence of the entity's being in reorganization. While certain allocations to the latter category are rather obvious, such as legal and accounting fees incurred, others are less clear. For example, the standard suggests that if the entity in reorganization earns interest income on funds which would normally have been used to settle obligations owed to creditors, such income will be deemed to be income arising as a consequence of the bankruptcy action.

Another interesting aspect of this standard is the accounting to be made for the emergence from reorganization (known as *confirmation of the plan of reorganization*). SOP 90-7 provides for so-called **fresh start** financial reporting in such instances. This accounting is similar to that applied to purchase business combinations under APB 16, with the total confirmed value of the entity upon its emergence from reorganization being analogous to the purchase price in an acquisition. In both cases, this total value is to be allocated to the identifiable assets and liabilities of the entity, with any excess being allocated to goodwill. In the case of entities emerging from bankruptcy, goodwill ("reorganization value in excess of amounts allocable to identifiable assets") is measured as the **excess** of liabilities existing at the plan confirmation date, computed at present value of future amounts to be paid, over the "reorganization value" of assets. Reorganization value is calculated with reference to a number of factors, including forecasted operating results and cash flows of the new entity.

SOP 90-7 applies only to entities undergoing formal reorganization under the Bankruptcy Code. Less formal procedures may still be accounted for under preexisting **quasi reorganization** accounting procedures.

Quasi reorganization. Generally, this procedure is applicable during a period of declining price levels. It is termed "quasi" since the accumulated deficit is eliminated at a lower cost and with less difficulty than a legal reorganization.

Per ARB 43, Ch. 7A, the procedures in a quasi reorganization involve the

1. Proper authorization from stockholders and creditors where required
2. Revaluation of assets to their current values. All losses are charged to retained earnings, thus increasing any deficit.
3. Elimination of any deficit by charging paid-in capital
    a. First, additional paid-in capital to the extent it exists
    b. Second, capital stock when additional paid-in capital is insufficient. The par value of the stock is reduced, creating the extra additional paid-in capital to which the remaining deficit is charged.

No retained earnings may be created by a reorganization. Any excess created by the reduction of par value is credited to "Paid-in capital from quasi reorganization."

ARB 46, para 2 requires that retained earnings be dated for 10 years (less than 10 years may be justified under exceptional circumstances) after a quasi reorganization takes place. Disclosure similar to "since quasi reorganization of June 30, 19XX" is appropriate.

Reporting by Limited Liability Companies and Partnerships

Accounting theory and practice have overwhelmingly developed within the context of businesses organized as normal corporations. Accordingly, there is little official guidance to entities organized as partnerships or other forms of business, which is generally not a serious concern given that most transactions entered into by such entities do not differ generically from those conducted by corporations. The primary differences relate to equity transactions and to the display of the equity section of the balance sheet.

The AICPA has recently released Practice Bulletin 14 to address certain issues pertaining to accounting and reporting by limited liability companies and partnerships. This pronouncement establishes that, when an entity restructures itself as a limited liability company or a limited liability partnership, the basis of all assets and liabilities from its predecessor entity are carried forward. Also, as suggested by SFAS 109, if the new entity is not a taxable one, any deferred tax assets or liabilities existing previously are to be written off at the time the change in tax status becomes effective; with the elimination of any debit or credit balance being effected by a charge or credit to current period tax expense.

With regard to financial statement display issues, the practice bulletin establishes that the headings of each statement identify the entity as being a limited liability company or a limited liability partnership, similar to the common practice of identifying partnership entities. The apparent logic is that this alerts the user to certain anomalies, such as (most commonly) an absence of income tax expense and a related liability, and the use of somewhat distinctive captions in the equity section of the balance sheet. In the case of limited liability companies and partnerships, the term "members' equity" has been prescribed, and the changes in members' equity is to be communicated either in a separate financial statement, in a combined statement of operations and changes in members' equity, or in the notes to the financial statements.

The bulletin recommends that, where there are several classes of members' equity, these be set forth separately in the equity section of the balance sheet, although this is not a firm requirement. If not set forth in the balance sheet, however, the notes must provide adequate disclosure about the different classes of equity outstanding. This is entirely analogous to the existing GAAP requirements concerning disclosure about common and preferred stock of typical corporations, which has been analogized further to apply to classes of partnership equity in limited partnerships.

A deficit, if one exists, should be reported in the members' equity account(s), even if there is limited liability for the members. This is consistent with the "going concern" assumption which underlies GAAP. It is not required to disaggregate members' equity into separate components (undistributed earnings, unallocated capital, etc.) on the face of the balance sheet or in the notes, although this is of course permissible.

Amounts due from members for capital contributions, if any remain unpaid at the balance sheet date, should be shown as deductions from members' equity. This is entirely consistent with practice for unpaid stock subscriptions receivable, as discussed earlier in this chapter.

GAAP presumes that comparative financial statements are more useful than those for a single period, and accordingly that comparative statements should normally be presented. However, for such financial statements to be meaningful, the information for the earlier period must be truly comparable to that of the more recent period. If the formation of the limited liability company or the limited liability partnership results in a new reporting entity being created, the guidance of APB 20 dealing with changes in accounting entities should be consulted.

Practice Bulletin 14 sets forth certain disclosures to be made in the financial statements of limited liability companies or limited liability partnerships. There should be a description of any limitations on members' equity and of the different classes of members' interests and the respective rights, preferences, and privileges of each class and amounts thereof. If the entity will cease to exist at a stipulated date, this must be disclosed. As suggested above, any change in tax status, and the impact of eliminating any tax liability or benefit from the entity's balance sheet, must be adequately explained in the notes to the financial statements in the period the change in status occurs.

In the period in which a limited liability company or a limited liability partnership is formed by combining entities under common control, or by conversion from another type of entity, the bulletin requires disclosures about the assets and liabilities previously held by the predecessor entity or entities. Entities created by combining predecessors under common control are encouraged, but not required, to make disclosures set forth by APB 16 applicable to poolings.

EMERGING ISSUES TASK FORCE CONSENSUS SUMMARIES

84-18 Stock Option Pyramiding

In cases in which an employee exercises a stock option by exchanging shares held instead of cash, some holding period of shares exchanged is necessary to avoid treating the exercise as a SAR. A majority of task force members agreed that is should be at least 6 months. This EITF only applies to APB 25.

85-1 Classifying Notes Received for Capital Stock

A consensus was reached regarding the classification of a contribution to a company's equity in the form of a note receivable. These notes should generally not be reported as an asset unless circumstances indicate both the ability and intent to pay in a short period of time. The Task Force noted that the most widespread practice is to report these notes as a reduction of equity. However, if the cash is received prior to the issuance of the financial statements, the note may be reported as an asset.

85-25 Sale of Preferred Stocks with a Put Option

The Task Force agreed that when the sale of perpetual preferred stock includes a put option that allows the purchaser to later transfer the stocks back to the seller at a fixed price, the proper accounting depends on the probability of exercise of the put option. If it is not probable, then recognition as a sale is appropriate. If probable, the transaction is recognized as a borrowing and the difference between the sale price and the put price is amortized over the period from the sale date to the first allowable put date.

87-6 Adjustments Relating to Stock Compensation Plans

A. Changes to Stock Option Plans Arising from the Tax Reform Act of 1986

As a result of tax law changes, a company may receive a significant tax deduction by disqualifying outstanding incentive stock options (ISO). The discussion focused on whether these changes to the option plan created a new measurement date for accounting purposes. A consensus was reached that minor technical changes, because of the tax reforms, would not create a new measurement date if the total effect on the value of the option is minimal from the perspective of the employee.

B. Stock Option Plan with Tax-Offset Cash Bonus

The issue was how to account for the cash bonus paid to reimburse employees for the tax liability they incur after exercising their options. The consensus was reached that split accounting treatment, in which the measurement date for the option is the date of grant and for the cash bonus is the date of exercise, should be applied **only** to grants outstanding as of April 4, 1987. The discussion also lists additional characteristics and restrictions which apply to the cash bonus. If these are not met, the plan would be accounted for as a variable plan, compensation measured at the date of exercise.

C. Use of Stock Option Shares to Cover Tax Withholdings

A consensus was reached that such an option plan would be considered a fixed plan if it meets all the other requirements of APB 25. No compensation expense would need to be recorded for the shares used to meet the tax withholding requirements.

D. "Phantom" Stock-for-Stock Exercise

Instead of paying cash to exercise the price of an option, some individuals may exchange shares already owned. The issue in this "phantom" stock-for-stock issue is how to account for this arrangement. A consensus was reached that the plan remains a fixed plan, compensation measured from date of grant, if employee meets the necessary holding period for the shares owned.

87-31 Sale of Put Options on Issuer's Stock

This involves the sale by an enterprise of put options on its common shares; when issued, these are "out of the money" but will be traded for some period and may ultimately result in the holder requiring the issuing entity to buy back its shares above the current market price. A consensus was reached that the proceeds of the sale of the puts would be reported in equity, with a concurrent transfer from equity to a "temporary equity" account of an amount equal to the redemption price of the stock. ("Temporary equity" is an SEC concept for publicly held companies; there is not at the present time any analog for private companies.) The EITF did not suggest that subsequent changes in the price of the stock be reflected (although presumably the later SFAS 107 would require that the fair value of this financial instrument be disclosed). The potentially dilutive effect on EPS would have to be disclosed at any balance sheet date when the options are "in the money" using a reverse of the so-called treasury stock method required under APB 15.

87-33 Stock Compensation Issues Related to Market Decline

A number of technical issues arising in the context of the October 1987 market crash were addressed here. There was a consensus that if existing options are repriced downward or are cancelled and replaced with less costly options, none of the previous compensation recognized should be reversed. Any remaining unamortized or unaccrued compensation should be amortized or accrued, and any additional compensation should be measured using current market and exercise prices. The added compensation should be amortized over the remaining service period. In addition, a consensus was reached that para 11(g) of APB 25 (recognition of additional compensation when cash is paid to settle an earlier option) would not apply to a buy back consummated pursuant to a reissuance of options. This interpretation applies equally to restricted stock awards. Another issue addressed by 87-33 related to tandem fixed awards involving a further grant of options, which was interpreted as a conversion to a variable plan, since the employee has the option to exercise either the old or new options, which will cancel the ones not exercised. The consensus was to use the standard approach to measure compensation prospectively, based on the new grant, until the market price increases sufficiently to make exercise of the old options more attractive.

88-6 Book Value Stock Plans in an Initial Public Offering

This consensus extends that set forth in 87-23. For publicly held companies, a book value stock purchase plan is a performance plan akin to stock appreciation rights, and thus gives rise to compensation expense. For book value options outstanding during an initial public offering (IPO), any value change resulting from the IPO is deemed to be compensation expense, as are further value changes after the IPO. However, for book value options which are converted to fair market value option plans during an IPO, compensation is recognized only during the IPO. Book value shares which convert to market value stock issued at or within 1 year of IPO also give rise to compensation in the amount of any increase in value; however, no further compensation is recognized after the IPO takes place. Book value stock which remains book value stock does not result in compensation during the IPO, per se, but if issued in contemplation of the IPO then book value increase would be attributable to compensation. Pure market value plans are covered under the provisions of APB 25, and are not affected by this pronouncement.

89-11 Sponsor's Balance Sheet Classification of Capital Stock with a Put Option Held by an Employee Stock Ownership Plan

This pronouncement deals with those circumstances in which an employee participant in an ESOP has a put option (i.e., a right to demand redemption by the sponsoring company). While the ESOP can substitute for the sponsor as the purchaser of the employee's shares, the sponsor cannot legally require the plan to do so; therefore, the employer is obligated to repurchase shares. The issue was: if the sponsor's shares are shown outside of the equity section as a consequence, can the contra equity (unearned compensation) also be presented there? The consensus was that the contra equity should follow the capital stock account.

90-7 Accounting for a Reload Stock Option

A reload stock option should be accounted for as a fixed plan if (1) each reload grant is for exercise at the market price on the reload grant date and (2) shares tendered satisfy the holding period in EITF 84-18.

90-9 Changes to Fixed Employee Stock Option Plans as a Result of Restructuring

A new measurement date does not occur for determining compensation expense (and no additional compensation expense should be recognized) as a result of spin-offs or recapitalization in the form of special, large and nonrecurring dividends if the following criteria are met:

1. Cash or other consideration (excluding additional options) given.
   If given to restore the option holder's economic position, the amount should be recognized as compensation expense once the employer agrees to provide them.
2. No cash or other consideration given.
   Changes to outstanding fixed stock option grants to restore the option holder's economic position if the criteria below are met.
   a. The aggregate intrinsic value of the options immediately after the change is not greater than immediately before.
   b. The rates of exercise price per option to market value per share is not reduced.
   c. The vesting provisions and option period of the original grant remain the same.

The change in market value should exclude independent, determinable and verifiable effects of other events than the equity restructuring.

Compensation expense should be recognized and measured in accordance with the provisions of APB 25 if changes to outstanding fixed stock options do not meet all of the above criteria. The additional expense would not include the amount that the current market price exceeds the original exercise price per option if that excess was measured as compensation expense at the original measurement date.

Any compensation expense unamortized from the original measurement date should continue to be amortized and should not be reversed.

The above consensus applies whether or not the original fixed option grant provided for adjustments to the option terms in case of equity restructuring.

94-6 Accounting for the Buyout of Compensatory Stock Options

The issue addressed was how to measure compensation when stock options granted below current market value are later reacquired by the issuing company before being exercised. In its consensus, the task force concluded that compensation should be measured by the sum of the compensation cost amortized to the buy back date, plus the intrinsic value of the options at the buy back date in excess of that previously recognized, plus any payment to the holder in excess of the intrinsic value. This would not, however, apply if replacement options were granted at or near the time of the buy back. Another consensus, Issue 87-33, would apply if this consensus is not appropriate to the fact pattern.

95-16 Accounting for Stock Compensation Arrangements with Employer Loan Features under APB Opinion No. 25

This issue relates to the situation in which an employee exercises a stock option by issuing a nonrecourse note to the employer, secured by the stock itself. The question is whether, when the terms of the note include either a variable interest rate or fixed interest with a prepayment option, this in effect results in the granting of a new option. The consensus was that the exercise of the option is, in substance, the issuance of a new option having a new measurement date, unless certain conditions are met. Those conditions might include a term in the original option which permitted exercise by issuance of nonrecourse debt having a specified term, or a proviso that implies that such an exercise does not extend the original option period even where the original agreement did not address exercise with a nonrecourse note. Otherwise, there will be another measurement of the compensation implicit in the arrangement. The consensus also stated that if the terms of the original arrangement provided for exercise through the issuance of the note and the interest is determined to be part of the exercise price, then the original grant should be accounted for as a variable plan, since the exercise price is not known at grant date. Furthermore, this may cause a fixed option to be converted into a variable option at the exercise, as when interest on the note is nonrecourse and thus must be deemed part of the exercise price. Lastly, dividends paid during the term of the nonrecourse note are to be treated as additional compensation; and interest received which is deemed part of the exercise price will be accounted for as payment for the shares, not as interest income.

96-1 Sale of Put Options on Issuer's Stock That Require or Permit Cash Settlement

When a company writes put options on its own shares requiring cash settlement, these are liabilities, marked to fair value with gain or loss taken to earnings.

If the puts give the holder a choice of settlement in cash or shares, these are also liabilities to be measured at fair value, with gain or loss taken to earnings and not later reversed to equity even if settlement is made in shares. If the issuing company has the choice of settlement method, follow Issue 87-31; any cash settlement would be included in contributed capital.

96-3 Accounting for Equity Instruments That are Issued for Consideration Other Than Employee Services Under FASB Statement No. 123

The issues involve the date to use for the determination of fair value, and how to account for transactions when the number of shares is contingent on outcome of one or more events. The consensus was that fair value is to be based on the date the parties come to an understanding of the terms of the arrangement and agree to a binding contract. The number of shares should be based on the best available estimate of number of instruments expected to be issued, revised as new information becomes available.

97-14 Accounting for Deferred Compensation Arrangements Where Amounts Earned Are Held in a Rabbi Trust and Invested

Assets are placed in a grantor trust representing deferred compensation, invested either in employer securities or diversified; assets in a so-called "rabbi trust" are available to a grantor/employer's creditors in the event of bankruptcy. The tentative conclusion by the EITF is that assets of the trust should be consolidated with employer's financial statements; any employer's stock held would be treated as treasury stock. Also, before diversification of trust assets, amount of deferred compensation would be adjusted through earnings to reflect fair value of amount owed to employee.

98-2 Accounting by a Subsidiary for an Investment in Its Parent Company's Stock

The issue relates to the display of an investment by a subsidiary in the parent's or joint venture partner's stock in separate statements of the subsidiary or the joint venture; specifically, how the SFAS 115 rules affect this presentation. Questions to be answered are how to account for the investment as an asset to be accounted for at fair value; a distribution to the parent or joint venture partner (similar to treasury stock); or as an asset measured by the equity method, with an elimination of reciprocal ownership investments. No consensus has been reached yet.

FASB TECHNICAL BULLETINS

97-1 Accounting Under Statement 123 for Certain Employee Stock Purchase Plans With a Look-Back Option

This bulletin provides guidance for accounting for certain employee stock purchase plans that have a look-back option, which is a provision that sets the exercise price equal to the lesser of the market price at the grant date or the exercise date.

APPENDIX

FINANCIAL STATEMENT PRESENTATION

This appendix provides an illustration of the various financial statements which may be required to be presented and are related to the stockholders' equity section of the balance sheet.

Stockholders' Equity Section of a Balance Sheet

Capital stock:		
Preferred stock, $100 par, 7% cumulative, 30,000 shares authorized, issued, and outstanding		$ 3,000,000
Common stock, no par, stated value $10 per share, 500,000 shares authorized, 415,000 shares issued		4,150,000
Total capital stock		$ 7,150,000
Additional paid-in capital:		
Issued price in excess of par value--preferred	$ 150,000	
Issued price in excess of stated value--common	845,000	995,000
Total paid-in capital		$ 8,145,000
Retained earnings:		
Appropriated for plant expansion	$2,100,000	
Unappropriated	2,110,000	4,210,000
Accumulated other comprehensive income		165,000
Total capital, retained earnings, and accumulated other comprehensive income		$12,620,000
Less 10,000 common shares held in treasury, at cost		(120,000)
Total stockholders' equity		$12,500,000

Retained Earnings Statement

Balance at beginning of year, as reported	$ 3,800,000
Prior period adjustment--correction of an error in method of depreciation (less tax effect of $77,000)	115,000
Balance at beginning of year, restated	$ 3,915,000
Net income for the year	748,000
Cash dividends declared during the year	
Preferred stock	(210,000)
Common stock	(78,000)
Balance at end of year	$ 4,375,000

Statement of Changes in Stockholders' Equity

	Preferred stock Shares	Preferred stock Amount	Common stock Shares	Common stock Amount	Additional paid-in capital	Donated capital	Retained earnings	Accumulated other comprehensive income*	Treasury stock (common)	Total stockholders' equity
Balance, 12/31/99, as reported	--	--	400,000	$4,000,000	$840,000	$100,000	$3,800,000	$ 56,000	$(120,000)	$8,620,000
Correction of an error in method of depr.	--	--	--	--	--	--	115,000		--	115,000
Balance, 12/31/99, restated	--	--	400,000	$4,000,000	$840,000	$100,000	$3,915,000		$(120,000)	$8,735,000
Preferred stock issued in public offering	30,000	$3,000,000	--	--	150,000	--	--		--	3,150,000
Stock options exercised	--	--	15,000	150,000	5,000	--	--		--	155,000
Net income	--	--	--	--	--	--	748,000		--	748,000
Cash dividends declared:										
Preferred, $7.00 per share	--	--	--	--	--	--	(210,000)		--	(210,000)
Common, $.20 per share	--	--	--	--	--	--	(78,000)		--	(78,000)
Unrealized holding gains on available-for-sale securities arising during period								85,000		
Less: Reclassification for adjustment of gains included in net income								(12,000)		
Foreign currency translation adjustments								36,000		
Total other comprehensive income								109,000		
Balance, 12/31/00	30,000	$3,000,000	415,000	$4,150,000	$995,000	$100,000	$4,375,000	$165,000	$(120,000)	$12,500,000

* *Comprehensive income for the period:*

Net income	*$748,000*
Other comprehensive income	*109,000*
	$857,000

18 EARNINGS PER SHARE

PERSPECTIVE AND ISSUES

Earnings per share (EPS) is an index which is widely used by both actual and prospective investors to gauge the profitability of a corporation. Its purpose is to indicate how effective an enterprise has been in using the resources provided by common shareholders. In its simplest form, EPS is net income (loss) divided by the number of shares of outstanding common stock. The EPS computation becomes difficult with existence of securities that are not common stock but have the potential of causing additional shares of common stock to be issued (e.g., convertible preferred stock or convertible debt, and options or warrants). The computation of an EPS number which ignores these potentially dilutive securities can be very misleading. In addition, a lack of standardization in the way in which these securities are included in an EPS computation makes comparisons among corporations extremely difficult.

The profession's first attempt to provide guidance in this area was Accounting Research Bulletin 49 (1958). However, this pronouncement was generally ignored, and most firms still computed EPS by dividing net income minus preferred stock dividends by a weighted-average of the number of common shares outstanding. The distortion inherent in an EPS number computed without regard for potentially dilutive securities was highlighted by the merger and acquisition activity of the 1960s. Many of these mergers, which resulted in larger earnings for the combined entity, were accomplished by the issuance of convertible securities, options, or warrants and by the retirement of the common stock of the merged company. Thus, an entity which disregarded outstanding dilutive securities when computing EPS could show an increase in EPS without a corresponding increase in profitability. The increase was due to larger combined earnings being divided by a smaller number of common shares.

APB 9 (1966) advised corporations with potentially dilutive securities (convertible preferred stock, convertible debt, or outstanding options or warrants) that if "potential dilution was material, supplementary pro forma computations of earnings per share should be furnished, showing what the earnings would be if conversions or contingent issuances took place."

APB 15 (1969) expanded and more clearly defined those securities which have the potential to dilute EPS, provided more specific guidance in computational matters, and delineated the correct reporting and disclosure requirements. This opinion was not applicable to nonprofit corporations, government-owned corporations, registered investment companies, mutual companies without common stock or common stock equivalents, or nonpublic enterprises as defined in SFAS 21. However, if any of these entities present EPS information, it must be prepared and displayed in conformity with the requirements of APB 15.

However, APB 15 has not been without criticism. This criticism focuses on the complex and arbitrary nature in which potentially dilutive securities are treated. As a result, in mid-1993 the FASB began the process of looking for ways to revise APB 15 by inviting comment letters on the subject. A large majority of letters indicated a need to revise the denominator amount of the EPS calculation.

In an effort to integrate with international reporting standards and to simplify the current reporting practices on EPS, the FASB issued a proposed statement addressing the subject of EPS. The final statement, SFAS 128, was issued in February 1997 and it supersedes APB 15.

SFAS 128 establishes standards for computing and presenting EPS for public companies. If a nonpublic company chooses to disclose EPS it must do so in accordance with SFAS 128. This statement greatly simplifies the standards for computing EPS previously found in APB 15 and provides standards which are more comparable to international EPS standards. According to the FASB's statement, publicly traded corporations with a complex capital structure would be obligated to report basic EPS and diluted EPS. The dual presentation is required on the face of the corporation's income statement even if both of these computations result in the same EPS amount. In addition, it also requires a reconciliation of the numerator and the denominator of the basic EPS computation to the numerator and denominator of the diluted EPS computation.

Basic EPS, which would include no dilution, would be computed by dividing income available to common shareholders by the weighted-average number of shares outstanding for that particular period. In contrast, diluted EPS would consider the potential dilution that could occur from other financial instruments that would increase the total number of outstanding shares of common stock. Under this statement, the calculation of diluted EPS noted minor changes from its method of calculation under APB 15.

In February 1997, the FASB also released SFAS 129 which establishes standards for disclosing information about an entity's capital structure. This statement continues previous disclosure requirements found in APB 10 and 15 and SFAS 47; however, it isolates the standards related to the disclosure of information about an entity's capital structure to one pronouncement. Additionally, this pronouncement applies to all entities, public and nonpublic. The statement indicates that companies are required to disclose the rights and privileges of each type of security outstanding. Examples of disclosures include company policies on participation rights, on the liquidation of preferred stock, and on redeemable stock.

SFAS 128 and 129 are effective for all financial statements issued for periods ending after December 15, 1997. Earlier application of SFAS 128 is not permitted, and SFAS 128 requires restatement of all prior-period EPS data presented.

Sources of GAAP

APB	*SFAS*	*FASB I*	*FASB TB*	*EITF*
30	128, 129	28	79-8	92-3

DEFINITIONS OF TERMS

There are a number of terms used in discussion of earnings per share which have special meanings in that context. When used, they are intended to have the meanings given in the following definitions.

Antidilution (antidilutive). An increase in earnings per share or reduction in net loss per share resulting from the inclusion of a potentially dilutive security in EPS calculations.

Basic earnings per share (basic EPS). The amount of earnings for the period available to each share of common stock outstanding during the reporting period.

Call option. A contract that allows the holder to buy a specified quantity of stock from the writer of the contract at a fixed price for a given period. Refer to **option** and **purchased call option**.

Call price. The amount at which a security may be redeemed by the issuer at the issuer's option.

Common stock. A stock which is subordinate to all other stocks of the issuer.

Contingent issuance. A possible issuance of shares of common stock that is dependent upon the exercise of conversion rights, options or warrants, the satisfaction of certain conditions, or similar arrangements.

Contingent stock agreement. An agreement to issue common stock (usually in connection with a business combination accounted for by the purchase method) that is dependent on the satisfaction of certain conditions. Refer to **contingently issuable shares**.

Contingently issuable shares (contingently issuable stock). Shares issuable for little or no cash consideration upon the satisfaction of certain conditions pursuant to a contingent stock agreement. Refer to **contingent stock agreement**.

Conversion price. The price that determines the number of shares of common stock into which a security is convertible. For example, $100 face value of debt convertible into 5 shares of common stock would be stated to have a conversion price of $20.

Conversion rate. The ratio of (a) the number of common shares issuable upon conversion to (b) a unit of convertible security. For example, a preferred stock may be convertible at the rate of 3 shares of common stock for each share of preferred stock.

Convertible security. A security that is convertible into another security based on a conversion rate; for example, convertible preferred stock that is convertible into common stock on a two-for-one basis (two shares of common for each share of preferred).

Conversion value. The current market value of the common shares obtainable upon conversion of a convertible security, after deducting any cash payment required upon conversion.

Diluted earnings per share (diluted EPS). The amount of earnings for the period available to each share of common stock outstanding during the reporting period and to each share that would have been outstanding assuming the issuance of common shares for all dilutive potential common shares outstanding during the reporting period.

Dilution (Dilutive). A reduction in earnings per share or an increase in net loss per share resulting from the assumption that convertible securities have been converted or that options and warrants have been exercised or other shares have been issued upon the fulfillment of certain conditions.

Dual presentation. The presentation with equal prominence of two types of earnings per share amounts on the face of the income statement: one is basic earnings per share, the other is diluted earnings per share.

Earnings per (common) share. The amount of earnings attributable to each share of common stock. For convenience, the term is used in SFAS 128 to refer to either net income (earnings) per share or net loss per share. It should be used without qualifying language only when no potentially dilutive convertible securities, options, warrants, or other agreements providing for contingent issuances of common stock are outstanding.

Exercise price. The amount that must be paid for a share of common stock upon exercise of a stock option or warrant.

If-converted method. A method of computing earnings per share data that assumes conversion of convertible securities as of the beginning of the earliest period reported (or at time of issuance, if later).

Income available to common stockholders. Income (or loss) from continuing operations or net income (or net loss) adjusted for preferred stock dividends.

Option. Unless otherwise stated in SFAS 128, a call option that gives the holder the right to purchase shares of common stock in accordance with an agreement upon payment of a specified amount, including, but not limited to, options granted to and stock purchase agreements entered into with employees. Options are considered "securities" in SFAS 128. Refer to **call option**.

Potential common stock. A security or other contact that may entitle its holder to obtain common stock during the reporting period or after the end of the reporting period.

Preferred stock. A security that has rights that are preferential to common stock.

Purchased call option. A contract that allows the reporting entity to buy a specified quantity of its own stock from the writer of the contract at a fixed price for a given period. Refer to **call option**.

Put option. A contract that allows the holder to sell a specified quantity of stock to the writer of the contract at a fixed price during a given period.

Redemption price. The amount at which a security is required to be redeemed at maturity or under a sinking fund arrangement.

Reverse treasury stock method. A method of recognizing the dilutive effect on earnings per share of satisfying a put obligation. It assumes that the proceeds used to buy back common stock (pursuant to the terms of a put option) will be raised from issuing shares at the average market price during the period. Refer to **put option.**

Rights issue. An offer to existing shareholders to purchase additional shares of common stock in accordance with an agreement for a specified amount (which is generally substantially less than the fair value of the shares) for a given period.

Security. The evidence of a debt or ownership or related right. For purposes of SFAS 128, it includes stock options and warrants, as well as debt and stock.

Treasury stock method. A method of recognizing the use of proceeds that would be obtained upon exercise of options and warrants in computing diluted earnings per share. It assumes that any proceeds would be used to purchase common stock at average market prices during the period.

Two-class method. A method employed for securities that are not convertible into common stock and thus cannot use the if-converted method. This method computes earnings per share by treating participating securities (nonconvertible) as though they were common stocks with different dividend rates from that of the common stock.

Warrant. A security giving the holder the right to purchase shares of common stock in accordance with the terms of the instrument, usually upon payment of a specified amount.

Weighted-average number of shares. The number of shares determined by relating (a) the portion of time within a reporting period that a particular number of shares of a certain security has been outstanding to (b) the total time in that period. For example, if 100 shares of a certain security were outstanding during the first quarter of a fiscal year and 300 shares were outstanding during the balance of the year, the weighted-average number of outstanding shares would be 250[(100 x 1/4) + (300 x 3/4)]. In computing diluted EPS, equivalent common shares are considered for all dilutive potential common shares.

CONCEPTS, RULES, AND EXAMPLES

Simple Capital Structure

According to SFAS 128, simple capital structures are those "with only **common stock** outstanding." These entities will simply present basic EPS. All other entities are considered to have a complex capital structure. Entities with a complex capital structure will have **potential common stock** in the form of potentially dilutive **securities, options, warrants**, or other rights that upon conversion or exercise could, in the aggregate, dilute **earnings per common share**. **Dilutive** securities are essentially those that exhibit the rights of debtholders (including warrants and options) and which have the potential upon their issuance to reduce the earnings per share.

Computational guidelines. The basic EPS calculation is **income available to common stockholders** (the numerator) divided by the **weighted-average number of common shares outstanding** (the denominator) during the period. The objective of the basic EPS calculation is to measure the performance of an entity over the reporting period. Complexities arise because net income does not necessarily represent the earnings available to the common shareholder, and a simple weighted-average of common shares outstanding does not necessarily reflect the true nature of the situation.

Numerator. The income available to common stockholders figure used as the numerator in any of the EPS computations must reflect any preferential claims against it by other securities. The justification for this reduction is that the preferential claims of the other securities must be satisfied before any income is available to the common shareholder. These other securities are usually in the form of **preferred stock**, and the deduction from income is the amount of the dividend declared (whether or not paid) during the year on the preferred stock. If the preferred stock is cumulative, the dividend is to be deducted from income (added to the loss) whether or not earned. Dividends in arrears do not affect the calculation of EPS in the current period; such dividends have been included in prior periods' EPS computations. However, the amount in arrears should be disclosed, as should all of the effects of the rights given to preferential securities on the EPS calculation.

Denominator. The weighted-average number of common stock shares outstanding is "an arithmetical mean average of shares outstanding and assumed to be outstanding for EPS computations" (SFAS 128, para 45). The difficulty in computing the weighted-average exists because of the effect that various transactions have on the computation of common shares outstanding. While it is impossible to analyze all the possibilities, SFAS 128 provides discussion of some of the more common transactions affecting the number of common shares outstanding. The theoretical construct set forth in these relatively simple examples can be followed in all other situations.

If a company reacquires its stock (treasury stock), the number of shares reacquired should be excluded from EPS calculations as of the date of acquisition. The same theory holds for the issuance of common stock during the period. The number of shares newly issued is included in the computation only for the period after their issuance date. The logic for this treatment is that the consideration for the shares was not available to generate earnings until the shares were issued. This same logic applies to the reacquired shares because the consideration relative to those shares was no longer available to generate earnings after the acquisition date.

A **stock dividend or split** does not generate additional consideration, but it does increase the number of shares outstanding. SFAS 128 states that the increase in shares as a result of a stock split or dividend, or decrease in shares as a result of a reverse split, should be given retroactive recognition as an appropriate equivalent charge for all periods presented. Thus, even if a stock dividend or split occurs at the end of the period, it is considered outstanding for the entire period of **each** period presented. The reasoning is that a stock dividend or split has no effect on the ownership percentage of the common stockholder. As such, to show a dilution in the EPS reported would erroneously give the impression of a decline in profitability when in fact it was merely an increase in the shares outstanding due to the stock dividend or split. SFAS 128 carries this one step further by requiring the retroactive adjustment of outstanding shares for stock dividends or splits occurring after the end of the period, but before the release of the report. The reason given is that the primary interest of the financial statement user is considered to be the current capitalization. If this situation occurs, disclosure of both the end-of-year outstanding shares and those used to compute EPS is required.

Complications also arise when a **business combination** occurs during the period. The treatment of the additional shares depends upon the nature of the combination. If the business combination is recorded as a pooling of interests, then the additional shares are assumed to have been issued at the beginning of the year, regardless of when the combination occurred. Conversely, if the combination is accounted for as a purchase, the shares are considered issued and outstanding as of the date of acquisition. The reason for this varied treatment lies in the income statement treatment accorded a pooling and a purchase. In a pooling, the income of the acquired company is included in the statements for the entire year, whereas in a purchase, the income is included only for the period after acquisition.

Weighted-Average (WA) Computation

Transaction	*Effect on WA computation*
• Common stock outstanding at the beginning of the period	• Increase number of shares outstanding by the number of shares
• Issuance of common stock during the period	• Increase number of shares outstanding by the number of shares issued times the portion of the year outstanding
• Conversion into common stock	• Increase number of shares outstanding by the number of shares converted times the portion of the year outstanding
• Company reacquires its stock	• Decrease number of shares outstanding by number of shares reacquired times portion of the year outstanding
• Stock dividend or split	• Increase number of shares outstanding by number of shares issued for the dividend or resulting from the split
• Reverse split	• Decrease number of shares outstanding by decrease in shares
• Pooling of interest	• Increase number of shares outstanding by number of shares issued
• Purchase	• Increase number of shares outstanding by number of shares issued times portion of year since acquisition

These do not characterize all of the possible complexities arising in the EPS computation; however, most of the others occur under a complex structure. The complications arising under a complex capital structure are discussed in detail later in this chapter. The illustration below applies some of the foregoing concepts to a simple capital structure.

Example of EPS Computation--Simple Capital Structure

Assume the following information:

	Numerator information			*Denominator information*	
a.	Income from continuing operations before extraordinary items	$130,000	a.	Common shares outstanding 1/1/99	100,000
b.	Extraordinary loss (net of tax)	30,000	b.	Shares issued for cash 4/1/99	20,000
c.	Net income	100,000	c.	Shares issued in 10% stock dividend declared in July 1999	12,000
d.	6% cumulative preferred stock, $100 par, 1,000 shrs. issued and outstanding	100,000	d.	Shares of treasury stock purchased 10/1/99	10,000

When calculating the numerator, the claims related to the preferred stock should be deducted to arrive at the income available to the common shareholders. In this example, the preferred stock is cumulative. Thus, regardless of whether or not the board of directors declares a preferred dividend, holders of the preferred stock have a claim of $6,000 (1,000 shares x $100 x 6%) against 1999 earnings. Therefore, $6,000 must be deducted from the numerator to arrive at the income available to common shareholders. Note that any cumulative preferred dividends in arrears are ignored in computing this period's EPS since they would have been incorporated into previous periods' EPS calculations. Also note that this $6,000 would have been deducted for **non**cumulative preferred only if a dividend of this amount had been declared during the period.

The EPS calculations follow:

Earnings per common share:

On income from continuing operations before extraordinary item

$$\frac{\$130,000 - \$6,000}{\text{Common stock outstanding}}$$

On net income

$$\frac{\$100,000 - \$6,000}{\text{Common shares outstanding}}$$

The computation of the denominator is based upon the weighted-average number of common shares outstanding. Recall that a simple weighted-average is not considered appropriate because of the various complexities. The table below illustrates one way of computing the weighted-average number of shares outstanding.

Table 1

Item	*Number of shares actually outstanding*	*Fraction of the year outstanding*	*Shares times fraction of the year*
Number of shares as of beginning of the year 1/1/99	110,000 [100,000 + 10%(100,000)]	12/12	110,000
Shares issued 4/1/99	22,000 [20,000 + 10%(20,000)]	9/12	16,500
Treasury shares purchased 10/1/99	(10,000)	3/12	(2,500)
Weighted-average number of common shares outstanding			124,000

Recall that the stock dividend declared in July is considered to be retroactive to the beginning of the year. Thus, for the period 1/1 through 4/1, 110,000 shares are considered to be outstanding. When shares are issued, they are included in the weighted-average beginning with the date of issuance. The stock dividend applicable to these newly issued shares is also assumed to have existed for the same period. Thus, we can see that of the 12,000-share dividend, 10,000 shares relate to the beginning balance and 2,000 shares to the new issuance (10% of 100,000 and 20,000, respectively). The purchase of the treasury stock requires that these shares be excluded from the calculation for the remainder of the period after their acquisition date. The figure is subtracted from the calculation because the shares were purchased from those outstanding prior to acquisition.

To complete the example, we divided the previously derived numerator by the weighted-average number of common shares outstanding to arrive at EPS.

Earnings per common share:

On income from continuing operations before extraordinary item

$$\frac{\$130,000 - \$6,000}{124,000 \text{ common shares}} = \$1.00$$

On net income

$$\frac{\$100,000 - \$6,000}{124,000 \text{ common shares}} = \$\ .76$$

The numbers computed above are required presentations on the face of the income statement. Reporting a $.24 loss per share ($30,000 ÷ 124,000) due to the extraordinary item is required either on the face of the income statement or in the notes to the financial statements.

Complex Capital Structure

The computation of EPS under a complex capital structure involves all of the complexities discussed under the simple structure and many more. By definition, a simple capital structure is one that only has common stock outstanding; therefore, a complex capital structure is one that has securities which have the potential to be exercised and **reduce** EPS (dilutive securities). Any **antidilutive** securities (those that increase EPS) would not be included in the computation of EPS. Note that a complex structure requires **dual presentation** of both basic EPS and diluted EPS (DEPS). The common stock outstanding and all other dilutive securities are used to compute DEPS.

Diluted earnings per share (DEPS). DEPS has been identified as the earnings attributable to each share of common stock after giving effect to all potential common shares which were outstanding during the period and dilutive. The computation of DEPS requires that the following steps be performed:

1. Identify all potentially dilutive securities.
2. Compute the effect (dilution) of the other dilutive securities on net income and common shares outstanding.

Identification of potentially dilutive securities. The first step requires that we identify all potentially dilutive securities. As defined earlier, dilutive securities are those which have the potential of being exercised and reducing the EPS figure. Some examples of dilutive securities identified by SFAS 128 are convertible debt, convertible preferred stock, options, warrants, participating securities, two-class common stocks, and contingent shares.

Convertible securities. A **convertible security** is one type of potentially dilutive security. A security of this type has an inherent dual nature. Convertibles are comprised of two distinct elements: the right to receive interest **and** the right to potentially participate in earnings by becoming a common shareholder. Due to the later right, this security is included in the DEPS computation

Options and warrants. Specific mention is also given to options, warrants, and their equivalents. Options and warrants generally derive their entire value from the right to obtain common stock at specified prices over an extended period of time.

Participating securities and two-class common stocks. The capital structure of some entities include securities that may participate in dividends with common stocks according to a predetermined formula, or a class of common stock with different dividend rates from those of another class of common stock but without prior or senior rights. The if-converted method shall be used for those securities that are convertible into common stock if the effect is dilutive. For those securities that are not convertible into a class of common stock, the "two class" method of computing earnings per share shall be used.

The two-class method. The two-class method is an earnings allocation formula that determines earnings per share for each class of common stock and participating security according to dividends declared (or accumulated) and participation rights in undistributed earnings. Under this method income from continuing operations (or net income) shall be reduced by the amount of dividends declared in the current period for each class of stock and by the contractual amount of dividends that must be paid for the current period. The remaining earnings shall be allocated to common stock and participating securities to the extent that each security may share in earnings if all of the earnings for the period had been distributed. The total earnings allocated to each security shall be determined by adding together the amount allocated for dividends and the amount allocated for a participation feature. The total earnings allocated to each security shall be divided by the number of outstanding shares of the security to which the earnings are allocated to determine the earnings per share for the security.

Contingent issuances of common stock. Also mentioned are **contingent issuances** of common stock (e.g., stock subscriptions). If shares are to be issued in the future with no restrictions on issuance other than the passage of time, they are to be considered issued and treated as outstanding in the computation of dilutive EPS (SFAS 128, para 91). Other issuances that are dependent upon certain conditions being met are to be evaluated in a different respect. SFAS 128 uses as examples the maintenance of current earnings levels and the attainment of specified earnings increases. If the contingency is to merely maintain the earnings levels currently being attained, then the shares are considered outstanding for the entire period and considered in the computation of dilutive EPS if the effect is dilutive. If the requirement is to increase earnings over a period of time, the diluted EPS computation shall include those shares that would be issued based on the assumption that current amount of earnings will remain unchanged, if the effect is dilutive. Previously reported EPS should not be restated to give recognition to shares issued as a result of the earnings level attainment. If a contingent issuance is based upon the lapsing of time **and** the market price of the stock (generally affects the number of shares issued), both conditions must be met to include the contingently issuable shares in the DEPS computation. The Board prohibits restatement of EPS data should fluctuations in the market price occur in future periods.

Computation of DEPS. The second step in the process is the actual computation of DEPS. There are basically two methods used to incorporate the effects of other dilutive securities and EPS (excluding participating and two-class common securities):

(1) the treasury stock method, and
(2) the if-converted method

The treasury stock method. The treasury stock method which is used for the exercise of most warrants or options requires that EPS be computed as if the options or warrants were exercised at the beginning of the period (or date of issuance, if later), and that the funds obtained from the exercise were used to purchase common stock at the **average market price** for the period. For example, if a corporation has warrants outstanding for 1,000 shares of common stock exercisable at $10 per share and the average market price of the common stock is $16 per share, the following would occur: the company would receive $10,000 (1,000 x $10) and issue 1,000 shares from the exercise of the warrants which would enable it to purchase 625 shares ($10,000 ÷ $16) in the open market. The net increase in the denominator (which effects a dilution in EPS) is 375 shares (1,000 issued less 625 repurchased). If the **exercise price** is greater than the average market price, the exercise should not be assumed since the result of this would be antidilutive. In this case, EPS of prior periods presented in comparative form should **not** be restated to reflect a change in market price.

> Denominator must be increased by net dilution, as follows:
>
> Net dilution = Shares issued – Shares repurchased
>
> where
>
> Shares issued = Proceeds received ÷ Exercise price
>
> Shares repurchased = Proceeds received ÷ Average market price per share

The if-converted method. The if-converted method is used for those securities which are currently sharing in the earnings of the company through the receipt of interest or dividends as preferential securities, but which have the **potential** for sharing in the earnings as common stock. The if-converted method logically recognizes that the convertible security only can share in the earnings of the company as one or the other, not both. Thus, the dividends or interest less tax effects applicable to the convertible security as a preferential security are not recognized in the income available to common stockholders figure used to compute EPS, and the weighted-average number of shares is adjusted to reflect the conversion as of the beginning of the year (or date of issuance, if later).

> **If-Converted Method**
>
> *Numerator*
>
> Income available to common stockholders recomputed to reflect conversion
>
> - Add back interest expense less tax effects
> - Convertible preferred dividends no longer subtracted
> - Add back other expenses attributable to convertible issues
>
> ---
>
> *Denominator*
>
> Common stock outstanding if convertible securities were converted at beginning or date of issuance, if later

Summary. Generally, the if-converted method is used for convertible securities, while the treasury stock method is used for options and warrants. There are some situations specified by SFAS 128 for which this does not hold true.

1. When options or warrants contain provisions which permit or require that debt or other securities of the issuer be tendered for all or a portion of the exercise price, the if-converted method should be used.
2. If the terms of the options or warrants require that the proceeds from the exercise are to be used to retire existing debt, the if-converted method should be used.
3. For convertible securities which require cash payment upon conversion, and are, therefore, considered equivalent to warrants, the treasury stock method should be used.

Dual presentation of earnings per share. DEPS is a pro forma presentation which reflects the dilution of EPS that would have occurred if **all** contingent issuances of common stock that would individually reduce EPS had taken place at the beginning of the period (or the date issued, if later). The concept of the dual earnings per share presentation distinguishes between no dilution and potential dilution, providing the users with the most factually supportable range of EPS possibilities. Diluted earnings per share assumes that all issuances that have the legal right to become common stock exercise that right (unless such exercise would be antidilutive) and therefore anticipates and measures all **potential** dilution. The **dual presentation** of both basic EPS and DEPS is to be prominently disclosed on the face of the income statements. The underlying basis for the computation is that of conservatism. The DEPS considers all other dilutive securities but only those securities which are dilutive. Thus, in most cases, the DEPS is less than the basic EPS. An exception occurs when no dilutive securities exist. The DEPS can never be greater than the basic EPS, but it could possibly be the same if all of the dilutive securities were antidilutive.

NOTE: The FASB concluded that an entity that reports a discontinued operation, an extraordinary item, or the cumulative effect of an accounting change in a period shall use ***income from continuing operations*** *as the "control number" for determining whether including potential common shares in the diluted EPS computation would be dilutive or antidilutive. Income from continuing operations (or a similar line item above net income if it appears on the income statement) would be adjusted for preferred dividends. If necessary, refer to SFAS 128, para 15, footnote 8 for an example.*

Examples of EPS Computation--Complex Capital Structure

Each of the following independent examples is presented to illustrate the foregoing principles. The procedural guidelines are detailed so as to allow the reader to understand the computation without referring back to the text.

Example of the Treasury Stock Method

Assume that the net income is $50,000 and the weighted-average number of common shares outstanding has been computed as 10,000. Additional information regarding the capital structure is given as

1. 4% nonconvertible, cumulative preferred stock, par $100, 1,000 shares issued and outstanding the entire year
2. Options and warrants to purchase 1,000 shares of common stock at $8 per share. The average market price of common stock during the year was $10. The options and warrants were outstanding all year.

The first step in the solution of this problem is the determination of basic EPS. This calculation appears as follows:

$$\frac{\text{Net income - Preferred dividends}}{\text{Weighted-average number of common shares outstanding}} = \frac{\$50{,}000 - \$4{,}000}{10{,}000 \text{ shares}} = \$4.60$$

The second step is the calculation of diluted EPS which is based upon outstanding common stock and other dilutive securities. The options and warrants are the only potentially dilutive securities in the example. However, remember that only dilutive options (market price > exercise price) are included in the computation. The treasury stock method used to compute the number of shares to be added to the denominator is illustrated below.

Proceeds from assumed exercise of options and warrants (1,000 shares x $8)	$8,000
Number of shares issued	1,000
Number of shares reacquired ($8,000 ÷ $10)	800
Number of shares assumed issued and not reacquired	200*

**An alternative approach that can be used to calculate this number for dilutive EPS is demonstrated below.*

$$\frac{\text{Average market price – Exercise price}}{\text{Average market price}} \times \text{Number of shares under options/warrants} = \text{Shares not reacquired}$$

$$\frac{\$10 - \$8}{\$10} \times 1{,}000 \text{ shares} = 200 \text{ shares}$$

Diluted EPS can now be calculated as follows, including the effects of applying the treasury stock method:

$$\frac{\text{Net income - Preferred dividends}}{\text{Weighted-average of common shares outstanding + Number of shares not reacquired with proceeds from options and warrants}} = \frac{\$50{,}000 - \$4{,}000}{10{,}200 \text{ shares}} = \$4.51$$

Note also that the options and warrants are dilutive, as EPS is reduced from $4.60 to $4.51.

Table 2
Computations of Basic and Diluted Earnings Per Share

	EPS on outstanding common stock (Basic EPS)		*Diluted*	
Items	*Numerator*	*Denominator*	*Numerator*	*Denominator*
Net income	$50,000		$50,000	
Preferred dividend	(4,000)		(4,000)	
Common shs. outstanding		10,000 shs.		10,000 shs.
Options and warrants				200
Totals	$46,000	÷ 10,000 shs.	$46,000	÷ 10,200shs.
EPS	$4.60		$4.51	

Example of the if-converted method

Again we will assume a net income of $50,000 and a weighted-average number of common shares outstanding of 10,000. The following information is provided regarding the capital structure:

1. 7% convertible debt, 200 bonds each convertible into 40 common shares. The bonds were outstanding the entire year. The income tax rate is 40%. The bonds were issued at par ($1,000 per bond). No bonds were converted during the year.
2. 4% convertible, cumulative preferred stock, par $100, 1,000 shares issued and outstanding. Each preferred share is convertible into two common shares. The preferred which was issued at par was outstanding the entire year. No shares were converted during the year.

Once again the first step is to compute basic EPS. As with the other example, this figure is $4.60. The next step is the computation of DEPS. Diluted EPS includes other dilutive securities. In the example, the convertible bonds are assumed to have been converted at the beginning of the year. Again, the effects of the assumption are twofold. One, if the bonds are converted, there will be no interest expense of $14,000 (7% x $200,000 face value); and two, there will be an additional 8,000 shares (200 bonds x 40 shares) of common stock outstanding during the year. One note of caution, however, must be mentioned; namely, the effect of not having $14,000 of interest expense will increase income, but it will also increase tax expense. Consequently, the net effect of not having interest expense of $14,000 is $8,400 ([1 – .40] x $14,000). Diluted EPS is computed as follows, reflecting the effects noted above for the dilutive preferred stock and the convertible bonds.

$$\frac{\text{Net income + Interest expense (net of tax)}}{\text{Weighted-average of common shares outstanding + Shares issued upon conversion of preferred and conversion of bonds}} = \frac{\$50{,}000 - \$4{,}000 + \$8{,}400}{18{,}000 \text{ shares}} = \$3.02$$

The convertible debt is dilutive as it reduces EPS from $4.60 to $3.02.

To determine the dilutive effect of the preferred stock, an assumption (called the if-converted method) is made that all of the preferred stock is converted at the earliest date that it could have been during the year. In this example, the date would be January 1. The effects of this assumption are twofold. One, if the preferred is converted, there will be no preferred dividends of $4,000 for the year; and, two, there will be an additional 2,000 shares of common stock outstanding during the year (the **conversion rate** is 2 for 1 on 1,000 shares of preferred). DEPS considering the preferred stock is computed, as follows, reflecting these two assumptions:

$$\frac{\text{Net income}}{\text{Weighted-average of common shares outstanding + Shares issued upon conversion of preferred}} = \frac{\$50{,}000 + \$8{,}400}{20{,}000 \text{ shares}} = \$2.92$$

The convertible preferred is also dilutive because it reduced EPS from $4.60 to $2.92.

Together the convertible bonds and preferred both reduced EPS from $4.60 to $2.92. For a complete explanation of the sequencing process of including multiple dilutive securities in the computations of dilutive EPS, see the comprehensive example in Appendix A. In this example the convertible bonds must first be considered prior to the inclusion of the convertible preferred stock. Table 3 summarizes the computations made for this example.

Table 3
Computations of Basic and Diluted Earnings Per Share

	EPS on outstanding common stock (Basic EPS)		*Diluted*	
Items	*Numerator*	*Denominator*	*Numerator*	*Denominator*
Net income	$50,000		$50,000	
Preferred dividend	(4,000)			
Common shs. outstanding		10,000 shs.		10,000 shs.
Conversion of preferred				2,000
Conversion of bonds			8,400	8,000
Totals	$46,000	÷ 10,000 shs.	$58,400	÷ 20,000 shs.
EPS		$4.60		$2.92

In the preceding example all of the potentially dilutive securities were outstanding the entire year and no conversions or exercises were made during the year. If a potentially dilutive security was not outstanding the entire year, then the numerator and denominator effects would have to be "time-weighted." For instance, suppose the convertible bonds in the above example were issued during the current year on July 1. If all other facts remain unchanged, diluted EPS would be computed as follows:

$$\frac{\text{Net income + Interest expense (net of tax)}}{\text{Weighted-average of common shares outstanding + Shares issued upon conversion of preferred and conversion of bonds}} = \frac{\$50{,}000 + 1/2(8{,}400)}{10{,}000 + 2{,}000 + 1/2(8{,}000)} = \$3.39$$

In this case, the convertible debt is dilutive whether or not it is outstanding the entire year.

If actual conversions or exercises take place during a period, the common shares issued will be outstanding from their date of issuance and, therefore, will be included in the computation of the weighted-average number of common shares outstanding. These shares are then weighted from their respective times of issuance. Assume that all the bonds in the above example are converted on July 1 into 8,000 common shares; the following effects should be noted:

1. For basic earnings per share, the weighted-average of common shares outstanding will be increased by (8,000)(.5) or 4,000. Income will increase $4,200 net of tax, because the bonds are no longer outstanding.
2. For diluted earnings per share, the if-converted method is applied to the period January 1 to July 1 because it was during this period that the bonds were potentially dilutive. The interest expense, net of tax, of $4,200 is added to the income, and 4,000 shares (.5 of 8,000) are added to the denominator.
3. Interestingly, the net effect of items 1 and 2 is the same for the period whether these dilutive bonds were outstanding the entire period or converted during the period.

Presentation. The reason for the differentiation between simple and complex capital structures is that SFAS 128 requires different financial statement presentation for each. SFAS 128 mandates that EPS be shown on the face of the income statement for each of the following items (when applicable):

1. Income from continuing operations.
2. Net income.

An entity which reports a discontinued operation, an extraordinary item, or the cumulative effect of a change in accounting principle shall present basic and diluted EPS amounts for these line items either on the face of the income statement or in the notes to the financial statements. These requirements must be fulfilled regardless of whether the structure is simple or complex. The difference in the two structures is that a simple capital structure requires presentation of only a single EPS number for each item, while a complex structure requires the dual presentation of both basic EPS and diluted EPS (DEPS) for each item.

Year-to-date DEPS. If an entity has year-to-date income from continuing operations (Topic 62 in EITF Abstracts) that includes losses in one or more quarters, the calculation of year-to-date DEPS should include dilutive potential shares for all quarters on a quarterly weighted-average basis. Thus, options that are in the money in a quarter(s) in which a net loss(es) occur(s) should be included in the year-to-date denominator in the EPS calculation. Likewise, contingent shares excluded because of a loss from continuing operations in a quarter(s) should be included in year-to-date DEPS.

Other Disclosure Requirements

The following additional items shall be disclosed by an entity for each period an income statement is presented:

1. A reconciliation of the numerators and the denominators of the basic and diluted EPS computations for income from continuing operations. The reconciliation should include the effects of all securities that affect EPS.
2. The effect of preferred dividends in arriving at income available for common stockholders in computing basic EPS.
3. Securities which could potentially dilute basic EPS in future periods but which were not included in dilutive EPS for the period(s) presented since the results were antidilutive.

In addition for the latest period for which an income statement is presented, a description is required for transactions occurring after the balance sheet date which result in a material change in the number of shares outstanding at the balance sheet date.

EMERGING ISSUES TASK FORCE CONSENSUS SUMMARIES

92-3 EPS Treatment of Tax Benefits for Dividends on Unallocated Stock Held by an Employee Stock Ownership Plan

Under SFAS 109, the tax benefits related to dividends paid on unallocated ESOP common stock held by an ESOP that are charged to retained earnings should not be a deduction to net income when calculating EPS. Also note, this consensus applies to convertible ESOP preferred stock when calculating the if-converted EPS. However, under SOP 93-6, dividends paid on unallocated shares are not charged to retained earnings. Since the employers control the use of dividends on unallocated shares, these dividends are not considered dividends for financial reporting purposes. Consequently, the dividends do not affect the EPS computation. The transition provisions of SOP 93-6 do, however, allow employers to continue their current accounting methods for ESOP shares acquired on or prior to December 31, 1992.

APPENDIX

COMPREHENSIVE EXAMPLE

The examples within the text used a simplified approach for determining whether or not options, warrants, convertible preferred stock, or convertible bonds have a dilutive effect on diluted EPS. If the diluted EPS number computed was lower than the basic EPS, the security was considered dilutive. This approach is adequate so long as the firm has only **one** potentially dilutive security. If this is not the case and the firm has more than one potentially dilutive security, a more complex ranking procedure must be employed (SFAS 128, Appendix C, Illustration 4).

For example, assume the following facts concerning the capital structure of a firm:

1. Income from continuing operations and net income are both $50,000. Income from continuing operations is not displayed on the firm's income statement.
2. Weighted-average number of common shares outstanding is 10,000 shares.
3. Tax rate is 40%.
4. Options to purchase 1,000 shares of common stock at $8 per share. The options were outstanding all year.
5. Options to purchase 2,000 shares of common stock at $13 per share. The average market price of common stock during the year was $10.
6. 7% convertible bonds, 200 bonds each convertible into 40 common shares. The bonds were outstanding the entire year. The bonds were issued at par ($1,000 per bond) and no bonds were converted during the year.
7. 4% convertible, **cumulative** preferred stock, par $100, 1,000 shares issued and outstanding the entire year. Each preferred share is convertible into one common share. The preferred stock was issued at par and no shares were converted during the year.

Note that in the application of the procedures set forth below, reference is made to some of the tables included in the body of the chapter because the facts above represent a combination of the facts used for the examples in the chapter.

In order to determine both basic and diluted EPS, the following procedures must be performed:

1. Calculate a basic EPS number as if the capital structure were simple.
2. Identify other potentially dilutive securities.
3. Calculate the per share effects of assuming issuance or conversion of each potentially dilutive security on an individual basis.
4. Rank the per share effects from smallest to largest.
5. Recalculate EPS (step 1 above) adding the potentially dilutive securities one at a time in order, beginning with the one with the **smallest** per share effect.

6. Continue adding potentially dilutive securities until all have been added or until the addition of a security increases EPS (antidilution) from its previous level.

Applying these procedures to the facts above:

1. Basic EPS:

$$\frac{\text{Net income - Preferred dividends}}{\text{Weighted-average number of common shares outstanding}} = \frac{\$50{,}000 - \$4{,}000}{10{,}000} = \$4.60$$

2. Identification of other potentially dilutive securities:
   a. Options (2 types).
   b. 7% convertible bonds.
   c. 4% convertible preferred stock.

Diluted EPS

3. Per share effects of conversion or issuance of other potentially dilutive securities:

   a. Options--Only the options to purchase 1,000 shares at $8.00 per share are dilutive. The options to purchase 2,000 shares of common stock are antidilutive. Thus, they are not included.

   Proceeds if options exercised:

   1,000 shares x $8 = $8,000

   Shares that could be acquired:

   $8,000 ÷ $10 = 800

   Dilutive shares: 1,000 – 800 = 200

$$\frac{\text{Increase/decrease in net income}}{\text{Increase in weighted-average number of common shares outstanding}} = \frac{\$0}{200 \text{ shs.}} = \$0$$

   b. 4% convertible preferred--The outstanding shares increase by 1,000 when all shares are converted. This results in total dividends of $4,000 not being paid.

$$\frac{\text{Increase/decrease in net income}}{\text{Increase in weighted-average number of common shares outstanding}} = \frac{\$4{,}000}{1{,}000 \text{ shs.}} = \$4.00$$

   c. 7% convertible bonds (see Table 3).

$$\frac{\text{Increase/decrease in net income}}{\text{Increase in weighted-average number of common shares}} = \frac{\$8{,}400}{8{,}000 \text{ shs.}} = \$1.05$$

4. Rank the per share effects:

a.	Options	$ 0
b.	7% convertible bonds	1.05
c.	4% convertible preferred stock	4.00

5. Recalculate the EPS adding in rank order one potentially dilutive security at a time:

   a. Diluted EPS--options added

$$\frac{\text{Net income} - \text{Preferred dividends}}{\text{Weighted-average number of common stock outstanding} + \text{Shares not acquired with proceeds of options}} = \frac{\$50{,}000 - \$4{,}000}{10{,}200 \text{ shs.}} = \$4.51$$

   b. Diluted EPS--options and 7% convertible bonds added

$$\frac{\text{Net income} - \text{Preferred dividends} + \text{Interest expense (net of tax)}}{\text{Weighted-average number of common stock outstanding} + \text{Shares not acquired with proceeds of options} + \text{Shares issued upon conversion of bonds}} = \frac{\$50{,}000 - \$4{,}000 + \$8{,}400}{10{,}200 + 8{,}000 \text{ shs.}} = \$2.99$$

   c. Diluted EPS--options, 7% convertible bonds and 4% convertible preferred added

$$\frac{\text{Net income} + \text{Interest expense (net of tax)}}{\text{Weighted-average number of common stock outstanding} + \text{Shares not acquired with proceeds of options} + \text{Shares issued upon conversion of bonds and preferred stock}} = \frac{\$50{,}000 + 8{,}400}{10{,}200 + 8{,}000 + 1{,}000 \text{ shs.}} = \$3.04$$

Diluted EPS = $2.99

Since the addition of the 4% convertible preferred stock raises diluted EPS from $2.99 to $3.04, the 4% convertible preferred is antidilutive and is therefore excluded from the diluted EPS.

A dual presentation of basic and diluted EPS is required. The dual presentation on the face of the income statement would appear as follows:

Net income	$50,000
Earnings per common share* (Note X)	$4.60
Earnings per common share, assuming dilution* (Note X)	$2.99

Note X: Earnings Per Share

Earnings per common share were computed by dividing income available to common stockholders by the weighted-average number of common shares outstanding during the year.

Diluted earnings per share was computed assuming the conversion of all options, the 4% cumulative preferred stock, and the 7% convertible bonds. Consequently, the income available to common stockholders figure is adjusted to reflect

**Basic earnings per share and diluted earnings per share may be substituted, respectively.*

the elimination of the preferred dividend; and the interest expense (net of tax) related to the convertible bonds and the number of common shares issuable assuming conversion of the preferred stock and convertible bonds, and complete exercise of the options as of the beginning of the year, were added to the number of common shares outstanding.

19 INTERIM AND SEGMENT REPORTING

INTERIM REPORTING

PERSPECTIVE AND ISSUES

Interim reporting is financial reporting for periods of less than a year, generally for a period of 3 months (quarterly reporting). The purpose of quarterly reports is to provide financial statement users with more timely information for investment and credit decisions. Additionally, quarterly reports can yield significant information concerning business points and seasonality, both of which could be "buried" in annual reports.

For over 60 years, the New York Stock Exchange has required quarterly financial reporting in its listing agreement. Since 1970, the SEC has required companies subject to its periodic reporting requirements to file quarterly financial information on a form 10-Q. Until 1973, however, there was no promulgated GAAP for publicly held companies issuing interim reports to their stockholders. The general guidelines are now set forth in APB 28, SFAS 3, and FASB Interpretation 18. Today, interim reporting generally takes the form of quarterly earnings reports.

The basic objective of interim reporting is to provide frequent and timely assessments of enterprise performance. However, interim reporting has inherent limitations. As the reporting period is shortened, the effects of errors in estimation and allocation are magnified. The proper allocation of annual operating expenses is a significant concern. Because progressive tax rates are applied to total annual income and various tax credits may arise, the determination of quarterly income tax expense is often difficult. Other annual operating expenses are often concentrated in one interim period, yet benefit the entire year's operations. Examples include advertising expenses and major repairs or maintenance of equipment. The effects of seasonal fluctuations and temporary market conditions further limit the reliability, comparability, and predictive value of interim reports. Because of this reporting environment, the issue of independent auditor association with interim financial reports is subject to continuing controversy.

Two distinct views of interim reporting have developed. Under the first view, the interim period is considered to be an **integral** part of the annual accounting period. Annual operating expenses are estimated and then allocated to the interim periods based on forecasted annual activity levels such as sales volume. The results of subsequent interim periods must be adjusted to reflect estimation errors. Under the second view, the interim period is considered to be a **discrete** accounting period. Thus, there are no estimations or allocations different from those used for annual reporting. The same expense recognition rules apply as under annual reporting, and no special interim accruals or deferrals are applied. Annual operating expenses are recognized in the interim period incurred, irrespective of the number of interim periods benefited.

Proponents of the **integral** view argue that the unique expense recognition procedures are necessary to avoid misleading fluctuations in period-to-period results. Using the **integral** view results in interim earnings which are indicative of annual earnings and, thus, useful for predictive purposes. Proponents of the **discrete** view argue that the smoothing of interim results for purposes of forecasting annual earnings has undesirable effects. For example, a turning point during the year in an earnings trend may be obscured.

In response to inconsistencies in interim reporting practices and problems in implementing interim reporting GAAP, the FASB undertook a comprehensive study of the issue. In 1978, the FASB Discussion Memorandum, *Interim Financial Accounting and Reporting*, was issued. A fundamental objective of this project was to resolve the **integral/discrete** debate. However, the FASB has made no recommendations and removed the project from its agenda.

Sources of GAAP

APB	*SFAS*	*FASB I*	*FASB TB*	*EITF*
28	3, 16	18	79-9	86-13 98-9

DEFINITIONS OF TERMS

Discrete view. An approach to measuring interim period income by viewing each interim period separately.

Estimated annual effective tax rate. An expected annual tax rate which reflects estimates of annual earnings, tax rates, tax credits, etc.

Integral view. An approach to measuring interim period income by viewing each interim period as an integral part of the annual period. Expenses are recognized in proportion to revenues earned through the use of special accruals and deferrals.

Interim reporting. Financial reporting for a period of less than a year, generally for a period of 3 months.

Last-12-months reports. Financial reporting for the 12-month period which ends on a given interim date.

Liquidation of LIFO inventories. The situation which occurs when quarterly sales exceed purchases and base-period costs are released into cost of goods sold.

Seasonality. The normal, expected occurrence of a major portion of revenues or costs in one or two interim periods.

Year-to-date reports. Financial reporting for the period which begins on the first day of the fiscal year and ends on a given interim date.

CONCEPTS, RULES, AND EXAMPLES

Revenues

Revenues are to be recognized as earned during an interim period using the same basis followed in annual reports. This rule applies to both product sales and service revenues. For example, product sales cutoff procedures should be applied at the end of each quarter as is done at year end, and revenue from long-term construction contracts should be recognized at interim dates using the same method used at year end.

Product Costs and Direct Costs

Product costs (and costs directly associated with service revenues) should be treated in interim reports as they are in annual reports (the discrete approach). However, APB 28 provides for four integral view exceptions, described below.

1. The gross profit method may be used to estimate cost of goods sold and ending inventory for interim periods.
2. When inventory consisting of LIFO layers or a portion of the base period is liquidated at an interim date, but is expected to be replaced by year end, cost of sales should include the expected cost of replacing the liquidated inventory.
3. An inventory market decline reasonably expected to be restored by year end (i.e., a decline deemed to be **temporary** in nature) need not be recognized

in the interim period. The Emerging Issues Task Force (Issue 86-13) has reached a consensus that situations not requiring a write-down are generally limited to seasonal price fluctuations. If an inventory loss from a market decline that is recognized in one period is followed by a market price recovery, such reversal should be recognized as a gain. Recognition of this gain is limited to the extent of loss previously recognized, in the later interim period.

4. Firms using standard cost accounting systems ordinarily should report purchase price, wage rate, and usage or efficiency variances in the same manner as used at year end. Planned purchase price and volume variances should be deferred if expected to be absorbed by year end.

The first exception above eliminates the need for a physical inventory count at the interim date. The other three exceptions attempt to synchronize the quarterly statements with the annual report. For example, consider the LIFO liquidation exception. Without this exception, interim cost of goods sold could include low base-period costs, while annual cost of goods sold would include only current year costs.

Several additional problems are encountered when using LIFO for interim reporting.

1. What is the best approach to estimating interim LIFO cost of sales?
2. As noted above, when an interim liquidation occurs that is expected to be replaced by year end, cost of sales should include the expected cost of replacement. How should this adjustment be treated on the interim balance sheet?
3. How should an interim liquidation that is **not** expected to be replaced by year end be recorded?

These problems are not addressed in APB 28. The only literature related to these problems is the AICPA Task Force Issues Paper, *Identification and Discussion of Certain Financial Accounting and Reporting Issues Concerning LIFO Inventories.*

The Issues Paper describes two acceptable approaches to measuring the interim LIFO cost of sales. The first approach makes specific quarterly computations of the LIFO effect based on year-to-date amounts. This is accomplished by reviewing quarterly price level changes and inventory levels. The second approach projects the expected **annual** LIFO effect and then allocates that projection to the quarters. The allocation can be made equally to each quarter or can be made in relation to certain operating criteria per quarter.

The Issues Paper also describes two acceptable approaches to treating the interim liquidation replacement on the balance sheet. The first approach is to record the adjustment for the pretax income effect of the replacement as a deferred credit in the current liabilities section. The second approach is to instead record the adjustment as a credit to inventory.

When an interim LIFO liquidation occurs that is not expected to be reinstated by year end, the Task Force believes that a company should recognize the effect of the liquidation in the period in which it occurs to the extent that this can reasonably be determined. They also believe, however, that a company using dollar-value LIFO may allocate the expected effect of the liquidation to the quarters.

Other Costs and Expenses

Most other costs and expenses are recognized in interim periods as incurred. However, an expenditure which **clearly benefits** more than one interim period (e.g., annual repairs or property taxes) may be allocated among the periods benefited. The allocation is to be based on estimates of time expired, benefit received, or activity related to the periods. Such allocation procedures should be consistent with those used by the firm at year-end reporting dates. However, if cost or expense cannot be readily associated with other interim periods, such costs should not be arbitrarily assigned to those periods. Application of these interim reporting expense principles is illustrated in the examples below.

1. Costs expensed at year-end dates that benefit two or more interim periods (e.g., annual major repairs) should be assigned to interim periods through use of deferrals or accruals.
2. Quantity discounts given customers based on annual sales volume should be apportioned to interim periods on the basis of sales to customers during the interim period relative to estimated annual sales.
3. Property taxes (and like costs) may be deferred or accrued at a year-end date to reflect a full year's charge to operations. Charges to interim periods should follow similar procedures.
4. Advertising costs may be deferred to subsequent interim periods within the same fiscal year if such costs clearly benefit the later interim periods. Advertising costs may be accrued and charged to interim periods preceding the time the service is received if there is an advertising program clearly implicit in the sales arrangement.

Costs and expenses subject to year-end adjustment, such as bad debts expense and discretionary bonuses, should be estimated and assigned to interim periods in a reasonable manner.

Income Taxes

At each interim date, the company should make its best **estimate of the effective tax rate** expected for the full fiscal year. This estimate should reflect expected federal and state tax rates, tax credits, and other tax planning techniques. However, changes in tax legislation are reflected only in interim periods after the effective date of the legislation.

The tax effect of losses in early quarters of the year should be recognized only when such losses can be carried back, or when the realization of the carryforward is reasonably assured. In the absence of contrary evidence, an established seasonal pattern of early-year losses offset by income later in the year constitutes reasonable assurance.

The accounting for income taxes in interim periods is discussed extensively in Appendix A to Chapter 15, Accounting for Income Taxes.

Discontinued Operations and Extraordinary Items

Extraordinary items and the effects of disposal of a segment should be reported separately in the interim period in which they occur. The same treatment is given to other unusual or infrequently occurring events. No attempt should be made to allocate such items over the entire fiscal year. Materiality is determined by relating the item to the annual results of operations.

Accounting Changes

Retroactive changes in accounting principle are handled on the same basis as in annual reports. Previously issued interim financial statements are retroactively restated.

When a cumulative effect type change occurs in the first quarter, the cumulative effect is included in the first quarter's net income. However, if the cumulative effect change occurs in later quarters, it is treated as if it occurred in the first quarter (to conform with the annual treatment). Therefore, previous quarters' financial statements are restated to reflect the change, and the cumulative effect as of the beginning of the year is included in the first quarter's net income.

The treatment of accounting changes in interim reports is covered extensively in the Appendix to Chapter 20, Accounting Changes.

Earnings Per Share

The same procedures used at year end are used for earnings per share computations and disclosures in interim reports. Note that annual earnings per share generally will not equal the sum of the interim earnings per share amounts, due to such factors as stock issuances during the year and market price changes.

Contingent Items

In general, contingencies at an interim date should be accrued or disclosed in the same manner required for annual reports. The materiality of the contingency is to be evaluated in relation to the expected annual results.

Certain items which are adjustments related to prior interim periods, such as a settlement of litigation or an income tax dispute, are accorded special treatment in interim reports. If such items are material, directly related to prior interim periods of the current fiscal year, and become reasonably estimable in the current interim period, they should be reported as follows:

1. The portion directly related to the current interim period is included in that period's income.
2. Prior interim periods are restated to reflect the portions directly related to those periods.

3. The portion directly related to **prior years** is recognized in the restated first quarter income of the current year.

Seasonality

The operations of many businesses are subject to material seasonal variations. Such businesses should disclose the seasonality of their activities to avoid the possibility of misleading interim reports. APB 28 also suggests that such businesses supplement their disclosures with information for 12-month periods ending at the interim date of the current and preceding year.

Fourth Quarter Adjustments

When the fourth quarter results are not separately reported, material year-end adjustments as well as disposals of segments, extraordinary items, and unusual or infrequently occurring items for the quarter should be disclosed in a footnote to the annual report.

EMERGING ISSUES TASK FORCE CONSENSUS SUMMARIES

98-9 Accounting for Contingent Rent in Interim Financial Periods

A consensus was reached that lessors should not recognize contingent rental income until the target that causes the contingent rental income is reached.

A consensus was also reached that lessees should recognize contingent rental income in the period that the cause of contingent rental income is probable before the end of the fiscal year. Previously recognized rental expense should be reversed if an assessment deemed probable changes during the year.

SEGMENT REPORTING

PERSPECTIVE AND ISSUES

Segment reporting, the disclosure of information about different components of an enterprise's operations as well as information related to the enterprise's products and services, its geographic areas, and its major customers, is a relatively recent development in financial reporting.

During the late 1960s, a large number of business combinations resulted in highly diversified corporations. Some of these companies voluntarily disclosed segment financial information in their annual reports, but the extent and nature of the disclosure varied widely. APB Statement 2, issued in 1967, recommended further voluntary disclosure. In addition, professional organizations, such as the FEI and the NAA, sponsored research studies that generally supported the desirability and feasibility of segment reporting.

Although the SEC began requiring "line-of-business" information in registrants' 10-K reports in 1970, many diversified companies still had no segment information in their annual reports issued to stockholders. By 1974, the SEC required registrants to include some of the line-of-business information in their annual reports to stockholders. Other companies began segment disclosure to gain the approval of investors. SFAS 14, issued in December 1976, established specific guidelines for the required disclosure of segment information on financial reports issued to stockholders, generally using an industry approach. SFAS 18 suspended the requirement for segment reporting in interim reports, and SFAS 21 further limited the required disclosures to the annual reports of publicly held companies. It should be noted that other pronouncements dealt indirectly with information on a less than total-enterprise basis. APB 18, for example, requires information on unconsolidated equity investees, and APB 30 requires information on discontinued segment operations.

The primary benefit of segment reporting is the release of "hidden data" from consolidated financial information. Different operating segments may possess different levels of profitability, risk, and growth. This important information is merged in the consolidated amounts. Assessing future cash flows and their associated risks can be aided by segmental data. For example, knowledge of the level of enterprise operations in a growth or declining product line can help cash flow predictions, while knowledge of the level of enterprise operations in an unstable geographic area can help assess risk. In general, information about the nature and relative size of an enterprise's various businesses is considered useful.

Still, several arguments, listed below, have been offered against segment reporting.

1. Comparison of segment data between companies is misleading due to the wide variety of measurement techniques in use.

2. Lack of user knowledge could render segment information meaningless or misleading.
3. Disclosure of such information to competitors, labor unions, etc. could harm the enterprise.
4. Such disclosure may discourage management from taking reasonable business risks to avoid reporting unsatisfactory segment data.
5. The investor invests in the entire company and has no right to expect segment information.
6. Accounting classification and allocation problems may be inherent in segment reporting.
7. Information overload--Financial reports have become too detailed and complex for the average user.

Despite the potential disadvantages listed above, segment reporting has become more important as the number and size of conglomerates increase, as foreign operations increase, and as companies continue to diversify. In addition, over the years financial analysts have consistently requested that financial statement data be more disaggregated than is currently required by SFAS 14. Also, financial statement users have suggested that standard setters should improve segment reporting.

As a result, the FASB has recently issued a new accounting statement, SFAS 131, *Disclosures About Segments of an Enterprise and Related Information*. This statement supersedes SFAS 14, 18, 21, 24, and 30, and changes the way public businesses are required to report disaggregated information in financial reports to shareholders, including interim reports. The statement defines operating segments as distinct revenue-producing components of the enterprise about which separate financial information is produced internally, and whose operating results are regularly reviewed by the enterprise. The approach used in SFAS 131 is a "management approach," meaning it is based on the way management organizes segments internally to make operating decisions and assess performance. The management approach will facilitate consistent descriptions of an enterprise for both internal and external reporting and, in general, provides that external financial reporting will more closely conform to internal reporting.

Practitioners of public companies can segment their financial information by products or services, by geography, by legal entity, or by type of customer. The statement requires that each of these operating segments report on segment profit or loss, on certain specific revenue and expense items, and on segment assets, among other items. The entity would then be required to reconcile segment information with general-purpose financial statements.

In addition, the statement requires that all public enterprises report information about revenues for each product and service, about countries in which the enterprise earns revenues and holds assets, and about major customers, even if this information is not used by the enterprise in making operating decisions.

The statement would not restrict segment reporting to purely financial information. The statement also requires a description of the company's rationale or methods employed in determining the composition of the operating segments. Included with this description would be the products or services produced by the segment, differences in measurement practices between a segment and the complete entity, and differences in measurement practices in a segment between periods. The statement is effective for all public companies for years beginning after December 15, 1997.

Sources of GAAP

APB	*SFAS*	*FASB TB*
18	69, 131	79-4, 79-5

DEFINITIONS OF TERMS

Assets test. One of the three 10% tests; used to determine reportability of operating segments.

Chief operating decision maker. A person whose general function (not specific title) is to allocate resources to, and assess the performance of, the segments of an enterprise.

Common costs. Operating expenses incurred by the enterprise for the benefit of more than one segment.

Corporate assets. Assets maintained for general corporate purposes and not used in the operations of any segment.

Expenditures for segment assets. Additions to a segment's long-lived assets; generally, property, plant, and equipment.

Financial report. Includes any compilation of information that includes one or more complete sets of financial statements, such as in an annual report to stockholders or in a filing with the Securities and Exchange Commission.

Foreign operations. Operations located outside of the enterprise's home country that generate either unaffiliated or intraenterprise revenues.

General corporate expenses. Expenses incurred for the benefit of the corporation as a whole, which cannot be reasonably allocated to any segment.

Geographic area. An individual country (domestic or foreign).

Intersegment sales. Transfers of products or services, similar to those sold to unaffiliated customers, between operating segments.

Major customer. A customer responsible for at least 10% of an enterprise's revenues.

Management approach. The method chosen by the FASB to determine what information should be reported; it is based on the way that management organizes the segments internally for making operating decisions and assessing performance.

Nonpublic enterprise. An enterprise other than one (1) whose debt or equity securities trade in a public market on a foreign or domestic stock exchange or in the over-the-counter market (including securities quoted only locally or regionally) or (2) that is required to file financial statements with the Securities and Exchange Commission. An enterprise is no longer considered a nonpublic enterprise when its financial statements are issued in preparation for the sale of any class of securities in a public market. Nonpublic enterprises include certain mutual associations, cooperatives, nonbusiness organizations, and partnerships that often make their financial statements available to a broad class, such as insurance policyholders, depositors, members, contributors, or partners.

Operating profit and loss test. One of the three 10% tests; used to determine reportability of operating segments.

Operating segment. A component of an enterprise which may earn revenues and incur expenses, about which separate financial information is available that is evaluated regularly by the chief operating decision maker in deciding how to allocate resources and in assessing performance.

Profit center. Those components of an enterprise that sell primarily to outside markets and for which information about revenue and profitability is accumulated. They are the smallest units of activity for which revenue and expense information is accumulated for internal planning and control purposes.

Reportable segments. Segments considered to be significant to an enterprise's operations; a segment which has passed one of three 10% tests or has been identified as being reportable through other criteria (e.g., aggregation, etc.).

Revenues test. One of three 10% tests; used to determine reportability of operating segments and major customers.

Segment assets. Those tangible and intangible assets directly associable or used by a segment, including any allocated portion of assets used jointly by more than one segment.

Segment operating profit or loss. All of a segment's revenue minus all operating expenses, including any allocated revenues or expenses (e.g., common costs).

Segment reporting. Disclosure of information about different components of an enterprise's operations as well as information related to the enterprise's products and services, its geographic areas, and its major customers.

Segment revenue. Revenue from sales to unaffiliated customers and from intersegment sales or transfers.

75% test. A test used to determine whether the reportable segments of an enterprise represent a substantial portion of the enterprise's total operations.

Transfer pricing. The pricing of products or services between industry segments or geographic areas.

CONCEPTS, RULES, AND EXAMPLES

Applicability of SFAS 131

SFAS 131 applies to public business enterprises. The statement does not apply to not-for-profit organizations or to **nonpublic enterprises**. However, entities other than public business enterprises are encouraged to provide the disclosures described in SFAS 131.

Operating Segments

In SFAS 131, an **operating segment** is defined as

> *A component of an enterprise engaged in business activity for which it may earn revenues and incur expenses, about which separate financial information is available that is evaluated regularly by the* ***chief operating decision makers*** *in deciding how to allocate resources and in assessing performance.*

This general definition leaves it up to management's judgment to determine operating segment classifications. However, the FASB believes meaningful segment information will be provided in external **financial reports** because the externally reported segment information must conform with the segment information that is used internally. The FASB does provide standards to assist enterprises in determining which operating segments are reportable segments.

Reportable Segments

A segment is considered to be reportable if it is significant to the enterprise as a whole. A segment is to be regarded as significant if it satisfies **one** of the three quantitative **10% tests** described below.

Revenues test. Segment revenue (unaffiliated and intersegment) is at least 10% of the combined revenue (unaffiliated and intersegment) of all reported operating segments.

Operating profit and loss test. Segment operating profit (loss) is revenues minus operating expenses. Both revenues and operating expenses consist of unaffiliated and intersegment components. The absolute amount of segment operating profit or loss is at least 10% of the **greater**, in absolute amount, of

1. Combined operating **profits** of all operating segments reporting a profit.
2. Combined operating **losses** of all operating segments reporting a loss.

Assets test. Segment assets are at least 10% of combined assets of all operating segments. **Segment assets** are those assets used exclusively by the segment and any allocated portion of assets shared by two or more segments. Assets held for general corporate purposes are not assigned to segments.

Interperiod comparability must be considered in conjunction with the results of the 10% tests. If a segment fails to meet the tests, but has satisfied the tests in the past and is expected to in the future, it should be considered reportable in the current year for the sake of comparability. Similarly, if a segment which rarely passes the tests does so in the current year as the result of an unusual event, that segment may be excluded to preserve comparability.

After the 10% tests are completed, a **75% test** must be performed. The combined **unaffiliated** revenue of all **reportable** segments must be at least 75% of the combined unaffiliated revenue of all operating segments. If the 75% test is not satisfied, additional segments must be designated as reportable until the test is satisfied. The purpose of this test is to ensure that reportable segments account for a substantial portion of the entity's operations.

The following example illustrates the three 10% tests and the 75% test.

Segment	*Unaffiliated revenue*	*Intersegment revenue*	*Total revenue*	*Operating profit (loss)*	*Assets*
A	$ 90	$ 90	$ 180	$ 20	$ 70
B	120		120	10	50
C	110	20	130	(40)	90
D	200		200	0	140
E	330	110	440	(100)	230
F	380	——	380	60	260
Total	$1,230	$220	$1,450	$ (50)	$840

Revenues test: (10%)($1,450) = $145

Reportable segments: A, D, E, F

Operating profit or loss test: (10%)($140) = $14

Reportable segments: A, C, E, F

[NOTE: Total operating loss ($140) is greater than total operating profit ($90)]

Assets test: (10%)($840) = $84

Reportable segments: C, D, E, F

Reportable segments are those which pass **at least one** of the 10% tests. Segments A, C, D, E, and F are reportable in this example.

75% test: (75%)($1,230) = $922.50

Segments A, C, D, E, and F have total unaffiliated revenue of $1,110, which is greater than $922.50. The 75% test is satisfied; no additional segments need be reported.

Certain other factors must be considered when identifying reportable segments. An enterprise may consider aggregating two or more operating segments if they have similar economic characteristics and if the segments are similar in each of the following areas:

1. The nature of the products and services
2. The nature of the production processes
3. The type of customer for their products and services
4. The methods used to distribute their products or provide their services
5. The nature of the regulatory environment (SFAS 131, para 17)

This aggregation can occur prior to performing the 10% tests if the enterprise desires.

Additionally, the enterprise may combine information on operating segments that do not meet any of the 10% tests to produce a reportable segment, but only if the segments meet a majority of the aggregation criteria discussed above. It should be noted that information about operating segments that do not meet any of the 10% thresholds may still be disclosed separately. By utilizing the aggregation criteria and quantitative thresholds (10% tests) for determining reportable segments, the statement uses a modified **management approach**.

However, the number of reportable segments should not be so great as to decrease the usefulness of segment reporting. As a rule of thumb, the FASB suggests that if the number of reportable segments exceeds 10, segment information may become too detailed. In this situation, the most closely related operating segments should be combined into broader reportable segments.

Accounting Problems

Since segment revenue as defined by SFAS 131 includes **intersegment sales**, **transfer pricing** becomes an issue. Rather than establishing a basis for setting transfer prices, the FASB required companies to use the same transfer prices for segment reporting purposes as are used internally. Since most segments are organizational **profit centers**, internal transfer prices would generally reflect market prices.

Another problem in determining operating profit or loss is the **allocation of common costs.** Common costs are operating expenses incurred by the enterprise for the benefit of more than one operating segment. These costs should only be allocated to a segment for external reporting purposes, if they are included in the measure of the segments profit or loss that is used internally by the chief operating decision maker.

A problem can arise in distinguishing common costs from **general corporate expenses**. General corporate expenses are not operating expenses from the point of view of any operating segment; they are incurred for the benefit of the corporation as a whole and cannot be reasonably allocated to any operating segment.

Similarly, only those assets that are included internally in the measure of the segment's assets used to make operating decisions, shall be reported as assets of the segment in external financial reports. If management does allocate amounts to segment profit or assets internally and those amounts are used by the chief operating decision maker, then those amounts shall be allocated on a reasonable basis and disclosed.

Segment Disclosures

SFAS 131 requires several disclosures regarding the enterprise's reportable segments. They include

1. **General information**--An explanation of how management identified the enterprise's reportable segments, including whether operating segments have been aggregated. Additionally, a description of the types of products and services from which each reportable segment derives its revenues.
2. **Certain information about reported segment profit and loss, segment assets and the basis of measurement**--This will include certain revenue and expense items included in segment profit and loss, as well as certain amounts related to the determination of segment assets. Also, the basis of measurement for these items must be disclosed.
3. **Reconciliations**--The enterprise will need to reconcile the segment amounts disclosed to the corresponding enterprise amounts.
4. **Interim period information**--Although the interim disclosures are not as extensive as in the annual financial report, certain segment disclosures are required in interim financial reports (SFAS 131, para 33).

See Appendix for an illustrative example of the disclosures required for segments reporting. Additionally, SFAS 131 also provides an illustrative example.

Restatement of Previously Reported Segment Information

Segment reporting is required on a comparative basis. Therefore, the information must be restated to preserve comparability, whenever the enterprise has changed the structure of its internal organization in a manner that causes a change to its reportable segments. The enterprise must explicitly disclose that it has restated the segment information of earlier periods.

Enterprise-Wide Disclosures About Products and Services, Geographic Areas, And Major Customers

The enterprise-wide disclosures are required for all enterprises, even those that have a single reportable segment.

Products and services. Revenue from external customers for each product and service shall be reported by the enterprise. If the company's reportable segments have been organized around products and services, then this disclosure will generally not be required.

Geographic areas. An enterprise shall report revenues from external customers and long-lived assets attributable to its domestic operations and **foreign operations**. If the company's reportable segments have been organized around geographic areas, then these disclosures will generally not be required.

An enterprise's domestic operations are those operations located in the enterprise's home country that generate either unaffiliated or intraenterprise revenues.

The enterprise's foreign operations are similar operations located outside of the enterprise's home country.

If the enterprise functions in two or more foreign **geographic areas**, to the extent revenues or assets of an individual foreign geographic area are material, then these amounts should be separately disclosed. In addition, the enterprise's basis for attributing revenue to different geographic areas shall be disclosed. A geographic area is defined as an individual country.

Information about major customers. If an enterprise earns 10% or more of its revenue on sales to a single external customer, that fact and the amount of revenue from each such customer must be disclosed. Also, the segment making these sales must be disclosed. This disclosure provides information on concentration risk.

A group of customers under common control, such as subsidiaries of a parent, is regarded as a single customer. Similarly the various agencies of a government are considered to be a single customer. An insuring entity (such as Blue Cross) should not be considered the customer unless that entity (rather than the patient) controls the decision as to the doctor, type of service, etc.

EMERGING ISSUES TASK FORCE CONSENSUS SUMMARIES

86-13 Recognition of Inventory Market Declines at Interim Reporting Dates

A consensus was reached that in accordance with APB 28 inventory should be written down to the lower of cost or market unless substantial evidence is available that the market value will recover before the inventory is sold or, when LIFO is used, that the inventory level will be restored by year end. Task Force members noted that generally a write-down is required unless the decline is due to seasonal price fluctuations.

FASB TECHNICAL BULLETINS

79-4 Segment Reporting of Puerto Rican Operations

Puerto Rican operations of U.S. enterprises are not considered to be foreign operations subject to the disclosure requirements of SFAS 14. However, such additional disclosures are not prohibited.

APPENDIX

COMPREHENSIVE ILLUSTRATION

The following illustration is provided for a hypothetical company called Resources Unlimited. The illustration provides segment disclosures by legal entity. *(NOTE: An illustration in SFAS 131 provides segment disclosures by product line).* References to SFAS 131 paragraphs which require the disclosure are provided.

Description of the types of products and services from which each reportable segment derives its revenues [SFAS 131, para 25(b)].

Resources Unlimited has four reportable segments: Wholesale Corporation, Retail Stores Corporation, Library Corporation, and Software Corporation. The Wholesale Corporation buys and resells used elementary and college textbooks. The Retail Stores Corporation operates 200 college book stores selling both new and used college textbooks, trade books, sports apparel, and other sundries. The Library Corporation sells library books primarily to elementary school libraries. Software Corporation develops and sells library system application software.

Measurement of segment profit or loss and segment assets (SFAS 131, para 31).

The accounting policies of the segments are the same as those described in the summary of significant accounting policies except the first-in-first-out (FIFO) method of inventory valuation is used. In addition, for segment reporting, Resources Unlimited allocates interest expense to each segment based on the segment's average borrowings from the corporate office. However, the related debt is not allocated to the segments and remains on the corporate books. Resources Unlimited evaluates performance based on profit or loss before income taxes not including nonrecurring gains and losses.

Resources Unlimited accounts for intersegment sales and transfers as if the sales or transfers were to third parties (i.e., at current market prices).

Factors management used to identify the enterprise's reportable segments [SFAS 131 para 26(a)].

Resources Unlimited's business is conducted through four separate legal entities. At the company's inception, each entity was established by a different Resources Unlimited family member. Each corporation is still managed separately, as each business has a distinct customer base and requires different strategic and marketing efforts.

Information about profit and loss and assets (SFAS 131, para 27 and 28)

The amounts in the illustration are assumed to be the amounts in reports used by the chief operating decision maker. Resources Unlimited does allocate interest expense to the segments, however income taxes and other unusual items are not allocated.

(Table in thousands)

	Wholesale Corporation	*Retail Stores Corporation*	*Library Corporation*	*Software Corporation*	*Totals*
Revenues from external customers	$197,500	$263,000	$182,300	$102,200	$745,000
Intersegment revenues	23,000	--	--	--	23,000
Interest revenue	250	150	--	--	400
Interest expense	1,570	2,150	1,390	2,700	7,810
Depreciation & amortization	8,600	13,100	7,180	6,070	34,950
Segment profit	12,100	13,500	9,900	5,100	40,600
Segment assets	121,200	153,350	100,600	85,000	460,150
Expenditures for segment assets	7,200	12,700	5,600	6,700	32,200

Reconciliations (SFAS 131, para 32)

Illustrations of reconciliations for revenues, profit and loss, assets, and other significant items are shown below. In general, this illustration assumes that there are no unreported operating segments, but there is a corporate headquarters, thus most reconciling items relate to corporate profit and loss accounts.

As discussed previously, the company recognizes and measures inventory based on FIFO valuation. The company's financials are assumed not to include discontinued operations or the cumulative effect of a change in accounting principle.

Revenue	
Total revenues for reportable segments	$768,000
Elimination of intersegment revenue	(23,000)
Total consolidated revenue	$745,000

Profit and loss	
Total profit and loss for reportable segments	$40,600
Elimination of intersegment profits	(6,100)
Unallocated amounts relating to corporate headquarters:	
Interest revenue	500
Interest expense	(800)
Depreciation	(1,900)
Unrealized gain on trading securities	1,865
Income before income taxes and extraordinary items	$30,435

Assets	
Total assets for reportable segments	$460,150
Corporate short-term investments, land and building	25,100
Adjustment for LIFO reserve in consolidation	(9,200)
	$476,050

Other significant items

	Segment totals	*Adjustments*	*Consolidated totals*
Expenditures for segment assets	$32,200	800	$33,000

The reconciling adjustment is the amount of expenditures incurred for additions to the corporate headquarters building, which is not included in the segment information.

Products and services (SFAS 131, para 37)

Used textbooks	$296,125
New textbooks	72,150
Trade books	45,700
Sports Apparel	41,325
Sundries	5,200
Library books	182,300
Library software	102,200
Total revenue	$745,000

Geographic information (SFAS 131, para 38)

	Revenues[a]	*Long-lived assets*
United States	$687,400	$253,200
Foreign countries	57,600	18,800
Total	$745,000	$272,000

[a] *Revenues are attributed to countries based on the shopping location of customer*

Major customers (SFAS 131, para 39)

An illustration of the required disclosures is not provided in this example as Resources Unlimited has no major customers.

20 ACCOUNTING CHANGES AND CORRECTION OF ERRORS

PERSPECTIVE AND ISSUES

Financial statements are the results of choices among different accounting principles and methodologies. Companies select those principles and methods that they believe depict, in their financial statements, the economic reality of their financial position, results of operations, and changes in financial position. Changes take place because of changes in the assumptions and estimates underlying the application of these principles and methods, changes in the acceptable principles by a promulgating authority, or other types of changes.

Accounting for and reporting of these changes is a problem which has faced the accounting profession for years. Much financial analysis is based on the consistency and comparability of annual financial statements. Any type of accounting change creates an inconsistency; thus, a primary focus of management in making the decision to change should be to consider its effect on financial statement comparability. APB 20 was issued so accounting changes could be reported and disclosed in a manner that would improve analysis and understanding of the financial statements.

In APB 20 the Board defined an accounting change as being a change in

1. Accounting principle
2. Accounting estimate
3. Reporting entity

Even though the correction of an error in previously issued financial statements is not considered an accounting change, it is discussed in the opinion and, therefore, will be covered in this chapter.

The Board concluded that in the preparation of the financial statements there is an underlying presumption that an accounting principle, once adopted, should not be changed in accounting for events and transactions of a similar type. This consistent use of accounting principles was believed to enhance the utility of the financial statements. The presumption that an entity should not change an accounting principle may be overcome only if the enterprise justifies the use of an alternative acceptable accounting principle on the basis that it is preferable.

APB 20 contained no definition of preferability or criteria by which to make such assessments. Because there was no universally agreed-upon set of objectives for external financial reporting, what was preferable to one industry or company was not necessarily considered preferable to another. This led to some of the same consistency problems in reporting that existed prior to the issuance of APB 20. However, this consistency problem did not cause great concern in the accounting profession because the justification of preferability rested with the enterprise. The independent accountant was responsible only for reviewing the rationale for preferability and determining its reasonableness.

In September of 1975 the Securities and Exchange Commission (SEC) radically changed the accounting profession's view of preferability by issuing Accounting Series Release (ASR) 177. In this ASR, the SEC mandated that each change in accounting principle, for purposes of SEC filing, must be accompanied by a letter from the independent accountant "...indicating whether or not the change is to an alternative principle which in his judgment is preferable under the circumstances." The lack of a uniform set of objectives for external reporting necessitated making individual determinations as to the preferability of accounting principles. In order to avoid this practice, accountants began using industry audit guides to assist in their decision because this was indicated as acceptable practice in APB 20. The FASB formalized this process by issuing SFAS 32 in 1979. This statement indicated that certain Statements of Position (SOP) and Industry Audit Guides were considered preferable accounting principles (these are listed in the appendixes of SFAS 32 and 56).

SFAS 56 and 83 amended SFAS 32 to include additional SOP and many of the recent SFAS have been issued to establish single, acceptable accounting policies for various industries to help eliminate the preferability question. SFAS 111 rescinds SFAS 32, 56, and 83. These are no longer needed because SAS 69 (discussed in Chapter 1) requires an entity to adopt the accounting principles in pronouncements whose effective date is after March 15, 1992. An entity initially applying an accounting principle after that date (including those making an accounting change) must follow the applicable hierarchy set forth in SAS 69. An entity following an established accounting principle that was effective as of March 15, 1992, need not change its accounting until a new pronouncement is issued.

Sources of GAAP

APB	*SFAS*	*FASB I*
20, 28	3, 16, 111	1, 20

DEFINITIONS OF TERMS

Change in accounting estimate. A revision of an accounting measurement based on new events, additional experience, subsequent developments, better insight, and improved judgment. Such revisions are an inherent part of the accounting process.

Change in accounting principle. A switch from one generally accepted accounting principle to another generally accepted accounting principle, including the methods of applying these principles. This does not include selection of an accounting principle to account for events occurring for the first time.

Change in reporting entity. A special type of change in accounting principle that results in financial statements which, in effect, are those of a different reporting entity. Financial statements are prepared for an entity that is different from the one reported on in previous financial statements.

Comparability. The quality of information that enables users to identify similarities in and differences between two sets of economic phenomena. Normally, comparability is a quantitative assessment of a common characteristic.

Consistency. Conformity from period to period with unchanging policies and procedures. Enhances the utility of financial statements to users by facilitating analysis and understanding of comparative accounting data.

Cumulative effect. The difference between the beginning retained earnings balance of the year in which the change is reported and the beginning retained earnings balance that would have been reported if the new principle had been applied retroactively for all prior periods which would have been affected.

Error. Results from mathematical mistakes, mistakes in applying accounting principles, oversight or misuse of available facts, and use of unacceptable GAAP.

Pro forma. "As if" basis. Disclosure of the required numbers computed on the assumption that certain events have transpired.

Restatement of financial reports. The recasting of a previously determined and published balance sheet or operating statement and its republication where there has been a substantial change in accounting principles or policies.

CONCEPTS, RULES, AND EXAMPLES

APB 20 describes three ways of reporting accounting changes and the type of change for which each should be used. These are

1. Retroactively
2. Currently
3. Prospectively

Retroactive treatment requires an adjustment to all current and prior period financial statements for the effect of the accounting change. Prior period financial statements presented currently are to be restated on a basis consistent with the newly adopted principle.

Current treatment requires reporting the cumulative effect of the accounting change in the current year's income statement as a special item. Prior period financial statements are **not** restated.

Prospective treatment of accounting changes requires **no** restatement of prior financial statements and **no** computing or reporting of the accounting change's cumulative effect in the current period's income statement. Only current and/or future periods' financial report data will reflect the accounting change.

Each of the types of accounting changes and the proper treatment prescribed for them is discussed in detail in the following sections.

Change in Accounting Principle

According to APB 20 the term "accounting principle" includes the accounting principles and practices used as well as the methods of applying them. FASB Interpretation 1 sets a base for the application of this statement by ruling that a change in the components used to cost a firm's inventory is a change in accounting principle. The Interpretation also stated that the preferability assessment must be made from the perspective of financial reporting basis and not from the income tax perspective. The Opinion indicates that changes in accounting principles should be accounted for currently using the cumulative effect method; however, there are a few specific exceptions to this general rule. One of these occurs when an authoritative body issues a new standard. The adoption of the standard will require accounting for the change as prescribed by the new pronouncement. Each new SFAS has its own transition rules. However, APB 20 requires that the cumulative effect method be used for most changes in accounting principles, and no restatement is to occur in the prior period financial statements.

The **cumulative effect** method is to be applied as follows:

1. Previously issued financial statements are **not** to be restated.
2. The cumulative effect of changing to the new accounting principle on the amount of retained earnings at the beginning of the period in which the change occurs should be included in the net income of the period of the change.
3. The effect of adopting the new principle on income before extraordinary items and net income, including per share amounts of the period of change, should be disclosed in the notes to the statements.
4. Income before extraordinary items and net income computed on a pro forma basis (defined below) should be shown on the face of the income statements for all periods presented as if the newly adopted principle had been applied during all periods affected. The nature of and justification for

> the change shall be disclosed in the financial statements in which the change is made.

According to the Board's conclusions, **income for the period of the change is to be computed using the newly adopted principle** while all other periods are to be presented as they originally appeared (step 1). **Restatement will occur only in the disclosures and the pro forma calculations.**

The cumulative effect of a change in accounting principle is to appear as a single amount on the income statement between extraordinary items and net income (step 2). The amount shown should be the difference between

1. The amount of retained earnings at the beginning of the period, and
2. The amount of retained earnings that would have been reported at that date if the new accounting principle had been applied retroactively to all prior periods affected.

The cumulative effect is generally determined by first calculating income before taxes for both the new principle and the old principle for all prior periods affected. Second, the difference between the two incomes for each prior period is determined. Third, these differences are adjusted for tax effects. Finally, the net of tax differences for each prior period are totaled. This total represents the cumulative effect adjustment at the beginning of the current period. The cumulative effect will either be an addition to or a subtraction from current income depending on how the change to the new principle affects income. Generally, only the direct effects of the change and the related income tax effect should be included in the cumulative effect calculation (i.e., if the company changes its method of computing depreciation, only the effects of the change in depreciation expense, net of tax, are considered to be direct effects). Indirect effects, such as the effect on a profit sharing contribution or bonus payments that would have occurred as a result of the change in net income, are not included in the cumulative effect computation unless these are to be recorded by the firm (i.e., the expense is actually incurred).

Step 3 requires that the effects of the change on income before extraordinary items and net income be disclosed for the year of the change. This is the difference between the old principle and the new principle on an after tax basis. The amount shall be disclosed for both the total effect and the per share amounts. In addition, the nature of and justification for the change must be disclosed, clearly indicating why the newly adopted principle is preferable.

The computation of income on a pro forma basis must be made for each period currently presented. The objective is to present income before extraordinary items and net income as if the new principle were being applied. This is achieved by adjusting each period's income before extraordinary items as previously reported (i.e., applying the old principle). The adjustment is made by adding or subtracting the difference in income net of tax for the period to income before extraordinary items as previously reported. The difference, net of tax, is the change in income that occurs when the new principle is applied instead of the old principle. This results in an income before extraordinary items figure that reflects the application of the new principle. Net income is then calculated as normally done from the adjusted income before extraordinary items. The per share amounts required are based upon the pro forma income before extraordinary items and net income amounts.

The pro forma calculation required by step 4 differs from that of the cumulative effect. It is to include both the direct effects of the change and the "nondiscretionary" adjustments of items **based** on income before taxes or net income. Examples of nondiscretionary items would be profit sharing expense or certain royalties. Both of these expenses are in some way based on net income, generally as a specified percentage. The related tax effects should be recognized for **both** the direct and nondiscretionary adjustments. The pro forma calculation is to be shown on the face of the financial statements for income before extraordinary items and net income. The earnings per share amounts (both basic and diluted as defined in APB 15) for both should also be computed and shown. According to SFAS 128, if space is not available on the face of the financial statements, the pro forma information may be disclosed prominently in the notes to the financial statements.

The following example will illustrate the computations and disclosures necessary when applying the cumulative effect method. This particular example is adapted from the one which is included in Appendix A of APB 20.

Example of cumulative effect (example from APB 20, Appendix A)

ABC Co. decides in 1999 to adopt the straight-line method of depreciation for plant equipment. The straight-line method will be used for all new acquisitions as well as for previously acquired plant equipment for which depreciation had been provided on an accelerated method.

The following assumptions are being made:

1. The direct effect of the change is limited to the change in accumulated depreciation.
2. The tax rate is a constant 40%.
3. The executive incentive bonus is the only nondiscretionary item affected by the change. It is 10% of the pretax accounting income.
4. There are 1,000,000 shares of common stock outstanding throughout the entire period affected by the change.
5. An additional 100,000 shares would be issued if all the outstanding bonds were converted. Annual interest on this bond obligation is $25,000 (net of tax).
6. For 1998 and 1999 the income before extraordinary item is given as $1,100,000 and $1,200,000 respectively. There is an extraordinary item in each year amounting to $100,000 for 1998 and ($35,000) for 1999. The extraordinary items are included to illustrate the proper positioning of the cumulative effect adjustment on the income statement.

Year	Excess of accelerated depreciation over straight-line depreciation	Direct effects of change, net of tax	Nondiscretionary item, net of tax	Pro forma amounts
Prior to 1995	$ 20,000	$ 12,000	$ 1,200	$ 10,800
1995	80,000	48,000	4,800	43,200
1996	70,000	42,000	4,200	37,800
1997	50,000	30,000	3,000	27,000
1998	30,000	18,000	1,800	16,200
Total at beg. of 1999	$250,000	$150,000	$15,000	$135,000

The following narrative provides assistance in grasping the computational aspects of the information given above. The "excess of...depreciation" is given in this example. It is generally determined by recomputing the depreciation under the new method and obtaining the difference between the two methods. The "direct...tax" represents the effect of the actual change (i.e., depreciation) upon income before extraordinary items adjusted for the tax effects. For example, in the years prior to 1995 the change in depreciation methods (from accelerated **to** straight-line) resulted in a $20,000 reduction in depreciation expense (or an increase in income). The net of tax number is $12,000 because the $20,000 increase in income is reduced by an $8,000 (40% x $20,000) increase in income tax expense.

The "nondiscretionary item, net of tax" represents the income statement items affected indirectly as a result of the change. In this case, it was given that the executive incentive bonus equal to 10% of pretax accounting income was the only "nondiscretionary item" affected. Thus, in years prior to 1995, when pretax accounting income increased by $20,000, the bonus expense would have been $2,000 higher ($20,000 x 10%). APB 20 indicates that this should also be computed net of tax, and because the expense would have increased by $2,000, the taxes would have decreased by $800 ($2,000 x 40%). The net of tax increase in expense is $1,200. The **pro forma** amounts are to include both the direct and indirect effects of the change. The computation for this example is as follows:

	Increase (decrease) in net income
Reduction in depreciation expense	$20,000
Increase in taxes (depreciation)	(8,000)
Increase in compensation expense	(2,000)
Reduction in taxes (compensation)	800
	$10,800

The pro forma amount is needed for disclosure purposes so that 1998 income can be shown on a comparative basis with 1999 net income (i.e., adding the 1998 income before the change. The pro forma increase or decrease will result in an income figure which reflects the same accounting principles as the 1999 income figure).

Below are the necessary disclosures required by APB 20 for the aforementioned situation.

On the Face of the Income Statement

	1999	1998
Income before extraordinary item and cumulative effect of a change in accounting principle	$1,200,000	$1,100,000
Extraordinary item (description)	(35,000)	100,000
Cumulative effect on prior years (to December 31, 1998) of changing to a different depreciation method	150,000	--
Net income	$1,315,000	$1,200,000
Per share amounts:		
Earnings per common share--assuming no dilution:		
Income before extraordinary item and cumulative effect of a change in accounting principle	$1.20	$1.10
Extraordinary item	(0.04)	0.10
Cumulative effect on prior years (to December 31, 1998) of changing to a different depreciation method	0.15	--
Net income	$1.31	$1.20
Earnings per common share--assuming dilution:		
Income before extraordinary item and cumulative effect of a change in accounting principle	$1.11	$1.02
Extraordinary item	(0.03)	0.09
Cumulative effect on prior years (to December 31, 1998) of changing to a different depreciation method	0.14	--
Net income	$1.22	$1.11
Pro forma amounts assuming the new depreciation method is applied retroactively:		
Income before extraordinary item and cumulative effect of a change in accounting principle	$1,200,000	$1,116,200
Earnings per common share--assuming no dilution	$1.20	$1.12
Earnings per common share--assuming dilution	$1.11	$1.01
Net income	$1,165,000	$1,216,200
Earnings per common share--assuming no dilution	$1.17	$1.22
Earnings per common share--assuming dilution	$1.08	$1.11

In the Notes to the Financial Statements

Note A: Change in Depreciation Method for Plant Equipment

During 1999 the company decided to change its method of computing depreciation on plant equipment from sum-of-the-years' digits (SYD) to the straight-line method. The company made the change because the straight-line method better matches revenues and cost amortization and, therefore, is a preferable accounting principle. The new method has been applied retroactively to equipment acquisitions of prior years. The effect of the change in 1999 was to increase income before extraordinary items by approximately $10,000 (or $.01 per share). The adjustment of $150,000 (net of $100,000 in taxes) included in 1999 income is the cumulative effect of applying the new method retroactively. The pro forma amounts shown on the income statement have been adjusted for the effect of the retroactive application of the new depreciation method, the change in the provisions for incentive compensation which would have been made had the new method been used, and the related income taxes for both.

If the company elected to disclose the pro forma amounts in notes to the financial statements and not on the face of the income statement, the following disclosure would have been included as part of Note A.

The following pro forma amounts show the effect of the retroactive application of the change from the SYD to straight-line method of depreciation.

	Actual	Pro forma
1999		
Income before extraordinary items	$1,200,000	$1,200,000
Basic earnings per share*	$1.20	$1.20
Diluted earnings per share*	$1.11	$1.11
Net income	$1,315,000	$1,165,000
Basic earnings per share	$1.31	$1.17
Diluted earnings per share	$1.22	$1.08
1998		
Income before extraordinary items	$1,100,000	$1,116,200
Basic earnings per share	$1.10	$1.12
Diluted earnings per share	$1.02	$1.01
Net income	$1,200,000	$1,216,200
Basic earnings per share	$1.20	$1.22
Diluted earnings per share	$1.11	$1.11

Notice how in the above example the four steps provided in APB 20 are followed:

Step 1 -- No restatement takes place on the face of the income statements. The 1998 figures provided for comparative purposes are the same as those originally reported.

Step 2 -- The cumulative effect of the change is included on the face of the income statement as a single amount. The $150,000 shown in 1999 represents the total direct effect net of tax for all years prior to 1999. The effect of the change in 1999 is included in the computation of operating income for 1999.

Step 3 -- The required disclosure of the 1999 effects of the change, both in total and the per share amounts, is usually done in the notes to the financial statements. This is assumed to be $10,000 in the example above or $.01 per share.

Step 4 -- The pro forma amounts are used to make the statements from the 2 years comparable. 1998 income before extraordinary items is increased by $16,200 to $1,116,200. This is the amount found in the original table across from 1998. Notice also how the 1999 net income figure no longer contains a cumulative effect adjustment. This is because 1999 and 1998 earnings, under the pro forma computations, are derived using the same accounting principles.

As was mentioned earlier, there are several cases for which the (FASB) APB has determined that a change in accounting principle should be accounted for retro-

---

* *SFAS 128 uses these captions but allows for alternatives such as those on the previous page.*

actively in the financial statements. There are five instances which require retroactive treatment.

1. Change from LIFO to another inventory method (APB 20, para 27)
2. A change in the method of accounting for long-term contracts (APB 20, para 27)
3. A change to or from the full cost method of accounting for exploration costs in the extractive industries (APB 20, para 27)
4. Any change made by a company first issuing financial statements for the purpose of obtaining additional equity capital, effecting a business combination, or registering securities (APB 20, para 29)
5. Any changes mandated by authoritative pronouncements (while this case is not specified by APB 20, the promulgating bodies have in most instances thus far required that the change be made retroactively). FASB Interpretation 20 has also indicated that AICPA SOP may mandate the treatment given the change.

The process of restating the financial statements in these situations was favored because it did not require that the cumulative effect of the change be included in net income. Rather, each of the years presented is adjusted to reflect the new accounting principle. The cumulative effect is calculated in the same manner shown earlier for accounting changes receiving nonretroactive treatment. **The cumulative effect of all periods prior to such period presented is treated as an adjustment to beginning retained earnings of the period.** The net income of each period presented is recomputed applying the new principle. Thus, the adjustment to beginning retained earnings includes all income effects prior to each period presented, and the recomputed net income includes the effect of the new principle on income for each period presented. Together these two adjustments restate the retained earnings ending balance for the period presented to the amount it would have been had the new principle always been applied. This restatement process is consistently followed for all periods presented. According to APB 20, the nature of and justification for the change must be disclosed in the year that the change is made. In addition, the effect of the change on income before extraordinary items, net income, and the related per share amounts should be disclosed for all periods presented. Again, subsequent financial statements do not need to repeat the disclosures.

The restatement need only reflect the direct effects of the change in accounting principle. The exception to this statement arises if the direct effect results in a change in a nondiscretionary item that will be recorded on the books. For example, assume that profit sharing expense is based on net income. The company changes its method of accounting for long-term construction contracts which results in an increase in income in all of the prior years. This increase in income would have changed the amount of the profit sharing expense required during the applicable years. However, the expense would only be changed for the purpose of the restatement if it is to be paid. If the profit sharing agreement does not require an adjustment to the actual contribution, the increase in expense would not be recognized on the restated financial statements.

The following illustration is an adaption of Appendix B in APB 20 and illustrates the proper restatement in a situation where the company changes its method of accounting for long-term construction contracts. As mentioned above, this is one of the five situations for which APB 20 requires retroactive treatment.

Example of retroactive treatment (example from APB 20, Appendix B)

During 1999 XYZ Company decided to adopt the percentage-of-completion method in accounting for all of its long-term construction contracts. The company had used the completed contract method in previous years and had maintained records which were adequate to retroactively apply the percentage-of-completion method.

The following assumptions are made for this example:

1. A constant tax rate of 40%.
2. There are 1,000,000 common shares outstanding in all periods affected by the change.
3. An additional 100,000 shares would be issued if all of the outstanding bonds, which are not common stock equivalents, were converted. The annual interest on this bond obligation is $15,000 (net of tax).

	Pretax accounting income		*Difference in income*	
Year	*Percentage-of-completion method*	*Completed contract method*	*Direct*	*Net of tax effect*
Prior to 1995	$1,800,000	$1,300,000	$500,000	$300,000
1995	900,000	800,000	100,000	60,000
1996	700,000	1,000,000	(300,000)	(180,000)
1997	800,000	600,000	200,000	120,000
1998	1,000,000	1,100,000	(100,000)	(60,000)
Total at beg. of 1999	$5,200,000	$4,800,000	$400,000	$240,000
1999	1,100,000	900,000	200,000	120,000
Total	$6,300,000	$5,700,000	$600,000	$360,000

Following is the proper method of disclosing this type of change as prescribed by APB 20.

On the Face of the Income Statement

	1999	*As adjusted See Note A 1998*
Income before extraordinary item	$ 660,000	$ 600,000
Extraordinary item (description)	--	(80,000)
Net income	$ 660,000	$ 520,000

Per share amounts:		
Basic earnings per common share:		
Income before extraordinary item	$.66	$.60
Extraordinary item	--	(.08)
Net income	$.66	$.52
Diluted earnings per common share:		
Income before extraordinary item	$.61	$.56
Extraordinary item	--	(.07)
Net income	$.61	$.49

On the Statement of Retained Earnings

	1999	*As adjusted See Note A 1998*
Balance at beginning of year, as previously reported	$17,910,000	$17,330,000
Add adjustment for the cumulative effect on prior years of applying retroactively the new method of accounting for long-term contracts (Note A)	240,000	300,000*
Balance at beginning of year	$18,150,000	$17,630,000
Net income	660,000	520,000
Balance at end of year	$18,810,000	$18,150,000

**This is the resultant amount of the change less the tax effect through 1997.*

In the Notes to the Financial Statements

Note A: Change in Method of Accounting for Long-term Construction Contracts

In 1999 the company changed its method of accounting for long-term construction contracts from the completed contract method to the percentage-of-completion method. The change was made because the company felt that the new method resulted in a more accurate recognition of revenue and a better matching of revenue and costs. The financial statements of prior periods have been restated to apply the new method retroactively. The company will continue to use the completed contract method for income tax purposes. The effect of the accounting change in income of 1999 and on income previously reported for 1998 is

	Increase (decrease)	
	1999	*1998*
Effect on:		
Income before extraordinary item and net income	$120,000	$(60,000)
Basic earnings per common share	.12	(.06)
Diluted earnings per common share	.11	(.05)

The balances of retained earnings for 1998 and 1999 have been adjusted for the effect (net of income taxes) of retroactively applying the new method of accounting.

Notice that the income statement does not highlight the change. This lack of disclosure has been the major argument surrounding the use of this method. While both periods reflect the increase in income resulting from the change, it is assumed that the average user of the financial statements may not refer to the notes in order to understand the change.

The only change shown "on" the financial statements is the cumulative adjustment which is part of the Statement of Retained Earnings. This amount is determined by totaling the effect of the change for all periods prior to the period presented in the financial statements. This amount is reflected as an adjustment to the beginning balance of retained earnings.

The notes to the financial statements must disclose the nature of and reason for the change. In addition, the effect of the change on income before extraordinary items and net income including the related per share amounts should be disclosed for all of the years presented. In this case, the change for 1999 and 1998 is to increase (decrease) net income by $100,000 and ($50,000), respectively.

Cumulative effect not determinable. The Board also realized that there would be certain circumstances in which the pro forma accounts or the cumulative effect amount would not be available. If the pro forma amounts cannot be determined or reasonably estimated for the individual prior periods, the cumulative effect should be shown on the income statement and the reason for not showing the pro forma amounts disclosed in the notes to the financial statements. In an instance where the cumulative effect cannot be determined disclosure will be limited to showing the effect of the change on the results of operations for the period of the change (including per share data) and to explaining the reason for omitting accounting for the cumulative effect and disclosure of pro forma results. The Board specified the change from the FIFO to LIFO method of inventory pricing as one circumstance under which it would be impossible to determine the cumulative effect.

Example of change from FIFO to LIFO

During 1999 Ramirez, Inc. decided to change the method used for pricing its inventories from FIFO to LIFO. The inventory values are as listed below for both FIFO and LIFO cost. Sales for the year amounted to $15,000,000 and the company's total purchases were $11,000,000. Other expenses amounted to $1,200,000 for the year. The company had 1,000,000 shares outstanding throughout the year.

Inventory values

	FIFO	*LIFO*
12/31/98	2,000,000	N/A
12/31/99	4,000,000	1,800,000

The computations would be as follows:

		FIFO	*LIFO*
Net income:			
	Sales	$15,000,000	$15,000,000
Less:	Cost of goods sold	9,000,000	11,200,000
	Gross margin	$ 6,000,000	$ 3,800,000
	Other expenses	1,200,000	1,200,000
	Net income	$ 4,800,000	$ 2,600,000

The following footnote would be an example of the required disclosure in this circumstance:

Note A: Change in Method of Accounting for Inventories

During 1999, the company changed its method of accounting for all of its inventories from first-in, first-out (FIFO) to last-in, first-out (LIFO). The change was made because management believes that the LIFO method provides a better matching of costs and revenues. In addition, the adoption of LIFO conforms the company's inventory pricing policy to the one which is predominant in the industry. The change and its effect on net earnings ($000 omitted except for per share) and earnings per share for 1999 are as follows:

	Net earnings	*Earnings per share*
Net earnings before the change	$4,800	$4.80
Reduction of earnings by the change	2,200	2.20
Net earnings	$2,600	$2.60

There is no cumulative effect of the change on prior years because beginning inventory on January 1, 1999, at LIFO is the same as that which was reported on a FIFO basis at December 31, 1998. As a result of this change, the current period's financial statements are not comparable with those of any prior periods.

The current cost of inventories valued at LIFO exceeds the carrying amount by $2,200,000 at December 31, 1999.

Change in amortization method. Another special case in accounting for a change in principle takes place when a company chooses to change the systematic pattern of amortizing the costs of long-lived assets to expense. When a company adopts a new method of amortization for newly acquired identifiable long-lived assets and uses that method for all new assets of the same class without changing the method used previously for existing assets of the same class, there is a change in accounting principle. Obviously, there is no adjustment required to the financial statements or any cumulative-type adjustment. In these special cases, a description of the nature of the method changed and the effect on net income, income before extraordinary items, and related per share amounts should be disclosed in the period of the change. Should the new method be adopted for all assets, both old and new, then the change in accounting principle would be the usual one and would require a cumulative effect adjustment.

Change in Accounting Estimate

The preparation of financial statements requires frequent use of estimates for such items as asset service lives, salvage values, collectibility of accounts receivable, warranty costs, pension costs, etc. These future conditions and events and their effects cannot be perceived with certainty; therefore, changes in estimates will be inevitable as new information and more experience is obtained. APB 20 requires that changes in estimates be handled currently and prospectively. "The effect of the change in accounting estimate should be accounted for in (1) the period of change if the change affects that period only or (2) the period of change and future periods if the change affects both." For example, on January 1, 1999, a machine purchased for $10,000 was originally estimated to have a 10-year life. On January 1, 2004 (5 years later), the asset is expected to last another 10 years. As a result, both the current period and the subsequent periods are affected by the change. The annual depreciation charge over the remaining life would be computed as follows:

$$\frac{\text{Book value of asset} - \text{Salvage value}}{\text{Remaining useful life}} = \frac{\$5{,}000 - 0}{10 \text{ yrs.}} = \$500/\text{yr.}$$

A permanent impairment affecting the cost recovery of an asset should not be handled as a change in accounting estimate but should be treated as a loss of the period. (See the discussion in Chapter 9.)

The Board concluded that a change in accounting estimate that is in essence effected by a change in accounting principle should be reported as a change in accounting estimate, the rationale being that the effect of the change in accounting principle is inseparable from the effect of the change in estimate. For example, a company may change from deferring and amortizing a cost to recording it as an expense when incurred because the future benefits of the cost have become doubtful. In this instance, the company is changing its accounting principle (from deferral to immediate recognition) because of its change in the estimate of the future value of a particular cost. The amount of the cumulative effect would be the same as that attributable to the current or future periods. Because the two are indistinguishable, changes of this type are to be considered changes in estimates according to APB 20. However, the change must be clearly indistinguishable to be combined. The ability to compute each element independently would preclude combining them as a single change. Also, for generally accepted auditing standards such a change is deemed a change in accounting principle for purposes of applying the consistency standard.

Change in Reporting Entity

An accounting change which results in financial statements that are, in effect, the statements of a different reporting entity should be reported by restating the financial statements of all prior periods presented in order to show financial information for the new reporting entity for all periods. The following qualify as changes in reporting entity:

1. Consolidated or combined statements in place of individual statements
2. Change in group of subsidiaries for which consolidated statements are prepared
3. Change in companies included in combined statements
4. Business combination accounted for as a pooling of interests

Correction of an Error

While good internal control and the exercise of due care will serve to minimize the number of **errors** made, these safeguards cannot be expected to completely eliminate errors in the financial statements. As a result, it was necessary for the accounting profession to promulgate standards that would insure uniform treatment of accounting for error corrections. APB 20 and SFAS 16 are the promulgated GAAP regarding the accounting for error corrections. APB 20 identifies examples of some errors and indicates that they are to be treated as prior period adjustments. SFAS 16 reiterates this treatment for accounting errors and provides guidance for the disclosing of prior period adjustments.

APB 20, para 13, identifies examples of errors as resulting from mathematical mistakes, mistakes in the application of accounting principles, or the oversight or misuse of facts known to the accountant at the time the financial statements were prepared. APB 20 also states that the change from an unacceptable (or incorrect) accounting principle to a correct principle **is** considered a correction of an error, not a change in accounting principle. This should not be confused with the preferability dilemma discussed earlier which involves two or more acceptable principles. While errors occur that affect both current and future periods, we are primarily concerned with the reporting of the correction of an error occurring in previously issued financial statements. Errors affecting current and future periods require correction but do not require disclosure as they are presumed to be discovered prior to the issuance of financial statements. According to APB 20, the correction of an error in the financial statements of a prior period discovered subsequent to their issuance should be reported as a prior period adjustment. The essential distinction between a change in estimate and the correction of an error depends upon the availability of information. An estimate requires correction because by its nature it is based upon incomplete information. Later data will either confirm or contradict the estimate and any contradiction will require correction. An error **misuses** existing information available at the time of the decision and is discovered at a later date. However, this discovery is not a result of additional information.

The required disclosure regarding the correction of an error is set forth by APB 20 and includes the nature of the error and the effect of its correction on income before extraordinary items, net income, and the related per share amounts in the period in which the error was discovered and corrected. This disclosure does not need to be repeated in subsequent periods.

The major criterion for determining whether or not to report the correction of the error is the materiality of the correction. According to APB 20, there are many factors to be considered in determining the materiality of the error correction. Materiality should be considered for each correction individually, as well as for all corrections in total. If the correction is determined to have a material effect on income before extraordinary items, net income, or the trend of earnings, it should be disclosed in accordance with the requirements set forth in the preceding paragraph.

Thus, the prior period adjustment should be presented in the financial statements as follows:

Retained earnings, 1/1/99, as previously reported	xxx
Correction of error (description) in prior period(s) (net of $___ tax)	xxx
Adjusted balance of retained earnings at 1/1/99	xxx
Net income	xxx
Retained earnings, 12/31/99	xxx

In comparative statements, prior period adjustments should also be shown as adjustments to the beginning balances in the retained earnings statements. The amount of the adjustment on the earliest statement shall be the cumulative effect of the error on periods prior to the earliest period presented. The later retained earnings statements presented should also show a prior period adjustment for the cumulative amount as of the beginning of the period being reported on.

Example of prior period adjustment

Assume that ABC Company had overstated its depreciation expense by $50,000 in 1996 and $40,000 in 1999, both due to a mathematical mistake. The errors which affected both the income statement and the tax return in 1998 and 1999 are found in 2000.

The following prior period adjustment would be required in 2000 to correct the accounts (assuming a 40% tax rate):

Accumulated depreciation	90,000	
Income taxes payable		36,000
Retained earnings		54,000

Assuming that we are presenting 2-year comparative statements, the resulting effects of the prior period adjustment should be included in each statement presented. The comparative statement of retained earnings would appear as follows (all figures other than corrections are assumed):

	2000	*1999*
Retained earnings, 1/1 (as previously reported)	$305,000	$250,000
Adjustments (See Note 1)	54,000	30,000
Restated as of 1/1	$359,000	$280,000
Net income	90,000	104,000
	$449,000	$384,000
Dividends	45,000	25,000
Retained earnings	$404,000	$359,000

Note 1: The balance of retained earnings at the end of 1999 has been restated from amounts previously reported to reflect a retroactive credit of $54,000 ($90,000 net of $36,000 tax) for overstatement of depreciation in the previous periods. Of this amount, $24,000 ($40,000 net of $16,000 tax) is applicable to 1999 and has been reflected as an increase in income for that year, and the balance (applicable to years prior to 1999) has been credited to 1999 beginning retained earnings.

The retained earnings as previously reported in 1999 and as it would have appeared in 2000 if no adjustments were made is as follows:

	2000	*1999*
Retained earnings, 1/1	$305,000	$250,000
Net income	90,000	80,000
	$395,000	$330,000
Dividends	45,000	25,000
Retained earnings, 12/31	$350,000	$305,000

Summary of Accounting for Accounting Changes and Error Correction

(See the following page.)

SUMMARY OF ACCOUNTING FOR ACCOUNTING CHANGES AND ERROR CORRECTION

	Reporting on financial statements						Recording in books	
	Footnote disclosures				Statement disclosures			
			Effect on income before x-items, NI, EPS					
	Nature of item	Justification*	Current yr. only	All periods presented	Retroactive treatment; previous financial statements restated	Cumulative effect treatment: pro formas shown for all years	Direct dr./cr. to retained earnings	Cumulative effect account
Accounting Changes								
In Principle								
General--change in principle or method of application from one acceptable GAAP to another. (Change from unacceptable GAAP is correction of error.)	x	x	x			x		x
Special • LIFO to another method • Change in method of accounting for long-term construction contracts. • Change to or from "full cost" method of accounting in the extractive industries.	x	x		x	x		x	
Special Exemptions for closely held corporation when it changes principles before its initial public offering.	x	x			x		x	
FASB Mandated Examples: equity method, R&D costs, inflation accounting.	x			x	x		x	
In Estimate** Natural occurrences because judgment is used in preparation of statements. New events, more experience, and additional information affect earlier good faith esitmates.				x***				
In Reporting Entity*** Includes consolidated or combined statements in place of individual statements, change in group of subsidiaries for which consolidated statements are prepared, change in companies included in combined statements, and business combination accounted for as a pooling of interests.	x	x		x	x			
Error Correction Mathematical mistakes, mistakes in applying principles, oversight or misuse of available facts, change from unacceptable to acceptable GAAP.	x			x	x		x	

*Should clearly explain why the newly adopted accounting principle is preferable.

**Change in estimate effected by a change in principle is accounted for as a change in estimate.

***For **material** changes affecting more than just the current year.

APPENDIX

ACCOUNTING CHANGES IN INTERIM PERIODS

APB 28 is concerned with interim reporting. APB 28 indicates that accounting changes are to be reported in interim periods in accordance with the provisions set forth in APB 20. The FASB then issued SFAS 3 in order to clarify the interim treatment of an accounting change and to provide examples. Of particular concern in SFAS 3 was the treatment to be accorded cumulative-effect-type accounting changes (including a change to LIFO for which no cumulative effect can be determined) and accounting changes made in the fourth quarter by publicly traded companies.

The treatment of a cumulative effect change in an interim period depends upon the quarter in which the change is made. If the cumulative-effect-type accounting change is made in the first quarter, then the cumulative effect on the beginning balance of retained earnings should be included in the net income of the first quarter. Again, the income for the first quarter of the current period is computed using the newly adopted method, and the cumulative effect of the change shall be shown on the income statement after extraordinary items and before net income. In accordance with APB 20, the comparative periods are not to be restated.

If the cumulative-effect-type accounting change is made in a period other than the first quarter, then no cumulative effect of the accounting change should be included in the net income of the period. Rather, the prechange interim periods of the year in which the change is made should be restated to reflect the newly adopted accounting principle. The cumulative effect on the beginning balance of retained earnings is then shown in the first interim period of the year in which the change is made. This includes any year-to-date or other financial statements that include the first interim period.

SFAS 3 requires that the following disclosures be made regarding a cumulative-effect-type accounting change in an interim period in addition to the treatment described above for the actual amount of the cumulative effect:

1. In the financial statements for the period in which the change is made, the nature and justification of the change
2. Disclosure of the effect of the change on income from continuing operations, net income, and related per share amounts for the interim period in which the change is made. If the change is made in other than the first interim period, then they shall also disclose the effect of the change on income from continuing operations, net income, and related per share amounts for each prechange interim period, and income from continuing operations, net income, and related per share amounts for each prechange interim period restated.

3. In the period in which the change is made, the pro forma amounts for income from continuing operations, net income, and the related per share amounts should be disclosed for

   a. The interim period in which the change is made
   b. Any interim periods of prior years for which financial information is presented

   If no prior year fiscal information is presented, then disclosure should be made, in the period of the change, of the actual and pro forma amounts of income from continuing operations, net income, and related per share amounts for the interim period of the immediately preceding fiscal year that corresponds to the interim period in which the change is made. The pro forma amounts are to be calculated in accordance with APB 20 (discussed earlier).
4. The same disclosures described in 1. and 2. above shall be made regarding any year-to-date or last-12-months financial statements that include the period of the change.
5. For a postchange interim period (same fiscal year), disclosure shall be made of the effect of the change on income from continuing operations, net income, and the related per share amounts for the postchange period.

As mentioned earlier, a change to the LIFO method of pricing inventories generally results in a situation where the cumulative effect is not determinable. If such a change occurs in the first interim period, then the same disclosures described above for the cumulative effect type accounting change shall be made with the exception of the pro forma amounts. If the change is made in a period other than the first interim period, the disclosures should include those mentioned above **and** restatement of the financial information presented for prechange interim periods of that year reflecting the adoption of the new accounting principle.

The following examples will illustrate the foregoing principles relative to a cumulative-effect-type accounting change made in both the first interim period and other than the first period. We will use the same facts and assumptions for both examples.

Example of accounting change in first interim period

In 1999 ABC Company decided to adopt the straight-line method of depreciation for plant equipment. The new method was to be used for both new acquisitions and previously acquired plant equipment. In prior periods, the company had used an accelerated method of computing depreciation on plant equipment. The following assumptions are made:

1. The effects of the change are limited to the direct effect on depreciation and the indirect effect on the incentive compensation, as well as the related tax effects.
2. The incentive compensation is 10% of pretax accounting income.

3. There is a constant tax rate of 50%.
4. There were 1,000,000 shares issued and outstanding throughout the periods covered, with no potential for dilution.
5. The company presents comparative interim statements.
6. Assume that the following information is given for years 1998 and 1999:

Period	*Net income on the basis of old accounting principle (accelerated depreciation)*	*Gross effect of change to straight-line depreciation*	*Gross effect less income taxes*	*Net effect after incentive compensation and related income taxes*
Prior to first qtr. 1998		$ 20,000	$ 10,000	$ 9,000
First quarter 1998	$1,000,000	30,000	15,000	13,500
Second quarter 1998	1,200,000	70,000	35,000	31,500
Third quarter 1998	1,100,000	50,000	25,000	22,500
Fourth quarter 1998	1,100,000	80,000	40,000	36,000
Total at beg. of 1999	$4,400,000	$250,000	$125,000	$112,500
First quarter 1999	$1,059,500*	$ 90,000	$ 45,000	$ 40,500*
Second quarter 1999	1,255,000	100,000	50,000	45,000
Third quarter 1999	1,150,500	110,000	55,000	49,500
Fourth quarter 1999	1,146,000	120,000	60,000	54,000
	$4,611,000	$420,000	$210,000	$189,000

**The net income for 1999 has been broken down into income based on the old accounting principle and the effect of the change. These numbers are unrealistic in the sense that the 1999 income figure would be computed based on the new principle (e.g., the 1st quarter net income is $1,100,000 which is $1,059,500 + 40,500).*

In the first example we apply the SFAS 3 criteria applicable to a change made in the first quarter. Notice that in interim reporting the same principles are followed as were set for annual financial reporting. The cumulative effect is considered to be a change in the beginning balance of retained earnings and, therefore, effective at the beginning of the year. To include the cumulative effect in any interim period other than the first, or year-to-date including the first, would be misleading. In this case we are dealing with the first period and the $125,000, representing the direct effects net of tax, is presented on the face of the income statement. Also, as with the annual reporting, the pro forma amounts reflecting the direct and indirect effects of the change are also presented. In this case the 1999 number already reflects the change, and from the given information we can see that the total effect on the first quarter of 1998 was to increase net income by $13,500.

The notes, as required, state the nature and justification of the change. Also included in the notes are the total cumulative effect, the effect on the earnings of the first quarter of the year in which the change is made (this disclosure makes allowable a comparison between statements), and the nature of the pro forma amounts. Essentially, if the change is made in the first quarter, the reporting and disclosure requirements are very similar to those in the annual financial statements.

The following quarterly financial statements and note illustrate the foregoing principles:

	Three months ended March 31,	
	1999	*1998*
Income before cumulative effect of a change in accounting principle	$1,100,000	$1,000,000
Cumulative effect on prior years (to December 31, 1998) of changing to a different depreciation method (Note A)	125,000	--
Net income	$1,225,000	$1,000,000
Amounts per common share:		
Income before cumulative effect of a change in accounting principle	$1.10	$1.00
Cumulative effect on prior years (to December 31, 1998) of changing to a different depreciation method (Note A)	0.13	--
Net income	$1.23	$1.00
Pro forma amounts assuming the new depreciation method is applied retroactively (Note A):		
Net income	$1,100,000	$1,013,500
Net income per common share	$1.10	$1.01

Note A: Change in Depreciation Method for Plant Equipment

During the first quarter of 1999, the company decided to change the method of computing depreciation on plant assets from the accelerated method used in previous periods to the straight-line method. The change was made to better match the amortized cost of the asset to the revenue produced by it. The retroactive application of the new method resulted in a cumulative effect of $125,000 (net of $125,000 in income taxes) which is included in the income for the first quarter of 1999. The effect of the change on the first quarter of 1999 was to increase income before cumulative effect of a change in accounting principle by $40,500 ($.04 per share) and net income by $165,500 ($.17 per share). The pro forma amounts reflect the effect of retroactive application on depreciation, the change in provisions for incentive compensation that would have been made in 1998 had the new method been in effect, and the related income taxes.

Example of accounting change in other than first interim period

In this case, we assume that the change is made in the third quarter of the year and that the company is presenting comparative financial information for both the current quarter and year-to-date. As mentioned above, the cumulative effect is not necessarily to be presented in the period of the change because it relates to the beginning of the year. Thus, in the illustration below the 3 months ended September 30 do not include an amount for the cumulative effect; however, the 9-month statements do. The presentation of the 3-month statements reflects the effect of the accounting change for 1999 and does not reflect this change for 1998. The 1998 statement is the same as it was presented in the prior year. The pro forma amounts and the disclosure in the notes provide the information necessary to make these two interim periods comparable.

The 9-month statement for 1999 reflects the effect of the change for the entire 9-month period. Thus, the results of the 6-month period for 1999 added to the 3-month results would not equal the amounts shown in the 9-month statement. This is because the prior statement for the 6-month period would not have reflected the new principle that the 3-month and 9-month figures do. Again, the 1998 numbers are presented as they were in the previous year. The remainder of the example is really no different from the disclosure required by another accounting change, with one exception. The exception is that the effect of the change on the preceding interim periods must also be disclosed. Note that the cumulative effect is included in the first period. The total of the three individual quarters will now equal the total income shown in the 9-month statement.

	Three months ended September 30,		*Nine months ended September 30,*	
	1999	*1998*	*1999*	*1998*
Income before cumulative effect of a change in accounting principle	$1,200,000	$1,100,000	$3,600,000	$3,300,000
Cumulative effect on prior years (to December 31, 1998) of changing to a different depreciation method (Note A)	--	--	125,000	--
Net income	$1,200,000	$1,100,000	$3,725,000	$3,300,000
Amounts per common share:				
Income before cumulative effect of a change in accounting principle	$1.20	$1.10	$3.60	$3.30
Cumulative effect on prior years (to December 31, 1998) of changing to a different depreciation method (Note A)	--	--	0.13	--
Net income	$1.20	$1.10	$3.73	$3.30
Pro forma amounts assuming the new depreciation method is applied retroactively (Note A):				
Net income	$1,200,000	$1,122,500	$3,600,000	$3,367,500
Net income per common share	$1.20	$1.12	$3.60	$3.37

Note A: Change in Depreciation Method for Plant Equipment

During the third quarter of 1999, the company decided to change the method of computing depreciation on plant assets from the accelerated method used in previous periods to the straight-line method. The change was made to better match the amortized cost of the asset to the revenue produced by it. The retroactive application of the new method resulted in a cumulative effect of $125,000 (net of $125,000 in income taxes) which is included in the income for the 9 months ended September 30, 1999. The effect of the change on the 3 months ended September 30, 1999, was to increase net income by $49,500 ($.05 per share); the effect of the change on the 9 months ended September 30,

1999, was to increase income before cumulative effect of a change in accounting principle by $135,000 ($.14 per share) and net income by $260,000 ($.26 per share). The pro forma amounts reflect the effect of retroactive application on depreciation, the change in the provisions for incentive pay that would have been made in 1998 had the new method been in effect, and the related income taxes.

The effect of the change on the first and second quarters of 1999 is as follows:

	Three months ended	
	March 31, 1999	*June 30, 1999*
Net income as originally reported	$1,059,500	$1,255,000
Effect of change in depreciation method	40,500	45,000
Income before cumulative effect of a change in accounting principle	1,100,000	1,300,000
Cumulative effect on prior years (to December 31, 1998) of changing to a different depreciation method	125,000	--
Net income as restated	$1,255,000	$1,300,000
Per share amounts:		
Net income as originally reported	$1.06	$1.26
Effect of change in depreciation method	0.04	0.04
Income before cumulative effect of a change in accounting principle	1.10	1.30
Cumulative effect on prior years (to December 31, 1998) of changing to a different depreciation method	0.13	--
Net income as restated	$1.23	$1.30

21 FOREIGN CURRENCY

PERSPECTIVE AND ISSUES

Since World War II, international activity by US corporations has increased significantly. Not only are transactions consummated with independent foreign entities, but also with foreign subsidiaries of US firms. In order for the users of these firms' financial statements to properly analyze the foreign involvement, the transactions entered into must be expressed in terms the users can understand (i.e., US dollars). The generally accepted accounting principles governing the translation of foreign currency financial statements and foreign currency transactions into US dollars are found primarily in SFAS 52, which superseded both SFAS 8 and 20. Additional guidance in this area is provided by FASB Interpretation 37. As stated in SFAS 52, these principles apply to the translation of:

1. Foreign currency transactions (e.g., exports, imports, and loans) which are denominated in other than a company's functional currency
2. Foreign currency financial statements of branches, divisions, subsidiaries, and other investees which are incorporated in the financial statements of a US company by combination, consolidation, or the equity method

The objectives of translation are to provide:

1. Information relative to the expected economic effects of rate changes on an enterprise's cash flows and equity
2. Information in consolidated statements relative to the financial results and relationships of each individual foreign consolidated entity as reflected by the functional currency of each reporting entity

Sources of GAAP

SFAS	*FASB I*	*EITF*
52	37	91-1, 92-4, 92-8, 93-9, 95-2

DEFINITIONS OF TERMS

Conversion. The exchange of one currency for another.

Current exchange rate. The current exchange rate is the rate at which one unit of a currency can be exchanged for (converted into) another currency. For purposes of translation of financial statements referred to in SFAS 52, the current exchange rate is the rate as of the end of the period covered by the financial statements or as of the dates of recognition in those statements in the case of revenues, expenses, gains, and losses.

Discount or premium on a forward contract. The foreign currency amount of the contract multiplied by the difference between the contracted forward rate and the spot rate at the date of inception of the contract.

Foreign currency. A currency other than the functional currency of the entity being referred to (for example, the dollar could be a foreign currency for a foreign entity). Composites of currencies, such as the Special Drawing Rights on the International Monetary Fund (SDR), used to set prices or denominate amounts of loans, etc., have the characteristics of foreign currency for purposes of applying SFAS 52.

Foreign currency statements. Financial statements that employ as the unit of measure a functional currency that is not the reporting currency of the enterprise.

Foreign currency transactions. Transactions whose terms are denominated in a currency other than the entity's functional currency. Foreign currency transactions arise when an enterprise (1) buys or sells on credit goods or services whose prices are denominated in foreign currency, (2) borrows or lends funds and the amounts payable or receivable are denominated in foreign currency, (3) is a party to an unperformed forward exchange contract, or (4) for other reasons, acquires or disposes of assets or incurs or settles liabilities denominated in foreign currency.

Foreign currency translation. The process of expressing in the reporting currency of the enterprise those amounts that are denominated or measured in a different currency.

Forward exchange contract. An agreement to exchange at a specified future date currencies of different countries at a specified rate (forward rate).

Functional currency. An entity's functional currency is the currency of the primary economic environment in which the entity operates; normally, that is the currency of the environment in which an entity primarily generates and expends cash.

Local currency. The currency of a particular country being referred to.

Monetary items. Cash, claims to receive a fixed amount of cash, and obligations to pay a fixed amount of cash.

Nonmonetary items. All balance sheet items other than cash, claims to cash, and cash obligations.

Remeasurement. If an entity's books and records are not kept in its functional currency, remeasurement into the functional currency is required. Monetary balances are translated by using the current exchange rate, and nonmonetary balances are translated by using historical exchange rates. If the US dollar is the functional currency, remeasurement into the reporting currency (the US dollar) obviates translation.

Reporting currency. The currency in which an enterprise prepares its financial statements.

Reporting enterprise. An entity or group whose financial statements are being referred to. In this statement, those financial statements reflect (1) the financial statements of one or more foreign operations by combination, consolidation, or equity accounting; (2) foreign currency transactions; or (3) both of the foregoing.

Spot rate. The exchange rate for immediate delivery of currencies exchanged.

Transaction date. The date at which a transaction (for example, a sale or purchase of merchandise or services) is recorded in accounting records in conformity with generally accepted accounting principles. A long-term commitment may have more than one transaction date (for example, the due date of each progress payment under a construction contract is an anticipated transaction date).

Transaction gain or loss. Transaction gains or losses result from a change in exchange rates between the functional currency and the currency in which a foreign currency transaction is denominated. They represent an increase or decrease in (1) the actual functional currency cash flows realized upon settlement of foreign currency transactions and (2) the expected functional currency cash flows on unsettled foreign currency transactions.

Translation adjustments. Translation adjustments result from the process of translating financial statements from the entity's functional currency into the reporting currency.

CONCEPTS, RULES, AND EXAMPLES

Translation of Foreign Currency Financial Statements

Selection of the functional currency. Before the financial statements of a foreign branch, division, or subsidiary are translated into US dollars, the management of the US company must make a decision as to which currency is the **functional currency** of the foreign entity. Once chosen, the functional currency cannot be changed unless it is clear that economic facts and circumstances have changed. Additionally, previously issued financial statements are not restated for any changes in the functional currency. The functional currency decision is crucial because different translation methods are applied which may have a material effect on the US company's financial statements.

The Financial Accounting Standards Board defines functional currency but does not list definitive criteria which, if satisfied, would result in the selection of an entity's functional currency. Rather, realizing that such criteria did not exist, the Board listed various factors which were intended to give management guidance in making the functional currency decision. These factors include

1. Cash flows (Do the foreign entity's cash flows directly affect the parent's cash flows and are they immediately available for remittance to the parent?)
2. Sales prices (Are the foreign entity's sales prices responsive to exchange rate changes and to international competition?)
3. Sales markets (Is the foreign entity's sales market the parent's country or are sales denominated in the parent's currency?)
4. Expenses (Are the foreign entity's expenses incurred in the parent's country?)
5. Financing (Is the foreign entity's financing primarily from the parent or is it denominated in the parent's currency?)
6. Intercompany transactions (Is there a high volume of intercompany transactions between the parent and the foreign entity?)

If the answers to the questions above are predominantly yes, the functional currency is the **reporting currency** of the parent company (i.e., the US dollar). If the answers are predominantly no, the functional currency would most likely be the **local currency** of the foreign entity, although it is possible for a foreign currency other than the local currency to be the functional currency.

Translation methods. In deciding upon the method used to translate assets and liabilities of a company's foreign subsidiary, the Board had four from which to choose. The primary distinction among the methods was the classification of assets and liabilities which would be translated at either the current or historical rate.

The first method is known as the **temporal method.** This method translates cash, receivables, payables, and assets and liabilities carried at present or future values at the current rate, with the remaining assets and liabilities carried at historical costs translated at the applicable historical rates. In essence, the accounting principles used to measure the assets and liabilities in the foreign statements are retained. However, the foreign exchange gains or losses which arise from this method do so because of this method and not because the economic events which affect the foreign entity's operations are reflected.

In most cases, the temporal method produces the same results as the second approach, the **monetary/nonmonetary method**. The **remeasurement** technique, required per SFAS 52 when the books and records are not maintained in the functional currency, is essentially the same as the monetary/nonmonetary method. This method remeasures nonmonetary assets and liabilities at the proper historical rates.

Under this method, it is the characteristics of assets and liabilities which are used as the basis for classification rather than the method of accounting, as under the first approach. It is by mere coincidence that assets and liabilities are measured on bases which approximately coincide with the monetary/nonmonetary classification which produces the aforementioned similar results. A problem with thismethod is that not all items may be classified as **monetary** or **nonmonetary**, and some arbitrary decisions must be made.

The third method is the **current/noncurrent method,** which, as implied, stresses balance sheet classification as the basis for translation. Current assets and liabilities are translated at the current rate and noncurrent assets and liabilities at the applicable historical rates. A major weakness under this approach is the treatment of inventory and long-term debt. Inventory, a current asset, would be translated at its current cost, a major departure from traditional GAAP. The translation of foreign-denominated long-term debt under this approach would be misleading to users, as it would be translated at its historical value. If the dollar weakens internationally, it will take more dollars to repay this obligation, a fact which would not be apparent from the parent's financial statements. Furthermore, some balance sheets are not classified and variations between current and noncurrent classifications of classified balance sheets may be arbitrarily based upon management's intentions.

The last approach is known as the **current rate method** and is the approach mandated by SFAS 52 when the functional currency is the **foreign currency**. All assets and liabilities are translated at the current rate. The basis of this method is the "net investment concept" wherein the foreign entity is viewed as a separate entity which the parent invested into, rather than it being considered as part of the parent's operations. The Board's reasoning was that users can benefit most when the information provided about the foreign entity retains the relationships and results created in the environment (economics, legal, and political) in which the entity operates.

Under this approach, the reasoning follows that foreign-denominated debt is used to purchase assets which create foreign-denominated revenues. These assets act as a hedge against the debt from changes in the exchange rate. The excess (net) assets will, however, be affected by this foreign exchange risk, and this is the effect which is recognized by the parent.

If the foreign entity's local currency is the functional currency, the Board requires the current rate method when translating the foreign entity's financial statements. If, on the other hand, the US dollar is the functional currency, the Board requires the remeasurement method when translating the foreign entity's financial statements. Both of these methods will be illustrated below.

Application of the Current Rate Method

Assume that a US company has a 100% owned subsidiary in Germany that commenced operations in 1999. The subsidiary's operations consist of leasing space in an office building. This building, which cost 500 deutsche marks (DM), was financed primarily by German banks. All revenues and cash expenses are received and paid in deutsche marks. The subsidiary also maintains its books and records in

DM. As a result, management of the US company has decided that the DM is the functional currency.

The subsidiary's balance sheet at December 31, 1999, and its combined statement of income and retained earnings for the year ended December 31, 1999, are presented below in DM.

German Company
Balance Sheet
At December 31, 1999

Assets		*Liabilities and Stockholders' Equity*	
Cash	DM 50	Accounts payable	DM 30
Note receivable	20	Unearned rent	10
Land	100	Mortgage payable	400
Building	500	Common stock	40
Accumulated depreciation	(10)	Additional paid-in capital	160
		Retained earnings	20
Total assets	DM 660	Total liabilities and stockholders' equity	DM 660

German Company
Combined Statement of Income and Retained Earnings
For the Year Ended December 31, 1999

Revenues	DM 200
Operating expenses (including depreciation expense of 10)	170
Net income	DM 30
Add retained earnings, January 1, 1999	--
Deduct dividends	(10)
Retained earnings, December 31, 1999	DM 20

Various exchange rates for 1999 are as follows:

1 DM = $.40 at the beginning of 1999 (when the common stock was issued and the land and building were financed through the mortgage)
1 DM = $.43 weighted-average for 1999
1 DM = $.42 at the date the dividends were declared and the unearned rent was received
1 DM = $.45 at the end of 1999

Since the DM is the functional currency, the German Company's financial statements must be translated into US dollars by the **current rate method**. This translation process is illustrated below.

German Company
Balance Sheet Translation
(DM is the functional currency)
At December 31, 1999

Assets	DM	Exchange rate	US dollars
Cash	DM 50	.45	$ 22.50
Accounts receivable	20	.45	9.00
Land	100	.45	45.00
Building (net)	490	.45	220.50
Total assets	DM 660		$297.00

Liabilities and Stockholders' Equity			
Accounts payable	DM 30	.45	$ 13.50
Unearned rent	10	.45	4.50
Mortgage payable	400	.45	180.00
Common stock	40	.40	16.00
Additional paid-in capital	160	.40	64.00
Retained earnings	20	See income statement	8.70
Translation adjustments	--	--	10.30
Total liabilities and stockholders' DM equity	660		$297.00

German Company
Combined Income and Retained Earnings
Statement Translation
For the Year Ended December 31, 1999

	DM	*Exchange rate*	*US dollars*
Revenues	DM 200	.43	$86.00
Expenses (including DM10 depreciation expense)	170	.43	73.10
Net income	DM 30	.43	$12.90
Add retained earnings, January 1	--	--	--
Deduct dividends	(10)	.42	(4.20)
Retained earnings, December 31	DM 20		$ 8.70

German Company
Statement of Cash Flows
For the Year Ended December 31, 1999

	Local currency	*Exchange rate*	*Reporting currency*
Operating activities			
Net income	DM 30	.43	$ 12.90
Adjustments to reconcile net income to net cash provided by operating activities:			
Depreciation	10	.43	4.30
Increase in accounts receivable	(20)	.43	(8.60)
Increase in accounts payable	30	.43	12.90
Increase in unearned rent	10	.42	4.20
Net cash provided by operating activities	60		$ 25.70
Investing activities			
Purchase of land	(100)	.40	(40.00)
Purchase of building	(500)	.40	(200.00)
Net cash used by investing activities	(600)		(240.00)

Financing activities				
Common stock issue		200	.40	80.00
Mortgage payable		400	.40	160.00
Dividends paid		(10)	.42	(4.20)
Net cash provided by financing		590		235.80
Effect on exchange rate changes on cash		N/A		1.00
Increase in cash and equivalents	DM	50		$ 22.50
Cash at beginning of year		-0-		-0-
Cash at end of year	DM	50	.45	$ 22.50

The following points should be noted concerning the current rate method:

1. All **assets and liabilities** are translated using the **current exchange rate** at the balance sheet date (1 DM = $.45). All revenues and expenses should be translated at the rates in effect when these items are recognized during the period. Due to practical considerations, however, weighted-average rates can be used to translate revenues and expenses (1 DM = $.43).
2. **Stockholders' equity** accounts are translated by using historical exchange rates. Common stock was issued at the beginning of 1996 when the exchange rate was 1 DM = $.40. The translated balance of retained earnings is the result of the weighted-average rate applied to revenues and expenses and the specific rate in effect when the dividends were declared (1 DM = $.42).
3. **Translation adjustments** result from translating all assets and liabilities at the current rate, while stockholders' equity is translated by using historical and weighted-average rates. The adjustments have no direct effect on cash flows; however, changes in exchange rate will have an indirect effect upon sale or liquidation. Prior to this time the effect is uncertain and remote. Also, the effect is due to the net investment rather than the subsidiary's operations. For these reasons, the translation adjustments balance is reported as a separate component in the stockholders' equity section of the US company's consolidated balance sheet. This balance essentially equates the total debits of the subsidiary (now expressed in US dollars) with the total credits (also in dollars). It also may be determined directly, as shown next, to verify the translation process.
4. The translation adjustments credit of $10.30 is calculated as follows:

Net assets at the beginning of 1999 (after common stock was issued and the land and building were acquired through mortgage financing)	200 DM (.45 – .40)	=	$10.00 credit
Net income	30 DM (.45 – .43)	=	.60 credit
Dividends	10 DM (.45 – .42)	=	.30 debit
Translation adjustment			$10.30 credit

5. The translation adjustments balance that appears as a separate component of stockholders' equity is cumulative in nature. Consequently, the change in

this balance during the year should be disclosed in the financial statements. In the illustration, this balance went from zero to $10.30 at the end of 1999. The analysis of this change was presented previously. In addition, assume the following occurred during 2000:

German Company
Balance Sheet
December 31

Assets		*2000*		*1999*		*Increase/(Decrease)*
Cash	DM	100	DM	50	DM	50
Accounts receivable		-0-		20		(20)
Land		150		100		50
Building (net)		480		490		(10)
	DM	730	DM	660	DM	70
Liabilities and Stockholders' Equity						
Accounts payable	DM	50	DM	30	DM	20
Unearned rent		-0-		10		(10)
Mortgage payable		450		400		50
Common stock		40		40		-0-
Additional paid-in capital		160		160		-0-
Retained earnings		30		20		10
Total liabilities and stockholders' equity	DM	730	DM	660	DM	70

German Company
Combined Statement of Income and Retained Earnings
For the Year Ended December 31, 2000

Revenues	DM	220
Operating expenses (including depreciation exp. of DM 10)		170
Net income	DM	50
Add: Retained earnings, Jan. 1, 2000		20
Deduct dividends		(40)
Retained earnings, Dec. 31, 2000	DM	30

Exchange rates were:

1 DM = $.45 at the beginning of 2000
1 DM = $.48 weighted-average for 2000
1 DM = $.50 at the end of 2000
1 DM = $.49 when dividends were paid in 2000 and land bought by incurring mortgage

The translation process for 2000 is illustrated below.

German Company
Balance Sheet Translation
(DM is the functional currency)
At December 31, 2000

Assets		*DM*	*Exchange rate*	*US dollars*
Cash	DM	100	.50	$ 50.00
Land		150	.50	75.00
Building		480	.50	240.00
	DM	730		$365.00

Liabilities and Stockholders' Equity				
Accounts payable	DM	50	.50	$ 25.00
Mortgage payable		450	.50	225.00
Common stock		40	.40	16.00
Addl. paid-in capital		160	.40	64.00
Retained earnings		30	(see income statement)	13.10
Translation adjustments		--		21.90
Total liabilities and stockholders' equity	DM	730		$365.00

German Company
Combined Income and Retained Earnings
Statement Translation
For the Year Ended December 31, 2000

	DM		Exchange rate	US dollars
Revenues	DM	220	.48	$105.60
Operating expenses (including depreciation of DM 10)		170	.48	81.60
Net income	DM	50	.48	$ 24.00
Add: Retained earnings 1/1/00		20	--	8.70
Less: dividends		(40)	.49	(19.60)
Retained earnings 12/31/00	DM	30		$ 13.10

German Company
Statement of Cash Flows
For the Year Ended December 31, 2000

	Local currency		Exchange rate	Reporting currency
Operating activities				
Net income	DM	50	.48	$24.00
Adjustments to reconcile net income to net cash provided by operating activities:				
Depreciation		10	.48	4.80
Decrease in accounts receivable		20	.48	9.60
Increase in accounts payable		20	.48	9.60
Decrease in unearned rent		(10)	.48	(4.80)
Net cash provided by operating activities	DM	90		$43.20
Investing activities				
Purchase of land		(50)	.49	(24.50)
Net cash used by investing activities		(50)		(24.50)
Financing activities				
Mortgage payable		50	.49	24.50
Dividends		(40)	.49	(19.60)
Net cash provided by financing		10		4.90
Effect of exchange rate changes on cash		NA		3.90
Increase in cash and equivalents	DM	50		$27.50
Cash at beginning of year		50		22.50
Cash at end of year	DM	100	.50	$50.00

Using the analysis that was presented before, the translation adjustment attributable to 2000 would be computed as follows:

Net assets at January 1, 2000	220 DM (.50 – .45)	=	$ 11.00 credit
Net income for 2000	50 DM (.50 – .48)	=	1.00 credit
Dividends for 2000	40 DM (.50 – .49)	=	.40 debit
Total			$11.60 credit

The balance in the translation adjustment account at the end of 2000 would be $21.90. ($10.30 from 1999 and $11.60 from 2000.)

6. The use of the equity method by the US company in accounting for the subsidiary would result in the following journal entries, based upon the information presented above:

	1999		*2000*	
Original investment				
Investment in German subsidiary	80*		--	
Cash		80		--

**$.40 x common stock of 40 DM plus additional paid-in capital of 160 DM*

	1999		*2000*	
Earnings pickup				
Investment in German subsidiary	12.90		24**	
Equity in subsidiary income		12.90		24

***$.48 x net income of 50 DM*

	1999		*2000*	
Dividends received				
Cash	4.20		19.60	
Investment in German subsidiary		4.20		19.60
Translation adjustments				
Investment in German subsidiary	10.30		11.60	
Translation adjustments		10.30		11.60

Note that the stockholders' equity of the US company should be the same whether or not the German subsidiary is consolidated (APB 18, para 19). Since the subsidiary does not report the translation adjustments on its financial statements, care should be exercised so that it is not forgotten in the application of the equity method.

7. If the US company disposes of its investment in the German subsidiary, the translation adjustments balance becomes part of the gain or loss that results from the transaction and must be eliminated. For example, assume that on January 2, 2001, the US company sells its entire investment for 300 DM. The exchange rate at this date is 1 DM = $.50. The balance in the investment account at December 31, 2001 is $135 as a result of the entries made previously.

Investment in German Subsidiary

	Debit	Credit
1/1/99	80.00	
	12.90	4.20
	10.30	
Total	103.20	4.20
1/1/00	99.00	
	24.00	
	11.60	19.60
Total	115.00	

The following entries would be made to reflect the sale of the investment:

Cash (300 DM x $.50)	150	
Investment in German subsidiary		115
Gain from sale of subsidiary		35
Translation adjustments	21.90	
Gain from sale of subsidiary		21.90

If the US company had sold a portion of its investment in the German subsidiary, only a pro rata portion of the translation adjustments balance would have become part of the gain or loss from the transaction (FASB Interpretation 37). To illustrate, if 80% of the German subsidiary was sold for 250 DM on January 2, 2001, the following journal entries would be made:

Cash	125	
Investment in German subsidiary (.8 x $115)		92
Gain from sale of subsidiary		33
Translation adjustments (.8 x $21.90)	17.52	
Gain from sale of subsidiary		17.52

Application of the Remeasurement Method

In the previous situation, the DM was the functional currency because the German subsidiary's cash flows were primarily in DM. Assume, however, that the financing of the land and building was in US dollars instead of DM and that the mortgage payable is denominated in US dollars (i.e., must be paid in US dollars). Although the rents collected and the majority of the cash flows for expenses are in DM, management has decided that, due to the manner of financing, the US dollar is the functional currency. The books and records, however, are maintained in DM.

The remeasurement of the German financial statements is accomplished by use of the **remeasurement method** (also known as the monetary/nonmonetary method). This method is illustrated below using the same information that was presented before for the German subsidiary.

German Company
Balance Sheet Translation (Remeasurement Method)
(US dollar is the functional currency)
At December 31, 1999

Assets	DM	Exchange rate	US dollars
Cash	DM 50	.45	$ 22.50
Note receivable	20	.45	9.00
Land	100	.40	40.00
Building (net)	490	.40	196.00
Total assets	DM 660		$267.50
Liabilities and Stockholders' Equity			
Accounts payable	DM 30	.45	$ 13.50
Unearned rent	10	.42	4.20
Mortgage payable	400	.45	180.00
Common stock	40	.40	16.00
Additional paid-in capital	160	.40	64.00
Retained earnings	20	See income statement	(10.20)
Total liabilities and stockholders' equity	DM 660		$267.50

German Company
Combined Income and Retained Earnings Statement Translation
(Remeasurement Method)
(US dollar is the functional currency)
For the Year Ended December 31, 1999

	DM	Exchange rate	US dollars
Revenues	DM 200	.43	$86.00
Expenses (not including depreciation)	(160)	.43	(68.80)
Depreciation expense	(10)	.40	(4.00)
Translation loss	--	See analysis below	(19.20)
Net income (loss)	DM 30	--	$ (6.00)
Retained earnings, January 1	--	--	--
Dividends paid	(10)	.42	(4.20)
Retained earnings, December 31	DM 20		(10.20)

German Company
Translation (Remeasurement Method) Loss
For the Year Ended December 31, 1999

	DM			US dollars	
	Debit	Credit	Exchange rate	Debit	Credit
Cash	DM 50		.45	$22.50	
Note receivable	20		.45	9.00	
Land	100		.40	40.00	
Building (net)	490		.40	196.00	
Accounts payable		DM 30	.45		$ 13.50
Unearned rent		10	.42		4.20
Mortgage payable		400	.45		180.00
Common stock		40	.40		16.00
Additional paid-in capital		160	.40		64.00
Retained earnings		--	--		--
Dividends declared	10		.42	4.20	
Revenues		200	.43		86.00
Operating expenses	160		.43	68.80	
Depreciation expenses	10		.40	4.00	
Totals	DM 840	DM 840		$344.50	$363.70
Remeasurement loss				19.20	
Totals				$363.70	$363.70

The following observations should be noted about the remeasurement method:

1. **Assets and liabilities** which have historical cost balances (nonmonetary assets and liabilities) are remeasured by using historical exchange rates (i.e., the rates in effect when the transactions occurred). Monetary assets and monetary liabilities, on the other hand, are remeasured by using the current exchange rate at the balance sheet date.
2. **Revenues and expenses** that occur frequently during a period are remeasured, for practical purposes, by using the weighted-average exchange rate for the period. Revenues and expenses that represent allocations of historical balances (e.g., depreciation) are remeasured by using historical exchange rates. Note that this is a different treatment as compared to the current rate method. Note also that in 2000, the unearned rent from 1999 of 10 DM would be remeasured at the rate of 1 DM = \$.42. The unearned rent at the end of 1999 is not considered a monetary liability. Therefore, the \$.42 historical exchange rate should be used for all applicable future years. See the appendix at the end of this chapter for a listing of accounts that are remeasured using historical exchange rates.
3. If the functional currency is the US dollar rather than the local foreign currency, the amounts of specific line items presented in the reconciliation of net income to net cash flow from operating activities will be different for nonmonetary items (e.g., depreciation). Note, however, that the **net** cash flow from operating activities will be the same in the reporting currency regardless of the applicable functional currency.
4. The calculation of the remeasurement gain (loss), in a purely mechanical sense, is the amount needed to make the dollar debits equal the dollar credits in the German company's trial balance.
5. The remeasurement loss of \$19.20 is reported on the US company's consolidated income statement because the US dollar is the functional currency. When the reporting currency is the functional currency, as it is in this example, it is assumed that all of the foreign entity's transactions occurred in US dollars. Accordingly, remeasurement gains and losses are taken immediately to the income statement in the year in which they occur as they can be expected to have direct cash flow effects. They are not deferred in a translation adjustments account as they were when the functional currency was the DM (current rate method).
6. The use of the equity method of accounting for the subsidiary would result in the following entries by the US company during 1999:

Original investment

Investment in German subsidiary	80	
Cash		80

Earnings (loss) pickup

Equity in subsidiary loss	6	
Investment in German subsidiary		6

Dividends received

Cash	4.20	
Investment in German subsidiary		4.20

Note that remeasurement gains and losses are included in the subsidiary's net income (net loss) as determined in US dollars before the equity pickup is made by the US company.

7. In highly inflationary economies, those in which cumulative inflation is greater than 100% over a 3-year period, the functional currency is the reporting currency, that is, the US dollar (SFAS 52, para 11). The remeasurement method must be used in this situation even though the factors indicate the local currency is the functional currency. The Board made this decision in order to prevent the evaporation of the foreign entity's fixed assets, a result that would occur if the local currency was the functional currency.

Summary of Current Rate and Remeasurement Methods

1. Before **foreign currency financial statements** can be translated into US dollars, management of the US entity must select the functional currency for the foreign entity whose financial statements will be incorporated into theirs by consolidation, combination, or the equity method. As the example illustrated, this decision is crucial because it may have a material effect upon the financial statements of the US company.
2. If the functional currency is the local currency of the foreign entity, the current rate method is used to translate foreign currency financial statements into US dollars. All assets and liabilities are translated by using the current exchange rate at the balance sheet date. This method insures that all financial relationships remain the same in both local currency and US dollars. Owners' equity is translated by using historical rates, while revenues (gains) and expenses (losses) are translated at the rates in existence during the period when the transactions occurred. A weighted-average rate can be used for items occurring numerous times throughout the period. The translation adjustments (debit or credit) which result from the application of these rules are reported as a separate component in owners' equity of the US company's consolidated balance sheet (or parent-only balance sheet if consolidation was not deemed appropriate).
3. If the functional currency is the reporting currency (the US dollar), the foreign currency financial statements are remeasured into US dollars. All foreign currency balances are restated to US dollars using both historical and current exchange rates. Foreign currency balances which reflect prices from past transactions are remeasured by using historical rates, while foreign currency balances which reflect prices from current transactions are remeasured by using the current exchange rate. Remeasurement

gains/losses that result from the remeasurement process are reported on the US company's consolidated income statement.

The above summary can be arranged in tabular form as shown below:

Functional currency	*Functional currency determinants*	*Translation method*	*Reporting*
Local currency of foreign company	a. Operations not integrated with parent's operations b. Buying and selling activities primarily in local currency c. Cash flows not immediately available for remittance to parent d. Financing denominated in local currency	Current rate (all assets/liabilities translated using current exchange rate; revenues/expenses use weighted-average rate; equity accounts use historical rates)	Translation adjustments are reported in equity section of the US company's consolidated balance sheet. Analysis of changes in accumulated transaction adjustments disclosed via footnote or separate schedule
US dollar	a. Operations integrated with parent's operations b. Buying and selling activities primarily in the US and/or US dollars c. Cash flows immediately available for remittance to parent d. Financing denominated in US dollars	Remeasurement (monetary assets/liabilities use current exchange rate; historical cost balances use historical rates; revenues/expenses use weighted-average rates and historical rates, the latter for allocations like depr. exp.).	Remeasurement gain/loss is reported on the US company's consolidated income statement.

Foreign Operations in the US

With the world economy as interconnected as it is, entities in the US are sometimes the subsidiaries of parent companies domiciled elsewhere in the world. The financial statements of the local company may be presented separately in the US or may be combined as part of the financial statements in the foreign country.

In general, financial statements of US companies are prepared in accordance with US generally accepted accounting principles. However, adjustments may have to be made to these statements in order to conform them to the accounting principles where they will be combined or consolidated into local companies.

Translation of Foreign Currency Transactions

According to SFAS 52, a **foreign currency transaction** is a transaction "... denominated in a currency other than the entity's functional currency." Denominated means that the amount to be received or paid is fixed in terms of the number of units of a particular foreign currency regardless of changes in the exchange rate. From the viewpoint of a US company, a foreign currency transaction results when it imports or exports goods or services to a foreign entity or makes a loan involving a foreign entity and agrees to settle the transaction in currency other than the US dollar (the functional currency of the US company). In these situations, the US company has "crossed currencies" and directly assumes the risk of fluctuating exchange rates of the foreign currency in which the transaction is denominated. This risk may lead to recognition of foreign exchange **transaction gains or losses** in the income statement of the US company. Note that transaction gains or losses can result only when the foreign currency transactions are denominated in a foreign currency. When a US company imports or exports goods or services and the transaction is to be settled in US dollars, the US company will incur neither gain nor loss because it bears no risk due to exchange rate fluctuations.

The following example will illustrate the terminology and procedures applicable to the translation of foreign currency transactions. Assume that US Company, an exporter, sells merchandise to a customer in Germany on December 1, 1999, for 10,000 DM. Receipt is due on January 31, 2000, and US Company prepares financial statements on December 31, 1999. At the transaction date (December 1, 1999), the spot rate for immediate exchange of foreign currencies indicates that 1 DM is equivalent to $.50. To find the US dollar equivalent of this transaction, the foreign currency amount, 10,000 DM, is multiplied by $.50 to get $5,000. At December 1, 1999, the foreign currency transaction should be recorded by US Company in the following manner:

Accounts receivable--Germany	5,000	
Sales		5,000

The accounts receivable and sales are measured in US dollars at the **transaction date** using the spot rate at the time of the transaction. While the accounts receivable is measured and reported in US dollars, the receivable is denominated or fixed in DM. This characteristic may result in foreign exchange transaction gains or losses if the spot rate for DM changes between the transaction date and the date the transaction is settled (January 31, 2000).

If financial statements are prepared between the transaction date and the settlement date, all receivables and liabilities which are denominated in a currency other than the functional currency (the US dollar) must be restated to reflect the spot rates in existence at the balance sheet date. Assume that, on December 31, 1999, the spot rate for DM is 1 DM = $.52. This means that the 10,000 DM are now worth $5,200 and that the accounts receivable denominated in DM should be increased by $200. The following journal entry would be recorded as of December 31, 1999:

Accounts receivable--Germany	200	
Foreign currency transaction gain		200

Note that the sales account, which was credited on the transaction date for $5,000, is not affected by changes in the spot rate. This treatment exemplifies the two-transaction viewpoint adopted by the FASB. In other words, making the sale is the result of an operating decision, while bearing the risk of fluctuating spot rates is the result of a financing decision. Therefore, the amount determined as sales revenue at the transaction date should not be altered because of a financing decision to wait until January 31, 2000, for payment of the account. The risk of a foreign exchange transaction loss can be avoided either by demanding immediate payment on

December 1 or by entering into a **forward exchange contract** to hedge the exposed asset (accounts receivable). The fact that US Company, in the example, did not act in either of these two ways is reflected by requiring the recognition of foreign currency transaction gains or losses in its income statement (reported as financial or nonoperating items) in the period during which the exchange rates changed. This treatment has been criticized, however, because both the unrealized gain and/or loss are recognized in the financial statements, a practice which is at variance with traditional GAAP. Furthermore, earnings will fluctuate because of changes in exchange rates and not because of changes in the economic activities of the enterprise.

On the settlement date (January 31, 2000), assume the **spot rate** is 1 DM = $.51. The receipt of 10,000 DM and their conversion into US dollars would be journalized in the following manner:

Foreign currency	5,100	
Foreign currency transaction loss	100	
Accounts receivable--Germany		5,200
Cash	5,100	
Foreign currency		5,100

The net effect of this foreign currency transaction was to receive $5,100 from a sale which was measured originally at $5,000. This realized net foreign currency transaction gain of $100 is reported on two income statements--a $200 gain in 1999 and a $100 loss in 2000. The reporting of the gain in two income statements causes a temporary difference between pretax accounting and taxable income. This results because the transaction gain of $100 is not taxable until 2000, the year the transaction was completed or settled. Accordingly, interperiod tax allocation is required for foreign currency transaction gains or losses.

Intercompany Transactions and Elimination of Intercompany Profits

Gains or losses from intercompany transactions should be reported on the US company's consolidated income statement unless settlement of the transaction is not planned or anticipated in the foreseeable future. In this case, gains and losses arising from intercompany transactions should be reflected in the translations adjustments component of the US entity's stockholders' equity. In the typical situation (i.e., gains and losses reported on the US entity's income statement) note that gains and losses result whether the functional currency is the US dollar or the foreign entity's local currency. When the US dollar is the functional currency, foreign currency transaction gains and losses result because of one of the two situations below.

1. The intercompany foreign currency transaction is denominated in US dollars. In this case, the foreign subsidiary has a payable or receivable denominated in US dollars. This may result in a foreign currency transaction gain or loss which would appear on the foreign subsidiary's income statement. This gain or loss would be translated into US dollars and would appear on the US entity's consolidated income statement.

2. The intercompany foreign currency transaction is denominated in the foreign subsidiary's local currency. In this situation, the US entity has a payable or receivable denominated in a foreign currency. Such a situation may result in a foreign currency transaction gain or loss that should be reported on the US entity's income statement.

The above two cases can be easily altered to reflect what happens when the foreign entity's local currency is the functional currency.

The elimination of intercompany profits due to sales and other transfers between related entities should be based upon exchange rates in effect when the sale or transfer occurred. Reasonable approximations and averages are allowed to be used if intercompany transactions occur frequently during the year.

Hedging

Foreign currency transaction gains or losses on assets and liabilities which are denominated in a currency other than the functional currency can be hedged if the US company enters into a forward exchange contract. Hedges and other futures contracts that are not entered into with respect to a foreign currency transaction are accounted for in accordance with SFAS 133, *Accounting for Derivative Instruments and Hedging Activities* (See Chapter 6). In the previous example, which illustrated the accounting for foreign currency transactions, US Company could have entered into a forward exchange contract on December 1 to sell 10,000 DM for a negotiated amount to a foreign exchange broker for future delivery on January 31, 2000. This forward contract is a hedge against the exposed asset position created by having an account receivable denominated in DM.

The negotiated rate referred to above is called a futures or forward rate. In most cases, this futures rate is not identical to the spot rate at the date of the forward contract. The difference between the futures rate and the spot rate at the date of the forward contract is referred to as a **discount or a premium**. Any discount or premium must be amortized over the term of the forward contract, generally on a straight-line basis (SFAS 52, para 18). Under SFAS 133 if the hedge is ineffective, the premium/discount should be charged to expense immediately. The amortization of discount or premium is reflected in a separate revenue or expense account, not as an addition or subtraction to the foreign currency transaction gain or loss amount. It is important to observe that under this treatment, no net foreign currency transaction gains or losses result if assets and liabilities denominated in foreign currency are completely hedged at the transaction date.

To illustrate a hedge of an exposed asset, consider the following additional information for the German transaction:

> On December 1, 1999, US Company entered into a forward exchange contract to sell 10,000 DM on January 31, 2000 at $.505 per DM. The spot rate on December 1 is $.50 per DM.

The journal entries which reflect the sale of goods and the forward exchange contract appear as follows:

Sale transaction entries			*Forward exchange contract entries (futures rate 1 DM = $.505)*		
12/1/99 (spot rate 1 DM = $.50)					
Accounts receivable--			Due from exchange broker	5,050	
Germany	5,000		Due to exchange broker		5,000
Sales		5,000	Premium on forward contract		50
12/31/99 (spot rate 1 DM = $.52)					
Accounts receivable--			Foreign currency transaction loss	200	
Germany			Due to exchange broker		200
Foreign currency transac-	200		Premium on forward contract	25	
tion gain			Financial revenue		
		200	($25 = $50/2 months)		25
1/31/00 (spot rate 1 DM = $.51)					
Foreign currency			Due to exchange broker	5,200	
Foreign currency transac-	5,100		Foreign currency		5,100
tion loss			Foreign currency transaction		
Accounts receivable--	100		gain		100
Germany			Cash	5,050	
		5,200	Due from exchange broker		5,050
			Premium on forward contract	25	
			Financial revenue		25

The following points should be noted from the entries above:

1. The net foreign currency transaction gain or loss is zero. The account "Due from exchange broker" is fixed in terms of US dollars, and this amount is not affected by changes in spot rates between the transaction and settlement dates. The account "Due to exchange broker" is fixed or denominated in DM. The US company owes the exchange broker 10,000 DM, and these must be delivered on January 31, 2000. Because this liability is denominated in DM, its amount is determined by spot rates. Since spot rates change, this liability changes in amount equal to the changes in accounts receivable because both of the amounts are based on the same spot rates. These changes are reflected as foreign currency transaction gains and losses which net out to zero.
2. The premium on forward contract is fixed in terms of US dollars. This amount is amortized to a financial revenue account over the life of the forward contract on a straight-line basis.
3. The net effect of this transaction is that $5,050 was received on January 31, 2000, for a sale originally recorded at $5,000. The $50 difference was taken into income via amortization.

SFAS 52 does not require a forward exchange contract in order for a hedge to take place. For example, it is possible for a foreign currency transaction to act as an economic hedge against a parent's net investment in a foreign entity if

1. The transaction is designated as a hedge.

2. It is effective as a hedge.

To illustrate, assume that a US parent has a wholly owned British subsidiary which has net assets of 2 million pounds. The US parent can borrow 2 million pounds to hedge its net investment in the British subsidiary. Assume further that the British pound is the functional currency and that the 2-million-pound liability is denominated in pounds. Fluctuations in the exchange rate for pounds will have no net effect on the parent company's consolidated balance sheet because increases (decreases) in the translation adjustments balance due to the translation of the net investment will be offset by decreases (increases) in this balance due to the adjustment of the liability denominated in pounds.

EMERGING ISSUES TASK FORCE CONSENSUS SUMMARIES

91-1 Hedging Intercompany Foreign Currency Risks

Transactions between members of a consolidated group with different functional currencies can present foreign currency risks that may be hedged. All formal exchange contracts and similar agreements are subject to the hedge accounting provisions of SFAS 52. An intercompany foreign currency commitment is considered firm if there is a commitment to a third party or, lacking that, if performance is probable because of sufficiently large disincentives (fiduciary responsibilities, existing laws, or significant economic penalties) for nonperformance. In the latter case, the facts and circumstances of the intercompany transaction must be examined closely. The provisions of EITF 90-17 are applicable to intercompany transactions also.

92-4 Accounting for a Change in Functional Currency When an Economy Ceases to be Considered Highly Inflationary

When a foreign subsidiary's economy is no longer considered highly inflationary, the entity should convert the reporting currency values into the local currency at the exchange rates on the date of change, in which these values become the new functional currency accounting bases for nonmonetary assets and liabilities.

92-8 Accounting for the Income Tax Effects Under FASB Statement No. 109 of a Change in Functional Currency When an Economy Ceases to be Considered Highly Inflationary

The Task Force reached a consensus that, deferred taxes on the temporary differences that arise as a result of a change in the functional currency are treated as an adjustment to the cumulative translation adjustments portion of stockholders' equity. If the change occurs before initial adoption of SFAS 109, then this deferred tax effect must be included in the cumulative effect of adoption of the Statement.

93-9 Application of FASB Statement No. 109 in Foreign Financial Statements Restated for Price-Level-Adjusted Financial Statements

Accounting Principles Board Statement 3 states that price-level-adjusted financial statements are preferred for foreign currency financial statements of entities operating in highly inflationary economies when they are intended for readers in the United States. The result is that the tax bases of the assets and liabilities in these financial statements are often restated for inflation. This statement provides guidance on the asset-and-liability approach of SFAS 109 as it relates to these financial statements. A consensus was reached on the following issues: (1) how temporary differences should be computed under SFAS 109 and (2) how deferred income tax expense or benefit for the year should be determined. With regard to the first issue, temporary differences are the difference between the indexed tax basis amount and the related price-level restated amount of the asset or liability. The consensus reached on the second issue is that the deferred income tax expense or benefit is the difference between the deferred tax assets and liabilities reported at the end of the current year and those reported at the end of the prior year. The deferred tax assets and liabilities of the prior year should be recalculated in units of the current year-end purchasing power.

95-2 Determination of What Constitutes a Firm Commitment for Foreign Currency Transactions Not Involving a Third Party

The Task Force reached a consensus in defining significant economic penalty as it appears in Issue 91-1 with respect to consolidated entities. Such penalty exists only when the penalty imposed by an unrelated party provides a compelling disincentive for nonperformance such that performance of the intercompany foreign currency commitment is probable, even if the anticipated transactions do not occur. If this penalty exists, a foreign currency commitment is considered a firm commitment as defined in Issue 91-1.

APPENDIX

ACCOUNTS TO BE REMEASURED USING HISTORICAL EXCHANGE RATES

1. Marketable securities carried at cost
   a. Equity securities
   b. Debt securities not intended to be held until maturity
2. Inventories carried at cost
3. Prepaid expenses such as insurance, advertising, and rent
4. Property, plant, and equipment
5. Accumulated depreciation on property, plant, and equipment
6. Patents, trademarks, licenses, and formulas
7. Goodwill
8. Other intangible assets
9. Deferred charges and credits, except deferred income taxes and policy acquisition costs for life insurance companies
10. Deferred income
11. Common stock
12. Preferred stock carried at issuance price
13. Revenues and expenses related to nonmonetary items
    a. Cost of goods sold
    b. Depreciation of property, plant, and equipment
    c. Amortization of intangible items such as goodwill, patents, licenses, etc.
    d. Amortization of deferred charges or credits, except deferred income taxes and policy acquisition costs for life insurance companies

Source: SFAS 52, para 48.

22 PERSONAL FINANCIAL STATEMENTS

PERSPECTIVE AND ISSUES

AICPA Statement of Position (SOP) 82-1, *Personal Financial Statements,* addresses the preparation and presentation of personal financial statements, or, more specifically, financial statements of individuals or groups of related individuals (i.e., family). Personal financial statements are generally prepared to organize and plan an individual's financial affairs on a more formal basis. Specific purposes deal with the obtaining of credit, income tax planning, retirement planning, gift and estate planning, or the public disclosure of financial affairs. The aforementioned purposes are such that the users of personal financial statements rely on them in determining whether to grant credit, in assessing the financial activities of individuals, in assessing the financial affairs of public officials and candidates for public office, and for similar purposes.

The 1968 AICPA Industry Audit Guide, *Audits of Personal Financial Statements*, used historical cost as the primary basis of measurement for personal financial statements. However, the guide recommended the presentation of estimated current values as additional information. The increasing use of personal financial statements created the need to reassess the conclusions found in the Industry Audit Guide due to the purposes for which personal financial statements are prepared, the users to whom they are directed, and the ways in which they are used. That reassessment resulted in SOP 82-1 which is discussed and illustrated in this chapter.

Sources of GAAP

<u>*SOP*</u>
82-1

DEFINITIONS OF TERMS

Estimated current value of an asset. The amount for which an item could be exchanged between a buyer and a seller, each of whom is well informed and willing, and neither of whom is compelled to buy or sell.

Estimated current amount of liabilities. Payables and other liabilities should be presented at the discounted amounts of cash to be paid. The discount rate should be the rate implicit in the transaction in which the debt was incurred. If, however, the debtor is able to discharge the debt currently at a lower amount, the debt should be presented at the lower amount.

CONCEPTS, RULES, AND EXAMPLES

Personal financial statements may be prepared for an individual, husband and wife, or family. Personal financial statements consist of

1. **Statement of financial condition**--Presents estimated current values of assets, estimated current amounts of liabilities, estimated income taxes and net worth at a specified date
2. **Statement of changes in net worth**--Presents main sources of increases (decreases) in net worth and is **optional**

Assets and liabilities, including changes therein, should be recognized using the accrual basis of accounting. In the Statement of Financial Condition, assets and liabilities should be listed by order of liquidity and maturity, not on a current/noncurrent basis.

In personal financial statements, **assets** should be presented at their **estimated current value**. This is an amount at which the item could be exchanged assuming both parties are well-informed, neither party is compelled to buy or sell, and material disposal costs are deducted to arrive at current values. A specialist may have to be consulted in the determination of the current value of certain types of assets (e.g., works of art, jewelry, restricted securities, investments in closely held businesses, and real estate). **Liabilities** should be presented at the lesser of the discounted amount of cash to be paid or the current cash settlement amount. The use of recent transactions involving similar types of assets and liabilities, in similar circumstances, constitutes a satisfactory means of determining the estimated current value of an asset and the **estimated current amount of a liability**. If recent information cannot be obtained, other methods can be used (e.g., capitalization of past or prospective earnings, the use of liquidation values, the adjustment of historical cost based on changes in a specific price index, the use of appraisals, and the use of the discounted amounts of projected cash receipts and payments). The methods used should be followed consistently from period to period unless the facts and circumstances dictate a change to different methods. Income taxes payable should include

Assets and liabilities	Discounted cash flow	Market price	Appraised value	Other
• Receivables	x			
• Marketable securities		x		If traded on valuation day: closing price. If not traded: valuation must fall in range (bid and asked price)
• Options--securities		x		Difference between exercise price and current value of asset; if material, discount the difference
• Options--other assets*				
• Investment in life insurance				Cash value less outstanding loans
• Investment in closely held business	x		x	Liquidation value, multiple of earnings, reproduction value, adjustment of book value or cost
• Real estate	x		x	Sales of similar property
• Intangible assets	x			Net proceeds from current sale or discounted cash flows from asset; otherwise, may use cost of asset
• Future interests (nonforfeitable rights)**	x			
• Payables and other liabilities	x			Discharge amount if lower than discounted amount
• Noncancelable commitments***	x			
• Income taxes payable				Unpaid income tax for completed tax years and estimated income tax for elapsed portion of current tax year to date of financial statements
• Estimated income tax on difference between current values of assets and current amounts of liabilities and their respective tax bases				Computed as if current value of assets and liabilities had been respectively realized or liquidated considering applicable tax laws and regulations, recapture provisions and carryovers.
• Uncertain obligations*				Not covered by SOP 82-1; follow SFAS 5

* *Taken from: "Personal Financial Statements," Michael D. Kinsman and Bruce Samuelson,* ***Journal of Accounting***, *September, 1987, pp. 138-148.*

** *Rights have all of the following attributes: (1) are for fixed or determinable amounts; (2) are not contingent on holder's life expectancy or occurrence of a particular event (e.g., disability/death), and (3) do not require future performance of service by holder.*

*** *Commitments have all of the following attributes: (1) are for fixed or determinable amounts; (2) are not contingent on others' life expectancies or occurrence of a particular event (e.g., disability/death); and (3) do not require future performance of service by others.*

unpaid income taxes for completed tax years and the estimated amount for the elapsed portion of the current tax year. Additionally, personal financial statements should include the estimated income tax on the difference between the current value (amount) of assets (liabilities) and their respective tax bases as if they had been realized or liquidated. The table above summarizes the methods of determining "estimated current values" for assets and "estimated current amounts" for liabilities.

Business interests which comprise a large portion of a person's total assets should be shown separately from other investments. An investment in a separate entity which is marketable as a going concern (e.g., closely held corporation) should be presented as one amount. If the investment is a limited business activity, not conducted in a separate business entity, separate asset and liability amounts should be shown (e.g., investment in real estate and related mortgage; of course, only the person's beneficial interest in the investment is included in their personal financial statements).

The CPA must decide whether to valuate the net investment him/herself or to defer valuation to a specialist. Because of the risk of litigation and the liability coverage limitations on valuation functions many CPAs prefer using a specialist. If the CPA does the valuation s/he must ensure that s/he has attained a sufficient level of competence to perform the engagement. The possible valuation methods available are discounted cash flow, appraised value, liquidation value, multiple of earnings, reproduction value, adjustment of book value (e.g., equity method), or cost.

APPENDIX

HYPOTHETICAL SET OF PERSONAL FINANCIAL STATEMENTS

Marcus and Kelly Imrich
Statements of Financial Condition
December 31, 2000 and 1999

	2000	*1999*
Assets		
Cash	$ 381,437	$ 207,621
Securities		
Marketable (Note 2)	128,787	260,485
Tax-exempt bonds (Note 3)	1,890,222	986,278
Certificate of deposit	20,000	10,000
Loans receivable (Note 4)	262,877	362,877
Partnership and venture interests (Note 5)	935,000	938,000
Real estate interests (Note 6)	890,000	2,500,000
David Corporation (Note 7)	2,750,687	2,600,277
Cash surrender value of life insurance (Note 8)	388,000	265,000
Personal residences (Note 9)	2,387,229	2,380,229
Deferred losses from partnerships	68,570	60,830
Vested interest in David Corporation benefit plan	545,960	530,960
Personal jewelry and furnishings (Note 10)	513,000	6,700
Total assets	$11,161,769	$11,109,257
Liabilities		
Mortgage payable (Note 11)	$ 254,000	$ 267,000
Security deposits--rentals	--	5,700
Income taxes payable--current year balance	9,800	10,680
Total liabilities	263,800	283,380
Estimated income taxes on difference between estimated current values of assets and estimated current amounts of liabilities and their tax bases (Note 12)	555,400	731,000
Net Worth	10,342,569	10,094,877
Total liabilities and net worth	$11,161,769	$11,109,257

Marcus and Kelly Imrich
Statement of Changes in Net Worth
For the Years Ended December 31, 2000 and 1999

	Year ended December 31, 2000	1999
Realized increases in net worth		
Salary and bonus	$ 200,000	$ 175,000
Dividends and interest income	184,260	85,000
Distribution from limited partnerships	280,000	260,000
Gain on sales of marketable securities	58,240	142,800
	722,500	662,800
Realized decreases in net worth		
Income taxes	180,000	140,000
Interest expense	25,000	26,000
Real estate taxes	21,000	18,000
Personal expenditures	242,536	400,000
	468,536	584,000
Net realized increase in net worth	253,964	78,800
Unrealized increases in net worth		
Marketable securities (net of realized gains on securities sold)	37,460	30,270
Benefit plan--David Corporation	15,000	14,000
Personal jewelry and furnishings	20,000	18,000
	72,460	62,270
Unrealized decreases in net worth		
Estimated income taxes on the difference between the estimated current values of assets and the estimated current amounts of liabilities and their tax bases	78,732	64,118
Net unrealized decrease in net worth	(6,272)	(1,848)
Net increase in net worth	247,692	76,952
Net worth at the beginning of year	10,094,877	10,017,925
Net worth at the end of year	$10,342,569	$10,094,877

Marcus and Kelly Imrich
Notes to Financial Statements

Note 1: The accompanying financial statements include the assets and liabilities of Marcus and Kelly Imrich. Assets are stated at their estimated current values, and liabilities at their estimated current amounts.

Note 2: The estimated current values of marketable securities are either (1) their quoted closing prices or (2) for securities not traded on the financial statement date, amounts that fall within the range of quoted bid and asked prices.

Marketable securities consist of the following:

	December 31, 2000		*December 31, 1999*	
	Number of shares	*Estimated current values*	*Number of shares*	*Estimated current values*
Stocks				
Susan Schultz, Inc.			1,000	$122,000
Ripley Robotics Corp.	500	$ 51,927	1,000	120,485
L.A.W. Corporation	300	20,700	100	5,000
Jay & Kelly Corp.	300	20,700	200	5,000
J.A.Z. Corporation	200	35,460	200	8,000
		$128,787		$260,485

Note 3: The interest income from state and municipal bonds is not subject to federal income taxes but is, except in certain cases, subject to state income tax.

Note 4: The loan receivable from Carol Parker, Inc. matures January 2007 and bears interest at the prime rate.

Note 5: Partnership and venture interests consist of the following:

	Percent owned	*Cost*	*Estimated current value 12/31/2000*	*Estimated current value 12/31/1999*
East Third Partnership	50.0%	$ 50,000	100,000	100,000
631 Lucinda Venture	20.0	10,000	35,000	38,000
27 Wright Partnership	22.5	10,000	40,000	50,000
Eannarino Partnership	10.0	40,000	60,000	50,000
Sweeney Venture	30.0	100,000	600,000	600,000
Kelly Parker Group	20.0	20,000	100,000	100,000
707 Lucinda Venture	50.0	(11,000)	--	--
			$935,000	$938,000

Note 6: Mr. and Mrs. Imrich own a one-half interest in an apartment building in DeKalb, Illinois. The estimated fair market value was determined by Mr. and Mrs. Imrich. Their basis in the apartment building was $1,000,000 for both 2000 and 1999.

Note 7: Kelly Imrich owns 75% of the common stock of the David Corporation. A condensed statement of assets, liabilities, and stockholders' equity (income tax basis) of David Corporation as of December 31, 2000 and 1999 is summarized below.

	2000	*1999*
Current assets	$2,975,000	$3,147,000
Investments	200,000	200,000
Property and equipment (net)	145,000	165,000
Loans receivable	110,000	120,000
Total assets	$3,430,000	$3,632,000
Current liabilities	$2,030,000	$2,157,000
Other liabilities	450,000	400,000
Total liabilities	2,480,000	2,557,000
Stockholders' equity--	950,000	1,075,000
Total liabilities and stockholders' equity	$3,430,000	$3,632,000

Note 8: At December 31, 2000 and 1999, Marcus Imrich owned a $1,000,000 whole life insurance policy.

Note 9: The estimated current values of the personal residences are their purchase prices plus their cost of improvements. Both residences were purchased in 1998.

Note 10: The estimated current values of personal effects and jewelry are the appraised values of those assets, determined by an independent appraiser for insurance purposes.

Note 11: The mortgage (collateralized by the residence) is payable in monthly installments of $1,083 a month, including interest at 10% a year through 2016.

Note 12: The estimated current amounts of liabilities at December 31, 2000, and December 31, 1999, equaled their tax bases. Estimated income taxes have been provided on the excess of the estimated current values of assets over their tax bases as if the estimated current values of the assets had been realized on the statement date, using applicable tax laws and regulations. The provision will probably differ from the amounts of income taxes that eventually might be paid because those amounts are determined by the timing and the method of disposal or realization and the tax laws and regulations in effect at the time of disposal or realization.

The estimated current values of assets exceeded their tax bases by $1,850,000 at December 31, 2000, and by $1,770,300 at December 31, 1999. The excess of estimated current values of major assets over their tax bases are

	December 31,	
	2000	*1999*
Investment in David Corporation	$1,400,000	$1,350,000
Vested interest in benefit plan	350,000	300,000
Investment in marketable securities	100,000	120,300

23 SPECIALIZED INDUSTRY GAAP

BANKING AND THRIFT INDUSTRIES

PERSPECTIVE AND ISSUES

The pronouncements below are incorporated in the Audit and Accounting Guide, *Banks and Savings Institutions* (1998). Special accounting rules are stated that permit an accelerated method of amortization for goodwill arising from the purchase of a savings and loan association if certain conditions are met. An accelerated method may be used if goodwill represents amounts paid for items for which there is not a satisfactory basis for assigning amounts to individual factors and the benefits from these factors decline over their expected lives. The period of amortization should not be longer than the discount on long-term interest-bearing assets acquired and recognized as interest income. In the cash flow statement, banks, savings institutions, and credit unions are not required to report gross amounts of cash receipts and payments for deposits and withdrawals with other financial institutions, time deposits activities, loans made, and loan payments received from customers.

Lenders often incur a sizable number of costs directly related to the origination or purchase of loans, and normally receive different nonrefundable fees at the inception of the loans.

In accounting practice, disparate accounting procedures emerged for the accounting for these costs and fees. The FASB responded with the issuance of SFAS 91, *Accounting for Nonrefundable Fees and Costs Associated with Originating or Acquiring Loans and Initial Direct Costs of Leases*. The standard points out various examples of these costs and fees, and the different accounting for each of them.

The Board recently issued SFAS 114, which is applicable to all creditors, which supersedes SFAS 15 and which substantially revises the accounting for impairments of loans. Under the earlier standard no impairment was recognized if the revised **un**discounted projected cash flows would be at least equal in amount to the carrying value of the loan. SFAS 114, however, requires loss recognition when the **discounted** present value of the anticipated collections are less than the carrying amount of the loan.

Sources of GAAP

APB	*SFAS*	*FASB I*	*TB*	*EITF*	*SOP*
23	72, 91, 104, 109, 114, 115, 118	9	85-1, 87-3,	84-4, 84-9, 84-19, 84-20, 84-21, 84-22, 84-31, 85-7, 85-8, 85-13, 85-18, 85-20, 85-24, 85-26, 85-31, 85-41, 85-42, 85-44, 86-21, 86-31, 86-38, 87-22, 87-34, 88-17, 88-19, 88-20, 88-25, 89-3, 89-9, 89-19, 90-18, 90-21, 92-5	93-1

DEFINITIONS OF TERMS

Carrying amount. The face amount of the interest-bearing asset plus (or minus) the unamortized premium (or discount).

Commitment fees. Fees charged for entering into an agreement that obligates the enterprise to make or acquire a loan or to satisfy an obligation of the other party under a specified condition. For purposes of this Statement, the term **commitment fees** includes fees for letters of credit and obligations to purchase a loan or group of loans and pass-through certificates.

General reserve. Used in the context of the special meaning this term has in regulatory pronouncements and in the US Internal Revenue Code.

Incremental direct costs. Costs to originate a loan that (1) result directly from and are essential to the lending transaction and (2) would not have been incurred by the lender had that lending transaction not occurred.

Long-term interest-bearing assets. For purposes of this section, these are interest-bearing assets with a remaining term to maturity of more than 1 year.

Net-spread method. Under this method, the acquisition of a savings and loan association is viewed as the acquisition of a leveraged whole rather than the acquisition of the separate assets and liabilities of the association.

Origination fees. Fees charged to the borrower in connection with the process of originating, refinancing, or restructuring a loan. This term includes, but is not limited to, points, management, arrangement, placement, application, underwriting, and other fees pursuant to a lending or leasing transaction and also includes syndication and participation fees to the extent they are associated with the portion of the loan retained by the lender.

Pretax accounting income. Represents income or loss for a period, exclusive or related income tax expense, determined in conformity with generally accepted accounting principles.

Reserve for bad debts. Term is used in the context of the special meaning this term has in regulatory pronouncements and in the US Internal Revenue Code.

Separate-valuation method. Under this method, each of the identifiable assets and liabilities (assumed) of the acquired savings and loan association is accounted for in the consolidated financial statements at an amount based on fair value at the date of acquisition, either individually or by types of assets and types of liabilities.

Taxable income. Represents pretax accounting income (1) adjusted for reversal of provisions of estimated losses on loans and property acquired in settlement of loans, gains or losses on the sales of such property, and adjusted for permanent differences and (2) after giving effect to the bad debt deduction allowable by the US Internal Revenue Code assuming the applicable tax return were to be prepared based on such adjusted pretax accounting income.

CONCEPTS, RULES, AND EXAMPLES

Justifying a Change in Accounting Principle

The following sources are preferred for banking and thrift industries that must justify a change in accounting principle:

1. Audit and Accounting Guide, *Banks and Savings Institutions* (1998)
2. Statement of Position 83-1, *Reporting by Banks of Investment Securities Gains or Losses*

Acquisition of a Banking or Thrift Institution

This section applies not only to the acquisition of a savings and loan association, but also to acquisition of savings and loan holding companies, commercial banks, mutual savings banks, credit unions, and other depository institutions with assets and liabilities of the same type.

Purchase method. In accounting for the acquisition of a banking and thrift institution, the fair value of the assets and liabilities acquired must be determined using the **separate-valuation method**. Under this method, each of the identifiable assets and liabilities acquired are accounted for individually, or by type, at their fair value at the date of acquisition. The total amount is reported in the consolidated financial statements.

Note that use of the **net-spread method** is **not** considered appropriate for this type of business combination. The net-spread method, which views acquisition of the institution as a leveraged whole, does not appropriately recognize the fair value of individual, or types of, assets and liabilities.

Liabilities acquired are accounted for at their present value at the date of acquisition. The present value of savings deposits due on demand equals the face amount plus interest accrued or accruable at the acquisition date. The present value of other liabilities assumed is calculated by using interest rates for similar liabilities in effect at the date of acquisition.

Identified intangible assets. The purchase price of a banking or thrift institution may include intangible benefits from the purchase, such as the capacity of acquired assets to generate new business. Intangible assets that can be separately identified at a determinable fair value should be assigned a portion of the total purchase price and should be amortized over their estimated lives. Any portion of the purchase price that cannot be identified with specific tangible and intangible assets (less liabilities assumed) should be assigned to goodwill. Goodwill is amortized on a straight-line basis unless the benefits expected to be received decline over the expected life of the goodwill received.

Unidentifiable intangible asset. An unidentifiable intangible asset arises when the fair value of liabilities assumed exceeds the fair value of tangible and identified intangible assets acquired. This asset is amortized over a period no greater than the estimated remaining life of any **long-term interest-bearing assets** acquired. Amortization is applied to the **carrying amount** of the interest-bearing assets expected to be outstanding at the beginning of each subsequent period. If, however, the assets acquired do **not** include a significant portion of long-term interest-bearing assets, the unidentifiable intangible asset is amortized over a period not exceeding the estimated average remaining life of the existing customer base acquired. Amortization in any case shall not exceed 40 years.

In the sale or liquidation of a large segment, or separable group, of the operating assets of an acquired banking or thrift institution, the portion of the unidentifiable intangible asset identified with that segment, or separable group, shall be included in the cost of the assets sold. If the sale or liquidation of a large portion of the interest-bearing assets significantly reduces the benefits of the unidentifiable intangible asset, any reduction shall be recognized as a charge to income.

Regulatory-assisted combinations. A regulatory authority may grant financial assistance to either party involved in the acquisition of a banking or thrift institution. The amount of assistance should be accounted for as part of the combination if receipt of the assistance is probable and the amount to be received is reasonably estimable. Otherwise, assistance should be reported as a reduction of the unidentifiable intangible asset with any excess reported in income. Note that assets and liabilities transferred to or assumed by a regulatory authority are **not** recognized in the acquisition. Any agreement by the grantee to repay all or a portion of the assistance shall require recognition of a liability and a charge to income by the grantee. Any assistance received by an enterprise shall be disclosed in the financial statements.

Bad-Debt Reserves

Both stock and mutual savings and loan associations are required by regulatory authorities to place a portion of their earnings into a **general reserve** as protection for depositors. Savings and loan associations are allowed by the IRS to maintain a **bad-debt reserve** and to deduct any additions to their reserve in determining taxable income. Since this method differs from the method for determining bad debt expense, **pretax accounting income** and **taxable income** will differ. Savings and loan associations, however, are not allowed to recognize deferred tax on this difference in tax years beginning before December 31, 1987. This restriction occurs because associations could manipulate their bad-debt reserve, thus controlling events leading to the tax consequence.

Accounting by Creditors for Impairment of a Loan

The issuance of SFAS 114, as amended by SFAS 118, has significantly altered the accounting for impairments of loans, including those evidenced by formal restructurings. This standard affects all creditors, although financial institutions are likely to be the most heavily impacted.

The FASB deemed that a loan is impaired when it is probable that a creditor will be unable to collect all amounts due according to the loan's contractual terms. To make this determination, a creditor would apply its normal loan review procedures. Once it has been determined that the loan's value has been impaired, the creditor must compute the present value of the estimated future cash flows. In determining the present value, the cash flows should be discounted using the loan's effective interest rate. The effective interest rate is represented by the contractual interest rate adjusted for any deferred loan fees or costs, premiums, or discounts.

If the computed present value of the expected future cash flows is less than the carrying amount of the loan, an impairment will be recognized and recorded in a valuation allowance. Significant changes in the amount and/or timing of future estimated cash flows require that the creditor recalculate the amount of the loan's impairment. Adjustments, subject to the LCM criteria, will be reflected through changes in the valuation allowance.

In the event of a formal loan restructuring through a troubled debt restructuring, the loan is remeasured at the fair market value at the date of the restructuring. This treatment differs from an impairment because it is assumed that a new, formally restructured loan reflects current market conditions; therefore, no impairment is deemed to exist.

The new standard, as amended, provides that impairment losses be recognized as bad debts when measured; however, no guidance is provided on the recognition and measurement of amounts later recovered.

Nonrefundable Loan Fees and Costs

Loan origination fees. These fees should be **deferred** and recognized over the life of the loan as an adjustment of interest income. If there are any related direct loan origination costs, the **origination fees** and origination costs should be **netted**, and only the net amount should be deferred and amortized via the interest method. Origination costs include those **incremental costs** such as credit checks and security arrangements, among others, pertaining to a specific loan.

The only exception to the foregoing rule would be in the instance of certain loans which also qualify as debt instruments under SFAS 115. For those carried in the "trading securities" portfolio, related loan origination fees should be charged to expense when incurred; the requirement that these be carried at fair value would make adding these costs to the asset carrying amounts a useless exercise.

Example 1

Debtor Corp. wishes to take out a loan with Klein Bank for the purchase of new machinery. The fair market value of the machinery is $614,457. The loan is for 10 years, designed to give Klein an implicit return of 10% on the loan. The annual payment is calculated as follows:

$$\text{Annual payment} = \frac{\$614,457}{PV_{10,\ 10\%}} = \frac{614,457}{6.14457} = \$100,000$$

Unearned interest on the loan would be $385,543 [(10 x $100,000) – $614,457].

Klein also is to receive a "nonrefundable origination fee" of $50,000. Klein incurred $20,000 of direct origination costs (for credit checks, etc.). Thus, Klein has **net** nonrefundable origination fees of $30,000. The new net investment in the loan is calculated below.

Gross investment in loan (10 x $100,000)	$1,000,000
Less: Unamortized net nonrefundable origination fees	(30,000)
	970,000
Less: Unearned interest income (from above)	385,543
Net investment in loan	$ 584,457

The new net investment in the loan can be used to find the new implicit interest rate.

$$\frac{100,000}{(1+i)^1} + \frac{100,000}{(1+i)^2} + \ . \ . \ . \ + \frac{100,000}{(1+i)^{10}} = \$584,457$$

where i = implicit rate

Thus, the implicit interest rate is 11.002%. The amortization table for the first 3 years is set up as follows:

(a) *Loan payments*	*(b)* *Reduction in unearned interest*	*(c)* *Interest revenue (PV x implicit rate of 11.002%)*	*(d)* *Reduction in net orig. fees (c-b)*	*(e)* *Reduction in PV of net invest (a-c)*	*(f)* *PV of net loan investment*
					$584,457
$100,000	$61,446*	$64,302	$2,856	$35,689	548,759
100,000	57,590**	60,374	2,784	39,626	509,133
100,000	53,349***	56,015	2,666	43,985	465,148

* *($614,457 x 10%) = $61,446*
** *[$614,457 – ($100,000 – $61,446)] x 10% = $57,590*
*** *[$575,900 – ($100,000 – $57,590)] x 10% = $53,349*

Commitment fees and costs. Often fees are received in advance in exchange for a **commitment** to originate or purchase a loan. These fees should be deferred and recognized upon exercise of the commitment as an adjustment of interest income over the life of the loan, as in example 1 for origination costs and fees. If a commitment expires unexercised, the fees should be recognized as income upon expiration.

As with loan origination fees and costs, if **both** commitment fees are received and commitment costs are incurred relating to a commitment to originate or purchase a loan, the **net** amount of fees or costs should be deferred and recognized over the life of the loan.

If there is a **remote** possibility of exercise, the commitment fees may be recognized on a straight-line basis over the commitment period as "service fee income." If there is a subsequent exercise, the unamortized fees at the date of exercise shall be recognized over the life of the loan as an adjustment of interest income, as in example 1.

In certain cases, commitment fees are determined retroactively as a percentage of available lines of credit. If the commitment fee percentage is nominal in relation to the stated rate on the related borrowing, with the borrowing earning the market rate of interest, the fees shall be recognized in income as of the determination date.

Example 2

Glass Corp. has a $2 million, 10% line of credit outstanding with Ritter Bank. Ritter charges its annual commitment fee as 0.1% of any available balance as of the end of the prior period. Ritter will report $2,000 ($2 million x 0.1%) as service fee income in its current income statement.

Fees and costs in refinancing or restructurings. (Assume not a troubled-debt restructuring) When the terms of a refinanced/restructured loan are as favorable to the lender as the terms for loans to customers with similar risks who are not in a restructuring, the refinanced loan is treated as a **new** loan, and all prior fees of the old loan are recognized in interest income when the new loan is made.

When the above situation is not satisfied, the fees or costs from the old loan become part of the net investment in the new loan.

Example 3

Jeffrey Bank refinanced a loan receivable to $1,000,000, at 10% interest, with annual interest receipts for 10 years. Jeffrey's "normal" loan in its portfolio to debtors with similar risks is for $500,000 at 9% interest for 5 years. Jeffrey had loan origination fees from the original loan of $20,000. These fees are recognized in income **immediately** because the terms of the restructuring are as favorable to Jeffrey as a loan to another debtor with similar risks.

Example 4

Assume the same facts as in example 3 except that the refinanced terms are $500,000 principal, 7% interest for 3 years. Since the terms of the restructuring are **not** as favorable to Jeffrey as a loan to another debtor with similar risks, the $20,000 origination fees become part of the new investment in the loan and recognized in interest income over the life of the new loan, as in example 1.

Purchase of a loan or group of loans. Fees paid or fees received when purchasing a loan or group of loans should normally be considered part of the initial investment; to be recognized in income over the lives of the loans. However, if the loans qualify as debt securities under SFAS 115 and are held in the lender's "trading securities" portfolio, these fees should be reported in income when paid or received, and not added to the cost of the loans.

Special arrangements. Often lenders provide demand loans (loans with no scheduled payment terms). In this case, any net fees or costs should be recognized on a straight-line basis over a period determined by mutual agreement of the parties, usually over the estimated length of the loan.

Under a revolving line of credit, any net fees or costs are recognized in income on a straight-line basis over the period that the line of credit is active. If the line of credit is terminated due to the borrower's full payment, any unamortized net fees or costs are recognized in income.

Example 5

Green Bank received $50,000 as a nonrefundable origination fee on a $2 million demand loan. Green's loan dictates that any fees are to be amortized over a period of 10 years. Therefore, $5,000 ($50,000 x 1/10) of origination fees will be recognized as an addition to interest income each year for the next 10 years.

Financial statement presentation. The unamortized balance of origination, commitment, and other fees/costs that are recognized as an adjustment of interest income shall be reported on the balance sheet as part of the loan balance to which they relate. Except for any special cases as noted in the above paragraphs, the amount of net fees/costs recognized each period as an adjustment will be reported in the income statement as part of interest income.

Cash Flow Statement

Banks, savings institutions, and credit unions are **not** required to report gross cash receipts and payments for the following:

1. Deposits placed with other financial institutions
2. Withdrawals of deposits
3. Time deposits accepted
4. Repayments of deposits
5. Loans made to customers
6. Principal collections of loans

If an enterprise is part of a consolidated enterprise, net cash receipts and payments of the enterprise should be reported separate from the gross cash receipts and payments of the consolidated enterprise.

EMERGING ISSUES TASK FORCE CONSENSUS SUMMARIES

84-4 Acquisition, Development, and Construction Loans

The Task Force discussed the treatment of ADC loans as loans, investments, or interests in a joint venture and the accounting for a partial sale of the arrangement. These issues were resolved by the issuance of the AICPA Notice to Practitioners, ADC Arrangements, which covers ADC arrangements in which the lender expects to participate in residual profit and gives guidance on accounting and reporting concerns.

84-9 Deposit Float of Banks

The Task Force agreed that to allow banks to delay recording assets and liabilities for checks deposited until collection is made from the drawee bank would constitute an accounting change. However, a consensus was reached that the change would be difficult to justify because this approach is conceptually flawed.

84-19 Mortgage Loan Payment Modifications

The Task Force discussed agreements in which the lender allows the borrower to make larger payments for some period (at least 12 payments) and is then relieved of his remaining obligation. A consensus was reached that the loss related to the forgiven portion should be accrued over the period of the larger payments.

84-20 GNMA Dollar Rolls

A consensus was reached on the treatment of only one of the four types of GNMA rolls. The Task Force agreed that forward commitment dollar rolls should be marked to market. The remaining issues were resolved by SOP 85-2, which was subsequently amended by SOP 90-3.

84-21 Sale of a Loan With a Partial Participation Retained

In some instances, an enterprise may sell a loan but retain a share in the interest income as well as servicing rights. The Task Force debated whether the present value of the future interest inflows should be recognized immediately or over the life of the loan and agreed that the accounting treatment specified in the AICPA Audit and Accounting Guide, *Savings and Loan Associations*, should be followed.

84-22 Prior Years' Earnings per Share Following a Savings and Loan Association Conversion and Pooling

The Task Force agreed that when a mutual savings and loan association converts to stock ownership and pools with another S&L, its EPS should be excluded from the restated combined EPS for years before the date of conversion. The method of presentation must be disclosed.

84-31 Equity Certificates of Deposit

The Task Force concluded that contingent interest expense resulting from equity certificates of deposit is recognized concurrently with gains relating to the assets upon which the equity is given.

85-7 Federal Home Loan Mortgage Corporation Stock

The Task Force debated the proper accounting for the new class of nonvoting, participating preferred stock issued on December 6, 1984, to members of the Federal Home Loan Banking System. A consensus was not reached, although the majority opinion was that the stock is a nonmonetary asset which should be accounted for at fair value in accordance with APB 29. The issue was subsequently resolved by FASB TB 85-1, which concurred with the Task Force and further stated that the resulting income is extraordinary.

85-8 Amortization of Thrift Intangibles

When a banking or thrift institution is acquired, the excess of the fair value of liabilities over the fair value of assets should be amortized to expense in accordance with SFAS 72. Any other goodwill resulting from the combination should be amortized according to APB 17.

85-13 Sale of Mortgage Service Rights on Mortgages Owned by Others

The Task Force agreed that a gain should be recognized upon the sale of mortgage service rights which include participation in the future interest stream of the loans.

85-18 Earnings per Share Effect of Equity Commitment Notes

The Task Force concluded that neither equity commitment notes nor equity contract notes should be included in earnings per share computations.

85-20 Recognition of Fees for Guaranteeing a Loan

A consensus was reached that a guarantor should recognize loan guarantee fees as revenue over the term of the guarantee. Any direct costs related to the guarantee must be recognized in the same manner. If material, footnote disclosure is required, and the probability of loss should be continually assessed.

85-24 Distribution Fees by Distributors of Mutual Funds That Do Not Have a Front-End Sales Charge

The Task Force concluded that the currently used cost deferral method should be maintained. Under this method, fees expected to be received over some future period should be recognized upon receipt. Deferred incremental direct costs are amortized while indirect costs are expensed as incurred.

85-26 Measurement of Servicing Fees Under FASB Statement 65 When a Loan Is Sold With Servicing Retained

The Task Force debated whether mortgage bankers should consider servicing fee rates set by secondary market makers (GNMA, FHLMC, FNMA) to be the minimum for a normal servicing fee rate. A consensus was not reached, but the issue was subsequently resolved by Technical Bulletin 87-3, which states that these rates should be considered normal for transactions with those agencies.

85-31 Comptroller of the Currency's Rule on Deferred Tax Debits

The Task Force reached a consensus that the Comptroller's Banking Circular 202, which limits the net deferred tax debits allowable on a bank's statement of condition, applies only for regulatory purposes and does not affect GAAP financial statements.

85-41 Accounting for Savings and Loan Associations Under FSLIC Management Consignment Program

When a troubled thrift is closed under the Management Consignment Program (MCP), its assets (tangible and identifiable intangible) and liabilities are transferred at fair value to a newly chartered federal mutual association. FV constitutes the new cost basis, which should not be adjusted to market on a continuing basis but instead maintained according to GAAP. Any excess of liabilities over assets is recorded as deficit equity. The proper accounting is the same for both stock and mutual institutions, and the transfer does not constitute a business combination.

85-42 Amortization of Goodwill Resulting From Recording Time Savings Deposits at Fair Values

When a financial institution is acquired by purchase, the excess of the fair value of liabilities over the fair value of assets (Statement 72 goodwill) should be amortized over a period up to the remaining life of the long-term interest-bearing assets acquired. Any other goodwill resulting from the combination should be amortized according to APB Opinion 17.

85-44 Differences Between Loan Loss Allowances for GAAP and RAP

The Task Force reached a consensus that loan loss allowances recorded by S&Ls may differ under regulatory accounting principles (RAP) and GAAP. However, auditors must make certain that any differences are justifiable.

86-21 Application of the AICPA Notice to Practitioners Regarding Acquisition, Development, and Construction Arrangements to Acquisition of an Operating Property

The Task Force concluded that AICPA Notice to Practitioners, *ADC Arrangements*, which deals with real estate ADC arrangements of financial institutions, should also be considered in relation to ADC arrangements transacted by nonfinancial institutions, shared appreciation mortgages, and loans on operating real estate. The Task Force also reached consensus that paras 3-5 of that Notice should be consulted in determining the nature of expected residual profit on the arrangement.

86-31 Reporting the Tax Implications of a Pooling of a Bank and a Savings and Loan Association

A consensus was reached regarding the tax effects of a required reduction in bad debt reserves (for tax purposes) in a merger of a savings and loan association and a banking, insurance, or other financial institution. The tax effects should be accounted for as an expense in the current period's combined financial statements of the merged entity.

The Task Force also reached a consensus that after the bad debt reserves are adjusted for the merger transaction, deferred taxes should be recorded for the difference between bad debt reserves for tax and financial purposes.

86-38 Implications of Mortgage Prepayments on Amortization of Servicing Rights

An excess service fee receivable (resulting from a higher than normal servicing fee) must be written down to the present value of the remaining future excess service fee revenue discounted with the same factor used to calculate the original receivable.

87-22 Prepayment to the Secondary Reserve of the FSLIC

The secondary reserve of the FSLIC was eliminated as of December 31, 1986, although member institutions were not notified until May 1987. The Task Force agreed that this represents a subsequent event and that the related amounts should be written off as a loss against 1987 operating income.

87-34 Sale of Mortgage Servicing Rights With a Subservicing Agreement

The Task Force discussed events in which a mortgage loan servicer (transferor) transfers the servicing rights and related risks to an unaffiliated enterprise (transferee), which then makes a subservicing agreement whereby the transferor services the loans for a fixed fee. A consensus was reached that income recognition should be deferred and that treatment as a sale or a financing depends on the circumstances surrounding the transaction. However, this consensus does not apply to temporary subservicing agreements. In addition, a loss should be recognized currently if loan prepayments may result in future servicing losses.

88-17 Accounting for Fees and Costs Associated With Loan Syndications, and Loan Participations

The Task Force agreed that there are no material differences between loan syndications and some loan participations and thus both should receive the same accounting treatment. In addition, a transaction structured legally as a participation which actually constitutes an in-substance syndication should be accounted for as a syndication. A transaction structured legally as a syndication must also meet certain criteria to be accounted for as such by the lead syndicator.

88-19 FSLIC-Assisted Acquisitions of Thrifts

The Task Force reached a consensus on several issues, which are listed below.

1. In a tax-sharing agreement, the Thrift acts as a conduit for tax benefits accruing to the FSLIC and records only its net benefit in accordance with GAAP.
2. In applying SFAS 72, assets covered by yield maintenance assistance are considered interest-bearing, even if they are not.
3. When allocating the purchase price, the stated interest rate is considered the market rate and is used to determine the fair value of the acquired assets.
4. The basis of an asset covered by yield maintenance assistance is carried over to any new covered asset to which it is converted.
5. Contingency losses related to the acquisition are recorded net of reimbursements under indemnification provisions of the assistance agreement.
6. If the assistance includes a note receivable from the FSLIC and the sale of equity securities to the FSLIC, the note should be offset against that equity.
7. If issue 6 applies, then the Thrift should net divided payments made to the FSLIC against cash received from the FSLIC as interest on the note. This net amount is recorded as regulatory assistance.

SFAS 109 and SEC Staff Accounting Bulletin provide additional guidance.

88-20 Difference Between Initial Investment and Principal Amount of Loans in a Purchased Credit Card Portfolio

The Task Force agreed that the excess of the purchase price of a credit card portfolio including cardholder relationships over the amounts due should be allocated between the credit card loans acquired and the cardholder relationships acquired. The premium related to cardholder relationships is an identifiable intangible asset and is amortized over the period of benefit. The premium related to the loans is amortized over the life of the loans.

88-25 Ongoing Accounting and Reporting for a Newly Created Liquidating Bank

The Task Force concluded that the assets and liabilities of liquidating banks should be reported at fair value as of the date of the financial statements, with subsequent increases and decreases in fair value included in the results of each period. The initial valuation method should be used to determine fair value each period. SEC Staff Accounting Bulletin 82 provides additional guidance.

89-3 Balance Sheet Presentation of Savings Accounts in Financial Statements of Credit Unions

The Task Force agreed that the savings accounts deposited in a credit union must be unequivocally listed as a liability if the financial statements of the credit union are to comply with the AICPA Credit Union Guide. The statement of financial condition must present savings accounts either as the first item in the liabilities and equity section or as a separate subtotal before total liabilities.

89-9 Accounting for In-Substance Foreclosures

The Task Force reached a consensus that the collateral seized in an in-substance foreclosure, which has a fair value less than the amount of the loan, must be recorded at fair value. This value becomes the new cost basis and is not adjusted for subsequent increases in fair value. Subsequent to the issuance of SFAS 114, the EITF decided not to change the provisions of this EITF consensus due to the practical problems of accounting for the operations of an asset the creditor does not possess.

89-19 Accounting for a Change in Goodwill Amortization for Business Combinations Initiated Prior to the Effective Date of FASB Statement 72

A consensus was reached that an enterprise can adopt the provisions of SFAS 72 to account for goodwill obtained in a purchase-type business combination occurring prior to the effective date of the statement. As the adoption of Statement 72 results in a change in accounting principle, it should be recorded as a cumulative effect adjustment.

The Task Force noted that this consensus applies specifically to SFAS 72 and should not be applied to other situations.

Additionally, the consensus on this issue does not prevent an enterprise from applying the special exemption for an initial public distribution.

90-18 Effect of a "Removal of Accounts" Provision on the Accounting for a Credit Card Securitization

The Task Force concluded that credit card securitizations with "removal of accounts" provisions should be recognized as sales transactions under SFAS 77 as long as the removal meets any specified terms, doesn't reduce the interests of the investor in the pool, and doesn't reduce the seller's percentage interest below a contractually specified level.

90-21 Balance Sheet Treatment of a Sale of Mortgage Servicing Rights With a Subservicing Agreement

The Task Force agreed that such transactions (discussed in Issue 87-34) should be accounted for as a sale if substantially all the risks and rewards of ownership have been transferred to the buyer. If substantially all the risks and rewards have **not** been transferred, then the transaction must be accounted for as a financing.

92-5 Amortization Period for Net Deferred Credit Card Origination Fees

A consensus was reached that credit card origination costs which qualify for deferral in accordance with para 6, SFAS 91, should be netted against the credit card fee charged, if any, and the net amount should be amortized on a straight-line basis over the term of the credit card or one year, depending on the significance of the fee.

Additionally, for both purchased and originated credit cards, the accounting policies; the net amount capitalized; and the amortization period should be disclosed.

FASB TECHNICAL BULLETINS

87-3 Accounting for Mortgage Servicing Fees and Rights

Normal servicing fee rates for mortgage loans are those set by federally sponsored secondary market makers (GNMA, FHLMC, FNMA). For transactions with those agencies or for mortgage loans sold to private sector investors where the seller retains servicing rights, normal servicing rates should be considered. In the latter case, a stated servicing fee rate which differs from the normal rate requires adjustment to the sales price to yield the normal rate. In either case, a loss should be accrued if expected servicing costs exceed anticipated fees based on the stated servicing fee rate. If the servicer refinances a mortgage loan and actual prepayments differ from any anticipated prepayments, then the servicing asset must be adjusted.

STATEMENTS OF POSITION

93-1 Accounting for Individual Credit Card Acquisitions

A consensus was reached that credit card accounts acquired individually should be accounted for as originations under SFAS 91 and EITF Issue 92-5.

BROADCASTING INDUSTRY

PERSPECTIVE AND ISSUES

SFAS 63 sets forth accounting and reporting standards for the broadcasting industry. A broadcaster is an enterprise or an affiliated group of enterprises that transmits radio or television program material. Broadcasters acquire program exhibition rights through license agreements. A typical license agreement for program material (e.g., features, specials, series, or cartoons) covers several programs (a package) and grants a television station, group of stations, network, pay television, or cable television system (licensee) the right to broadcast either a specified number or an unlimited number of showings over a maximum period of time (license period) for a specified fee. Ordinarily, the fee is paid in installments over a period generally shorter than the license period. The agreement usually contains a separate license for each program in the package. The license expires at the earlier of the last allowed telecast or the end of the license period. The licensee pays the required fee whether or not the rights are exercised. If the licensee does not exercise the contractual rights, the rights revert to the licensor with no refund to the licensee. The license period is not intended to provide continued use of the program material throughout that period but rather to define a reasonable period of time within which the licensee can exercise the limited rights to use the program material.

Sources of GAAP
SFAS
63

DEFINITIONS OF TERMS

Barter. The exchange of unsold advertising time for products or services. The broadcaster benefits (providing the exchange does not interfere with its cash sales) by exchanging otherwise unsold time for such things as programs, fixed assets, merchandise, other media advertising privileges, travel and hotel arrangements, entertainment, and other services or products.

Broadcaster. An enterprise or an affiliated group of enterprises that transmits radio or television program material.

Daypart. An aggregation of programs broadcast during a particular time of day (e.g., daytime, evening, late night) or programs of a similar type (e.g., sports, news, children's shows). Broadcasters generally sell access to viewing audiences to advertisers on a daypart basis.

License agreement for program material. A typical license agreement for program material (e.g., features, specials, series, or cartoons) covers several programs (a package) and grants a television station, group of stations, network, pay television, or cable television system (licensee) the right to broadcast either a specified number or an unlimited number of showings over a maximum period of time (license period) for a specified fee. Ordinarily, the fee is paid in installments over a period generally shorter than the license period. The agreement usually contains a separate license for each program in the package. The license expires at the earlier of the last allowed telecast or the end of the license period. The licensee pays the required fee whether or not the rights are exercised. If the licensee does not exercise the contractual rights, the rights revert to the licensor with no refund to the licensee. The license period is not intended to provide continued use of the program material throughout that period but rather to define a reasonable period of time within which the licensee can exercise the limited rights to use the program material.

Network affiliation agreement. A broadcaster may be affiliated with a network under a network affiliation agreement. Under the agreement the station receives compensation for the network programming that it carries based on a formula designed to compensate the station for advertising sold on a network basis and included in network programming. Program costs, a major expense of television stations, are generally lower for a network affiliate than for an independent station because an affiliate does not incur program costs for network programs.

CONCEPTS, RULES, AND EXAMPLES

Accounting for License Agreements

A broadcaster should account for a license agreement for program material as a purchase of rights. Thus, an asset and a liability for the program rights purchased and the liability assumed should be reported when the license period begins and the broadcaster

1. Knows or can reasonably determine the cost of each program
2. Has accepted the program material according to the license agreement
3. Has access to the program for the first telecast (unless an agreement with another licensor prevents the telecast)

The asset may be capitalized and the liability reported at the gross amount of the liability for program rights. Alternatively, the broadcaster may choose to record the asset and liability at the present value of the liability, which should be calculated using an imputed rate of interest. In this case, the difference between the gross and net amounts is reported as interest. Under either method, the capitalized costs are allocated to each program within a package based on the relative value of each program to the broadcaster.

The asset recorded should be separated into current and noncurrent portions based on expected time of program usage. The liability should likewise be segregated according to the terms of payment.

Amortizing Capitalized Costs

The capitalized costs should be amortized to expense as the program rights are used; generally according to the estimated number of program telecasts. However, licenses granting the right to unlimited broadcasts of programs such as cartoons should be amortized over the license period, since the number of telecasts may be indeterminable.

Feature programs and program series require specific treatment. Feature programs should be amortized program-by-program, unless amortization as a package produces approximately the same result. Syndicated programs should be amortized as a series. If the broadcaster considers the first showing to be more valuable than reruns, the series should be amortized using an accelerated method. If each showing is equally valuable, straight-line amortization should be used.

Accounting for Network Affiliation Agreements

A broadcaster may be affiliated with a network under a network affiliation agreement. Under the agreement, the station receives compensation for the network programming that it carries based on a formula designed to compensate the station for advertising sold on a network basis and included in network programming. Program costs, a major expense of television stations, are generally lower for a network affiliate than for an independent station because an affiliate does not incur program costs for network programs.

Upon termination of a network affiliation agreement, immediate replacement or an agreement to replace the affiliation will allow the broadcaster to recognize a loss measured by the unamortized cost of the previous affiliation less the fair value of the new affiliation. No gain is recognized if the fair value exceeds the unamortized cost. If the terminated affiliation is not replaced, its unamortized cost should be charged to expense.

Accounting for Barter Transactions

Broadcasters may exchange unsold advertising time for products or services. The broadcaster benefits (providing the exchange does not interfere with its cash sales) by exchanging otherwise unsold time for such things as programs, fixed assets, merchandise, other media advertising privileges, travel and hotel arrangements, entertainment, and other services or products. Such transactions should be reported at the fair value of the services or products (except when advertising time is exchanged for programs).

Barter revenue is recognized as the commercials are broadcast. The products or services received in exchange are reported when received or used. A liability results if products or services are received before the commercial is aired, and a receivable results if the commercial is aired first.

Reporting and Disclosure

The capitalized cost of program rights is reported in the balance sheet at the lower of unamortized cost or net realizable value. Net realizable value is estimated on a package, series, program-by-program, or daypart basis. Daypart is an aggregation of programs broadcast during a particular time of day (e.g, daytime, evening, late night) or programs of a similar type (e.g., sports, news, children's shows). Broadcasters generally sell access to viewing audiences to advertisers on a daypart basis. If the broadcaster expects the usefulness of a program to diminish, the program may have to be written down from unamortized cost to estimated net realizable value. This establishes a new cost basis for the program.

Network affiliations agreements are reported in the balance sheet as intangible assets.

Present value method. Each payment is discounted at 12% from the first day of the license period to the date of payment as follows:

	Payment		*Discount period*			
Film	*Date*	*Amount*	*From*	*To*	*PV factor*	*Discounted Present value*
A & B	7/31/98	$2,000			1.0000	$2,000
	1/1/99	4,000	9/1/98	1/1/99	.9615	3,846
		$6,000				$5,846
C	1/1/00	$4,000	11/1/98	1/1/00	.9804	
					x .8929	$3,502

When each film's license period begins, an asset and a liability are recorded at the present value of the liability. Since the first two payments apply to both film A and film B, the $5,846 must be allocated to these films according to their relative values (the stated license fees), or 4/6 to film A and 2/6 to film B.

Film	*Asset and liability recognized*
A	$3,897
B	1,949
C	3,502

In this case, all costs are capitalized in 1998 because all the license periods begin in 1998 (assuming the three conditions are met).

The amount capitalized as an asset is amortized according to the percentage of revenues to be earned each year from each film. Interest is accrued on the unpaid balance of the liability for each film. Note that for films A and B, the **unpaid** balance in 1998 is $3,846 ($5,846 – $2,000).

Film	1998	Year of expense recognition 1999	2000
A - Accrued interest	$103(a)		
Amortization	2,728(b)	$1,169(f)	
B - Accrued interest	51(c)		
Amortization	1,169(d)	780(g)	
C - Accrued interest	70(e)	428(h)	
Amortization	___	2,276(i)	$1,226(j)
	$4,121	$4,653	$1,226

(a) $3,846 x 12% x 4/12 x 4/6
(b) $3,897 x 70%
(c) $3,846 x 12% x 4/12 x 2/6
(d) $1,949 x 60%
(e) $3,502 x 12% x 2/12
(f) $3,897 x 30%
(g) $1,949 x 40%
(h) ($3,502 + $70) x 12%
(i) $3,502 x 65%
(j) $3,502 x 35%

Note that interest expense equals the gross amount minus the present value (A & B: $6,000 – $5,846 = $154 and C: $4,000 – $3,502 = $498).

Gross method. Costs are capitalized at the gross amount of the liability.

Film	Asset and liability recognized
A	$4,000
B	2,000
C	4,000

Again, since the license period for all the films begins in 1998, the assets and liabilities are recognized in 1998.

Under the gross approach, no interest is accrued on the unpaid liability. Thus, the only expense is amortization of program cost.

Film	1998	Year of expense recognition 1999	2000
A	$2,800 (a)	$1,200 (c)	
B	1,200 (b)	800 (d)	
C	___	2,600 (e)	$1,400 (f)
	$4,000	$4,600	$1,400

(a) $4,000 x 70%
(b) $2,000 x 60%
(c) $4,000 x 30%
(d) $2,000 x 40%
(e) $4,000 x 65%
(f) $4,000 x 35%

CABLE TELEVISION INDUSTRY

PERSPECTIVE AND ISSUES

SFAS 51 sets forth accounting and reporting standards for the cable television industry. These standards apply to cable television systems in the prematurity period. During the prematurity period, the cable television system is partially under construction and partially in service. The prematurity period begins with the first earned subscriber revenue. Its end will vary with circumstances of the system but will be determined based on plans for completion of the first major construction period or achievement of a specified predetermined subscriber level at which no additional investment will be required for other than cable television plants. The length of the prematurity period varies with the franchise development and construction plans. Except in the smallest systems, programming is usually delivered to portions of the system, and some revenues are obtained before construction of the entire system is complete. Thus, virtually every cable television system experiences a prematurity period during which it is receiving some revenue while continuing to incur substantial costs related to the establishment of the total system.

Sources of GAAP

SFAS
51, 121

DEFINITIONS OF TERMS

Cable television plant. The cable television plant required to render service to the subscriber includes the following equipment:

Head-end. This includes the equipment used to receive signals of distant television or radio stations, whether directly from the transmitter or from a microwave relay system. It also includes the studio facilities required for operator-originated programming, if any.
Cable. This consists of cable and amplifiers (which maintain the quality of the signal) covering the subscriber area, either on utility poles or underground.
Drops. These consist of the hardware that provides access to the main cable, the short length of cable that brings the signal from the main cable to the subscriber's television set, and other associated hardware, which may include a trap to block particular channels.
Converters and descramblers. These devices are attached to the subscriber's television sets when more than 12 channels are provided or when special services are provided, such as "pay cable" or two-way communication.

Direct selling costs. Direct selling costs include commissions, the portion of a salesperson's compensation other than commissions for obtaining new subscribers, local advertising targeted for acquisition of new subscribers, and costs of processing documents related to new subscribers acquired. Direct selling costs do not include supervisory and administrative expenses or indirect expenses, such as rent and costs of facilities.

Subscriber-related costs. These are costs incurred to obtain and retain subscribers to the cable television system and include costs of billing and collection, bad debts, and mailings; repairs and maintenance of taps and connections; franchise fees related to revenues or number of subscribers; general and administrative system costs, such as salary of the system manager and office rent; programming costs for additional channels used in the marketing effort or costs related to revenues from, or number of subscribers to, per channel or per program service; and direct selling costs.

CONCEPTS, RULES, AND EXAMPLES

Accounting During the Prematurity Period

Before the first subscriber revenue is earned by the cable company, the beginning and end of the prematurity period must be established by management. This period generally will not exceed 2 years. Once the prematurity period has been established, it may not be changed except in extraordinary circumstances.

Separate accounting is required for any part of a cable television system that is in the prematurity period and that is distinct from the rest of the system. This distinction may be made if the portion is characterized by a majority of the following differences:

- Accountability (e.g., separate forecasts, budgets, etc.)
- Investment decisions (e.g., separate ROI, breakeven, etc.)
- Geographical (e.g., separate franchise area)
- Mechanical (e.g., separate equipment)
- Timing (e.g., separate inception of construction or marketing)

If the portion meets these requirements, it will be charged costs of the entire system only if these costs are directly traceable to that portion. Separate projections should also be developed for that portion.

During the prematurity period, costs incurred by the plant should be capitalized as usual. General and administrative expenses and subscriber-related costs are considered period costs. Subscriber-related costs are costs incurred to obtain and retain subscribers to the cable television system.

System costs that will benefit the cable system upon completion (e.g., programming costs), and that will remain fairly constant despite changes in the number of subscribers, should be separated into current and noncurrent portions. A fraction is calculated each month and multiplied by the total of these costs for the month to determine the amount of current cost. The fraction is computed as follows:

Current portion of system costs benefitting future periods	=	Greatest of a) Average # of subscribers expected that month as estimated at beginning of prematurity period, b) Average # of subscribers assuming straight-line progress towards estimated subscribers at end of prematurity period, or c) Average # of actual subscribers ——————————————— Total # of subscribers expected at end of prematurity period

During the prematurity period, interest cost is capitalized using an interest capitalization rate as described in SFAS 34, paras 13 and 14. The amount of interest cost to be capitalized is determined as follows:

Interest cost capitalized	=	Interest capitalization rate	x	Average amount of qualifying assets during the period

SFAS 34, paras 16 and 18, defines qualifying assets. The amount of capitalized interest cost may not exceed actual interest cost for the period.

Depreciation and amortization during the prematurity period are determined as follows:

Depr. and amort. expense	=	Monthly depr. and amort. expected after prematurity period (using depr. method to be used then)	x	Fraction used to determine current portion of system costs benefitting future periods

Amortizing Capitalized Costs

Capitalization based on timing differences. Costs that have been capitalized for a portion of a cable television system that is in the prematurity period and that is clearly distinguishable on the basis of timing differences should be amortized over the same depreciation period used by the main cable plant.

Installation revenues and costs. A cable television system recognizes initial hookup revenue to the extent of the direct selling costs associated with that revenue. The deferred portion is amortized to income over the average expected period that subscribers will continue to receive cable service.

Initial installation costs are capitalized and depreciated over a period that does not exceed the period used to depreciate the cable plant. After the initial installation, any costs incurred to disconnect or reconnect subscribers are charged to expense.

Franchise applications. The treatment of franchise costs depends upon whether or not the franchise is successful. If successful, the costs are capitalized and amortized as intangible assets. If unsuccessful, all costs are charged to expense.

Recoverability of capitalized costs. Capitalized plant and certain identifiable intangible assets are subject to the impairment provisions outlined in SFAS 121. A separate evaluation should be made for the portion of the cable television system that is in the prematurity period. If total capitalized cost reaches the maximum recoverable amount, capitalization should continue. However, the provision to reduce capitalized costs to recoverable value is increased.

COMPUTER SOFTWARE COSTS AND REVENUES

PERSPECTIVE AND ISSUES

Accounting standards have previously dealt with the questions of computer software developed for sale or lease to customers (in SFAS 86, issued in 1985) and with the general issues related to research and development expenditures (in SFAS 2, issued in 1974, and Interpretation 6, issued in 1975). However, the increasingly important question of how to account for the cost of software developed internally or acquired from outside vendors to be used internally, rather than sold to customers or included in final products sold to customers, has not been definitively dealt with in the past. While SFAS 86 applies to software which is sold, leased, or "part of a product or process" but does not define that term, some have attempted to apply that standard to internal use software as well, although that does not seem to be what was intended when that pronouncement was promulgated. In some cases, of course, the same software is both used internally and incorporated as part of a product or service to be sold to customers.

When SFAS 86 was promulgated, it was commonly the case that reporting entities were expensing the costs of developing software for internal use. Over the years, however, as internal development of software became more prevalent, there was a greater divergence of practices. The project to provide guidance culminated with SOP 98-1.

While today the costs of acquired (and to a lesser extent, internally created) software are frequently being accounted for as assets, with appropriate capitalization and amortization, there has been substantial variation in practice regarding (1) the defining of which costs (for internally generated software) qualify for capitalization, (2) identifying when asset recognition should commence, and (3) determining when the asset is impaired and how it should be accounted for thereafter. In response, the AICPA's Accounting Standards Executive Committee (AcSEC) has issued SOP 98-1.

In 1991, the AICPA's Accounting Standards Executive Committee (AcSEC) issued guidance on the principles of revenue recognition for software developers and marketers, in SOP 91-1, *Software Revenue Recognition*. This standard was intended to end the diverse practices which had developed as the market for custom and standardized software products. Additionally such typical corollary services as maintenance agreements, training assistance, and on-line help (hot lines), exploded over the prior decade or so. SOP 91-1 established a typology of sales and leasing and licensing transactions. Under this SOP, the accounting for software revenues was determined by the specific conditions of each particular transaction.

Categories of software revenue-producing transactions were defined by SOP 91-1 to include (1) software licenses with no attendant obligations by seller; (2) software licenses with minor seller obligations; (3) software licenses with significant, ongoing vendor obligations; (4) software transactions structured as leases; (5) software customization or modification projects necessitating the use of contract accounting; (6) service transactions; and (7) postcontract customer support. SOP 91-1 set forth the conceptual bases for dealing with the timing and amounts of revenues to be recognized by entities which license, sell, lease, or otherwise market computer software. However, after the standard had been implemented it was determined that the guidance was incomplete; conflicting procedures were developing in practice, particularly in the very common circumstances in which contracts provided for multiple deliverables, often including postcontract customer support (PCS). For that reason, the AICPA undertook a project that was originally intended to amend SOP 91-1. Ultimately, this led to the development of SOP 97-2, which entirely replaces and supersedes the former statement. It is effective for transactions entered into in fiscal years beginning after December 15, 1997. SOP 98-4 deferred the effective date of SOP 97-2 for 1 year with regard to provisions which limit what is considered vendor-specific objective evidence of the fair value of the various elements in a multiple-element arrangement.

Sources of GAAP

SFAS	*AICPA SOP*
2, 86	97-2, 98-1, 98-4

DEFINITIONS OF TERMS

Coding. Generating detailed instructions in a computer language to carry out the requirements described in the detail program design. The coding of a computer software product may begin prior to, concurrent with, or subsequent to the completion of the detail program design.

Customer support. Services performed by an enterprise to assist customers in their use of software products. Those services include any installation assistance, training classes, telephone question and answer services, newsletters, on-site visits, and software or data modifications.

Detail program design. The detail design of a computer software product that takes product function, feature, and technical requirements to their most detailed, logical form and is ready for coding.

Maintenance. Activities undertaken after the product is available for general release to customers to correct errors or keep the product updated with current information. Those activities include routine changes and additions.

Product design. A logical representation of all product functions in sufficient detail to serve as product specifications.

Product enhancement. Improvements to an existing product that are intended to extend the life or improve significantly the marketability of the original product. Enhancements normally require a product design and may require a redesign of all or part of the existing product.

Product masters. A completed version, ready for copying, of the computer software product, the documentation, and the training materials that are to be sold, leased, or otherwise marketed.

Testing. Performing the steps necessary to determine whether the coded computer software product meets function, feature, and technical performance requirements set forth in the product design.

Working model. An operative version of the computer software product that is completed in the same software language as the product to be ultimately marketed, performs all the major functions planned for the product, and is ready for initial customer testing (usually identified as **beta testing**).

CONCEPTS, RULES, AND EXAMPLES

Developed Software for Internal Use

SOP 98-1 was developed to provide guidance for internally developed software. Software must meet two criteria to be accounted for as internally developed software. First, the software's specifications must be designed or modified to meet the reporting entity's internal needs, including costs to customize purchased software. Second, during the period in which the software is being developed, there can be no plan or intent to market the software externally, although development of the software can be jointly funded by several entities that each plan to use the software internally.

In order to justify capitalization of related costs, it is necessary for management to conclude that it is probable that the project will be completed and that the software will be used as intended. Absent that level of expectation, costs must be expensed currently as research and development costs are required to be. Entities which historically were engaged in both research and development of software for internal use and for sale to others would have to carefully identify costs with one or the other activity, since the former would (if all conditions are met) be subject to capitalization, while the latter might be expensed as research and development costs until technological feasibility had been demonstrated, per SFAS 86.

Costs Subject to Capitalization

Under terms of the proposed standard, cost capitalization commences when an entity has completed the conceptual formulation, design, and testing of possible project alternatives, including the process of vendor selection for purchased software, if any. These early-phase costs (referred to as "preliminary project stage" in SOP 98-1) are analogous to research and development costs and must be expensed as incurred. These cannot be later restored to an asset account if the development proves to be successful.

Costs incurred subsequent to the preliminary stage, and which meet the criteria under GAAP as long-lived assets, can be capitalized and amortized over the asset's expected economic life. Capitalization of costs will begin when both of two conditions are met. First, management having the relevant authority authorizes and commits to funding the project and believes that it is probable that it will be completed and that the resulting software will be used as intended. Second, the conceptual formulation, design, and testing of possible software project alternatives (i.e., the preliminary project stage) have been completed.

Costs to be capitalized include those of the "program instructions stage" and the "implementation stage" of the software development process. These include coding and testing activities and various implementation costs. In particular, the SOP notes that such costs will be limited to (1) external direct costs of materials and services consumed in developing or obtaining internal-use computer software; (2) payroll and payroll-related costs for employees who are directly associated with and who devote time to the internal-use computer software project to the extent of the time spent directly on the project; and (3) interest costs incurred while developing internal-use computer software, consistent with the provisions of SFAS 34.

As expected, the standard requires that general and administrative costs, overhead costs, and training costs not be capitalized. Even though these may be costs which are associated with the internal development or acquisition of software for internal use, under GAAP those costs relate to the period in which incurred. The issue of training costs is particularly important, since internal-use computer software purchased from third parties often includes, as part of the purchase price, training for the software (and often maintenance fees for routine maintenance as well). Per the SOP, when the amount of training or maintenance fees is not specified in the contract, entities are required to allocate the cost among training, maintenance, and amounts representing the capitalizable cost of computer software. Training costs must be recognized in expense as incurred. (Maintenance fees will be recognized in expense over the maintenance period.)

The SOP provides examples of when computer software is acquired or developed for internal use. Some of these are: when modifications are made to software controlling robots acquired for use in the manufacturing process; software is developed for cash management, payroll processing, or accounts payable system purposes; a bank develops an on-line account status inquiry system for customers to utilize; a travel agency invests in software to give it access to an airline reservation system; a communications provider develops computerized systems to manage customer services such as voice-mail; or when a publisher invests in computerized systems to produce a product which is then sold to customers.

On the other hand, software which does not qualify under the standard as being for internal use includes software sold by a robot manufacturer to purchasers of its products; the cost of developing programs for microchips used in automobile electronic systems; software developed for both sale to customers and internal use; computer programs written for use in research and development efforts; and costs of developing software under contract with another entity.

Impairment

The SOP makes it clear that, consistent with the treatment of other long-lived assets, possible impairment of capitalized internal use software will need to be recognized and measured in accordance with the provisions of SFAS 121. Circumstances which might suggest that an impairment has occurred include (1) a realization that the internal-use computer software is not expected to provide substantive service potential; (2) there has been a significant change in the extent or manner in which the software is used; (3) a significant change has been made or is being anticipated to the software program; or (4) the costs of developing or modifying the internal-use computer software significantly exceeds the amount originally expected. These conditions are analogous to those generically provided in SFAS 121.

In some instances, ongoing software development projects will become troubled before being aborted. The SOP provides that management will have to assess the likelihood of successful completion of projects in process. When it becomes no longer probable that the computer software being developed will be completed and placed in service, the asset should be written down at the lower of the carrying amount or fair value, if any, less costs to sell. Importantly, it will be a rebuttable presumption that any uncompleted software has a zero fair value. The SOP suggests indications that the software is no longer expected to be completed and placed in service. These include (1) a lack of expenditures budgeted or incurred for the project; (2) programming difficulties that cannot be resolved on a timely basis; (3) significant cost overruns; (4) information indicating that the costs of internally developed software will significantly exceed the cost of comparable third-party software or software products, suggesting that management intends to obtain the third-party software instead of completing the internal development effort; (5) the introduction of new technologies which increase the likelihood that management will elect to obtain third-party software instead of completing the internal project; and (6) a lack of profitability of the business segment or unit to which the software relates or actual or potential discontinuation of that segment.

Amortization of Capitalized Costs of Software for Internal Use

As for other long-lived assets, the costs of computer software developed or obtained for internal use should be amortized in a systematic and rational manner over its estimated useful life. The nature of the asset exacerbates the difficulty of developing a meaningful estimate, however. Among the factors to be weighed are the effects of obsolescence, technology, and competition. Entities would especially need to consider if rapid changes are occurring in the development of software products, software operating systems, or computer hardware, and whether management had intentions to replace any technologically obsolete software or hardware.

Amortization of each module or component of a software project should commence when the computer software is ready for its intended use, without regard to whether the software is to be placed in service in planned stages that might extend beyond a single reporting period. The SOP stipulates that computer software is to be deemed ready for its intended use after substantially all testing has been completed.

Other Matters

In some cases internal use software is later sold or licensed to third parties, notwithstanding the original intention of management that the software was acquired or developed solely for internal use. In such cases, the SOP provides that any proceeds received would be applied against the carrying amount of that software. No profit is recognized until the aggregate proceeds from sales exceed the carrying amount of the software. After the carrying value is fully recovered, any subsequent proceeds would be recognized in revenue as earned.

This standard does not add any new disclosure requirements. Relevant standards addressing disclosures include APB 12 and 22, SFAS 121, and SOP 94-6.

Software Development Costs Developed Internally for Sale or Lease

A separate set of accounting issues arise in connection with the costs of computer software developed internally for leasing or sale to others. The principal issue relates to the point in the development process at which efforts are no longer characterized as research and development (and thus expensed currently), but rather may be deferred (i.e., inventoried) and later classified as cost of sales as the finished products are disposed of.

SFAS 86 established the concept of **technological feasibility** to demarcate the point at which it is proper to begin to defer costs. According to this standard, all costs of development are considered to be research and development costs until technological feasibility has been established. This point is reached when all the necessary planning, designing, **coding**, and testing activities have been completed, to the extent these activities are necessary to establish that the product in question can meet its design specifications. Design specifications, in turn, may include such product aspects as functions, features, and technical performance requirements.

If the process of creating the software involves **detail program design**, evidence of having achieved technological feasibility includes having performed these steps.

1. The product design (the logical representation of the product) and detailed program design have been completed. This step includes having demonstrated that the necessary skills, hardware, and software technologies are accessible to the entity for it to complete the product development effort.
2. The detailed program design has been documented and traced to product specifications, thus demonstrating completeness and consistency.
3. The detailed program design has been reviewed for any high risk elements, such as unproven functions or product innovations, and any such high risk elements have been resolved through coding and testing.

If the software development effort does **not** involve detailed program design, then the following steps would need to have been completed to demonstrate technological feasibility:

1. A product design and a working model of the software have been completed.
2. The completeness of the working model and its consistency with the product design have been confirmed by testing.

If all the foregoing steps in either of the above listings have been completed as applicable, then technological feasibility has been shown, and costs incurred thereafter are to be capitalized. Such costs could include, but are not limited to, additional product development and the costs of producing product masters (which may include not only the master copy of the software itself but also related training materials and other such items). Capitalization of software costs is to cease, however, once the product is available for general release to customers of the entity. Period costs, such as maintenance and ongoing **customer support** efforts, are to be expensed as incurred in all cases.

The deferred computer software development costs must be amortized, beginning when the product is first available for general release to customers. Amortization is to be computed on a product by product basis, which means that costs related to development of earlier products cannot be "rolled forward" into the costs of newer products, thereby delaying expense recognition. Periodic amortization must be the greater of (1) an amount determined with reference to total estimated revenues to be generated by the product, or (2) an amount computed on a straight-line basis with reference to the product's expected life cycle.

Example of amortization of deferred computer software development costs

Assume total costs of $340,000 have been deferred at the point product sales begin. Management estimates that the product will eventually generate revenues of $5,100,000 over a period of 4 years. For the current period (one-half of a year), revenues of $600,000 have been realized. Deferred costs of $42,500 must be amortized, which is the greater of the pro rata amount based on estimated total revenues to be derived from product sales [($340,000 ÷ $5,100,000) x $600,000 = $40,000] or the amount determined on a straight-line basis ($340,000 ÷ 4 x 1/2 = $42,500).

Other costs, such as product duplication and training material publication costs, are to be capitalized and expensed on a unit specific basis as sales of product occur. All deferred costs are subject an annual evaluation for net realizable value; if inventoried costs are adjusted for this reason at any reporting date, such amount becomes the cost basis for further amortization purposes, as well as for comparison to net realizable value in the following period.

The Board is considering a change to SFAS 86 regarding development costs for personal computer software. Perhaps because there has been a very short life cycle for much of these products, and a high failure rate for new products that are marketed, the concern is that capitalization of costs may not be warranted in many cases. Reportedly, therefore, the change, if there is to be one, would be to require that all costs to develop software for personal computers be expensed as incurred, as research and development costs. Presumably this would not alter the accounting for software development costs for computers other than personal (micro) computers.

Software Revenue Recognition

The basic principles underlying SOP 97-2 are set forth in the following paragraphs.

Licensing vs. sales. AcSEC was concerned that transfers of rights to software by licenses rather than by outright sales--a technique widely employed to protect vendors from the unauthorized duplication of their products--were being accounted for differentially. It concluded that any legal distinction between a license and a sale should not cause revenue recognition to differ.

Product may not equate with delivery of software. AcSEC observed that arrangements to deliver software, whether alone or in conjunction with other products, often include services. Services to be provided in such contexts commonly involve significant production, modification, or customization of the software. AcSEC therefore concluded that in such circumstances the software, even if physically delivered, might not constitute the **delivery** of the product contracted for, absent those alterations. This resulted in the new requirement that such arrangements be accounted for as construction-type or production-type contracts, to be accounted for in conformity with ARB 45 and SOP 81-1. However, if the services do not entail significant production, modification, or customization of software, the service element should be accounted for as a separate element.

Delivery is the key threshold issue for revenue recognition. Consistent with the principles set forth in FASB Concepts Statement 5, *Recognition and Measurement in Financial Statements of Business Enterprises*, which states that "An entity's revenue-earning activities involve delivering or producing goods, rendering services, or other activities that constitute its ongoing major or central operations, and revenues are considered to have been earned when the entity has substantially accomplished what it must do to be entitled to the benefits represented by the revenues. . . [t]he two conditions (being realized or realizable and being earned) are usually met by the time the product or merchandise is delivered. . . to customers, and revenues. . .are commonly recognized at time of sale (usually meaning delivery)."

Revenue must be allocated to all elements of the sales arrangement, with recognition dependent upon meeting the criteria on an element-by-element basis. In SOP 91-1, the accounting for vendor obligations remaining after delivery of software was dependent upon whether or not the obligation was deemed to be significant. Under the new standard, all obligations are to be accounted for and the revenue form an arrangement should be allocated to each element of the arrangement, based on vendor-specific objective evidence of the fair values of the elements. Revenue associated with a particular element is not to be recognized until the revenue-recognition conditions established by the SOP are met, as the earnings process related to that element will not be considered complete until that time.

Fair values for revenue allocation purposes must be vendor-specific. When there are multiple elements of an arrangement, revenue is generally recognized on an element-by-element basis as individual elements are delivered. Revenue is to be allocated to the various elements in proportion to relative fair values. Under SOP 97-2, this allocation process requires that vendor-specific objective evidence of fair value be employed, regardless of any separate prices stated in the contract for each element, since prices stated in a contract may not represent fair value and, accordingly, might result in an unreasonable allocation of revenue. AcSEC concluded that this approach would be consistent with the accounting for commingled revenue as set forth in the current standard on accounting for franchise fee revenue (SFAS 45). The use of surrogate prices, such as those published by the competitors or industry averages, was rejected because of the wide differences in products and services offered by vendors. Separate transaction prices for the elements comprising the arrangement, if they are also being sold on that basis, would be the best such evidence, although under some circumstances (such as when prices in the arrangement are based on multiple users rather than the single user pricing of the element on a standalone basis) even that information could conceivably be invalid for revenue allocation purposes. Relative sales prices of the elements as included in the arrangement should be used whenever possible.

The earnings process is not complete if fees are subject to forfeiture. Even when the product has been delivered, if fees allocated to those products are subject to forfeiture, refund, or other concession if the vendor does not fulfill its delivery responsibilities relative to other parts of the arrangement, those fees should not be treated as having been earned. The potential concessions indicate the customer would not have licensed the delivered products without also licensing the undelivered products. For that reason, there must be persuasive evidence that fees allocated to delivered products are not subject to forfeiture, refund, or other concessions before revenue recognition can be justified. Thus, for example, in determining the persuasiveness of the evidence, the vendor's history of making concessions that were not required by the provisions of an arrangement is more persuasive than are terms included in the arrangement that indicate that no concessions are required.

Operational Rules Established By SOP 97-2

1. If an arrangement to deliver software or a software system, either alone or together with other products or services, requires significant production, modification, or customization of software, the entire arrangement should be accounted for in conformity with Accounting Research Bulletin (ARB) 45, *Long-Term Construction-Type Contracts*, and SOP 81-1, *Accounting for Performance of Construction-Type and Certain Production-Type Contracts*.

2. If the arrangement does not require significant production, modification, or customization of software, revenue should be recognized when **all** of the following criteria are met:

   a. Persuasive evidence of an arrangement exists;
   b. Delivery has occurred;
   c. The vendor's fee is fixed or determinable; and
   d. Collectibility is probable.

3. For software arrangements which provide licenses for multiple software deliverables (multiple elements), some of which may be deliverable only on a when-and-if available basis, these deliverables should be considered in determining whether an arrangement includes multiple elements. The requirements with respect to arrangements that consist of multiple elements should be applied to all additional products and services specified in the arrangement, including those described as being deliverable only on a when-and-if available basis.
4. For arrangements having multiple elements, the fee should be allocated to the various elements based on vendor-specific objective evidence of fair value, regardless of any separate prices stated for each element within the contract. Vendor-specific objective evidence of fair value is limited to the following:

   a. The price charged when the same element is sold separately; or
   b. For an element not yet being sold separately, the price established by management, if it is probable that the price, once established, will not change before the separate introduction of the element into the marketplace.

   The revenue allocated to undelivered elements cannot later be adjusted. However, as is traditional under GAAP, if it becomes probable that the amount allocated to an undelivered element will result in a loss on that element of the arrangement, the loss must be recognized. When a vendor's pricing is based on multiple factors such as the number of products and the number of users, the amount allocated to the same elements when sold separately must consider all the salient factors of the vendor's pricing structure.
5. If a discount is offered in a multiple-element arrangement, a proportionate amount thereof should be applied to each element included in the arrangement, based on each element's fair value without regard to the discount. However, no portion of the discount should be allocated to any upgrade rights.
6. If sufficient vendor-specific objective evidence does not exist for the allocation of revenue to the various elements of the arrangement, all revenue from the arrangement should be deferred until the earlier of the point at which (1) such sufficient vendor-specific objective evidence does exist, or (2) all ele-

ments of the arrangement have been delivered. The exceptions to this guidance, as provided in SOP 97-2, are as follows:

a. If the only undelivered element is postcontract customer support (PCS), the entire fee should be recognized ratably.
b. If the only undelivered element is services that do not involve significant production, modification, or customization of software (e.g., training or installation), the entire fee should be recognized over the period during which the services are expected to be performed.
c. If the arrangement is in substance, the entire fee should be recognized ratably.
d. If the fee is based on the number of copies, how the arrangement should be accounted for depends on whether the total fee is fixed, and on whether the buyer can alter the composition of the copies to be received, as follows:

    (1) If the arrangement provides customers with the right to reproduce or obtain copies of two or more software products at a specified price per copy (**not** per product) up to the total amount of the fixed fee, an allocation of the fee to the individual products generally cannot be made, because the total revenue allocable to each software product is unknown and depends on the choices to be made by the customer and, sometimes, on future vendor development activity. Nevertheless, certain arrangements that include products that are not deliverable at the inception impose a maximum number of copies of the undeliverable product(s) to which the customer is entitled. In such arrangements, a portion of the arrangement fee should be allocated to the undeliverable product(s). This allocation should be made assuming that the customer will elect to receive the maximum number of copies of the undeliverable product(s).
    (2) In arrangements in which no allocation can be made, until the first copy or product master of each product covered by the arrangement has been delivered to the customer, and assuming the four conditions set forth above are met, revenue should be recognized as copies of delivered products either (a) are reproduced by the customer, or (b) are furnished to the customer if the vendor is duplicating the software. Once the vendor has delivered the product master or the first copy of all products covered by the arrangement, any licensing fees not previously recognized should be recognized, since only duplication of the software is required to satisfy the vendor's delivery requirement and such duplication is incidental to the arrangement, so that delivery is deemed to have occurred upon delivery of the product master or first copy. When the arrangement terminates, the vendor should recognize any licensing fees not previously recognized. Revenue should not be recognized fully until at least one

of the following conditions is met: either (a) delivery is complete for all products covered by the arrangement, or (b) the aggregate revenue attributable to all copies of the software products delivered is equal to the fixed fee, provided that the vendor is not obligated to deliver additional software products under the arrangement.

(3) If the arrangement includes products that are not deliverable at inception and it imposes a maximum number of copies of the undeliverable product(s) to which the customer is entitled, then a portion of the arrangement fee should be allocated to the undeliverable product(s). This allocation should be made assuming that the customer will elect to receive the maximum number of copies of the undeliverable product(s).

(4) The revenue allocated to the delivered products should be recognized when the product master or first copy is delivered. If, during the term of the arrangement, the customer reproduces or receives enough copies of these delivered products so that revenue allocable to the delivered products exceeds the revenue previously recognized, such additional revenue should be recognized as the copies are reproduced or delivered. The revenue allocated to the undeliverable product(s) should be reduced by a corresponding amount.

7. The portion of the fee allocated to a contract element should be recognized when the four revenue recognition criteria are met with respect to the element. In applying those criteria, the delivery of an element is considered not to have occurred if there are undelivered elements that are essential to the functionality of the delivered element, because functionality of the delivered element would be impaired.
8. No portion of the fee can be deemed to be collectible if the portion of the fee allocable to delivered elements is subject to forfeiture, refund, or other concession if any of the undelivered elements are not delivered. If management represents that it will not provide refunds or concessions that are not required under the provisions of the arrangement, this assertion must be evaluated by reference to all available evidence. This evidence may include the following:

   a. Acknowledgment in the arrangement regarding products not currently available or not to be delivered currently;
   b. Separate prices stipulated in the arrangement for each deliverable element;
   c. Default and damage provisions as defined in the arrangement;
   d. Enforceable payment obligations and due dates for the delivered elements that are not dependent on the delivery of future deliverable elements, coupled with the intent of the vendor to enforce rights of payment;
   e. Installation and use of the delivered software; and

f. Support services, such as telephone support, related to the delivered software being provided currently by the vendor.

EMERGING ISSUES TASK FORCE CONSENSUS SUMMARIES

97-13 Accounting for Costs Incurred in Connection With a Consulting Contract or an Internal Project That Combines Business Process Reengineering and Information Technology Transformation

A consensus was reached that all expenditures incurred for business processs engineering activities (either by insiders or outsiders) should be expensed immediately. Guidance also applies when business engineering processing activities are part of development or implementation of internal-use software. Finally, the accounting for internal-use software development and acquisition of property, plant, and equipment are not affected by this consensus.

Another consensus was reached that in cases where a third party is engaged for a business process engineering project, the entire consulting contract price should be allocated to each activity on the basis of the relative fair values of the separate components. Finally, there was a consensus that any previously capitalized costs should be written off in the quarter in which November 20, 1997, falls. The write-off should be reported as a cumulative effect.

EMPLOYEE BENEFIT PLANS

PERSPECTIVE AND ISSUES

The purpose of *Audits of Employee Benefit Plans* is to assist in the auditing of and reporting on the financial statements of employee benefit plans, such as defined benefit pension plans, defined contribution plans, and employee health and welfare benefit plans. This guide applies to financial statements that are subject to ERISA and to those that are not. Accounting and reporting by defined benefit pension plans is presented in accordance with SFAS 35. Although SFAS 35 does not apply to defined contribution plans and employee health and welfare benefit plans, this audit guide describes the specialized accounting principles and practices for these plans in a manner consistent with SFAS 35. Information regarding statutory rules and regulations applicable to employee benefit plans is also included. Guidance in this publication is generally more detailed than in other audit guides. Illustrations of plan financial statements and auditors' reports are presented.

SFAS 130 requires enterprises that issue a complete set of general-purpose financial statements to report and display comprehensive income. However, entities that are not required to issue a statement of cash flows per SFAS 102 are not exempt if SFAS 130 applies otherwise. SFAS 130 does not apply to not-for-profits that follow SFAS 117 nor does it apply to enterprises with no items of other comprehensive income. The component entitled "other comprehensive income" shall classify items by their nature and should be displayed separately and prominently.

Sources of GAAP

AICPA Audit and Accounting Guide	SFAS	SOP
Audits of Employee Benefit Plans, 1998	35, 75, 102, 110, 130	92-6, 94-4

DEFINITIONS OF TERMS

Defined benefit pension plans. Determinable benefits are promised to participants based on factors such as compensation, years of service, and age.

Defined contribution plans. Each participant has an individual account. Benefits are based on amounts contributed, investment experience, and allocated forfeitures.

Health and welfare benefit plans. Plans that provide benefits such as medical, insurance, disability, vacation, education, and child care.

CONCEPTS, RULES, AND EXAMPLES

Employee benefit plans have become increasingly important and diverse. They may consist of a single employer or multiemployer plan. Contributory plans require contributions from employers and from participants whereas noncontributory plans receive contributions from employers only. Self-insured plans fund benefits from accumulated contributions and income, insured plans fund benefits through insurance contracts, and split-funded plans use a combination of both. Plans that have IRS approval are available.

Operation

An employee benefit plan is established and maintained by a plan sponsor. The plan's provisions deal with such matters as eligibility, entitlement, funding, plan amendments, operation and administration, allocation of responsibilities among specified fiduciaries, and delegation of duties. ERISA requires the plan to be in writing.

Accounting Records

The function of the accounting records is to provide information that will facilitate effective management and reliable financial reporting. The type of plan, number of employer contributors, benefit formula, benefit payment options, and delegation of administrative duties will determine the degree of complexity. The accounting records may be maintained at a variety of locations by trustees, insurance companies, consulting actuaries, service bureaus, the plan administrator, and plan sponsors.

The records of a plan should include

1. **Investment asset records**--ERISA requires detailed and extensive reporting.
2. **Participants' records**--These records are found in personnel and payroll and are used by the plan's actuary to determine eligibility for benefits. Periods of service, earnings, production, contributions, age, and breaks in service are factors to be considered by the actuary.
3. **Contribution records**--Separate records are used to record contributions and payments and to determine delinquencies and errors.
4. **Claim records**--Health and welfare plans use these records to determine benefit limits, types and amounts of claims, amounts paid, and timing of claims.
5. **Distribution records**--These records should support all distributions and should identify entitlements, amounts, commencement data, terminations, forfeitures, transfers, and information to determine the tax consequences of distributions.
6. **Separate participants' accounts**--Records which reflect each participant's share of the total net assets of the plan are required by defined contribution plans. The plan determines how changes in the value of net assets are allocated to the participants' accounts.

Defined Benefit Pension Plans

Since users of the plan's financial statements are likely to be most interested in the plan's ability to pay benefits when they become due, assets should be presented at fair value rather than at historical cost. An exception had previously been made for certain investment contracts (so-called GIC) issued by insurance companies and banks, which had been reportable at contract values. However, SFAS 110 eliminated this exception. Information about the participants' accumulated benefits should also be presented in the financial statements of these plans. Accrual basis financial statements should include

1. A statement of the net assets available for benefits (end of plan year)
2. A statement of changes in net assets available for benefits (end of plan year)
3. The actuarial present value of accumulated plan benefits
4. The significant effects of factors affecting the year-to-year change in accumulated plan benefits

Defined Contribution Plans

The financial statements should provide information about plan resources and stewardship responsibility, the results of transactions and events that affect those resources, and other factors necessary to understand the information provided. Accrual basis financial statements for benefits of the plan should include

1. A statement that includes information on net assets available as of the financial statement date
2. A statement of changes in net assets during the period

SOP 94-4 requires reporting of investment contracts with fully benefit-responsive features at contract value; other investment contracts should be reported at fair value. If these contracts incorporate mortality or morbidity risk, contract value may be used.

Health and Welfare Benefit Plans

The financial statements should provide information that is useful in assessing the plan's present and future ability to pay its benefit obligations when due. This objective is met by providing information about plan resources and stewardship responsibility, the results of transactions and events that affect the information about those resources and obligations, and other factors necessary to understand the information provided. Accrual basis financial statements should include

1. A statement of net assets of the plan, presenting assets and liabilities as of the end of the period
2. A statement of changes in net assets during the year

In addition, defined benefit plans should include

1. Information concerning end of the year benefit obligations

2. Information concerning significant factors affecting year-to-year changes in benefit obligations

This information should appear on the face of the financial statements and should identify the nature and classification of the obligations.

SOP 94-4, discussed above, also applies to Health and Welfare Plans.

FINANCE COMPANIES

PERSPECTIVE AND ISSUES

The specialized accounting and reporting principles and practices contained in *Audits of Finance Companies* (Audit and Accounting Guide, 1998); and SOP 92-3, *Accounting for Foreclosed Assets*, are preferable accounting principles for purposes of justifying a change of accounting principles.

Finance companies provide lending and financing services to consumers (consumer financing) and to business enterprises (commercial financing). Some financing companies engage solely in consumer or commercial financing activities; others engage in both types.

Manufacturers, retailers, wholesalers and other business enterprises may provide financing to encourage customers to buy their products or services. Such financing is known as captive financing activity, and may be provided by those companies or affiliated companies. Although most companies originally financed only their own products and services, many have expanded their financing activities to include a wide variety of products and services sold by unaffiliated businesses.

Consumer financing activities include direct consumer loans, retail sales contracts, and insurance services.

Commercial financing enterprises often provide a wide range of services, including factoring arrangements, revolving loans, installment and term loans, floor plan loans, and lease financing.

Sources of GAAP

SFAS	*FASB I*	*SOP*	*EITF*
91, 124, 127	41, 42	92-3, 96-1	95-22

DEFINITIONS OF TERMS

Accounts receivable loan. A loan collateralized by the accounts receivable of the borrower.

Dealer reserves. Finance company liabilities for dealers' shares of finance charges on retail contracts purchased from dealers.

Direct consumer loan. A two-party transaction in which the finance company lends funds directly to the borrower; such a loan may or may not be collateralized.

Discount. Amount deducted from the face value in advance as a charge for the loan or a deduction for interest at the time of the loan or any charge for credit that is precomputed and included in the face of the instrument.

Discount factoring. See **advance factoring**.

Discount loan. A loan that is written with the interest or finance charges included in the face amount of the note. Discount loans are also called **precompute** or **add-on loans.**

Effective interest rate. The implicit rate of interest based on the amount advanced and the amount and timing of the specified repayments over the period of the contract.

Factor. A company that engages primarily in factoring.

Factoring. Purchase, usually without recourse, of individual accounts receivable arising in the client's ordinary course of business. Under a factoring agreement, the finance company also provides credit checking, collection, and recordkeeping services.

Floor plan checking. Physical inspection of dealer's inventories that are collateral for advances to the dealer to be repaid from the proceeds from sale of specific items. Sometimes referred to as floor plan auditing.

Floor planning. Financing of dealers' inventories, particularly automobiles and other consumer goods, sometimes referred to as **wholesaling**. The dealers are obliged to repay the supplier or manufacturer from proceeds of sale of specific items, or after an elapsed period even though inventory is not sold.

Interest-bearing loan. A loan that is written at the principal amount advanced to the borrower and bearing interest computed monthly on the unpaid balance.

Interest method. A method of computing income under which interest income on a fixed-rate obligation is accrued over the life of the loan based on a constant rate (percent) of interest applied to the outstanding loan balance. As a result, the amount of income recognized at a given time is directly proportional to the outstanding loan balance. Also called the **actuarial method**.

Inventory loan. A loan collateralized by inventory of the borrower.

Nonrefundable fee. Any charge made in connection with a loan that does not have to be refunded to the borrower when the loan is prepaid.

Origination fee. An amount charged by finance companies for originating, refinancing, or restructuring a loan. The amount may be intended to cover costs such as underwriting, loan application processing, and reviewing legal title to property involved.

Overadvance (in factoring). An amount advanced to a client in excess of the amount of uncollected receivables purchased by the factor.

Points. Amounts, generally expressed as a percent of the loan, charged for granting loans, that primarily are adjustments of yield but also may be intended to cover costs such as underwriting, loan application processing, and reviewing title to collateral.

CONCEPTS, RULES, AND EXAMPLES

Finance Receivables

Finance receivables include both interest-bearing and discount loans. The face amount of an interest-bearing or simple interest loan is equal to the loan amount; no unearned interest is computed. Conversely, for discount loans the amount loaned is less than the face value of the loan. This difference represents unearned interest income to the borrower, and as such, it is recognized by the lender over the life of the loan.

Allowance for Loan Losses

The allowance for loan losses decreases the book value or carrying amount of loans receivable to net realizable value. SFAS 5, *Accounting for Contingencies*, and SFAS 14, *Reasonable Estimation of the Amount of a Loss*, provide accounting guidance on these issues. SFAS 5 requires that an allowance be established when it is probable that an asset has been impaired and an amount can be reasonably estimated.

Interest Income and Nonrefundable Loan Fees

The interest method should be used to account for interest income in accordance with SFAS 91, *Accounting for Nonrefundable Fees and Costs Associated with Originating or Acquiring Loans and Initial Direct Costs of Leases*. Under this method, often called the actuarial method, interest on installment loans is computed and accrued over the lives of the loans to arrive at constant interest rates throughout the loans' lives. Use of this method produces loans which are carried at amounts equal to future receipts discounted at original implicit interest rates. The accounting for nonrefundable loan fees is also covered in SFAS 91. (See the treatment of this area under the section on Banking and Thrift Industries p. 797).

Other Items

The accounting treatment for other items germane to finance companies is fully described in the Audit and Accounting Guide, *Audits of Finance Companies*. Such items include factoring commissions, advances and overadvances to factoring clients, repossessed assets acquired in liquidation of receivables, dealer reserves and holdbacks, and sales of receivables.

GOVERNMENT CONTRACTS

PERSPECTIVE AND ISSUES

ARB 43 (ch 11) covers the accounting and income recognition problems concerning cost-plus-fixed-fee and fixed-price supply contracts. The fees under government cost-plus-fixed-fee contracts may be recognized as income on the basis of partial performance if there is reasonable assurance of realization. Fees may also be accrued as they are billable unless this accrual is not reasonably related to the proportionate performance of total work to be performed.

This pronouncement also covers renegotiation (refunds of excessive profits) and contracts terminated for the convenience of the government.

Sources of GAAP
<u>*ARB*</u> 43, ch 11

DEFINITIONS OF TERMS

Contractors. Include prime contractors and subcontractors.

Contracts. Refer to prime contracts and subcontracts.

Cost-plus-fixed-fee contracts. Provide for contractors to receive a specified fixed fee and to be reimbursed for their allowable costs. Because title passes to the government and the contractor obtains an unconditional right to partial payment prior to delivery, delivery of the finished product is not necessarily evidence of performance.

Disposal credits. Deductions from the termination claim receivable for approved retention or sale of inventory previously included in the claim.

No-cost settlements. Settlements in which the contractor waives the right to make a claim. No sale should be recorded and applicable costs should retain their usual classification

Service contracts. Contracts in which the contractor acts only as an agent.

Supply contracts. Contract in which the contractor's services extend beyond that of an agent. Contracts include services such as the use of the contractor's own facilities and responsibility to creditors for material and services, and to employees for salaries.

Subcontractor's claims. Claims made in conjunction with a terminated contract are costs for the terminated contract that do not result in the transfer of billable materials or services to the contractor before termination.

CONCEPTS, RULES, AND EXAMPLES

Cost-plus-fixed-fee contracts (CPFFC) are used for the manufacture and delivery of products, the construction of plants and other facilities, and for management and other services. The amount of the flat fee payment is usually determined by the ratio of the actual expenditures to the total estimated expenditures. Because CPFFC may be cancelled and terminated by the government, the **contractor** is entitled to reimbursement for expenditures and an appropriate portion of the fixed fee.

Normally, profits are recognized when the right to full payment is unconditional. However, revenues can be accrued and profits recognized for partial performance when total profit can be reasonably estimated and realization is reasonably assured. The fees are usually accrued as they become billable. Because risk is minimal and there is no credit problem, billable amounts are indicative of realization. The contractor's fee is considered earned when it is billable and when the costs are incurred or paid. Accrual based on billable amounts is an application of the percentage-of-completion method, rather than a deviation from the accrual method. The fee is considered billable when approved by the government. An alternative date should be used when a determination is made that estimated and final costs are significantly different. Accrual of the fee upon delivery or based on percentage of completion would be more appropriate when excess costs are extensive.

For **supply contracts**, reimbursable costs and fees should be included in sales. For **service contracts**, only fees should be included in sales. Unbilled amounts should be included in the balance sheet as a receivable, but should be distinguished from billed items. Advances in CPFFC should be offset against **contract** receivables only when there is an expectation that the advances will be applied against those specific charges. Such offsets should be disclosed.

Renegotiation

Renegotiation typically addresses a refund of "excessive" profits. In reality, it is more of an adjustment of the selling price. The financial statement should indicate when a substantial portion of a contractor's business consists of contracts that are subject to renegotiation. When a reasonable estimate of renegotiation refunds can be made, a provision should be shown as a deduction from sales in the income statement and as a current liability on the balance sheet. Taxes should be adjusted accordingly. When a reasonable estimate cannot be made, disclosure is required along with the reasons for the inability to make an estimate. Footnote disclosure may also be required regarding material uncertainties and their significance, and regarding the basis for determining the renegotiation provision.

Terminated Defense Contracts

These contracts are contracts terminated for the convenience of the government. Profits accrue as of the effective date of termination and should be included in financial statements after the termination. Disclosure should be made of all material facts and circumstances. Termination claims should be recorded in one account and classified as current assets. They should be disclosed separately. Pretermination contract advances may be shown as a deduction from claims receivable, if adequately explained. Loans are current liabilities.

Termination claims should be accounted for as sales with separate disclosure, if material. When inventory is reacquired, after including it in a termination claim, it should be recorded as a purchase. The credit can be applied against the termination claim receivable.

INSURANCE INDUSTRY TRANSACTIONS

PERSPECTIVE AND ISSUES

The two major types of insurance companies are life and property and casualty. Each category is further subdivided into stock companies and mutual associations. Due to the regulated nature of the insurance industry, financial reporting may be in conformity to **statutory accounting principles (SAP)** or GAAP. Furthermore, publicly held companies subject to SEC accounting rules will account for certain transactions and events in other manners dictated by those requirements. While accounting principles under GAAP are broadly applicable to all types of insurance companies (including those dealing in such specialized products as mortgage insurance, title insurance, and reinsurance), the nature of the estimation process (such as for claims liabilities) differs substantially depending upon the character of the risks assumed.

The main contrasts between SAP and GAAP arise from the more conservative nature of SAP, which is a reflection of the insurance regulatory agencies' concern with protection of the policyholders' interests, and hence with the liquidity and solvency of the insurance companies. Accordingly, under SAP certain costs, such as policy acquisition expenses, are written off as incurred; certain nonliquid assets, such as property and furniture, are not recognized; and claims liabilities are very conservatively estimated. In contrast to this essentially short-term perspective, financial statements prepared on the GAAP basis are more concerned with the value of the companies' investments and net worth on a going concern basis.

The primary source of insurance industry GAAP is SFAS 60. Although mutual insurance companies and certain other organizations were not required to apply this standard, SFAS 120 extends its requirements to these enterprises. Insurance contracts are categorized as short duration (which includes most property and liability insurance) or long duration (which includes most life, mortgage, and title insurance). Nominal insurance contracts which are effectively investment contracts, however, are not accounted for as insurance. The Audit and Accounting Guide, *Audits of Property and Liability Insurance Companies*, was issued in June 1998.

Sources of GAAP

SFAS	FASB I	SOP	EITF
5, 60, 91, 97, 109, 113, 114, 115, 120, 124	40	92-4, 92-5, 94-5, 95-1, 97-3	92-9, 93-6, 93-14

CONCEPTS, RULES, AND EXAMPLES

Premium Income

Premium income is recognized differently for short and long duration contracts. For short duration contracts, premium income is recognized over the contract term in proportion to the amount of insurance provided. In the case of long duration contracts, revenue is accrued as the premiums become due from policyholders, except for contracts which provide benefits over a term longer than the premium payment term (such as 20-year life policies), in which case income is recognized over the longer period during which benefits may be provided.

Claim Cost Recognition

Costs of benefits are recognized when insured events such as property damage occur. Estimated costs are accrued for as claims incurred but not yet reported. For long duration contracts, the present values of estimated future benefits are accrued, net of the present values of future net premiums to be collected. Accrual of these benefit obligations generally involves actuarial determinations. Accountants may be dependent on the services of specialists in such cases, as they are in computing costs related to defined benefit pension plans. Recognition of other expenses is governed by the matching concept. For example, costs which vary with acquisition activity are capitalized and amortized over the period during which premium income is earned. Catastrophic losses (as from natural disasters such as hurricanes) are accrued under the guidelines of SFAS 5: when impairment of the asset or incurring of a liability is probable and the amount is reasonably estimable.

Investments

The other major concern of GAAP for insurance enterprises relates to the presentation of investments held. Prior GAAP (SFAS 60) has been revised by the issuance of SFAS 115, which establishes the accounting requirements for investments in debt and marketable equity securities. Briefly, those investments must be categorized as being either held-for-trading, available-for-sale, or held-to-maturity. Investments falling within the first two categories should be reported at fair value, with value changes affecting the trading securities portfolio being reflected in income, while changes in the available-for-sale portfolio are reported in a separate equity account. Securities to be held to maturity are accounted for at amortized historical cost, absent a permanent decline in value. Equity securities which do not meet the definition of "marketable" are also to be reported at fair value, with gains or losses reported in stockholders' equity.

Deferred Income Taxes

GAAP requires that deferred income taxes be provided for temporary differences. An exception was previously provided under the "indefinite reversal criterion," for stock life insurance companies only, for differences designated as policyholders' surplus. However, SFAS 109 provides that, for such differences arising after 1992, deferred taxes must be provided, consistent with the accounting prescribed for all other temporary differences. Furthermore, if changed circumstances suggest that pre-1993 differences are in fact differences which are likely to reverse, deferred taxes are to be provided, with the provision reflected in current period tax expense.

Other Matters

Another specialized topic area pertinent to insurance companies is that of reinsurance. After a lengthy period of development and discussion, a new standard, SFAS 113, was promulgated. This standard, which amends SFAS 60, eliminates the former practice of reporting assets and liabilities net of the effects of reinsurance. It requires that reinsurance receivables, including amounts related to claims incurred but not reported, be reported as assets, consistent with the manner in which liabilities relating to the underlying reinsured contracts are accounted for. The standard also establishes criteria for recognition as reinsurance, and sets forth detailed accounting for long and short duration contracts, as well as new disclosure requirements. The Board also ended another long-standing controversy by releasing Interpretation 40, which clarifies that GAAP applies essentially equally to mutual insurance companies as it does to stock companies, unless explicit exceptions were established. Regulatory reporting can no longer, therefore, be deemed to be in accordance with GAAP.

The AICPA has also been actively reviewing insurance company accounting practices and auditing issues. SOP 92-4 addressed matters relating to estimation of loss reserves, and a number of auditing concerns relating to reserves, reinsurance, loss adjustment expenses, and other topics. SOP 92-5 concerns accounting for foreign property and liability reinsurance, and concludes that except for special circumstances, only the periodic method is acceptable in accounting for foreign reinsurance premiums. SOP 94-5 requires disclosures where permission was received from the National Association of Insurance Commissioners to use different accounting practices. SOP 95-1 covers capitalization and amortization costs and several other matters for mutual life insurance companies. SFAS 120 requires that the provision of this SOP be applied to assessment enterprises, fraternal benefit societies, and stock life insurance companies.

A recently issued SOP addresses matters pertaining to guaranty funds and certain other insurance-related assessments. Existing practice has been quite diverse, but the new SOP essentially applies the criteria of SFAS 5, *Accounting for Contingencies*, to these matters, with the exception that practice can be substantially conformed. The key elements of SOP 97-3 are discussed in the following paragraphs.

Under the new standard, guaranty fund and similar assessments would be recognized when (1) is has been imposed or is deemed probable of being imposed, (2) the event obligating an entity to pay the assessment has occurred, and (3) the amount of the assessment can be reasonably estimated. All three conditions would have to be fulfilled before a liability could be accrued. Discounting to present value will be permitted. The SOP offers specific guidance regarding the ability to reasonably estimate the liability for assessments.

Guaranty funds are essentially state-mandated insurance funds used to settle claims against insolvent insurers and, typically, all licensed insurers are assessed premiums based on the volume of defined lines of business they conduct in the given state. A variety of methods have been applied in determining the amounts of guaranty fund assessments (e.g., retrospectively, based on premiums written over the past 2 years; or prospectively, based on business written over the next several years following an insolvency of a failed insurer), with the result that entities upon which assessments are being levied have been inclined to use different methods of recognizing the cost and related obligation. In general, to warrant accrual under SOP 97-3, an insolvency of another insurer would have to have occurred, since the presumption would be that the assessments would become probable (the threshold criterion) when there has been a formal determination of another entity's insolvency. An example of an exception would be when the state uses prospective premium-based guaranty fund assessments; if the reporting entity **cannot** avoid the obligation by ceasing to write policies, the obligating event would be the determination of insolvency, but if it **could** avoid the assessment, the obligating event is the writing of premiums **after** the insolvency.

A recent AICPA practice bulletin affects accounting by certain insurance companies which issue a security known as surplus notes. Practice Bulletin 15, *Accounting by the Issuer of Surplus Notes*, requires that these instruments be accounted for as debt and included in the liabilities caption of the balance sheet. Furthermore, interest must be accrued over the term of the notes, whether or not payment of interest and/or principal has been approved by an insurance company. However, disclosure is required as to the status of the request for approval.

A number of other insurance-industry-related projects are being pursued by the AICPA at this time. One of these is to complete a replacement for the 1972 Audit and Accounting Guide applicable to life and health insurance entities. This reportedly is near completion and will not contain any new accounting guidance, although it will impose new or expanded audit requirements. Another project, to produce an industry accounting guide for insurance agents and brokers, was dropped after several years of development, when the intended beneficiaries could not agree on a number of key matters.

The AICPA is deliberating on an important issue, the application of deposit accounting for certain insurance and reinsurance contracts, which was made necessary by the issuance of SFAS 113 and the resolution of several EITF issues. It has been observed that existing guidance on the use of deposit accounting does not provide adequate assistance regarding the application of this accounting technique to insurance or reinsurance contracts, and that existing guidance is difficult to analogize to those other situations. Accordingly, a proposed SOP would provide instruction on how to apply deposit accounting to insurance and reinsurance contracts; it would not offer rules as to when deposit accounting would be required, however. Reportedly, the project would affect all entities which enter into insurance and reinsurance contracts that do not indemnify against both underwriting and timing risks, but would exclude long duration life on health insurance contracts that do not indemnify against mortality or morbidity risk, since guidance is provided by SFAS 97 and 113. Also, the SOP is expected to provide that, once a loss is incurred that will be reimbursed under a reinsurance or insurance agreement which transfers significant underwriting risk only, the deposit would be measured by the present value of expected future cash flows discounted at the current risk-free rate available in the market, adjusted for default risk, and this rate would be used for the duration of the contract. A revised exposure draft is expected before year-end 1998, with a final standard also promised in 1998.

Finally, the AICPA is contemplating issuing either an SOP or an industry audit and accounting guide on mass tort exposure of insurance enterprises. This would include guidance on accounting issues that arise in connection with such mass tort exposures as asbestos and environmental claims and address how the various components of such liabilities are to be measured. Further, it would deal with application of present value concepts to mass tort liabilities and consider the methods used to estimate these obligations. Disclosure requirements would also be established.

EMERGING ISSUES TASK FORCE CONSENSUS SUMMARIES

92-9 Accounting for the Present Value of Future Profits Resulting From the Acquisition of a Life Insurance Company

The Task Force noted that industry practice is to amortize the present value of future profits (PVP) using an interest method with accrual of interest added to the unamortized balance. In the past, there has been some diversity in the application of this method in practice, and so the EITF has worked to standardize this practice. The first consensus reached was that the interest rate used to amortize PVP should be the liability or contract rate. The second consensus was that changes in estimates of future gross profits on SFAS 97 contracts should be accounted for as a catch-up adjustment. And finally, PVP and any related liability should be subject to the premium deficiency test required in SFAS 60 and 97.

93-6 Accounting for Multiple-Year Retrospectively-Rated Contracts by Ceding and Assuming Enterprises

A number of issues involving retrospective rating provisions contained in reinsurance contracts were resolved in this set of consensuses. These address criteria for the recognition and amounts of assets and liabilities by the assuming and ceding enterprises, respectively, and accounting for changes in coverage during the reinsurance period. A number of conditions were identified, satisfaction of which are necessary for a contract to be treated as reinsurance, and in their absence such contracts are to be accounted for by the deposit method.

93-14 Accounting for Multiple-Year Retrospectively-Rated Insurance Contracts by Insurance Enterprises and Other Enterprises

This EITF addresses how enterprises other than insurance companies should account for contracts with insurance companies covering various types of risks such as product and environmental liability risks. This EITF also addresses "pooled risk" contracts and reinsurance contracts entered into by a captive insurer. A consensus was reached that in order for a contract to be considered insurance it must indemnify the insured party as this would result in a transfer of risk. If no transfer of risk exists (SFAS 5, paragraph 45), then the contract is not considered insurance, and the balance of the premium less any amount to be retained by the insurer should be accounted for as a deposit. Other consensuses follow those reached in EITF Issue 93-6.

STATEMENTS OF POSITION

94-5 Disclosures of Certain Matters in the Financial Statements of Insurance Enterprises

Supplements the disclosure requirements in other FASB and SEC pronouncements. Required disclosures are set forth for insurance enterprises which have received permission by the insurance department in their domiciliary states to use accounting practices other than those prescribed by state laws, regulations, and rules and by the National Association of Insurance Commissioners (NAIC). This statement also defines liability for unpaid claims and claims adjustment expenses and lists the related disclosures required.

95-1 Accounting for Certain Insurance Activities of Mutual Life Insurance Enterprises

Provides guidance on applying SFAS 60, 97, and 113 in accounting for mutual life insurance contracts. Capitalization and amortization of acquisition costs is discussed. Premiums are to be reported as revenue when due from policyholders. Death and surrender benefits are reported as expenses, and annual dividends are reported separately as expenses. The calculation of estimated gross margin and liability for future policy benefits is described.

INVESTMENT COMPANIES

PERSPECTIVE AND ISSUES

The specialized accounting and reporting principles and practices contained in *Audits of Investment Companies* (Audit and Accounting Guide, 1998); SOP 74-11, *Financial Accounting and Reporting by Face-Amount Certificate Companies*; SOP 77-1, *Financial Accounting and Reporting by Investment Companies*; and SOP 79-1, *Accounting for Municipal Bond Funds*, are preferable accounting principles for purposes of justifying a change in accounting principles. Highly liquid investment companies may be exempt from the requirement to provide a statement of cash flows as a part of a full set of financial statements. Investment companies subject to the Investment Company Act of 1940 or having essentially the same characteristics as those subject to the 1940 Act are exempted from providing a statement of cash flows. Additionally, common trust funds, variable annuity accounts, and other similar funds are exempted.

An investment company pools shareholders' funds to provide shareholders with professional investment management. Investment companies' activities include selling capital shares to the public, investing the proceeds in securities, and distributing net income and net realized gains to its shareholders.

Sources of GAAP

SFAS	*SOP*
102, 126	93-1, 93-2, 93-4, 95-2, 95-3

DEFINITIONS OF TERMS

Closed-end fund. An investment company having a fixed number of shares outstanding, which it does not stand ready to redeem. Its shares are traded similarly to those of other public corporations.

Closed-up fund. An open-ended investment company that no longer offers its shares for sale to the general public but still stands ready to redeem its outstanding shares.

Equalization. An accounting method used to prevent a dilution of the continuing shareholders' per share equity in undistributed net investment income caused by the continuous sales and redemptions of capital shares.

Ex-dividend or ex-distribution. Synonym for **shares being traded without dividend or without capital gains distribution**. The buyer of a stock selling ex-dividend does not acquire a right to receive a previously declared but not-yet-paid dividend. Dividends are payable on a fixed date to shareholders recorded on the stock transfer books of the disbursing company as of a previous date of record. For example, a dividend may be declared as payable to holders of record on the books of the disbursing company on a given Friday. Because five business days are allowed for delivery of the security in regular-way transactions on a stock exchange or over-the-counter, the exchange or the NASD declares the stock ex-dividend as of the opening of the market on the preceding Monday or on one business day earlier for each intervening nontrading day. Therefore, anyone buying the stock on and after Monday is not entitled to the dividend. In the case of nontraded shares of mutual funds, the ex-dividend date is the same as the record date.

Open-end investment company. A mutual fund that is ready to redeem its shares at any time and that usually offers its shares for sale to the public continuously.

CONCEPTS, RULES, AND EXAMPLES

Accounting Policies

The accounting policies for an investment company result from the company's role as a vehicle through which investors can invest as a group. These policies are largely governed by the SEC, Small Business Administration, and specific provisions of the Internal Revenue Code relating to investment companies.

Investment companies report all investment securities at market value, or if quoted market values are not available, at fair values as determined by management. Along with other industry groups for which specialized GAAP already existed, calling for presentation of all investments at market value (a group that includes broker-dealers and defined benefit pension plans), investment companies were exempted from the provisions of SFAS 115.

Security purchases and sales are generally recorded at the trade date; therefore, the effects of all securities trades entered into by the investment company to the date of the financial statements are included in the financial report.

Investment companies record dividend income on the ex-dividend date, not on the later record or payable date. The rationale for this treatment is that the market price of market securities may be affected by the exclusion of the declared dividend. Additionally, investment companies record a liability for dividends payable on the ex-dividend date because mutual fund shares are purchased and redeemed at prices equal to or based on net asset value. If investors purchase shares between the declaration and ex-dividend dates they are entitled to receive dividends; however, investors purchasing shares after the ex-dividend date are not entitled to receive dividends.

Open-end investment companies often employ the practice of equalization. This theory states that the net asset value of each share of capital stock sold comprises the par value of the stock, undistributed income, and paid-in capital and other surplus. When shares are sold or repurchased, the investment company calculates the amount of undistributed income available for distribution to its shareholders. Based on the number of shares outstanding, the investment company determines the per share amount; this amount is credited to an equalization account when shares are sold. Conversely, the equalization account is charged when shares are repurchased.

Accounting for High-Yield Debt Securities

An amendment to the Industry Audit and Accounting Guide, *Audits of Investment Companies*, addresses accounting by creditors for investments in "step interest" and "PIK" debt securities, if these qualify as "high-yield" securities. Step interest bonds are generally unsecured debentures which pay no interest for a specified period after issuance, then pay a stipulated rate for a period, then a higher rate for another period, etc., until maturity. Thus, they combine some of the characteristics of zero-coupon bonds with some features of current interest bonds. PIK (payment in kind) bonds pay some or all interest in the form of other debt instruments ("baby" or "bunny" bonds), which in turn may also pay interest in the form of baby bonds. All babies mature at the due date of the parent bond.

The Guide, as amended, requires that the effective interest method should be used for step interest bonds; to the extent that interest income is not expected to be realized, a reserve against the income should be established. A previously employed technique, the bifurcation method, is no longer acceptable. For PIK bonds, the effective interest method is also required; the market value method, which was widely used in the past, can no longer be employed.

Exemptions From the Requirement to Provide a Statement of Cash Flows

The following conditions must be met for an investment company to be exempted from providing a statement of cash flows:

1. Substantially all of the entity's investments were highly liquid.
2. The entity's investments are carried at market value.
3. The entity had little or no debt, based on average debt outstanding during the period, in relation to average total assets.
4. The entity provides a statement of changes in net assets.

Taxes

Investment companies that distribute all taxable income and taxable realized gains qualifying under Subchapter M of the Internal Revenue Code are not required to record a provision for federal income taxes. If the investment company does not distribute all taxable income and taxable realized gains, a liability should be recorded at the end of the last day of the taxable year. The rationale for recording on the last day of the year is that only shareholders of record at that date are entitled to credit for taxes paid.

STATEMENTS OF POSITION

93-1 Financial Accounting and Reporting for High-Yield Debt Securities by Investment Companies

The Division concluded that for PIK and step bonds, (1) the effective-interest method should be used to determine interest income; (2) a reserve against income should be established for interest income not expected to be realized; (3) the cost plus any discount should not exceed undiscounted future cash collections; (4) SEC yield-formula calculations must be made; and (5) all high-yield and restricted debt securities whose values were estimated should be indicated in the portfolio. For defaulted debt securities, any interest receivable written off that had been recognized as income constitutes a reduction of income. Write-offs of purchased interest increase the cost basis and represent an unrealized loss until the security is sold. "Capital infusions" are accounted for as an addition to the cost basis, while related "workout expenditures" are recorded as unrealized losses. Any ongoing expenditures to protect the value of the investment are recorded as operating expenses. Auditors should consider additional pricing valuation audit procedures.

93-2 Determination, Disclosure, and Financial Statement Presentation of Income, Capital Gain, and Return of Capital Distributions by Investment Companies

This statement was developed to clarify the reporting of shareholder distributions that exceed the tax-basis current and accumulated earnings and profits in GAAP financial statements. The statement recommends that the caption "tax return of capital" be used to report such distributions.

93-4 Foreign Currency Accounting and Financial Statement Presentation for Investment Companies

Transactions denominated in a foreign currency must originally be measured in that currency. Reporting exchange rate gains and losses separately from any gain/loss on the investment due to changes in market price is allowable but not required.

95-2 Financial Reporting by Nonpublic Investment Partnerships

This statement pertains to investment partnerships which are exempt from SEC registration under the Investment Company Act of 1940. Specifically, the statement requires that the financial statements include a condensed schedule of securities which categorizes investments by type, country or geographic region, and industry; discloses pertinent information concerning investments comprising greater than 5% of net assets; and aggregates any securities holdings less than the 5% of net assets threshold. The statement of operations for nonpublic investment companies shall be presented in conformity with requirements for public investment companies per the *Audit Guide* so as to reflect their comparable operations. The financial statements shall also present management fees and disclose their computation.

95-3 Accounting for Certain Distribution Costs of Investment Companies

This statement requires investment companies with enhanced 12b-1 plans or board-contingent plans for which the board has committed to pay costs to recognize a liability and the related expense, for the amount of excess costs. This liability should be discounted at an appropriate current rate if the amount and timing of cash flows are reliably determinable and if distribution costs are not subject to a reasonable interest charge. Excess costs are recorded as a liability as the fund has assumed an obligation to pay the 12b-1 fee after the termination of the plan to the extent that the distributor has excess costs.

MORTGAGE BANKING ACTIVITIES

PERSPECTIVE AND ISSUES

Mortgage banking comprises two activities.

1. The origination or purchase of mortgage loans and subsequent sale to **permanent investors**, and
2. Long-term **servicing** of the mortgage loan.

Mortgage loans and mortgage-backed securities held for sale, origination costs, premiums paid to acquire mortgage loans, loan origination fees, and other fees are accounted for in accordance with SFAS 65, 91, and FASB Technical Bulletin 87-3. These pronouncements also apply to other companies that conduct operations similar to the operations of a mortgage banking entity. However, these pronouncements do not apply to the normal lending activities of those other enterprises. Mortgage loans held for sale are valued at lower of cost or market. Mortgage-backed securities are reported under SFAS 115, loan origination fees and related direct costs for loans held for sale are capitalized as part of the related loan and shall not be amortized. Fees and costs for loans held for investment are deferred and recognized as an adjustment to the yield.

The FASB is working on a proposed amendment to SFAS 65. The Mortgage Banker's Association of America requested a reconsideration of the provisions of SFAS 65 as amended by SFAS 115 and 125. Under these provisions, in a securitization of a mortgage held for sale, the resulting mortgage-backed securities shall be classified as a trading security. The problem is that classification as a trading security is required even if the mortgage banker does not intend to sell such securities in the near term. An exposure draft is scheduled for release in the third quarter of 1998.

Sources of GAAP

SFAS	*FASB TB*	*SOP*
65, 91	87-3	97-1

DEFINITIONS OF TERMS

Affiliated enterprise. An enterprise that directly or indirectly controls, is controlled by, or is under common control with another enterprise; also, a party with which the enterprise may deal if one party has the ability to exercise significant influence over the other's operating and financial policies.

Current (normal) servicing fee rate. A servicing fee rate that is representative of servicing fee rates most commonly used in comparable servicing agreements covering similar types of mortgage loans.

Federal Home Loan Mortgage Corporation (FHLMC). Often referred to as "Freddie Mac," FHLMC is a private corporation authorized by Congress to assist in the development and maintenance of a secondary market in conventional residential mortgages. FHLMC purchases mortgage loans and sells mortgages principally through mortgage participation certificates (PC) representing an undivided interest in a group of conventional mortgages. FHLMC guarantees the timely payment of interest and the collection of principal on the PC.

Federal National Mortgage Association (FNMA). Often referred to as "Fannie Mae," FNMA is an investor-owned corporation established by Congress to support the secondary mortgage loan market by purchasing mortgage loans when other investor funds are limited and selling mortgage loans when other investor funds are available.

Gap commitment. A commitment to provide interim financing while the borrower is in the process of satisfying provisions of a permanent loan agreement, such as obtaining a designated occupancy level on an apartment project. The interim loan ordinarily finances the difference between the floor loan (the portion of a mortgage loan commitment that is less than the full amount of the commitment) and the maximum permanent loan.

Government National Mortgage Association (GNMA). Often referred to as "Ginnie Mae," GNMA is a US governmental agency that guarantees certain types of securities (mortgage-backed securities) and provides funds for and administers certain types of low-income housing assistance programs.

Internal reserve method. A method for making payments to investors for collections of principal and interest on mortgage loans by issuers of GNMA securities. An issuer electing the internal reserve method is required to deposit in a custodial account an amount equal to one month's interest on the mortgage loans that collateralize the GNMA security issued.

Mortgage-backed securities. Securities issued by a governmental agency or corporation (e.g., GNMA or FHLMC) or by private issuers (e.g., FNMA, banks, and mortgage banking enterprises). Mortgage-backed securities generally are referred to as **mortgage participation certificates** or **pass-through certificates** (PC). A PC represents an undivided interest in a pool of specific mortgage loans. Periodic payments on GNMA PC are backed by the US government. Periodic payments on FHLMC and FNMA PC are guaranteed by those corporations, but are not backed by the US government.

Mortgage banking enterprise. An enterprise that is engaged primarily in originating, marketing, and servicing real estate mortgage loans for other than its own account. Mortgage banking enterprises, as local representatives of institutional lenders, act as correspondents between lenders and borrowers.

Permanent investor. An enterprise that invests in mortgage loans for its own account, for example, an insurance enterprise, commercial or mutual savings bank, savings and loan association, pension plan, real estate investment trust, or FNMA.

Servicing. Mortgage loan servicing includes collecting monthly mortgagor payments, forwarding payments and related accounting reports to investors, collecting escrow deposits for the payment of mortgagor property taxes and insurance, and paying taxes and insurance from escrow funds when due.

Standby commitment. A commitment to lend money with the understanding that the loan probably will not be made unless permanent financing cannot be obtained from another source. Standby commitments ordinarily are used to enable the borrower to obtain construction financing on the assumption that permanent financing will be available on more favorable terms when construction is completed. Standby commitments normally provide for an interest rate substantially above the market rate in effect when the commitment is issued.

CONCEPTS, RULES, AND EXAMPLES

Mortgage Loans and Mortgage-Backed Securities

Valuation. Mortgage loans held for sale are reported at the lower of cost or market as of the balance sheet date. Any excess of cost over market should be accounted for as a valuation allowance, changes in which are to be included in income currently. During the period such loans are held for sale, any related purchase discounts may not be amortized as interest revenue.

Mortgage-backed securities held for sale are to be accounted for as trading securities as defined by SFAS 115. The securitization of mortgage loans held for sale should be accounted for as a sale of the mortgage loans and the purchase of mortgage-backed securities, which are to be classified as trading securities and accounted for at fair value.

The market value of mortgage loans and mortgage-backed securities held for sale is to be determined by type of loan; at a minimum, separate determinations must be made for residential and commercial loans. Either an aggregate or individual loan basis may be used in determining the lower of cost or market for each type. Market values for loans subject to investor purchase commitments (committed loans) and loans held for speculative purposes (uncommitted loans) must be determined separately.

For committed loans and mortgage-backed securities, market value is defined by the commitment prices. For committed mortgage-backed securities, if the fair value exceeds the commitment price, the implicit loss must be taken into income. If the commitment price for committed loans provides for servicing fee rates materially different from current fee rates, the price must be adjusted as described under "Servicing Fees," below.

Fair value for uncommitted mortgage-backed securities collateralized by the entity's own loans ordinarily should be based on the market value of the securities. If the trust holding the loans may be terminated and the loans sold directly, fair value for the securities should be based on the market value of the loans or the securities, depending on the entity's intentions. Fair value for other uncommitted mortgage-backed securities should be based on published yield data.

The capitalized costs of servicing rights are excluded from loan cost in calculating lower of cost or market values.

A mortgage loan or mortgage-backed security may not be reported as a long-term investment unless the mortgage banker is both able to and intends to hold the loan or security to maturity or at least into the foreseeable future. These assets are transferred to a long-term investment classification at the lower of cost or market on the date of transfer. If the carrying amount differs from the outstanding principal balance, then the yield is adjusted by the interest method.

Uncollectibility. If full recovery of the carrying amount of a mortgage loan or mortgage-backed security held as a long-term investment is permanently impaired, then the carrying amount should be written down to its expected recoverable amount. This amount becomes the new cost basis and the amount of the write-down is a period loss. Any recovery from the new basis may be reported as a gain **only** upon the maturity or disposition of the loan or security.

Repurchase agreements. Mortgage loans or mortgage-backed securities held for sale may be temporarily transferred by a mortgage banker to another financial institution under a formal or informal agreement which serves as a means of financing these assets. Loans and securities transferred under such agreements are accounted for as collateralized financing arrangements and are still reported as held for sale.

A formal repurchase agreement specifies that the mortgage banker retains control over future economic benefits and also the risk of loss relating to the loans or securities transferred. These assets are subsequently reacquired from the financial institution upon the sale of the assets by the mortgage banking enterprise to permanent investors.

An informal repurchase agreement exists when no formal agreement has been made but loans or securities are transferred by a mortgage banking enterprise which

1. Is the sole marketer of the assets
2. Retains any interest spread on the assets
3. Retains risk of loss in market value
4. Reacquires uncollectible loans
5. Regularly reacquires most or all of the assets and sells them to permanent investors.

When mortgage loans held for sale are transferred under a repurchase arrangement, they should continue to be reported by the transferor as loans held for sale. Mortgage-backed securities sold under agreements to repurchase should be reported as trading securities as defined in SFAS 115.

Servicing Mortgage Loans

Rights to service mortgage loans for others must be recognized as separate assets by mortgage banking enterprises. If the enterprise acquires such rights through purchase or origination of mortgage loans and retains them upon sale or securitization, the total cost of the mortgage loans must be allocated between the rights and the loans (sans the rights) based on their relative fair market values. If it is impossible to determine the fair value of the mortgage servicing rights apart from the mortgage, the transferor shall record the mortgage servicing rights at zero value (SFAS 12, para 45). Mortgage servicing rights are capitalized at their fair value and recognized as a net asset if the benefits of servicing the mortgage are expected to be more than adequate compensation to the server for performing the duties. If the benefits of servicing the mortgage are not expected to adequately compensate the server, then the server recognizes a liability. The asset Mortgage Servicing Contract Rights is initially measured at its fair market value and subsequently impaired in the following manner:

1. The mortgage servicing assets are stratified based on predominant risk characteristics.
2. Impairment is recognized through a valuation allowance for an individual stratum. The amount of impairment equals the carrying amount for a particular stratum minus their fair market value.
3. The valuation allowance is adjusted to reflect changes in the measurement of impairment after the initial measurement of impairment.

Servicing fees. Servicing fees are usually based on a percentage of the outstanding principal balance of the mortgage loan. When a mortgage loan is sold with servicing rights retained, the sales price must be adjusted if the stated rate is materially different from the **current (normal) servicing fee rate** so that the gain or loss on the sale may be determined. The adjustment is

$$\text{Adjustment} = \begin{array}{c}\text{Actual}\\ \text{Sales}\\ \text{Price}\end{array} - \begin{array}{c}\text{Estimated sales price}\\ \text{obtainable if normal}\\ \text{servicing fee rate had}\\ \text{been used}\end{array}$$

This adjustment allows for recognition of normal servicing fees in subsequent years.

The adjustment and any recognized gain or loss are determined as of the sale date. If estimated normal servicing fees are less than total expected servicing costs, then this loss should be accrued on the sale date as well.

Sales to Affiliated Enterprises

When mortgage loans or mortgage-backed securities are sold to an **affiliated enterprise**, the carrying amount of the assets must be adjusted to lower of cost or market as of the date that management decides that the sale will occur. This date is evidenced by formal approval by a representative of the affiliated enterprise (purchaser), issuance of a purchase commitment, and acceptance of the purchase commitment by the seller. Any adjustment is charged to income.

If a group of (or all) mortgage loans are originated specifically for an affiliate, then the originator is an agent of the affiliated enterprise. In this case, the loans are transferred at the originator's cost of acquisition. This treatment does not apply to "right of first refusal" or similar contracts in which the originator retains all risks of ownership.

Issuance of GNMA

An issuer of GNMA securities who elects the **internal reserve method** must pay 1-month's interest cost to a trustee. This cost is capitalized (at no greater than the present value of net future servicing income) and amortized.

Loan and Commitment Fees and Costs

Mortgage bankers may pay or receive loan and commitment fees as compensation for various loan administration services. These fees and costs are accounted for as described in the following paragraphs.

Loan origination. Loan origination fees and direct costs must be deferred. If the loan is later held for resale, these fees and costs are recognized upon sale of the loan. If the loan is held for investment, loan origination fees and costs are recognized as an adjustment of yield.

Services rendered. Fees for specific services rendered by third parties as part of a loan origination (e.g., appraisal fees) are recognized as revenue when the services are performed.

Loans held for sale. Residential or commercial loan commitment fees paid to permanent investors are recognized as expense when the loans are sold or when it is determined that the commitment will not be used. Since residential loan commitment fees typically cover groups of loans, the amount of fees recognized as revenue or expense relating to an individual transaction is calculated as

$$\text{Revenue or expense recognized on individual transaction} = \text{Total residential loan commitment fee} \times \frac{\text{Amount of individual loan}}{\text{Total commitment amount}}$$

Loan placement fees (fees for arranging a commitment directly between investor and borrower) are recognized as revenue once all significant services have been performed. In some cases, a mortgage banker secures a commitment from a permanent investor before or at the same time as a commitment is made to a borrower and the latter commitment requires

1. Simultaneous assignment to the investor, and
2. Simultaneous transfer to the borrower of amounts paid by the investor.

The fees related to such transactions are also accounted for as loan placement fees.

Expired commitments or early repayment of loans. At the time that a loan commitment expires unused or is repaid before repayment is due, any related fees which had been deferred are recognized as revenue or expense.

Reporting

Mortgage banking enterprises must, on the balance sheet, distinguish between mortgage loans and mortgage-backed securities which are held for sale and those which are held for long-term investment.

STATEMENT OF POSITION

97-1 Accounting by Participating Mortgage

Establishes the borrower's accounting for a participating mortgage loan if the lender participates in increases in the market value of the mortgaged real estate project, the results of operations of that mortgaged real estate project, or both. It requires that certain disclosures must be made in the financial statements. In addition, this SOP requires the following: (1) At origination, if the lender is entitled to participate in appreciation in the market value of the mortgaged real estate project, the borrower should determine the fair value of the participation feature and should recognize a participation liability for that amount. A corresponding debit should then be recorded to a debt-discount account. The debt discount should be amortized by the interest method, using the effective interest rate. (2) At the end of each reporting period, the balance of the participation liability should be adjusted if necessary, so that the liability equals the fair value of the participation feature at that point in time. The corresponding debit or credit should be adjusted to the related debt-discount account. The revised debt discount should then be amortized prospectively.

MOTION PICTURE INDUSTRY

PERSPECTIVE AND ISSUES

SFAS 53 sets forth accounting and reporting standards for the motion picture industry. These standards apply to film producers (motion picture enterprises) independent producers, and distributors (licensors). Independent producers receive advance funds or guaranteed loans from motion picture companies for the production of films. Distributors own the rights to distribute films. This definition excludes syndicators or other independent sales organizations that act only as sales agents or owners of films under agreements that do not call for sharing of profits. Motion picture films may be licensed to movie theaters, to television broadcasters, or for use in the home viewing market.

Sources of GAAP

SFAS	*EITF*
53	87-10

DEFINITIONS OF TERMS

Distributor (film distributor). [Owner of] the rights to distribute films, which are sold (licensed) to movie theaters, individual television stations, groups of stations, networks, or others. This definition excludes syndicators or other independent sales organizations that act only as sales agents for producers or owners of films under agreements that do not call for the sharing of profits.

Exploitation costs. Costs incurred during the final production phase and during the release periods of films in both primary and secondary markets. Examples of such costs are film prints, advertising, rents, salaries, and other distribution expenses.

Home viewing market. Includes all means by which films are sold or otherwise made available to residential viewers for a fee. Examples are video cassettes and disks and all forms of pay television, including cable and over-the-air transmission.

Independent producer. Motion picture companies frequently advance funds or guarantee loans for the production of films by independent producers. Certain legal rights of ownership, including the copyright, may be retained by the independent producer. The motion picture company frequently has a participation in the net revenues from the film and generally has additional attributes of ownership, such as the right to exploit the film and the risk of loss. The financing arrangement usually provides that the production loan by the motion picture company (or the guaranteed loan) is repayable only from the revenues from the particular film. The independent producer does not have general liability with respect to such a loan. Consequently, the motion picture company bears substantially all the risks of ownership.

License agreement for television program material. A typical license agreement for television program material covers several films (a package) and grants a broadcaster (licensee) the right to telecast either a specified number or an unlimited number of showings over a maximum period of time (license period) for a specified fee. Ordinarily, the fee is paid in installments over a period generally shorter than the license period. The agreement usually contains a separate license for each film in the package. The license expires at the earlier of the last allowed telecast or the end of the license period. The licensee pays the required fee whether or not the rights are exercised. If the licensee does not exercise the contractual rights, the rights revert to the licensor with no refund to the licensee. The license period generally is not intended to provide continued use of the film throughout that period but rather to define a reasonable period of time within which the licensee can exercise the limited rights to use the film.

Market. The first market in which a film is exploited is called the primary market because that is the market for which a film principally is produced. All other exploitation is in the secondary market. Generally, the markets are mutually exclusive; that is, a film cannot be exploited in more than one market at a time because of the contract terms or sound marketing techniques.

There is only one first-run telecast of a particular film in a given market, and film rights are marketed in a manner to avoid conflict in a given market. For example, conflict may exist in a market between (1) theaters and television stations, (2) premium cable or broadcast subscription television and network television, (3) network television and local stations, and (4) two or more local stations within the market area. To avoid conflict between theaters and television, a producer may impose restrictions on distribution that would prohibit the licensing of the film for television while the film is being shown in movie theaters.

The market in which a film is exhibited is a prime determinant of the value of the film. A film's previous exposure in a market will generally have an effect on the price the exhibitor is willing to pay for exhibition rights. In addition, the size and demographics of a particular market and the audience's acceptance of the film affect the price that a telecaster can charge for advertising time.

Motion picture film. The term **film** refers to all types of films and video cassettes and disks, including features, television specials, series, and cartoons that are (1) exhibited in theaters; (2) licensed for exhibition by individual television stations, groups of stations, networks, cable television systems, or other means; or (3) licensed for the home viewing market.

Net realizable value. Net realizable value is the estimated selling price (rental value) in the ordinary course of business less estimated costs to complete and exploit in a manner consistent with realization of that income.

Participation. Frequently, persons involved in the production of a motion picture film are compensated, in part or in full, with a participation in the income from the film. Determination of the amount of compensation payable to the participant is usually based on percentages of revenues or profits from the film from some or all sources. Television residuals are comparable to participations and are generally based on the number of times the film is exhibited on television or as a percentage of revenues from such exhibition.

Producer. An individual or motion picture enterprise that produces films for exhibition in movie theaters, on television, or elsewhere.

Production costs. Production costs include the cost of a story and scenario to be used for a film and other costs to produce a film, for example, salaries of cast, directors, producers, extras, and miscellaneous staff; cost of set construction and operations, wardrobe, and all accessories; cost of sound synchronization; production overhead, including depreciation and amortization of studio equipment and leasehold improvements used in production; and rental of facilities on location. Production costs ordinarily are accumulated by individual films in four chronological steps: (1) acquisition of the story rights; (2) preproduction, which includes script development, costume design, and set design and construction; (3) principal photography, which includes shooting the film; and (4) postproduction, which includes sound synchronization and editing, culminating in a completed master negative.

CONCEPTS, RULES, AND EXAMPLES

Accounting for Film Revenue

License revenues are recognized as the licensee is able to exercise exhibition rights and in order of the film's market-by-market exploitation. The licensee's rights are exercisable either when the license period begins or upon expiration of a conflicting license. Market-by-market exploitation involves two markets. The first market in which a film is exploited is called the primary market because that is the market for which a film principally is produced. All other exploitation is in the secondary market. Generally, the markets are mutually exclusive; that is, a film cannot be exploited in more than one market at a time because of the contract terms or sound marketing techniques. For example, to avoid conflict between theaters and television, a producer may impose restrictions on distribution that would prohibit the licensing of the film for television while the film is being shown in movie theaters. The market in which a film is distributed is a prime determinant of the value of the film.

The amount of revenue recognized is the sales price for each film, which is computed as the present value of the license fee.

Revenue From Movie Theaters

Film exhibition rights are usually licensed to movie theaters for a percentage of box office receipts or for a stated fee. In either case, these revenues are recognized by the licensor on the dates of film exhibition.

In some cases, the licensor receives a nonrefundable guarantee of a certain percentage of the box office receipts. This guarantee is most often deferred and recognized as revenue on the film exhibition dates. However, a guarantee is sometimes considered an outright sale because the licensor cannot expect to receive any additional revenue. In this instance, revenue is recognized when the conditions listed under Revenue from Television Broadcasters are met.

Revenue From Television Broadcasters

A license agreement for television program material is considered a sale of rights by producers and distributors. These parties recognize revenue when the license period begins and

1. The license fee is known for each film in the package
2. There is reasonable assurance that the license fee is fully collectible
3. The licensor knows or can reasonably determine the cost of each film
4. The licensee has accepted each film according to the license agreement
5. The licensee has access to the films for the first telecast (unless an agreement with another licensor prevents the telecast)

When these conditions are met, a contractual obligation between the licensor and licensee is created. However, if the ability of either party to perform becomes doubtful, revenue recognition is delayed until doubt ceases to exist. Only significant factors are sufficient to delay revenue recognition.

Revenue From the Home Viewing Market

The home viewing market includes all means by which films are sold or made available to residential viewers for a fee. Examples are video cassettes and disks and all forms of pay television, including cable and over-the-air transmission. Transactions in which motion picture companies license films to the home viewing market may be similar either to films licensed to movie theaters or films licensed to television. Thus, revenues earned from such transactions should be accounted for by the appropriate method.

Accounting for Costs and Expenses

Story costs. Film inventory costs include the cost of properties such as film rights to books, plays, etc. Any costs incurred to adapt these scenarios for motion picture production is included in the cost of the property. Upon periodic review, if it is decided not to use a particular property then the cost of that story is charged to current production overhead. Once a property has been held for 3 years and not used, story costs should be charged to production overhead. Once story costs are charged off they cannot be restored even if the property is subsequently used.

Film production costs. Production costs are capitalized as film cost inventory and amortized using one of two methods. The individual-film-forecast-computation method is recommended but the periodic-table-computation method may be used if approximately the same result is achieved. Under either method, the amortization should relate film costs to gross revenues in such a way that a constant rate of gross profit is reported. Film cost amortization begins when a film is released and the related revenues are recognized.

Under the individual-film-forecast-computation method, film costs are amortized in the ratio of current gross revenues to expected total gross revenues as follows:

$$\text{Amortization for the period} = \frac{\text{Gross film revenues for the period}}{\text{Expected total gross film revenues from exploitation in all markets during film's useful life}}$$

Revenue from sales to television broadcasters of long-term, noninterest-bearing exhibition rights are included in this fraction at the present value of the revenues as of the expected date of recognition. The numerator includes only the portion of such revenues that were recognized during the period, while the denominator includes the total estimated revenues from such sales (all at present value).

Periodically, estimates of total gross revenues should be reviewed and adjusted to reflect current expectations. If an adjustment is made, the denominator of the preceding fraction must be revised to the new estimate of total gross revenues as of the beginning of the current period. The numerator is not affected.

Under the periodic-table-computation method, film costs are amortized using tables which reflect the past revenue patterns of many films. It is assumed that these patterns can reasonably predict revenues of new films which are similarly produced and distributed. This method is generally used only for the portion of film costs which relates to exhibition rights licensed to movie theaters. Thus, film costs must be allocated between those markets included in the table and any other markets exploited.

The periodic tables must be reviewed often and revised when revenue patterns change considerably. Such tables should not be used to amortize films whose distribution patterns do not reflect the patterns underlying the table.

Exploitation costs. Exploitation costs are costs incurred during the final production phase and during the release periods of films in both primary and secondary markets. Examples are film prints, advertising, rents, salaries, and other distribution expenses. Exploitation costs that benefit future periods, such as prerelease and early release advertising, are capitalized as film cost inventory and amortized as described for production costs. Distribution expenses not expected to benefit future periods are expensed currently.

Participation agreements. Frequently, persons involved in the production of a motion picture film are compensated, in part or in full, with a participation in the income from the film. Determination of the amount of compensation payable to the participant is usually based on percentage of revenues or profits from the film from some or all sources. Television residuals are comparable to participations and are generally based on the number of times the film is exhibited on television or as a percentage of revenues from such exhibition. Total expected participation, including residuals, should be expensed in the ratio of current gross revenues to expected total gross revenues as described for amortization of production costs.

Valuation of film cost inventory. Each period, unamortized film inventory costs for each film should be compared with net realizable value. If expected gross revenues from a particular film are sufficient to recover unamortized film costs, participations, and direct distribution expenses, the film should be recorded at cost. However, if expected gross revenues are less than unamortized costs, the film costs should be written down to net realizable value. This adjustment is recorded in the interim period in which the revision is made; previous interim amounts should not be restated. In some cases, such as changing consumer demand or excessive costs, a film may be written down before it is released. If estimates of gross revenue increase, film costs may be written back up **only** during the same fiscal year of the write-down and in an amount not exceeding the write-down.

Investments in Independent Productions

Motion picture companies sometimes make cash advances to or guarantee the loans of independent producers. These transactions are recorded by the motion picture company as follows:

Cash advance		
Film cost inventory	xxx	
Cash		xxx

Loan guarantee		
Film cost inventory	xxx	
Liability under loan guarantee		xxx

Reporting

Agreements to license film rights to television broadcasters are not reported on the balance sheet until the related revenue is recognized. Any amounts received before revenue is recognized are considered advance payments and, if related to the current assets portion of film cost inventory, are reported as current liabilities.

The balance sheet may be classified or unclassified. If it is classified, current assets include the following: unamortized film inventory costs relating to the primary market, completed but unreleased films (minus the portion relating to secondary markets), and uncompleted television films under contracts of sale. Noncurrent assets include all remaining capitalized film costs. The portion of film costs relating to secondary markets is classified as a noncurrent asset and amortized as revenues are recognized.

Example: Individual-film-forecast-computation method

Assume that a licensor incurs film costs and earns revenue as follows:

Film cost	$15,000
Actual gross revenues:	
Year 1	18,000
Year 2	5,000

Year 3	2,000
Year-end estimated total gross revenues:	
Year 1	36,000
Years 2 and 3	30,000

Under this method, film costs are amortized in the ratio of current period gross revenues to anticipated total gross revenues.

Year 1 Amortization:

$$\frac{\$18,000}{\$36,000} \times \$15,000 = \$7,500$$

Since anticipated total gross revenues are reduced in year 2, anticipated total gross revenues and unamortized film costs must be recomputed from the beginning of the period.

Anticipated total gross revenues at beginning of the year:

$$\$30,000 - \$18,000 = \$12,000$$

Unamortized film costs:

$$\$15,000 - \$7,500 = \$7,500$$

Year 2 Amortization:

$$\frac{\$\ 5,000}{\$12,000} \times \$7,500 = \$3,125$$

Year 3 Amortization:

$$\frac{\$\ 2,000}{\$12,000} \times \$7,500 = \$1,250$$

EMERGING ISSUES TASK FORCE CONSENSUS SUMMARIES

87-10 Revenue Recognition by Television "Barter" Syndicators

A consensus was reached that revenue from the sale of advertising time acquired from a barter would be recognized when the criteria of SFAS 53 are met and either a noncancelable contract is signed by both parties or the advertisement has been aired.

NOT-FOR-PROFIT ORGANIZATIONS

PERSPECTIVE AND ISSUES

The purpose of *Not-for-Profit Organizations, Audit and Accounting Guide* (1998) is to assist in the auditing of and the reporting on the financial statements of **not-for-profit organizations for which there are no audit guides**. These organizations include cemetery, civic, fraternal, religious, performing arts, research and scientific organizations, labor unions, libraries, museums and other cultural institutions, political parties, private and community foundations, private elementary schools, professional and trade associations, public broadcasting stations, social and country clubs, and zoological and botanical societies. This Audit Guide does **not** apply to organizations that are primarily commercial businesses operated to benefit their members or stockholders, such as employee benefit and pension plans, mutual insurance companies, mutual banks, trusts, and farm cooperatives.

SFAS 116 establishes standards of accounting and reporting for contributions. It applies to **all** organizations that receive or make contributions. SFAS 117 addresses not-for-profit organizations, establishes standards for their general-purpose external statements and designates the statement of financial position, the statement of activities, the statement of cash flows and the accompanying notes as a complete set of financial statements. Inconsistent provisions in the SOP or AICPA Guides are no longer acceptable specialized accounting and reporting.

SFAS 105 was the first in a series of disclosure statements about financial instruments. Its focus is on the extent, nature, and terms of financial instruments with **off-balance-sheet** credit or market risk. In addition, the statement addresses concentrations of credit risk for **all** financial instruments.

SFAS 107 requires entities to disclose the fair value of **all** (recognized and unrecognized) financial instruments that it is practicable to estimate, including liabilities. Pertinent descriptive information as to the fair value of the instrument is to be disclosed if an estimate of fair value cannot be made without incurring excessive costs. In paragraph 8, the statement excludes certain types of financial instruments including pensions, postretirement benefits, deferred compensation, defeased debt, insurance contracts, lease contracts, warranty obligations and others. Fair value disclosure requirements specified by GAAP are acceptable for purposes of this statement.

SFAS 119, entitled *Disclosure about Derivative Financial Instruments and Fair Value of Financial Instruments*, requires issuers and holders of derivative financial instruments (DFI) to disclose information about those instruments. It also amends the disclosure requirements of SFAS 105 and SFAS 107. SFAS 132 will supersede SFAS 119 (see Chapter 6).

SFAS 124 requires that investments in all debt securities and in equity securities that have a readily determinable fair value be reported at fair value. In addition, certain disclosures are required for each period for which a balance sheet or statement of activities is presented. This statement also establishes standards for reporting losses on investments in a donor-restricted endowment fund.

SFAS 125 uses a financial-components approach that relies on control to establish standards for transfers and servicing of financial assets and extinguishments of liabilities. Derivatives and liabilities resulting from a transfer of financial assets are measured at fair value. In-substance defeasance does not result in the extinguishment of a liability. This statement is to be applied prospectively and is effective December 31, 1996. Early or retroactive application is not permitted.

SFAS 126 makes SFAS 107 disclosures optional for enterprises meeting the following criteria:

1. Enterprise is nonpublic.
2. Total enterprise assets are less than $100 million on financial statement date.
3. During the reporting period, enterprise has not held or issued any financial instruments as defined in SFAS 119.

SFAS 127 amends SFAS 125 to require deferral for 1 year of paragraph 15 (secured borrowings and collateral) and paragraphs 9-12 (dollar-rolls, repurchase agreements, securities lending, and similar transactions).

SFAS 129 applies to all enterprises and requires disclosing information about an enterprise's capital structure. It is effective December 15, 1997.

SFAS 130 requires enterprises that issue a complete set of general-purpose financial statements to report and display comprehensive income. However, entities that are not required to issue a statement of cash flows per SFAS 102 are not exempt if SFAS 130 applies otherwise. SFAS 130 does not apply to not-for-profits that follow SFAS 117 nor does it apply to enterprises with no items of other comprehensive income. The component entitled "other comprehensive income" should classify items by their nature and should be displayed separately and prominently. December 15, 1997, is the effective date.

Sources of GAAP

AICPA Audit and Accounting Guide	*SFAS*	*FASB I*	*SOP*
Not-For-Profit Organizations, 1998	93, 105, 107, 116, 117, 119, 124, 125, 126, 127, 129, 130	42	94-3

DEFINITIONS OF TERMS

Control. The ability to determine the direction of management and policy for purposes of presenting combined financial statements.

CONCEPTS, RULES, AND EXAMPLES

Financial Statements

In addition to reporting the nature and amount of available resources, the uses made of the resources, and the net change in fund balances, the financial statements of not-for-profit organizations also should identify the organization's primary programs and their costs, disclose the control of donors over the use of assets, and help the user to evaluate the organization's ability to accomplish its objectives.

Not-for-profit organizations prepare the following financial statements:

1. Statement of financial position
2. Statement of activities
3. Statement of cash flows

The financial statement title and format should be appropriate for the organization and should be prepared on an accrual basis.

Cash basis may be used if there are no material differences from the accrual basis.

SFAS 117 requires the statement of financial position to show total assets, total liabilities and net assets. Net assets must be categorized as to (1) unrestricted, (2) temporarily restricted, or (3) permanently restricted. The same categories above are used in the statement of activities to show the **changes** in net assets. The statement of cash flows should report the change in **cash and cash equivalents**.

Not-for-profit organizations must present in the financials all information required by GAAP (unless specifically exempted) and all information required by specialized principles. This information includes display and disclosure provisions of

1. Financial instruments
2. Loss contingencies
3. Extraordinary, unusual, and infrequent events
4. Accounting changes

Aggregation and order of presentation should, generally, be similar to those of a business enterprise.

In the year of application, SFAS 117 does not need to be applied to interim periods. If reported with annual statements, however, interim periods should be reclassified for that year. In the initial year, disclosure is required, for each year presented, of (1) the nature of any restatements and (2) their effect on the change in net assets.

Restatement to reflect retroactive application is necessary if comparative financials are presented for earlier periods.

Fund Accounting

Other not-for-profit organizations usually use fund accounting to comply with donor and grantor restrictions and to distinguish unrestricted resources from restricted resources. Funds consist of a self-balancing group of accounts composed of assets, liabilities, and a fund balance (net assets). Organizations that have restricted resources and do not use fund accounting must comply with the requirements of this audit and accounting guide and must disclose all material restrictions in their financial statements. Nontraditional fund classifications may be used if the audit and accounting guide's required disclosures are made. For external reporting, a particular fund balance may fall totally into one of the three net asset classes or may be allocated among more than one class per SFAS 117.

Financially Interrelated Organizations

A combined financial statement should be used when one organization **controls** another and any of the following exist:

1. An organization solicits funds for the reporting organization and the donor intends or requires the funds to be transferred or used by the reporting organization.
2. An organization receives resources from the reporting organization to be used for the reporting organization.
3. An organization, funded by nonpublic contributions, is assigned responsibilities by the reporting organization.

Disclosure of the basis for the combination is required. The combined financial statement should include all resources of the related organization. Organizations which are affiliated, but do not meet the requirements for combination, should be disclosed.

In some instances a not-for-profit will be financially interrelated with another not-for-profit organization. Under the provisions of SOP 94-3, the entity should be consolidated if 50% or more of the outstanding voting shares are owned, unless control is likely to be temporary or does not rest with the majority owner. Further, consolidated financial statements should be prepared, unless control is likely to be temporary or does not rest with the majority owner, if there is **both** control through a majority ownership interest by other than outstanding voting shares or control through a majority voting interest in the board **and** an economic beneficial interest.

In addition to the foregoing rules, under this standard consolidation is permitted, unless control is likely to be temporary, but not required if there is control through other than a majority ownership or voting interest (e.g., contract or affiliation) and an economic beneficial interest. If consolidated financial statements are not presented, the reporting entity must identify the other organization and the nature of its relationship that results in control, present summarized financial data of the other organization, and include the disclosures required by SFAS 57.

If there is control or an economic beneficial interest but not both, consolidated financial statements should not be prepared. However, the related-party disclosures required by SFAS 57 should be made; the other organization and the nature of its relationship with the reporting organization that results in control should be identified, summarized financial data of the other organization should be presented, and any transactions between the organizations should be described and quantified.

If consolidated financial statements are presented, disclosure should be made of any restrictions made by entities outside of the reporting entity on distributions from the controlled not-for-profit organization to the reporting organization, and of any results which make net assets unavailable for use by the reporting organization.

Revenue, Support, and Capital

The primary sources and amounts of revenue, support, and capital funds should be disclosed in the statement of activity. Capital additions restricted for plant assets should be shown as deferred capital support in the balance sheet until they are used.

Current restricted funds should be reported as revenue and support to the extent that expenses conforming to the grantor's restrictions have been incurred. Any remaining funds should be reported as deferred revenue or support in the balance sheet until the restrictions are met and the expenses incurred.

Unrestricted funds are reported in the unrestricted fund.

Legally enforceable pledges should be reported as assets at the estimated realizable value and should be recognized as support when so designated by the donor. If that designation occurs after the balance sheet date, these pledges would be shown as deferred support in the balance sheet. If no designation is made, pledges should be reported when they are expected to be received.

Revenue from the sale of goods or services is recognized when goods are sold or services are performed. Revenue from membership dues should be allocated over the dues period.

Investments

SFAS 124 established standards for investments by not-for-profit enterprises in equity securities having readily determinable fair values, except for those accounted for by the equity method and investments in consolidated subsidiaries, and investments in any debt securities. In sharp contrast to the standard applicable to commercial enterprises, not-for-profits must account for all such investments at fair value (even if debt securities are to be held to maturity) and the gains and losses must be taken to results of operations (generally, unrestricted net assets, unless use is temporarily or permanently restricted) and reported in the statement of activities.

Dividend, interest and other investment income should be reported as earned. Generally, these are to be reported as increases in unrestricted net assets unless use of assets received is limited by donor-imposed restrictions, in which case they would be reported as increases in temporarily or permanently restricted net assets. Gains and investment income that are limited to specific uses by donor-imposed restrictions may be reported as increases in unrestricted net assets if the conditions are met in the same period as the gains are recognized, but only if the entity follows the same policy for contributions received, and reports consistently from one period to the next, with an adequate disclosure of its accounting policy.

If a donor stipulates that a gift be invested in perpetuity or for a specified term, this creates an endowment fund. Unless gains and losses are temporarily or permanently restricted by explicit stipulation or by law, these represent changes in the unrestricted net assets of the enterprise. If the gift requires that a particular security be held in perpetuity, then the gains or losses are subject to the same restriction as the security, unless the donor stipulates otherwise. If the donor allows the entity to choose suitable investments, then the gains and losses are not restricted and become part of unrestricted net assets if income is unrestricted, and part of temporarily restricted net assets if investment income is temporarily restricted by the donor.

Unless there are stipulations or law to the contrary, losses on the investments of a donor-restricted endowment fund should temporarily reduce restricted net assets to the extent that donor-imposed restrictions on net appreciation of the fund have not been met prior to occurrence of the loss. Any remaining loss would reduce unrestricted net assets. If losses reduce assets below the level required by donor stipulations or the law, gains that restored the fair value to the required level should be classified as increases in unrestricted net assets.

The new standard also establishes a number of disclosure requirements. For each period for which a statement of financial position is presented, the aggregate carrying value of investments, by major types (e.g., equity, real estate, treasury bonds) must be disclosed; the basis for determining the carrying value of other investments must be stated; the methods and significant assumptions used to estimate the fair values of investments other than financial instruments if those were reported on the basis of fair value must be given; and the aggregate amount of the deficiencies for all donor restricted endowment funds for which fair value of assets at reporting date is less than the level required by donor stipulations or law must be noted. For each period for which a statement of activities is presented, the composition of investment return must be set forth, including, at the minimum, (1) investment income, (2) realized gains and losses on investments reported at other than fair value, and (3) net gains or losses on investments reported at fair value and a reconciliation of investment return to amounts reported in the statement of activities. Additionally, if investment return is separated into operating and nonoperating amounts, the entity must present a description of the policy used to determine the amount that is included in the measure of operations and a discussion of circumstances leading to a change, if any, in the policy.

For the most recent statement of financial position only, the nature of any carrying amount for each individual investment or group of investments that represents a significant concentration of market risk should also be disclosed.

This standard became effective for years beginning after December 1995, with early application encouraged and retroactive application permitted. The expiration of restrictions on previously unrecognized gains and losses should be applied prospectively. If initial adoption is not applied retroactively, the effect of the adoption should be reported as the cumulative effect of an accounting change on each class of net assets, to be presented on the statement of activities between extraordinary items (if any) and change in unrestricted, temporarily restricted, and permanently restricted net assets, respectively.

Contributions

SFAS 116 specifies that unconditional promises to give and contributions received (made) are recognized at fair value in the period received (made). When conditions are substantially met, conditional promises to give are recognized. FASB I 42 specifies when a reporting entity acts as an agent, trustee, or intermediary, rather than as both a donee and donor.

Not-for-profits are required to differentiate increases in net assets from contributions between (1) permanently restricted, (2) temporarily restricted, and (3) unrestricted. In the period of expiration, recognition of the expiration of donor-imposed restrictions on contributions must be given. Service contributions should not be recognized **unless** (1) nonfinancial assets are created or enhanced or (2) qualified individuals provide specialized skills that would otherwise need to be purchased. Collections held for public exhibition, education or research in furtherance of public service and comprised of works of art, historical treasures, etc., are not required to be capitalized and recognized as revenue.

In the year of change, retroactive application or recognition of a cumulative effect may be used. Recognition of restriction expirations may be prospectively applied.

Expenses

Expenses should be identified by function unless another basis would be useful to the users of the financial statement. Expenses for specific program services and for supporting services such as management and general costs and fund-raising costs should be presented separately for each significant program or activity (such as fund-raising, membership development, and unallocated management and general expenses). Classification of expenditure by type may be presented also. Costs which are attributable to more than one function should be allocated on a reasonable basis.

An expense and a liability should be reported when grant recipients are entitled to receive the grant. Grants to be made over several years should be reported in the year the grant is first made, unless the grantor retains the right to revoke the grant or unless grants are subject to periodic renewal.

Tax Allocation

Interperiod tax allocations should be made when temporary differences occur with respect to federal or state income taxes or federal excise taxes.

Transfers

Interfund transfers are reported as changes in fund balances rather than as revenues or expenses. Third-party agreements and term endowment fund expirations that require transfers should be disclosed.

Depreciation

Depreciation should be recognized. SFAS 93 also requires the disclosure of depreciation expense, balances of the major classes of depreciable assets, accumulated depreciation at the balance sheet date, and a description of the depreciation method used.

STATEMENTS OF POSITION

94-3 Reporting of Related Entities by Not-for-Profit Organizations

This SOP makes guidance uniform in regard to not-for-profit (NFP) reporting of investments in for-profit (FP) entities and in regard to financial interrelationships with other NFP. It does not apply to entities covered by the *Audits of Providers of Health Care Services* Audit Guide.

If ARB 51, as amended by SFAS 94 applies, a NFP with a controlling financial interest through ownership of a majority voting interest should consolidate FP entities. The nature of the FP's activities will govern the manner of its presentation in the NFP's financials. If APB 18 applies, a NFP should use the equity method to report FP investments. An exception to the use of the equity method is made for NFP reporting investments at market value in conformity with AICPA audit guides.

If SFAS 94 paragraph 13 applies (temporary control or lack of control by majority ownership), consolidation is prohibited. Otherwise, a NFP should consolidate another NFP if

1. It has a controlling financial interest through ownership of a majority interest.
2. It has both control (through majority ownership or majority voting on the board) and an economic interest.

Economic interest is present when

a. Other entities solicit funds on behalf of the reporting organization (RO).
b. A RO transfers significant resources to another entity to be maintained for benefit of RO.
c. A RO delegates some significant functions to another entity.
d. A RO gives or is committed to give funds to the other entity or guarantees material debt of the other entity.

Any restrictions imposed by outside entities regarding distributions and any resulting unavailability of net assets of the controlled NFP should be disclosed if consolidated statements are presented.

The existence of control or economic interest, but not both, precludes consolidation but requires SFAS 57 disclosures.

This SOP will be reconsidered when the FASB completes its consolidation project.

98-2 Accounting for Costs of Activities of Not-For-Profit Organizations and State and Local Governmental Entities That Include Fund-Raising

This SOP makes guidance uniform in regard to not-for-profits (NFP). This SOP requires joint costs of fund-raising and the appropriate program or management or general function be allocated to those functions if the criteria of purpose, audience, and content are met as defined in the SOP.

In cases where some of the criteria of purpose, audience, and content are not met, the SOP requires expensing of all fund-raising costs, including costs that otherwise might be considered program or management and general costs. An exception is the cost of goods or services provided in an exchange transaction that are part of joint activities, such as costs of direct donor benefits of a special event (for example, a meal), should not be reported as fund-raising.

OIL AND GAS PRODUCING ACTIVITIES

PERSPECTIVE AND ISSUES

SFAS 19 is the financial accounting and reporting standard for oil and gas **producing** activities. It does not address refining, marketing, or transportation issues. SFAS 19 adheres to the traditional historical cost basis. This statement prescribes a form of the successful efforts method of accounting for oil and gas producing activities.

SFAS 25 subsequently amended SFAS 19 to suspend the effective date indefinitely. Thus, the use of the successful efforts method was not required. At the time, the SEC was permitting a prescribed form of the full cost method to be used and the conflict was resolved by suspension of SFAS 19.

SFAS 69 amended the disclosure requirements of SFAS 19 and established, in its place, a comprehensive set of disclosures. The method used for accounting for costs incurred and the manner of disposing of capitalized costs was a required disclosure for all enterprises. The other disclosures are only required for publicly traded companies.

FASB I 33 addresses the application of SFAS 34 to enterprises using the full cost method of accounting. If the oil and gas producing operation is engaged in earning activities with assets being depreciated, depleted, or amortized, it does not qualify for interest capitalization. Qualifying assets are those with in-progress exploration or development activities taking place, but which are not yet engaged in earning pursuits and which are not presently being depreciated, depleted, or amortized.

FASB I 36 addresses the problem of accounting for exploratory wells or tests that are in progress at the end of the period. If, subsequent to the end of the period, but before the financial statements are issued, the well or test is found to be unsuccessful, the incurred costs, less salvage, should be expensed. Retroactive financial statements should not be issued.

Sources of GAAP

SFAS	FASB I
19, 25, 69	33, 36

CONCEPTS, RULES, AND EXAMPLES

The costs of the special types of assets used in oil and gas producing activities should be capitalized when incurred. Some examples include

1. Mineral interests in properties
   a. Unproved
   b. Proved

2. Wells and related equipment and facilities
3. Support equipment and facilities
4. Uncompleted wells, equipment, and facilities

These costs should be amortized as reserves are produced and, along with lifting costs, should become costs of production. Periodically, unproved properties should be evaluated for impairment. If impaired, a loss should be recognized.

Acquisition costs incurred to obtain oil and gas properties through purchase, lease, etc., should be capitalized.

Geological and geophysical costs, unproved properties' carrying costs, and the costs of dry hole and bottom hole contributions should be expensed. Drilling costs should be capitalized until a determination has been made as to the success of the well. If successful, these costs are transferred to uncompleted wells, related equipment, and facilities. The cost of drilling, less residual value, is charged to expense if proved reserves are not found.

Development costs are incurred in order to

1. Get access to and prepare well locations
2. Drill and equip development wells
3. Set up production facilities
4. Provide better recovery systems

These costs are capitalized as a cost in uncompleted equipment and facilities until drilling or construction is completed.

The cost of support equipment is to be capitalized and depreciated. This depreciation, along with other operating costs, is allocated to exploration, development, or production costs, as appropriate.

Production involves different costs ranging from lifting to field storage. These costs, together with depreciation, depletion, and amortization of capitalized acquisition, exploration, and development costs, are part of the cost of the oil and gas produced.

Unproved properties are reclassified to proved properties upon discovery of proved reserves. When proved reserves are found, the costs capitalized as uncompleted wells, equipment, and facilities are reclassified as completed wells, equipment, and facilities. Capitalized costs are to be amortized or depleted by the unit of production method. Estimated residual values must be considered when determining amortization and depreciation rates.

Any information that becomes available between the end of the period and the date when the financial statements are issued is to be considered in the evaluation of conditions existing at the balance sheet date. With respect to the costs of a company's wells, related equipment, facilities and the costs of related proved properties, the provisions for impairment as outlined in SFAS 121 are applicable.

PENSION FUNDS

PERSPECTIVE AND ISSUES

SFAS 35 is the principal standard involving the accounting and reporting by private sector defined benefit pension plans. These plans usually provide pension benefits but may provide death and disability benefits or termination of employment benefits. This statement applies both to plans that are subject to ERISA and those that are not. SFAS 35 applies to ongoing plans, but not to ones that are expected to be terminated and not to government sponsored social security plans. This standard emphasizes aspects of particular importance to pension plans and aspects that differ from existing GAAP for other types of entities.

SFAS 75 amended SFAS 35 and indefinitely deferred its application to pension plans of state and local government units.

SFAS 102 amended SFAS 95 and provided that a statement of cash flows was not required for defined benefit pension plans and certain other employee benefit plans that present similar information to that required by SFAS 35.

SFAS 110 amended SFAS 35 to require all investment contracts issued to be reported at fair value. Only contracts that incorporate mortality or morbidity risk should be reported at contract value.

SFAS 130 requires enterprises that issue a complete set of general-purpose financial statements to report and display comprehensive income. However, entities that are not required to issue a statement of cash flows per SFAS 102 are not exempt if SFAS 130 applies otherwise. SFAS 130 does not apply to not-for-profits that follow SFAS 117 nor does it apply to enterprises with no items of other comprehensive income. The component entitled "other comprehensive income" should classify items by their nature and should be displayed separately and prominently. December 15, 1997 is the effective date.

Sources of GAAP

<u>SFAS</u>
35, 75, 102, 110, 130

CONCEPTS, RULES, AND EXAMPLES

The most important goal of the financial statements of a pension plan is to communicate information that is relevant in determining the plan's capability to pay benefits. Thus, the statements should report

1. Plan resources
2. Stewardship responsibilities
3. Participants' accumulated plan benefits

4. Results of transactions and events regarding the resources and benefits
5. Any other significant information that will aid the users in assessing accomplishments or lack thereof

Financial Statements

The plan's annual financial statements should include

1. A statement of end-of-the-year net assets available
2. A statement of period changes in net assets available
3. Information concerning actuarial present value of accumulated plan benefits (APVAPB) as of either the end or beginning of the plan year
4. Information concerning significant factors affecting the year-to-year changes in the APVAPB

Net assets available and APVAPB should be reported as of the same date and information regarding their changes should be for the same period. End-of-the-year benefit information is preferable.

Net Assets

The accrual basis of accounting is required.

Contributions receivable include those due from formal commitments, legal requirements, or contractual requirements. These amounts are due as of the reporting date from plan participants, employers, and other sources.

Investments of the plan are to be reported at fair value. If there is an active market, market price should be used. Otherwise, the selling price of similar investments or discounted cash flows could be useful in estimating fair value. Plan investments should be identified by type of investment and should indicate how fair value was determined.

Insurance company contracts were to be reported in a manner required by ERISA. SFAS 110 amended this provision of SFAS 35 to require investment contracts with an insurance company or other financial institution to be reported at fair value. The effective date was December 31, 1992. Certain contracts entered into prior to March 20, 1992, are reported as before. Restatement is required if prior year financials are presented with statements for plan years beginning after December 15, 1992.

Buildings, equipment, and other fixed assets should be reported at cost less accumulated depreciation or amortization.

Changes in Net Assets

Disclosure of significant changes in net assets should include

1. Contributions from
   a. Employer(s)--Indicate cash and noncash
   b. Participants, including sponsor

   c. Other identified sources

2. Paid benefits
3. Payments to insurance companies to purchase contracts that are excluded from plan assets
4. Each significant class of investment should show its net appreciation or depreciation in fair value presented by
   a. Investments measured by market price in an active market
   b. Investments measured by some other means
5. Investment income (not including appreciation or depreciation in fair value)
6. Administrative expenses

Actuarial Present Value of Accumulated Plan Benefits (APVAPB)

The provisions of the plan should be used, to the extent possible, to measure the accumulated plan benefits. If the plan is unclear on this aspect, one of two ratios should be used. If the benefit it **includable** in vested benefits, then the ratio is

$$\frac{\text{Number of years of service completed to date}}{\text{Number of years of service needed for full vesting}}$$

If the benefit is **not** includable in vested benefits, then the applicable ratio is

$$\frac{\text{Number of years of service completed to date}}{\text{Projected number of years of service completed until separation from covered employment}}$$

The following are applicable in the measurement of accumulated plan benefits (APB):

1. APB as of the benefit information date should be based on
   a. Pay and service history of employees
   b. Other significant factors that are relevant
2. In determining expected eligibility for particular benefits, projected years of service may be used
3. If the plan specifies automatic benefit increases, they should be recognized
4. Payments to insurance companies should be excluded if the related contracts to provide benefits is excluded from plan assets
5. Amendments to the plan effective after the information date should not be recognized
6. Employee compensation is assumed not to change beyond the information date for the determination of social security benefits. Wage base increases and benefit level increases should not be recognized

The APVAPB should be separated into the following reporting categories:

1. Vested benefits--Participants receiving payments
2. Other vested benefits
3. Nonvested benefits

As of the benefit information date

1. Category 1. above should include benefits due and payable
2. Employees' accumulated contributions (including interest) should be disclosed
3. Interest rates in 2., if applicable, should be disclosed

Actuarial assumption changes are considered changes in estimates. Significant factors affecting the change of APVAPB during the period should be identified. Such factors include plan amendments, actuarial assumption changes, and plan mergers or spin-offs.

Cash Flows Statement Exemption

SFAS 102 exempted defined benefit pension plans from the requirement that a statement of cash flows be provided. Other employee benefit plans that report similar financial information (including reporting plan investments at fair value) were also exempted. Although exempted, a presentation of a statement of cash flows was encouraged if it would provide useful information about the plan's ability to pay future liabilities.

RECORD AND MUSIC INDUSTRY

PERSPECTIVE AND ISSUES

SFAS 50 sets forth accounting and reporting standards for the record and music industry. In this industry, business is transacted through contractual arrangements entered into by an owner (licensor) of a record master or music copyright. The licensor grants the licensee the right to sell or distribute records or music for a fixed fee paid to the licensor or for a fee based on sales of records or music. License agreements are modifications of the compulsory provisions of the copyright law. This section presents the proper accounting by both the licensor and the licensee for license agreements in the record and music industry.

Sources of GAAP
SFAS
50

DEFINITIONS OF TERMS

Advance royalty. An amount paid to music publishers, record producers, songwriters, or other artists in advance of their earning royalties from record or music sales. Such an amount is based on contractual terms and is generally nonrefundable.

License agreements. Contractual arrangements entered into by an owner (licensor) of a record master or music copyright with a licensee granting the licensee the right to sell or distribute records or music for a fixed fee paid to the licensor or for a fee based on sales of records or music. License agreements are modifications of the compulsory provisions of the copyright law.

Minimum guarantee. An amount paid in advance by a licensee to a licensor for the right to sell or distribute records or music.

Record master. The master tape resulting from the performance of the artist. It is used to produce molds for commercial record production and other tapes for use in making cartridges, cassettes, and reel tapes.

Royalties. Amounts paid to record producers, songwriters, or other artists for their participation in making records and to music publishers for their copyright interest in music. Amounts for artists are determined by the terms of personal service contracts negotiated between the artists and record companies and usually are determined based upon a percentage of sales activity and license fee income, adjusted for estimated sales returns. Royalties for publishing are based on the copyright or other applicable laws, but the requirements of the law may be modified by licenses issued by the publishers.

CONCEPTS, RULES, AND EXAMPLES

Accounting by Licensors

Revenues. A license agreement is considered an outright sale when the licensor has

1. Signed a noncancelable contract
2. Agreed to accept a specified fee
3. Transferred the music rights to the licensee, who is able to use them
4. Fulfilled all significant duties owed the licensee

When these conditions are met, the earnings process is complete and revenue may be recognized if there is reasonable assurance that the license fee is fully collectible.

In some cases the licensee pays a minimum guarantee, which is an amount paid in advance to a licensor for the right to sell or distribute records or music. A minimum guarantee is first recorded as a liability and then amortized to income as the license fee is earned. If the amount of the fee that is earned is indeterminable, then straight-line recognition of revenue from the guarantee is required over the license period.

Example

A licensor receives a $10,000 minimum guarantee on a license agreement which spans a 5-year period. The entry to record the receipt of cash is

Cash	$10,000	
Liability under license agreement		$10,000

The licensor will recognize revenue from the guarantee on a straight-line basis. At the end of each year of the license period, the licensor will record the following entry:

Liability under license agreement	$2,000	
License fees earned		$2,000

A licensor may charge fees for such items as free records beyond a certain number given away by a record club. The amount of such fees is not determinable when the license agreement is made. Therefore, the licensor can recognize revenue only when the amount can be reasonably estimated or when the license agreement expires.

Cost of artist compensation. Royalties are paid to record producers, songwriters, or other artists for their participation in making records and to music publishers for their copyright interest in music. Amounts for artists are determined by the terms of personal service contracts negotiated between the artists and record companies and usually are determined based upon a percentage of sales activity and license fee income, adjusted for estimated sales returns. Publishing royalties are generally based on copyright or other applicable laws. Royalties paid to artists are charged off as a period expense of the licensor.

Advance royalties are amounts paid to music publishers, record producers, songwriters, or other artists in advance of their earning royalties from record or music sales. Such royalties are based on contractual terms and are generally nonrefundable. Advance royalties are recorded as assets if the licensor expects that the artist's recording will be successful enough to provide for full recovery of the advance from future royalties due the artist. As royalties are subsequently earned by the artist, the capitalized advance is charged to expense. The advance must be apportioned between current and noncurrent assets according to how soon each portion will be charged to expense. If it later appears that the advance will not be fully recovered from subsequent royalties earned by the artist, then the unrecoverable portion should be charged to expense in the period in which the loss becomes apparent.

Cost to produce record masters. A record master is the master tape resulting from the performance of the artist. The costs of producing a record master include (1) the cost of the musical talent (musicians, vocal background, and arrangements); (2) the cost of the technical talent for engineering, directing, and mixing; (3) costs for the use of the equipment to record and produce the master; and (4) studio facility charges. Under the standard type of artist contract, the record company bears a portion of the costs and recovers a portion of the cost from the artist out of designated royalties earned. However, either party may bear all or most of the cost.

The portion of the cost that is paid by the record company is recorded as an asset if the company expects that sales of the artist's recording will be successful enough to provide for full recovery of costs. If this is not the case, then these costs should be expensed. Any amount capitalized should be amortized over the useful life of the recording in such a way that relates the costs to estimated net revenue to be realized. Costs to produce record masters which are recoverable from the artist's royalties should be treated as advanced royalties by the record company.

Accounting by Licensees

When a licensee pays a minimum guarantee in advance, the guarantee is recorded as an asset and then amortized to expense according to the terms specified in the license agreement. If it later appears that the minimum guarantee is not fully recoverable through use of the rights received under the agreement, then the unrecoverable portion should be charged to expense.

Fees for which the amount is indeterminable before the agreement expires are sometimes stipulated in the license agreement. An example is a fee charged to a record club for free records beyond a certain number given away. The licensee must estimate the amount of such fees and accrue them on a license-by-license basis.

REGULATED OPERATIONS

PERSPECTIVE AND ISSUES

Although various businesses are subject to regulatory oversight to greater or lesser degrees, as used in GAAP the term **regulated operations** refers primarily to public utilities, whose ability to set selling prices for the goods or services they offer is constrained by government actions. Generally, the regulatory process has been designed to permit such enterprises to recover the costs they incur, plus a reasonable rate of return to stockholders. However, given the political process of rate-setting by regulatory authorities, and the fact that costs such as those for plant construction escalated greatly during the past decade or so, the ability to recover all costs through rate increases has become less certain. For this and other reasons, specialized GAAP has been promulgated.

Sources of GAAP

SFAS	*TB*	*EITF*
71, 90, 92, 98, 101	87-2	92-7, 92-12, 93-4, 97-4

CONCEPTS, RULES, AND EXAMPLES

These accounting principles apply to regulated enterprises only if they continue to meet certain criteria, which relate to the intended ability to recover all costs through the rate-setting process. When and if these conditions no longer are met, due to deregulation or a shift to rate-setting which is not based on cost recovery, then application of the specialized GAAP is to terminate.

Asset Recognition

If certain costs are not recognized for current rate-setting purposes, but it is probable that the costs will be recovered through future revenue, then these costs can be capitalized even though a nonregulated enterprise would be required to expense these costs currently. Deferred costs can include an imputed cost of equity capital, if so accounted for rate-setting purposes, even though this would not normally be permitted under GAAP. Thus, the regulatory process can result in the accounting recognition of an asset which would not otherwise be recognized. If at any time it becomes apparent that the incurred cost will not be recovered through generation of future revenue, that cost should be charged to earnings. If a regulator subsequently excludes specific costs from allowable costs, the carrying value of the asset recognized shall be reduced to the extent of the excluded costs. Should the regulator allow recovery of these previously excluded costs or any additional costs, a new asset shall be recognized and classified as if these costs had been initially included in allowable costs.

Imposition of Liabilities

In other situations, the regulatory process can result in the accounting recognition of a liability. This usually occurs when regulators mandate that refunds be paid to customers, which must be accrued when probable and reasonably estimable, per SFAS 5. Furthermore, regulatory rates may be set at a higher level, in order to recover costs expected to be incurred in the future, subject to the caveat that such amounts will be refunded to customers if it later becomes apparent that actual costs incurred were less than expected. In such cases, the incremental rate increase related to recovery of future costs must be accounted for as a liability (unearned revenue), until the condition specified is satisfied. Finally, regulators may stipulate that a gain realized by the utility will be returned to customers over a specified future period; this will be accounted for by accrual of a liability rather than by recognition of the gain for accounting purposes.

Phase-in Plans

Special rules apply to so-called phase-in plans, as defined in SFAS 92. If a phase-in plan was ordered by regulators for a plant which had been substantially constructed before 1988, then all allowable costs which are deferred for regulatory purposes, subject to the phase-in plan, are also deferred for financial reporting purposes. However, imputed cost of capital permitted by regulators (in effect, interest on the deferred costs) cannot be capitalized for financial reporting. Specific criteria must be met in order to utilize phase-in accounting, and the method cannot be employed for plants not constructed until after 1987.

Abandonment

Accounting for abandonments is also stipulated for regulated enterprises. If an abandonment occurs or becomes probable, any costs which are probable of not being recovered should be written off as a loss. Furthermore, if the return on the investment which will be recoverable will not be equal to the normal rate of return, then an additional loss accrual must be recognized currently. This loss is measured by the difference between the projected future revenues, discounted at the enterprise's incremental borrowing rate, and the remaining costs to be recovered. The amount of loss to be recognized obviously depends on the enterprise's estimate of time to elapse until rate increases are effective, and the length of time over which the increases will remain in effect. These estimates may change over time, and the effect of revisions in the estimate will be reflected in earnings in the periods the new estimates are made.

The carrying value of the costs of an abandoned plant is increased during the period from the abandonment until recovery occurs through rate increases as promised by the regulatory authorities. If full return of investment is anticipated, the cost of abandoned assets is accreted at the rate (the enterprise's overall cost of capital) permitted for rate-setting purposes. If partial or no return on investment is expected, the asset value is accreted at the same rate which was used to compute the loss accrual, which is the enterprise's incremental borrowing rate. During the recovery period, the costs of the abandoned plant are amortized. If full return on investment is expected, this amortization should be computed on the same basis as is permitted for rate-setting purposes. If partial or no return is expected, amortization should be such as to provide a constant rate of return on the unamortized balance of the investment in the costs of the abandoned plant.

Deferred Income Taxes

Deferred taxes must be provided consistent with SFAS 109. There are no exemptions or special provisions for income tax accounting for regulated enterprises. Assets or liabilities related to future rate increases or decreases are temporary differences within the meaning of SFAS 109.

Accounting for Liabilities Related to Closure or Removal

Perhaps the most significant development arising from concerns about regulated enterprises is the proposed FASB statement which has been broadened in applicability to all types of entities. This proposal has as its origins concerns about the decommissioning costs for nuclear power generation plants, which was the sole focus when the project began in 1984. It later was expanded to address similar concerns applicable to industries having potential for environmental damage, such as offshore oil drilling and landfills. The project addresses all costs incurred in the acquisition, construction, development or early operation of long-lived assets, relating to subsequent closure or removal of assets, which costs cannot be satisfied until the current operation or use of the assets cease and which cannot realistically be avoided. The project does not address costs incurred as a consequence of improper use of the assets, or costs incurred over the assets' useful lives for operations or maintenance.

If the new standard is ultimately approved, legal and unavoidable constructive obligations will have to be recognized as liabilities and accrued when incurred. The time when these obligations will be deemed to have been incurred will generally be at the inception of the use of the related assets. Thus, the recorded amount of the assets will be grossed up to include another class of "costs" related to the usage thereof. Future periods' depreciation will include a pro rata share of the extra costs.

The proposal stipulates that the correct basis for measurement of the liability will be discounted present value of the cash needed to ultimately satisfy the obligation. This assumes, of course, that the timing of these expenditures can be reasonably estimated--which is likely, given that by definition these are costs to be incurred upon closure or removal, and the choice of depreciable useful lives is similarly based on this same expectation as to timing. In estimating the future cash cost of closure or removal, factors such as future inflation, the effects of technology changes in the near term, efficiencies to be gained from moving down the learning curve, the impact of unforeseen circumstances which can be assumed from past experience, and internal costs related to the closure or removal activities, are all to be taken into account. Finally, in computing present value, the proposal states that the market rates on Treasury bonds that have maturities corresponding to the expected timing of the cash flows related to the closure or removal activities are to be used.

In the past, various methods were used to account for costs similar to those addressed in this proposal (although, in most cases, no accruals were being made at all). The proposal states that such alternatives as accruing extra depreciation expense (thereby ultimately causing the net book values of the assets in question to "go negative" and have credit balances, which implies that such a balance would be the amount of the net liability at the end of the assets' useful lives) would no longer be acceptable.

The FASB has expanded the scope of this project since the initial exposure draft was issued (in early 1996), and now plans to issue a revised exposure draft in late 1998. As part of its current deliberations, the Board has reaffirmed that asset retirement costs should be capitalized as part of the cost of the related assets. The expanded scope standard, if adopted, will also apply to indefinite-lived assets, as well as to component parts of larger asset systems. Retirements, as defined, would exclude temporary removals from active service. The Board has also tentatively concluded that, for there to be recognition of removal costs based on a constructive (rather than legal) obligation, the entity's past practices would have to suggest that such actions would in fact be taken, that other parties are relying on such an expectation, and that a failure to continue past practices would have a significant adverse effect on the reporting entity.

Accounting for Deregulation and "Stranded Costs"

In recent years the utilities industries have been undergoing vast changes in the regulatory environment. The wholesale electricity markets were essentially deregulated in 1996, and the apparent intent is to fully deregulated public utilities entirely within the next several years. This will have significant effects on the financial reporting of many of the entities operating in these industries, since under GAAP many had recognized so-called regulatory assets and regulatory liabilities which will no longer be recognizable once full deregulation occurs. Also, certain costs may no longer be recoverable in a deregulated environment, transforming certain assets into so-called "stranded costs."

A consensus in EITF 97-4 has addressed the matter of deregulation. When deregulatory legislation has been enacted affecting all or a portion of the entity's operations, it should cease applying SFAS 71 to the affected operations. In cases in which the effects of deregulation are imposed by means of a rate order, such an order would have to be sufficiently detailed so that the entity would be able to determine how it will be affected. Regulatory assets would not, however, be immediately written off; instead, an evaluation of regulatory cash flows would be conducted to determine whether an impairment had occurred and to determine whether the portion of the business from which the regulatory cash flows are derived is still subject to SFAS 71. Only if the asset is impaired (applying SFAS 121 criteria) or if SFAS 71 is no longer applicable would the asset be written off before being recovered. Similarly, regulatory liabilities would not be written into income until the obligation is eliminated by the regulatory authority.

A related concern is whether the new regulatory assets or liabilities must be given recognition to reflect expenses and obligations that will arise from the portion of the business being deregulated. The same "source of cash flow" type of analysis noted above is to be applied to make these determinations. Thus, a cost or obligation is recognized as a regulatory asset or liability, respectively, once it is expensed or incurred after SFAS 101 is applied to that portion of the operations, if it has been designated for recovery or settlement, respectively, via regulated cash flows.

EMERGING ISSUES TASK FORCE CONSENSUS SUMMARIES

92-7 Accounting for Rate-Regulated Utilities for the Effects of Certain Alternative Revenue Programs

A consensus was reached regarding the treatment of additional revenues of rate-regulated utility companies which are to be billed in the future under alternative revenue programs. The EITF abstract identifies two types of alternative revenue programs, defined as Type A and Type B. The revenues from alternative revenue programs should be recognized when the events permitting billing of the revenues have occurred and three specific criteria which are discussed in the abstract are met.

The Task Force also notes that rate-regulated utilities recognizing revenues from an alternative revenue program which do not meet the conditions of this EITF must amend the plan or change the program to meet the conditions.

92-12 Accounting for OPEB Costs by Rate-Regulated Enterprises

If the regulator includes other postemployment benefits, (OPEB), costs in rates on a pay-as-you-go basis, the regulatory asset relating to the cost under SFAS 106 should not be recognized. The Task Force also reached a consensus that the regulatory asset for a rate-regulated enterprise should recognize the difference between SFAS 106 costs and the OPEB costs if future revenue will at least offset the deferred cost and meet four specific criteria. The four specific criteria are discussed in detail in the EITF Abstracts.

93-4 Accounting for Regulatory Assets

The Task Force reached a consensus that a rate-regulated enterprise that fails to initially meet the asset recognition criteria can recognize a regulatory asset for other postemployment benefits costs in a future period when applicable criteria are met. This consensus applies also to all regulatory assets recognized pursuant to SFAS 71 criteria.

Additionally, the Task Force noted that the carrying amount of the regulatory asset to be recognized should be reduced by any impairment which may have occurred.

TITLE PLANT

PERSPECTIVE AND ISSUES

SFAS 61 presents accounting and reporting standards for costs relating to the construction and operation of title plants. A title plant comprises a record of all transactions or conditions that affect titles to land located in a specified area. The length of time spanned by a title plant depends upon regulatory requirements and the time frame required to gather sufficient information to efficiently issue title insurance. Updating occurs frequently as documentation of the current status of a title is added to the title plant.

This pronouncement applies to enterprises such as title insurance companies, title abstract companies, and title agents that use a title plant in their operations. The standard provides that costs directly incurred to construct a title plant should be capitalized when the entity can use the title plant to do title searches and that such capitalized costs are not normally depreciated. The statement also requires that the costs of maintaining a title plant and of doing title searches be expensed as incurred.

Sources of GAAP
SFAS
61

DEFINITIONS OF TERMS

Title plant. Consists of (1) indexed and catalogued information for a period concerning the ownership of, and encumbrances on, parcels of land in a particular geographic area; (2) information relating to persons having an interest in real estate; (3) maps and plats; (4) copies of prior title insurance contracts and reports; and (5) other documents and records. In summary, a title plant constitutes a historical record of all matters affecting title to parcels of land in a particular geographic area.

CONCEPTS, RULES, AND EXAMPLES

Acquisition Costs

The cost of constructing a title plant includes the cost of obtaining, organizing, and summarizing historical information pertaining to a particular tract of land. Costs incurred to assemble a title plant should be capitalized until the record is usable for conducting title searches. Costs incurred to construct a backplant (a title plant that antedates the time span of an existing title plant) must also be capitalized. However, an enterprise may capitalize only those costs that are directly related to and traceable to the activities performed in constructing the title plant or backplant.

The purchase of a title plant or an undivided interest in title plant (the right to its joint use) is recorded at cost as of the date acquired. If title plant is acquired separately, it is recorded at the fair value of consideration given. Backplant may also be purchased.

Capitalized title plant costs are not amortized or depreciated unless an impairment in the carrying amount of the title plant occurs. The following events or changes in circumstances, provided in para 5 of SFAS 121, can indicate that the carrying amount may not be recoverable. An impairment may be indicated by the following circumstances:

1. Changing legal or statutory requirements
2. Economic factors, such as changing demand
3. Loss of competitive advantage
4. Failure to maintain an up-to-date title plant
5. Circumstances that indicate obsolescence, such as abandonment of title plant

The provisions of SFAS 121 apply to any such impairment.

Operating Costs

Costs of title plant maintenance and of conducting title searches must be expensed currently. A title plant is maintained through frequent, often daily, updating which involves adding reports on the current status of specific real estate titles and documentation of security or other ownership interests in such land. A title search entails a search for all information or documentation pertaining to a particular parcel of land. This information is found in the most recently issued title report.

Once a title plant is operational, costs may be incurred to convert the record from one storage and retrieval system to another or to modify the current storage and retrieval system. These costs may **not** be capitalized as title plant. However, they may be separately capitalized and amortized using a systematic and rational method.

Reporting Title Plant Sales

The sale of a title plant should be reported separately. The amount to be reported is determined by the circumstances surrounding the sale as follows:

Terms of sale	*Amount reported*
Sells title plant and waives all rights to future use	Amount received less adjusted cost of title plant
Sells undivided ownership interest (rights to joint use)	Amount received less pro rata portion of adjusted cost of title plant
Sells copies of title plant or the right to use it	Amount received

Note that in the last instance the amount reported is simply the amount received. In this case, no cost is allocated to the item sold unless the title plant's value drops below its adjusted cost as a result of the sale.

APPENDIX

DISCLOSURE CHECKLIST

The disclosure checklist presented below provides a quick reference to the disclosures common to the financial statements of most business enterprises and includes certain common references to items required by the SEC for public companies only.

DISCLOSURE CHECKLIST INDEX

General

A. Basis of Reporting
B. Accounting Policies
C. Accounting Changes
D. Related Parties
E. Contingencies and Commitments
F. Risks and Uncertainties
G. Nonmonetary Transactions
H. Subsequent Events, if Material
I. Rights and Privileges of Various Securities Outstanding
J. Other

Balance Sheet

A. Cash and Cash Equivalents
B. Receivables
C. Marketable Securities
D. Inventories
E. Investments--Equity Method
F. Other Investments
G. Property, Plant, and Equipment
H. Intangibles
I. Accounting for Transfers and Servicing of Assets and Extinguishment of Liabilities
J. Current Liabilities
K. Deferred Tax Assets and Liabilities
L. Notes Payable and Debt
M. Financial Instruments and Derivatives
N. Pensions and Other Postretirement Benefits
O. Leases--Lessees
P. Leases--Lessors
Q. Other Liabilities
R. Stockholders' Equity

Income Statement

A. Basic Disclosure
B. Marketable Securities
C. Income Taxes
D. Extraordinary Items
E. Discontinued Operations
F. Interim Financial Information
G. Segment Data
H. Development Stage Enterprises
I. Long-Term Construction Contracts
J. Research & Development
K. Sales Where Collection Is Uncertain
L. Revenues When Right of Return Exists
M. Other Reporting
N. Foreign Currency
O. Business Combinations and Consolidations
P. Earnings per Share
Q. Comprehensive Income

Statement of Cash Flows

A. Basis
B. Format

Specialized GAAP

A. Banking and Thrift Industries
B. Broadcasting Industry
C. Computer Software Costs and Revenues
D. Franchisor Accounting
E. Insurance Industry Transactions
F. Mortgage Banking Activities
G. Motion Picture Industry
H. Oil and Gas Producing Activities
I. Pension Funds
J. Record and Music Industry
K. Regulated Operations

GENERAL

A. Basis of Reporting and Nature of Operations

1. Name of entity for whom statements are being presented ____
2. Titles of statements should be appropriate (certain titles denote GAAP statements; other titles denote comprehensive basis of accounting) ____
3. Dates and periods covered should be clearly stated ____
4. If comparative statements are presented, repeat footnotes from prior years to extent appropriate ____
5. Differences between "economic" entity and entity being presented (e.g., consolidated or not? subsidiaries included and excluded, combined statements?, etc.) Disclose summarized financial information for previously unconsolidated subsidiaries ____
6. For SEC--New accounting principles not yet adopted and impact of adoption ____
7. Description of major products and services and principle markets and locations ____
8. Relative importance of operations in each business and basis for determination (assets, revenue, earnings) ____

B. Accounting Policies

1. Description of business unless otherwise apparent from statements themselves ____
2. Description of all significant accounting policies involving inventory; marketable securities and investments; property, plant, and equipment; income taxes; revenue recognition; and cost allocation methods ____
3. For SEC only
   a. Adoption of a new standard ____
   b. Methods available under new standard and method chosen ____
   c. Impact of adoption ____
   d. Other significant items ____

C. Accounting Changes

1. Nature and justification of change and its effects on statements ____
2. Change in principle--Regular
   a. Cumulative effect adjustment between extraordinary items and net income on income statement ____
   b. Pro forma effects on net income, income before extraordinary items, and per share ____

c. Effect of new principle on current and future income ____

3. Change in principle--Retroactive

   a. Restate prior period for the following changes: from LIFO; in long-term contract accounting; to or from full cost in extractive industries; in connection with initial public offering; in accounting entity ____
   b. Follow transition rules in all SFAS which might vary from APB 20 ____

4. Change in principle--No cumulative effect (such as change in depreciation method for current and future asset acquisitions)

   a. Statement that cumulative effect either does not exist or cannot be computed ____

5. Change in estimate

   a. Effect on current and future income, if material ____

6. Correction of error--Adjust retained earnings

   a. Nature of error ____
   b. Effect on income before extraordinary item, net income and per share amounts ____

D. Related Parties

1. Nature of relationship and amounts due to or from related parties with terms and matter of settlement ____
2. For each income statement: description and dollar amounts of transactions ____
3. Economic dependency and significant customers ____
4. Nature and extent of related-party leases ____

E. Contingencies and Commitments

1. Accruals **not** made because probable loss could not be estimated ____
2. Upper limit of range of estimates for cases in which lower limit is accrued because **no** best estimate exists ____
3. Nature of reasonably possible losses and one of the following:

   a. Estimated amount of loss ____
   b. Statement that **no** estimate is possible ____

4. Unasserted claims for which it is

   a. Probable that a claim will be asserted, and ____
   b. Reasonably possible that an unfavorable outcome will result ____

5. Events occurring after balance sheet date that may give rise to a loss contingency may be disclosed in either a footnote or pro forma presentation ____
6. Gain contingencies described such that the likelihood of realization is not overstated ____
7. Guarantees of affiliates' obligations ____
8. Indirect guarantees of others' indebtedness ____
9. Material commitments, guarantees, and purchase obligations (SFAS 47) ____
10. Renegotiation of government contracts ____
11. Pending litigation ____
12. Tax disputes ____
13. Unused letters of credit ____
14. Environmental risks and liabilities ____

F. Risks and Uncertainties

1. Nature of operations including major products, services, locations ____
2. Use of estimates in financial statements by management ____
3. Significant estimates and impact of possible changes in estimate ____
4. Vulnerability due to concentrations in business, revenue, sources of supply or labor and market area ____

G. Nonmonetary Transactions

1. Nature of transaction ____
2. Gain or loss and basis of accounting for assets transferred ____

H. Subsequent Events, if Material

1. Adjust financial statements for conditions existing at balance sheet date ____
2. Disclose for conditions subsequent (consider pro forma) ____

I. Rights and Privileges of Various Securities Outstanding

1. Liquidation preferences ____
2. Participations ____
3. Call, conversion and exercise data ____
4. Redeemable preferred stock ____

J. Other

1. Asset valuation allowances ____
2. Pledged and encumbered assets ____
3. Current and noncurrent classifications ____
4. Derivatives (hedge or trading objectives and policy) ____

BALANCE SHEET

A. Cash and Cash Equivalents

1. Segregate and classify the amount of restricted cash according to the nature of the restriction ____
2. Compensating balances disclosed as to their nature and amount ____
3. Overdrafts presented as a current liability ____
4. For SEC, foreign bank balances ____
5. Credit risk for significant concentrations of cash deposits in excess of federally insured limits ____

B. Receivables

1. Receivables involving officers, employees, and other related parties separated as to the amount and nature of the transactions ____
2. The amount of unearned finance charges and interest deducted from the face amount of the receivables ____
3. The amount and nature of pledged or assigned receivables and receivables sold without recourse ____
4. The amount of the valuation allowance including the current period provision ____
5. Credit balances reclassified as a current liability ____
6. Concentrations of credit risk ____
7. Transfers of receivables with recourse ____
8. For impaired loans
    a. For each balance sheet
        (1) Investment in impaired loans ____
        (2) Amount of allowance for credit losses ____
        (3) Policy of income recognition for interest ____
    b. For each income statement
        (1) Average investment in impaired loans, interest income recognized and activity in the allowance for credit losses account ____
9. For noninterest-bearing notes or inappropriate stated interest rates
    a. Discount or premium ____
    b. Effective interest rate and face amount ____
    c. Amortization ____
    d. Issue costs ____

C. Marketable Securities

Classification as trading, available-for-sale, or held-to-maturity

1. Fair value ____
2. Gross unrealized gains ____
3. Gross unrealized losses ____
4. Amortized cost for each major security type ____
5. Maturity date for those debt instruments held to maturity ____
6. For each period for which the results of operations are presented
   a. The proceeds from sales of available-for-sale securities and the gross realized gains and gross realized losses on those sales ____
   b. The basis on which cost was determined in computing realized gain or loss ____
   c. The gross gains and gross losses included in earnings from transfers of securities from the available-for-sale category into the trading category ____
   d. The change in net realized holding gain or loss on available-for-sale securities that has been included in the separate component of shareholders' equity during the period ____
   e. The change in net unrealized holding gain or loss on trading securities that has been included in earnings during the period ____
7. For any sales/transfers from held to maturity
   a. Cost of security ____
   b. Realized or unrealized gain or loss ____
   c. Circumstances leading to decision to sell or transfer ____
8. Significant concentrations of credit risks from securities of a particular issuer ____
9. For SEC--Substantial post-balance-sheet market decline ____

D. Inventories

1. The dollar amount assigned to inventory (cost, lower of cost or market, etc.) ____
2. The cost flow assumption (FIFO, LIFO, etc.) ____
3. The basis of valuation ____
4. Classification (materials, work in process, etc.) ____
5. Principles peculiar to a particular industry ____
6. Pledging of inventories in borrowing agreements ____
7. Product financing arrangements ____
8. Firm purchase commitments ____
9. Liquidation of LIFO inventories and effects on income ____
10. Lower of cost or market "losses," if material ____

E. Investments--Equity Method

1. The name of each investee and the percentage of ownership of common stock ____
2. The accounting policies with respect to each of the investments ____
3. The difference between the carrying amount for each investment and its underlying equity in the investee's net assets and the accounting treatment of the difference between these amounts ____
4. For those investments which have a quoted market price, the aggregate value of each investment ____
5. If investments in investees are considered to have a material effect on the investor's financial position and operating results, summarized data for the investor's assets, liabilities, and results of operations ____
6. If potential conversion of convertible securities and exercise of options and warrants would have material effects on the investor's percentage of the investee ____

F. Other Investments

For equity and debt securities

1. Classification as a held-to-maturity or an available-for-sale investment ____
2. Related basis of accounting ____
3. Any valuation accounts in stockholders' equity which reflect unrealized gains and losses and any income statement effects ____

G. Property, Plant, and Equipment

1. Classes of assets ____
2. The basis of valuation ____
3. The method of computing depreciation ____
4. The amount of accumulated depreciation ____
5. A description of and the amount of any assets pledged as collateral ____
6. Capitalized interest cost

   a. The total amount of interest cost incurred during the period ____
   b. The amount which has been capitalized ____

7. Impairments

   a. If impairment loss is recognized

      (1) Description of impaired assets and situation surrounding impairment ____

(2) Amount of impairment loss and method of determining fair value ____
(3) If impairment losses are not reported separately or parenthetically, the caption where losses are aggregated ____
(4) The business segment affected, if applicable ____

b. In the case of assets to be disposed of

(1) The initial loss ____
(2) Gains or losses resulting from subsequent revision in estimates of fair value less cost to sell ____
(3) If they can be identified and to the extent they are included in entity's operations for the period, results of operations for disposed assets ____
(4) If not reported separately or parenthetically, caption where gains and losses are aggregated ____
(5) Description of the assets and situation surrounding disposal, the carrying amount of assets and expected date of disposal ____
(6) The business segment affected (for public companies) ____

H. Intangibles

1. A description of the nature of the assets ____
2. The amount of amortization expense for the period and the method used ____
3. The amortization period used ____
4. The amount of accumulated amortization ____
5. R&D expenditures

a. The total research and development costs charged to expense for each period for which an income statement is presented ____
b. For contractual agreements

(1) The terms of significant agreements under the R&D arrangements as of the date of each balance sheet presented ____
(2) The amount of compensation earned and costs incurred under contract for each period for which an income statement is presented ____

6. Deferred charges and other assets

a. Segregated by type ____
b. Carrying value of capitalized computer software ____

7. Amount and reason for significant impairment ____
8. Computer software

a. Capitalized value ____
b. Amortization ____
c. Write-downs to realizable value ____

9. Capitalized direct-response advertising ____
10. For obligations to service financial assets

a. Amounts of servicing assets/liabilities recognized and amortized ____
b. Fair value of items (methods and assumptions) ____
c. Risk and amounts of impairment ____

I. Accounting for Transfers and Servicing of Assets and Extinguishment of Liabilities

1. For all servicing assets and liabilities

a. The amounts recognized and amortized during the period ____
b. Fair value of such recognized items including methods and assumptions ____
c. Risk characteristics of assets used to measure impairment ____
d. Activity in the valuation allowance for impairment ____
e. Assets set aside solely to satisfy payments of a specific obligation ____

2. Other disclosures

a. Security required for repurchase agreements or security lending transactions ____
b. Remaining debt outstanding previously extinguished by SFAS 76 ____
c. Restriction on assets set aside to pay specific obligations ____
d. Fair value of assets transferred or description and reasons why fair value cannot be measured ____

J. Current Liabilities

1. Accounts payable

a. Trade ____
b. Nontrade ____
c. Related parties separate disclosure (affiliates; investees for which the equity method is used; employee trusts; principal owners; management, immediate families of owners and management; or any party capable of significantly influencing a transaction) ____

2. Callable obligations

   For long-term callable obligations containing a violation of debt agreement

   a. Description of covenants violated ____
   b. In unclassified balance sheet, include surrounding circumstances with disclosure of long-term debt maturities ____
   c. Obligation that will be classified as noncurrent because it is probable that a violation of debt agreement will be cured within a grace period or a waiver has been obtained ____

3. Income taxes payable

   a. Current ____
   b. Deferred ____

4. Notes payable

   a. Description of note ____
   b. Classified by type

      (1) Trade ____
      (2) Bank ____
      (3) Assets used as security ____
      (4) Related parties (see Accounts payable, 1.c.) ____

   c. Interest rate ____
   d. Aggregate maturities and for 5 years in future ____

5. Other current liabilities

   a. Accruals ____
   b. Advances or deposits ____
   c. Current portions of long-term liabilities ____
   d. Compensated absences ____
   e. Liabilities not recorded because amounts could **not** be estimated ____
   f. Short-term debt expected to be refinanced

      (1) Terms of new obligation incurred or expected to be incurred ____
      (2) Terms of equity securities issued or expected to be issued ____

   g. Bank overdrafts ____
   h. Special termination benefits ____
   i. Credit balances in accounts receivable ____
   j. Terms, interest rates, collateral, and other significant information about the underlying obligation ____

K. Deferred Tax Assets and Liabilities

1. Assets are limited to amounts that could be realized by loss carry-backs segregated by tax jurisdiction ____
2. Classify as current if related to asset or liability that is current or will result in net taxable or deductible amounts next year. Otherwise classify as noncurrent. ____
3. Total deferred tax liabilities ____
4. Total deferred tax assets ____
5. Valuation allowance for deferred tax assets based upon more-likely-than-not recoverability ____
6. Tax effect of each type of temporary difference and carryforward included in deferred taxes ____

L. Notes Payable and Debt

1. Notes and bonds

   a. The aggregate amount of debt shown as a long-term liability on the face of the financial statements net of the current portion due within 1 year and any discount or premium ____

   b. The detail relating to each debt issue in the notes to the financial statements, including

      (1) Nature of the liabilities ____
      (2) Maturity dates ____
      (3) Interest rates (effective and stated) ____
      (4) Call provisions ____
      (5) Conversion privileges ____
      (6) Restrictive covenants (i.e., sinking fund requirements, restrictions on retained earnings, etc.) ____
      (7) Assets pledged as collateral. These assets are shown in the asset section of the balance sheet ____
      (8) Amounts due to related parties including officers, directors, and employees, and terms of settlement (SFAS 57, para 2) ____
      (9) Disclosure of notes or bonds issued subsequent to the balance sheet date ____
      (10) Amounts of unused letters of credit ____

   c. The current portion of the long-term debt is shown as a current liability unless other than current assets will be used to satisfy the obligation ____

   d. Long-term debt is classified as current if the debtor is in violation of a debt covenant at the balance sheet date which

      (1) Makes the obligation callable within 1 year, or ____

(2) Will make the obligation callable within 1 year if the violation is not cured within a specified grace period ____

e. The debt referred to in d. above need not be reclassified if either of the following conditions are met:

(1) The creditor has waived or has subsequently lost the right to demand repayment for 1 year (or, if longer, the operating cycle) from the balance sheet date ____
(2) It is probable (likely) that the violation will be cured by the debtor within the grace period stated in the terms of the debt agreement, thus preventing the obligation from being called ____

2. Induced conversions of convertible debt

a. Nature of any restatement and its effect on income before extraordinary items, net income, and related per share amounts in year SFAS 84 first applied ____

3. Extinguishment of debt

a. Gains or losses resulting from the extinguishment of debt are to be aggregated and unconditionally classified as extraordinary items and the following information provided either on the face of the financial statements or in the notes:

(1) A description of the extinguishment transaction, including the sources of the funds used, if practicable ____
(2) The income tax effect of the transaction ____
(3) The per share amount of the aggregate gain or loss, net of tax ____

b. Defeasance of debt requires footnote disclosure as long as that debt remains outstanding. Disclose the nature of the transaction and the amount of debt held in trust and treated as extinguished. ____

4. Troubled debt restructurings

a. Debtor

(1) A description of the changes in terms and/or major features of settlement ____
(2) The aggregate gain on restructuring and the related tax effect ____
(3) The aggregate net gain or loss on the transfer of assets recognized during the period ____

(4) The per share amount of the aggregate gain on restructuring, net of tax ____
(5) Information on any contingent payments ____

b. Creditor

(1) For the outstanding restructured receivables

(a) The aggregate recorded investment ____

(2) The amount of commitments to lend additional funds to debtors owing receivables whose terms have been modified by restructurings ____
(3) The recorded investment amount for which impairment has been recognized, including the total allowance for credit losses related to those impaired loans, and recorded investments not requiring an allowance ____
(4) The activity in the allowance for credit losses account, including the balance in the allowance for credit losses account at the beginning and end of each period, additions charged to operations, direct write-downs charged against the allowance, and recoveries of amounts previously charged off ____
(5) The creditor's interest income recognition policy on impaired loans, including how cash receipts are recorded ____
(6) For each period of operations, the amount of interest income related to impaired loans, the average investment impaired, and if practical, the amount of interest income using a cash-basis method ____

5. Unconditional purchase obligations

In order to qualify as such an obligation and to be subject to disclosure, the contract must meet the following criteria:

a. It is noncancelable, or cancelable only

(1) Upon the occurrence of some remote contingency ____
(2) With the permission of the other party ____
(3) If a replacement agreement is signed between the same parties ____
(4) Upon payment of a penalty in an amount such that continuation of the agreement appears reasonably assured ____

b. It is negotiated as part of a supplier's product financing arrangement for the facilities that will provide the contracted goods or services or for costs related to those goods or services (e.g., carrying costs for contracted goods) ____

c. It has a remaining term in excess of 1 year ____

d. If the obligation fulfills the foregoing criteria and is recorded on the balance sheet, the following disclosures are required:

(1) Aggregate amount of payments to be made ____

(2) Aggregate amount of maturities and sinking fund requirements for all long-term borrowings ____

e. If the obligation is **not** recorded on the balance sheet, then the following footnote disclosures are required:

(1) The nature and term of the obligation(s) ____

(2) The total amount of the fixed or determinable portion of the obligation(s) at the balance sheet date in the aggregate and for each of the next 5 years, if determinable ____

(3) The nature of any variable components of the obligation(s) ____

(4) The amounts purchased under the obligation(s) (as in take-or-pay or through-put contracts) for each period for which an income statement is presented ____

M. Financial Instruments and Derivatives (SFAS 133)

1. Extent, nature, and terms of financial instruments and derivatives with off-balance-sheet risk by class of instrument

a. Face or contract amount (or notional principal amount if there is no face or contract amount) ____

b. Credit and market risk ____

c. Cash requirements ____

d. Related accounting policy pursuant to the requirements of APB 22 ____

e. Leverage features and effects on the above ____

f. Disclosed by class or category of financial instrument in body of financial statements or in the accompanying notes ____

g. Exceptions

(1) Insurance contracts, other than financial guarantees and investment contracts, as discussed in SFAS 60 and SFAS 97 ____

(2) Unconditional purchase obligations subject to SFAS 47 ____

(3) Employers' and plans' obligations for pension benefits, postretirement health care and life insurance benefits, and employee stock option and stock purchase plans, as reported by SFAS 35, 43, 81, and 87, as well as APB 12 and 25 ____

(4) Financial instruments of a pension plan, when subject to SFAS 87 ____

(5) Substantively extinguished debt subject to SFAS 76 ____
(6) Lease contracts, as defined in SFAS 13 ____
(7) Payables and obligations denominated in foreign currencies and included in the statement of financial position at translated or remeasured amounts according to SFAS 52, *Foreign Currency Translation*, except

(a) Obligations that have additional off-balance-sheet risk from other risks, and ____
(b) Obligations under foreign currency exchange contracts ____

2. Credit risk of financial instruments with off-balance-sheet credit risk

a. Amount of accounting loss entity would incur should any party to the financial instrument fail to perform according to terms of the contact and collateral or security, if any, is of no value ____
b. Entity's policy of requiring collateral or security, entity's access to that collateral or security, and the nature and brief description of collateral or security ____
c. To be disclosed by class of financial instrument in the body of the financial statements or in the accompanying notes ____
d. Exceptions: Same as in 1.f. above ____

3. Concentrations of credit risk of all financial instruments

a. All significant concentrations of credit risk from **all** financial instruments, whether from an individual counterparty or groups of counterparties ____
b. Group concentrations exist if a number of counterparties are engaged in similar activities and have similar economic characteristics such that they would be similarly affected by changes in conditions ____
c. Each significant concentration

(1) Information about the (shared) activity, region, or economic characteristics ____
(2) Same as 2.a. ____
(3) Same as 2.b. ____

d. Exceptions: Same as 1.g.(1)--1.g.(5) ____

4. Derivatives

a. Trading

(1) Averaging fair value during period ____

(2) Gains or losses by category of item ____

b. Nontrading

(1) Class, objectives and strategies ____
(2) Description of reporting in financial statements including recognition and measurement policies ____
(3) For hedges--Information about transaction hedged and amounts deferred ____

c. Hedging activities

(1) Objectives for hedging and risk management policy ____
(2) Differences between fair value and foreign currency derivatives hedging instruments ____
(3)
(a) Fair value hedges ____
1] The net gain or loss recognized in earnings during the reporting period representing (1) the amount of the hedges' ineffectiveness and (2) the component of the derivative instruments' gain or loss, if any, excluded from the assessment of hedge effectiveness, and a description of where the net gain or loss is reported in the statement of income or other statement of financial performance ____
2] The amount of net gain or loss recognized in earnings when a hedged firm commitment no longer qualifies as a fair value hedge ____

(b) Cash flow hedges ____

1] The net gain or loss recognized in earnings during the reporting period representing (1) the amount of the hedges' ineffectiveness and (2) the component of the derivative instruments' gain or loss, if any, excluded from the assessment of hedge effectiveness, and a description of where the net gain or loss is reported in the statement of income or other statement of financial performance ____
2] A description of the transactions or other events that will result in the reclassification into earning of gains and losses that are reported in accumulated other comprehensive income, and the estimated net amount of the existing gains or losses at the reporting date that is expected to be reclassified into earnings within the next 12 months ____

3] The maximum length of time over which the entity is hedging its exposure to the variability in future cash flows for forecasted transactions excluding those forecasted transactions related to the payment of variable interest on existing financial instruments ____

4] The amount of gains and losses reclassified into earnings as a result of the discontinuance of cash flow hedges ____

(c) Hedges of the net investment in a foreign operation

For derivative instruments, as well nonderivative instruments that may give rise to foreign currency transaction gains or losses under Statement 52, that have been designated and have qualified as hedging instruments for hedges of the foreign currency exposure of a net investment in a foreign operation, the net amount of gains or losses included in the cumulative translation adjustment during the reporting period

1] Futures contracts

a] If hedges--nature of assets, liabilities commitments, etc. hedged ____

b] Method of accounting ____

N. Pensions and Other Postretirement Benefits

1. Defined benefit plans require the following disclosures:

a. A reconciliation of beginning and ending balances of the benefit obligation with the effects of the following shown separately:

(1) Service cost ____
(2) Interest cost ____
(3) Contributions by plan participants ____
(4) Actuarial gains and losses ____
(5) Foreign currency exchange rate changes ____
(6) Benefits paid ____
(7) Plan amendments ____
(8) Business combinations ____
(9) Divestitures ____
(10) Curtailments ____
(11) Settlements ____
(12) Special termination benefits ____

b. A reconciliation of beginning and ending balances of the fair value of plan assets with the effects of the following shown separately:
   (1) Actual return on plan assets ____
   (2) Foreign currency exchange rate changes ____
   (3) Contributions by the employer ____
   (4) Contributions by plan participants ____
   (5) Benefits paid ____
   (6) Business combinations ____
   (7) Divestitures ____
   (8) Settlements ____
c. The funded status of the plans ____
d. The amounts recognized and the amounts not recognized in the statement of financial position such as
   (1) Any unamortized service cost ____
   (2) Any unrecognized net gain or loss ____
   (3) Any unamortized net obligation or net asset existing at the initial date of prior Statement 87 or 106 that are still unrecognized ____
   (4) Prepaid assets or accrued liabilities of the net pension or other postretirement benefits ____
   (5) Any intangible asset ____
   (6) The amount of other comprehensive income recognized ____
e. The recognized amount of the net periodic benefit cost with the components shown separately ____
f. The amount caused from a change in the additional minimum pension liability that was included in other comprehensive income ____
g. Rates for
   (1) Assumed discount rate ____
   (2) Rate of compensation increase ____
   (3) Expected long-term rate of return on plan assets ____
h. Trend rates assumed for health care cost for the next year and thereafter ____
i. The effects of a one-percentage point increase or decrease of the trend rates for health care costs on ____
   (1) The aggregate of the service and interest cost components ____
   (2) The accumulated postretirement benefit obligation ____
j. If applicable

(1) The amounts and types of securities of the employer or a related party in plan assets ____
(2) The amount of future benefits covered by insurance contracts issued by the employer or a related party ____
(3) Any significant transactions between the plan and the employer or a related party ____
(4) An amortization method used not pursuant to prior standards ____
(5) Any substantive commitment used as the basis for accounting for the benefit obligation ____
(6) The cost of special or contractual termination benefits recognized during the period with a description of the event ____

k. An explanation of significant changes in the benefit obligation or plan assets that is not apparent in the other disclosures required ____

2. Disclosures for employers with more than one plan ____

a. Disclosures required in this statement may be disclosed in aggregate for an employer's defined benefit pension plans and in aggregate for an employer's defined benefit postretirement plans but must still present separately prepaid benefit costs and accrued benefit liabilities recognized in the statement of financial position. ____
b. An employer may not combine the disclosures of plans outside the US and plans in the US if the benefit obligation of the plans outside the US represent a significant portion of the total benefit obligation and significant differences exist in the assumptions used. ____

3. Disclosure requirements for nonpublic entities ____

a. Nonpublic entities may choose to disclose the following instead of the disclosures stated in 1.: ____

(1) Benefit obligation ____
(2) Fair value of plan assets ____
(3) Funded status of the plan ____
(4) Contributions by the employer and the participant ____
(5) Amounts recognized in the statement of financial position of

(a) Prepaid assets or accrued liabilities ____
(b) Any intangible asset ____

(6) Amount of accumulated other comprehensive income recognized and the amount resulting from a change in the minimum pension liability recognized ____
(7) Net periodic benefit cost recognized ____
(8) Rates for

(a) Assumed discount rate ____
(b) Rate of compensation increase ____
(c) Expected long-term rate of return on plan assets ____

(9) Trend rates assumed for health care cost for the next year and thereafter ____
(10) If applicable

(a) Amounts and types of securities of the employer or a related party ____
(b) Future annual benefits covered by insurance contracts issued by the employer or a related party ____
(c) Any significant transactions between the plan and the employer or a related party ____

(11) Nature and effect of significant nonroutine events ____

4. Disclosures for defined contribution plans

a. Amount of cost recognized for pension or postretirement benefit plans must be separate from the cost recognized for defined benefit plans ____
b. Nature and effect of any significant changes that affect comparability must be disclosed ____

5. Disclosures for multiemployer plans

a. Amount of contributions to multiemployer plans ____
b. Nature and effect of changes which affect comparability ____
c. If withdrawals made by an employer from a multiemployer plan will result in an obligation for a portion of the unfunded benefit obligation or the unfunded accumulated postretirement benefit obligation, follow the provision of SFAS 5, *Accounting for Contingencies* ____

6. Defined contribution plans require the following separate disclosures:

a. Description of the plan and an indication of the groups covered ____
b. Basis for determining contributions ____

c. Acknowledgment of matters of significance that have affected the comparability of the accounting periods presented and comments as to their nature and effect ____
d. Amount of cost recognized during the period ____
e. For multiemployer plans: types of benefits provided ____
f. Compliance with minimum funding requirements of ERISA, if applicable ____
g. Receipt of minimum funding waiver by IRS, if applicable ____

O. Leases--Lessees

1. For capital leases

   a. The gross amount of assets recorded under capital leases presented by major classes according to function or nature ____
   b. Future minimum lease payments in the aggregate and for each of the next 5 fiscal years with separate deductions made for executory costs (including any profit thereon) included in the minimum lease payments, and the amount of imputed interest needed to reduce the net minimum lease payments to present value ____
   c. Total of minimum sublease rentals to be received in the future under noncancelable subleases ____
   d. Total contingent rentals actually incurred for each period for which an income statement is presented ____
   e. Depreciation on capital leases should be separately disclosed ____

2. For sale-leaseback transactions

   a. In addition to requirements of SFAS 13 and 66, financials of seller-lessee shall describe terms of sale-leaseback transaction, including future commitments, obligations, provisions, or circumstances requiring or resulting in seller-lessee's involvement ____
   b. Where seller-lessee has accounted for transaction by deposit method or as a financing per SFAS 98, para 17

      (1) The obligation for future minimum lease payments as of the date of the latest balance sheet presented in the aggregate and for each of the 5 succeeding fiscal years ____
      (2) The total of minimum sublease rentals, if any, to be received in the future under noncancelable subleases in the aggregate and for each of the 5 succeeding fiscal years ____

3. For operating leases having a remaining noncancelable term in excess of 1 year

a. Future minimum lease payments in the aggregate and for each of the next 5 fiscal years ____
b. Total of minimum rentals that will be received under noncancelable subleases ____

4. For all operating leases

a. Present rental expense disclosing separately the amount for minimum rentals, contingent rentals, and sublease rentals ____
b. Rental payments for leases with terms of a month or less that were not renewed may be excluded ____

5. General description required of lessee's leasing arrangements including, but not limited to

a. Basis of computing contingent rental payments ____
b. Existence and terms of renewal or purchase options and escalation clauses ____
c. Restrictions imposed by leasing agreements such as on dividends, additional debt, and further leasing arrangements ____

P. Leases--Lessors

1. For sales-type and direct financing leases

a. Components of the net investment in leases include the following:

(1) Future minimum lease payments to be received with separate deductions for amount representing executory costs (including any profit thereon), and the accumulated allowance for uncollectible lease payments ____
(2) Unguaranteed residual values accruing to benefit of lessor ____
(3) For direct financing leases only, initial direct costs ____
(4) Unearned interest revenue ____

b. Future minimum lease payments to be received for each of the next 5 fiscal years ____
c. Total contingent rentals included in income for each period for which an income statement is presented ____

2. For operating leases

a. The cost and carrying amount (if different) of property leased or held for leasing segregated by major classes of property according to function or nature, and the total amount of accumulated depreciation ____

b. Minimum rentals on noncancelable leases in the aggregate and for each of the next 5 fiscal years ____
c. Total contingent rentals included in income for each period for which an income statement is presented ____

3. A general description of the lessor's leasing arrangements ____
4. Leveraged leases ____

Q. Other Liabilities

1. Deferred compensation ____

R. Stockholders' Equity

1. General

The stockholders' equity section of the balance sheet provides information to interested parties concerning the stewardship function and the efficiency of the firm's management. In addition, it provides information concerning the historical and prospective economic interests of the groups holding a specific or general interest in the firm. The following should be disclosed:

a. The sources of capital supplied to the firm ____
b. The legal restrictions on the distribution of invested capital ____
c. The legal, contractual, managerial, and financial restrictions on the distribution of dividends to stockholders ____
d. The priorities of the classes of stockholders in a partial or final liquidation ____

2. Capital stock and additional paid-in capital

a. For each class of stock

(1) Par, stated, or assigned value ____
(2) Number of shares authorized, issued, and outstanding ____
(3) Number of shares held in treasury ____
(4) Conversion terms of preferred, if applicable, including call prices, rates, and dates. Additionally, the amount of redemption requirements for all issues of stock that are redeemable at fixed or determinable prices on fixed or determinable dates must be disclosed for each of the 5 years following the date of the latest balance sheet presented. ____
(5) Changes in the number of shares authorized, issued, and outstanding during the year and changes in the equity accounts ____
(6) Liquidation values, if different than par, in the aggregate for preferred ____

(7) For preferred, any dividend preferences, special privileges, arrearages in dividends, etc. ____
(8) Any unusual voting rights ____
(9) Rights and privileges (dividend, liquidation, participation, call prices/dates, conversion or exercise rights, involuntary liquidation rights) ____

b. The amount of cumulative dividends in arrears, per share and in aggregate ____
c. Aggregate securities issuable under rights or warrants, as well as their prices, and exercise and expiration dates ____
d. Any discount on capital stock ____
e. The amount of subscribed shares not yet issued ____
f. Deferred compensation expense offset against the paid-in capital account, "Stock options outstanding" (see 6. a.) ____
g. Stock dividends distributable in total or at par or stated value with the excess included in additional paid-in capital. Also acceptable is deferment of their recording until issuance. However, disclosure is necessary in the notes. ____
h. The amount of capital stock issued in business combinations (purchase or pooling) or agreements to issue additional shares at a later date ____
i. Transactions affecting equity subsequent to the date of the financial statements (recapitalization, sales of stock, etc.) ____
j. Additional paid-in capital, listed by source, along with any changes during the period ____
k. Any changes in the capital accounts of partners or sole proprietors ____

3. Retained earnings

a. Appropriation and segregation of retained earnings, as well as their nature, cause, and amount. Changes in these accounts should be disclosed. ____
b. Nature and dollar amounts of restrictions on retained earnings (treasury stock, lease covenants, etc.) ____
c. Date retained earnings for 10 years following quasi reorganization ____
d. Increase/decrease results from combination by pooling of interests (revenues, expenses, extraordinary items, and net income) ____
e. Prior period adjustments, net of tax and in gross. For correction of an error, in the period discovered

(1) Nature of the error on previous statements ____

(2) Effect of correction on income before extraordinary items, net income, and related per share amounts ____

4. Dividends

a. Dividends in aggregate and per share as well as the nature and extent of any restrictions on retained earnings limiting availability of dividends ____
b. The amount of dividends in arrears, per share and in aggregate ____
c. Dividends declared after balance sheet date, prior to opinion date, unless a long-established history of regular payment dates exists and the dividend is not abnormal in amount ____
d. For stock dividends and stock splits, disclosure of the amounts capitalized, per share and in total. Historical presentations of earnings per share should be restated in an equivalent number of shares so the figures are presented on a comparable basis. ____

5. Treasury stock

a. Treasury stock, cost method--Present total cost of treasury stock as a deduction from total stockholders' equity. Disclose number of shares held in treasury. ____
b. Treasury stock, par value method--Present par value of treasury stock as a deduction from par value of issued shares of same class. Any related additional paid-in capital from treasury stock is netted with corresponding additional paid-in capital without separate disclosure. Disclose number of shares held in treasury. ____

6. Compensatory stock plans

a. **Plan description**, including general terms of awards such as vesting requirements, maximum term of options granted, and the number of shares authorized for grants of options or other equity instruments. ____
b. For each year for which an income statement is provided

(1) **Number and weighted-average exercise prices** of the following options: those outstanding at the beginning and at the end of the year; those exercisable at the end of the year; and those granted, exercised, forfeited, or expired during the year ____
(2) **Weighted-average grant-date fair value** of options granted during the year and additional required disclosures if exercise prices of some options differ from the market price of the stock on the grant date ____

(3) **Number and weighted-average grant-date fair value of equity instruments** other than options, such as shares of nonvested stock, granted during the year ____
(4) **Description of method and significant assumptions used** during the year **to estimate the fair value of options** ____
(5) **Total compensation cost** recognized for stock-based employee compensation awards ____
(6) Terms of **significant modifications** of outstanding awards ____

c. For options outstanding at the latest balance sheet date, the **range of exercise prices** and the weighted-average remaining contractual life ____

7. Employee stock ownership plans (ESOP)

a. Description of the plan, including basis for determining contributions, groups covered, nature and effect of matters affecting comparability of information across periods ____
b. The basis for releasing shares by leveraged and pension reversion ESOP ____
c. Accounting policies pertinent to ESOP transactions ____
d. Compensation cost recognized during the period ____
e. Numbers of shares allocated, committed to be released, and held in suspense by the ESOP ____
f. Fair value amount of unearned compensation at year end ____
g. Nature of any repurchase obligations and aggregate fair value thereof ____

8. For SEC only

a. Dividend payout restrictions ____
b. Stock subscriptions ____
c. Redemption requirements on redeemable stock ____
d. Separate classification for redeemable preferred stock ____

INCOME STATEMENT

A. Basic Disclosures

1. Sales, costs, and expenses ____
2. Income or loss before extraordinary items ____
3. Extraordinary items ____
4. Income taxes ____
5. Discontinued segments ____
6. Depreciation ____
7. Interest costs ____
8. Early extinguishment of debt ____
9. Foreign currency gains and losses ____
10. Marketable securities gains and losses ____
11. Research and development expenses ____
12. S Corporation election--No income tax effect ____

B. Marketable Securities

1. Proceeds from sales of available-for-sale securities and the gross realized gains and gross realized losses on those sales ____
2. Basis on which cost was determined in computing realized gain or loss ____
3. The gross gains and gross losses included in earnings from transfers of securities from the available-for-sale category into the trading category ____
4. The change in net unrealized holding gain or loss on available-for-sale securities that has been included in other comprehensive income during the period ____
5. The change in net unrealized holding gain or loss on trading securities that has been included in earnings during the period ____

C. Income Taxes

1. State if entity is not subject to income taxes because income is taxed directly to owners. State the net difference between tax and book bases of assets and liabilities. ____
2. State amounts allocated to

   a. Current tax expense or benefit ____
   b. Deferred tax expense or benefit (exclusive of the effects of other components listed below) ____
   c. Investment tax credits ____
   d. Government grants (to the extent recognized as a reduction of income tax expense) ____
   e. The benefits of operating loss carryforwards ____

f. Tax expense that results from allocating certain tax benefits either directly to contributed capital or to reduce goodwill or other noncurrent intangible assets of an acquired entity ____
g. Adjustments of a deferred tax liability or asset for enacted changes in tax laws or rates or a change in the tax status of the enterprise ____
h. Adjustments of the beginning-of-the-year balance of a valuation allowance because of a change in circumstances that causes a change in judgment about the realizability of the related deferred tax asset in future years ____

3. Amounts allocated to

a. Continuing operations ____
b. Discontinued operations ____
c. Extraordinary items ____
d. Cumulative effect of accounting changes ____
e. Prior period adjustments ____
f. Gains and losses included in comprehensive income but excluded from net income ____
g. Capital transactions ____

4. Reconcile statutory tax rates to actual rates for significant items (nonpublic enterprises need only disclose the nature of significant reconciling items) ____
5. Amounts and expiration dates for operating loss and tax credit carryforward for financial reporting ____
6. If consolidated return filed, separately issued financial statements should state

a. Amount of current and deferred tax expense for each income statement ____
b. Tax-related balances due to or from affiliates for each balance sheet ____
c. The method of allocating consolidated amounts of current and deferred tax expense and effects of any change in that methodology ____

7. Effect of adopting new pronouncement for restated prior years' financial statements ____
8. Cumulative effect of change (similar to change in accounting principle) for earliest restated financial statements ____
9. When a deferred tax liability is not recognized because of the exceptions to comprehensive recognition of deferred taxes, the following information shall be disclosed:

a. A description of the types of temporary differences for which a deferred tax liability has not been recognized and the types of events that would cause those temporary differences to become taxable ____
b. The cumulative amount of each type of temporary difference ____
c. The amount of the unrecognized deferred tax liability for temporary differences related to investments in foreign subsidiaries and foreign corporate joint ventures that are essentially permanent in duration if determination of that liability is practicable or a statement that determination is not practicable ____
d. The amount of the deferred tax liability for temporary differences other than those in c. above (i.e., undistributed domestic earnings, the bad-debt reserve for tax purposes of a US savings and loan association or other qualified thrift lender, the policyholders' surplus of a life insurance enterprise, and the statutory reserve funds of a US steamship enterprise) that is not recognized. ____

D. Extraordinary Items

1. Segregated and shown net of tax ____
2. Adequate explanations of nature ____
3. Infrequent or unusual items shown separately although not extraordinary; not shown net of tax ____

E. Discontinued Operations

1. Assets and operations segregated ____
2. Gain/loss from disposal ____
3. Expected loss on future disposal--date and manner ____

F. Interim Financial Information

1. Minimum disclosures are required by APB 28 when publicly traded entities report summarized interim financial information. These required disclosures are

   a. Sales or gross revenues, provision for income taxes, extraordinary items, cumulative effect of a change in principle, and net income ____
   b. Primary and fully diluted earnings per share ____
   c. Seasonal revenues, costs, and expenses ____
   d. Significant changes in income tax estimates ____
   e. Discontinued operations and extraordinary, unusual, or infrequently occurring items ____
   f. Contingencies ____

   g. Changes in accounting principles or estimates ____
   h. Significant changes in financial position ____

2. When summarized financial information is reported on a regular quarterly basis, the above disclosures should be presented for the current year and the current year-to-date (or preceding 12 months), with comparable data for the preceding year ____

G. Segment Data

1. Factors identifying reportable segments (products, geography, regulatory environment or combination of factors) ____
2. Types of products and services for each segment ____
3. Segment profit or loss including
   a. Revenue from external customers ____
   b. Revenue from other customers ____
   c. Interest income ____
   d. Interest expense ____
   e. Depreciation, depletion and amortization ____
   f. Unusual items per APB 30 ____
   g. Equity method income ____
   h. Income tax expense or benefit ____
   i. Extraordinary items ____
   j. Significant noncash items not included above ____
   k. Measurement methods for each segment's data ____
4. Basis of accounting for transactions between segments ____
5. Differences between segment data and consolidated data, both assets and income ____
6. Changes from prior periods in methods of measurement and data ____
7. Geographic information ____
8. Reliance on single customer for entity when 10% or more of revenue ____

H. Development Stage Enterprises

1. Cumulative revenue, expenses and losses, and cash flows ____
2. Identification as development stage enterprise ____
3. Description of activities ____

I. Long-Term Construction Contracts

1. The method of recognizing income (percentage-of-completion or completed-contract) ____

2. If the percentage-of-completion method is used, the method of computing percentage of completion (e.g., cost-to-cost, efforts-expended) ____
3. If the completed-contract method is used, the justification for its use should be indicated ____
4. Length of the operating cycle; if greater than 1 year, the range of contract durations should be disclosed ____
5. The basis of recording inventory ____
6. The effect of changes in estimates ____
7. The accounting for deferred costs ____
8. The accounting for general and administrative expenses ____
9. Criteria for determining substantial completion (e.g., compliance with specifications, acceptance by customer) ____
10. Information on revenues and costs arising from claims ____
11. Effects of accounting changes to conform to SOP 81-1 (retroactive restatements of prior periods' financial statements) ____

J. Research and Development

1. Expenditures (See Intangibles) ____
2. R&D arrangements
    a. Terms including royalties, purchase provisions, license agreements and funding ____
    b. Amounts earned and costs incurred each period for which an income statement is presented ____

K. Sales Where Collection Is Uncertain

1. Method and justification of accounting for installment basis sales ____
2. Yearly gross profit rates ____
3. Contractual terms such as interest and repossession provisions ____
4. Average length of installment contracts ____

L. Revenue Recognition When Right of Return Exists

1. Basis for recognizing revenue and cost of sales ____
2. Estimated amount of returns ____
3. Description of return privilege granted to customers ____
4. Length of time covered by the return privilege ____

M. Other Reporting

1. Financing arrangements--Real estate and product financing ____
2. Real estate sales ____
3. Futures contracts ____
4. Service sales transaction

a. The revenue recognition method used and its justification ____
b. Information concerning unearned revenues ____
c. Information concerning deferred costs ____
d. Periods over which services are to be performed ____

5. Advertising costs including policy and any amounts classified as assets ____

N. Foreign Currency

1. Aggregate transaction gain or loss that is included in the entity's net income ____
2. Analysis of changes in accumulated translation adjustments which are reported as other comprehensive income. At a minimum, the disclosures should include

   a. Beginning and ending amounts of the translation adjustments account ____
   b. Aggregate adjustment for the period resulting from translation adjustments, and gains and losses from certain hedges and intercompany balances ____
   c. Amount of income taxes for the period allocated to translation adjustments ____
   d. Amounts transferred from the translation adjustments account and included in determining net income as a result of the (partial) sale or liquidation of the foreign operation ____

3. Significant rate changes subsequent to the date of the financial statements including effects on unsettled foreign currency transactions. Rate changes subsequent to the balance sheet date are not incorporated into the financial statements for the period just ended. ____
4. Accounts to be remeasured using historical exchange rates

   a. Marketable securities carried at cost

      (1) Equity securities ____
      (2) Debt securities not intended to be held until maturity ____

   b. Inventories carried at cost ____
   c. Prepaid expenses such as insurance, advertising, and rent ____
   d. Property, plant, and equipment ____
   e. Accumulated depreciation on property, plant, and equipment ____
   f. Patents, trademarks, licenses, and formulas ____
   g. Goodwill ____
   h. Other intangible assets ____
   i. Deferred charges and credits, except deferred income taxes and policy acquisition costs for life insurance companies ____

j. Deferred income ____
k. Common stock ____
l. Preferred stock carried at issuance price ____
m. Revenues and expenses related to nonmonetary items

(1) Cost of goods sold ____
(2) Depreciation of property, plant, and equipment ____
(3) Amortization of intangible items such as goodwill, patents, licenses, etc. ____
(4) Amortization of deferred charges or credits, except deferred income taxes and policy acquisition costs for life insurance companies ____

O. Business Combinations and Consolidations

1. Nature and policy of combinations ____
2. Intercompany eliminations ____
3. Detailed purchase disclosures

a. Name and description of acquired company ____
b. Acquisition was a purchase ____
c. Period that acquired results of operations are consolidated ____
d. Cost of acquired and shares issued ____
e. Plan of amortization and goodwill ____
f. Contingent payments ____
g. Net operating loss/carryforward ____

4. Detailed pooling disclosures

a. Name and description of pooling companies ____
b. Pooling accounting was used ____
c. Description and number of shares issued ____
d. Details of operations of separate companies for period prior to pooling included in first year's operation ____
e. Accounting adjustments to achieve uniform accounting methods ____
f. Explanation of change in retained earnings caused by change in fiscal year ____
g. Reconciliation of individual company operating results to combined results ____

5. Remeasure purchase combinations for prior year financial statements restated for deferred income taxes payable ____
6. Summarize disclosures of balance sheets and income statements previously provided for formerly unconsolidated majority-owned subsidiaries ____

7. Segregation of minority interest ____
8. Material differences caused by different financial reporting periods of subsidiaries ____

P. Earnings per Share

1. For each income statement presented

   a. Simple capital structure
   b. Basic earnings per share for
      (1) Income from continuing operations ____
      (2) Net income ____

   c. Complex capital structure (potential common stock issuances such as options, warrants, convertible securities or contingent stock agreements). Required disclosure for both basic and diluted earnings per share for both income from continuing operation and net income. ____

2. Other disclosures

   a. Per share amounts for discontinued operations, extraordinary items or cumulative change in accounting principle for both basic and diluted may be disclosed in the income statement or in the footnotes. ____
   b. Reconciliation of numerators and denominators of basic and diluted per share calculations for income from continuing operation. ____
   c. Effect given to preferred dividends. ____
   d. Potentially dilutive securities not included in per share calculations because they are antidilutive. ____

Q. Comprehensive Income

1. All components and total comprehensive income ____
2. Net income as separate component ____
3. Foreign currency, pension liability, unrealized gains and losses (net of tax) ____

STATEMENT OF CASH FLOWS

A. Basis

1. Definition of cash and cash equivalents adopted ____
2. Summarize noncash investing and financing activities ____

B. Format

1. Reconcile net income to net cash flow ____

2. If direct method used, display major categories of gross cash receipts and cash payments ____

   a. Cash receipts

      (1) Cash receipts from sale of goods or services ____
      (2) Interest and dividends received ____
      (3) Other operating cash receipts ____

   b. Cash payments

      (1) Payments to employees and other suppliers of goods or services ____
      (2) Income taxes paid ____
      (3) Interest paid ____
      (4) Other operating cash payments ____

3. If indirect method used, state both interest and income taxes paid ____

SPECIALIZED GAAP

A. Banking and Savings Institutions

(See the AICPA Audit and Accounting Guide: *Banks and Savings Institutions*, 1997)

B. Broadcasting Industry

1. License agreements for program material not reported due to failure to meet the specified conditions ____

C. Computer Software Costs and Revenues

1. Amount of research and development costs charged to expense during the period ____
2. Amount of capitalized computer software costs amortized to expense during the period ____
3. Unamortized computer software costs at the end of the period ____
4. For software costs developed or obtained for internal use disclosure requirements of APB 12 and 22, SFAS 2 and 121, and SOP 94-6. ____

D. Franchisor Accounting

1. Nature of all significant commitments resulting from franchise agreements ____
2. Description of services not yet substantially performed ____
3. If collectibility is uncertain

   a. Use of installment or cost recovery method ____

b. Sales price of franchises including deferral of both costs and revenue ____
c. Amounts originally deferred but later recognized due to resolution of uncertainty ____

4. Initial franchise fees segregated from other franchise fee revenue and contribution to net income of such initial fees ____
5. Saturation point of locations or other expectation of decline in future initial franchise fee revenue ____
6. Segregation of franchisor owned outlet revenues and expenses from other activities ____
7. Other

   a. Franchises sold or purchased or operated ____
   b. Franchisor owned outlets ____
   c. Significant changes in the outlets during the period ____

E. Insurance Industry

1. Liabilities for claims and claim adjustment expenses

   a. Basis for estimating liabilities ____
   b. For short-term contracts carried at present value

      (1) Carrying amount ____
      (2) Discount rate used ____
      (3) Claim adjustment expenses ____
      (4) Consideration of anticipated investment income in determining if a premium deficiency exists ____

2. Future policy benefits owed

   a. Methods and assumptions ____
   b. Average rate of expected investment yields ____

3. Capitalized acquisition costs

   a. Nature ____
   b. Method of amortization ____
   c. Amount amortized during the period ____

4. Reinsurance transactions

   a. Nature, purpose and effect of ceded transactions ____
   b. Methods of income recognition on reinsurance contracts ____
   c. Short-term contracts--Premiums from direct business, reinsurance assumed and ceded ____

d. Long-term contracts--Premiums and amounts assessed against policyholders, reinsurance assumed and ceded, premiums and amounts earned ____
e. Concentration of credit risk on reinsurance receivables and premiums ____

5. Participating insurance

a. Relative percentage ____
b. Method of accounting for dividends ____
c. Amount of dividends ____
d. Additional income allocated to participating policyholders ____

6. Statutory accounting practices

a. Statutory capital and surplus

(1) Actual amount ____
(2) Amount required by statute (if significant compared to actual) ____

b. Statutory restrictions of the payment of dividends

(1) Nature ____
(2) Amount of retained earnings restricted ____

7. Income tax disclosures ____

F. Mortgage Banking Activities

1. Method used to determine lower of cost or market value

a. Aggregate vs. individual loan basis ____

2. Servicing rights capitalized during the period

a. Amount ____
b. Method of amortization ____
c. Amount of amortization for the period ____

3. Fair value of capitalized servicing rights, including methods and assumptions used and explanation of reasons if not practical to estimate ____
4. Risk characteristics for stratifying servicing rights in measuring impairment ____
5. Changes in servicing rights valuation allowance ____

G. Motion Picture Industry

1. Components of film inventories

a. Scenarios and story rights ____

b. Films in production ____
c. Films completed but unreleased ____
d. Films released ____

H. Oil and Gas Activities

SFAS 69 requires publicly traded enterprises to disclose the following oil and gas producing data as **supplementary** (not part of the financial statements) information:

1. Proved oil and gas reserves ____
2. Capitalized costs ____
3. Acquisition, exploration, and development costs ____
4. Results of operations ____
5. Standardized measure of discounted future cash flows relating to proved reserves ____

I. Pension Funds

The plan's accounting policies should disclose a description of methods and assumptions

1. Used to determine fair value ____
2. Used to determine APVAPB ____
3. Changed during the current period ____

The financial statements should disclose the following:

1. Plan descriptions--Including vesting and benefit provisions ____
2. Significant plan amendment descriptions--Indicate if APVAPB does not include the effects of the amendments ____
3. Priority order of participants' claims to assets ____
4. Benefits guaranteed by Pension Benefit Guaranty Corp. ____
5. Funding policy and any period changes. In addition, the following should make the disclosure indicated:

   a. Contributory plan--Method of determining contributions ____
   b. ERISA--Whether minimum funding requirements were met ____

   Disclosure of a minimum funding waiver or a request for one from the IRS is required.

6. Policy concerning insurance companies and the purchase of contracts that are excluded from plan assets. Disclosure should be made of the amount of dividend income related to excluded contracts. ____
7. Income status of the plan ____
8. Investments that are 5% or more of plan assets should be identified ____

9. Significant real estate or other transactions between the plan and the sponsor, the employer, or the employee organization ____
10. Infrequent or unusual events that occur between the benefit information date and the issuance of statements that would aid in the determination of the plan's ability to pay benefits ____

Use of averages is acceptable if substantially the same results are obtained.

J. Record and Music Industry

1. Licensors
   a. Commitments to pay advance royalties in the future ____
   b. Future royalty guarantees ____
   c. Cost of record masters borne by the record company and capitalized as assets (disclose separately) ____

K. Regulated Operations

1. Refunds
   a. Effect on net income, when recognized in period(s) different than related revenue
      (1) Not recognized as an extraordinary item ____
2. Discontinuation of specialized accounting
   a. Reasons for discontinuation ____
   b. Portion of operations to which the discontinuation applies ____
   c. Net adjustment reported as an extraordinary item ____

GAAP

INTERPRETATION AND APPLICATION OF GENERALLY ACCEPTED ACCOUNTING PRINCIPLES

1999 EDITION

SELF-STUDY CPE PROGRAM

Unit I
Chapters 1-7

Unit II
Chapters 8-11

Unit III
Chapters 12-15

Unit IV
Chapters 16-22

JOHN WILEY & SONS, INC.

New York • Chichester • Weinheim • Brisbane • Toronto • Singapore

About this Course

We are pleased that you have selected our course. A course description that is based on the 1999 edition of *GAAP: Interpretation and Application* follows:

Prerequisites:	**None**
Recommended CPE credits:	**10 hours per unit**
Knowledge level:	**Basic**
Area of study:	**Accounting and Auditing**

The credit hours recommended are in accordance with the AICPA Standards for CPE Programs. Since CPE requirements are set by each state, you need to check with your State Board of Accountancy concerning required CPE hours and fields of study.

If you decide to take this course follow the directions on the following page. Each course unit costs $59.00. Methods of payment are shown on the answer forms.

Each CPE exam is graded no later than 2 weeks after receipt. The passing score is at least 70%. John Wiley & Sons, Inc. will issue a certificate of completion to successful participants to recognize their achievement.

Photocopy one copy of the answer sheet for each additional participant who wishes to take the CPE course. Each participant should complete the answer form and return it with the $59 fee for each self-study course.

The enclosed self-study CPE program will expire on December 31, 2000. Completed exams must be postmarked by that date.

Directions for the CPE Course

Each course unit includes reading assignments and objectives, discussion questions and answers, and a publisher-graded examination. For those units that you intend to have graded by the publisher, follow these steps:

1. Read the chapter learning objectives.
2. Study the respective chapter in the *1999 GAAP: Interpretation and Application.*
3. Answer the discussion questions and refer to the answers to assess your understanding of the respective chapter.
4. Study material in any weak areas again.
5. Upon completion of all chapters in a unit, do the publisher graded examination for that unit. Record your answers by writing true, false, or a letter (a-e) on the line for that question on the answer form.
6. Upon completion of the examination, cut out the answer sheet, put it in a stamped envelope, and mail to the address below:

GAAP CPE Program Director
ValuSource
7222 Commerce Center Drive
Suite 210
Colorado Springs, CO 80919

CONTINUING PROFESSIONAL EDUCATION: SELF-STUDY

UNIT I

OBJECTIVES

Chapter 1: Researching GAAP Problems

Studying Chapter 1 should enable you to:

- Understand the development of generally accepted accounting principles
- Differentiate between the levels of GAAP
- Understand the sources of GAAP for both business entities and state and local government
- Identify the authoritative publications of the FASB
- Distinguish between mandatory and preferable GAAP
- Describe and explain materiality
- Learn how to research established GAAP
- Learn how to use this book in researching answers to questions about GAAP

Read Chapter 1 and answer discussion questions 1 through 4.

Chapter 2: Balance Sheet

Studying Chapter 2 should enable you to:

- Understand the purpose of the balance sheet
- Define assets, liabilities, and equity
- Understand the limitations of balance sheets
- Understand the classifications on the balance sheet
- Learn about the disclosures that accompany balance sheets
- Learn about the form and measurement of items on the balance sheet

Read Chapter 2 and answer discussion questions 5 through 8.

Chapter 3: Income Statement

Studying Chapter 3 should enable you to:

- Understand the purpose of the income statement
- Understand the elements comprising the income statement
- Differentiate between the concepts of income

- Define revenues and the realization concept
- Explain the characteristics of expenses
- Learn the criteria for extraordinary items
- Define comprehensive income and learn about required disclosure of it
- Learn about prior period adjustments
- Learn about special requirements for development stage companies
- Learn about comprehensive income
- Learn about accounting for start-up costs

Read Chapter 3 and answer discussion questions 9 through 14.

Chapter 4: Statement of Cash Flows

Studying Chapter 4 should enable you to:

- Understand the purpose of the statement of cash flows
- Define cash equivalents
- Classify cash flows as operating, investing, or financing activities
- Describe the preparation of the operating activities section under the
    - Direct method
    - Indirect method
- Describe the preparation of the investing activities section
- Describe the preparation of the financing activities section
- Describe the disclosure of noncash financing and investing activities

Read Chapter 4 and answer discussions questions 14 through 18.

Chapter 5: Cash, Receivables, and Prepaid Expenses

Studying Chapter 5 should enable you to:

- Classify items as cash
- Describe the accounting for receivables
- Understand how bad debt expense is estimated
- Understand pledging, assigning, and factoring of receivables and the differences between them
- Understand the requirements of SFAS 125, *Accounting for Transfers and Servicing of Financial Assets and Extinguishment of Liabilities*

- Requirements for recognition of transfer
- Derecognition of liabilities

Read Chapter 5 and answer discussion questions 19 through 23.

Chapter 6: Short-Term Investments and Financial Instruments

Studying Chapter 6 should enable you to:

- Understand the accounting for short-term investments
- Classify short-term investments
- Describe derivative financial instruments
- Know the disclosure requirements for financial instruments
- Know the disclosure requirements for derivative financial instruments
- Describe the SFAS 125 amendment dealing with held-to-maturity securities of SFAS 115, *Accounting for Certain Investments in Debt and Equity Securities*
- Be familiar with SFAS 133 concerning derivatives and its tentative effective date

Read Chapter 6 and answer discussion questions 24 through 31.

Chapter 7: Inventory

Studying Chapter 7 should enable you to:

- Determine ownership of goods
- Identify inventoriable costs
- Understand differences in financial statement amounts among cost flow assumptions
- Understand the application of the dollar-value LIFO method
- Describe the lower of cost or market valuation method
- Discuss the acceptability and workings of estimation methods
  - Gross profit
  - Retail
- Account for purchase commitments
- Apply the LIFO conformity rule

Read Chapter 7 and answer discussion questions 32 through 38.

DISCUSSION QUESTIONS

1. What is the content of the conceptual framework pronouncements by the FASB?
2. What is GAAP and what are its sources?
3. What is the hierarchy of GAAP?
4. Discuss materiality.
5. Define the elements of a balance sheet.
6. What are the three conditions for an item to qualify as an asset?
7. What are the three conditions for an item to qualify as a liability?
8. Discuss some of the disclosures that accompany balance sheets.
9. What is the difference between the economic and accounting definitions of income?
10. What are the recognition criteria for revenue?
11. What is the realization concept?
12. What are the criteria for an event to be classified as extraordinary on the statement of income?
13. What is the difference between an "expense" and a "loss"?
14. What is comprehensive income and how is it reported?
15. What information is provided for users in the statement of cash flows?
16. Under the indirect method of presentation, how should dividends received and income recognized from an investment accounted for under the equity method be treated?
17. Describe how to determine cash paid for interest.
18. During an accounting period some bonds were retired and new bonds were issued. How should these transactions be accounted for in a statement of cash flows?
19. Discuss the disclosure of a capital lease transaction in a statement of cash flows, both at inception and when payments are made under the lease agreement.
20. What is promulgated GAAP for accounting for cash and what are the criteria for inclusion?
21. Describe how receivables should be presented on the balance sheet.

22. What are two popular techniques used to estimate bad debts expense? Which is oriented toward the income statement and which is oriented toward the balance sheet?
23. Describe pledging, assigning, and factoring of receivables. Which is the most significant in terms of accounting requirements?
24. What is the basic accounting problem addressed by SFAS 125 and what is the principal issue?
25. What three categories are used to classify securities under SFAS 115 and how is each category valued?
26. What is the determination of current or noncurrent status for individual held-to-maturity and individual available-for-sale securities based on?
27. What is the balance sheet classification of trading securities and what items are included in income from continuing operations?
28. What value is used for transfers among the three categories used in SFAS 115?
29. How should the cash flows resulting from the sales, purchases, or maturity of securities be accounted for on the cash flow statement?
30. How does the FASB exposure draft entitled "Accounting for Derivative and Similar Financial Instruments and for Hedging Activities" recommend that derivatives be shown on the balance sheet?
31. What are derivatives?
32. SFAS 107 requires entities to disclose what basic information?
33. Under what circumstances does an entity not have ownership of goods in its possession?
34. Under what circumstances does the use of the LIFO cost flow assumption result in lower net income than FIFO?
35. How is the cost of a dollar-value LIFO layer determined for a manufacturer's inventory?
36. Describe the workings of the link-chain method.
37. Discuss the objective and implementation of the lower of cost or market valuation process.
38. Explain how dollar-value LIFO is applied under the retail method.
39. What are three ways of measuring the effect of a LIFO liquidation on net income under IRS requirements?

ANSWERS TO DISCUSSION QUESTIONS

1. The conceptual framework pronouncements cover the objectives of financial reporting, qualitative characteristics of accounting information, elements of financial statements, and recognition and measurement in financial statements.

2. GAAP is the conventions, rules and procedures that define accepted accounting practice and comes primarily from the FASB and its predecessors.

3. The hierarchy of GAAP consists of four levels specified in SAS 69 as establishing GAAP. These levels are: Accounting principles promulgated by a body designated by the AICPA Council to establish such principles, pursuant to rule 203 (ET section 203.01) of the AICPA Code of Professional Conduct; pronouncements of bodies that are exposed for public comment prior to issuance; pronouncements of bodies that are not exposed prior to issuance; and industry or other general practices.

4. Materiality is both quantitative and qualitative. It involves the use of judgment in evaluating the significance and importance of events.

5. Assets (future economic benefits controlled by an entity), liabilities (probable future sacrifices of economic benefits from present obligations) and equity (residual interest in assets).

6. Assets provide probable future benefits in the form of cash flows, the benefit is restricted solely to the entity, and the benefit arose out of a past event.

7. Liabilities require probable future transfers of assets, the obligation cannot be avoided, and the event obligating the entity has previously occurred.

8. Disclosures include accounting policies, related parties, subsequent events, contingencies, and risks and uncertainties.

9. Accountants define income as that created by events subject to recognition criteria while economists use a wealth maintenance concept.

10. The four criteria are
    a. The item must be defined as an element of financial statements.
    b. The item must be measurable in monetary units.
    c. Relevance.
    b. Reliability.

11. Realization states that revenue is recognized only when the earning process is complete or virtually complete and an exchange transaction has taken place.

12. For an item to be extraordinary, it must have an unusual nature (e.g., abnormal and not related to ordinary activities) and be of infrequent occurrence (e.g., not expected to recur in the foreseeable future).

13. Both expenses and losses are decreases in assets or increases in liabilities, but expenses relate to the entity's central operations while losses involve peripheral transactions.
14. Comprehensive income is the change in equity of a business enterprise during a period from all transactions and other events and circumstances from numerous sources. Under SFAS 130, changes in components of comprehensive income should be reported in the financial statements. Net income and total other comprehensive income should be displayed as part of the income statement, a separate statement of comprehensive income where the beginning number is net income, or in a separate statement of changes in equity.
15. The statement of cash flows discloses increases and decreases of cash and classifies cash flows into operating, investing, and financing activities.
16. Dividends received increase cash and must be added to net income to arrive at cash from operating activities; income recognized must be deducted from net income because no cash was received.
17. Cash paid for interest is equal to interest expense plus a decrease (or minus an increase) in accrued interest payable less bond discount amortization (or plus premium amortization).
18. Bonds issued should be shown with the cash resulting therefrom and bonds retired should be shown with the cash used.
19. In the period of inception, a capital lease should be disclosed as a noncash financing and investing activity either following the statement or in the footnotes. As payments are made on the lease, part of each payment represents a principal reduction and part represents interest expense. The former is shown under financing activities and the latter in operating activities.
20. The promulgated GAAP for accounting for cash is ARB 43, Chapter 3. To be included as cash in the balance sheet, funds must be represented by actual coins and currency on hand or demand deposits available without restriction. It must be management's intention that the cash be available for current purposes.
21. Receivables should be presented at **net realizable** (i.e., realistically anticipated collectible) amounts.
22. The **percentage-of-sales** method is principally oriented towards achieving the best possible matching of revenues and expenses. **Aging the accounts** is more oriented toward the presentation of the correct net realizable value of the trade receivables in the balance sheet. Both methods are acceptable and widely employed.

23. Pledging is an agreement where accounts receivable are used as collateral for loans. The assignment of accounts receivable is a more formalized transfer of the asset to the lending institution. Factoring traditionally has involved the outright sale of receivables to a financing institution known as a factor. This category of financing is the most significant in terms of accounting implications.

24. The basic accounting problem addressed by SFAS 125 involves instances of possible continuing involvement through recourse, repurchase agreements, options generated, servicing, and collateral. The issue is whether the transfer has resulted in a sale or a secured borrowing.

25. SFAS 115 is GAAP regarding investments in all debt securities and in equity securities that have a readily determinable fair value. It classifies these securities into one of the following three categories:

    1. Held-to-maturity - Debt securities reported at amortized cost
    2. Trading - Debt and equity securities reported at fair value
    3. Available-for-sale - Debt and equity securities not classified as 1 or 2, reported at fair value

26. The determination of current or noncurrent status for individual held-to-maturity and individual available-for-sale securities is made on the basis of whether or not the securities are considered working capital available for current operations (ARB 43, ch 3A).

27. Trading securities are required to be carried at fair value on the balance sheet as current assets. All applicable interest and dividends, realized gains and losses, and unrealized gains and losses are included in income from continuing operations.

28. Fair value is used for transfers between categories.

29. Cash flows resulting from sales, purchases, or maturity of securities should be accounted for as follows:

    1. Trading - Operating activity
    2. Held-to-maturity - Investing activity
    3. Available-for-sale - Investing activity

30. The FASB exposure draft on derivatives specifies recognition of all derivatives in the balance sheet as assets or liabilities measured at fair value. Derivatives could be specifically designated as hedges.

31. Derivatives are financial instruments that derive their value from changes in a benchmark based on stock prices, interest rates, mortgage rates, currency rates, commodity prices or some other agreed-upon base.

32. SFAS 107 requires entities to disclose the fair value of all (recognized and unrecognized) financial instruments that it is practicable to estimate, including liabilities. Pertinent descriptive information as to the fair value of the instrument is to be disclosed if an estimate of fair value cannot be made without incurring excessive costs.

33. An entity does not have ownership of goods that are in its possession when goods are on **consignment** from another entity or the transaction is a **product financing arrangement.**

34. The LIFO cost flow assumption results in lower net income than FIFO in periods of rising prices. This result is obtained because higher costs are matched with revenue. When prices are declining the opposite result is obtained.

35. The amount of a dollar-value LIFO layer is determined for a manufacturer's inventory by expressing both beginning and ending inventory in base-year costs in terms of total dollars. The difference is the amount of the layer in base-year dollars. An index is calculated by dividing the ending inventory at current-year cost by the ending inventory at base-year cost. Finally, if a layer is added, the layer at base-year prices is extended at the current index.

36. Each period a link (index number for the period) is calculated which is determined by dividing the inventory priced at end-of-year prices by the ending inventory priced at beginning-of-year prices. Next, the current-year index number is multiplied by the cumulative index number to arrive at a new cumulative index number. This index is then used to restate the inventory to base-year cost by dividing the inventory in end-of-year dollars by the cumulative index. From this point, accounting for a decrement or increment is basically the same as the double-extension method.

37. The objective of the lower of cost or market valuation process is to determine the inventory amount (lower of cost or market) which most clearly reflects periodic income. A departure from the cost basis of pricing the inventory is required when the utility of the goods is no longer as great as its cost. The implementation of lower of cost or market requires that three steps be followed.

    a. Determine market--where market is the replacement cost limited to the ceiling (net realizable value) or floor (net realizable value less normal profit)
    b. Determine cost
    c. Select the lower of cost or market for either an individual item or for the inventory as a whole

38. Under dollar-value retail LIFO the first step is to divide the ending inventory at selling price by a government published index number to arrive at a base retail amount which is compared to the beginning base retail amount. The difference is a layer to be added or a decrement to be removed. A layer added is determined by extending the layer at base-period retail by both the cost to retail ratio and the current-year government published index number.

39. The three ways of measuring the effect of a LIFO liquidation on net income under IRS tax requirements are

    a. The difference between actual costs of sales and what cost of sales would have been had the inventory been reinstated under the entity's normal pricing procedure.
    b. The difference between actual costs of sales and what cost of sales would have been had the inventory been reinstated at year-end replacement cost.
    c. The amount of the LIFO reserve at the beginning of the year which was credited to income (excluding the increase in the reserve due to current-year price changes).

UNIT I

PUBLISHER-GRADED EXAMINATION

True/False 1. EITF pronouncements are integrated with FASB Statements and Interpretations in the Current Text--FASB Professional Standards.

True/False 2. The levels of GAAP were determined by a pronouncement of the FASB.

True/False 3. Materiality is both a quantitative and qualitative term.

True/False 4. Assets and liabilities exist as a result of past economic events.

True/False 5. Balance sheets are a mixture of current value and historical cost.

True/False 6. Current liabilities are not classified strictly on the basis of maturity.

True/False 7. All balance sheets should be classified so as to distinguish current from noncurrent items.

True/False 8. Long-term investments intended to be held for an extended period of time cannot be classified as available-for-sale.

True/False 9. Offsetting assets against liabilities are acceptable when the right of setoff is legally enforceable.

True/False 10. Disclosures to the financial statements can only be either parenthetical or footnotes.

True/False 11. Related party transactions should be disclosed even if there is no accounting recognition to transactions.

True/False 12. Loss contingencies should be accrued if it is probable that an asset is impaired or liability incurred.

True/False 13. Recognition and realization are the same term in income determination.

True/False 14. Comprehensive income does not include net income.

True/False 15. Expected gains from a disposal of a segment are not recognized until disposal date.

True/False 16. Only items which are both unusual and infrequent can ever be classified as extraordinary.

Multiple-choice 17. Cash flows resulting from the purchase of debt or equity instruments classified as trading securities are classified as

a. Operating cash flows.
b. Investing cash flows.
c. Financing cash flows.
d. Operating or investing cash flows.

True/False 18. Items that have quick turnovers, large amounts, and short maturities may not be shown as net cash flows if pertaining to investments or loans receivable.

True/False 19. The indirect method reports only items that affect cash flow and ignores items that do not affect cash flow.

True/False 20. The primary purpose of the statement of cash flows is to provide information about investing and financing activities during the period.

True/False 21. The cash flows from principal collections of loans from other entities' debt instruments that were held as available-for-sale are classified as investing cash flows.

True/False 22. The formula to convert net sales to the cash basis is

Net sales + Ending AR – Beginning AR = Cash received from
AR written off customers

True/False 23. In an aging of accounts receivable, the adjustment entry for bad debts expense will be the amount computed by the aging.

True/False 24. Under SFAS 125, in general, the more the transferor of assets retains an interest, the more likely the transaction will be classified as a sale and the less likely the transaction will be classified as a secured borrowing.

True/False 25. Securitization is the transformation of financial assets into securities (asset-backed securities).

True/False 26. In accounting for collateral under SFAS 125, ordinarily, the transferor should not carry the collateral as an asset and the transferee should record the pledged assets.

True/False 27. Under SFAS 133, derivative instruments represent rights and obligations and must be reported as assets and liabilities at book value.

True/False 28. Under SFAS 133, gains and losses not designated as hedges are recognized in Other Comprehensive Income.

True/False 29. Like SFAS 119, SFAS 133 defined derivative instruments by classes or categories of financial instruments.

True/False 30. Under SFAS 133, an underlying is commonly a number of units such as shares of stock, principal amount, face value, etc.

True/False 31. Under SFAS 133, two basic forms of derivative instruments are futures contracts and options.

True/False 32. Regular-way security trades and normal purchases and normal sales are subject to SFAS 133 requirements.

True/False 33. Under SFAS 133, the effective portion of all hedges must be reported immediately in earnings.

True/False 34. In a perpetual inventory system, periodic physical counts are necessary for tax regulations but not to determine the cost of goods sold.

True/False 35. Lost discounts on purchases are included in cost of goods sold.

Multiple-choice 36. Small inventory quantities that have high unit values and low turnover rates should use which of the following methods to determine cost of goods sold?

a. FIFO.
b. LIFO.
c. Specific Identification.
d. Dollar-Value LIFO.

True/False 37. The advantage of using the LIFO method of inventory valuation is that it most closely parallels the actual physical flow of goods in most industries.

Multiple-choice 38. When determining market price under the lower of cost or market inventory valuation method, the ceiling is

a. Selling price minus miscellaneous costs.
b. Net realizable value.
c. Net realizable value minus profit margin.
d. Net realizable value minus income from operations.

True/False 39. When comparing LIFO, FIFO, and weighted-average methods, the results from the weighted-average method will fall between results using LIFO and FIFO.

Multiple-choice

40. If ending inventory is destroyed in a fire, which method can be used to estimate the cost?
    a. LIFO.
    b. FIFO.
    c. Retail method.
    d. Weighted-average.

GAAP 1999 CPE Course

UNIT I

Record your CPE answers on the answer form provided below and return this page for grading.

Mail to:

***GAAP 1999* CPE Director**

ValuSource, 7222 Commerce Center Drive, Suite 210, Colorado Springs, CO 80919

PAYMENT OPTIONS

☐ **Payment enclosed ($59.00 per Unit).**
(Make checks payable to John Wiley & Sons, Inc.)
Please add appropriate sales tax.
Be sure to sign your order below.

Charge my:

☐ American Express ☐ MasterCard ☐ Visa

Account number ____________________

Expiration date ____________________

Please sign below for all credit card orders.

Signature ____________________

NAME ____________________

FIRM NAME ____________________

ADDRESS ____________________

____

PHONE (   ) ____________________

CPA STATE LICENSE # ____________________

SEE THE OTHER SIDE OF THIS PAGE FOR THE CPE FEEDBACK FORM.

UNIT I CPE ANSWERS

1. ____	2. ____	3. ____	4. ____	5. ____	6. ____	7. ____	8. ____	9. ____	10. ____
11. ____	12. ____	13. ____	14. ____	15. ____	16. ____	17. ____	18. ____	19. ____	20. ____
21. ____	22. ____	23. ____	24. ____	25. ____	26. ____	27. ____	28. ____	29. ____	30. ____
31. ____	32. ____	33. ____	34. ____	35. ____	36. ____	37. ____	38. ____	39. ____	40. ____

GAAP 1999 CPE Feedback

1. Were you informed in advance of the
   a. Course objectives? **Y N**
   b. Requisite experience level? **Y N**
   c. Course content? **Y N**
   d. Type and degree of preparation necessary? **Y N**
   e. Instruction method? **Y N**
   f. CPE credit hours? **Y N**

2. Do you agree with the publisher's determination of
   a. Course objectives? **Y N**
   b. Requisite experience level? **Y N**
   c. Course content? **Y N**
   d. Type and degree of preparation necessary? **Y N**
   e. Instruction method? **Y N**
   f. CPE credit hours? **Y N**

3. Was the content relevant? **Y N**

4. Was the content displayed clearly? **Y N**

5. Did the course enhance your professional competence? **Y N**

6. Was the course content timely and effective? **Y N**

How can we make the course better? If you have any suggestions please summarize them in the space below. We will consider them in developing future courses.

CONTINUING PROFESSIONAL EDUCATION: SELF-STUDY

UNIT II

OBJECTIVES

Read Chapter 8: Special Revenue Recognition Areas

Studying Chapter 8 should enable you to:

- Understand the unique elements in accounting for long-term construction contracts
- Explain revenue measurement under percentage-of-completion and completed-contract
- Understand the various methods used to measure progress under the percentage-of-completion method
- Explain revenue recognition methods for service sale transactions
- Differentiate between various revenue recognition methods when collection is uncertain
- Understand the criteria that must be met for revenue to be recognized when the buyer has a return right
- Explain the conditions for use of the full accrual method for real estate sales
- Understand the condition for profit recognition on retail land sales
- Understand the adequacy tests for a buyers initial investment for real estate sale
- Explain the unique conditions that must be met for a franchisor to recognize revenue on sale of a franchise
- Learn about net realizable value

Read Chapter 8 and answer discussion questions 1 through 10.

Read Chapter 9: Long-Lived Assets

Studying Chapter 9 should enable you to:

- Determine the cost of fixed assets
- Calculate depreciation, depletion, and amortization
- Account for nonmonetary transactions
- Describe and record impairment
- Understand capitalization of interest

- Account for intangible assets and research and development costs

Read Chapter 9 and answer discussion questions 11 through 19.

Read Chapter 10: Investments

Studying Chapter 10 should enable you to:

- Understand accounting for marketable equity securities held as passive investments
- Understand accounting for debt securities held as investments
- Account for investments in common stock in which the investor has significant influence over the investee company
- Understand the difference between permanent impairments of investments and temporary declines in value
- Account for transfers of investments between portfolios
- Understand the deferred tax implications of investments in debt and equity securities
- Apply the equity method of accounting for intercorporate investments

Read Chapter 10 and answer discussion questions 20 through 26.

Chapter 11: Business Combinations and Consolidated Financial Statements

Studying Chapter 11 should enable you to:

- Understand and apply the differences between pooling of interest and purchase accounting for business combinations
- Allocate the purchase price of business acquisitions among tangible and intangible assets and liabilities, including goodwill and negative goodwill
- Understand and account for minority interests in business combinations
- Understand the circumstances when consolidated financial statements will be required
- Account for changes in ownership after initial acquisition of a subsidiary
- Account for contingent consideration paid in a business combination
- Understand the accounting for preacquisition contingencies
- Prepare combined financial statements

Read Chapter 11 and answer discussion questions 27 through 33.

DISCUSSION QUESTIONS

1. What are the two methods for recognition of revenue for long-term construction contracts?
2. What are the four types of pricing arrangements typical for long-term contracts?
3. How is progress toward completion usually measured under the percentage-of-completion method?
4. What conditions must be met for the recognition of contract revenue for claims?
5. What are the methods commonly used to measure performance for service sales transactions?
6. Under what circumstances should the installment method of revenue recognition be used?
7. Discuss the conditions for recognizing revenue when a customer may return the purchase.
8. Discuss the conditions for consummation of a sale for other than retail land sales of real estate.
9. What methods of income recognition should be used when the full accrual method of nonretail sales of real estate is not appropriate?
10. Discuss the accounting for amenities in connection with real estate operations.
11. GAAP regarding long-lived assets involves what two primary determinations?
12. What is the basic requirement regarding asset impairment per SFAS 121?
13. What costs are recorded as part of the cost of fixed assets?
14. What are the basic requirements that must result from the method of depreciation chosen?
15. Identify the three types of nonmonetary transactions.
16. What is the general rule established by APB 29?
17. Recoverability of long-lived assets should be assessed under what circumstances?
18. In general terms, what portion of interest should be capitalized?
19. When intangible assets are purchased, what should their cost be?
20. What are the three categories of investments defined by SFAS 115, and what types of securities can be classified in each of these?

21. How does the accounting for available-for-sale securities differ from those classified as held-to-maturity?
22. What is the reason for reporting unrealized gains and losses on available-for-sale securities in the equity section of the balance sheet?
23. Are market declines in available-for-sale or held-to-maturity securities never reflected in earnings prior to the disposition of the investment?
24. Can an entity transfer securities between the portfolios, and if so, what would be the accounting implications?
25. How are impairments to the value of investments which occur after the balance sheet date to be accounted for?
26. Why is the equity method sometimes called "one-line consolidation"?
27. What is the essential underlying concept of pooling of interests accounting?
28. In what situations will consolidated financial statements be required?
29. What is goodwill and what is so-called "negative goodwill"?
30. What are preacquisition contingencies and how are they accounted for?
31. In a purchase business combination the price is paid in stock, with additional shares to be issued if the market price declines within 1 year. If the extra shares are issued, does the purchase price have to be adjusted?
32. If additional shares are given after a purchase business combination due to an "earn out" provision being met, will there be an adjustment of the purchase price?
33. Can a pooling be effected by means of a swap of common stock for preferred stock?

ANSWERS TO DISCUSSION QUESTIONS

1. The two methods are percentage-of-completion and completed-contract.
2. The four types of pricing are: (a) fixed price, (b) time and materials, (c) cost type, and (d) unit price.
3. Progress toward completion is usually measured by the cost-to-cost method, efforts expanded method, units of delivery method, or units of work method.
4. For claim revenue to be recognized, (a) the contract must provide a legal basis for the claim (or a legal opinion has been obtained), (b) additional costs were caused by unforeseen circumstances, (c) costs are identified, and (d) evidence in support of the claim is objective and verifiable.

5. The methods commonly used to measure performance on service sale transactions are the specific performance method, the proportional performance method, the completed performance method, and the collection method.

6. The installment method of revenue recognition should be used when the length of the contract payment period or other such condition does not permit reliable estimation of uncollectibles.

7. When the right of return exists, recognition of revenue at the time of sale can only be met if: (a) the sale price is fixed or determinable, (b) the buyer has paid or is obligated to pay, (c) the buyer's obligation is unchanged by condition or theft of the product, (d) the buyer has separate economic substance from the seller, (e) the seller is not obligated to perform substantial future service, and (f) the amount of future returns can be reasonably estimated.

8. The conditions for a sale on real estate are met when the parties are bound by a contract, all consideration has been exchanged, permanent financing has been arranged, and all precedent conditions have been performed.

9. The methods of income recognition when the full accrual method cannot be used are: (a) deposit, (b) cost recovery, (c) installment, (d) reduced profit, and (e) percentage-of-completion methods.

10. Amenities that are to be sold, transferred, or retained should have all costs in excess of fair value changed as common costs, with the fair value treated as the asset.

11. GAAP regarding long-lived assets involves the determination of the appropriate cost at which to record the asset and the appropriate method to be used to allocate that cost over the periods benefiting.

12. SFAS 121 requires long-lived assets and certain identifiable intangible assets and any goodwill related to those assets to be reviewed for impairment whenever circumstances and situations change such that there is an indication that the carrying amount may not be recoverable.

13. All costs required to bring the asset into operating condition are recorded as part of the cost of the fixed assets. Examples include sales taxes, finders' fees, freight costs, installation costs, break-in costs, and set-up costs. Thus, any reasonable cost involved in bringing the asset to the buyer and incurred prior to using the asset in actual production is capitalized.

14. The method of depreciation chosen must result in the systematic and rational allocation of the cost of the asset (less its residual value) over the asset's expected useful life.

15. APB 29 governs the accounting for nonmonetary transactions. It identifies the following three types of nonmonetary transactions:

   a. Nonreciprocal transfers with owners
   b. Nonreciprocal transfers with other than owners
   c. Nonmonetary exchanges

16. The general rule established by APB 29 is that the accounting for nonmonetary transactions should be based on the fair values of the assets involved. The fair value to be used is that of the asset surrendered unless the fair value of the asset received is "more clearly evident."

17. Recoverability under SFAS 121 should be assessed under the following circumstances (among others):
    a. The asset market value decreases significantly
    b. The use of the asset is significantly changed in extent or manner
    c. Legal factors or business climate changes adversely affect asset value
    d. Regulator's adverse assessment or action
    e. Original expected costs are significantly exceeded
    f. A history of cash flow losses and continued asset losses are forecasted

18. The amount of interest to be capitalized is that portion which could have been avoided if the qualifying asset had not been acquired.

19. When intangible assets are purchased, their cost should be the cash or fair market value disbursed or the present value of the liability assumed in conjunction with the exchange. This amount represents the potential earning power of the intangible asset as of the date of its acquisition.

20. The three categories, or portfolios, of investments are trading, available-for-sale, and held-to-maturity; of these, marketable equity securities can be categorized in the first two only, while investments in debt securities may be in any of the three portfolios. The middle category, available-for-sale, is used for those investments which cannot be clearly categorized in the trading or held-to-maturity portfolios.

21. Available-for-sale securities are reported at fair market value, with unrealized gains or losses included in the equity section of the balance sheet; held-to-maturity investments are reported at amortized historical cost.

22. Reporting unrealized gains or losses in equity is done to avoid having periodic earnings affected by price changes which are, over the long run, expected to largely offset or net out. Since the intent is not clearly to sell the investments in the short term, the decision was made to not have reported income made volatile by including these items. However, since fair value is used to report the asset, it was necessary (due to the double entry nature of accounting) to report these unrealized gains or losses in the financials, and the solution was to create a new contra equity or additional equity account for them.

23. "Other than temporary" declines in value must be reported in earnings in all instances. Once such a decline is recorded, the adjusted carrying amount is the new cost basis and any increases in value would be disclosed in the manner prescribed for the portfolio in question: as additional equity if the change in value affects available-for-sale securities; as a footnote disclosure if it affects held-to-maturity investments.

24. Yes, transfers are permitted when management intent changes, although transfers from the held-to-maturity category are expected to be rare, since such transfers call into question management's originally stated intentions and might preclude classifying future investments in debt securities as being held-to-maturity. Transfers between portfolios are to be accounted for similarly to arm's-length transactions between unrelated parties.

25. If the decline in value occurred after the balance sheet date but before the financial statements are issued, it would be disclosed if material, but would not be recorded since it was truly a "subsequent event." If, however, a "confirming event" revealed that the investment was impaired as of the balance sheet date, the decline in value would be formally recorded and reported in earnings for the period.

26. The equity method is similar to consolidation since the impact on the reporting entity's net income and net worth will be identical to what it would have been had full consolidation been effected. However, instead of reporting the investor's share of each revenue and expense item, the investor's share of the net income of the investee is reported in a single line (with certain limited exceptions).

27. Poolings of interests are based on continuity of ownership after the combination has occurred. The same group of shareholders which controlled the combining entities must survive as owners after the combination.

28. Under current rules, consolidated financial statements will be required if one entity owns over 50% of another, unless control is temporary or control is absent. The former "nonhomogeneity" exceptions no longer apply.

29. Goodwill is the excess of the price paid in a purchase business combination over the fair value of the net identifiable assets acquired. Negative goodwill is the excess of the fair value of the net identifiable assets acquired over the cost.

30. Preacquisition contingencies are uncertainties existing at the date of the purchase acquisition. If resolved within 1 year the purchase price is reallocated; if after 1 year, these are accounted for as current period events.

31. No. Contingencies based on market value of shares given in a purchase business combination do not result in adjustment of the purchase price if more shares have to be issued pursuant to the terms of the agreement.
32. Yes. The additional consideration will be considered part of the purchase cost; allocation to assets acquired may need to be adjusted.
33. Poolings require that only voting common stock be given in exchange for voting common stock of the other entity.

UNIT II

PUBLISHER-GRADED EXAMINATION

True/False 1. For long term construction in contracts, the percentage-of-completion method of income recognition is preferable under all circumstances.

True/False 2. Contract costs are identifiable to specific contracts and exclude all allocated costs.

True/False 3. Progress towards completion is in general measured by either input or output measures.

True/False 4. The installment method of revenue recognition is acceptable under GAAP.

True/False 5. When the right of return exists, revenue recognition should be delayed until all material uncertainties are removed.

True/False 6. One of the conditions for a sale of real estate (nonland) to be considered consummated is when all consideration has been exchanged.

True/False 7. The minimum initial investment requirements for real estate sales (other than land) is 10%.

True/False 8. Net realizable value and fair market value are the same concept for real estate.

True/False 9. Indirect costs that relate to several projects should be capitalized and allocated to these projects.

True/False 10. An enterprise's reacquisition of its outstanding stock is a nonreciprocal transfer.

True/False 11. Ordinary maintenance and repair expenditures are capitalized and depreciated.

True/False 12. The determination of useful life should only take into consideration the actual physical usage.

True/False 13. Tax depreciation using MACRS is not considered to be in accordance with GAAP.

True/False 14. Differences between financial depreciation and tax depreciation must be used in the calculation of deferred taxes.

True/False 15. Unit depletion rates, once established, cannot be changed unless a cumulative effect of a change in accounting principle is calculated and reported on the income statement.

True/False 16. The general rule established by APB 29 is that the accounting for nonmonetary transactions should be based on the book value of the assets involved.

True/False 17. An exchange is considered the culmination of the earnings process when dissimilar assets are involved.

True/False 18. The general rule in the exchange of similar assets involving a gain is to value the transaction at the fair value of the asset given up.

True/False 19. In an exchange of similar real estate that is a monetary transaction under EITF 86-29 because boot is at least 25% of the fair value exchanged, the fair value would be allocated between the monetary and nonmonetary components based on relative fair values.

True/False 20. Significant influence over another entity does not alone necessitate accounting for equity investments on the equity method.

True/False 21. A sole general partner in a limited partnership would be deemed to have significant influence even if the 20% threshold is not achieved.

True/False 22. Occasional sales out of the held-to-maturity portfolio would not make it impossible to classify future securities purchases as held-to-maturity.

True/False 23. Permanent impairments of available-for-sale investments, unlike market value fluctuations, are reported in the income statement.

True/False 24. The tax rate used to compute deferred tax to be provided on temporary differences arising in connection with equity method investments should be that which would apply based on the expected means of distribution to the investor.

True/False 25. The investor using the equity method to report its interest in another corporation will record its share of the investee's income or loss, even if this creates a negative balance in its investment account.

True/False 26. The equity method of accounting is an alternative method of reporting financial results for subsidiaries when the presentation of consolidated financial statements is thought to be potentially misleading.

True/False 27. Held-to-maturity securities are carried at amortized historical cost, and therefore transfers to the available-for-sale portfolio of debt securities are made on that basis, with any changes in fair value from that date forward reported in comprehensive income.

True/False 28. When an equity method investor sells inventory or fixed assets to its investee, unrealized intercompany profit at the financial statement date must be eliminated pending realization through a third-party transaction.

True/False 29. Deferred taxes recorded in connection with unrealized gain or loss on securities which are classified as available-for-sale are reported in the income statement.

True/False 30. Depending upon the specific circumstances, in either a pooling of interests or a purchase business combination, a new basis of accountability can arise.

True/False 31. Legal and other expenses incurred in a purchase transaction must be allocated to goodwill.

True/False 32. Since the concept of a pooling is that two or more entities are being combined for the purpose of continuing all operations which were formerly carried out separately on a unified basis, the intention to dispose of some redundant assets after the transaction will disqualify it from being accounted for as a pooling.

True/False 33. When brother/sister corporations are controlled by the same parent corporation, presentation of combined financial statements is suggested, but not required, under GAAP.

True/False 34. In consolidated financial statements, minority interest must be presented as a special category between the liability and the equity sections of the balance sheet.

True/False 35. If there are contingencies such as lawsuits still to be resolved at the time a purchase business combination is consummated, resolution within 1 year of that date will result in adjustment of the purchase price.

True/False 36. A small intercompany holding of voting common stock immediately prior to a business combination will not preclude accounting for it as a pooling of interests.

True/False 37. In a pooling transaction, the retained earnings of the new combined company can be greater than that of the constituent entities if the aggregate par value of the new shares issued is less than the aggregate par values of the shares of the combining entities.

True/False 38. Goodwill in a purchase business combination is computed as the excess of price paid over the fair value of the net assets acquired.

True/False 39. To qualify for pooling of interests treatment, there can be no inter-company holdings of common shares prior to the planned transaction.

True/False 40. In a purchase business combination, the tax effect of net operating losses of the acquired entity are only given financial statement recognition if it is "beyond a reasonable doubt" that they are going to be realized.

GAAP 1999 CPE Course

UNIT II

Record your CPE answers on the answer form provided below and return this page for grading.

Mail to:

***GAAP 1999* CPE Director**

ValuSource, 7222 Commerce Center Drive, Suite 210, Colorado Springs, CO 80919

PAYMENT OPTIONS

☐ **Payment enclosed ($59.00 per Unit).**
(Make checks payable to John Wiley & Sons, Inc.)
Please add appropriate sales tax.
Be sure to sign your order below.

Charge my:

☐ American Express ☐ MasterCard ☐ Visa

Account number ______________________

Expiration date ______________________

Please sign below for all credit card orders.

NAME ______________________

FIRM NAME ______________________

ADDRESS ______________________

____

PHONE (   ) ______________________

CPA STATE LICENSE # ______________________

Signature ______________________

SEE THE OTHER SIDE OF THIS PAGE FOR THE CPE FEEDBACK FORM.

UNIT II CPE ANSWERS

1. ____	2. ____	3. ____	4. ____	5. ____	6. ____	7. ____	8. ____	9. ____	10. ____
11. ____	12. ____	13. ____	14. ____	15. ____	16. ____	17. ____	18. ____	19. ____	20. ____
21. ____	22. ____	23. ____	24. ____	25. ____	26. ____	27. ____	28. ____	29. ____	30. ____
31. ____	32. ____	33. ____	34. ____	35. ____	36. ____	37. ____	38. ____	39. ____	40. ____

GAAP 1999 CPE Feedback

1. Were you informed in advance of the

   a. Course objectives? **Y N**
   b. Requisite experience level? **Y N**
   c. Course content? **Y N**
   d. Type and degree of preparation necessary? **Y N**
   e. Instruction method? **Y N**
   f. CPE credit hours? **Y N**

2. Do you agree with the publisher's determination of

   a. Course objectives? **Y N**
   b. Requisite experience level? **Y N**
   c. Course content? **Y N**
   d. Type and degree of preparation necessary? **Y N**
   e. Instruction method? **Y N**
   f. CPE credit hours? **Y N**

3. Was the content relevant? **Y N**

4. Was the content displayed clearly? **Y N**

5. Did the course enhance your professional competence? **Y N**

6. Was the course content timely and effective? **Y N**

How can we make the course better? If you have any suggestions please summarize them in the space below. We will consider them in developing future courses.

CONTINUING PROFESSIONAL EDUCATION: SELF-STUDY

UNIT III

OBJECTIVES

Read Chapter 12: Current Liabilities and Contingencies

Studying Chapter 12 should enable you to:

- Record current liabilities
- Describe the accounting for due-on-demand obligations
- Account for short-term obligations expected to be refinanced
- Explain the accounting for compensated absences
- Describe, record, and disclose contingencies

Read Chapter 12 and answer discussion questions 1 through 5.

Read Chapter 13: Long-Term Debt

Studying Chapter 13 should enable you to:

- Record long-term debt
- Account for notes payable
- Amortize bond premiums and discounts
- Account for the extinguishment of debt
- Understand the requirements of SFAS 125 regarding extinguishment of liabilities
- Account for troubled debt restructurings
- Understand convertible debt issues

Read Chapter 13 and answer discussion questions 6 through 14.

Read Chapter 14: Accounting for Leases

Studying Chapter 14 should enable you to:

- Know the definitions of terms used in accounting for leases
- Classify a lessee's lease as a capital lease or an operating lease using the four criteria specified in SFAS 13

- Classify a lessor's lease as operating or as a sales-type, direct financing, or leveraged-lease using the same four criteria applicable to lessees and the two criteria applicable only to lessors
- Distinguish between sales-type and direct financing leases
- Account for each type of lessee's and lessor's lease that contains varying provisions
- Account for sale-leaseback transactions
- Account for leases involving real estate

Read Chapter 14 and answer discussion questions 15 through 25.

Read Chapter 15: Accounting for Income Taxes

Studying Chapter 15 should enable you to:

- Understand the differences between the liability and deferred approaches to deferred tax accounting
- Understand the concept of temporary differences
- Determine the deferred tax assets and liabilities to be recorded by a company which has temporary differences
- Compute the allowance to be provided for deferred tax benefits which are not more likely than not to be realized
- Determine the allocation of income tax expense among captions on the income statement (intraperiod allocation)
- Understand the accounting for operating loss carryforwards
- Understand the exceptions to the deferred tax provisions required under GAAP

Read Chapter 15 and answer discussion questions 26 through 34.

DISCUSSION QUESTIONS

1. Define current liabilities.
2. How should the current maturing portion of long-term debt be classified on the balance sheet?
3. What principal pronouncement governs the accounting for short-term obligations expected to be refinanced?
4. SFAS 5 states that a loss contingency must be accrued if what two conditions are met?

5. SFAS 43 states an employer must accrue a liability for employees' compensation of future absences if what conditions are met?
6. What is the proper valuation of long-term debt?
7. When the rate on a note is **not** considered fair, how should the note be recorded according to APB 21?
8. What is the preferred method of accounting for a discount or premium arising from a note or bond?
9. What costs may be incurred in connection with issuing bonds and how are they accounted for?
10. What SFAS will provide the accounting and reporting standard for extinguishments of liabilities after December 31, 1996?
11. What is the exception to the general rule that all gains and losses from extinguishment, if material in amount, receive extraordinary item treatment?
12. In what two ways can a troubled debt restructuring occur?
13. When convertible debt is issued, what value is apportioned to the conversion feature?
14. Under SFAS 84, what is the accounting specified for an induced conversion of debt to equity?
15. Define minimum lease payments.
16. What are the differences between sales-type and direct financing leases?
17. Describe the accounting treatment in cases where the fair value of the property exceeds the present value of the property's minimum lease payments at the inception of the lease.
18. Over what period of time should a leased asset be amortized (depreciated)?
19. How should lessors and lessees account for rental payments that are specified in a lease on other than a straight-line basis?
20. Describe the lessor's accounting for initial direct costs in an operating lease.
21. Describe the lessor's accounting for initial direct costs in a direct financing lease.
22. How should lessees account for guaranteed residual values in a capital lease?
23. How does the seller-lessee account for a gain in a sale-leaseback transaction?
24. How does the seller-lessee account for a loss in a sale-leaseback transaction in a case in which the sales price of the property is less than the book value and the fair market is greater than the book value?

25. What kind of continuing involvement indicates that a sale-leaseback of real estate transaction is a normal leaseback and, thus, sale-leaseback accounting treatment is appropriate?
26. What is the objective of the liability method of deferred tax accounting?
27. What are temporary differences?
28. How are the tax effects of temporary differences in the bases of assets acquired in purchase business combinations to be accounted for?
29. In measuring the tax effect of temporary differences, what tax rates should be utilized?
30. How is the valuation allowance for deferred tax assets determined?
31. How is the effect of changing tax rates on previously provided deferred tax assets and liabilities reported, and in what period?
32. What tax rates should be used to provide deferred taxes on undistributed earnings of equity method investees?
33. The "indefinite reversal" criterion of APB 23 was used to avoid the provision of deferred taxes on undistributed earnings of subsidiaries. Can this still be done, or must deferred taxes be provided?
34. How should income taxes be allocated among income from continuing operations, income from discontinued operations, extraordinary items and the cumulative effect of change in accounting principles?

ANSWERS TO DISCUSSION QUESTIONS

1. ARB 43, Chapter 3 defines current liabilities as those enterprise obligations whose liquidation is reasonably expected to require the use of existing resources properly classifiable as current assets or the creation of other current liabilities.
2. Current maturing portion of long-term debt is shown as a current liability if the obligation is to be liquidated by using assets classified as current. However, if the currently maturing debt is to be liquidated by using other than current assets (i.e., by using a sinking fund which is properly classified as an investment) then these obligations should be classified as long-term liabilities.
3. SFAS 6 specifies when it is acceptable to reclassify a currently maturing debt to a long-term liability. Either post-balance-sheet financing or both management's intent and ability to refinance as demonstrated in an agreement that extends due date of the currently maturing debt beyond 1 year are required.
4. SFAS 5 states that a loss must be accrued if both of the following conditions are met:

   a. It is probable that an asset has been impaired or a liability has been incurred at the date of the financial statements.
   b. The amount of loss can be reasonably estimated.

5. SFAS 43 states that an employer must accrue a liability for employee's compensation of future absences if all of the following conditions are met:

   a. The employee's right to receive compensation for future absences is attributable to employee services already rendered.
   b. The right vests or accumulates.
   c. Payment of the compensation is probable.
   d. The amount of the payment can be reasonably estimated.

6. The proper valuation of long-term debt is the present value of future payments using the market rate of interest, either stated or implied in the transaction, at the date the debt was incurred. An exception to the use of the market rate of interest stated or implied in the transaction in valuing long-term notes occurs when it is necessary to use an imputed interest rate (APB 21).

7. According to APB 21, when the rate on the note is **not** considered fair, the note is to be recorded at the "fair market value of the property, goods, or services received or at an amount that reasonably approximates the market value of the note, whichever is the more clearly determinable." When this amount differs from the face value of the note, the difference is to be recorded as a discount or premium and amortized to interest expense.

8. The effective interest method is the preferred method of accounting for a discount or premium arising from a note or bond, although some other method may be used (e.g., straight-line) if the results are not materially different.

9. Costs may be incurred in connection with issuing bonds. Examples include legal, accounting, and underwriting fees; commissions; and engraving, printing, and registration costs. Although these costs should be classified as a deferred charge and amortized using the effective interest method, generally the amount involved is such that use of the simpler straight-line method would not result in a material difference.

10. SFAS 125 provides accounting and reporting standards for extinguishments of liabilities.

11. Except for any gains and losses resulting from satisfying sinking fund requirements within 1 year of the date of the extinguishment (SFAS 64), all gains and losses from extinguishment, if material in amount, receive extraordinary item treatment (SFAS 4, para 8).

12. A troubled debt restructuring can occur one of two ways. The first is a settlement of the debt at less than the carrying amount. The second is a continuation of the debt with a modification of terms (i.e., a reduction in the interest rate,

face amount, accrued interest owed, or an extension of the payment date for interest or face amount).

13. When convertible debt is issued, no value is apportioned to the conversion feature when recording the issue (APB 14, para 12). The debt is treated as nonconvertible debt.

14. Upon conversion, the debtor must recognize, under SFAS 84, an expense for the excess of the fair value of all the securities and other consideration given over the fair value of the securities specified in the original conversion terms. The reported expense should not be classified as an extraordinary item.

15. Minimum lease payments are the payments that the lessor/lessee is or can be required to make in connection with leased property. Minimum lease payments include: (1) rent payments, (2) bargain purchase options over the lease term, (3) guarantee of residual value, and (4) failure to renew or extend penalties.

16. Sales-type leases occur when the lessor recognizes a profit or loss on the transaction in addition to interest revenue. This occurs when the fair value of the property differs from the carrying value. On the other hand, direct financing leases only have interest revenue to recognize in the transaction as profit or loss due to the cost of the item being the same as the fair value.

17. When the fair value of the property exceeds the present value of the minimum lease payments at the inception of the lease, the lease is classified as a sales-type lease. The present value of the property is booked as sales revenue and the excess of fair value over the present value (carrying amount) will be booked as unearned interest at the inception of the lease. Unearned interest will be amortized into income using the effective interest method, resulting in a constant periodic rate of return on the net investment. The journal entry to record the inception of the lease follows:

Lease Receivable	xxx	
Sales		xxx
Unearned Interest		xxx
Cost of Goods Sold	xxx	
Inventory		xxx

18. The lessee will amortize (depreciate) the leased asset over the lease term unless title transfers or a bargain purchase option exists, in which case, the lease is amortized (depreciated) over the useful life of the asset. The amortization (depreciation) method used should be consistent with the lessee's normal depreciation policy.

19. An alternative basis which is systematic and rational and is more representative of the time pattern of physical usage of the lease property may be used by lessors and lessees.

20. The lessor will amortize initial direct leasing costs over the lease term as the revenue is recognized for operating leases (usually straight-line).

21. The lessor will amortize the initial direct leasing costs over the lease term so that a constant periodic rate is earned on the net investment. The effect of the amortization is to reduce the implicit interest rate (yield) to the lessor over the life of the lease.

22. The guaranteed residual value is included in the minimum lease payments to reduce the periodic payments in cases where the property is to revert back to the lessor.

23. A gain on the sale of property in a sale-leaseback transaction is deferred by the lessee and amortized over the life of the asset at the same rate that the asset is being depreciated.

24. Such losses are termed artificial. A real loss would occur only if the fair market value were less than book value. Artificial losses shall be deferred and amortized as additional depreciation.

25. Active use of property in the seller-lessee's trade or business represents continuing involvement that does not preclude the use of sale-leaseback accounting.

26. The liability method has as its primary objective the presentation on the balance sheet of the best estimate of the amount of future tax benefits or the liability for future income taxes to be paid by the reporting entity. This is in contrast with the deferred method which was utilized by the earlier GAAP, APB 11, under which the principal goal was the matching of periodic revenue and expense on the income statement, with little concern about whether the deferred tax assets or liabilities represented actual claims or obligations.

27. Temporary differences include all differences between the tax and book bases of assets and liabilities; this definition includes timing differences as defined under prior GAAP, but also includes other differences.

28. Tax effects of differences in the bases of assets acquired in purchase business combinations are reflected as deferred tax assets or liabilities, and the assets acquired are "grossed up" for these differences in the purchase price allocation process. The formerly prescribed "net of tax" method is no longer acceptable.

29. Since deferred tax assets and liabilities should represent the amounts of benefits to be received or obligations to be settled when the temporary differences reverse, the tax rates expected to be effective at those times should be used, based on current law (not rumored tax rate cuts, for example).

30. The purpose of the valuation allowance is to reduce the net deferred tax asset to the amount which is "more likely than not" to be realized. This must be assessed at each financial statement date.

31. The effect of changing tax rates on previously provided deferred tax assets and liabilities must be reported as part of the current year deferred tax provision allocated to income from continuing operations, even if the deferred tax asset or obligation relates to items which did not affect income from continuing operations.

32. The tax rates to employ are dependent upon the method by which the enterprise intends to realize the earnings, as ordinary income or as capital gains, for example. This expectation may change from one period to the next.

33. SFAS 109 has eliminated the "indefinite reversal" exception to comprehensive interperiod income tax allocation. However, deferred taxes or existing temporary differences for which deferred taxes were not provided for this reason that arose in fiscal years beginning on or before December 15, 1992, are exempt. Deferred taxes must be provided on all differences arising after that date.

34. Intraperiod tax allocation should be determined by a "with and without" approach, which means that tax on total income is compared to tax on income from continuing operations, with the marginal amount allocated to all categories other than continuing operations. Generally, the effective rate of the marginal items is applied to all such items, unless it is clear that some specific portion of the marginal tax provision belongs to one or another item.

UNIT III

PUBLISHER-GRADED EXAMINATION

True/False 1. The ARB 43, Chapter 3 definition of current liabilities excludes from the current liability classifications any currently maturing obligations which will be satisfied by using long-term assets and currently maturing obligations expected to be refinanced.

Multiple-choice 2. Per FASB Technical Bulletin 88-2 the conditions to be met for a right of setoff are as follows:

a. Each of the two parties owes the other determinable amounts.
b. The reporting party has the right to set off.
c. The reporting party intends to set off.
d. The right of setoff is enforceable at law.

True/False 3. The most acceptable method of accounting for property taxes is to record the expense when the cash is paid.

True/False 4. SFAS uses the conditions of SFAS 43 to accrue an obligation for postemployment benefits other than pensions if employees' rights accumulate or vest, payment is probable, and the amount can be reasonably estimated.

True/False 5. SFAS 114 and SFAS 118 together specify the accounting by creditors for troubled debt restructurings involving a modification of terms.

True/False 6. The stated rate on a note or bond is usually the same as the market rate at the time of issuance.

True/False 7. When a note is issued solely for cash, an imputed interest rate must be used.

True/False 8. If the fair market value of the note is not determinable, then the present value of the note must be determined using an imputed interest rate.

True/False 9. SFAS 125 provides accounting and reporting standards for extinguishments of liabilities.

True/False 10. A troubled debt restructuring can occur in one of two ways. The first is a scttlement of the debt at less than the carrying amount. The second is a continuation of the debt with a modification of terms.

True/False 11. SFAS 114, as amended by SFAS 118, applies to all loans on leases.

True/False 12. If the book value approach is used upon the conversion of convertible debt, no gain or loss is recognized upon conversion.

True/False 13. When bonds with detachable warrants are issued, the purchase price is not allocated between the debt and the stock warrants.

True/False 14. If a lease contains a bargain purchase option, it should be classified as a capital lease on the books of the lessee.

True/False 15. A capital lease of a lessee should record the lease as both an asset and a liability on a balance sheet.

Multiple-choice 16. Minimum lease payments include
- a. Executory costs.
- b. Guarantee of the residual value.
- c. Both a. and b.
- d. None of the above.

True/False 17. Initial direct leasing costs should be amortized over the term of the lease.

True/False 18. A direct financing lease is the result of a manufacturer wanting a different means of financing the sale of his product.

Multiple-choice 19. Which type of lease results is the lessor recognizing a profit or loss in addition to interest revenue?
- a. Leveraged lease.
- b. Direct financing lease.
- c. Sales-type lease.
- d. Capital lease.

True/False 20. If the present value of the minimum lease payments at the beginning of the lease term is at least 80% of the fair market value to the lessor, the lease should be classified as a capital lease.

True/False 21. The interest rate to be used to compute the present value of a lease is the incremental borrowing rate of the lessor unless the implicit rate is available and lower.

Multiple-choice 22. Which one of the following is not a criterion for determining if a lease is an operating or a capital lease for the lessee?
- a. The lease contains a bargain purchase option.
- b. The lease term is equal to at least 75% of the estimated economic life of the leased property.
- c. Ownership transfers to the lessee at the end of the lease term.
- d. All of the above.

True/False 23. The rental payments for an operating lease are charged as expenses when made or payable.

True/False 24. A leased asset with a lease that qualifies as a capital lease because the lease had a bargain purchase option should be amortized over the estimated useful life of the leased asset, not the life of the lease.

True/False 25. In determining whether a valuation allowance will be required for deferred tax assets, absent evidence that the entity will generate future taxable income sufficient to absorb the temporary difference reversals, it would be necessary to establish at least a partial allowance.

True/False 26. Gross deferred tax assets should be provided only for the tax effects of all deductible temporary differences expected to be realized.

True/False 27. When a tax rate increase has been enacted to take effect in future periods, this would typically be used to compute the deferred tax provision in the current period.

True/False 28. The effect of tax rate changes on previously provided deferred taxes should be allocated among current operations, extraordinary items, discontinued operations and prior period adjustments, based on how the deferred taxes were initially provided.

True/False 29. In computing the current year's deferred tax provision, the normal approach is to determine the deferred tax balances required at the year end for as-yet unreversed temporary differences, and provide sufficient additional taxes to reach the indicated balance needed.

True/False 30. In determining the valuation allowance for deferred tax assets, evidence that the entity will generate future taxable income sufficient to absorb the temporary difference reversals would be considered.

True/False 31. In deciding how large a valuation reserve to provide against deferred tax assets, an entity could give consideration to the existence of assets whose fair values had appreciated over their respective tax bases.

True/False 32. Deferred taxes are sometimes provided in connection with goodwill or negative goodwill recorded pursuant to a purchase business combination.

True/False 33. A cumulative history of taxable losses would typically not influence the decision to provide a valuation allowance for deferred tax assets.

True/False 34. The tax effect of net operating loss carryforwards should be given current recognition only when it is deemed to be probable that it will ultimately be realized.

True/False 35. The deferred tax effects of voluntary changes in tax status of the reporting entity should not be reported in earnings until the change has become effective.

True/False 36. The deferred tax effects of a change in tax status from a C corporation to an S corporation can be reported as a contribution of capital by the stockholders to the entity, since the owners personally will be paying the taxes that otherwise would be paid by the company when temporary differences later reverse.

True/False 37. Taxes on extraordinary items should be determined by applying statutory rates to the extraordinary items individually.

True/False 38. Disclosure need only be made of the net amount of deferred tax assets as of the balance sheet date.

True/False 39. Payments made to the Internal Revenue Service to maintain a fiscal year are reported as an asset, not an expense.

True/False 40. Deferred taxes on undistributed earnings of investees must be provided for using either the rate applicable to dividend distributions or that applicable to capital gains, depending on how the earnings are expected to be realized by the reporting entity.

GAAP 1999 CPE Course

UNIT III

Record your CPE answers on the answer form provided below and return this page for grading.

Mail to:
***GAAP 1999* CPE Director**
ValuSource, 7222 Commerce Center Drive, Suite 210, Colorado Springs, CO 80919

PAYMENT OPTIONS

☐ **Payment enclosed ($59.00 per Unit).**
(Make checks payable to John Wiley & Sons, Inc.)
Please add appropriate sales tax.
Be sure to sign your order below.

Charge my:

☐ American Express ☐ MasterCard ☐ Visa

Account number ______________________

Expiration date ______________________
Please sign below for all credit card orders.

Signature ______________________

NAME ______________________

FIRM NAME ______________________

ADDRESS ______________________

____

PHONE ( ) ______________________

CPA STATE LICENSE # ______________________

SEE THE OTHER SIDE OF THIS PAGE FOR THE CPE FEEDBACK FORM.

UNIT III CPE ANSWERS

1. ____	2. ____	3. ____	4. ____	5. ____	6. ____	7. ____	8. ____	9. ____	10. ____
11. ____	12. ____	13. ____	14. ____	15. ____	16. ____	17. ____	18. ____	19. ____	20. ____
21. ____	22. ____	23. ____	24. ____	25. ____	26. ____	27. ____	28. ____	29. ____	30. ____
31. ____	32. ____	33. ____	34. ____	35. ____	36. ____	37. ____	38. ____	39. ____	40. ____

GAAP 1999 CPE Feedback

1. Were you informed in advance of the

   a. Course objectives? **Y N**
   b. Requisite experience level? **Y N**
   c. Course content? **Y N**
   d. Type and degree of preparation necessary? **Y N**
   e. Instruction method? **Y N**
   f. CPE credit hours? **Y N**

2. Do you agree with the publisher's determination of

   a. Course objectives? **Y N**
   b. Requisite experience level? **Y N**
   c. Course content? **Y N**
   d. Type and degree of preparation necessary? **Y N**
   e. Instruction method? **Y N**
   f. CPE credit hours? **Y N**

3. Was the content relevant? **Y N**

4. Was the content displayed clearly? **Y N**

5. Did the course enhance your professional competence? **Y N**

6. Was the course content timely and effective? **Y N**

How can we make the course better? If you have any suggestions please summarize them in the space below. We will consider them in developing future courses.

CONTINUING PROFESSIONAL EDUCATION: SELF-STUDY

UNIT IV

OBJECTIVES

Read Chapter 16: Accounting for Pensions

Studying Chapter 16 should enable you to:

- Understand the accrual basis of accounting for pension costs
- Know the six components of net periodic pension costs
- Calculate net periodic pension costs
- Describe the accounting for settlements and curtailments
- Account for postretirement benefits other than pensions
- Know GAAP regarding deferred compensation contracts

Read Chapter 16 and answer discussion questions 1 through 9.

Read Chapter 17: Stockholders' Equity

Studying Chapter 17 should enable you to:

- Understand the natures of preferred and common stock
- Account for contributed capital and retained earnings
- Understand accounting for treasury stock transactions
- Account for stock, cash and property dividends
- Account for stock splits and reverse splits
- Account for quasi reorganizations
- Account for employee stock options and related compensation arrangements
- Understand the use of the options pricing models for employee stock compensation arrangements
- Understand employer accounting for ESOP plans

Read Chapter 17 and answer discussion questions 10 through 17.

Read Chapter 18: Earnings Per Share

Studying Chapter 18 should enable you to:

- Differentiate between basic and fully diluted earnings per share

- Describe the treasury stock method and the if-converted method, and explain when these methods are utilized
- Describe the components of income for which EPS must be computed
- Calculate the income from continuing operations available for common stockholders (numerator) for basic EPS and fully diluted EPS
- Calculate the weighted-average number of shares outstanding (denominator) for basic EPS and fully diluted EPS
- Describe the treatment of stock splits and stock dividends in calculating EPS
- Describe the required EPS disclosures

Read Chapter 18 and answer discussion questions 18 through 20.

Read Chapter 19: Interim and Segment Reporting

Studying Chapter 19 should enable you to:

- Understand the discrete and integral views of reporting on interim periods
- Know the recognition criteria in interim periods for revenues, product costs, direct costs, and other costs and expenses
- Describe required interim reporting disclosures
- Know the definition of an industry segment
- Identify reportable operating segments

Read Chapter 19 and answer discussion questions 21 through 23.

Read Chapter 20: Accounting Changes and Correction of Errors

Studying Chapter 20 should enable you to:

- Differentiate among changes in accounting principle, changes in accounting estimate, and changes in reporting entity
- Describe the three ways of reporting accounting changes: retroactively, currently, and prospectively
- Describe implementation of the cumulative effect method, including disclosures and pro forma calculations
- Identify the changes in accounting principles that are accounted for retroactively
- Discuss implementation of retroactive-type changes in accounting principle
- Explain how to account for a change in accounting estimate
- Describe how to disclose a change in reporting entity

- Describe how to correct errors in previously issued financial statements

Read Chapter 20 and answer discussion questions 24 through 28.

Read Chapter 21: Foreign Currency

Studying Chapter 21 should enable you to:

- Differentiate between translation of foreign currency transactions and foreign currency financial statements
- Apply the factors from SFAS 52 that shall be used in identifying the functional currency of the foreign entity
- Apply the current rate method of translating balances of a foreign branch or subsidiary
- Apply the remeasurement method of translating balances of a foreign branch or subsidiary
- Describe the reporting of unrealized translation gains or losses
- Describe the accounting for hedges

Read Chapter 21 and answer discussion questions 29 through 33.

Read Chapter 22: Personal Financial Statements

Studying Chapter 22 should enable you to:

- Know which financial statements and the format thereof that constitute a set of personal financial statements
- Know the valuation bases for assets and liabilities

Read Chapter 22 and answer discussion questions 34 and 35.

DISCUSSION QUESTIONS

1. What are the sources of GAAP in the pension area?
2. Net periodic pension cost consists of the sum of what six components?
3. What is a major difference between the accumulated benefit obligation and the projected benefit obligation?
4. What do plan assets include?
5. What are service costs?
6. In SFAS 87, how is the additional minimum liability recognized?

7. What three criteria must all be met in order to constitute a pension obligation settlement?
8. What standard establishes the standard for employers' accounting for other than pension postretirement benefits (OPEB)?
9. If the aggregate deferred compensation contracts with individual employees are **not** equivalent to a pension plan, what governs the accounting?
10. What is the distinction between paid-in capital and retained earnings, and why is this considered to be important in financial reporting?
11. Why are stock subscriptions receivable generally reported as a contra equity account?
12. What is the distinction between a stock dividend and a stock split, and what is the proper accounting for each?
13. How are "gains" and "losses" on treasury stock transactions accounted for, and what is the underlying accounting principle?
14. What is the approach to accounting for employee stock options underlying the new rules of SFAS 123? How does this differ from the old approach of APB 25?
15. Under the options pricing models endorsed by SFAS 123, what attributes give value to employee stock options?
16. What are tandem stock plans and what is the basic concept of accounting for these under APB 25 and SFAS 123?
17. What is the objective of accounting for a "quasi reorganization"?
18. Why are shares issued during a period weighted so as to reflect the portion of a period that they are outstanding?
19. In calculating income available to common stockholders, how are dividends in arrears on cumulative preferred stock treated?
20. Explain the reason that stock splits or dividends are reflected in EPS as though they occurred at the beginning of the period and, in cases when comparative financial statements are presented, for all prior periods presented.
21. Discuss the rationale for the dual presentation of EPS (i.e., basic and fully diluted EPS) by companies with a complex capital structure.
22. Is it possible for the computations from the basic EPS and diluted EPS calculations to yield the same EPS figure?
23. Describe the treasury stock method and the if-converted method.
24. Discuss the difference between the discrete and integral views of reporting on interim periods.

25. Describe the treatment of inventory market declines in interim financial statements.
26. On what basis shall reportable operating segments be reported?
27. How are changes in amortization methods for long-lived assets accounted for if the change is adopted for all assets?
28. How must changes in accounting principle requiring the cumulative effect method be disclosed in the year the changes are made?
29. In what circumstances may cumulative effect not be determinable? How are these circumstances to be disclosed?
30. If the cumulative-effect-type of accounting change is made at an interim date, how is it accounted for on the financial statements?
31. Describe when a change in reporting entity occurs.
32. What are the factors to be considered by management when selecting the functional currency?
33. Under the current rate method of translation, which elements are translated at historical rates?
34. Compare and contrast the remeasurement method of translation with the current rate method.
35. Explain the accounting at the end of a reporting period if an entity has receivables and payables that are denominated in a foreign currency.
36. If the number of US dollars for each foreign currency unit increases between the transaction date and the balance sheet date, does the translation of receivables and payables denominated in the foreign currency result in gains or losses?
37. What basis of valuation should be used for liability in the statement of financial condition?
38. How should estimated income taxes related to unrealized gains and losses be measured?

ANSWERS TO DISCUSSION QUESTIONS

1. SFAS 87 and SFAS 88 are the sources of GAAP in the pension area.
2. Net periodic pension cost consists of the sum of the following six components:
   a. Service cost
   b. Interest cost on projected benefit obligation
   c. Actual return on plan assets
   d. Gain or loss
   e. Amortization of unrecognized prior service cost
   f. Amortization of unrecognized net assets or net obligation existing at date of initial application of SFAS 87
3. The accumulated benefit obligation does not include an assumption about future compensation levels, whereas the projected benefit obligation does include such an assumption.
4. Plan assets include contributions and asset earnings less benefits paid. They must be segregated and effectively restricted for pension benefits.
5. The service cost component of net periodic pension cost is the actuarial present value of benefits attributed during the current period. Under SFAS 87, the plan's benefit formula is the key to attributing benefits to employee service periods.
6. In SFAS 87, the additional minimum liability is recognized by an offset to an intangible asset up to the amount of unrecognized prior service cost. Any additional debit needed is considered a loss and is shown net of tax benefits (subject to the restrictions on recognition of deferred tax assets per SFAS 109) as a separate component reducing equity.
7. The following three criteria must all be met in order to constitute a pension obligation settlement:
   a. Must be irrevocable
   b. Must relieve the obligor of primary responsibility
   c. Must eliminate significant risks associated with elements used to effect it
8. SFAS 106 establishes the standard for employers' accounting for other (than pension) postretirement benefits (OPEB). This standard prescribes a single method for measuring and recognizing an employer's accumulated postretirement benefit obligation (APBO). It applies to all forms of postretirement benefits, although the most material benefit is usually postretirement health care.
9. If the aggregate deferred compensation contracts with individual employees are equivalent to a pension plan, the contracts should be accounted for according to

SFAS 87 and 88. All other deferred compensation contracts should be accounted for according to APB 12, para 6.

10. Paid-in capital represents the permanent owners' investment in the corporation, which in most jurisdictions represents legal capital which is available for the protection of creditors. Retained earnings is the accumulation of the earnings of the corporation since inception, less dividend distributions. Historically this distinction has been important since it reveals the amount of capital which will continue to be available for the satisfaction of creditors' claims, and is a measure of the cumulative success of the company over its entire history.

11. Subscriptions receivable are shown as offsets to subscribed stock to avoid an overstatement of the balance sheet simply as a result of promises to acquire shares which have yet to be substantiated by cash infusions. In rare cases (if the cash is collected after the balance sheet date but before the statements are issued) the receivable is shown as an asset, since it is known to have been collected.

12. Stock dividends and splits both are merely the change in evidences of ownership, without any distribution of assets from the company to the stockholders. However, stock dividends are generally viewed by the market as indications of earnings distributions, and are typically small (no more than 20% to 25%) while splits are universally seen as being merely bookkeeping events. Stock dividends often do not affect the market price of the outstanding shares (or do not affect it in proportion to the extent of the dividend) while splits are usually accompanied by proportionate declines in market value. For these reasons, stock dividends are accounted for as true dividends (retained earnings are transferred to paid-in capital) while splits do not affect retained earnings.

13. When treasury shares are resold for more than cost, the "gain" is credited to paid-in capital, while if the subsequent sale is for less than cost, the "loss" is charged to retained earnings (unless paid-in capital from prior similar transactions is available to absorb the loss). The principle is that an entity's transactions in its own equity cannot create income to be reported in the income statement or increase retained earnings, while losses will reduce retained earnings.

14. SFAS 123 adopts the "fair value" approach to measuring stock options, while the older APB 25 rules used the "intrinsic value" model. Under APB 25 most employee options did not give rise to accounting recognition of compensation expense, although clearly the purpose of granting options was to compensate employees. SFAS 123 rules will result in compensation expense in most cases. However, SFAS 123 is not mandatory, so companies may elect to continue to use APB 25.

15. The value assigned to options under the Black-Scholes and binomial models is a function of the spread between option price and market price at grant date, the

risk-free discount rate, the expected market price growth rate, the expected volatility in stock price, and the expected dividends to be paid on the stock during the service period. For nonpublic companies, the minimum value model is similar, but ignores the volatility of stock prices.

16. Tandem plans are simultaneous grants of stock options and stock appreciation rights or phantom shares, whereby the exercise of one cancels the other. Under APB 25, as amended by FASB Interpretation 28, the accounting is based on the expectation of which of the two will be elected by the holders, but under SFAS 123, the liability arising from the stock appreciation rights, if they can be settled in cash at the holders' option, is generally the basis for the accrual of compensation expense.

17. Quasi reorganizations were developed to deal with major, permanent declines in price levels, which would make it unlikely that an entity could recover the carrying value of long-term assets, and which result in recurring losses due to high amortization charges. Under those limited conditions, a write-down of fixed assets can be recorded, and the accumulated deficit in retained earnings absorbed against paid-in capital. For an extended period of time thereafter, retained earnings must be "dated" so financial statement readers are not misled about the entity's historical performance record. A quasi reorganization is an accounting, not a legal, process.

18. Shares issued during a period are weighted from the date of issuance because that is the period of time during which management had use of the resources to generate income.

19. Only the preferred dividends for 1 year would be deducted from net income; the amount of dividends for 1 year were deducted in each prior year.

20. The rationale for treating stock splits or dividends as of the beginning of the period, and in all earlier periods when comparative financial statements are presented, is to avoid distortion when comparing earlier periods' earnings per share amounts with later periods it would appear that earnings per share decreased, when in essence each shareholder's equity in the earnings of the enterprise are unchanged by a split or dividend.

21. The underlying basis for this presentation is conservatism. The range from basic to diluted EPS distinguishes between no dilution and potential dilution, thereby providing the users with the most factually supportable range of EPS possiblities. Diluted EPS considers all other dilutive securities (unless such exercise would be antidilutive).

22. It is possible for BEPS and DEPS to be the same, if the other potentially dilutive securities in the DEPS calculation are antidilutive. However, to the extent dilutive securities exist the DEPS figure will always be lower than the basic EPS figure.

23. Generally the treasury stock method is used for options and warrants, while the if-converted method is used for convertible securities. Each method requires certain pro forma assumptions. The treasury stock method requires that EPS be computed as if the options or warrants were exercised as of the beginning of the period (or date of issuance, if later), and that the funds obtained from the exercise were used to purchase common stock at the average market price. The if-converted method assumes the conversion of preferential securities with convertible features (e.g., convertible bonds or convertible preferred stock) to common stock. This method recognizes (via a pro forma assumption) that these securities share in the earnings of the common shareholder. Thus the dividends or net income effects applicable to the preferential security are not recognized in the income available to common stockholders figure, and the weighted-average number of shares is also adjusted.

24. According to the integral view of interim reporting, the resulting earnings figures for an interim period should give users information concerning annual earnings; these numbers should predict annual earnings. On the other hand, the discrete view is that each reporting period should stand by itself; estimates and allocations should not differ from those used in annual statements.

25. Market declines expected to be restored are deemed temporary and do not require recognition. Ordinarily, only seasonal gains may be deferred.

26. SFAS 131 requires reporting of information about operating segments on the same basis that it is provided for internal evaluation by the chief operating decision maker.

27. The change requires a cumulative effect adjustment. Newly acquired identifiable long-lived assets will use the new method of amortization. Long-lived assets already on the books will be adjusted based on the new amortization method.

28. The nature of and justification for the change and the effect of the change on income before extraordinary items, net income, and related per share amounts shall be disclosed for all periods presented.

29. The cumulative effect might not be determinable in a change from LIFO to FIFO. Disclosure will be limited to showing the effect and per share effect of the change in the period of change. It will also be necessary to explain the reason for omitting accounting for the cumulative effect and disclosure of the pro forma results.

30. No cumulative effect of the accounting change should be included in the net income of the period. The prechange interim periods of the year in which the change is made should be restated to reflect the newly adopted accounting principle.

31. A change in reporting entity occurs when a change in the structure of the organization is made which results in financial statements that represent a different or changed entity.

32. The factors are: effect of foreign entity's cash flow on parent, responsiveness of sales prices to exchange rates and global competition, location of sales market as reflected by currency in which denominated, country in which expenses incurred, source of financing, and volume of intercompany transactions.

33. Only stockholders' equity accounts are translated at historical rates.

34. Whereas all assets and liabilities are translated at current rates under the current rate method, only monetary assets and liabilities are translated at the current rate under the remeasurement method. Nonmonetary assets and liabilities use historical rates.

35. Each of the receivables and payables must be translated to dollars using the spot rate at the balance sheet date. Differences between the translated amounts and the carrying amounts result in unrealized gains or losses.

36. If the number of dollars per unit of foreign currency increases, there would be unrealized gains on receivables and losses on payables that are denominated in that foreign currency unit.

37. Liabilities should be measured at the lesser of the discounted amount of cash to be paid or the current cash settlement amount.

38. Estimated income taxes should be measured as if the current values of assets and liabilities had been realized or liquidated, respectively, and the provisions of current tax law were applied.

UNIT IV

PUBLISHER-GRADED EXAMINATION

True/False 1. SFAS 132 requires restatement for comparative purposes, unless the information is not readily available.

True/False 2. Among other things, SFAS 132 requires disclosure for defined benefit plans of amounts in Other Comprehensive Income for the period due to a change in the additional minimum pension liability.

True/False 3. The benefit formula incorporates many factors including employee compensation, employee service longevity, employee age, etc., and is considered to provide the best indication of pension obligations and costs.

True/False 4. The accounting for pension service costs should always be based solely on the benefit formula and should not be based on substantive commitments.

True/False 5. The interest cost on the projected benefit obligation results form multiplying the assumed settlement discount rate times the projected benefit obligation as of the start of the year.

True/False 6. Actuarial gains (losses) are not considered prior period adjustments but are considered changes in an estimate that should be recognized in current and future periods.

True/False 7. Any difference between the amount funded and the amount expensed must appear on the balance sheet as an additional minimum liability.

True/False 8. If there is a difference between the substantive plan and the written plan, SFAS 106 requires that the written plan be the basis for the accounting.

True/False 9. Dividends can be paid out of additional paid in capital and retained earnings, but not out of the common stock (aggregate par value) account.

True/False 10. Stock dividends reduce retained earnings but not total stockholders' equity.

True/False 11. Stock splits, as distinct from stock dividends, reduce neither retained earnings nor total stockholders' equity.

True/False 12. Treasury shares can be shown as an asset only in the balance sheets of companies operating in certain regulated industries.

True/False 13. Although stock subscribed but not paid for is reported in stockholders' equity, the subscription receivable is shown as an offset so that the net effect is to report no increase in equity form unpaid subscriptions.

True/False 14. Compensatory stock options granted to employees create compensation expense which does not have to be reported on the income statements.

True/False 15. The options pricing models prescribed by SFAS 123 are equally valid for publicly and privately held companies which grant compensatory stock options to employees.

True/False 16. Under the provisions of SFAS 123, no compensation expense will be reportable if options are granted with exercise prices at or above market price at grant date.

True/False 17. Although a company which issues employee stock options will receive tax benefits as a result of those options being exercised, these benefits will not impact the company's reported tax expense of any period.

True/False 18. When preferred stock contains mandatory redemption provisions, the stock must be presented on the balance sheet outside the equity section.

True/False 19. The details of the equity accounts pertaining to other comprehensive income need not be presented on the face of the balance sheet.

True/False 20. Under the provisions of APB 25, there will be no compensation expense to be reported if options are granted with exercise prices at or above market price at grant date.

True/False 21. Under GAAP for employee stock ownership plans (ESOP), compensation cost related to stock allocated to employees is measured by the cost of the shares to the employer at the time the shares are acquired, even if the values change before the shares are allocated.

True/False 22. Dividends paid on unallocated shares held by an ESOP are reported as dividends rather than as compensation expense.

True/False 23. The accounting for companies which are reorganized under the bankruptcy laws is similar to that for poolings of interests or mergers between affiliated entities.

True/False 24. Appropriations can be made from retained earnings for contingencies and other purposes, but if this is done, expenses or losses must not be charged against the appropriation account.

True/False 25. The inability to compel further capital contributions from the members of limited liability companies does not preclude the reporting of a deficit in members' equity.

True/False 26. A reverse split increases the number of shares outstanding.

True/False 27. Antidilutive securities are not included in the computation of the weighted-average number of shares outstanding.

True/False 28. An extraordinary item should be reported at the end of the year, not in an interim period.

True/False 29. Businesses that experience seasonal fluctuations should not create interim reports because of misleading users.

Multiple-choice 30. Which of the following is not a 10% test to determine if a segment is significant?
a. Liabilities test.
b. Revenues test.
c. Operating profit and loss test.
d. Assets test.

True/False 31. Prospective treatment of accounting changes requires no restatement of prior financial statements, but it does require reporting in the current period the cumulative effect of accounting changes.

True/False 32. The cumulative effect of a change in accounting principle is shown on the income statement as an extraordinary item.

Multiple-choice 33. Which of the following does not require retroactive treatment for a change in accounting principle?
a. A change for LIFO to FIFO.
b. A change mandated by authoritative pronouncements.
c. A change from FIFO to LIFO.
d. A change form the completed-contract method of accounting for long-term contracts to the percentage-of-completion method.

True/False 34. If the pro forma amounts of a cumulative effect of a change in accounting principle cannot be determined, then the cumulative effect should be reported on the income statement with disclosure in the notes stating the reasons the pro forma amounts were not disclosed.

True/False 35. Once the functional currency is chosen it can be changed only if economic facts or circumstances have changed.

True/False 36. A change in the functional currency requires a restatement of previous financial statements.

Multiple-choice 37. All of the following are translation methods that may be used by an entity except for

a. Monetary/nonmonetary method.
b. Current rate method.
c. Temporal method.
d. Functional currency method.

Multiple-choice 38. If the functional currency is a foreign currency, which translation method is required to be used?

a. Temporal method.
b. Current rate method.
c. Current/noncurrent method.
d. Monetary/nonmonetary method.

True/False 39. Translation adjustments that result from using the current method should be reported on the balance sheet as a separate component of owner's equity.

True/False 40. The statement of changes in net worth is a required statement.

GAAP 1999 CPE Course

UNIT IV

Record your CPE answers on the answer form provided below and return this page for grading.

Mail to:
***GAAP 1999* CPE Director**
ValuSource, 7222 Commerce Center Drive, Suite 210, Colorado Springs, CO 80919

PAYMENT OPTIONS

☐ **Payment enclosed ($59.00 per Unit).**
(Make checks payable to John Wiley & Sons, Inc.)
Please add appropriate sales tax.
Be sure to sign your order below.

Charge my:

☐ American Express ☐ MasterCard ☐ Visa

Account number ______________

Expiration date ______________

Please sign below for all credit card orders.

Signature ______________

NAME ______________

FIRM NAME ______________

ADDRESS ______________

____

PHONE ( ) ______________

CPA STATE LICENSE # ______________

SEE THE OTHER SIDE OF THIS PAGE FOR THE CPE FEEDBACK FORM.

UNIT IV CPE ANSWERS

1. ____	2. ____	3. ____	4. ____	5. ____	6. ____	7. ____	8. ____	9. ____	10. ____
11. ____	12. ____	13. ____	14. ____	15. ____	16. ____	17. ____	18. ____	19. ____	20. ____
21. ____	22. ____	23. ____	24. ____	25. ____	26. ____	27. ____	28. ____	29. ____	30. ____
31. ____	32. ____	33. ____	34. ____	35. ____	36. ____	37. ____	38. ____	39. ____	40. ____

GAAP 1999 CPE Feedback

1. Were you informed in advance of the

   a. Course objectives? **Y N**
   b. Requisite experience level? **Y N**
   c. Course content? **Y N**
   d. Type and degree of preparation necessary? **Y N**
   e. Instruction method? **Y N**
   f. CPE credit hours? **Y N**

2. Do you agree with the publisher's determination of

   a. Course objectives? **Y N**
   b. Requisite experience level? **Y N**
   c. Course content? **Y N**
   d. Type and degree of preparation necessary? **Y N**
   e. Instruction method? **Y N**
   f. CPE credit hours? **Y N**

3. Was the content relevant? **Y N**

4. Was the content displayed clearly? **Y N**

5. Did the course enhance your professional competence? **Y N**

6. Was the course content timely and effective? **Y N**

How can we make the course better? If you have any suggestions please summarize them in the space below. We will consider them in developing future courses.

E

New Corporate and Public Accounting Titles from John Wiley & Sons

OUTSOURCING: A Guide to
...Selecting the Correct Business Unit
...Negotiating the Contract
...Maintaining Control of the Process
STEVEN M. BRAGG
Paper, ISBN 1-25268-9, $59.95, 1998, 384 pp.
Gain practical understanding of why to outsource a function; how to choose your vendors; how to control, manage, and measure outsourced activities; how to bring outsourced functions back in house; plus much more.

HANDBOOK OF BUDGETING
Fourth Edition
ROBERT RACHLIN AND H.W. ALLEN SWEENY
Cloth, ISBN 1-18350-4
$150.00, Pub. date: 11/98, 976 pp.
Pre-pub $125 through 11/30/98
Completely updated, *Handbook of Budgeting 4th Edition*. can help you make your annual budgeting the most productive and well-managed process possible.

COLLECTION MANAGEMENT HANDBOOK
The Art of Getting Paid, Second Edition
A. MICHAEL COLEMAN
Cloth, ISBN 1-25414-2, $95.00
Pub. date: 10/98, 336 pp.
An all-in-one reference where you'll find: advanced collection techniques that work; strategies to produce profitable changes in your firm; and new methods that redefine the art of collection.

OPERATIONAL REVIEW
Maximum Results at Efficient Costs
Second Edition
ROB REIDER
Cloth, ISBN 1-25204-2, $130.00
Pre-pub $105 through 11/30/98
Pub. date: 11/98, 552 pp.
In clear and easy-to-read language, Rob Reider shows you how to approach the review and covers the important differences between an operational and financial review.

ACCOUNTANTS' HANDBOOK
Ninth Edition, 2-Volume Set
DOUGLAS CARMICHAEL, STEVEN B. LILIEN, MARTIN MELLMAN
Paper, ISBN 1-29122-6, $125.00, Pub. date: 2/98
Vol. 1: Financial Accounting and General Topics
ISBN 1-29594-9, $75.00
Vol. 2: Special Industries and Special Topics
ISBN 1-29595-7, $75.00

AUDITING INFORMATION SYSTEMS
A Comprehensive Reference Guide
JACK CHAMPLAIN
Cloth, ISBN 1-16890-4, $70.00, Pub. date: 10/98, 440 pp.

1998 GLOBAL TELECOMS TAX PROFILES:
A Resource for Business, Tax, and Market Strategies
PRICEWATERHOUSECOOPERS GLOBAL TELECOMS TAX NETWORK
Paper, ISBN 1-31841-8, $150.00, 1998, 446 pp.
This is a business planning guide for assessing foreign investment opportunities in the telecommunications industry—with profiles of the telecommunications environment, tax laws, and regulations of 43 countries around the world.

COST OF CAPITAL
Estimation and Applications
SHANNON PRATT
Cloth, ISBN 1-19751-3, $65.00, 1998, 256 pp.
These two books by nationally recognized expert, Shannon Pratt, provide a full range of practical answers to business valuation questions and issues.

BUSINESS VALUATION BODY OF KNOWLEDGE
Exam Review and Professional Reference
SHANNON PRATT
Paper, ISBN 1-25451-7, $89.95
Pub. date: 9/98, 336 pp.

ACTIVITY-BASED COSTING
Making it Work for Small and Midsized Companies, Second Edition
DOUGLAS HICKS
Cloth, ISBN 1-24959-9, $65.00
Pub. date: 12/98, 384 pp.

DRIVING VALUE USING ACTIVITY-BASED BUDGETING
JAMES R. BRIMSON, JOHN ANTOS, AND STEVEN R. PLAYER
Cloth, ISBN 1-08631-2, $65.00
Pub. date: 12/98, 288 pp.

ACTIVITY-BASED MANAGEMENT
Arthur Andersen's Lessons from the ABM Battlefield, Second Edition
STEVEN R. PLAYER AND DAVID KEYS
Cloth, ISBN 1-31288-6, $29.95
Pub. date: 2/99, 224 pp.

VALUE PLANNING
The New Approach to Building Value Every Day
LAWRENCE B. M. SERVEN
Cloth, ISBN 1-19955-9, $59.95
Pub. date: 11/98, 240 pp.
A practical, modern guide to assessing the control and security of virtually any type of computer information system.

To Order Call: 1-800-272-2100 or
Fax: 1-732-302-2300 (Please ref. CRPAD)
Visit our Web site at: www. wiley.com/accounting

WILEY
Publishers Since 1807